Street by Street

GLASGOW

EAST KILBRI OCK, PAISLEY

Alexandria, Carluke, Clydebar ıuld,
Gourock, Hamilton, Helensburg Kilmacolm,
Kilsyth, Lanark, Largs, Larkhall, Motherwell, Newton Mearns, Shotts

Key to map pages	ii-iii
Key to map symbols	iv–1
Enlarged map pages	2-9
Main map pages	10-137
Index – towns & villages	138
Index – streets	139-172
Index – featured places	172-176
Glasgow Underground	177
Acknowledgements	177

2nd edition October 2007

Original edition printed May 2001

Published by AA Publishing (a trading name of Automobile Association Developments Limited, whose registered office is Fanum House, Basing View, Basingstoke, Hampshire RG21 4EA. Registered number 1878835).

Produced by the Mapping Services Department of The Automobile Association. (A03384)

A CIP Catalogue record for this book is available from the British Library.

Printed by Oriental Press in Dubai

The contents of this atlas are believed to be correct at the time of the latest revision. However, the publishers cannot be held responsible or liable for any loss or damage occasioned to any person acting or refraining from action as a result of any use or reliance on any material in this atlas, nor for any errors, omissions or changes in such material. This does not affect your statutory rights. The publishers would welcome information to correct any errors or omissions and to keep this atlas up to date. Please write to Publishing, The Automobile Association, Fanum House (FH12), Basing View, Basingstoke, Hampshire, RG21 4EA. E-mail: *streetbystreet@theaa.com*

Ref: MX71z

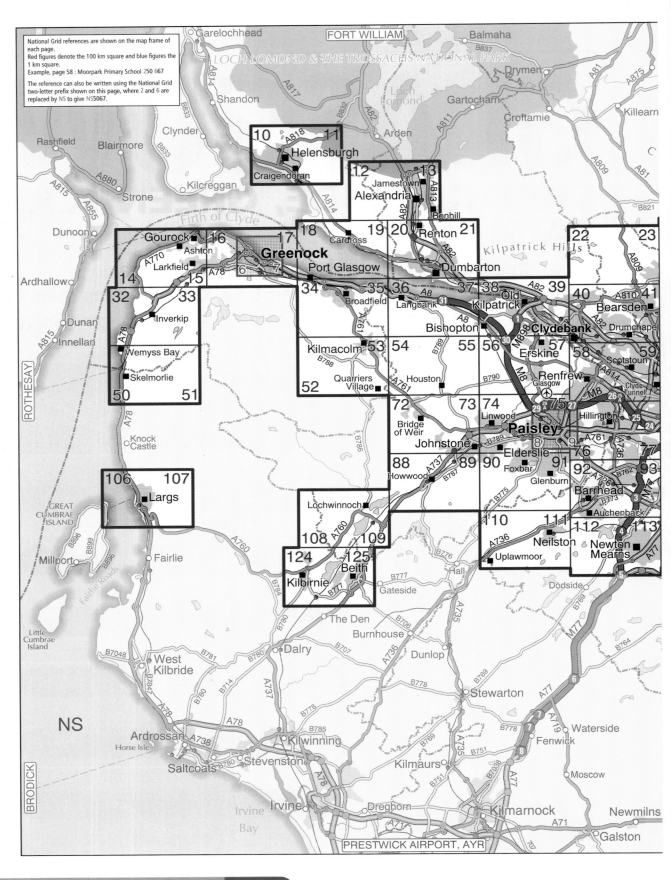

National Grid references are shown on the map frame of each page.
Red figures denote the 100 km square and blue figures the 1 km square.
Example, page 58 : Moorpark Primary School 250 667

The reference can also be written using the National Grid two-letter prefix shown on this page, where 2 and 6 are replaced by NS to give NS5067.

Scale of enlarged map pages 1:10,000 6.3 inches to 1 mile

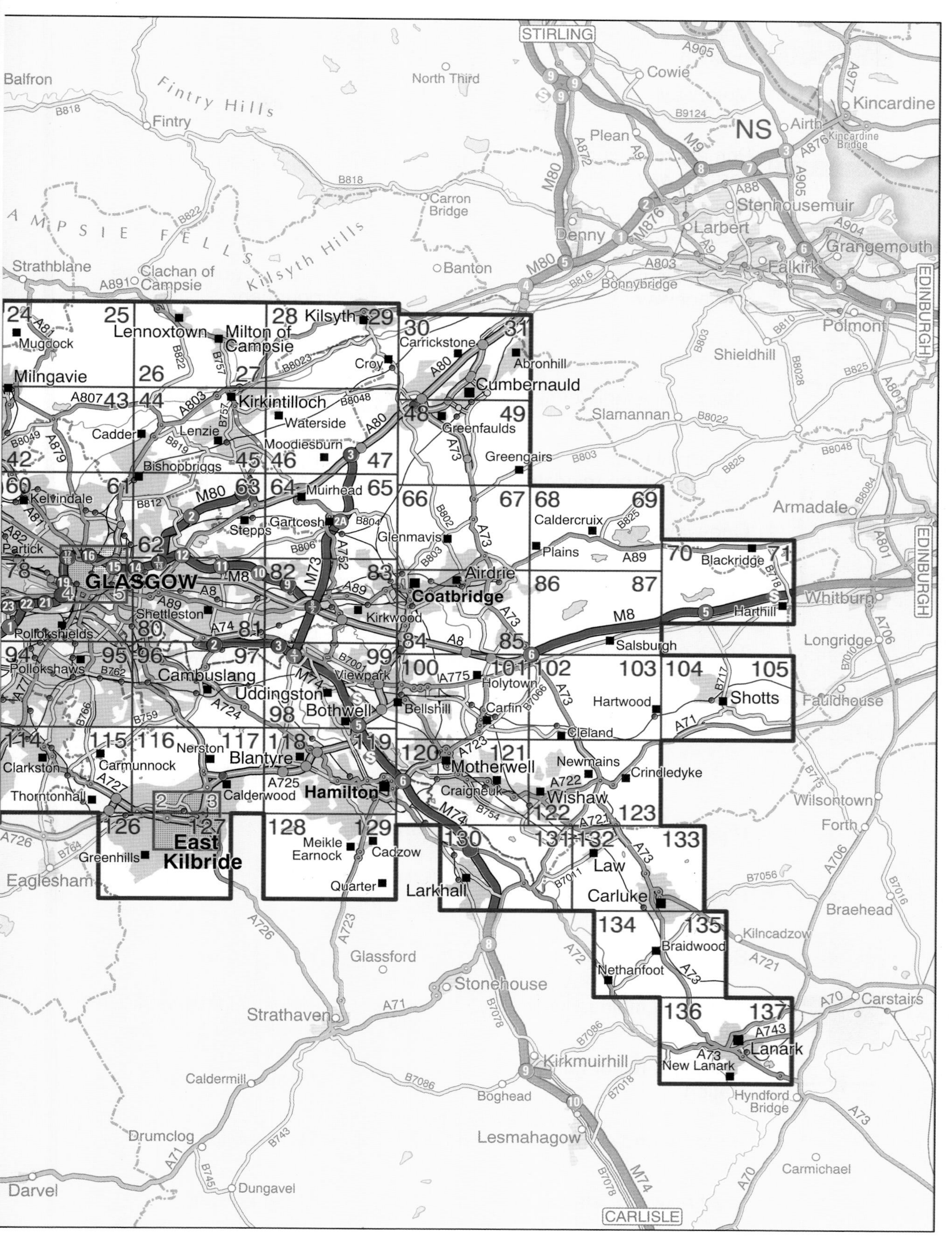

3.6 inches to 1 mile **Scale of main map pages 1:17,500**

Junction 9	Motorway & junction
Services	Motorway service area
	Primary road single/dual carriageway
Services	Primary road service area
	A road single/dual carriageway
	B road single/dual carriageway
	Other road single/dual carriageway
	Minor/private road, access may be restricted
← ←	One-way street
	Pedestrian area
	Track or footpath
	Road under construction
	Road tunnel
P	Parking
P+	Park & Ride
	Bus/coach station
	Railway & main railway station
	Railway & minor railway station
⊖	Underground station
⊖	Light railway & station
	Preserved private railway

LC	Level crossing
	Tramway
	Ferry route
	Airport runway
	County, administrative boundary
	Mounds
93	Page continuation 1:15,000
7	Page continuation to enlarged scale 1:10,000
	River/canal, lake
	Aqueduct, lock, weir
465 ▲ Winter Hill	Peak (with height in metres)
	Beach
	Woodland
	Park
	Cemetery
	Built-up area
	Industrial/business building
	Leisure building
	Retail building
	Other building
IKEA	IKEA store

Symbol	Description	Symbol	Description
	City wall		Castle
A&E	Hospital with 24-hour A&E department		Historic house or building
PO	Post Office	Wakehurst Place (NTS)	National Trust property
	Public library	M	Museum or art gallery
i	Tourist Information Centre		Roman antiquity
i	Seasonal Tourist Information Centre		Ancient site, battlefield or monument
	Petrol station, 24 hour Major suppliers only		Industrial interest
†	Church/chapel		Garden
	Public toilets		Garden Centre Garden Centre Association Member
	Toilet with disabled facilities		Garden Centre Wyevale Garden Centre
PH	Public house AA recommended		Arboretum
	Restaurant AA inspected		Farm or animal centre
Madeira Hotel	Hotel AA inspected		Zoological or wildlife collection
	Theatre or performing arts centre		Bird collection
	Cinema		Nature reserve
	Golf course		Aquarium
▲	Camping AA inspected	V	Visitor or heritage centre
	Caravan site AA inspected		Country park
	Camping & caravan site AA inspected		Cave
	Theme park		Windmill
	Abbey, cathedral or priory		Distillery, brewery or vineyard

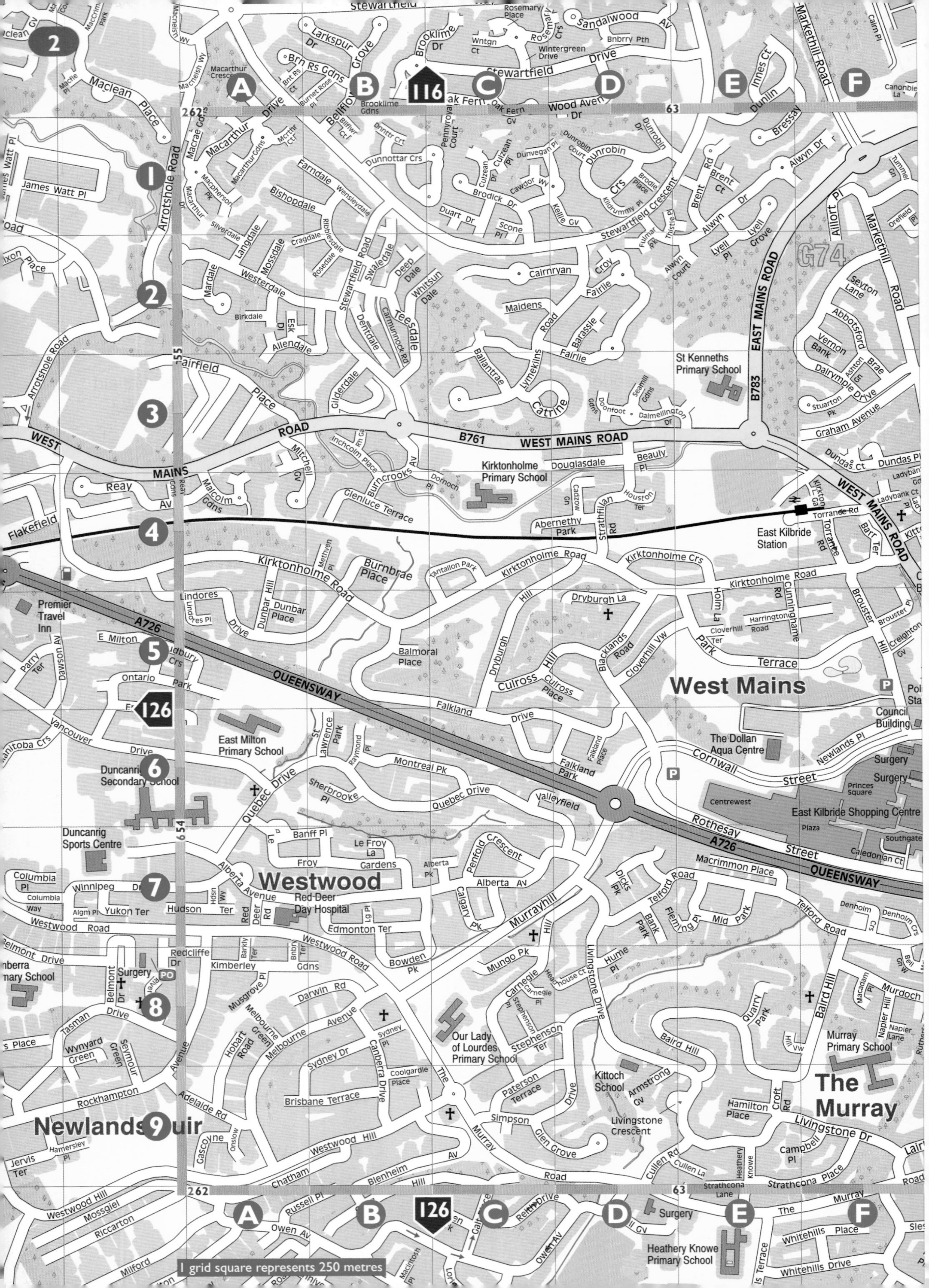

2
116
126
A
B
C
D
E
F
1
2
3
4
5
6
7
8
9
262
63
G74
West Mains
Westwood
Newlandsmuir
The Murray
WEST MAINS ROAD
B761
B783
EAST MAINS ROAD
A726
QUEENSWAY
Stewartfield Drive
Arrotshole Road
Maclean Place
James Watt Pl
Kirktonholme Road
Kirktonholme Primary School
St Kenneths Primary School
East Kilbride Station
East Milton Primary School
Duncanrig Secondary School
Duncanrig Sports Centre
Premier Travel Inn
The Dollan Aqua Centre
Council Building
East Kilbride Shopping Centre
Centrewest
Princes Square
Plaza
Southgate
Cornwall Street
Rothesay Street
Red Deer Day Hospital
Our Lady of Lourdes Primary School
Kittoch School
Murray Primary School
Heathery Knowe Primary School
Surgery
Westwood Road
Westwood Hill
Livingstone Drive
Murray Road
Falkland Drive
Quebec Drive
Alberta Avenue
Telford Road
Baird Hill
Strathcona Place
1 grid square represents 250 metres

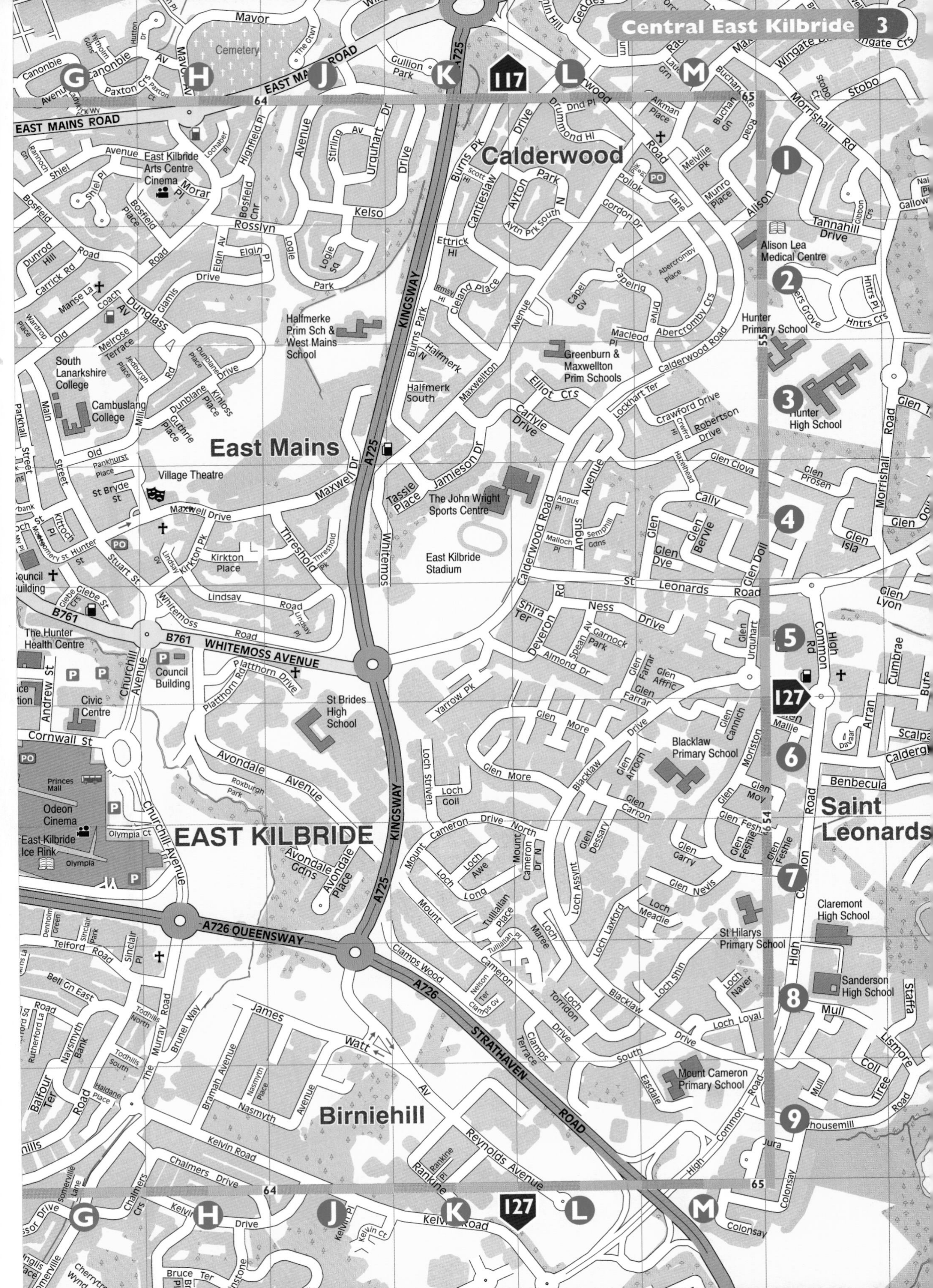
Central East Kilbride
3
Calderwood
East Mains
EAST KILBRIDE
Birniehill
Saint Leonards
Cemetery
East Kilbride Arts Centre Cinema
Halfmerke Prim Sch & West Mains School
South Lanarkshire College
Cambuslang College
Village Theatre
Greenburn & Maxwellton Prim Schools
The John Wright Sports Centre
East Kilbride Stadium
Alison Lea Medical Centre
Hunter Primary School
Hunter High School
The Hunter Health Centre
Council Building
Civic Centre
St Brides High School
Blacklaw Primary School
Princes Mall
Odeon Cinema
East Kilbride Ice Rink
Olympia
Claremont High School
St Hilarys Primary School
Sanderson High School
Mount Cameron Primary School
EAST MAINS ROAD
KINGSWAY
A725
A726 QUEENSWAY
A726
STRATHAVEN ROAD
B761
WHITEMOSS AVENUE
Calderwood Road
St Leonards Road
Maxwell Drive
Avondale Avenue
Churchill Avenue
Cornwall St
Kelvin Road
Reynolds Avenue
Chalmers Drive
Morrishall Rd
Tannahill Drive
Blacklaw Drive
High Common Road
Mount Cameron Drive North
Whitemoss Road
Lindsay Road
Rosslyn
Kelso
Old Coach Rd
Main Street
Telford Road
James Watt Av
Nasmyth Road
Brunel Way
Bramah Avenue
Alison Lea
Glen Clova
Ness Drive
64
65
117
127
G
H
J
K
L
M
1
2
3
4
5
6
7
8
9

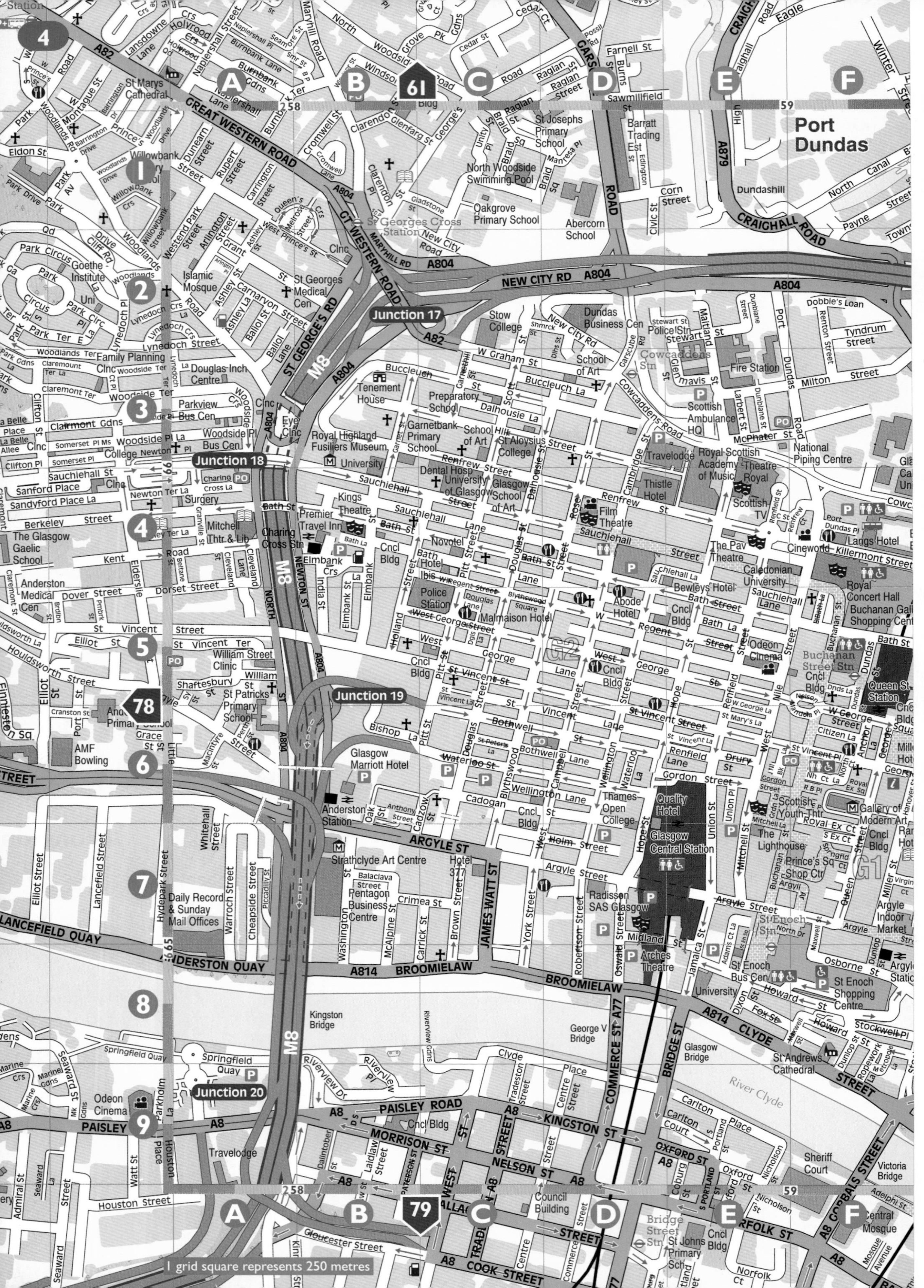

4
A
B
61
C
D
E
F
258
59
Port Dundas
1
2
3
4
5
6
7
8
9
78
79
GREAT WESTERN ROAD
A82
A804
A879
A8
A814
A77
M8
St Marys Cathedral
St Josephs Primary School
Barratt Trading Est
North Woodside Swimming Pool
Oakgrove Primary School
Abercorn School
Dundashill
CRAIGHALL ROAD
St Georges Cross Station
NEW CITY RD
Goethe Institute
Uni
Islamic Mosque
St Georges Medical Cen
Junction 17
ST GEORGE'S RD
Stow College
Dundas Business Cen
Police Stn
Fire Station
Cowcaddens Stn
Family Planning Clnc
Douglas Inch Centre
Tenement House
Preparatory School
School of Art
Scottish Ambulance HQ
National Piping Centre
Parkview Bus Cen
Woodside Pl Bus Cen
Junction 18
Royal Highland Fusiliers Museum
University
Garnetbank Primary School
St Aloysius College
Travelodge
Royal Scottish Academy of Music
Theatre Royal
Dental Hosp University of Glasgow
Glasgow School of Art
Thistle Hotel
Scottish TV
Film Theatre
Surgery
Mitchell Thtr & Lib
The Glasgow Gaelic School
Premier Travel Inn
Kings Theatre
Charing Cross Stn
Elmbank Crs
Novotel
Bath Hotel
Ibis
Cncl Bldg
The Pav Theatre
Cineworld
Langs Hotel
Caledonian University
Royal Concert Hall
Buchanan Galleries Shopping Centre
Anderston Medical Cen
Police Station
Malmaison Hotel
Abode Hotel
Bewleys Hotel
Odeon Cinema
Buchanan Street Stn
Queen St Station
William Street Clinic
St Patricks Primary School
Junction 19
AMF Bowling
Glasgow Marriott Hotel
Anderston Station
Quality Hotel
Glasgow Central Station
Thames Open College
Scottish Youth Thtr
Gallery of Modern Art
The Lighthouse
Prince's Sq Shop Ctr
Strathclyde Art Centre
Hotel 377
ARGYLE ST
JAMES WATT ST
Daily Record & Sunday Mail Offices
Pentagon Business Centre
Radisson SAS Glasgow
Midland
Arches Theatre
St Enoch Stn
Argyle Indoor Market
LANCEFIELD QUAY
ANDERSTON QUAY
BROOMIELAW
St Enoch Bus Cen
St Enoch Shopping Centre
University
Kingston Bridge
George V Bridge
Glasgow Bridge
St Andrews Cathedral
CLYDE STREET
River Clyde
Junction 20
Odeon Cinema
PAISLEY ROAD
KINGSTON ST
MORRISON ST
NELSON ST
COMMERCE ST
BRIDGE ST
Travelodge
Council Building
Sheriff Court
Victoria Bridge
Central Mosque
Bridge Street Stn
St Johns Primary Sch
Cncl Bldg
COOK STREET
NORFOLK ST
1 grid square represents 250 metres

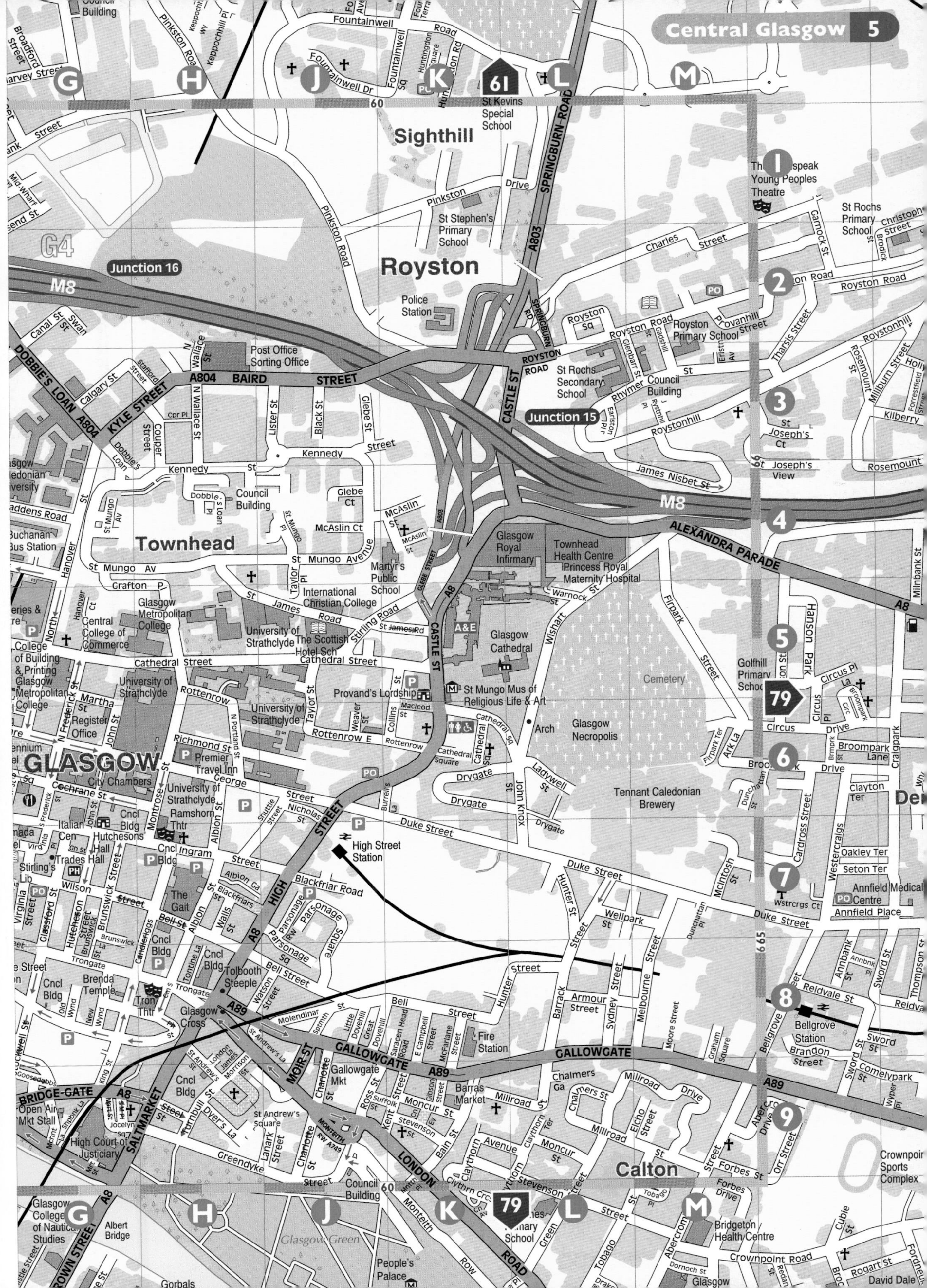

Central Glasgow
5
Sighthill
Royston
Townhead
GLASGOW
Calton
Glasgow Green
Gorbals
St Kevins Special School
Pinkston Drive
Springburn Road
A803
St Stephen's Primary School
Pinkston Road
Police Station
Junction 16
M8
Post Office Sorting Office
A804 Baird Street
Kyle Street
Dobbie's Loan
Castle St
Royston Road
St Rochs Secondary School
Council Building
Junction 15
Roystonhill
James Nisbet St
The Platform Young Peoples Theatre
St Rochs Primary School
Charles Street
Garnock St
Royston Primary School
Tharsis Street
Rosemount St
Millburn Street
Kilberry
St Joseph's Ct
St Joseph's View
Alexandra Parade
Glasgow Royal Infirmary
Townhead Health Centre
Princess Royal Maternity Hospital
Glasgow Caledonian University
Buchanan Bus Station
Council Building
McAslin Ct
St Mungo Avenue
Martyr's Public School
International Christian College
Glasgow Metropolitan College
Central College of Commerce
University of Strathclyde
The Scottish Hotel Sch
St James Road
Stirling Road
Cathedral Street
Glasgow Cathedral
A&E
Provand's Lordship
St Mungo Mus of Religious Life & Art
Glasgow Necropolis
Cemetery
Firpark Street
Golfhill Primary School
Hanson Park
Circus Drive
Broompark Drive
Tennant Caledonian Brewery
College of Building & Printing
Register Office
Premier Travel Inn
City Chambers
George Street
Duke Street
High Street Station
Ramshorn Thtr
Italian Cen
Hutchesons' Hall
Trades Hall
Stirling's Lib
Ingram Street
The Gait
Blackfriar Road
Trongate
Tolbooth Steeple
Tron Thtr
Glasgow Cross
Brenda Temple
A89 Gallowgate
Gallowgate Mkt
Barras Market
Fire Station
Bell Street
Moir St
London Road
Saltmarket
High Court of Justiciary
Bridge-Gate
Open Air Mkt Stall
St Andrew's Square
Council Building
Bellgrove Station
Annfield Medical Centre
Annfield Place
Crownpoint Sports Complex
Bridgeton Health Centre
Crownpoint Road
Glasgow College of Nautical Studies
Albert Bridge
People's Palace
Greendyke
Millroad Drive
Abercromby Drive
Forbes Drive
Westercraigs
Cardross Street

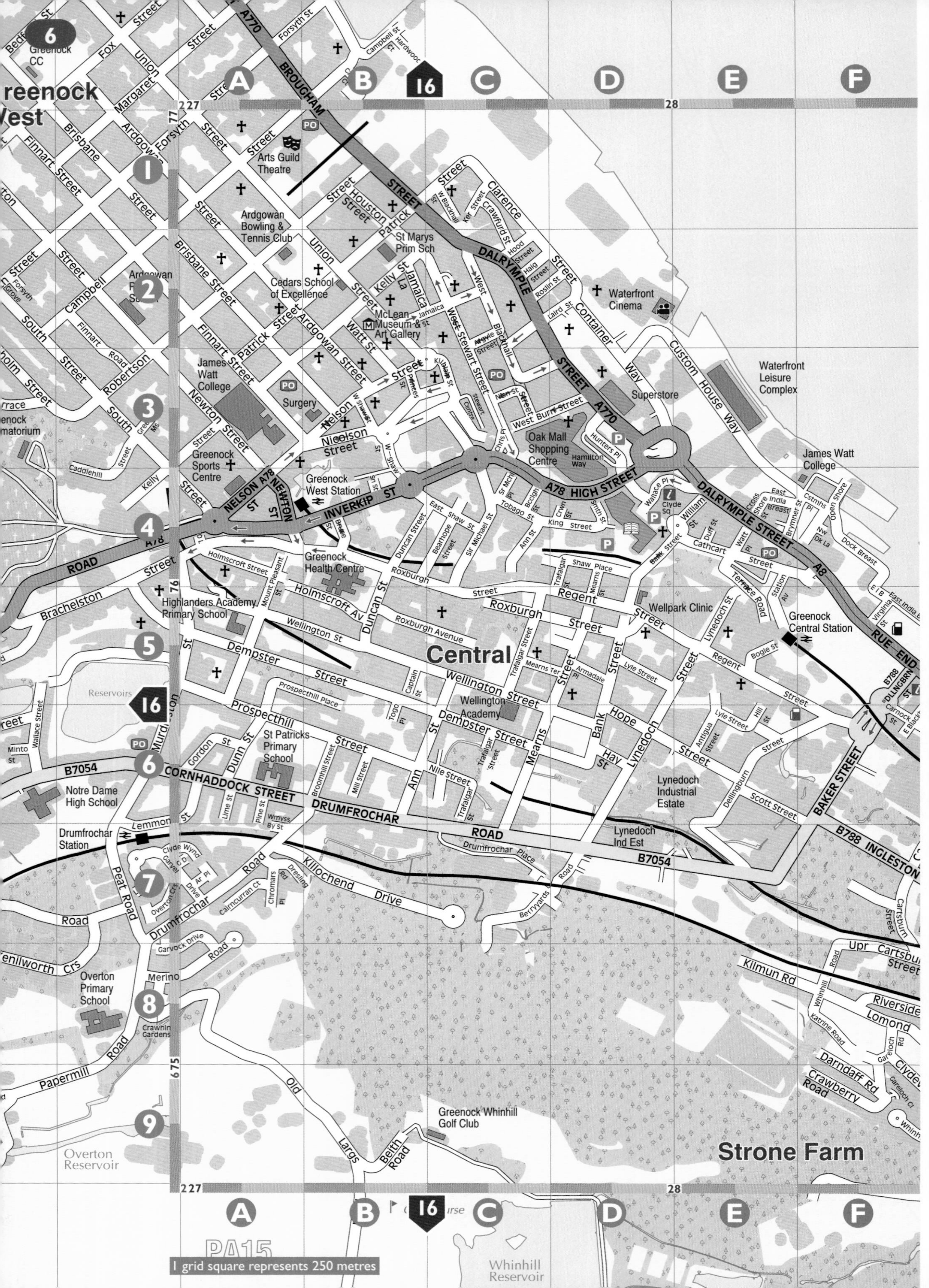
6
Greenock West
Greenock CC
A
B
16
C
D
E
F
227
28
1
2
3
4
5
6
7
8
9
76
77
675
A770
BROUGHAM STREET
DALRYMPLE STREET
Arts Guild Theatre
Ardgowan Bowling & Tennis Club
St Marys Prim Sch
Cedars School of Excellence
McLean Museum & Art Gallery
James Watt College
Surgery
Greenock Sports Centre
Greenock West Station
NELSON A78
NEWTON ST
INVERKIP ST
A78 HIGH STREET
Oak Mall Shopping Centre
Hamilton Way
Waterfront Cinema
Waterfront Leisure Complex
Superstore
Custom House Way
Container Way
James Watt College
Greenock Central Station
Wellpark Clinic
Greenock Health Centre
Highlanders Academy Primary School
Central
Wellington Academy
St Patricks Primary School
Notre Dame High School
B7054
CORNHADDOCK STREET
DRUMFROCHAR ROAD
Drumfrochar Station
Lynedoch Industrial Estate
Lynedoch Ind Est
BAKER STREET
B788 INGLESTON
RUE END
A8
Overton Primary School
Reservoirs
16
Greenock Whinhill Golf Club
Strone Farm
Overton Reservoir
Whinhill Reservoir
PA15
1 grid square represents 250 metres
Brachelston Street
Holmscroft Street
Roxburgh Street
Regent Street
Wellington Street
Dempster Street
Prospecthill Street
Kilmun Rd
Papermill Road
Peat Road
Old Largs Road
Belth Road
Killochend Drive
Kenilworth Crs
Upr Cartsburn Street

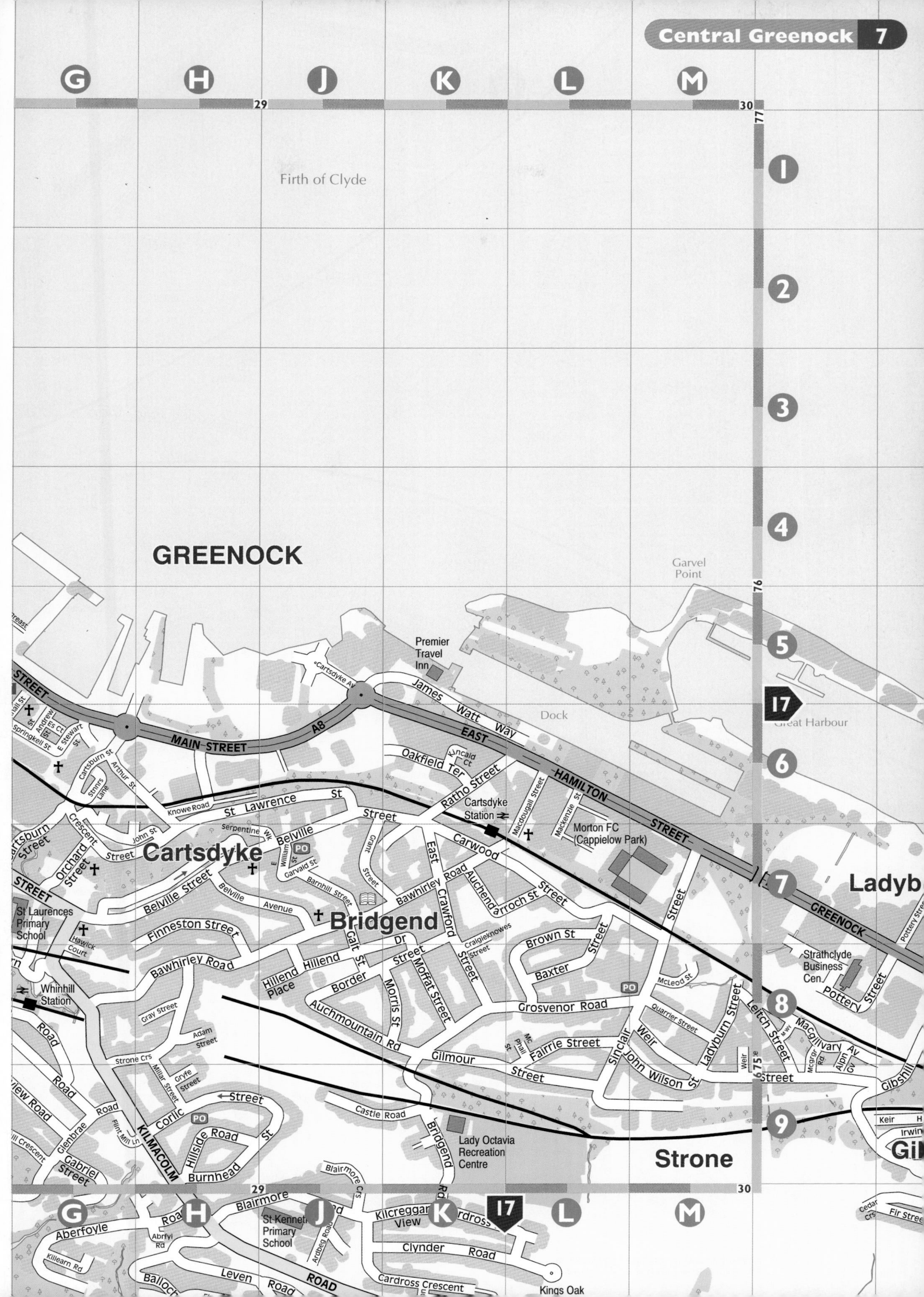

G H J K L M

Firth of Clyde

GREENOCK

Garvel
Point

Premier
Travel
Inn

James Watt Way

Dock

EAST

Great Harbour

Cartsdyke Av

Oakfield Ter

Kincaid
Ct

Ratho Street

Cartsdyke
Station

HAMILTON

STREET

Macdougall Street

Mackenzie St

Morton FC
(Cappielow Park)

STREET

MAIN STREET

A8

Knowe Road

St Lawrence St

Street

Street

Cartsburn
Crescent

Orchard
Street

John St

Cartsdyke

Belville
William
Garvald St

Serpentine Wk

Belville Street

Belville
Avenue

Barnhill Street

PO

Grant Street

East
Crawford Street
Bawhirley Road

Carwood
Auchenarroch St

Street

Ladyb

Cartsburn
Street

STREET

St Laurences
Primary
School

Hawick
Court

Finneston Street

Bridgend

Craigieknowes
Street

Brown St

Baxter
Street

McLeod St

PO

Bawhirley Road

Hillend
Place

Hillend
Border

Galt St

Moffat Street

Dr

Morris St

Street

Grosvenor Road

Quarrier Street

Sinclair St

Ladyburn Street

Leitch Street

Strathclyde
Business
Cen

Pottery Street

MacGillivray Av

Whinhill
Station

Gray Street

Adam
Street

Gryfe Street

Strone Crs

Millar Street

Auchmountain Rd

Fairlie Street

Gilmour
Street

John Wilson St

Weir St

MacGr
Av

Albn
Gv

Gibshill

View Road

Road

Road

KILMACOLM

Corlic
St

Hillside Road

Flint Mill Lane

PO

Street

Castle Road

Bridgend Rd

Lady Octavia
Recreation
Centre

Strone

Weir
Street

Gil

Keir
Irwin

Glenbrae

Gabriel
Street

Burnhead

Aberfoyle

Blairmore Crs

Blairmore
Road

St Kenneth
Primary
School

Abrfyl
Rd

Ardbeg Road

Kilcreggan
View

Ardross

17

Cedar
Crs

Fir Stree

Killearn Rd

Leven Road

ROAD

Clynder Road

Cardross Crescent

Kings Oak

G H J K L M

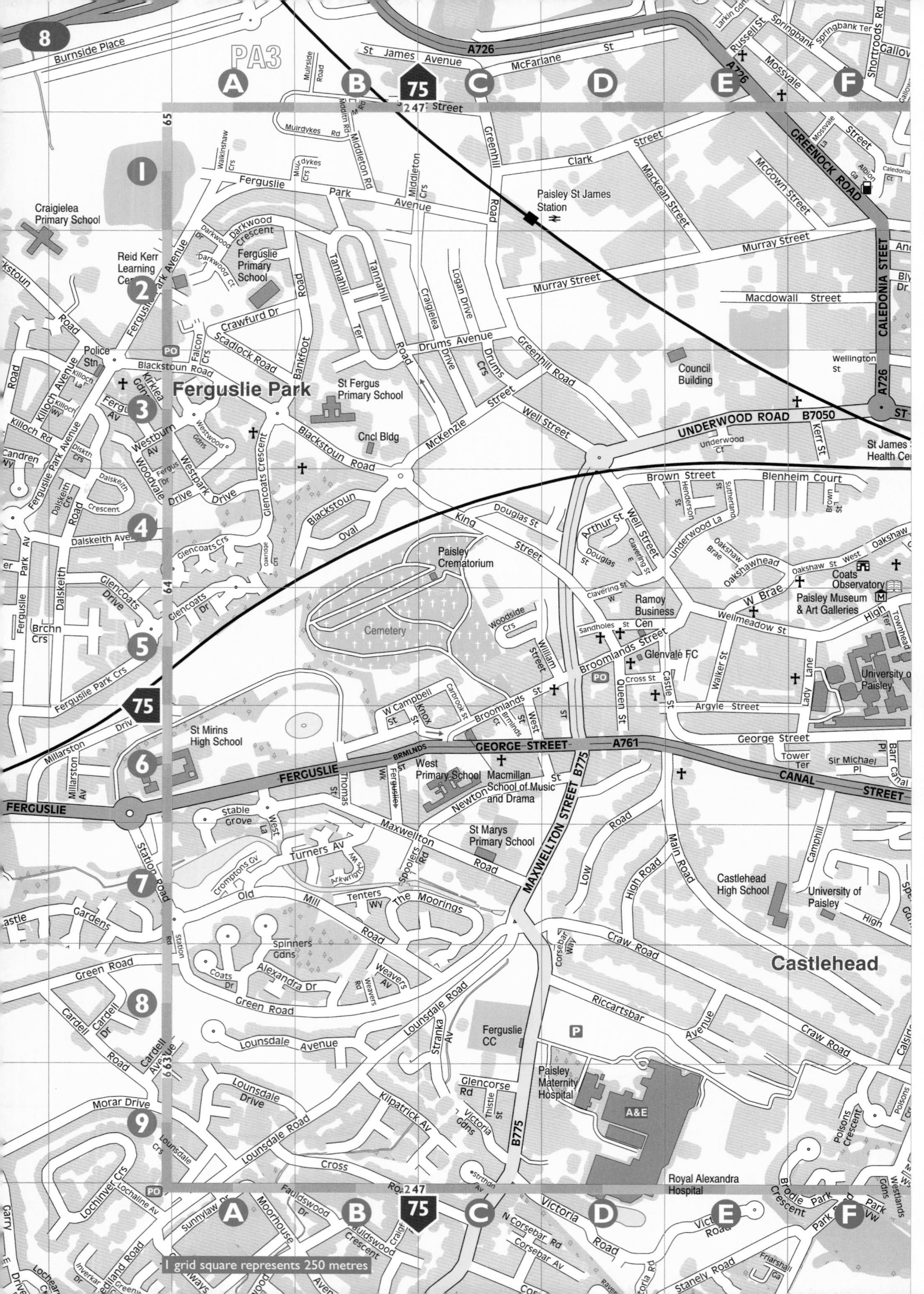

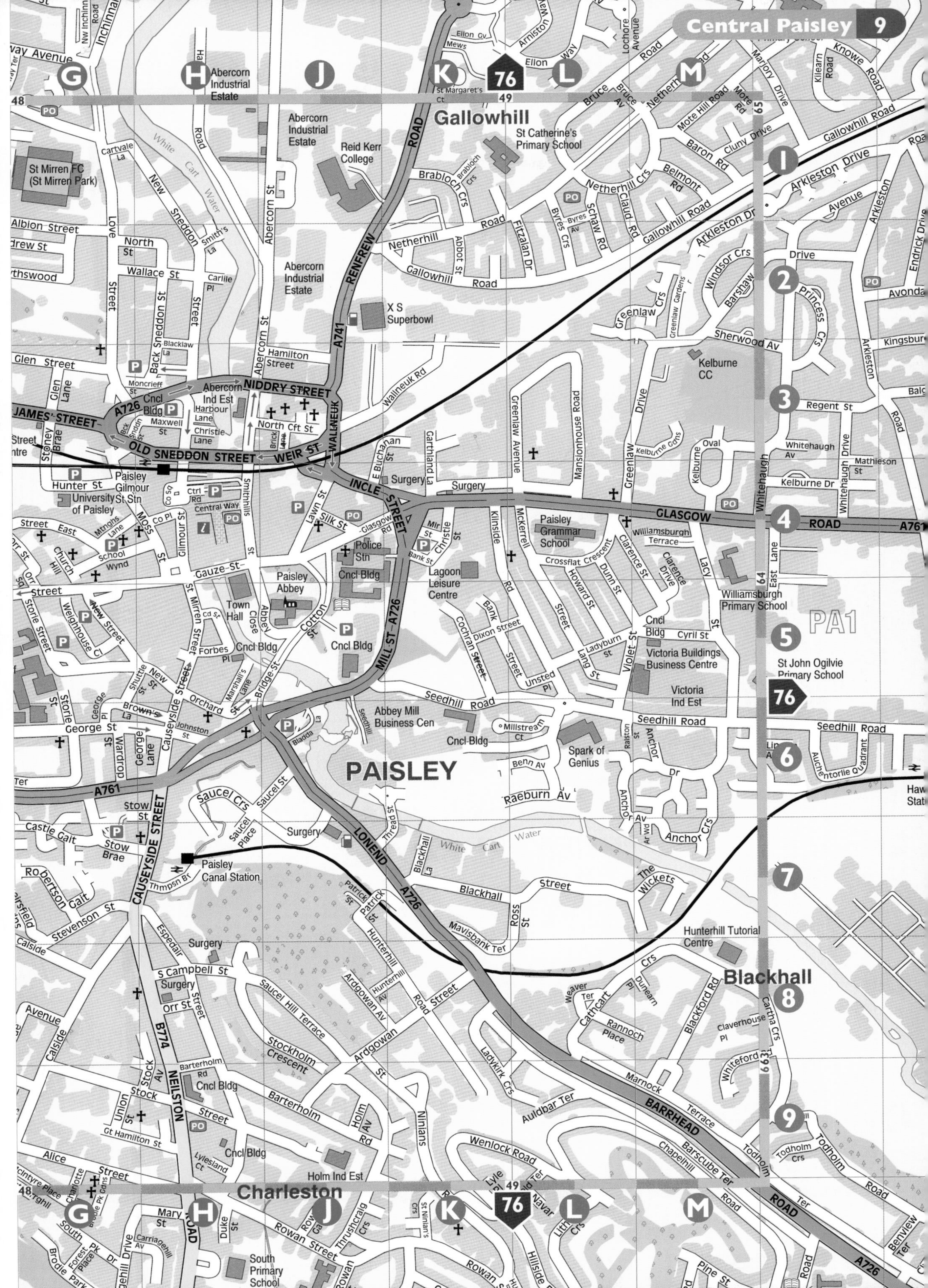
Gallowhill
Abercorn Industrial Estate
Reid Kerr College
St Catherine's Primary School
St Mirren FC (St Mirren Park)
White Cart Water
X S Superbowl
Hamilton Street
Niddry Street
Old Sneddon Street
Weir St
Wallneuk
Incle Street
Paisley Gilmour St Stn
University of Paisley
Central Way
Police Stn
Cncl Bldg
Paisley Abbey
Town Hall
Lagoon Leisure Centre
Paisley Grammar School
Kelburne CC
Glasgow Road
A761
A726
A741
Renfrew Road
Mill St
Williamsburgh Primary School
St John Ogilvie Primary School
PA1
Victoria Buildings Business Centre
Victoria Ind Est
Seedhill Road
Abbey Mill Business Cen
Spark of Genius
PAISLEY
Lonend
Paisley Canal Station
Causeyside Street
Blackhall Street
Hunterhill Tutorial Centre
Blackhall
Barrhead Road
Neilston Road
B774
Holm Ind Est
Charleston
South Primary School
Gallowhill Road
Arkleston Drive
Netherhill Road
Whitehaugh
Saucel Hill Terrace
Stockholm Crescent
Ardgowan St
Wenlock Road
Rowan Street
76
48
49

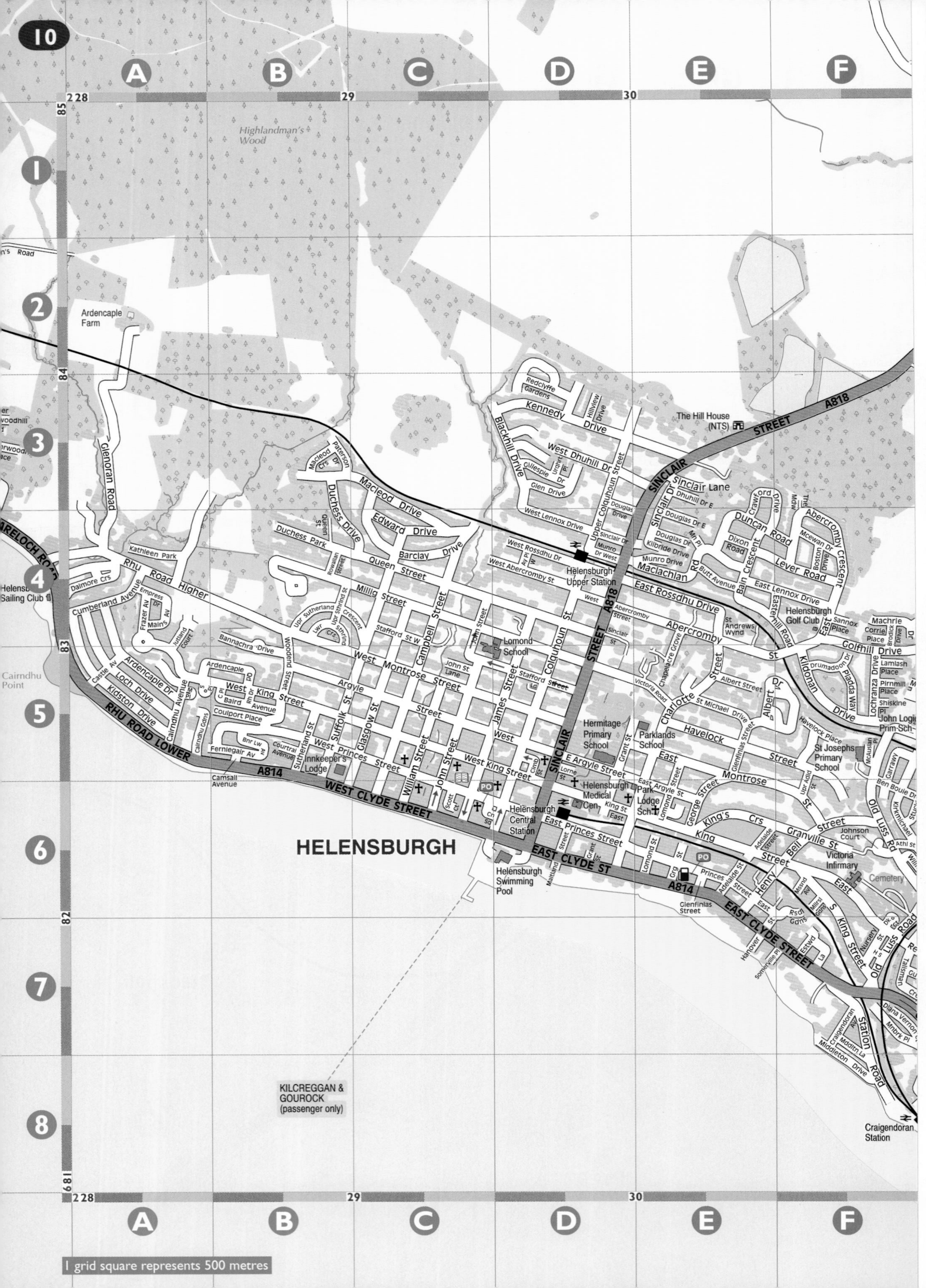
A
B
C
D
E
F
228
29
30
85
84
83
82
681
1
2
3
4
5
6
7
8
Highlandman's Wood
Ardencapple Farm
Glenoran Road
Kathleen Park
Rhu Road Higher
Dalmore Crs
Cumberland Avenue
Helensburgh Sailing Club
Cairndhu Point
Castle Av
Ardencaple Dr
Loch Drive
Kidston Drive
RHU ROAD LOWER
Cairndhu Avenue
Coulport Place
Ferniegair Av
Camsail Avenue
Courtrai Avenue
Sutherland St
West Princes Street
Innkeeper's Lodge
A814
WEST CLYDE STREET
HELENSBURGH
Macleod Drive
Duchess Drive
Edward Drive
Barclay Drive
Duchess Park
Queen Street
Millig Street
Campbell Street
Stafford St W
West Montrose Street
Argyle Street
Suffolk St
Glasgow St
William Street
John Street
West King Street
James Street
Colquhoun St
Lomond School
Bannachra Drive
Woodend Street
West King Street
Blackhill Drive
Kennedy Drive
Redclyffe Gardens
Hillview Drive
West Dhuhill Dr
Glen Drive
West Lennox Drive
Upper Colquhoun Street
West Rossdhu Dr
West Abercromby St
Helensburgh Upper Station
SINCLAIR STREET
A818
The Hill House (NTS)
Sinclair Lane
Duncan Road
Abercromby Crescent
Lever Road
Maclachlan Rd
Munro Drive
Kilbride Drive
East Rossdhu Drive
Abercromby Street
East Lennox Drive
Helensburgh Golf Club
Golfhill Drive
Kidonan Drive
Charlotte Street
Albert Street
Hermitage Primary School
Parklands School
Havelock Street
E Argyle Street
East Montrose Street
Helensburgh Medical Cen.
Park Lodge Sch.
Helensburgh Central Station
East Princes Street
EAST CLYDE ST
Helensburgh Swimming Pool
George Street
King Street
Granville St
Victoria Infirmary
St Josephs Primary School
John Logie Prim Sch
Old Luss Road
Cemetery
Glenfinlas Street
Adelaide St
Henry Bell Street
EAST CLYDE STREET
King Street
Station Road
Middleton Drive
Craigendoran Av
Craigendoran Station
KILCREGGAN & GOUROCK (passenger only)
1 grid square represents 500 metres

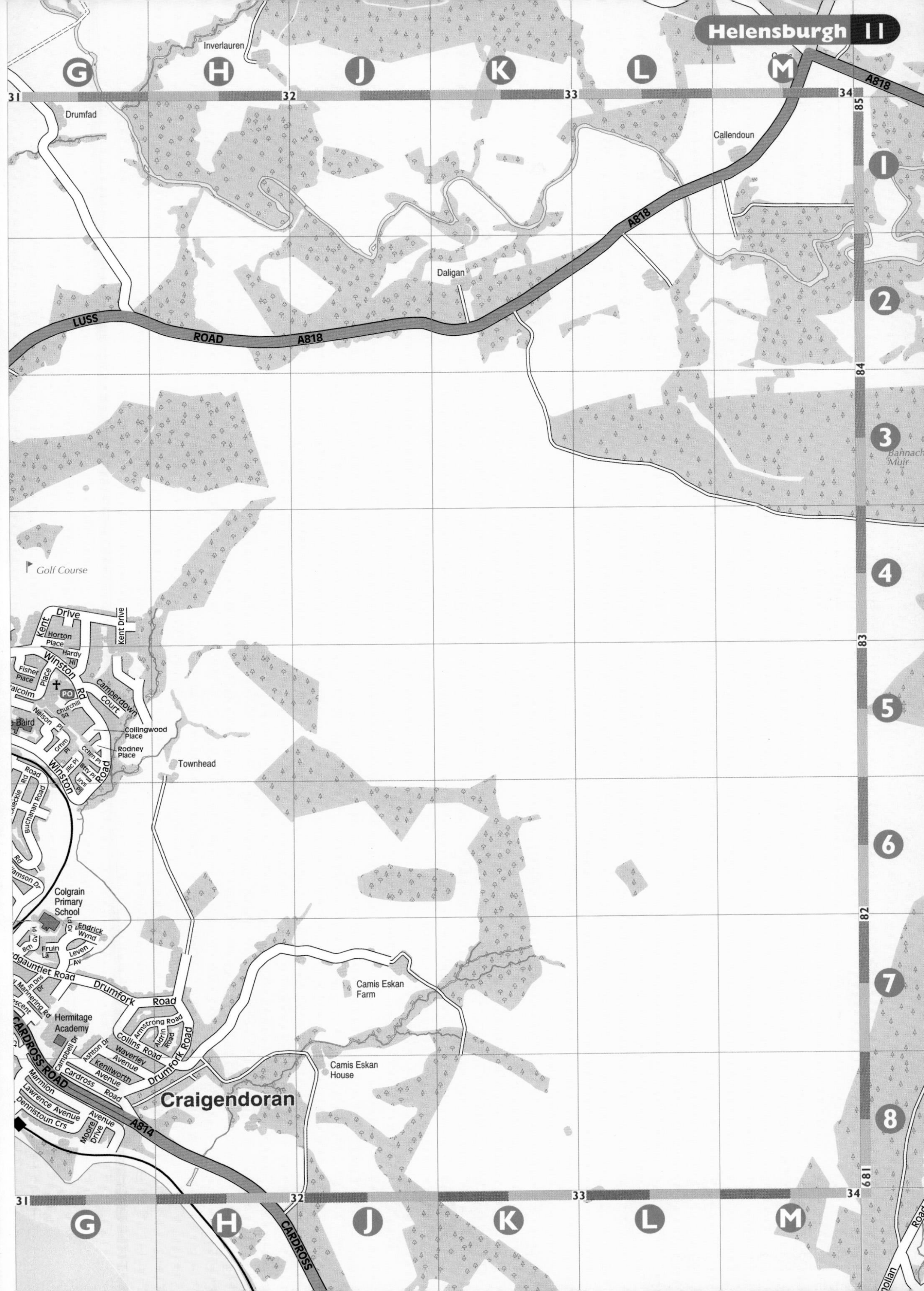

G H J K L M

Inverlauren

Drumfad

Callendoun

A818

1

Daligan

LUSS ROAD A818

2

84

3

Bannach Muir

Golf Course

4

83

Kent Drive

Horton Place
Hardy
Winston Rd   Kent Drive

Fisher Place

Camperdown Court

Malcolm

PO

Nelson Pl
Churchill Sq
Grimm Pl
Baird
Grimm Pl
Collingwood Place

Rodney Place

Townhead

5

Winston Road

6

82

Colgrain Primary School

Endrick Wynd

Fruin La
Leven
Av

7

Camis Eskan Farm

Drumfork Road

Hermitage Academy

Armstrong Road
Atorn Road
Collins Road
Waverley Avenue
Campbell Dr
Aston Dr
Kenilworth
Cardross Avenue
Cardross Road

Drumfork Road

Camis Eskan House

8

681

Lawrence Avenue
Marmion
Moore Drive
Dennistoun Crs

Craigendoran

A814

CARDROSS ROAD

G H J K L M

CARDROSS ROAD

31 32 33 34

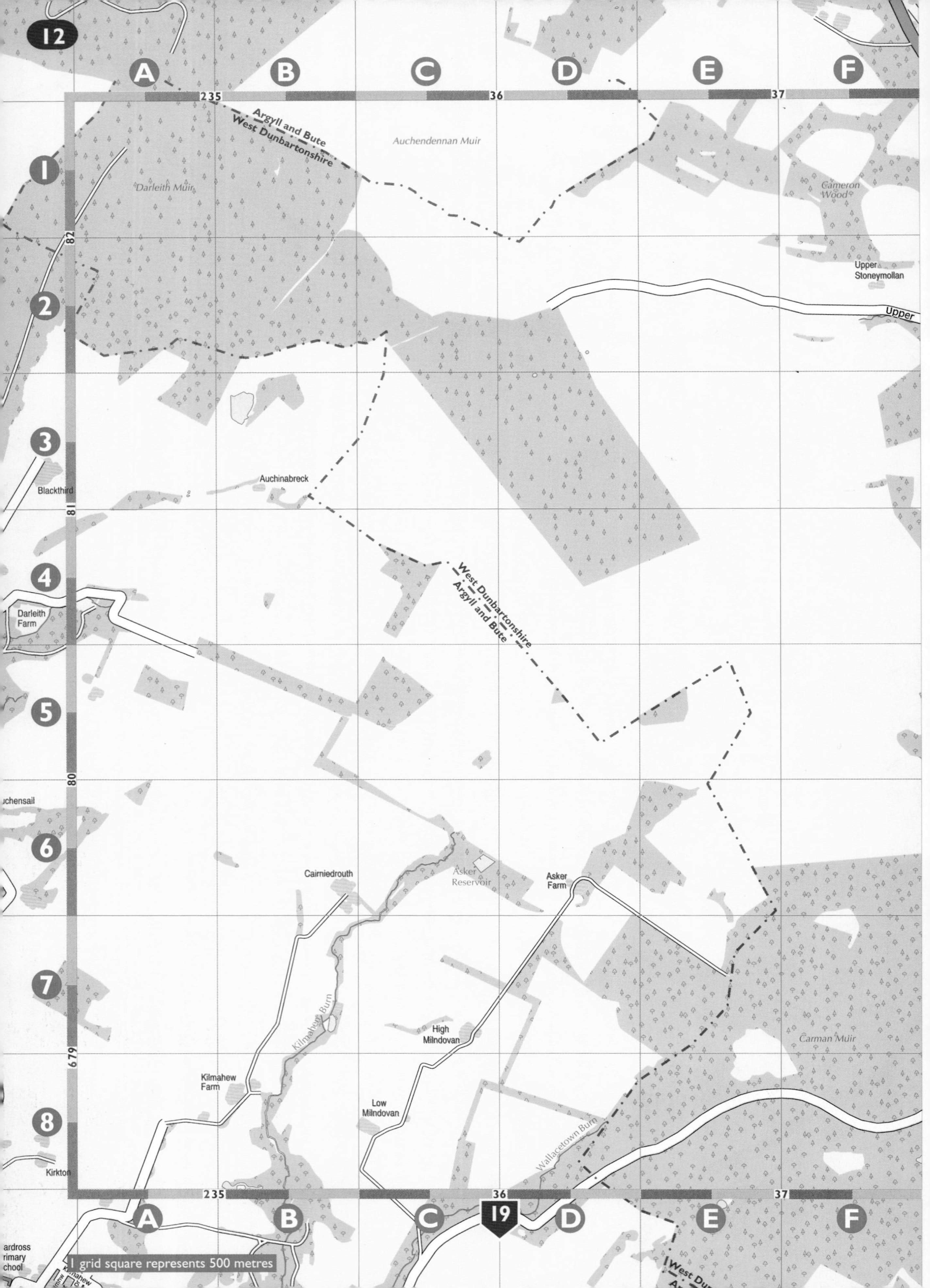

12

A   B   C   D   E   F

235   36   37

1

Argyll and Bute
West Dunbartonshire

Auchendennan Muir

Cameron
Wood

Darleith Muir

82

Upper
Stoneymollan

2

Upper

3

81

Blackthird

Auchinabreck

4

Darleith
Farm

West Dunbartonshire
Argyll and Bute

5

80

uchensail

6

Cairniedrouth

Asker
Reservoir

Asker
Farm

7

679

High
Milndovan

Carman Muir

Kilmahew Burn

Kilmahew
Farm

8

Low
Milndovan

Wallacetown Burn

Kirkton

235   36   37

A   B   C   19   D   E   F

ardross
rimary
chool

I grid square represents 500 metres

West Du
A

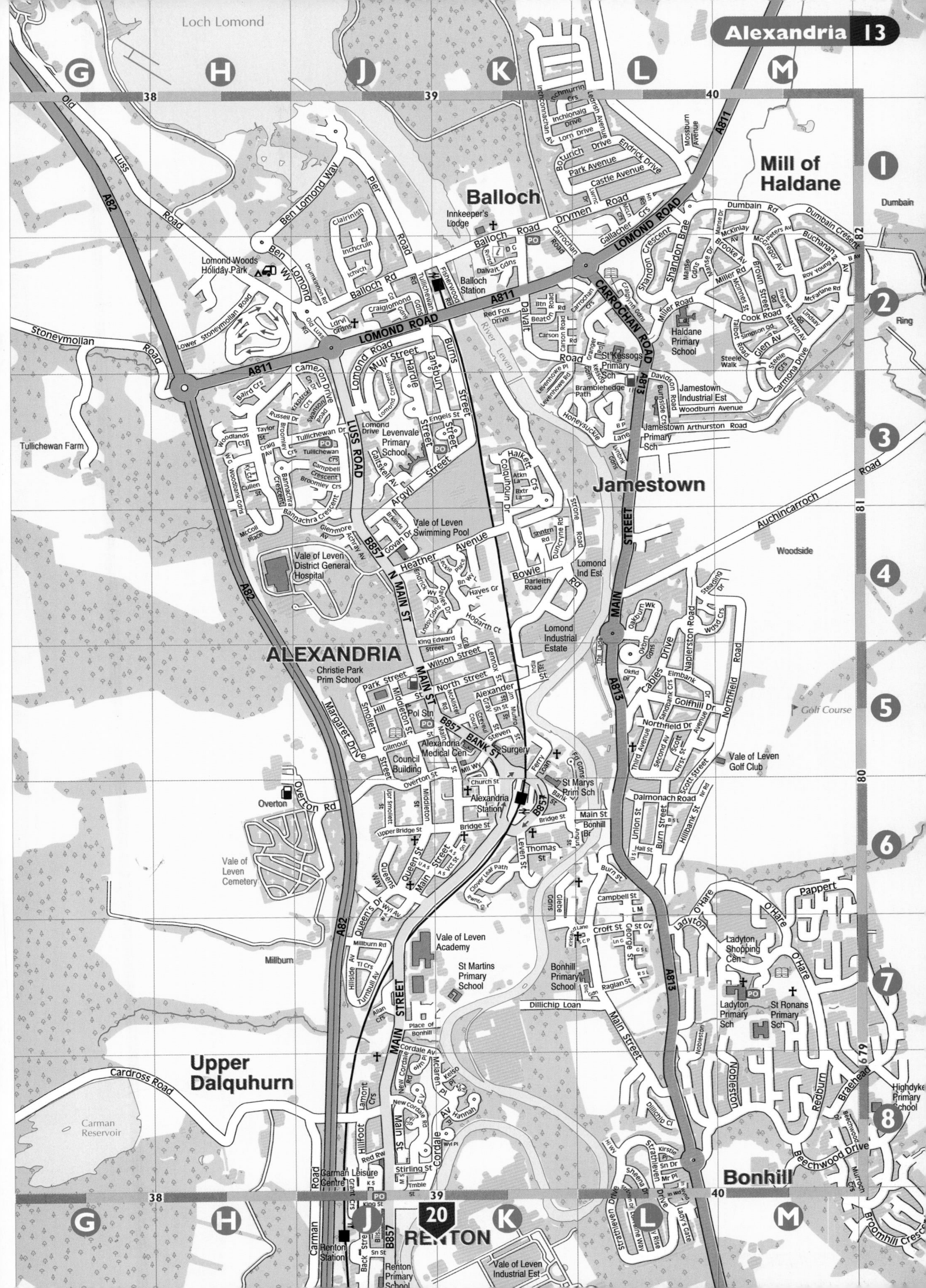
Loch Lomond
Balloch
Mill of Haldane
Dumbain
Ring
Innkeeper's Lodge
Balloch Station
Lomond Woods Holiday Park
LOMOND ROAD
A811
A82
A813
Haldane Primary School
St Kessogs Primary Sch
Jamestown Industrial Est
Jamestown Primary Sch
Jamestown
Tullichewan Farm
Levenvale Primary School
Vale of Leven Swimming Pool
Vale of Leven District General Hospital
Woodside
Lomond Ind Est
Lomond Industrial Estate
ALEXANDRIA
Christie Park Prim School
Pol Stn
Alexandria Medical Cen
Council Building
Surgery
Alexandria Station
St Marys Prim Sch
Golf Course
Vale of Leven Golf Club
Overton
Vale of Leven Cemetery
Vale of Leven Academy
St Martins Primary School
Bonhill Primary School
Ladyton Shopping Cen
Ladyton Primary Sch
St Ronans Primary Sch
Millburn
Upper Dalquhurn
Carman Reservoir
Carman Leisure Centre
Highdyke Primary School
Bonhill
RENTON
Renton Station
Renton Primary School
Vale of Leven Industrial Est
20

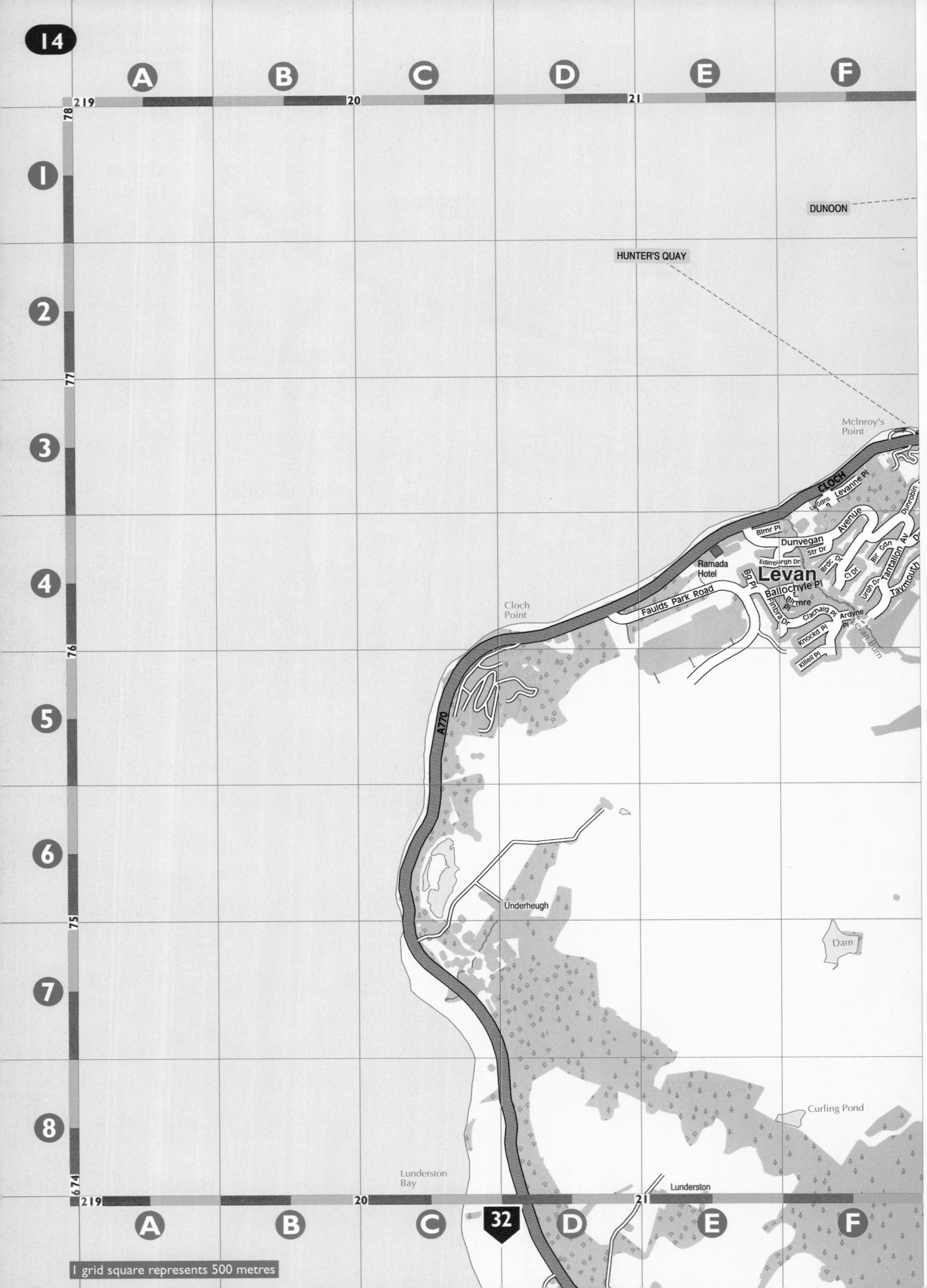

14

A　B　C　D　E　F

219
78

20

21

1

2

77

3

McInroy's
Point

CLOCH

Levanne Pl

La Gdns

Blmr Pl

76

4

Dunvegan

Ramada
Hotel

Cloch
Point

Faulds Park Road

Levan

Ballochyle Pl

Edinburgh Dr

Str Dr

Brdc Dr

Avenue

Dunrobin

Cl Dr

Tantallon AV

urgh Dr

Taymouth

Blmre

Pmbra Dr

Clachaig Pl

Ardyne

Knocka Pl

Levan Brun

Killelt Pl

5

A770

6

75

Underheugh

Dam

7

Curling Pond

8

674

Lunderston
Bay

Lunderston

219

20

21

32

A　B　C　D　E　F

HUNTER'S QUAY

I grid square represents 500 metres

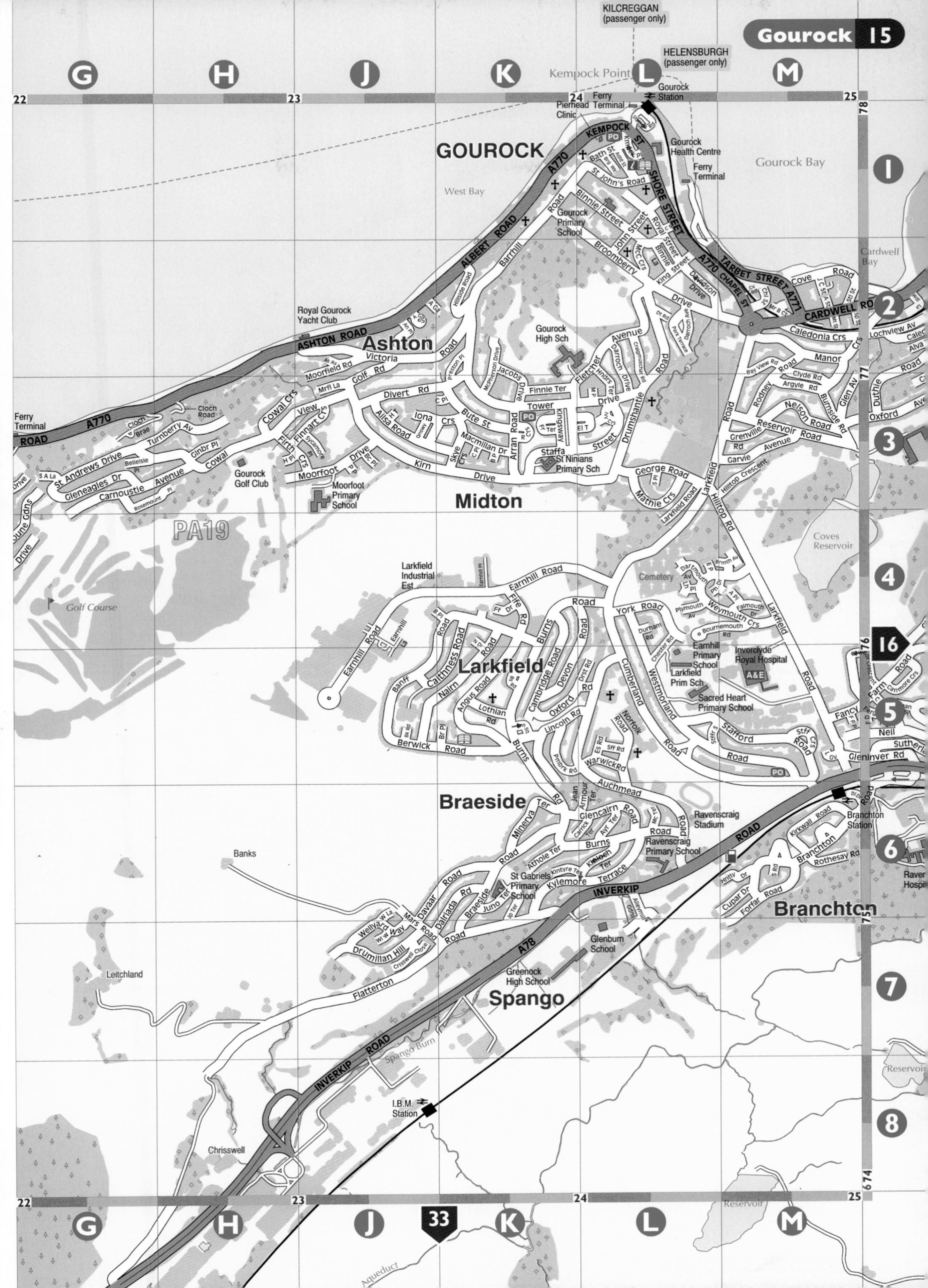

KILCREGGAN (passenger only)
HELENSBURGH (passenger only)
Kempock Point
Gourock Station
Ferry Terminal
Pierhead Clinic
GOUROCK
West Bay
Gourock Bay
Gourock Health Centre
Ferry Terminal
Cardwell Bay
Gourock Primary School
Royal Gourock Yacht Club
Ashton
Gourock High Sch
St Ninians Primary Sch
Gourock Golf Club
Moorfoot Primary School
Midton
PA19
Golf Course
Coves Reservoir
Cemetery
Larkfield Industrial Est
Larkfield
Earnhill Primary School
Larkfield Prim Sch
Inverclyde Royal Hospital
A&E
Sacred Heart Primary School
Braeside
Ravenscraig Stadium
Ravenscraig Primary School
St Gabriels Primary School
Branchton Station
Branchton
Banks
Glenburn School
Greenock High School
Spango
Leitchland
Spango Burn
I.B.M. Station
Chrisswell
Reservoir
Aqueduct
Ferry Terminal
ALBERT ROAD
ASHTON ROAD
CARDWELL ROAD
TARBET STREET A771
INVERKIP ROAD
A78
A770
16
33

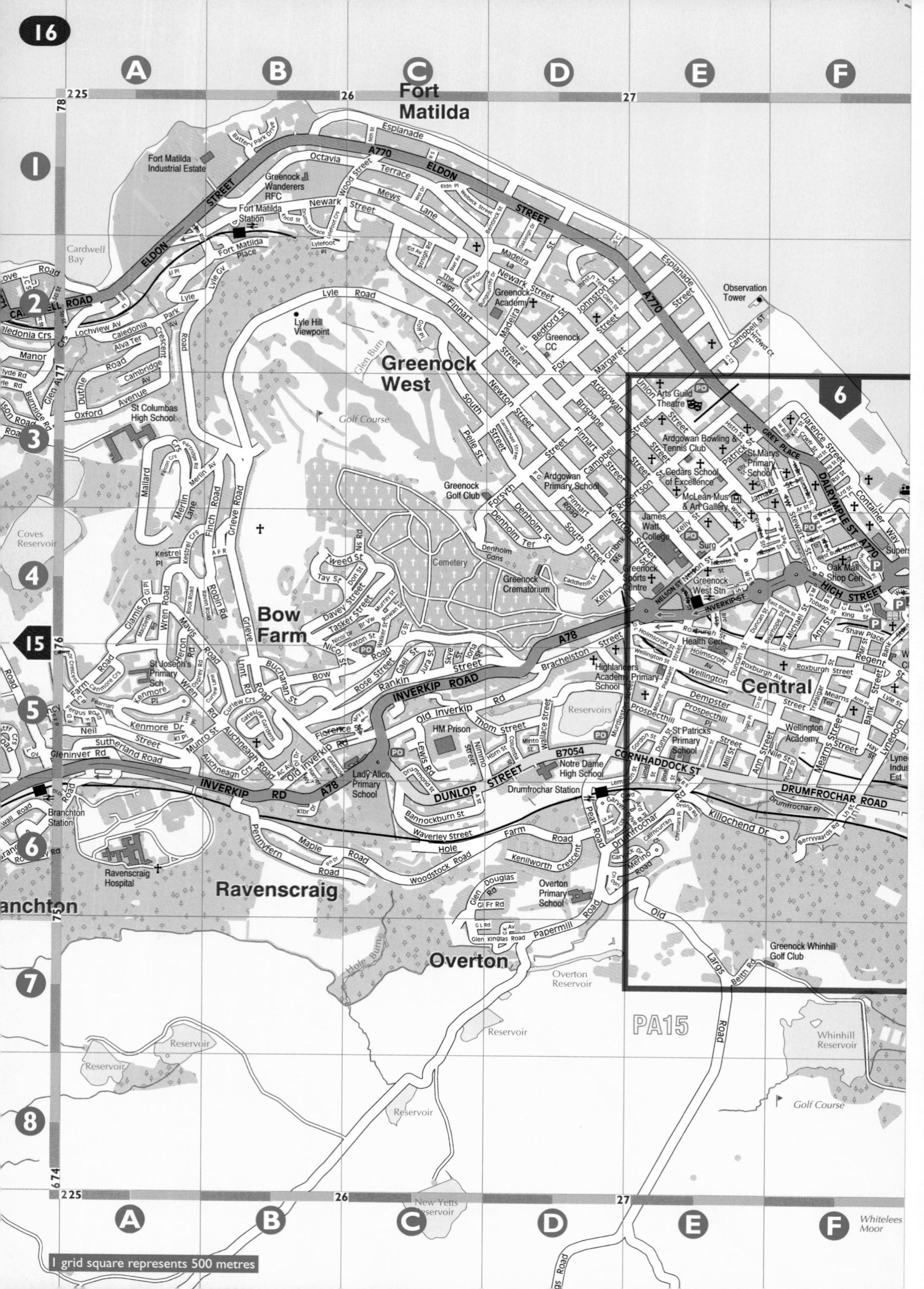
Fort Matilda
Greenock West
Bow Farm
Central
Ravenscraig
Overton
PA15
Fort Matilda Industrial Estate
Greenock Wanderers RFC
Fort Matilda Station
Cardwell Bay
Lyle Hill Viewpoint
Golf Course
Observation Tower
Arts Guild Theatre
Ardgowan Bowling & Tennis Club
St Marys Primary School
Cedars School of Excellence
McLean Mus & Art Gallery
James Watt College
Greenock Sports Centre
Greenock West Stn
Greenock Golf Club
Ardgowan Primary School
Greenock Academy
Greenock CC
Cemetery
Greenock Crematorium
St Columbas High School
Coves Reservoir
St Joseph's Primary Sch
HM Prison
Highlanders Academy Primary School
Reservoirs
Notre Dame High School
St Patricks Primary School
Wellington Academy
Health Cen
Oak Mall Shop Cen
Drumfrochar Station
Lady Alice Primary School
Branchton Station
Ravenscraig Hospital
Overton Primary School
Overton Reservoir
Greenock Whinhill Golf Club
Whinhill Reservoir
Reservoir
New Yetts Reservoir
Whitelees Moor
ELDON STREET
INVERKIP ROAD
INVERKIP RD
DUNLOP STREET
CORNHADDOCK ST
DRUMFROCHAR ROAD
DALRYMPLE ST
HIGH STREET
GREY PLACE
NELSON ST
A770
A78
B7054
1 grid square represents 500 metres

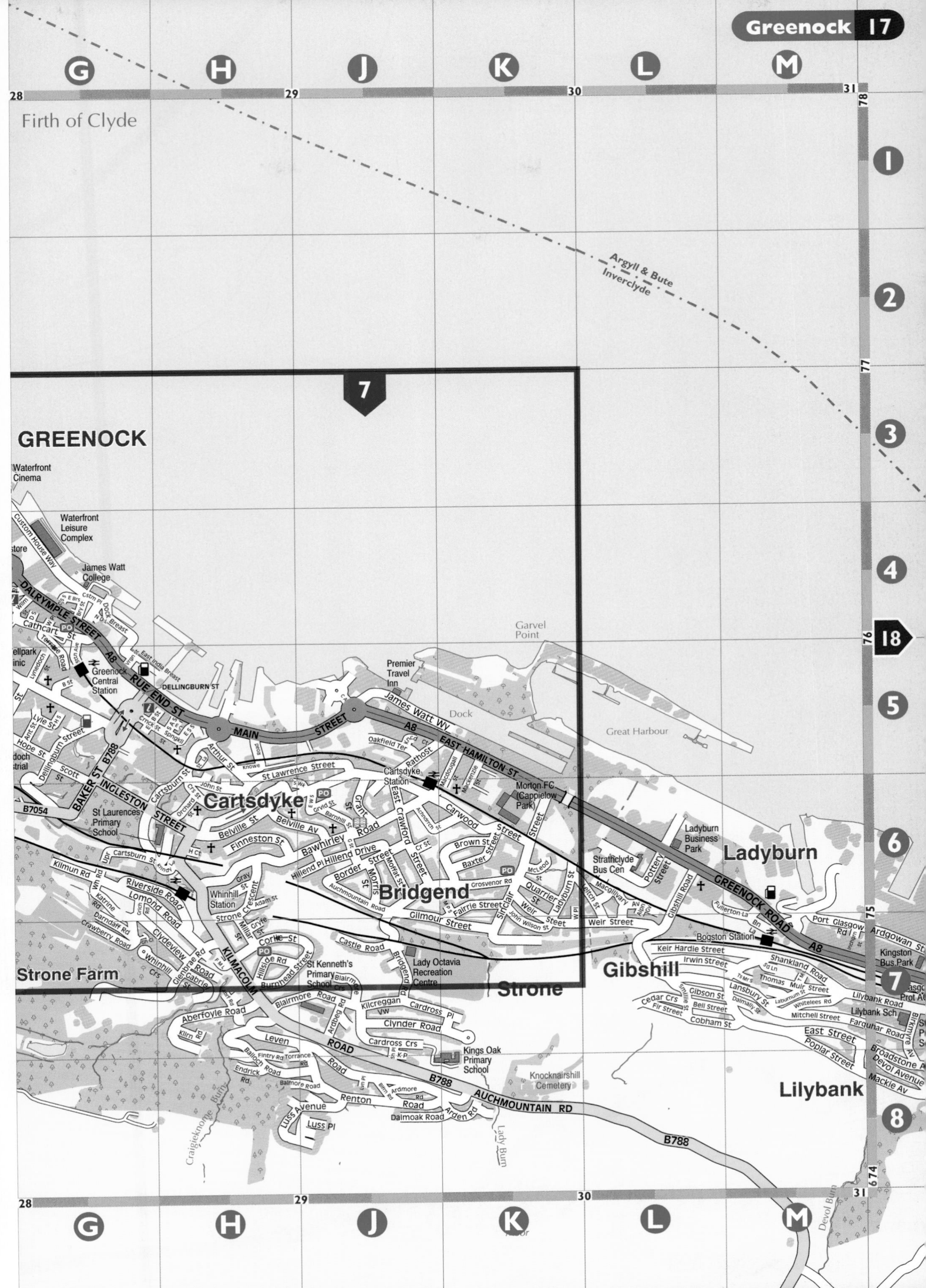

Firth of Clyde

G H J K L M

7

GREENOCK

Waterfront Cinema

Waterfront Leisure Complex

James Watt College

DALRYMPLE STREET

Cathcart

Bellpark Clinic

Greenock Central Station

RUE END ST

DELLINGBURN ST

Lyle St

Ant St

Hope St

Dellingburn Street

Scott St

BAKER ST

B788

INGLESTON STREET

B7054

St Laurences Primary School

Upr Cartsburn St

Cartsburn St

Orchard St

John St

H Ct

Kilmun Rd

Riverside Road

Lomond Road

Clydeview

Darnaff Rd

Crawberry Road

KILMACOLM

Strone Farm

Aberfoyle Road

Leven Road

Luss Avenue
Luss Pl

Craigieknowe Burn

Ballloch Road

Endrick Rd

Balmore Road

Fintry Rd

Torrance Rd

Renton Road

Ardmore Rd

Daimaok Road

Arden Rd

Cartsdyke

MAIN STREET

Arthur St

Crick St

St Lawrence street

Belville St
Belville Av

Finneston St

Bawhirley

Hiliend Pl

Whinhill Station

Strone Crescent

Corlic St

Castle Road

St Kenneth's Primary School

Blairmore Road

Cardross Pl

Clynder Road

Cardross Crs

ROAD

VW

B788

Knocknairshill Cemetery

Lady Burn

AUCHMOUNTAIN RD

B788

Premier Travel Inn

James Watt Wy

A8 EAST HAMILTON ST

Oakfield Ter

Rathost

Cartsdyke Station

Macdougall

Mackenzie

Bridgend

Hillend Drive

Grant Road

East Crawford Street

Border Street

Morris Street

Market Street

Baxter Street

Carwood Street

Brown Street

Quarrier Street

Grosvenor Rd

Fairrie Street

Sinclair St

John Wilson St

Weir Street

Gilmour Street

Auchmountain Road

Lady Octavia Recreation Centre

Strone

Kings Oak Primary School

Garvel Point

Dock

Great Harbour

Morton FC (Cappielow Park)

Strathclyde Bus Cen

McLeod

Potery Street

Ladyburn Business Park

Gibshill Road

GREENOCK ROAD

Ladyburn

Bogston Station

A8

Keir Hardie Street

Irwin Street

Shankland Road

Thomas Muir Street

Gibshill

Cedar Crs
Fir Street

Gibson St
Bell Street

Lansbury St
Daimally St

Mitchell Street

Cobham St

East Street
Poplar Street

Lilybank

Lilybank Road

Lilybank Sch

Farquhar Road

Whitelees Rd

Labuinum AV

Port Glasgow Rd

Ardgowan St

Kingston Bus Park

7

Devol Avenue

Mackie Av

Broadstone Av

8

Argyll & Bute
Inverclyde

1 2 3 4 18 5 6 7 8

78 77 76 75 674

28 29 30 31

G H J K L M

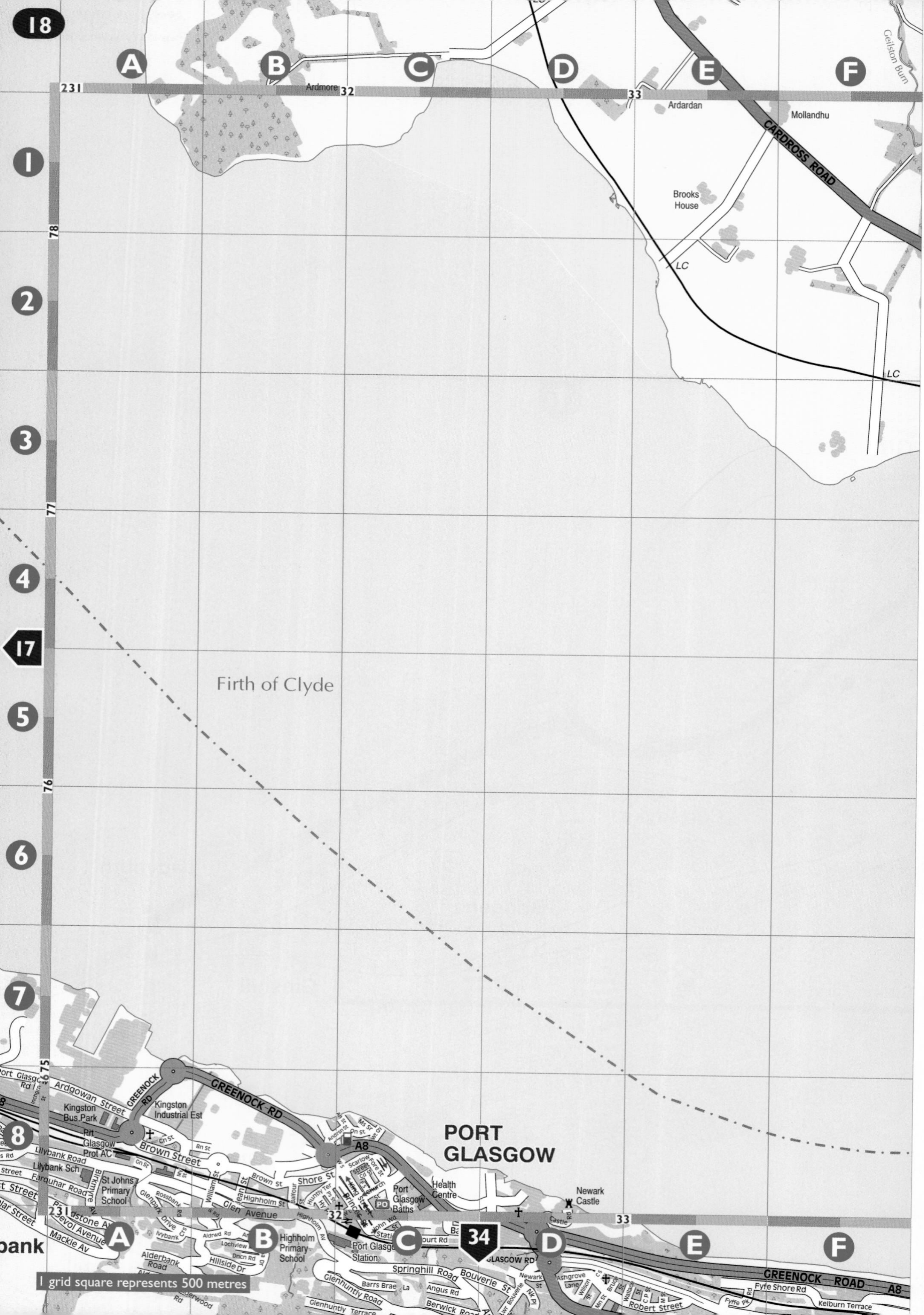

A   B   C   D   E   F

231

Ardmore 32   33   Ardardan   Mollandhu

CARDROSS ROAD

Brooks
House

LC

LC

1

78

2

3

77

4

17

Firth of Clyde

5

76

6

7

75

Port Glasgow
Rd   Ardgowan Street   GREENOCK
RD   GREENOCK RD

Kingston
Bus Park   Kingston
Industrial Est

Pitt
Glasgow
Prot AC   PO
A8   PORT
GLASGOW

8   Brown Street

Lilybank Road
Lilybank Sch
Farquhar Road   St Johns
Primary
School   William St   Glen Avenue   Port
Glasgow
Baths   Health
Centre   Newark
Castle

231   Mackie Av   A   Alderbank
Road   Hillside Dr   Highholm
Primary
School   B   Port Glasgow
Station   Springhill Road   C   Bouverie St   34   D GLASGOW RD   E   GREENOCK ROAD A8 F

1 grid square represents 500 metres   Glenhuntly Road   Barrs Brae La   Angus Rd   Berwick Road   Robert Street   Fyfe Shore Rd   Kelburn Terrace

bank

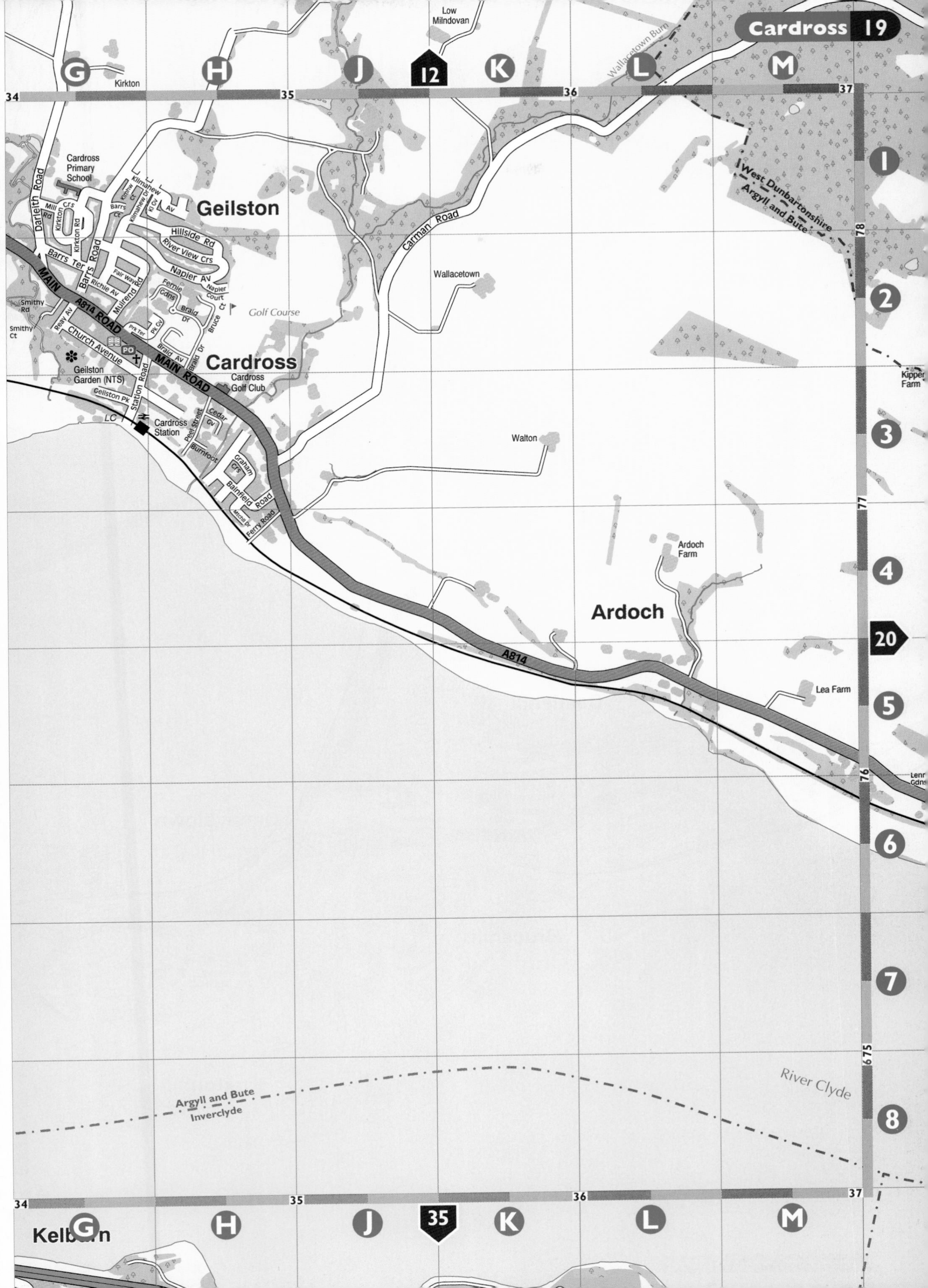

G   H   J   12   K   L   M

34   35   36   37

1

Kirkton

Cardross Primary School

Kilmahew Av
Kilmahew Dr

Geilston

Hillside Rd
River View Crs
Napier Av
Napier Court

Darleith Road

Mill Rd
Kirkton Crs
Kirkton Rd
Barrs Ter
Barrs Road
Richie Av
Mulrend Rd
Fernie Gdns
Braid Dr
Bruce Ct

Fair Ways Dr

Golf Course

Carman Road

Wallacetown

West Dunbartonshire
Argyll and Bute

78

I

2

Kipper Farm

Smithy Rd
Smithy Ct

MAIN
A814 ROAD
Reay Av
Church Avenue
PO
Geilston Garden (NTS)
Geilston Pk
Prk Ter
Pt Cv
Braid Av
MAIN ROAD
Cardross
Cardross Golf Club

LC
Station Road
Cedar Gv
Reed Street
Burnfoot
Graham Grs
Bainfield Road
Michell Dr
Ferry Road
Cardross Station

Walton

Walton

3

77

A814

Ardoch Farm

Ardoch

4

20

Lea Farm

5

Lenr Gdns

76

6

7

675

River Clyde

Argyll and Bute
Inverclyde

8

34   35   36   37

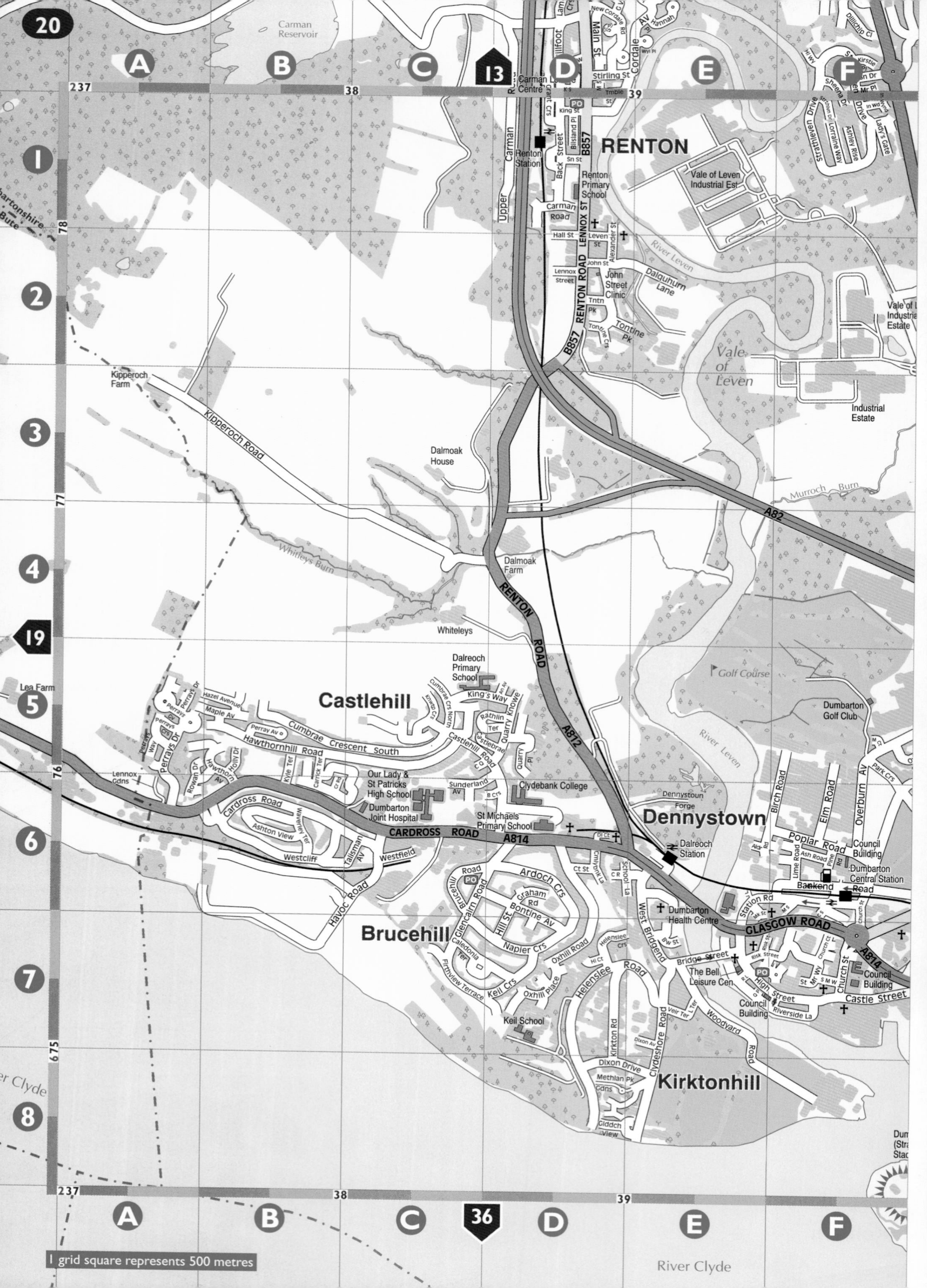

Carman Reservoir
13
RENTON
Renton Station
Renton Primary School
Vale of Leven Industrial Est
River Leven
John Street Clinic
Vale of Leven
Industrial Estate
Kipperoch Farm
Kipperoch Road
Dalmoak House
Dalmoak Farm
Whiteleys Burn
Murroch Burn
A82
RENTON ROAD
Whiteleys
19
Golf Course
Dumbarton Golf Club
Lea Farm
Castlehill
Dalreoch Primary School
Cumbrae Crescent South
Hawthornhill Road
Our Lady & St Patricks High School
Dumbarton Joint Hospital
Clydebank College
St Michaels Primary School
CARDROSS ROAD
A814
A812
Dennystoun Forge
Dennystown
Dalreoch Station
Dumbarton Central Station
Council Building
GLASGOW ROAD
Brucehill
Dumbarton Health Centre
The Bell Leisure Cen
High Street
Castle Street
Keil School
Kirktonhill
River Clyde
36
1 grid square represents 500 metres

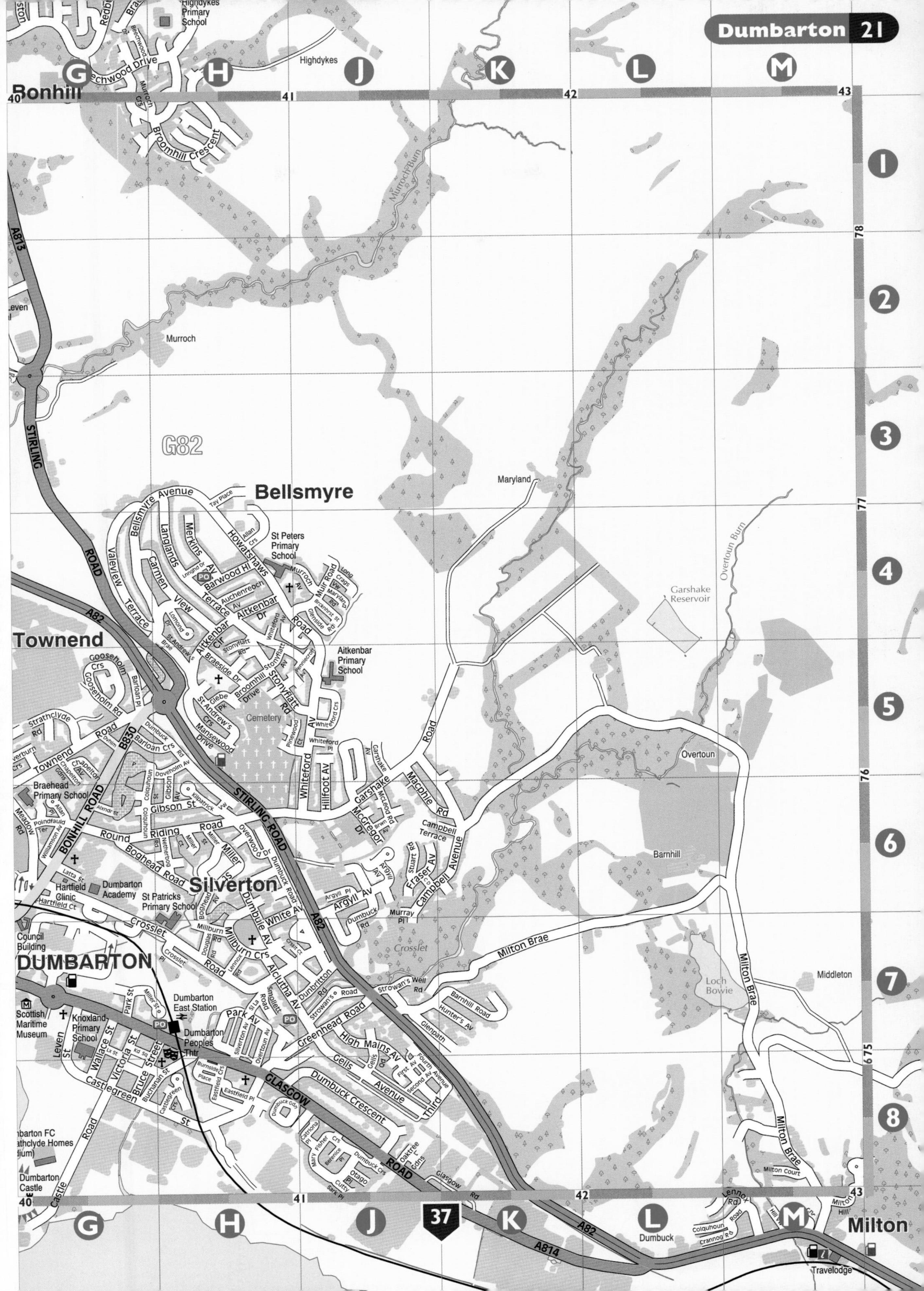

Bonhill
Highdykes
Murroch
Murroch Burn
G82
Bellsmyre
Maryland
Garshake Reservoir
Overtoun Burn
Overtoun
Barnhill
Townend
Silverton
DUMBARTON
Crosslet
Milton Brae
Loch Bowie
Middleton
Dumbuck
Milton
Travelodge
STIRLING ROAD
GLASGOW ROAD
A82
A813
A814
B850
St Peters Primary School
Aitkenbar Primary School
Braehead Primary School
Dumbarton Academy
St Patricks Primary School
Knoxland Primary School
Scottish Maritime Museum
Dumbarton East Station
Dumbarton Peoples Thtr
Council Building
Dumbarton Castle
Cemetery

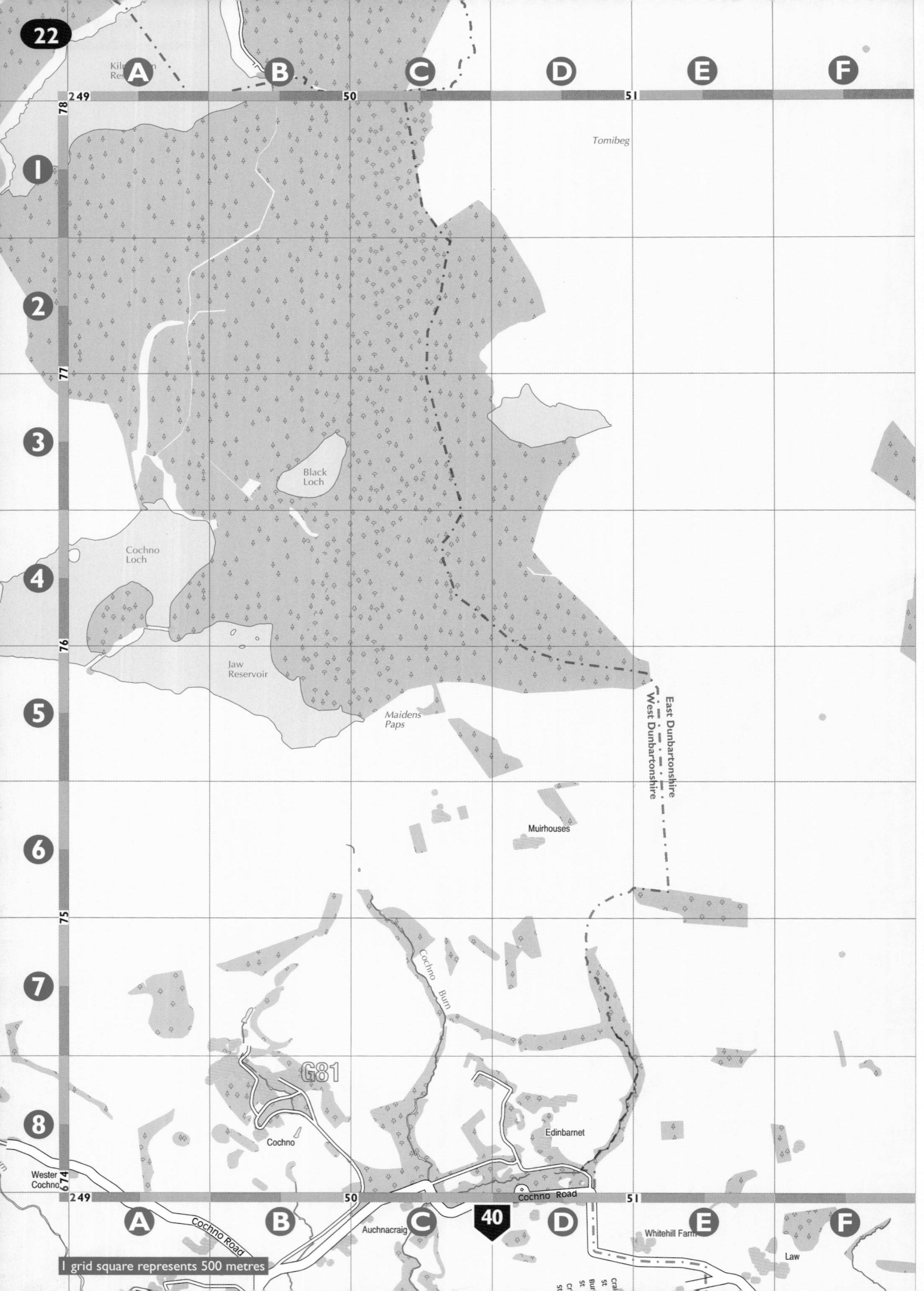

78

Kil... ...on
Res...

Tomibeg

I

77

2

3

Black
Loch

Cochno
Loch

4

76

Jaw
Reservoir

5

Maidens
Paps

East Dunbartonshire
West Dunbartonshire

Muirhouses

6

75

Cochno Burn

7

G81

8

Cochno

Edinbarnet

Wester
Cochno

674

249   50   Cochno Road   51

Cochno Road

Auchnacraig

Whitehill Farm

Law

1 grid square represents 500 metres

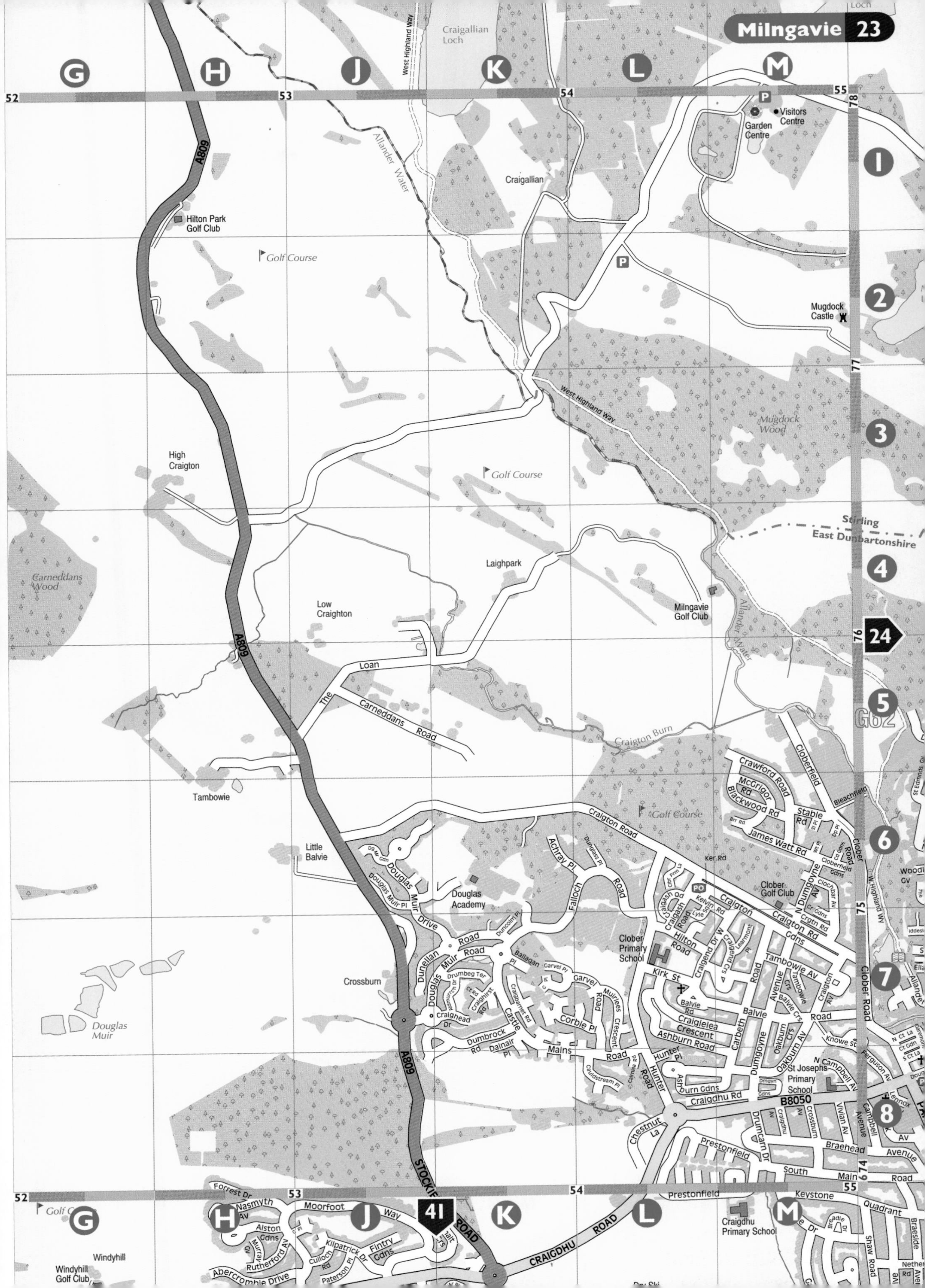
Craigallian Loch
West Highland Way
Allander Water
Visitors Centre
Garden Centre
Craigallian
Hilton Park Golf Club
Golf Course
A809
Mugdock Castle
West Highland Way
Mugdock Wood
High Craigton
Golf Course
Stirling
East Dunbartonshire
Carneddans Wood
Laighpark
Low Craighton
Milngavie Golf Club
Allander Water
The Loan
Carneddans Road
Craigton Burn
G62
Tambowie
Little Balvie
Craigton Road
Golf Course
Crawford Road
Cloberfield
McGrigor Rd
Blackwood Rd
Stable Rd
Bleachfield
James Watt Rd
Clober Road
Douglas Academy
Douglas Muir Drive
Achray Pl
Douglas Pl
Falloch Road
Clober Golf Club
Craigton Gdns
Clober Primary School
Hilton Road
Tambowie Av
Kirk St
Crossburn
Douglas Muir
Craighead Dr
Dunellan Road
Balvie Rd
Craiglelea Crescent
Ashburn Road
Dumbrock Rd
Dainair Pl
Mains Road
Corbie Pl
Hunter Road
St Josephs Primary School
B8050
Craigdhu Rd
Chestnut La
Drumcarn Dr
Prestonfield
Braehead Avenue
South Main Road
Keystone Quadrant
Craigdhu Primary School
STOCKIEMUIR ROAD
CRAIGDHU ROAD
Moorfoot Way
Nasmyth Av
Alston Gdns
Rutherford Av
Kilpatrick Dr
Fintry Gdns
Abercrombie Drive
Paterson Pl
Windyhill
Windyhill Golf Club
Forrest Dr
Shaw Road
Braeside
G H J K L M
1 2 3 4 5 6 7 8
52 53 54 55
78 77 76 75 674
24
41

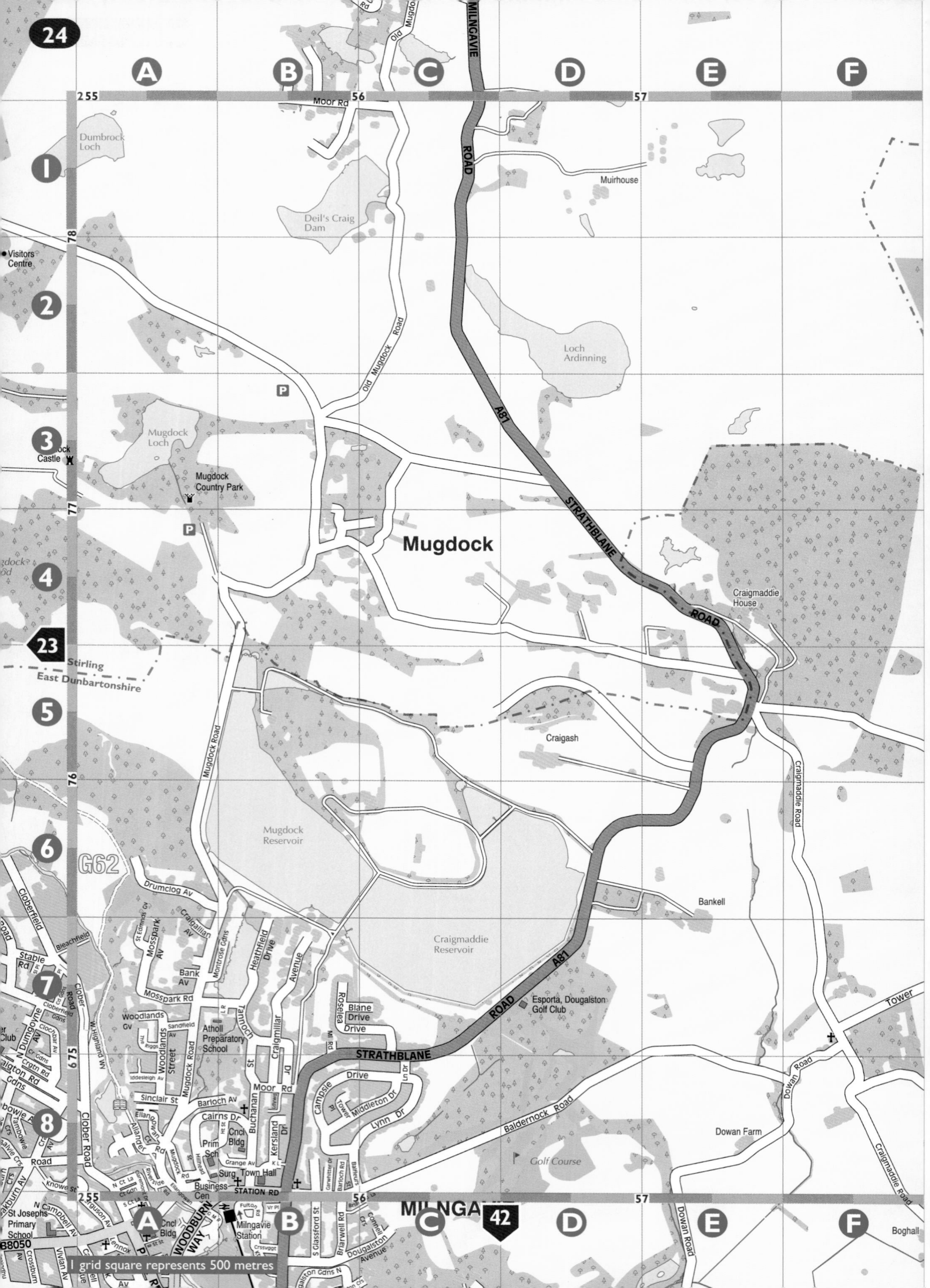
Mugdock
Dumbrock Loch
Deil's Craig Dam
Muirhouse
Visitors Centre
Loch Ardinning
Mugdock Loch
Mugdock Castle
Mugdock Country Park
Craigmaddie House
Stirling
East Dunbartonshire
Craigash
Mugdock Reservoir
Craigmaddie Reservoir
Bankell
Esporta, Dougalston Golf Club
Atholl Preparatory School
Dowan Farm
Golf Course
Milngavie Station
St Josephs Primary School
Boghall
MILNGAVIE ROAD
STRATHBLANE ROAD
A81
Old Mugdock Road
Mugdock Road
Craigmaddie Road
Baldernock Road
Dowan Road
Moor Rd
G62
1 grid square represents 500 metres

23
42

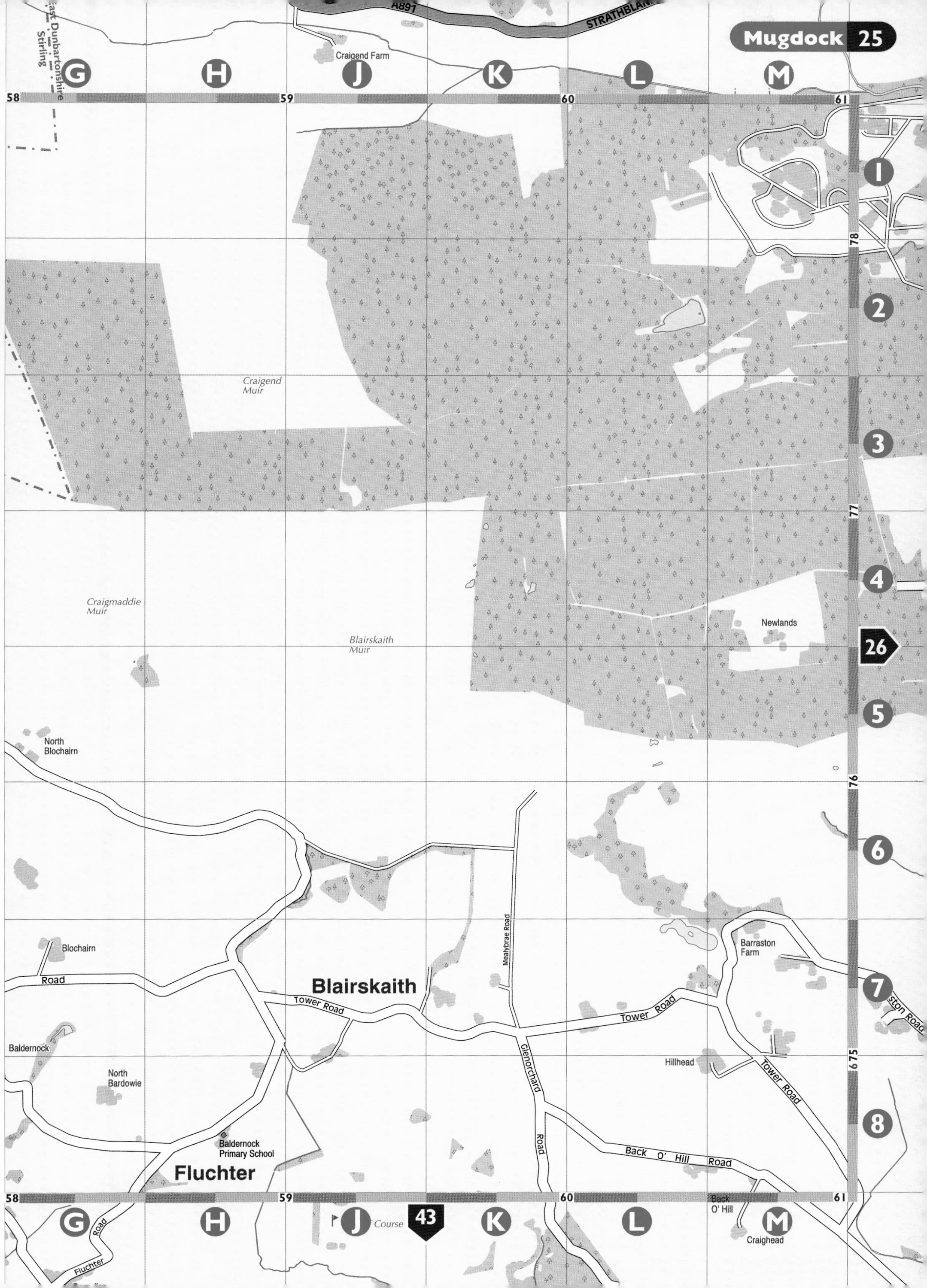

East Dunbartonshire
Stirling

G   H   J   K   L   M

58   59   60   61

78

I

2

77

3

4

Newlands

26

5

76

6

Craigend
Muir

Craigmaddie
Muir

Blairskaith
Muir

North
Blochairn

Blochairn

Road

Baldernock

North
Bardowie

Baldernock
Primary School

Fluchter

Blairskaith

Tower Road

Mealybrae Road

Glenorchard

Road

Tower   Road

Hillhead

Barraston
Farm

ston Road

7

675

Tower Road

Back O' Hill   Road

8

58   59   60   61

G   H   J   K   L   M

Course **43**

Back
O' Hill

Craighead

Fluchter

Road

Craigend Farm

A897

STRATHBLANE

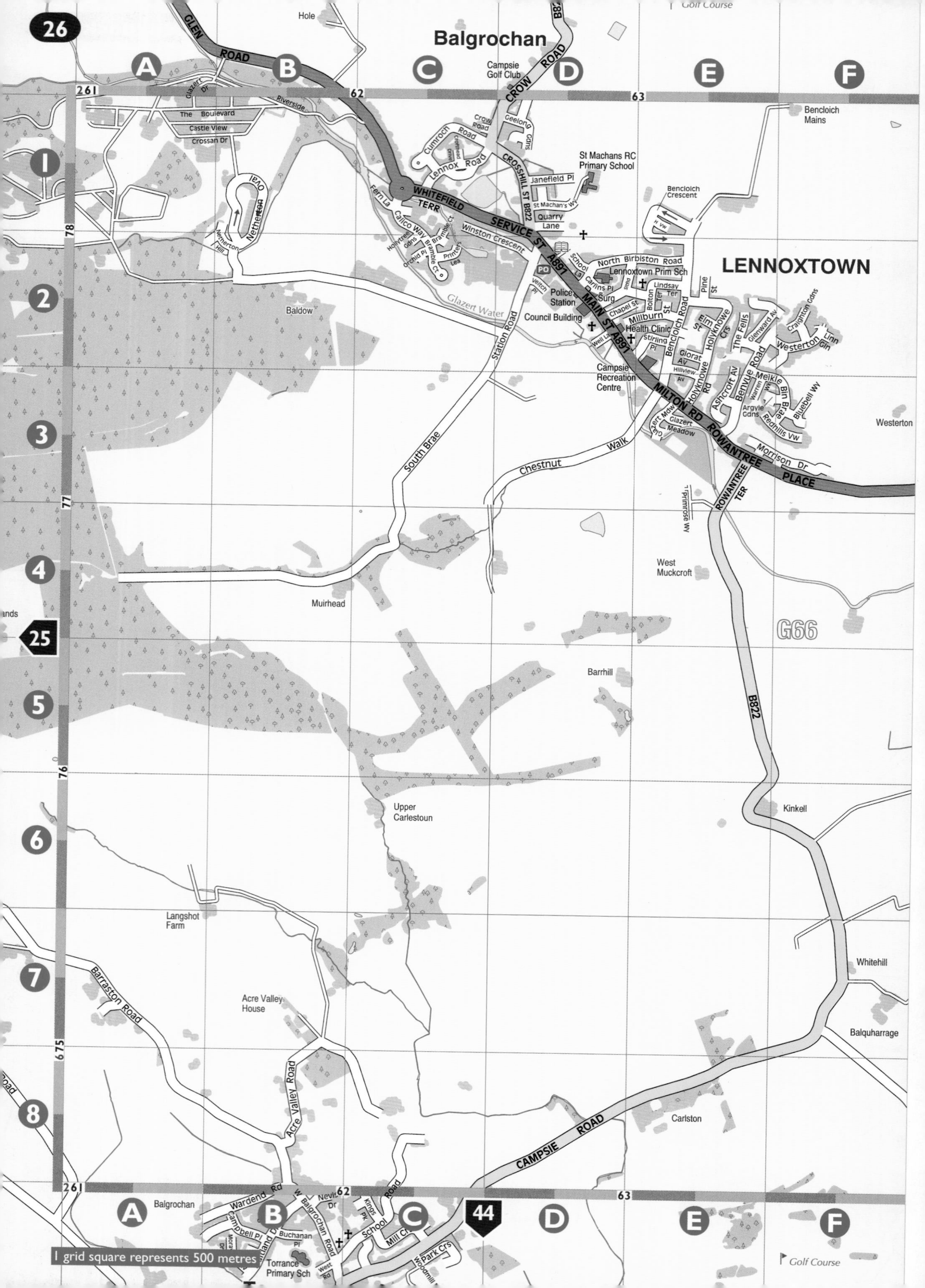

Balgrochan

A   B   C   D   E   F

261   62   63

Hole

GLEN ROAD
Glazert Dr
The Boulevard
Castle View
Crossan Dr
Riverside
Netherhead
Netherton Hill

Campsie Golf Club
Crow Road
Cumroch
Lennox Road
CROSSHILL ST B822
WHITEFIELD TERR
SERVICE ST A891
Winston Crescent
Calico Way
Fern La
Hollytree Gdns
Orchid Pl
Bramble Ct
Printers Lea

CROW ROAD
B822

Geelong Gdns

St Machans RC
Primary School
Janefield Pl
St Machan's Wy
Quarry Lane

Bencloich Mains

Bencloich Crescent
H Vw

LENNOXTOWN

North Birbiston Road
School La
Carlins Pl
Lennoxtown Prim Sch
Lindsay Ter
Chapel St
Millburn
Health Clinic
Well Grn
Stirling Pl
Glorat Av
Hillview Av
Glazert Meadow
Jeff Mdw

Pine St
Bolton St
Elm St
Bencloich Road
Holyknowe Crs
The Fells
Glenward Av
Westerton Av
Craigton Gdns
Linn
Westerton Gdn
Ashcroft Av
Benvue Road
Meikle Bin Brae
Redhills Vw
Bluebell Wy
Warren
Argyle Gdns
Morrison Dr

Westerton

MILTON RD
ROWANTREE PLACE
ROWANTREE TER
Primrose Wy

PO
Veitch Pl
Police Station
Council Building
MAIN ST A891
Surg
Campsie Recreation Centre

Glazert Water
Baldow
Station Road
South Brae
Chestnut Walk

Muirhead

Upper Carlestoun

West Muckcroft

Barrhill

G66

Kinkell

B822

Whitehill

Balquharrage

Langshot Farm

Ballraston Road

Acre Valley House

Acre Valley Road

Wardend Rd
Campbell Pl
Buchanan Pl
Balgrochan Road
Nevit Dr
School Rd
Kings Pk
Mill Cr
WePark Crs
Hillhead

CAMPSIE ROAD

Carlston

Balgrochan

Torrance Primary Sch

A   B   C   D   E   F

261   62   63

44

1
2
3
4
25
5
6
7
8

78   77   76   675   261

Golf Course
Golf Course

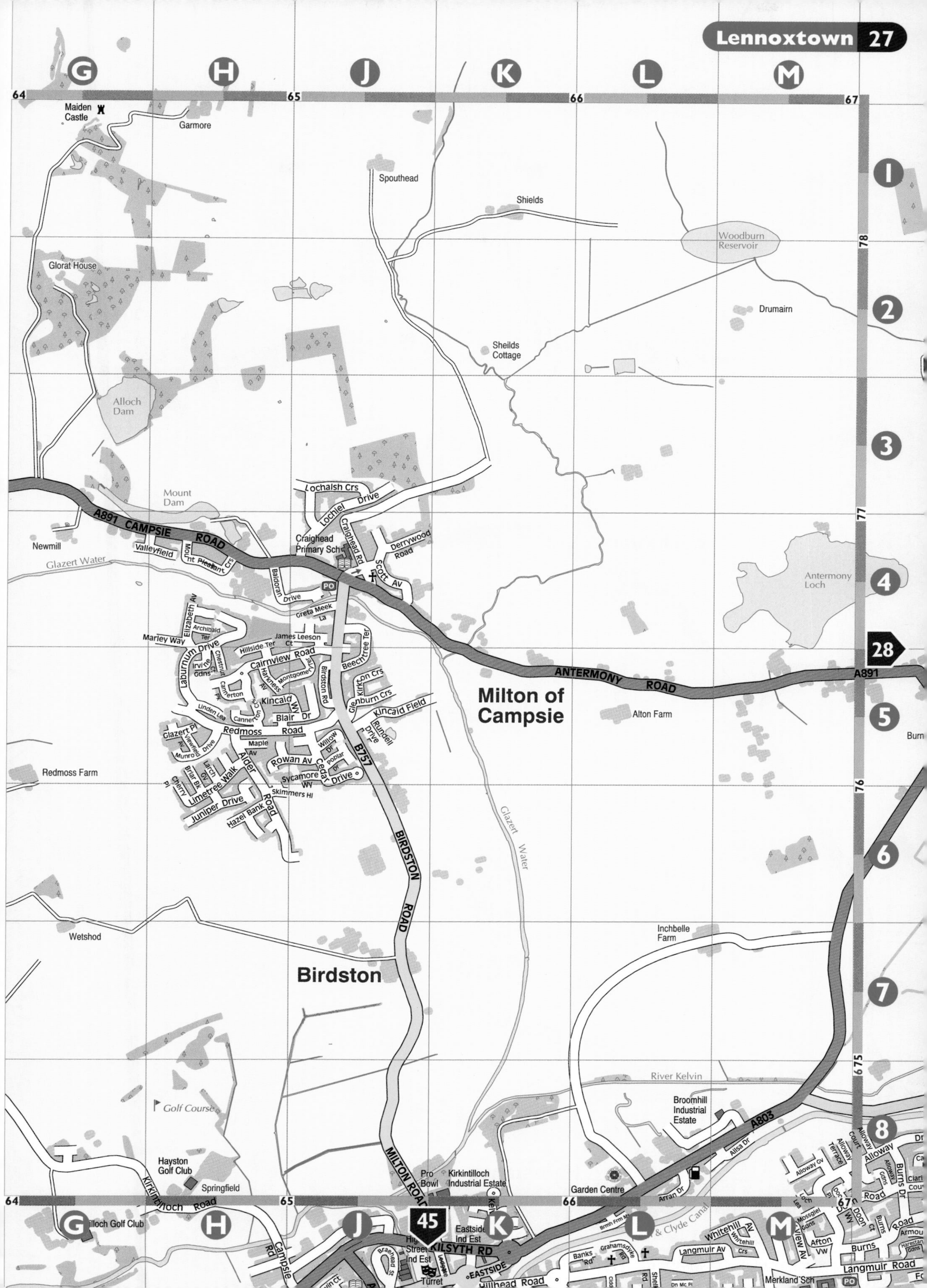

G H J K L M

64 65 66 67

Maiden Castle
Garmore

Spouthead

Shields

Woodburn Reservoir

Glorat House

Drumairn

Alloch Dam

Mount Dam

Sheilds Cottage

Newmill

A891 CAMPSIE ROAD

Glazert Water

Valleyfield

Mount Pleasant Crs

Baldoran Drive

Lochalsh Crs
Lochiel Drive
Craighead Rd

Craighead Primary Sch

Derrywood Road

Scott Av

Antermony Loch

PO

Greta Meek La

Elizabeth Av
Archibald Ter
Marley Way
Laburnum Drive
Irvine Gdns
Chestnut
Cameron
Hillside Ter
James Leeson Ct
Cairnview Road
Hawkes
Montgomerie
Birdston Rd
Beech Tree Ter
Kirk
Glenburn Crs

ANTERMONY ROAD

A891

28

Milton of Campsie

Alton Farm

Linden Lea
Glazert Pl
Viewfield Drive
Munro Rd
Larch
Redmoss
Maple Av
Kincaid Wy
Blair Dr
Canner
Kincaid Road
Willow
Cedar
Kincaid Field
Poplar
Klundell Drive

B757

Redmoss Farm

Cherry Pl
Brae Bk
Limetree Walk
Juniper Drive
Rowan Av
Alder
Sycamore Wy
Hazel Bank Road
Skimmers Hl
Crescent Drive

Glazert Water

Wetshod

Inchbelle Farm

Birdston

BIRDSTON ROAD

6

7

River Kelvin

Golf Course

Broomhill Industrial Estate

A803

675

8

Hayston Golf Club
Springfield

Kirkintilloch Road

MILTON ROAD

Pro Bowl
Kirkintilloch Industrial Estate

Garden Centre

Arran Dr
Ailsa Dr

Forth & Clyde Canal

Alloway Ter
Alloway Terrace
Alloway Gv
Alloway

Burns Road

64 65 66 67

G H J K L M

Killoch Golf Club
Campsie Rd

High Street
45
KILSYTH RD
Eastside Ind Est
Turret

EASTSIDE

Kilsyth Rd

Banks Rd
Grahamsdyke

Langmuir Av
Langmuir Crs

Whitehill
Montehill
View Av
Afton Av
Afton Vw

Doon
Loch Av

Mossgiel Gdns

Langmuir Road

Merkland Sch

Burns Road

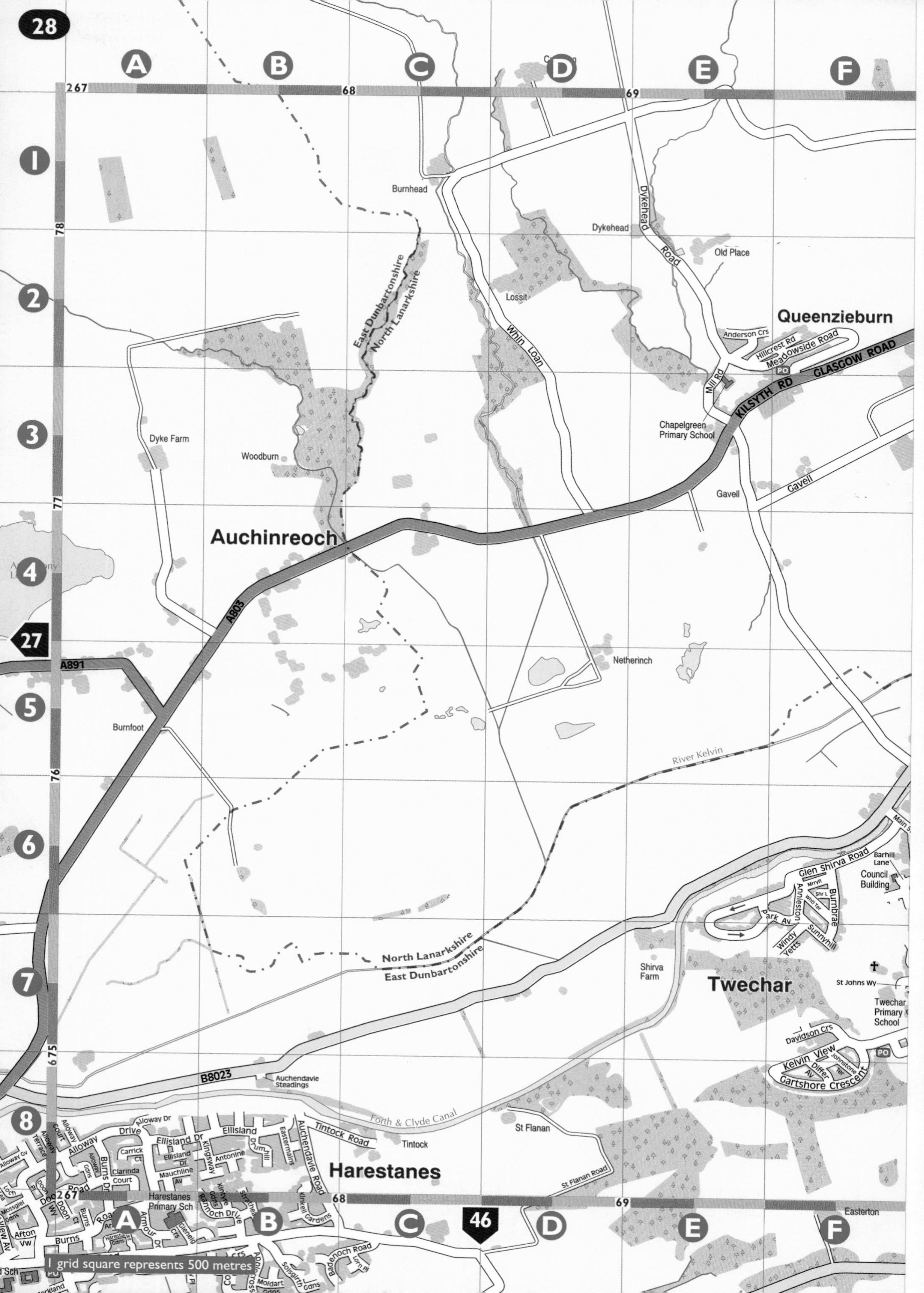

Burnhead
Dykehead
Dykehead Road
Old Place
Lossit
Whin Loan
Queenzieburn
Anderson Crs
Hillcrest Rd
Meadowside Road
Mill Rd
KILSYTH RD
GLASGOW ROAD
Chapelgreen Primary School
Gavell
East Dunbartonshire
North Lanarkshire
Dyke Farm
Woodburn
Auchinreoch
A803
A891
Burnfoot
Netherinch
River Kelvin
Glen Shirva Road
Barhill Lane
Council Building
Park Av
Burnbrae
Sunnyhill
Windy Yetts
Shirva Farm
Twechar
St Johns Wy
Twechar Primary School
Davidson Crs
Kelvin View
Gartshore Crescent
B8023
Auchendavie Steadings
Forth & Clyde Canal
St Flanan
St Flanan Road
Tintock Road
Tintock
Harestanes
Alloway Drive
Ellisland Dr
Kingsway
Antonine
Carrick Ct
Clarinda Court
Mauchline Av
Auchendavie Road
Harestanes Primary Sch
Rannoch Drive
Armour Dr
Kinkell Gardens
Badenoch Road
Afton Vw
Burns
Easterton
1 grid square represents 500 metres

27
46

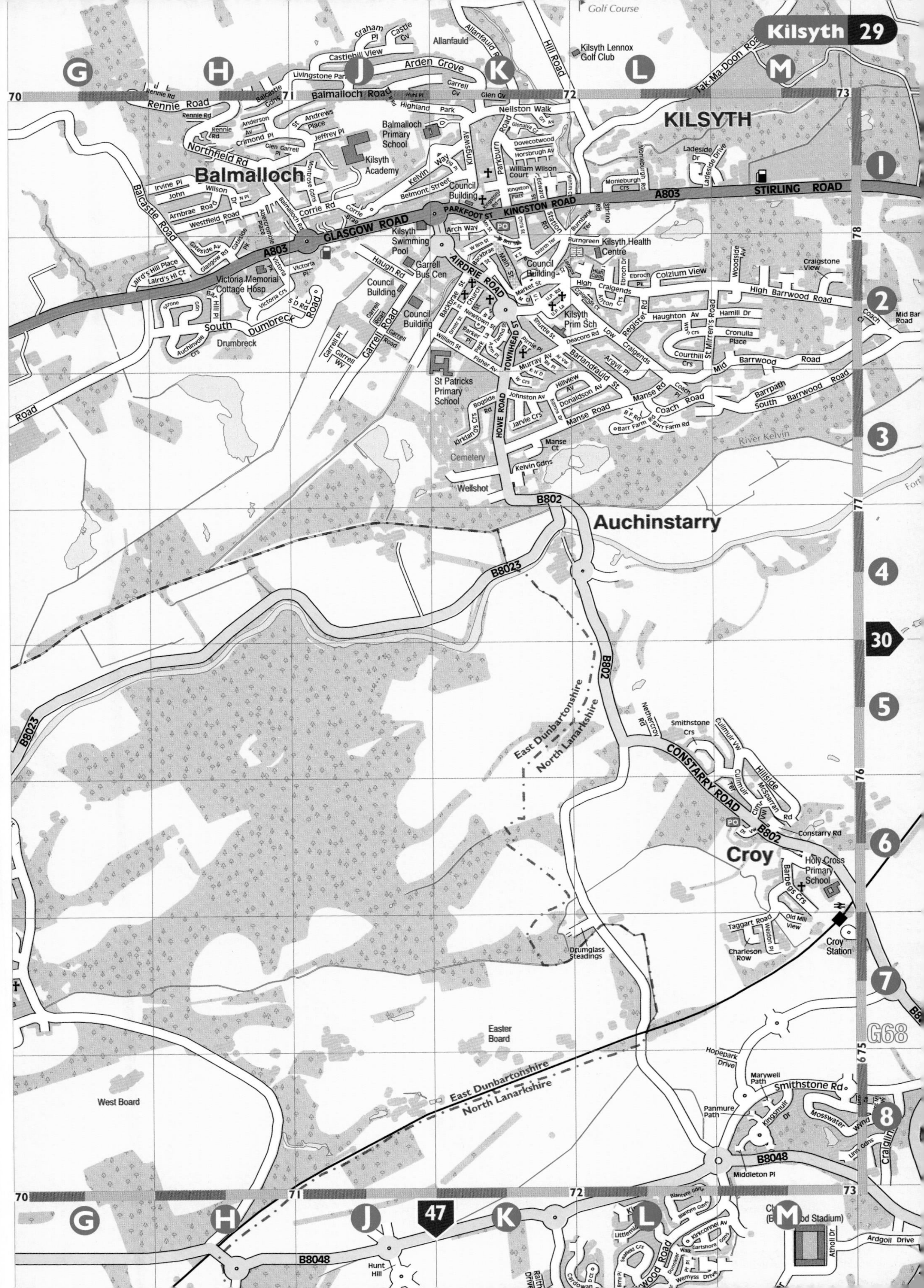
Golf Course
Kilsyth Lennox Golf Club
Allanfauld
KILSYTH
Balmalloch
Balmalloch Primary School
Kilsyth Academy
Council Building
Kilsyth Swimming Pool
Garrell Bus Cen
Victoria Memorial Cottage Hosp
Kilsyth Health Centre
Kilsyth Prim Sch
St Patricks Primary School
Cemetery
Wellshot
Drumbreck
Auchinstarry
River Kelvin
Rennie Road
Balmalloch Road
Northfield Rd
Arden Grove
Highland Park
Neilston Walk
Kingsway
Parkburn Road
Glasgow Road
Parkfoot St
Kingston Road
Stirling Road
A803
Airdrie Road
Townhead St
Howe Road
Garrell Road
Haugh Rd
South Dumbreck Road
Balcastle Road
Barwood Road
High Barrwood Road
South Barrwood Road
Colzium View
Craigends
Manse Road
Coach Road
Barlandfauld St
Westfield Road
Corrie Rd
Belmont Street
Kelvin Way
Tak-Ma-Doon Road
B802
B8023
Constarry Road
Croy
Holy Cross Primary School
Croy Station
Drumglass Steadings
Easter Board
West Board
East Dunbartonshire
North Lanarkshire
Smithstone Rd
Mosswater Wynd
Hopepark Drive
Maryweil Path
Panmure Path
Middleton Pl
B8048
Hunt Hill
Ardgoil Drive
Atholl Dr
Kirkconnel Av
G68
30
47
70
71
72
73
75
76
77
78
G
H
J
K
L
M
1
2
3
4
5
6
7
8

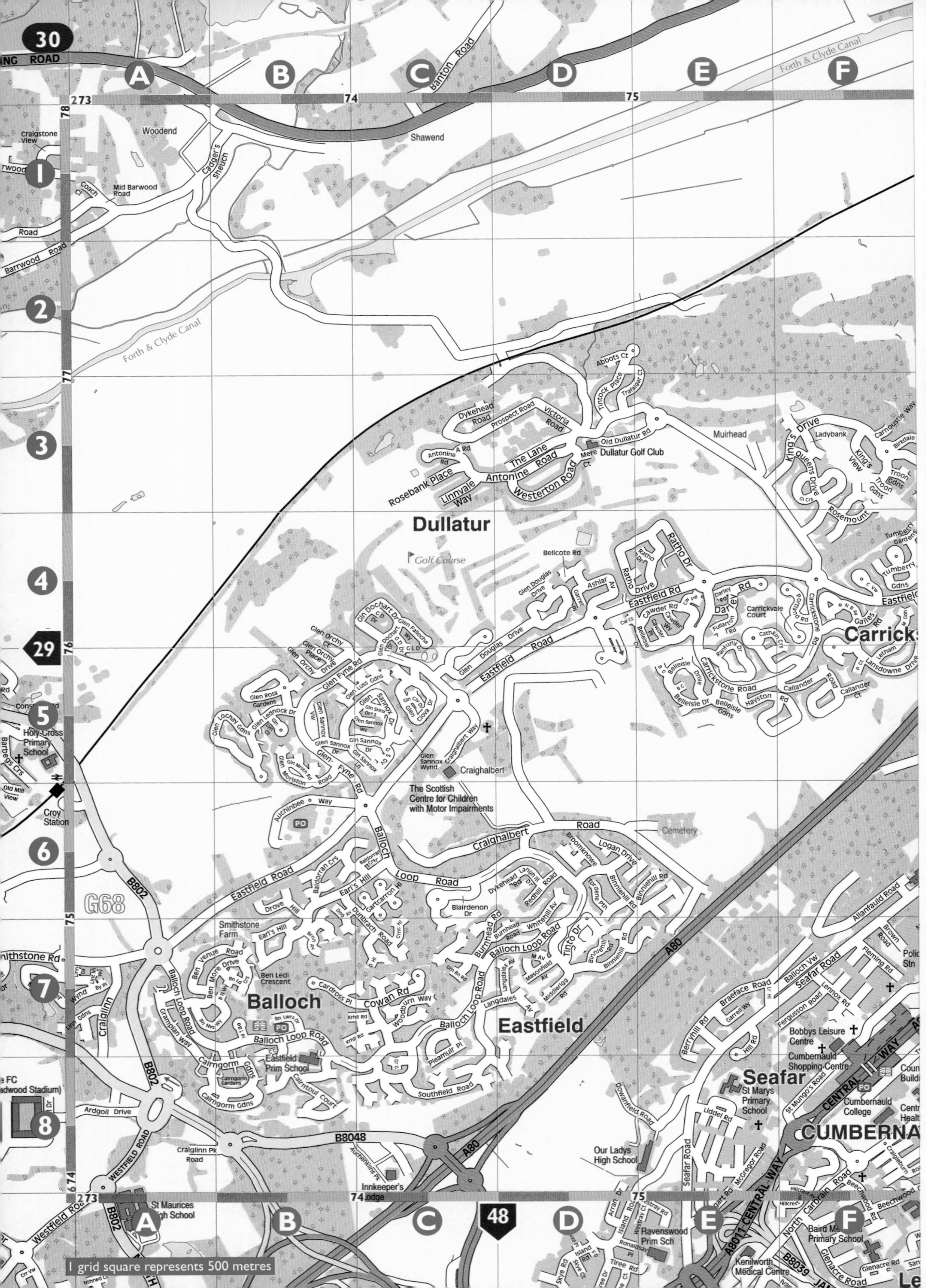

30
29
48
A
B
C
D
E
F
1
2
3
4
5
6
7
8
273
74
75
78
77
76
Forth & Clyde Canal
Banton Road
Woodend
Shawend
Cadger's Sheuch
Mid Barwood Road
Craigstone View
Coach Cl
Barwood Road
Muirhead
Abbots Ct
Tintock Place
Trafalgar Ct
Dykehead Road
Prospect Road
Victoria Road
Old Dullatur Rd
Dullatur Golf Club
Mere Ct
Antonine Rd
The Lane
Antonine Road
Westerton Road
Rosebank Place
Linnvale Way
Dullatur
Golf Course
Bellcote Rd
Ladybank
King's Drive
Queens Drive
King's View
Carnoustie Way
Troon Gdns
Rosemount
Turnberry Gardens
Turnberry Gdns
Ratho Dr
Ratho Drive
Ashlar Av
Glen Douglas Drive
Eastfield Rd
Eastfield Road
Cawder Rd
Darley Rd
Carrickvale Court
Fullarton Rd
Carrickstone Rd
Carrickstone Road
Cathkin Crs
Ranfurly Dr
Belleisle Drive
Belleisle Dr
Belleisle Gdns
Hayston Rd
Callander Road
Callander Ct
Lansdowne Drive
Letham
Galles Rd
Carricks
Glen Orchy Ct
Glen Orchy Place
Glen Orchy Drive
Glen Fyne Rd
Glen Dochart Dr
Glen Falloch Way
Glen Luss Gdns
Glen Sannox Dr
Glen Clova Dr
Glen Rosa Gardens
Glen Lednock Dr
Glen Lochay Gdns
Glen Moriston Road
Glen Sannox Wynd
Craighalbert Way
Craighalbert
The Scottish Centre for Children with Motor Impairments
Auchinbee Way
Craighalbert Road
Cemetery
Broomknowe
Logan Drive
Balloch Loop Road
Baldorran Crs
Earl's Hill
Gartcarron Hill
Dunbrach Road
Dykehead Rd
Langhill Dr
Redhill Road
Torbrex Pth
Binniehill Rd
Whitehill Av
Blairdenon Dr
Burnhead Rd
Burnhead Road
Tinto Dr
Drove Hill
Smithstone Farm
Ben Venue Road
Ben More Drive
Ben Ledi Crescent
Cardross Pl
Cowan Rd
Woodburn Way
Langdales Av
Masonfield Av
Middlerigg Rd
Balloch
Eastfield
Balloch Loop Road
Grampian Way
Cairngorm Gdns
Cairngorm Gardens
Eastfield Prim School
Cairntoul Court
Pleamuir Pl
Southfield Road
B802
B8048
A80
G68
Holy Cross Primary School
Croy Station
Old Mill View
Smithstone Rd
Craiglinn
Ardgoil Drive
Westfield Road
Craiglinn Pk Road
St Maurices High School
Innkeeper's Lodge
Auchenkilns Pk
Our Ladys High School
Dowanfield Road
Seafar Road
McGregor Road
A8011 Central Way
Seafar
St Marys Primary School
Liddel Rd
Berryhill Rd
Hill Rd
Braeface Road
Balloch Vw
Seafar Road
Fleming Rd
Allanfauld Road
Brown Road
Police Stn
Lennox Rd
Fergusson Road
Bobbys Leisure Centre
Cumbernauld Shopping Centre
St Mungo's Road
Central Way
Cumbernauld College
CUMBERNA
Craigieburn Rd
North Carbrain Road
Beechwood Rd
Baird Memorial Primary School
Glenacre Road
B8039
Ravenswood Prim Sch
Kenilworth Medical Centre
Arran Dr
Island Rd
Skye Rd
Tiree Rd
1 grid square represents 500 metres

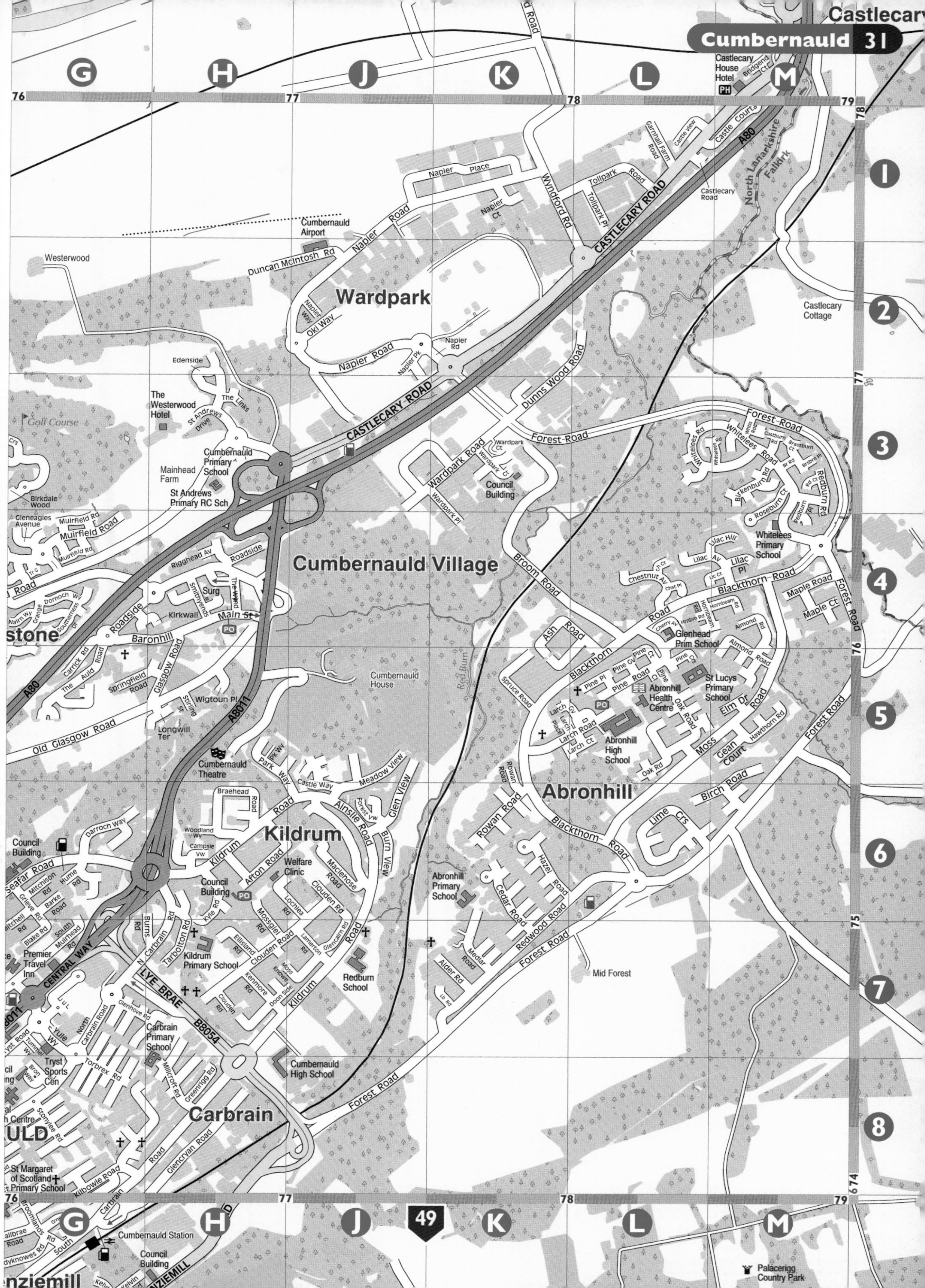
Castlecary
G
H
J
K
L
M
Castlecary House Hotel
Wardpark
Cumbernauld Airport
Westerwood
Napier Place
Napier Road
Duncan McIntosh Rd
Oki Way
Wyndford Rd
Tollpark Road
CASTLECARY ROAD
A80
North Lanarkshire
Falkirk
Castlecary Road
Castlecary Cottage
Edenside
The Westerwood Hotel
Golf Course
The Links
St Andrews Drive
Cumbernauld Primary School
Mainhead Farm
St Andrews Primary RC Sch
Birkdale Wood
Gleneagles Avenue
Muirfield Road
Dunns Wood Road
Forest Road
Wardpark Road
Council Building
Whitelees Rd
Whitelees Road
Redburn Rd
Rosebum Ct
Whitelees Primary School
Cumbernauld Village
Broom Road
Lilac Hill
Lilac Pl
Chestnut Av
Blackthorn Road
Maple Road
Maple Ct
Roadside
Rigghead Av
Main St
Baronhill
Kirkwall
Smithyends
The Wynd
Surg
stone
Carrick Rd
The Auld Road
Springfield Road
Glasgow Road
Wigtoun Pl
Stirling St
Longwill Ter
Old Glasgow Road
A8011
Cumbernauld House
Red Burn
Ash Road
Glenhead Prim School
Almond Road
Hornbeam Rd
Spruce Road
Pine Road
Pine Pl
Abronhill Health Centre
St Lucys Primary School
Oak Road
Elm Dr
Larch Road
Larch Ct
Abronhill High School
Rowan Road
Moss Road
Gean Court
Hawthorn Rd
Birch Road
Abronhill
Lime Crs
Cumbernauld Theatre
Park Way
Castle Way
Meadow View
Glen View
Braehead Road
Kildrum
Kildrum Road
Afton Road
Ainslie Road
Burn View
Darroch Way
Council Building
Seafar Road
Welfare Clinic
Maclehose Road
Clouden Rd
Abronhill Primary School
Hazel Road
Cedar Road
Redwood Road
Forest Road
Medlar Road
Alder Rd
Mid Forest
Kildrum Primary School
Redburn School
Premier Travel Inn
CENTRAL WAY
LYE BRAE
B8054
Carbrain Primary School
Tryst Sports Cen
Torbrex Rd
Cumbernauld High School
Carbrain
Glencryan Road
Kilbowie Road
St Margaret of Scotland Primary School
Cumbernauld Station
Council Building
Palacerigg Country Park
76
77
78
79
1
2
3
4
5
6
7
8
49

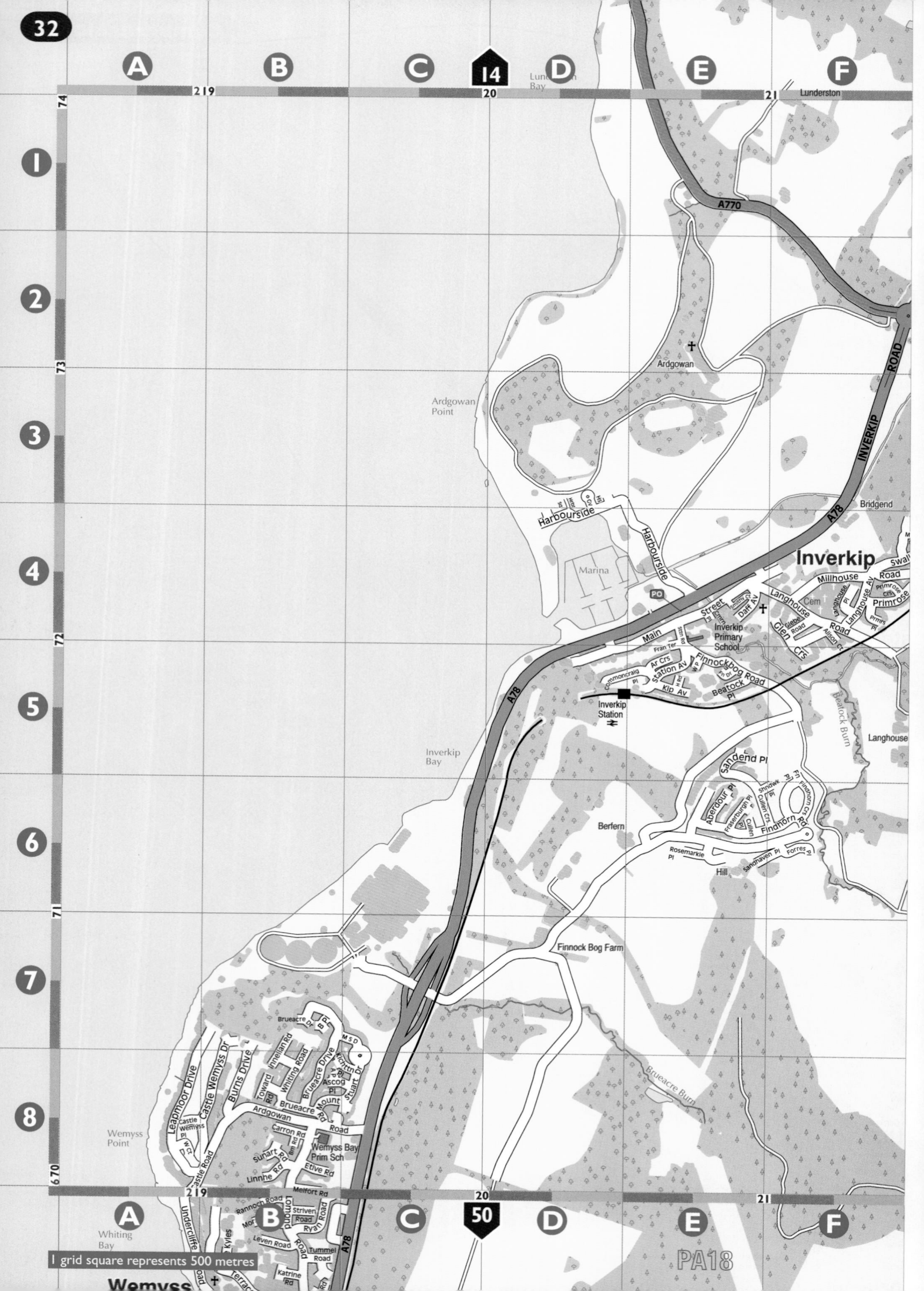

32

A   219   B   C   14   D   E   21   F
20   Lunderston Bay   Lunderston

1

2
73

Ardgowan
✝

Ardgowan
Point

3

INVERKIP ROAD

A770

Bridgend

Harbourside
A78

4

Marina
PO
Millhouse
Road
Primrose
Inverkip
Daff Av   ✝   Cem
Langhouse
Main
Street
Road
Glen Crs
Inverkip
Primary
School
Fran Ter
Ar Crs
Station Av
Kip Av
Finnockbog Road
Beatock
Pl
Commoncraig
Pl

5
72

Inverkip
Station

Inverkip
Bay
Sandend Pl
Beatock Burn
Langhouse

Arbour Pl
Findhorn
Findhorn Rd
Freemburgh Pl
Cullen Crs
Cullen
Findhorn Crs

A78

Berfern
Hill
Sandhaven Pl
Forres Pl
Rosemarkie
Pl

6
71

7

Finnock Bog Farm

Bruecre Dr
Brueacre Burn

MSD
Imelian Rd
Korttn Dr
Brueacre Drive
Ascog Pl
Mount
Scart
Castle Wemyss Dr
Leapmoor Drive
Burns Drive
Toyard
Whiting Road

8
670

Wemyss
Point
Castle
Wemyss
Ardgowan
Road
Carron Rd
Wemyss Bay
Prim Sch
Castle Road
WC
Sunart Rd
Linnhe
Melfort Rd
Etive Rd

A   219   B   C   20   D   E   21   F
Whiting
Bay
Underdiffe
Kyles
Moi
Ormond
Rannoch Road
Striven Road
Ry's
Leven Road
Tummel Road
50
A78
Katrine Rd
PA18

1 grid square represents 500 metres

Wemyss   ✝

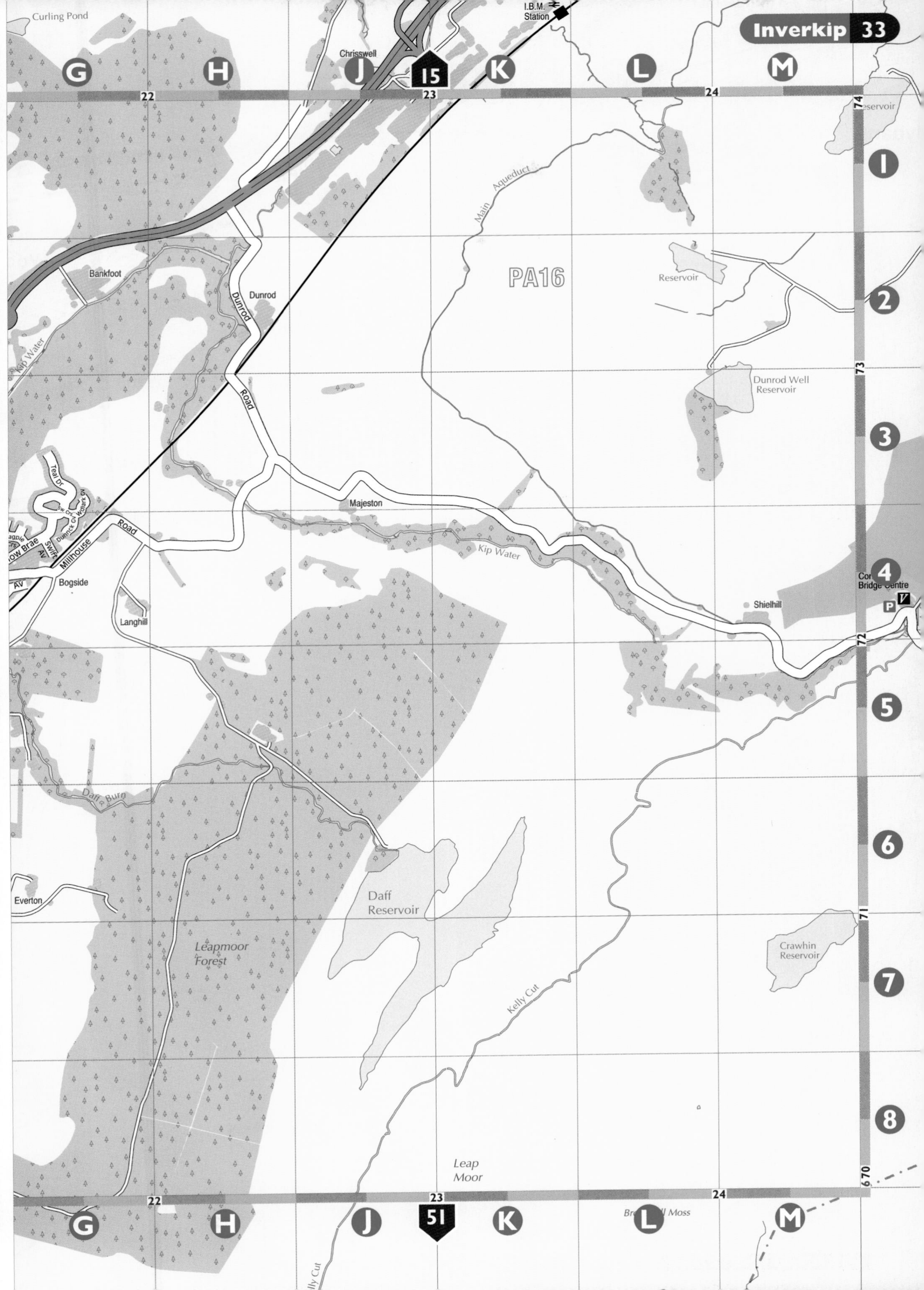

Curling Pond

G   H   J   15   K   L   M

22   23   24

I.B.M.
Station

Chrisswell

Bankfoot

Dunrod

Dunrod
Road

PA16

Reservoir

Dunrod Well
Reservoir

Main Aqueduct

Kip Water

Teal Dr

Magpie

Dunnet Wrens

Swift

Willow Brae

AV

Millhouse
Road

Road

Bogside

Langhill

Majeston

Kip Water

Shielhill

Cor
Bridge Centre

P   V

Daff Burn

Everton

Leapmoor
Forest

Daff
Reservoir

Kelly Cut

Crawhin
Reservoir

Leap
Moor

Kelly Cut

Brae Hill Moss

G   H   J   51   K   L   M

22   23   24

I   2   3   4   5   6   7   8

74   73   72   71   70

Reservoir

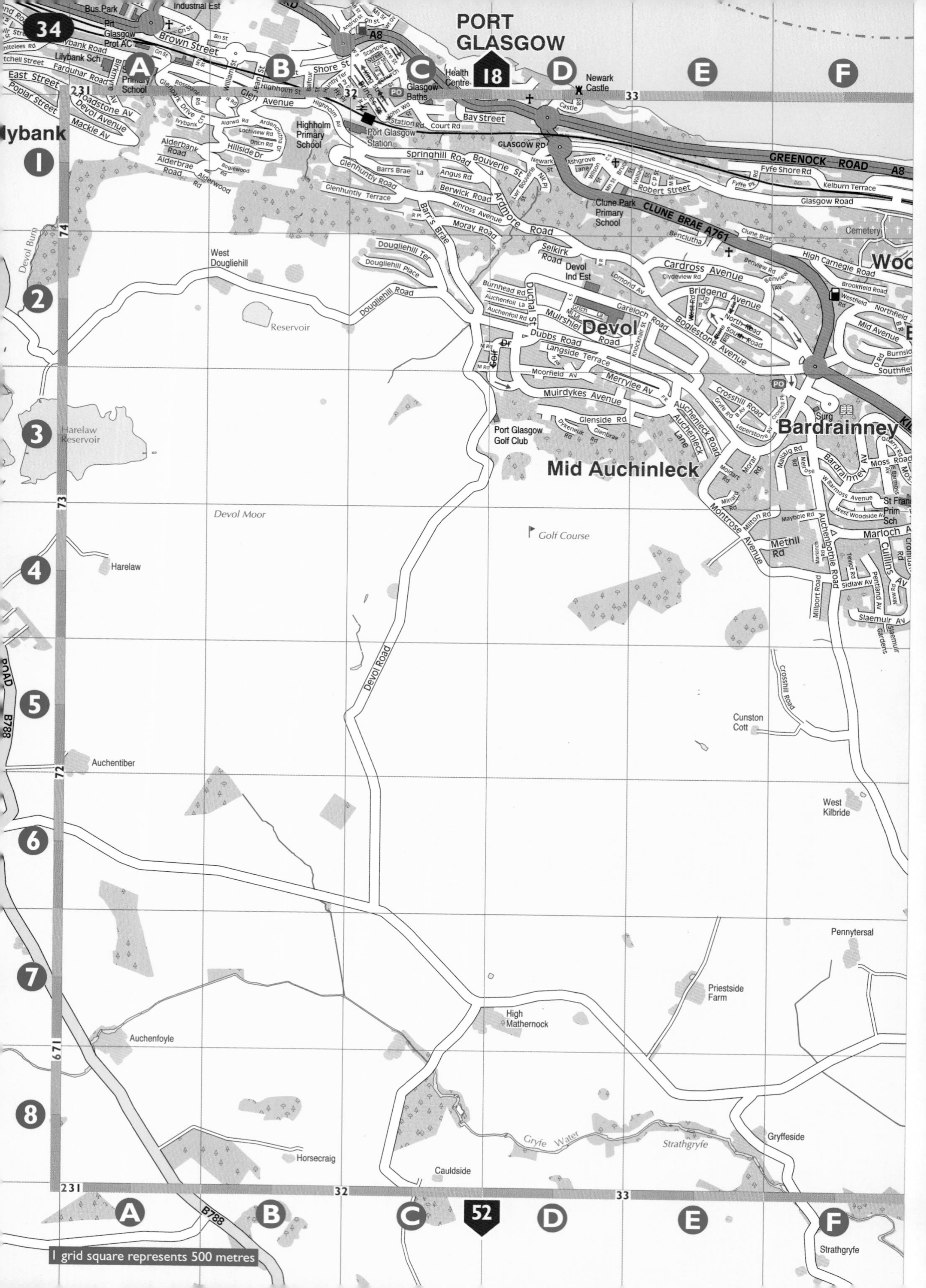
34
PORT GLASGOW
18
A
B
C
D
E
F
1
2
3
4
5
6
7
8
231
32
33
74
73
72
671
Bus Park
Industrial Est
Pt Glasgow Prot AC
Brown Street
Lilybank Road
Lilybank Sch
East Street
Poplar Street
Farquhar Road
Primary School
Glen Avenue
Highholm St
Shore St
Health Centre
Glasgow Baths
Newark Castle
Bay Street
Court Rd
Station Rd
Port Glasgow Station
Highholm Primary School
Broadstone Av
Devol Avenue
Mackie Av
Lilybank
Alderbank Road
Alderbrae Road
Hillside Dr
Glenhuntly Road
Glenhuntly Terrace
Springhill Road
Bouverie St
Barrs Brae
Angus Rd
Berwick Road
Kinross Avenue
Moray Road
Ardmore Road
Barr's Brae
GLASGOW RD
GREENOCK ROAD A8
Fyfe Shore Rd
Kelburn Terrace
Glasgow Road
Robert Street
Clune Park Primary School
CLUNE BRAE A761
Clune Brae
Benclutha
Cemetery
High Carnegie Road
Brookfield Road
Westfield Rd
Northfield
Mid Avenue
Southfield
West Dougliehill
Dougliehill Ter
Dougliehill Place
Dougliehill Road
Reservoir
Devol Burn
Selkirk Road
Devol Ind Est
Lomond Av
Cardross Avenue
Bridgend Avenue
Burnhead Rd
Auchenfoil La
Auchenfoil Rd
Duchal St
Muirshiel La
Devol
Dubbs Road
Gareloch Road
Knocknair St
Boglestone Avenue
North Road
South Road
Langside Terrace
Golf Dr
Moorfield Av
Merryvale Av
Muirdykes Avenue
Glenside Rd
Crosshill Road
Auchenleck Road
Auchenleck Lane
Harelaw Reservoir
Port Glasgow Golf Club
Mid Auchinleck
Bardrainney
Surg
Bardrainney Av
Moss Road
Mallaig Rd
W Barmoss Avenue
Moidart Rd
Morar Rd
Minard Rd
Montrose Avenue
Milton Rd
Methil Rd
Mayfield Rd
Auchenbothie Road
Marloch Av
Cuillins Av
Sidlaw Av
Pentland Av
Slaemuir Av
Slaemuir Gardens
Millport Road
Devol Moor
Golf Course
Harelaw
Devol Road
Crosshill Road
Cunston Cott
Auchentiber
B788
West Kilbride
Pennytersal
Priestside Farm
High Mathernock
Auchenfoyle
Gryfe Water
Strathgryfe
Gryffeside
Horsecraig
Cauldside
52
Strathgryfe
1 grid square represents 500 metres

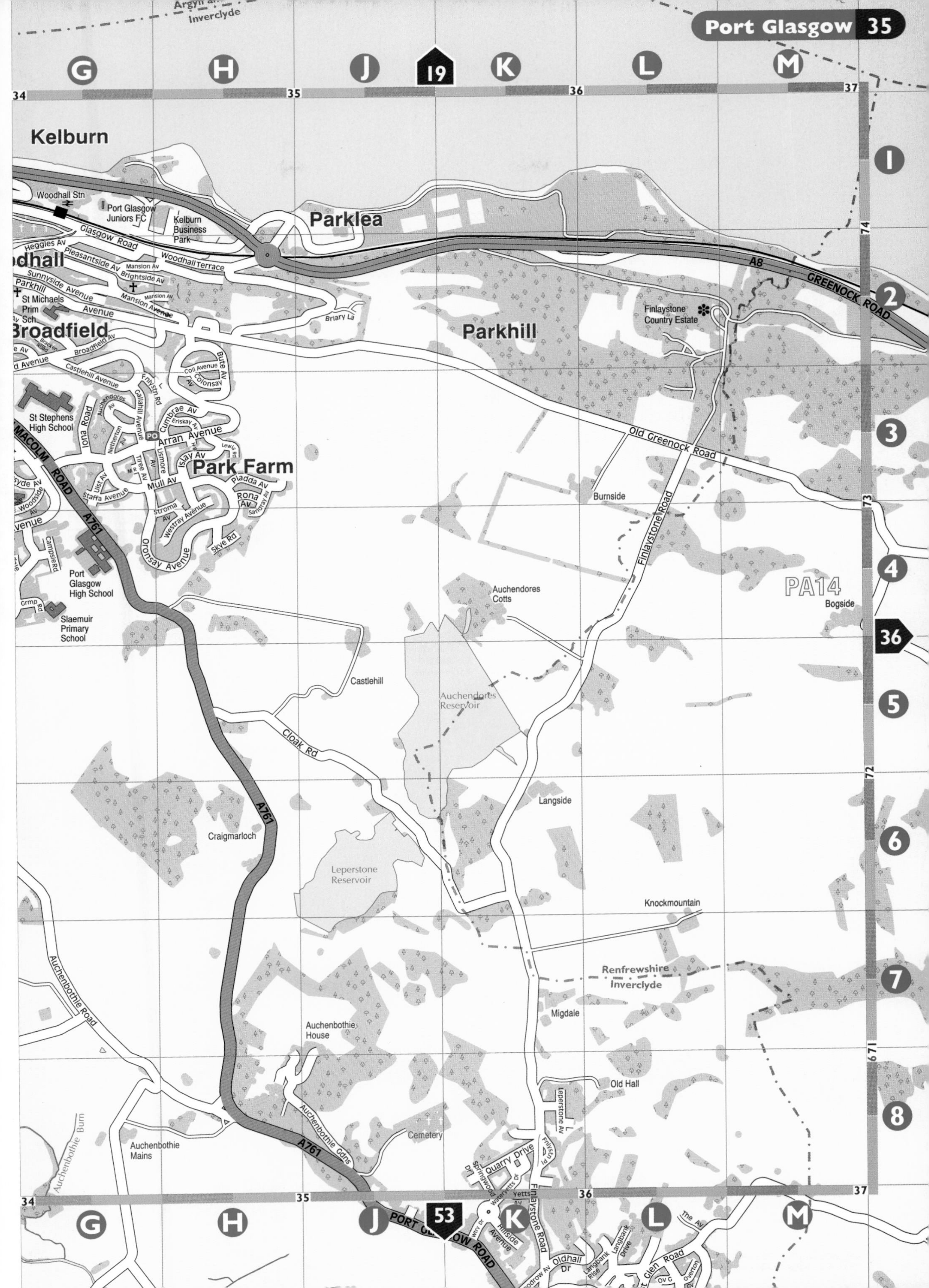
Kelburn
Woodhall Stn
Port Glasgow Juniors FC
Kelburn Business Park
Parklea
Glasgow Road
Heggles Av
Pleasantside Av
Woodhall Terrace
Brightside Av
Mansion Av
Sunnyside Avenue
Mansion Avenue
Parkhill
St Michaels Prim Sch
Broadfield
Broadfield Av
Castlehill Avenue
Briary La
Parkhill
Finlaystone Country Estate
A8
GREENOCK ROAD
Bute Av
Coll Avenue
Colonsay Av
St Stephens High School
Iona Road
Auchendores Av
Netherton Av
Callahill Avenue
Cumbrae Av
Eriskay Av
Arran Avenue
Lewis Rd
Islay Av
Lismore Av
Tiree Av
Park Farm
Old Greenock Road
Uist Av
Mull Av
Pladda Av
Rona Av
Staffa Avenue
Stroma Av
Westray Avenue
Sandray Av
Oronsay Avenue
Skye Rd
KILMACOLM ROAD
A761
Campsie Rd
Port Glasgow High School
Slaemuir Primary School
Burnside
Finlaystone Road
PA14
Bogside
Auchendores Cotts
Castlehill
Auchendores Reservoir
Cloak Rd
Langside
Craigmarloch
Leperstone Reservoir
Knockmountain
Renfrewshire
Inverclyde
Migdale
Auchenbothie Road
Auchenbothie House
Old Hall
Leperstone Av
Auchenbothie Burn
Auchenbothie Mains
Auchenbothie Gdns
Cemetery
Quarry Drive
Springwood Dr
Wateryetts Dr
Yetts Av
Hillside Avenue
Oldhall Dr
Langbank Rise
Langbank Drive
Glen Road
The Av
Overton
PORT GLASGOW ROAD
Argyll and Bute
Inverclyde
19
36
53
G H J K L M
1 2 3 4 5 6 7 8
34 35 36 37
74 73 72 671

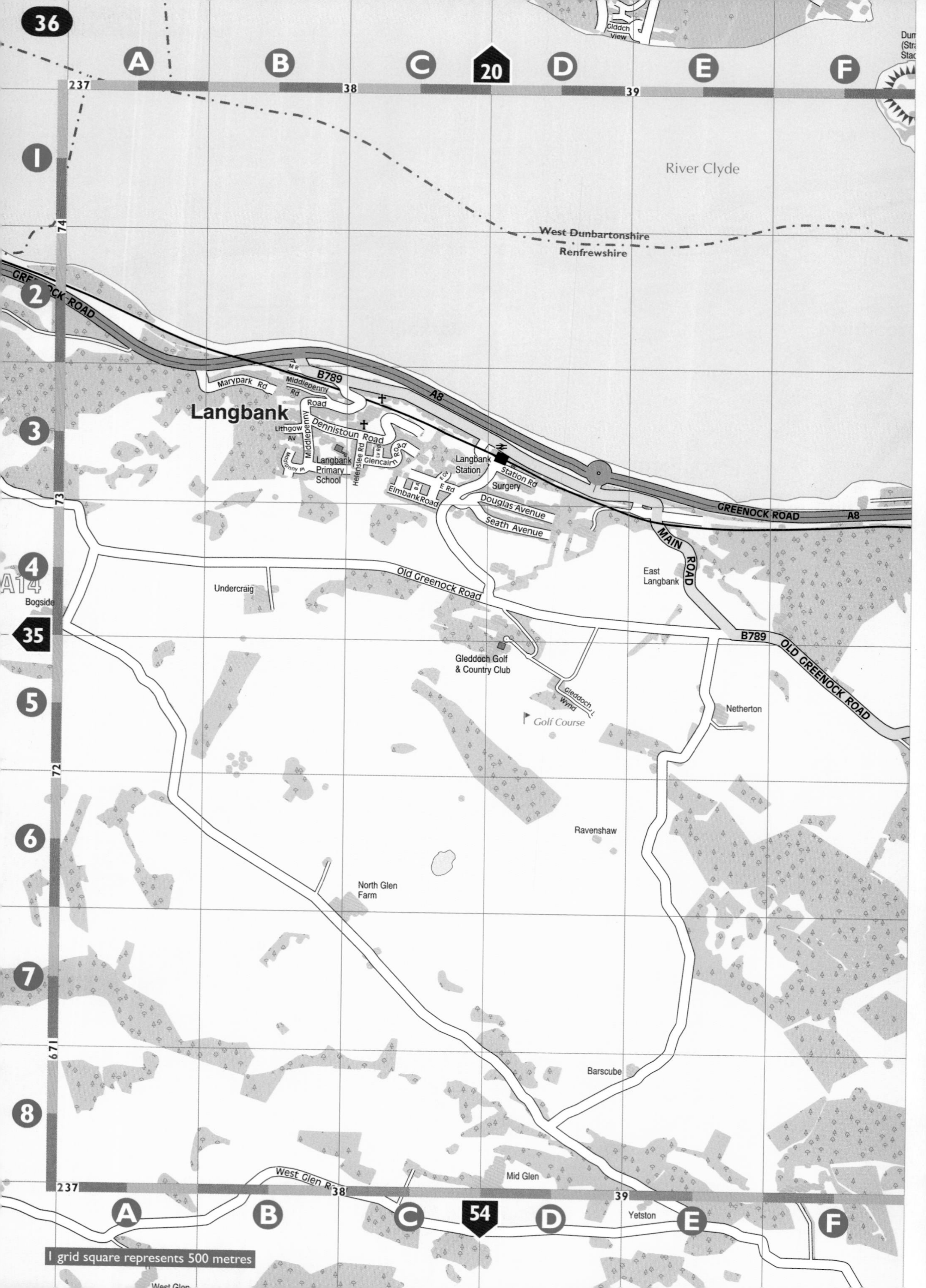

36

A · · · B · · · C **20** D · · · E · · · F

237 · · · 38 · · · 39

I

74

River Clyde

West Dunbartonshire
Renfrewshire

2 GREENOCK ROAD

M R

Marypark Rd B789

Middlepenny
Rd

Dennistoun Road

A8

3 **Langbank**

Lithgow
AV

Helenslee Rd

Glencairn

Langbank Station

Langbank
Primary
School

Elmbank Road

E Rd

Station Rd

Surgery

Douglas Avenue

Seath Avenue

GREENOCK ROAD A8

73

MAIN ROAD

4 A14

Bogside

Undercraig

Old Greenock Road

East
Langbank

35

Gleddoch Golf
& Country Club

B789 OLD GREENOCK ROAD

5

Gleddoch
Wynd

Netherton

Golf Course

72

6

Ravenshaw

North Glen
Farm

7

671

Barscube

8

West Glen R 38

Mid Glen

237 39

Yetston

A · · · B · · · C **54** D · · · E · · · F

I grid square represents 500 metres

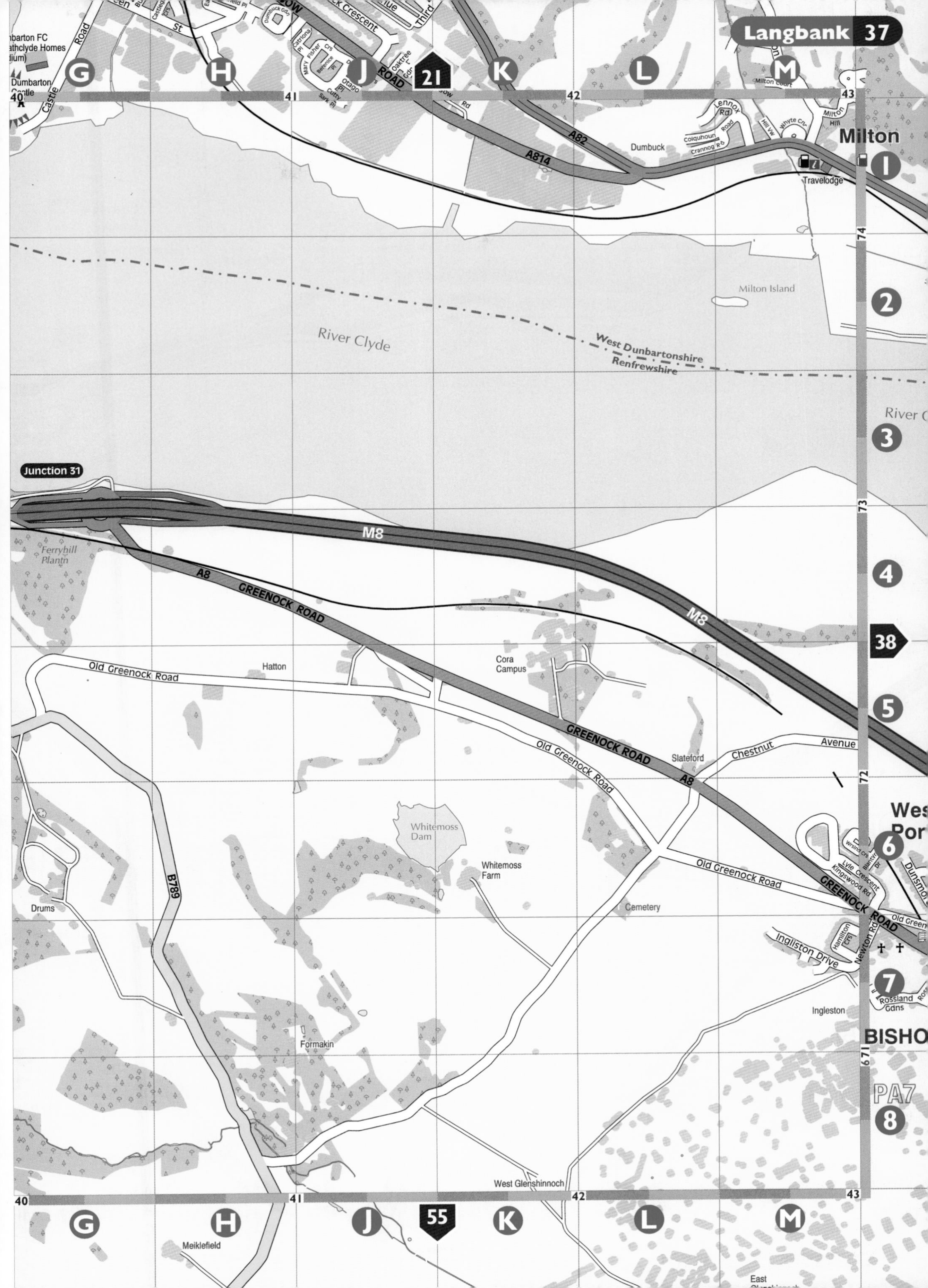
Dumbarton FC
Dumbarton Castle
Castle Road
St
Dumbuck Gdn
Crescent
Third
Catriona Pl
Mary Fisher Crs
Berenice Pl
Otago
Cutty Sark Pl
Oaktree Gdns
ROAD
21
Rd
A814
A82
Dumbuck
Milton Court
Lennox Rd
Colquhoun Road
Crannog Rd
Hill Vw
Whyte Crs
Milton Hill
Milton
Travelodge
G
H
J
K
L
M
40
41
42
43
74
73
72
71
1
2
3
4
5
6
7
8
Milton Island
River Clyde
West Dunbartonshire
Renfrewshire
Junction 31
M8
Ferryhill Plantn
A8
GREENOCK ROAD
38
Hatton
Old Greenock Road
Cora Campus
Slateford
Chestnut Avenue
Whitemoss Dam
Whitemoss Farm
B789
Drums
Cemetery
Wrsind Crs
Lyle Crescent
Blantyre Pl
Kingswood Rd
Hamilton Crs
Newton Rd
Ingliston Drive
Rossland Gdns
Ingleston
BISHO
PA7
Formakin
West Glenshinnoch
55
Meiklefield
East

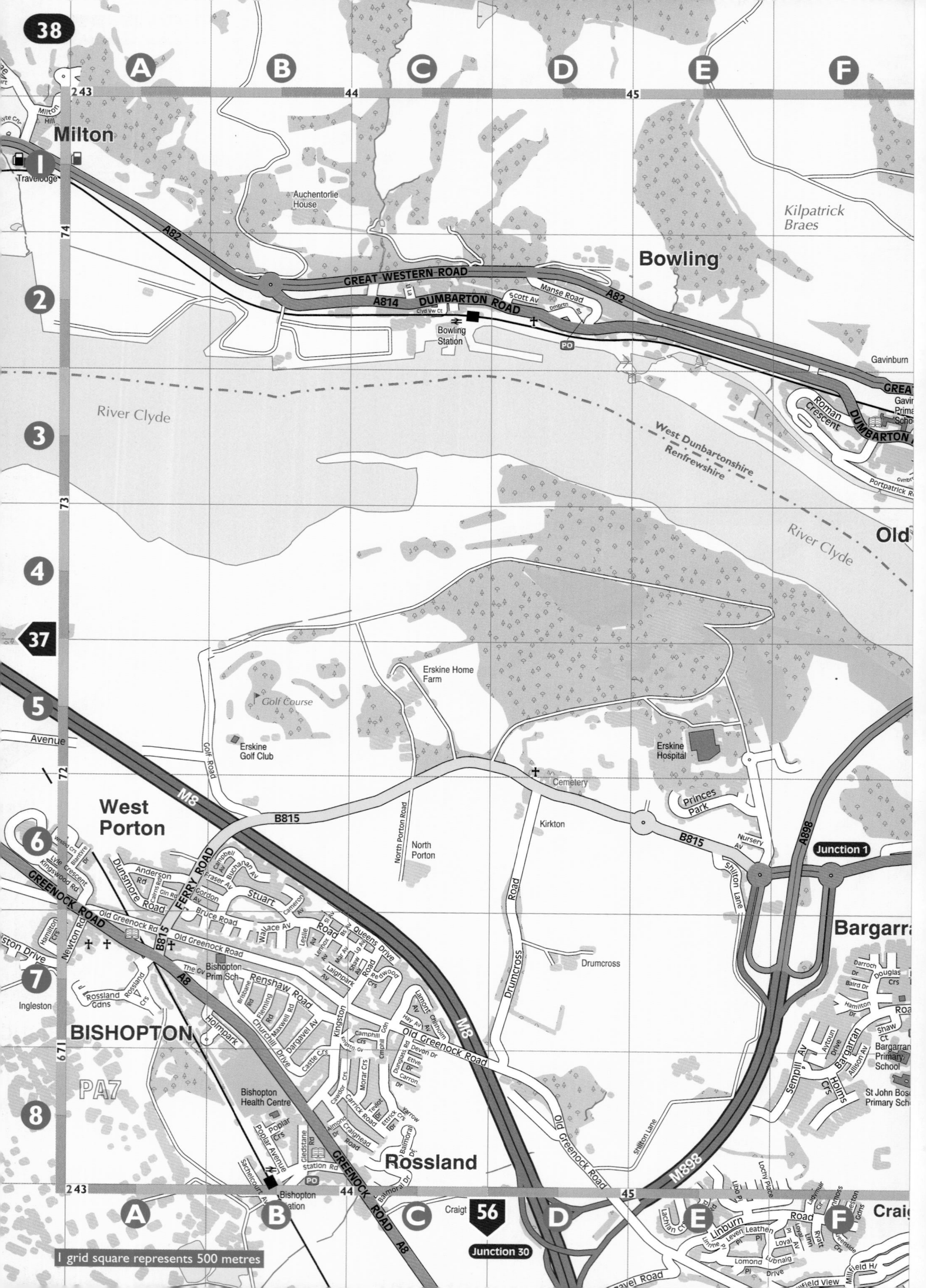
A
B
C
D
E
F
1
2
3
4
5
6
7
8
243
44
45
74
73
72
671
37
56
Milton
Travelodge
Auchentorlie House
A82
GREAT WESTERN ROAD
A814
DUMBARTON ROAD
Scott Av
Manse Road
Bowling Station
PO
Bowling
Kilpatrick Braes
Gavinburn
Roman Crescent
River Clyde
West Dunbartonshire
Renfrewshire
Portpatrick Rd
Old
Erskine Home Farm
Golf Course
Erskine Golf Club
Golf Road
Avenue
Erskine Hospital
Cemetery
Princes Park
Kirkton
B815
North Porton Road
North Porton
Nursery Av
Shilton Lane
A898
Junction 1
West Porton
M8
FERRY ROAD
Anderson Rd
Dunsmore Road
Buchanan Av
Fraser Av
Gordon Av
Stuart
Bruce Road
Wallace Av
Cameron Av
Leslie Av
Queens Drive
Redwood Crs
GREENOCK ROAD
Old Greenock Rd
Old Greenock Road
Lyle Crescent
Kingswood Rd
Hamilton Crs
Newton Rd
Bishopton Prim Sch
Renshaw Road
Laighpark Av
Drumcross Road
Drumcross
Bargarran
Ingleston
Rossland Gdns
Rossland Crs
BISHOPTON
Holmpark
Brisbane Rd
Fleming Rd
Maxwell Rd
Churchill Drive
Dargavel Av
Kingston
Castle Crs
Lamont Av
Chisholm Av
Campbell Crs
Old Greenock Road
Dunglass Rd
Devon Dr
Etive Dr
Carron Dr
Morar Crs
Cawdor Crs
Carrick Road
Craighead Road
Almond Dr
Balmoral Dr
Yarrow Crs
Ettrick Dr
Teviot Dr
PA7
Bishopton Health Centre
Poplar Crs
Poplar Avenue
Gledstane Rd
Station Rd
Sachelcourt Av
Bishopton Station
Rossland
Old Greenock Road
Shilton Lane
M898
Sempill Av
Aytoun Drive
Bargarran Road
Holms Crs
Allison Av
Douglas Crs
Darroch Dr
Baird Dr
Hamilton Dr
Shaw Ct
Bargarran Primary School
St John Bosco Primary School
Lochy Place
Linburn Road
Leven Pl
Leathen Pl
Loyal Av
Ryatt Linn
Lomond Pl
Lubnaig Drive
Craigton
Junction 30
A8
1 grid square represents 500 metres

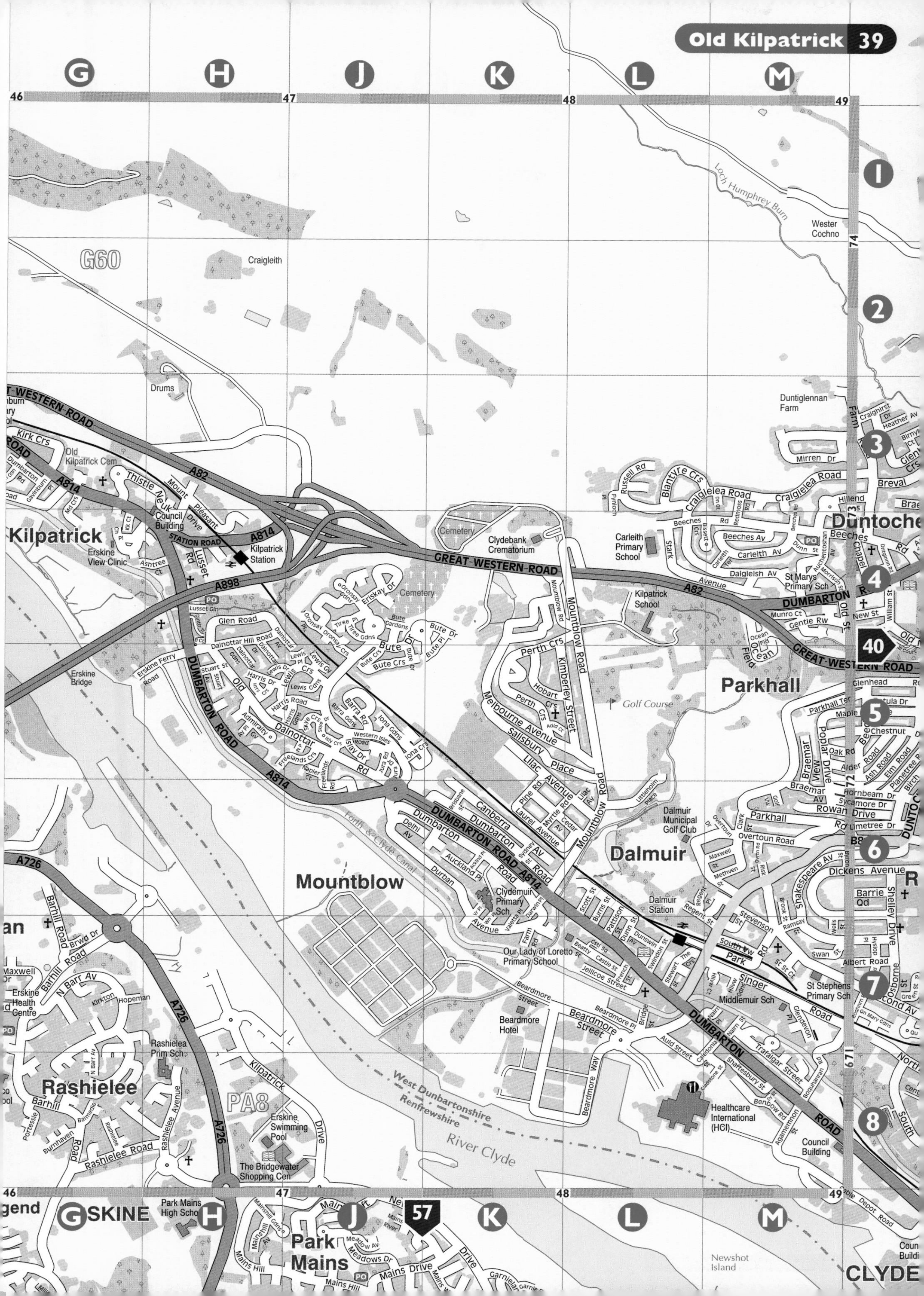

G | H | J | K | L | M

46 | **47** | **48** | **49**

I

G60

Craigleith

Loch Humphrey Burn

Wester Cochno

2

Drums

Duntiglennan Farm

WEST WESTERN ROAD

Kirk Crs

Old Kilpatrick Cem

Thistle Neuk

A82

Russell Rd

Blantyre Crs

Craiglelea Road

Craiglelea Road

Breval

Beeches

Craighirst Dr

Heather Rd

Birnyie

3

Mirren Dr

Hillend

A814

Council Building

Mount Pleasant Drive

STATION ROAD

Kilpatrick Station

GREAT WESTERN ROAD

Cemetery

Clydebank Crematorium

Carleith Primary School

Beeches Av

Carleith Av

Carleith

Stark Avenue

Dalgleish Av

St Marys Primary Sch

Beeches

PO

Auchentoshan

Duntoche

Kilpatrick

Erskine View Clinic

Ashtree

A898

A814

Glen Road

PO

Lusset Gln

Erskine Ferry Road

Erskine Bridge

DUMBARTON ROAD

Dalnottar Hill Road

Stuart St

Harris Dr

Harris Road

Admiralty

Old Dalnottar

Freelands Crs

Napiers

Barra Rd

Iona Gdns

Lewis Crs

Lewis Gdns

Jura Rd

Iona Crs

Western Isles Road

Islay Dr

Bute Cardens

Tiree Pl

Oronsay Crs

Oronsay Ct

Bute Dr

Bute Crs

Bute Dr

Cemetery

Mountblow Rd

Perth Crs

Hobart Crs

Perth Rd

Melbourne Avenue

Salisbury

Lilac Avenue

Laurel Avenue

Pine Rd

Myrtle

Kimberley Street

Kilpatrick School

Golf Course

Ocean Field

A82

DUMBARTON

Munro Ct

Gentle Rw

GREAT WESTERN ROAD

New St

Glenhead

Fistula Dr

Chestnut

Maple Dr

Braemar View

Oak Rd

Poplar Drive

Alder Rd

Ash Road

Elm Road

Planetree

Birch

Braemar AV

Hornbeam

Sycamore

Rowan Drive

Limetree Dr

Parkhall

Parkhall

40

4

5

6

DUMTOCH

A726

N Barr Av

Barhill Road

Erskine Health Centre

PO

Rashielee

Barhill

Rashielee Prim Sch

Hopeman

Kirkton

Rashielee Road

Rashielee Avenue

A726

Forth & Clyde Canal

Mountblow

Avenue

DUMBARTON ROAD A814

Canberra

Durban

Delhi

Dumbarton

Auckland Pl

Clydemuir Primary Sch

Farm

Our Lady of Loretto Primary School

Beardmore Street

Beardmore Hotel

Jellicoe Street

DUMBARTON ROAD A814

Scott St

Burns St

Pattison St

Castle St

Dunn St

Beatty St

French St

Swindon St

Dalmuir

Dalmuir Municipal Golf Club

Overtoun Road

Maxwell St

Methven

Clark St

Overtoun

Parkhall

Risk

B8

Dalmuir Station

Regent St

South Av

Stevenson

Singer

Middlemuir Sch

Shakespeare AV

Dickens Avenue

Barrie Qd

Shelley Drive

Albert Road

St Stephens Primary Sch

Osborne

Second Av

7

DUMBARTON ROAD

Stewart St

The

Auld Street

Beardmore Way

Beardmore Pl

Chelmsford

Shaftesbury St

Trafalgar Street

Bridge St

Benbow Rd

Aitkenhead Rd

Healthcare International (HCI)

Council Building

8

A726

Kilpatrick Drive

Erskine Swimming Pool

The Bridgewater Shopping Cen

PA8

West Dunbartonshire Renfrewshire

River Clyde

46 | **47** | **48** | **49**

Legend

SKINE

Park Mains High School

Park Mains

PO

57

Mains Drive

Meadow Dr

Meadows Dr

Garnieland

Newshot Island

Depot Road

Coun Build

CLYDE

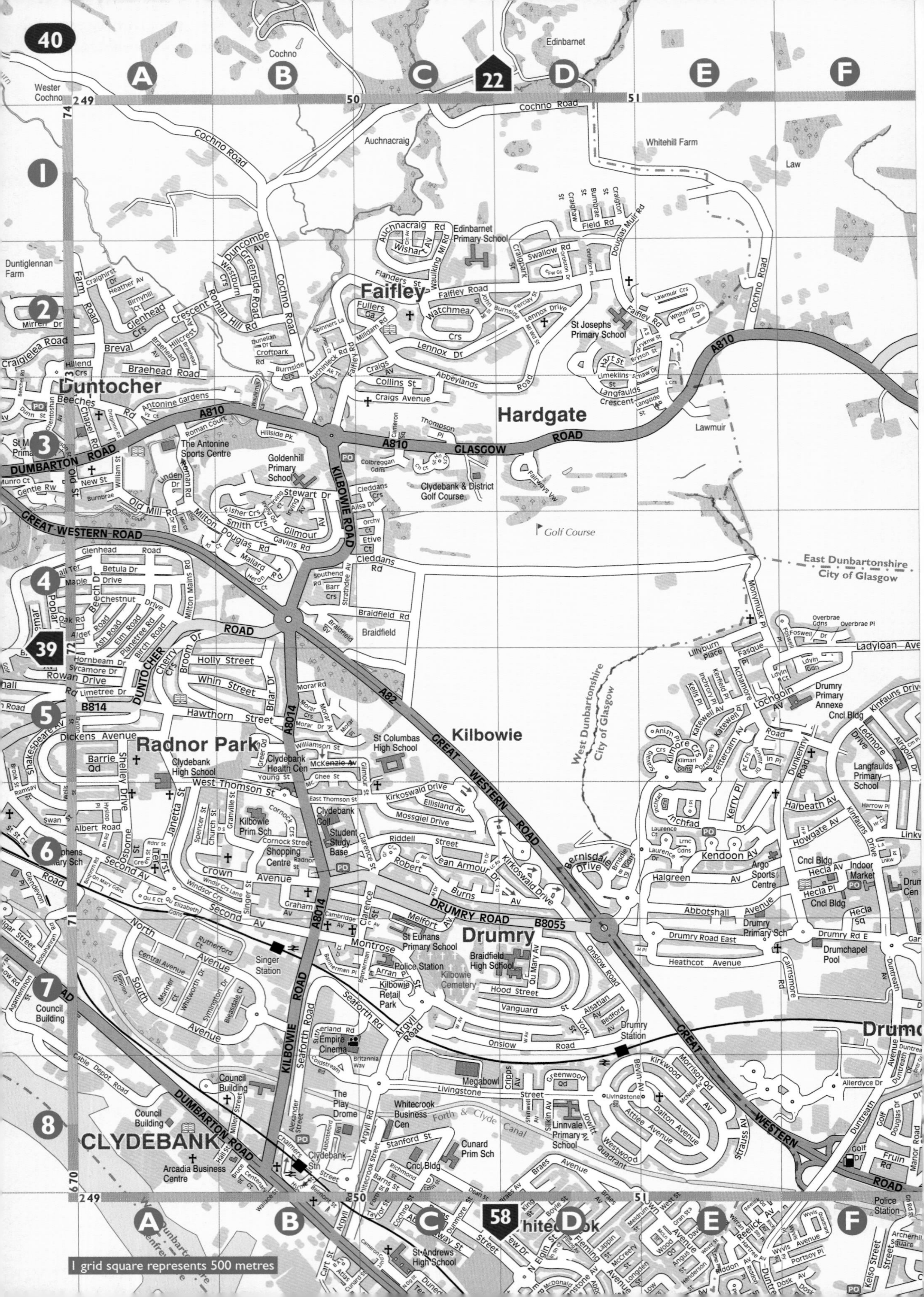
A
B
C
D
E
F
22
Cochno
Wester Cochno
Edinbarnet
Cochno Road
Auchnacraig
Whitehill Farm
Law
Duntiglennan Farm
Edinbarnet Primary School
Faifley
Faifley Road
Lennox Dr
Abbeylands
St Josephs Primary School
Duntocher
Antonine Gardens
Dumbarton Road
A810
Hardgate
Glasgow Road
The Antonine Sports Centre
Goldenhill Primary School
Kilbowie Road
Clydebank & District Golf Course
Golf Course
Great Western Road
Cleddans Rd
Braidfield
East Dunbartonshire
City of Glasgow
West Dunbartonshire
Lawmuir
Radnor Park
Clydebank High School
St Columbas High School
Kilbowie
A82
A8014
B814
Drumry Primary Annexe
Langfaulds Primary School
Kilbowie Prim Sch
Student Study Base
Argo Sports Centre
Indoor Market
Drumry
Drumry Road
B8055
St Eunans Primary Sch
Braidfield High School
Kilbowie Cemetery
Drumry Primary Sch
Drumchapel Pool
Singer Station
Police Station
Kilbowie Retail Park
Drumry Station
Empire Cinema
Megabowl
Council Building
The Play Drome
Whitecrook Business Cen
Forth & Clyde Canal
Cunard Prim Sch
Linnvale Primary School
CLYDEBANK
Clydebank Stn
Arcadia Business Centre
St Andrews High School
39
58
1 grid square represents 500 metres

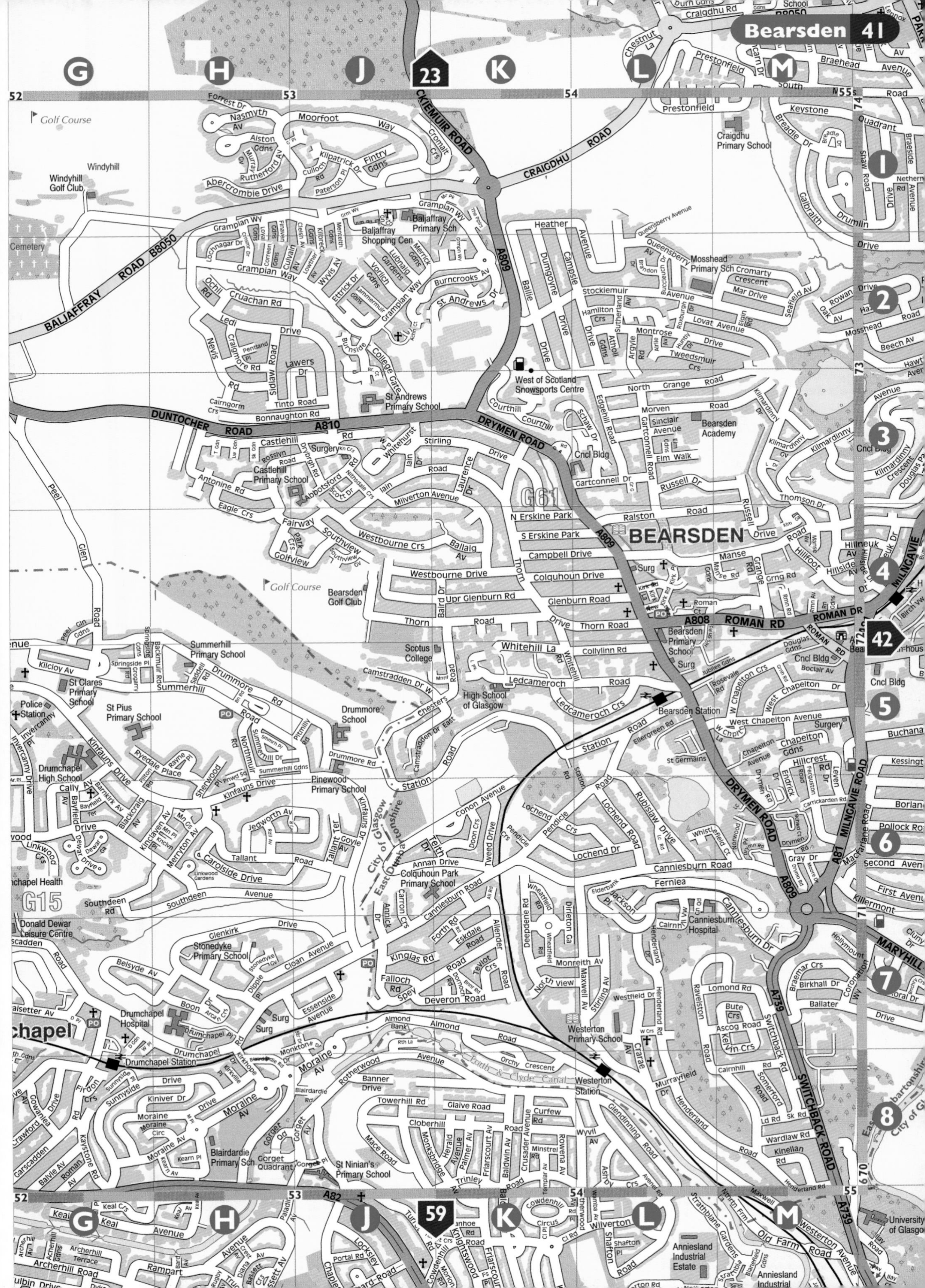

Bearsden 41
G
H
J
K
L
M
23
52
53
54
55
Golf Course
Windyhill
Windyhill Golf Club
Cemetery
BALJAFFRAY ROAD B8050
Forrest Dr
Nasmyth Av
Moorfoot Way
Alston Gdns
Murray Gv
Rutherford Av
Kilpatrick Dr
Fintry Gdns
Culloch Rd
Paterson Pl
Abercrombie Drive
Cromalt Crs
STOCKIEMUIR ROAD
CRAIGDHU ROAD
Craigdhu Rd
Prestonfield
Craigdhu Primary School
Braehead Avenue
Keystone Quadrant
Breadie Dr
Shaw Road
Braeside Av
Calbraith
Drumlin Drive
Grampian Wy
Grampian Way
Lochnagar Dr
Corrieen Gdns
Finlaven Gdns
Culvain Gdns
Lowther
Killbreck
Baljaffray Primary Sch
Baljaffray Shopping Cen
Merrick Gdns
Lubnaig Gardens
Wyvis Av
Vorlich Gdns
Ettrick Dr
Burncrooks Av
St Andrews Dr
Ochil Rd
Cruachan Rd
Ledi Drive
Nevis Rd
Craigmore Rd
Pendland Pl
Sidlaw Road
Lawers Dr
Cairngorm Crs
Tinto Road
Bonnaughton Rd
College Gate
Burnside
St Andrews Primary School
DUNTOCHER ROAD A810
A809
Heather Avenue
Queensberry Avenue
Dumgoyne Drive
Campsie Drive
Baile Drive
Mosshead Primary Sch
Cromarty Crescent
Mar Drive
Stockiemuir Avenue
Hamilton Crs
Sutherland Av
Atholl Gdns
Argyle Rd
Montrose Drive
Lovat Avenue
Tweedsmuir Crs
Seafield Av
Rowan Dr
Oak Av
Mosshead Road
Beech Av
West of Scotland Snowsports Centre
North Grange Road
Morven Road
Edgehill Road
Gartconnell Road
Sinclair Avenue
Elm Walk
Bearsden Academy
Kilmardinny Avenue
Kilmardinny Crescent
Douglas Pk
Courthill
DRYMEN ROAD
Castlehill Rd
Rossyln Road
Castlehill Primary School
Surgery
Whitehurst
Stirling Drive
Iain Road
Laurence Dr
Antonine Rd
Abbotsford
Scott Dr
Milverton Avenue
Eagle Crs
Fairway
Southview
Westbourne Crs
Ballaig Av
Golfview
Park Crs
Cncl Bldg
G61
Gartconnell Dr
Russell Dr
Thomson Dr
Ralston Road
N Erskine Park
S Erskine Park
BEARSDEN
Campbell Drive
Colquhoun Drive
Glenburn Road
Thorn Road
Thorn Drive
Manse Road
Grange Rd
Hillfoot Dr
Hillneuk Av
Hillside Av
MILNGAVIE
Golf Course
Bearsden Golf Club
Westbourne Drive
Baird Dr
Upr Glenburn Rd
ROMAN RD A808
ROMAN DR
Bearsden Primary School
42
Peel Glen Road
Peel Gdns
Kilcloy Av
Springside Pl
Backmuir Rd
Summerhill Primary School
Scotus College
Whitehill La
Whitehill Rd
Collylinn Rd
Douglas Gdns
Cncl Bldg
Boclair Av
St Clares Primary School
Police Station
Invercanny Pl
Summerhill Rd
Drummore Rd
Camstradden Dr W
Ledcameroch Road
High School of Glasgow
Ledcameroch Crs
Bearsden Station
Rosevale Rd
W Chapelton Crs
West Chapelton Dr
5
St Pius Primary School
Drummore School
Chesters
Camstradden Dr East
Station Road
Ellergreen Rd
West Chapelton Avenue
Surgery
Buchanan
Drumchapel High School
Kinfauns Drive
Ryedale Place
Rayne Pl
Sherwood Pl
Northmuir Rd
Summerhill Gdns
Pinewood Primary School
Drummore Rd
St Germains
Chapelton Gdns
Chapelton Avenue
Hillcrest Rd
Kessington
Cally Av
Barnkirk Av
Bayfield Drive
Blackcraig Av
Kinclaven Av
Merryton Av
Jedworth Av
Tallant Ter
Goyle Av
Conon Avenue
Doon Crs
Tweed Drive
Pendicle Crs
Lochend Road
Rubislaw Drive
Endrick Dr
Drymen Rd
Leven Dr
MILNGAVIE ROAD A81
Borland
Pollock Rd
Linkwood Crs
Dewar Drive
Carolside Drive
Tallant Road
City of Glasgow
East Dunbartonshire
Telfth Dr
Annan Drive
Lochend Dr
Whistlefield Ct
Gray Dr
MacFarlane Road
6
Second Avenue
Drumchapel Health
G15
Southdeen Avenue
Southdeen Rd
Colquhoun Park Primary School
Canniesburn Road
Fernlea
Elderbank
Jackson Pl
First Avenue
Killermont
Donald Dewar Leisure Centre
Glenkirk Drive
Stonedyke Primary School
Belsyde Av
Cloan Avenue
Carron Crs
Annick Dr
Forth Rd
Eskdale Road
Allender Road
Deepdene Rd
Dirleton Ga
Wheatfield
Canniesburn Hospital
Canniesburn Dr
MARYHILL
Cluny Dr
Hollymount
Braemar Crs
Birkhall Dr
Ballater Drive
Coronation Wy
7
Kinglas Rd
Teviot Crs
Falloch Rd
Spey
Deveron Road
Monreith Av
North View
Maxwell Av
Stirling Av
Henderland Rd
Lomond Rd
Bute Crs
Ascog Road
Kelvin Crs
Ravelston Road
Switchback Rd
A739
Boon Dr
Dipple Pl
Essenside Avenue
Drumchapel Hospital
Drumchapel Pl
Drumchapel Station
Surg
Almond Road
Monktone
Rth La
Orchy Crescent
Forth & Clyde Canal
Westerton Primary School
Westerton Station
Cairnhill Rd
Somerford Road
SWITCHBACK ROAD
Sunnyside Drive
Kiniver Dr
Moraine Circ
Moraine Av
Rotherwood Avenue
Banner Drive
Blairdardie Rd
Gorget Av
Towerhill Rd
Glaive Road
Cloberhill Road
Curfew Rd
Wyvil Av
Glendinning Road
Murrayfield Dr
Henderland Rd
8
Crawford Drive
Carscadden
Balvie Av
Roman Av
Kaystone Rd
Kearn Pl
Blairdardie Primary Sch
Gorget Quadrant
St Ninian's Primary School
Mace Road
Monksbridge Av
Herald Avenue
Palmer Av
Friarscourt Av
Baldwin Av
Crusader Avenue
Minstrel Rd
Rowena Av
Trinley Rd
Ld Rd
Sk Rd
Wardlaw Rd
Kinellan Rd
A82
Keal Crs
Keal Avenue
Archerhill Road
Archerhill Terrace
Rampart Av
59
Locksley Av
Portal Rd
Cowdenhill Circus
Wilverton Rd
Shafton Road
Anniesland Industrial Estate
Old Farm Road
Westerton Avenue
Maxwell
University of Glasgow

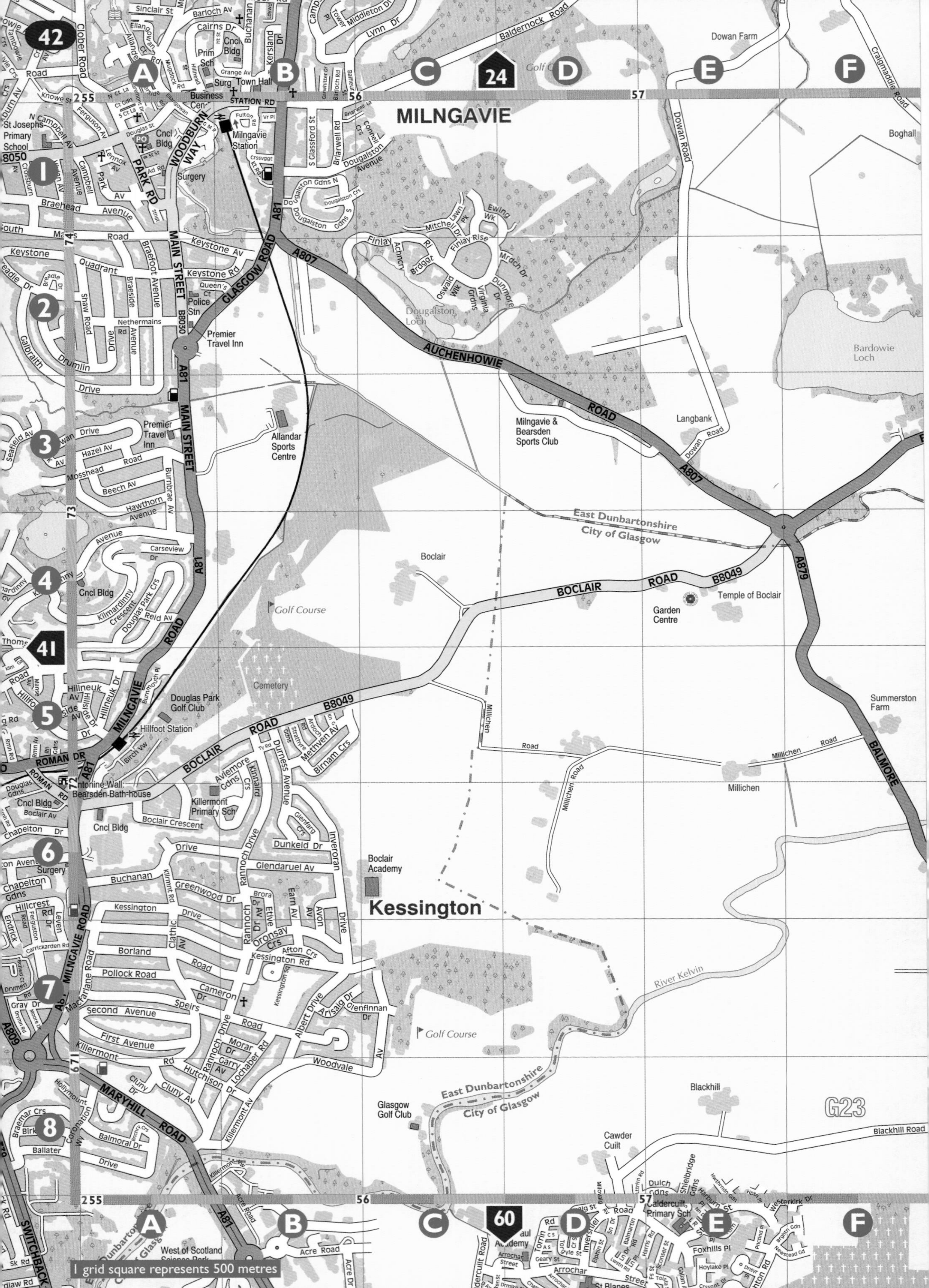

42
24
41
60
A
B
C
D
E
F
1
2
3
4
5
6
7
8
255
56
57
74
73
72
71
MILNGAVIE
Kessington
Clober Road
Sinclair St
Barloch Av
Cairns Dr
Buchanan
Kersland Dr
Lynn Dr
Middleton Dr
Baldernock Road
Golf Course
Dowan Farm
Craigmaddie Road
Boghall
Station Rd
Business Cen
Town Hall
Woodburn Way
Park Rd
Milngavie Station
Surgery
St Josephs Primary School
Braehead Avenue
Mains Road
Keystone Av
Keystone Rd
Keystone Quadrant
Main Street
Glasgow Road
Queen's Ct
Police Stn
Premier Travel Inn
Nethermains
Braefoot Avenue
Braeside Avenue
Shaw Road
Drumlin Drive
Galbraith
A81
A807
B8050
B8030
Dougalston Gdns N
Dougalston Gdns S
Dougalston Avenue
Dougalston Loch
Finlay Rise
Mitchell Dr
Ewing Wk
Oswald Wlk
Virginia Gdns
Dunmore Dr
Auchenhowie Road
Dowan Road
Langbank
Bardowie Loch
Milngavie & Bearsden Sports Club
Allandar Sports Centre
Hazel Av
Mosshead Road
Beech Av
Hawthorn Avenue
Burnbrae Av
Carseview Dr
Cncl Bldg
Kilmardinny Crescent
Douglas Park Crs
Reid Av
East Dunbartonshire
City of Glasgow
Boclair
Boclair Road
B8049
A879
Temple of Boclair
Garden Centre
Golf Course
Cemetery
Douglas Park Golf Club
Hillfoot Station
Milngavie Road
Roman Dr
Antonine Wall: Bearsden Bath-house
Boclair Crescent
Killermont Primary Sch
Aviemore Gdns
Kinnaird Crs
Durness Avenue
Methven Av
Birnam Crs
Millichen Road
Millichen
Summerston Farm
Balmore Road
Boclair Academy
Dunkeld Dr
Glendaruel Av
Inveroran Drive
Buchanan Drive
Greenwood Dr
Kessington Drive
Rannoch Drive
Borland Road
Pollock Road
Oronsay Crs
Afton Crs
Kessington Rd
Cameron Dr
Speirs Road
Second Avenue
First Avenue
Killermont Rd
Macfarlane Road
Morar Dr
Garry Av
Lochaber Rd
Hutchison Dr
Cluny Av
Cluny Dr
Albert Drive
Arisaig Dr
Glenfinnan Dr
Woodvale Av
Maryhill Road
River Kelvin
Golf Course
Glasgow Golf Club
Blackhill
Blackhill Road
Cawder Cuilt
G23
Chapelton Gdns
Hillcrest Rd
Surgery
A809
Braemar Crs
Ballater Drive
Balmoral Dr
Coronation Wy
Killermont Av
Acre Road
Acre Dr
A81
Switchback
West of Scotland Science Park
Caldercuilt Primary Sch
Foxhills Pl
Arrochar Street
St Blanes
1 grid square represents 500 metres

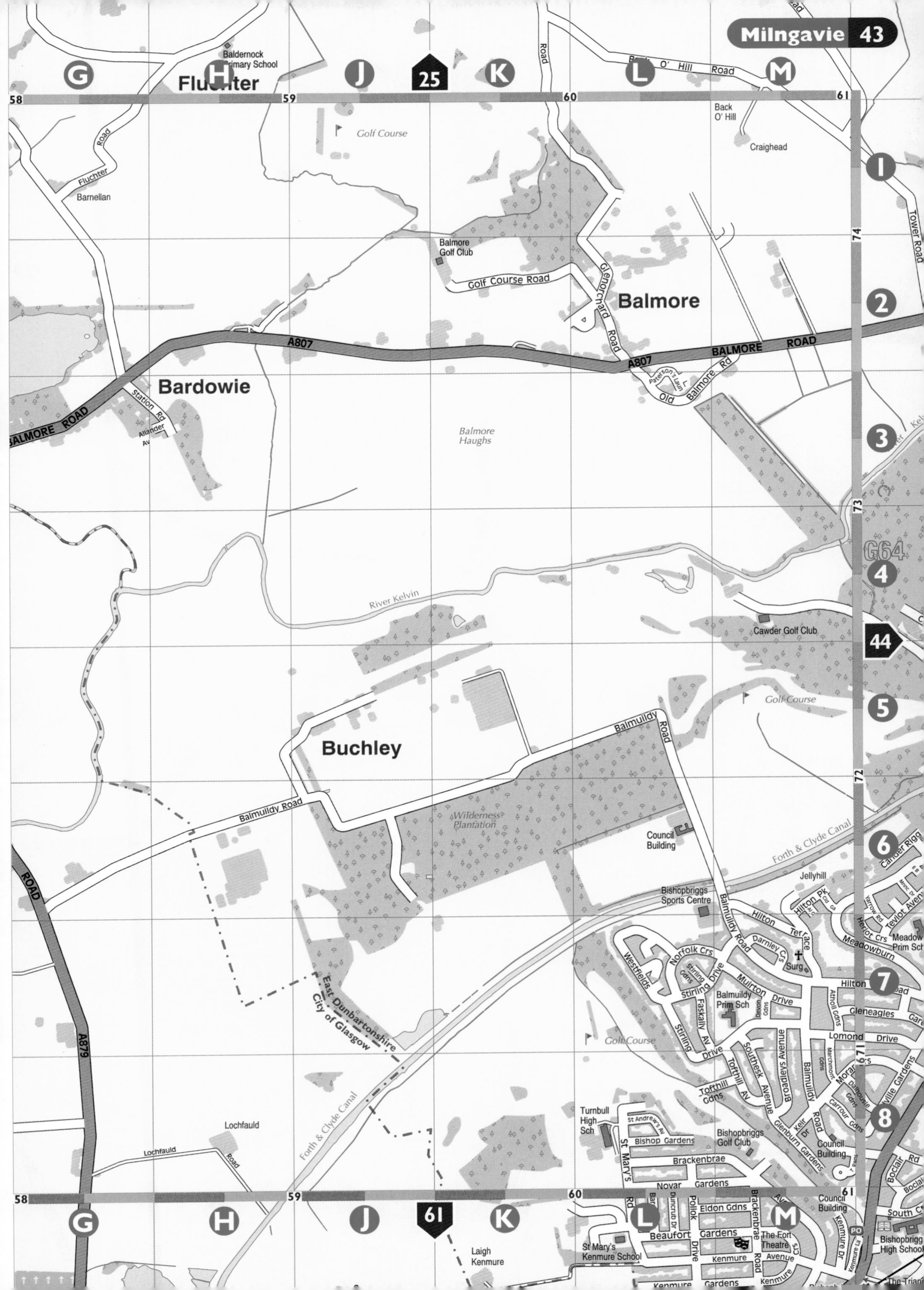

G   H   J   **25**   K   L   M

Fluchter

58   59   60   61

Golf Course

Baldernock Primary School

Fluchter

Barnellan

Road

I

Craighead

Back O' Hill

Back O' Hill Road

Balmore Golf Club

Golf Course Road

Balmore

Glenorchard Road

Tower Road

2

A807   BALMORE ROAD

Balmore Rd

A807

Bardowie

BALMORE ROAD

Station Rd

Allander Av

Old Balmore Rd

Paterson Lea

74   73   72

3

G64

4

Balmore Haughs

River Kelvin

Cawder Golf Club

44

Golf Course

5

Buchley

Balmulidy Road

Balmulidy Road

Wilderness Plantation

Council Building

Forth & Clyde Canal

Cander Rigg

6

Jellyhill

Bishopbriggs Sports Centre

Hilton Ter

Balmulidy Road

Hilton Pk

Yarrow Cr

Heriot Crs

Teviot Aven

Meadow Prim Sch

Meadowburn

ROAD

A879

East Dunbartonshire City of Glasgow

Norfolk Crs

Stirling Gdns

Westfields

Muirton Drive

Darnley Crs

Surg

Hilton

Atholl Gdns

Gleneagles

7

Faskally Av

Balmuildy Prim Sch

Stirling Drive

Stirling Av

Drive

Southesk Avenue

Broadleys Avenue

Balmuildy Road

Marchmont Gdns

Lomond   Drive

Morar

Carrour Gdns

Dunhope

Orville Gardens

8

Golf Course

Lochfauld

Tofthill Gdns

Tofthill Av

Turnbull High Sch

St Andrew's

Bishop Gardens

Bishopbriggs Golf Club

Glenburn Gardens

Council Building

Forth & Clyde Canal

Lochfauld   Road

St Mary's

Brackenbrae

Novar   Gardens

Eldon Gdns

Boclair

Brackenbrae Av

Council Building

South C

Bishopbriggs High School

58   59   60   61

G   H   J   **61**   K   L   M

Laigh Kenmure

St Mary's Kenmure School

Bishop Gardens

Duncrub Dr

Pollok

Beaufort Gardens

Kenmure Drive

The Fort Theatre

Kenmure Avenue

Kenmure Dr

The Triang

PO

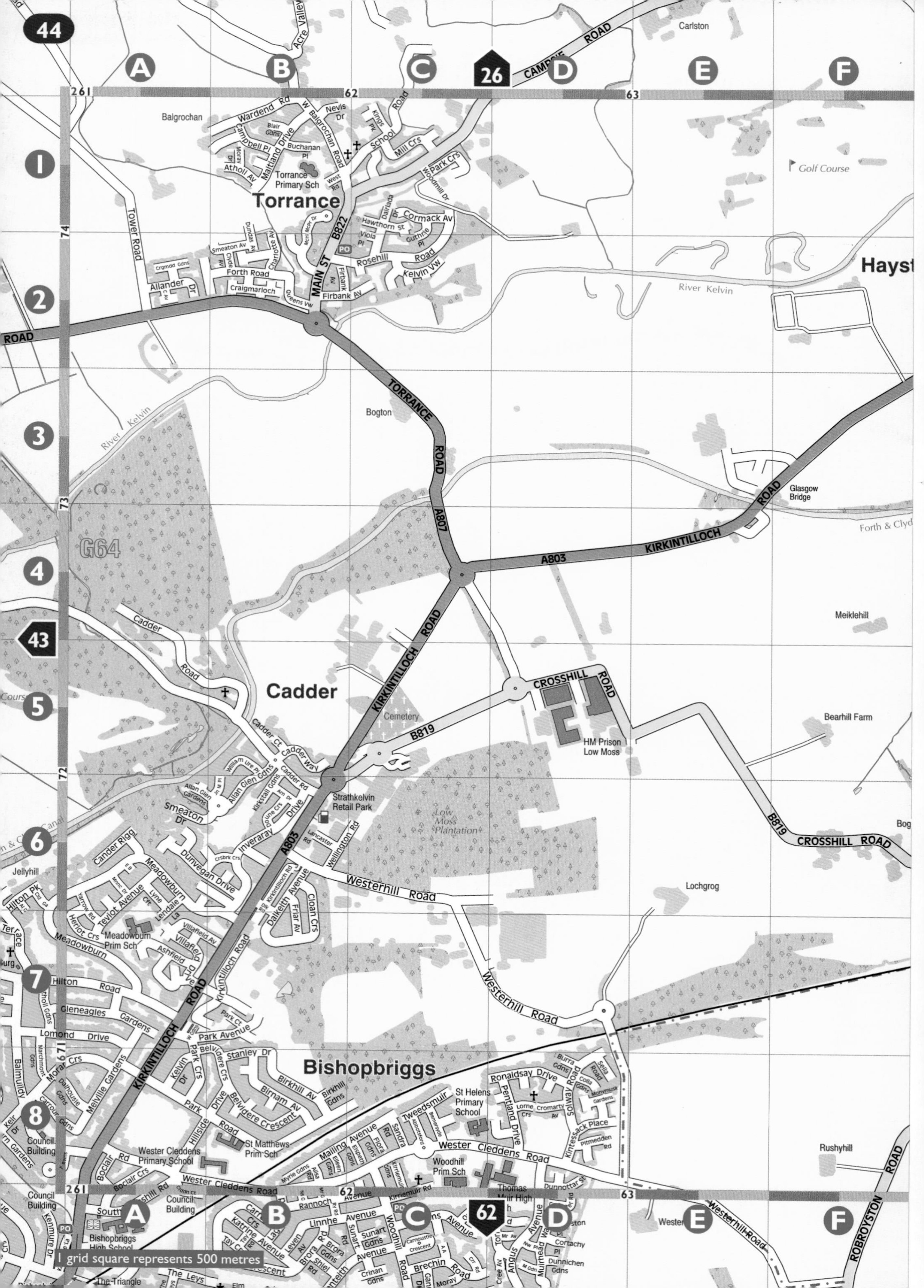
Torrance
Balgrochan
Torrance Primary Sch
Carlston
Golf Course
Hayst
River Kelvin
Bogton
Glasgow Bridge
Forth & Clyde
G64
Cadder
Cemetery
HM Prison Low Moss
Meiklehill
Bearhill Farm
Strathkelvin Retail Park
Low Moss Plantation
Lochgrog
Jellyhill
Meadowburn Prim Sch
Bishopbriggs
St Helens Primary School
St Matthews Prim Sch
Wester Cleddens Primary School
Woodhill Prim Sch
Thomas Muir High
Council Building
Bishopbriggs High School
Rushyhill
TORRANCE ROAD
A807
KIRKINTILLOCH ROAD
A803
CROSSHILL ROAD
B819
Westerhill Road
Wester Cleddens Road
ROBROYSTON ROAD
CAMPSIE ROAD
MAIN ST
B822
Cadder Road
Tower Road
43
26
62
1 grid square represents 500 metres

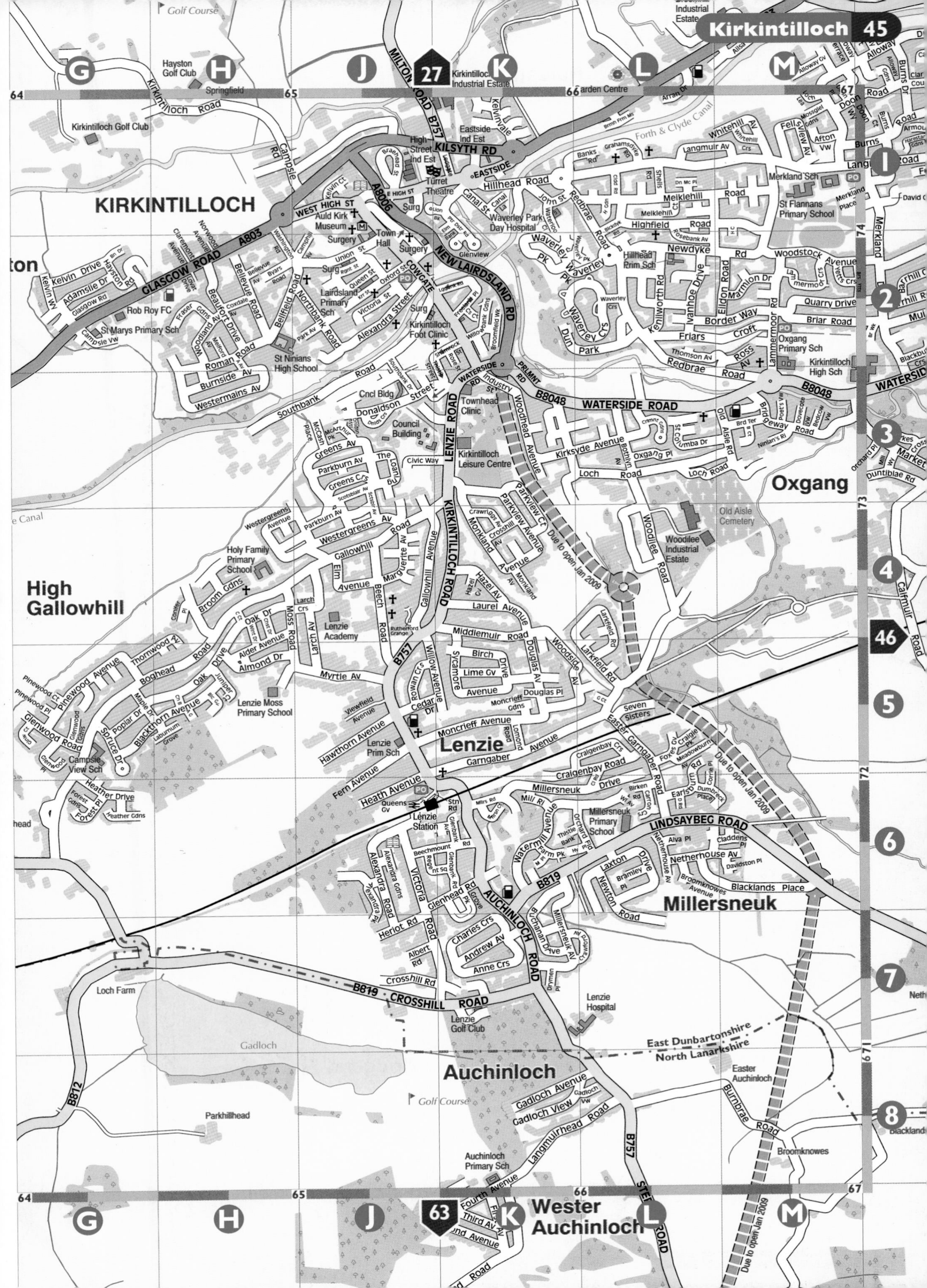
KIRKINTILLOCH
High Gallowhill
Lenzie
Oxgang
Millersneuk
Auchinloch
Wester Auchinloch
Golf Course
Hayston Golf Club
Springfield
Kirkintilloch Golf Club
Kirkintilloch Industrial Estate
Garden Centre
Industrial Estate
Forth & Clyde Canal
Eastside Ind Est
High Street Ind Est
Turret Theatre
KILSYTH RD
EASTSIDE
MILTON ROAD B757
NEW LAIRDSLAND RD
A8006
WEST HIGH ST
GLASGOW ROAD A803
Kirkintilloch Road
Campsie Rd
Auld Kirk Museum
Town Hall
Surgery
Lairdsland Primary Sch
Kirkintilloch Foot Clinic
Rob Roy FC
St Marys Primary Sch
St Ninians High School
Cncl Bldg
Council Building
Townhead Clinic
Kirkintilloch Leisure Centre
Waverley Park Day Hospital
Hillhead Prim Sch
Merkland Sch
St Flannans Primary School
Oxgang Primary Sch
Kirkintilloch High Sch
B8048 WATERSIDE ROAD
Old Aisle Cemetery
Woodilee Industrial Estate
Due to open Jan 2009
LENZIE ROAD
KIRKINTILLOCH ROAD
B757
Holy Family Primary School
Lenzie Academy
Lenzie Moss Primary School
Campsie View Sch
Lenzie Prim Sch
Lenzie Station
Millersneuk Primary School
LINDSAYBEG ROAD
B819
AUCHINLOCH ROAD
B819 CROSSHILL ROAD
Lenzie Golf Club
Lenzie Hospital
Loch Farm
Gadloch
Parkhillhead
East Dunbartonshire
North Lanarkshire
Easter Auchinloch
Burnbrae Road
Broomknowes
Auchinloch Primary Sch
Langmuirhead Road
Gadloch Avenue
Gadloch View
B812
Seven Sisters
27
46
63
G
H
J
K
L
M
1
2
3
4
5
6
7
8
64
65
66
67
71
72
73
74

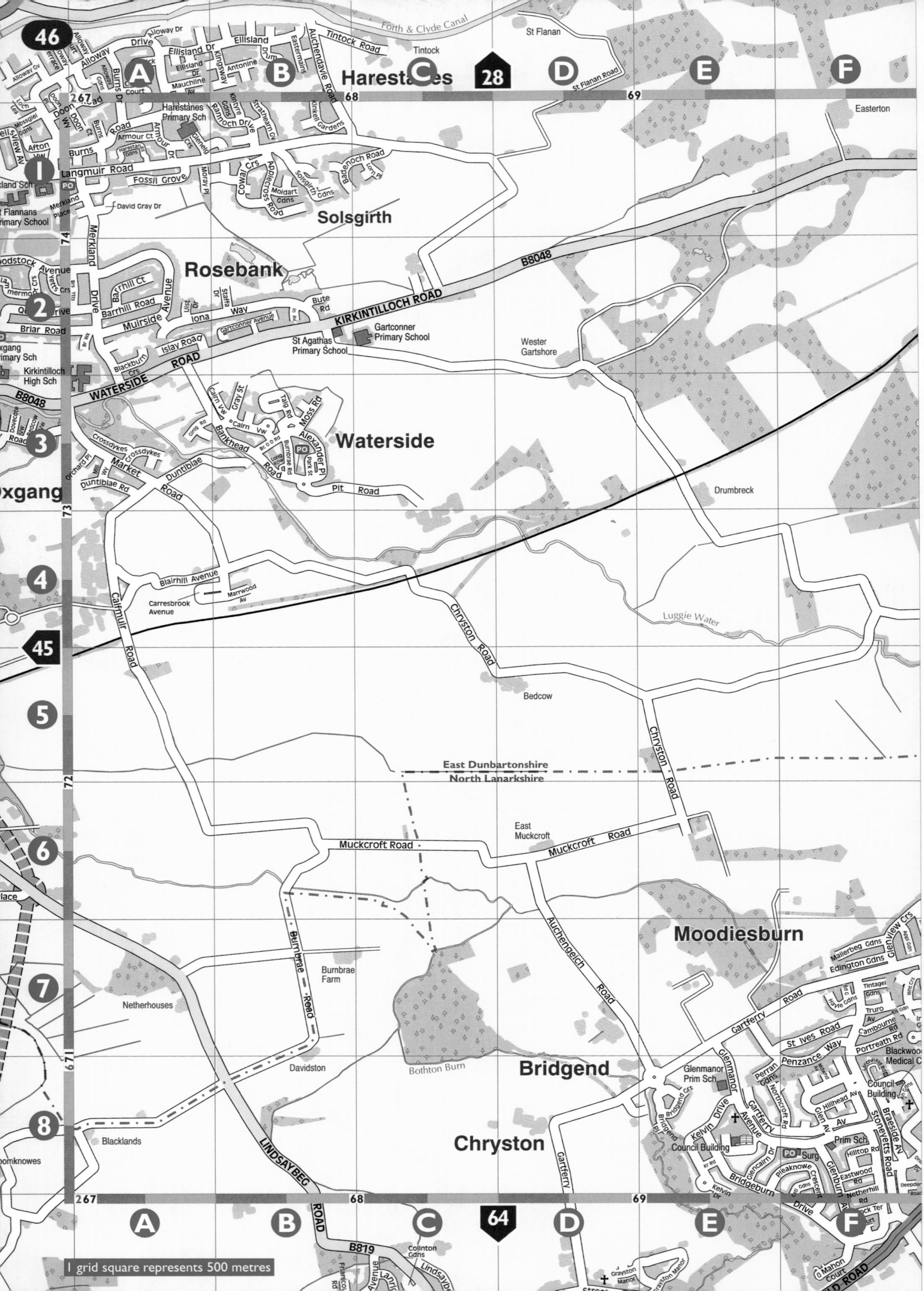
46
28
45
64
A
B
C
D
E
F
1
2
3
4
5
6
7
8
267
68
69
74
73
72
671
Forth & Clyde Canal
St Flanan
Tintock
Tintock Road
Harestanes
Harestanes Primary Sch
St Flanan Road
Easterton
Alloway Drive
Ellisland Dr
Ellisland
Kingsway
Antonine
Auchendavie Road
Eastermains
Kinkell Gardens
Strathearn Gv
Rannoch Drive
Kintyre Gdns
Glenelg Crs
Mauchline Av
Burns Dr
Burns Road
Doon Road
Afton Vw
Armour Ct
Armour Dr
Langmuir Road
Fossil Grove
Moray Pl
Cowal Crs
Applecross Road
Moidart Gdns
Solsgirth Gdns
Badenoch Road
Lorn Pl
David Gray Dr
Merkland Place
Merkland Drive
St Flannans Primary School
Solsgirth
Rosebank
B8048
KIRKINTILLOCH ROAD
Woodstock Avenue
Barrhill Ct
Barrhill Road
Muirside Avenue
Uist Dr
Staffa Dr
Iona Way
Gartconner Avenue
Bute Rd
Briar Road
Islay Road
Blackburn Crs
Gartconner Primary School
St Agathas Primary School
Wester Gartshore
Oxgang Primary Sch
Kirkintilloch High Sch
WATERSIDE ROAD
Cairn Vw
Gray St
Talg Rd
Moss Rd
Alexander Pl
Bankhead Road
Waterside
Crossdykes
Market Road
Duntiblae Road
Duntiblae Rd
Orchard Pl
Mill Wy
Pit Road
Oxgang
Drumbreck
Blairhill Avenue
Marrwood Av
Carresbrook Avenue
Calfmuir Road
Chryston Road
Luggie Water
Bedcow
East Dunbartonshire
North Lanarkshire
East Muckcroft
Muckcroft Road
Auchengeich Road
Moodiesburn
Burnbrae Road
Burnbrae Farm
Netherhouses
Gartferry Road
Mallerbeg Gdns
Edington Gdns
Glenview Crs
St Ives Road
Penzance Way
Cambourne Rd
Portreath Rd
Blackwood Medical C
Davidston
Bothton Burn
Bridgend
Glenmanor Prim Sch
Glenmanor Avenue
Gartferry Avenue
Kelvin Drive
Council Building
Hillhead Av
Stoneyetts Road
Braeside Av
Prim Sch
Hilltop Rd
Eastwood Rd
Netherhill Rd
Glenburn
Bridgeburn Drive
Pleaknowe Crescent
Surg
Blacklands
LINDSAYBEG ROAD
Chryston
Gartferry
B819
Colinton Gdns
Grayston Manor
Mahon Court
1 grid square represents 500 metres

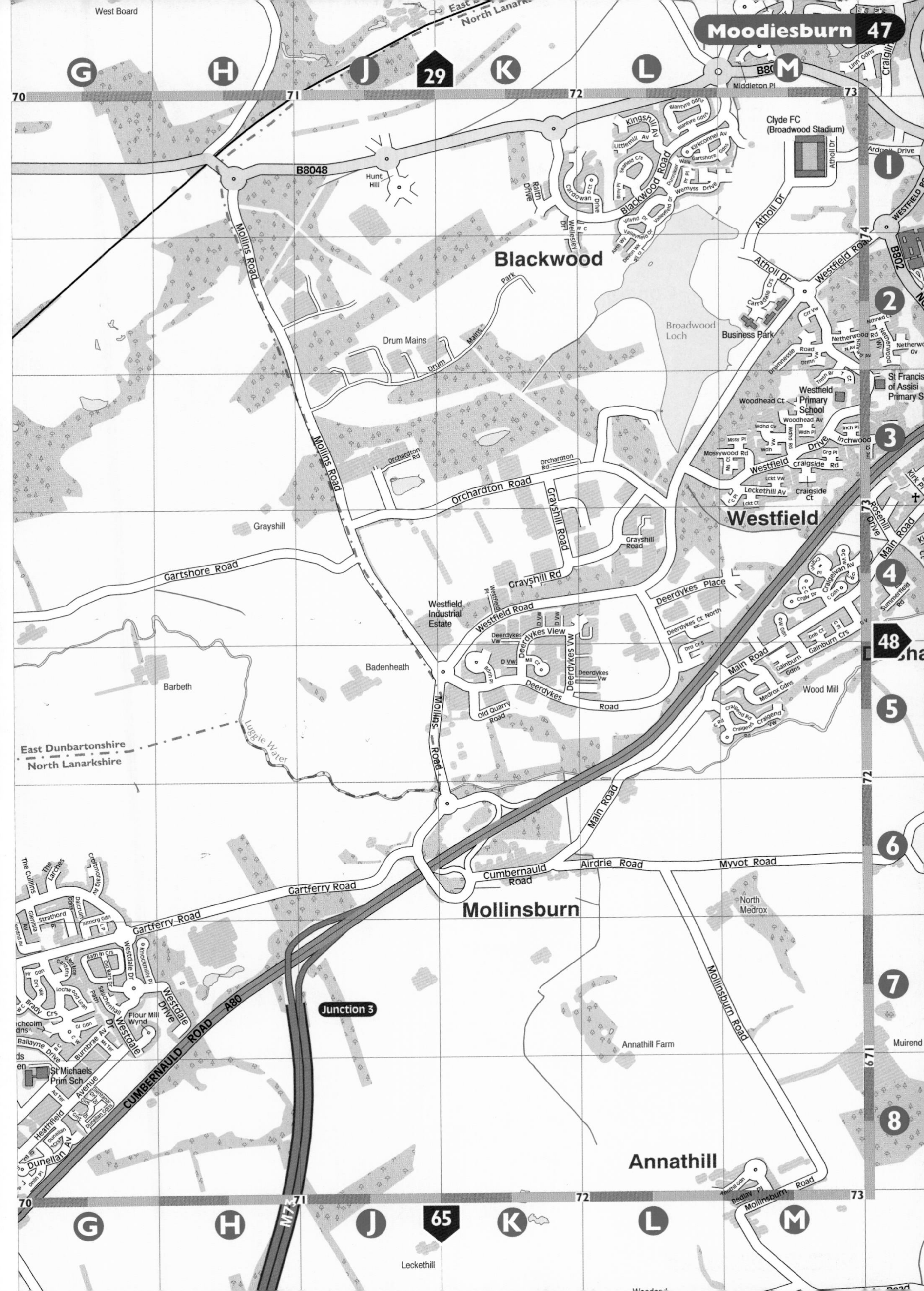

West Board

East
North Lanark

North Lanark

G   H   J   29   K   L   M

70   71   72   73

B8048

Middleton Pl
B80

Linn Gdns
Craiglin

Ardgoil Drive

1

Clyde FC
(Broadwood Stadium)

Kingshill Av
Littlehill Av
Kirkliston
Walls Crs
Gartshore Gdns
Blantyre Gdns
Blantyre Gdns
Kirkconnel Av
Wemyss Drive

Cyprowan Drive

Rain
Drive

Wellesley
Dr

Hunt
Hill

Blackwood

Atholl Dr

Atholl Dr

Westfield Road

Westfield Rd
B802

2

Netherwd Ct
Netherwood Rd
Netherw
Gv

Carracarr Crs

Drum Mains

Park

Drum Mains

Drum

Broadwood
Loch

Business Park

Crr Vw

Drummesdle
Road

St Francis
of Assisi
Primary S

Woodhead Ct

Westfield
Primary
School

Woodhead Av

Wdhd Gv
Wdn Dr

Wdh Pl

Grg Pl
Inch Ct

Inchwood

3

Mossywood Rd

Mssy Pl
Mil Ct
Wcth

Westfield

Orchardton Rd

Orchardton Rd

Orchardton Road

Grayshill Road

Leckethill Av
Lckt Vw
C Pk

Craigside Rd

Craigside
Ct

Westfield

Grayshill

Grayshill
Road

Craldovan Av

Rosehill
Drive

Main Road

4

Gartshore Road

Grayshill Rd

Deerdykes Place

Crglv Dr

Crlv Dr
C Gdn
G Ct

Summerfield

48 ha

Westfield Road

Deerdykes Ct North

Drd Crs

Main Road

Gainburn
Gdns

Gainburn Crs

Medrox Gdns

Wood Mill

5

Westfield
Industrial
Estate

Westfield
Pl

Deerdykes
Vw

D Vw

M Ct

Deerdykes Vw

Deerdykes Vw

Crglnd Rd
Rd
Crglend
Rd

Craigend
Vw

Badenheath

Barbeth

Mollins Road

Barn Pl

Deerdykes

Old Quarry
Road

Deerdykes
Road

East Dunbartonshire
North Lanarkshire

Luggie Water

6

North
Medrox

Cumbernauld
Road

Airdrie Road

Myvot Road

Main Road

Mollinsburn Road

7

Gartferry Road

The
Arches
The Cullins

Craigmochy Av

Gartferry Road

Strathord Pl
Altncrg Gdn
L Pl

Mollinsburn

Dalshannon Pl

Brady
Crs
Glenisa
Pl

Loch Vw

Westdale Dr

Rain In Ct
Gl Pl
P
Flour Mill
Wynd

Gl Gdn

8

Annathill Farm

CUMBERNAULD ROAD   A80

Junction 3

St Michaels
Prim Sch

Heathfield

Dunellan AV

Avenue
Dunellan AV

M73

Annathill

Bedlay Pl

Muirend

Mollinsburn
Road

70   71   72   73

G   H   J   65   K   L   M

Leckethill

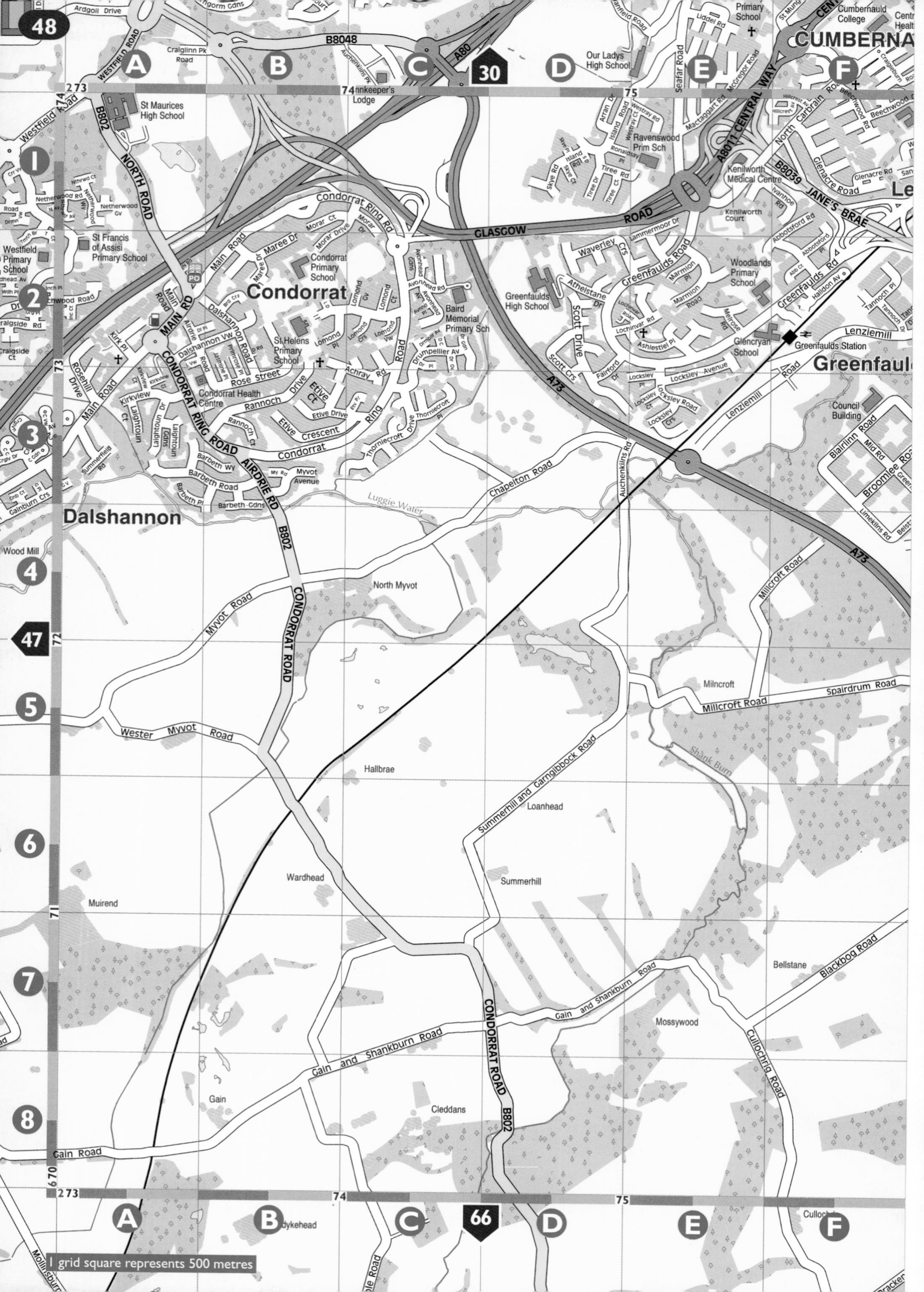

48

CUMBERNA

Cumbernauld College
Central Health

Primary School

St Mungo

CEN

Cumbernauld College

B8048

A80

30

Our Ladys
High School

E

F

273

Westfield Road

North Road

B802

Craiglinn Pk Road

St Maurices
High School

Condorrat Ring Rd

GLASGOW ROAD

A8011 CENTRAL WAY

JANE'S BRAE

B8039

Le

74

75

I

Netherwood

Westfield
Primary School

St Francis
of Assisi
Primary School

Main Road

Maree Dr

Morar Ct

Morar Drive

Condorrat
Primary
School

Baird
Memorial
Primary Sch

Greenfaulds
High School

Greenfaulds Road

Waverley Crs

Marmion

Woodlands
Primary
School

Greenfaulds Rd

Lenziemill

2

Condorrat

Main Rd

Dalshannon Road

Dalshannon Vw Rd

St Helens
Primary
School

Lomond

Achray

Avonhead Rd

Drumpellier Av

Atheistane Dr

Scott Crs

Marmion Road

Glencryan
School

Greenfaulds Station

Greenfaul

3

Rosehill Drive

Main Road

Laightoun

Kirkview

Condorrat Health Centre

Condorrat Ring Road

Rose Street

Etive Ct

Etive Drive

Ring Road

Rannoch

Etive Crescent

Thornliecroft Drive

Thornecroft Pl

Scott Drive

A73

Fairford Dr

Locksley

Locksley Avenue

Locksley Road

Council
Building

Blairlinn Road

Broomlee Ro

4

Dalshannon

Calnburn Crs

Barbeth Wy

Barbeth Road

Barbeth Pl

Barbeth Gdns

Condorrat Airdrie Rd

B802

Myvot
Avenue

Luggie Water

Chapelton Road

Auchenkilns Rd

Millcroft Road

A73

Wood Mill

North Myvot

Millcroft Road

Limekilns Ro

47

72

Myvot Road

Condorrat Road

Milncroft

Millcroft Road

Spairdrum Road

Shank Burn

5

Wester Myvot Road

Hallbrae

Muirend

71

Wardhead

Summerhill and Garngibbock Road

Loanhead

Summerhill

Bellstane

Blackbog Road

6

7

Gain

Gain and Shankburn Road

Condorrat Road

Cleddans

B802

Gain and Shankburn Road

Mossywood

Culloching Road

8

Gain Road

670

273

74

75

A

B

dykehead

C

66

D

E

F

Culloch

Mollinsburn

1 grid square represents 500 metres

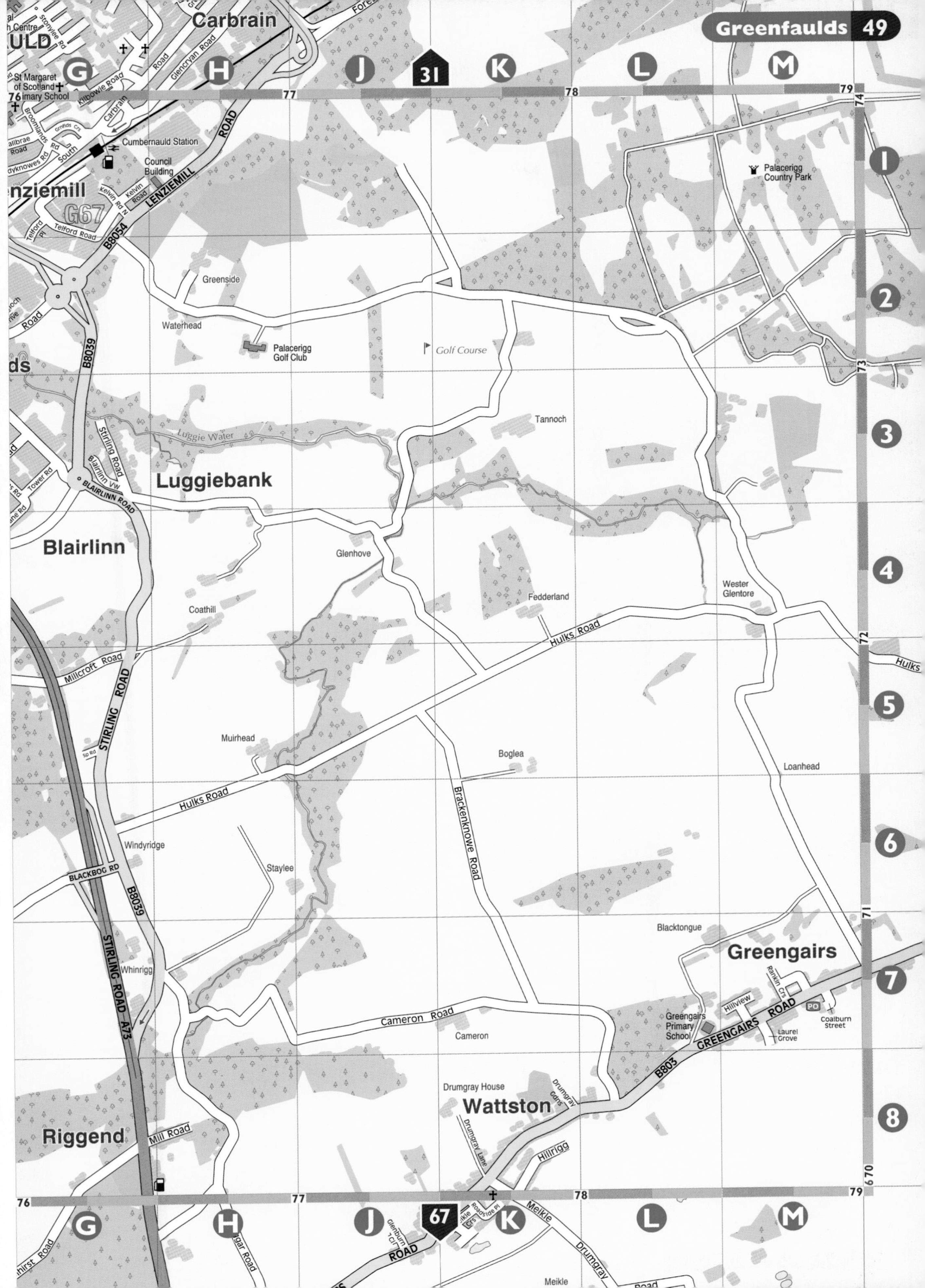

Carbrain

ULD

G H J 31 K L M

St Margaret
of Scotland
imary School

76

Cumbernauld Station

Council
Building

Glencryan Road

Carbrain

Kilbowie Road

LENZIEMILL ROAD

nziemill

G67

B8054

Telford Road

Kelvin

Kelvin Road

77 78 79 74

I

1

Palacerigg
Country Park

2

B8059

Greenside

Waterhead

Palacerigg
Golf Club

Golf Course

73

Blairlinn VW

BLAIRLINN ROAD

Stirling Road

Blairlinn VW

Luggie Water

Luggiebank

Tannoch

3

Blairlinn

Glenhove

Coathill

Fedderland

Wester
Glentore

4

Hulks Road

72

Hulks

Millcroft Road

STIRLING ROAD

Muirhead

Boglea

Loanhead

5

Hulks Road

Brackenknowe Road

Windyridge

Staylee

6

BLACKBOG RD

B8059

Blacktongue

71

Whinrigg

Greengairs

7

STIRLING ROAD A73

Cameron Road

Cameron

Greengairs
Primary School

Hillview

Rowan Crs

GREENGAIRS ROAD

PO

Coalburn
Street

Laurel
Grove

B803

Drumgray House

Drumgray Gdns

Wattston

Drumgray Lane

Hillrigg

8

Riggend

Mill Road

670

76 77 78 79

G H J 67 K L M

Stonehouse Road

Clenburn Crs

ROAD

Meikle

Drumgray Road

Meikle

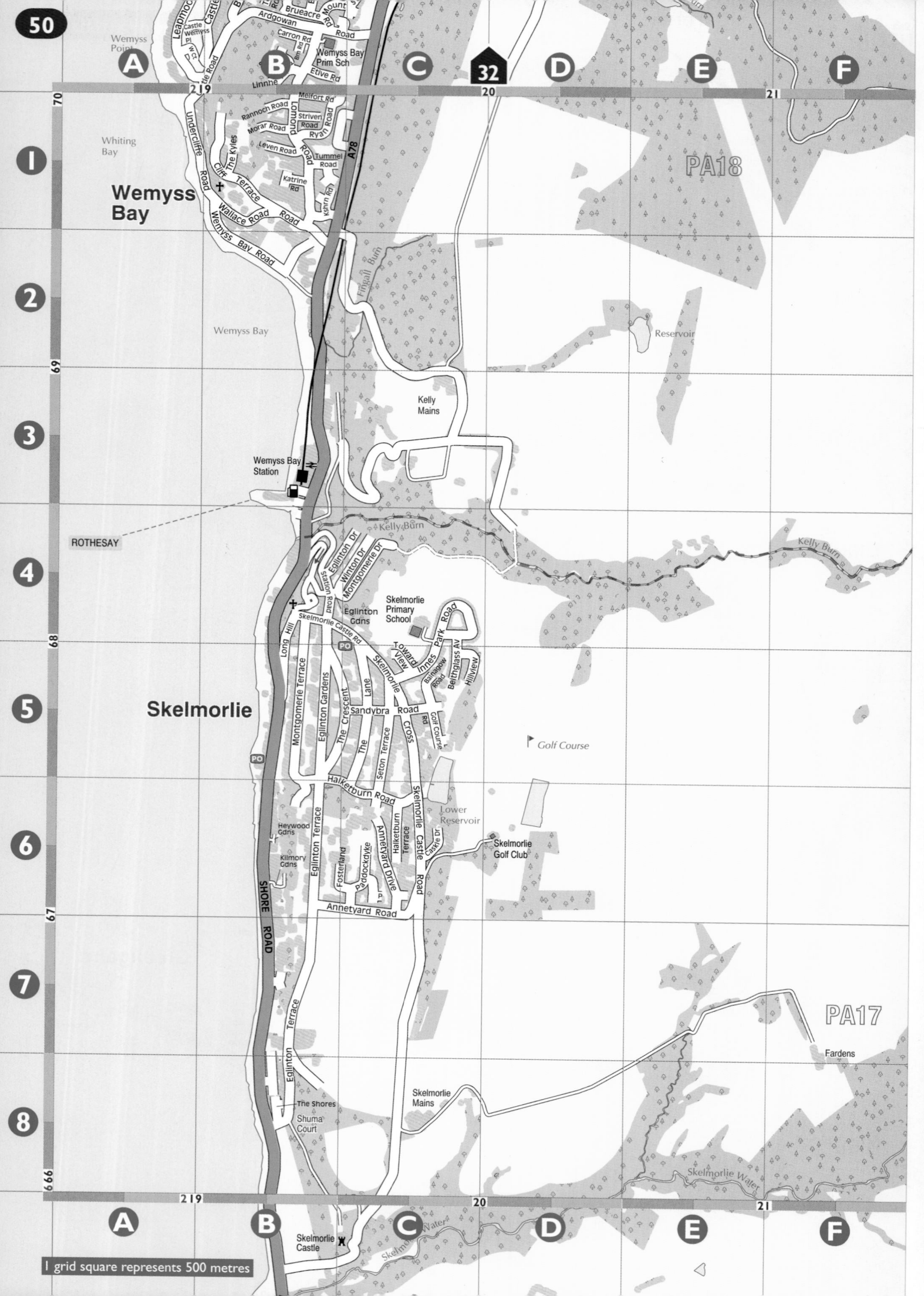

A   B   C   **32**   D   E   F

219   20   21

70

1

Whiting
Bay

**Wemyss
Bay**

PA18

69

2

Wemyss Bay

Kelly Mains

68

3

Wemyss Bay
Station

ROTHESAY

4

Skelmorlie
Primary
School

5

Skelmorlie

Golf Course

Lower
Reservoir

6

Skelmorlie
Golf Club

67

SHORE ROAD

7

PA17

Fardens

Skelmorlie
Mains

8

The Shores

Shuma
Court

666

219   20   21

A   B   C   D   E   F

Skelmorlie
Castle

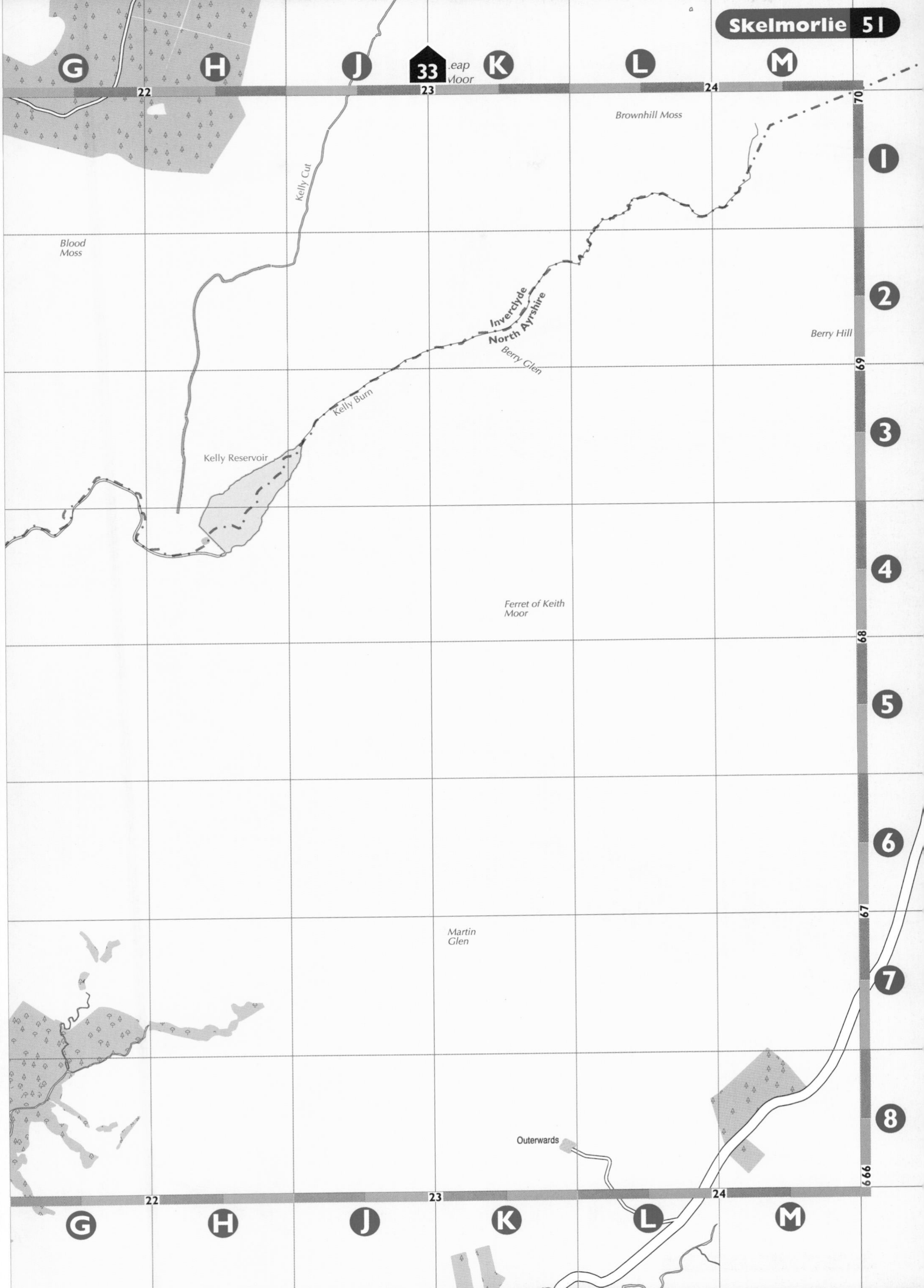

G H J 33 Leap Moor K L M

22 23 24

70

1

Brownhill Moss

Blood
Moss

2

Berry Hill

69

Kelly Cut

Inverclyde
North Ayrshire

Berry Glen

3

Kelly Burn

Kelly Reservoir

4

Ferret of Keith
Moor

68

5

6

67

Martin
Glen

7

8

Outerwards

666

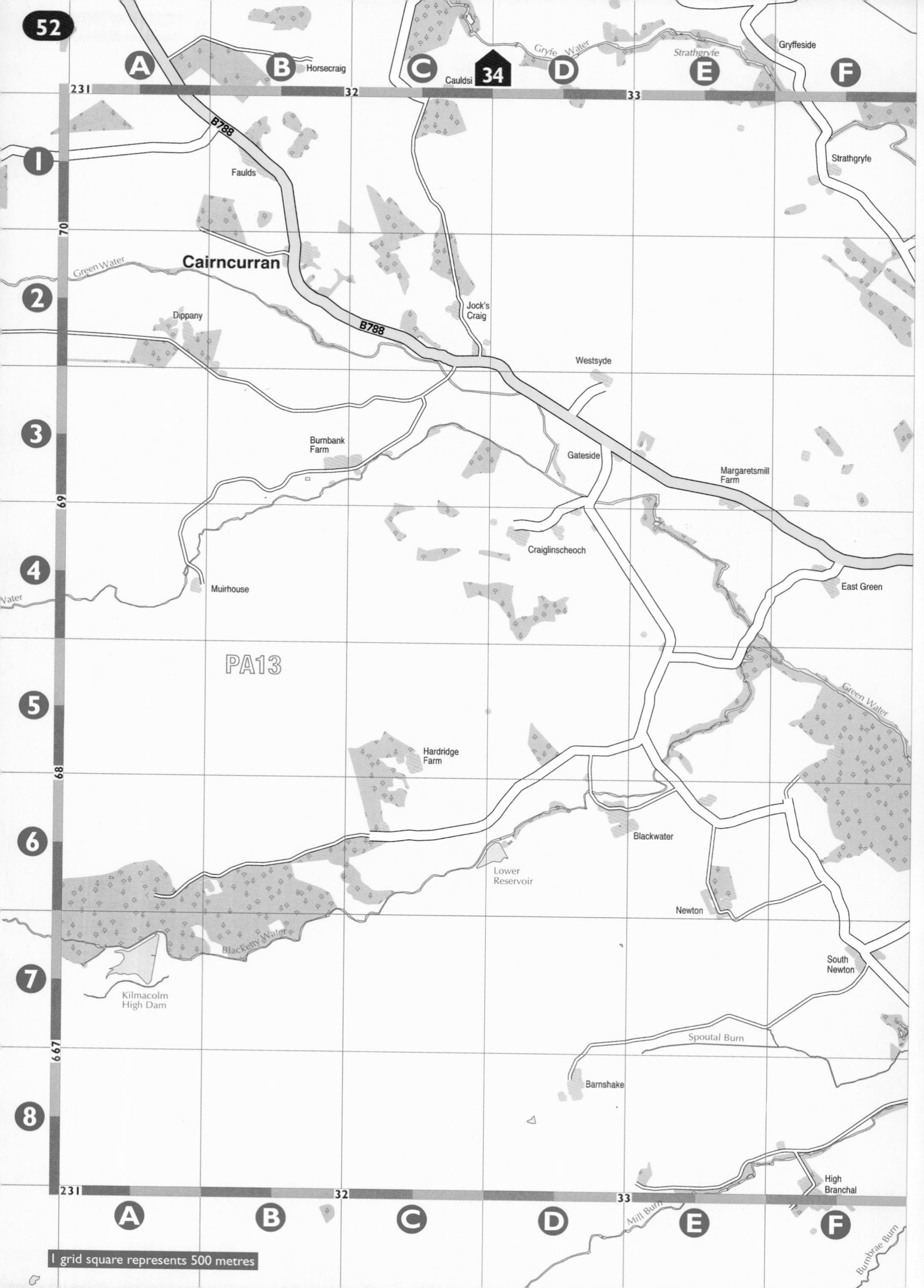

A
B
Horsecraig
C
Cauldsi
34
D
Gryfe Water
Strathgryfe
E
Gryffeside
F
231
32
33
B788
1
Faulds
Strathgryfe
70
Cairncurran
Green Water
2
Dippany
Jock's Craig
B788
Westsyde
3
Burnbank Farm
Gateside
Margaretsmill Farm
69
Craiglinscheoch
4
Muirhouse
East Green
PA13
5
Green Water
Hardridge Farm
68
6
Blackwater
Lower Reservoir
Newton
Blacketty Water
7
South Newton
Kilmacolm High Dam
667
Spoutal Burn
8
Barnshake
High Branchal
231
32
33
Mill Burn
A
B
C
D
E
F
Burnbrae Burn
1 grid square represents 500 metres

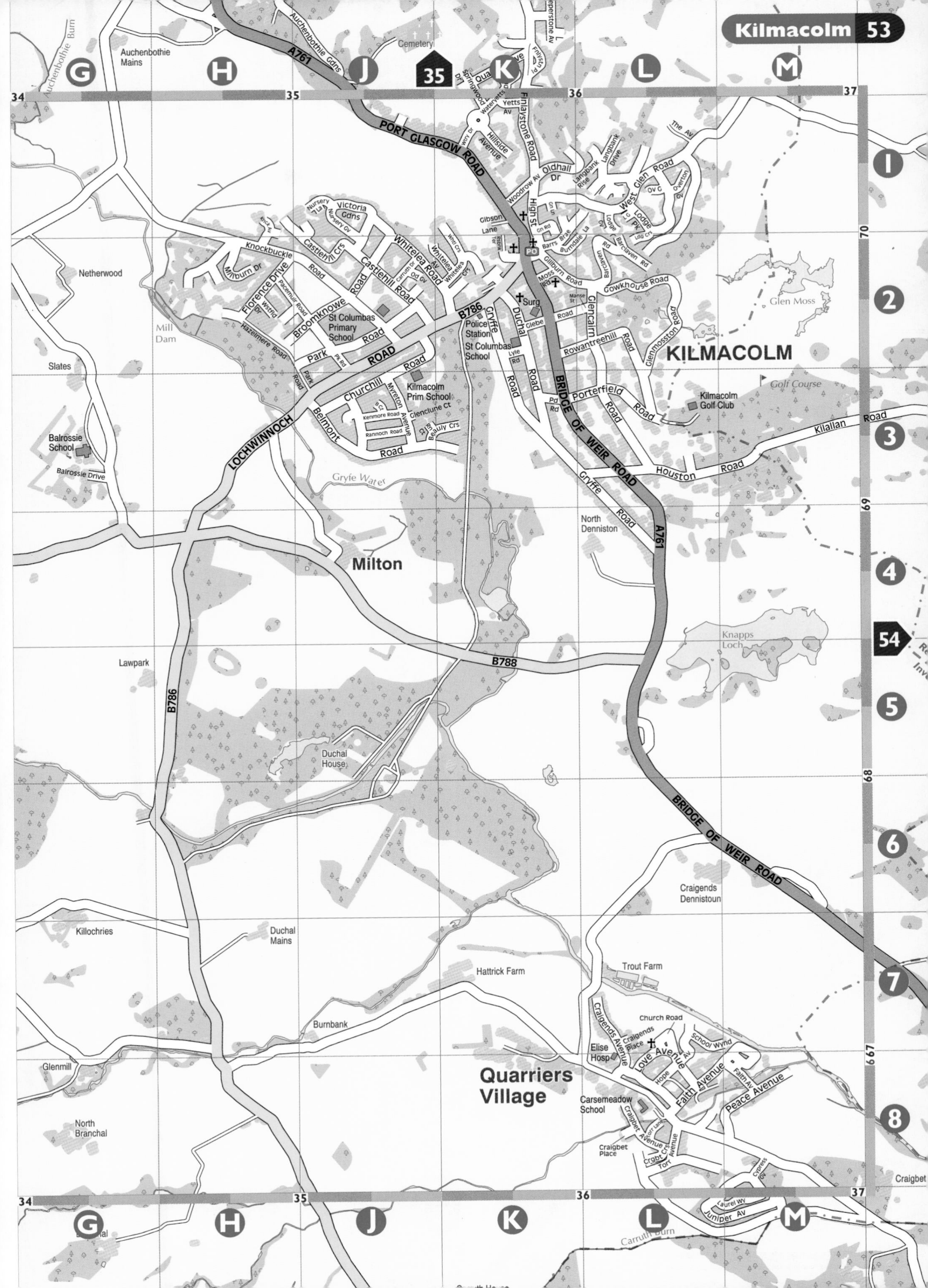

G H J 35 K L M

34 35 36 37

Auchenbothie Burn
Auchenbothie Gdns
A761
Cemetery
35
Qua
Finlaystone Road
Yetts Av
Woodrow Av
Hillside Avenue
High St
Waterstone
Oldhall Dr
West Glen Road
Langbank
Overton
Lodge
Glen Moss
Gibson Lane
PO
Gn Rd
Barrs
Brae
Burndale La
Balhaven Rd
Langbank

I
70
2

Auchenbothie Mains
Netherwood
Knockbuckle
Castlehill Crs
Whitelea Drive
Victoria Gdns
Nursery
Whitelea Av
Whitelea
Castlehill Road
Florence Drive
Milburn Dr
Broomknowe
Hazelmere Road
Park
Road
B786
Gryffe
Duchal
Gilburn Road
Mose
Manse St
Clencairn
Gowkhouse Road
Glenmosston Road
KILMACOLM
Golf Course

Mill Dam
St Columbas Primary School
St Columbas School
Police Station
Road
Lyle Rd
Glebe
Surg
Rowantreehill Road
Kilmacolm Golf Club
Kilmacolm Golf-Club

69
3

Slates
Churchill
Kilmacolm Prim School
Mireton Avenue
Glenclune ct
Beauly Crs
Kenmore Road
Rannoch Road
Belmont Road
LOCHWINNOCH
Pd Rd
BRIDGE OF WEIR ROAD
Porterfield Road
Road
Houston Road
Kilallan Road

Balrossie School
Balrossie Drive
Gryfe Water
Gryfe Road
North Denniston
A761

4

54
Knapps Loch

Lawpark
Milton
B786
B788

5
68

Duchal House

6

BRIDGE OF WEIR ROAD
Craigends Dennistoun

Killochries
Duchal Mains
Hattrick Farm
Trout Farm
Church Road

7
667

Burnbank
Elise Hosp
Craigends Avenue
Cragends Place
Love Avenue
School Wynd
Faith Av
Hope

Glenmill
Quarriers Village
Carsemeadow School
Faith Avenue
Peace Avenue

North Branchal
Craigbet Place
Crabet Avenue
Torr
Cypress
8

34 35 36 37
G H J K L M
Juniper Av
Laurel Wy
Craigbet
Carruth Burn

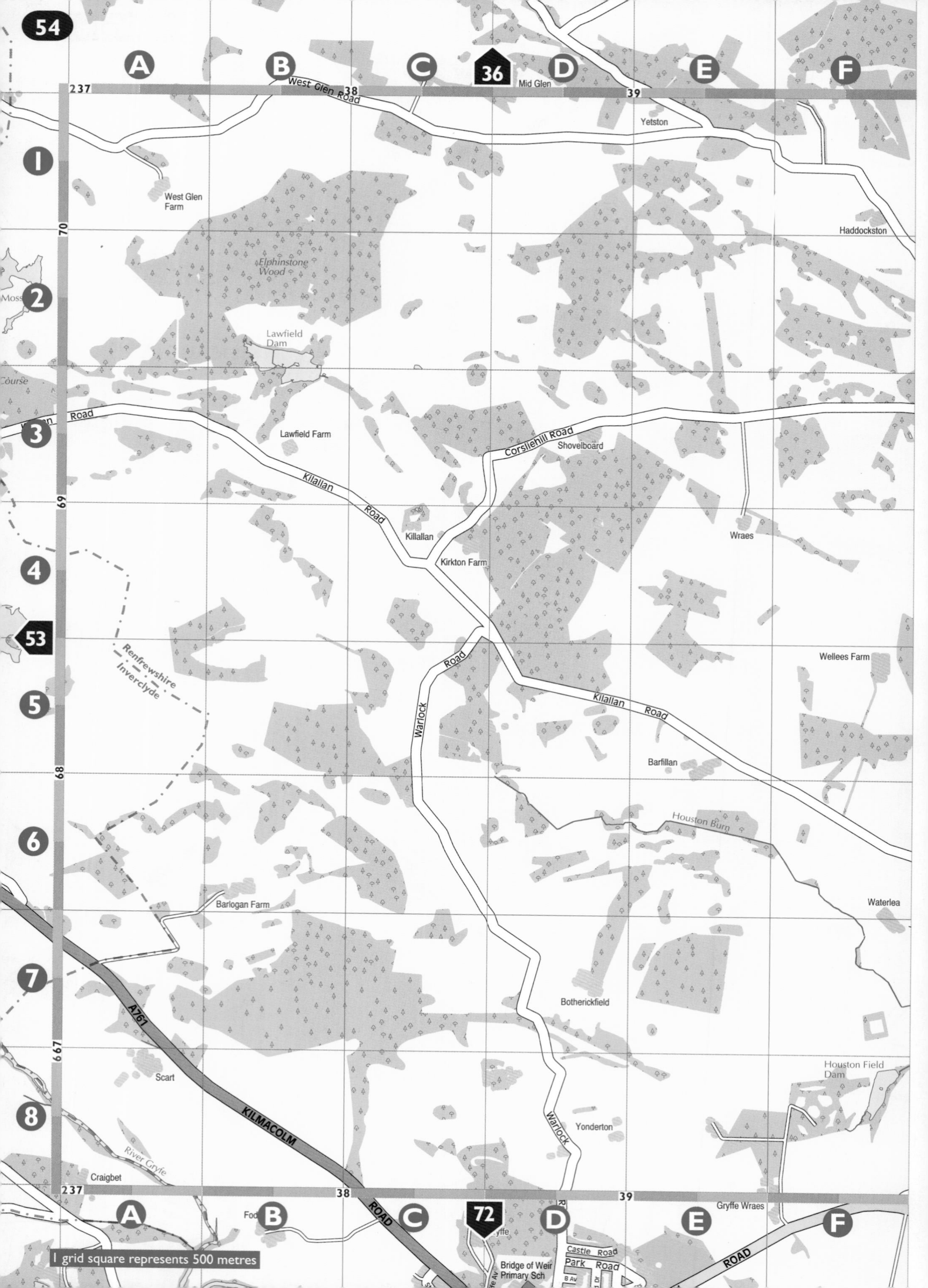

A B C **36** D E F

237 West Glen Road 38 39

Mid Glen

I

Yetston

West Glen
Farm

Haddockston

Elphinstone
Wood

2

Moss

70

Lawfield
Dam

Course

3

Road Lawfield Farm Corsliehill Road Shovelboard

Kilallan Road

69

Killallan Wraes

Kirkton Farm

4

53

Renfrewshire
Inverclyde

Wellees Farm

5

Warlock Road Kilallan Road

68

Barfillan

Houston Burn

6

Waterlea

Barlogan Farm

7 A761 Botherickfield

Houston Field
Dam

667

8 Scart

KILMACOLM Warlock Yonderton

River Gryfe

Craigbet

237 38 ROAD **72** 39 Gryffe Wraes

A B C D E F

Foo ryffe Castle Road Park Road ROAD

Bridge of Weir
Primary Sch

B Av

1 grid square represents 500 metres

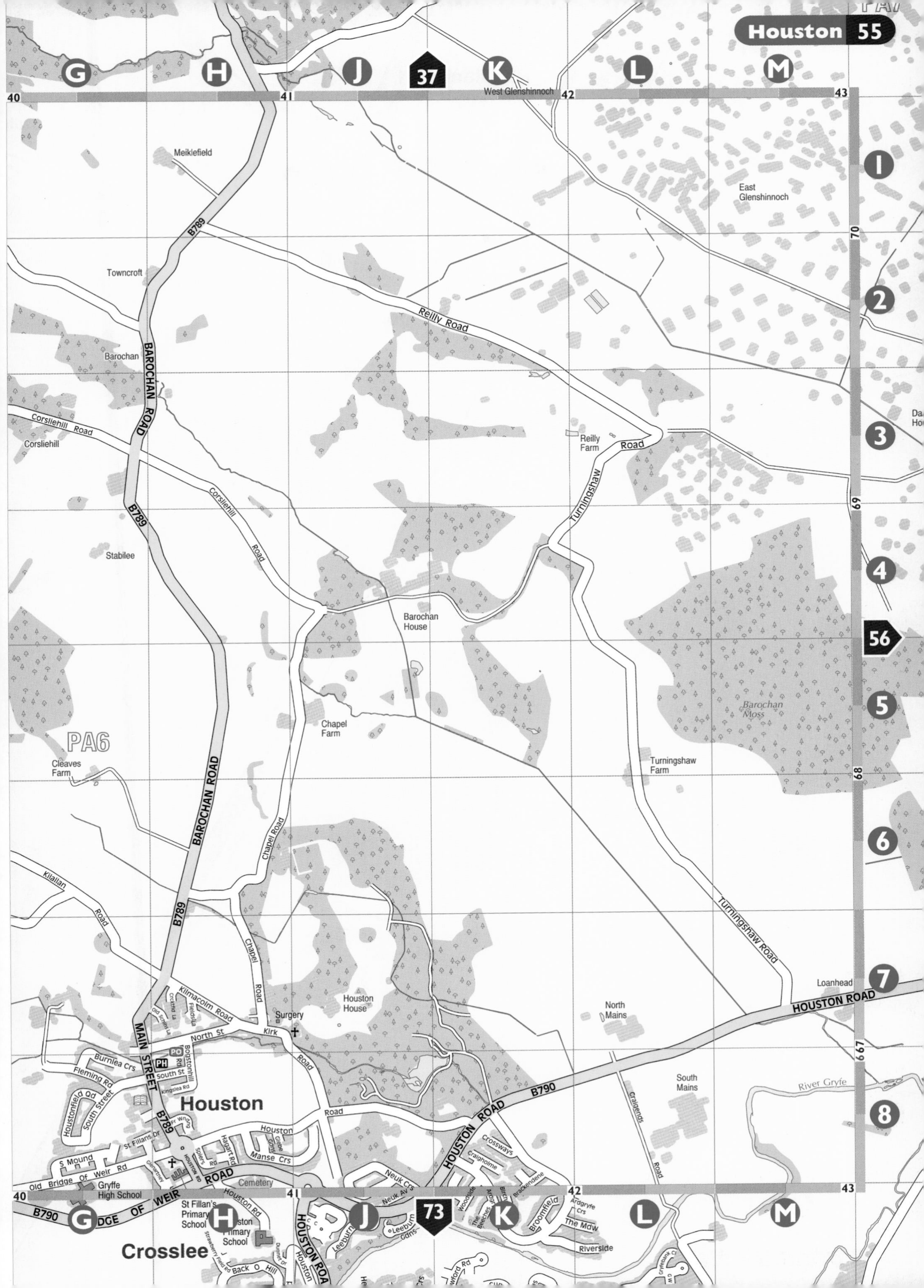
Meiklefield
West Glenshinnoch
East Glenshinnoch
Towncroft
Reilly Road
Barochan
BAROCHAN ROAD
B789
Corsliehill Road
Corsliehill
Reilly Farm
Turningshaw Road
Stabilee
Barochan House
Barochan Moss
Chapel Farm
PA6
Cleaves Farm
Turningshaw Farm
Chapel Road
Killallan Road
Kilmacolm Road
Houston House
Surgery
Loanhead
HOUSTON ROAD
North Mains
South Mains
River Gryfe
Craigends Road
B790
Houston
MAIN STREET
North St
Kirk Road
Burnlea Crs
Fleming Rd
South St
Kingslea Rd
Houstonfield Qd
South Street
St Fillans Dr
S Mound
Old Bridge Of Weir Rd
Gryffe High School
Cemetery
Manse Crs
Crossways
Craigholme
Neuk Cres
Neuk Av
Leeburn
Leeburn Gdns
Woodside
Birch
Brackendene
Broomfield
Ardgryfe Crs
The Mdw
Riverside
St Fillan's Primary School
Houston Primary School
Crosslee
Back O Hill
HOUSTON ROAD
BRIDGE OF WEIR ROAD
G
H
J
K
L
M
37
73
56
40
41
42
43
1
2
3
4
5
6
7
8
67
68
69
70

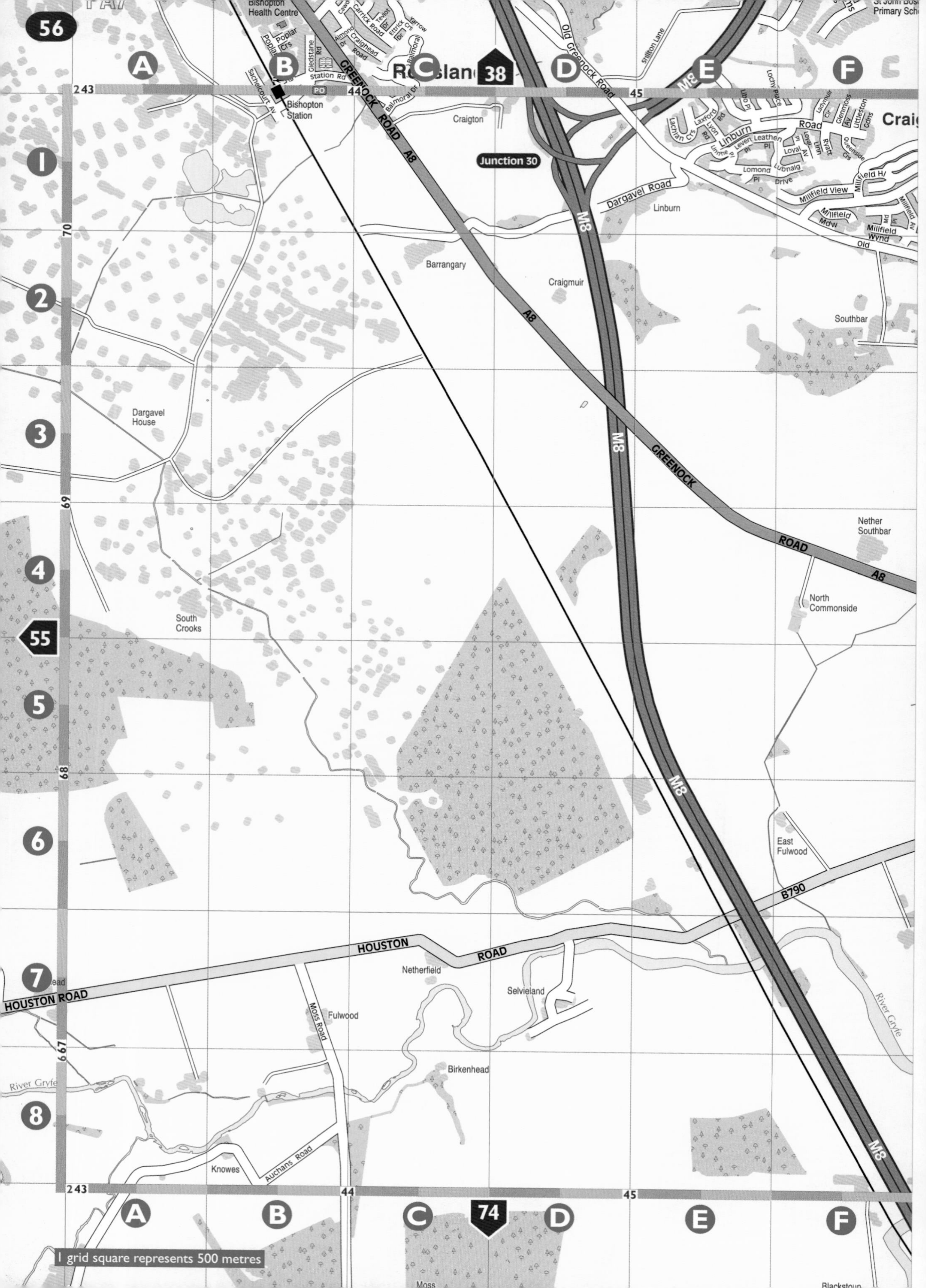

56

A   B   C   **38**   D   E   F

243   44   45

Bishopton
Health Centre

Poplar
Crs

Gledstane
Rd

Station Rd

PO

Sachelcourt Av

Bishopton
Station

GREENOCK ROAD A8

Almond Ct
Garrick Road
Teviot

Craighead Dr

Balmoral

Craignead
Road

Yarrow
Ettrick Crs

Roslanc

Craigton

Old Greenock Road

Stillton Lane

Junction 30

M8

A8

Barrangary

Craigmuir

Loch Place

Linburn

Lachlan Crs
Lawford
Cron Rd

Leven
Linnhe

Leathen

Loyal
PI

Lomond
PI

Loyal Av

Tubnaig
Drive

Dargavel Road

Linburn

Millfield View

Millfield
Mdw

Millfield
Wynd

Old

Craig

Southbar

St John Bosc
Primary Sch

Road

Leanmir

Glenmoss
Av

Littleston
Gdns

Queensido
Cres

Millfield H/

Millfield AV

Millfield

I

2

3

Dargavel
House

70

69

GREENOCK

M8

ROAD

Nether
Southbar

A8

4

55

South
Crooks

68

North
Commonside

5

6

East
Fulwood

B790

7

HOUSTON ROAD

HOUSTON

ROAD

Netherfield

Selvieland

Moss Road

Fulwood

Birkenhead

67

River Gryfe

River Gryfe

8

Knowes

Auchans Road

M8

243   44   45

A   B   C   **74**   D   E   F

Moss

Blackstoun

I grid square represents 500 metres

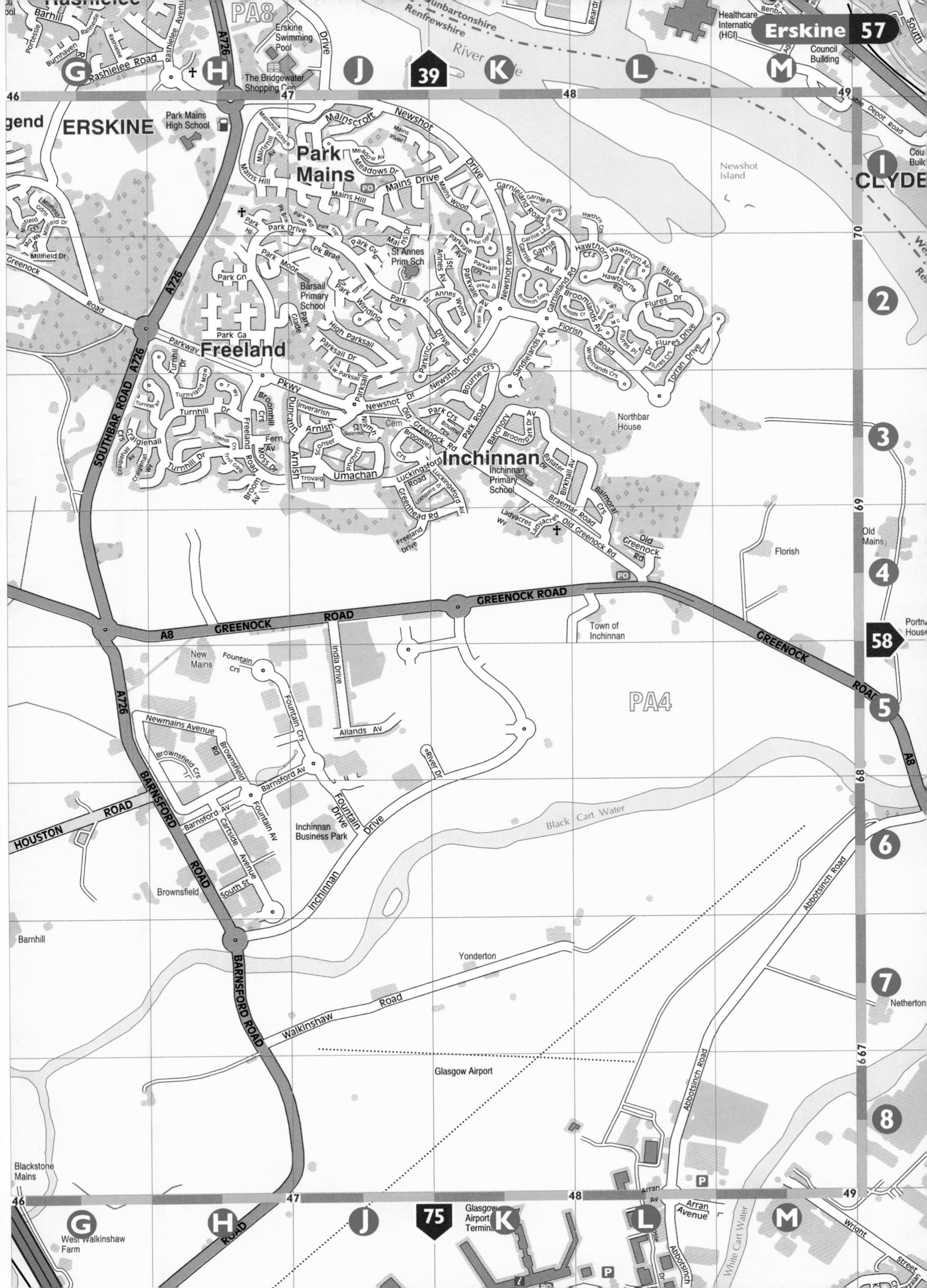
ERSKINE
Park Mains
Freeland
Inchinnan
Park Mains High School
Erskine Swimming Pool
The Bridgewater Shopping Cen
St Annes Prim Sch
Barsail Primary School
Inchinnan Primary School
Healthcare International (HCI)
Council Building
Newshot Island
CLYDE
River Clyde
Dunbartonshire
Renfrewshire
Northbar House
Old Mains
Florish
Town of Inchinnan
New Mains
Inchinnan Business Park
Black Cart Water
Brownsfield
Barnhill
Yonderton
Netherton
Glasgow Airport
Blackstone Mains
West Walkinshaw Farm
Glasgow Airport Terminal
White Cart Water
PA8
PA4
GREENOCK ROAD
A8
A726
SOUTHBAR ROAD
BARNSFORD ROAD
HOUSTON ROAD
Walkinshaw Road
Inchinnan Drive
Fountain Drive
Fountain Crs
India Drive
Allands Av
Newmains Avenue
Brownsfield Rd
Brownsfield Crs
Barnsford Av
Fountain Av
Cartside Avenue
South St
River Dr
Abbotsinch Road
Arran Avenue
Wright Street
Newshot Drive
Mains Drive
Mainscroft
Meadows Dr
Mains Hill
Park Drive
Park Moor
Pk Brae
High Parksail
Parksail Dr
Parkway
Pkwy
Turnhill Dr
Craigiehall Crs
Freeland Road
Broomhill Crs
Moss Dr
Duncarn
Arnish
Umachan
Old Greenock Rd
Luckingsford Road
Greenhead Rd
Freeland Drive
Park Road
Bourne Crs
Banchory Av
Broompark Dr
Birkhall Av
Balmoral Crs
Braemar Road
Ladyacres
Garnieland Road
Hawthorn Crs
Broomlands Av
Florish Road
Flures Dr
Flures Drive
Torran Drive
Sandielands Av
Rashielee Road
Rashielee Avenue
Barhill
Burnhaven
Millfield Dr
Cable Depot Road
46
47
48
49
67
68
69
70
G
H
J
K
L
M
2
3
4
5
6
7
8
39
58
75

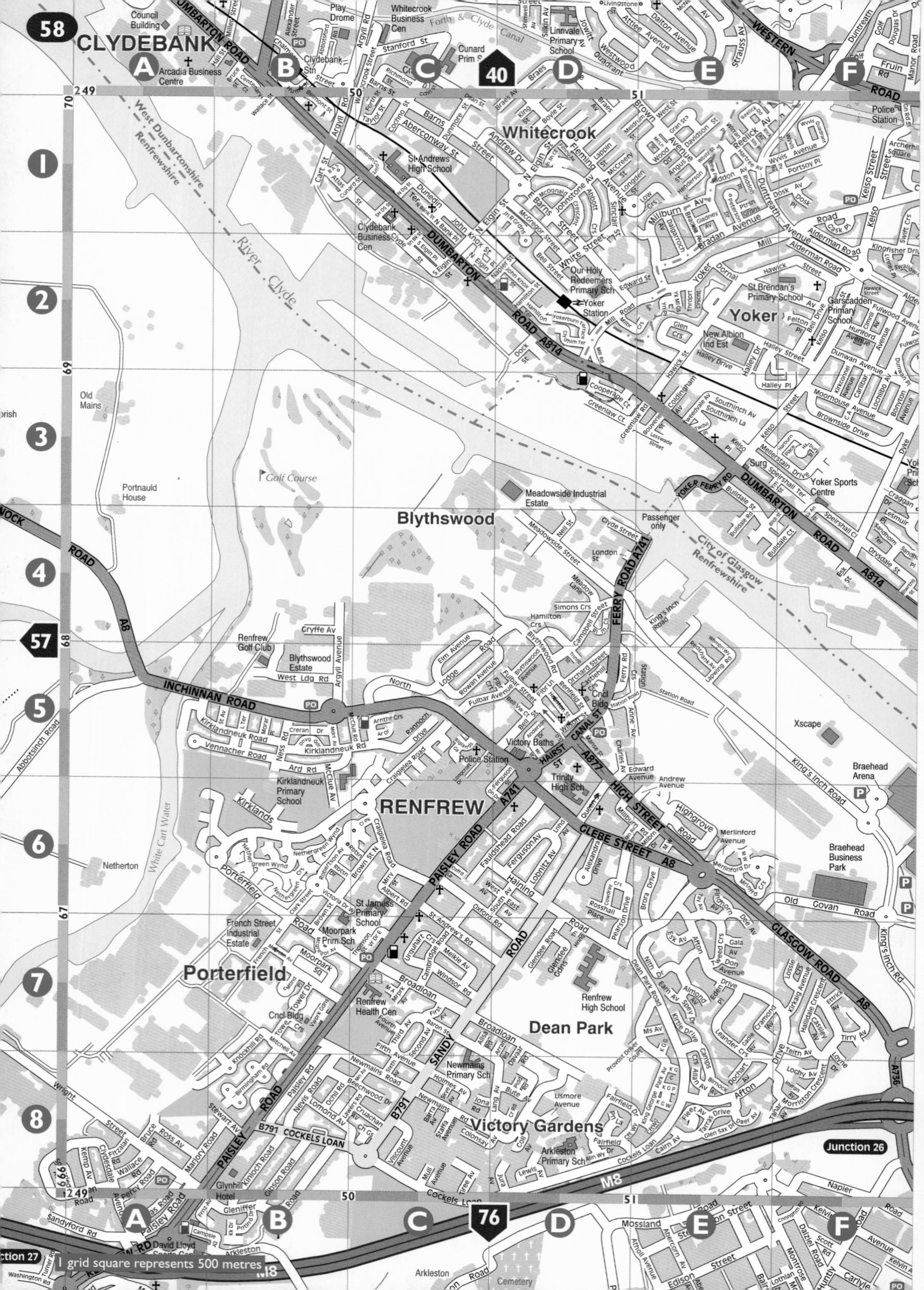

Map tile and grid references:

58 CLYDEBANK

Grid columns (top): A B C D E F
Grid columns (bottom): A B C D E F
Grid rows (left): 1 2 3 4 5 6 7 8

57
40
76

Place names and labels:

CLYDEBANK
Whitecrook
Yoker
Blythswood
RENFREW
Porterfield
Dean Park
Victory Gardens
Netherton
Old Mains
Portnauld House
Golf Course

Rivers / water:

River Clyde
White Cart Water
Forth & Clyde Canal

Major roads:

DUMBARTON ROAD A814
FERRY ROAD A741
YOKER FERRY RD
DUMBARTON ROAD A814
GLASGOW ROAD A8
CLEBE STREET A8
HIGH STREET A877
PAISLEY ROAD A741
SANDY ROAD
INCHINNAN ROAD
WESTERN ROAD
Old Govan Road
King's Inch Road
King's Inch Rd
B791
INCHINNAN ROAD
A8
M8

Junctions:

Junction 26
Junction 27

Selected streets and features:

Council Building
Arcadia Business Centre
Alexander Street
Play Drome
Argyll Rd
Whitecrook Business Cen
Linnvale Primary School
Police Station
Archerhill Square
Clydebank Stn
St Andrews High School
Clydebank Business Cen
Our Holy Redeemers Primary Sch
Yoker Station
St Brendan's Primary School
Garscadden Primary School
Meadowside Industrial Estate
Passenger only
City of Glasgow / Renfrewshire
Yoker Sports Centre
Renfrew Golf Club
Blythswood Estate
West Ldg Rd
Kirklandneuk Road
Kirklandneuk Primary School
Victory Baths
Police Station
Trinity High Sch
Xscape
Braehead Arena
King's Inch Road
Braehead Business Park
Merlinford Avenue
French Street Industrial Estate
Moorpark Prim Sch
St James's Primary School
St Andrews Rd
Renfrew Health Cen
Renfrew High School
Newmains Primary Sch
Glynhill Hotel
Arkleston Primary Sch
Cemetery
David Lloyd

I grid square represents 500 metres

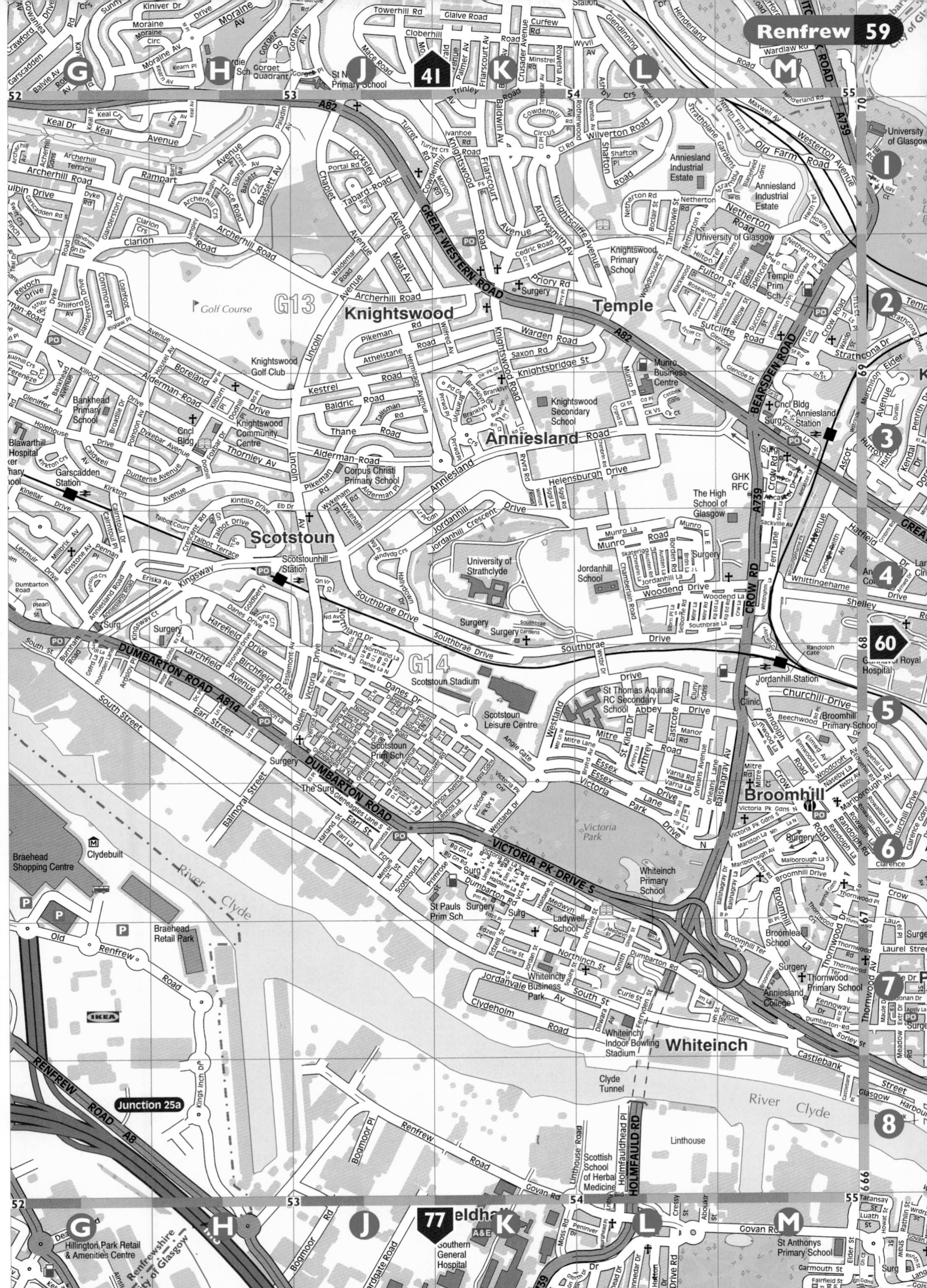

Renfrew 59
G
H
J
41
K
L
M
52
53
54
55
Knightswood
Temple
Anniesland
Scotstoun
Broomhill
Whiteinch
Linthouse
G13
G14
60
77
Junction 25a
University of Glasgow
Anniesland Industrial Estate
Knightswood Golf Club
Golf Course
Knightswood Primary School
Knightswood Secondary School
Knightswood Community Centre
Bankhead Primary School
Corpus Christi Primary School
University of Strathclyde
Jordanhill School
The High School of Glasgow
GHK RFC
Scotstoun Stadium
Scotstoun Leisure Centre
Scotstoun Prim Sch
St Thomas Aquinas RC Secondary School
Broomhill Primary School
Victoria Park
Whiteinch Primary School
Ladywell School
St Pauls Prim Sch
Whiteinch Business Park
Whiteinch Indoor Bowling Stadium
Broomlea School
Thornwood Primary School
Anniesland College
Clyde Tunnel
Scottish School of Herbal Medicine
Braehead Shopping Centre
Clydebuilt
Braehead Retail Park
IKEA
River Clyde
Hillington Park Retail & Amenities Centre
Southern General Hospital
A&E
St Anthonys Primary School
Gartnavel Royal Hospital
Blawarthill Hospital
Garscadden Station
Scotstounhill Station
Jordanhill Station
Anniesland Station
Munro Business Centre
Temple Prim Sch
GREAT WESTERN ROAD
A82
A739
A814
A8
DUMBARTON ROAD
VICTORIA PK DRIVE S
BEARSDEN ROAD
CROW RD
RENFREW ROAD
HOLMFAULD RD
Anniesland Road
Archerhill Road
Alderman Road
Southbrae Drive
Jordanhill Drive
Helensburgh Drive
Churchill Drive
Castlebank Street
South Street
Balmoral Street
Old Renfrew Road
Kings Inch Dr
Govan Rd
Renfrewshire
City of Glasgow

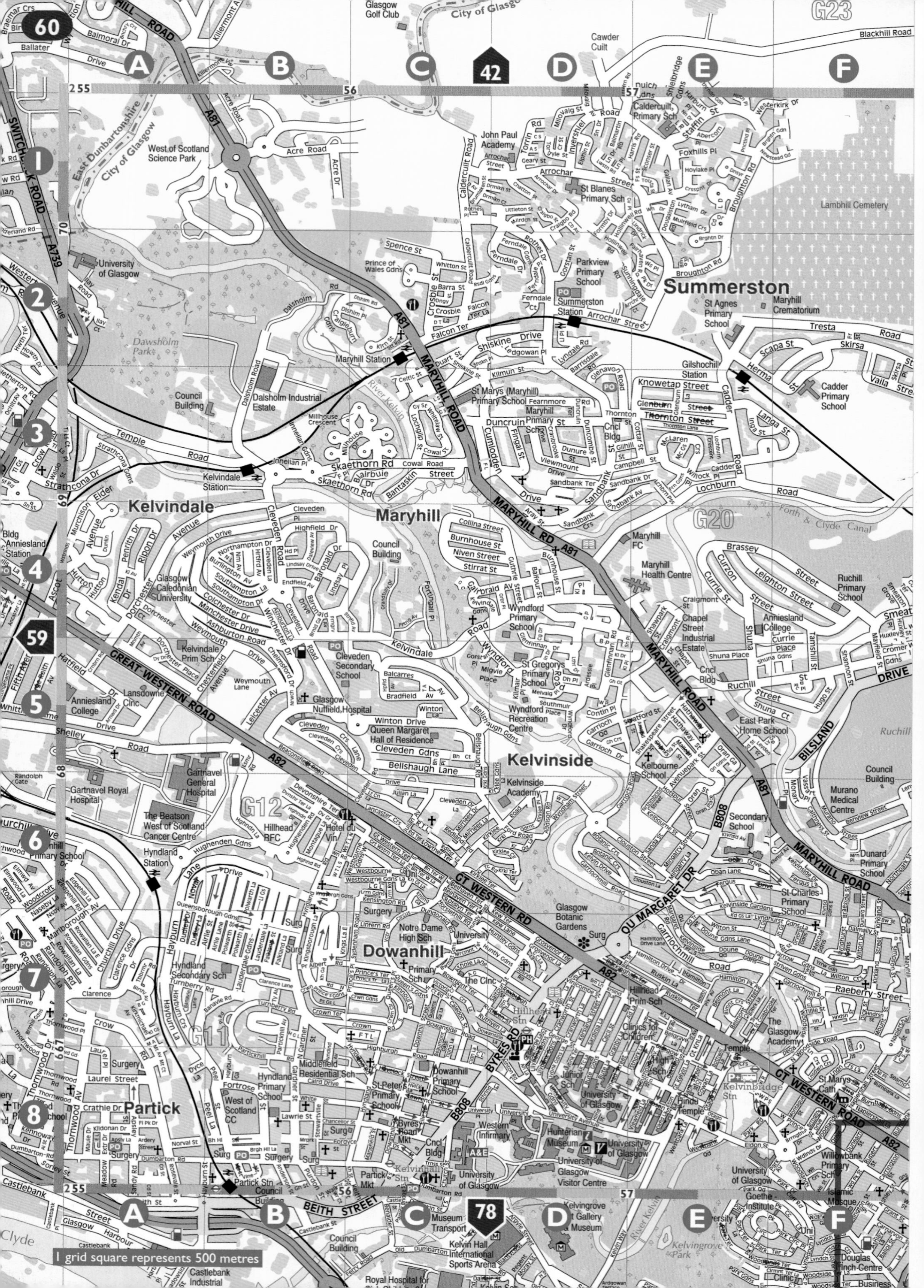

60
42
59
78
G23
G20
G12
G11
A
B
C
D
E
F
1
2
3
4
5
6
7
8
Summerston
Maryhill
Kelvindale
Kelvinside
Dowanhill
Partick
Lambhill Cemetery
Maryhill Crematorium
West of Scotland Science Park
University of Glasgow
Dawsholm Park
Dalsholm Industrial Estate
Council Building
Maryhill Station
Summerston Station
Gilshochill Station
Kelvindale Station
Hyndland Station
Partick Stn
Kelvinhall Stn
Kelvinbridge Stn
Hillhead Stn
Glasgow Caledonian University
Gartnavel Royal Hospital
Gartnavel General Hospital
The Beatson West of Scotland Cancer Centre
Glasgow Nuffield Hospital
Queen Margaret Hall of Residence
Kelvinside Academy
Glasgow Botanic Gardens
Maryhill Health Centre
Maryhill FC
Western Infirmary
Hunterian Museum
Glasgow Visitor Centre
Kelvin Hall International Sports Arena
Museum of Transport
Kelvingrove Art Gallery & Museum
Kelvingrove Park
Forth & Clyde Canal
River Kelvin
Clyde
MARYHILL ROAD
GREAT WESTERN ROAD
GT WESTERN RD
SWITCHBACK ROAD
BYRES RD
QU MARGARET DR
BEITH STREET
Blackhill Road
Tresta Road
Lochburn Road
Temple Road
Crow Road
Dumbarton Rd
Castlebank Street
Glasgow Harbour
A81
A82
A739
B808
1 grid square represents 500 metres

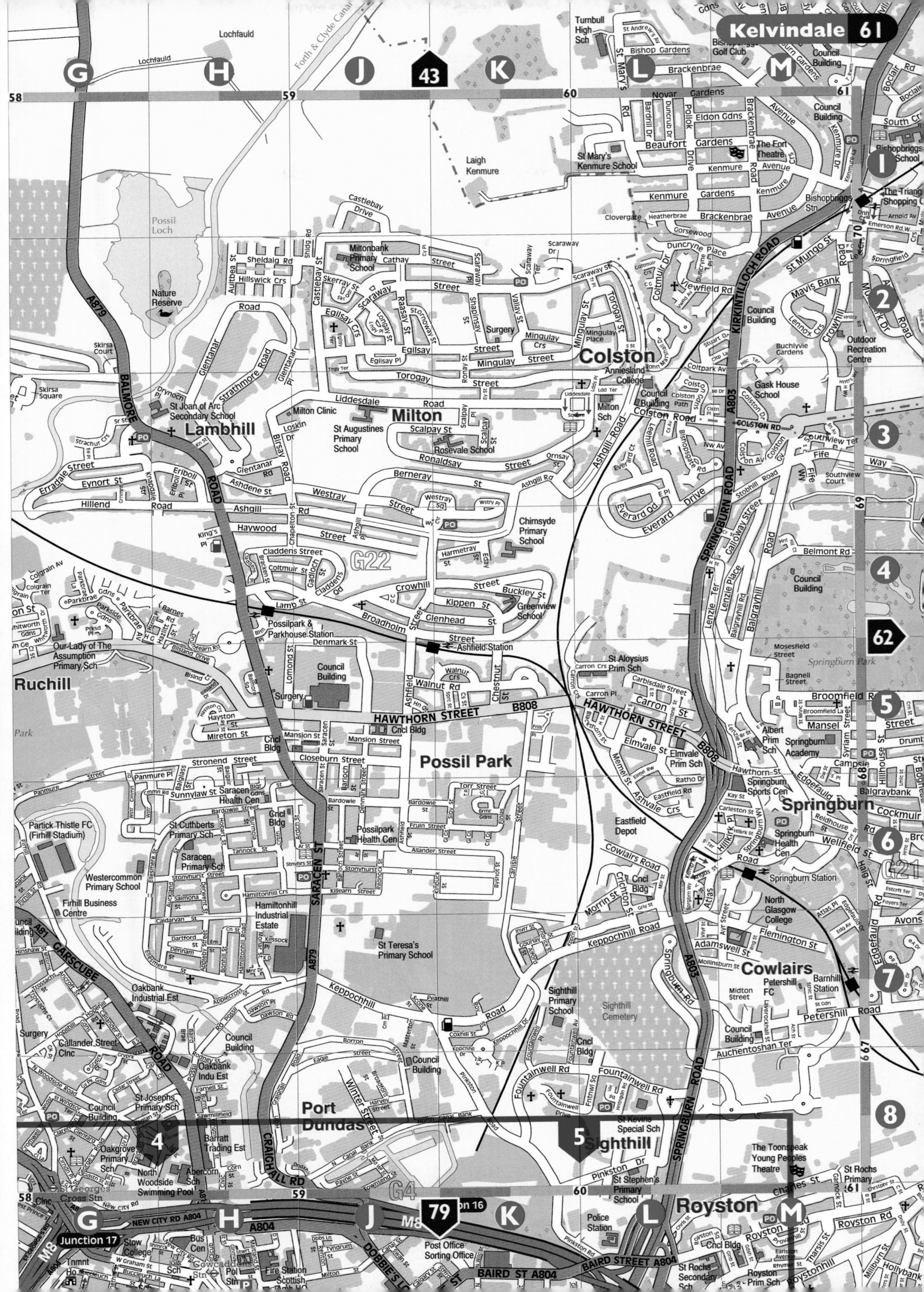

Kelvindale 61
43
62
79
4
5
G
H
J
K
L
M
58
59
60
61
Lochfauld
Forth & Clyde Canal
Turnbull High Sch
Bishop Gardens
Bishopbriggs Golf Club
Brackenbrae
Novar Gardens
Eldon Gdns
Beaufort Gardens
The Fort Theatre
Kenmure Gardens
Council Building
Bishopbriggs School
St Mary's Kenmure School
Laigh Kenmure
Bishopbriggs Stn
The Triangle Shopping C
Possil Loch
Nature Reserve
Castlebay Drive
Miltonbank Primary School
Scaraway Street
Colston
Annesland College
Milton
Milton Clinic
St Augustines Primary School
Rosevale School
Milton Sch
Liddesdale Road
Colston Road
Lambhill
St Joan of Arc Secondary School
Balmore Road
A879
Kirkintilloch Road
A803
Springburn Road
Mavis Bank
Council Building
Outdoor Recreation Centre
Gask House School
Buchlyvie Gardens
Southview Court
Fife Way
Chirnsyde Primary School
Greenview School
G22
Possilpark & Parkhouse Station
Ashfield Station
Our Lady of The Assumption Primary Sch
Ruchill
Park
Council Building
Surgery
Hawthorn Street
B808
Possil Park
St Aloysius Prim Sch
Elmvale Prim Sch
Springburn Sports Cen
Albert Prim Sch
Springburn Academy
Springburn
Springburn Park
Springburn Health Cen
Springburn Station
G21
Partick Thistle FC (Firhill Stadium)
St Cuthberts Primary Sch
Saracen Primary Sch
Westercommon Primary School
Firhill Business Centre
Hamiltonhill Industrial Estate
Possilpark Health Cen
Saracen St
St Teresa's Primary School
Eastfield Depot
Cowlairs Road
North Glasgow College
Keppochhill Road
Cowlairs
Petershill FC
Barnhill Station
Petershill Road
Sighthill Primary School
Sighthill Cemetery
Auchentoshan Ter
Garscube Road
A81
Oakbank Industrial Est
Oakbank Indu Est
Callander Street Clnc
St Josephs Primary Sch
Oakgrove Primary Sch
North Woodside Swimming Pool
Barratt Trading Est
Port Dundas
Craighall Rd
Sighthill
St Kevins Special Sch
St Stephen's Primary School
The Toonspeak Young Peoples Theatre
St Rochs Primary
Royston
Royston Rd
Police Station
New City Rd A804
Junction 17
Junction 16
M8
Stow College
Post Office Sorting Office
Baird Street A804
Dobbie's Ln
St Georges Cross Stn
Fire Station
St Rochs Secondary Sch
Royston Prim Sch

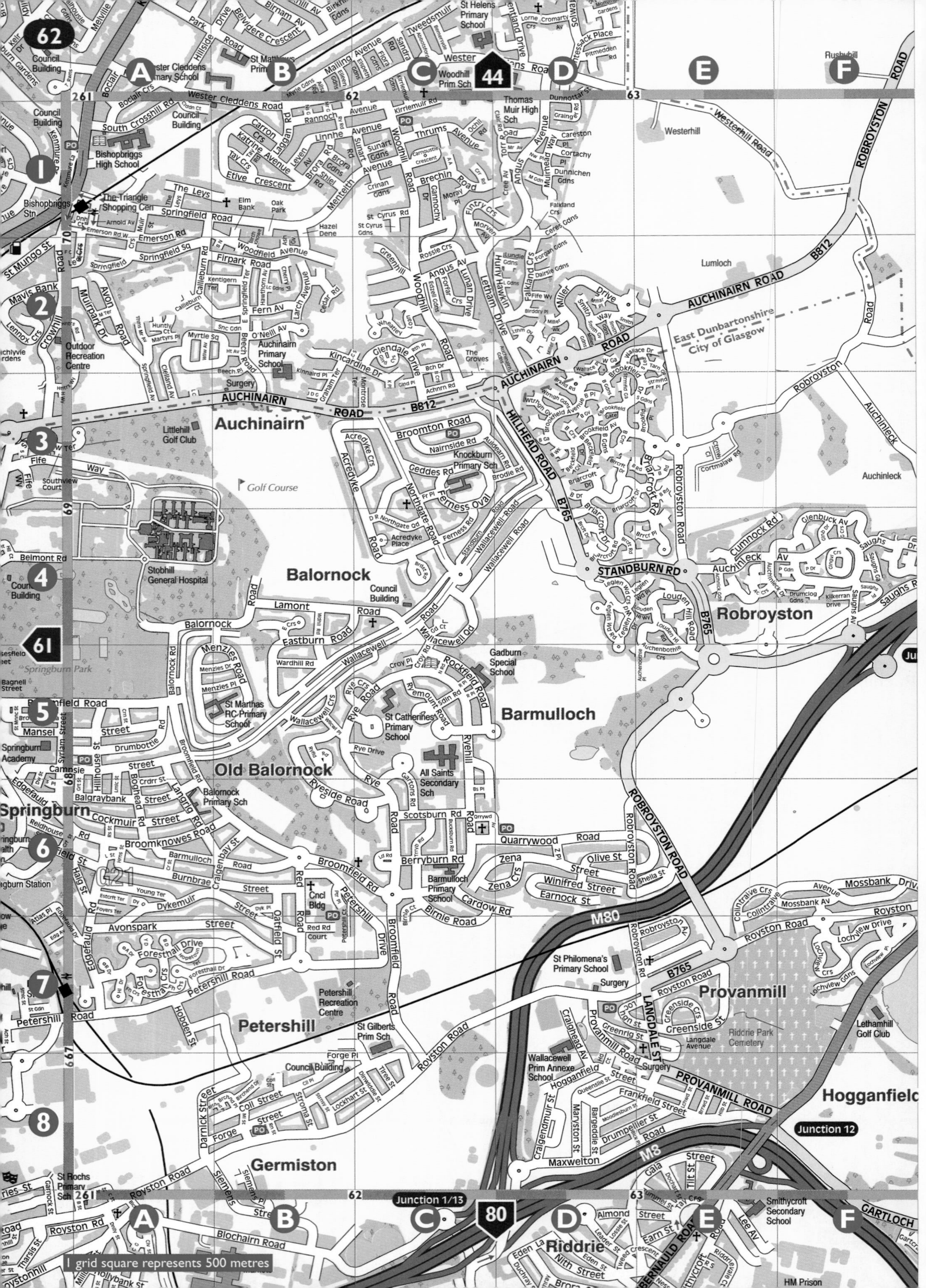

62
44
61
80
A
B
C
D
E
F
1
2
3
4
5
6
7
8
261
62
63
70
69
68
67
Auchinairn
Balornock
Robroyston
Barmulloch
Old Balornock
Springburn
Petershill
Provanmill
Germiston
Riddrie
Hogganfield
Lumloch
Westerhill
Auchinleck
Rushyhill
East Dunbartonshire
City of Glasgow
AUCHINAIRN ROAD
B812
HILLHEAD ROAD
B765
STANDBURN RD
ROBROYSTON ROAD
Robroyston Road
Westerhill Road
PROVANMILL ROAD
GARTLOCH
M80
M8
Junction 12
Junction 1/13
Wester Cleddens Road
South Crosshill Rd
Springfield Road
Woodfield Avenue
Firpark Road
Muirpark Dr
Crowhill
Lennox Crs
Mavis Bank
St Mungo St
Woodhill Road
Menteith Avenue
Etive Crescent
Katrine Avenue
Carron Crs
Thrums Avenue
Brechin Road
Angus Avenue
Lethnam Drive
Lunan Drive
Kincardine Dr
Glendale Drive
Beech Road
O'Neill Av
Myrtle Sq
Fern Av
Larch Avenue
Cedar Rd
Broomton Road
Nairnside Rd
Geddes Rd
Acredyke Crs
Acredyke Road
Northgate Road
Ferness Oval
Wallacewell Road
Wallacewell Qd
Lamont Road
Eastburn Road
Wardhill Rd
Balornock Road
Menzies Road
Broomfield Road
Rye Road
Ryemount Road
Rockfield Road
Ryehill Road
Rye Drive
Ryeside Road
Scotsburn Road
Quarrywood Road
Olive St
Zena Street
Zena Crs
Winifred Street
Earnock St
Birnie Road
Cardow Rd
Berryburn Rd
Robroyston Av
Royston Road
Mossbank Drive
Mossbank Av
Lochview Drive
Lochview Crs
Lochview Gdns
Royston
Greenside Crs
Greenside St
Langdale St
Provanmill Road
Greenrig St
Hogganfield Street
Frankfield Street
Drumpellier St
Barcaple St
Maryston St
Craigendmuir St
Maxwelton
Darnick Street
Coll Street
Forge Street
Stroma St
Lockhart St
Siemens
Bluchairn Road
Hobden St
Petershill Road
Petershill Drive
Forestfall Drive
Avonspark Street
Dykemuir Street
Burnbrae Street
Barmulloch Road
Broomknowes Road
Cockmuir Street
Balgraybank Street
Drumbottie Rd
Craigenbay St
Mansel Street
Syriam Street
Edgefauld Rd
Hillhouse St
Bishopbriggs High School
Bishopbriggs Stn
The Triangle Shopping Cen
Council Building
Outdoor Recreation Centre
Auchinairn Primary School
Surgery
Littlehill Golf Club
Golf Course
Stobhill General Hospital
Knockburn Primary Sch
Gadburn Special School
St Catherines Primary School
St Marthas RC Primary School
All Saints Secondary Sch
Balornock Primary Sch
Barmulloch Primary School
St Philomena's Primary School
Wallacewell Prim Annexe School
Petershill Recreation Centre
St Gilberts Prim Sch
Springburn Academy
Springburn Park
Riddrie Park Cemetery
Lethamhill Golf Club
Smithycroft Secondary School
St Rochs Primary Sch
St Helens Primary School
Thomas Muir High Sch
Woodhill Prim Sch
Cncl Bldg
The Groves
Auchenbothie Crs
HM Prison
1 grid square represents 500 metres

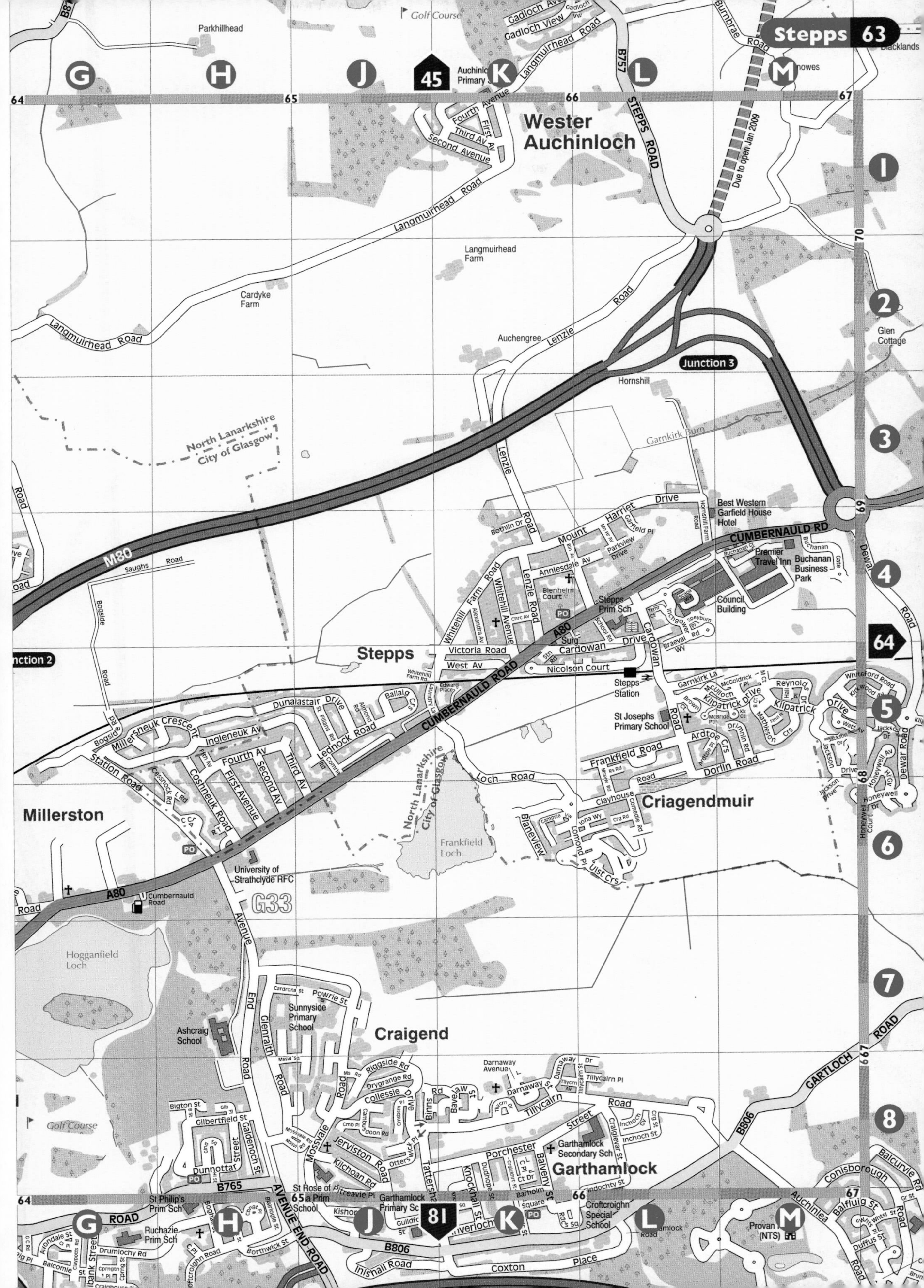
Wester Auchinloch
Stepps
Millerston
Criagendmuir
Craigend
Garthamlock
M80
A80
CUMBERNAULD ROAD
STEPPS ROAD
Langmuirhead Road
Lenzie Road
Junction 3
Junction 2
North Lanarkshire
City of Glasgow
Hogganfield Loch
Frankfield Loch
Garnkirk Burn
Stepps Station
St Josephs Primary School
Sunnyside Primary School
Ashcraig School
Garthamlock Secondary Sch
University of Strathclyde RFC
Best Western Garfield House Hotel
Premier Travel Inn
Buchanan Business Park
Council Building
Langmuirhead Farm
Cardyke Farm
Auchengree
Hornshill
Parkhillhead
Glen Cottage
Blacklands
Golf Course
Due to open Jan 2009
GARTLOCH ROAD
AVENUE-END ROAD
Provan (NTS)
G33
45
64
81

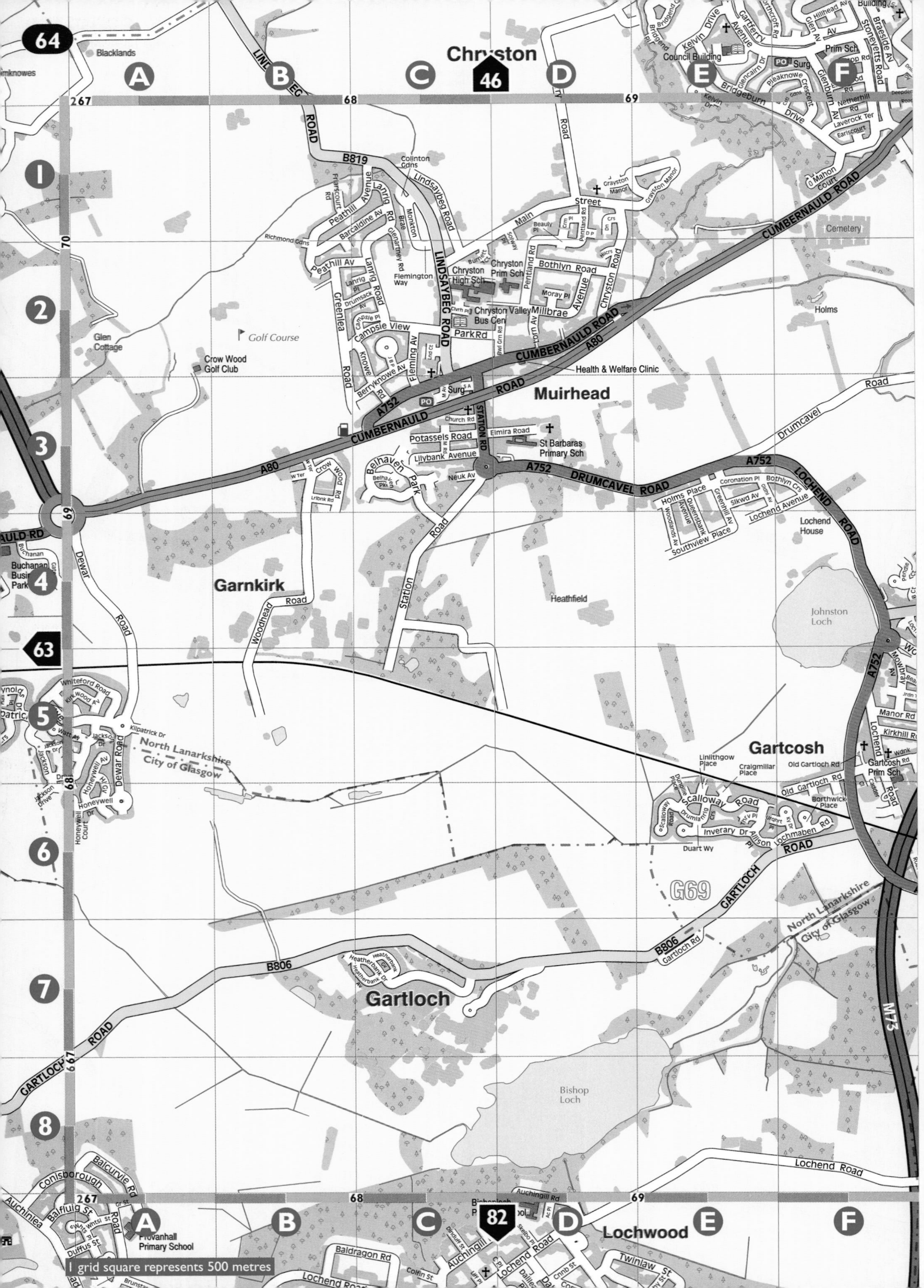

64
46
63
82
Chryston
Muirhead
Garnkirk
Gartcosh
Gartloch
Lochwood
Blacklands
Golf Course
Crow Wood Golf Club
Glen Cottage
Chryston High Sch
Chryston Prim Sch
Chryston Valley Bus Cen
Health & Welfare Clinic
St Barbaras Primary Sch
Heathfield
Lochend House
Johnston Loch
Bishop Loch
Holms
Cemetery
Council Building
Gartcosh Prim Sch
Provanhall Primary School
Buchanan Business Park
North Lanarkshire
City of Glasgow
G69
CUMBERNAULD ROAD
LINDSAYBEG ROAD
STATION RD
DRUMCAVEL ROAD
LOCHEND ROAD
GARTLOCH ROAD
Dewar Road
Woodhead Road
Station Road
Lochend Road
Main Street
A80
A752
B819
B806
M73
1 grid square represents 500 metres

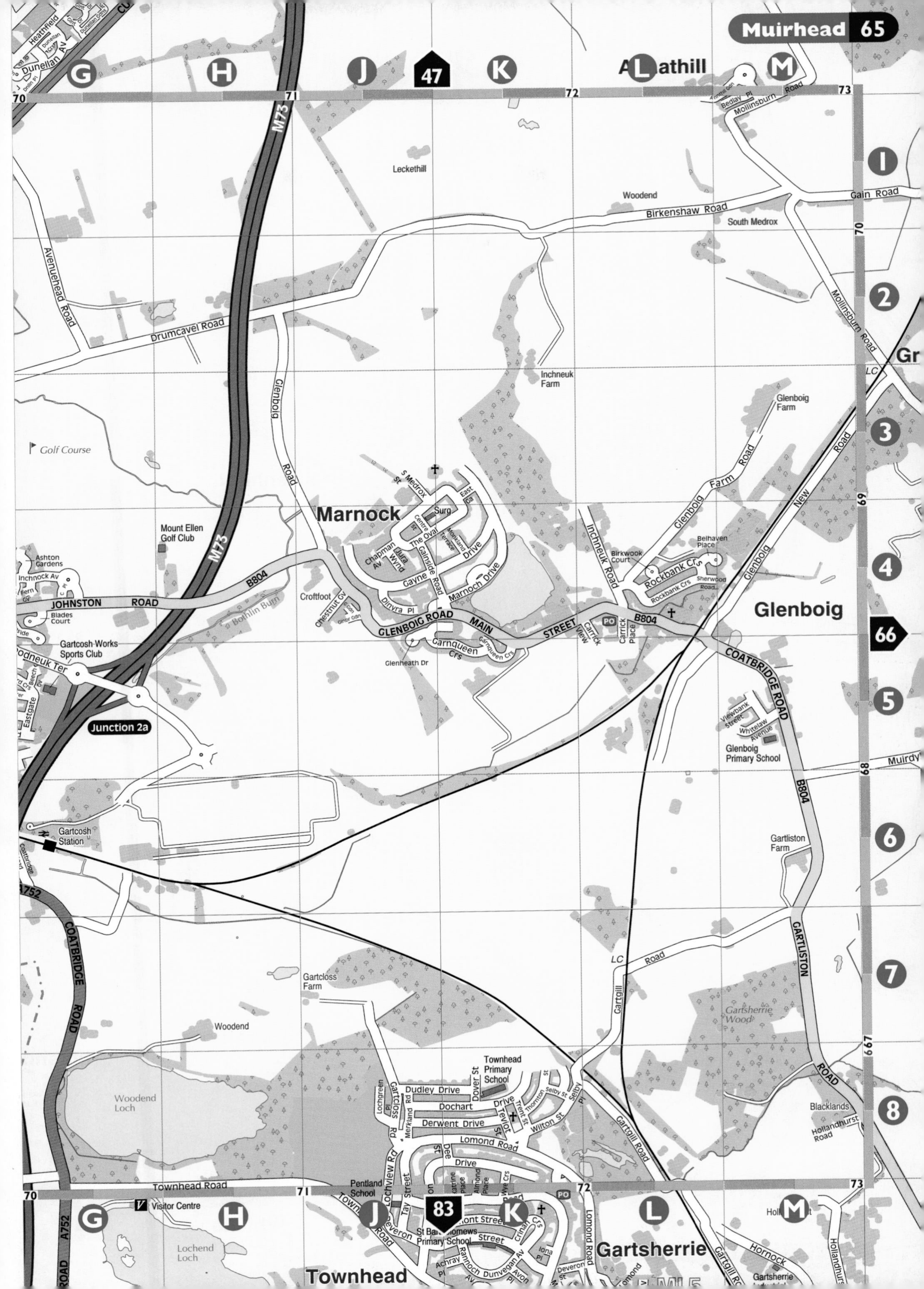

Lathill
Leckethill
Woodend
Birkenshaw Road
Gain Road
South Medrox
Mollinsburn Road
Avenuehead Road
Drumcavel Road
M73
Inchneuk Farm
Glenboig Farm
Golf Course
Glenboig Road
Marnock
Mount Ellen Golf Club
Ashton Gardens
Inchnock Av
JOHNSTON ROAD
B804
Blades Court
Croftfoot
GLENBOIG ROAD
MAIN STREET
Carnqueen Crs
Glenheath Dr
Inchneuk Road
Birkwook Court
Rockbank Crs
Belhaven Place
Sherwood Road
Glenboig
New Road
COATBRIDGE ROAD
Gartcosh Works Sports Club
Junction 2a
Viewbank Street
Whitelaw Avenue
Glenboig Primary School
Gartcosh Station
Gartliston Farm
GARTLISTON ROAD
Gartgill Road
Gartclose Farm
Woodend
Gartsherrie Wood
Woodend Loch
Townhead Primary School
Dudley Drive
Dochart Drive
Derwent Drive
Lomond Road
Blacklands
Hollandhurst Road
Gartgill Road
Townhead Road
Pentland School
Visitor Centre
Lochend Loch
St Bartholomews Primary School
Gartsherrie
Townhead
Hornock

47
66
83

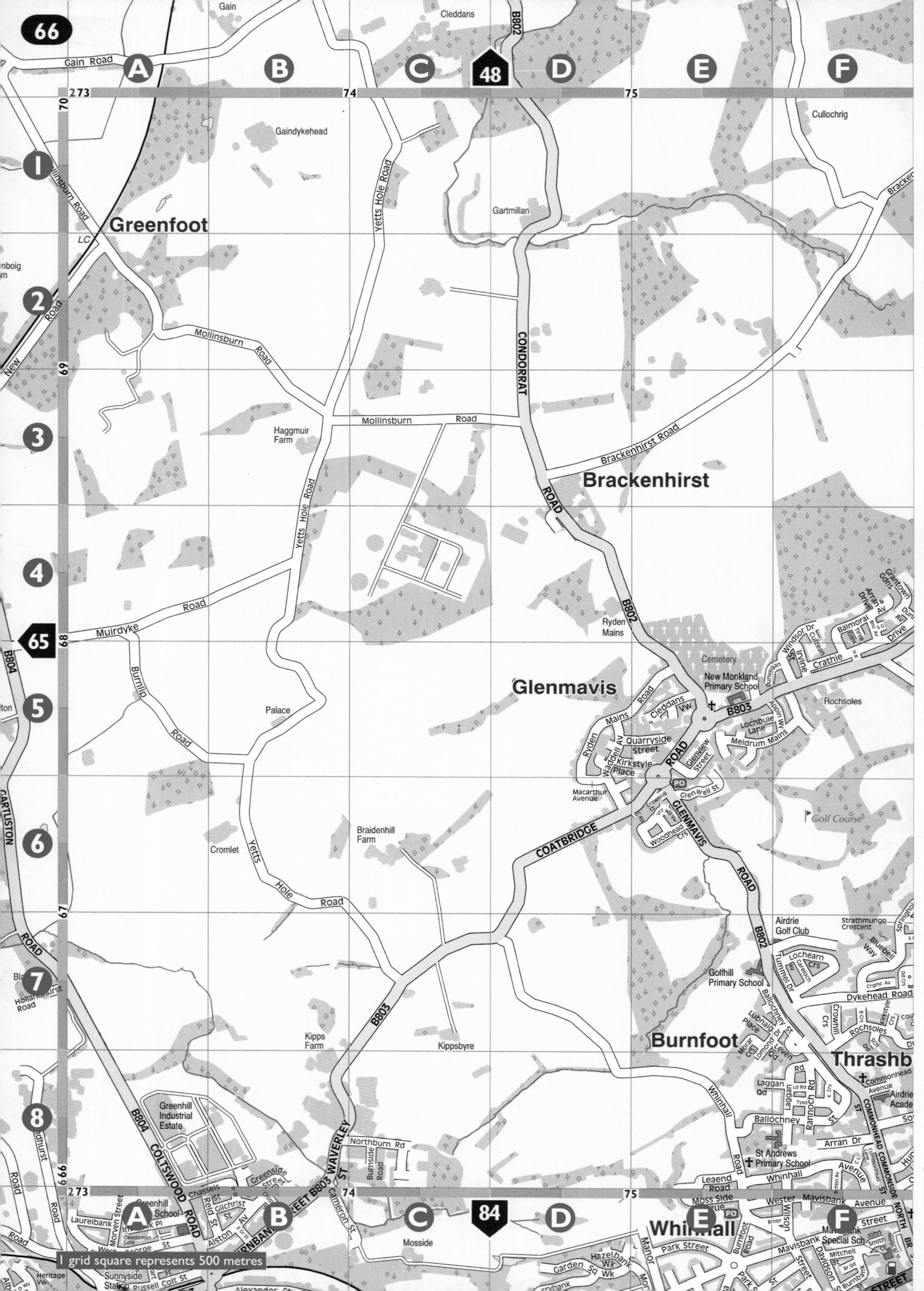
Gain
Gain Road
Cleddans
B802
48
A
B
C
D
E
F
Gaindykehead
Cullochrig
Yetts Hole Road
Mollinsburn Road
Greenfoot
Gartmillan
New Road
Mollinsburn Road
CONDORRAT ROAD
Haggmuir Farm
Brackenhirst Road
Brackenhirst
Yetts Hole Road
Muirdyke Road
B802
Ryden Mains
Cemetery
New Monkland Primary School
Glenmavis
B803
Rochsoles
Burnlip Road
Palace
Ryden Mains Road
Cleddans Vw
Quarryside Street
Kirkstyle Place
Glenview Street
Meldrum Mains
Lochbule Lane
Crathie
Irvine
Windsor Dr
Balmoral
Drive
Macarthur Avenue
PO
Glen Well St
Woodhead Crs
COATBRIDGE ROAD
GLENMAVIS ROAD
Golf Course
Braidenhill Farm
Cromlet
Yetts Hole Road
GARTLISTON ROAD
B804
65
Airdrie Golf Club
Strathmungo Crescent
Lochearn Crs
Tummel Dr
Golfhill Primary School
Dykehead Road
Bluebell Way
Rochsoles
Crowhill
B803
Kipps Farm
Kippsbyre
Burnfoot
Thrashb
Ballochney St
Lubnaig Place
Commonhead Avenue
Airdrie Acade
Laggan Rd
Rannoch St
Ballochney
Arran Dr
Whinhall Road
St Andrews Primary School
Whinhall Avenue
COMMONHEAD ST
COMMONSIDE ST
NORTH BR
Greenhill Industrial Estate
B804
COLTSWOOD ROAD
Greenside Street
Chassels St
WAVERLEY ST
B803
Northburn Rd
Burnside Road
Leaend Road
Moss Side
Wester Mavisbank Avenue
Greenhill School
Reid St
Gilchrist St
Alston Av
Cameron St
Laurelbank
Morven Street
Caledonian Gate
West George St
84
Mosside
Whinhall
Park Street
Burnfoot Road
Wilson St
Mavisbank Street
Mavisbank Special Sch
Davidson St
Mitchell St
Manor
Hazelbank Wk
Garden Sq Wk
Sunnyside Station
Russell Colt St
Heritage Vw
STREET
1 grid square represents 500 metres
273
74
75
70
69
68
67
666
1
2
3
4
5
6
7
8

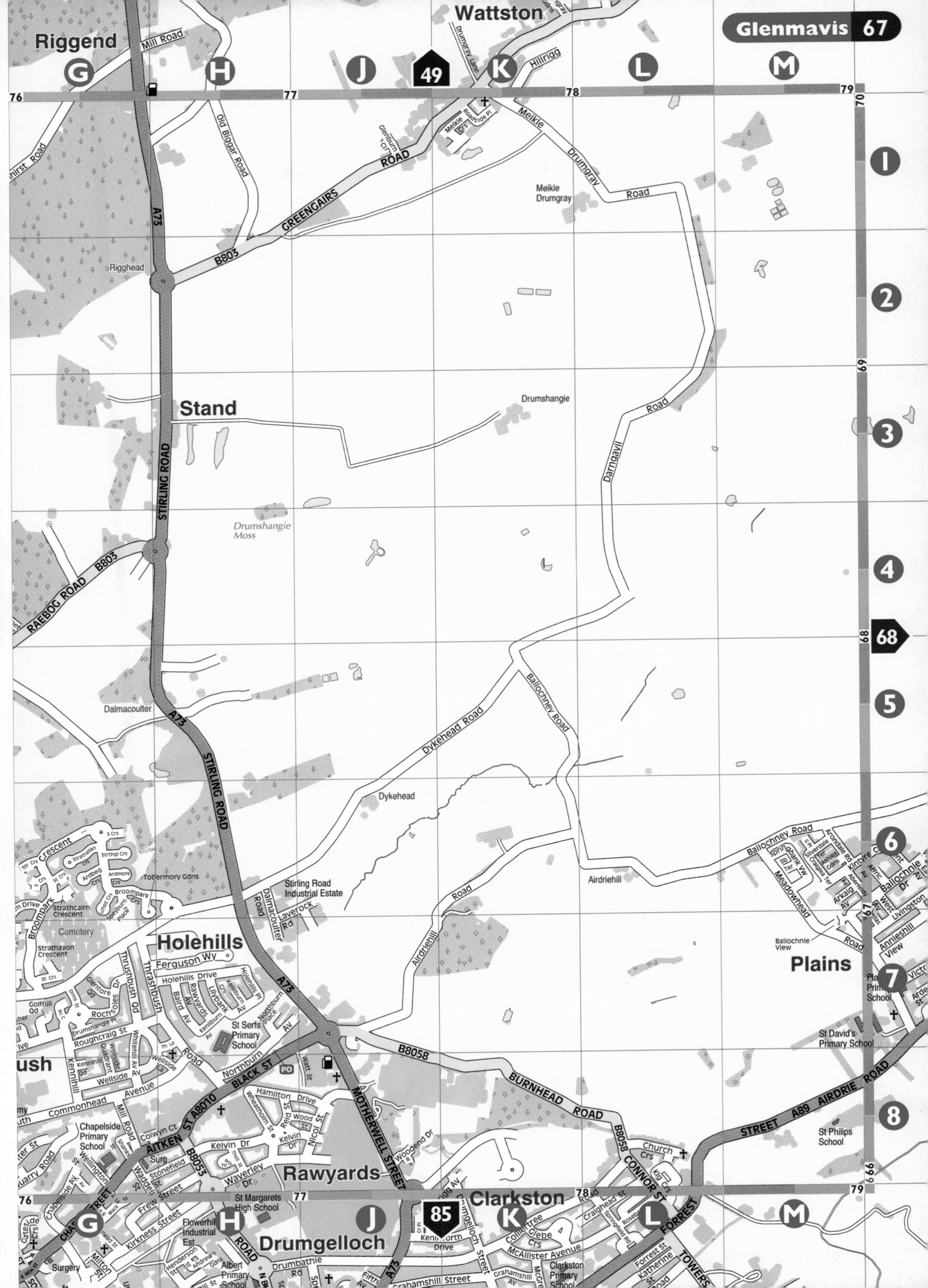

Wattston
Riggend
Mill Road
Old Biggar Road
GREENGAIRS ROAD
B803
Meikle Drumgray
Drumgray Road
Rigghead
Stand
STIRLING ROAD
A73
Drumshangie
Darngavil Road
Drumshangie Moss
RAEBOG ROAD
Dalmacoulter
Dykehead Road
Ballochney Road
Dykehead
Airdriehill
Airdriehill Road
Stirling Road Industrial Estate
Tobermory Gdns
Holehills
Ferguson Wy
Holehills Drive
Plains
St Serfs Primary School
St David's Primary School
B8058
BURNHEAD ROAD
AIRDRIE ROAD
A89
St Philips School
Chapelside Primary School
Commonhead
Rawyards
Clarkston
Drumgelloch
St Margarets High School
Flowerhill Industrial Est
Albert Primary School
Clarkston Primary School
FORREST STREET
TOWERS ROAD
CONNOR ST
MOTHERWELL STREET
AITKEN ST A8010
BLACK ST
Cemetery
Meadowhead

49
68
85

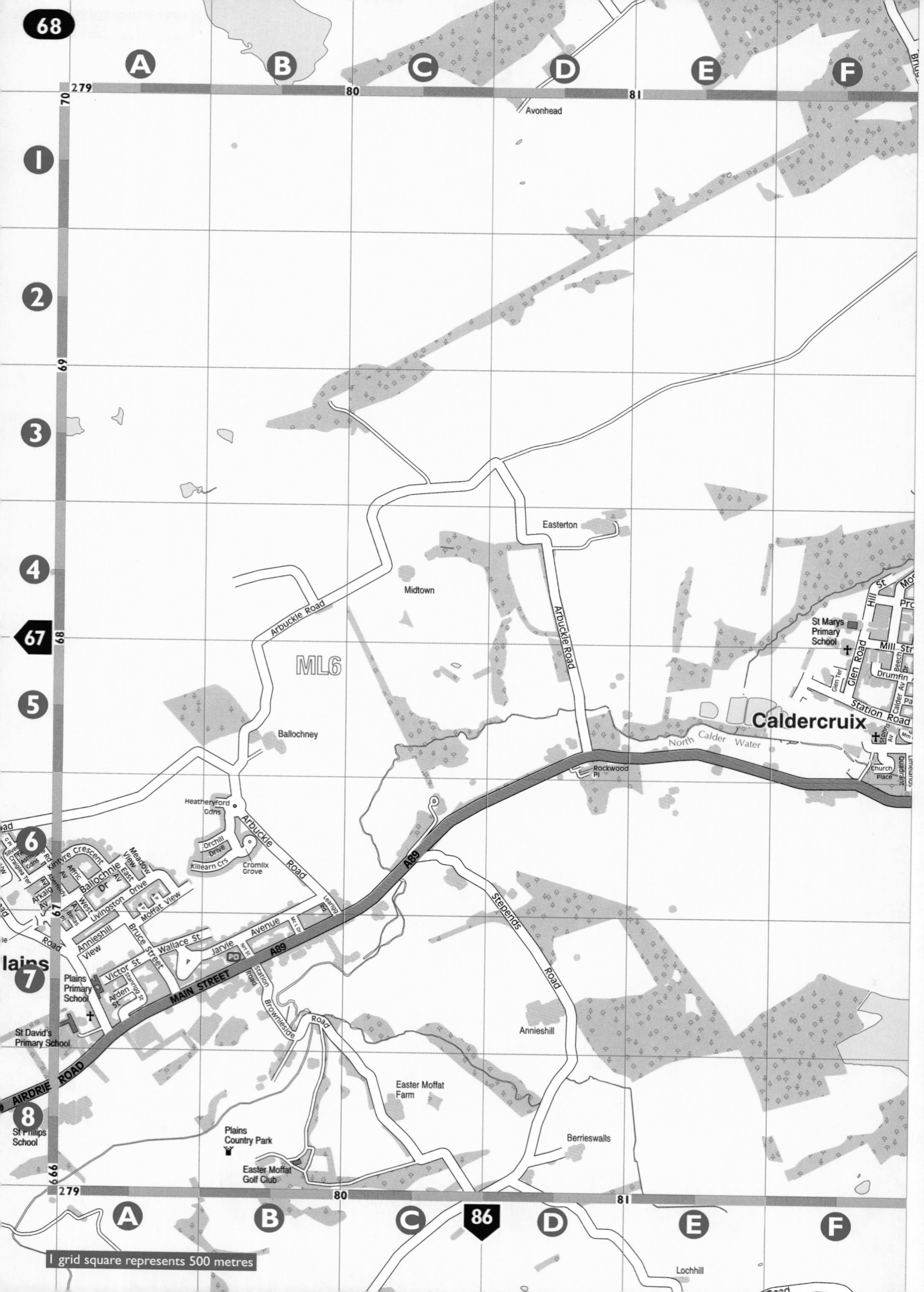

A B C D E F

279
70 80 81

Avonhead

1

2

69

3

Easterton

4

Arbuckle Road

Midtown

67 68

ML6

5

Ballochney

St Marys
Primary
School

Drumfin

Caldercruix

North Calder Water

Rockwood
Pl

Church
Place

Heatheryford
Gdns

Arbuckle Road

6

Kintyre Crescent

Orchill
Drive

Ballochnie
Dr

Meadow
View East

Killearn Crs

Cromlix
Grove

Arbuckle Road

Livingston Drive

Moffat View

67

A89

Stepends Road

Arkalg

Annieshill
View

Bruce Street

Wallace St

Jarvie
Avenue

Lennox
Drive

PO

A89

An+N

lains

7

Plains
Primary
School

Victor St

Arden
St

Main Street

Station
Road

Brownieside
Road

Anniesfield

St David's
Primary School

AIRDRIE ROAD

Easter Moffat
Farm

8

St Philips
School

Plains
Country Park

Berrieswalls

Easter Moffat
Golf Club

666

279
70 80 81

A B C 86 D E F

1 grid square represents 500 metres

Lochhill

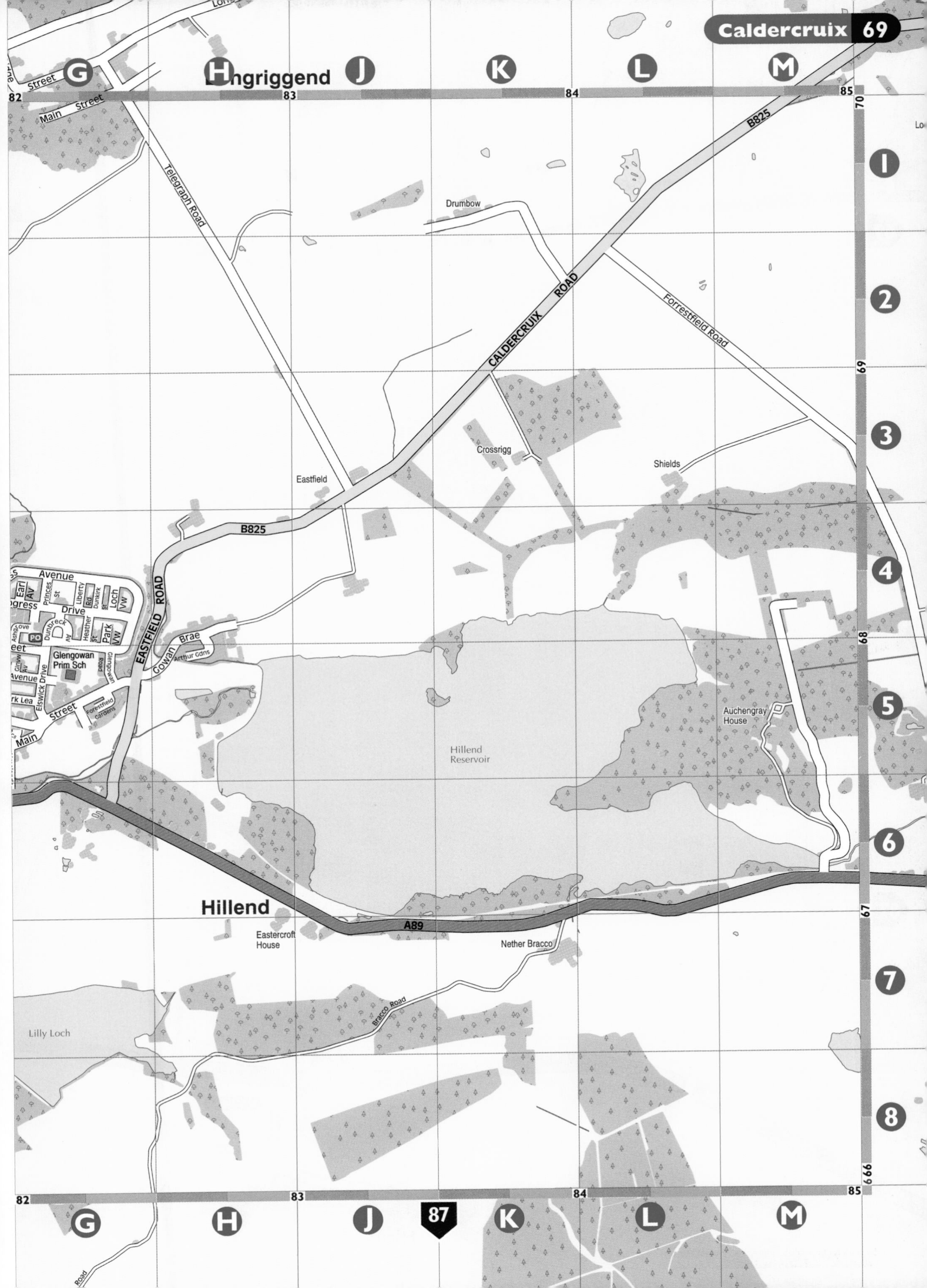

G
H ngriggend
J
K
L
M

82
83
84
85
70

Street
Main Street

Telegraph Road

B825

Drumbow

CALDERCRUIX ROAD

Forrestfield Road

1

2

69

3

Crossrigg

Shields

Eastfield

B825

Avenue
Earl
Av
Princes
St
Liberty
Rd
Dunkirk
St
Loch
VW
ngress
Drive
Heather
St
Park
VW
Dunbreck
Av
EASTFIELD ROAD
Glengowan Drive
PO
Gowan Brae
Arthur Gdns
Glengowan
Prim Sch
Street
Elswick Drive
rk Lea
Forrestfield
Gardens
Main
Street

4

68

Auchengray
House

5

Hillend
Reservoir

6

67

Hillend

A89

Eastercroft
House

Nether Bracco

7

Bracco Road

Lilly Loch

8

666

82
83
84
85

G
H
J
87
K
L
M

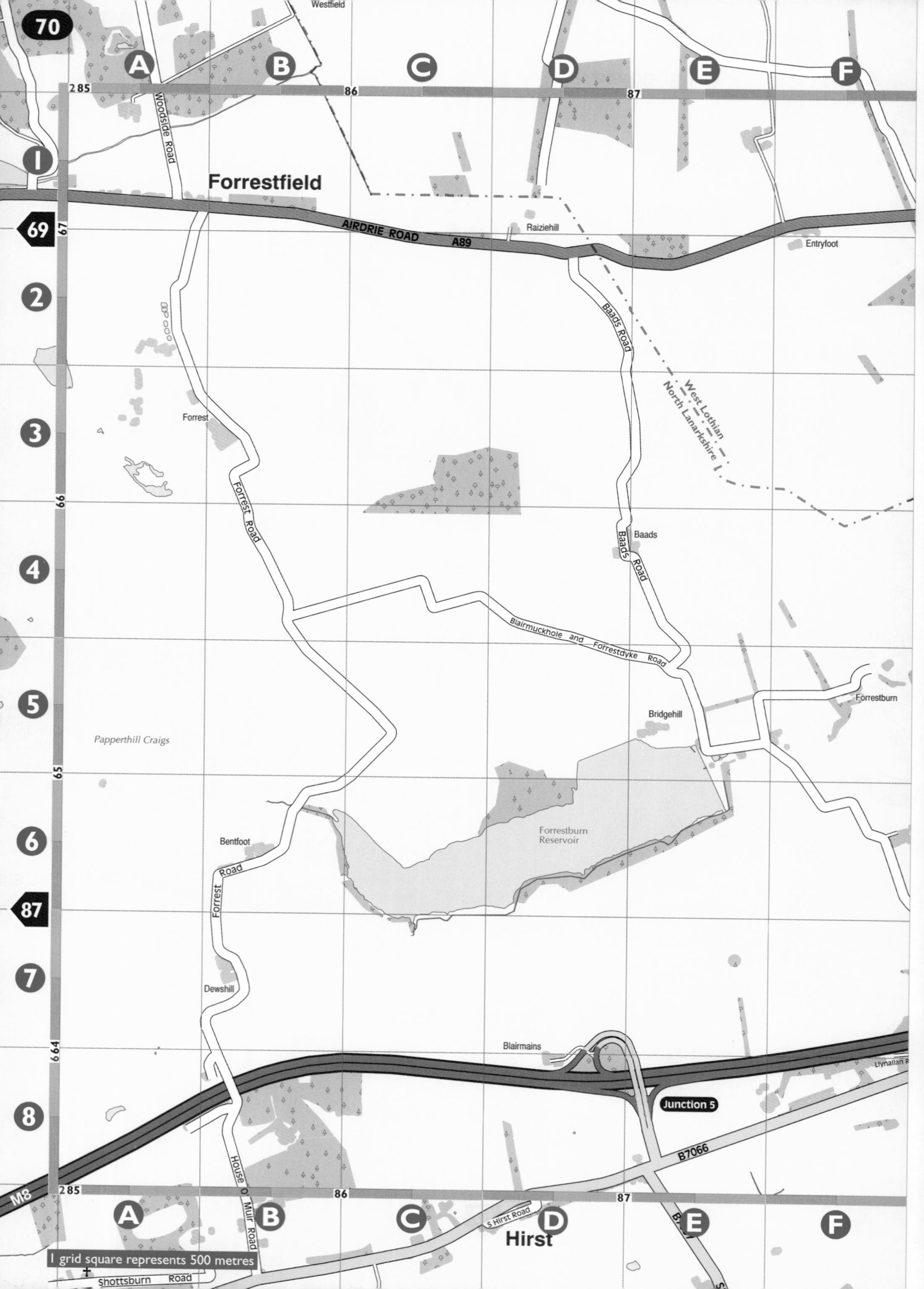

70

A   B   C   D   E   F

285   86   87

I

Forrestfield

69   67   AIRDRIE ROAD   A89   Raiziehill   Entryfoot

2

Baads Road

3   Forrest   West Lothian
North Lanarkshire

66

4   Baads Road   Baads

Blairmuckhole and Forrestdyke Road

5   65   Bridgehill   Forrestburn

Papperthill Craigs

6   Bentfoot   Forrestburn
Road   Reservoir

87   Forrest
Road

7   Dewshill

664

Blairmains   Llynallan R

8   Junction 5

M8   285   B7066   86   87

A   B   C   D   E   F

Hirst

House O Muir Road

S Hirst Road

1 grid square represents 500 metres

Shottsburn   Road

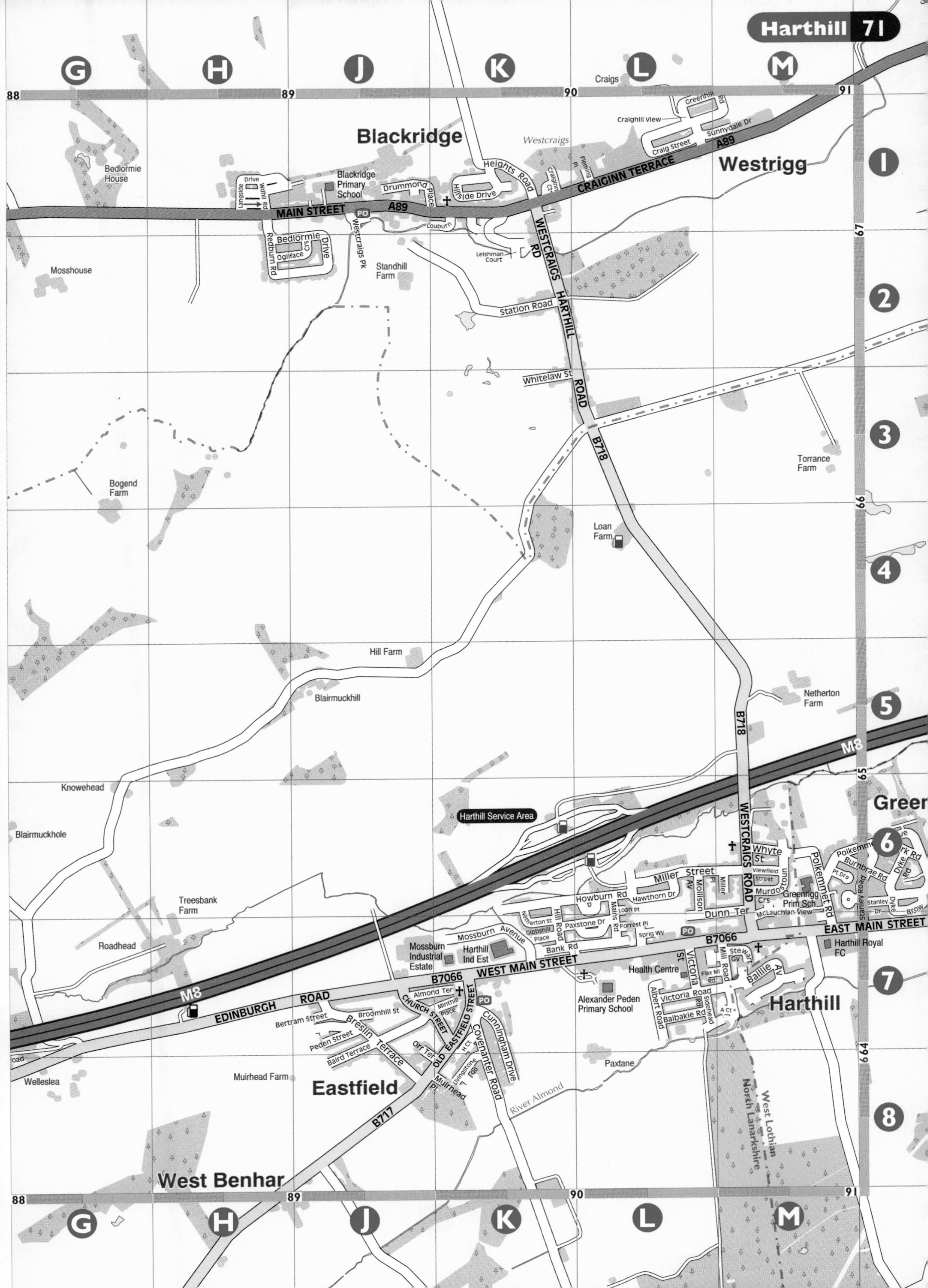

G GH H J K L M

88 89 90 91

Blackridge

Craigs

Westcraigs

Craighill View

Greenhill Rd

Craig Street

Sunnydale Dr

A89

Westrigg

1

Heights Road

CRAIGINN TERRACE

Fleming

Craighill Ct

Drive

Wahli Rd

Blackridge Primary School

Drummond Place

Hillside Drive

Bedlormie House

MAIN STREET A89

PO

Louburn

WESTCRAIGS RD

Mosshouse

Bedlormie Drive

Redburn Rd Ogilface Crs

Westcraigs Pk

Leishman Court

Standhill Farm

2

HARTHILL ROAD

Station Road

Whitelaw St

3

B718

Torrance Farm

66

Bogend Farm

Loan Farm

4

Hill Farm

Blairmuckhill

B718

Netherton Farm

5

M8

65

Knowehead

Greer

Harthill Service Area

6

Blairmuckhole

Whyte St

Viewfield Street

Polkemmet Rd

Dyke Rd

Greenrig Prim Sch

Burnbrae Rd

Pt Dra

Stanley Road

Dyke BfDW

Treesbank Farm

Miller Street

Mollison Av

Miller

Murdoch

McLauchlan View

Stanley Dr

Howburn Rd

Hawthorn Dr

Crs

Dunn Ter

Roadhead

Nelherton St

Gibbshill Place

Loan Pl

Mains Rd

Paxstone Dr

Forrest Pl

sprig Wy

PO

EAST MAIN STREET

Mossburn Avenue

Hill Road

Bank Rd

B7066

Stew art (GV)

Mill Road

Harthill Royal FC

Mossburn Industrial Estate

Harthill Ind Est

WEST MAIN STREET

Health Centre

Victoria St

Flax Mill

Baillie Av

Harthill

7

664

M8

EDINBURGH ROAD

Almord Ter

B7066

CHURCH STREET

Minthill Place

PO

Alexander Peden Primary School

Albert Road

Victoria Road

Solehead

A Ct

Wesleslea

Bertram street

Broomhill St

Breslin Terrace

Minthill

H Crs

Balbakie Rd

Paxtane

West Lothian North Lanarkshire

Peden Street

Baird Terrace

Orr Ter

OLD EASTFIELD STREET

Covenanter Drive

Livingstone St

Muirhead Pl

Muirhead Farm

Eastfield

River Almond

Paxtane

8

B717

West Benhar

88 89 90 91

G GH H J K L M

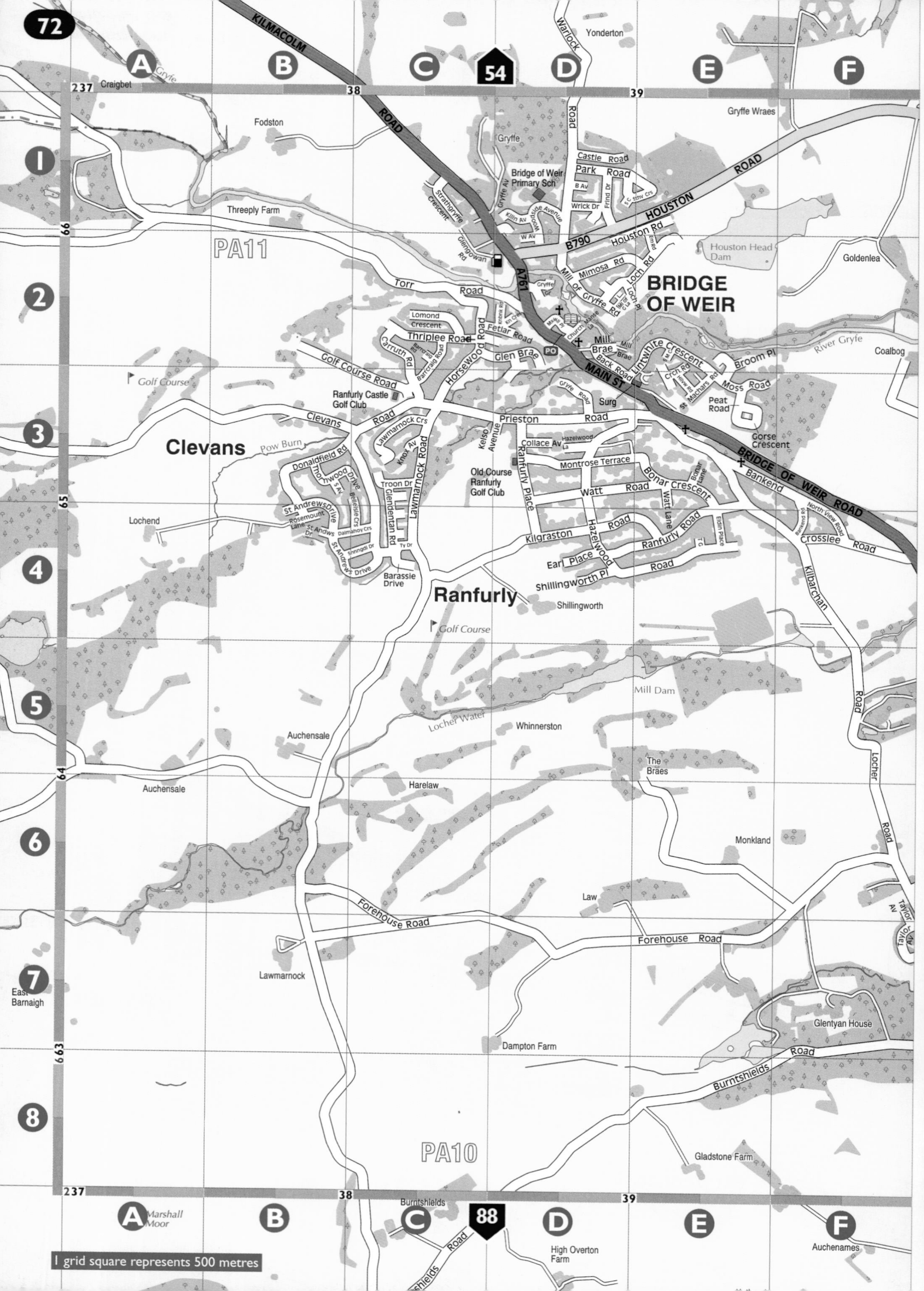

KILMACOLM ROAD
Yonderton
Warlock Road
Craigbet
Gryfe
Fodston
Gryffe Wraes
Castle Road
Park Road
Bridge of Weir Primary Sch
HOUSTON ROAD
B790
Houston Rd
Threeply Farm
PA11
Houston Head Dam
Goldenlea
Glengowan Rd
A761
Mimosa Rd
Loch Rd
Mill of Gryffe Rd
BRIDGE OF WEIR
Torr Road
Lomond Crescent
Thriplee Road
Fetlar Road
Horsewood Road
Glen Brae
Golf Course Road
Carruth Rd
Barrcraig Road
River Gryfe
Coalbog
Mill Brae
Back Road
MAIN ST
Lintwhite Crescent
Broom Pl
Moss Road
Peat Road
Golf Course
Ranfurly Castle Golf Club
Clevans Road
Prieston Road
Surg
Gorse Crescent
Clevans
Pow Burn
Lawmarnock Crs
Knox Av
Kelso Avenue
Collace Av
Hazelwood La
Montrose Terrace
BRIDGE OF WEIR ROAD
Bankend
Donaldfield Rd
Thornwood Drive
Lawmarnock Road
Old Course Ranfurly Golf Club
Ranfurly Place
Watt Road
Bonar Crescent
Bonar Lane
Watt Lane
Troon Dr
Glendentan Rd
Lochend
St Andrews Drive
Rosemount Lane
Kilgraston Road
Hazelwood
Ranfurly Road
Eldin Place
Crosslee Road
North View Road
Earl Place
Shillingworth Pl
Barassie Drive
Ranfurly
Shillingworth
Kilbarchan Road
Golf Course
Mill Dam
Locher Water
Whinnerston
Auchensale
The Braes
Harelaw
Auchensale
Locher Road
Monkland
Law
Forehouse Road
Forehouse Road
Taylor Av
Lawmarnock
East Barnaigh
Glentyan House
Dampton Farm
Burntshields Road
PA10
Gladstone Farm
Burntshields
Marshall Moor
High Overton Farm
Auchenames
1 grid square represents 500 metres

54
88

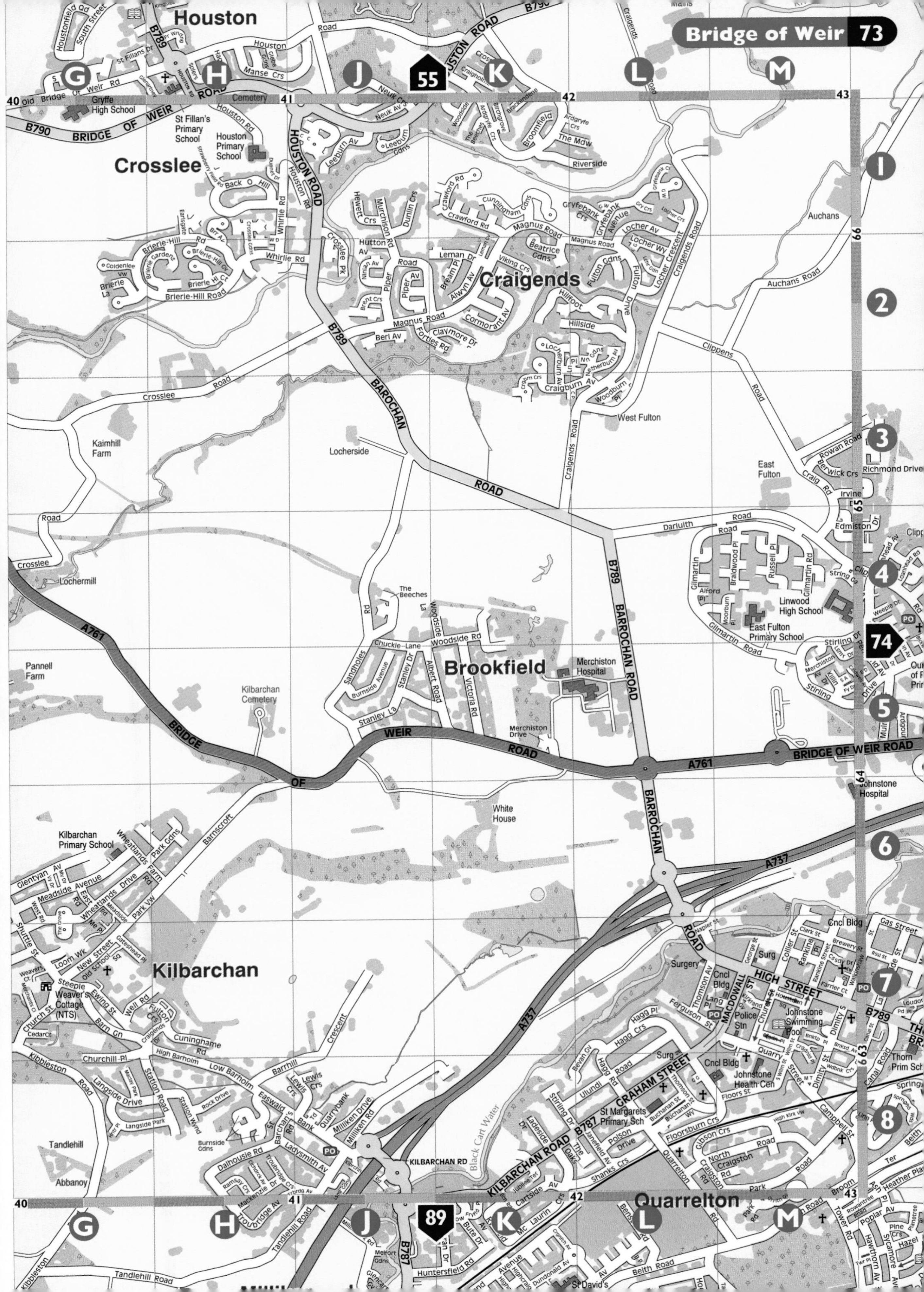
Bridge of Weir 73
Houston
Crosslee
Craigends
Brookfield
Kilbarchan
Quarrelton
B790 BRIDGE OF WEIR ROAD
HOUSTON ROAD
B789
BARROCHAN ROAD
BRIDGE OF WEIR ROAD
A761
A737
B787
KILBARCHAN ROAD
Crosslee Road
Gryffe High School
St Fillan's Primary School
Houston Primary School
Cemetery
Magnus Road
Crawford Rd
Cunningham Gdns
Gryfebank Avenue
Locher Crescent
Craigends Road
Fulton Drive
Hillside
Craigburn Av
Woodburn Pl
West Fulton
Auchans
Auchans Road
Clippens Road
East Fulton
Darluith Road
Linwood High School
East Fulton Primary School
Gilmartin Road
Stirling Drive
Kaimhill Farm
Locherside
Lochermill
Pannell Farm
Kilbarchan Cemetery
The Beeches
Chuckie Lane
Woodside Rd
Sandholes Rd
Burnside Avenue
Stanley Dr
Albert Road
Victoria Rd
Merchiston Hospital
Merchiston Drive
White House
Johnstone Hospital
Barnscroft
Kilbarchan Primary School
Wheatlands Farm Rd
Meadside Avenue
Weaver's Cottage (NTS)
Steeple
High Barholm
Low Barholm
Churchill Pl
Station Road
Langside Drive
Tandlehill
Abbanoy
Tandlehill Road
Kibbleston Road
Cuninghame Rd
Crescent
Barrhill
Lewis Crs
Quarrybank
Milliken Drive
Ladysmith Av
KILBARCHAN RD
Black Cart Water
HIGH STREET
MACDOWALL ST
Johnstone Swimming Pool
Police Stn
Johnstone Health Cen
GRAHAM STREET
St Margarets Primary Sch
Floorsburn Crs
North Craigston Rd
Surgery
Cncl Bldg
Thorn Prim Sch
Huntersfield Rd
Beith Road
Hawthorn Av
Tower Rd
G H J K L M
55 74 89
40 41 42 43
1 2 3 4 5 6 7 8
63 64 65 66

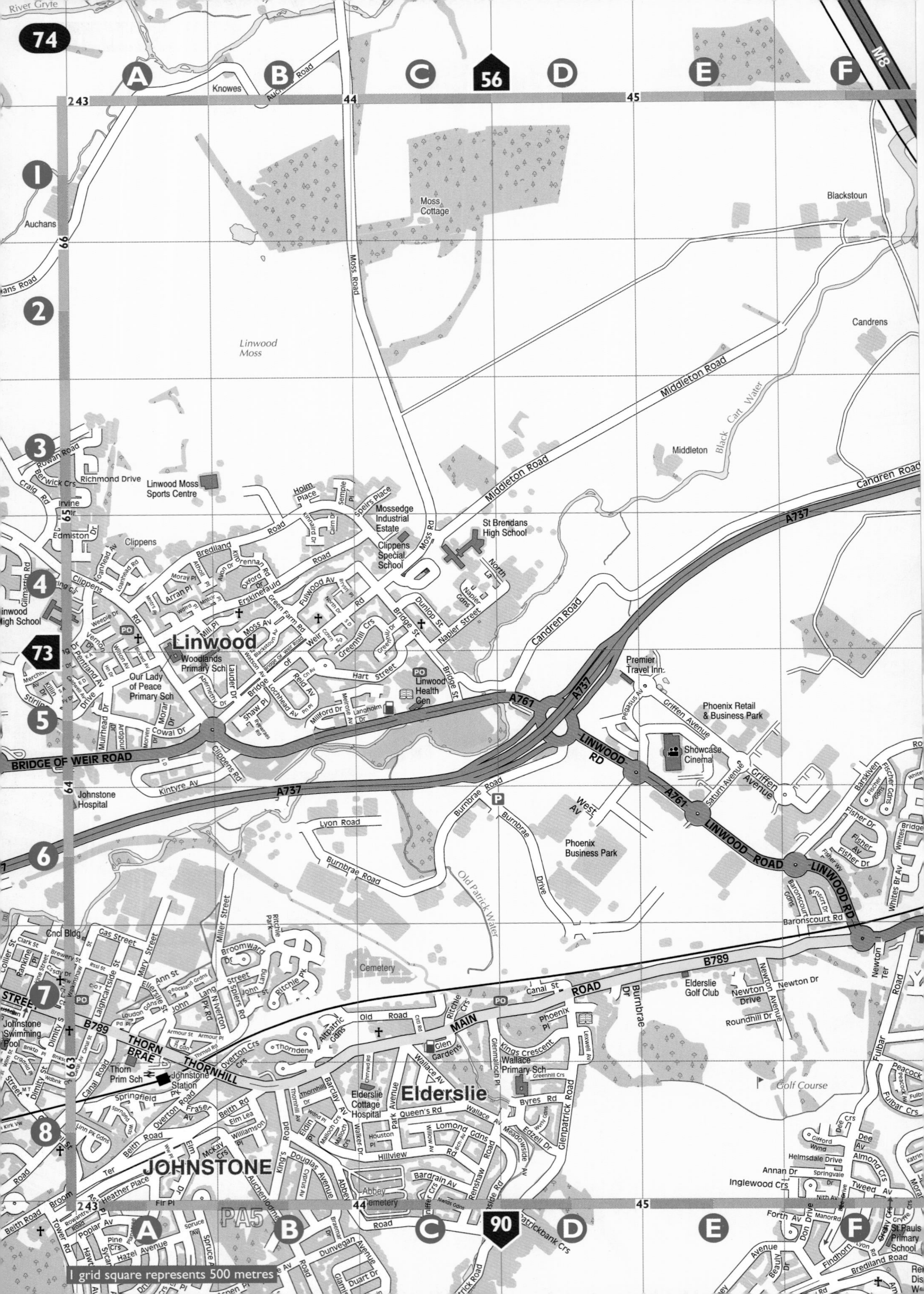

74
56
73
90
A
B
C
D
E
F
1
2
3
4
5
6
7
8
2 43
44
45
65
66
64
63
M8
River Gryfe
Knowes
Auchans Road
Auchans
Moss Cottage
Blackstoun
Moss Road
Linwood Moss
Candrens
Middleton Road
Black Cart Water
Middleton
Rowan Road
Berwick Crs
Richmond Drive
Craig Rd
Irvine Dr
Edmiston Dr
Linwood Moss Sports Centre
Holm Place
Semple Pl
Speirs Place
Mossedge Industrial Estate
Kinnaird Dr
Cairn Dr
St Brendans High School
Candren Road
A737
Clippens
Clippens Special School
Brediland Road
Kilbrennan Rd
Oxford Dr
Moray Pl
Arran Pl
Erskinefauld Rd
Green Farm Rd
Fulwood Av
Loanhead Av
Loanhead Rd
North La
Napier Gdns
Napier Street
Dunlop St
Bridge St
Gilmartin Rd
Linwood High School
Weepie Dr
Mill Pl
Moss Av
Greenhill Crs
Linwood
Woodlands Primary Sch
Our Lady of Peace Primary Sch
Hart Street
Linwood Health Cen
Lauder Dr
Abernethy Dr
Bridge of Weir Road
Reid Av
Lochhead Av
Shaw Pl
Millford Dr
Langholm Dr
Premier Travel Inn
Pegasus Av
Griffen Avenue
Phoenix Retail & Business Park
Showcase Cinema
Saturn Avenue
A761
Pentland Av
Stirling Dr
Muirhead Dr
Ardgour Dr
Morven Dr
Morar Dr
Cowal Dr
BRIDGE OF WEIR ROAD
Clippens Rd
Kintyre Av
LINWOOD RD
Burnbrae Road
West Av
Barskiven Rd
Fischer Gdns
Fisher Dr
Fisher Wy
Whites Br Av
Johnstone Hospital
Lyon Road
Phoenix Business Park
LINWOOD ROAD
Old Patrick Water
Burnbrae Drive
Baronscourt Gdns
Baronscourt Rd
Cncl Bldg
Gas Street
Miller Street
Ritchie Park
Broomward Dr
Mary Street
Collier St
Clark St
Rankine Pl
Brewery St
Cemetery
B789
Canal St
Elderslie Golf Club
Newton Drive
Newton Avenue
Newton Dr
Newton Ter
Roundhill Dr
Ann St
Ellerslie St
John Lang St
Speirs Rd
Ritchie Pk
MAIN ROAD
Old Road
Phoenix Pl
Lexwell Av
Johnstone Swimming Pool
Dimity St
Laighcartside St
Loudon Gdns
Armour St
Armour Pl
Overton Crs
Thorndene
Altpatric Gdns
THORN BRAE
THORNHILL
Thorn Prim Sch
Johnstone Station
Kings Crescent
Wallace Primary Sch
Glen Gardens
Wallace Av
Glenpatrick Road
Golf Course
Fulbar Av
Peacock Dr
Springfield Pk
Canal Road
Overton Road
Fraser Av
Beith Rd
Elm Lea
Williamson Pl
Elderslie Cottage Hospital
Elderslie
Queen's Rd
Byres Rd
Edzell Dr
Meadowside Av
Dee Crs
Dee Av
Almond Crs
Gifford Wynd
Helmsdale Drive
Annan Dr
Springvale Dr
Inglewood Crs
Tweed Av
Beith Road
Elm Dr
McKay Crs
JOHNSTONE
King's Road
Douglas Avenue
Houston Pl
Hillview
Lomond Gdns
Renshaw Road
Bargrain Av
Abbey Cemetery
Heather Place
Fir Pl
Broom Rd
PA5
Tower Rd
Poplar Av
Pine Crs
Hazel Avenue
Spruce Av
Spruce Avenue
Braemar Dr
Dunvegan Avenue
Duart Dr
Glenpatrickbank Crs
Forth Av
Don Drive
Findhorn
Brediland Road
St Pauls Primary School
1 grid square represents 500 metres

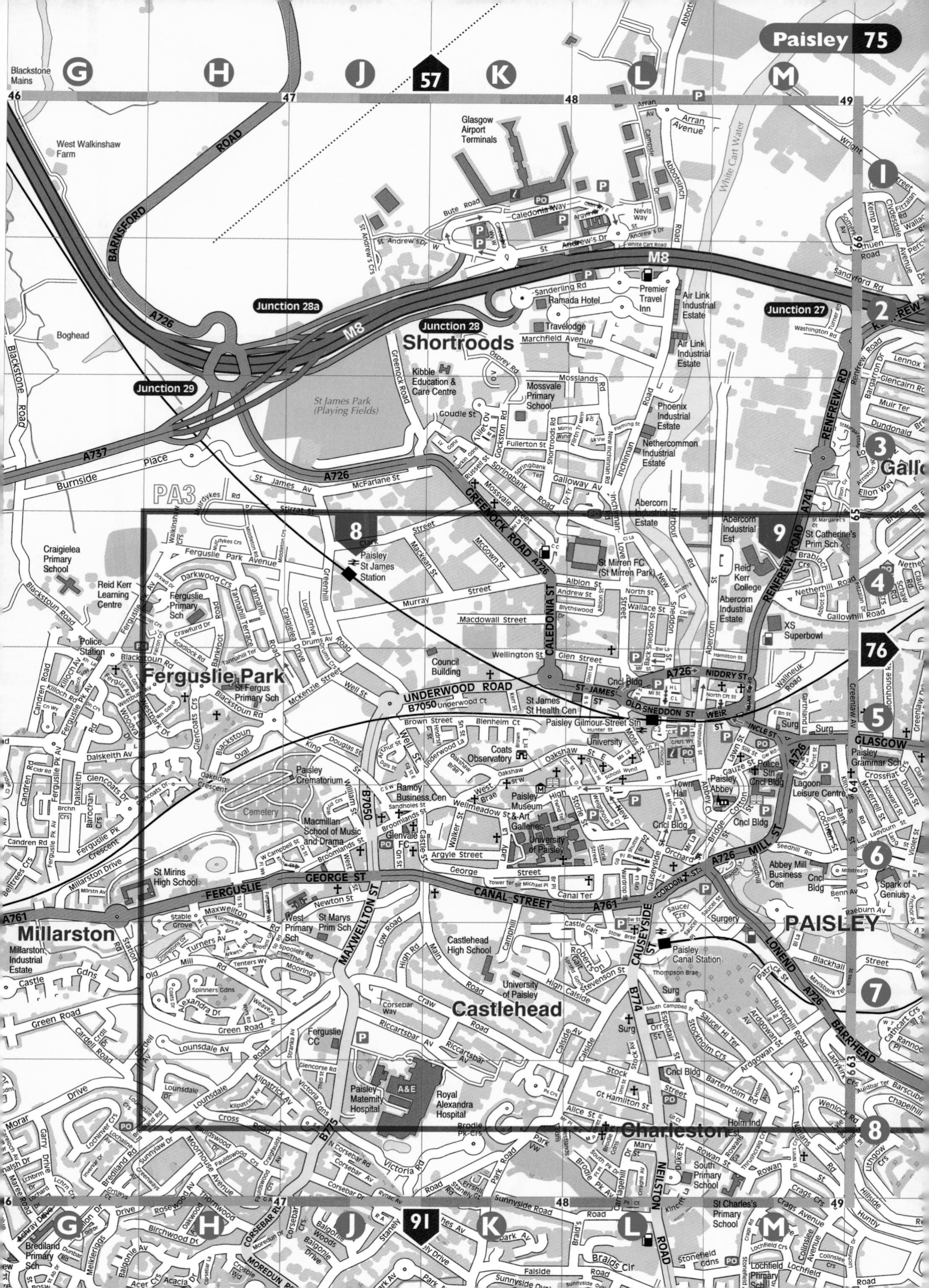
G
H
J
57
K
L
M
Blackstone Mains
West Walkinshaw Farm
Boghead
Glasgow Airport Terminals
BARNSFORD ROAD
A726
M8
Junction 28a
Junction 28
Junction 29
Junction 27
Shortroods
Ramada Hotel
Travelodge
Premier Travel Inn
Air Link Industrial Estate
Kibble Education & Care Centre
St James Park (Playing Fields)
Mossvale Primary School
Phoenix Industrial Estate
Nethercommon Industrial Estate
Abercorn Industrial Estate
A737
Burnside Place
PA3
8
9
Paisley St James Station
St Mirren FC (St Mirren Park)
Reid Kerr College
XS Superbowl
Craigielea Primary School
Reid Kerr Learning Centre
Ferguslie Primary Sch
Police Station
Ferguslie Park
St Fergus Primary Sch
Council Building
GREENOCK ROAD
CALEDONIA ST
RENFREW ROAD
UNDERWOOD ROAD
Paisley Gilmour Street Stn
University
Coats Observatory
Paisley Crematorium
Cemetery
Ramoy Business Cen
Paisley Museum & Art Galleries
University of Paisley
Paisley Abbey
Town Hall
Macmillan School of Music and Drama
Glenvale FC
Lagoon Leisure Centre
Paisley Grammar Sch
Abbey Mill Business Cen
St Mirins High School
GEORGE ST
CANAL STREET
A761
Millarston
Millarston Industrial Estate
West Primary Sch
St Marys Prim Sch
MAXWELLTON ST
Castlehead High School
Castlehead
University of Paisley
Paisley Canal Station
CAUSEYSIDE ST
PAISLEY
LONEND
BARRHEAD
Ferguslie CC
Paisley Maternity Hospital
A&E
Royal Alexandra Hospital
Charleston
South Primary School
NEILSTON ROAD
St Charles's Primary School
Bredilland Primary Sch
Lochfield Primary Sch
91
76
1
2
3
4
5
6
7
8
46
47
48
49

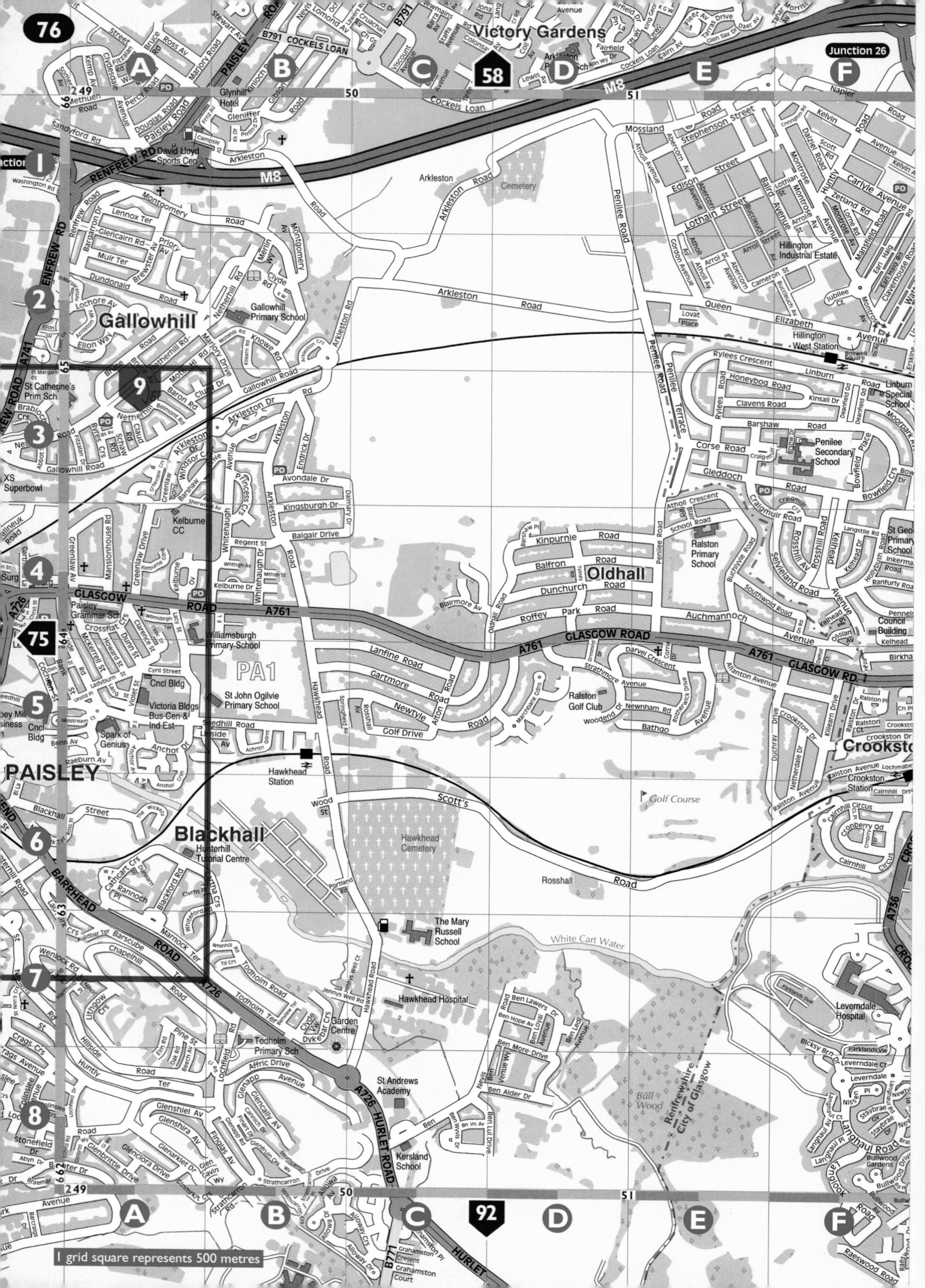

Victory Gardens

58

Gallowhill

9

Oldhall

PAISLEY

PA1

Blackhall

Crookston

Levendale Hospital

92

CARDONALD

JOHNSTONE

01505   6|9 323

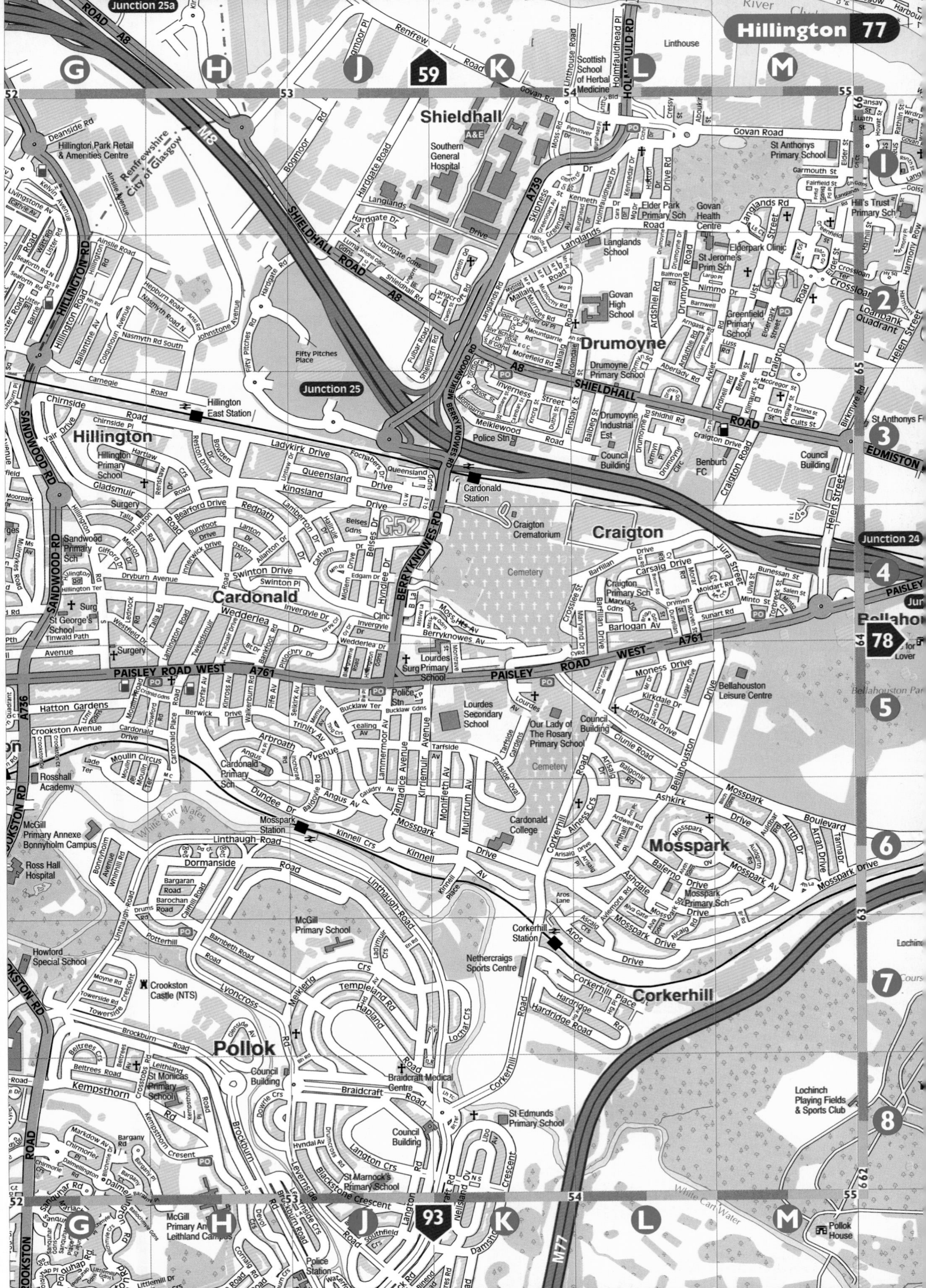

Hillington 77
Junction 25a
Junction 25
Junction 24
59
78
93
Shieldhall
Southern General Hospital
Hillington Park Retail & Amenities Centre
Renfrewshire
City of Glasgow
Fifty Pitches Place
Hillington East Station
Hillington
Hillington Primary School
Cardonald
Cardonald Station
Craigton Crematorium
Cemetery
Craigton
Craigton Primary Sch
Drumoyne
Drumoyne Primary School
Govan High School
Elder Park Primary Sch
Govan Health Centre
Elderpark Clinic
St Jerome's Prim Sch
Greenfield Primary School
St Anthonys Primary School
Hill's Trust Primary Sch
Langlands School
Scottish School of Herbal Medicine
Linthouse
Meiklewood Police Stn
Drumoyne Industrial Est
Council Building
Benburn FC
Sandwood Primary Sch
St George's School
Lourdes Primary School
Lourdes Secondary School
Our Lady of The Rosary Primary School
Bellahouston Leisure Centre
Bellahouston Park
Cardonald Primary Sch
Cardonald College
Rosshall Academy
McGill Primary Annexe Bonnyholm Campus
Ross Hall Hospital
Mosspark Station
Mosspark
Mosspark Primary Sch
Corkerhill Station
Corkerhill
Nethercraigs Sports Centre
McGill Primary School
Howford Special School
Crookston Castle (NTS)
Pollok
St Monicas Primary School
Braidcraft Medical Centre
St Edmunds Primary School
St Marnock's Primary School
McGill Primary Annexe Leithland Campus
Police Station
Lochinch Playing Fields & Sports Club
Pollok House
White Cart Water
River Clyde
M8
M77
A8
A739
A761
A736
PAISLEY ROAD WEST
SHIELDHALL ROAD
EDMISTON
HILLINGTON RD
SANDWOOD RD
BERRYKNOWES RD
MEIKLEWOOD RD
HOLMFAULD RD
Govan Road
Mosspark Boulevard
Mosspark Drive
Linthaugh Road
Dormanside Road
Brockburn Road
Crookston Road
Helen Street
Birkmyre Rd
G51
G52
G H J K L M
52 53 54 55
1 2 3 4 5 6 7 8
66 65 64 63 62

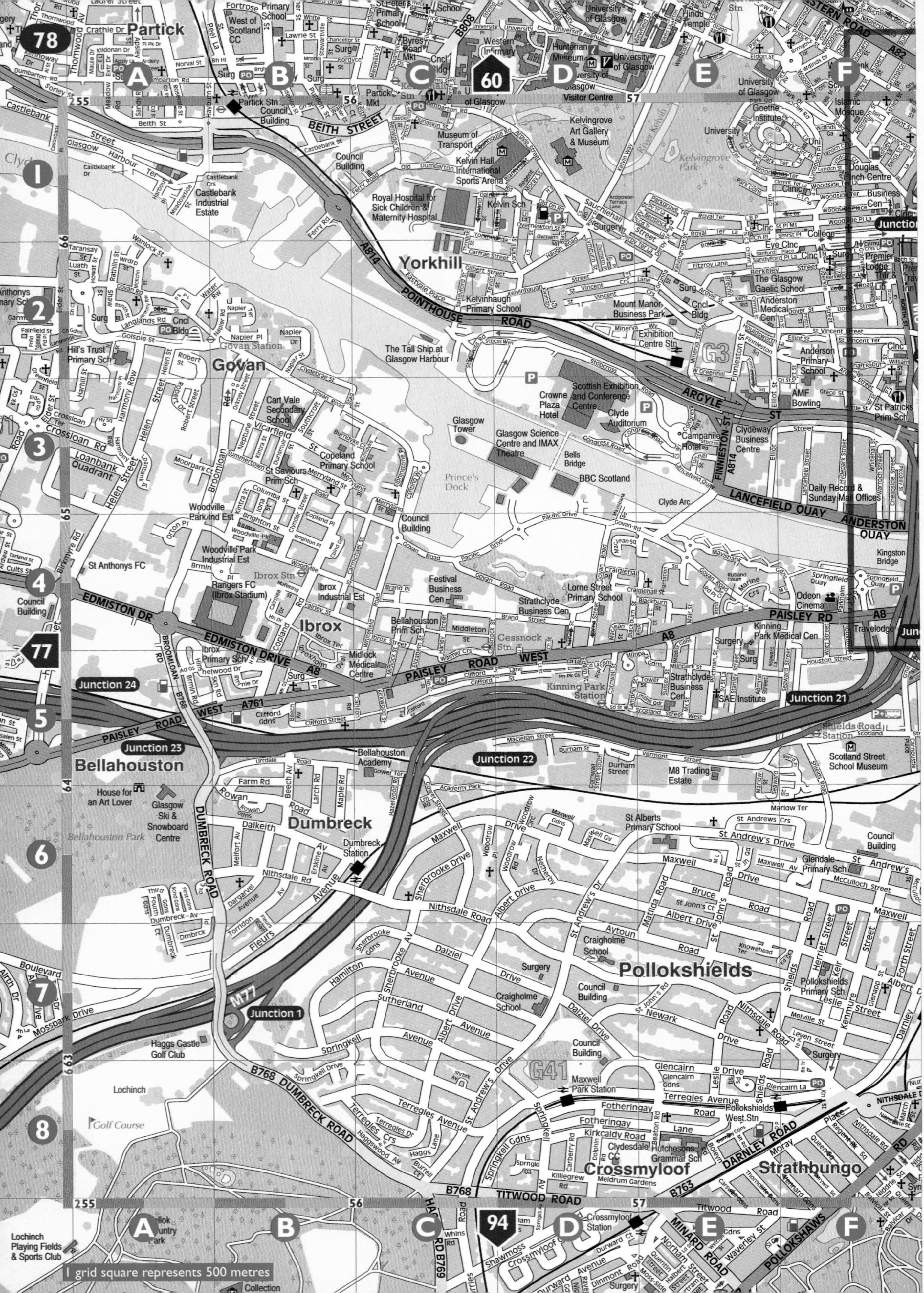
78
Partick
60
77
94
255
56
57
66
65
64
663
Partick Stn
Beith Street
Museum of Transport
Kelvingrove Art Gallery & Museum
Kelvingrove Park
University of Glasgow
Hunterian Museum
Western Infirmary
Kelvin Hall International Sports Arena
Royal Hospital for Sick Children & Maternity Hospital
Yorkhill
Pointhouse Road
A814
Castlebank Industrial Estate
Govan
Govan Station
Hill's Trust Primary Sch
Crossloan Rd
Helen Street
The Tall Ship at Glasgow Harbour
Exhibition Centre Stn
Scottish Exhibition and Conference Centre
Crowne Plaza Hotel
Clyde Auditorium
Glasgow Tower
Glasgow Science Centre and IMAX Theatre
Bells Bridge
BBC Scotland
Prince's Dock
Argyle St
Finnieston St
Lancefield Quay
Anderston Quay
Kingston Bridge
Daily Record & Sunday Mail Offices
Clydeway Business Centre
AMF Bowling
Anderston Primary School
The Glasgow Gaelic School
Cart Vale Secondary School
Copeland Primary School
St Saviours Prim Sch
Woodville Park Ind Est
Woodville Park Industrial Est
St Anthonys FC
Rangers FC (Ibrox Stadium)
Ibrox Stn
Ibrox
Ibrox Industrial Est
Festival Business Cen
Strathclyde Business Cen
Lorne Street Primary School
Cessnock Stn
Kinning Park Station
Paisley Road West
Paisley Rd
A8
Edmiston Drive
Junction 24
Junction 23
Junction 22
Junction 21
Junction 1
M77
A761
B768
Bellahouston
Bellahouston Park
House for an Art Lover
Glasgow Ski & Snowboard Centre
Bellahouston Academy
Dumbreck
Dumbreck Station
Dumbreck Road
Nithsdale Road
Haggs Castle Golf Club
Lochinch
Golf Course
Pollokshields
Craigholme School
Maxwell Park Station
Pollokshields West Stn
Hutchesons' Grammar Sch
Crossmyloof
Crossmyloof Station
Strathbungo
Titwood Road
Darnley Road
Shields Road Station
Scotland Street School Museum
M8 Trading Estate
St Alberts Primary School
Glendale Primary Sch
Pollokshields Primary Sch
Odeon Cinema
Travelodge
Kinning Park Medical Cen
SAE Institute
Pollok Country Park
Lochinch Playing Fields & Sports Club
Minard Road
Pollokshaws
1 grid square represents 500 metres

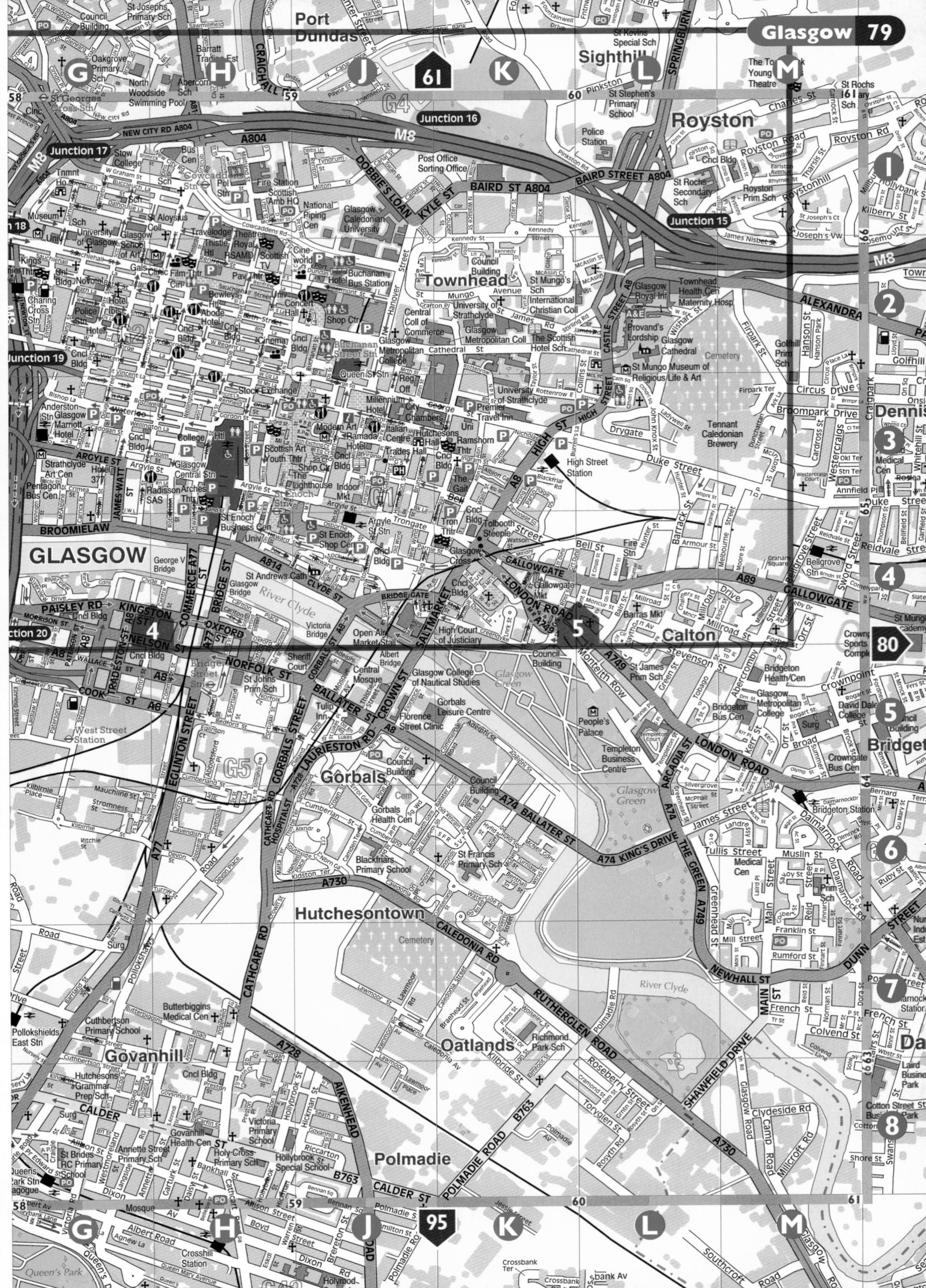

Port Dundas
Sighthill
Royston
Townhead
GLASGOW
Calton
Gorbals
Hutchesontown
Oatlands
Govanhill
Polmadie
Bridgeton
Dennistoun
61
80
95
G
H
J
K
L
M
2
3
4
5
6
7
8
58
59
60
61
Junction 15
Junction 16
Junction 17
Junction 18
Junction 19
Junction 20
M8
NEW CITY RD A804
BAIRD ST A804
BAIRD STREET A804
ALEXANDRA PARADE
DOBBIE'S LOAN
KYLE ST
CASTLE STREET A8
HIGH STREET
HIGH ST A8
ARGYLE ST
BROOMIELAW
CLYDE ST
GALLOWGATE
LONDON ROAD
PAISLEY RD
KINGSTON ST
NELSON ST
OXFORD ST
NORFOLK ST
BALLATER ST
CROWN ST
GORBALS STREET
SALTMARKET
LAURIESTON RD
ECLINTON STREET
CATHCART RD
AIKENHEAD ROAD
CALDER ST
POLMADIE ROAD B763
RUTHERGLEN ROAD
SHAWFIELD DRIVE
CALEDONIA RD
KING'S DRIVE
THE GREEN A749
NEWHALL ST
DUNN STREET
SPRINGBURN
CRAIGHALL RD
River Clyde
Glasgow Green
Tennant Caledonian Brewery
Glasgow Cathedral
Glasgow Royal Inf
Provand's Lordship
St Mungo Museum of Religious Life & Art
University of Strathclyde
Glasgow Caledonian University
Queen St Stn
Buchanan Bus Station
Buchanan Street Stn
Glasgow Central Stn
Argyle St Stn
High Street Station
Bellgrove Stn
Bridgeton Station
West Street Station
Pollokshields East Stn
Crosshill Station
Queens Park Stn
Charing Cross Stn
Anderston Stn
Cowcaddens Stn
St Enoch Stn
Bridge Street Stn
St Georges Cross Stn
People's Palace
Barras Mkt
Trongate
Glasgow Cross
Tolbooth Steeple
City Chambers
Royal Concert Hall
Theatre Royal
Gorbals Leisure Centre
Glasgow College of Nautical Studies
Templeton Business Centre
Butterbiggins Medical Cen
Hutchesons' Grammar Prep Sch
Richmond Park Sch
Victoria Bridge
Albert Bridge
Glasgow Bridge
George V Bridge
Queen's Park

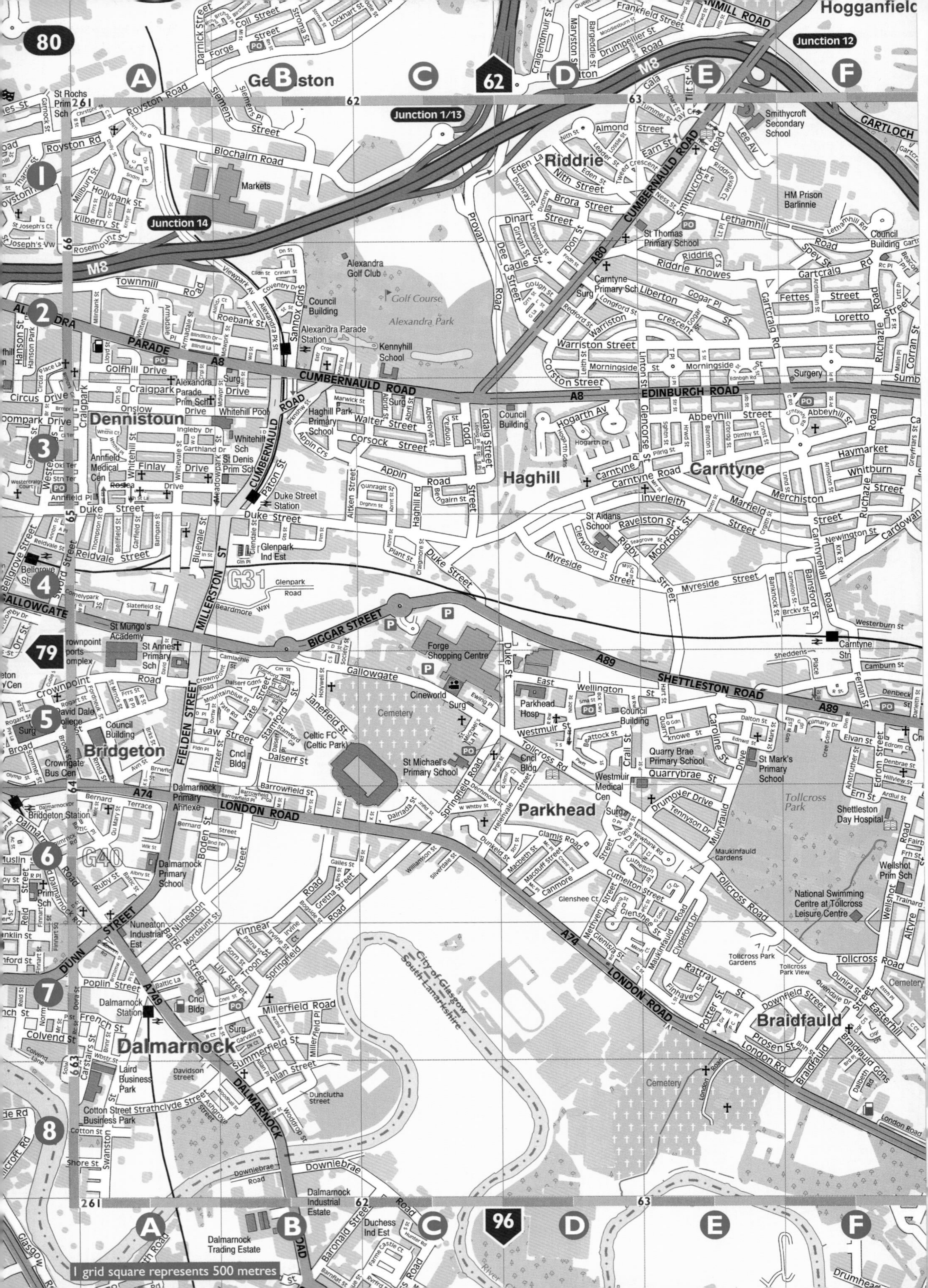

80
Hogganfield
Junction 12
Junction 1/13
Junction 14
62
79
96
A
B
C
D
E
F
1
2
3
4
5
6
7
8
M8
Royston Road
Blochairn Road
Markets
Riddrie
Smithycroft Secondary School
HM Prison Barlinnie
St Thomas Primary School
Carntyne Primary Sch
Council Building
Alexandra Golf Club
Golf Course
Alexandra Park
Alexandra Parade Station
Kennyhill School
Alexandra Parade
Cumbernauld Road
A8
Edinburgh Road
A80
Dennistoun
Haghill
Carntyne
Haghill Primary School
Whitehill Pool
Anniefield Medical Cen
Duke Street Station
Duke Street
Glenpark Ind Est
G31
Gallowgate
Biggar Street
Forge Shopping Centre
St Mungo's Academy
Cineworld
Cemetery
Celtic FC (Celtic Park)
St Michael's Primary School
Parkhead Hosp
Parkhead
Shettleston Road
A89
Carntyne Stn
Bridgeton
Bridgeton Station
G40
London Road
A74
Dalmarnock Primary School
Nuneaton Industrial Est
Dalmarnock Station
Dalmarnock
Laird Business Park
Cotton Street Business Park
Tollcross Park
Tollcross Park Gardens
National Swimming Centre at Tollcross Leisure Centre
Shettleston Day Hospital
Braidfauld
City of Glasgow
South Lanarkshire
Dalmarnock Industrial Estate
Dalmarnock Trading Estate
Duchess Ind Est
1 grid square represents 500 metres

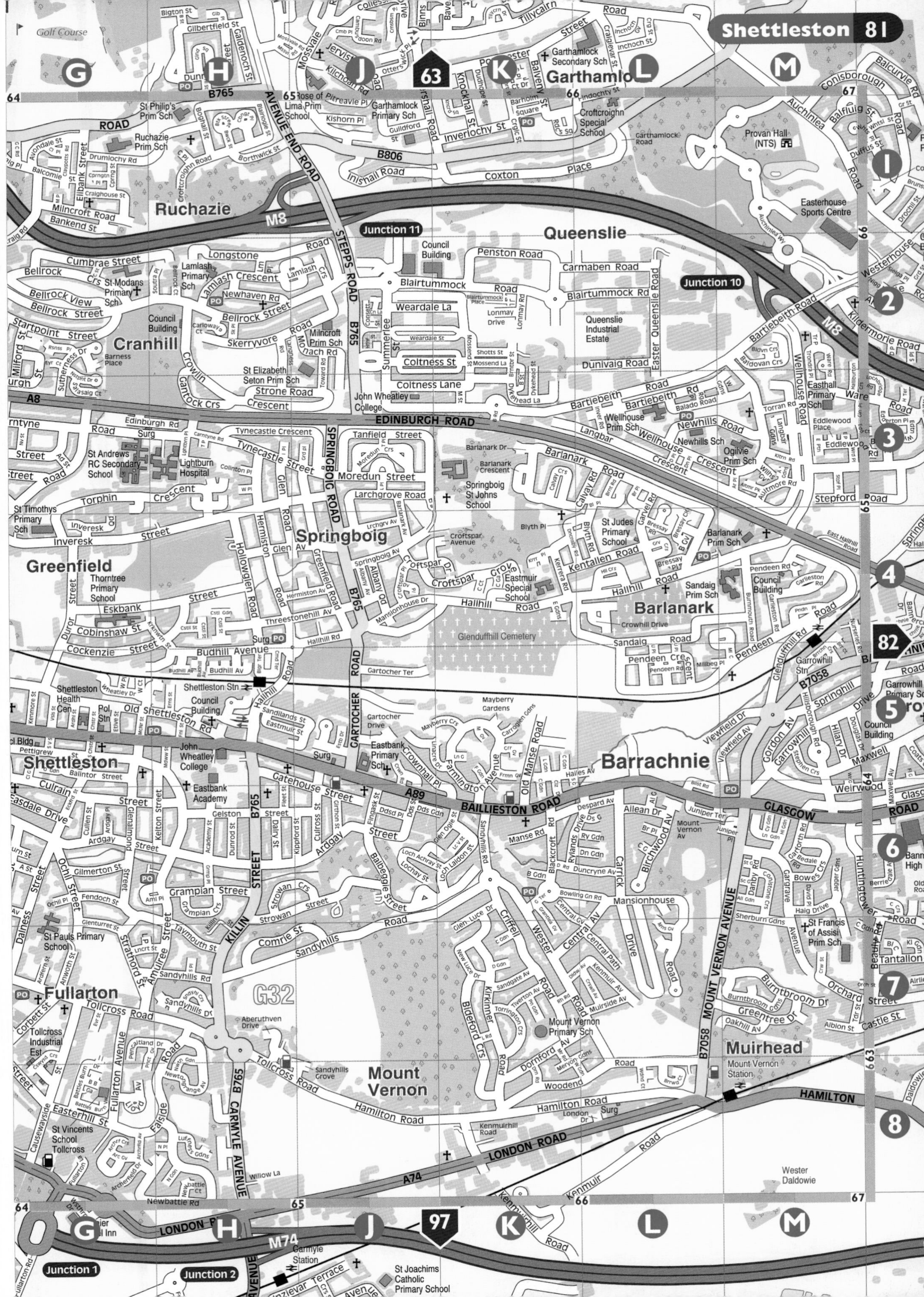

Golf Course
G
H
J
63
K
L
M
Garthamlock
Garthamlock Secondary Sch
Tillycairn Road
Gilbertfield St
Bigton St
Gadlenoch St
B765
64
65
66
67
St Philip's Prim Sch
Rose of Lima Prim School
Garthamlock Primary Sch
Kishorn Pl
Pitreavie Pl
Guildford St
Inverlochy St
Croftcroighn Special School
Garthamlock Road
Ruchazie Prim Sch
Ruchazie Road
Boghall St
Blairtoggle St
Borthwick St
Croftcroighn Road
Drumlochy Rd
Avondale St
Balcomie St
Elibank Street
Craighouse St
Milncroft Road
Bankend St
Ruchazie
AVENUE END ROAD
B806
Inishail Road
Coxton Place
Auchinlea Road
Provan Hall (NTS)
Conisborough Rd
Balcurvie Rd
Balfluig St
Duffus St
1
Easterhouse Sports Centre
Auchinlea Wy
M8
Junction 11
Queenslie
STEPPS ROAD
Council Building
Penston Road
Carmaben Road
Junction 10
Westerhouse Rd
Longstone Road
Lamlash Primary Sch
Lamlash Crescent
Lamlash Crs
Cumbrae Street
Bellrock Crs
St Modans Primary Sch
Bellrock View
Bellrock Street
Newhaven Rd
Blairtummock Road
Blairtummock Rd
Weardale La
Weardale St
Lonmay Drive
Queenslie Industrial Estate
Easter Queenslie Road
Bartiebeith Road
Kildermorie Road
2
Startpoint Street
Council Building
Cranhill
Carlowaygate
Skerryvore Road
Milncroft Prim Sch
Monach Rd
Barness Place
Crowlin Cres
Summerlee St
Coltness St
Shotts St
Mossend La
Dunivaig Road
Bartiebeith Road
Baldovan Crs
Wellhouse Road
Easthall Primary Sch
Ware Road
Milford St
Sutherness Dr
St Elizabeth Seton Prim Sch
Strone Road
Gartock Crs
Crescent
Coltness Lane
John Wheatley College
Dykehead La
Bartiebeith Rd
Wellhouse Prim Sch
Balado Road
Newhills Road
Torran Rd
Edgewood Place
Eddlewood Rd
3
A8
EDINBURGH ROAD
Edinburgh Rd
Tynecastle Crescent
Tanfield Street
Barlanark Dr
Barlanark Crescent
Langbar Crs
Wellhouse Crescent
Newhills Sch
Ogilvie Prim Sch
Crescent
Aultmore Rd
Stepford Road
St Andrews RC Secondary School
Lightburn Hospital
Tynecastle Street
Moredun Street
Larchgrove Road
Springboig St Johns School
Calvay Rd
Barlanark Road
Torphin Crescent
St Timothys Primary Sch
Inveresk Street
Hermiston Road
Glen Road
SPRINGBOIG ROAD
Springboig
Croftspar Avenue
Blyth Pl
St Judes Primary School
Bressay Rd
Barlanark Prim Sch
East Hallhill Road
Greenfield
Thorntree Primary School
Hollowglen Road
Glen Av
Greenfield Road
B765
Springboig Av
Croftspar Dr
Croftspar Grove
Eastmuir Special School
Kentallen Road
Hallhill Road
Sandaig Prim Sch
Pendeen Rd
Council Building
4
Eskbank Street
Cobinshaw St
Duror Street
Threestonehill Av
Mansionhouse Dr
Hallhill Road
Glenduffhill Cemetery
Barlanark
Crowhill Drive
Sandaig Road
Pendeen Road
Cockenzie Street
Budhill Avenue
Budhill Av
Surg
Hallhill Rd
GARTOCHER ROAD
Gartocher Ter
Pendeen Crescent
Glenduffhill Rd
Garrowhill Stn
B7058
82
Shettleston Health Cen
Shettleston Stn
Council Building
Old Shettleston Rd
Sandilands St
Eastmuir St
Mayberry Gardens
Gartocher Drive
Mayberry Crs
Carrogien Gdns
Old Manse Road
Viewfield Dr
Viewfield Av
Springhill Drive
Garrowhill Primary Sch
5
Council Building
Shettleston
John Wheatley College
Eastbank Academy
Eastbank Primary Sch
Crownhall Pl
Farmington Avenue
Barrachnie
Gordon Av
Hillsborough Rd
Maxwell Av
Culrain St
Balintor Street
Easdale Drive
Gatehouse Street
A89
BAILLIESTON ROAD
Juniper Ter
Mount Vernon Av
GLASGOW ROAD
Weirwood Av
Ardgay Pl
Gelston Street
Dairy St
Kelton Street
Glenalmond Street
Ardgay Street
B765
Fingask Street
Manse Rd
Despard Av
Ailean Dr
Birchwood Av
Carrick
6
Gilmerton St
Ochil Street
Fendoch St
Grampian Street
Grampian Crs
STREET
Strowan Crs
Strowan Street
Balbeggie Street
Loch Achray St
Lochay St
Loch Laidon St
Glen Ogle St
Sandyhills Rd
Duncryne Av
Blackcroft Rd
Rylands Drive
Bowling Gn Rd
Mansionhouse Drive
MOUNT VERNON AVENUE
Garforth Rd
Gargrave Avenue
Haig Drive
Sherburn Gdns
St Francis of Assisi Prim Sch
St Pauls Primary School
Glenturret St
Strathord St
Taymouth St
Amulree St
KILLIN STREET
Comrie St
Sandyhills Road
Glen Luce Dr
Criffell
Wester Road
Central Av
Central Path
Kenmuir Av
Huntingtower
Tantallon
7
Fullarton
Tollcross Road
Sandyhills Rd
Sandyhills Crs
G32
New Luce Dr
Sandgate Av
Torrington Crs
Tiverton Av
Muirside Av
Burntbroom Dr
Greentree Dr
Orchard Street
Castle St
Albion St
Oakhill Av
Tollcross Industrial Est
Corbett St
Aberuthven Drive
Sandyhills Grove
Mount Vernon
Bideford Crs
Kirkinner Road
Mount Vernon Primary Sch
Dornford Av
Meryon Gdns
Woodend
B7058
Muirhead
Mount Vernon Station
HAMILTON
663
Fullarton Avenue
Newtongrange Av
Easterhill St
Tollcross Road
Hamilton Road
Kenmuirhill Road
Hamilton Road
London Road
Surg
8
Causewayside
St Vincents School Tollcross
Fullarton
Archerfield Dr
CARMYLE AVENUE
Willow La
A74
LONDON ROAD
Kenmuir Road
Wester Daldowie
Newbattle Rd
Newbattle Ct
G
H
J
97
K
L
M
LONDON ROAD
M74
Carmyle Station
Junction 1
Junction 2
St Joachims Catholic Primary School

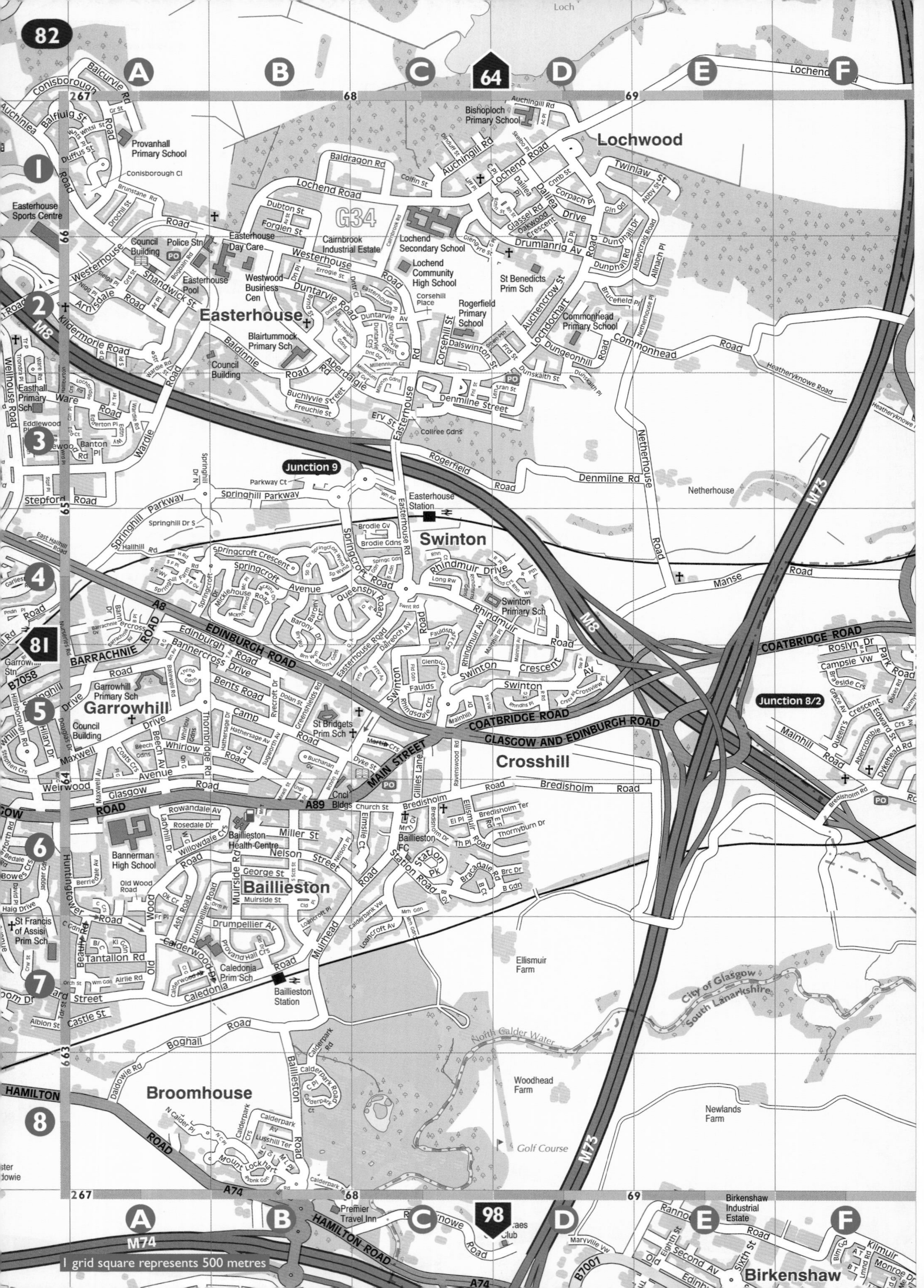
82
64
81
98
A
B
C
D
E
F
1
2
3
4
5
6
7
8
267
68
69
66
65
64
663
G34
Lochwood
Easterhouse
Swinton
Garrowhill
Crosshill
Baillieston
Broomhouse
Birkenshaw
Netherhouse
Junction 9
Junction 8/2
M8
M73
M74
A8
A89
A74
B7058
B7001
EDINBURGH ROAD
BARRACHNIE ROAD
COATBRIDGE ROAD
GLASGOW AND EDINBURGH ROAD
MAIN STREET
HAMILTON ROAD
Provanhall Primary School
Easterhouse Sports Centre
Council Building
Police Stn
Easterhouse Day Care
Easterhouse Pool
Westwood Business Cen
Blairtummock Primary Sch
Cairnbrook Industrial Estate
Lochend Secondary School
Lochend Community High School
Bishoploch Primary School
Rogerfield Primary School
St Benedicts Prim Sch
Commonhead Primary School
Easthall Primary Sch
Easterhouse Station
Swinton Primary Sch
Garrowhill Primary Sch
St Bridgets Prim Sch
Bannerman High School
Baillieston Health Centre
Baillieston FC
Caledonia Prim Sch
Baillieston Station
St Francis of Assisi Prim Sch
Ellismuir Farm
Woodhead Farm
Newlands Farm
Golf Course
North Calder Water
City of Glasgow
South Lanarkshire
Premier Travel Inn
Birkenshaw Industrial Estate
1 grid square represents 500 metres

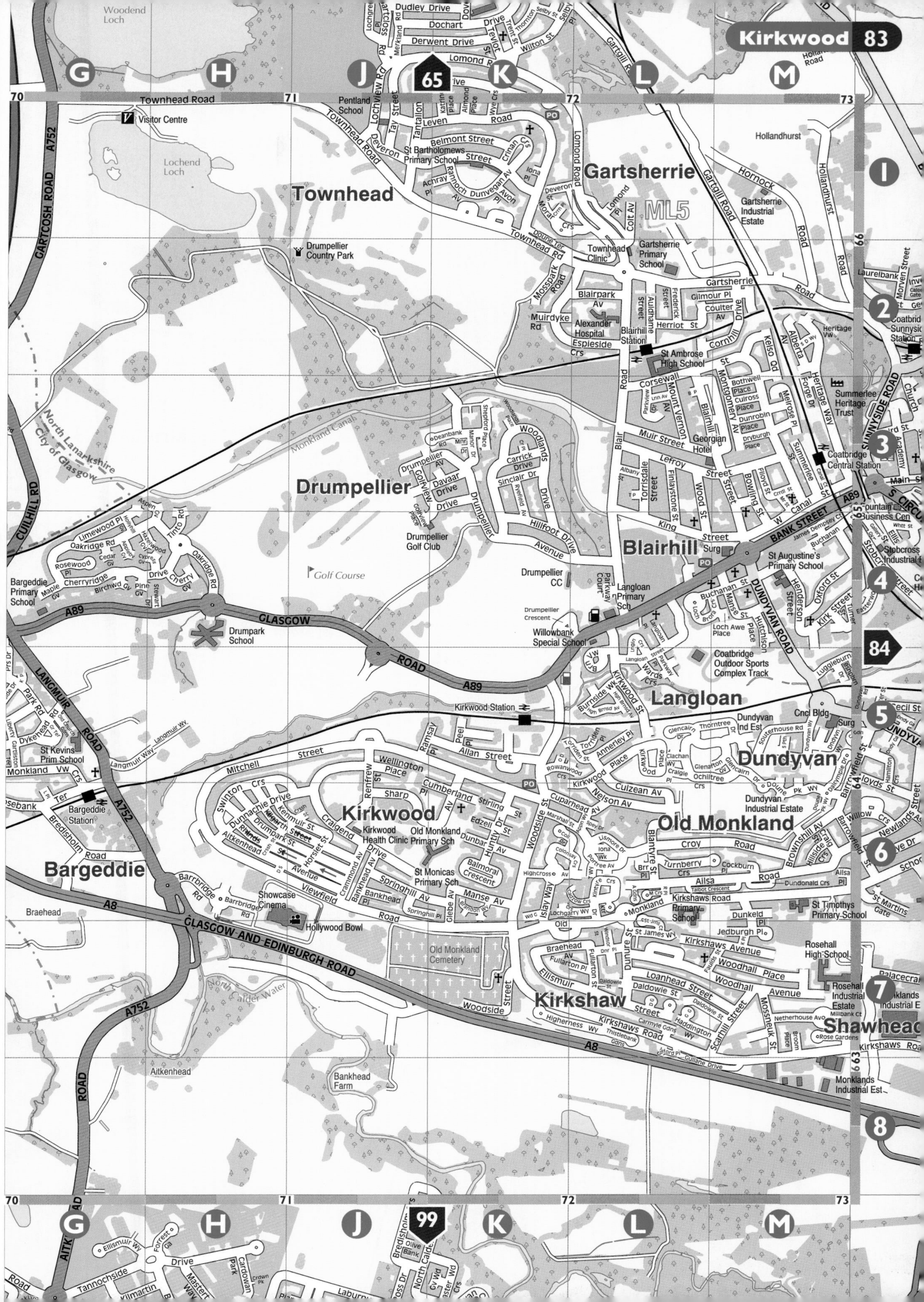
Townhead
Gartsherrie
Drumpellier
Blairhill
Langloan
Dundyvan
Kirkwood
Old Monkland
Bargeddie
Kirkshaw
Shawhead
ML5
Woodend Loch
Lochend Loch
Townhead Road
Visitor Centre
Drumpellier Country Park
Golf Course
Drumpellier Golf Club
Drumpark School
Glasgow Road
A89
A8
Glasgow and Edinburgh Road
A752
Gartcosh Road
Langmuir Road
Aitkenhead Road
Kirkwood Station
Blairhill Station
Coatbridge Central Station
Bargeddie Station
Summerlee Heritage Trust
Gartsherrie Industrial Estate
Dundyvan Industrial Estate
Rosehall Industrial Estate
Monklands Industrial Est
Old Monkland Cemetery
Showcase Cinema
Hollywood Bowl
Monkland Canal
North Calder Water
North Lanarkshire
City of Glasgow
Hollandhurst
Aitkenhead
Braehead
Bankhead Farm
65
84
99

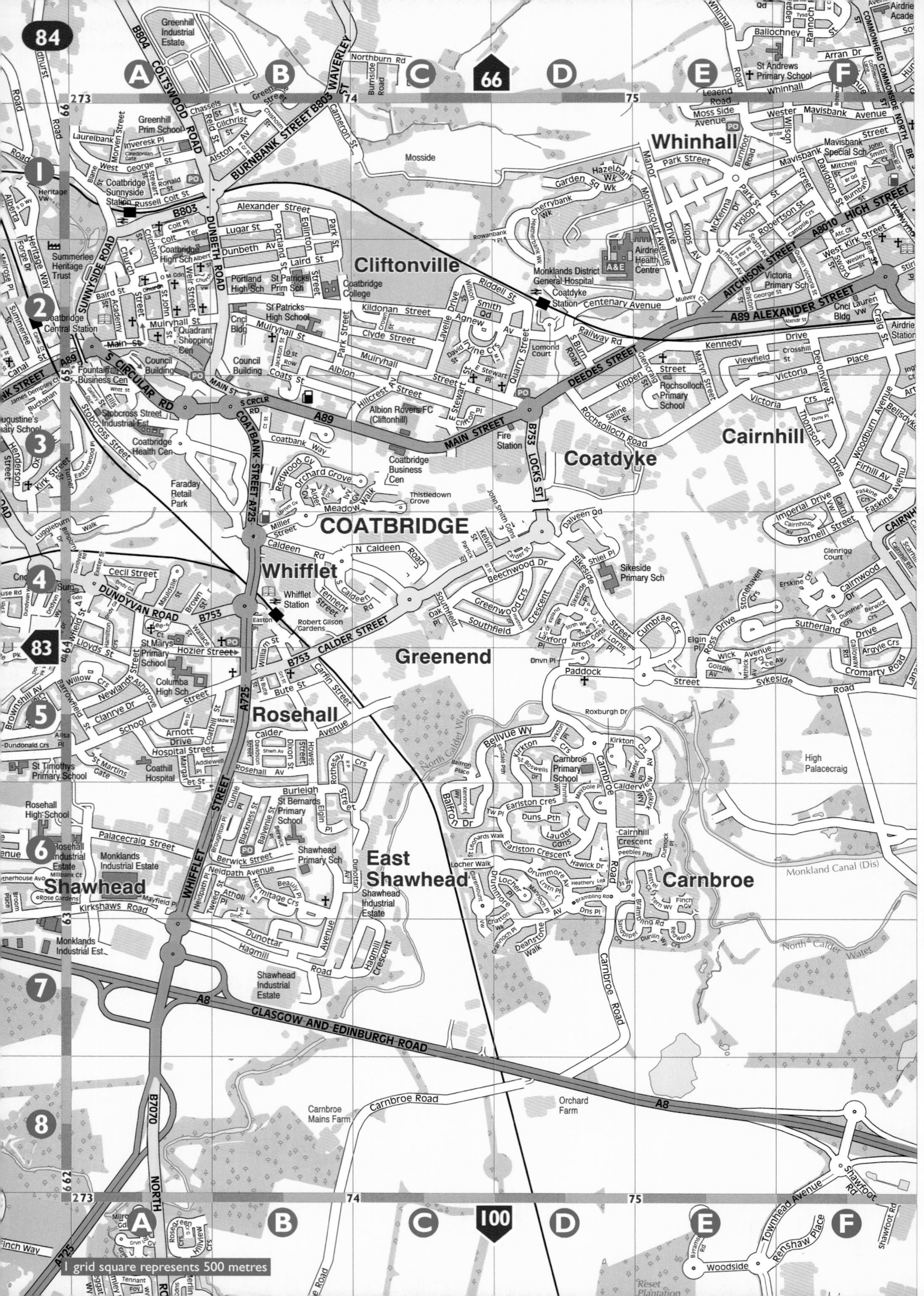
66
A
B
C
D
E
F
273
74
75
Greenhill Industrial Estate
B804
COLTSWOOD ROAD
WAVERLEY ST
Northburn Rd
Burnside Road
BURNBANK STREET B803
Cameron St
Mosside
Whinhall
Ballochney
St Andrews Primary School
Arran Dr
Leaend Road
Whinhall
Moss Side Avenue
Wester
Mavisbank Avenue
Wilson
COMMONHEAD COMMONSIDE NORTH
Greenhill Prim School
Laurelbank
Inveresk Pl
West George St
Coatbridge Sunnyside Station
Russell Colt St
B803
Alexander Street
Lugar St
Dunbeth Av
Portland St
Eglinton St
Park St
Laird St
Cliftonville
Coatbridge College
Portland High Sch
St Patricks Prim Sch
DUNBETH ROAD
SUNNYSIDE ROAD
Coatbridge High Sch
Summerlee Heritage Trust
Heritage Way
Baird St
Academy St
Church St
Muiryhall St
Quadrant Shopping Cen
Coatbridge Central Station
Main St
Council Building
Fountain Business Cen
S CIRCULAR RD
A89
Stobcross Street Industrial Est
Coatbridge Health Cen
Stobcross Street
Faraday Retail Park
St Patricks High School
Muiryhall St
Cncl Bldg
Council Building
Coats St
Kildonan Street
Clyde Street
Muiryhall
Albion
Hillcrest Av
Albion Rovers FC (Cliftonhill)
Coatbank Way
Coatbridge Business Cen
MAIN STREET
A89
S CRCLR RD
COATBANK STREET A725
Orchard Grove
Meadow Walk
Thistledown Grove
Miller Street
COATBRIDGE
Riddell St
Smith Qd
Agnew Av
Irvine Crs
Quarry Street
Lomond Court
Fire Station
B753 LOCKS ST
Coatdyke
Park Street
Hazelbank Wk
Garden Sq Wk
Cherrybank Wk
Monksourt Avenue
Manor Drive
Kipps Av
Airdrie Health Centre
A&E
Monklands District General Hospital
Coatdyke Station
Centenary Avenue
Railway Rd
DEEDES STREET
A89 ALEXANDER STREET
AITCHISON STREET
A8010 HIGH STREET
Mavisbank Special Sch
Victoria Primary Sch
Airdrie Station
Kennedy Drive
Viewfield St
Crosshill St
Victoria Place
Victoria Crs
Rochsolloch Primary School
Rochsolloch Road
Saline St
Cairnhill
Thomson Drive
Woodburn Avenue
Firhill Av
Faskine Avenue
Imperial Drive
Parnell Street
Glenrigg Court
Whifflet
Whifflet Station
Caldeen Rd
N Caldeen Road
Tennent Street
Beechwood Dr
Greenwood Crs
Southfield Crescent
Sikeside Primary Sch
Sikeside Street
Dalveen Qd
Cecil Street
DUNDYVAN ROAD
B753
Hozier Street
St Marys Primary School
Columba High Sch
Robert Gilson Gardens
B753 CALDER STREET
Greenend
Cumbrae Crs
Ross Drive
Wick Avenue
Sutherland Drive
Argyle Crs
Cromarty Road
Sykeside Road
Paddock Street
Erskine Crs
Cairnwood Dr
Stonehaven Crs
Rosehall
Bute St
Carfin Street
Calder Avenue
Rosehall Av
School Street
Clanrye Dr
Newlands St
Arnott Drive
Hospital Street
Coathill Hospital
St Timothys Primary School
St Martins Gate
Rosehall High School
Palacecraig Street
Rosehall Industrial Estate
Monklands Industrial Estate
Shawhead
Kirkshaws Road
Monklands Industrial Est
WHIFFLET STREET
A725
Burleigh St
St Bernards Primary School
Berwick Street
Neidpath Avenue
Shawhead Primary Sch
East Shawhead
Shawhead Industrial Estate
Dunottar Av
Hagmill Road
Hagmill Crescent
Rothesay Crs
North Calder Water
Bellvue Wy
Kirkton Crs
Carnbroe Primary School
Carnbroe Road
Earlston Cres
Duns Pth
Lauder Gdns
Earlston Crescent
Cairnhill Crescent
Drummore Av
Deanstone Walk
Carnbroe
Roxburgh Dr
High Palacecraig
Monkland Canal (Dis)
A8
GLASGOW AND EDINBURGH ROAD
Carnbroe Road
Carnbroe Mains Farm
Orchard Farm
B7070
NORTH
Townhead Avenue
Renshaw Place
Shawfoot Rd
Woodside
Reset Plantation
Finch Way
A725
1
2
3
4
5
6
7
8
83
65
64
63
662
100
1 grid square represents 500 metres

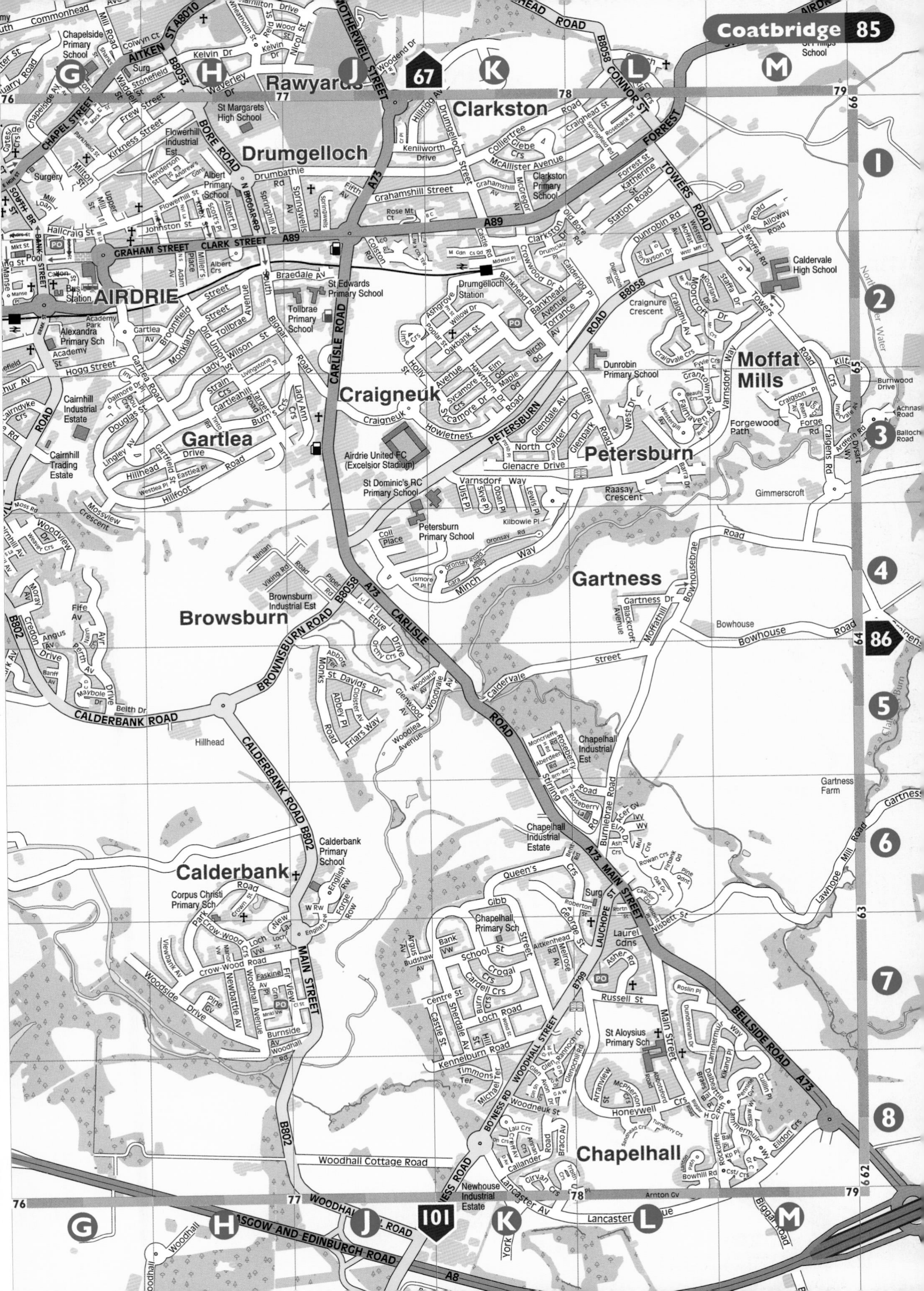
Rawyards
Clarkston
Drumgelloch
AIRDRIE
Craigneuk
Gartlea
Petersburn
Moffat Mills
Gartness
Browsburn
Calderbank
Chapelhall
Chapelside Primary School
St Margarets High School
Flowerhill Industrial Est
Albert Primary School
Clarkston Primary School
Caldervale High School
Drumgelloch Station
St Edwards Primary School
Tollbrae Primary School
Alexandra Primary Sch
Dunrobin Primary School
Cairnhill Industrial Estate
Cairnhill Trading Estate
Airdrie United FC (Excelsior Stadium)
St Dominic's RC Primary School
Petersburn Primary School
Browsburn Industrial Est
Chapelhall Industrial Est
Chapelhall Industrial Estate
Calderbank Primary School
Corpus Christi Primary Sch
Chapelhall Primary Sch
St Aloysius Primary Sch
Newhouse Industrial Estate
Gimmerscroft
Bowhouse
Gartness Farm
Hillhead
Woodhall
GRAHAM STREET
CLARK STREET
A89
CARLISLE ROAD
A73
MOTHERWELL STREET
PETERSBURN ROAD
B8058
BROWNSBURN ROAD
CALDERBANK ROAD
B802
MAIN STREET
BELLSIDE ROAD
FORREST STREET
TOWERS ROAD
CONNOR ST
AITKEN ST A8010
CHAPEL STREET
BORE ROAD
B8053
Bowhouse Road
Lawhope Mill Road
Woodhall Cottage Road
WOODHALL STREET
B799
LAUCHOPE ST
BO'NESS RD
GLASGOW AND EDINBURGH ROAD
A8
Lancaster Av
Grahamshill Street
Drumbathie Rd
Hogg Street
Caldervale Street
67
86
101
G
H
J
K
L
M
I
2
3
4
5
6
7
8
76
77
78
79
66
65
64
63
662

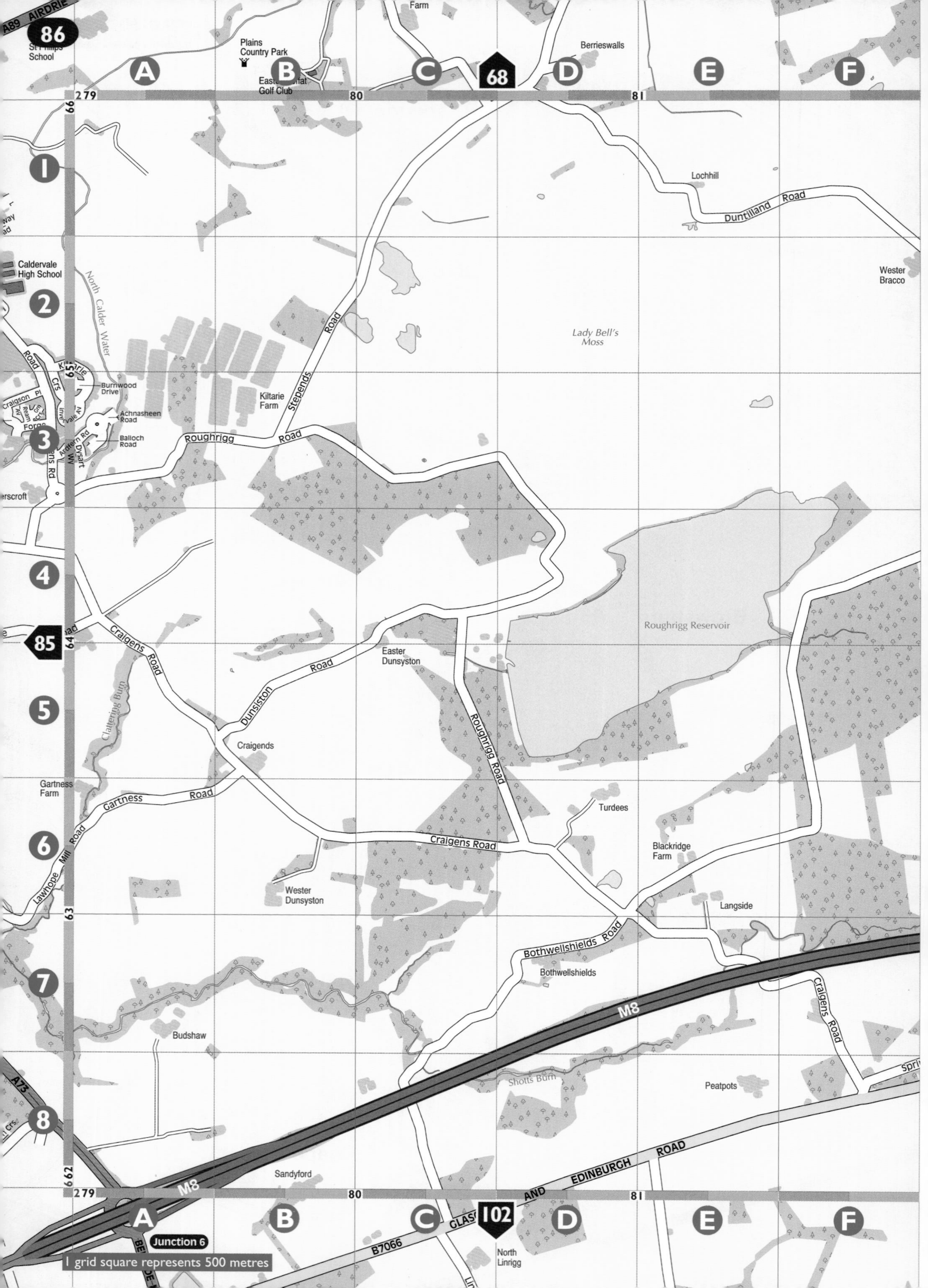

A89 AIRDRIE
St Philips School
Plains Country Park
Easter Moffat Golf Club
Farm
68
Berrieswalls
Lochhill
Duntilland Road
Wester Bracco
Caldervale High School
North Calder Water
Lady Bell's Moss
Stepends Road
Kiltarie Farm
Burnwood Drive
Achnasheen Road
Balloch Road
Roughrigg Road
Roughrigg Reservoir
85
Craigens Road
Easter Dunsyston
Dunsiston Road
Clattering Burn
Craigends
Roughrigg Road
Gartness Farm
Gartness Road
Turdees
Lawhope Mill Road
Craigens Road
Blackridge Farm
Wester Dunsyston
Langside
Bothwellshields Road
Bothwellshields
M8
Craigens Road
Budshaw
Shotts Burn
Peatpots
A73
GLASGOW AND EDINBURGH ROAD
Sandyford
M8
102
B7066
North Linrigg
Junction 6
1 grid square represents 500 metres

G   H   J   **69**   K   L   M

82   83   84   85

66

I

2

Papperth

65 **70**

3

283
▲
Torrance

4

64

Mountcow

5

Duntilland Road

M8

Shottsburn

Duntilland
Farm

6
Shott

63

Kirk O'Shotts
Prim Sch

Gibson
Street

HIRST ROAD

Manse Road

Kirk of Shotts

7

PQ

Reid Street
Cross St.

Lorne
Gdns

Muirhall Terrace

David Rd

Terrace
Muirmead
Gdns

Kirkview Av.

Newmill and Canthill Road

B7066

Blackcroft

Duntilland Av.

Sighthill

Carvale Av.

Avenue

Glebe
Farm

ngfield   Road

Kate
St.
Wyle
Drumbo Dr.
Drumbo Cr.

Crs

Carvale

Salsburgh

662

Bostock

Road

82   83   84   85

G   H   J   **103**   K   L   M

Westfield

Manse Road

Road

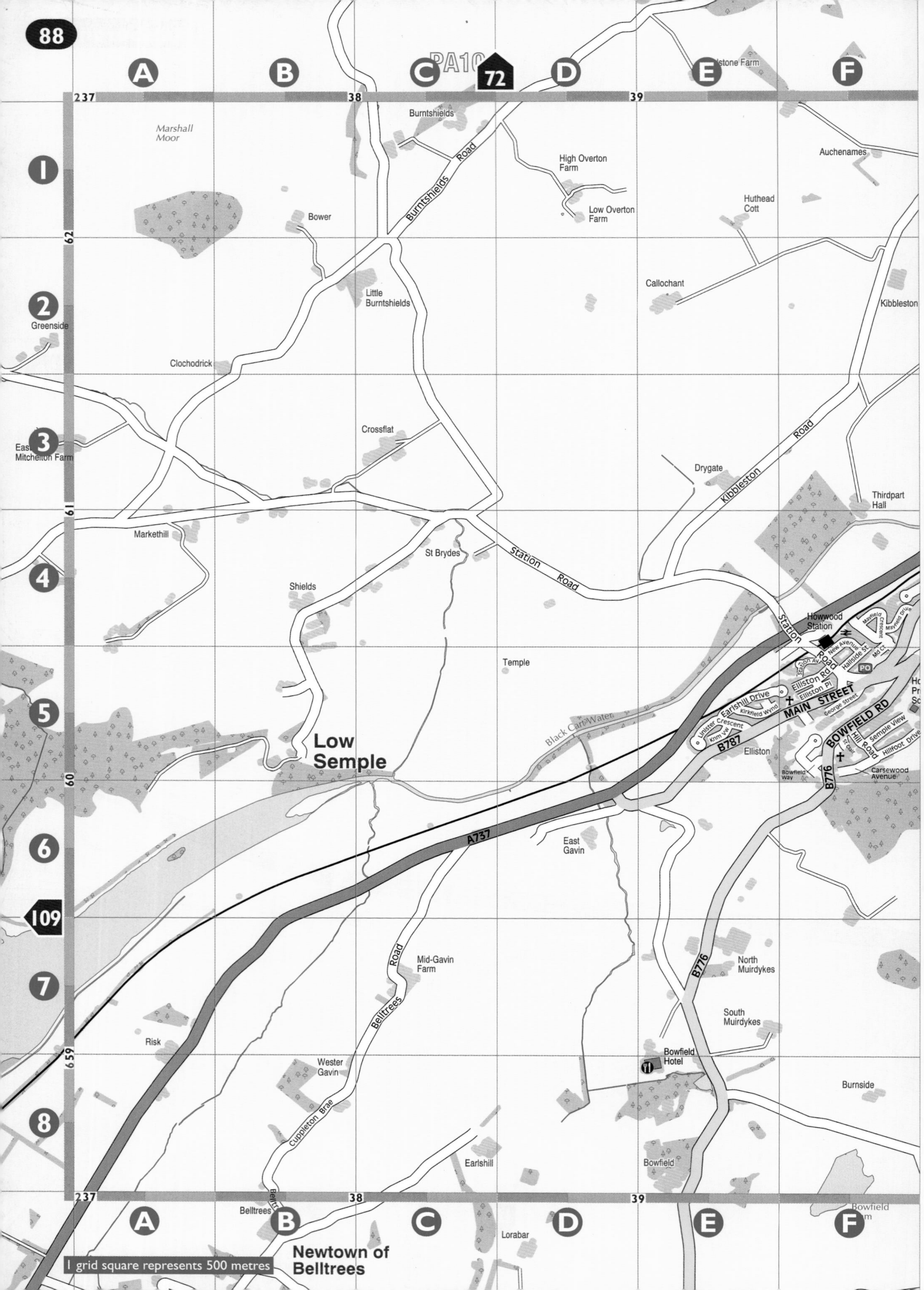

PA10
72
A
B
C
D
E
F
237
38
39
1
2
3
4
5
6
7
8
62
61
60
659
109
Marshall Moor
Burntshields
Burntshields Road
High Overton Farm
Low Overton Farm
Auchenames
Huthead Cott
Bower
Callochant
Little Burntshields
Kibbleston
Greenside
Clochodrick
Crossflat
Kibbleston Road
East Mitchelton Farm
Drygate
Thirdpart Hall
Markethill
St Brydes
Station Road
Shields
Howwood Station
Temple
Elliston Rd
Elliston Pl
Earlshill Drive
Kirkfield Wynd
MAIN STREET
George Street
BOWFIELD RD
Semple View
Unlster Crescent
Black Cart Water
B787
Elliston
Hill Road
Hillfoot Drive
Low Semple
Bowfield Way
Carsewood Avenue
B776
A737
East Gavin
Mid-Gavin Farm
Belltrees Road
North Muirdykes
South Muirdykes
Risk
Bowfield Hotel
Wester Gavin
Burnside
Cuppleton Brae
Earlshill
Bowfield
Belltrees
Lorabar
Newtown of Belltrees
I grid square represents 500 metres

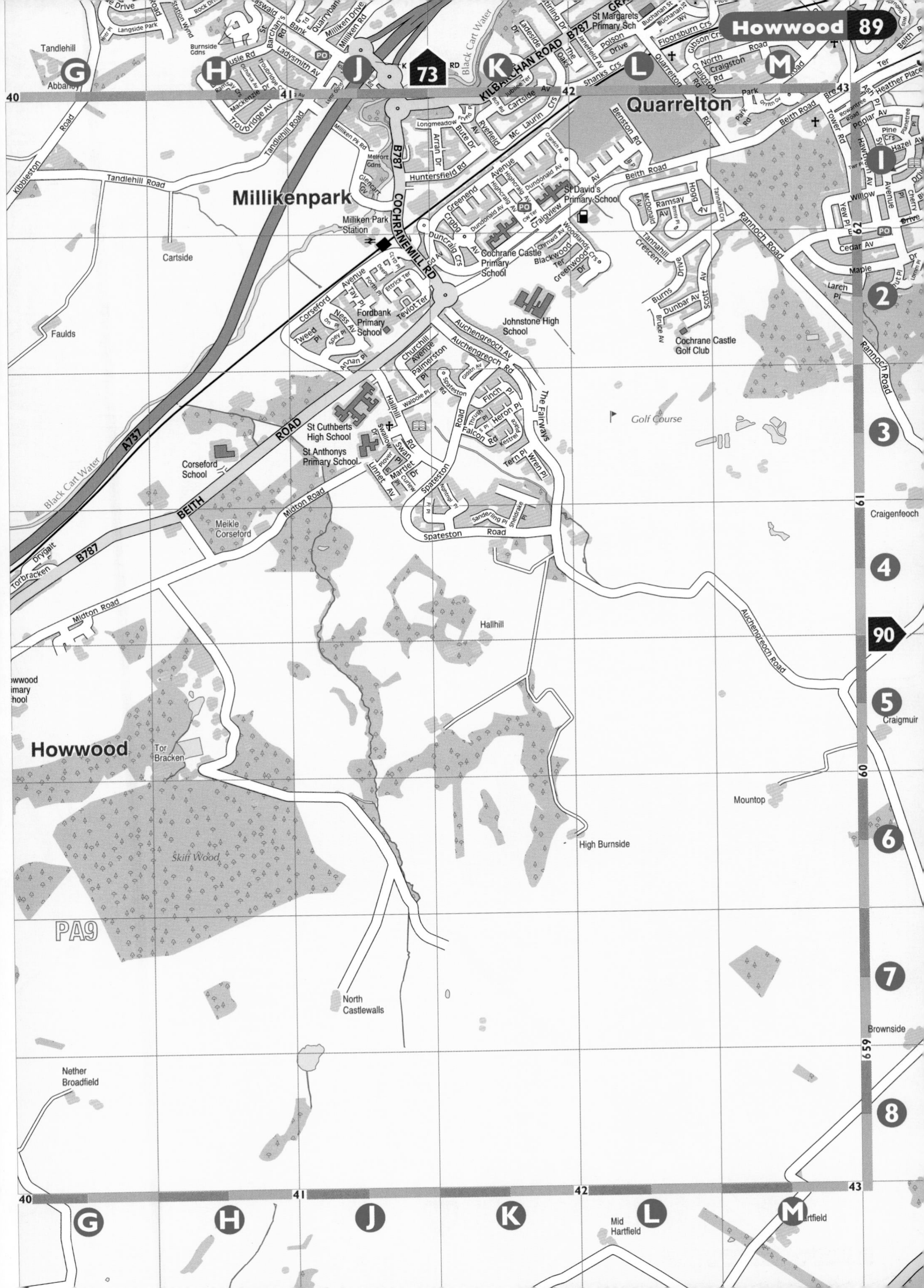
Millikenpark
Quarrelton
Howwood
Tandlehill
Cartside
Faulds
Milliken Park Station
Cochrane Castle Primary School
Fordbank Primary School
Johnstone High School
Cochrane Castle Golf Club
St David's Primary School
St Margarets Primary Sch
St Cuthberts High School
St Anthonys Primary School
Corseford School
Meikle Corseford
Golf Course
Hallhill
High Burnside
Mountop
Craigenfeoch
Craigmuir
Brownside
Skiff Wood
Tor Bracken
North Castlewalls
Nether Broadfield
Mid Hartfield
Black Cart Water
PA9
A737
B787
BEITH ROAD
KILBARCHAN ROAD
COCHRANEMILL RD
Tandlehill Road
Kibbleston Road
Midton Road
Spateston Road
Auchengreoch Road
Auchengreoch Av
Beith Road
Rannoch Road
Huntersfield Rd
The Fairways
73
90
G H J K L M
40 41 42 43
2 3 4 5 6 7 8

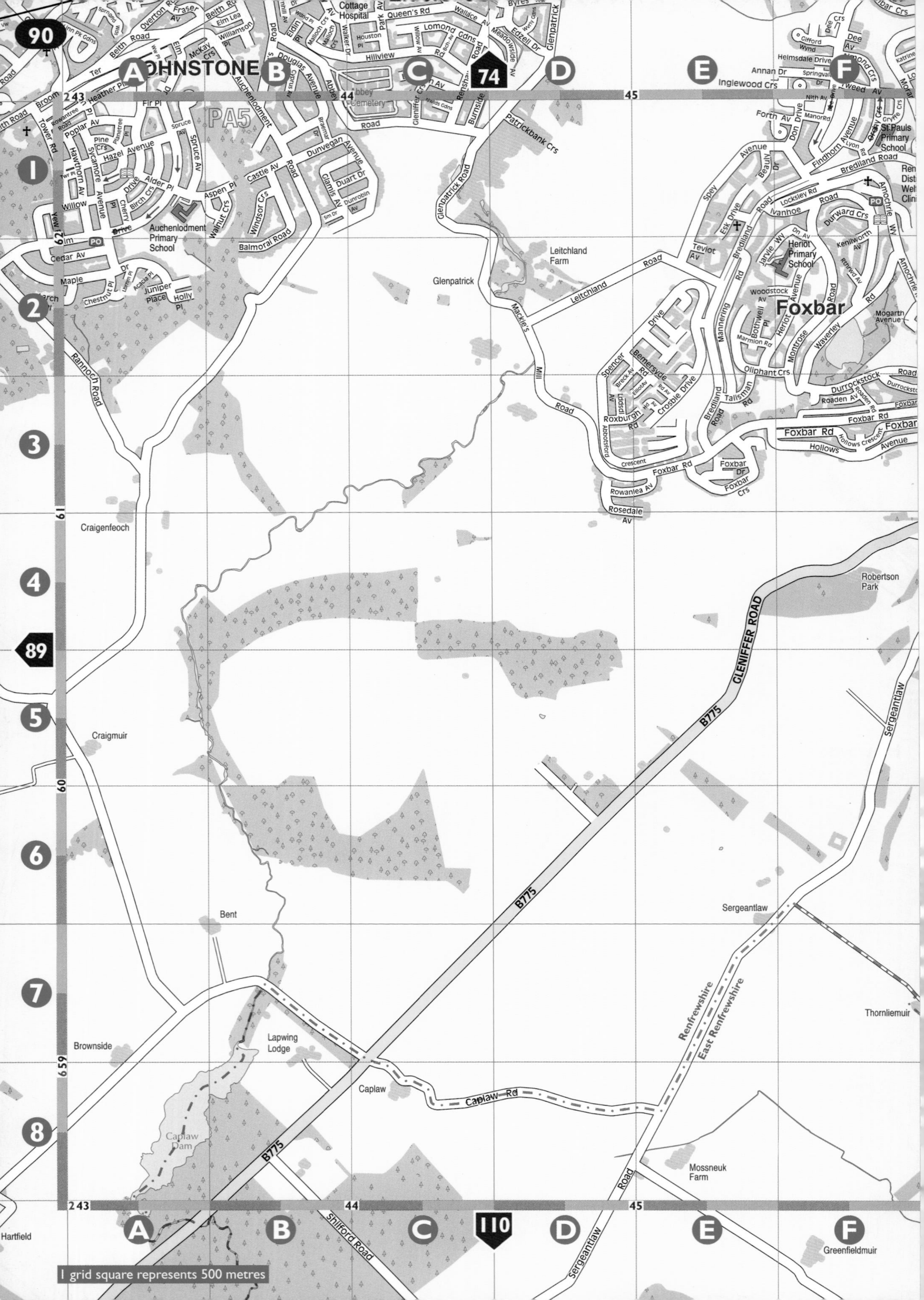

90

JOHNSTONE

74

PA5

89

Foxbar

1 grid square represents 500 metres

110

Hartfield

Greenfieldmuir

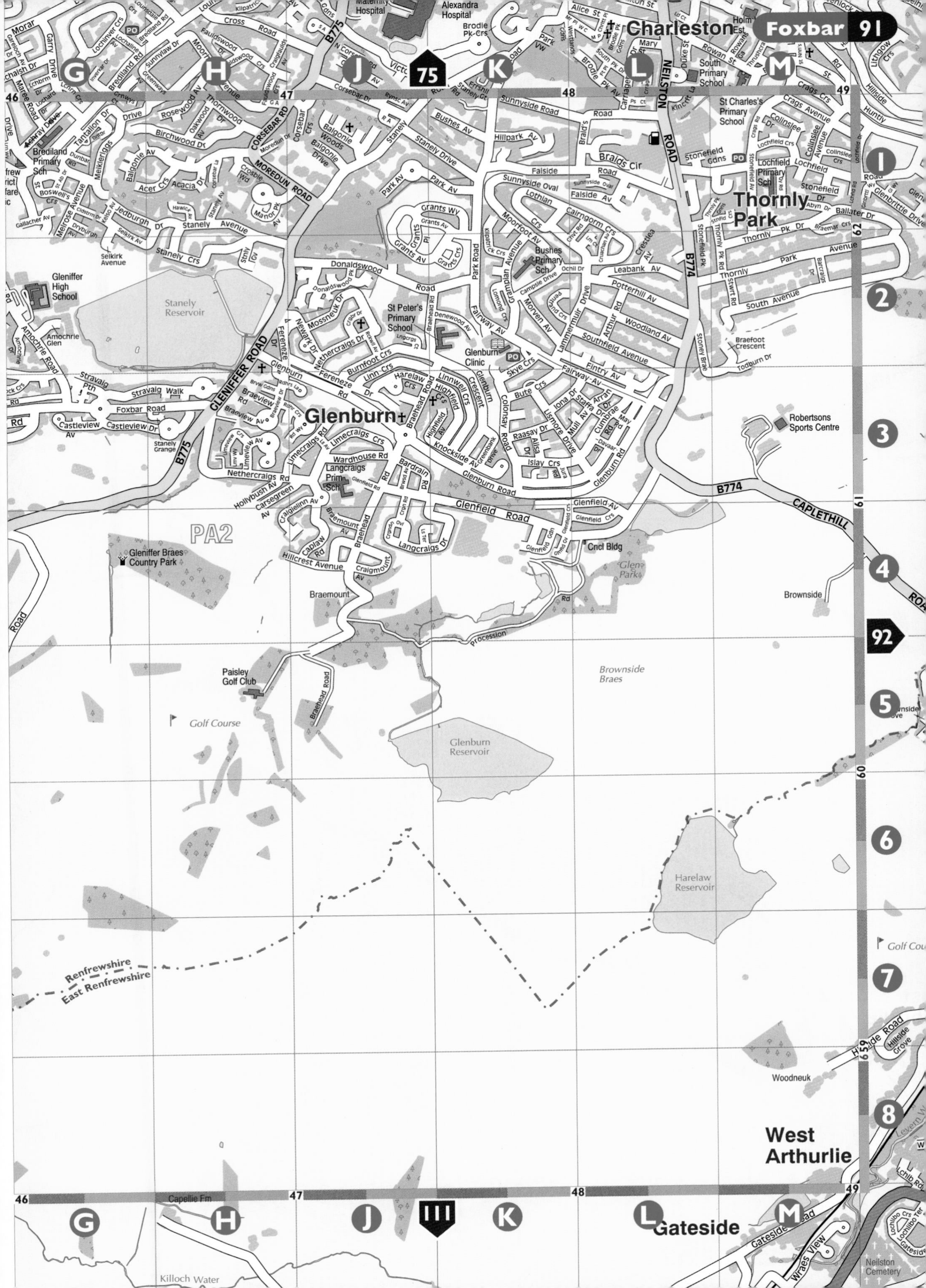
Charleston
Thornly Park
Glenburn
West Arthurlie
Gateside
PA2
Stanely Reservoir
Glenburn Reservoir
Harelaw Reservoir
Brownside Braes
Gleniffer Braes Country Park
Paisley Golf Club
Golf Course
Gleniffer High School
Alexandra Hospital
St Peter's Primary School
Bushes Primary Sch
Langcraigs Prim Sch
Glenburn Clinic
Robertsons Sports Centre
St Charles's Primary School
South Primary School
Lochfield Primary Sch
Brediland Primary Sch
Cncl Bldg
Glen Park
Braemount
Brownside
Woodneuk
Renfrewshire
East Renfrewshire
Procession Rd
Capellie Fm
Killoch Water
Neilston Cemetery
GLENIFFER ROAD
NEILSTON ROAD
CAPLETHILL ROAD
MOREDUN ROAD
CORSEBAR RD
B775
B774
75
92
111

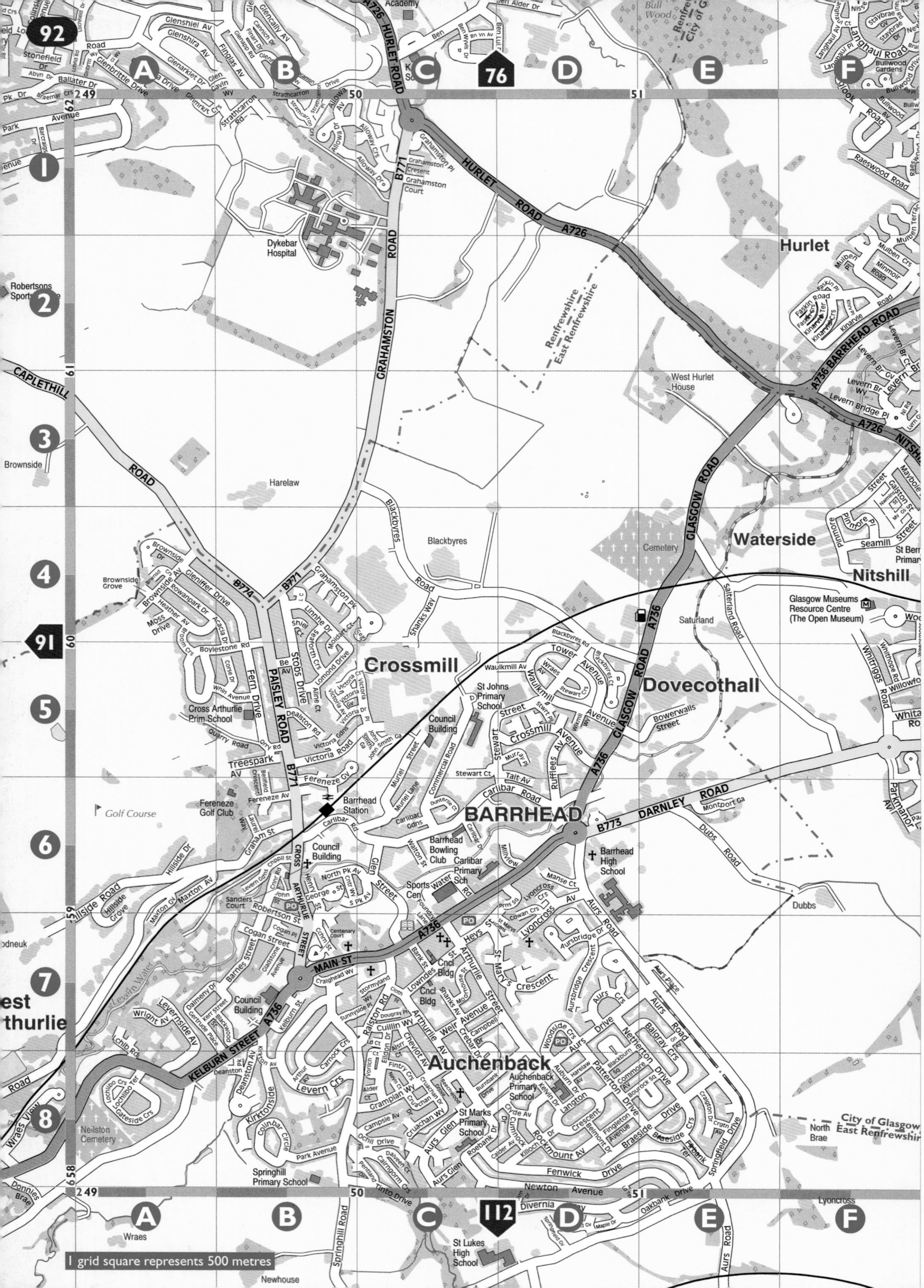
92
76
91
112
A
B
C
D
E
F
1
2
3
4
5
6
7
8
Dykebar Hospital
Robertsons Sports
Brownside
Harelaw
Blackbyres
Hurlet
West Hurlet House
Waterside
Nitshill
Cemetery
Saturland
Glasgow Museums Resource Centre (The Open Museum)
Crossmill
Dovecothall
St Johns Primary School
Council Building
Cross Arthurlie Prim School
Barrhead Station
Fereneze Golf Club
Golf Course
BARRHEAD
Barrhead Bowling Club
Carlibar Primary Sch
Sports Cen
Barrhead High School
Dubbs
Auchenback
Auchenback Primary School
St Marks Primary School
Springhill Primary School
Neilston Cemetery
North Brae
City of Glasgow
East Renfrewshire
Renfrewshire
Lyoncross
Wraes
Newhouse
St Lukes High School
GRAHAMSTON ROAD
HURLET ROAD
GLASGOW ROAD
DARNLEY ROAD
CAPLETHILL ROAD
PAISLEY ROAD
KELBURN STREET
MAIN ST
A736 BARRHEAD ROAD
1 grid square represents 500 metres

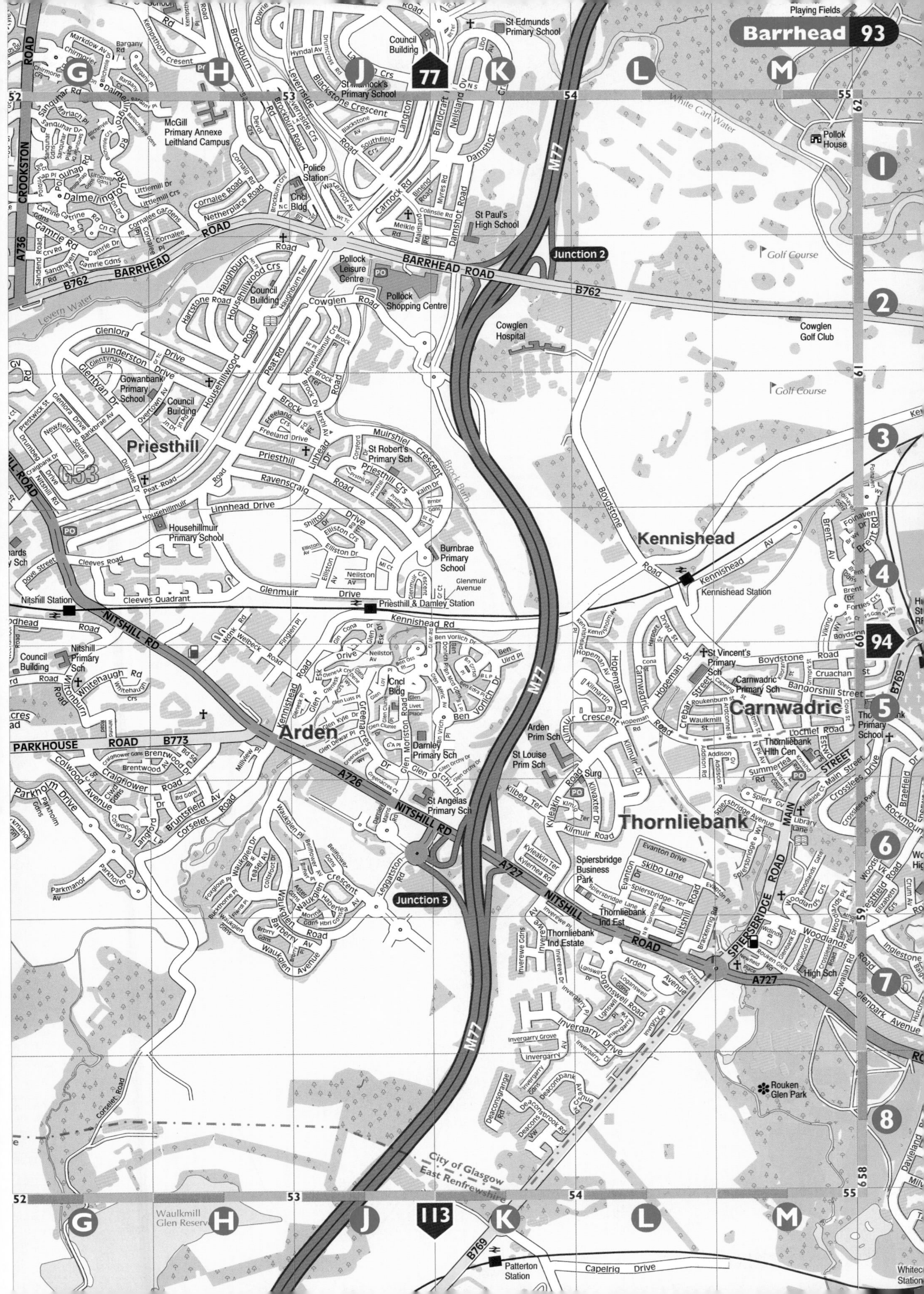

77
94
113
G
H
J
K
L
M
52
53
54
55
1
2
3
4
5
6
7
8
Priesthill
Arden
Kennishead
Carnwadric
Thornliebank
Junction 2
Junction 3
M77
BARRHEAD ROAD
B762
A736
CROOKSTON ROAD
NITSHILL RD
A726
A727
B773
B769
PARKHOUSE ROAD
SPIERSBRIDGE ROAD
MAIN STREET
Levern Water
White Cart Water
Brock Burn
Council Building
St Edmunds Primary School
St Marnock's Primary School
McGill Primary Annexe Leithland Campus
Police Station
Cncl Bldg
St Paul's High School
Pollock Leisure Centre
Pollock Shopping Centre
Pollok House
Golf Course
Cowglen Hospital
Cowglen Golf Club
Gowanbank Primary School
St Robert's Primary Sch
Househillmuir Primary School
Burnbrae Primary School
Nitshill Station
Priesthill & Damley Station
Kennishead Station
Nitshill Primary Sch
Darnley Primary Sch
St Angelas Primary Sch
Arden Prim Sch
St Louise Prim Sch
St Vincent's Primary Sch
Carnwadric Primary Sch
Thornliebank Hlth Cen
Thornliebank Primary School
Library Lane
Spiersbridge Business Park
Thornliebank Ind Est
Thornliebank Ind Estate
High Sch
Rouken Glen Park
City of Glasgow
East Renfrewshire
Waulkmill Glen Reservoir
Patterton Station
Capelrig Drive
Playing Fields

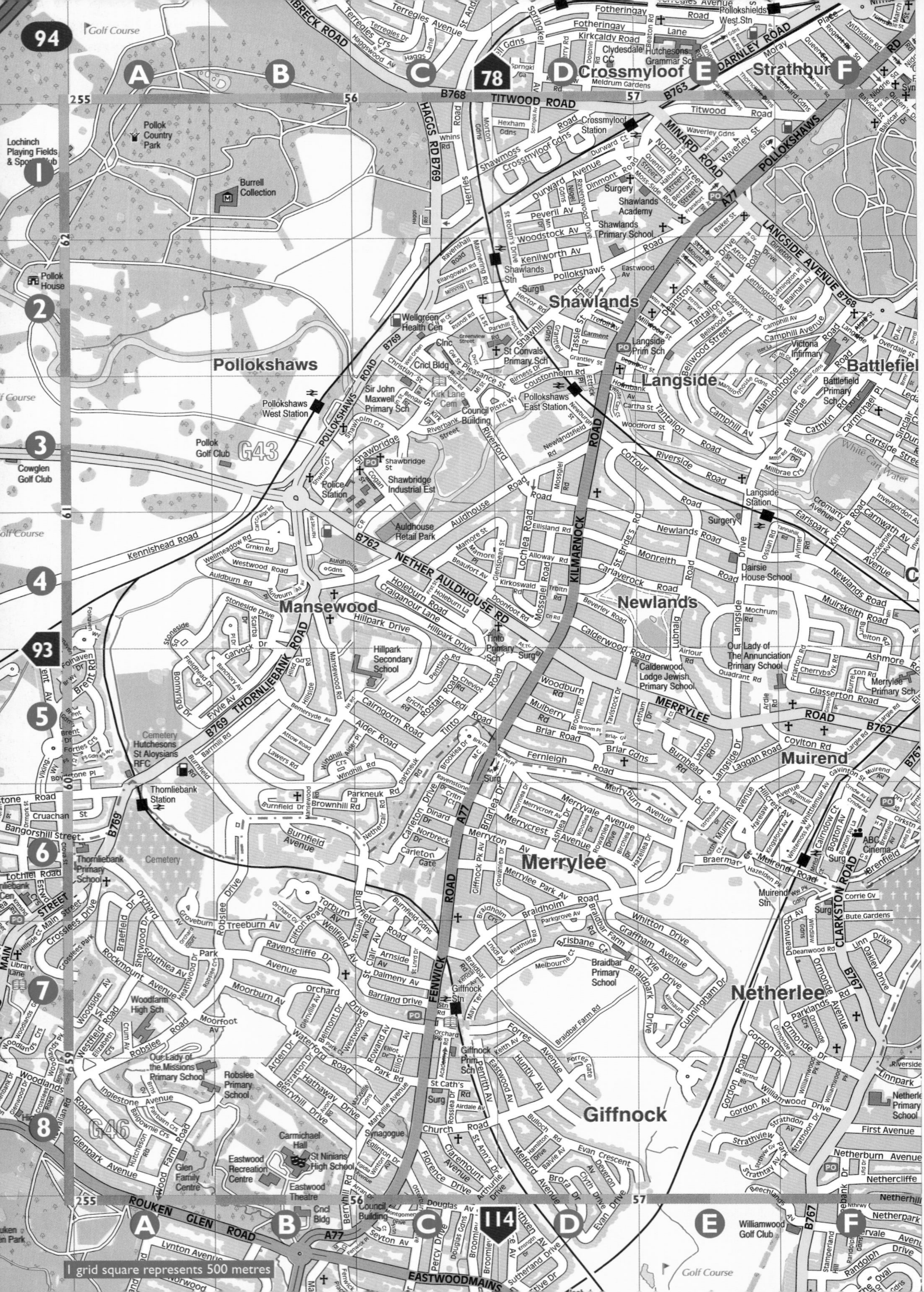
94
93
78
114
A
B
C
D
E
F
1
2
3
4
5
6
7
8
255
56
57
62
61
60
59
Crossmyloof
Strathbungo
Pollokshaws
Shawlands
Langside
Battlefield
Mansewood
Newlands
Merrylee
Muirend
Netherlee
Giffnock
Pollok Country Park
Burrell Collection
Pollok House
Lochinch Playing Fields & Sports Club
Pollok Golf Club
Cowglen Golf Club
Golf Course
Williamwood Golf Club
Pollokshaws West Station
Pollokshaws East Station
Shawlands Stn
Crossmyloof Station
Langside Station
Thornliebank Station
Muirend Stn
Giffnock Stn
Pollokshields West Stn
Hutchesons' Grammar Sch
Clydesdale CC
Shawlands Academy
Shawlands Primary School
Langside Prim Sch
St Convals Primary Sch
Sir John Maxwell Primary Sch
Victoria Infirmary
Battlefield Primary Sch
Wellgreen Health Cen
Kirk Lane Cem
Council Building
Police Station
Shawbridge Industrial Est
Auldhouse Retail Park
Hillpark Secondary School
Tinto Primary Sch
Calderwood Lodge Jewish Primary School
Our Lady of The Annunciation Primary School
Merrylee Primary Sch
Dairsie House School
Cemetery
Hutchesons St Aloysians RFC
Thornliebank Primary School
Woodfarm High Sch
Our Lady of the Missions Primary School
Robslee Primary School
Braidbar Primary School
Giffnock Prim Sch
Netherlee Primary School
Carmichael Hall
St Ninians High School
Synagogue
Eastwood Recreation Centre
Eastwood Theatre
Glen Family Centre
Cncl Bldg
Council Building
ABC Cinema
G43
G46
TITWOOD ROAD
B768
B769
B762
B763
B767
A77
DARNLEY ROAD
MINARD ROAD
POLLOKSHAWS ROAD
LANGSIDE AVENUE
KILMARNOCK ROAD
NETHER AULDHOUSE RD
THORNLIEBANK ROAD
MERRYLEE ROAD
FENWICK ROAD
CLARKSTON ROAD
ROUKEN GLEN ROAD
EASTWOODMAINS
HAGGS RD
Kennishead Road
Auldhouse Road
Riverside Road
Newlands Road
Muirend Road
Braidholm Road
Whitton Drive
Rouken Glen Park
1 grid square represents 500 metres

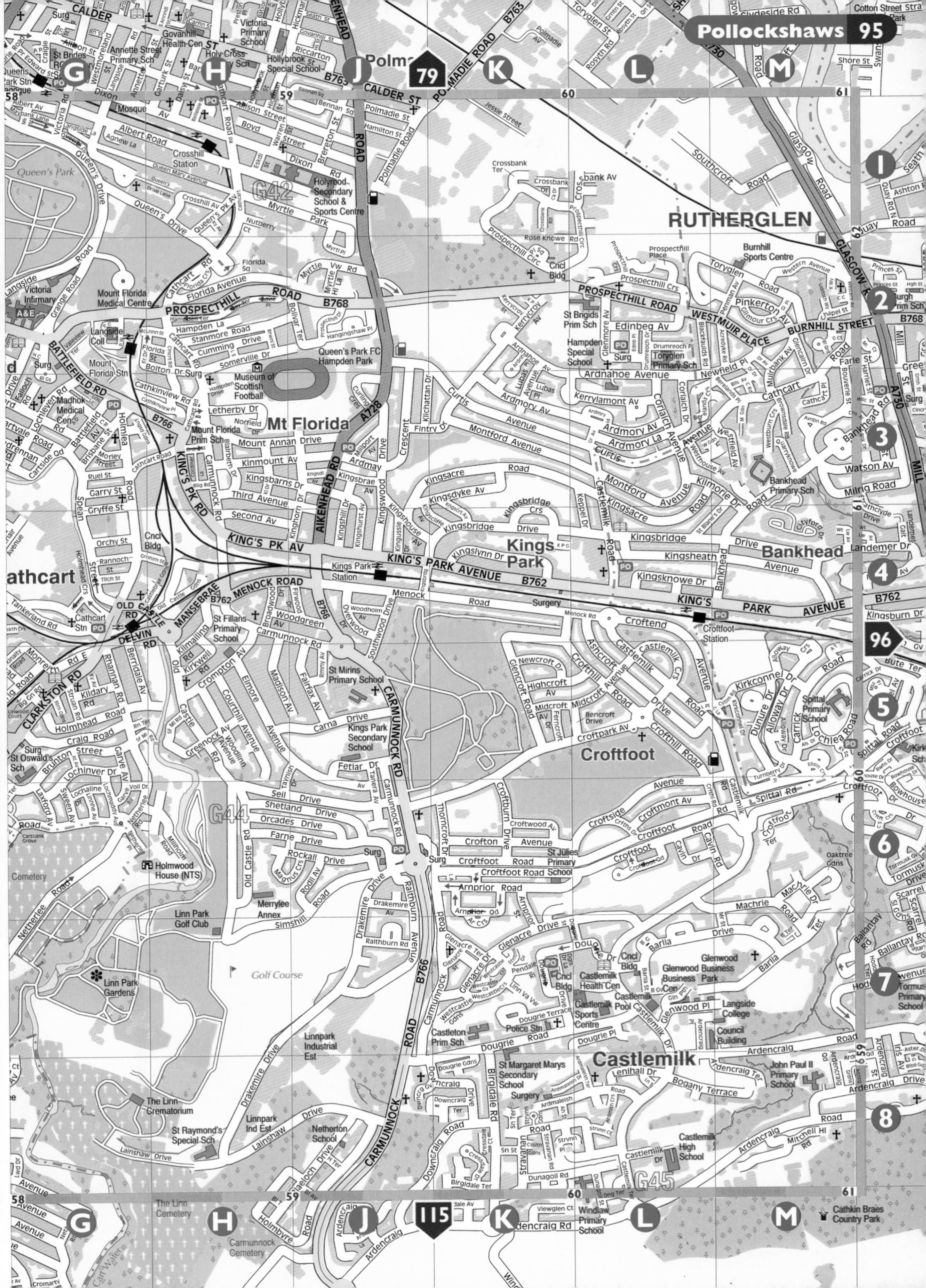

Pollockshaws 95
79
96
115
RUTHERGLEN
Mt Florida
Kings Park
Bankhead
Croftfoot
Castlemilk
Cathcart
G42
G44
G45
Queen's Park
Victoria Infirmary
A&E
Mount Florida Medical Centre
Crosshill Station
Holyrood Secondary School & Sports Centre
Queen's Park FC Hampden Park
Museum of Scottish Football
Hampden Special School
St Brigids Prim Sch
Toryglen Primary Sch
Burnhill Sports Centre
Bankhead Primary Sch
Kings Park Station
Croftfoot Station
Cathcart Stn
Mount Florida Stn
Langside Coll
St Fillans Primary School
St Mirins Primary School
Kings Park Secondary School
St Julies Primary School
Spittal Primary School
Holmwood House (NTS)
Linn Park Golf Club
Golf Course
Linn Park Gardens
The Linn Crematorium
St Raymond's Special Sch
Netherton School
Linnpark Industrial Est
Linnpark Ind Est
Merrylee Annex
Castleton Prim Sch
Police Stn
Castlemilk Health Cen
Castlemilk Sports Centre
Castlemilk Pool
Glenwood Business Park
Glenwood Business Cen
Langside College
Council Building
St Margaret Marys Secondary School
John Paul II Primary School
Castlemilk High School
Windlaw Primary School
Tormusk Primary School
Cathkin Braes Country Park
The Linn Cemetery
Carmunnock Cemetery
Cemetery
PROSPECTHILL ROAD
B768
KING'S PARK AVENUE
B762
AIKENHEAD RD
A728
CARMUNNOCK RD
B766
CALDER ST
POLMADIE ROAD
B763
BURNHILL STREET
WESTMUIR PLACE
GLASGOW RD
A730
BATTLEFIELD RD
KING'S PK RD
KING'S PK AV
MENOCK ROAD
MANSEBRAE
OLD CASTLE RD
DELVIN RD
CLARKSTON RD
Southcroft Road
Curtis Avenue
Montford Avenue
Kingsbridge Drive
Croftfoot Road
Dougrie Road
Ardencraig Road
Glenacre Drive
Simshill Road
Netherlee Road

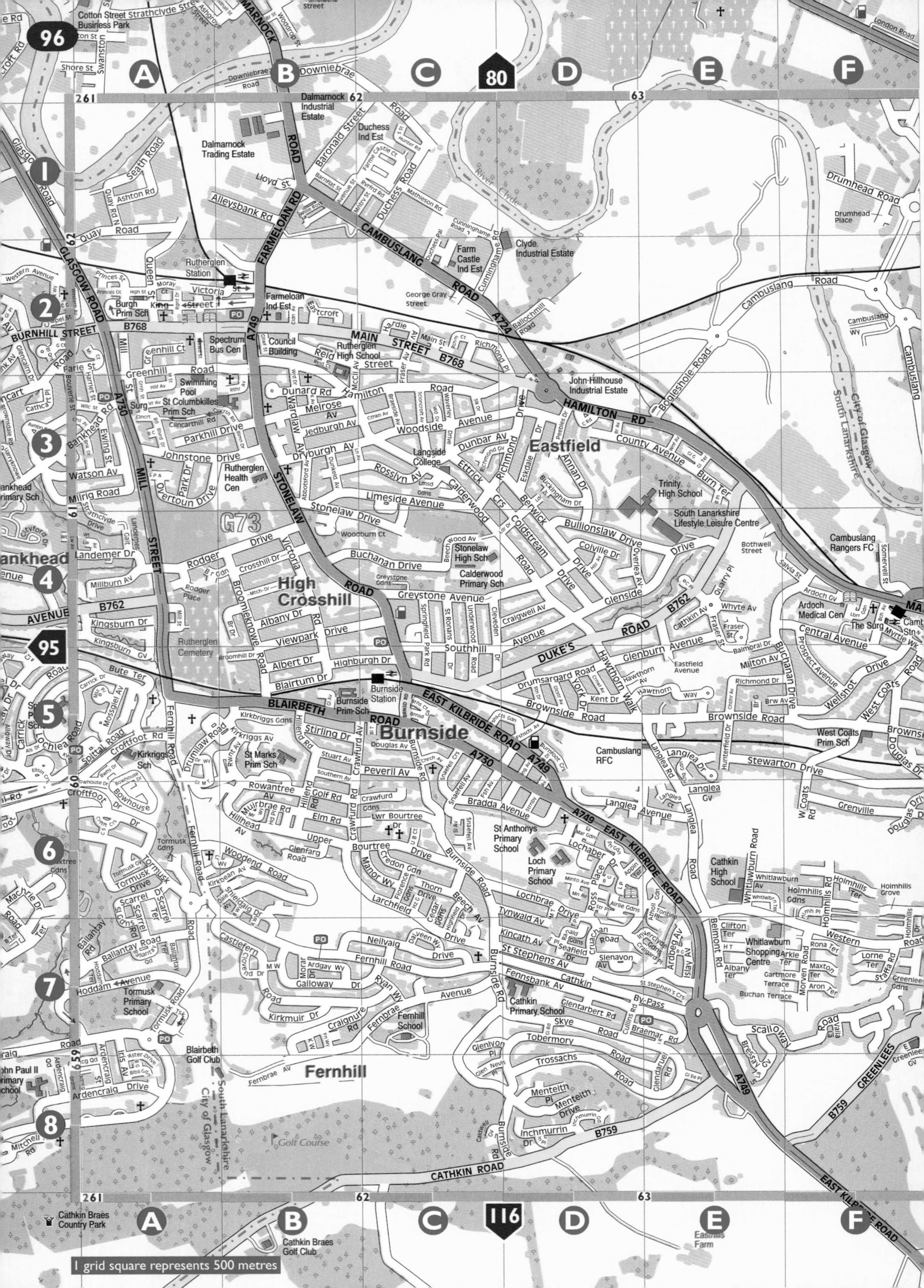

96
80
95
116
A
B
C
D
E
F
1
2
3
4
5
6
7
8
261
62
63
Cotton Street Strathclyde Street Business Park
Shore St
Swanston Street
Downiebrae Road
Dalmarnock Road
Dalmarnock Industrial Estate
Dalmarnock Trading Estate
Baronald Street
Duchess Ind Est
Duchess Road
Seath Road
Ashton Rd
Quay Rd N
Lloyd St
Alleysbank Rd
Quay Road
Farmeloan Rd
Cambuslang Road
Mathieson Rd
Cunninghame Road
River Clyde
Farm Castle Ind Est
Clyde Industrial Estate
Drumhead Road
Drumhead Place
Glasgow Road
Western Avenue
Princes St
Rutherglen Station
Queen St
Moray Ct
Victoria St
King St
Burgh Prim Sch
Farmeloan Ind Est
Eastcroft
George Gray Street
Ballochmill Road
Cambuslang Road
Cambuslang Wy
Burnhill Street
B768
Main Street
Council Building
Spectrum Bus Cen
Greenhill Ct
Rutherglen High School
Reid Street
Hardie Av
Richmond Pl
Fraser Av
Greenhill Road
Swimming Pool
St Columbkilles Prim Sch
Farie St
Dunard Rd
Hamilton Road
John Hillhouse Industrial Estate
Bogleshole Road
Hamilton Rd
Melrose Av
Jedburgh Av
Woodside Avenue
Parkhill Drive
Clincarthill Rd
Bankhead Rd
Ewing St
Watson Av
Johnstone Drive
Dryburgh Av
Dunbar Av
Eastfield
County Avenue
Burn Ter
Rosslyn Av
Langside College
Rutherglen Health Cen
Park Dr
Overtoun Drive
Milrig Road
Stonelaw Road
Limeside Avenue
Calderwood Rd
Ettrick Crs
Richmond Dr
Berwick Dr
Coldstream Rd
Trinity High School
South Lanarkshire Lifestyle Leisure Centre
City of Glasgow
South Lanarkshire
Bullionslaw Drive
Stonelaw Drive
Woodburn Ct
G73
Bankhead Primary Sch
Landemer Dr
Rodger Drive
Crosshill Dr
Victoria Rd
Buchanan Drive
Stonelaw High Sch
Calderwood Primary Sch
Colville Dr
Overlea Av
Glenside Drive
Bothwell Street
Cambuslang Rangers FC
Somervell St
Millburn Av
Rodger Place
High Crosshill
Greystone Gdns
Greystone Avenue
Craigwell Av
Quarry Pl
Whyte Av
Ardoch Gv
Ardoch Medical Cen
The Surg
Cambuslang Stn
B762
Avenue
Kingsburn Dr
Kingsburn Gv
Albany Dr
Broomieknowe Rd
Viewpark Drive
Springfield Park Rd
St Ronans Dr
Underwood Rd
Clevedon Dr
Southhill Av
Duke's Road
Catkin Av
Fraser St
Central Avenue
Prospect Avenue
Rutherglen Cemetery
Broomhill Dr
Albert Dr
Highburgh Dr
Glenburn Avenue
Eastfield Avenue
Milton Av
Buchanan Drive
Wellshot Drive
West Coats Road
Bute Ter
Blairtum Dr
Burnside Station
East Kilbride Road
A730
A749
Drumsargard Road
York Dr
Hawthorn Walk
Hawthorn Way
Kent Dr
Richmond Dr
Brownside Road
Blairbeth Road
Burnside Prim Sch
Burnside
Stirling Dr
Carrick Dr
Mossgiel Av
Fernhill Road
Kirkbriggs Gdns
Kirkriggs Av
Douglas Av
Stuart Av
Crawfurd Av
Peveril Av
Burnside Rd
Southern Av
St Marks Prim Sch
Spittal Road
Croftfoot Rd
Kirkriggs Sch
Drumilaw Road
Cambuslang RFC
Langlea Rd
Langlea Dr
Hunterfield Dr
Stewarton Drive
West Coats Prim Sch
Douglas Dr
Lochlea Road
Bowhouse Dr
Croftfoot Dr
Rowantree Av
Golf Rd
Muirbrae Rd
Hillhead Av
Elm Rd
Lwr Bourtree Dr
Snaefell Av
Bradda Avenue
Langlea Avenue
Langlea Gv
Grenville Dr
W Coats Rd
Tormusk Gdns
Upper Bourtree Drive
Glenfarg Road
St Anthonys Primary School
Loch Primary School
Lochaber Dr
Whitlawburn Road
Cathkin High School
Holmhills Ter
Holmhills Grove
Woodend Road
Kirkbean Av
Manor Wy
Credon Gdn
Thorn Drive
Larchfield
Beech Av
Lochbrae Drive
Ross Place
Tormusk Drive
Scarrel Dr
Scarrel Ter
Ballantay Rd
Ballantay Road
Castlefern Rd
Neilvaig Drive
Tynwald Av
Kincath Av
Seafield Dr
Cruachan Road
Ardbeg Av
Islay Av
Belmont Rd
Clifton Ter
Whitlawburn Shopping Centre
Western Road
Rona Ter
Lorne Ter
Staffa Rd
Hoddam Avenue
Tormusk Primary School
Tormusk Road
Morar Dr
Ardgay Wy
Galloway Dr
Fernhill Road
St Stephens Av
Slenavon Av
Cathkin By-Pass
Fennsbank Av
Albany Ter
Gartmore Terrace
Buchan Terrace
Maxton Ter
Aron Ter
Greenlees Gdns
Ryan Wy
Avenue
Kirkmuir Dr
Craignure Rd
Fernbrae Av
Fernhill School
Cathkin Primary School
Glentarbert Rd
Skye Road
Braemar Rd
Cullins Rd
Scalloway Rd
Bressay Gv
Blairbeth Golf Club
Ardencraig Rd
Iris Av
Ardencraig Drive
John Paul II Primary School
Glenlyon Pl
Glen Nevis Pl
Tobermory Road
Trossachs Road
Glendaruel Rd
A749
B759
Greenlees Road
Fernhill
Menteith Pl
Menteith Drive
Inchmurrin Dr
Golf Course
Mitchell Rd
Cathkin Road
East Kilbride Road
Cathkin Braes Country Park
Cathkin Braes Golf Club
Eastfield Farm
1 grid square represents 500 metres

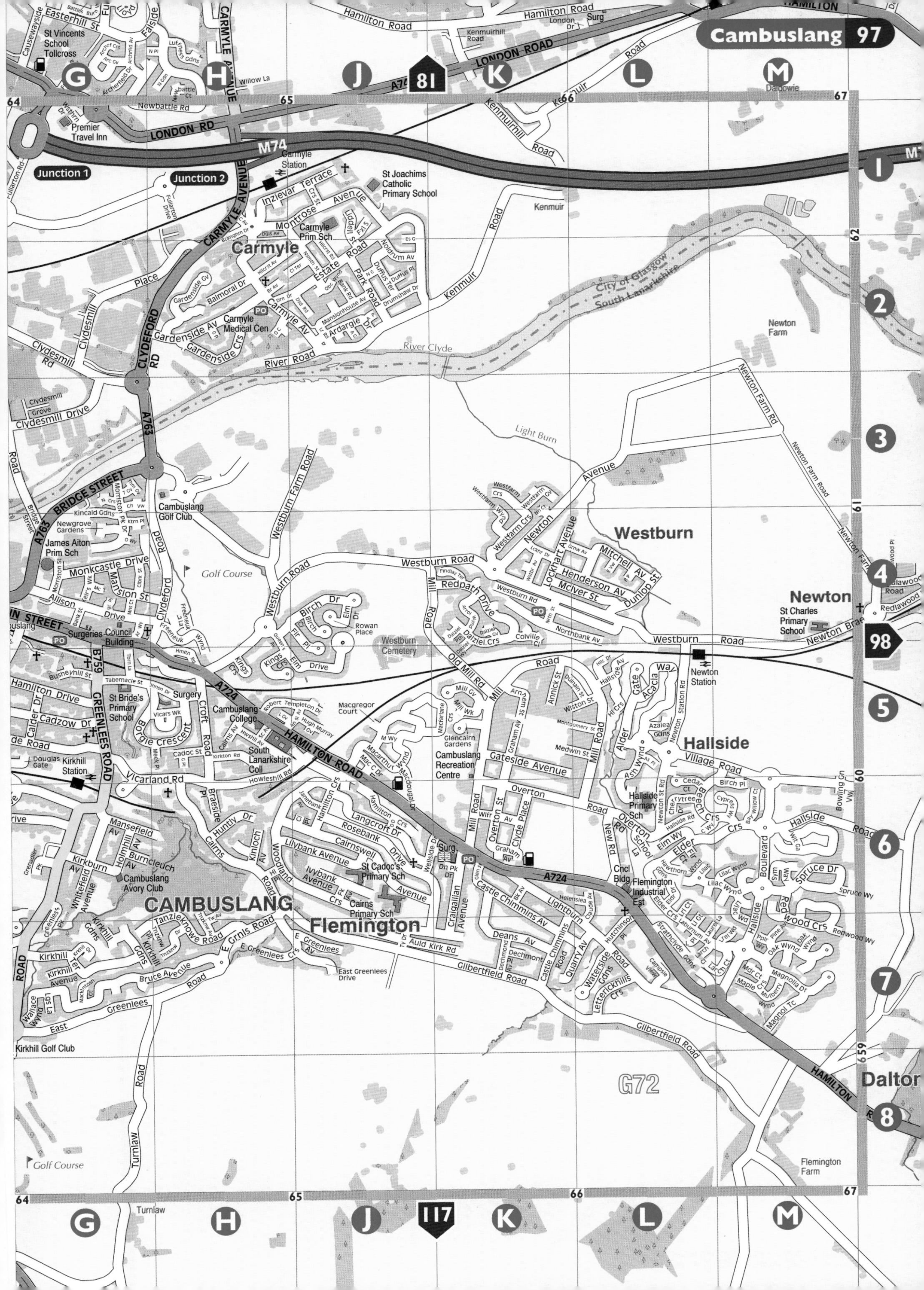
81
98
117
G
H
J
K
L
M
1
2
3
4
5
6
7
8
64
65
66
67
62
61
60
659
M74
Junction 1
Junction 2
LONDON ROAD
LONDON RD
Hamilton Road
Carmyle
Carmyle Station
St Joachims Catholic Primary School
Carmyle Prim Sch
Carmyle Medical Cen
St Vincents School Tollcross
Premier Travel Inn
Kenmuir
City of Glasgow
South Lanarkshire
River Clyde
River Road
Newton Farm
Newton Farm Rd
Light Burn
CARMYLE AVENUE
CLYDEFORD RD
A763
BRIDGE STREET
Clydesmill Drive
Cambuslang Golf Club
Golf Course
James Aiton Prim Sch
Newgrove Gardens
Monkcastle Drive
Westburn Farm Road
Westburn Road
Westburn
Westburn Cemetery
Rowan Place
Newton
St Charles Primary School
Newton Station
Newton Brae
Hallside
Hallside Primary Sch
Village Road
Hallside Road
Hallside Boulevard
Surgeries
Council Building
St Bride's Primary School
Cambuslang College
South Lanarkshire Coll
Kirkhill Station
GREENLEES ROAD
HAMILTON ROAD
A724
B759
Cambuslang Recreation Centre
Glencairn Gardens
Macgregor Court
Gateside Avenue
Mill Road
Overton Road
St Cadoc's Primary Sch
Cairns Primary Sch
CAMBUSLANG
Flemington
Flemington Industrial Est
Cambuslang Avory Club
Gilbertfield Road
Kirkhill Golf Club
East Greenlees
Turnlaw Road
Turnlaw
G72
Flemington Farm
Dalton
HAMILTON

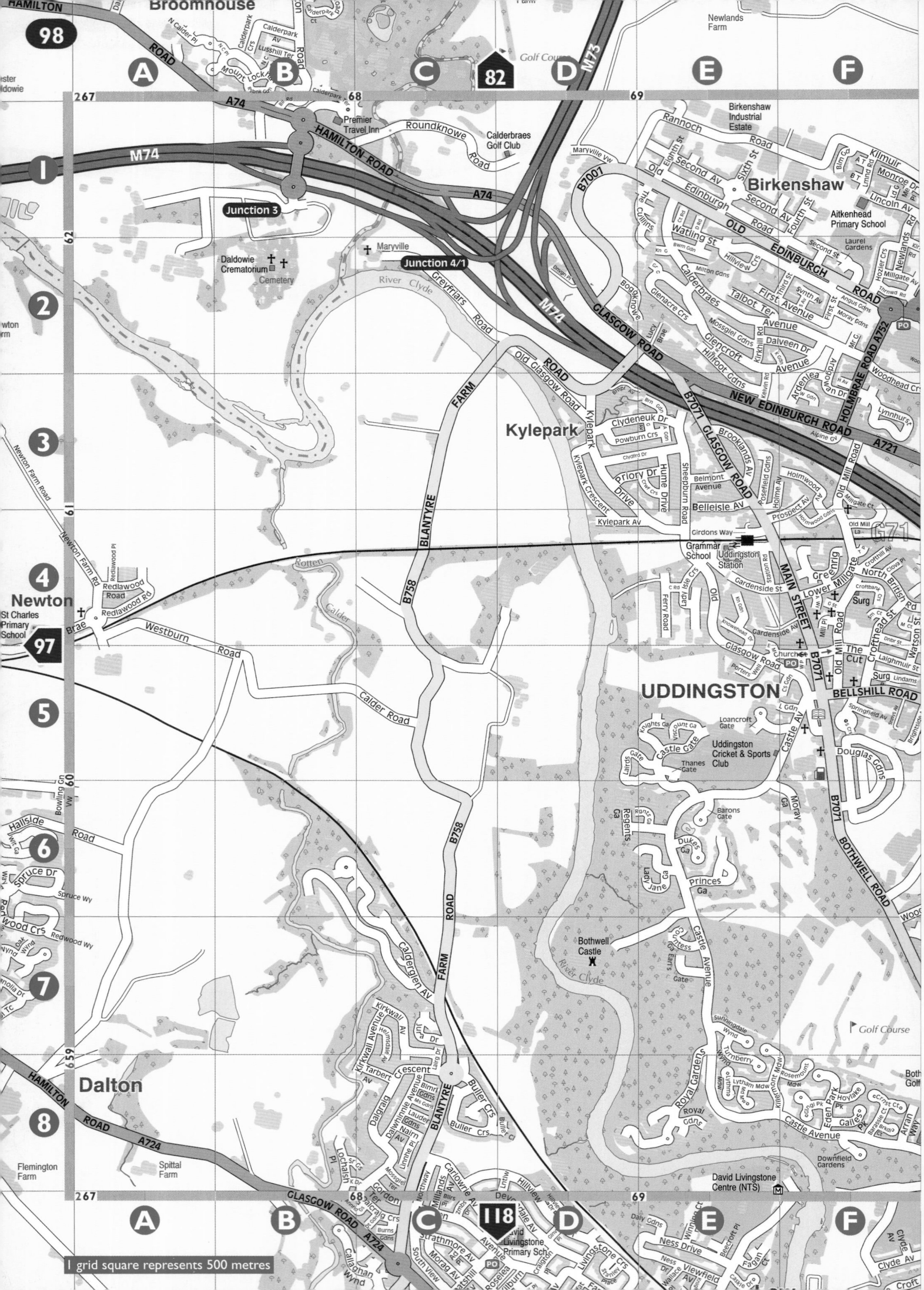

98

A **B** **C** **82** **D** **E** **F**

I

2

3

4 Newton
97

5

6

7

8

Broomhouse

HAMILTON ROAD
N Calder Pl
Calderpark Av
Lusshill Ter
Mount Lock Rd
Calderpark Ct

A74
Premier Travel Inn
HAMILTON ROAD
Roundknowe Road
Calderbraes Golf Club
M74
Junction 3
Daldowie Crematorium
Cemetery
Maryville
River Clyde
Junction 4/1
Greyfriars Road
Old Glasgow Road
Kylepark
ROAD
BLANTYRE FARM ROAD
Rotten Calder
Westburn Road
Calder Road
B758
B758 FARM ROAD

Newlands Farm

Rannoch
Birkenshaw Industrial Estate
Kilmuir
Monroe Dr
Lincoln Av
Eighth St
Second Av
Sixth St
Old Edinburgh Road
Birkenshaw
OLD EDINBURGH ROAD
Aitkenhead Primary School
Laurel Gardens
Watling St
Hillview Cres
First Avenue
Millgate Rd
Second St
Calderbraes
Talbot Ter
Avenue
Moray Gdns
Mossgiel Gdns
Glencroft
Glencroft
Kirkhill Rd
Dalveen Dr
Hilfoot Gdns
Ardenlea
Woodhead Cr
Lynnhurst
NEW EDINBURGH ROAD
Holmbrae Road A721
Glasgow Road
GLASGOW ROAD
B7071 GLASGOW ROAD
Clydeneuk Dr
Powburn Crs
Priory Dr
Hume Drive
Sheepburn Road
Belmont Avenue
Belleisle Av
Kylepark Crescent
Kylepark Av
Girdons Way
Grammar School
Uddingston Station
Gardenside St
Rosefield Gdns
Holme Av
Prospect Av
Holmwood
Old Mill Road
Old Mill La
G71
North British Rd
Greenrig
Lower Millgate
MAIN STREET
Ferry Road
Gardenside St
Gardenside Av
Glasgow Road
Church
PO
B7071
The Cut
BELLSHILL ROAD
UDDINGSTON
Loancroft Gate
Castle Gate
Thanes Gate
Uddingston Cricket & Sports Club
Knights Gate
Castle Av
Douglas Gdns
Springfield Av
B7071 BOTHWELL ROAD
Barons Ga
Regents Ga
Dukes Ga
Lady Jane Ga
Princes Ga
Castle Avenue
Countess Gate
Earl's Gate
Bothwell Castle
River Clyde
Golf Course
Sunningdale Wynd
Turnberry
Royal Gardens
Royal Gdns
Castle Avenue
Lytham Mdw
Eden Park
Hoylake
Arran
Downfield Gardens

Dalton
HAMILTON ROAD
A724
Flemington Farm
Spittal Farm
Halside Road
Bowling Cr
Spruce Dr
Spruce Wy
Redwood Crs
Redwood Wy
Magnolia Dr
St Charles Primary School
Redlawood Pl
Redlawood Road
Redlawood Rd
Newton Farm Road
Newton Farm Rd
Brae

Kirkwall Avenue
Tarbert Av
Dalgraig Crescent
Dalwhinnie Av
Narn Av
Blantyre
Buller Crs
Buller Cl
Carlowrie Av
Millands Av
Kirkwall Av
Caldergien Av
GLASGOW ROAD A724
118
David Livingstone Primary Sch
Strathmore Av
Moray Av
South View
Hillview Av
Dale Av
Avenue
David Livingstone Centre (NTS)
Ness Drive
Viewfield
Clyde Av

1 grid square represents 500 metres

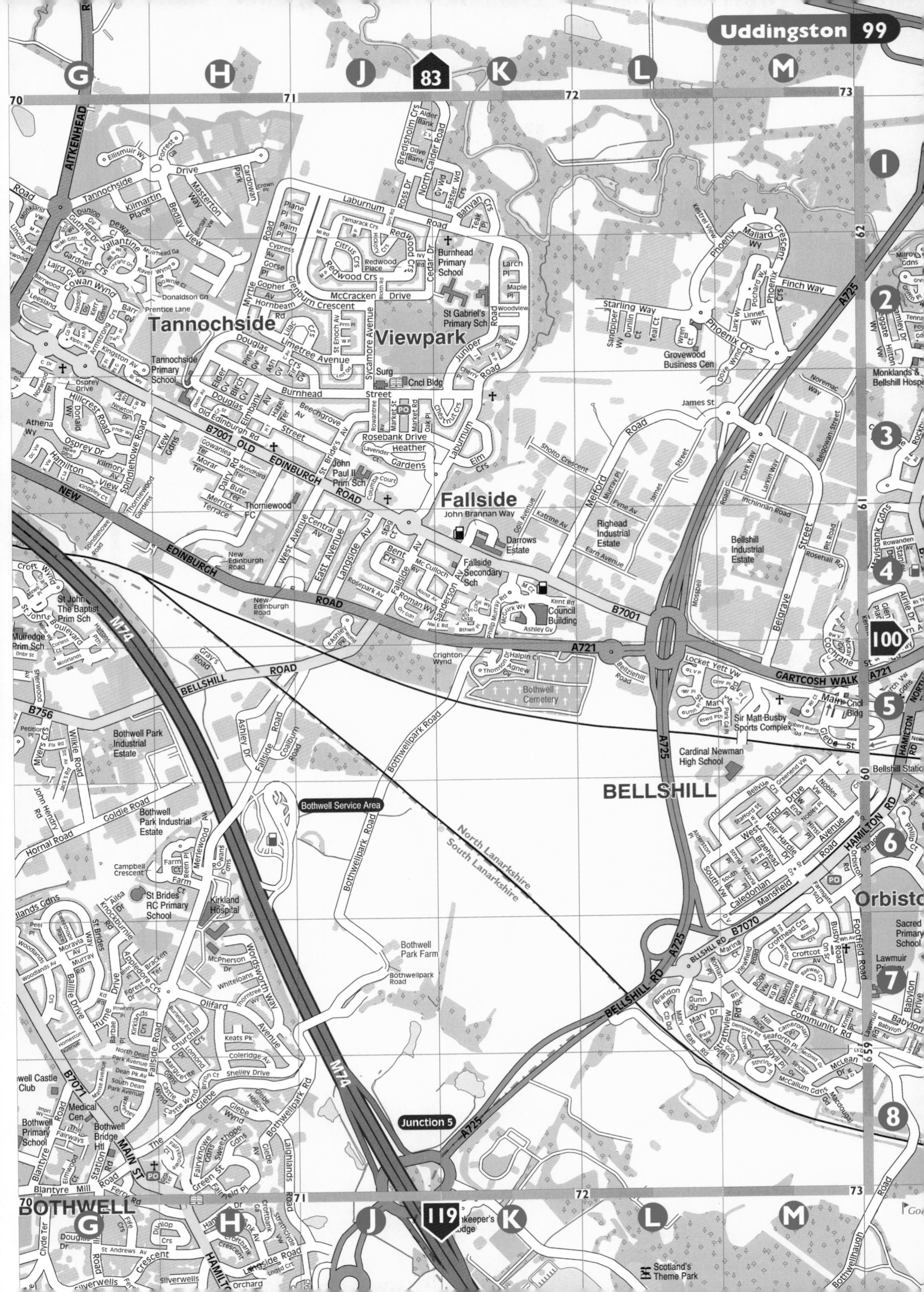
G
H
J
83
K
L
M
70
71
72
73
AITKENHEAD
Tannochside
Viewpark
Fallside
BELLSHILL
Orbiston
BOTHWELL
Tannochside Primary School
Burnhead Primary School
St Gabriel's Primary Sch
Grovewood Business Cen
John Paul II Prim Sch
Thorniewood FC
John Brannan Way
Darrows Estate
Fallside Secondary Sch
Council Building
Righead Industrial Estate
Bellshill Industrial Estate
Monklands & Bellshill Hospital
St John The Baptist Prim Sch
Muiredge Prim Sch
Bothwell Park Industrial Estate
Bothwell Cemetery
Sir Matt Busby Sports Complex
Cardinal Newman High School
Bellshill Station
Bothwell Service Area
North Lanarkshire
South Lanarkshire
St Brides RC Primary School
Kirkland Hospital
Bothwell Park Farm
Bothwellpark Road
Sacred Primary School
Lawmuir Primary
Bothwell Castle Club
Medical Cen
Bothwell Primary School
Bothwell Bridge Htl
Junction 5
Scotland's Theme Park
M74
A725
A721
B7001
B7070
B7071
B756
NEW EDINBURGH ROAD
OLD EDINBURGH ROAD
BELLSHILL ROAD
GARTCOSH WALK
HAMILTON ROAD
MAIN ST
100
119
I
2
3
4
5
6
7
8
62
61
60
59

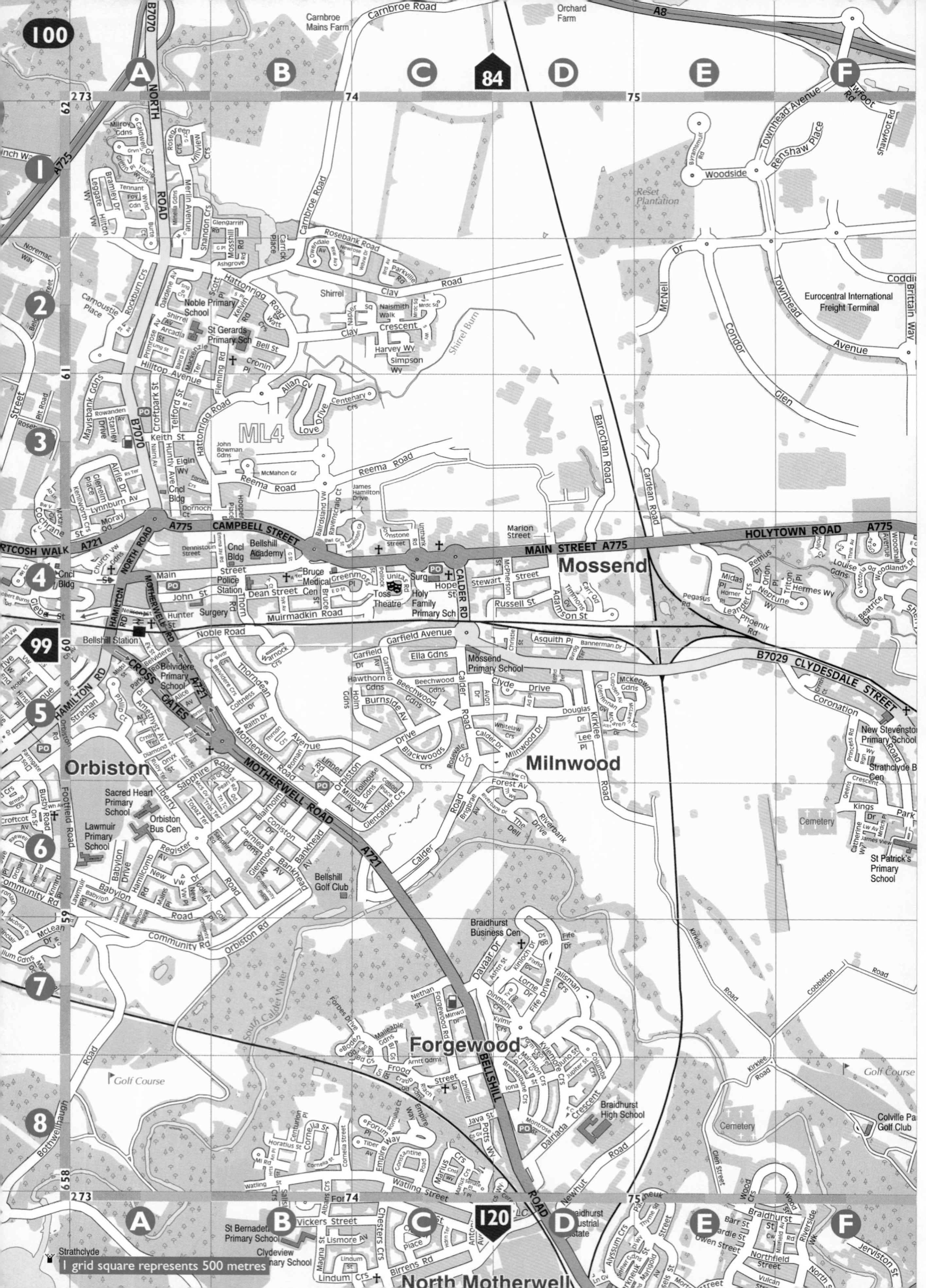
100
84
99
120
Mossend
Milnwood
Orbiston
Forgewood
North Motherwell
ML4
Carnbroe Road
Carnbroe Mains Farm
Orchard Farm
A8
NORTH ROAD
B7070
A725
Reset Plantation
Woodside
Townhead Avenue
Renshaw Place
Shawfoot Rd
Eurocentral International Freight Terminal
Condor Glen
McNeil Dr
Rosebank Road
Clay Road
Clay Crescent
Shirrel
Shirrel Burn
Noble Primary School
St Gerards Primary Sch
Hattonrigg Road
Hilltop Avenue
Allan Gv
Love Drive
Centenary Crs
Reema Road
Barochan Road
Cardean Road
A775 CAMPBELL STREET
MAIN STREET A775
HOLYTOWN ROAD
Bellshill Academy
Police Station
Dean Street
Bruce Medical Cen
Muirmadkin Road
Toss Theatre
Holy Family Primary Sch
CALDER RD
Stewart Street
Russell St
Adamson St
Bellshill Station
Noble Road
Garfield Avenue
Mossend Primary School
B7029 CLYDESDALE STREET
Coronation
New Stevenston Primary School
Cemetery
St Patrick's Primary School
HAMILTON RD
CROSS GATES
MOTHERWELL RD
A721
MOTHERWELL ROAD
Sacred Heart Primary School
Lawmuir Primary School
Orbiston Bus Cen
Bellshill Golf Club
Footfield Road
Community Rd
Orbiston Rd
Golf Course
Braidhurst Business Cen
Braidhurst High School
BELLSHILL ROAD
Colville Park Golf Club
Kirklee Road
Cobbleton Road
St Bernadette's Primary School
Clydeview Primary School
Vickers Street
Lismore Av
Watling Street
Braidhurst Industrial Estate
Jerviston St
Strathclyde
1 grid square represents 500 metres

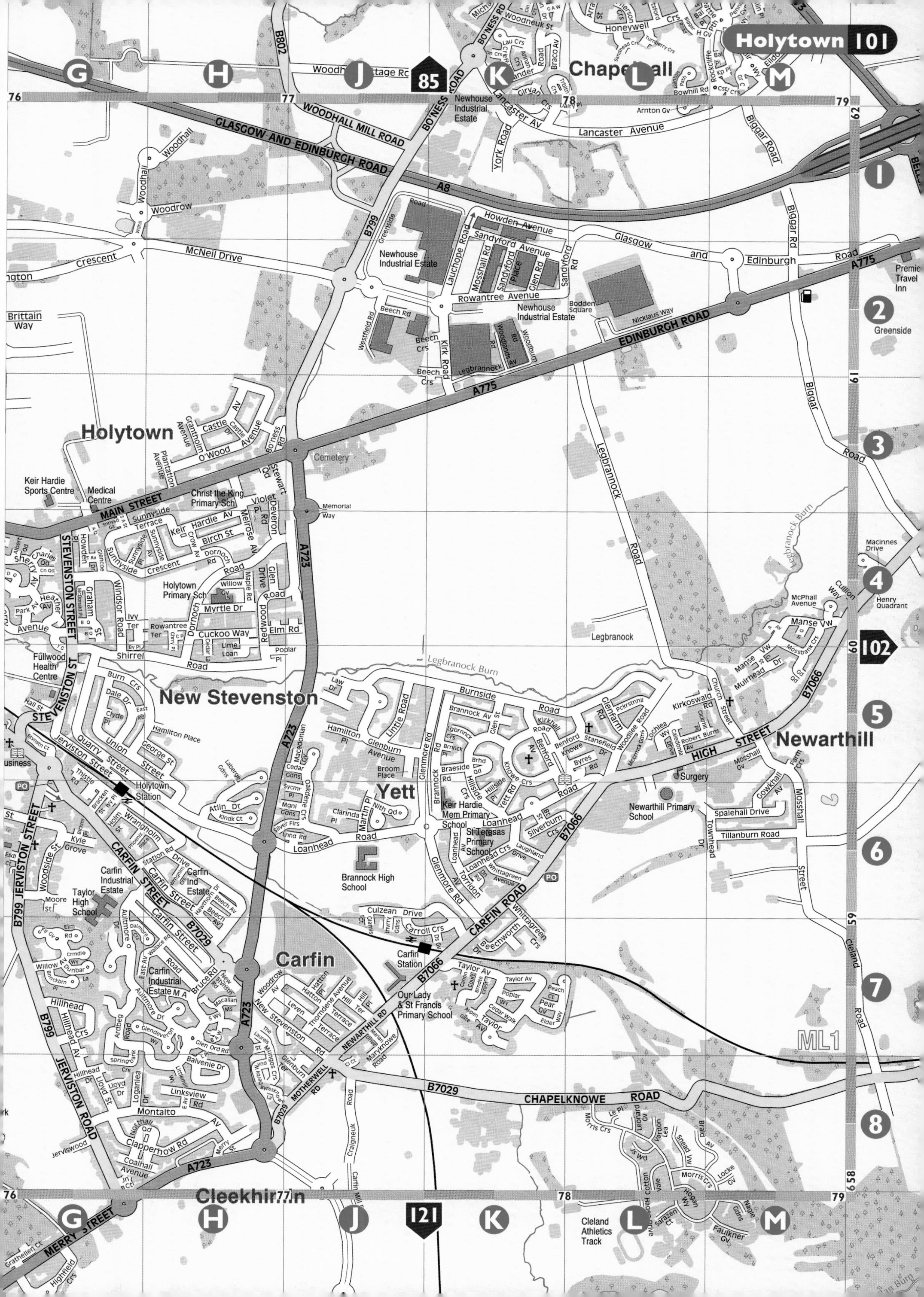
85
Chapelhall
Newhouse Industrial Estate
Woodhall Mill Road
Glasgow and Edinburgh Road
A8
Bo'ness Road
B799
B802
Lancaster Avenue
York Road
Biggar Road
Howden Avenue
Sandyford Avenue
Rowantree Avenue
Lauchope Road
Mosshall Rd
Sandyford Place
Glen Rd
Kirk Road
Beech Rd
Westfield Rd
Woodlands Av
Woodburn Rd
Legbrannock Rd
Bodden Square
Nicklaus Way
Edinburgh Road
A775
Premier Travel Inn
Greenside
McNeil Drive
Crescent
Woodrow
Woodhall
Brittain Way
Holytown
Castle Dr
O'Wood Avenue
Grantholm Avenue
Plantation Avenue
Cemetery
Keir Hardie Sports Centre
Medical Centre
Main Street
Christ the King Primary Sch
Memorial Way
A723
Legbrannock Road
Legbrannock
Legbrannock Burn
Sunnyside Terrace
Keir Hardie Av
Birch St
Sunnyside Crescent
Dornoch Rd
Holytown Primary Sch
Myrtle Dr
Cuckoo Way
Elm Rd
Redwood Rd
Shirrel Road
Stevenston Street
Windsor Road
Graham St
Fullwood Health Centre
New Stevenston
Hamilton Place
Quarry Street
Union Street
George St
Jerviston Street
Holytown Station
Wrangholm
Burnside Road
Lintie Road
Glenburn Avenue
Glenmore Rd
Brannock Rd
Yett
Loanhead Road
Keir Hardie Mem Primary School
St Teresas Primary School
Brannock High School
Benford Knowe
Kirkoswald Rd
High Street
Newarthill
Surgery
Newarthill Primary School
Spalehall Drive
Tillanburn Road
Mosshall Street
Townhead Dr
Manse Vw
Cullion Way
Macinnes Drive
McPhail Avenue
Henry Quadrant
B7066
102
Carfin Street
Carfin Ind Estate
Carfin Industrial Estate
Taylor High School
Woodside St
Kyle Grove
B7029
Carfin
Carfin Station
Carfin Road
Culzean Drive
Carroll Crs
Beechworth
Whittagreen Crs
Taylor Av
Our Lady & St Francis Primary School
Newarthill Rd
New Stevenston Rd
Thorndene Avenue
Hatton Terrace
Maryknowe Road
Motherwell Rd
Chapelknowe Road
Cleland Road
ML1
Hillhead Crs
Jerviston Road
Montalto Av
Linksview Rd
Clapperhow Rd
Coalhall Avenue
Balvenie Dr
Craigneuk Road
Carfin Mill Rd
Morris Crs
Cleekhimin
Merry Street
Cleland Athletics Track
121
G
H
J
K
L
M
1
2
3
4
5
6
7
8
76
77
78
79
62
61
60
59
658

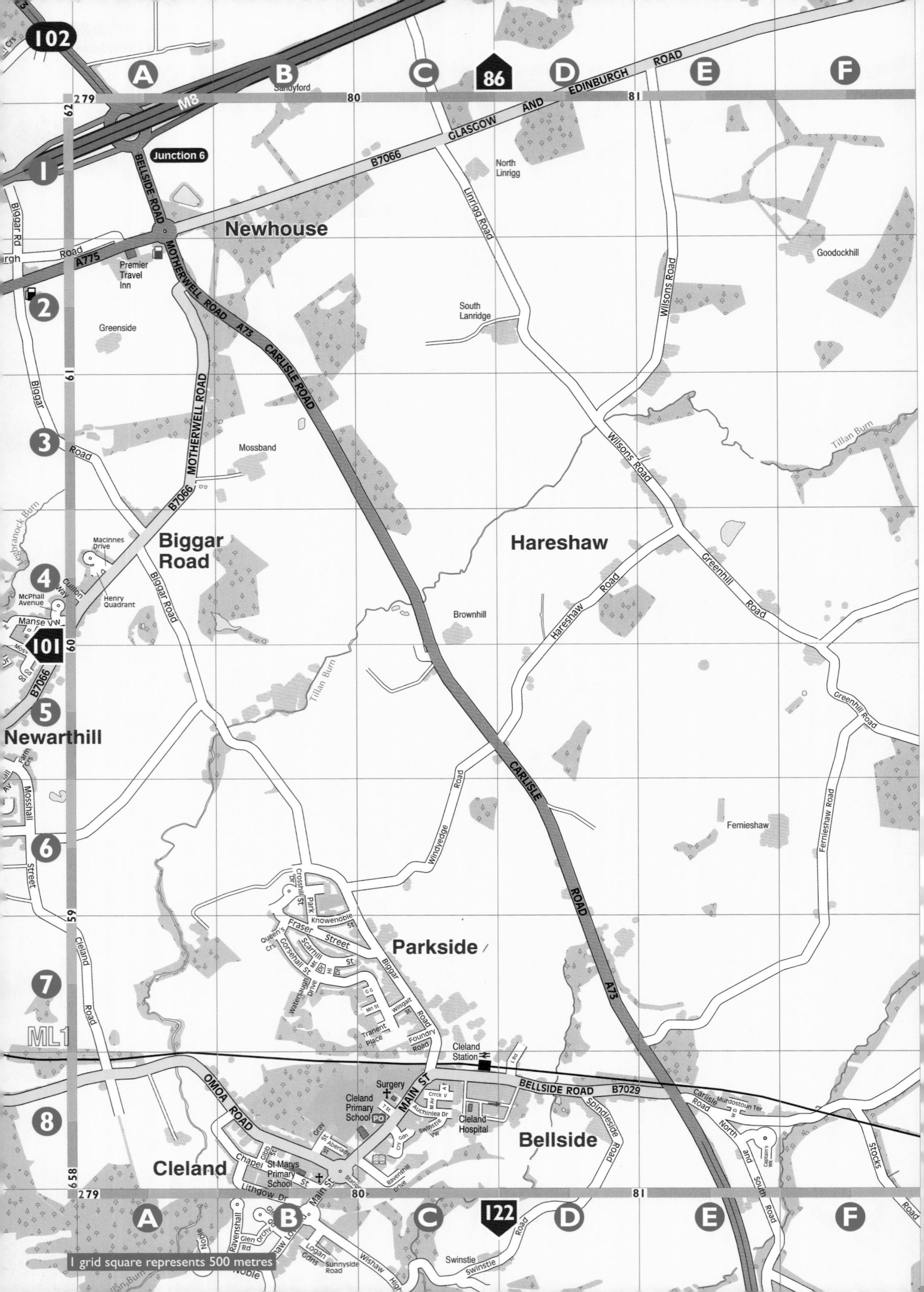

102
86
101
122
A
B
C
D
E
F
1
2
3
4
5
6
7
8
279
80
81
62
61
60
59
658
M8
Junction 6
Sandyford
GLASGOW AND EDINBURGH ROAD
B7066
BELLSIDE ROAD
North Linrigg
Linrigg Road
Newhouse
Premier Travel Inn
A775
Road
Biggar Rd
MOTHERWELL ROAD
A73
CARLISLE ROAD
South Lanridge
Wilsons Road
Goodockhill
Greenside
Biggar Road
Mossband
Tillan Burn
Biggar Road
Macinnes Drive
Cullion Way
McPhail Avenue
Henry Quadrant
Manse Vw
Hareshaw
Hareshaw Road
Greenhill Road
Brownhill
Newarthill
Mosshall
Street
Windyedge Road
CARLISLE
Fernieshaw
Fernieshaw Road
ROAD
Crosshill Dr
Park
Knowenoble St
Fraser Street
Queen's Crs
Scarhill
Corsehall St
Watersaugh Drive
Wilsgait St
Biggar Road
Tranent Place
Foundry Road
Parkside
A73
Cleland Road
ML1
Cleland Station
OMOA ROAD
Surgery
Cleland Primary School
MAIN ST
BELLSIDE ROAD
B7029
Cleland Hospital
Spindleside Road
Carlisle Road
Murdostoun Ter
North and South Road
Bellside
Stocks
Captain's W
Aberlady
Gray St
Gibb St
Chapel St
St Marys Primary School
Cleland
Lithgow Dr
Main St
Station
Ravenshill Drive
Ravenshall
Glen Orchy
Glen Rd
Noble
Logan Gdns
Sunnyside Road
Wishaw High
Swinstie
Swinstie Road
1 grid square represents 500 metres

G   H   J   87   K   L   M

82   83   84   85

1

Manse Road

Westfield

Roughdike   Muiredge and Jersy Road

Jersay

Muiredge and Jersy Road

2

Birniehill Road

3

Muiredge and Jersy Road

4

104

5

Newmill and Canthill Road

Hartwood Road

Homefarm Road

Ashgrove   Hartwood Road

Hartwood Station

Canthill

6   Hartw

Newmill Gdns

Hartwood Gardens

Penty

Hartwood Hospital

Foulburn Road

7   Bowhou or Lique

Bowho

Hill of Murdostoun

Shawstonfoot Road

Foulburn Road

Castlerigg

8

Murdostoun

Mill Road

Allan Bank

82   83   84   85

G   H   J   123   K   L   M

PO

Caider Rd

Coltness Avenue

Allan Street

Hawthorn Place

Springbank Road

Kingshi

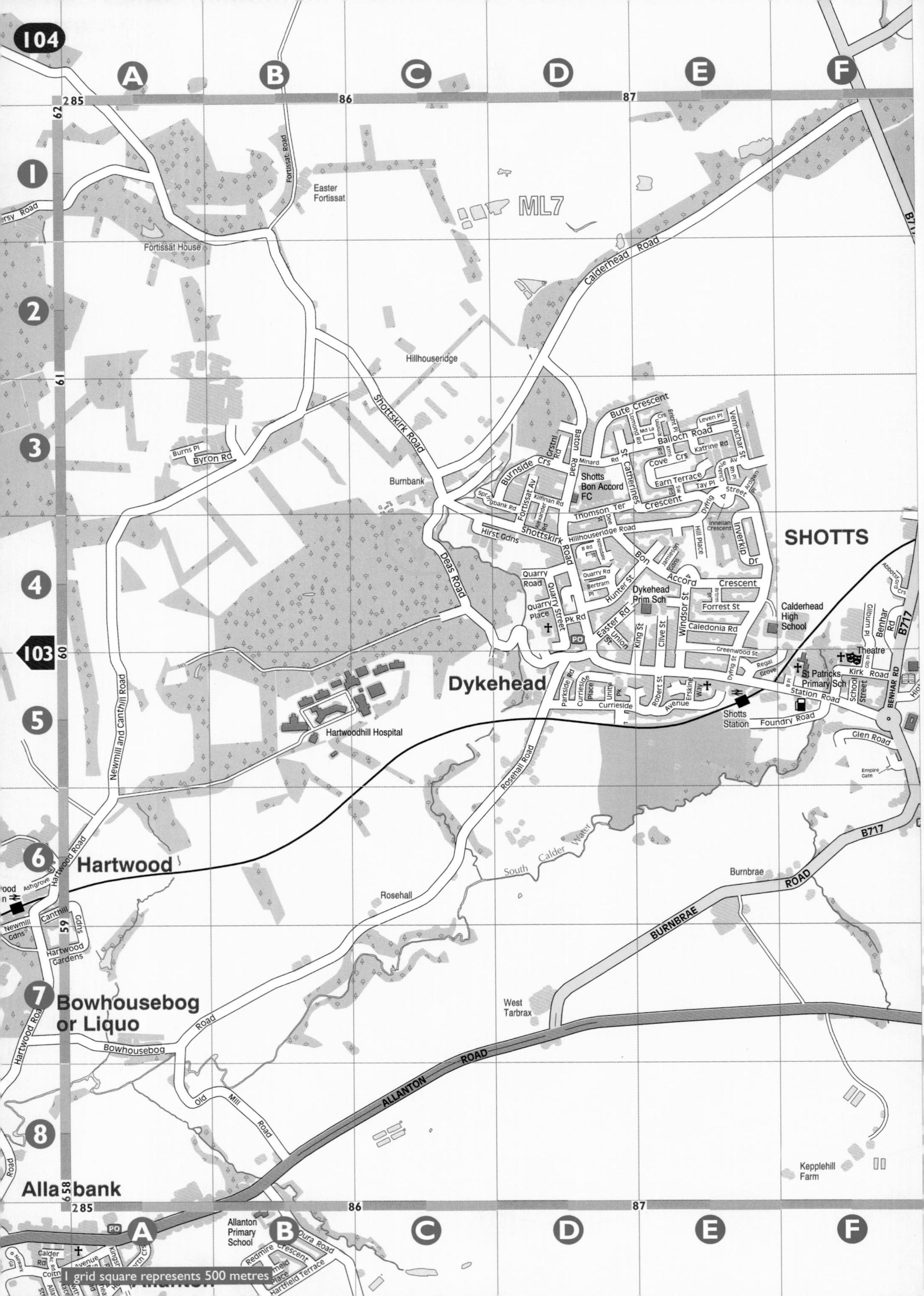

104
103
A
B
C
D
E
F
285
86
87
62
61
60
59
658
1
2
3
4
5
6
7
8
ML7
SHOTTS
Dykehead
Hartwood
Bowhousebog or Liquo
Allanbank
Easter Fortissat
Fortissat House
Fortissat Road
Calderhead Road
Hillhouseridge
Burnbank
Shottskirk Road
Deas Road
Newmill and Canthill Road
Burns Pl
Byron Rd
Bute Crescent
Balloch Road
Vennachar St
Katrine Rd
Cove Crs
Earn Terrace
Tay Pl
Minard Rd
St Catherines Crescent
Baton Road
Burnside Crs
Shotts Bon Accord FC
Thomson Ter
Springbank Rd
Fortissat Av
Kilfinan Rd
Hirst Gdns
Hillhouseridge Road
Dyfrig Street
Innellan Crescent
Hill Place
Inverkip Dr
Quarry Road
Quarry Place
Quarry Street
Quarry Rd
Bertram Pl
Hunter St
Bon Accord Crescent
Dykehead Prim Sch
Forrest St
Caledonia Rd
Windsor St
Clive St
King St
Easter Rd
Union St
Pk Rd
Greenwood St
Calderhead High School
Regal Grove
Theatre
St Patricks Primary Sch
Kirk Road
Station Road
School Street
Benhar Rd
BENHAR RD
B717
Shotts Station
Foundry Road
Glen Road
Empire Gate
Parkside Rd
Curriefside Place
Unity Pk
Curriefside Avenue
Robert St
Erskine Way
Hartwoodhill Hospital
Rosehall Road
Rosehall
South Calder Water
Burnbrae
BURNBRAE ROAD
West Tarbrax
ALLANTON ROAD
Hartwood Road
Ashgrove
Canthill Gdns
Newmill Gdns
Hartwood Gardens
Bowhousebog Road
Old Mill Road
Kepplehill Farm
Allanton Primary School
Redmire Crescent
Oura Road
Hartfield Terrace
Calder Rd
1 grid square represents 500 metres

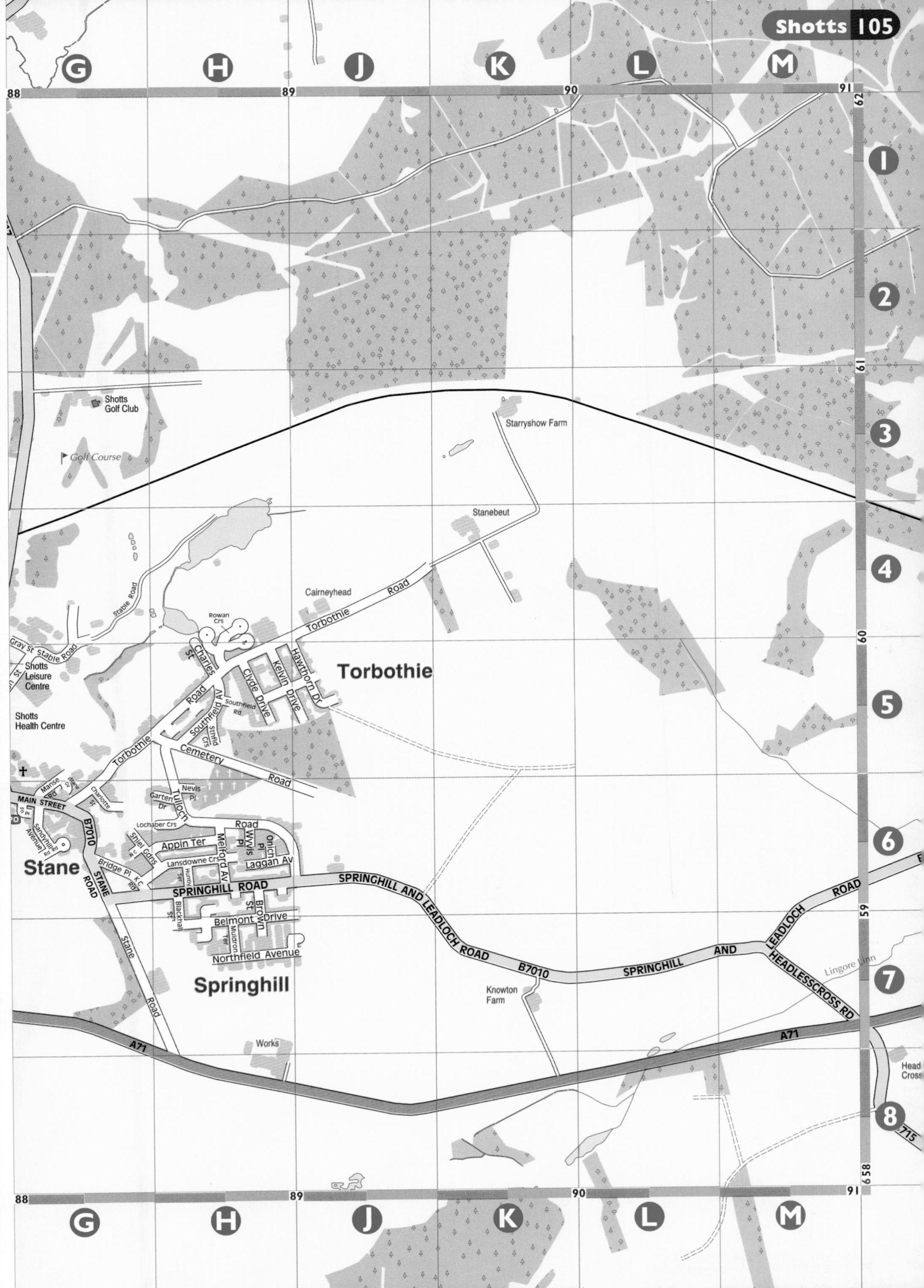

G H J K L M

88 89 90 91

62

1

2

Shotts
Golf Club

3

▶ *Golf Course*

Starryshow Farm

Stanebeut

61

4

Cairneyhead Road

Torbothie Road

Rowan
Crs

Gray St Stable Road

Stable Road

Charles St

Kelvin Drive

Hawthorn Dr

Clyde Drive

Southfield Av

Southfield Rd

Torbothie

60

5

Shotts
Leisure
Centre

Shotts
Health Centre

Road

Stmd Crs

Cemetery Road

Torbothie

Nevis
Pl

Manse
Rd

Charlotte

Garten
Dr

Tulloch Ct

Lochaber Crs

Shiel Gdns

Bridge Pl

K C

Stane

6

MAIN STREET

Sandyhill Rd

Avenue

B7010

STANE ROAD

Appin Ter

Lansdowne Cres

Melfort Av

Huntly Ter

Road

Wyvis Pl

Onich Pl

Laggan Av

SPRINGHILL AND LEADLOCH ROAD

SPRINGHILL AND

LEADLOCH ROAD

59

Springhill

SPRINGHILL ROAD

Blackhall St

Mugdon Ter

Belmont

Brown St

Drive

Northfield Avenue

B7010

HEADLESSCROSS RD

Lingore Linn

7

Stane Road

A71

Knowton
Farm

A71

Head
Cross

8

B7158

Works

658

88 89 90 91

G H J K L M

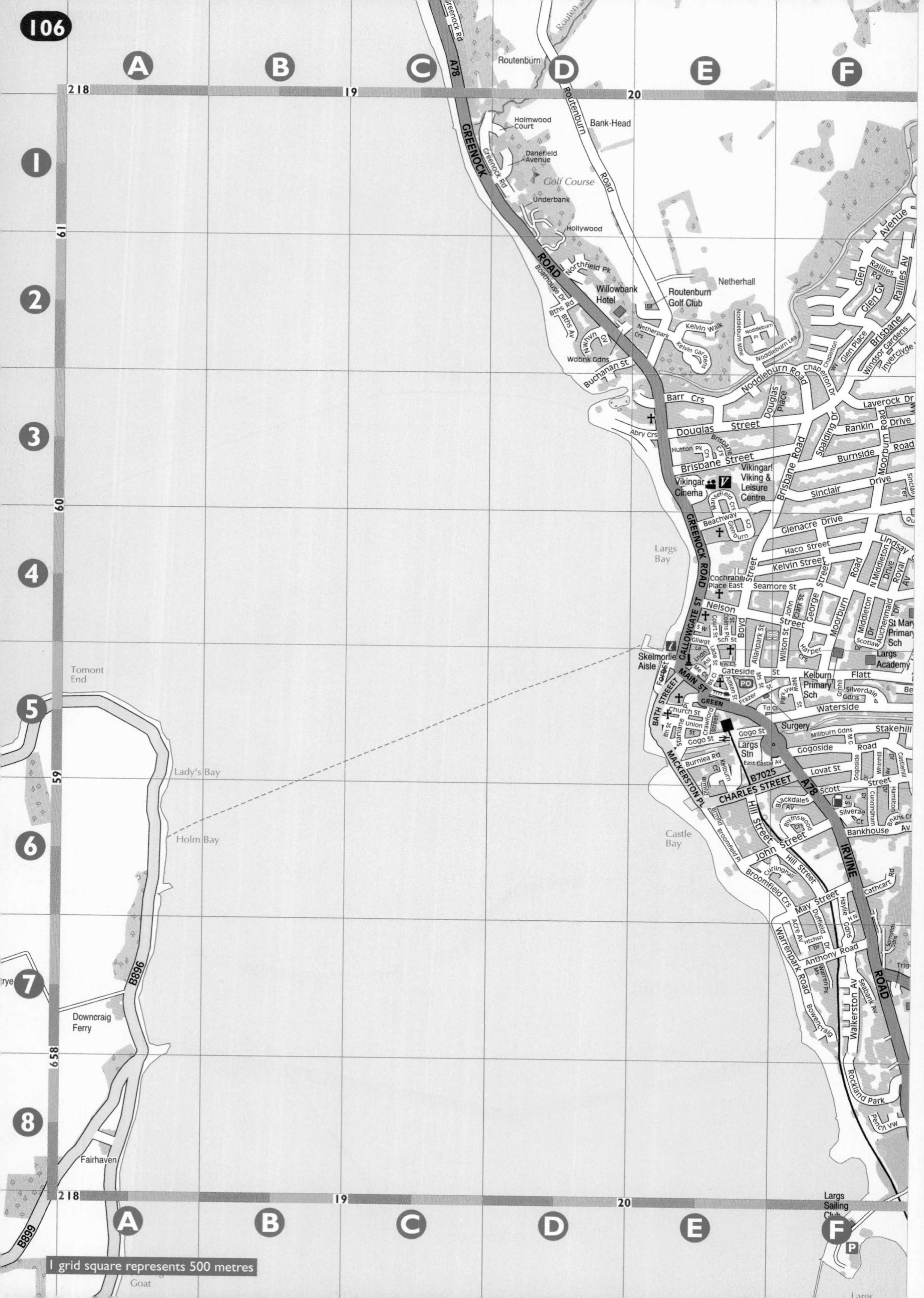

A B C D E F

218 19 20

61

60

59

658

I

2

3

4

5

6

7

8

Routenburn

A78

GREENOCK

Holmwood
Court

Bank-Head

Danefield
Avenue

Golf Course

Routenburn Road

Underbank

Hollywood

ROAD

Greenock Rd

Northfield Pk

Willowbank
Hotel

Routenburn
Golf Club

Netherhall

Boathouse Dr

Bths Rd

Bths Av

Hvn

Hvn

Netherpark
Crs

Kelvin Walk

Kelvin Gardens

Noddleburn Msn

Noddleburn Les

Netherhall

Glen

Glen Gv

Railies Rd

Railies Av

Avenue

Brisbane

Windsor Gardens

Inverclyde

W Glen Place

Chapelton

Wdbnk Gdns

Buchanan St

Barr Crs

Noddleburn Road

Noddleburn Pl

Douglas Place

Laverock Dr

Rankin

Abry Crs

Douglas Street

Brisbane Rd

Spalding Dr

Burnside Road

Moorburn Road

Drive

Hutton Pk

Brisbane Street

Sinclair

Drive

Sinclair

Largs
Bay

GREENOCK ROAD

Brisbane
Vikingar!
Cinema

Vikingar!
Viking &
Leisure
Centre

Beachway

Glen

Haco Street

Glenacre Drive

Lindsay

Kelvin Street

N Middleton Dr

Royal Av

Harper

Cochrane
Place East

Nelson

Seamore St

George

John
Street

Street

Moorburn

Middleton
Dr

Auchenmaid

St Mary
Primary
Sch

GALLOWGATE ST

Boyd

Wilson Dr

Allanpark St

Scotlaw

Drive

Largs
Academy

Skelmorlie
Aisle

Forbes

MAIN ST

Gateside

Kelburn
Primary
Sch

Flatt

Silverdale
Gdns

Largs
Be

Tomont
End

BATH STREET

PO

New

Frazer

Waterside

Church St

GREEN

Gogo St

Surgery

Millburn Gdns

Stakehill
Road

Lady's Bay

Station

Union St

Gogo St

Largs
Stn

Burnlea Rd

East Castle Av

Gogoside

Lovat St

Warren

Holm Bay

MACKERSTON PL

B7025

CHARLES STREET

Blackdales
Av

Scott

Street

Bankhouse

Hill Street

Bythswood

Duffield

Silverae
Ct

Cunningham

Castle
Bay

John

Street

Curlinghall

IRVINE

Broomfield Crs

May Street

Hill Street

Broomfield Rd

Cathcart

Frye

Downcraig
Ferry

Warrenpark Road

Acre Av

Haylie Gdns

Seabank AV

ROAD

Anthony Road

Walkerston AV

Bowencraig

Rockland Park

Fairhaven

B899

Goat

A B C D E F

218 19 20

Largs
Sailing
Club

P

1 grid square represents 500 metres

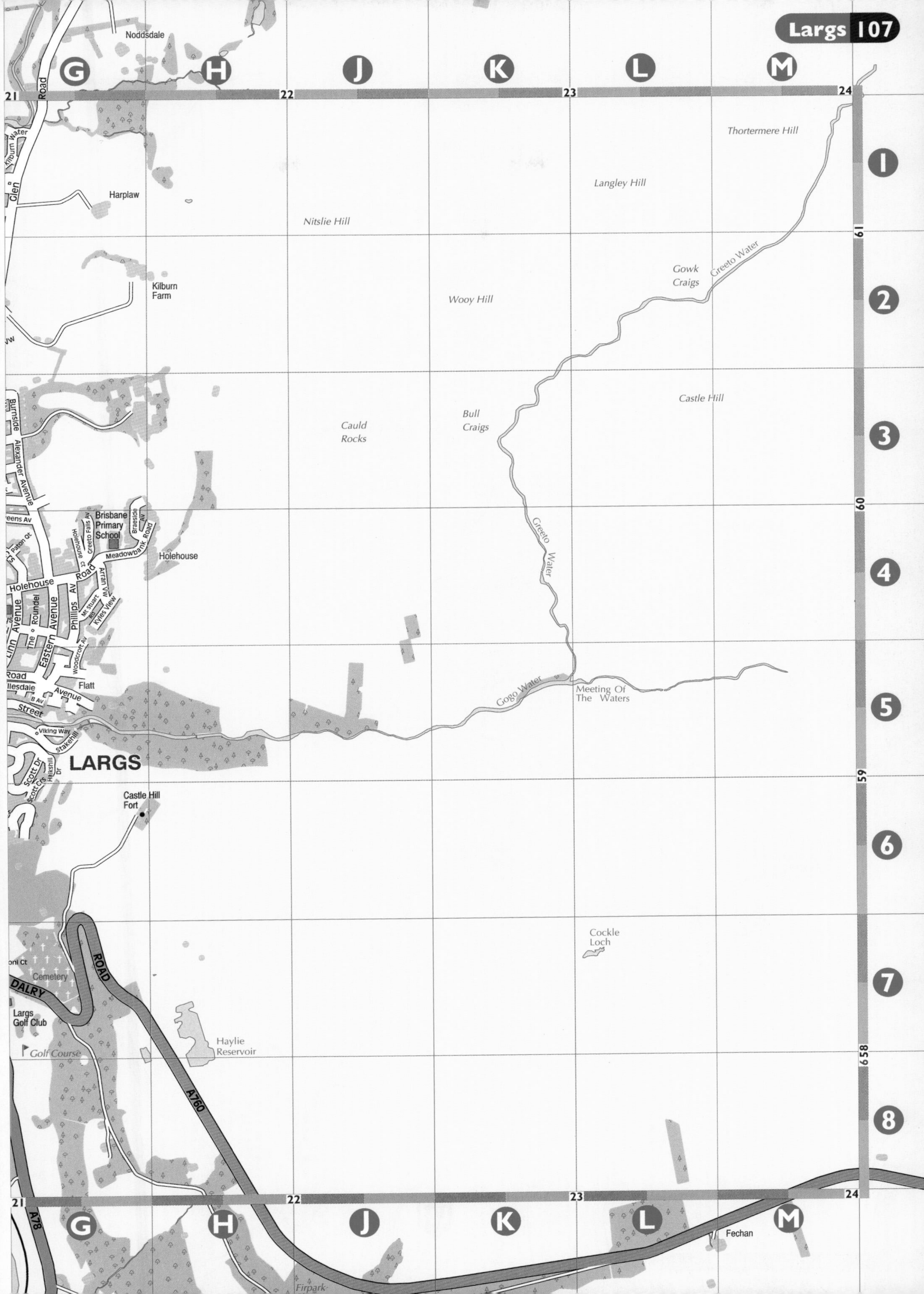

G   H   J   K   L   M

21   22   23   24

I

2

3

4

5

6

7

8

19

60

59

658

Noddsdale

Thortermere Hill

Langley Hill

Harplaw

Nitslie Hill

Gowk Craigs

Creeto Water

Kilburn Farm

Wooy Hill

Castle Hill

Burnside

Alexander Avenue

Cauld Rocks

Bull Craigs

Greens Av

Paton Ct

Brisbane Primary School

Braeside

Meadowbank Road

Holehouse

Creeto Water

Holehouse Ct

Mt Stuart

Arran Av

Phillips Av

Woodcroft Av

Kyles View

Holehouse Avenue

The Roundel

Eastern Avenue

Linn Avenue

Flatt

B Av

Avenue

llesdale Road

Gogo Water

Meeting Of The Waters

Street

Viking Way

Stravenhill

Scott Dr

Scott Cres

Halkhill Dr

LARGS

Castle Hill Fort

Cockle Loch

oni Ct

Cemetery

ROAD

DALRY

Largs Golf Club

Haylie Reservoir

Golf Course

A760

A78

Fechan

G   H   J   K   L   M

21   22   23   24

Firpark

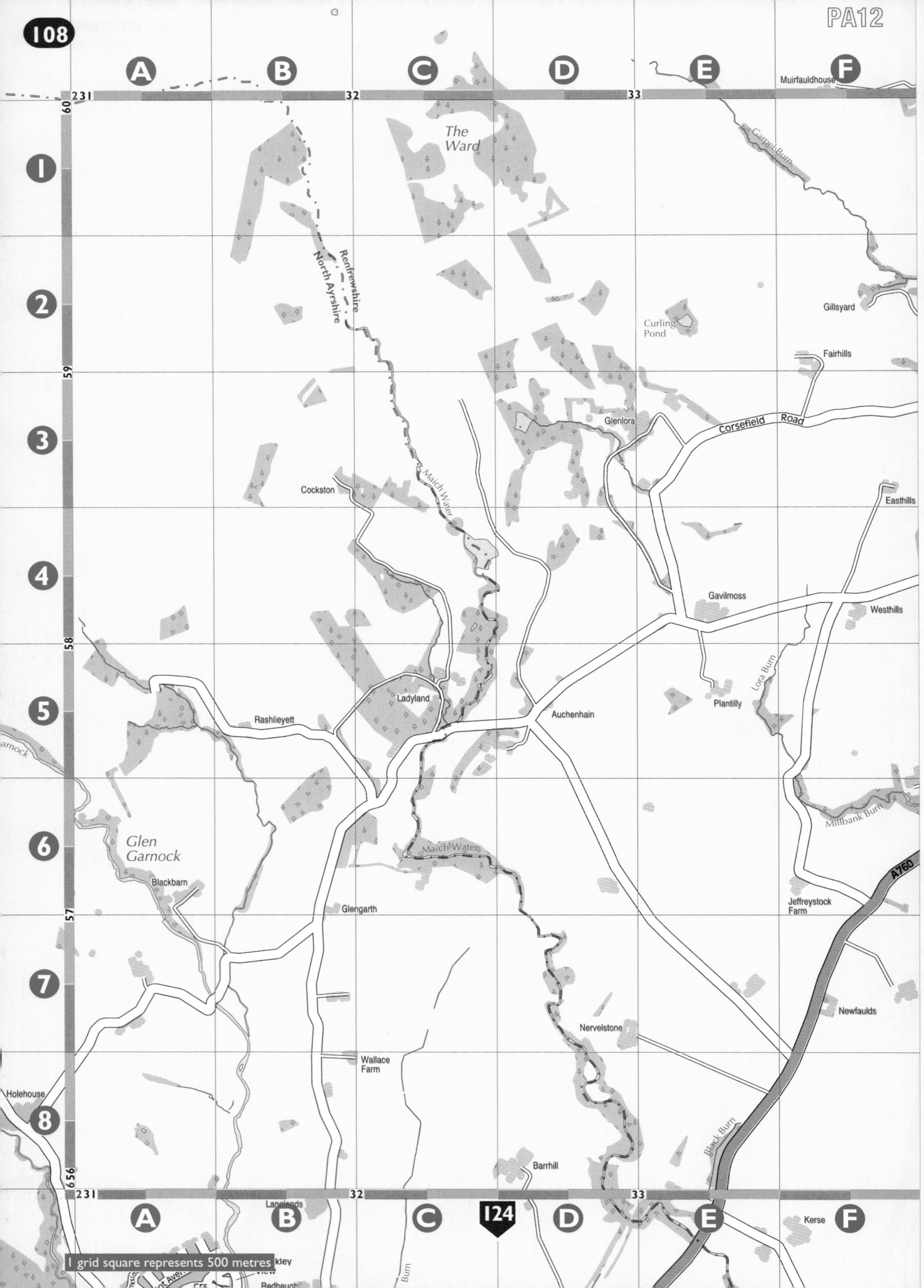
A
B
C
D
E
F
231
32
33
Muirfauldhouse
The Ward
Carpel Burn
Renfrewshire
North Ayrshire
Curling Pond
Gillsyard
Fairhills
Glenlora
Corsefield Road
Cockston
Maich Water
Easthills
Gavilmoss
Westhills
Lora Burn
Ladyland
Plantilly
Rashlieyett
Auchenhain
Millbank Burn
Glen Garnock
Blackbarn
Glengarth
Jeffreystock Farm
A760
Newfaulds
Nervelstone
Wallace Farm
Holehouse
Black Burn
Barrhill
Langlands
Kerse
Burn
Redheugh
1
2
3
4
5
6
7
8
60
59
58
57
656

124

1 grid square represents 500 metres

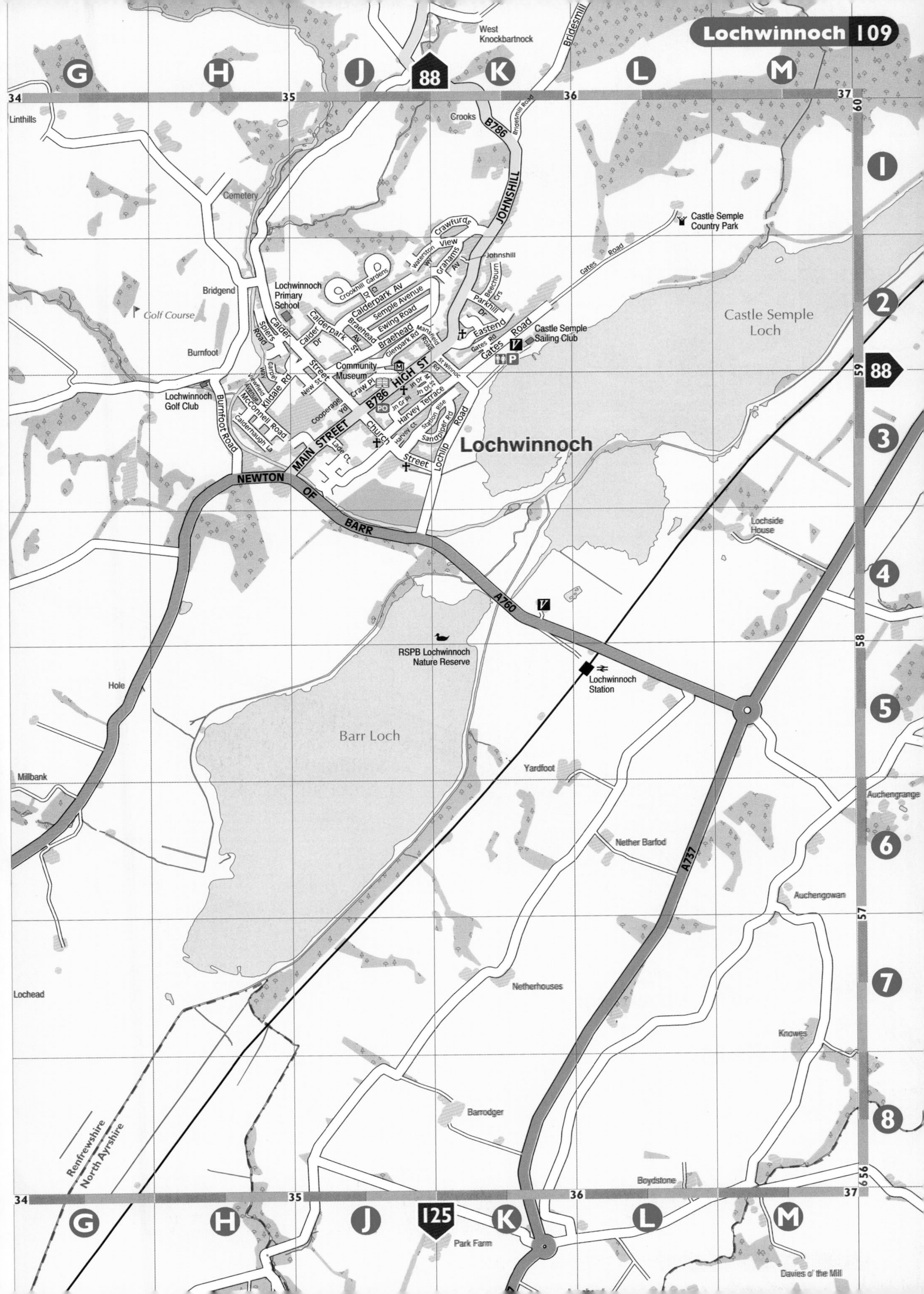

West Knockbartnock

Linthills

Crooks

B786

Bridesmill Road

JOHNSHILL

Castle Semple Country Park

Cemetery

Crawfurds View

Bridgend

Golf Course

Waterton

Crookhill Gardens

Lochwinnoch Primary School

Calderpark Av

Grahams Av

Johnshill

Semple Avenue

Calderpark Av

Braehead

Beechburn Crs

Burnfoot

Calder Dr

Ewing Road

Parkhill

Castle Semple Loch

Calder Street

Braehead

Glenpark Rd

Eastend

Gates Road

Castle Semple Sailing Club

Lochwinnoch Golf Club

Spiers Road

Calders Road

Kildale Rd

New Street

Community Museum

Craw Pl

Gates Rd

Cates Road

Burnfoot Road

McConnell Road

Caldernaugh La

Cooperage Yd

HIGH ST

B786

PO

Harvey Terrace

St Winnoc

Jn Cr Pl

Jn Dr St

Harvey Pl

School Brae

Sandpiper Rd

Lochlip Road

Lochwinnoch

MAIN STREET

Lade

Church Street

NEWTON

OF

BARR

A760

Lochside House

Hole

RSPB Lochwinnoch Nature Reserve

Barr Loch

Lochwinnoch Station

Millbank

Yardfoot

Auchengrange

Lochead

Nether Barfod

Auchengowan

A737

Netherhouses

Knowes

Renfrewshire / North Ayrshire

Barrodger

Boydstone

125

Park Farm

Davies o' the Mill

G H J K L M
I 2 3 88 4 5 6 7 8
60 59 58 57 656
34 35 88 36 37

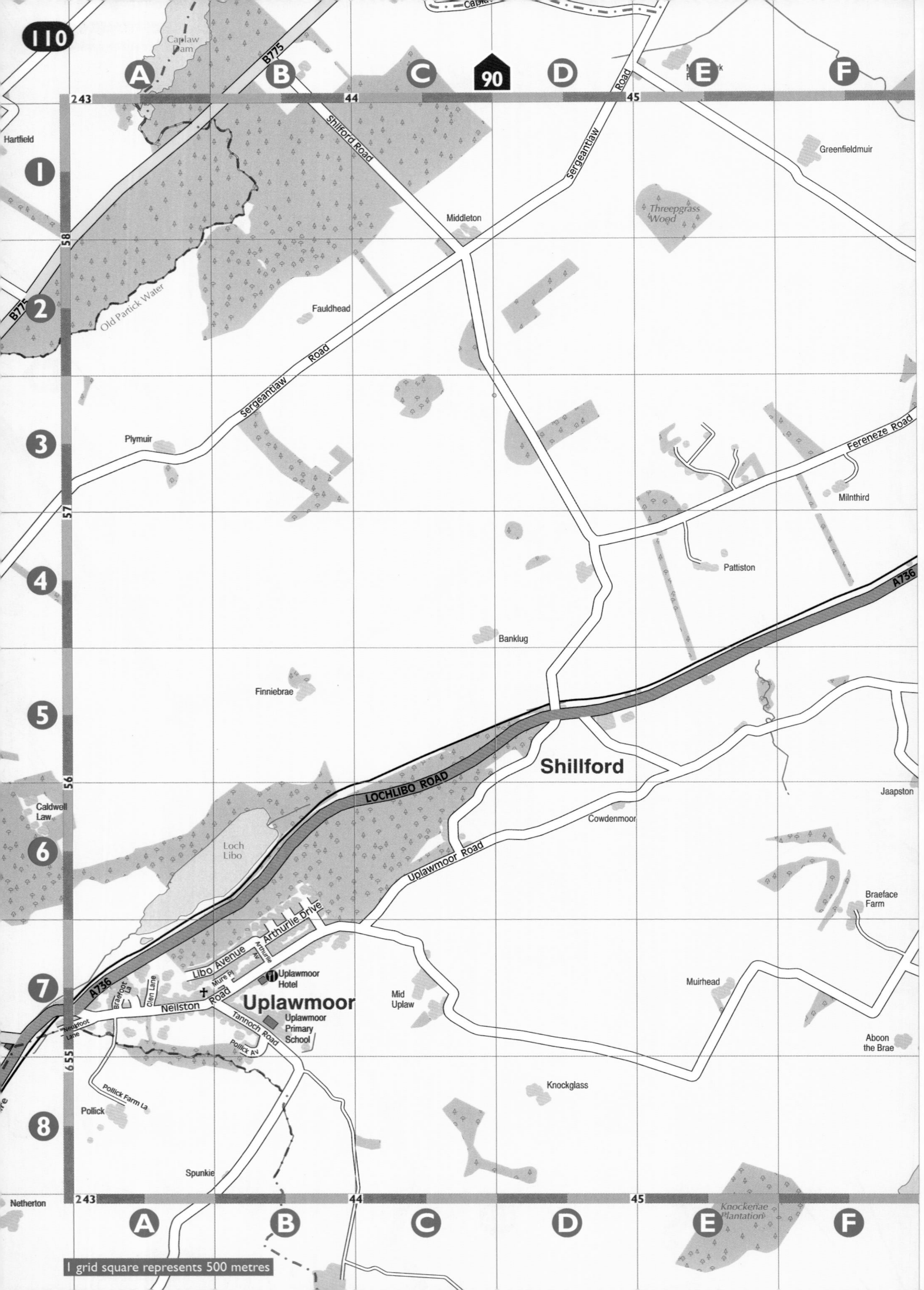

90

A B C D E F

243 44 45

Hartfield

1

58

B775

2

Caplaw Dam

Old Partick Water

Shilford Road

Middleton

Sergeantlaw Road

Threepgrass Wood

Greenfieldmuir

Fauldhead

3

57

Plymuir

Sergeantlaw Road

Fereneze Road

Milnthird

4

Pattiston

A736

Banklug

Finniebrae

5

56

Shillford

Jaapston

Caldwell Law

6

Loch Libo

LOCHLIBO ROAD

Uplawmoor Road

Cowdenmoor

Braeface Farm

7

A736

Libo Avenue

Arthurlie Drive

Arthurlie Av

Mure Pl

Glen Lane

Brigurcot La

Neilston Road

Uplawmoor Hotel

Uplawmoor

Mid Uplaw

Muirhead

Aboon the Brae

Tannoch Road

Uplawmoor Primary School

Pollick Av

Knockglass

8

655

Neilsroot Lane

Pollick Farm La

Pollick

Spunkie

Knockenae Plantation

Netherton

243 44 45

A B C D E F

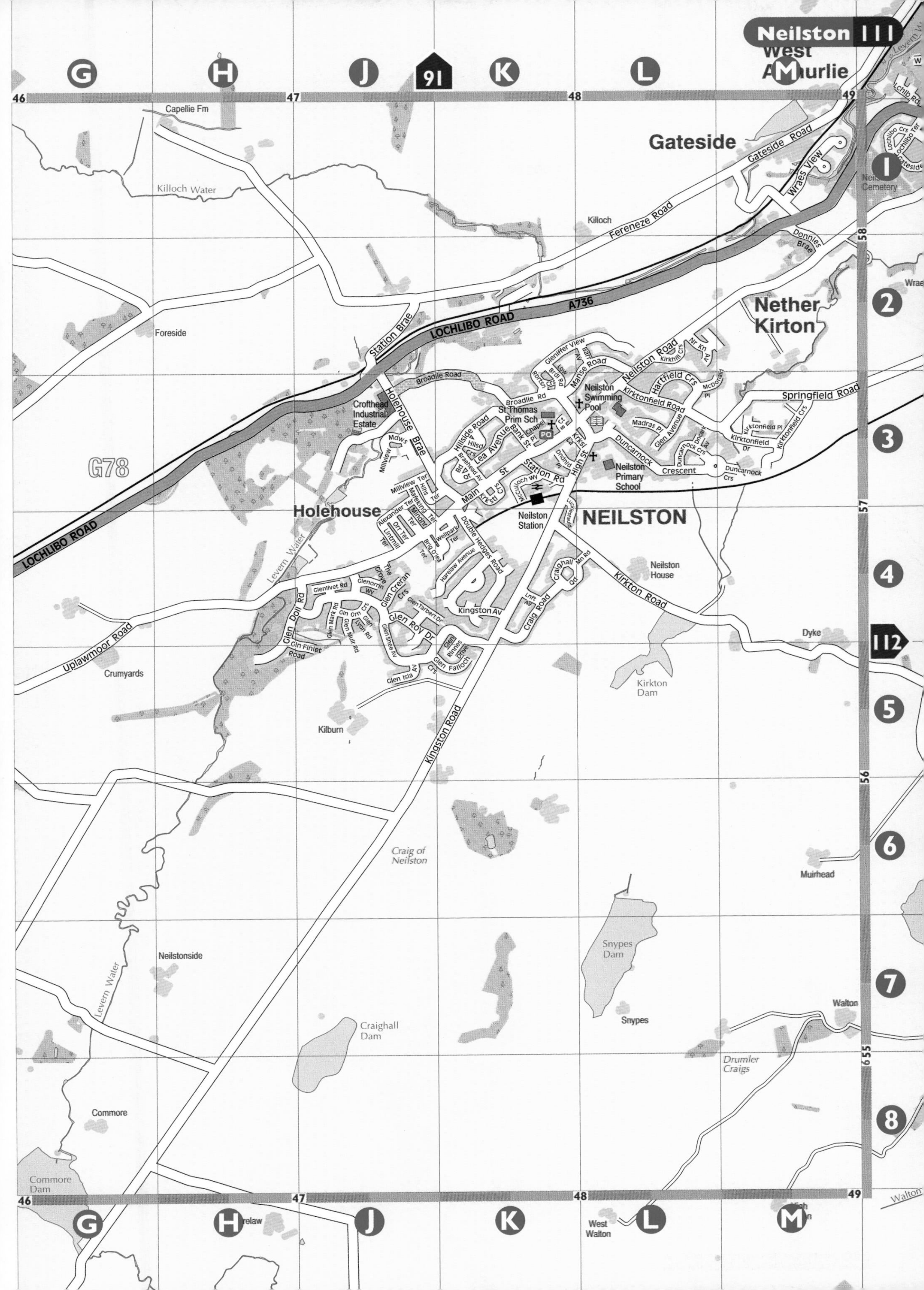
91
112
G
H
J
K
L
M
1
2
3
4
5
6
7
8
46
47
48
49
58
57
56
655
West Arthurlie
Gateside
Gateside Road
Wraes View
Neilston Cemetery
Capellie Fm
Killoch Water
Killoch
Fereneze Road
Donnies Brae
Nether Kirton
Station Brae
LOCHLIBO ROAD
A736
Foreside
Broadlie Road
Crofthead Industrial Estate
Holehouse Brae
G78
St Thomas Prim Sch
Neilston Swimming Pool
Neilston Road
Manse Road
Gleniffer View
Harfield Crs
Kirktonfield Road
Springfield Road
Madras Pl
Glen Avenue
Duncarnock Crescent
Kirktonfield Dr
Kirktonfield Crs
Duncarnock Crs
Neilston Primary School
Hillside Road
Lea Avenue
Bank St
Station Rd
High St
Main St
Holehouse
Neilston Station
NEILSTON
Millview Ter
Mafeking Ter
Alexander Ter
Orr Ter
Lintmill Ter
Wellpark Ter
Double Hedges Road
Harelaw Avenue
Kingston Av
Craig Road
Craighall Qd
Levern Water
Kirkton Road
Neilston House
Glenlivet Rd
Glenorrin Wy
The Grove
Glen Creran Crs
Glen Doll Rd
Glen Mark Rd
Glen Muir Rd
Glen Tarbert Dr
Glen Roy Dr
Glen Finlet Road
Glen Rinnes Drive
Glen Falloch Crs
Glen Isla Av
Glen Shee Av
Uplawmoor Road
Crumyards
Kilburn
Kingston Road
Dyke
Kirkton Dam
Craig of Neilston
Muirhead
Snypes Dam
Snypes
Neilstonside
Levern Water
Craighall Dam
Walton
Drumler Craigs
Commore
Commore Dam
West Walton

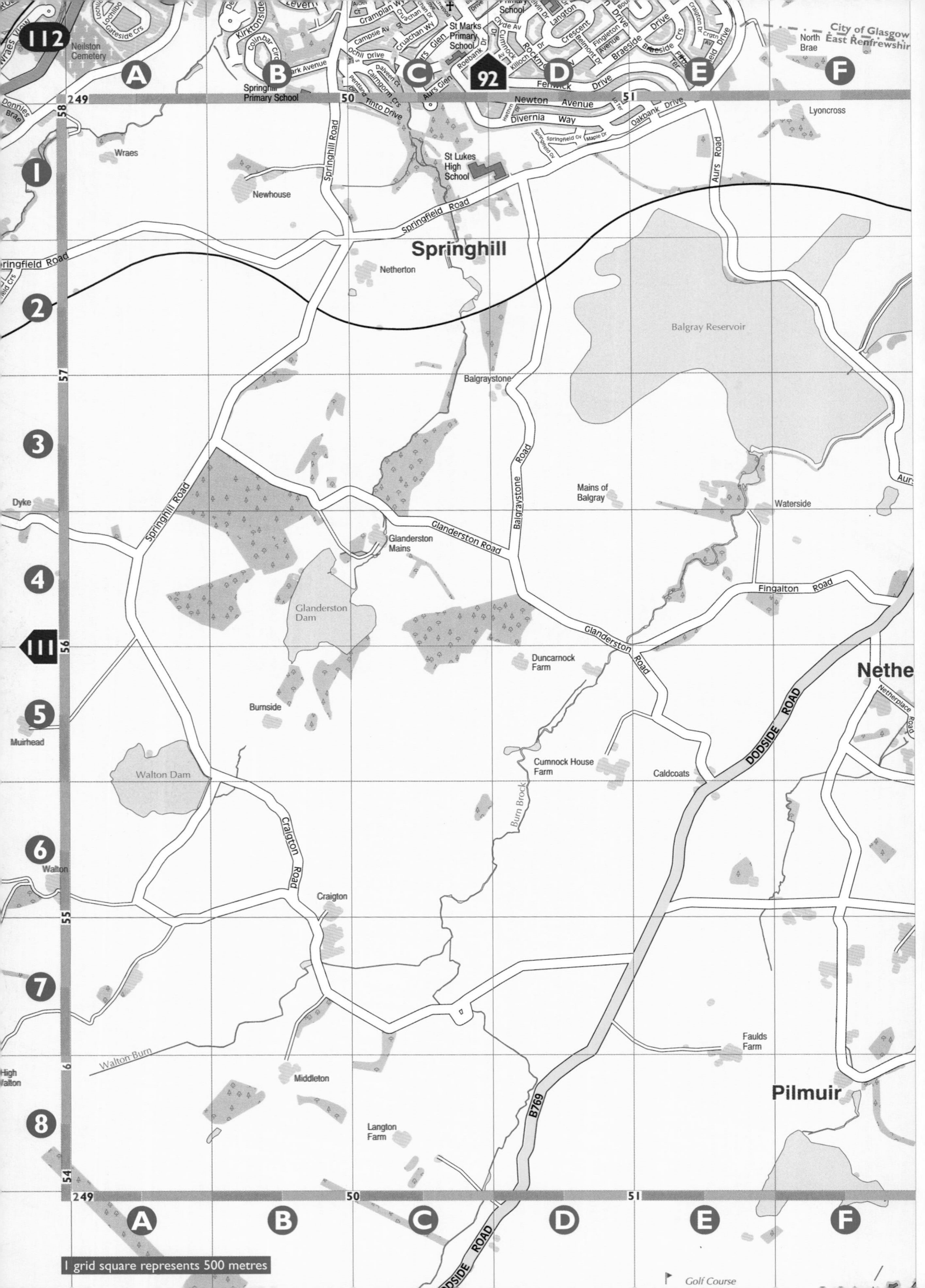

112
92
111
City of Glasgow
East Renfrewshire
Neilston Cemetery
Springhill Primary School
St Marks Primary School
St Lukes High School
Springhill
Springhill Road
Springfield Road
Newton Avenue
Divernia Way
Fenwick Drive
Oakbank Drive
Aurs Road
Lyoncross
North Brae
Wraes
Newhouse
Netherton
Balgray Reservoir
Balgraystone
Balgraystone Road
Mains of Balgray
Waterside
Dyke
Glanderston Road
Glanderston Mains
Glanderston Dam
Fingalton Road
Duncarnock Farm
Burnside
Muirhead
Walton Dam
Cumnock House Farm
Caldcoats
Burn Brock
DODSIDE ROAD
Craigton Road
Craigton
Walton
Walton Burn
Faulds Farm
High Walton
Middleton
Pilmuir
Langton Farm
B769
Netherplace Road
Golf Course
1 grid square represents 500 metres

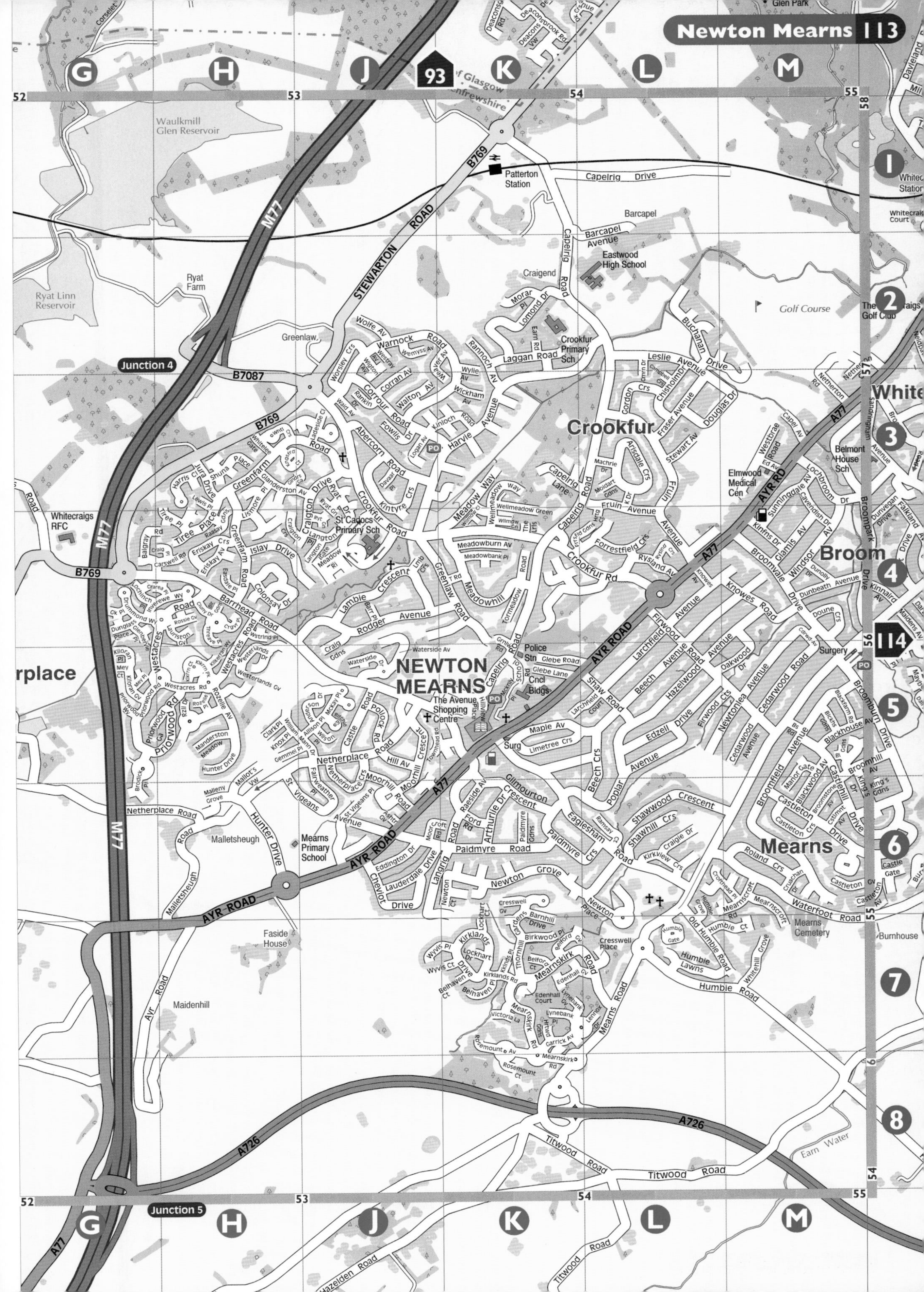
NEWTON MEARNS
Crookfur
Broom
Mearns
Junction 4
Junction 5
M77
A77
AYR ROAD
STEWARTON ROAD
B769
B7087
A726
Patterton Station
Capelrig Drive
Barcapel
Eastwood High School
Craigend
Crookfur Primary Sch
Waulkmill Glen Reservoir
Ryat Linn Reservoir
Ryat Farm
Greenlaw
Whitecraigs RFC
St Cadocs Primary Sch
The Avenue Shopping Centre
Police Stn
Cncl Bldgs
Mearns Primary School
Malletsheugh
Faside House
Maidenhill
Mearns Cemetery
Elmwood Medical Cen
Belmont House Sch
Golf Course
The Whitecraigs Golf Club
Surgery
Titwood Road
Humbie Road
Earn Water
Hazelden Road
Netherplace Road
Hunter Drive
Barrhead Road
Crookfur Rd
Mearns Road
Broompark Drive
Waterfoot Road
93
114

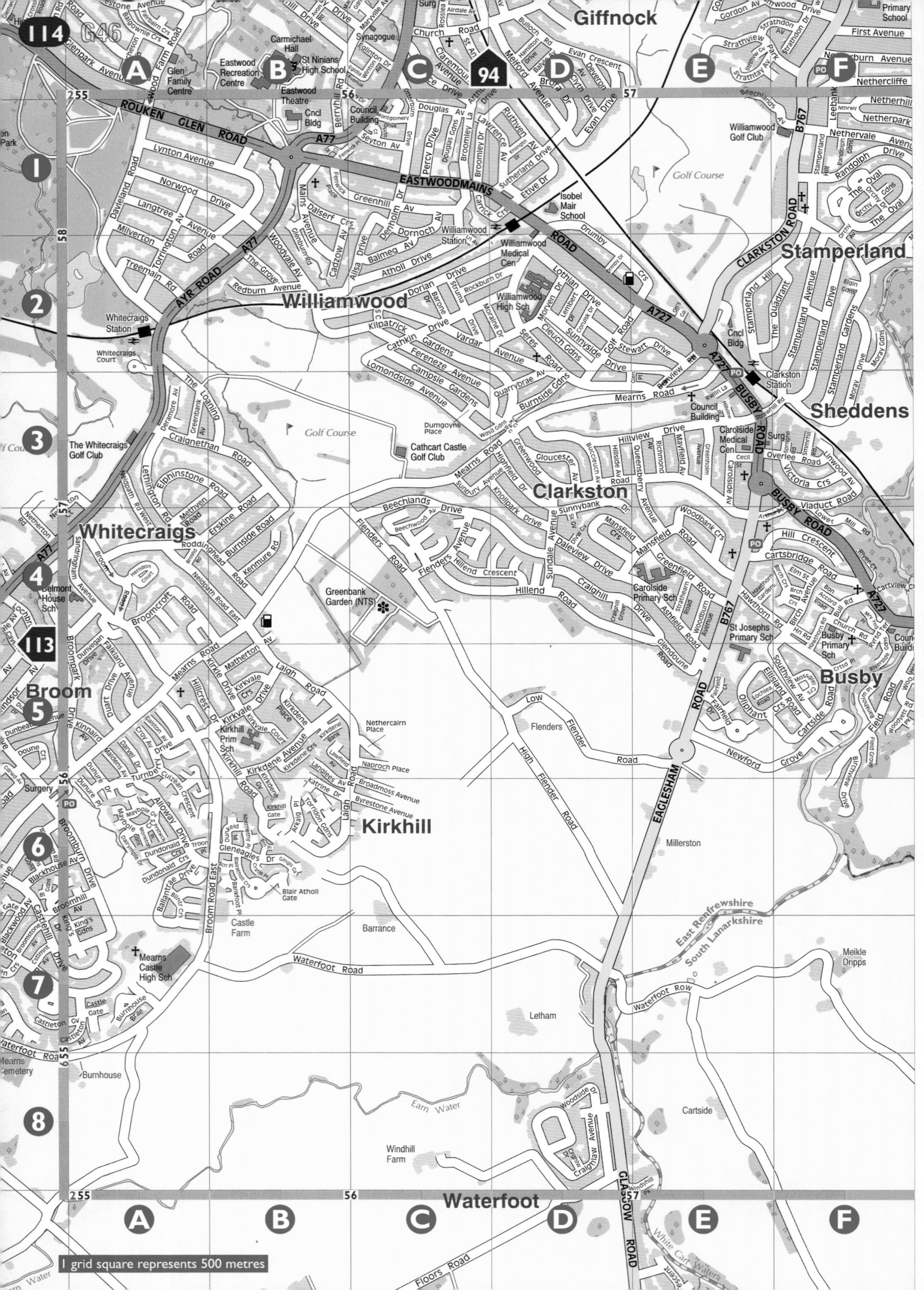

114
G46
94
113
Giffnock
Williamwood
Stamperland
Sheddens
Clarkston
Whitecraigs
Broom
Kirkhill
Busby
Waterfoot
A
B
C
D
E
F
1
2
3
4
5
6
7
8
255
56
57
58
655
ROUKEN GLEN ROAD
EASTWOODMAINS ROAD
AYR ROAD
CLARKSTON ROAD
BUSBY ROAD
EAGLESHAM ROAD
GLASGOW ROAD
A77
A727
B767
Eastwood Recreation Centre
St Ninians High School
Eastwood Theatre
Carmichael Hall
Glen Family Centre
Synagogue
Council Building
Cncl Bldg
Williamwood Station
Williamwood Medical Cen
Williamwood High Sch
Isobel Mair School
Whitecraigs Station
Whitecraigs Court
The Whitecraigs Golf Club
Golf Course
Cathcart Castle Golf Club
Williamwood Golf Club
Dumgoyne Place
Greenbank Garden (NTS)
Clarkston Station
Carolside Medical Cen
Carolside Primary Sch
St Josephs Primary Sch
Busby Primary Sch
Kirkhill Prim Sch
Mearns Castle High Sch
Belmont House Sch
Nethercairn Place
Castle Farm
Barrance
Millerston
Letham
Meikle Dripps
Burnhouse
Windhill Farm
Cartside
Flenders
Earn Water
White Cart Water
East Renfrewshire
South Lanarkshire
Waterfoot Road
Waterfoot Row
Floors Road
Low Flender Road
High Flender Road
Newford Grove
Mearns Road
Broom Road East
Broomburn Drive
Broompark Drive
Stamperland Gardens
Stamperland Avenue
Stamperland Drive
Stamperland Hill
The Quadrant
The Oval
Nethervale Avenue
Netherhill
Netherpark
Nethercliffe
First Avenue
Primary School
1 grid square represents 500 metres

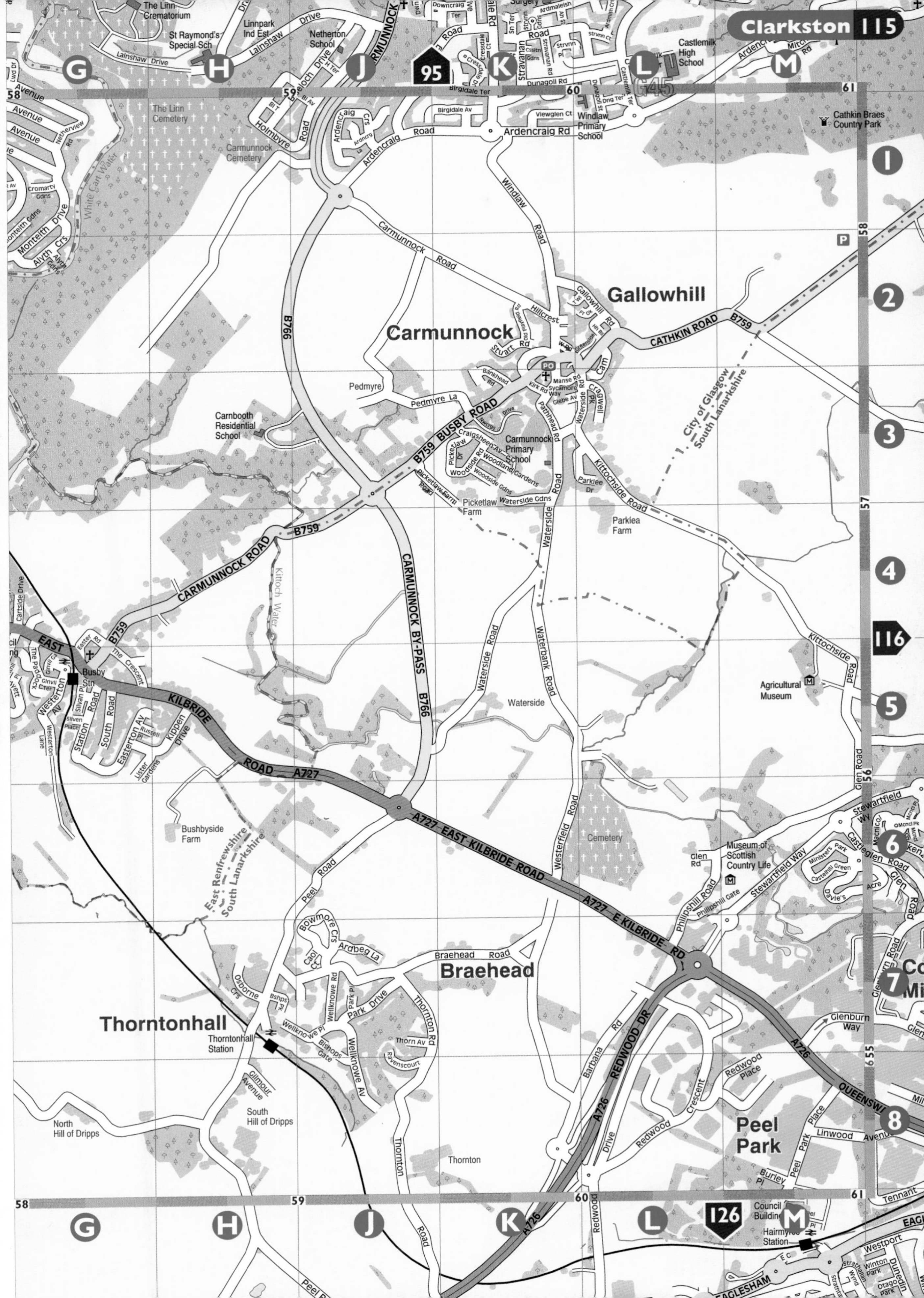

Carmunnock
Gallowhill
Braehead
Thorntonhall
Peel Park
Pedmyre
Waterside
Thornton
North Hill of Dripps
South Hill of Dripps
Bushbyside Farm
Picketlaw Farm
Parklea Farm
Carnbooth Residential School
Carmunnock Primary School
Windlaw Primary School
Castlemilk High School
Netherton School
St Raymond's Special Sch
The Linn Crematorium
Linnpark Ind Est
The Linn Cemetery
Carmunnock Cemetery
Cemetery
Cathkin Braes Country Park
Agricultural Museum
Museum of Scottish Country Life
Thorntonhall Station
Busby Stn
Hairmyres Station
Council Buildings
City of Glasgow
South Lanarkshire
East Renfrewshire
South Lanarkshire
B759 BUSBY ROAD
CATHKIN ROAD B759
CARMUNNOCK ROAD B759
CARMUNNOCK BY-PASS B766
B766
A727 EAST KILBRIDE ROAD
A727 E KILBRIDE RD
EAST KILBRIDE ROAD A727
A726
REDWOOD DR
QUEENSWAY
Carmunnock Road
Windlaw Road
Ardencraig Road
Ardencraig Rd
Waterside Road
Waterbank Road
Westerfield Road
Kittochside Road
Kittochside Road
Peel Road
Thornton Road
Thornton Rd
Braehead Road
Philipshill Road
Philipshill Gate
Stewartfield Way
Glen Road
Barbana Rd
Redwood Crescent
Redwood Place
Redwood Drive
Peel Park Place
Linwood Avenue
Burley Pl
Wellknowe Rd
Wellknowe Av
Park Drive
Bowmore Crs
Ardbeg La
Osborne Crs
Gilmour Avenue
Kittoch Water
White Cart Water
95
116
126
G H J K L M
1 2 3 4 5 6 7 8
58 59 60 61
55 56 57 58

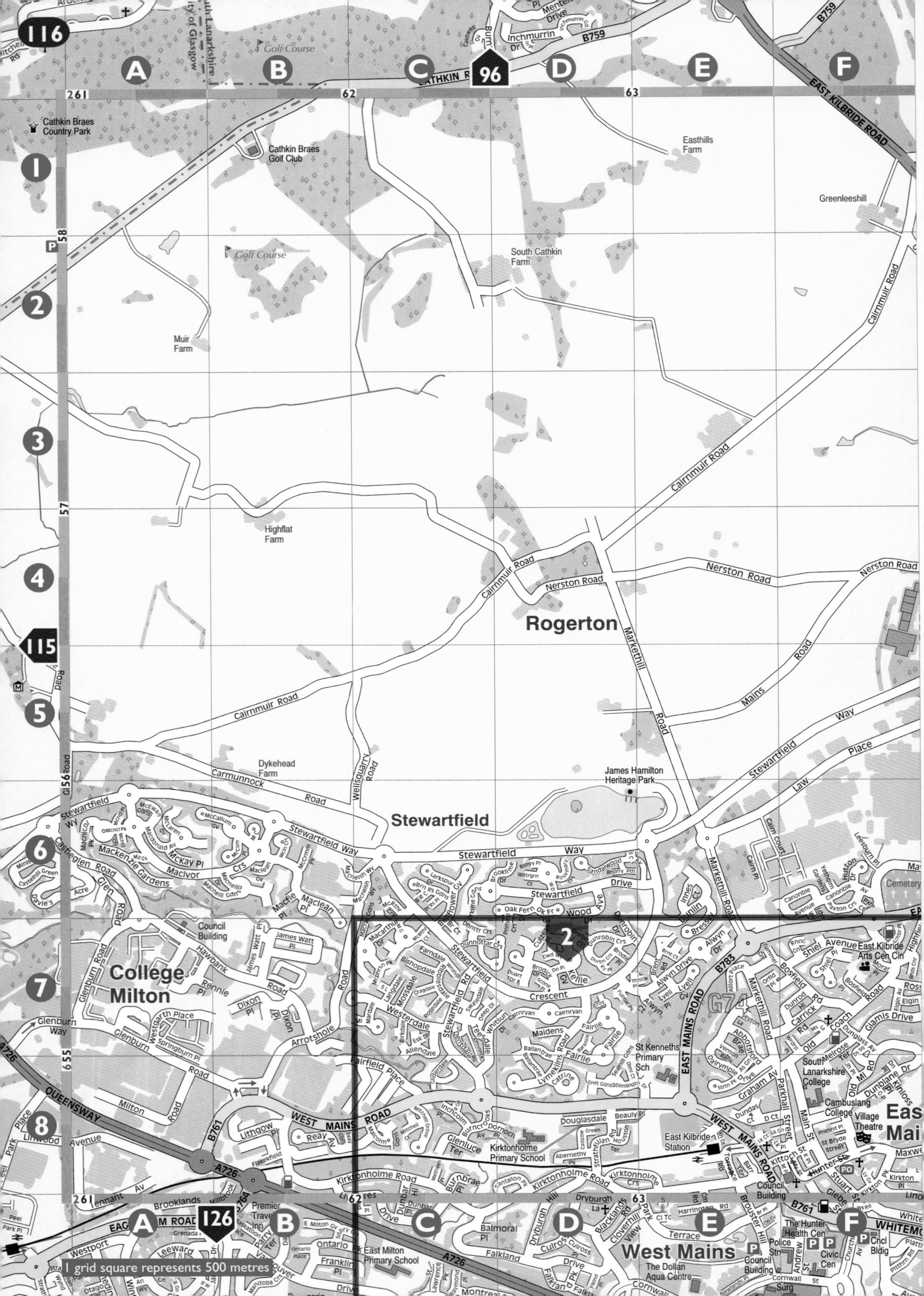
116
A
B
C
D
E
F
Golf Course
CATHKIN RD
96
B759
EAST KILBRIDE ROAD
Cathkin Braes Country Park
Cathkin Braes Golf Club
Easthills Farm
Greenleeshill
South Cathkin Farm
Muir Farm
Cairnmuir Road
Highflat Farm
Nerston Road
Rogerton
Markethill Road
Mains Road
115
Dykehead Farm
Carmunnock Road
Wellsquarry Road
James Hamilton Heritage Park
Stewartfield
Stewartfield Way
Law Place
Stewartfield Drive
Council Building
College Milton
Hawbank Road
Glenburn Road
Arrotshole Road
Westerdale
Crescent
St Kenneths Primary Sch
EAST MAINS ROAD
B783
WEST MAINS ROAD
Kirktonholme Road
Kirktonholme Primary School
East Kilbride Station
South Lanarkshire College
Cambuslang College
East Kilbride Arts Cen Cin
Village Theatre
Cemetery
QUEENSWAY
A726
B761
Milton Road
Premier Travel Inn
126
East Milton Primary School
Balmoral Pl
West Mains
The Dollan Aqua Centre
The Hunter Health Cen
Civic Cen
Police Stn
WHITEMOSS
1 grid square represents 500 metres
261
62
63
58
57
56
655

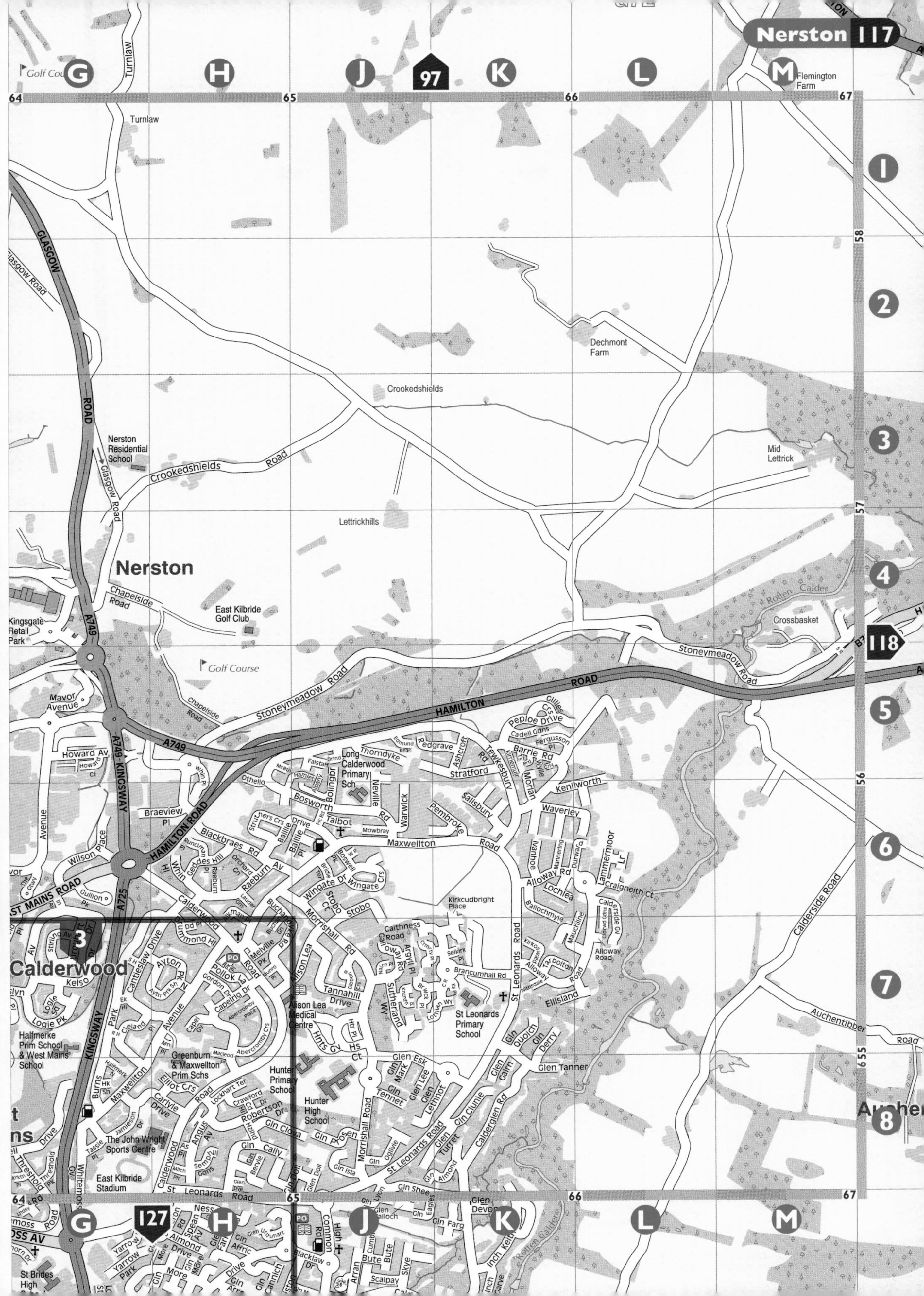
Nerston
Calderwood
Turnlaw
Flemington Farm
Dechmont Farm
Crookedshields
Mid Lettrick
Lettrickhills
Crossbasket
Nerston Residential School
East Kilbride Golf Club
Golf Course
Kingsgate Retail Park
GLASGOW ROAD
Glasgow Road
Crookedshields Road
Chapelside Road
Stoneymeadow Road
HAMILTON ROAD
A749
KINGSWAY
A725
EAST MAINS ROAD
Rotten Calder
Calderside Road
Auchentibber Road
Long Calderwood Primary Sch
Kirkcudbright Place
St Leonards Primary School
St Leonards Road
Alison Lea Medical Centre
Hunter Primary School
Hunter High School
Halfmerke Prim School & West Mains School
Greenburn & Maxwellton Prim Schs
The John Wright Sports Centre
East Kilbride Stadium
St Brides High
Maxwellton Road
Morrishall Road
Calderwood Road
Caithness Road
Brancumhall Rd
Alloway Road
Glen Tanner
Calderglen Rd
97
118
127
3
G H J K L M
64 65 66 67
I 2 3 4 5 6 7 8
58 57 56 655

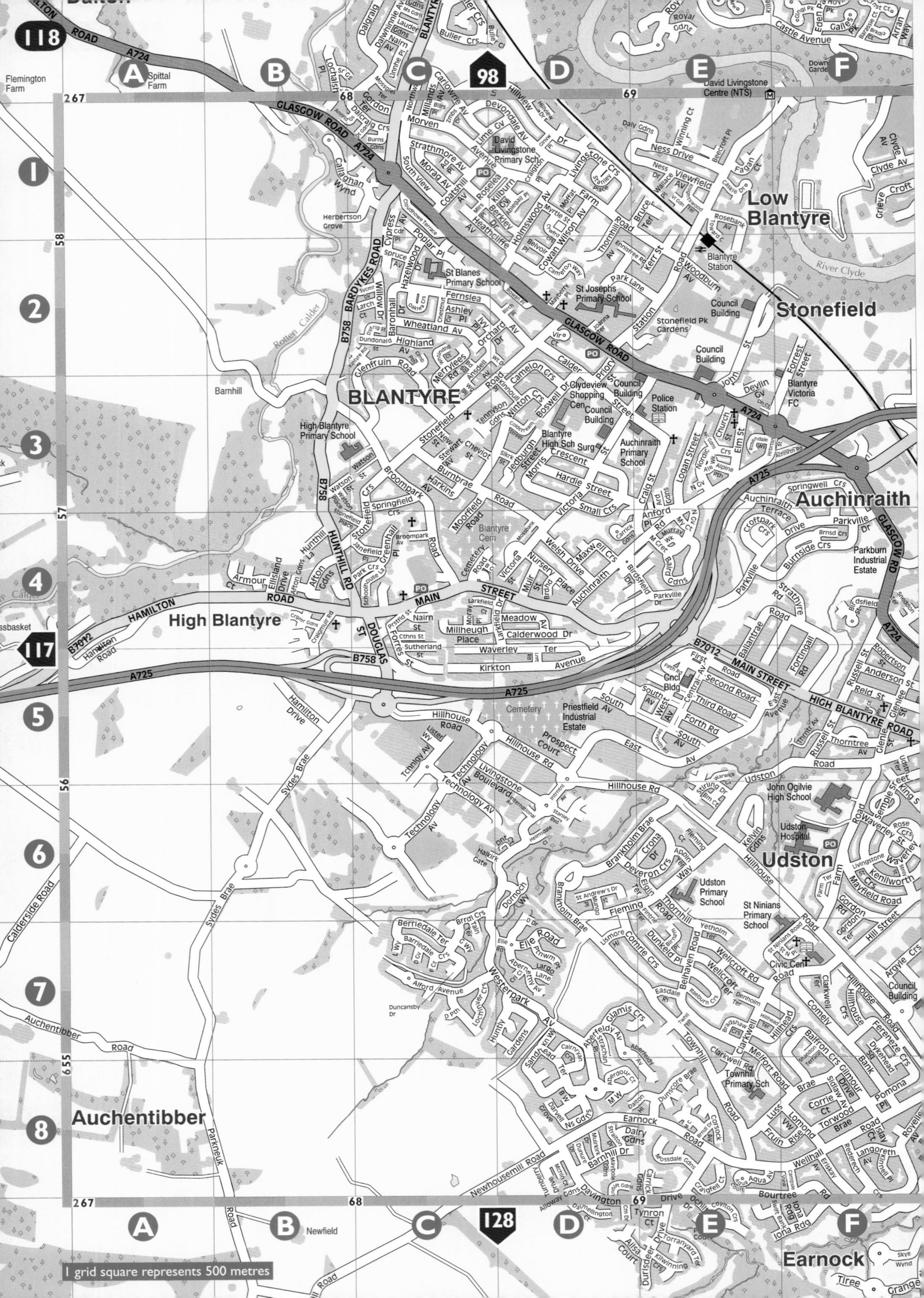

118
98
117
128
A
B
C
D
E
F
1
2
3
4
5
6
7
8
267
68
69
58
57
56
655
BLANTYRE
Low Blantyre
Stonefield
Auchinraith
High Blantyre
Udston
Auchentibber
Earnock
Flemington Farm
Spittal Farm
Barnhill
Herbertson Grove
Newfield
David Livingstone Centre (NTS)
David Livingstone Primary Sch
St Blanes Primary School
St Josephs Primary School
High Blantyre Primary School
Blantyre High Sch
Auchinraith Primary School
Clydeview Shopping Cen
Police Station
Council Building
Blantyre Station
Stonefield Pk Gardens
Blantyre Victoria FC
Parkburn Industrial Estate
Priestfield Industrial Estate
Blantyre Cem
Cemetery
John Ogilvie High School
Udston Hospital
Udston Primary School
St Ninians Primary School
Townhill Primary Sch
Civic Cen
River Clyde
Rotten Calder
GLASGOW ROAD
A724
A725
B758
B7012
HAMILTON ROAD
MAIN STREET
HIGH BLANTYRE ROAD
BARDYKES ROAD
HUNTHILL RD
DOUGLAS ST
Hillhouse Rd
Technology Av
Livingstone Boulevard
Sydes Brae
Calderside Road
Auchentibber Road
Parkneuk Road
Newhousemill Road
Westerpark Av
Brankholm Brae
Hillhouse Road
Udston Road
Station Road
Stonefield Road
Victoria Street
Glenfruin Road
Kirkton Avenue
Calderwood Dr
Waverley Ter
Earnock Road
Townhill Road
Clarkwell Rd
Wellhall Rd
1 grid square represents 500 metres

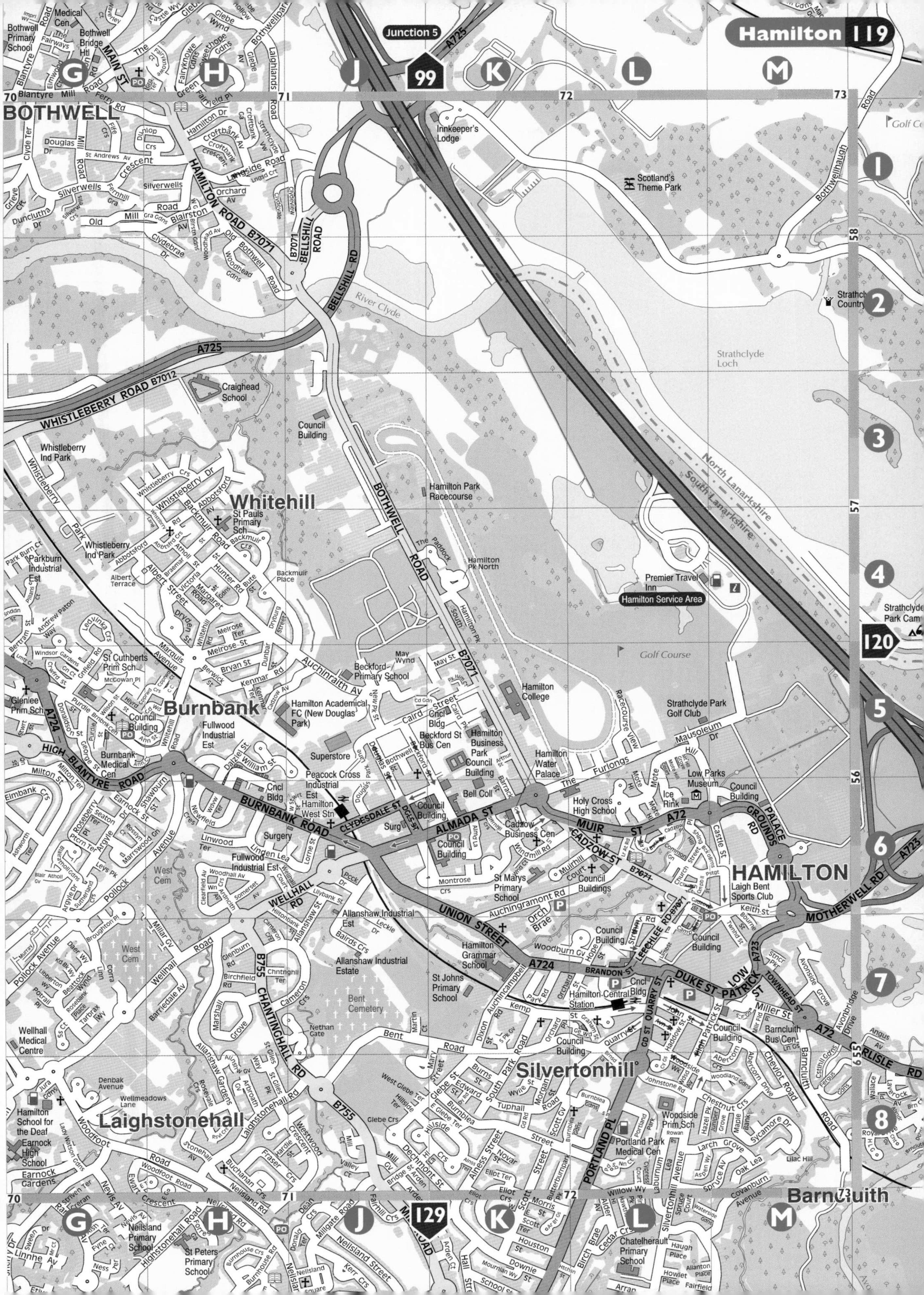
Junction 5
99
A725
BOTHWELL
Bothwell Primary School
Medical Cen.
Bothwell Bridge Htl
MAIN ST
HAMILTON ROAD B7071
BELLSHILL ROAD
BELLSHILL RD
Innkeeper's Lodge
Scotland's Theme Park
River Clyde
Strathclyde Loch
WHISTLEBERRY ROAD B7012
Craighead School
Council Building
Whistleberry Ind Park
Whitehill
St Pauls Primary Sch
BOTHWELL ROAD
Hamilton Park Racecourse
The Paddock
Hamilton Pk North
North Lanarkshire
South Lanarkshire
Premier Travel Inn
Hamilton Service Area
Golf Course
120
Parkburn Industrial Est
Albert Terrace
Backmuir Place
St Cuthberts Prim Sch
Beckford Primary School
Hamilton College
Burnbank
Hamilton Academical FC (New Douglas Park)
Glenlee Prim Sch
A724
HIGH BLANTYRE ROAD
Council Building
Fullwood Industrial Est
Burnbank Medical Cen
Superstore
Peacock Cross Industrial Est
Hamilton West Stn
Cncl Bldg
Beckford St Bus Cen
Hamilton Business Park
Council Building
Strathclyde Park Golf Club
Mausoleum Dr
Hamilton Water Palace
The Furlongs
Holy Cross High School
Low Parks Museum
Council Building
BURNBANK ROAD
CLYDESDALE ST
ALMADA ST
Bell Coll
MUIR ST
A72
PALACE GROUNDS RD
Ice Rink
Cadzow Business Cen
CADZOW ST
Surgery
Surg
Council Building
Fullwood Industrial Est
West Cem
St Marys Primary School
Council Buildings
HAMILTON
Laigh Bent Sports Club
MOTHERWELL RD
A723
UNION STREET
WELLHALL RD
Allanshaw Industrial Est
Allanshaw Industrial Estate
Auchingramont Rd
Council Building
Council Building
B755
CHANTINGHALL RD
Hamilton Grammar School
BRANDON ST
DUKE ST
LOW PATRICK ST
TOWNHEAD ST
West Cem
Bent Cemetery
St Johns Primary School
Hamilton Central Station
Cncl Bldg
QUARRY ST
Barncluith Bus Cen
Council Building
Nethan Gate
Bent Road
Wellhall Medical Centre
Denbak Avenue
Wellmeadows Lane
Silvertonhill
Council Building
CARLISLE RD
Hamilton School for the Deaf
Laighstonehall
Earnock High School
Earnock Gardens
Woodside Prim Sch
Portland Park Medical Cen
PORTLAND PL
Lilac Hill
Barncluith
129
Neilsland Primary School
St Peters Primary School
Chatelherault Primary School
G H J K L M
1 2 3 4 5 6 7 8
70 71 72 73
55 56 57 58

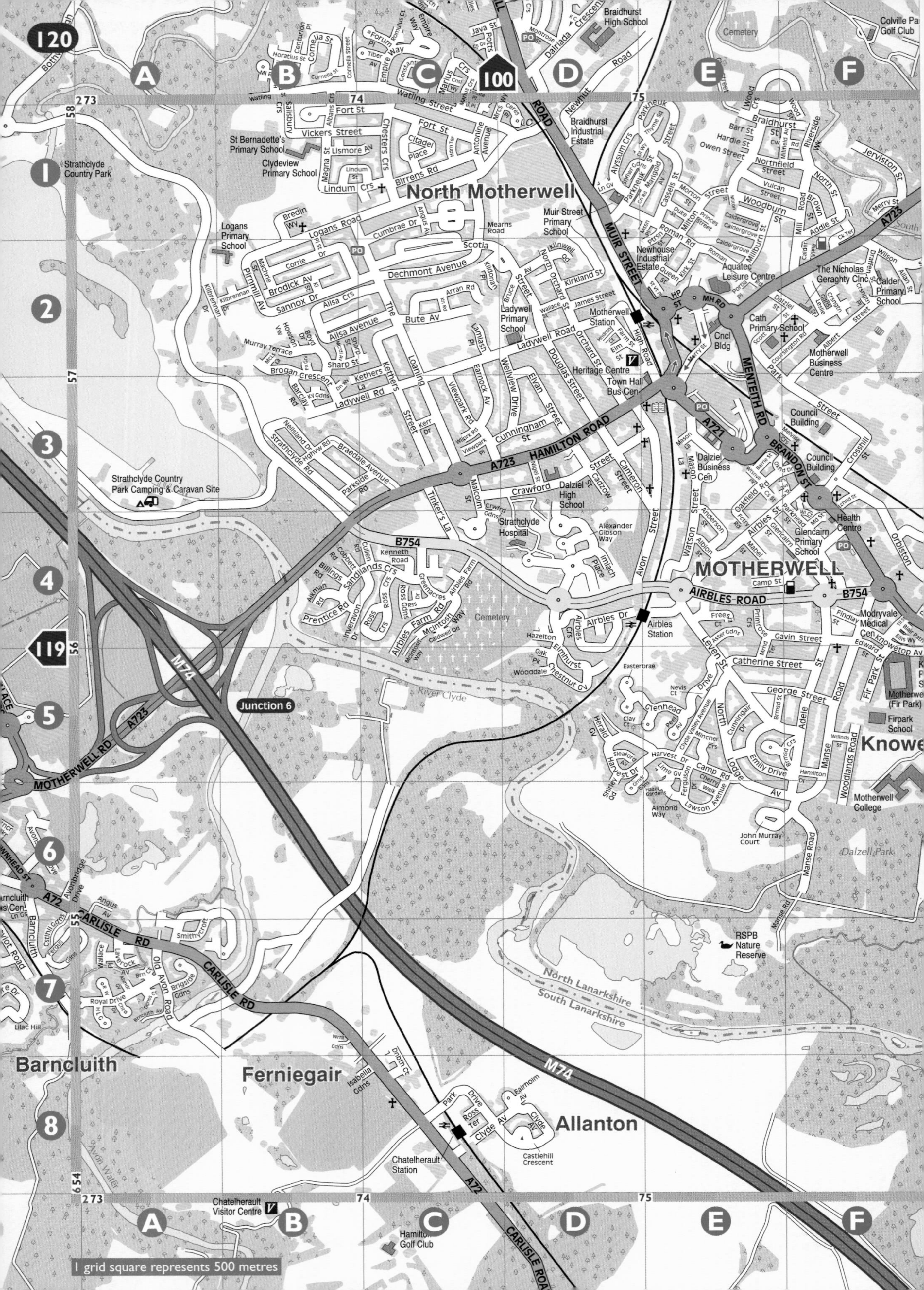

120
100
119
A
B
C
D
E
F
1
2
3
4
5
6
7
8
273
74
75
58
57
56
55
654
North Motherwell
MOTHERWELL
Barncluith
Ferniegair
Allanton
Knowe
Strathclyde Country Park
Strathclyde Country Park Camping & Caravan Site
St Bernadette's Primary School
Clydeview Primary School
Logans Primary School
Braidhurst High School
Braidhurst Industrial Estate
Muir Street Primary School
Newhouse Industrial Estate
Aquatec Leisure Centre
The Nicholas Geraghty Clnc
Calder Primary School
Cath Primary School
Motherwell Business Centre
Ladywell Primary School
Motherwell Station
Heritage Centre
Town Hall
Bus Cen
Cncl Bldg
Council Building
Dalziel Business Cen
Dalziel High School
Strathclyde Hospital
Glencairn Primary School
Health Centre
Airbles Station
Modryvale Medical Cen
Motherwell (Fir Park)
Firpark School
Motherwell College
Cemetery
Colville Park Golf Club
RSPB Nature Reserve
Dalzell Park
John Murray Court
Chatelherault Station
Chatelherault Visitor Centre
Hamilton Golf Club
River Clyde
Avon Water
Lilac Hill
North Lanarkshire
South Lanarkshire
Junction 6
M74
A723
A721
A72
B754
HAMILTON ROAD
AIRBLES ROAD
MUIR STREET
MENTEITH RD
BRANDON ST
MOTHERWELL RD
CARLISLE RD
CARLISLE ROAD
Watling Street
Fort St
Vickers Street
Birrens Rd
Logans Road
Dechmont Avenue
Ladywell Road
Brogan Crescent
Ailsa Avenue
Bute Av
Loaning
Tinker's La
Cunningham St
Douglas Street
Orchard St
High Road
Crawford
Cameron Street
Avon Street
Watson Street
Leven St
Catherine Street
George Street
Gavin Street
Woodlands Road
Manse Road
Camp Rd
Lawson Avenue
Harvest Dr
Glenhead
Sandilands Crs
Airbles Farm Rd
Prentice Rd
Kenneth Road
Braedale Avenue
Parkside Rd
Strathclyde Rd
Woodburn St
Northfield Street
Braidhurst St
Jerviston St
Newhut Road
Dalnada Crescent
Smithycroft
Royal Drive
Old Avon Road
Barncluith Rd
Isabella Gdns
Park Drive
Ross Ter
Clyde Av
Fairholm Av
Castlehill Crescent
1 grid square represents 500 metres

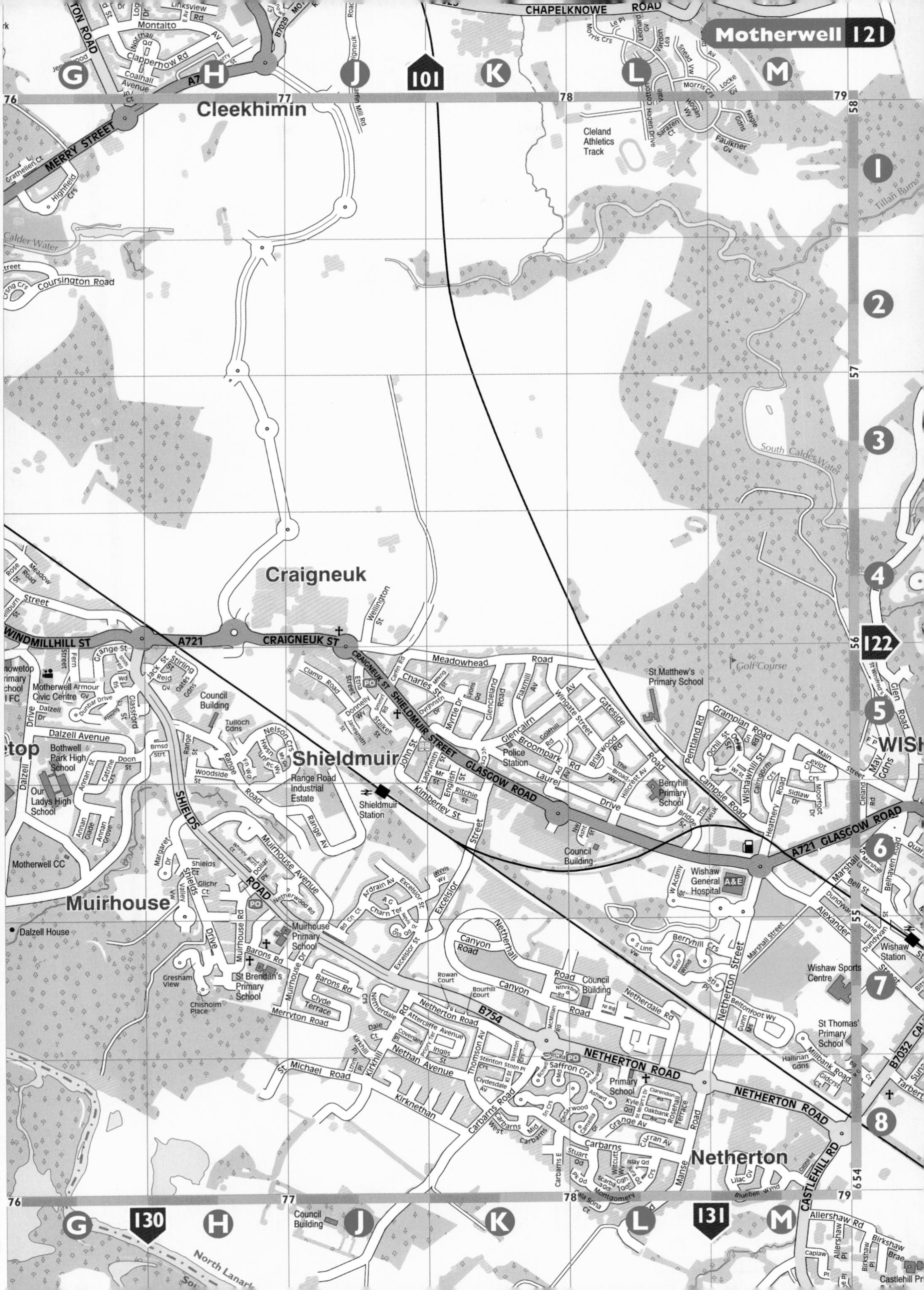
Cleekhimin
Craigneuk
Shieldmuir
Muirhouse
Netherton
CHAPELKNOWE ROAD
MERRY STREET
WINDMILLHILL ST
A721
CRAIGNEUK ST
SHIELDMUIR STREET
GLASGOW ROAD
A721 GLASGOW ROAD
SHIELDS ROAD
NETHERTON ROAD
B754
CASTLEHILL RD
Cleland Athletics Track
Calder Water
South Calder Water
Tillan Burn
Coursington Road
St Matthew's Primary School
Golf Course
Council Building
Range Road Industrial Estate
Shieldmuir Station
Police Station
Berryhill Primary School
Wishaw General Hospital
A&E
Bothwell Park High School
Our Ladys High School
Motherwell Civic Centre
Motherwell CC
Dalzell House
Muirhouse Primary School
St Brendan's Primary School
Primary School
Wishaw Sports Centre
Wishaw Station
St Thomas' Primary School
Dalzell Avenue
Meadowhead Road
Netherton Street
Marshall Street
Canyon Road
Kirknethan
St Michael Road
Nethan Avenue
Merryton Road
Muirhouse Avenue
Excelsior Street
Kimberley St
Allershaw Rd
Birkshaw Brae
Castlehill Pr
North Lanark
G
H
J
K
L
M
76
77
78
79
101
122
130
131
1
2
3
4
5
6
7
8
54
55
56
57
58

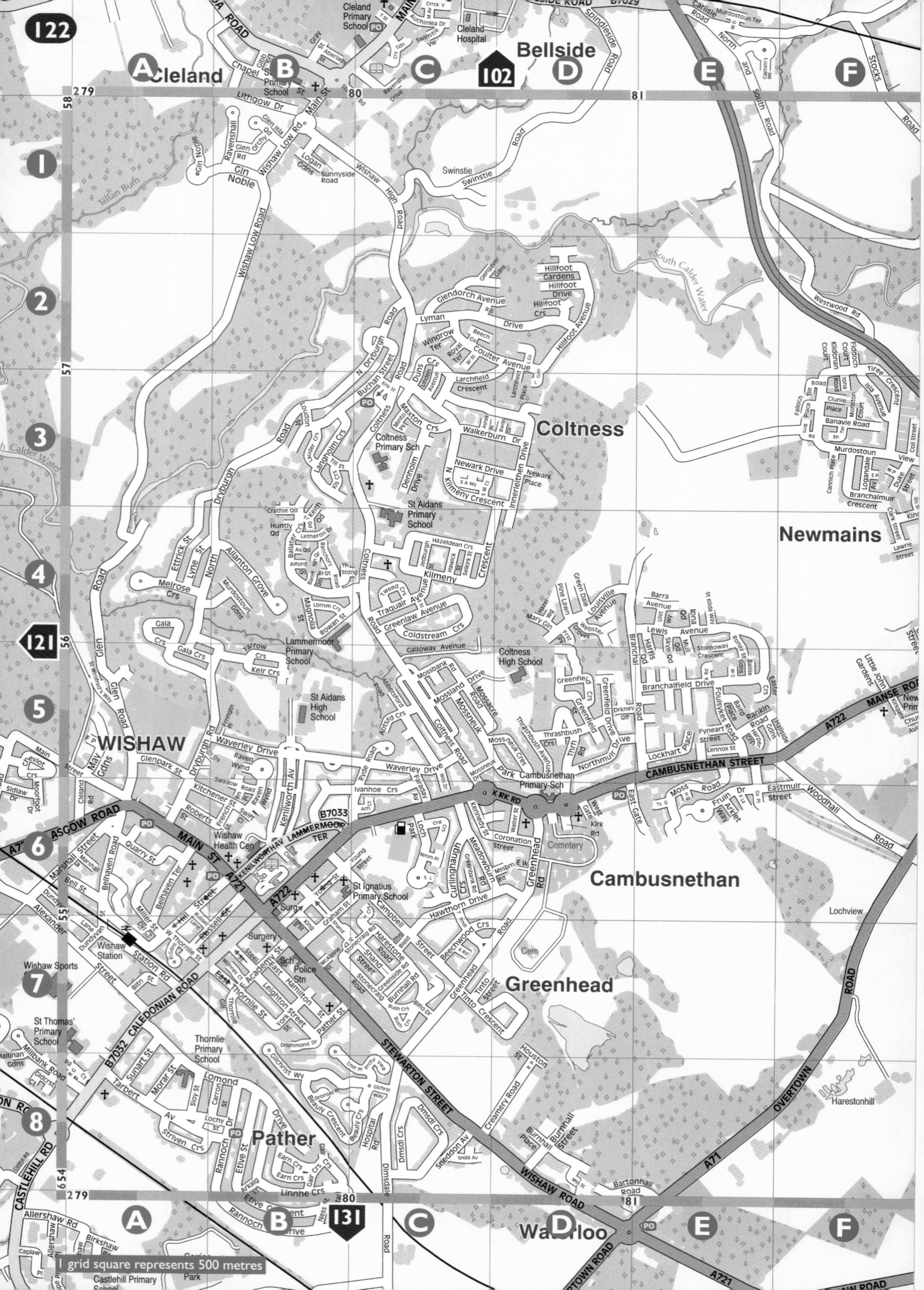
Cleland
Bellside
Coltness
Newmains
WISHAW
Cambusnethan
Greenhead
Pather
Waterloo
102
121
131
A
B
C
D
E
F
1
2
3
4
5
6
7
8
279
80
81
58
57
56
55
654
Cleland Primary School
Cleland Hospital
St Mary's Primary School
Coltness Primary Sch
St Aidans Primary School
Lammermoor Primary School
St Aidans High School
Coltness High School
Cambusnethan Primary Sch
Wishaw Health Cen
St Ignatius Primary School
Wishaw Station
Wishaw Sports
St Thomas' Primary School
Thornlie Primary School
Castlehill Primary School
Police Stn
Cemetery
Swinstie
South Calder Water
Tillan Burn
Lochview
Harestonhill
Wishaw Low Road
Wishaw High Road
Dryburgh Road
Coltness Road
Glen Road
Lyman Drive
Glendorch Avenue
Hillfoot Avenue
Coulter Avenue
Larchfield Crescent
Walkerburn Dr
Newark Drive
Kilmeny Crescent
Innerleithen Drive
Waverley Drive
Glenpark St
Kenilworth Av
Galloway Avenue
Mossland Drive
Mossneuk Road
Branchal Road
Branchalfield Drive
Lewis Avenue
Louisville Avenue
Northmuir Drive
CAMBUSNETHAN STREET
MANSE ROAD
A722
A721
B7033
B7032
B7029
A71
MAIN ST
GLASGOW ROAD
CALEDONIAN ROAD
STEWARTON STREET
WISHAW ROAD
OVERTOWN ROAD
CASTLEHILL RD
Station Rd
Hill Street
Russell St
Kirk Rd
Hawthorn Drive
Beechwood Crs
Greenhead Rd
Tinto Crescent
Creamery Road
Burnhall Street
Hospital Rd
Dimsdale Road
Beauly Crescent
Thornlie St
East Thornlie St
Academy St
Pather St
York Street
Lomond
Tarbert Av
Morar St
Rannoch Dr
Etive St
Woodhall Road
Eastmuir Street
Murdostoun View
Westwood Rd
Carlisle Road
North and South Road
Stocks Road
1 grid square represents 500 metres

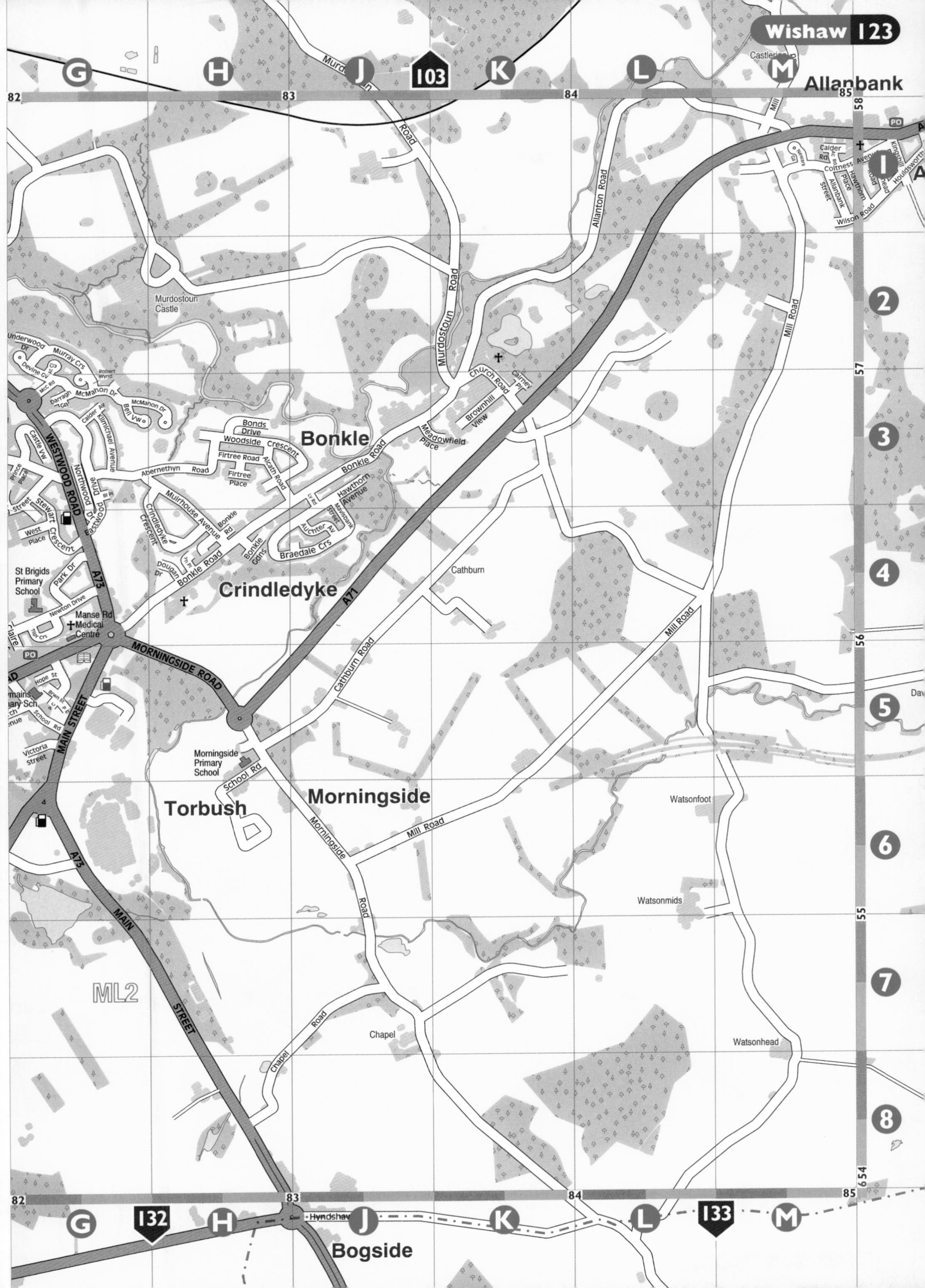

G H J K L M

82 83 84 85

103

Allanbank

Castlehill

Murdostoun Castle

Murdo...n
Road

Murray Crs
Underwood Dr
Devine Gv
McC Rd
Darragh
Hall
Calder Av
Yuinichael Avenue
Ben VW
McMahon Dr
McMahon Dr
Robert Wynd
Castle VW
Prince Road
Stewart Crescent
Northwood Drive
WESTWOOD ROAD
West Place
Street

Bonds Drive
Woodside Crescent
Firtree Road
Firtree Place
Abernethyn Road
Alcath Road
Bonkle
Bonkle Road
Hawthorn Avenue
Auchter Av
Manshore
Bonkle Gdns
Bonkle Rd
Braedale Crs
Muirhouse Avenue
Crindledyke Crescent
Dougan Dr
Bonkle Road
Newton Drive

St Brigids Primary School
Park Dr
Manse Rd
Medical Centre
PO
Hope St
mains ary Sch
School Rd
Victoria Street

A73

Crindledyke

MORNINGSIDE ROAD

A71

Murdostoun Road

Church Road
Meadowfield Place
Brownhill View
Carmel Pl

Allanton Road

Mill Road

Cathburn

Cathburn Road

Morningside Primary School
School Rd

Torbush

Morningside

Morningside Road

Mill Road

Watsonfoot

Watsonmids

MAIN STREET

A73

ML2

Chapel Road

Chapel

Watsonhead

Calder Rd
Coirness Place
Hawthorn Avenue
Allanbank Street
Wilson Road
Kinneil
Avenue
Houldsworth
PO

Dav...

82 2

57 3

56 4

5

55 6

7

654 8

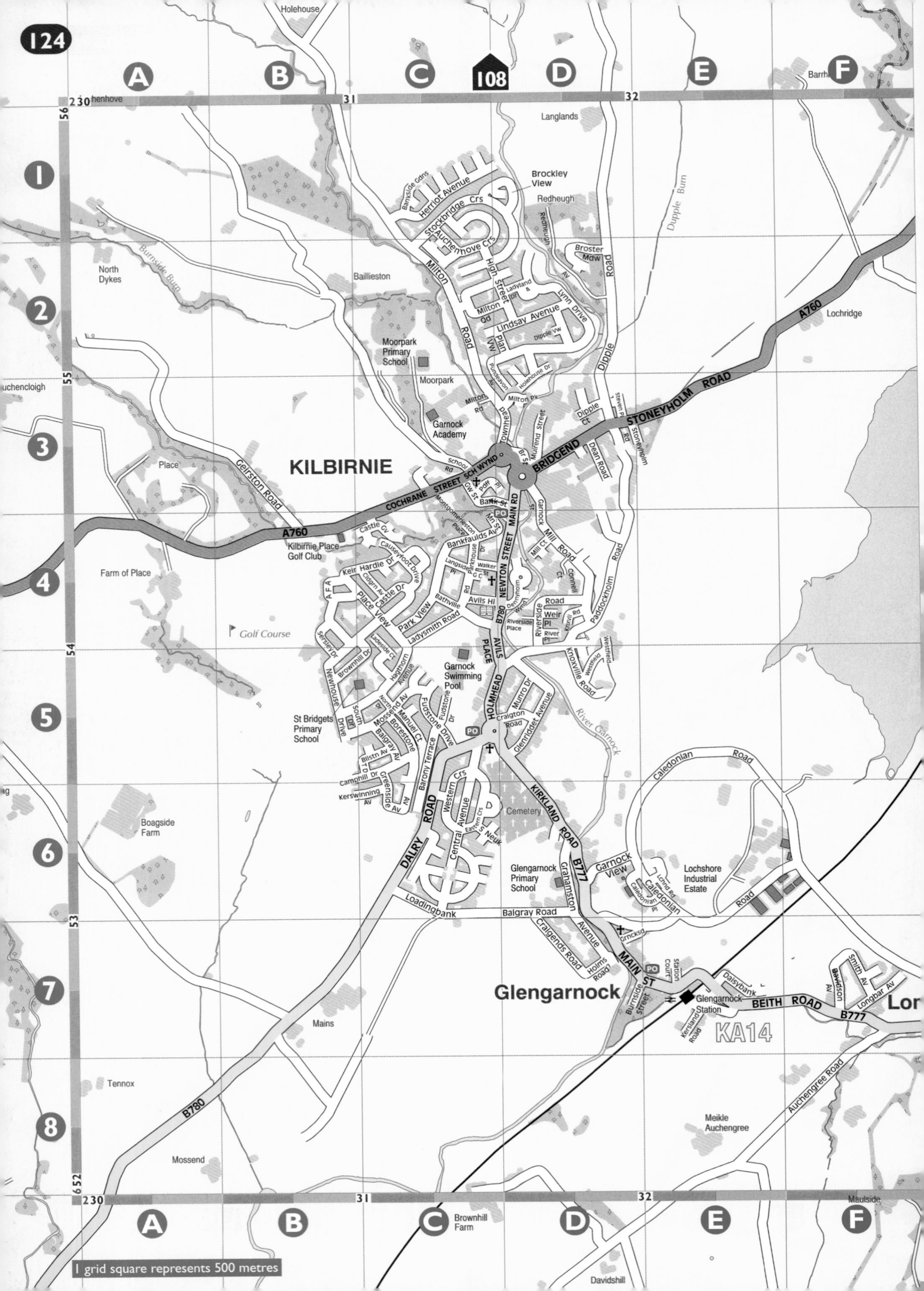

108

A B C D E F

1

2

3

4

5

6

7

8

Holehouse

henhove

Langlands

Brockley
View

Redheugh

Broster
Maw

Dipple Burn

Burnside Gdns

Herriot Avenue

Stockbridge Crs

Auchenhove Crs

Milton Road

High Street

Milton Rd
PW

Milton
Rd

Ladyland
Drive

Dipple Vw

Lindsay Avenue

Lynn Drive

Punchkean

Holenhouse Dr

Steven St

Dipple
Road

A760 Lochridge

STONEYHOLM ROAD

Steven St

Stoneyholm

Dipple
Ct

North
Dykes

Burnside Burn

Baillieston

Moorpark
Primary
School

Moorpark

Garnock
Academy

Milton
Rd

Milton Pk.

School
Rd

Townhead

Mulrend Street

Dean Road

Auchencloigh

Place

Gelrston Road

KILBIRNIE

COCHRANE STREET SCH WYND

BRIDGEND

NEWTON STREET MAIN RD

Garnock Mill Road

Mill Ct

Connell

Paddockholm Road

A760

Castle Cv

Kilbirnie Place
Golf Club

Montgomeriecton

Bank St

PO

Paff

CW St

By Pl

Bankraulds Av

Langside
Pl

Parkhouse

Walker
St

Bathville

Avils HI

B780

Denholm

Road

Weir
Pl

River

Farm of Place

Keir Hardie Dr

Causeyfoot Drive

Park View

Castle Dr

Logan Av

Ladysmith Road

Riverside
Place

Knoxville Road

Westfield

Riverside Pl

AFA

Place View

Brownhill Dr

Lawacre Ct

Haghorn
Avenue

Garnock
Swimming
Pool

Avils PLACE

Munro Dr

Glenriddet Avenue

River Garnock

Golf Course

Newhouse

Sersioss Dr

South

Mossfend Av

Garrstone

Manuel Ct

Holmhead

Fudstone Drive

Fudstone
Dr

Craigton
Road

Caledonian Road

St Bridgets
Primary
School

Balgray Av

Bilstn Av

Barony Terrace

Greenside Av

Campnill Dr

Kerswinning Av

Western Crs

Central Avenue

Eastern Crs

St Neuk

Cemetery

KIRKLAND ROAD B777

Grahamston

Garnock
View

Caledonian Pl

Lochra Rd

Lochshore Industrial
Estate

Boagside
Farm

DALRY ROAD

Glengarnock
Primary
School

Loadingbank

Balgray Road

Craigends Road

Holms
Road

Avenue

MAIN ST

PO

X Grnckscd

Station
Court

Daisybank

Smith Av

Longbar Av

Samuelston

Glengarnock

Burnside
Street

Glengarnock
Station

Kersland
Road

BEITH ROAD B777

Lor

KA14

Mains

Tennox

B780

Meikle
Auchengree

Auchengree Road

Mossend

Brownhill
Farm

Davidshill

Maulside

230 31 32

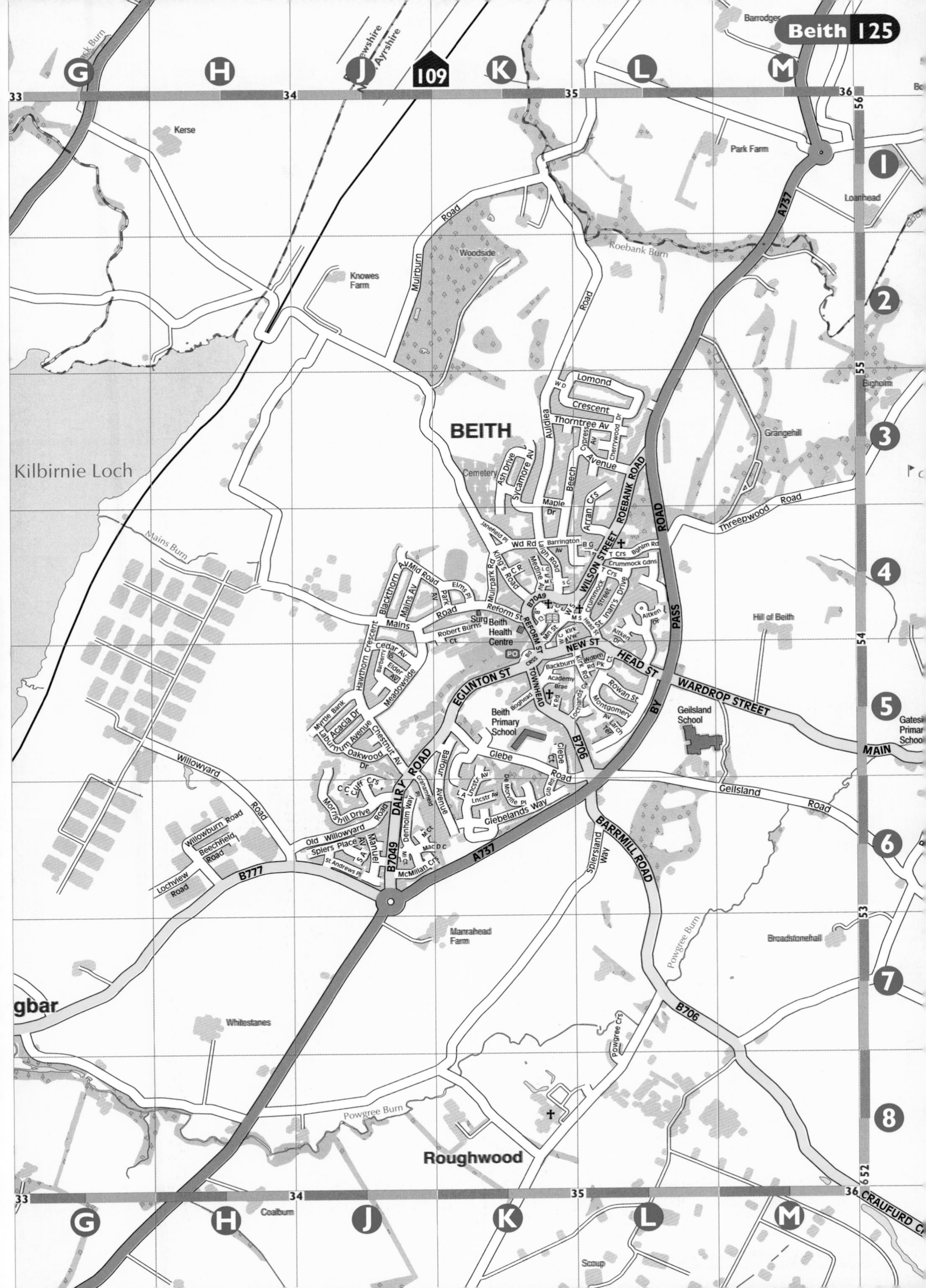

Barrodger

Park Farm

Loanhead

Bigholm

Grangehill

Roebank Burn

Woodside

Knowes Farm

Muirburn

Kerse

Threepwood Road

BEITH

Lomond Crescent

Thorntree Av

Cypress Av

Cherrywood Dr

Hill of Beith

Kilbirnie Loch

Cemetery

Ash Drive

Sycamore Av

Alpine

Beech Avenue

Arran Crs

Maple Dr

ROEBANK ROAD

Barrington Av

Crummock Gdns

Crummock Street

WILSON STREET

T Crs

B G

Bgrim Rd

Mains Burn

Blackthorn Av

Mid Road

Mains Av

Elms Pl

Park Av

Muirpark Rd

King's Road

C R

Wd Rd

Medine

Laigh Road

ROAD

PASS

St Inan's Drive

Aitken Dr

Grangehill

Mains

Reform St

Robert Burns Ct.

Surg

Beith Health Centre

B1049

Kirk St

M S

Aitken Pl

Hawthorn Crescent

Cedar Av

Barberry

Elder Av

Meadowside

PO

Backburn

Academy Brae

NEW ST

Reform Rd Pk

HEAD ST

BY

WARDROP STREET

Geilsland School

Gatesi Primary Scho

Myrtle Bank

Acacia Dr

Laburnum Avenue

Chestnut Av

Oakwood

EGLINTON ST

TOWNEND

Boghead

Beith Primary School

Lomands

Rowan St

Montgomery Av

MAIN

Geilsland Road

C C

Cliff Crs

Morris

Mill Drive

DALRY

Balfour Avenue

Glenholm Way

Channelhead

Glebe Road

B706

Glebe Road

De Morvilla

McMorine Pl

Glebelands Way

Spiersland Way

BARRMILL ROAD

Broadstonehall

Willowburn Road

Beechfield Road

Willowyard Road

Lochview Road

B777

Old Willowyard Road

Spiers Place

Manuel

B7049

St Andrews Pl

McMillan Crs

A737

Powgree Burn

B706

Mamrahead Farm

Whitestanes

gbar

Powgree Crs

Powgree Burn

Roughwood

Coalburn

Scoup

CRAUFURD C

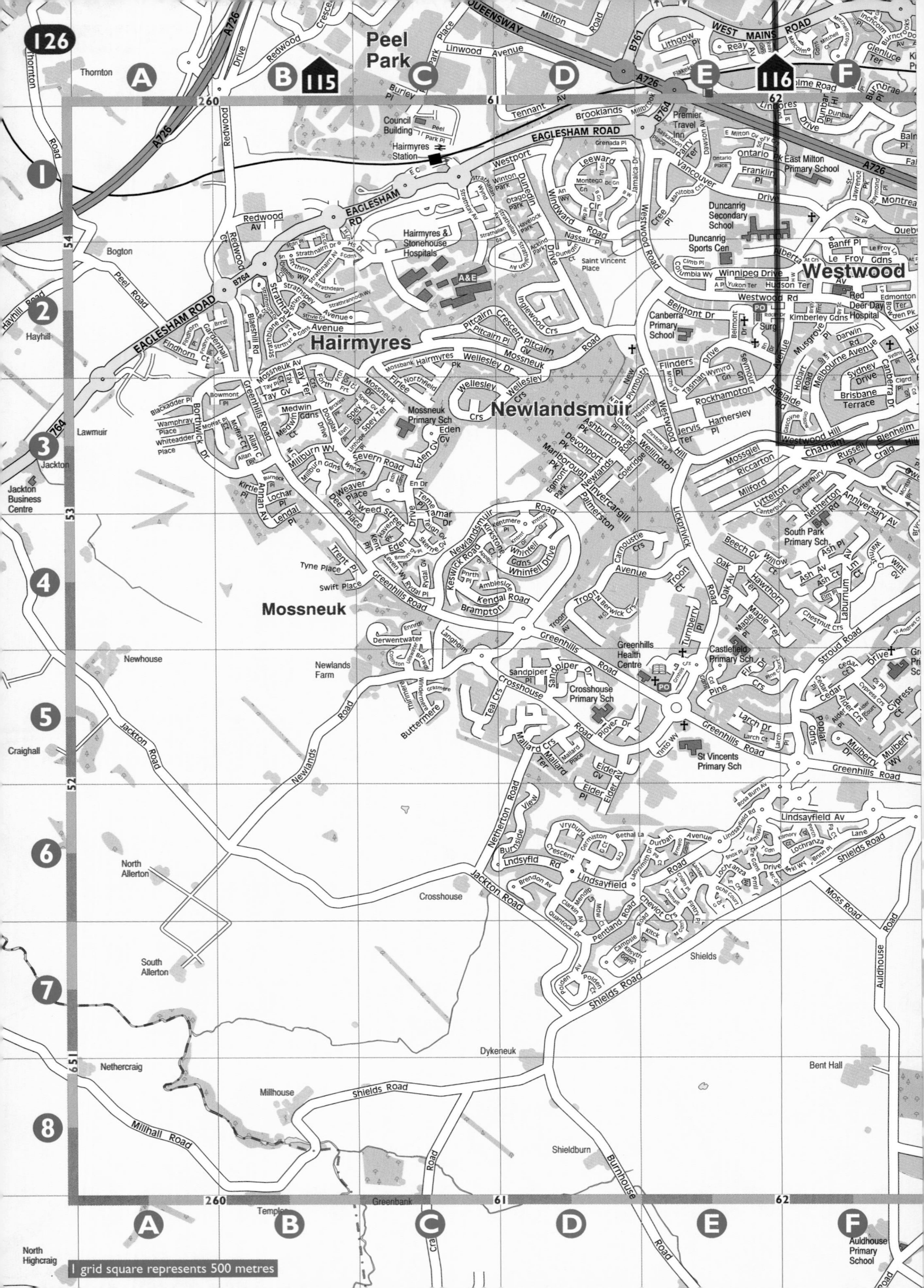

115
116
A
B
C
D
E
F
1
2
3
4
5
6
7
8
260
61
62
54
53
52
651
Peel Park
Hairmyres
Newlandsmuir
Westwood
Mossneuk
Thornton
Bogton
Hayhill
Lawmuir
Jackton
Jackton Business Centre
Newhouse
Newlands Farm
Craighall
North Allerton
South Allerton
Crosshouse
Nethercraig
Millhouse
Dykeneuk
Shieldburn
Shields
Bent Hall
Templeton
Greenbank
North Highcraig
Council Building
Hairmyres Station
Hairmyres & Stonehouse Hospitals
A&E
Premier Travel Inn
East Milton Primary School
Duncanrig Secondary School
Duncanrig Sports Cen
Canberra Primary School
Red Deer Day Hospital
Mossneuk Primary Sch
South Park Primary Sch
Greenhills Health Centre
Castlefield Primary Sch
Crosshouse Primary Sch
St Vincents Primary Sch
Auldhouse Primary School
Saint Vincent Place
EAGLESHAM ROAD
QUEENSWAY
WEST MAINS ROAD
A726
B764
B761
Thornton Road
Redwood Drive
Redwood Crescent
Redwood Av
Peel Road
Hayhill Road
Linwood Avenue
Milton Road
Tennant Av
Brooklands
Westport
Dunedin Drive
Windward Road
Westwood Road
Vancouver Drive
Ontario Pk
Franklin Pl
Alberta Av
Winnipeg Drive
Westwood Rd
Belmont Dr
Kimberley Gdns
Melbourne Avenue
Sydney Drive
Brisbane Terrace
Canberra Dr
Rockhampton
Hamersley Pl
Jervis Ter
Adelaide Rd
Westwood Hill
Chatham
Mossgiel
Riccarton
Milford
Lyttelton
Canterbury
Netherton Rd
Anniversary Av
Beech Gv
Oak Pl
Hawthorn Ter
Maple Ter
Ash Av
Laburnum Lm
Chestnut Crs
Stroud Road
Cedar Drive
Cypress Ct
Poplar Gdns
Mulberry Dr
Larch Dr
Pine Crs
Greenhills Road
Lickprivick Road
Troon Av
Carnoustie Crs
Turnberry Pl
Sandpiper Dr
Crosshouse Road
Plover Dr
Mallard Crs
Elder Av
Teal Crs
Netherton Road
Burnside View
Lindsayfield Av
Lindsayfield Road
Lochranza Drive
Durban Avenue
Vryburg Crescent
Pentland Road
Cheviot Crs
Polden Av
Shields Road
Moss Road
Auldhouse Road
Burnhouse Road
Jackton Road
Newlands Road
Millhall Road
Craigend Road
Pitcairn Crescent
Wellesley Dr
Wellesley Crs
Mossneuk Drive
Mossneuk Av
Tay Gv
Tay Ter
Strathspey Avenue
Strathtay Avenue
Greenhills Road
Borthwick Dr
Allan Ct
Millburn Wy
Medwin Gdns
Spey Ter
Severn Road
Eden Gv
Weaver Place
Dee Place
Tweed Street
Teme Dr
Tamar Dr
Kirtle Pl
Annan Av
Lochar Pl
Lendal Pl
Trent Pl
Tyne Place
Swift Place
Newlandsmuir Road
Keswick Road
Kirkstone Ct
Whinfell Drive
Kendal Road
Brampton
Ambleside
Derwentwater
Buttermere
Inglewood Crs
New Plymouth
Ashburton Road
Devonport Pk
Marlborough Pk
Invercargill
Palmerston
Wellington
Coleridge
Flinders Pl
Tasman Drive
Seymour Gn
Gardenhall
Blaeshill Rd
Findhorn
Lindsayfield
Brendon Av
Quantock Dr
1 grid square represents 500 metres

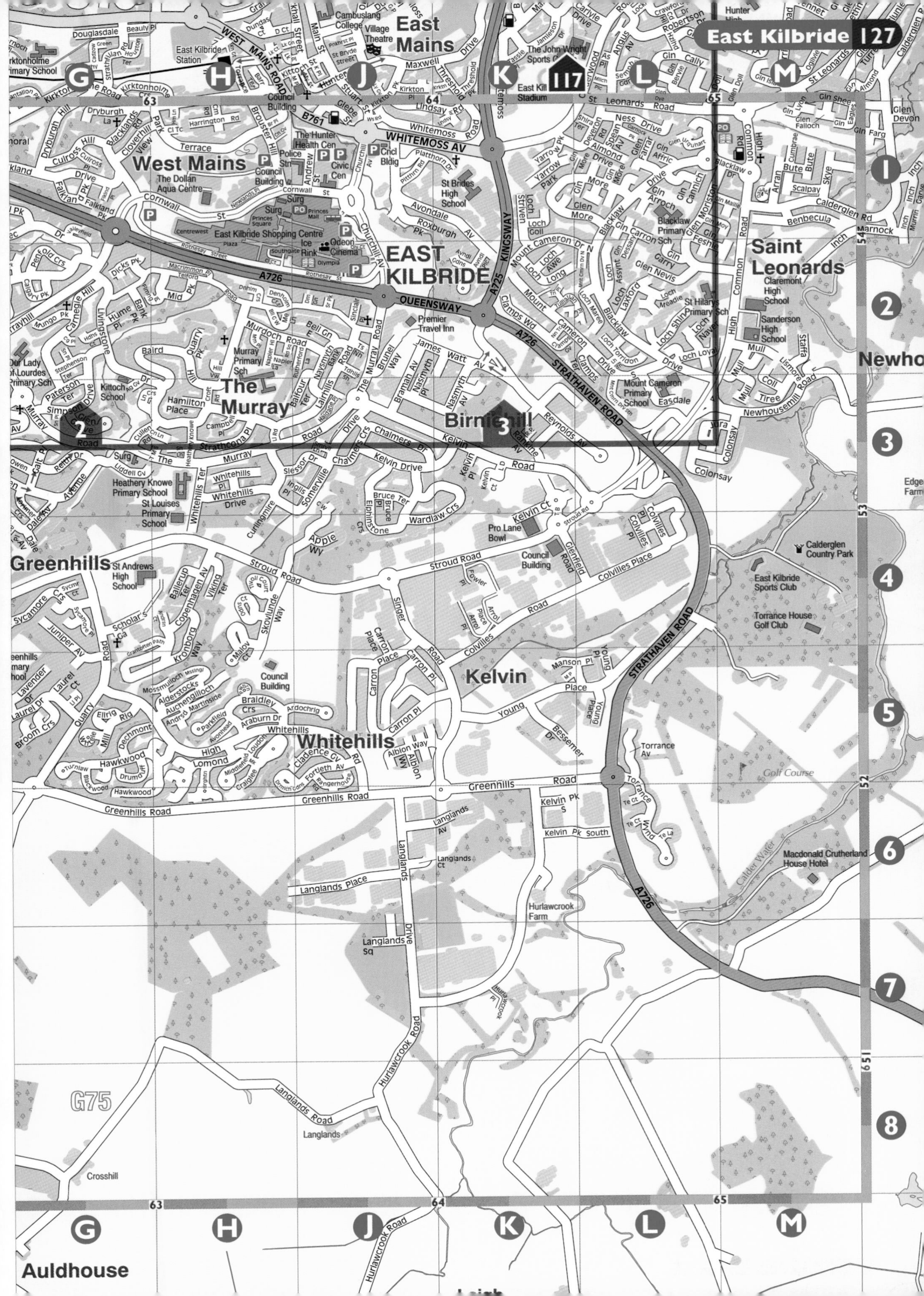
East Mains
West Mains
EAST KILBRIDE
Saint Leonards
The Murray
Birniehill
Greenhills
Kelvin
Whitehills
Auldhouse
Newhouse
G75
G
H
J
K
L
M
1
2
3
4
5
6
7
8
63
64
65
117
East Kilbride Station
WEST MAINS ROAD
Cambuslang College
Village Theatre
Maxwell Drive
Kirktonholme Primary School
Kirktonholme Rd
Douglasdale
Council Building
B761
Whitemoss Road
WHITEMOSS AV
St Leonards Road
The John Wright Sports Centre
East Kilbride Stadium
The Hunter Health Cen
Police Stn
Civic Cen
Cncl Bldg
St Brides High School
The Dollan Aqua Centre
Cornwall St
East Kilbride Shopping Centre
Princes Mall
Centrewest
Princes Square
Plaza
Southgate
Olympia
Odeon Cinema
Ice Rink
Rothesay Street
A726
QUEENSWAY
A725
KINGSWAY
Churchill Av
Avondale Av
Roxburgh Pk
Premier Travel Inn
Murdoch Road
Murray Primary Sch
Kittoch School
Our Lady of Lourdes Primary Sch
Hamilton Place
James Watt Av
Nasmyth Av
Brunel Way
The Murray Road
Strathcona Pl
STRATHAVEN ROAD
Mount Cameron Primary School
Blacklaw Primary
Glen Moriston
St Hilarys Primary Sch
Claremont High School
Sanderson High School
Calderglen Rd
Newhousemill Road
Colonsay
Kelvin Drive
Kelvin Road
Heathery Knowe Primary School
St Louises Primary School
Whitehills Drive
Pro Lane Bowl
Kelvin Ct
Stroud Road
Council Building
Colvilles Place
Colvilles Road
St Andrews High School
Calderglen Country Park
East Kilbride Sports Club
Torrance House Golf Club
Golf Course
Carron Place
Young Place
Bessemer Dr
Torrance Av
Greenhills Road
Kelvin Pk South
Langlands Place
Langlands Drive
Langlands Sq
Hurlawcrook Farm
Hurlawcrook Road
Langlands Road
Langlands
Crosshill
Calder Water
Macdonald Crutherland House Hotel

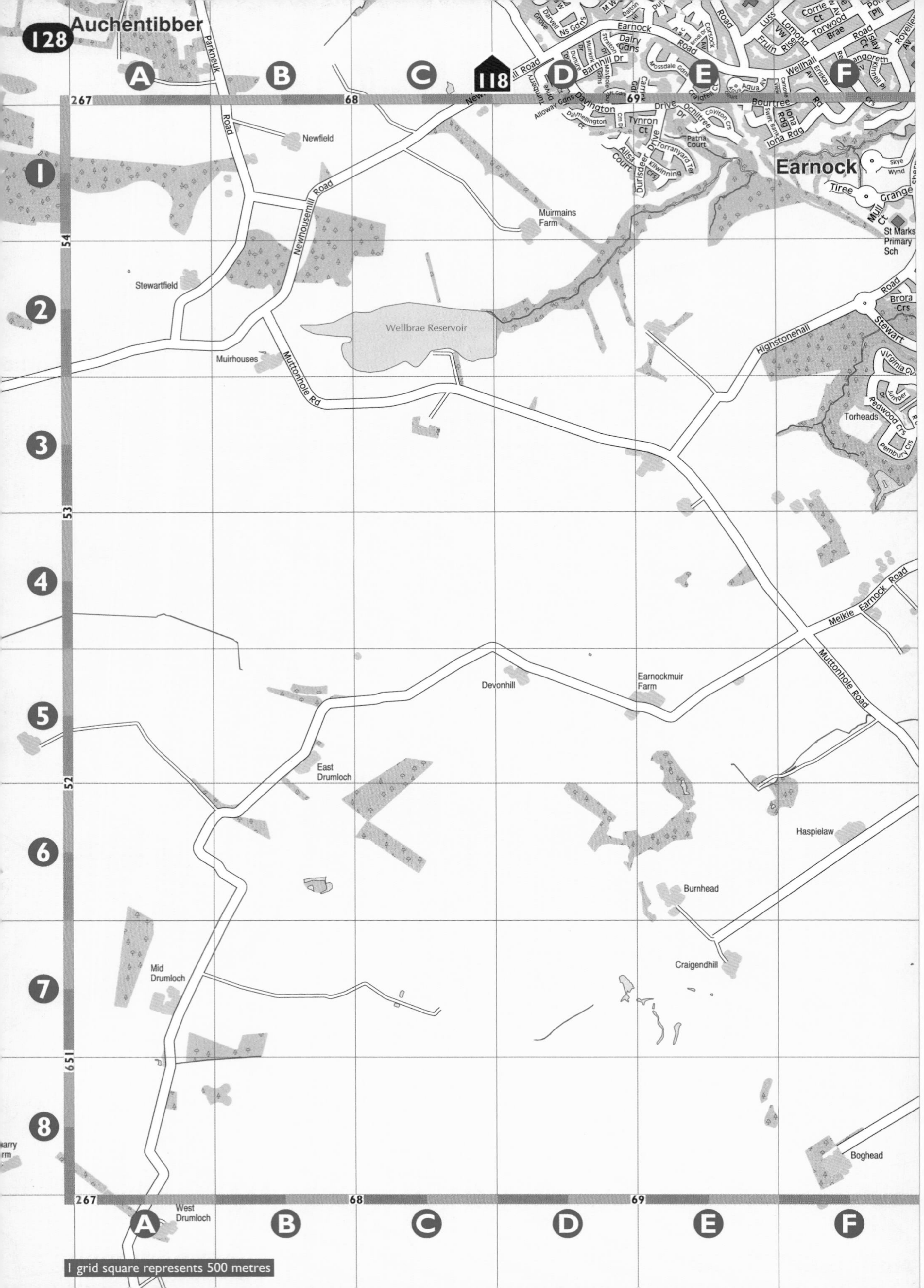

Auchentibber

Earnock

Newfield

Stewartfield

Muirhouses

Wellbrae Reservoir

Muirmains Farm

Highstonehall

St Marks Primary Sch

Tiree

Torheads

Devonhill

Earnockmuir Farm

Meikle Earnock Road

Haspielaw

East Drumloch

Burnhead

Craigendhill

Mid Drumloch

Boghead

West Drumloch

118

1 grid square represents 500 metres

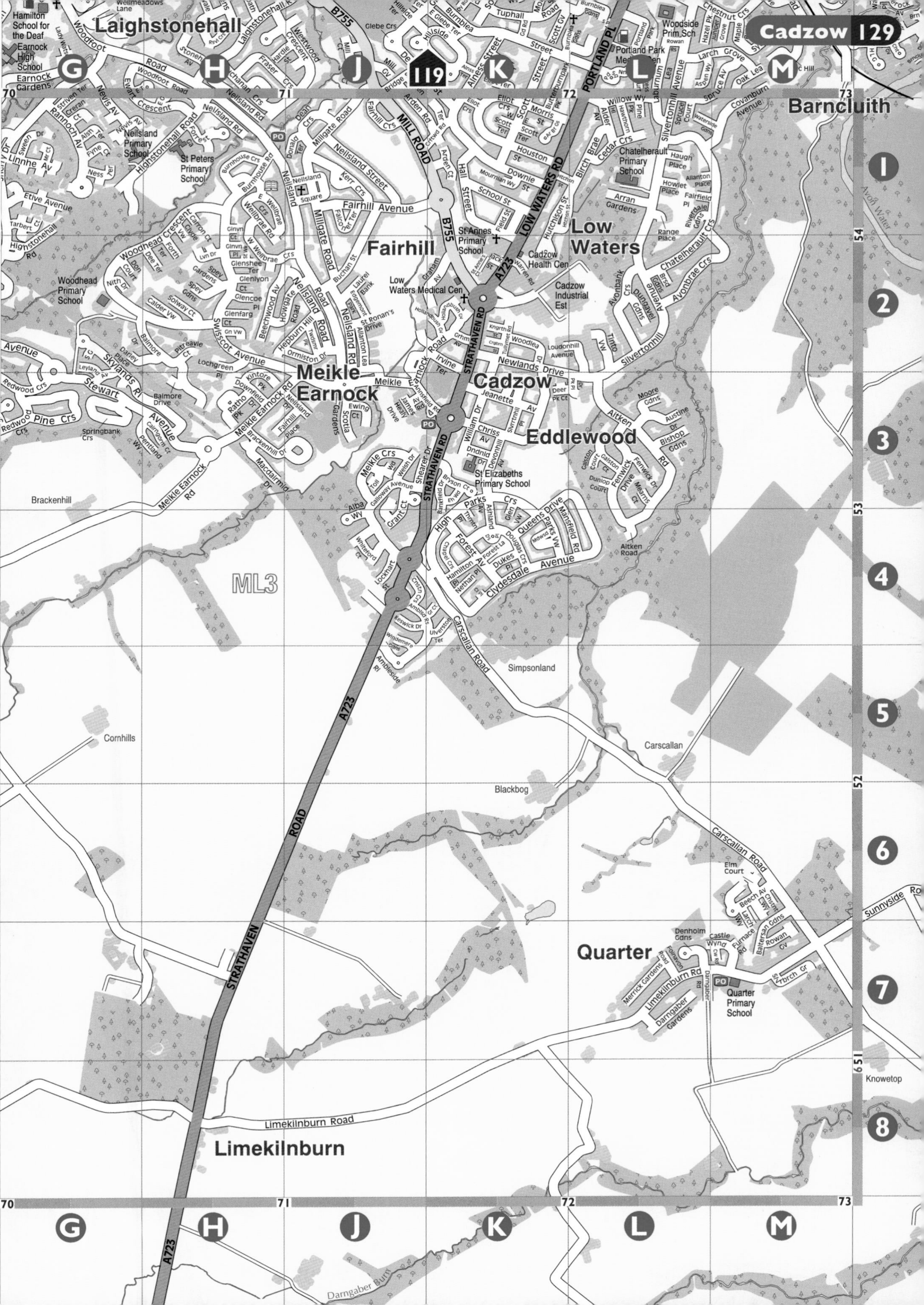

Laighstonehall

G H J 119 K L M

70 71 72 73

Barncluith

Hamilton
School for
the Deaf
Earnock
High
School
Earnock
Gardens

B755

I

54

Fairhill

MILL ROAD

B755

St Peters
Primary
School

Neilsland
Primary
School

Woodhead
Primary
School

Fairhill Avenue

St Annes
Primary
School

Low Waters Medical Cen

Cadzow
Health Cen

Low
Waters

Cadzow
Industrial
Est

Chatelherault
Primary
School

Arran
Gardens

LOW WATERS RD

A723

2

Meikle
Earnock

Cadzow

Eddlewood

Newlands Drive

Loudonhill
Avenue

Silvertonhill

3

53

Brackenhill

STRATHAVEN RD

St Elizabeths
Primary
School

Aitken
Road

Aitken
Road

ML3

4

Simpsonland

A723

5

52

Cornhills

Carscallan

Blackbog

Carscallan Road

6

Quarter

Elm
Court

STRATHAVEN ROAD

Quarter
Primary
School

Limekilnburn Rd

7

651

Knowetop

Limekilnburn

Limekilnburn Road

8

70 71 72 73

G H J K L M

A723

Darngaber Burn

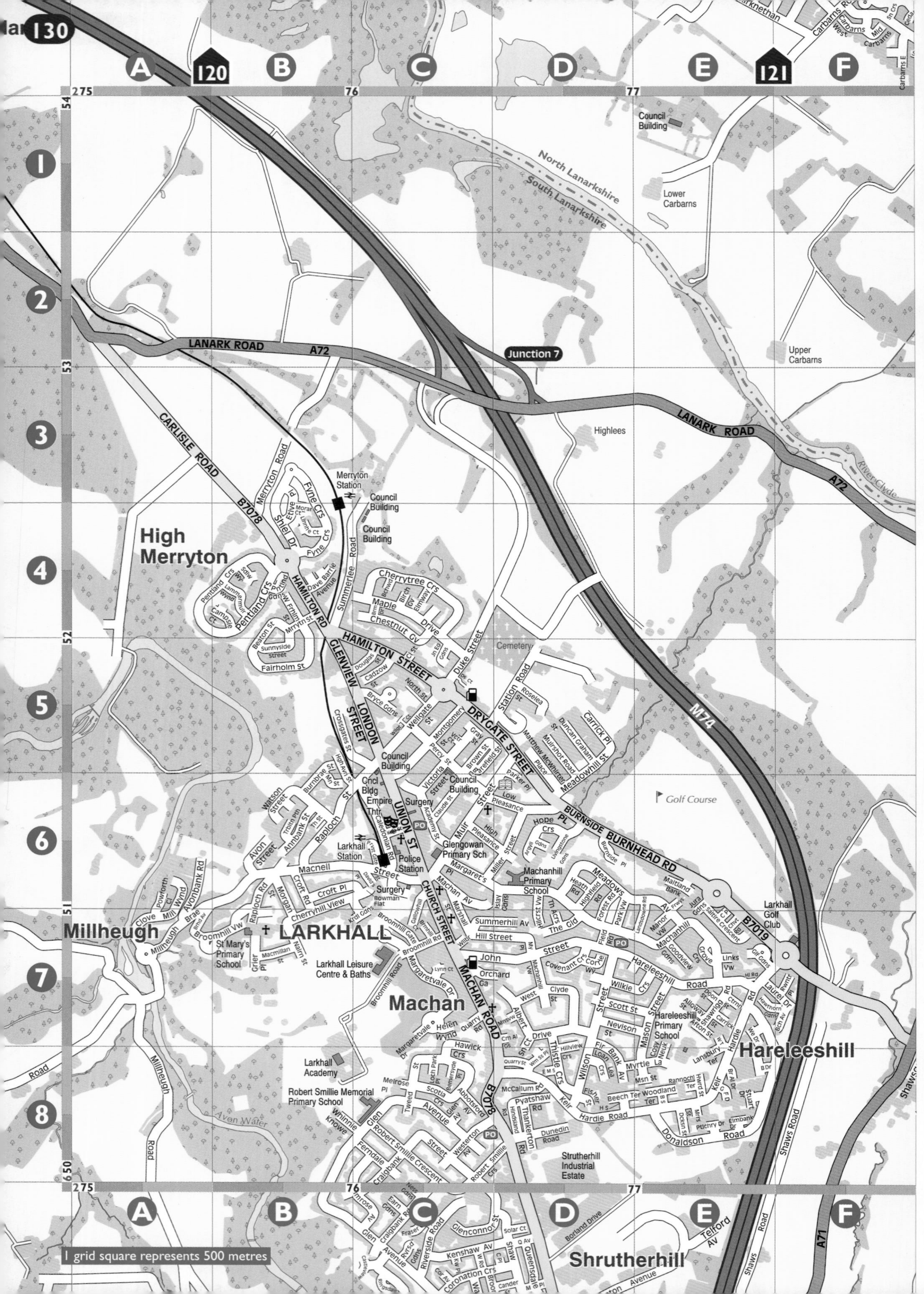

130
120
121
A
B
C
D
E
F
275
76
77
54
53
52
51
650
1
2
3
4
5
6
7
8
Council Building
North Lanarkshire
South Lanarkshire
Lower Carbarns
Upper Carbarns
LANARK ROAD
A72
Junction 7
Highlees
River Clyde
CARLISLE ROAD
B7078
Merryton Road
Merryton Station
High Merryton
Fyne Crs
Shiel Dr
Pentland Crs
HAMILTON RD
Dave Barrie Avenue
Summerlee Road
Cherrytree Crs
Maple
Chestnut Gv
Drive
HAMILTON STREET
GLENVIEW
LONDON STREET
Duke Street
Cemetery
Station Road
DRYGATE STREET
Fairholm St
Beaton St
Sunnyside Street
Bryce Gdns
Wellgate St
Montgomery St
North St
Crossgates St
Carrick Pl
Muirshot Road
Meadowhill St
Matthew McWhirter Place
M74
Council Building
Cncl Bldg
Empire Thtr
UNION ST
Surgery
Victoria Street
Low Pleasance
High Pleasance
Parker Pl
Golf Course
BURNSIDE PL
BURNHEAD RD
Hope Crs
Watson Street
Burnbrae St
Annbank St
Raploch St
Avon Street
Larkhall Station
Caledonian Rd
Police Station
Glengowan Primary Sch
Miller Street
Machanhill Primary School
Meadows
Maitland Bank
Larkhall Golf Club
B7019
Macneil Street
Croft Pl
Cherryhill View
Surgery
Bowman Flat
CHURCH STREET
Machan Av
Summerhill Av
Hill Street
Millheugh
LARKHALL
Broomhill Rd
St Mary's Primary School
Larkhall Leisure Centre & Baths
Margaretvale Dr
MACHAN ROAD
John Street
Orchard Ga
Hareleeshill Road
Wilkie Crs
Scott St
Nevison St
Hareleeshill Primary School
Machan
Helen Wynd
Quarry Rd
Drive
Thistle Crs
Wilson Street
Myrtle La
Hareleeshill
Larkhall Academy
Hawick Crs
Robert Smillie Memorial Primary School
Scotia Avenue
Abbotsford
McCallum Rd
Pyatshaw Rd
Keir Hardie Road
Beech Ter
Woodland Ter
Donaldson Road
Dunedin Road
Strutherhill Industrial Estate
Robert Smillie Crescent
Avon Water
Road
Shaws Road
Borland Drive
Telford Av
Glenconnor St
Riverside Road
Shrutherhill
Coronation Crs
A71
1 grid square represents 500 metres

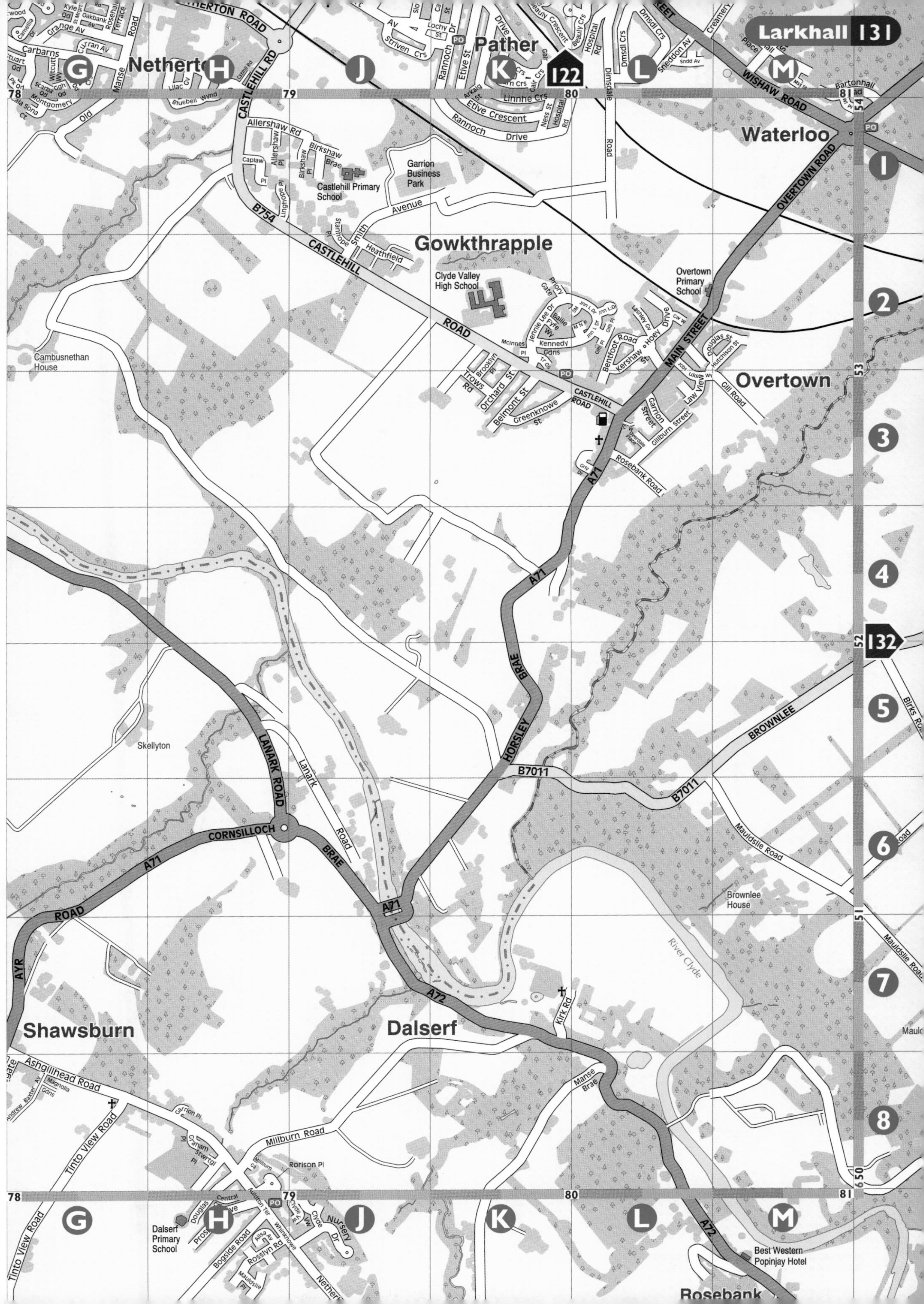

Netherton
Pather
Waterloo
Gowkthrapple
Overtown
Shawsburn
Dalserf
Rosebank
Castlehill Primary School
Garrion Business Park
Clyde Valley High School
Overtown Primary School
Cambusnethan House
Skellyton
Brownlee House
Dalserf Primary School
Best Western Popinjay Hotel
River Clyde
CASTLEHILL RD
CASTLEHILL ROAD
B754
MAIN STREET
OVERTOWN ROAD
WISHAW ROAD
HORSLEY BRAE
LANARK ROAD
CORNSILLOCH BRAE
AYR ROAD
BROWNLEE
B7011
A71
A72
Mauldslie Road
Ashgillhead Road
Tinto View Road
Millburn Road
Rosebank Road
Gill Road
Kirk Rd
Manse Brae
Lanark Road
Smith Avenue
Rannoch Drive
Etive Crescent
Dimsdale Road
122
132

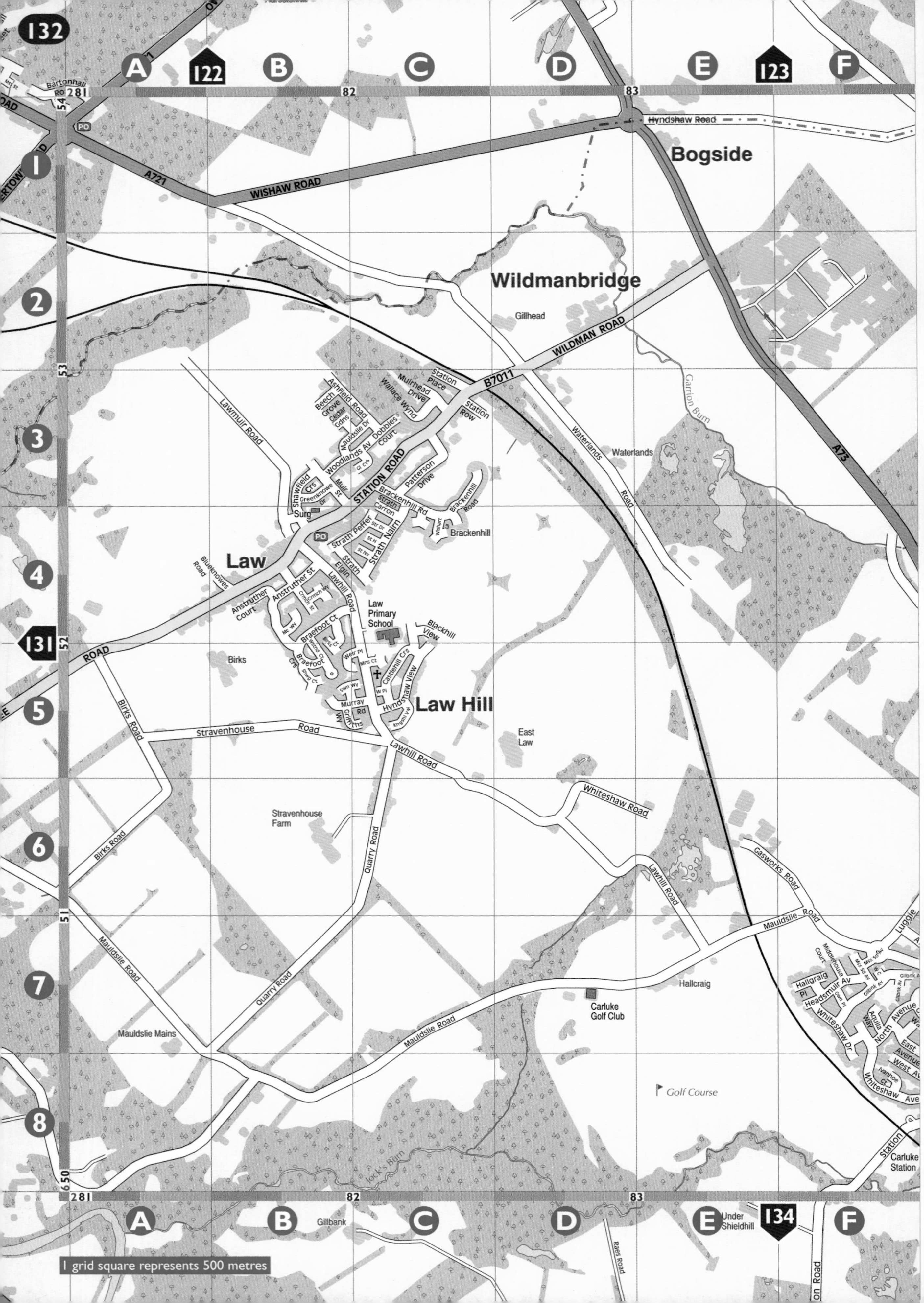

132
122
123
131
134
A
B
C
D
E
F
1
2
3
4
5
6
7
8
281
82
83
54
53
52
51
650
Bartonhall Rd
PO
A721
WISHAW ROAD
Hyndshaw Road
Bogside
Wildmanbridge
Gillhead
WILDMAN ROAD
B7011
A73
Garrion Burn
Waterlands
Waterlands Road
Lawmuir Road
Station Place
Station Row
Muirhead Drive
Wallace Wynd
Ashfield Road
Beech Grove
Cedar Gdns
Mauldslie Dr
Dobbies Court
Woodlands Av
STATION ROAD
Patterson Drive
Shawfield Crs
Greenknowe Dr
Muir St
Brackenhill Rd
Brackenhill Road
Brackenhill
Strath Carron
Strath Peffer
Strath Nairn
Strath Elgin
Surg
Law
Blueknowes Road
Anstruther Court
Anstruther St
Lawhill Road
Law Primary School
Blackhill View
Braefoot Ct
Braefoot Crs
Birks
Weir Pl
Castlehill Crs
Hyndshaw View
Murray Rd
Griffiths Wy
Law Hill
East Law
ROAD
Birks Road
Stravenhouse Road
Lawhill Road
Whiteshaw Road
Stravenhouse Farm
Quarry Road
Gasworks Road
Mauldslie Road
Hallcraig
Carluke Golf Club
Mauldslie Mains
Hallcraig Pl
Headsmuir Av
Middlehouse Court
Whiteshaw Dr
Aquila Way
North Avenue
East Avenue
West Av
Ivanhoe Ct
Whiteshaw Ave
Luggie
Golf Course
Station Road
Carluke Station
Jock's Burn
Gillbank
Under Shieldhill
Raes Road
1 grid square represents 500 metres

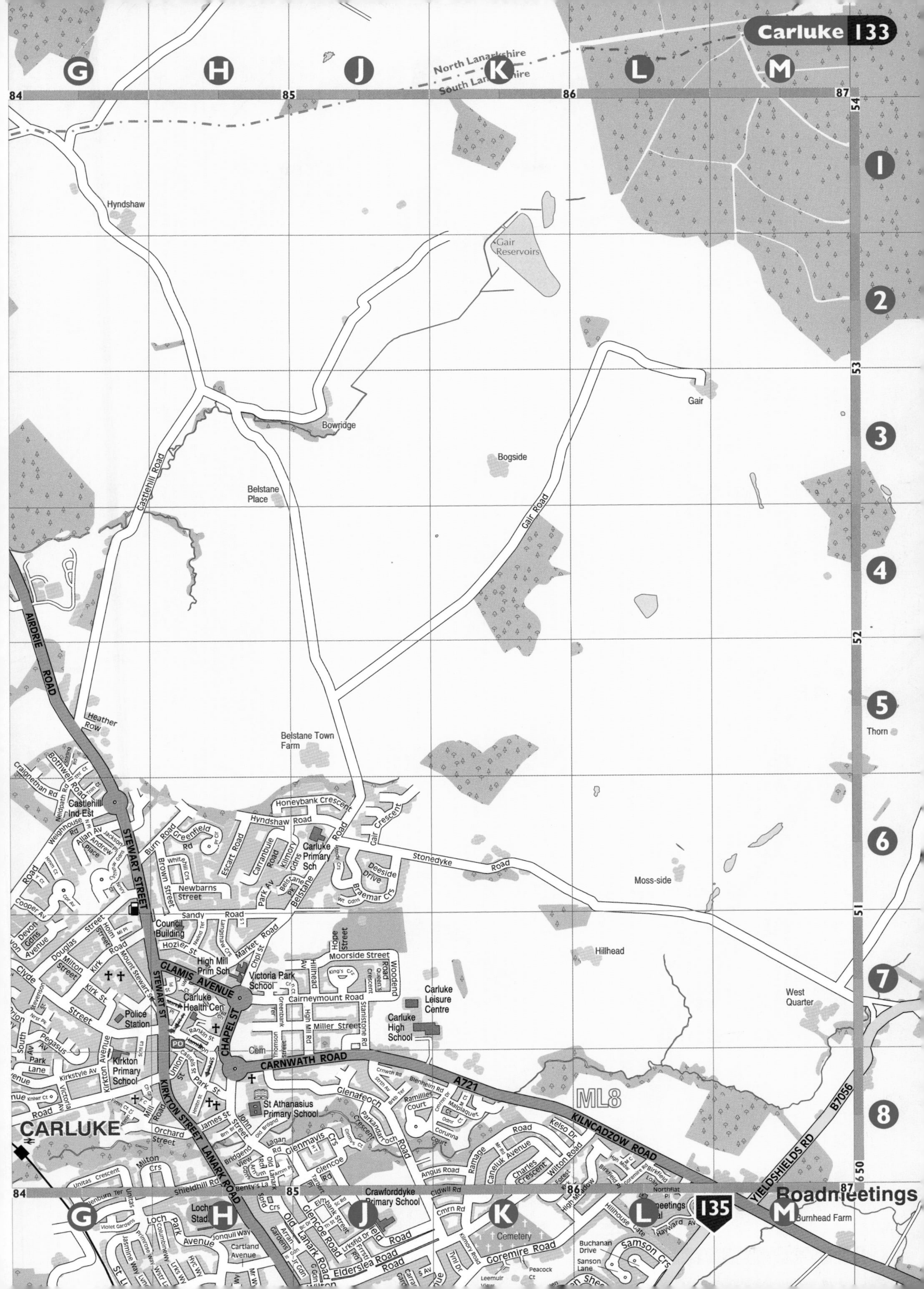

G **H** **J** **K** **L** **M**

84   85   86   87

North Lanarkshire
South Lanarkshire

54

1
2
3
4
5
6
7
8

53

52

51

50

Hyndshaw

Gair
Reservoirs

Gair

Bowridge

Bogside

Belstane
Place

Belstane Town
Farm

Thorn

Moss-side

Hillhead

West
Quarter

AIRDRIE ROAD

Castlehill Road

Gair Road

Heather
Row

Craignethan Rd

Castlehill
Ind Est

STEWART STREET

Bothwell Rd

Weighhouse
Rd

Alan Av

Andrew
Place

Greenfield

Burn Road

Brown Street

White Hill Crs

Newbarns
Street

Honeybank Crescent

Hyndshaw Road

Escart Road

Carrantoule

Kindry

Gdns

Carluke
Primary
Sch

Belstane Road

Gair Crescent

Park Av

Belstane

Deeside
Drive

Braemar Crs

Wt. Gdns

Stonedyke Road

Sandy Road

Hozier St

Council
Building

High Mill Prim Sch

Market St

Chpl St

Hope
Street

Moorside Street

King's Crs

Woodend Road

Cooper Av

Devon Gdns

Avenue

Douglas
Street

Milton
Street

Kirk St

Kirk
Street

Clyde
Street

South

Pegasus

Park
Lane

Kirkstyle Av

Kirkton Avenue

Kirkton
Primary
School

GLAMIS AVENUE

STEWART ST

Victoria Park
School

Hillhead Av

Cairneymount Road

Greenbank

Miller Street

Stanistone Road

Crescent

Carluke
Health Cen

CHAPEL ST

Cem

Thomson Street

High Mill Rd

Police
Station

PO

Ranken St

James St

Union St

Cassels St

Park St

St Athanasius
Primary School

Glenafeoch

Carkman

Crescent

Ramillies
Court

Blenheim Rd

Malplaquet

Corunna
Court

Carluke
Leisure
Centre

Carluke
High
School

A721

KILNCADZOW ROAD

ML8

CARNWATH ROAD

KIRKTON STREET

LANARK ROAD

Orchard
Street

Milton
Crs

Bridgend
View

Bentys's La

Glenmavis Crs

Glencoe
Rd

John Street

Lagan

Loch Road

Angus Road

Kelso Dr

Canteluk Avenue

Charles
Crescent

Wilton Road

B7056

YIELDSHIELDS RD

CARLUKE

Shieldhill Rd

Unitas Crescent

Violet Gardens

Loch
Stad

Loch
Park
Avenue

Jonquil Way

Cartland
Avenue

Crawforddyke
Primary School

OLD LANARK ROAD

Glencoe Road

Elderslee Road

Goremire Road

Cemetery

Buchanan
Drive

Sanson
Lane

Samson Crs

Burnhead Farm

Northflat
Pl

Roadmeetings
Hospital

I 35

Roadmeetings

84   85   86   87

G **H** **J** **K** **L** **M**

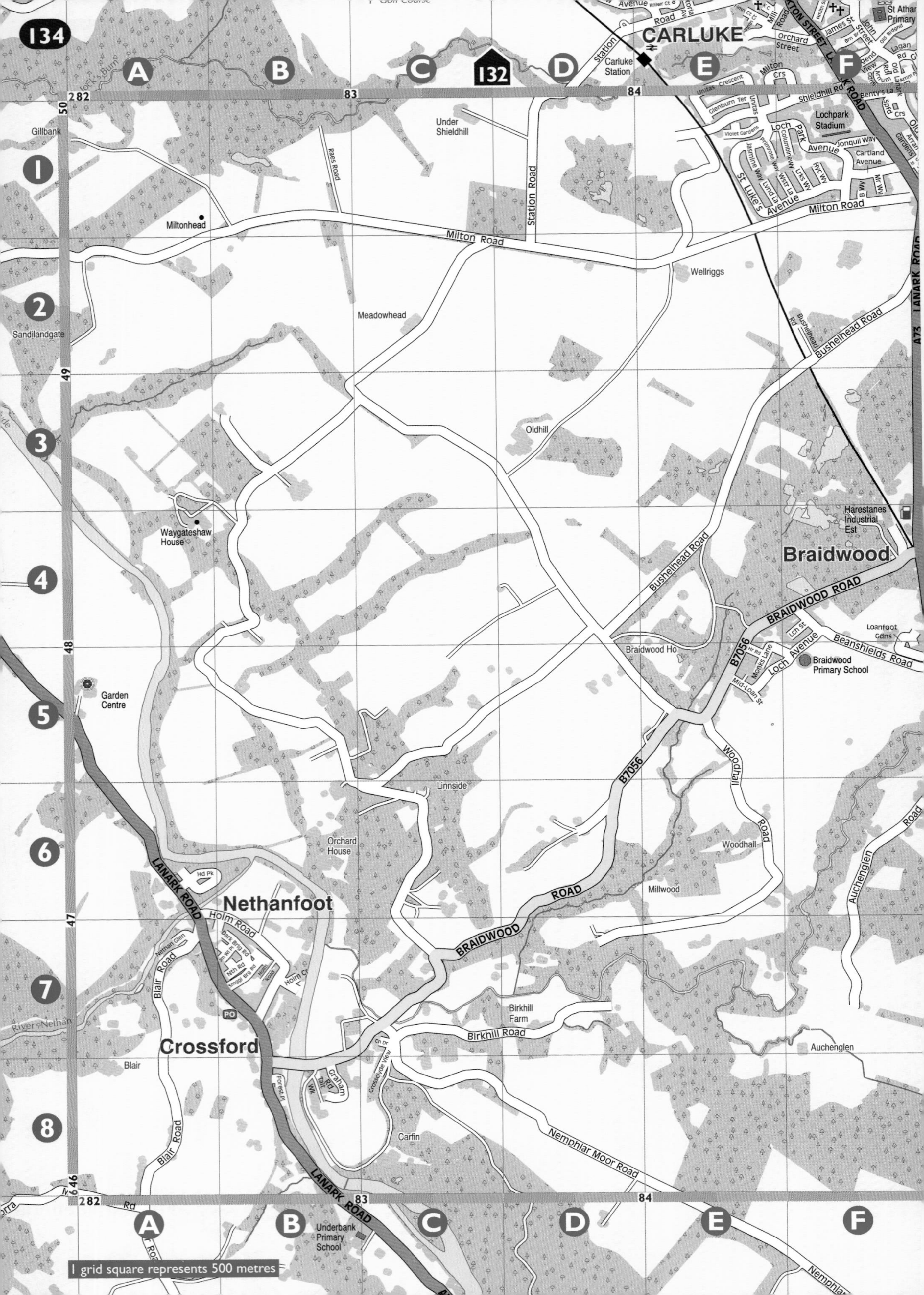

CARLUKE
Carluke Station
Under Shieldhill
Station Road
Raes Road
Gillbank
Miltonhead
Milton Road
Loch Park Avenue
St Luke's Avenue
Lochpark Stadium
Cartland Avenue
Wellriggs
Meadowhead
Sandilandgate
Busheihead Road
A73 LANARK ROAD
Oldhill
Waygateshaw House
Harestanes Industrial Est
Braidwood
BRAIDWOOD ROAD
Braidwood Ho
Braidwood Primary School
Beanshields Road
Loch Avenue
Monks Lane
Mid-Loan St
B7056
Garden Centre
Linnside
Woodhall Road
Woodhall
Orchard House
Millwood
Auchenglen Road
LANARK ROAD
Nethanfoot
Holm Road
Blair Road
Birkhill Farm
Birkhill Road
River Nethan
Crossford
Blair
Auchenglen
Crossdyke View
Graham Rd
Carfin
Nemphlar Moor Road
Underbank Primary School
1 grid square represents 500 metres

132

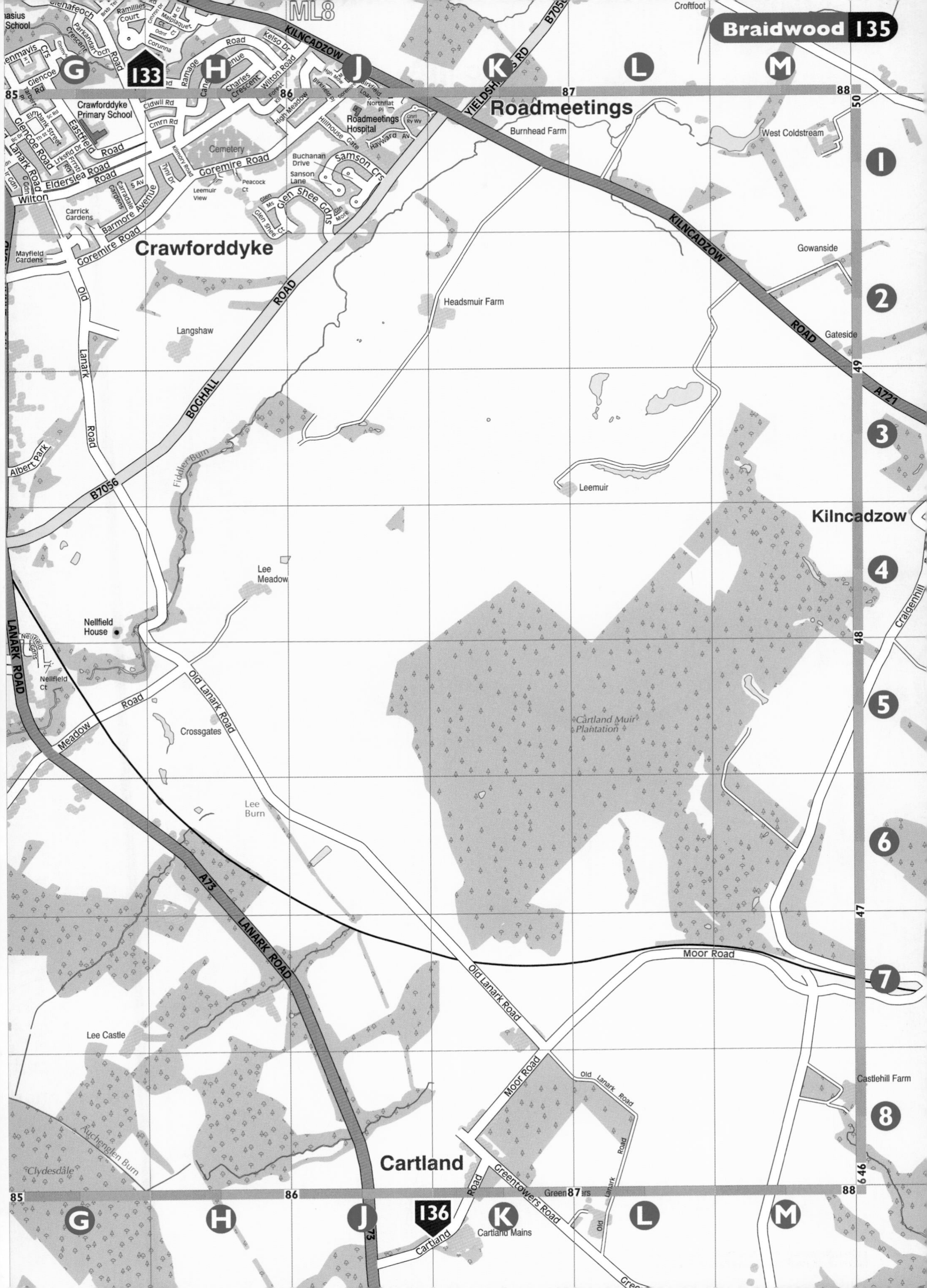

ML8

G 133 H J K L M

Kilncadzow Road
B705 RD
B705

85 86 87 88 50

Croftfoot

Roadmeetings

Burnhead Farm

West Coldstream

I

Glenafeoch
School
Ramillies Ct
Maplaque
Odir
Coruna

Crawfordyke
Primary School

Cidwll Rd
Cmrn Rd

Kelso Dr
Ramage Road

Wilton Road
Charles Crescent

High Meadow
Forest

Northflat
Pl
Glnrt Wy
Logan

KILNCADZOW

Gowanside

2

Eastfield
Lanark Road
Road
Elderslea Road
Road
Wilton

Cemetery
Goremire Road

Buchanan
Drive
Sanson
Lane

Roadmeetings
Hospital
Hillhouse
Cafe

Hayward Av

ROAD

Gateside

49

Carrick Gardens
Barmore Avenue
Goremire Road

Lefsield Dr

Tyrdl Ct

S Av
Carradale
Crescent

Peacock
Ct

Leemuir
View

Glen Shee Gdns

Samson Crs

Mfr
Glen
Mfr
Glen Shee Ct
Glen Shee Dr

A721

3

Mayfield
Gardens

Crawforddyke

Old
Lanark
Road

BOGHALL

ROAD

Headsmuir Farm

Leemuir

Kilncadzow

Albert
Park

B7096

Langshaw

Fidder Burn

4

Craigenhill

48

Lee
Meadow

5

LANARK
ROAD

Nellfield
House

Nellfield
Ct

Old Lanark Road
Road

Meadow

Crossgates

Lee
Burn

Cartland Muir
Plantation

6

47

A73
LANARK ROAD

Moor Road

7

Lee Castle

Old Lanark Road

Castlehill Farm

8

Auchenglen Burn

Clydesdale

Moor Road
Road

Moor Road

Old Lanark Road

Old Lanark Road

46

Cartland

Greentowers Road

Green 87 rs

85 86 87 88

G H J 136 K L M
73
Cartland
Cartland Mains
Green

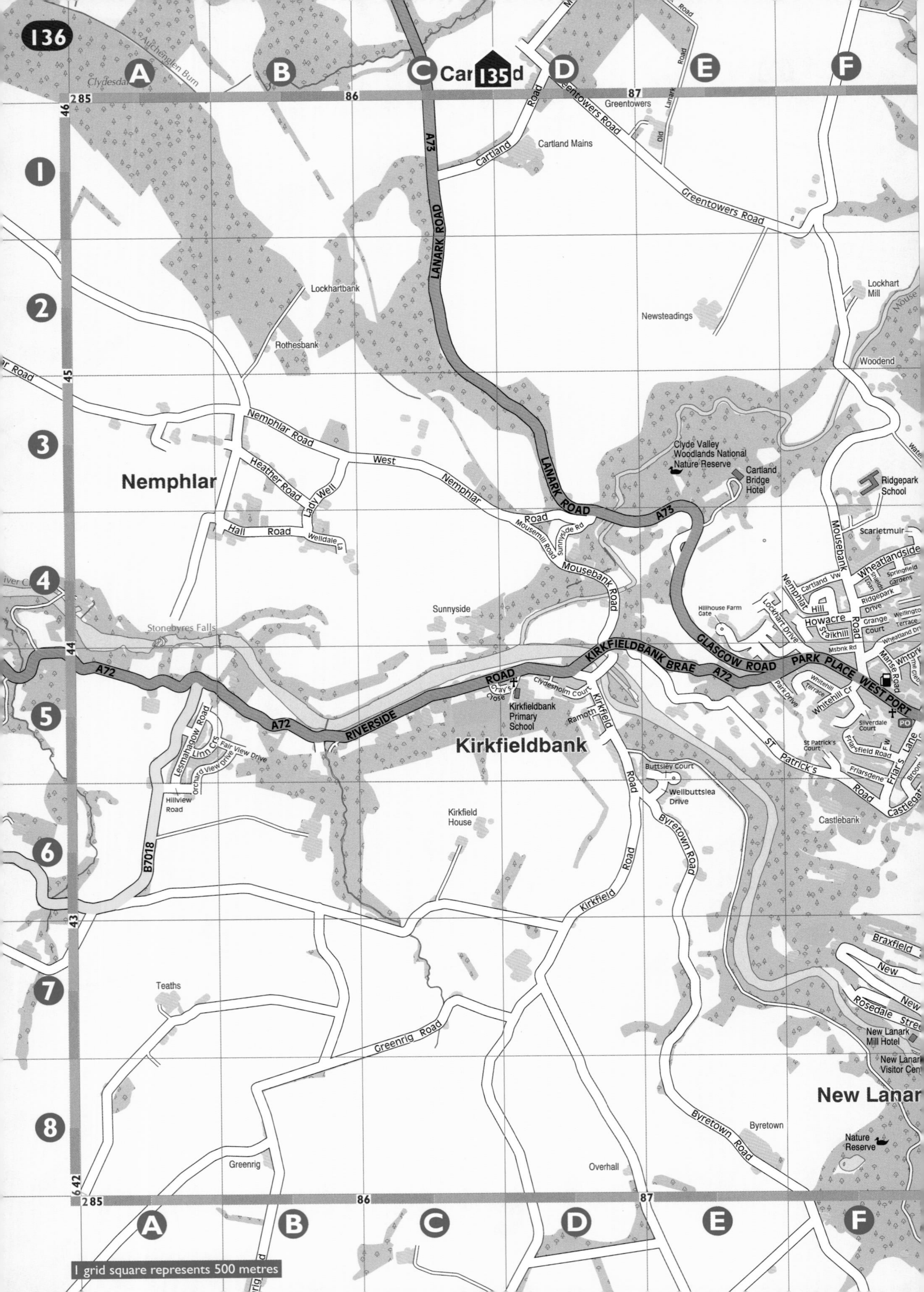
Cartland 135
Nemphlar
Kirkfieldbank
New Lanark
Lockhartbank
Rothesbank
Newsteadings
Greentowers
Cartland Mains
Clyde Valley Woodlands National Nature Reserve
Cartland Bridge Hotel
Ridgepark School
Lockhart Mill
Woodend
Sunnyside
Stonebyres Falls
Kirkfieldbank Primary School
Kirkfield House
Castlebank
Teaths
Greenrig
Overhall
Byretown
New Lanark Mill Hotel
New Lanark Visitor Centre
Nature Reserve
LANARK ROAD
A73
A72
RIVERSIDE ROAD
KIRKFIELDBANK BRAE
GLASGOW ROAD
PARK PLACE
WEST PORT
Nemphlar Road
West Nemphlar Road
Heather Road
Lady Well
Hall Road
Welldale La
Mousemill Road
Sunnyside Rd
Mousebank Road
Greentowers Road
Cartland Road
Old Lanark Road
Kirkfield Road
Byretown Road
Greenrig Road
Lesmahagow Road
Linn Crs
Fair View Drive
Orchard View Drive
Hillview Road
B7018
Clydesholm Court
Cray's Close
Ramoth
Buttsley Court
Wellbuttslea Drive
St Patrick's Road
Braxfield
Rosedale Street
1 grid square represents 500 metres

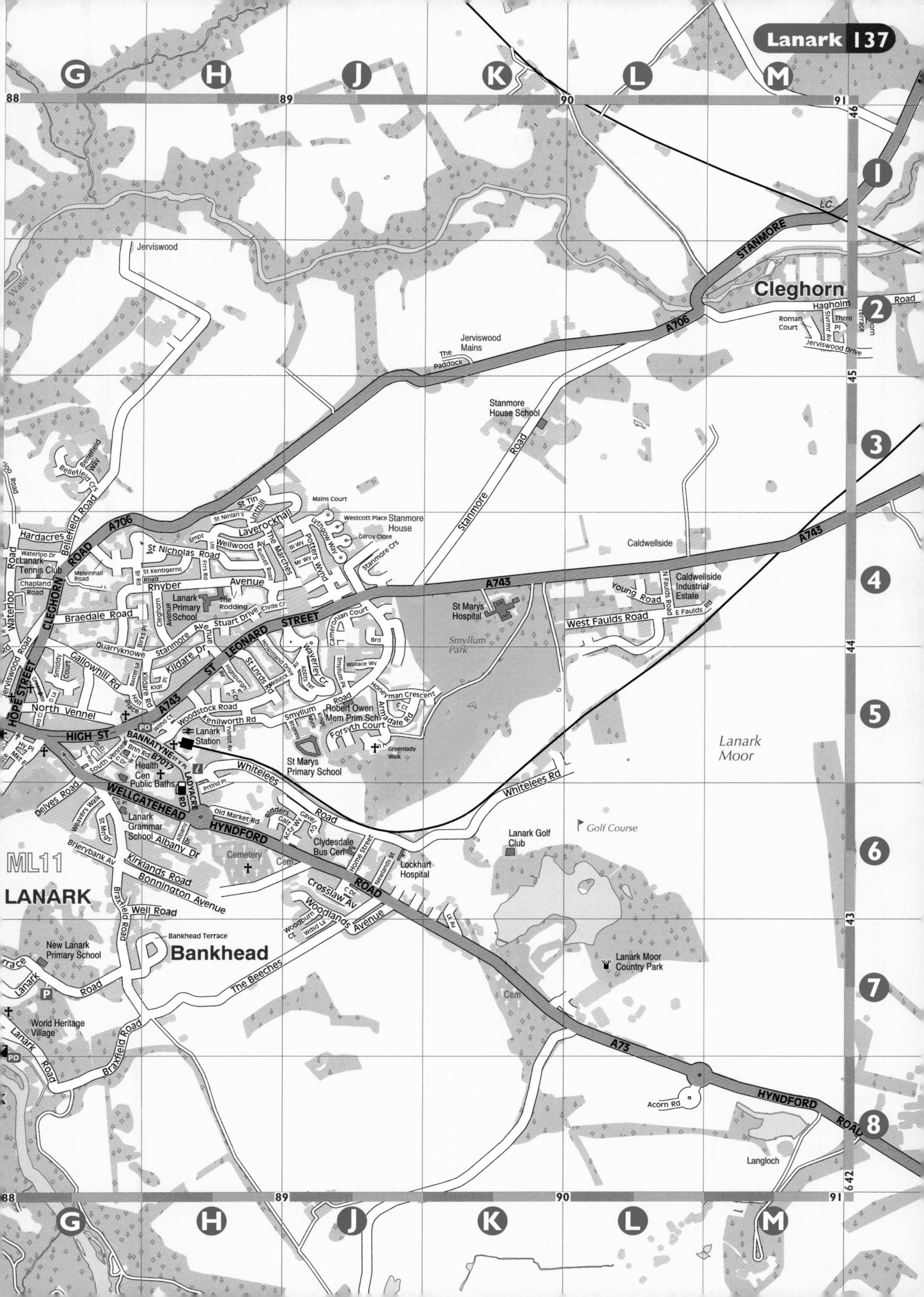

G H J K L M

88 89 90 91 46

1

STANMORE

Cleghorn

Hagholm
Terrace

Roman
Court

Thrnl
Pl

Silvrmr Av

Jerviswood drive

Road

2

45

Jerviswood

A706

Jerviswood Mains

The Paddock

Jerviswood
Road

Stanmore
House School

A706

Stanmore Road

Caldwellside

A743

3

Hardacres

Bellefield Way
Bellefield Cr

Bellefield Road

CLEGHORN ROAD

A706

St Tin

St Ninian's

Mains Court

Westcott Place Stanmore
House

Gilroy Close

Stanmore Crs

Lychgoon Way

Caldwellside
Industrial
Estate

N Faulds Road

E Faulds Rd

44

Waterloo Dr
Lanark
Tennis Club

Chapland
Road

Waterloo Road

St Nicholas Road

Melvinhall
Road

Wellwood Av

St Kentigerns

Rhyber
Avenue

The
Marches

Patters Wynd

LAVEROCKHALL

Mr Wy

Mr Y

Young Road

St Marys
Hospital

West Faulds Road

4

Braedale Road

Quarryknowe

Gallowhill Rd

Smiddy
Court

Stanmore Avenue

Cleghorn Avenue

Kildare Dr

Kildt Pl

ST LEONARD STREET

Stuart Drive

The
Rodding

Clyde Cr

Cameronian Court

Brd

Waverley Cr

Smyllum
Park

Road

5

HOPE STREET

North Vennel

A743

St Lnrds Rd

Woodstock Road

Kenilworth Rd

Smyllum Road

Robert Owen
Mem Prim Sch

Arngdale

Honeyman Crescent

Forsyth Court

6 42

HIGH ST

BANNATYNE

LADYACRE

Lanark Station

Health
Cen

Public Baths

Whitelees

Whitelees Rd

Greenlady
Walk

St Marys
Primary School

**Lanark
Moor**

5

Delves Road

WELLGATEHEAD

HYNDFORD

Lanark
Grammar
School

Albany Dr

Old Market Rd

Road

Clydesdale
Bus Cen

Home Street

Newlands St

Lockhart
Hospital

Golf Course

Lanark Golf
Club

6

ML11

LANARK

Brierybank Av

Braxfield Road

Kirklands Road

Bonnington Avenue

Well Road

Cemetery

Crosslaw Av

ROAD

43

New Lanark
Primary School

Bankhead Terrace

Bankhead

The Beeches

Woodlands
Avenue

Woodburn
Ct

Cem

Lanark Moor
Country Park

7

World Heritage
Village

Lanark Road

P

Braxfield Road

A73

HYNDFORD ROAD

Acorn Rd

8

Langloch

88 89 90 91 6 42

G H J K L M

Place	Page	Ref
Abronhill	31	K6
Airdrie	85	G2
Alexandria	13	H5
Allanbank	105	M8
Allanton	120	D8
Annathill	47	L8
Anniesland	59	K3
Arden	93	H5
Ardoch	19	L4
Ashton	15	J2
Auchenback	92	C8
Auchentibber	118	A8
Auchinairn	62	B3
Auchinloch	45	K8
Auchinraith	118	F3
Auchinreoch	28	B4
Auchinstarry	29	L4
Baillieston	82	B6
Balloch	13	K1
Balloch	30	B7
Balmalloch	29	H1
Balmore	43	L2
Balornock	62	B4
Bankhead	95	M4
Bankhead	137	H7
Bardowie	43	H3
Bardrainney	34	F3
Bargarran	38	F7
Bargeddie	83	G6
Barlanark	81	L4
Barmulloch	62	D5
Barncluith	129	M1
Barrachnie	81	L5
Barrhead	92	C6
Battlefield	94	F2
Bearsden	41	L4
Beith	125	K3
Bellahouston	78	A5
Bellshill	99	L6
Bellside	102	D8
Bellsmyre	21	H3
Biggar Road	102	A4
Birdston	27	J7
Birkenshaw	98	E1
Birniehill	3	J9
Bishopbriggs	44	B8
Bishopton	38	A7
Blackhall	9	M8
Blackridge	71	J1
Blackwood	47	K2
Blairhill	83	L4
Blairlinn	49	G4
Blairskaith	25	J7
Blantyre	118	B3
Blythswood	58	C4
Bogside	132	E1
Bonhill	13	M8
Bonkle	123	J5
Bothwell	118	F1
Bow Farm	16	B4
Bowhousebog or Liquo	103	M7
Bowling	38	E2
Brackenhirst	66	D3
Braehead	115	K7
Braeside	15	K6
Braidfauld	80	E7
Braidwood	134	F4
Branchton	15	M6
Bridgend	7	J7
Bridgend	46	D8
Bridge of Weir	72	F3
Bridgeton	80	A5
Broadfield	34	F2
Brookfield	73	K5
Broom	113	M4
Broomhill	59	M6
Broomhouse	82	A8
Browsburn	85	H4
Brucehill	20	C7
Buchley	43	J5
Burnbank	119	H5
Burnfoot	66	E7
Burnside	96	C5
Busby	114	F5
Cadder	44	B5
Cadzow	129	K3
Cairncurran	52	A2
Cairnhill	84	E3
Calderbank	85	H6
Caldercruix	68	C3
Calderwood	3	K1
Calton	5	L9
Cambuslang	97	G6
Cambusnethan	122	D6
Carbrain	31	H8
Cardonald	77	H4
Cardross	19	H2
Carfin	101	H7
Carluke	133	C8
Carmunnock	115	J2
Carmyle	97	H2
Carnbroe	84	E6
Carntyne	80	E3
Carnwadric	93	M5
Carrickstone	30	F4
Cartland	135	J8
Cartsdyke	7	H7
Castlehead	8	E8
Castlehill	20	B5
Castlemilk	95	L8
Cathcart	94	F4
Central	6	B5
Chapelhall	85	M8
Charleston	75	L8
Chryston	46	C8
Clarkston	85	K1
Clarkston	114	D3
Cleekhimin	121	H1
Cleghorn	137	M2
Cleland	102	A8
Clevans	72	A3
Cliftonville	84	C2
Clydebank	40	A8
Coatbridge	84	B4
Coatdyke	84	D3
College Milton	116	A7
Colston	61	L2
Coltness	122	D3
Condorrat	48	B2
Corkerhill	77	L7
Cowlairs	61	M7
Craigend	56	F1
Craigend	63	J7
Craigendoran	11	H8
Craigends	73	K2
Craigneuk	85	J3
Craigneuk	121	H4
Craigton	77	L4
Cranhill	81	G2
Crawforddyke	135	G2
Criagendmuir	63	L6
Crindledyke	123	H4
Croftfoot	95	L5
Crookfur	113	K3
Crookston	76	F5
Crossford	134	A7
Crosshill	82	D5
Crosslee	73	C1
Crossmill	92	C5
Crossmyloof	78	D8
Croy	29	M6
Cumbernauld	30	F8
Cumbernauld Village	31	J4
Dalmarnock	80	A7
Dalmuir	39	L6
Dalserf	131	J7
Dalshannon	48	A4
Dalton	98	A8
Dean Park	58	D7
Dennistoun	80	A3
Dennystown	20	E6
Devol	34	D2
Dovecothall	92	E5
Dowanhill	60	C7
Drumchapel	40	F7
Drumgelloch	85	H1
Drumpellier	83	J3
Drumry	40	C7
Dullatur	30	C4
Dumbarton	21	G7
Dumbreck	78	B6
Dundyvan	83	M5
Duntocher	39	M4
Dykehead	104	C5
Earnock	128	F1
Easterhouse	82	A2
Eastfield	30	C7
Eastfield	71	J8
Eastfield	96	D3
East Kilbride	3	H7
East Mains	3	H5
East Shawhead	84	C6
Eddlewood	129	K3
Elderslie	74	C8
Erskine	57	G1
Faifley	40	C2
Fairhill	129	J2
Fallside	99	K3
Ferguslie Park	8	A3
Fernhill	96	B8
Ferniegair	120	B8
Flemington	97	J7
Fluchter	25	H8
Forgewood	100	C7
Forrestfield	70	A1
Foxbar	90	F2
Freeland	57	H2
Fullarton	81	G7
Gallowhill	9	K1
Gallowhill	115	L2
Garnkirk	64	B4
Garrowhill	82	A5
Gartcosh	64	E5
Garthamlock	63	K8
Gartlea	85	H3
Gartloch	64	C7
Gartness	85	L4
Gartsherrie	83	L1
Gateside	111	L1
Gellston	19	H1
Germiston	62	B8
Gibshill	17	L7
Giffnock	94	B8
Glasgow	5	C6
Glenboig	65	M4
Glenburn	91	J3
Glengarnock	124	C7
Glenmavis	66	D5
Gorbals	79	G7
Gourock	15	K1
Govan	78	B2
Govanhill	79	G7
Gowkthrapple	131	J2
Greenend	84	C5
Greenfaulds	48	F2
Greenfield	81	G4
Greenfoot	66	A1
Greengairs	49	M7
Greenhead	122	D7
Greenhills	126	F4
Greenock	7	H4
Greenock West	16	C2
Haghill	80	D3
Hairmyres	126	B2
Hallside	97	L5
Hamilton	119	M6
Hardgate	40	D3
Hareleeshill	130	E8
Hareshaw	102	D4
Harestanes	28	B8
Harthill	71	M7
Hartwood	104	A6
Hayston	44	F2
Helensburgh	10	B6
High Blantyre	118	A4
High Crosshill	96	B4
High Gallowhill	45	G4
High Merryton	130	A4
Hillend	69	H6
Hillington	77	G3
Hogganfield	62	F8
Holehills	67	H7
Holehouse	111	H4
Holytown	101	G3
Houston	55	H8
Howwood	89	G5
Hurlet	92	F2
Hutchesontown	79	J6
Ibrox	78	B4
Inchinnan	57	K3
Inverkip	32	F4
Jamestown	13	L3
Johnstone	74	A8
Kelburn	35	C1
Kelvin	127	K5
Kelvindale	60	A4
Kelvinside	60	D5
Kennishead	93	L4
Kessington	42	C6
Kilbarchan	73	G7
Kilbirnie	124	B3
Kilbowie	40	C5
Kildrum	31	H6
Kilmacolm	53	L2
Kilncadzow	135	M4
Kilsyth	29	L1
Kings Park	95	K4
Kirkfieldbank	136	C5
Kirkhill	114	C6
Kirkintilloch	45	G1
Kirk of Shotts	87	K7
Kirkshaw	83	K7
Kirktonhill	20	E8
Kirkwood	83	J6
Knightswood	59	J2
Knowetop	120	F5
Kylepark	98	D5
Ladyburn	17	M6
Laighstonehall	119	G8
Lambhill	61	H3
Lanark	137	G6
Langbank	36	A3
Langloan	83	L5
Langside	94	E3
Largs	107	G5
Larkfield	15	K5
Larkhall	130	B7
Law	132	B4
Law	132	C5
Lennoxtown	26	E2
Lenzie	45	K5
Lenziemill	48	F1
Levan	14	E4
Lilybank	17	M8
Limekilnburn	129	H8
Linwood	74	A4
Lochwinnoch	109	K3
Lochwood	82	D1
Longbar	124	F7
Low Blantyre	118	E1
Low Semple	88	B5
Low Waters	129	L1
Luggiebank	49	H3
Machan	130	C7
Mansewood	94	B4
Marnock	65	J4
Maryhill	60	C4
Mearns	113	M6
Meikle Earnock	129	K3
Merrylee	94	D6
Mid Auchinleck	34	D3
Midton	15	K3
Millarston	75	G7
Millersneuk	45	L6
Millerston	63	G6
Millikenpark	89	H1
Mill of Haldane	13	M1
Milngavie	42	C1
Milnwood	100	D5
Milton	37	M1
Milton	53	J4
Milton	61	J3
Milton of Campsie	27	K5
Moffat Mills	85	M2
Mollinsburn	47	K6
Moodiesburn	46	E7
Morningside	123	J6
Mossend	100	D4
Mossneuk	126	B4
Mosspark	77	L6
Motherwell	120	E4
Mountblow	39	J6
Mount Vernon	81	J8
Mt Florida	95	H3
Mugdock	24	C4
Muirend	94	F5
Muirhead	64	D3
Muirhead	81	M7
Muirhouse	121	G6
Neilston	111	L4
Nemphlar	136	A3
Nerston	117	G4
Nethanfoot	134	B6
Nether Kirton	111	M2
Netherlee	94	E7
Netherplace	112	F5
Netherton	121	L8
Newarthill	101	M5
Newhouse	102	B1
New Lanark	136	F8
Newlands	94	D4
Newlandsmuir	126	C3
Newmains	122	F4
New Stevenston	101	H5
Newton	97	M4
Newton Mearns	113	J4
Nitshill	92	F4
North Motherwell	120	C1
Oatlands	79	K7
Old Balornock	62	B5
Oldhall	76	D4
Old Kilpatrick	38	F4
Old Monkland	83	L6
Orbiston	99	M6
Overton	16	C7
Overtown	131	M3
Oxgang	45	M3
Paisley	9	J6
Park Farm	35	H3
Parkhall	39	M5
Parkhead	80	D6
Parkhill	35	K2
Parklea	35	J1
Park Mains	57	J1
Parkside	102	C7
Partick	60	A8
Pather	122	B8
Peel Park	115	M8
Petersburn	85	L3
Petershill	62	B7
Pilmuir	112	E8
Plains	67	M7
Pollok	77	H7
Pollokshaws	94	B2
Pollokshields	78	D7
Polmadie	79	J8
Port Dundas	4	F1
Porterfield	58	A7
Port Glasgow	18	C8
Possil Park	61	J5
Priesthill	93	G3
Provanmill	62	E7
Quarrelton	89	L1
Quarriers Village	53	K8
Quarter	129	L7
Queenslie	81	M2
Queenzieburn	28	F2
Radnor Park	40	A5
Ranfurly	72	C4
Rashielee	39	G8
Ravenscraig	16	B6
Rawyards	67	H8
Renfrew	58	C6
Renton	20	D1
Riddrie	80	D1
Riggend	49	G8
Roadmeetings	135	K1
Robroyston	62	E4
Rogerton	116	D4
Rosebank	46	A2
Rosehall	84	B5
Rossland	38	C8
Roughwood	125	J8
Royston	5	K2
Ruchazie	81	H1
Ruchill	61	G5
Rutherglen	95	L1
Saint Leonards	127	M2
Salsburgh	87	J8
Scotstoun	59	H4
Seafar	30	E8
Shawhead	83	M7
Shawlands	94	D2
Shawsburn	131	G2
Sheddens	114	F3
Shettleston	81	G5
Shieldhall	77	J1
Shieldmuir	121	J5
Shillford	110	D5
Shortroods	75	J2
Shotts	104	F4
Sighthill	5	K1
Silverton	21	H6
Silvertonhill	119	K8
Skelmorlie	50	A5
Solsgirth	46	B1
Spango	15	K7
Springboig	81	J4
Springburn	61	M6
Springhill	105	H7
Springhill	112	C2
Stamperland	114	F2
Stand	67	H3
Stane	105	G6
Stepps	63	J5
Stewartfield	116	C6
Stonefield	118	F2
Strathbungo	78	E8
Strone	7	M9
Strone Farm	6	E9
Summerston	60	E2
Swinton	82	C4
Tannochside	99	G2
Temple	59	L2
The Murray	2	F9
Thornliebank	93	L6
Thornly Park	91	M1
Thorntonhall	115	G7
Thrashbush	66	F8
Torbothie	105	J5
Torbush	123	H6
Torrance	44	B1
Townend	21	G4
Townhead	5	H4
Townhead	83	J1
Twechar	28	E7
Uddingston	98	C5
Udston	118	E6
Uplawmoor	110	B7
Upper Dalquhurn	13	H8
Victory Gardens	58	C8
Viewpark	99	J2
Wardpark	31	J2
Waterloo	131	M1
Waterside	46	B3
Waterside	92	E4
Wattston	49	K8
Wemyss Bay	50	A1
West Arthurlie	91	M8
West Benhar	71	H8
Westburn	97	L4
West Drumoyne	77	L2
Wester Auchinloch	63	K1
Westfield	47	M4
West Mains	2	D5
West Porton	38	A4
Westrigg	71	M1
Westwood	2	A1
Whifflet	84	B4
Whinhall	84	E1
Whitecraigs	114	A4
Whitecrook	58	D1
Whitehill	119	H3
Whitehills	127	J5
Whiteinch	59	L7
Wildmanbridge	132	C2
Williamwood	114	B2
Wishaw	122	A5
Woodhall	34	F2
Yett	101	J6
Yoker	58	E2
Yorkhill	78	C2

USING THE STREET INDEX

Street names are listed alphabetically. Each street name is followed by its postal town or area locality, the Postcode District, the page number, and the reference to the square in which the name is found.

Standard index entries are shown as follows:

Abbey Cl *PSLY* PA1 .... **9** J5

Street names and selected addresses not shown on the map due to scale restrictions are shown in the index with an asterisk:

Arran Pl *CTBR* ML5 * **84** D5

GENERAL ABBREVIATIONS

ACC .... ACCESS	BRK .... BROOK	CHYD .... CHURCHYARD	CON .... CONVENT	CTS .... COURTS	
ALY .... ALLEY	BTM .... BOTTOM	CIR .... CIRCLE	COT .... COTTAGE	CTYD .... COURTYARD	
AP .... APPROACH	BUS .... BUSINESS	CIRC .... CIRCUS	COTS .... COTTAGES	CUTT .... CUTTINGS	
AR .... ARCADE	BVD .... BOULEVARD	CL .... CLOSE	CP .... CAPE	CV .... COVE	
ASS .... ASSOCIATION	BY .... BYPASS	CLFS .... CLIFFS	CPS .... COPSE	CYN .... CANYON	
AV .... AVENUE	CATH .... CATHEDRAL	CMP .... CAMP	CR .... CREEK	DEPT .... DEPARTMENT	
BCH .... BEACH	CEM .... CEMETERY	CNR .... CORNER	CREM .... CREMATORIUM	DL .... DALE	
BLDS .... BUILDINGS	CEN .... CENTRE	CO .... COUNTY	CRS .... CRESCENT	DM .... DAM	
BND .... BEND	CFT .... CROFT	COLL .... COLLEGE	CSWY .... CAUSEWAY	DR .... DRIVE	
BNK .... BANK	CH .... CHURCH	COM .... COMMON	CT .... COURT	DRO .... DROVE	
BR .... BRIDGE	CHA .... CHASE	COMM .... COMMISSION	CTRL .... CENTRAL	DRY .... DRIVEWAY	

DWGS DWELLINGS
E EAST
EMB EMBANKMENT
EMBY EMBASSY
ESP ESPLANADE
EST ESTATE
EX EXCHANGE
EXPY EXPRESSWAY
EXT EXTENSION
F/O FLYOVER
FC FOOTBALL CLUB
FK FORK
FLD FIELD
FLDS FIELDS
FLS FALLS
FM FARM
FT FORT
FTS FLATS
FWY FREEWAY
FY FERRY
GA GATE
GAL GALLERY
GDN GARDEN
GDNS GARDENS
GLD GLADE
GLN GLEN
GN GREEN
GND GROUND
GRA GRANGE
GRG GARAGE
GT GREAT
GTWY GATEWAY
GV GROVE
HGR HIGHER
HL HILL
HLS HILLS
HO HOUSE
HOL HOLLOW
HOSP HOSPITAL
HRB HARBOUR
HTH HEATH
HTS HEIGHTS
HVN HAVEN
HWY HIGHWAY
IMP IMPERIAL
IN INLET
IND EST INDUSTRIAL ESTATE
INF INFIRMARY
INFO INFORMATION
INT INTERCHANGE
IS ISLAND
JCT JUNCTION
JTY JETTY
KG KING
KNL KNOLL
L LAKE
LA LANE
LDG LODGE
LGT LIGHT
LK LOCK
LKS LAKES
LNDG LANDING
LTL LITTLE
LWR LOWER
MAG MAGISTRATE
MAN MANSIONS
MD MEAD
MDW MEADOWS
MEM MEMORIAL
MI MILL
MKT MARKET
MKTS MARKETS
ML MALL
MNR MANOR
MS MEWS
MSN MISSION
MT MOUNT
MTN MOUNTAIN
MTS MOUNTAINS
MUS MUSEUM
MWY MOTORWAY
N NORTH
NE NORTH EAST
NW NORTH WEST
O/P OVERPASS
OFF OFFICE
ORCH ORCHARD
OV OVAL
PAL PALACE
PAS PASSAGE
PAV PAVILION
PDE PARADE
PH PUBLIC HOUSE
PK PARK
PKWY PARKWAY
PL PLACE
PLN PLAIN
PLNS PLAINS
PLZ PLAZA
POL POLICE STATION
PR PRINCE
PREC PRECINCT
PREP PREPARATORY
PRIM PRIMARY
PROM PROMENADE
PRS PRINCESS
PRT PORT
PT POINT
PTH PATH
PZ PIAZZA
QD QUADRANT
QU QUEEN
QY QUAY
R RIVER
RBT ROUNDABOUT
RD ROAD
RDG RIDGE
REP REPUBLIC
RES RESERVOIR
RFC RUGBY FOOTBALL CLUB
RI RISE
RP RAMP
RW ROW
S SOUTH
SCH SCHOOL
SE SOUTH EAST
SER SERVICE AREA
SH SHORE
SHOP SHOPPING
SKWY SKYWAY
SMT SUMMIT
SOC SOCIETY
SP SPUR
SPR SPRING
SQ SQUARE
ST STREET
STN STATION
STR STREAM
STRD STRAND
SW SOUTH WEST
TDG TRADING
TER TERRACE
THWY THROUGHWAY
TNL TUNNEL
TOLL TOLLWAY
TPK TURNPIKE
TR TRACK
TRL TRAIL
TWR TOWER
U/P UNDERPASS
UNI UNIVERSITY
UPR UPPER
V VALE
VA VALLEY
VIAD VIADUCT
VIL VILLA
VIS VISTA
VLG VILLAGE
VLS VILLAS
VW VIEW
W WEST
WD WOOD
WHF WHARF
WK WALK
WKS WALKS
WLS WELLS
WY WAY
YD YARD
YHA YOUTH HOSTEL

POSTCODE TOWNS AND AREA ABBREVIATIONS

AIRDRIE Airdrie
ALEX/LLW Alexandria/Loch Lomond west
BAIL/MDB/MHD Baillieston/Moodiesburn/Muirhead
BALLOCH Balloch
BEITH Beith
BLSH Bellshill
BLTYR/CAMB Blantyre/Cambuslang
BNYBR/BNK Bonnybridge/Banknock
BRHD/NEIL Barrhead/Neilston
BRWEIR Bridge of Weir
BSDN Bearsden
BSHPBGS Bishopbriggs
BSHPTN Bishopton
BTHG/ARM Bathgate/Armadale
CAR/SHTL Carmyle/Shettleston
CARD/HILL/MSPK Cardonald/Hillington/Mosspark
CARLUKE Carluke
CGLE Central Glasgow east
CGLW Central Glasgow west
CLYDBK Clydebank
CMPF/LLE Campsie Fells/Loch Lomond east
COWCAD Cowcaddens
CRG/CRSL/HOU Craigends/Crosslee/Houston
CRMNK/CLK/EAG Carmunnock/Clarkston/Eaglesham
CSMK Castlemilk
CTBR Coatbridge
CUMB Cumbernauld
DALRY Dalry
DEN/PKHD Dennistoun/Parkhead
DMBTN Dumbarton
DMNK/BRGTN Dalmarnock/Bridgeton
DRUM Drumchapel
EKILN East Kilbride north
EKILS East Kilbride south
ERSK Erskine
ESTRH Easterhouse
FAIRLIE Fairlie
FLK Falkirk
GBLS Gorbals
GIF/THBK Giffnock/Thornliebank
GLGNK Glengarnock
GOV/IBX Govan/Ibrox
GRK Gourock
GRNK Greenock
GRNKW/INVK Greenock West/Inverkip
GTCI Great Cumbrae Island
GVH/MTFL Govanhill/Mount Florida
HBR/GL Helensburgh/Gare Loch
HMLTN Hamilton
HWWD Howwood
JNSTN Johnstone
KBRN Kilbirnie
KKNTL Kirkintilloch
KLBCH Kilbarchan
KLMCLM Kilmacolm
KNTSWD Knightswood
KSYTH Kilsyth
KVD/HLHD Kelvindale/Hillhead
KVGV Kelvingrove
LARGS Largs
LNK/LMHG Lanark/Lesmahagow
LNPK/KPK Linn Park/King's Park
LOCHW Lochwinnoch
LRKH Larkhall
MLNGV Milngavie
MRYH/FIRH Maryhill/Firhill
MTHW Motherwell
NMRNS Newton Mearns
OLDK Old Kilpatrick
PGL Port Glasgow
PLK/PH/NH Pollock/Priesthill/Nitshill
PLKSD/SHW Pollockshields/Shawlands
PLKSW/MSWD Pollockshaws/Mansewood
PPK/MIL Possil Park/Milton
PSLY Paisley
PSLYN/LNWD Paisley north/Linwood
PSLYS Paisley south
PTCK Partick
RNFRW Renfrew
RUTH Rutherglen
SCOT Scotstoun
SHOTTS Shotts
SKLM Skelmorlie
SMSTN Summerston
SPRGB/BLRNK Springburn/Balornock
STPS/GTHM/RID Stepps/Garthamlock/Riddrie
STRHV Strathaven
UD/BTH/TAN Uddingston/Bothwell/Tannochside
WHIT/BBN/FH Whitburn/Blackburn/Fauldhouse
WISHAW Wishaw
WMYSB Wemyss Bay

Index - streets

A

Abbey Cl *PSLY* PA1 **9** J5
Abbeycraig Rd *ESTRH* G34 **82** E2
Abbey Dr *SCOT* G14 **59** L5
Abbeygreen St *ESTRH* G34 **82** E1
Abbeyhill St *CAR/SHTL* G32 **80** F3
Abbeylands Rd *CLYDBK* G81 **40** C3
Abbey Pl *AIRDRIE* ML6 **85** J5
Abbey Rd *JNSTN* PA5 **74** B8
Abbots Ct *BALLOCH* G68 **30** D2
Abbotsford *BSHPBGS* G64 **44** C8
Abbotsford Av *HMLTN* ML3 **119** H4
LRKH ML9 **130** C8
RUTH G73 **96** B3
Abbotsford Brae *EKILN* G74 **2** F3
Abbotsford Ct *CUMB* G67 **48** F2
Abbotsford Crs *HMLTN* ML3 **119** H4
PSLYS PA2 **90** D3
SHOTTS ML7 **104** F4
WISHAW ML2 **122** C5
Abbotsford La *BLSH* ML4 **99** M4
Abbotsford Pl *CUMB* G67 **48** F2
GBLS G5 **79** H6
Abbotsford Rd
AIRDRIE ML6 **85** L8
BSDN G61 **41** J3
CLYDBK G81 **40** B8
CUMB G67 **48** F2
HMLTN ML3 **119** G4
WISHAW ML2 **122** C5
Abbotsford Ter
LNK/LMHG ML11 **137** J5
Abbotshall Av *DRUM* G15 **40** E6
Abbotsinch Rd
PSLYN/LNWD PA3 **75** L1
RNFRW PA4 **57** M6
Abbots Ter *AIRDRIE* ML6 **85** J5
Abbot St *GRNKW/INVK* PA16 **16** C6
PLKSD/SHW G41 **94** E1
PSLYN/LNWD PA3 **9** K2
Abbott Crs *CLYDBK* G81 **58** D1
Aberconway St *CLYDBK* G81 **58** C1
Abercorn Av
CARD/HILL/MSPK G52 **76** E2
Abercorn Crs *HMLTN* ML3 **119** M8
Abercorn Dr *HMLTN* ML3 **119** M7
Abercorn Pl *SMSTN* G23 **60** E1
Abercorn Rd *NMRNS* G77 **113** J3
Abercorn St *CLYDBK* G81 **40** E2
PSLYN/LNWD PA3 **9** J3
Abercrombie Crs
BAIL/MDB/MHD G69 **82** F5
Abercrombie Dr *BSDN* G61 **41** H1
Abercrombie Pl *KSYTH* G65 **29** H1
Abercromby Crs *EKILN* G74 **3** M2
HBR/GL G84 **10** F4
Abercromby Dr
DMNK/BRGTN G40 **5** M9
Abercromby Pl *EKILN* G74 **3** M2
Abercromby Pl West
HBR/GL G84 **10** D4
Abercromby St
DMNK/BRGTN G40 **79** M5
Abercromby St East
HBR/GL G84 **10** F4
Aberdalgie Gdns *ESTRH* G34 **82** B2
Aberdalgie Rd *ESTRH* G34 **82** B2
Aberdeen Rd *AIRDRIE* ML6 **85** K5
Aberdour Ct *BLTYR/CAMB* G72 **118** D8
Aberdour Pl *GRNKW/INVK* PA16 **32** E6
Aberdour St *DEN/PKHD* G31 **80** C3
Aberfeldy Av *AIRDRIE* ML6 **67** M6
BLTYR/CAMB G72 **118** D8
Aberfeldy St *DEN/PKHD* G31 **80** C3
Aberfoyle Rd *GRNK* PA15 **17** H7
Aberfoyle St *DEN/PKHD* G31 **80** C3
Aberlady Rd *GOV/IBX* G51 **77** L3
Aberlady St *MTHW* ML1 **102** B8
Abernethy Av
BLTYR/CAMB G72 **118** D7
Abernethy Dr
PSLYN/LNWD PA3 **74** A5
Abernethyn Rd *WISHAW* ML2 **123** G3
Abernethy Pk *EKILN* G74 **2** D4
Abernethy Pl *NMRNS* G77 **114** B6
Abernethy St *DEN/PKHD* G31 **80** C3
Aberuthven Dr *CAR/SHTL* G32 **81** H7
Abiegail Pl *BLTYR/CAMB* G72 **118** D1
Aboukir St *GOV/IBX* G51 **77** L1
Aboyne Dr *PSLYS* PA2 **91** M1
Acacia Dr *BEITH* KA15 **125** J5
BRHD/NEIL G78 **92** A4
PSLYS PA2 **91** H1
Acacia Pl *JNSTN* PA5 **90** A2
Acacia Wy *BLTYR/CAMB* G72 **97** L5
Academy Brae *BEITH* KA15 **125** K5
Academy Pk *AIRDRIE* ML6 **85** G2
PLKSD/SHW G41 **78** C6
Academy Rd *GIF/THBK* G46 **94** C8
Academy St *AIRDRIE* ML6 **85** G2
CAR/SHTL G32 **81** H6
CTBR ML5 **84** A2
LRKH ML9 **130** C6
Academy Ter *BLSH* ML4 **100** B4
Acer Crs *PSLYS* PA2 **91** G1
Acer Gv *AIRDRIE* ML6 **85** L6
Achamore Crs *DRUM* G15 **40** E5
Achamore Dr *DRUM* G15 **40** E5
Achamore Rd *DRUM* G15 **40** E5
Acherhill Gdns *KNTSWD* G13 **59** G1
Achnasheen Rd *AIRDRIE* ML6 **86** A3
Achray Av *ALEX/LLW* G83 **13** J4
Achray Dr *PSLYS* PA2 **91** G1
Achray Pl *CTBR* ML5 **83** J1
MLNGV G62 **23** K6
Achray Rd *CUMB* G67 **48** B3
Acorn Rd *LNK/LMHG* ML11 **137** L8
Acorn St *DMNK/BRGTN* G40 **79** M6
Acre Av *LARGS* KA30 **106** F6
Acre Dr *MRYH/FIRH* G20 **60** B1
Acredyke Crs
SPRGB/BLRNK G21 **62** B3
Acredyke Pl *SPRGB/BLRNK* G21 **62** C4
Acredyke Rd *RUTH* G73 **95** M2
SPRGB/BLRNK G21 **62** B3
Acre Rd *MRYH/FIRH* G20 **60** B1
The Acres *LRKH* ML9 **130** D6
Acre Valley Rd *BSHPBGS* G64 **26** B8
Adam Av *AIRDRIE* ML6 **85** H2
Adams Court La *CGLE* G1 **4** E8
Adamslie Dr *KKNTL* G66 **45** G2
Adamson St *BLSH* ML4 **100** D4
Adams Pl *KSYTH* G65 **29** K2
Adam St *GRK* PA19 **15** M2
GRNK PA15 **7** H8
Adamswell St
SPRGB/BLRNK G21 **61** L7
Adamswell Ter
BAIL/MDB/MHD G69 **47** G8
Addie St *MTHW* ML1 **120** F1
Addiewell Pl *CTBR* ML5 **84** A5
Addiewell St *CAR/SHTL* G32 **81** G3
Addison Gv *GIF/THBK* G46 **93** L5
Addison Pl *GIF/THBK* G46 **93** M5
Addison Rd *GIF/THBK* G46 **93** L5
KVD/HLHD G12 **60** D6
Adelaide Ct *CLYDBK* G81 **39** K5
Adelaide Rd *EKILS* G75 **126** E3
Adelaide St *GRK* PA19 **15** L1
HBR/GL G84 **10** E6
Adele St *MTHW* ML1 **120** F5
Adelphi St *GBLS* G5 **79** K5
Admiral St *PLKSD/SHW* G41 **78** E5
Admiralty Gv *OLDK* G60 **39** H5
Admiralty Pl *OLDK* G60 **39** H5
Advie Pl *GVH/MTFL* G42 **95** H2
Affric Av *AIRDRIE* ML6 **68** A6
Affric Dr *PSLYS* PA2 **76** B8
Afton Crs *BSDN* G61 **42** B7
Afton Dr *RNFRW* PA4 **58** E8
Afton Gdns *BLTYR/CAMB* G72 **118** B4
CTBR ML5 **84** D4
Afton Rd *CUMB* G67 **31** H6
Afton St *LRKH* ML9 **130** E7
PLKSD/SHW G41 **94** E2
Afton Vw *KKNTL* G66 **45** M1
Agamemnon St *CLYDBK* G81 **39** M8
Agnew Av *CTBR* ML5 **84** D2
Agnew Gv *BLSH* ML4 **99** K5
Agnew La *GVH/MTFL* G42 **95** G1
Aikenhead Rd *GVH/MTFL* G42 **79** J8
LNPK/KPK G44 **95** J4
Aikman Pl *EKILN* G74 **3** M1
Aikman Rd *MTHW* ML1 **120** B4
Ailean Dr *CAR/SHTL* G32 **81** L6
Ailean Gdns *CAR/SHTL* G32 **81** L6
Aileymill Gdns
GRNKW/INVK PA16 **15** L6
Ailort Pl *EKILN* G74 **2** F2
Ailort Av *LNPK/KPK* G44 **95** G5
Ailsa Av *MTHW* ML1 **120** B2
Ailsa Ct *HMLTN* ML3 **128** D1
Ailsa Crs *MTHW* ML1 **120** B2
Ailsa Dr *CLYDBK* G81 **40** B3
GIF/THBK G46 **114** C2
GVH/MTFL G42 **94** F3
KKNTL G66 **27** M8
PSLYS PA2 **91** K3
RUTH G73 **95** M5
UD/BTH/TAN G71 **99** G6
Ailsa Pl *CTBR* ML5 **83** M6
Ailsa Rd *BSHPBGS* G64 **44** B8
CTBR ML5 **83** L6
GRK PA19 **15** J3
RNFRW PA4 **58** C7
Ainslie Av
CARD/HILL/MSPK G52 **77** G1
Ainslie Rd
CARD/HILL/MSPK G52 **77** H2
CUMB G67 **31** J6
Airbles Crs *MTHW* ML1 **120** D4
Airbles Dr *MTHW* ML1 **120** D4
Airbles Farm Rd *MTHW* ML1 **120** C5
Airbles Rd *MTHW* ML1 **120** E4
Airbles St *MTHW* ML1 **120** E4
Airdale Av *GIF/THBK* G46 **94** C8
Airdriehill Rd *AIRDRIE* ML6 **67** J7
Airdrie Rd *AIRDRIE* ML6 **67** M8
BTHG/ARM EH48 **70** C2
CARLUKE ML8 **133** G4
CUMB G67 **47** L6
KSYTH G65 **29** K2
Airgold Dr *DRUM* G15 **40** F5
Airlie Av *BSDN* G61 **41** L2
Airlie Dr *BLSH* ML4 **100** A3
Airlie Gdns *RUTH* G73 **96** D6
Airlie La *KVD/HLHD* G12 **60** B7
Airlie Rd *BAIL/MDB/MHD* G69 **82** A7
Airlie St *KVD/HLHD* G12 **60** B7
Airlour Rd *PLKSW/MSWD* G43 **94** E5
Airth Dr *CARD/HILL/MSPK* G52 **77** M6
Airth La *CARD/HILL/MSPK* G52 **77** M6
Airthrey Av *SCOT* G14 **59** L5
Airthrey La *SCOT* G14 **59** L5
Airth Wy *BALLOCH* G68 **47** L2
Aitchison Ct *AIRDRIE* ML6 **84** F1
Aitchison St *AIRDRIE* ML6 **84** E2
Aitkenbar Cir *DMBTN* G82 **21** H5
Aitkenbar Dr *DMBTN* G82 **21** H4
Aitken Cl *WISHAW* ML2 **123** G2
Aitken Dr *BEITH* KA15 **125** L5
Aitkenhead Av *CTBR* ML5 **83** H6
Aitkenhead Rd *AIRDRIE* ML6 **85** K7
UD/BTH/TAN G71 **99** G1
Aitken La *ALEX/LLW* G83 **13** K3
Aitken Rd *HMLTN* ML3 **129** L4
Aitken St *AIRDRIE* ML6 **67** G8
DEN/PKHD G31 **80** B4
LARGS KA30 **106** E5
Alasdair Ct *BRHD/NEIL* G78 **92** C7
Albans Crs *MTHW* ML1 **120** B1
Albany *EKILN* G74 **117** J6
Albany Av *CAR/SHTL* G32 **81** J4
Albany Dr *LNK/LMHG* ML11 **137** H6
RUTH G73 **96** B4
Albany Qd *CAR/SHTL* G32 **81** J4
Albany Rd *HMLTN* ML3 **129** J3
Albany St *CTBR* ML5 **83** L3
DMNK/BRGTN G40 **80** A6
Albany Ter *BLTYR/CAMB* G72 **96** E7
Alba Wy *HMLTN* ML3 **129** J4
Alberta Av *CTBR* ML5 **83** M2
EKILS G75 **2** A7
Alberta Pk *EKILS* G75 **2** B7
Albert Av *GVH/MTFL* G42 **95** G1
Albert Br *GBLS* G5 **79** J5
Albert Crs *AIRDRIE* ML6 **85** H2
Albert Dr *BSDN* G61 **42** B7
HBR/GL G84 **10** E5
LRKH ML9 **130** D7
PLKSD/SHW G41 **78** E6
RUTH G73 **96** B5
Albert Pk *CARLUKE* ML8 **135** G3
Albert Pl *AIRDRIE* ML6 **85** H1
Albert Qd *MTHW* ML1 **101** G4
Albert Rd *CLYDBK* G81 **39** M7
GRK PA19 **15** K2
GVH/MTFL G42 **95** G1
JNSTN PA5 **73** J5
KKNTL G66 **45** J7
RNFRW PA4 **58** C6
SHOTTS ML7 **71** L7
Albert St *ALEX/LLW* G83 **13** K6
CTBR ML5 **84** A2
HBR/GL G84 **10** E5
HMLTN ML3 **119** H4
MTHW ML1 **120** F2
Albert Ter *HMLTN* ML3 **119** G4
Albion Ga *CGLE* G1 **5** H7
PSLYN/LNWD PA3 **8** F1
Albion St *BAIL/MDB/MHD* G69 **81** M7
CGLE G1 **5** H7
CTBR ML5 **84** B2
MTHW ML1 **120** E4
PSLYN/LNWD PA3 **9** G2
Albion Wy *EKILS* G75 **127** J5
Alcaig Rd *CARD/HILL/MSPK* G52 **77** L7
Alcath Rd *WISHAW* ML2 **123** H3
Alclutha Av *DMBTN* G82 **21** H7
Alder Av *HMLTN* ML3 **129** L1
KKNTL G66 **45** H5
Alder Bank *UD/BTH/TAN* G71 **99** J1
Alderbank Rd *PGL* PA14 **34** A1
Alderbrae Rd *PGL* PA14 **34** A1
Alder Ct *BRHD/NEIL* G78 **92** C8
EKILS G75 **126** F5
Alder Crs *EKILS* G75 **126** F5
Alder Gdns *MTHW* ML1 **121** J6
Alder Ga *BLTYR/CAMB* G72 **97** L5
Alder Gv *CTBR* ML5 **84** B3
Alderman Pl *KNTSWD* G13 **59** J3
Alderman Rd *KNTSWD* G13 **58** F2
Alder Pl *EKILS* G75 **126** F5
JNSTN PA5 **90** A1
PLKSW/MSWD G43 **94** B5
Alder Rd *CLYDBK* G81 **39** M5
CUMB G67 **31** K7
DMBTN G82 **20** E6
KKNTL G66 **27** H5
PLKSW/MSWD G43 **94** C5
Alderside Av *WISHAW* ML2 **121** K5
Alderside Gdns
UD/BTH/TAN G71 **98** E3
Alderstocks *EKILS* G75 **127** H5
Alderston Pl *BLSH* ML4 **99** L6
Aldersyde Pl *BLTYR/CAMB* G72 **118** C1
Aldersyde Ter *MTHW* ML1 **102** C8
Alderwood Rd *PGL* PA14 **34** B1
Aldrin Rd *HBR/GL* G84 **11** H7
Alexander Av *LARGS* KA30 **107** G3
UD/BTH/TAN G71 **99** J4
Alexander Balfour Gdns
HMLTN ML3 **129** K1
Alexander Crs *GBLS* G5 **79** J6
Alexander Fleming Av
KBRN KA25 **124** B4
Alexander Gdns *HMLTN* ML3 **120** A7

Alexander Gibson Wy
MTHW ML1 120 D4
Alexander Pl *KKNTL* G66 46 B3
Alexander Rd *SHOTTS* ML7 104 D4
Alexander St *ALEX/LLW* G83 13 K5
CLYDBK G81 40 B8
CTBR ML5 84 B1
DMBTN G82 20 D2
WISHAW ML2 121 M6
Alexander Ter *BRHD/NEIL* G78 111 J4
Alexandra Av
STPS/GTHM/RID G33 63 K4
Alexandra Ct *DEN/PKHD* G31 80 B2
Alexandra Dr *PSLYS* PA2 8 A8
RNFRW PA4 58 D6
Alexandra Gdns *KKNTL* G66 45 J6
Alexandra Pde *DEN/PKHD* G31 5 M4
Alexandra Pk *KKNTL* G66 45 J6
Alexandra Park St
DEN/PKHD G31 80 B2
Alexandra Rd *KKNTL* G66 45 J6
Alexandra St *KKNTL* G66 45 J2
Alexandria Qd *MTHW* ML1 101 G4
Alford Av *BLTYR/CAMB* G72 118 C7
KKNTL G66 45 H2
Alford Pl *PSLYN/LNWD* PA3 73 L4
Alford Qd *WISHAW* ML2 122 B4
Alford St *SPRGB/BLRNK* G21 61 K7
Alfred La *KVD/HLHD* G12 60 E7
Algie St *GVH/MTFL* G42 94 F2
Algoma Pl *EKILS* G75 126 E2
Alice Av *BLSH* ML4 100 A5
Alice St *PSLYS* PA2 9 G9
Aline Ct *BRHD/NEIL* G78 92 B5
Alison Ct *GRNKW/INVK* PA16 32 F4
Alison Lea *EKILN* G74 3 M1
Allan Av *CARLUKE* ML8 133 G6
RNFRW PA4 58 E8
Allanbank St *SHOTTS* ML7 123 M1
Allan Ct *EKILS* G75 126 B3
Allan Crs *DMBTN* G82 13 J7
Allandale Av *MTHW* ML1 101 M4
Allander Av *MLNGV* G62 43 G3
Allander Dr *BSHPBGS* G64 44 A2
Allander Gdns *BSHPBGS* G64 43 M6
Allander Rd *MLNGV* G62 24 A8
Allander St *PPK/MIL* G22 61 J6
Allands Av *RNFRW* PA4 57 J5
Allanfauld Rd *CUMB* G67 30 F7
Allan Glen Gdns *BSHPBGS* G64 44 B6
Allan Gv *BLSH* ML4 100 B3
Allanpark St *LARGS* KA30 106 E5
Allan Pl *DMBTN* G82 21 G6
DMNK/BRGTN G40 80 B7
EKILS G75 126 B3
Allanshaw Gdns *HMLTN* ML3 119 H7
Allanshaw Gv *HMLTN* ML3 119 H8
Allanshaw St *HMLTN* ML3 119 J7
Allan St *CTBR* ML5 83 K5
DMNK/BRGTN G40 80 B8
MTHW ML1 120 F2
Allanton Av *PSLY* PA1 76 E5
Allanton Dr
CARD/HILL/MSPK G52 77 H4
Allanton Gv *WISHAW* ML2 122 B4
Allanton Lea *HMLTN* ML3 129 J2
Allanton Pl *HMLTN* ML3 129 L1
Allanton Rd *SHOTTS* ML7 123 L1
Allbany Crs *MTHW* ML1 100 F4
Allendale Av *EKILN* G74 2 A2
Allender Rd *BSDN* G61 41 K7
Allen Wy *RNFRW* PA4 58 D8
Allerdyce Dr *DRUM* G15 40 F8
Allershaw Pl *WISHAW* ML2 131 H1
Allershaw Rd *WISHAW* ML2 131 H1
Allerton Gdns
BAIL/MDB/MHD G69 81 M6
Alleysbank Rd *RUTH* G73 96 A1
Allison Av *ERSK* PA8 38 F8
Allison Dr *BLTYR/CAMB* G72 97 G4
Allison Pl *BAIL/MDB/MHD* G69 64 E6
GVH/MTFL G42 79 G8
NMRNS G77 113 J5
Allison St *GVH/MTFL* G42 79 G8
Allnach Pl *ESTRH* G34 82 E2
Alloway Av *PSLYS* PA2 92 B1
Alloway Ct *KKNTL* G66 28 A8
Alloway Crs *PSLYS* PA2 92 C1
RUTH G73 95 M5
Alloway Dr *CLYDBK* G81 40 C6
KKNTL G66 28 A8
NMRNS G77 114 A6
PSLYS PA2 92 C1
RUTH G73 95 M5
Alloway Gdns *HMLTN* ML3 128 D1
KKNTL G66 28 A8
Alloway Gv *KKNTL* G66 27 M8
Alloway Rd *AIRDRIE* ML6 85 M1
EKILN G74 117 L7
PLKSW/MSWD G43 94 D4
Alloway St *LRKH* ML9 130 E7
Alloway Ter *KKNTL* G66 27 M8
Almada La *HMLTN* ML3 119 K6
Almada St *HMLTN* ML3 119 K6
Almond Av *RNFRW* PA4 58 E7
Almond Bank *BSDN* G61 41 J7
Almond Crs *PSLYS* PA2 74 F8
Almond Dr *BSHPTN* PA7 38 B8
EKILN G74 3 L5
KKNTL G66 45 H5
Almond Pl *CTBR* ML5 83 K1
Almond Rd *BSDN* G61 41 J7
CUMB G67 31 M4
STPS/GTHM/RID G33 63 J5
Almond St *STPS/GTHM/RID* G33 80 D1
Almond Ter *SHOTTS* ML7 71 J7
Almond V *UD/BTH/TAN* G71 99 G3
Almond Wy *MTHW* ML1 120 E6
Alness Crs
CARD/HILL/MSPK G52 77 K6
Alness St *HMLTN* ML3 119 K8
Alness Ter *HMLTN* ML3 119 K8
Alpine Gv *GRNK* PA15 17 L7
UD/BTH/TAN G71 98 F3
Alpine Pth *BLTYR/CAMB* G72 118 E3
Alpine Wk *BLTYR/CAMB* G72 118 E3
Alsatian Av *CLYDBK* G81 40 D7
Alsh Ter *HMLTN* ML3 129 G1
Alston Av *CTBR* ML5 84 B1
Alston Gdns *BSDN* G61 41 H1
Altnacreag Gdns
BAIL/MDB/MHD G69 47 G7
Alton Rd *PSLY* PA1 76 C5
Altpatrick Gdns *JNSTN* PA5 74 B7
Altyre St *CAR/SHTL* G32 80 F7
Alva Gdns
CARD/HILL/MSPK G52 77 L7
Alva Ga *CARD/HILL/MSPK* G52 77 L6
Alva Pl *KKNTL* G66 45 L6
Alva Ter *GRK* PA19 16 A2
Alwyn Av *CRG/CRSL/HOU* PA6 73 K2
Alwyn Ct *EKILN* G74 2 D2
Alwyn Dr *EKILN* G74 2 E2
Alyssum Crs *MTHW* ML1 120 D1
Alyth Crs
CRMNK/CLK/EAG G76 115 G2
Alyth Gdns
CARD/HILL/MSPK G52 77 L6
CRMNK/CLK/EAG G76 115 G2
Amber Ter *BLSH* ML4 100 A5
Ambleside *EKILS* G75 126 C4
Ambleside Ri *HMLTN* ML3 129 J5
Amethyst Av *BLSH* ML4 100 A5
Amisfield St *MRYH/FIRH* G20 60 E5
Amochrie Dr *PSLYS* PA2 91 G2
Amochrie Gln *PSLYS* PA2 91 G2
Amochrie Rd *PSLYS* PA2 90 F2
Amochrie Wy *PSLYS* PA2 90 F1
Amulree Pl *CAR/SHTL* G32 81 G6
Amulree St *CAR/SHTL* G32 81 G7
Ancaster Dr *KNTSWD* G13 59 M3
Ancaster La *KNTSWD* G13 59 M3
Anchor Av *PSLY* PA1 9 L6
Anchor Crs *PSLY* PA1 9 M7
Anchor Dr *PSLY* PA1 9 M6
Anchor La *CGLE* G1 4 F6
Anchor Wynd *PSLY* PA1 9 M7
Ancroft St *MRYH/FIRH* G20 61 G7
Andersen Ct *EKILS* G75 127 H4
Anderside *EKILS* G75 127 H5
Anderson Av *KSYTH* G65 29 H1
Anderson Ct *BLSH* ML4 100 B4
Anderson Crs *KSYTH* G65 28 E2
Anderson Dr *NMRNS* G77 113 J5
RNFRW PA4 58 D5
Anderson La *AIRDRIE* ML6 85 G1
Anderson Rd *BSHPTN* PA7 38 A6
Anderson St *AIRDRIE* ML6 85 G1
HMLTN ML3 118 F5
MTHW ML1 120 E4
PGL PA14 18 B8
PTCK G11 60 B8
Anderston Quay *KVGV* G3 78 F4
Andrew Av *KKNTL* G66 45 K7
RNFRW PA4 58 E5
Andrew Baxter Av *LRKH* ML9 131 G8
Andrew Dr *CLYDBK* G81 58 C1
Andrew Paton Wy *HMLTN* ML3 119 G4
Andrew Pl *CARLUKE* ML8 133 G6
Andrew Sillars Av
BLTYR/CAMB G72 97 J5
Andrew St *EKILN* G74 3 G6
PSLYN/LNWD PA3 8 F2
Anford Gdns *BLTYR/CAMB* G72 118 E3
Anford Pl *BLTYR/CAMB* G72 118 E4
Angela Wy *UD/BTH/TAN* G71 98 F4
Angle Ga *SCOT* G14 59 K5
Angus Av *AIRDRIE* ML6 85 G4
BSHPBGS G64 62 D1
CARD/HILL/MSPK G52 77 J6
EKILN G74 3 L4
HMLTN ML3 120 A6
Angus Gdns *UD/BTH/TAN* G71 98 F2
Angus Ov *CARD/HILL/MSPK* G52 77 H5
Angus Pl *CARD/HILL/MSPK* G52 77 H5
EKILN G74 3 L4
Angus Rd *CARLUKE* ML8 133 J8
GRNKW/INVK PA16 15 K5
PGL PA14 34 C1
Angus St *ALEX/LLW* G83 13 K6
CLYDBK G81 58 E1
SPRGB/BLRNK G21 61 L6
Anish Pl *DRUM* G15 40 E5
Annan Av *EKILS* G75 126 B3
Annan Crs *AIRDRIE* ML6 85 K8
Annandale St *GVH/MTFL* G42 79 H7
Annan Dr *BSDN* G61 41 J6
PSLYS PA2 74 E8
RUTH G73 96 D3
Annan Gld *MTHW* ML1 121 G6
Annan Gv *MTHW* ML1 121 G6
Annan Pl *JNSTN* PA5 89 J2
Annan St *MTHW* ML1 121 G6
Annathill Gdns *CTBR* ML5 65 L1
Annbank Pl *DEN/PKHD* G31 79 M4
Annbank St *DEN/PKHD* G31 79 M4
LRKH ML9 130 B6
Ann Ct *HMLTN* ML3 119 G5
Anne Av *RNFRW* PA4 58 D5
Anne Crs *KKNTL* G66 45 K7
Annerley Pl *CTBR* ML5 83 L5
Annette St *GVH/MTFL* G42 79 H8
Annetyard Dr *SKLM* PA17 50 C6
Annetyard Rd *SKLM* PA17 50 B6
Annfield Gdns
BLTYR/CAMB G72 118 B1
Annfield Pl *DEN/PKHD* G31 79 M3
Annick Dr *BSDN* G61 41 J6
Annick St *BLTYR/CAMB* G72 97 K5
Anniesdale Av
STPS/GTHM/RID G33 63 K4
Anniesbill Vw *AIRDRIE* ML6 68 A7
Anniesland Crs *SCOT* G14 59 G4
Anniesland Rd *SCOT* G14 59 G4
Annieston *KSYTH* G65 28 F6
Anniversary Av *EKILS* G75 126 F3
Annsfield Rd *HMLTN* ML3 129 K3
Ann St *GRNK* PA15 6 B6
HMLTN ML3 119 G5
JNSTN PA5 74 A7
Ansdell Av *BLTYR/CAMB* G72 118 C3
Anson St *DMNK/BRGTN* G40 79 M6
Anstruther Ct *CARLUKE* ML8 132 B4
Anstruther St *CAR/SHTL* G32 80 E5
CARLUKE ML8 132 B4
Antermony Rd *KKNTL* G66 27 K5
Anthony Rd *LARGS* KA30 106 F7
Anthony St *CGLW* G2 4 B6
Antigua St *GRNK* PA15 6 E6
Antigua Wy *EKILS* G75 126 D1
Anton Crs *KSYTH* G65 29 L2
Antonine *KKNTL* G66 28 B8
Antonine Av *MTHW* ML1 120 C1
Antonine Gdns *CLYDBK* G81 40 A3
Antonine Rd *BALLOCH* G68 30 C3
BSDN G61 41 H3
Anwoth St *CAR/SHTL* G32 81 G7
Appian Pl *MTHW* ML1 100 B8
Appin Crs *DEN/PKHD* G31 80 B3
Appin Rd *DEN/PKHD* G31 80 C3
Appin Ter *HMLTN* ML3 118 E6
RUTH G73 96 D6
SHOTTS ML7 105 H6
Appin Wy *AIRDRIE* ML6 66 E5
CTBR ML5 83 L6
Appleby Cl *EKILS* G75 126 C4
Appleby Gv
BAIL/MDB/MHD G69 83 G4
Appleby St *PPK/MIL* G22 61 H7
Applecross Gdns
BAIL/MDB/MHD G69 46 F7
Applecross Qd *WISHAW* ML2 122 B4
Applecross Rd *KKNTL* G66 46 B1
Applecross St *COWCAD* G4 61 H7
Appledore Crs
UD/BTH/TAN G71 99 G7
Apple Wy *EKILS* G75 127 J4
Apsley La *PTCK* G11 60 A8
Apsley St *PTCK* G11 60 A8
Aqua Av *HMLTN* ML3 118 E8
Aqua Ct *HMLTN* ML3 118 E8
Aquila Wy *CARLUKE* ML8 132 F7
Araburn Dr *EKILS* G75 127 H5
Aranthrue Crs *RNFRW* PA4 58 C5
Aranthrue Dr *RNFRW* PA4 58 C5
Aray St *MRYH/FIRH* G20 60 D4
Arbroath Av
CARD/HILL/MSPK G52 77 H5
Arbroath Gv *HMLTN* ML3 119 H8
Arbuckle Pl *AIRDRIE* ML6 68 A6
Arbuckle Rd *AIRDRIE* ML6 68 B4
Arcadia Pl *DMNK/BRGTN* G40 79 L5
Arcadia St *BLSH* ML4 100 A2
DMNK/BRGTN G40 79 L6
Arcan Crs *DRUM* G15 41 H7
Archerfield Av *CAR/SHTL* G32 81 G8
Archerfield Crs *CAR/SHTL* G32 81 G8
Archerfield Dr *CAR/SHTL* G32 81 G8
Archerfield Gv *CAR/SHTL* G32 81 G8
Archerhill Av *KNTSWD* G13 59 G1
Archerhill Crs *KNTSWD* G13 59 H1
Archerhill Rd *KNTSWD* G13 59 J2
Archerhill Sq *KNTSWD* G13 58 F1
Archerhill Ter *KNTSWD* G13 59 G1
Archibald Ter *KKNTL* G66 27 H4
Archiebald Pl *BLSH* ML4 100 D5
Arch Wy *KSYTH* G65 29 K1
Ardargie Dr *CAR/SHTL* G32 97 J2
Ardargie Gv *CAR/SHTL* G32 97 J2
Ardargie Pl *CAR/SHTL* G32 97 J2
Ardbeg Av *BSHPBGS* G64 62 C1
RUTH G73 96 E7
Ardbeg Crs *AIRDRIE* ML6 67 G6
Ardbeg La *EKILN* G74 115 J7
GVH/MTFL G42 79 G8
Ardbeg Rd *GRNK* PA15 17 J7
MTHW ML1 101 G7
Ardbeg St *GVH/MTFL* G42 79 G8
Ardconnel St *GIF/THBK* G46 93 M5
Arden Av *GIF/THBK* G46 93 L7
Ardencaple Dr *HBR/GL* G84 10 A5
Ardencaple Qd *HBR/GL* G84 10 A5
Ardenclutha Av *HMLTN* ML3 119 H6
Ardenclutha Dr *PGL* PA14 34 B1
Arden Ct *HMLTN* ML3 129 K1
Ardencraig Crs *CSMK* G45 115 J1
Ardencraig Dr *CSMK* G45 95 M8
Ardencraig Gdns *CSMK* G45 95 M8
Ardencraig La *CSMK* G45 115 J1
Ardencraig Pl *CSMK* G45 95 L7
Ardencraig Qd *CSMK* G45 95 M8
Ardencraig Rd *CSMK* G45 115 K1
Ardencraig St *CSMK* G45 96 A8
Ardencraig Ter *CSMK* G45 95 L8
Arden Dr *GIF/THBK* G46 94 B8
Ardenlea *UD/BTH/TAN* G71 98 F3
Ardenlea St *DMNK/BRGTN* G40 80 B7
Arden Pl *GIF/THBK* G46 93 L7
Arden Rd *GRNK* PA15 17 K8
HMLTN ML3 119 J8
Arden St *AIRDRIE* ML6 68 A7
Arden Ter *HMLTN* ML3 119 J8
Ardery St *PTCK* G11 60 A8
Ardessie Pl *MRYH/FIRH* G20 60 D5
Ardessie St *SMSTN* G23 60 D1
Ardfern Rd *AIRDRIE* ML6 85 M3
Ardfern St *CAR/SHTL* G32 81 G7
Ardgay Pl *CAR/SHTL* G32 81 G6
Ardgay St *CAR/SHTL* G32 81 G6
Ardgay Wy *RUTH* G73 96 B7
Ardgoil Dr *BALLOCH* G68 30 A8
Ardgour Dr *PSLYN/LNWD* PA3 74 A5
Ardgowan Av *PSLYS* PA2 9 J8
Ardgowan Crs
GRNKW/INVK PA16 32 E5
Ardgowan Dr
UD/BTH/TAN G71 98 F2
Ardgowan Pl *SHOTTS* ML7 104 E3
Ardgowan Rd *WMYSB* PA18 32 B8
Ardgowan St *GRNKW/INVK* PA16 6 A2
PGL PA14 18 A8
PSLYS PA2 9 J9
Ardgowan Terrace La *KVGV* G3 78 D1
Ardgryfe Crs
CRG/CRSL/HOU PA6 73 L1
Ardholm St *CAR/SHTL* G32 81 G5
Ardhu Pl *DRUM* G15 40 F5
Ardlaw St *GOV/IBX* G51 77 M3
Ardle Rd *PLKSW/MSWD* G43 94 E5
Ardlui St *CAR/SHTL* G32 80 F6
Ardmaleish Crs *CSMK* G45 95 L8
Ardmaleish Dr *CSMK* G45 95 K8
Ardmaleish Rd *CSMK* G45 95 L8
Ardmaleish St *CSMK* G45 95 K8
Ardmaleish Ter *CSMK* G45 95 L8
Ardmay Crs *LNPK/KPK* G44 95 J3
Ardmillan St
STPS/GTHM/RID G33 80 F2
Ardmore Crs *AIRDRIE* ML6 67 G6
Ardmore Pl *GRNK* PA15 6 A7
Ardmore Rd *GRNK* PA15 17 J8
PGL PA14 34 D1
Ardmory Av *GVH/MTFL* G42 95 L3
Ardmory La *LNPK/KPK* G44 95 L3
Ardmory Pl *GVH/MTFL* G42 95 L3
Ardnahoe Av *GVH/MTFL* G42 95 L3
Ardnahoe Pl *GVH/MTFL* G42 95 L3
Ardneil Rd *GOV/IBX* G51 77 M3
Ardnish St *GOV/IBX* G51 77 K2
Ardoch Crs *DMBTN* G82 20 D6
Ardoch Gv *BLTYR/CAMB* G72 96 F4
Ardochrig *EKILS* G75 127 H5
Ardoch Rd *BSDN* G61 42 B5
Ardoch St *PPK/MIL* G22 61 J6
Ardo Gdns *GOV/IBX* G51 78 A5
Ardrain Av *MTHW* ML1 121 J6
Ard Rd *RNFRW* PA4 58 B5
Ardshiel Rd *GOV/IBX* G51 77 L2
Ardsloy Pl *SCOT* G14 59 G5
Ard St *CAR/SHTL* G32 81 G6
Ardtoe Crs *STPS/GTHM/RID* G33 63 L5
Ardtoe Pl *STPS/GTHM/RID* G33 63 L5
Arduthie Rd *GOV/IBX* G51 77 L2
Ardwell Rd
CARD/HILL/MSPK G52 77 L6
Ardyne Pl *GRK* PA19 14 F4
Argus Av *AIRDRIE* ML6 85 J7
Argyle Crs *AIRDRIE* ML6 84 F5
HMLTN ML3 118 F7
Argyle Dr *HMLTN* ML3 119 G6
Argyle Gdns *KKNTL* G66 26 E3
Argyle Rd *BSDN* G61 41 L2
GRK PA19 15 M3
Argyle St *CGLW* G2 4 B7
GRNK PA15 6 C3
KVGV G3 78 E2
PSLY PA1 8 E6
Argyle St West *HBR/GL* G84 10 B5
Argyll Arc *CGLE* G1 4 E7
Argyll Av *DMBTN* G82 21 J6
PSLYN/LNWD PA3 75 L1
RNFRW PA4 58 B5
Argyll Ct *SHOTTS* ML7 71 M7
Argyll Gdns *CTBR* ML5 83 L6
LRKH ML9 130 D6
Argyll Pl *BLSH* ML4 99 M7
DMBTN G82 21 J6
EKILN G74 117 J7
KSYTH G65 29 L2
Argyll Rd *CLYDBK* G81 40 C8
Argyll St *ALEX/LLW* G83 13 J3
Arisaig Dr *BSDN* G61 42 B7
CARD/HILL/MSPK G52 77 L6
Arisaig Pl *CARD/HILL/MSPK* G52 77 L6
Arisdale Crs *NMRNS* G77 113 L3
Arkaig Av *AIRDRIE* ML6 67 M7
Arkaig Pl *NMRNS* G77 114 B6
Arkaig St *WISHAW* ML2 131 K1
Ark La *DEN/PKHD* G31 5 M6
Arkleston Crs *PSLYN/LNWD* PA3 76 B2
Arkleston Dr *PSLY* PA1 9 M2
Arkleston Rd *PSLY* PA1 76 B3
Arkle Ter *BLTYR/CAMB* G72 96 E7
Arklet Rd *GOV/IBX* G51 77 L3
Arklet Wy *WISHAW* ML2 122 E6
Arkwrights Wy *PSLY* PA1 8 B7
Arlington Pl *KVGV* G3 4 A2
Arlington St *KVGV* G3 4 A2
Armadale Pl *DEN/PKHD* G31 80 A2
GRNK PA15 6 D5
Armadale Rd *LNK/LMHG* ML11 137 J5
Armadale St *DEN/PKHD* G31 80 A2
Armour Av *AIRDRIE* ML6 84 E2
Armour Ct *BLTYR/CAMB* G72 118 B4
KKNTL G66 46 A1
Armour Dr *KKNTL* G66 46 A1
Armour Gv *MTHW* ML1 121 G5
Armour Pl *JNSTN* PA5 74 A7
Armour St *COWCAD* G4 5 L8
JNSTN PA5 74 A7
Armstrong Crs
UD/BTH/TAN G71 99 G2
Armstrong Gv *EKILS* G75 2 D9
Armstrong Rd *HBR/GL* G84 11 G7
Arnbrae Rd *KSYTH* G65 29 H1
Arngask Rd *GOV/IBX* G51 77 L2
Arnhall Pl
CARD/HILL/MSPK G52 77 L6
Arnhem St *BLTYR/CAMB* G72 97 K5
Arnholm Pl
CARD/HILL/MSPK G52 77 L6
Arnisdale Pl *ESTRH* G34 82 A2
Arnisdale Rd *ESTRH* G34 82 A2
Arnisdale Wy *RUTH* G73 96 B7
Arnish *ERSK* PA8 57 J3
Arniston St *CAR/SHTL* G32 80 F3
Arniston Wy *PSLYN/LNWD* PA3 76 A2
Arnold Av *BSHPBGS* G64 62 A1
Arnol Pl *STPS/GTHM/RID* G33 81 M3
Arnott Dr *CTBR* ML5 84 A5
Arnott Qd *MTHW* ML1 100 C8
Arnott Wy *BLTYR/CAMB* G72 97 G4
Arnprior Crs *CSMK* G45 95 K7
Arnprior Qd *CSMK* G45 95 K6
Arnprior Rd *CSMK* G45 95 K6
Arnprior St *CSMK* G45 95 K6
Arnside Av *GIF/THBK* G46 94 C7
Arnton Gv *AIRDRIE* ML6 101 L1
Arnum Gdns *CARLUKE* ML8 133 H8
Arnum Pl *CARLUKE* ML8 133 H8
Arnwood Dr *KVD/HLHD* G12 60 A5
Arondale Rd *AIRDRIE* ML6 67 M6
Aron Ter *BLTYR/CAMB* G72 96 F7
Aros Dr *CARD/HILL/MSPK* G52 77 K7
Aros La *CARD/HILL/MSPK* G52 77 K6
Arran *EKILN* G74 127 M1
Arran Av *DMBTN* G82 20 D5
PGL PA14 35 H3
PSLYN/LNWD PA3 75 L1
Arran Crs *BEITH* KA15 125 L4
Arran Dr *AIRDRIE* ML6 66 F8
CARD/HILL/MSPK G52 77 M6
CUMB G67 48 D1
GIF/THBK G46 94 B8
JNSTN PA5 89 K1
KKNTL G66 45 L1
PSLYS PA2 91 L3
Arran Gdns *CARLUKE* ML8 134 F1
HMLTN ML3 129 L1
Arran Pl *CLYDBK* G81 40 C7
CTBR ML5 * 84 D5
PSLYN/LNWD PA3 74 A4
Arran Rd *GRK* PA19 15 K3
MTHW ML1 120 C2
RNFRW PA4 58 D7
Arran Ter *RUTH* G73 95 M5
Arran Vw *KSYTH* G65 29 K2
LARGS KA30 107 G4
Arranview St *AIRDRIE* ML6 85 L8
Arran Wy *UD/BTH/TAN* G71 98 F8
Arrochar Ct *SMSTN* G23 60 E2
Arrochar Dr *SMSTN* G23 60 D1
Arrochar St *MRYH/FIRH* G20 60 D2
Arrol Pl *EKILS* G75 127 K4
Arrol St *CARD/HILL/MSPK* G52 76 F1
Arrol Wynd *BLTYR/CAMB* G72 97 K4
Arrotshole Rd *EKILN* G74 116 B7
Arrowsmith Av *KNTSWD* G13 59 K1
Arthur Av *AIRDRIE* ML6 85 H4
BRHD/NEIL G78 92 B8
Arthur Gdns *AIRDRIE* ML6 69 H5
Arthurlie Av *BRHD/NEIL* G78 92 C7
BRHD/NEIL G78 110 B7
Arthurlie Dr *BRHD/NEIL* G78 110 B7
GIF/THBK G46 114 C1
NMRNS G77 113 K6
Arthurlie St *BRHD/NEIL* G78 92 C7
Arthur Rd *PSLYS* PA2 91 L2
Arthurston Rd *ALEX/LLW* G83 13 M3
Arthur St *ALEX/LLW* G83 13 K6
CRMNK/CLK/EAG G76 114 E4
GRNK PA15 7 G6
HMLTN ML3 119 K5
KVGV G3 78 D1
PSLY PA1 8 D4
Arundel Dr *BSHPBGS* G64 44 B6
GVH/MTFL G42 95 G3
Ascaig Crs
CARD/HILL/MSPK G52 77 L7
Ascog Pl *WMYSB* PA18 32 B8
Ascog Rd *BSDN* G61 41 M7
Ascog St *GVH/MTFL* G42 79 G8
Ascot Av *KVD/HLHD* G12 59 M3
Ash Av *EKILS* G75 126 F4
Ashbank Crs *AIRDRIE* ML6 85 L6
Ashburn Gdns *GRK* PA19 15 J2
MLNGV G62 23 L8
Ashburn Ga *GRK* PA19 15 J2
Ashburn Rd *MLNGV* G62 23 L7
Ashburton La *KVD/HLHD* G12 60 B4
Ashburton Pk *EKILS* G75 126 D3
Ashburton Rd *KVD/HLHD* G12 60 A4
Ashby Crs *KNTSWD* G13 41 L8
Ash Ct *EKILS* G75 126 F4
Ashcroft *EKILN* G74 117 K5
Ashcroft Av *KKNTL* G66 26 E3
Ashcroft Dr *LNPK/KPK* G44 95 L4
Ashdale Dr
CARD/HILL/MSPK G52 77 L6
Ashdene St *PPK/MIL* G22 61 H3
Ash Dr *BEITH* KA15 125 K3
Asher Rd *AIRDRIE* ML6 85 L7
Ashfield *BSHPBGS* G64 44 A7
Ashfield Rd *CARLUKE* ML8 132 B3
CRMNK/CLK/EAG G76 114 E4
MLNGV G62 42 A1
Ashfield St *PPK/MIL* G22 61 J6
Ashgillhead Rd *LRKH* ML9 131 G8
Ashgill Pl *PPK/MIL* G22 61 J4
Ashgill Rd *PPK/MIL* G22 61 H4
Ash Gv *BSHPBGS* G64 62 B2
KKNTL G66 45 H5
UD/BTH/TAN G71 99 H2
Ashgrove *AIRDRIE* ML6 69 G4
CTBR ML5 84 A5
SHOTTS ML7 103 M6
Ashgrove Av *GRK* PA19 15 J2
Ashgrove La *PGL* PA14 34 D1
Ashgrove Rd *BLSH* ML4 100 B2
Ashgrove St *DMNK/BRGTN* G40 80 A8
Ashiestiel Pl *CUMB* G67 48 E2
Ashkirk Dr
CARD/HILL/MSPK G52 77 L6
Ashkirk Pl *WISHAW* ML2 122 C3
Ashland Av *HMLTN* ML3 129 K3
Ashlar Av *BALLOCH* G68 30 D4
Ashlea Dr *GIF/THBK* G46 94 D6
Ashlea Gdns *AIRDRIE* ML6 67 M6
Ashley Dr *UD/BTH/TAN* G71 99 H5
Ashley Gv *BLSH* ML4 99 K4
Ashley La *KVGV* G3 4 A2
Ashley Pk *UD/BTH/TAN* G71 99 J5
Ashley Pl *BLTYR/CAMB* G72 118 C2
Ashley Ri *ALEX/LLW* G83 20 F1
Ashley St *KVGV* G3 4 A2
Ashmore Rd *PLKSW/MSWD* G43 94 F5
Ash Pl *EKILS* G75 126 F4
JNSTN PA5 74 A8
Ash Rd *BAIL/MDB/MHD* G69 82 A7
CLYDBK G81 40 A4
CUMB G67 31 K4
DMBTN G82 20 F6
Ashton Dr *HBR/GL* G84 11 G8
Ashton Gdns
BAIL/MDB/MHD G69 65 G4
Ashton Gn *EKILN* G74 2 F3
Ashton La *KVD/HLHD* G12 60 D8
Ashton Pl *GRK* PA19 15 J2
Ashton Rd *GRK* PA19 15 J2
KVD/HLHD G12 60 D8
RUTH G73 96 A1
Ashton St *MTHW* ML1 100 C7
Ashton Vw *DMBTN* G82 20 B6
Ashtree Ct *OLDK* G60 39 H4
Ashtree Gv *NMRNS* G77 113 J6
Ashtree Rd *PLKSW/MSWD* G43 94 C3
Ashvale Crs *SPRGB/BLRNK* G21 61 L6
Ashwood *WISHAW* ML2 121 L8
Ashwood Gdns *KNTSWD* G13 59 M4
Ashworth Ter *HMLTN* ML3 119 G6
Ash Wynd *BLTYR/CAMB* G72 97 L6
Aspen Dr *SPRGB/BLRNK* G21 62 A7
Aspen Ga *MTHW* ML1 101 K7
Aspen Gv *BAIL/MDB/MHD* G69 83 G3
Aspen Pl *BLTYR/CAMB* G72 97 L5
JNSTN PA5 90 A1
Aspen Wy *HMLTN* ML3 119 L8
Asquith Pl *BLSH* ML4 100 D4
Aster Dr *CSMK* G45 96 A8
Aster Gdns *MTHW* ML1 120 E4
PLK/PH/NH G53 93 J6
Athelstane Dr *CUMB* G67 48 D2
Athelstane Rd *KNTSWD* G13 59 J2
Athena Wy *UD/BTH/TAN* G71 99 G3
Athole Gdns *KVD/HLHD* G12 60 C7
Athole La *KVD/HLHD* G12 60 C7
Athole St *HBR/GL* G84 10 F6
Athole Ter *GRNKW/INVK* PA16 15 K6
Atholl Av *BSHPBGS* G64 44 B1
CARD/HILL/MSPK G52 76 E2
Atholl Crs *PSLY* PA1 76 E4
Atholl Dr *BALLOCH* G68 47 M2
GIF/THBK G46 114 C2
Atholl Gdns *BSDN* G61 41 L2
BSHPBGS G64 43 M7
GIF/THBK G46 93 M7
RUTH G73 96 E7
Atholl Pl *CTBR* ML5 84 B6
GIF/THBK G46 93 M7
PSLYN/LNWD PA3 74 A4
Atholl St *HMLTN* ML3 119 H4
Atholl Ter *UD/BTH/TAN* G71 98 F1
Atlas Pl *SPRGB/BLRNK* G21 61 M7
Atlas Rd *SPRGB/BLRNK* G21 61 L6
Atlas St *CLYDBK* G81 58 B1
Atlin Dr *MTHW* ML1 101 H6
Attercliffe Av *WISHAW* ML2 121 J7
Attlee Av *CLYDBK* G81 40 E8
Attow Rd *PLKSW/MSWD* G43 94 B5
Aubery Crs *LARGS* KA30 106 E3
Auburn Dr *BRHD/NEIL* G78 92 D8
Auchans Rd
CRG/CRSL/HOU PA6 73 M2
Auchenbothie Crs
STPS/GTHM/RID G33 62 E5

Auchenbothie Gdns KLMCLM PA13 35 J8
Auchenbothie Pl STPS/GTHM/RID G33 62 E5
Auchenbothie Rd KLMCLM PA13 35 G7
PGL PA14 34 F4
Auchencrow St ESTRH G34 82 D2
Auchencruive MLNGV G62 42 C2
Auchendarroch St GRNK PA15 7 K7
Auchendavie Rd KKNTL G66 28 B8
Auchendavie Steadings KKNTL G66 28 B8
Auchendores Av PGL PA14 35 G3
Auchenfoil La PGL PA14 34 C2
Auchenfoil Rd PGL PA14 34 C2
Auchengeich Gdns BAIL/MDB/MHD G69 46 F8
Auchengeich Rd BAIL/MDB/MHD G69 46 D6
Auchengilloch EKILS G75 127 H5
Auchenglen Rd CARLUKE ML8 134 F6
Auchengree Rd GLGNK KA14 124 F8
Auchengreoch Av JNSTN PA5 89 K2
Auchengreoch Rd JNSTN PA5 89 K2
Auchenhove Crs KBRN KA25 124 C1
Auchenhowie Rd MLNGV G62 42 C2
Auchenkilns Pk BALLOCH G68 30 B8
Auchenkilns Rd CUMB G67 48 D3
Auchenleck La PGL PA14 34 E3
Auchenleck Rd PGL PA14 34 E3
Auchenlodment Rd JNSTN PA5 74 B8
Auchenmaid Dr LARGS KA30 106 F4
Auchenreoch Av DMBTN G82 21 H4
Auchenstewart Ct WISHAW ML2 122 C6
Auchentibber Rd BLTYR/CAMB G72 117 M7
Auchentorlie Qd PSLY PA1 76 B5
Auchentorlie St PTCK G11 59 M7
Auchentoshan Av CLYDBK G81 39 M4
Auchentoshan Ter SPRGB/BLRNK G21 61 L8
Auchinairn Gdns BSHPBGS G64 62 D2
Auchinairn Rd BSHPBGS G64 62 C3
Auchinbee Farm Rd BALLOCH G68 * 30 B5
Auchinbee Wy BALLOCH G68 30 B6
Auchincampbell Rd HMLTN ML3 119 K7
Auchincarroch Rd ALEX/LLW G83 13 M4
Auchineden Ct BSDN G61 41 J2
Auchingill Pl ESTRH G34 82 D1
Auchingill Rd ESTRH G34 82 D1
Auchingramont Rd HMLTN ML3 119 K7
Auchinlea Dr MTHW ML1 102 C8
Auchinlea Rd ESTRH G34 81 M1
Auchinlea Wy ESTRH G34 81 M1
Auchinleck Av STPS/GTHM/RID G33 62 E4
Auchinleck Crs STPS/GTHM/RID G33 62 E4
Auchinleck Dr STPS/GTHM/RID G33 62 E4
Auchinleck Gdns STPS/GTHM/RID G33 62 E4
Auchinleck Rd CLYDBK G81 40 B3
STPS/GTHM/RID G33 62 F3
Auchinleck Ter CLYDBK G81 40 B2
Auchinloch Rd KKNTL G66 45 K6
Auchinloch St SPRGB/BLRNK G21 61 M7
Auchinraith Av HMLTN ML3 119 J5
Auchinraith Rd BLTYR/CAMB G72 118 D4
Auchinraith Ter BLTYR/CAMB G72 118 E4
Auchinvole Crs KSYTH G65 29 H2
Auchmannoch Av PSLY PA1 76 E4
Auchmead Rd GRNKW/INVK PA16 15 L6
Auchmountain Rd GRNK PA15 7 J8
Auchnacraig Rd CLYDBK G81 40 C2
Auchneagh Av GRNKW/INVK PA16 16 B5
Auchneagh Crs GRNKW/INVK PA16 16 A5
Auchneagh Farm Rd GRNKW/INVK PA16 16 B4
Auchneagh Rd GRNKW/INVK PA16 16 B5
Auchter Av WISHAW ML2 123 J4
Auchterburn Rd SHOTTS ML7 123 M1
Auchter Rd WISHAW ML2 122 E5
Auckland Pk EKILS G75 126 D2
Auckland Pl CLYDBK G81 39 K6
Auckland St PPK/MIL G22 61 H6
Auctioneers Wy LNK/LMHG ML11 137 J6
Auldbar Rd CARD/HILL/MSPK G52 77 M6
Auldbar Ter PSLYS PA2 9 L9
Auldburn Pl PLKSW/MSWD G43 94 B4
Auldburn Rd PLKSW/MSWD G43 94 A4
Auldearn Rd SPRGB/BLRNK G21 62 C3
Auldgirth Rd CARD/HILL/MSPK G52 77 M6
Auldhame St CTBR ML5 83 L2
Auldhouse Av PLKSW/MSWD G43 94 B4
Auldhouse Gdns PLKSW/MSWD G43 94 B4
Auldhouse Rd EKILS G75 126 F7
PLKSW/MSWD G43 94 C4
Auldhouse Ter PLKSW/MSWD G43 94 D4
Auld Kirk Rd BLTYR/CAMB G72 97 J7
Auldlea Rd BEITH KA15 125 K3
Auldmurroch Dr MLNGV G62 23 K7
The Auld Rd CUMB G67 31 G5
Auld's Brae AIRDRIE ML6 85 G1
Auld St CLYDBK G81 39 L7
Auldton Ter LRKH ML9 131 H8
Aultbea St PPK/MIL G22 61 H2
Aultmore Dr MTHW ML1 101 G7
Aultmore Gdns STPS/GTHM/RID G33 81 M3
Aultmore Pk STPS/GTHM/RID G33 81 M3
Aultmore Rd STPS/GTHM/RID G33 81 M3
Aursbridge Crs BRHD/NEIL G78 92 D7
Aursbridge Dr BRHD/NEIL G78 92 D7
Aurs Crs BRHD/NEIL G78 92 D7
Aurs Dr BRHD/NEIL G78 92 D8
Aurs Gln BRHD/NEIL G78 92 C8
Aurs Pl BRHD/NEIL G78 92 E7
Aurs Rd BRHD/NEIL G78 92 E7
NMRNS G77 112 F3
Austen La KNTSWD G13 59 L4
Austen Rd KNTSWD G13 59 L4
Austine Dr HMLTN ML3 129 L3
Avenel Rd KNTSWD G13 41 L8
Avenue End Rd STPS/GTHM/RID G33 63 H8
Avenuehead Rd BAIL/MDB/MHD G69 65 G2
Avenuepark St MRYH/FIRH G20 60 E6
Avenue St DMNK/BRGTN G40 80 A5
RUTH G73 96 B1
The Avenue KLMCLM PA13 53 L1
Aviemore Gdns BSDN G61 42 B6
Aviemore Rd CARD/HILL/MSPK G52 77 L7
Avils Hl KBRN KA25 124 C4
Avils Pl KBRN KA25 124 C5
Avoch St ESTRH G34 82 B1
Avon Av BSDN G61 42 B6
CARLUKE ML8 132 F7
Avonbank Crs HMLTN ML3 129 L2
Avonbank Rd LRKH ML9 130 A7
RUTH G73 95 M3
Avonbrae Crs HMLTN ML3 129 L2
Avonbridge Dr HMLTN ML3 119 M7
Avondale Av EKILN G74 3 H6
Avondale Dr PSLY PA1 76 B3
Avondale Gdns EKILN G74 3 J7
Avondale Pl EKILN G74 3 J7
Avondale St STPS/GTHM/RID G33 81 G1
Avon Dr BLSH ML4 100 C5
PSLYN/LNWD PA3 74 B4
Avonhead EKILS G75 127 H5
Avonhead Av CUMB G67 48 C2
Avonhead Gdns CUMB G67 48 C2
Avonhead Pl CUMB G67 48 C2
Avonhead Rd CUMB G67 48 C2
Avonmouth Pl GRK PA19 15 M4
Avon Pl CTBR ML5 83 K1
Avon Rd BSHPBGS G64 62 A2
GIF/THBK G46 94 B8
Avonside Gv HMLTN ML3 119 M7
Avonspark St SPRGB/BLRNK G21 62 A7
Avon St HMLTN ML3 119 L7
LRKH ML9 130 B6
MTHW ML1 120 D4
Aylmer Rd PLKSW/MSWD G43 94 F4
Ayr Dr AIRDRIE ML6 85 G4
Ayr Rd GIF/THBK G46 114 A2
LRKH ML9 131 G7
NMRNS G77 113 H7
Ayr St SPRGB/BLRNK G21 61 M7
Ayr Ter GRNKW/INVK PA16 15 L6
Ayton Pk North EKILN G74 3 L1
Ayton Pk South EKILN G74 3 K2
Aytoun Dr ERSK PA8 38 F7
Aytoun Rd PLKSD/SHW G41 78 D7
Azalea Gdns BLTYR/CAMB G72 97 L5

B

Baads Rd BTHG/ARM EH48 70 D2
Babylon Av BLSH ML4 100 A6
Babylon Dr BLSH ML4 100 A6
Babylon Pl BLSH ML4 100 A7
Babylon Rd BLSH ML4 100 A6
Backbrae St KSYTH G65 29 K2
Backburn BEITH KA15 125 K5
Back Cswy DEN/PKHD G31 80 D5
Backmuir Crs HMLTN ML3 119 H4
Backmuir Pl HMLTN ML3 119 H4
Backmuir Rd DRUM G15 41 H4
HMLTN ML3 119 H3
Back O Barns HMLTN ML3 119 L6
Back O Dykes Rd KKNTL G66 46 B3
Back O Hl CRG/CRSL/HOU PA6 73 H1
Back O' Hill Rd BSHPBGS G64 25 M8
Back Rd BRWEIR PA11 72 D2
Back Rw HMLTN ML3 119 L6
Back Sneddon St PSLYN/LNWD PA3 9 H3
Back St DMBTN G82 20 D1
Badenheath Pl BALLOCH G68 47 K5
Badenoch Rd KKNTL G66 46 B1
Bagnell St SPRGB/BLRNK G21 61 M5
Bahamas Wy EKILS G75 126 D1
Bailie Dr BSDN G61 41 K2
Bailie Fyfe Wy WISHAW ML2 131 K2
Bailie Av SHOTTS ML7 71 M7
Baillie Dr EKILN G74 117 H6
UD/BTH/TAN G71 99 G7
Baillie Gdns WISHAW ML2 122 E5
Baillie Pl EKILN G74 117 J6
Baillies La AIRDRIE ML6 85 G1
Bailliesmuir Pl WISHAW ML2 123 G3
Baillieston Av KBRN KA25 124 C5
Baillieston Rd CAR/SHTL G32 81 L6
UD/BTH/TAN G71 98 B1
Baillie Wynd UD/BTH/TAN G71 99 G3
Bain Crs HBR/GL G84 10 E4
Bainfield Rd DMBTN G82 19 H3
Bainsford St CAR/SHTL G32 80 F4
Bain St DMNK/BRGTN G40 5 K9
Bain Wy ALEX/LLW G83 13 K4
Baird Av AIRDRIE ML6 67 H7
CARD/HILL/MSPK G52 76 E1
HBR/GL G84 10 B5
Baird Brae COWCAD G4 61 H7
Baird Crs ALEX/LLW G83 13 H3
CUMB G67 48 B2
Baird Dr BSDN G61 41 K4
ERSK PA8 38 F7
Baird Gdns BLTYR/CAMB G72 118 E4
Baird Hl EKILS G75 2 D8
Baird Pl BLSH ML4 100 A2
WISHAW ML2 122 E5
Bairds Crs HMLTN ML3 119 J7
Bairdsland Vw BLSH ML4 100 B4
Baird St COWCAD G4 5 H3
CTBR ML5 84 A2
Baird Ter SHOTTS ML7 71 J8
Baker St GRNK PA15 6 F6
PLKSD/SHW G41 94 E1
Bakewell Rd BAIL/MDB/MHD G69 82 A5
Balaclava St KVGV G3 4 B7
Balado Rd STPS/GTHM/RID G33 81 L3
Balbakie Rd SHOTTS ML7 71 L7
Balbeggie St CAR/SHTL G32 81 J6
Balbeg St GOV/IBX G51 77 L3
Balblair Rd CARD/HILL/MSPK G52 77 M6
Balcarres Av KVD/HLHD G12 60 C5
Balcary Pl AIRDRIE ML6 85 L8
Balcastle Gdns KSYTH G65 29 H1
Balcastle Rd KSYTH G65 29 G1
Balcomie St STPS/GTHM/RID G33 81 G1
Balcurvie Rd ESTRH G34 64 A8
Baldernock Rd MLNGV G62 24 D8
Baldinnie Rd ESTRH G34 82 B2
Baldoran Dr KKNTL G66 27 H4
Baldorran Crs BALLOCH G68 30 C6
Baldovan Crs STPS/GTHM/RID G33 81 M2
Baldovie Rd CARD/HILL/MSPK G52 77 J6
Baldragon Rd ESTRH G34 82 B1
Baldric Rd KNTSWD G13 59 J3
Baldwin Av KNTSWD G13 41 K8
Balerno Dr CARD/HILL/MSPK G52 77 L6
Balfleurs St MLNGV G62 24 B8
Balfluig St ESTRH G34 81 M1
Balfour Av BEITH KA15 125 K6
Balfour St MRYH/FIRH G20 60 D4
PGL PA14 18 B8
Balfour Ter EKILS G75 3 G9
Balfron Crs HMLTN ML3 118 F7
Balfron Dr CTBR ML5 84 C6
Balfron Pl CTBR ML5 84 C5
Balfron Rd GOV/IBX G51 77 L2
GRNK PA15 17 J8
PSLY PA1 76 D4
Balgair Dr PSLY PA1 76 B4
Balgair Gdns PPK/MIL G22 61 H6
Balgair St PPK/MIL G22 61 H5
Balgair Ter CAR/SHTL G32 81 H5
Balglass St PPK/MIL G22 61 H6
Balgonie Av PSLYS PA2 91 G1
Balgonie Dr PSLYS PA2 91 J1
Balgonie Rd CARD/HILL/MSPK G52 77 L6
Balgonie Woods PSLYS PA2 91 J1
Balgownie Crs GIF/THBK G46 94 A8
Balgray Av KBRN KA25 124 C5
Balgraybank St SPRGB/BLRNK G21 62 A6
Balgray Crs BRHD/NEIL G78 92 E7
Balgrayhill Rd SPRGB/BLRNK G21 61 M4
Balgray Rd KBRN KA25 124 D6
NMRNS G77 113 G4
Balgraystone Rd NMRNS G77 112 D4
Balintore St CAR/SHTL G32 81 G5
Baliol La KVGV G3 4 A3
Baliol St KVGV G3 4 A2
Baljaffray Rd BSDN G61 41 G2
Ballagan Pl MLNGV G62 23 K7
Ballaig Av BSDN G61 41 K4
Ballaig Crs STPS/GTHM/RID G33 63 J5
Ballantay Qd CSMK G45 96 A7
Ballantay Rd CSMK G45 96 A7
Ballantay Ter CSMK G45 96 A7
Ballantine Av CARD/HILL/MSPK G52 77 G2
Ballantrae EKILN G74 2 C2
Ballantrae Crs NMRNS G77 114 A6
Ballantrae Dr NMRNS G77 114 A6
Ballantrae Rd BLTYR/CAMB G72 118 E5
Ballater Crs WISHAW ML2 122 B4
Ballater Dr BSDN G61 41 M7
PSLYS PA2 91 M1
RNFRW PA4 57 K3
Ballater Pl GBLS G5 79 K6
Ballater St GBLS G5 79 K6
Ballayne Dr BAIL/MDB/MHD G69 47 G7
Ballerup Ter EKILS G75 127 H4
Ballindalloch Dr DEN/PKHD G31 80 A2
Ballindalloch La DEN/PKHD G31 80 A2
Balloch Gdns CARD/HILL/MSPK G52 77 M6
Balloch Loop Rd BALLOCH G68 30 A7
Ballochmill Rd RUTH G73 96 D2
Ballochmyle EKILN G74 117 K6
Ballochmyle Crs PLK/PH/NH G53 93 G1
Ballochmyle Dr PLK/PH/NH G53 77 G8
Ballochmyle Gdns PLK/PH/NH G53 93 G1
Ballochmyle Pl PLK/PH/NH G53 93 G1
Ballochney Rd AIRDRIE ML6 67 K5
Ballochney St AIRDRIE ML6 66 E8
Ballochnie Dr AIRDRIE ML6 68 A6
Ballochnie Vw AIRDRIE ML6 67 M7
Balloch Rd AIRDRIE ML6 86 A3
ALEX/LLW G83 13 K2
GRNK PA15 17 H7
SHOTTS ML7 104 E3
Balloch Vw CUMB G67 30 F7
Ballochyle Pl GRK PA19 14 E4
Ballogie Rd LNPK/KPK G44 95 H3
Balmalloch Rd KSYTH G65 29 H1
Balmartin Rd SMSTN G23 60 D1
Balmedie ERSK PA8 39 G8
Balmeg Av GIF/THBK G46 114 C2
Balmoral Av AIRDRIE ML6 66 F4
Balmoral Crs CTBR ML5 83 K6
RNFRW PA4 57 L3
Balmoral Dr BLTYR/CAMB G72 96 E5
BSDN G61 42 A8
BSHPTN PA7 56 C1
CAR/SHTL G32 97 H2
Balmoral Gdns BLTYR/CAMB G72 98 C8
Balmoral Pl EKILN G74 2 B5
GRK PA19 14 E4
Balmoral Rd JNSTN PA5 90 B2
Balmoral St SCOT G14 59 H6
Balmore Ct KLMCLM PA13 53 J3
Balmore Dr HMLTN ML3 129 H3
Balmore Pl PPK/MIL G22 61 H4
Balmore Rd BSHPBGS G64 43 M2
GRNK PA15 17 H8
SMSTN G23 42 F5
Balmore Sq PPK/MIL G22 61 H5
Balmuildy Rd SMSTN G23 43 H6
Balnagowan Rd SKLM PA17 50 C5
Balornock Rd SPRGB/BLRNK G21 62 A5
Balrossie Dr KLMCLM PA13 53 G3
Balruddery Pl BSHPBGS G64 62 D2
Balshagray Av PTCK G11 59 M6
Balshagray Crs PTCK G11 59 L7
Balshagray Dr PTCK G11 59 M6
Balshagray La PTCK G11 59 M6
Balshagray Pl PTCK G11 59 M6
Baltersan Gdns HMLTN ML3 129 M7
Baltic Ct DMNK/BRGTN G40 80 A7
Baltic La DMNK/BRGTN G40 80 A7
Baltic Pl DMNK/BRGTN G40 79 M6
Baltic St DMNK/BRGTN G40 80 A7
Balure Pl DEN/PKHD G31 80 C3
Balure St DEN/PKHD G31 80 C3
Balvaird Crs RUTH G73 96 A3
Balvaird Dr RUTH G73 96 A3
Balvenie Dr MTHW ML1 101 H8
Balvenie St CTBR ML5 84 B6
Balveny St STPS/GTHM/RID G33 63 K8
Balvicar Dr GVH/MTFL G42 94 F1
Balvicar St GVH/MTFL G42 78 F8
Balvie Av DRUM G15 41 G8
GIF/THBK G46 94 D8
Balvie Crs MLNGV G62 23 M7
Balvie Rd MLNGV G62 23 M7
Banavie La PTCK G11 60 A7
Banavie Rd PTCK G11 60 B7
WISHAW ML2 122 F3
Banchory Av AIRDRIE ML6 66 F4
PLKSW/MSWD G43 94 B5
RNFRW PA4 57 K3
Banchory Crs BSDN G61 42 A8
Banchory Rd WISHAW ML2 122 B4
Baneberry Pth EKILN G74 116 D6
Banff Av AIRDRIE ML6 85 G5
Banff Pl EKILS G75 2 A7
GRNKW/INVK PA16 15 J4
Banff Qd WISHAW ML2 122 B4
Banff Rd GRNKW/INVK PA16 15 J5
Banff St STPS/GTHM/RID G33 63 H8
Bangorshill St GIF/THBK G46 93 M5
Bank Av MLNGV G62 24 A7
Bankbrae Av PLK/PH/NH G53 93 G3
Bankend BRWEIR PA11 72 E3
Bankend Rd BRWEIR PA11 72 F4
DMBTN G82 20 F6
Bankend St STPS/GTHM/RID G33 81 G1
Bankfaulds Av KBRN KA25 124 C4
Bankfield Dr HMLTN ML3 129 K4
Bankfoot Dr CARD/HILL/MSPK G52 77 H5
Bankfoot Pl NMRNS G77 114 B6
Bankfoot Rd CARD/HILL/MSPK G52 77 H5
PSLYN/LNWD PA3 8 B3
Bankglen Rd DRUM G15 41 H5
Bankhall St GVH/MTFL G42 79 H8
Bankhead Av AIRDRIE ML6 85 K2
BLSH ML4 100 B6
CTBR ML5 83 J6
KNTSWD G13 59 G3
Bankhead Dr RUTH G73 96 A3
Bankhead Pl AIRDRIE ML6 85 K2
CTBR ML5 83 J6
Bankhead Rd CRMNK/CLK/EAG G76 115 K3
KKNTL G66 46 B3
RUTH G73 95 M4
Bankhead Ter LNK/LMHG ML11 137 H7
Bankholm Pl CRMNK/CLK/EAG G76 114 F5
Bankhouse Av LARGS KA30 106 F6
Bankhouse Crs LARGS KA30 106 F6
Banknock St CAR/SHTL G32 80 E4
Bank Pk EKILS G75 2 D7
Bank Pl SHOTTS ML7 104 F5
Bank Rd CAR/SHTL G32 97 J2
SHOTTS ML7 71 K7
Bankside Av JNSTN PA5 73 M7
Bankside Gdns KBRN KA25 124 C1
Banks Rd KKNTL G66 45 L1
Bank St AIRDRIE ML6 85 G1
ALEX/LLW G83 13 K6
BLTYR/CAMB G72 97 G4
BRHD/NEIL G78 92 C7
CTBR ML5 83 M4
GRNK PA15 6 D6
KBRN KA25 124 C3
KVD/HLHD G12 60 E8
PSLY PA1 9 K5
Banktop Pl JNSTN PA5 73 M7
Bank Vw AIRDRIE ML6 85 K7
Bankview Dr KKNTL G66 45 G2
Bannachra Crs ALEX/LLW G83 13 H4
Bannachra Dr HBR/GL G84 10 B5
Bannatyne St LNK/LMHG ML11 137 G5
Bannercross Av BAIL/MDB/MHD G69 82 A5
Bannercross Dr BAIL/MDB/MHD G69 82 A4
Bannercross Gdns BAIL/MDB/MHD G69 82 A5
Banner Dr KNTSWD G13 41 J8
Bannerman Dr BLSH ML4 100 D4
Bannerman Pl CLYDBK G81 40 C7
Banner Rd BSDN G61 41 K7
Bannockburn Dr LRKH ML9 130 E8
Bannockburn Pl MTHW ML1 101 G7
Bannockburn St GRNKW/INVK PA16 16 C6
Bantaskin St MRYH/FIRH G20 60 C3
Banton Pl STPS/GTHM/RID G33 82 A3
Banyan Crs UD/BTH/TAN G71 99 K1
Barassie EKILN G74 2 D2
Barassie Ct UD/BTH/TAN G71 98 F8
Barassie Dr BRWEIR PA11 72 C4
Barbados Gn EKILS G75 126 D1
Barbae Pl UD/BTH/TAN G71 99 G7
Barbana Rd EKILN G74 115 L8
Barbegs Crs KSYTH G65 29 M6
Barberry Av PLK/PH/NH G53 93 H7
Barberry Dr BEITH KA15 125 J5
Barberry Gdns PLK/PH/NH G53 93 H7
Barberry Pl PLK/PH/NH G53 93 J7
Barbeth Gdns CUMB G67 48 B4
Barbeth Pl CUMB G67 48 A3
Barbeth Rd CUMB G67 48 A3
Barbeth Wy CUMB G67 48 B3
Barbreck Rd PLKSD/SHW G41 78 F8
Barcaldine Av BAIL/MDB/MHD G69 64 C1
Barcaldine Ter PLKSD/SHW G41 78 F8
Barcapel Av NMRNS G77 113 L2
Barclaven Rd KLMCLM PA13 53 L2
Barclay Av JNSTN PA5 74 B8
Barclay Ct OLDK G60 39 H4
Barclay Dr HBR/GL G84 10 C4
Barclay Rd MTHW ML1 120 B3
Barclay St SPRGB/BLRNK G21 61 M5
Barcloy Pl AIRDRIE ML6 85 M8
Barcraigs Dr PSLYS PA2 91 M2
Bard Av KNTSWD G13 59 H1
Bardowie St PPK/MIL G22 61 J6
Bardrain Av JNSTN PA5 74 C8
Bardrainney Av PGL PA14 34 F3
Bardrain Rd PSLYS PA2 91 J3
Bardrill Dr BSHPBGS G64 61 L1
Bardykes Rd BLTYR/CAMB G72 118 C2
Barefield St LRKH ML9 130 C5
Barfillan Dr CARD/HILL/MSPK G52 77 L4
Bargany Ct PLK/PH/NH G53 77 G8
Bargany Pl PLK/PH/NH G53 93 G1
Bargany Rd PLK/PH/NH G53 77 G8
Bargaran Rd PLK/PH/NH G53 77 H6
Bargarran Rd ERSK PA8 38 F8
Bargarron Dr PSLYN/LNWD PA3 76 A2
Bargeddie St STPS/GTHM/RID G33 62 D8
Barhill La KSYTH G65 28 F6
Bar Hill Pl KSYTH G65 29 H2
Barhill Rd ERSK PA8 39 G8
Barholm Sq STPS/GTHM/RID G33 81 K1
Barke Rd CUMB G67 31 G6
Barkly Ter EKILS G75 2 A8
Barlanark Av CAR/SHTL G32 81 J3
Barlanark Crs STPS/GTHM/RID G33 81 K3
Barlanark Dr STPS/GTHM/RID G33 81 K3
Barlanark Pl STPS/GTHM/RID G33 81 L3
Barlanark Rd STPS/GTHM/RID G33 81 K3
Barlandfauld St KSYTH G65 29 L3
Barlia Dr CSMK G45 95 L7
Barlia Gdns CSMK G45 95 L7
Barlia Gv CSMK G45 95 L7
Barlia St CSMK G45 95 L7
Barlia Ter CSMK G45 95 M7
Barloan Crs DMBTN G82 21 G5
Barloan Pl DMBTN G82 21 G5
Barloch Av MLNGV G62 24 A8
Barloch Rd MLNGV G62 24 B8
Barloch St PPK/MIL G22 61 J6
Barlogan Av CARD/HILL/MSPK G52 77 L4
Barlogan Qd CARD/HILL/MSPK G52 77 L4
Barmore Av CARLUKE ML8 135 G1
Barmouth Av GRK PA19 15 L4
Barmulloch Rd SPRGB/BLRNK G21 62 A6
Barnbeth Rd PLK/PH/NH G53 77 H7
Barncluith Av HMLTN ML3 120 A7
Barncluith Rd HMLTN ML3 119 M7
Barnes Rd MRYH/FIRH G20 61 H4
Barness Pl STPS/GTHM/RID G33 81 G2
Barnes St BRHD/NEIL G78 92 B7
Barnflat St RUTH G73 96 B1
Barn Gn KLBCH PA10 73 G7
Barnhill Dr HMLTN ML3 118 D8
NMRNS G77 113 K7
SPRGB/BLRNK G21 62 A7
Barnhill Rd DMBTN G82 21 K7
Barnhill St GRNK PA15 7 J7
Barnkirk Av DRUM G15 41 G6
Barnscroft KLBCH PA10 73 H6
Barnsford Av RNFRW PA4 57 G6
Barnsford Rd PSLYN/LNWD PA3 75 G2
RNFRW PA4 57 G5
Barns St CLYDBK G81 58 C1
Barnton St CAR/SHTL G32 80 E3
Barnwell Ter GOV/IBX G51 77 L2
Barochan Crs PSLYN/LNWD PA3 75 G6
Barochan Rd BLSH ML4 100 D3
CRG/CRSL/HOU PA6 55 G2
PLK/PH/NH G53 77 H6
Baronald Dr KVD/HLHD G12 60 B4
Baronald Ga KVD/HLHD G12 60 B4
Baronald St RUTH G73 96 B1
Baron Ct HMLTN ML3 120 A7
Barone Dr CRMNK/CLK/EAG G76 114 C2
Baronhall Dr BLTYR/CAMB G72 118 C2
Baronhill CUMB G67 31 G4
Baron Rd PSLYN/LNWD PA3 9 M1
Baronscourt Dr PSLY PA1 74 F6
Baronscourt Gdns PSLY PA1 74 F6
Baronscourt Rd PSLY PA1 74 F7
Barons Ga UD/BTH/TAN G71 98 E6
Barons Rd MTHW ML1 121 J7
Baron St RNFRW PA4 58 C7
Barony Ct BAIL/MDB/MHD G69 82 B4
Barony Dr BAIL/MDB/MHD G69 82 B4
Barony Gdns BAIL/MDB/MHD G69 82 B5
Barony Pl BALLOCH G68 47 L1
Barony Ter KBRN KA25 124 C6
Barony Wynd BAIL/MDB/MHD G69 82 B5
Barra Av RNFRW PA4 58 C8
WISHAW ML2 122 E4
Barrachnie Av BAIL/MDB/MHD G69 82 A5
Barrachnie Ct BAIL/MDB/MHD G69 81 M5
Barrachnie Crs BAIL/MDB/MHD G69 81 M5
Barrachnie Gv BAIL/MDB/MHD G69 82 A4
Barrachnie Pl BAIL/MDB/MHD G69 82 A4
Barrachnie Rd BAIL/MDB/MHD G69 82 A5
Barrack St COWCAD G4 5 L8
HMLTN ML3 119 K6
Barra Dr AIRDRIE ML6 85 L3
Barra Gdns OLDK G60 39 J5
Barra Pl CTBR ML5 83 L6
Barra Rd OLDK G60 39 J5
Barraston Rd BSHPBGS G64 26 A7
Barra St MRYH/FIRH G20 60 C2
Barr Av BRHD/NEIL G78 111 L2
Barrbridge Rd BAIL/MDB/MHD G69 83 H6
Barrcraig Rd BRWEIR PA11 72 C3
Barr Crs CLYDBK G81 40 B4
LARGS KA30 106 E3
Barr Farm Rd KSYTH G65 29 L3
Barr Gv UD/BTH/TAN G71 99 G2

Barrhead Rd *NMRNS* G77 **113** H4
PLK/PH/NH G53 **92** F2
PSLYS PA2 **9** M9
Barrhill Ct *KKNTL* G66 **46** A2
Barrhill Crs *KLBCH* PA10 **73** H8
Barrhill Rd *GRK* PA19 **15** K2
KKNTL G66 **46** A2
Barriedale Av *HMLTN* ML3 **119** H7
Barriedale Crs
BLTYR/CAMB G72 **118** C7
Barrie Qd *CLYDBK* G81 **40** A5
Barrie Rd *CARD/HILL/MSPK* G52 **77** G2
EKILN G74 **117** K5
Barrie St *MTHW* ML1 **120** E3
Barrington Av *BEITH* KA15 **125** K4
Barrington Dr *COWCAD* G4 **60** F8
Barrington Gdns *BEITH* KA15 **125** L4
Barrisdale Rd *MRYH/FIRH* G20 **60** D3
WISHAW ML2 **122** F3
Barrisdale Wy *RUTH* G73 **96** B6
Barrland Dr *GIF/THBK* G46 **94** C7
Barrland St *PLKSD/SHW* G41 **79** G7
Barrmill Rd *BEITH* KA15 **125** L6
PLKSW/MSWD G43 **94** A5
Barrochan Rd *JNSTN* PA5 **73** L7
Barrowfield Ga
DMNK/BRGTN G40 **80** B6
Barrowfield Pl
DMNK/BRGTN G40 **80** B6
Barrowfield St *CTBR* ML5 **83** M6
DMNK/BRGTN G40 **80** B6
Barrpath *KSYTH* G65 **29** M3
Barr Pl *NMRNS* G77 **113** J4
PSLY PA1 **8** F6
Barrs Brae *KLMCLM* PA13 **53** K2
PGL PA14 **34** C1
Barrs Brae La *PGL* PA14 **34** C1
Barrs Ct *DMBTN* G82 **19** G1
Barrs Rd *DMBTN* G82 **19** G2
Barrs Ter *DMBTN* G82 **19** G2
Barr St *MRYH/FIRH* G20 **61** G7
MTHW ML1 **120** E1
Barr Ter *EKILN* G74 **2** F4
Barrwood Pl *UD/BTH/TAN* G71 **99** G2
Barrwood St
STPS/GTHM/RID G33 **62** E8
Barry Gdns *BLTYR/CAMB* G72 **118** C4
Barscube Av *PGL* PA14 **34** E3
Barscube Ter *PSLYS* PA2 **9** M9
Barshaw Ct
CARD/HILL/MSPK G52 **76** F3
Barshaw Dr
CARD/HILL/MSPK G52 **76** F3
PSLY PA1 **9** M2
Barshaw Pl *PSLY* PA1 **76** D4
Barshaw Rd
CARD/HILL/MSPK G52 **76** E3
Barskiven Rd *PSLY* PA1 **74** F6
Barterholm Rd *PSLYS* PA2 **9** J9
Bartholomew St
DMNK/BRGTN G40 **80** A7
Bartiebeith Rd
STPS/GTHM/RID G33 **81** L3
Barton Av *ALEX/LLW* G83 **13** M2
Bartonhall Rd *WISHAW* ML2 **122** D8
Barty's Rd *BLSH* ML4 * **100** C4
Barwood Dr *ERSK* PA8 **39** G7
Barwood Hl *DMBTN* G82 **21** H4
Bassett Av *KNTSWD* G13 **59** H1
Bassett Crs *KNTSWD* G13 **59** H1
Bathgate St *DEN/PKHD* G31 **80** A4
Bathgo Av *PSLY* PA1 **76** E5
Bath La *CGLW* G2 **4** B4
Bathlin Crs *BAIL/MDB/MHD* G69 **47** G7
Bath St *GRK* PA19 **15** L1
KVGV G3 **4** A4
LARGS KA30 **106** E5
Bathville Rd *KBRN* KA25 **124** C4
Baton Rd *SHOTTS* ML7 **104** D4
Batson St *GVH/MTFL* G42 **79** H8
Battery Park Dr
GRNKW/INVK PA16 **16** B1
Battismains *LNK/LMHG* ML11 **137** J5
Battlefield Av *GVH/MTFL* G42 **95** G3
Battlefield Gdns *GVH/MTFL* G42 **95** G3
Battlefield Rd *GVH/MTFL* G42 **95** G2
Battles Burn Dr *CAR/SHTL* G32 **81** G8
Battles Burn Ga *CAR/SHTL* G32 **81** G8
Battles Burn Vw *CAR/SHTL* G32 **81** G8
Bavelaw St
STPS/GTHM/RID G33 **63** K8
Bawhirley Rd *GRNK* PA15 **7** H8
Baxter La *ALEX/LLW* G83 **13** K3
LNK/LMHG ML11 **137** G5
Baxter St *GRNK* PA15 **7** L8
Baxter Wynd *WISHAW* ML2 **121** L7
Bayfield Av *DRUM* G15 **41** G6
Bayfield Ter *DRUM* G15 **41** G6
Bay St *PGL* PA14 **34** C1
Bay View Rd *GRK* PA19 **15** M3
Bay Willow Ct
BLTYR/CAMB G72 **97** M6
Beachway *LARGS* KA30 **106** E4
Beacon Pl *STPS/GTHM/RID* G33 **80** F2
Beaconsfield Rd
KVD/HLHD G12 **60** B5
Beanshields Rd *CARLUKE* ML8 **134** F4
Beard Crs *BAIL/MDB/MHD* G69 **64** E4
Beardmore Pl *CLYDBK* G81 **39** L7
Beardmore St *CLYDBK* G81 **39** L7
Beardmore Wy *CLYDBK* G81 **39** L8
DEN/PKHD G31 **80** B4
Bearford Dr
CARD/HILL/MSPK G52 **77** H4
Bearhope St *GRNK* PA15 **6** C4
Bearsden Rd *KNTSWD* G13 **59** M3
Beatock Pl *GRNKW/INVK* PA16 **32** E5
Beaton Rd *ALEX/LLW* G83 **13** K2
PLKSD/SHW G41 **78** E8
Beaton St *LRKH* ML9 **130** B5
Beatrice Dr *MTHW* ML1 **100** F4
Beatrice Gdns
CRG/CRSL/HOU PA6 **73** K2
Beatson Wynd
UD/BTH/TAN G71 **99** G1
Beattock St *DEN/PKHD* G31 **80** D5
Beattock Wynd *HMLTN* ML3 **119** G7
Beatty Pl *HBR/GL* G84 **11** G5
Beatty St *CLYDBK* G81 **39** L7
Beaufort Av
PLKSW/MSWD G43 **94** C4
Beaufort Dr *KKNTL* G66 **45** H2
Beaufort Gdns *BSHPBGS* G64 **61** L1
Beauly Crs *AIRDRIE* ML6 **85** L3
KLMCLM PA13 **53** J3
WISHAW ML2 **122** B8
Beauly Dr *PSLYS* PA2 **90** F1
Beauly Pl *BAIL/MDB/MHD* G69 **64** D1
CTBR ML5 **84** B6
EKILN G74 **2** D3
MRYH/FIRH G20 **60** D5
MTHW ML1 **101** G5
Beauly Rd *BAIL/MDB/MHD* G69 **82** A7
Beaumont Ga *KVD/HLHD* G12 **60** C8
Beckfield Crs
STPS/GTHM/RID G33 **62** D3
Beckfield Dr
STPS/GTHM/RID G33 **62** D3
Beckfield Ga
STPS/GTHM/RID G33 **62** D3
Beckfield Gv
STPS/GTHM/RID G33 **62** D3
Beckfield Wk
STPS/GTHM/RID G33 **62** D3
Beckford St *HMLTN* ML3 **119** J5
Bedale Rd *BAIL/MDB/MHD* G69 **81** M6
Bedcow Vw *KKNTL* G66 **45** M3
Bedford Av *CLYDBK* G81 **40** D7
Bedford La *GBLS* G5 **79** H5
GRNKW/INVK PA16 **16** D2
Bedford St *GBLS* G5 **79** H5
GRNKW/INVK PA16 **16** D2
Bedlay Ct *BAIL/MDB/MHD* G69 **47** G7
Bedlay Pl *CTBR* ML5 **65** M1
Bedlay Vw *UD/BTH/TAN* G71 **99** H1
Bedlormie Dr *BTHG/ARM* EH48 **71** H2
Beech Av *BAIL/MDB/MHD* G69 **82** A5
BEITH KA15 **125** K3
BRWEIR PA11 **72** D1
BSDN G61 **42** A3
HMLTN ML3 **129** M6
JNSTN PA5 **74** C8
LRKH ML9 **130** F7
MTHW ML1 **101** H7
NMRNS G77 **113** L5
PLKSD/SHW G41 **78** B6
PSLYS PA2 **76** A8
RUTH G73 **96** C6
Beechbank Av *AIRDRIE* ML6 **84** F1
Beechburn Crs *LOCHW* PA12 **109** K2
Beech Crs *BLTYR/CAMB* G72 **97** L6
MTHW ML1 **101** J3
NMRNS G77 **113** L6
Beech Dr *AIRDRIE* ML6 **68** F5
CLYDBK G81 **40** A4
Beeches Av *CLYDBK* G81 **39** M4
Beeches Rd *CLYDBK* G81 **39** M4
The Beeches *JNSTN* PA5 **73** J4
LNK/LMHG ML11 **137** H7
Beechfield Dr *CARLUKE* ML8 **135** G1
Beechfield Rd *BEITH* KA15 **125** H6
Beech Gdns
BAIL/MDB/MHD G69 **82** A5
Beech Gv *BAIL/MDB/MHD* G69 **65** G5
CARLUKE ML8 **132** B3
EKILS G75 **126** E4
WISHAW ML2 **122** C2
Beechgrove Av
UD/BTH/TAN G71 **99** J3
Beech Grove Pl *HBR/GL* G84 **11** G7
Beechgrove Qd *MTHW* ML1 **101** G4
Beechgrove St
DMNK/BRGTN G40 * **80** B8
Beechlands Av *LNPK/KPK* G44 **94** E8
Beechlands Dr
CRMNK/CLK/EAG G76 **114** C4
Beechmount Rd *KKNTL* G66 **45** K6
Beech Pl *BSHPBGS* G64 **62** B2
GRK PA19 **15** J3
Beech Rd *BSHPBGS* G64 **62** B2
JNSTN PA5 **89** K1
KKNTL G66 **45** J4
MTHW ML1 **101** J2
Beech Ter *LRKH* ML9 **130** D8
Beechtree Ter *KKNTL* G66 **27** J5
Beechwood *LRKH* ML9 **130** C4
WISHAW ML2 **121** K8
Beechwood Av
CRMNK/CLK/EAG G76 **114** C4
HMLTN ML3 **129** H2
PGL PA14 **36** C3
RUTH G73 **96** C4
Beechwood Ct *BSDN* G61 **41** M6
CUMB G67 **48** F1
Beechwood Crs *WISHAW* ML2 **122** C7
Beechwood Dr *ALEX/LLW* G83 **13** M8
CTBR ML5 **84** C4
PTCK G11 **59** M5
RNFRW PA4 **58** C8
Beechwood Gdns *BLSH* ML4 **100** C5
Beechwood Gv *BRHD/NEIL* G78 **92** C5
Beechwood Pl *PTCK* G11 **59** M5
Beechwood Rd *CUMB* G67 **30** F8
Beechworth Dr *MTHW* ML1 **101** K7
Beecroft Pl *BLTYR/CAMB* G72 **118** E1
Beil Dr *KNTSWD* G13 **58** F2
Beith Dr *AIRDRIE* ML6 **85** G5
Beithglass Av *SKLM* PA17 **50** C5
Beith Rd *GLGNK* KA14 **124** F7
GRNKW/INVK PA16 **6** B9
JNSTN PA5 **89** M1
Beith St *PTCK* G11 **78** B1
Beith Wy *BLTYR/CAMB* G72 **118** D8
Belford Ct *NMRNS* G77 **113** K7
Belford Gv *NMRNS* G77 **113** K7
Belgowan St *BLSH* ML4 **99** M3
Belgrave La *KVD/HLHD* G12 **60** E7
Belgrave St *BLSH* ML4 **99** M4
Belhaven Ct *NMRNS* G77 **113** J7
Belhaven Pk
BAIL/MDB/MHD G69 **64** C3
Belhaven Pl *CTBR* ML5 **65** L4
NMRNS G77 **113** K7
Belhaven Rd *HMLTN* ML3 **118** E7
WISHAW ML2 **122** A6
Belhaven St *PGL* PA14 **18** B8
Belhaven Ter *KVD/HLHD* G12 **60** C6
WISHAW ML2 **122** A6
Belhaven Terrace La
KVD/HLHD G12 **60** C6
Belhaven Ter West
KVD/HLHD G12 **60** C6
Belhaven Terrace West La
KVD/HLHD G12 **60** C6
Bellahouston Dr
CARD/HILL/MSPK G52 **77** L6
Bellairs Pl *BLTYR/CAMB* G72 **118** C1
Bellas Pl *AIRDRIE* ML6 **68** A7
Bellcote Rd *BALLOCH* G68 **30** D4
Belleaire Dr *GRNKW/INVK* PA16 **16** C2
Bellefield Crs *LNK/LMHG* ML11 **137** G3
Bellefield Rd *LNK/LMHG* ML11 **137** G4
Bellefield Wy *LNK/LMHG* ML11 **137** G3
Belleisle Av *UD/BTH/TAN* G71 **98** E4
Belleisle Ct *BALLOCH* G68 **30** E5
Belleisle Crs *BRWEIR* PA11 **72** B3
Belleisle Dr *BALLOCH* G68 **30** E5
Belleisle Gdns *BALLOCH* G68 **30** E5
Belleisle Gv *BALLOCH* G68 **30** E5
Belleisle Pl *GRK* PA19 **15** G3
Belleisle St *GVH/MTFL* G42 **95** H1
Bellesdale Av *LARGS* KA30 **106** F5
Bellevue Av *KKNTL* G66 **45** H2
Bellevue Rd *KKNTL* G66 **45** H2
Bellfield Crs *BRHD/NEIL* G78 **92** B5
Bellfield Dr *WISHAW* ML2 **122** C7
Bellfield Rd *KKNTL* G66 **45** H2
Bellfield St *DEN/PKHD* G31 **80** A4
Bellflower Av *PLK/PH/NH* G53 **93** J6
Bellflower Ct *EKILN* G74 **2** B1
Bellflower Gdns
PLK/PH/NH G53 **93** J6
Bellflower Gv *EKILN* G74 **2** B1
Bellflower Pl *PLK/PH/NH* G53 **93** J6
Bell Gn East *EKILS* G75 **3** G8
Bell Gn West *EKILS* G75 **2** F8
Bellgrove St *DEN/PKHD* G31 **79** M4
Bellman's Cl *BEITH* KA15 **125** K4
LARGS KA30 **106** E5
Bellrock Ct
STPS/GTHM/RID G33 **81** H2
Bellrock Crs
STPS/GTHM/RID G33 **81** G2
Bellrock St
STPS/GTHM/RID G33 **81** H2
Bellrock Vw
STPS/GTHM/RID G33 **81** G2
Bells Br *KVGV* G3 **78** D3
Bellscroft Av *RUTH* G73 **95** M3
Bellsdyke Rd *AIRDRIE* ML6 **84** F3
Bellshaugh Ct *KVD/HLHD* G12 **60** C5
Bellshaugh Gdns
KVD/HLHD G12 **60** C5
Bellshaugh La *KVD/HLHD* G12 **60** C5
Bellshaugh Pl *KVD/HLHD* G12 **60** C5
Bellshaugh Rd *KVD/HLHD* G12 **60** C5
Bellshill Rd *MTHW* ML1 **100** C7
UD/BTH/TAN G71 **98** F5
Bellside Rd *AIRDRIE* ML6 **85** M7
MTHW ML1 **102** A1
Bellsmyre Av *DMBTN* G82 **21** G4
Bell St *AIRDRIE* ML6 **84** F2
BLSH ML4 **100** B2
CGLE G1 **5** H7
GRNK PA15 **17** L7
RNFRW PA4 **58** D5
WISHAW ML2 **121** M6
Bells Wynd *LNK/LMHG* ML11 **137** J4
Belltrees Crs *PSLY* PA1 **75** G6
Belltrees Rd *HWWD* PA9 **88** C7
Bell Vw *WISHAW* ML2 **123** G3
Bell View Ct *RNFRW* PA4 **58** D5
Bellvue Crs *BLSH* ML4 **99** M6
Bellvue Wy *CTBR* ML5 **84** C5
Bellwood St *PLKSD/SHW* G41 **94** E3
Bellziehill Rd *BLSH* ML4 **99** L5
Belmont Av *UD/BTH/TAN* G71 **98** E3
Belmont Crs *KVD/HLHD* G12 **60** E7
Belmont Dr *BRHD/NEIL* G78 **92** D8
EKILS G75 **126** E2
GIF/THBK G46 **94** B7
RUTH G73 **96** B3
SHOTTS ML7 **105** H7
Belmont La *KVD/HLHD* G12 **60** E7
Belmont Rd *BLTYR/CAMB* G72 **96** E7
KLMCLM PA13 **53** J3
PSLYN/LNWD PA3 **9** M1
SPRGB/BLRNK G21 **61** M4
Belmont St *CLYDBK* G81 **40** B8
CTBR ML5 **83** J1
KSYTH G65 **29** J1
KVD/HLHD G12 **60** E7
WISHAW ML2 **131** K3
Belses Dr
CARD/HILL/MSPK G52 **77** J4
Belses Gdns
CARD/HILL/MSPK G52 **77** J4
Belstane Pk *CARLUKE* ML8 **133** J6
Belstane Pl *UD/BTH/TAN* G71 **99** G7
Belstane Rd *CARLUKE* ML8 **133** J6
CUMB G67 **48** F4
Belsyde Av *DRUM* G15 **41** G7
Beltane St *KVGV* G3 **4** A4
WISHAW ML2 **122** A7
Beltonfoot Wy *WISHAW* ML2 **121** M7
Beltrees Av *PLK/PH/NH* G53 **77** G8
Beltrees Crs *PLK/PH/NH* G53 **77** G8
Beltrees Rd *PLK/PH/NH* G53 **77** G8
Belvidere Crs *BLSH* ML4 **100** B5
BSHPBGS G64 **44** B8
Belvidere Rd *BLSH* ML4 **100** A5
Belville Av *GRNK* PA15 **7** H7
Belville St *GRNK* PA15 **7** J7
Belvoir Pl *BLTYR/CAMB* G72 **118** D2
Bemersyde *BSHPBGS* G64 **44** C8
Bemersyde Av
PLKSW/MSWD G43 **94** B5
Bemersyde Pl *LRKH* ML9 **130** C8
Bemersyde Rd *PSLYS* PA2 **90** E2
Ben Alder Dr *PSLYS* PA2 **76** D8
Benalder St *PTCK* G11 **78** C1
Benbecula *EKILN* G74 **127** M1
Ben Bouie Dr *HBR/GL* G84 **10** F6
Benbow Rd *CLYDBK* G81 **39** M8
Bencloich Crs *KKNTL* G66 **26** E1
Bencloich Rd *KKNTL* G66 **26** E1
Benclutha *PGL* PA14 **34** E1
Bencroft Dr *LNPK/KPK* G44 **95** L5
Ben Donich Pl *PLK/PH/NH* G53 **93** K4
Ben Edra Pl *PLK/PH/NH* G53 **93** K5
Benford Av *MTHW* ML1 **101** K5
Benford Knowe *MTHW* ML1 **101** K5
Bengairn St *DEN/PKHD* G31 **80** C3
Bengal Pl *PLKSW/MSWD* G43 **94** C3
Bengal St *PLKSW/MSWD* G43 **94** C3
Ben Garrisdale Pl
PLK/PH/NH G53 **93** K5
Benhar Pl *STPS/GTHM/RID* G33 **80** F3
Benhar Rd *SHOTTS* ML7 **104** F5
Benholm St *CAR/SHTL* G32 **80** F7
Ben Hope Av *PSLYS* PA2 **76** D7
Ben Laga Pl *PLK/PH/NH* G53 **93** K5
Ben Lawers Dr *BALLOCH* G68 **30** B7
PSLYS PA2 **76** D7
Ben Ledi Av *PSLYS* PA2 **76** D7
Ben Ledi Crs *BALLOCH* G68 **30** B7
Ben Lomond Wy *ALEX/LLW* G83 **13** H2
Ben Loyal Av *PSLYS* PA2 **76** D7
Ben Lui Dr *PSLYS* PA2 **76** D8
Ben Lui Pl *BALLOCH* G68 **30** B7
PLK/PH/NH G53 **93** K5
Ben Macdui Gdns
PLK/PH/NH G53 **93** K5
Ben More Dr *BALLOCH* G68 **30** A7
PSLYS PA2 **76** D7
Bennan Pl *EKILS* G75 **126** F6
Bennan Sq *GVH/MTFL* G42 **95** J1
Benn Av *PSLY* PA1 **9** L6
Ben Nevis Rd *PSLYS* PA2 **76** D7
Ben Nevis Wy *BALLOCH* G68 **30** B7
Benny Lynch Ct *GBLS* G5 **79** J5
Ben Oss Pl *PLK/PH/NH* G53 **93** J5
Benson St *CTBR* ML5 **84** A5
Benston Pl *JNSTN* PA5 **89** L1
Benston Rd *JNSTN* PA5 **89** L1
Bent Crs *UD/BTH/TAN* G71 **99** J4
Bentfoot Rd *WISHAW* ML2 **131** L3
Benthall St *GBLS* G5 **79** K6
Bentinck St *GRNKW/INVK* PA16 **16** D1
KVGV G3 **78** E1
Bent Rd *AIRDRIE* ML6 **85** K6
HMLTN ML3 **119** J7
Bents Rd *BAIL/MDB/MHD* G69 **82** B5
Benty's La *CARLUKE* ML8 **134** F1
Ben Uird Pl *PLK/PH/NH* G53 **93** K5
Ben Vane Av *PSLYS* PA2 **76** C8
Ben Venue Rd *BALLOCH* G68 **30** A7
Ben Venue Wy *PSLYS* PA2 **76** D8
Benview Av *PGL* PA14 **34** F2
Benview Rd
CRMNK/CLK/EAG G76 **114** E3
PGL PA14 **34** E2
Benview St *MRYH/FIRH* G20 **60** F6
Benview Ter *PSLYS* PA2 **76** B7
Ben Vorlich Dr *PLK/PH/NH* G53 **93** K5
Ben Vorlich Pl *PLK/PH/NH* G53 **93** K5
Benvue Rd *KKNTL* G66 **26** E3
Ben Wyvis Dr *PSLYS* PA2 **76** C8
Berelands Crs *GVH/MTFL* G42 **95** L3
Berelands Pl *RUTH* G73 **95** M3
Berenice Pl *DMBTN* G82 **21** J8
Beresford Av *SCOT* G14 **59** L5
Berkeley St *KVGV* G3 **78** E2
Berkeley Terrace La *KVGV* G3 **78** F2
Berkley Dr *BLTYR/CAMB* G72 **118** C1
Berl Av *CRG/CRSL/HOU* PA6 **73** J2
Bernadette Crs *MTHW* ML1 **101** K7
Bernadette St *MTHW* ML1 **101** K6
Bernard St *DMNK/BRGTN* G40 **80** B6
Bernard's Wynd
LNK/LMHG ML11 **137** G5
Bernard Ter *DMNK/BRGTN* G40 **80** A6
Berneray St *PPK/MIL* G22 **61** J3
Bernisdale Dr *DRUM* G15 **40** D6
Bernisdale Gdns *DRUM* G15 **40** D6
Bernisdale Pl *DRUM* G15 **40** D6
Berridale Av *LNPK/KPK* G44 **95** G5
Berriedale *EKILS* G75 **126** B2
Berriedale Av
BAIL/MDB/MHD G69 **82** A6
Berriedale Crs
BLTYR/CAMB G72 **118** C7
Berriedale Qd *WISHAW* ML2 **122** B4
Berriedale Ter
BLTYR/CAMB G72 **118** C7
Berryburn Rd
SPRGB/BLRNK G21 **62** C6
Berryhill Crs *WISHAW* ML2 **121** L7
Berryhill Dr *GIF/THBK* G46 **94** B8
Berryhill Rd *CUMB* G67 **30** E8
GIF/THBK G46 **114** B1
Berryknowe Av
BAIL/MDB/MHD G69 **64** C3
Berryknowes Av
CARD/HILL/MSPK G52 **77** J4
Berryknowes La
CARD/HILL/MSPK G52 **77** J4
Berryknowes Rd
CARD/HILL/MSPK G52 **77** J4
Berryyards Rd *GRNK* PA15 **6** C7
Bertram Dr *SHOTTS* ML7 **87** H7
Bertram Pl *SHOTTS* ML7 **104** D4
Bertram St *HMLTN* ML3 **119** G5
LRKH ML9 **130** E8
PLKSD/SHW G41 **94** E1
SHOTTS ML7 **104** E4
Bervie St *GOV/IBX* G51 **77** M3
Berwick Crs *AIRDRIE* ML6 **84** F4
PSLYN/LNWD PA3 **73** M3
Berwick Dr
CARD/HILL/MSPK G52 **77** H5
RUTH G73 **96** D3
Berwick Pl *CTBR* ML5 **84** B6
EKILN G74 **117** J7
GRNKW/INVK PA16 **15** K5
Berwick Rd *GRNKW/INVK* PA16 **15** J5
PGL PA14 **34** C1
Berwick St *CTBR* ML5 **84** B6
HMLTN ML3 **119** H5
Bessemer Dr *EKILS* G75 **127** K5
Bethal La *EKILS* G75 **126** D6
Betula Dr *CLYDBK* G81 **40** A4
Bevan Gv *JNSTN* PA5 **73** L8
Beveridge Ter *BLSH* ML4 **100** D5
Beverley Rd
PLKSW/MSWD G43 **94** D4
Bevin Av *CLYDBK* G81 **40** D8
Bidders Gait *LNK/LMHG* ML11 **137** H6
Bideford Crs *CAR/SHTL* G32 **81** K7
The Bield *WISHAW* ML2 **122** C7
Bigfoot Rd *SHOTTS* ML7 **87** G6
Biggar Rd *MTHW* ML1 **101** M3
Biggar St *DEN/PKHD* G31 **80** B4
Bigholm Rd *BEITH* KA15 **125** L4
Bigton St *STPS/GTHM/RID* G33 **63** H8
Billings Rd *MTHW* ML1 **120** B4
Bilsland Ct *MRYH/FIRH* G20 **61** H5
Bilsland Dr *MRYH/FIRH* G20 **60** F5
Bilsland Pl *DMBTN* G82 **20** D1
Binend Rd *PLK/PH/NH* G53 **93** J1
Binniehill Rd *BALLOCH* G68 **30** E6
Binnie La *GRK* PA19 **15** L2
Binnie Pl *DMNK/BRGTN* G40 **79** L5
Binnie St *GRK* PA19 **15** K1
Binns Rd *STPS/GTHM/RID* G33 **63** J8
Birch Av *CRMNK/CLK/EAG* G76 **114** F4
Birch Brae *HMLTN* ML3 **129** L1
Birch Cl *BLTYR/CAMB* G72 **97** J4
Birch Crs *CRMNK/CLK/EAG* G76 **114** F4
JNSTN PA5 **90** A1
Birch Dr *BLTYR/CAMB* G72 **97** J4
KKNTL G66 **45** K5
Birchend Dr *SPRGB/BLRNK* G21 **62** B8
Birchend Pl *SPRGB/BLRNK* G21 **62** B8
Birchfield Dr *SCOT* G14 **59** H5
Birchfield Rd *HMLTN* ML3 **119** H7
Birchgrove
CRG/CRSL/HOU PA6 **73** K1
Birch Gv *LRKH* ML9 **130** C4
UD/BTH/TAN G71 **99** H3
Birch Knowe *BSHPBGS* G64 **62** B2
Birchlea Dr *GIF/THBK* G46 **94** D6
Birchmount Ct *AIRDRIE* ML6 **85** K1
Birch Pl *BLTYR/CAMB* G72 **118** D2
Birch Qd *AIRDRIE* ML6 **85** K2
Birch Rd *CLYDBK* G81 **40** A5
CUMB G67 **31** L6
DMBTN G82 **20** F6
Birch St *GBLS* G5 **79** K7
MTHW ML1 **101** H4
Birch Vw *BSDN* G61 **42** A5
Birchview Dr
CRMNK/CLK/EAG G76 **114** F5
Birchwood Av *CAR/SHTL* G32 **81** L6
Birchwood Dr *PSLYS* PA2 **91** H1
Birchwood Gv
BAIL/MDB/MHD G69 **83** G4
Birchwood Pl *CAR/SHTL* G32 **81** L6
Birdsfield Dr *BLTYR/CAMB* G72 **118** D4
Birdsfield St *HMLTN* ML3 **118** F4
Birdston Rd *KKNTL* G66 **27** J6
SPRGB/BLRNK G21 **62** C4
Birgidale Av *CSMK* G45 **115** K1
Birgidale Rd *CSMK* G45 **95** K8
Birgidale Ter *CSMK* G45 **95** K8
Birkdale *EKILN* G74 **2** A2
Birkdale Ct *UD/BTH/TAN* G71 **98** F8
Birkdale Crs *BALLOCH* G68 **30** F3
Birkdale Wd *BALLOCH* G68 **31** G3
Birkenburn Rd *CUMB* G67 **31** M3
Birken Rd *KKNTL* G66 **45** L6
Birkenshaw Rd *CTBR* ML5 **65** L1
Birkenshaw St *DEN/PKHD* G31 **80** B3
Birkfield Loan *CARLUKE* ML8 **133** L8
Birkfield Pl *CARLUKE* ML8 **133** L8
Birkhall Av
CARD/HILL/MSPK G52 **76** F5
RNFRW PA4 **57** K3
Birkhall Dr *BSDN* G61 **41** M7
Birkhill Av *BSHPBGS* G64 **44** B8
Birkhill Gdns *BSHPBGS* G64 **44** B8
Birkhill Rd *CARLUKE* ML8 **134** C7
Birkmyre Av *PGL* PA14 **18** A8
Birkmyre Rd *GOV/IBX* G51 **77** M3
Birks Ct *CARLUKE* ML8 **132** B4
Birkshaw Brae *WISHAW* ML2 **131** J1
Birkshaw Pl *WISHAW* ML2 **131** J1
Birks Pl *LNK/LMHG* ML11 **137** G5
Birks Rd *CARLUKE* ML8 **132** A6
Birkwood Pl *NMRNS* G77 **113** K7
Birkwood St *DMNK/BRGTN* G40 **80** B8
Birkwook Ct *CTBR* ML5 **65** L4
Birmingham Rd *RNFRW* PA4 **58** B8
Birnam Av *BSHPBGS* G64 **44** B8
Birnam Crs *BSDN* G61 **42** B5
Birnam Pl *HMLTN* ML3 **118** E7
NMRNS G77 **114** B6
Birnam Rd *DEN/PKHD* G31 **80** D7
Birness Dr *PLKSW/MSWD* G43 **94** D3
Birnie Ct *SPRGB/BLRNK* G21 **62** C7
Birniehill Rd *MTHW* ML1 **103** H4
Birnie Rd *SPRGB/BLRNK* G21 **62** C6
Birnock Av *RNFRW* PA4 **58** E8
Birnyhill Ct *CLYDBK* G81 **40** A2
Birrell Rd *MLNGV* G62 **23** M6
Birrens Rd *MTHW* ML1 **120** C1
Birsay Rd *PPK/MIL* G22 **61** H3
Bishopburn Dr *CTBR* ML5 **83** M5
Bishopdale *EKILN* G74 **2** A1
Bishop Gdns *BSHPBGS* G64 **43** L8
HMLTN ML3 **129** L3
Bishop La *CGLW* G2 **4** B6
Bishopmill Pl
SPRGB/BLRNK G21 **62** C6
Bishops Ga *EKILN* G74 **115** J7
Bishopsgate Rd
SPRGB/BLRNK G21 **61** L3
Bishops Pk *EKILN* G74 **115** H7
Bissett Crs *CLYDBK* G81 **39** L4
Blackadder Pl *EKILS* G75 **126** A3
Blackbog Rd *AIRDRIE* ML6 **48** F7
Blackbraes Rd *EKILN* G74 **117** H6
Blackburn Crs *DMBTN* G82 **20** D6
KKNTL G66 **46** A3
Blackburn Sq *BRHD/NEIL* G78 **92** D8
Blackburn St *GOV/IBX* G51 **78** E4
Blackbyres Ct *BRHD/NEIL* G78 **92** C4
Blackbyres Rd *BRHD/NEIL* G78 **92** D4
Blackcraig Av *DRUM* G15 **41** G6
Blackcroft Av *AIRDRIE* ML6 **85** L4
Blackcroft Gdns *CAR/SHTL* G32 **81** K6
Blackcroft Rd *CAR/SHTL* G32 **81** K6
Blackcroft Ter *SHOTTS* ML7 **87** H7
Blackdales Av *LARGS* KA30 **106** F6
Blackdyke Rd *KKNTL* G66 **45** L2
Blackfarm Rd *NMRNS* G77 **113** M5
Blackfaulds Rd *RUTH* G73 **95** L2
Blackford Rd *PSLYS* PA2 **9** M8
Blackfriar Rd *CGLE* G1 **5** J7
Blackfriars St *CGLE* G1 **5** H7
Blackhall La *PSLY* PA1 **9** K7
Blackhall St *PSLY* PA1 **9** K7
SHOTTS ML7 **105** H6
Blackhill Dr *HBR/GL* G84 **10** D3
Blackhill Pl
STPS/GTHM/RID G33 **62** D8
Blackhill Rd *SMSTN* G23 **42** F8
Blackhill Vw *CARLUKE* ML8 **132** C4
Blackhouse Av *NMRNS* G77 **113** M5
Blackhouse Gdns *NMRNS* G77 **113** M5
Blackhouse Rd *NMRNS* G77 **113** M5
Blackie St *KVGV* G3 **78** D2
Blacklands Pl *KKNTL* G66 **45** M6
Blacklands Rd *EKILN* G74 **2** D5
Blacklaw Dr *EKILN* G74 **3** L6
Blacklaw La *PSLYN/LNWD* PA3 **9** H3
Blackmoor Pl *MTHW* ML1 **101** G6
Blackmoss Dr *BLSH* ML4 **99** M6
Blackness St *CTBR* ML5 **84** B6
Blacksey Burn Dr
PLK/PH/NH G53 **76** F7
Blackstone Av *PLK/PH/NH* G53 **93** J1
Blackstone Crs *PLK/PH/NH* G53 **77** J8
Blackstone Rd
PSLYN/LNWD PA3 **75** G2
Blackstoun Av
PSLYN/LNWD PA3 **74** B5
Blackstoun Ov
PSLYN/LNWD PA3 **8** B4
Blackstoun Rd
PSLYN/LNWD PA3 **8** B3
Black St *AIRDRIE* ML6 **67** H8
COWCAD G4 **5** J3
Blackthorn Av *BEITH* KA15 **125** J4
KKNTL G66 **45** G5

Blackthorn Gv *KKNTL* G66 45 H5
Blackthorn Rd *CUMB* G67 31 L6
UD/BTH/TAN G71 99 J2
Blackthorn St *PPK/MIL* G22 61 L5
Blackwood *EKILS* G75 127 G5
Blackwood Av *NMRNS* G77 113 M6
PSLYN/LNWD PA3 74 A4
Blackwood Gdns *MTHW* ML1 100 C8
Blackwood Rd *BALLOCH* G68 47 L1
MLNGV G62 23 M6
Blackwoods Crs *BLSH* ML4 100 C5
Blackwood St *BRHD/NEIL* G78 92 A7
KNTSWD G13 59 L2
Blackwood Ter *JNSTN* PA5 89 K2
Bladda La *PSLY* PA1 9 J6
Blades Ct *BAIL/MDB/MHD* G69 65 G4
Bladnoch Dr *DRUM* G15 41 J7
Blaeberry Pl *BALLOCH* G68 30 A7
Blaeloch Av *CSMK* G45 115 J1
Blaeloch Dr *CSMK* G45 115 J1
Blaeloch Ter *CSMK* G45 115 H1
Blaeshill Rd *EKILS* G75 126 B2
Blairatholl Av *PTCK* G11 60 A7
Blairatholl Crs *NMRNS* G77 114 B6
Blair Atholl Dr *LRKH* ML9 130 E8
Blairatholl Gdns *HMLTN* ML3 119 G6
PTCK G11 60 A7
Blair Atholl Ga *NMRNS* G77 114 B6
Blair Atholl Gv *HMLTN* ML3 119 G6
Blair Atholl Wynd *MTHW* ML1 101 H7
Blairbeg Pl *GRK* PA19 14 E4
Blairbeth Dr *LNPK/KPK* G44 95 H3
Blairbeth Rd *RUTH* G73 96 B5
Blairbeth Ter *RUTH* G73 96 C5
Blairbuie Dr *MRYH/FIRH* G20 60 C3
Blair Crs *BAIL/MDB/MHD* G69 82 A7
Blairdardie Rd *DRUM* G15 41 J8
Blairdenan Av
BAIL/MDB/MHD G69 46 F7
Blairdenon Dr *BALLOCH* G68 30 C6
Blair Dr *KKNTL* G66 27 H5
Blair Gdns *BSHPBGS* G64 44 B1
GRK PA19 14 F4
NMRNS G77 113 H4
Blairgowrie Rd
CARD/HILL/MSPK G52 77 J5
Blairhall Av *PLKSD/SHW* G41 94 F2
Blairhill Av *KKNTL* G66 46 A4
Blairhill Pl *CTBR* ML5 83 L3
Blairhill St *CTBR* ML5 83 M3
Blairholm Dr *BLSH* ML4 100 B6
Blairlinn Rd *CUMB* G67 48 F3
Blairlinn Vw *CUMB* G67 49 G3
Blairlogie St
STPS/GTHM/RID G33 81 H1
Blairmore Av *PSLY* PA1 76 C4
Blairmore Crs *GRNK* PA15 7 J9
Blairmore Pl *GRK* PA19 14 F4
Blairmore Rd *GRNK* PA15 17 J7
Blairmuckhole & Forrestdyke Rd *SHOTTS* ML7 70 E5
Blairpark Av *CTBR* ML5 83 L2
Blair Pth *MTHW* ML1 120 F4
Blair Rd *CARLUKE* ML8 134 A8
CTBR ML5 83 L3
PSLY PA1 76 E3
Blairston Av *UD/BTH/TAN* G71 119 H1
Blairston Gdns
UD/BTH/TAN G71 119 H1
Blair St *CAR/SHTL* G32 80 F5
Blairtum Dr *RUTH* G73 96 B5
Blairtummock Pl
STPS/GTHM/RID G33 81 K2
Blairtummock Rd
STPS/GTHM/RID G33 81 K2
Blake Rd *CUMB* G67 31 G7
Blane Dr *MLNGV* G62 24 B7
Blanefield Gdns *KNTSWD* G13 59 M1
Blane St *CTBR* ML5 84 A1
Blaneview *STPS/GTHM/RID* G33 63 K6
Blantyre Crs *CLYDBK* G81 39 L3
Blantyre Dr *BSHPTN* PA7 38 A6
Blantyre Farm Rd
BLTYR/CAMB G72 98 C8
Blantyre Gdns *BALLOCH* G68 47 L1
Blantyre Mill Rd
UD/BTH/TAN G71 99 G8
Blantyre Rd *UD/BTH/TAN* G71 99 G8
Blantyre St *CTBR* ML5 83 L6
KVGV G3 78 D1
Blaven Ct *BAIL/MDB/MHD* G69 82 C6
Blawarthill St *SCOT* G14 58 F4
Bleachfield *MLNGV* G62 23 M6
Bleasdale Ct *CLYDBK* G81 40 B7
Blenheim Av
STPS/GTHM/RID G33 63 K4
Blenheim Ct *KSYTH* G65 29 K1
PSLY PA1 8 E4
STPS/GTHM/RID G33 63 K4
Blenheim Rd *CARLUKE* ML8 133 J8
Blochairn Rd
SPRGB/BLRNK G21 80 B1
Bluebell Gdns *CSMK* G45 96 A8
MTHW ML1 100 C7
Bluebell Wy *AIRDRIE* ML6 66 F7
CARLUKE ML8 134 F1
KKNTL G66 26 F3
Bluebell Wynd *WISHAW* ML2 131 H1
Blueknowes Rd *CARLUKE* ML8 132 A4
Bluevale St *DEN/PKHD* G31 80 A4
Blythe Pl *STPS/GTHM/RID* G33 81 L3
Blyth Pl *STPS/GTHM/RID* G33 81 K4
Blyth Rd *STPS/GTHM/RID* G33 81 L4
Blythswood Av *RNFRW* PA4 58 D5
Blythswood Crs *LARGS* KA30 106 F6
Blythswood Dr
PSLYN/LNWD PA3 8 F2
Blythswood Rd *RNFRW* PA4 58 D4
Blythswood Sq *CGLW* G2 4 C5
Blythswood St *CGLW* G2 4 C6
The Boardwalk *EKILS* G75 127 K4
Boathouse Av *LARGS* KA30 106 D2
Boathouse Rd *LARGS* KA30 106 D2
Boclair Av *BSDN* G61 41 M5
Boclair Crs *BSDN* G61 42 A6
BSHPBGS G64 62 A1
Boclair Rd *BSDN* G61 42 A5
BSHPBGS G64 44 A8
Boclair St *KNTSWD* G13 59 L1
Bodden Sq *MTHW* ML1 101 L2
Boden Qd *MTHW* ML1 100 C7
Boden St *DMNK/BRGTN* G40 80 A6
Bodmin Gdns
BAIL/MDB/MHD G69 46 F7
Bogany Ter *CSMK* G45 95 L8
Bogbain Rd *ESTRH* G34 82 A2
Boggknowe *UD/BTH/TAN* G71 98 D2
Boghall Rd
BAIL/MDB/MHD G69 82 A7
CARLUKE ML8 135 H3
Boghall St *STPS/GTHM/RID* G33 81 H1
Boghead *BEITH* KA15 125 K5
Boghead Av *DMBTN* G82 21 H6
Boghead Rd *DMBTN* G82 21 G6
KKNTL G66 45 G5
SPRGB/BLRNK G21 62 A5
Bogiewood Rd *PGL* PA14 34 B1
Bogleshole Rd
BLTYR/CAMB G72 96 E3
Boglestone Av *PGL* PA14 34 E2
Bogle St *GRNK* PA15 6 E5
Bogmoor Pl *GOV/IBX* G51 59 J8
Bogmoor Rd *GOV/IBX* G51 77 J1
Bogside Rd *KSYTH* G65 29 K3
PGL PA14 34 F2
STPS/GTHM/RID G33 63 G5
Bogside St *DMNK/BRGTN* G40 80 B6
Bogstonhill Rd
CRG/CRSL/HOU PA6 55 H8
Bogston La *GRNK* PA15 17 M7
Bogs Vw *BLSH* ML4 99 M7
Bogton Av *LNPK/KPK* G44 94 F6
Bogton Avenue La
LNPK/KPK G44 94 F6
Boleyn Rd *PLKSD/SHW* G41 78 E8
Bolingbroke *EKILN* G74 117 J6
Bolivar Ter *GVH/MTFL* G42 95 J2
Bolton Dr *GVH/MTFL* G42 95 G2
Bolton Ter *KKNTL* G66 26 E2
Bon Accord Crs *SHOTTS* ML7 104 E4
Bon Accord Rd
CRMNK/CLK/EAG G76 114 F4
Bon Accord Sq *CLYDBK* G81 58 B1
Bonar Crs *BRWEIR* PA11 72 E3
Bonar La *BRWEIR* PA11 72 E3
Bonar Law Av *HBR/GL* G84 10 B5
Bonawe St *MRYH/FIRH* G20 60 F7
Bonds Dr *WISHAW* ML2 123 H3
Bo'Ness Rd *AIRDRIE* ML6 85 K8
MTHW ML1 101 H3
Boness St *DMNK/BRGTN* G40 80 B6
Bonhill Br *ALEX/LLW* G83 13 L6
Bonhill Rd *DMBTN* G82 21 G6
Bonhill St *PPK/MIL* G22 61 H7
Bonkle Gdns *WISHAW* ML2 123 H4
Bonkle Rd *WISHAW* ML2 123 J3
Bonnar St *DMNK/BRGTN* G40 80 A7
Bonnaughton Rd *BSDN* G61 41 H3
Bonnet Rd *LNK/LMHG* ML11 137 G5
Bonnington Av
LNK/LMHG ML11 137 G6
Bonnyholm Av
PLK/PH/NH G53 77 G6
Bonnyrigg Dr
PLKSW/MSWD G43 94 A5
Bontine Av *DMBTN* G82 20 D6
Bonyton Av *KNTSWD* G13 58 F3
Boon Dr *DRUM* G15 41 H7
Boquhanran Rd *CLYDBK* G81 39 M8
Borden La *KNTSWD* G13 59 L4
Borden Rd *KNTSWD* G13 59 L4
Border St *GRNK* PA15 7 J8
Border Wy *KKNTL* G66 45 L2
Boreland Dr *HMLTN* ML3 118 E8
KNTSWD G13 59 H2
Boreland Pl *KNTSWD* G13 59 H3
Bore Rd *AIRDRIE* ML6 85 H1
Borestone Av *KBRN* KA25 124 C6
Borgie Crs *BLTYR/CAMB* G72 97 G5
Borland Rd *BSDN* G61 42 A7
Borron St *COWCAD* G4 61 H8
Borrowdale *EKILS* G75 126 C5
Borthwick Dr *EKILS* G75 126 A3
Borthwick Pl
BAIL/MDB/MHD G69 64 F6
Borthwick St
STPS/GTHM/RID G33 81 H1
Bosfield Cnr *EKILN* G74 3 H1
Bosfield Pl *EKILN* G74 3 G1
Bosfield Rd *EKILN* G74 3 G1
Boston Dr *HBR/GL* G84 10 F4
Boswell Ct *GVH/MTFL* G42 94 F3
Boswell Dr *BLTYR/CAMB* G72 118 D3
Boswell Pk *EKILN* G74 117 J6
Boswell Sq
CARD/HILL/MSPK G52 76 F2
Bosworth Rd *EKILN* G74 117 J6
Botanic Crs *MRYH/FIRH* G20 60 D6
Bothlin Dr *STPS/GTHM/RID* G33 63 K4
Bothlyn Av *KKNTL* G66 45 L3
Bothlyn Crs
BAIL/MDB/MHD G69 64 E3
Bothlyn Rd
BAIL/MDB/MHD G69 64 D2
Bothwellhaugh Qd *BLSH* ML4 99 M7
Bothwellhaugh Rd
MTHW ML1 119 M1
Bothwell La *CGLW* G2 4 C6
KVD/HLHD G12 60 E8
Bothwellpark Pl *BLSH* ML4 99 K4
Bothwellpark Rd
UD/BTH/TAN G71 99 H8
Bothwell Pl *CTBR* ML5 83 M3
PSLYS PA2 90 E2
Bothwell Rd *CARLUKE* ML8 133 G5
HMLTN ML3 119 J3
UD/BTH/TAN G71 98 F6
Bothwellshields Rd *MTHW* ML1 86 D7
Bothwell St *BLTYR/CAMB* G72 96 E4
CGLW G2 4 C6
HMLTN ML3 119 J5
Boturich Dr *ALEX/LLW* G83 13 K1
The Boulevard *KKNTL* G66 26 A1
Bourhill Ct *WISHAW* ML2 121 K7
Bourne Ct *RNFRW* PA4 57 K3
Bourne Crs *RNFRW* PA4 57 K3
Bournemouth Rd *GRK* PA19 15 M4
Bourne St *HMLTN* ML3 119 M7
Bourock Sq *BRHD/NEIL* G78 92 D8
Bourtree Rd *HMLTN* ML3 128 E1
Bouverie St *PGL* PA14 34 C1
RUTH G73 95 M2
SCOT G14 58 E3
Bowden Dr
CARD/HILL/MSPK G52 77 H3
Bowden Gv *WISHAW* ML2 122 D3
Bowden Pk *EKILS* G75 2 B8
Bowencraig *LARGS* KA30 106 F7
Bower St *KVD/HLHD* G12 60 E7
Bowerwalls St *BRHD/NEIL* G78 92 E5
Bowes Crs
BAIL/MDB/MHD G69 81 M6
Bowfield Crs
CARD/HILL/MSPK G52 76 F3
Bowfield Dr
CARD/HILL/MSPK G52 76 F3
Bowfield Pl
CARD/HILL/MSPK G52 76 F3
Bowfield Rd *HWWD* PA9 88 F5
Bowfield Wy *HWWD* PA9 88 F5
Bowhill Rd *AIRDRIE* ML6 85 L8
Bowhousebog Rd
SHOTTS ML7 104 A7
Bowhousebrae Rd
AIRDRIE ML6 85 L4
Bowhouse Dr *CSMK* G45 95 M6
Bowhouse Rd *AIRDRIE* ML6 85 M5
Bowie Rd *ALEX/LLW* G83 13 K4
Bowie St *DMBTN* G82 20 E7
Bowling Green La *SCOT* G14 59 K6
Bowling Green Rd
BAIL/MDB/MHD G69 64 D2
CAR/SHTL G32 81 K6
LNPK/KPK G44 95 G5
SCOT G14 59 K6
Bowling Green St *BLSH* ML4 100 B4
Bowling Green Vw
BLTYR/CAMB G72 97 M6
Bowling St *CTBR* ML5 83 M3
Bowman Flat *LRKH* ML9 130 C6
Bowman St *GVH/MTFL* G42 79 G8
Bowmont Pl *EKILS* G75 126 B3
Bowmont Ter *KVD/HLHD* G12 60 C7
Bowmore Crs *EKILN* G74 115 J7
Bowmore Gdns *RUTH* G73 96 E7
UD/BTH/TAN G71 98 E2
Bowmore Rd
CARD/HILL/MSPK G52 77 L4
Bowmount Gdns
KVD/HLHD G12 60 C7
Bow Rd *GRNKW/INVK* PA16 16 B5
Bowyer Vennel *BLSH* ML4 99 M4
Boyd Dr *MTHW* ML1 120 B2
Boydstone Pl *GIF/THBK* G46 93 M4
Boydstone Rd
PLKSW/MSWD G43 93 L3
Boyd St *GVH/MTFL* G42 95 H1
LARGS KA30 106 E4
Boylestone Rd *BRHD/NEIL* G78 92 B5
Boyle St *CLYDBK* G81 58 D1
Boyndie St *ESTRH* G34 82 B2
Brabloch Crs *PSLYN/LNWD* PA3 9 K1
Bracadale Dr
BAIL/MDB/MHD G69 82 D6
Bracadale Gdns
BAIL/MDB/MHD G69 82 D6
Bracadale Gv
BAIL/MDB/MHD G69 82 C6
Bracadale Rd
BAIL/MDB/MHD G69 82 C6
Bracco Rd *AIRDRIE* ML6 87 G1
Brachelston St
GRNKW/INVK PA16 16 D5
Brackenbrae Av *BSHPBGS* G64 43 L8
Brackenbrae Rd *BSHPBGS* G64 61 M1
Brackendene
CRG/CRSL/HOU PA6 73 K1
Brackenhill Dr *HMLTN* ML3 129 H3
Brackenhill Rd *CARLUKE* ML8 132 C4
Brackenhirst Rd *AIRDRIE* ML6 66 D3
Brackenhurst St *DMBTN* G82 21 J4
Brackenknowe Rd *AIRDRIE* ML6 49 K6
Brackenrig Rd *GIF/THBK* G46 93 L7
Bracken Rd *PGL* PA14 35 G2
Bracken St *MTHW* ML1 101 G6
PPK/MIL G22 61 H6
Bracken Ter *UD/BTH/TAN* G71 99 G7
Brackla Av *CLYDBK* G81 58 E1
Braco Av *AIRDRIE* ML6 85 K8
Bradan Av *KNTSWD* G13 58 E2
Bradda Av *RUTH* G73 96 C6
Bradfield Av *KVD/HLHD* G12 60 C5
Bradley Ct
STPS/GTHM/RID G33 63 M5
Bradshaw Crs *HMLTN* ML3 118 E7
Brady Crs *BAIL/MDB/MHD* G69 47 G7
Braedale Av *AIRDRIE* ML6 85 H2
MTHW ML1 120 B3
Braedale Crs *WISHAW* ML2 123 H4
Braedale Rd *LNK/LMHG* ML11 137 G4
Braeface Rd *CUMB* G67 30 E7
Braefield Dr *GIF/THBK* G46 94 A7
Braefoot Av *MLNGV* G62 42 A2
Braefoot Ct *CARLUKE* ML8 132 B5
Braefoot Crs *CARLUKE* ML8 132 B5
PSLYS PA2 91 M2
Braefoot La *BRHD/NEIL* G78 110 A7
Braehead *ALEX/LLW* G83 13 M8
BEITH KA15 125 K5
BLTYR/CAMB G72 118 D4
LOCHW PA12 109 J2
Braehead Av *BRHD/NEIL* G78 111 K3
CLYDBK G81 40 A2
CTBR ML5 83 K7
LOCHW PA12 109 J2
LRKH ML9 130 A7
MLNGV G62 23 M8
Braehead Crs *CLYDBK* G81 40 A2
Braehead Dr *BLSH* ML4 99 M6
Braehead Pl *BLSH* ML4 99 M6
Braehead Qd *BRHD/NEIL* G78 111 K3
MTHW ML1 101 K5
Braehead Rd *CLYDBK* G81 40 A2
CUMB G67 31 H6
EKILN G74 115 J7
PGL PA14 34 E2
PSLYS PA2 91 J5
Braehead St *GBLS* G5 79 K7
KKNTL G66 45 J1
Braemar Av *CLYDBK* G81 39 M6
Braemar Ct *LNPK/KPK* G44 94 E6
Braemar Crs *BSDN* G61 41 M7
CARLUKE ML8 133 J6
PSLYS PA2 91 M1
Braemar Dr *JNSTN* PA5 90 B1
Braemar Rd *RNFRW* PA4 57 K3
RUTH G73 96 D7
Braemar St *GVH/MTFL* G42 94 F3
HMLTN ML3 119 H4
Braemar Vw *CLYDBK* G81 39 M6
Braemore Gdns *PPK/MIL* G22 61 K6
Braemount Av *PSLYS* PA2 91 J4
Braes Av *CLYDBK* G81 58 D1
Braesburn Ct *CUMB* G67 31 M3
Braesburn Pl *CUMB* G67 31 M3
Braesburn Rd *CUMB* G67 31 M3
Braeside Av
BAIL/MDB/MHD G69 46 F8
LARGS KA30 107 G4
MLNGV G62 42 A2
RUTH G73 96 C3
Braeside Crs
BAIL/MDB/MHD G69 82 F5
BRHD/NEIL G78 92 E8
Braeside Dr *BRHD/NEIL* G78 92 D8
DMBTN G82 21 H5
Braeside Gdns *HMLTN* ML3 129 L2
Braeside Pl *BLTYR/CAMB* G72 97 H6
Braeside Rd *GRNKW/INVK* PA16 15 K6
MTHW ML1 101 K5
Braeside St *MRYH/FIRH* G20 60 F7
Braes O' Yetts *KKNTL* G66 46 A2
Braeval Wy
STPS/GTHM/RID G33 63 L5
Brae Vw *GRNKW/INVK* PA16 16 C4
Braeview Av *PSLYS* PA2 91 H3
Braeview Dr *PSLYS* PA2 91 H3
Braeview Gdns *PSLYS* PA2 91 H3
Braeview Pl *EKILN* G74 117 H6
Braeview Rd *PSLYS* PA2 91 H3
Braid Av *DMBTN* G82 19 H2
MTHW ML1 101 L8
Braidbar Farm Rd
GIF/THBK G46 94 D7
Braidbar Rd *GIF/THBK* G46 94 C7
Braidcraft Rd *PLK/PH/NH* G53 93 K1
Braidcraft Ter *PLK/PH/NH* G53 77 K8
Braid Dr *DMBTN* G82 19 H2
Braidfauld Gdns *CAR/SHTL* G32 80 F7
Braidfauld Pl *CAR/SHTL* G32 80 F8
Braidfauld St *CAR/SHTL* G32 80 F8
Braidfield Gv *CLYDBK* G81 40 B4
Braidfield Rd *CLYDBK* G81 40 C4
Braidfute *LNK/LMHG* ML11 137 J4
Braidholm Crs *GIF/THBK* G46 94 C6
Braidholm Rd *GIF/THBK* G46 94 D6
Braidhurst St *MTHW* ML1 120 E1
Braidley Crs *EKILS* G75 127 H5
Braidpark Dr *GIF/THBK* G46 94 D7
Braids Cir *PSLYS* PA2 91 L1
Braids Dr *PLK/PH/NH* G53 76 F8
Braid Sq *COWCAD* G4 4 D1
Braid's Rd *PSLYS* PA2 91 L1
Braid St *COWCAD* G4 4 C1
Braidwood Pl
PSLYN/LNWD PA3 73 M4
Braidwood Rd *CARLUKE* ML8 134 C7
Braidwood St *WISHAW* ML2 122 C2
Bramah Av *EKILS* G75 3 H9
Bramble Ct *KKNTL* G66 26 C2
Bramblehedge Pth
ALEX/LLW G83 13 L3
Brambling Ct *WISHAW* ML2 121 M8
Brambling Rd *CTBR* ML5 84 E6
Bramley Dr *BLSH* ML4 100 A1
Bramley Pl *AIRDRIE* ML6 85 L3
KKNTL G66 45 L6
Brampton *EKILS* G75 126 C4
Branchalfield Dr *WISHAW* ML2 122 E5
Branchalmuir Crs
WISHAW ML2 122 F3
Branchal Rd *WISHAW* ML2 122 D4
Branchock Av
BLTYR/CAMB G72 97 K6
Branchton Rd
GRNKW/INVK PA16 15 M6
Brancumhall Rd *EKILN* G74 117 K7
Brandon Dr *BSDN* G61 41 L2
Brandon Gdns
BLTYR/CAMB G72 96 E5
Brandon Ga *BLSH* ML4 100 B4
Brandon Pl *BLSH* ML4 99 L7
Brandon St *DEN/PKHD* G31 79 M4
HMLTN ML3 119 L7
MTHW ML1 120 E3
Brandon Wy *CTBR* ML5 83 K6
Brand Pl *GOV/IBX* G51 78 C4
Brand St *GOV/IBX* G51 78 D4
Brankholm Brae *HMLTN* ML3 118 D6
Branklyn Cl *KNTSWD* G13 59 K3
Branklyn Ct *KNTSWD* G13 59 K3
Branklyn Crs *KNTSWD* G13 59 K3
Branklyn Gv *KNTSWD* G13 59 K3
Branklyn Pl *KNTSWD* G13 59 K3
Brannock Av *MTHW* ML1 101 K5
Brannock Pl *MTHW* ML1 101 K5
Brannock Rd *MTHW* ML1 101 K6
Brassey St *MRYH/FIRH* G20 60 E4
Braxfield Rd *LNK/LMHG* ML11 137 G6
Braxfield Ter *LNK/LMHG* ML11 136 F7
Breadalbane Crs *MTHW* ML1 100 D8
Breadalbane Gdns *RUTH* G73 96 D6
Breadalbane St *KVGV* G3 78 F2
Breadie Dr *MLNGV* G62 41 M1
Breamish Pl *EKILS* G75 126 C4
Bream Pl *CRG/CRSL/HOU* PA6 73 K2
Brechin Rd *BSHPBGS* G64 62 C1
Brechin St *KVGV* G3 78 E2
Breck Av *PSLYS* PA2 90 D3
Brediland Rd *PSLYN/LNWD* PA3 74 A4
PSLYS PA2 90 E3
Bredin Wy *MTHW* ML1 120 B1
Bredisholm Crs
UD/BTH/TAN G71 99 J1
Bredisholm Dr
BAIL/MDB/MHD G69 82 C6
Bredisholm Rd
BAIL/MDB/MHD G69 82 D6
Bredisholm Ter
BAIL/MDB/MHD G69 82 C6
Brendon Av *EKILS* G75 126 D6
Brenfield Av *LNPK/KPK* G44 94 F6
Brenfield Dr *LNPK/KPK* G44 94 F6
Brenfield Rd *LNPK/KPK* G44 94 F6
Brent Av *GIF/THBK* G46 93 M4
Brent Ct *EKILN* G74 2 E1
Brent Crs *CRG/CRSL/HOU* PA6 73 J2
Brent Dr *GIF/THBK* G46 93 M4
Brent Gdns *GIF/THBK* G46 93 M4
Brent Rd *EKILN* G74 2 E1
GIF/THBK G46 94 A5
Brent Wy *GIF/THBK* G46 93 M4
Brentwood Av *PLK/PH/NH* G53 93 G5
Brentwood Dr *PLK/PH/NH* G53 93 G5
Brentwood Sq *PLK/PH/NH* G53 93 H5
Brereton St *GVH/MTFL* G42 95 J1
Breslin Ter *SHOTTS* ML7 71 J7
Bressay *EKILN* G74 2 E1
Bressay Cl *STPS/GTHM/RID* G33 81 L4
Bressay Gv *BLTYR/CAMB* G72 96 E7
STPS/GTHM/RID G33 81 L4
Bressay Pl *STPS/GTHM/RID* G33 81 L4
Bressay Rd
STPS/GTHM/RID G33 81 L4
Breval Crs *CLYDBK* G81 40 A2
Brewery St *JNSTN* PA5 73 M7
Brewster Av *PSLYN/LNWD* PA3 76 A2
Briar Bank *KKNTL* G66 27 H5
Briarcroft Dr
STPS/GTHM/RID G33 62 D4
Briarcroft Pl
STPS/GTHM/RID G33 62 E4
Briarcroft Rd
STPS/GTHM/RID G33 62 E3
Briar Dr *CLYDBK* G81 40 B5
Briar Gdns *PLKSW/MSWD* G43 94 D5
Briar Gv *PLKSW/MSWD* G43 94 D5
Briarlea Dr *GIF/THBK* G46 94 C6
Briar Neuk *BSHPBGS* G64 62 B2
Briar Pl *GRK* PA19 15 K3
Briar Rd *KKNTL* G66 45 M2
PLKSW/MSWD G43 94 D5
Briar Wk *KKNTL* G66 46 A2
Briarwell La *MLNGV* G62 42 B1
Briarwell Rd *MLNGV* G62 42 B1
Briarwood Ct *CAR/SHTL* G32 81 L8
Briarwood Rd *WISHAW* ML2 121 L5
Briary La *PGL* PA14 35 J2
Brick La *PSLYN/LNWD* PA3 9 J3
Bridesmill Rd *LOCHW* PA12 109 K1
Bridgeburn Dr
BAIL/MDB/MHD G69 46 E8
Bridgeford Av *BLSH* ML4 100 C2
Bridgegait *MLNGV* G62 42 C2
Bridge-gate *CGLE* G1 5 G9
Bridgend *KBRN* KA25 124 D3
Bridgend Av *PGL* PA14 34 E2
Bridgend Crs
BAIL/MDB/MHD G69 46 E8
Bridgend Pl
BAIL/MDB/MHD G69 46 E8
Bridgend Rd *GRNK* PA15 7 K9
Bridgend Vw *CARLUKE* ML8 133 H8
Bridge of Weir Rd
BRWEIR PA11 72 E3
CRG/CRSL/HOU PA6 73 H1
KLMCLM PA13 53 K3
PSLYN/LNWD PA3 74 B5
Bridge Pl *SHOTTS* ML7 105 G6
Bridge Rd *PGL* PA14 34 E2
Bridge St *ALEX/LLW* G83 13 K6
BLTYR/CAMB G72 97 G4
CLYDBK G81 39 L7
DMBTN G82 20 E7
GBLS G5 4 E9
HMLTN ML3 119 J8
KBRN KA25 124 D3
PSLY PA1 9 H5
PSLYN/LNWD PA3 74 C5
WISHAW ML2 121 L6
Bridgeton Cross
DMNK/BRGTN G40 79 M5
Bridgeway Ct *KKNTL* G66 45 M3
Bridgeway Rd *KKNTL* G66 45 M3
Bridgeway Ter *KKNTL* G66 45 M3
Bridie Ter *EKILN* G74 117 J6
Brierie Av *CRG/CRSL/HOU* PA6 73 H1
Brierie Gdns
CRG/CRSL/HOU PA6 73 H2
Brierie Hill Ct
CRG/CRSL/HOU PA6 73 H2
Brierie-Hill Gv
CRG/CRSL/HOU PA6 73 H2
Brierie-Hill Rd
CRG/CRSL/HOU PA6 73 H2
Brierie La *CRG/CRSL/HOU* PA6 73 G2
Brierybank Av
LNK/LMHG ML11 137 G6
Brigbrae Av *BLSH* ML4 100 C6
Brigham Pl *SMSTN* G23 60 E2
Brighton Pl *GOV/IBX* G51 78 B4
Brighton St *GOV/IBX* G51 78 B4
Brightside Av *PGL* PA14 35 H2
UD/BTH/TAN G71 98 F5
Brig O'Lea Ter *BRHD/NEIL* G78 111 J4
Brigside Gdns *HMLTN* ML3 120 A7
Brisbane Ct *GIF/THBK* G46 94 D7
Brisbane Crs *LARGS* KA30 106 E3
Brisbane Glen Rd *LARGS* KA30 106 F2
Brisbane Rd *BSHPTN* PA7 38 B7
LARGS KA30 106 F3
Brisbane St *CLYDBK* G81 39 K6
GRNKW/INVK PA16 16 D3
GVH/MTFL G42 95 G3
LARGS KA30 106 E3
Brisbane Ter *EKILS* G75 2 A9
Brittain Wy *MTHW* ML1 100 F2
Britannia Wy *CLYDBK* G81 40 B8
Broad Cairn Ct *MTHW* ML1 121 J7
Broadfield Av *PGL* PA14 35 G2
Broadford St *COWCAD* G4 61 J8
Broadholm St *PPK/MIL* G22 61 J4
Broadleys Av *BSHPBGS* G64 43 M8
Broadlie Ct *BRHD/NEIL* G78 111 K3
Broadlie Dr *KNTSWD* G13 59 G3
Broadlie Rd *BRHD/NEIL* G78 111 K3
Broadloan *RNFRW* PA4 58 C7
Broadmoss Av *NMRNS* G77 114 C6
Broad Sq *BLTYR/CAMB* G72 118 C2
Broadstone Av *PGL* PA14 34 A1
Broad St *DMNK/BRGTN* G40 79 M5
The Broad Wy *WISHAW* ML2 121 L5
Broadwood Dr *LNPK/KPK* G44 95 H4
Brockburn Crs *PLK/PH/NH* G53 93 H1
Brockburn Rd *PLK/PH/NH* G53 77 H8
Brockburn Ter *PLK/PH/NH* G53 93 J1
Brockley Vw *KBRN* KA25 124 D1
Brocklinn Pk *EKILS* G75 126 B3
Brock Ov *PLK/PH/NH* G53 93 J3
Brock Pl *PLK/PH/NH* G53 93 J2
Brock Rd *PLK/PH/NH* G53 93 H3
Brock Ter *PLK/PH/NH* G53 93 J3
Brockville St *CAR/SHTL* G32 80 F4
Brodick Av *MTHW* ML1 120 B2
Brodick Dr *EKILN* G74 2 C1
GRK PA19 14 F4
HBR/GL G84 10 F5
Brodick Pl *NMRNS* G77 113 G6
Brodick St *SPRGB/BLRNK* G21 80 A1
Brodie Gdns
BAIL/MDB/MHD G69 82 C4
Brodie Gv *BAIL/MDB/MHD* G69 82 C4
Brodie Park Av *PSLYS* PA2 75 L8
Brodie Park Crs *PSLYS* PA2 8 E9
Brodie Park Gdns *PSLYS* PA2 75 L8
Brodie Pl *EKILN* G74 2 D1
Brodie Rd *SPRGB/BLRNK* G21 62 C3
Brogan Crs *MTHW* ML1 120 B2
Bron Wy *CUMB* G67 31 G8
Brookbank Ter *CARLUKE* ML8 133 J8
Brooke Av *ALEX/LLW* G83 13 M2
Brookfield Av
STPS/GTHM/RID G33 62 D3
Brookfield Cnr
STPS/GTHM/RID G33 62 D3

Brookfield Dr
STPS/GTHM/RID G33 62 D3
Brookfield Gdns
STPS/GTHM/RID G33 62 D3
Brookfield Ga
STPS/GTHM/RID G33 62 D3
Brookfield Pl
STPS/GTHM/RID G33 62 E3
Brookfield Rd PGL PA14 34 F2
STPS/GTHM/RID G33 62 D3
Brooklands ALEX/LLW G83 13 J4
EKILN G74 126 D1
Brooklands Av
UD/BTH/TAN G71 98 E3
Brooklea Dr GIF/THBK G46 94 C5
Brooklime Dr EKILN G74 116 D6
Brooklyn Pl WISHAW ML2 131 K3
Brookside St DMNK/BRGTN G40 80 A5
Brook St CLYDBK G81 39 M6
DMNK/BRGTN G40 79 M5
Broom Av ERSK PA8 57 H3
Broomberry Dr GRK PA19 15 L2
Broomburn Dr NMRNS G77 113 M5
Broom Crs BRHD/NEIL G78 92 A4
EKILS G75 127 G5
Broomcroft Rd NMRNS G77 114 A4
Broom Dr CLYDBK G81 40 A5
LRKH ML9 130 C4
Broomfield CRG/CRSL/HOU PA6 73 K1
LARGS KA30 106 E6
Broomfield Av
BLTYR/CAMB G72 96 D3
NMRNS G77 113 M6
Broomfield Crs LARGS KA30 106 E6
Broomfield La
SPRGB/BLRNK G21 61 M5
Broomfield Pl LARGS KA30 106 E6
SPRGB/BLRNK G21 61 M5
Broomfield Rd GIF/THBK G46 114 A4
SPRGB/BLRNK G21 61 M5
Broomfield St AIRDRIE ML6 85 H2
Broomfield Ter
UD/BTH/TAN G71 98 F1
Broomfield Wk KKNTL G66 45 K2
Broom Gdns KKNTL G66 45 H4
Broomgate LNK/LMHG ML11 136 F6
Broomhill Av CAR/SHTL G32 97 H2
NMRNS G77 113 M5
PTCK G11 59 M7
Broomhill Ct LRKH ML9 130 C7
Broomhill Crs ALEX/LLW G83 21 H1
BLSH ML4 99 M7
ERSK PA8 57 H3
Broomhill Dr DMBTN G82 21 H5
PTCK G11 59 M6
RUTH G73 96 B5
Broomhill Farm Ms KKNTL G66 45 L1
Broomhill Gdns NMRNS G77 113 M5
PTCK G11 59 M6
Broomhill Ga LRKH ML9 130 C7
Broomhill La PTCK G11 59 M6
Broomhill Pl PTCK G11 59 M7
Broomhill Rd LRKH ML9 130 C7
Broomhill St GRNK PA15 6 B6
SHOTTS ML7 71 J7
Broomhill Ter PTCK G11 59 M7
Broomhill Vw LRKH ML9 130 A7
Broomieknowe Dr RUTH G73 96 B4
Broomieknowe Gdns
RUTH G73 96 A4
Broomieknowe Rd RUTH G73 96 B4
Broomielaw CGLW G2 4 B8
Broomknoll St AIRDRIE ML6 85 G2
Broomknowe BALLOCH G68 30 D6
Broomknowe Rd KLMCLM PA13 53 J2
Broomknowes Av KKNTL G66 45 L6
Broomknowes Rd
SPRGB/BLRNK G21 62 A6
Broomlands Av ERSK PA8 57 K2
Broomlands Ct PSLY PA1 8 C6
Broomlands Crs ERSK PA8 57 K2
Broomlands Gdns ERSK PA8 57 K2
Broomlands Rd CUMB G67 49 G1
Broomlands St PSLY PA1 8 B6
Broomlands Wy ERSK PA8 57 L2
Broomlea Crs RNFRW PA4 57 J3
Broomlee Rd CUMB G67 48 F3
Broomley Crs ALEX/LLW G83 13 J3
Broomley Dr GIF/THBK G46 114 C1
Broomley La GIF/THBK G46 114 C1
Broomloan Pl GOV/IBX G51 78 B4
Broomloan Rd GOV/IBX G51 78 A5
Broompark Av
BLTYR/CAMB G72 118 C4
Broompark Circ
DEN/PKHD G31 79 M2
Broompark Crs AIRDRIE ML6 67 G7
Broompark Dr DEN/PKHD G31 5 M6
NMRNS G77 113 M3
RNFRW PA4 57 K3
Broompark La DEN/PKHD G31 79 M3
Broompark Rd
BLTYR/CAMB G72 118 C3
WISHAW ML2 121 K5
Broompark St DEN/PKHD G31 79 M3
Broom Pl BRWEIR PA11 72 E2
CTBR ML5 83 M7
MTHW ML1 101 J5
PLKSW/MSWD G43 94 D5
Broom Rd CUMB G67 31 K4
NMRNS G77 114 A4
PLKSW/MSWD G43 94 D5
WMYSB PA18 32 B8
Broom Rd East NMRNS G77 114 B7
Broomside Crs MTHW ML1 120 F5
Broomside St MTHW ML1 120 E5
Broomstone Av NMRNS G77 113 M6
Broom Ter JNSTN PA5 89 M1
Broomton Rd
SPRGB/BLRNK G21 62 C3
Broomvale Dr NMRNS G77 113 M4
Broomward Dr JNSTN PA5 74 B7
Brora Crs HMLTN ML3 128 F2
Brora Dr BSDN G61 42 B6
GIF/THBK G46 94 D8
RNFRW PA4 58 E6
Brora Gdns BSHPBGS G64 62 B1
Brora Rd BSHPBGS G64 62 B1
Brora St STPS/GTHM/RID G33 80 D1
Broster Mdw KBRN KA25 124 D2
Broughton EKILS G75 127 H6
Broughton Dr SMSTN G23 60 E2
Broughton Gdns SMSTN G23 60 E1
Broughton Pl CTBR ML5 84 B6
HMLTN ML3 119 G7
Broughton Rd SMSTN G23 60 E2
Brouster Hl EKILN G74 2 F5
Brouster Pl EKILN G74 2 F5
Brown Av CLYDBK G81 58 D1
DMBTN G82 21 J6
Brown Ct STPS/GTHM/RID G33 63 J6
Brownhill Dr KBRN KA25 124 B5
Brownhill Rd
PLKSW/MSWD G43 94 B6
Brownhill Vw WISHAW ML2 123 K3
Brownieside Pl AIRDRIE ML6 68 A6
Brownieside Rd AIRDRIE ML6 68 B7
Brownlee Rd CARLUKE ML8 131 M5
Brownlie St GVH/MTFL G42 95 H2
Brown Pl BLTYR/CAMB G72 97 G4
Brown Rd CUMB G67 30 F7
Brownsburn Rd AIRDRIE ML6 85 H5
Brownsdale Rd RUTH G73 95 M3
Brownsfield Crs RNFRW PA4 57 H5
Brownsfield Rd RNFRW PA4 57 H5
Brownshill Av CTBR ML5 83 M6
Brownside Av
BLTYR/CAMB G72 96 E5
BRHD/NEIL G78 92 A4
Brownside Crs BRHD/NEIL G78 92 A4
Brownside Dr BRHD/NEIL G78 92 A4
KNTSWD G13 58 F3
Brownside Gv BRHD/NEIL G78 92 A4
Brownside Rd RUTH G73 96 D5
Brownsland Ct
BAIL/MDB/MHD G69 65 G4
Brown's La PSLY PA1 9 G6
Brown St ALEX/LLW G83 13 M2
CARLUKE ML8 133 H6
CGLW G2 4 C7
CTBR ML5 84 A4
GRNK PA15 7 L8
LRKH ML9 130 C5
MTHW ML1 120 F1
PGL PA14 18 B8
PSLY PA1 8 D4
RNFRW PA4 58 B7
SHOTTS ML7 105 H6
WISHAW ML2 123 G5
Brown St North RNFRW PA4 58 C6
Browside Av PSLYS PA2 91 J3
Bruce Av BLTYR/CAMB G72 97 G7
JNSTN PA5 89 L2
MTHW ML1 120 D2
PSLYN/LNWD PA3 76 A2
Bruce Ct DMBTN G82 19 H2
Brucefield Pl ESTRH G34 82 D2
Brucehill Rd DMBTN G82 20 C6
Bruce Pl EKILS G75 127 J3
Bruce Rd BSHPTN PA7 38 A7
MTHW ML1 101 H7
PLKSD/SHW G41 78 E6
PSLYN/LNWD PA3 9 L1
RNFRW PA4 58 A8
Bruce St AIRDRIE ML6 68 A7
BLSH ML4 100 B4
CLYDBK G81 40 B8
CTBR ML5 84 B1
DMBTN G82 21 G8
GRNK PA15 6 B4
PGL PA14 34 D1
Bruce Ter BLTYR/CAMB G72 118 E1
EKILS G75 127 J3
Brueacre Dr WMYSB PA18 32 B8
Brueacre Pl WMYSB PA18 32 B7
Brueacre Rd WMYSB PA18 32 B8
Brunel Wy EKILS G75 3 H8
Brunstane Rd ESTRH G34 82 A1
Brunswick La CGLE G1 5 G8
Brunswick St CGLE G1 5 G8
Brunton St LNPK/KPK G44 95 G5
Brunton Ter LNPK/KPK G44 94 F6
Bruntsfield Av PLK/PH/NH G53 93 H6
Bruntsfield Gdns
PLK/PH/NH G53 93 H6
Bryan St HMLTN ML3 119 H5
Bryce Gdns LRKH ML9 130 C5
Bryce Pl EKILS G75 126 F4
Brydson Pl PSLYN/LNWD PA3 74 B4
Brymner St GRNK PA15 6 E4
Bryon Ct UD/BTH/TAN G71 99 H8
Bryson Ct HMLTN ML3 129 K3
Bryson St CLYDBK G81 40 D2
Buccleuch Av
CARD/HILL/MSPK G52 76 F2
CRMNK/CLK/EAG G76 114 D3
Buccleuch Dr BSDN G61 41 L2
Buccleuch La KVGV G3 4 C3
Buccleuch St KVGV G3 4 B3
Buccleugh St GRNK PA15 6 C4
Buchanan Av ALEX/LLW G83 13 M2
BSHPTN PA7 38 B6
Buchanan Ct
STPS/GTHM/RID G33 63 M4
Buchanan Crs BSHPBGS G64 62 C2
HMLTN ML3 119 H8
Buchanan Dr BSDN G61 42 A6
BSHPBGS G64 62 C2
CARLUKE ML8 * 132 C3
CARLUKE ML8 135 J1
KKNTL G66 45 K6
NMRNS G77 113 L2
RUTH G73 96 B4
Buchanan Ga
STPS/GTHM/RID G33 63 M4
Buchanan Gv
BAIL/MDB/MHD G69 82 B5
Buchanan Pl BSHPBGS G64 44 B1
Buchanan Rd HBR/GL G84 11 G6
Buchanan St AIRDRIE ML6 85 G1
BAIL/MDB/MHD G69 82 B6
CGLE G1 4 E7
CTBR ML5 83 M4
DMBTN G82 21 G8
GRNKW/INVK PA16 16 B5
JNSTN PA5 73 L8
LARGS KA30 106 D3
MLNGV G62 24 B8
Buchanan Wy JNSTN PA5 73 L8
Buchandyke Rd EKILN G74 117 H6
Buchan Gn EKILN G74 3 M1
Buchan Rd MTHW ML1 101 H7
Buchan St HMLTN ML3 129 J2
WISHAW ML2 122 C3
Buchan Ter BLTYR/CAMB G72 96 E7
Buchlyvie Gdns BSHPBGS G64 61 M2
Buchlyvie Rd PSLY PA1 76 E4
Buchlyvie St ESTRH G34 82 B3
Buckingham Ct HMLTN ML3 118 E6
Buckingham Dr CAR/SHTL G32 97 H2
RUTH G73 96 D3
Buckingham St KVD/HLHD G12 60 D7
Buckingham Ter
KVD/HLHD G12 60 D7
Bucklaw Gdns
CARD/HILL/MSPK G52 77 J5
Bucklaw Pl
CARD/HILL/MSPK G52 77 J5
Bucklaw Ter
CARD/HILL/MSPK G52 77 J5
Buckley St PPK/MIL G22 61 K4
Bucksburn Rd
SPRGB/BLRNK G21 62 C6
Buckthorne Pl PLK/PH/NH G53 93 H7
Buddon St DMNK/BRGTN G40 80 C6
Budhill Av CAR/SHTL G32 81 H5
Budshaw Av AIRDRIE ML6 85 J7
Bulldale Ct SCOT G14 58 F4
Bulldale Rd SCOT G14 58 E4
Bulldale St SCOT G14 58 E4
Buller Cl BLTYR/CAMB G72 98 D8
Buller Crs BLTYR/CAMB G72 98 C8
Bullionslaw Dr RUTH G73 96 D4
Bulloch Rd GIF/THBK G46 94 D8
Bull Rd CRMNK/CLK/EAG G76 114 F4
Bullwood Av PLK/PH/NH G53 92 F1
Bullwood Ct PLK/PH/NH G53 92 F1
Bullwood Dr PLK/PH/NH G53 76 F8
Bullwood Gdns PLK/PH/NH G53 76 F8
Bullwood Pl PLK/PH/NH G53 76 F8
Bunbury Ter EKILS G75 2 A8
Bunessan St
CARD/HILL/MSPK G52 77 M4
Bunhouse Rd KVGV G3 78 C1
Burghead Dr GOV/IBX G51 77 L1
Burghead Pl GOV/IBX G51 77 L1
Burgher St DEN/PKHD G31 80 C5
Burgh Hall La PTCK G11 60 B8
Burgh Hall St PTCK G11 60 B8
Burgh La KVD/HLHD G12 60 D7
Burgh Wk GRK PA19 15 L1
Burleigh Rd UD/BTH/TAN G71 99 H7
Burleigh St CTBR ML5 84 B6
GOV/IBX G51 78 A2
Burley Pl EKILN G74 115 M8
Burlington Av KVD/HLHD G12 60 B4
Burmola St PPK/MIL G22 61 H6
Burnacre Gdns
UD/BTH/TAN G71 98 E3
Burnawn Gdns
STPS/GTHM/RID G33 62 D3
Burnawn Gv
STPS/GTHM/RID G33 62 D3
Burnawn Pl
STPS/GTHM/RID G33 62 D3
Burnbank Braes CARLUKE ML8 133 H8
Burnbank Centre HMLTN ML3 119 G5
Burnbank Dr BRHD/NEIL G78 92 C8
Burnbank Gdns
MRYH/FIRH G20 60 F8
Burnbank La MRYH/FIRH G20 60 F8
Burnbank Pl MRYH/FIRH G20 61 G8
Burnbank Qd AIRDRIE ML6 84 F1
Burnbank Rd HMLTN ML3 119 H6
Burnbank St CTBR ML5 84 B1
Burnbank Ter COWCAD G4 4 A1
KSYTH G65 29 L1
Burnblea Gdns HMLTN ML3 119 L8
Burnblea St HMLTN ML3 119 K8
Burnbrae CLYDBK G81 40 A3
KSYTH G65 28 F6
Burnbrae Av
BAIL/MDB/MHD G69 47 G8
BSDN G61 42 A3
Burnbrae Dr JNSTN PA5 74 D7
RUTH G73 96 D5
Burnbrae Gdns PLK/PH/NH G53 93 J4
Burnbrae Pl EKILN G74 2 B4
Burnbrae Rd BLTYR/CAMB G72 118 C3
KKNTL G66 45 M8
PSLYN/LNWD PA3 74 C6
SHOTTS ML7 71 M6
SHOTTS ML7 104 E7
Burnbrae St CLYDBK G81 40 D1
LRKH ML9 130 B6
SPRGB/BLRNK G21 62 A6
Burncleuch Av
BLTYR/CAMB G72 97 G6
Burn Crs AIRDRIE ML6 85 K7
MTHW ML1 101 G5
Burncrooks Av BSDN G61 41 K2
EKILN G74 2 B4
Burndale La KLMCLM PA13 53 L1
Burndyke Ct GOV/IBX G51 78 C3
Burndyke Sq GOV/IBX G51 78 C3
Burnet Rose Ct EKILN G74 116 C6
Burnet Rose Gdns EKILN G74 116 C6
Burnet Rose Pl EKILN G74 116 C6
Burnett Ct BAIL/MDB/MHD G69 64 C2
Burnett Rd
STPS/GTHM/RID G33 81 L3
Burnfield Av GIF/THBK G46 94 B6
Burnfield Dr PLKSW/MSWD G43 94 B6
Burnfield Gdns GIF/THBK G46 94 C6
Burnfield Rd GIF/THBK G46 94 A5
Burnfoot DMBTN G82 19 H3
Burnfoot Crs PSLYS PA2 91 J3
RUTH G73 96 D5
Burnfoot Dr
CARD/HILL/MSPK G52 77 H4
Burnfoot Rd AIRDRIE ML6 84 E1
LOCHW PA12 109 H3
Burngreen KSYTH G65 29 K2
Burnhall Pl WISHAW ML2 122 D8
Burnhall Rd WISHAW ML2 122 C7
Burnhall St WISHAW ML2 122 D8
Burnham Rd SCOT G14 59 G5
Burnhaven ERSK PA8 39 G8
Burnhead Rd AIRDRIE ML6 67 K8
BALLOCH G68 30 D7
LRKH ML9 130 D6
PGL PA14 34 C2
PLKSW/MSWD G43 94 E5
Burnhead St GRNK PA15 7 H9
UD/BTH/TAN G71 99 H3
Burnhill Qd RUTH G73 95 M2
Burnhill St RUTH G73 95 M2
Burnhouse Av BALLOCH G68 30 B7
Burnhouse Brae NMRNS G77 114 A7
Burnhouse Crs HMLTN ML3 129 H1
Burnhouse Rd EKILS G75 126 D8
HMLTN ML3 129 H1
Burnhouse St MRYH/FIRH G20 60 D4
Burniebrae AIRDRIE ML6 84 E1
Burniebrae Rd AIRDRIE ML6 85 L6
Burnlea Crs CRG/CRSL/HOU PA6 55 G8
Burnlea Rd LARGS KA30 106 E5
Burnlip Rd AIRDRIE ML6 66 A5
Burnmouth Pl BSDN G61 42 A5
Burnmouth Rd
STPS/GTHM/RID G33 81 M4
Burnock Pl EKILS G75 126 B3
Burnpark Av UD/BTH/TAN G71 98 D3
Burn Pl BLTYR/CAMB G72 96 E3
Burn Rd CARLUKE ML8 133 G6
Burns Av BSHPTN PA7 38 B7
Burns Ct KKNTL G66 46 A1
Burn's Crs AIRDRIE ML6 85 H3
Burns Dr JNSTN PA5 89 L2
KKNTL G66 28 A8
WMYSB PA18 32 B8
Burns Gdns BLTYR/CAMB G72 118 C1
Burns Gv GIF/THBK G46 94 A8
Burnside BSDN G61 41 J2
Burnside Av AIRDRIE ML6 85 H7
BLSH ML4 100 C5
BRHD/NEIL G78 92 B5
JNSTN PA5 73 J5
KKNTL G66 45 H3
PGL PA14 34 F2
Burnside Ct BSDN G61 41 J2
RUTH G73 96 C5
Burnside Crs ALEX/LLW G83 13 L3
BLTYR/CAMB G72 118 F4
CLYDBK G81 40 B3
SHOTTS ML7 104 D3
Burnside Gdns
CRMNK/CLK/EAG G76 114 D3
KLBCH PA10 73 H8
Burnside Ga RUTH G73 96 C5
Burnside La HMLTN ML3 119 L8
Burnside Pl DMBTN G82 21 H8
LRKH ML9 130 D6
PSLYN/LNWD PA3 75 G3
Burnside Qd MTHW ML1 101 G4
Burnside Rd CTBR ML5 66 C8
GIF/THBK G46 114 B4
GRK PA19 15 M3
JNSTN PA5 90 C1
LARGS KA30 106 F3
MTHW ML1 101 K5
RUTH G73 96 C8
Burnside St GLGNK KA14 124 D7
MTHW ML1 121 H5
Burnside Vw CTBR ML5 83 L5
EKILS G75 126 D6
Burnside Wk CTBR ML5 83 L5
Burnside Wy LARGS KA30 107 G3
Burns La AIRDRIE ML6 85 K6
Burns Pk EKILN G74 3 K1
Burns Pl SHOTTS ML7 104 A3
Burns Rd AIRDRIE ML6 85 K6
CUMB G67 31 G6
GRNKW/INVK PA16 15 K4
KKNTL G66 45 M1
Burns Sq GRNKW/INVK PA16 15 K5
Burns St ALEX/LLW G83 13 K2
CLYDBK G81 39 L7
COWCAD G4 61 H8
HMLTN ML3 119 K8
Burn St ALEX/LLW G83 13 L6
Burn Street La ALEX/LLW G83 13 L6
Burntbroom Dr
BAIL/MDB/MHD G69 81 M7
Burntbroom Gdns
BAIL/MDB/MHD G69 81 M7
Burntbroom St
STPS/GTHM/RID G33 81 K3
Burn Ter BLTYR/CAMB G72 96 E3
Burntshields Rd KLBCH PA10 88 C1
Burn Vw CUMB G67 31 J6
Burnwood Dr AIRDRIE ML6 86 A3
Burra Gdns BSHPBGS G64 44 D8
Burrell Ct PLKSD/SHW G41 78 C8
Burrell's La COWCAD G4 5 K6
Burrelton Rd
PLKSW/MSWD G43 94 F5
Burte Ct BLSH ML4 100 A1
Busby Rd BLSH ML4 99 M7
CRMNK/CLK/EAG G76 114 E3
Bush Crs WISHAW ML2 122 C7
Bushelhead Rd CARLUKE ML8 134 E4
Busheyhill St BLTYR/CAMB G72 97 G5
Bute EKILN G74 127 M1
Bute Av MTHW ML1 120 C2
PGL PA14 35 H2
RNFRW PA4 58 D8
Bute Crs BSDN G61 41 M7
OLDK G60 39 J5
PSLYS PA2 91 K3
SHOTTS ML7 104 D3
Bute Dr JNSTN PA5 89 K1
OLDK G60 39 K4
Bute Gdns KVD/HLHD G12 60 D8
LNPK/KPK G44 94 F7
OLDK G60 39 J4
Bute La KVD/HLHD G12 60 D8
Bute Pl OLDK G60 39 K5
Bute Rd KKNTL G66 46 B2
PSLYN/LNWD PA3 75 K1
Bute St CTBR ML5 84 B5
GRK PA19 15 K3
HMLTN ML3 119 H4
Bute Ter RUTH G73 96 A5
UD/BTH/TAN G71 99 H3
Butt Av HBR/GL G84 10 E4
Butterbiggins Rd
GVH/MTFL G42 79 H7
Butterburnpark Pk
HMLTN ML3 129 K1
Butterfield Pl GVH/MTFL G42 79 G7
Buttermere EKILS G75 126 C5
Buttsley Ct LNK/LMHG ML11 136 E5
Byars Rd KKNTL G66 45 H2
By-Pass Rd BEITH KA15 125 L5
Byramsmuir Rd MTHW ML1 100 E1
Byrebush Rd PLK/PH/NH G53 77 J8
Byres Av PSLYN/LNWD PA3 9 L2
Byres Crs PSLYN/LNWD PA3 9 L1
Byresknowe La MTHW ML1 101 H8
Byres Rd JNSTN PA5 74 D8
KVD/HLHD G12 60 D8
MTHW ML1 101 L5
Byrestone Av NMRNS G77 114 C6
Byretown Rd LNK/LMHG ML11 136 E6
Byron Rd SHOTTS ML7 104 A3
Byron St CLYDBK G81 39 M6
PTCK G11 59 M7
Byshot St PPK/MIL G22 61 K6

C

Cable Depot Rd CLYDBK G81 40 A8
Cables Dr ALEX/LLW G83 13 L5
Cadder Cl BAIL/MDB/MHD G69 64 F5
Cadder Ct BSHPBGS G64 44 B5
Cadder Pl MRYH/FIRH G20 60 E3
Cadder Rd BSHPBGS G64 44 A4
MRYH/FIRH G20 60 E3
Cadder Wy BSHPBGS G64 44 B5
Caddlehill St GRNKW/INVK PA16 16 D4
Cadell Gdns EKILN G74 117 K5
Cadger's Sheuch KSYTH G65 30 B1
Cadoc St BLTYR/CAMB G72 97 H5
Cadogan St CGLW G2 4 C6
Cadzow Av GIF/THBK G46 114 B2
HMLTN ML3 119 H5
Cadzow Crs CTBR ML5 83 K6
Cadzow Dr BLTYR/CAMB G72 97 G5
Cadzow Gn EKILN G74 2 D4
Cadzow Pk HMLTN ML3 119 L6
Cadzow Rd HMLTN ML3 129 M7
Cadzow St CGLW G2 4 C6
HMLTN ML3 119 L6
LRKH ML9 130 C5
MTHW ML1 120 D3
Caird Av GRNKW/INVK PA16 16 C2
Caird Dr PTCK G11 60 B8
Caird Gdns HMLTN ML3 119 J5
Caird Pk HMLTN ML3 119 K5
Caird St HMLTN ML3 119 K5
Cairn Av RNFRW PA4 58 E8
Cairnban St GOV/IBX G51 77 K3
Cairnbrook Rd ESTRH G34 82 C2
Cairn Ct EKILN G74 116 E6
Cairncurran Ct GRNK PA15 6 A7
Cairndhu Av HBR/GL G84 10 A5
Cairndhu Gdns HBR/GL G84 10 A5
Cairndow Av LNPK/KPK G44 94 F6
Cairndow Avenue La
LNPK/KPK G44 94 F6
Cairndow Ct LNPK/KPK G44 94 F6
Cairn Dr PSLYN/LNWD PA3 74 B4
Cairndyke Crs AIRDRIE ML6 85 G3
Cairneymount Rd
CARLUKE ML8 133 H7
Cairney Pl WISHAW ML2 123 K3
Cairngorm Ct HMLTN ML3 129 H3
Cairngorm Crs BRHD/NEIL G78 92 C8
BSDN G61 41 H3
PSLYS PA2 91 K1
WISHAW ML2 121 M6
Cairngorm Gdns BALLOCH G68 30 B8
Cairngorm Pl EKILS G75 126 E6
Cairngorm Rd
PLKSW/MSWD G43 94 C5
Cairnhill Av AIRDRIE ML6 84 F4
Cairnhill Circ
CARD/HILL/MSPK G52 76 F6
Cairnhill Ct CARLUKE ML8 133 H7
Cairnhill Crs CTBR ML5 84 D6
Cairnhill Dr
CARD/HILL/MSPK G52 76 F6
Cairnhill Pl
CARD/HILL/MSPK G52 76 F6
Cairnhill Rd AIRDRIE ML6 84 F4
BSDN G61 41 M8
Cairnhill Vw BSDN G61 41 L7
Cairnhope Av AIRDRIE ML6 84 F4
Cairnlea Dr GOV/IBX G51 78 B4
Cairnlea Gdns BLSH ML4 100 B6
Cairnlea Rd MLNGV G62 23 L8
Cairnmuir Rd
CRMNK/CLK/EAG G76 116 B5
Cairnoch Hl BALLOCH G68 30 C7
Cairn Pl EKILN G74 116 E6
Cairnryan EKILN G74 2 C2
Cairnryan Crs
BLTYR/CAMB G72 118 D7
Cairns Av BLTYR/CAMB G72 97 H5
Cairns Dr MLNGV G62 24 A8
Cairnsmore Dr BSDN G61 41 H2
Cairnsmore Rd DRUM G15 40 F7
Cairns Rd BLTYR/CAMB G72 97 H6
BSHPTN PA7 38 A6
Cairns St MTHW ML1 120 E3
Cairn St SPRGB/BLRNK G21 61 M4
Cairnswell Av BLTYR/CAMB G72 97 J6
Cairnswell Pl BLTYR/CAMB G72 97 J6
Cairntoul Ct BALLOCH G68 30 B8
Cairntoul Dr SCOT G14 59 G3
Cairntoul Pl SCOT G14 59 G4
Cairn Vw AIRDRIE ML6 84 F3
KKNTL G66 46 B3
Cairnview Rd KKNTL G66 27 H5
Cairnwood Dr AIRDRIE ML6 84 F4
Caithness Rd EKILN G74 117 K7
GRNKW/INVK PA16 15 J5
Caithness St BLTYR/CAMB G72 118 C4
MRYH/FIRH G20 60 F6
Cala Sona Ct WISHAW ML2 131 G1
Calcots Pl ESTRH G34 82 C1
Caldarvan St PPK/MIL G22 61 H7
Caldeen Rd CTBR ML5 84 B4
Calder Av AIRDRIE ML6 68 F5
BRHD/NEIL G78 92 D8
CTBR ML5 84 B5
WISHAW ML2 123 G3
Calderbank Rd AIRDRIE ML6 85 H5
Calderbank Ter MTHW ML1 120 F2
Calderbank Vw
BAIL/MDB/MHD G69 82 B7
Calderbraes Av
UD/BTH/TAN G71 98 E2
Caldercruix Rd AIRDRIE ML6 69 K2
Caldercuilt Rd MRYH/FIRH G20 60 C2
Calder Dr BLSH ML4 100 C5
BLTYR/CAMB G72 97 G5
LOCHW PA12 109 J2
Calder Ga BSHPBGS G64 43 M6
Calderglen Av
BLTYR/CAMB G72 98 C7
Calderglen Rd EKILN G74 117 K8
Caldergrove MTHW ML1 120 E2
Calderhaugh La LOCHW PA12 109 H3
Calderhead Rd SHOTTS ML7 104 D2
Calderigg Pl AIRDRIE ML6 85 K2
Calderpark Av LOCHW PA12 109 J2
UD/BTH/TAN G71 82 B8
Calderpark Ct UD/BTH/TAN G71 82 B8
Calderpark Pl UD/BTH/TAN G71 82 B8
Calderpark Rd
UD/BTH/TAN G71 82 B8
Calderpark St LOCHW PA12 109 J2
Calderpark Ter
UD/BTH/TAN G71 82 B8
Calder Pl BAIL/MDB/MHD G69 82 B6
Calder Rd BLSH ML4 100 C6
BLTYR/CAMB G72 98 C5
PSLYN/LNWD PA3 75 G5
SHOTTS ML7 123 M1
Calderside Gv EKILN G74 117 L6

Calderside Rd
BLTYR/CAMB G72 117 M7
Calder St AIRDRIE ML6 85 J7
BLTYR/CAMB G72 118 D2
CTBR ML5 84 B5
GVH/MTFL G42 79 G8
LOCHW PA12 109 H2
Caldervale St AIRDRIE ML6 85 L5
Calder Vw HMLTN ML3 129 H2
MTHW ML1 120 F2
Calderview Av CTBR ML5 84 E5
Calderwood Av
BAIL/MDB/MHD G69 82 A7
Calderwood Dr
BAIL/MDB/MHD G69 82 A7
BLTYR/CAMB G72 118 D4
Calderwood Gdns
BAIL/MDB/MHD G69 82 A7
EKILN G74 117 L7
Calderwood Rd EKILN G74 3 L5
PLKSW/MSWD G43 94 D4
RUTH G73 96 C3
Caldwell Av KNTSWD G13 59 G3
PSLYN/LNWD PA3 73 M5
Caldwell Gv BLSH ML4 100 A1
RUTH G73 96 C8
Caldwell Qd MTHW ML1 120 C4
Caldwell Rd CARLUKE ML8 135 G1
Caledonia Av GBLS G5 79 J7
RUTH G73 96 B2
Caledonia Ct PSLYN/LNWD PA3 8 F1
Caledonia Crs GRK PA19 15 M2
Caledonia Dr
BAIL/MDB/MHD G69 82 B7
MTHW ML1 101 L5
Caledonian Av BLSH ML4 99 M6
Caledonian Ct EKILN G74 2 F7
Caledonian Crs KVD/HLHD G12 60 E8
Caledonian Ga CTBR ML5 84 A1
Caledonian Pl GLGNK KA14 124 E6
Caledonian Rd GLGNK KA14 124 E6
LRKH ML9 130 C6
WISHAW ML2 122 A7
Caledonia Rd
BAIL/MDB/MHD G69 82 B7
BEITH KA15 125 K4
GBLS G5 79 J7
SHOTTS ML7 104 E4
Caledonia St CLYDBK G81 39 M8
GBLS G5 79 K7
PGL PA14 34 D1
PSLYN/LNWD PA3 8 F2
Caledonia Ter DMBTN G82 20 C7
Caledonia Wy
PSLYN/LNWD PA3 75 K1
Caledonia Wy East
PSLYN/LNWD PA3 75 L1
Caledonia Wy West
PSLYN/LNWD PA3 75 K1
Caledon La KVD/HLHD G12 60 C8
Caledon St KVD/HLHD G12 60 C7
Calfhill Rd PLK/PH/NH G53 77 H6
Calfmuir Rd KKNTL G66 46 A4
Calgary Pk EKILS G75 2 C7
Calgary St COWCAD G4 5 G3
Calico Wy KKNTL G66 26 C1
Callaghan Wynd
BLTYR/CAMB G72 118 B1
Callander Ct BALLOCH G68 30 F5
Callander Rd AIRDRIE ML6 85 K8
BALLOCH G68 30 F5
Callander St MRYH/FIRH G20 61 G7
Callieburn Ct BSHPBGS G64 62 A2
Callieburn Rd BSHPBGS G64 62 A2
Callon St AIRDRIE ML6 85 G2
Cally Av DRUM G15 41 G6
Calside PSLYS PA2 9 G8
Calside Av PSLYS PA2 8 F8
Calton Entry DMNK/BRGTN G40 5 K9
Calvay Crs STPS/GTHM/RID G33 81 K3
Calvay Rd STPS/GTHM/RID G33 81 L3
Cambourne Rd
BAIL/MDB/MHD G69 46 F7
Cambridge Av CLYDBK G81 40 C7
GRK PA19 16 A3
Cambridge Rd
GRNKW/INVK PA16 15 K5
RNFRW PA4 58 C7
Cambridge St KVGV G3 4 D4
Camburn St CAR/SHTL G32 80 F5
Cambusdoon Rd
STPS/GTHM/RID G33 63 J8
Cambuskenneth Gdns
CAR/SHTL G32 81 K5
Cambuslang Rd RUTH G73 96 C1
Cambuslang Wy CAR/SHTL G32 96 F2
Cambusnethan St
WISHAW ML2 122 E5
Cambus Pl STPS/GTHM/RID G33 63 J8
Camden Ter GBLS G5 79 J6
Camellia Dr WISHAW ML2 121 L8
Camelon Crs BLTYR/CAMB G72 118 D3
Camelon St CAR/SHTL G32 80 F4
Cameron Av BSHPTN PA7 38 B7
Cameron Ct CLYDBK G81 58 C1
Cameron Crs
CRMNK/CLK/EAG G76 115 L3
HMLTN ML3 119 J7
Cameron Dr ALEX/LLW G83 13 J3
BSDN G61 42 A7
NMRNS G77 113 L3
UD/BTH/TAN G71 99 G2
Cameronian Ct
LNK/LMHG ML11 137 J4
Cameronian Dr CARLUKE ML8 133 K8
Cameronian Pl BLSH ML4 99 M7
Cameron Pl GRNKW/INVK PA16 32 E4
Cameron Rd AIRDRIE ML6 49 J7
CARLUKE ML8 135 H1
Cameron Sq CLYDBK G81 40 C3
Cameron St
CARD/HILL/MSPK G52 76 E2
CTBR ML5 84 B1
MTHW ML1 120 D3
Cameron Wy
BLTYR/CAMB G72 118 D2
Camlachie St DEN/PKHD G31 80 B5
Campbell Av BSHPTN PA7 38 B6
DMBTN G82 21 J6
MLNGV G62 42 A1
Campbell Ct GRNKW/INVK PA16 16 E2
Campbell Crs ALEX/LLW G83 13 J3
NMRNS G77 113 L3
UD/BTH/TAN G71 99 G6
Campbell Dr BRHD/NEIL G78 92 C7
BSDN G61 41 K4
DMBTN G82 21 J6
HBR/GL G84 11 G8
Campbell La HMLTN ML3 119 L7
Campbell Pl BSHPBGS G64 44 B1
EKILS G75 2 E9
Campbell St ALEX/LLW G83 13 L6
BLSH ML4 100 B4
GRNKW/INVK PA16 16 E2
HBR/GL G84 10 C5
HMLTN ML3 119 L6
JNSTN PA5 73 M8
MRYH/FIRH G20 60 E3
RNFRW PA4 58 D5
WISHAW ML2 122 C6
Campbell Ter DMBTN G82 21 J6
Camperdown Ct HBR/GL G84 11 G5
Camphill PSLY PA1 8 F7
Camphill Av KKNTL G66 45 J2
PLKSD/SHW G41 94 E3
Camphill Crs BSHPTN PA7 38 C7
Camphill Dr KBRN KA25 124 B6
Camphill Gdns BSHPTN PA7 38 C8
Campion Rd MTHW ML1 120 E1
Camp Rd BAIL/MDB/MHD G69 82 B5
MTHW ML1 120 E5
RUTH G73 79 M8
Camps Crs RNFRW PA4 58 E7
Campsie Av BRHD/NEIL G78 92 C8
Campsie Ct LRKH ML9 130 A4
Campsie Crs AIRDRIE ML6 84 F1
Campsie Dr BSDN G61 41 K2
MLNGV G62 24 B8
PSLYN/LNWD PA3 75 L1
PSLYS PA2 91 K2
RNFRW PA4 76 A1
Campsie Gdns
CRMNK/CLK/EAG G76 114 C2
Campsie Pl
BAIL/MDB/MHD G69 64 C2
Campsie Rd BSHPBGS G64 26 D8
EKILS G75 126 D7
KKNTL G66 27 G4
PGL PA14 35 G4
WISHAW ML2 121 L5
Campsie St
SPRGB/BLRNK G21 61 M5
Campsie Vw
BAIL/MDB/MHD G69 64 C2
BLTYR/CAMB G72 97 L7
CUMB G67 31 H6
HMLTN ML3 118 F8
KKNTL G66 45 G2
STPS/GTHM/RID G33 63 K6
UD/BTH/TAN G71 99 G2
Campston Pl
STPS/GTHM/RID G33 81 H1
Camp St MTHW ML1 120 E4
Camsail Av HBR/GL G84 10 B5
Camsbusmore Pl
STPS/GTHM/RID G33 63 J8
Camsdale Av SHOTTS ML7 87 H7
Camstradden Dr East
BSDN G61 41 J5
Camstradden Dr West
BSDN G61 41 J5
Camus Pl DRUM G15 40 F5
Canal Av JNSTN PA5 74 A8
Canal Ct CTBR ML5 83 M3
Canal La KKNTL G66 45 K1
Canal Rd JNSTN PA5 74 A8
Canal St COWCAD G4 5 G2
JNSTN PA5 74 A7
KKNTL G66 45 K1
PSLY PA1 8 E6
RNFRW PA4 58 D5
Canal Ter PSLY PA1 8 F6
Canberra Av CLYDBK G81 39 K6
Canberra Dr EKILS G75 2 B8
Cander Rigg BSHPBGS G64 44 A6
Candleriggs CGLE G1 5 H8
Candren Rd PSLYN/LNWD PA3 74 D4
Candren Wy PSLYN/LNWD PA3 75 G5
Caneluk Av CARLUKE ML8 133 K8
Canmore Crs
GRNKW/INVK PA16 16 A5
Canmore Pl DEN/PKHD G31 80 D6
Canmore St DEN/PKHD G31 80 D6
Cannerton Crs KKNTL G66 27 H5
Cannerton Pk KKNTL G66 27 H5
Cannich Dr PSLYS PA2 76 B8
Cannich Pl WISHAW ML2 122 F3
Canniesburn Dr BSDN G61 41 M6
Canniesburn Qd BSDN G61 41 L7
Canniesburn Rd BSDN G61 41 J7
Canonbie Av EKILN G74 116 F6
Canonbie St ESTRH G34 82 D1
Canon Ct MTHW ML1 101 K7
Canterbury EKILS G75 126 F3
Canthill Gdns SHOTTS ML7 103 M6
Cantieslaw Dr EKILN G74 3 K2
Canting Wy GOV/IBX G51 78 C3
Canyon Rd WISHAW ML2 121 K7
Caol Ct EKILN G74 115 J7
Capel Av NMRNS G77 113 M3
Capel Gv EKILN G74 3 L2
Capelrig Dr EKILN G74 3 L2
NMRNS G77 113 L1
Capelrig La NMRNS G77 113 K3
Capelrig Rd NMRNS G77 113 K5
Capelrig St GIF/THBK G46 93 M5
Caplaw Pl WISHAW ML2 131 H1
Caplaw Rd BRHD/NEIL G78 90 C8
PSLYS PA2 91 J4
Caplethill Rd PSLYS PA2 91 M4
Caprington Pl
STPS/GTHM/RID G33 81 G1
Caprington St
STPS/GTHM/RID G33 81 G1
Captain St GRNK PA15 6 B5
Captain's Wk MTHW ML1 102 E8
Cara Dr GOV/IBX G51 77 L1
Carbarns WISHAW ML2 121 L8
Carbarns East WISHAW ML2 121 K8
Carbarns Rd WISHAW ML2 121 K8
Carbarns West WISHAW ML2 121 K8
Carberry Rd PLKSD/SHW G41 78 D8
Carbeth Rd MLNGV G62 23 M8
Carbeth St PPK/MIL G22 61 H6
Carbisdale St PPK/MIL G22 61 L5
Carbost St SMSTN G23 60 D1
Carbrook St PSLY PA1 8 C5
SPRGB/BLRNK G21 80 A1
Cardarrach St
SPRGB/BLRNK G21 62 A6
Cardean Rd BLSH ML4 100 E3
Cardell Av PSLYS PA2 75 G7
Cardell Crs AIRDRIE ML6 85 K7
Cardell Dr PSLYS PA2 75 G7
Cardell Rd PSLYS PA2 75 G7
Cardonald Dr
CARD/HILL/MSPK G52 77 G5
Cardonald Gdns
CARD/HILL/MSPK G52 77 G5
Cardonald Place Rd
CARD/HILL/MSPK G52 77 H5
Cardowan Dr BALLOCH G68 47 L1
STPS/GTHM/RID G33 63 K5
Cardowan Pk UD/BTH/TAN G71 99 H1
Cardowan Rd CAR/SHTL G32 80 F4
STPS/GTHM/RID G33 63 L4
Cardow Rd SPRGB/BLRNK G21 62 C6
Cardrona St
STPS/GTHM/RID G33 63 H7
Cardross Av PGL PA14 34 E2
Cardross Crs GRNK PA15 17 J7
Cardross Pl BALLOCH G68 30 B7
GRNK PA15 17 K7
Cardross Rd DMBTN G82 18 E1
HBR/GL G84 10 F7
Cardross St DEN/PKHD G31 79 M3
Cardwell Rd GRK PA19 15 M2
Cardwell St GBLS G5 79 G6
Cardyke St SPRGB/BLRNK G21 62 A6
Careston Pl BSHPBGS G64 62 D1
Carey Gdns MTHW ML1 102 C8
Carfin Dr CARLUKE ML8 134 C7
Carfin Mill Rd MTHW ML1 121 J1
Carfin Rd MTHW ML1 101 K7
WISHAW ML2 121 J5
Carfin St CTBR ML5 84 B5
GVH/MTFL G42 79 H8
MTHW ML1 101 H6
Carfrae St KVGV G3 78 C2
Cargill Sq BSHPBGS G64 62 C2
Carham Dr
CARD/HILL/MSPK G52 77 J4
Carillon Rd GOV/IBX G51 78 C5
Carisbrooke Crs BSHPBGS G64 44 B6
Carlaverock Rd
PLKSW/MSWD G43 94 D4
Carleith Av CLYDBK G81 39 M4
Carleith Qd GOV/IBX G51 77 K2
Carleith Ter CLYDBK G81 39 M4
Carleston St SPRGB/BLRNK G21 61 M6
Carleton Ct GIF/THBK G46 94 C6
Carleton Dr GIF/THBK G46 94 C6
Carleton Ga GIF/THBK G46 94 C6
Carlibar Av KNTSWD G13 58 F3
Carlibar Dr BRHD/NEIL G78 92 C6
Carlibar Gdns BRHD/NEIL G78 92 C6
Carlibar Rd BRHD/NEIL G78 92 C6
Carlile Pl PSLYN/LNWD PA3 9 H2
Carlins Pl KKNTL G66 26 D2
Carlisle Rd AIRDRIE ML6 85 J4
HMLTN ML3 119 M7
LRKH ML9 130 A3
MTHW ML1 102 B2
Carlisle St PPK/MIL G22 61 K6
Carloway Ct
STPS/GTHM/RID G33 81 H2
Carlowrie Av BLTYR/CAMB G72 98 C8
Carlton Ct GBLS G5 4 D9
Carlton Pl GBLS G5 4 E9
Carlyle Av
CARD/HILL/MSPK G52 76 F1
Carlyle Dr EKILN G74 3 L3
Carmaben Rd
STPS/GTHM/RID G33 81 K2
Carman Rd DMBTN G82 19 J2
Carment Dr PLKSD/SHW G41 94 D2
Carmen Vw DMBTN G82 21 G4
Carmichael Ct
LNK/LMHG ML11 137 J5
Carmichael Pl GVH/MTFL G42 94 F3
Carmichael St CARLUKE ML8 132 B4
GOV/IBX G51 78 B4
GRNKW/INVK PA16 16 D3
Carmichael Wy CARLUKE ML8 132 B4
Carmona Dr ALEX/LLW G83 13 M3
Carmunnock By-pass
CRMNK/CLK/EAG G76 115 J4
Carmunnock Rd EKILN G74 2 B2
LNPK/KPK G44 95 H4
Carmyle Av CAR/SHTL G32 97 H2
Carmyle Gdns CTBR ML5 83 L7
Carna Dr LNPK/KPK G44 95 J5
Carnarvon St KVGV G3 4 A2
Carnbroe Rd BLSH ML4 84 C8
BLSH ML4 100 B1
Carneddans Rd MLNGV G62 23 J5
Carnegie Hl EKILS G75 2 C8
Carnegie Pl EKILS G75 2 C8
Carnegie Rd
CARD/HILL/MSPK G52 77 G3
Carnoch St SMSTN G23 60 D1
Carnock Crs BRHD/NEIL G78 92 B8
Carnock Rd PLK/PH/NH G53 93 J1
Carnock St GRNK PA15 6 F6
Carnoustie Av GRK PA19 15 G3
Carnoustie Ct UD/BTH/TAN G71 98 F8
Carnoustie Crs BSHPBGS G64 62 C1
EKILS G75 126 D4
Carnoustie Pl BLSH ML4 100 A2
GBLS G5 78 F5
Carnoustie St GBLS G5 78 F5
Carnoustie Wy BALLOCH G68 30 F3
Carntynehall Rd CAR/SHTL G32 80 F4
Carntyne Pl CAR/SHTL G32 80 D3
Carntyne Rd CAR/SHTL G32 80 D3
Carnwadric Rd GIF/THBK G46 93 L5
Carnwath Av
PLKSW/MSWD G43 94 F4
Carnwath Rd CARLUKE ML8 133 J8
Caroline St DEN/PKHD G31 80 E5
Carolside Av
CRMNK/CLK/EAG G76 114 E3
Carolside Dr DRUM G15 41 H6
Carousel Crs WISHAW ML2 122 C6
Carradale Crs BALLOCH G68 47 M2
Carradale Gdns CARLUKE ML8 135 G1
Carradale St CTBR ML5 83 M3
Carranbuie Rd CARLUKE ML8 133 H6
Carrbridge Dr MRYH/FIRH G20 60 D4
Carresbrook Av KKNTL G66 46 A4
Carriagehill Av PSLYS PA2 75 L8
Carriagehill Dr PSLYS PA2 91 L1
Carrickarden Rd BSDN G61 41 M6
Carrick Ct KKNTL G66 28 A8
Carrick Crs GIF/THBK G46 114 C1
Carrick Dr CAR/SHTL G32 81 L6
CTBR ML5 83 K3
RUTH G73 96 A5
Carrick Gdns BLSH ML4 100 A1
BLTYR/CAMB G72 118 D4
CARLUKE ML8 135 G1
Carrick Gv CAR/SHTL G32 81 L6
Carrick Pl BLSH ML4 100 B1
CTBR ML5 83 K3
LRKH ML9 130 D5
Carrick Rd BSHPBGS G64 62 C1
BSHPTN PA7 38 C8
CUMB G67 31 G5
EKILN G74 3 G2
RUTH G73 95 M5
Carrickstone Rd BALLOCH G68 30 F4
Carrickstone Vw BALLOCH G68 30 F4
Carrick St CGLW G2 4 C8
LRKH ML9 130 E7
Carrick Ter DMBTN G82 20 B6
GRNKW/INVK PA16 15 L6
Carrick V MTHW ML1 102 C8
Carrickvale Ct BALLOCH G68 30 E4
Carrick Vw CTBR ML5 65 L4
Carrington St COWCAD G4 4 A1
Carrochan Crs ALEX/LLW G83 13 L2
Carrochan Rd ALEX/LLW G83 13 L2
Carroglen Gdns CAR/SHTL G32 81 K5
Carroglen Gv CAR/SHTL G32 81 K5
Carroll Crs MTHW ML1 101 J7
Carron Ct HMLTN ML3 129 H1
Carron Crs BSDN G61 41 J6
BSHPBGS G64 62 B1
KKNTL G66 45 L6
PPK/MIL G22 61 L5
Carron Dr BSHPTN PA7 38 C8
Carron Pl CTBR ML5 83 K1
EKILS G75 127 J5
PPK/MIL G22 61 L5
Carron Rd WMYSB PA18 32 B8
Carron St PPK/MIL G22 61 L5
WISHAW ML2 122 B8
Carrour Gdns BSHPBGS G64 43 M8
Carr Qd BLSH ML4 100 D4
Carruth Dr KLMCLM PA13 53 J2
Carruth Rd BRWEIR PA11 72 C2
Carsaig Dr
CARD/HILL/MSPK G52 77 L4
Carscallan Rd HMLTN ML3 129 K4
Carsegreen Av PSLYS PA2 91 H4
Carseview Dr BSDN G61 42 A4
Carsewood Av HWWD PA9 88 F5
Carson Rd ALEX/LLW G83 13 K2
Carstairs St DMNK/BRGTN G40 80 A8
Carswell Gdns PLKSD/SHW G41 78 E8
Carswell Rd NMRNS G77 113 G4
Cartbank Gv LNPK/KPK G44 95 G6
Cartcraigs Rd
PLKSW/MSWD G43 94 B4
Cartha St PLKSD/SHW G41 94 D3
Cartland Av CARLUKE ML8 134 F1
Cartland Rd LNK/LMHG ML11 136 C1
Cartland Vw LNK/LMHG ML11 136 F4
Cartsbridge Rd
CRMNK/CLK/EAG G76 114 E4
Cartsburn St GRNK PA15 6 F7
Cartsdyke Av GRNK PA15 7 J5
Cartside Av JNSTN PA5 89 K1
RNFRW PA4 57 H6
Cartside Dr
CRMNK/CLK/EAG G76 115 G4
Cartside Pl
CRMNK/CLK/EAG G76 114 F5
Cartside Qd GVH/MTFL G42 95 G3
Cartside Rd
CRMNK/CLK/EAG G76 114 F5
Cartside St GVH/MTFL G42 94 F3
Cart St CLYDBK G81 58 B1
Cartvale La PSLYN/LNWD PA3 9 G1
Cartvale Rd GVH/MTFL G42 94 F3
Cartview Ct
CRMNK/CLK/EAG G76 114 F4
Carvale Av SHOTTS ML7 87 H8
Carwood St GRNK PA15 7 K7
Caskie Dr BLTYR/CAMB G72 118 E1
SKLM PA17 50 C6
Cassels Gv MTHW ML1 100 C8
Cassels St CARLUKE ML8 133 H8
MTHW ML1 120 E1
Cassidy Dr JNSTN PA5 73 M7
Cassiltoun Gdns CSMK G45 95 K8
Cassley Av RNFRW PA4 58 F7
Castburn Rd CUMB G67 31 M3
Castle Av ALEX/LLW G83 13 L1
HBR/GL G84 10 A5
JNSTN PA5 90 B1
MTHW ML1 101 H3
UD/BTH/TAN G71 98 F8
Castlebank Ct KNTSWD G13 59 L3
Castlebank Crs PTCK G11 78 A1
Castlebank Dr PTCK G11 78 A1
Castlebank Gdns KNTSWD G13 59 L3
Castlebank Pl PTCK G11 59 M8
Castlebank St PTCK G11 59 M8
PTCK G11 78 B1
Castlebank Vls KNTSWD G13 59 L3
Castlebay Dr PPK/MIL G22 61 J1
Castlebay Pl PPK/MIL G22 61 J2
Castlebay St PPK/MIL G22 61 J2
Castlebrae DMBTN G82 20 C5
Castlebrae Gdns LNPK/KPK G44 95 H4
Castlecary Rd BALLOCH G68 31 J3
Castle Chimmins Av
BLTYR/CAMB G72 97 K6
Castle Chimmins Rd
BLTYR/CAMB G72 97 K7
Castle Ct BALLOCH G68 31 M1
KKNTL G66 45 K2
Castle Crs BSHPTN PA7 38 B8
Castlecroft Gdns
UD/BTH/TAN G71 98 F5
Castle Dr KBRN KA25 124 C4
MTHW ML1 101 H3
Castlefern Rd RUTH G73 96 A7
Castlefield Gdns EKILS G75 126 E5
Castle Gait PSLY PA1 9 G7
Castle Gdns
BAIL/MDB/MHD G69 64 F1
PSLYS PA2 75 G7
Castlegate LNK/LMHG ML11 136 F6
Castle Ga NMRNS G77 114 A7
UD/BTH/TAN G71 98 E5
Castleglen Rd EKILN G74 115 M6
Castlegreen Crs DMBTN G82 21 H8
Castlegreen St DMBTN G82 21 G8
Castle Gv KBRN KA25 124 C4
Castlehill Av PGL PA14 35 G2
Castlehill Crs AIRDRIE ML6 85 M8
CARLUKE ML8 132 C5
HMLTN ML3 120 D8
KLMCLM PA13 53 J2
RNFRW PA4 58 D5
Castlehill Dr LARGS KA30 106 F5
NMRNS G77 113 M5
Castlehill Gdns HMLTN ML3 119 M8
Castlehill Gn EKILN G74 115 M6
Castlehill Qd DMBTN G82 20 C5
Castlehill Rd BSDN G61 41 H3
CARLUKE ML8 133 G4
DMBTN G82 20 C5
KLMCLM PA13 53 J2
WISHAW ML2 121 M8
Castleknow Gdns
CARLUKE ML8 133 G6
Castlelaw Gdns CAR/SHTL G32 81 H4
Castlelaw St CAR/SHTL G32 81 H4
Castle Mains Rd MLNGV G62 23 L8
Castlemilk Crs LNPK/KPK G44 95 L5
Castlemilk Dr CSMK G45 95 L8
Castlemilk Rd LNPK/KPK G44 95 L3
Castlemilk Ter CSMK G45 95 L8
Castlemount Av NMRNS G77 113 M6
Castle Qd AIRDRIE ML6 85 K2
Castle Rd AIRDRIE ML6 85 K2
BRWEIR PA11 72 D1
DMBTN G82 37 G1
GRNK PA15 7 J9
JNSTN PA5 74 C7
NMRNS G77 113 J5
PGL PA14 34 D1
WMYSB PA18 50 A1
Castle Sq CLYDBK G81 39 L7
Castle St AIRDRIE ML6 85 J7
BAIL/MDB/MHD G69 81 M7
CLYDBK G81 39 L7
COWCAD G4 5 K5
DMBTN G82 20 F7
HMLTN ML3 119 M6
PSLY PA1 8 D5
PTCK G11 78 C1
RUTH G73 96 B2
Castleton Av NMRNS G77 113 M6
SPRGB/BLRNK G21 61 L3
Castleton Crs NMRNS G77 113 M6
Castleton Dr NMRNS G77 113 M6
Castleton Gv NMRNS G77 113 M6
Castleview BALLOCH G68 31 L1
Castle Vw KKNTL G66 26 A1
WISHAW ML2 123 G3
Castleview Av PSLYS PA2 91 G3
Castleview Dr PSLYS PA2 91 G3
Castle Wy CUMB G67 31 J6
Castle Wemyss Dr
WMYSB PA18 32 B8
Castle Wemyss Pl WMYSB PA18 32 A8
Castle Wynd HMLTN ML3 129 L7
UD/BTH/TAN G71 99 H8
Cathay St PPK/MIL G22 61 J2
Cathburn Rd WISHAW ML2 123 J5
Cathcart Crs PSLYS PA2 9 L8
Cathcart Pl RUTH G73 95 M3
Cathcart Rd GVH/MTFL G42 95 K1
LARGS KA30 106 F6
Cathcart St GRNK PA15 6 E4
Cathedral Sq COWCAD G4 5 K6
Cathedral St CGLE G1 5 G5
Catherine St MTHW ML1 120 E5
Catherine Wy MTHW ML1 100 F6
Cathkin Av RUTH G73 96 C3
Cathkin By-Pass RUTH G73 96 D7
Cathkin Crs BALLOCH G68 30 E4
Cathkin Dr
CRMNK/CLK/EAG G76 114 C2
Cathkin Pl BLTYR/CAMB G72 96 E4
Cathkin Rd
CRMNK/CLK/EAG G76 115 L2
GVH/MTFL G42 94 F3
RUTH G73 96 C8
UD/BTH/TAN G71 98 E1
Cathkinview Pl GVH/MTFL G42 95 G3
Cathkinview Rd GVH/MTFL G42 95 G3
Catrine EKILN G74 2 C3
Catrine Ct PLK/PH/NH G53 93 G1
Catrine Crs MTHW ML1 121 G5
Catrine Gdns PLK/PH/NH G53 93 G1
Catrine Pl PLK/PH/NH G53 93 G1
Catrine Rd PLK/PH/NH G53 93 G1
Catrine St LRKH ML9 130 E7
Catriona Pl DMBTN G82 21 J8
Cauldstream Pl MLNGV G62 23 L8
Causewayside Crs
CAR/SHTL G32 81 G8
Causewayside St CAR/SHTL G32 81 G8
Causeyfoot Dr KBRN KA25 124 C4
Causeyside St PSLY PA1 9 H7
Cavendish Dr NMRNS G77 113 M3
Cavendish Pl GBLS G5 79 H6
Cavendish St GBLS G5 79 H6
Cavin Dr CSMK G45 95 L6
Cavin Rd CSMK G45 95 L6
Cawder Ct BALLOCH G68 30 D4
Cawder Pl BALLOCH G68 30 E4
Cawder Rd BALLOCH G68 30 E4
Cawder Vw BALLOCH G68 30 E4
Cawder Wy BALLOCH G68 30 E4
Cawdor Crs AIRDRIE ML6 85 L6
BSHPTN PA7 38 B8
GRNKW/INVK PA16 15 M5
Cawdor Pl GRNKW/INVK PA16 16 A5
Cawdor Wy EKILN G74 2 C1
Cayton Gdns
BAIL/MDB/MHD G69 81 M6
Cecil St CRMNK/CLK/EAG G76 114 E3
CTBR ML5 84 A4
KVD/HLHD G12 60 D7
Cedar Av BEITH KA15 125 J5
CLYDBK G81 39 K6
JNSTN PA5 89 M2
UD/BTH/TAN G71 99 H2
Cedar Ct BLTYR/CAMB G72 97 L6
EKILS G75 126 F5
KLBCH PA10 73 G7
MRYH/FIRH G20 61 H8
Cedar Crs GRNK PA15 17 L7
HMLTN ML3 129 L1
Cedar Dr EKILS G75 126 F5
KKNTL G66 45 J5
UD/BTH/TAN G71 99 K2
Cedar Gdns CARLUKE ML8 132 B3
MTHW ML1 101 J5
RUTH G73 96 C7
Cedar Gv BAIL/MDB/MHD G69 83 G4
DMBTN G82 19 H3
Cedar La MTHW ML1 101 H4
Cedar Pl BLTYR/CAMB G72 118 C2
EKILS G75 126 F5
GRK PA19 15 K3
Cedar Rd BSHPBGS G64 62 B2
CUMB G67 31 K6
Cedar St MRYH/FIRH G20 61 G8

Cedar Wk *MTHW* ML1 .... 101 K7
Cedarwood *WISHAW* ML2 .... 121 K8
Cedarwood Av *NMRNS* G77 .... 113 M5
Cedarwood Rd *NMRNS* G77 .... 113 M5
Cedric Pl *KNTSWD* G13 .... 59 K2
Cedric Rd *KNTSWD* G13 .... 59 K2
Celtic St *MRYH/FIRH* G20 .... 60 C3
Cemetery Rd
BLTYR/CAMB G72 .... 118 C4
CARD/HILL/MSPK G52 .... 77 K5
SHOTTS ML7 .... 105 H5
Centenary Av *AIRDRIE* ML6 .... 84 D2
Centenary Ct *BRHD/NEIL* G78 .... 92 B7
CLYDBK G81 .... 40 B8
Centenary Crs *BLSH* ML4 .... 100 B3
Centenary Gdns *CTBR* ML5 .... 83 M5
HMLTN ML3 .... 119 L8
Centenary Qd *MTHW* ML1 .... 101 G4
Central Av *BLTYR/CAMB* G72 .... 96 F4
BLTYR/CAMB G72 .... 118 E5
CAR/SHTL G32 .... 81 K7
CLYDBK G81 .... 40 A7
KBRN KA25 .... 124 C6
MTHW ML1 .... 100 F4
PTCK G11 .... 59 M7
UD/BTH/TAN G71 .... 99 J4
Central Gv *CAR/SHTL* G32 .... 81 K6
Central Pth *CAR/SHTL* G32 .... 81 L7
Central Rd *PSLY* PA1 .... 9 H4
Central Wy *CUMB* G67 .... 48 E1
PSLY PA1 .... 9 H4
Centre St *AIRDRIE* ML6 .... 85 J7
CTBR ML5 .... 65 J4
GBLS G5 .... 4 D9
Centre Wy *BRHD/NEIL* G78 .... 92 B6
Centrewest *EKILS* G75 .... 2 E6
Centurion Pl *MTHW* ML1 .... 100 B8
Ceres Gdns *BSHPBGS* G64 .... 62 D1
Ceres Pl *MTHW* ML1 .... 120 D1
Cessnock Rd
STPS/GTHM/RID G33 .... 63 G5
Cessnock St *GOV/IBX* G51 .... 78 C5
Chalmers Crs *EKILS* G75 .... 127 J3
Chalmers Dr *EKILS* G75 .... 3 H9
Chalmers Ga *DMNK/BRGTN* G40 .... 5 L9
Chalmers St *CLYDBK* G81 .... 40 B8
DMNK/BRGTN G40 .... 5 L9
GRK PA19 .... 15 M2
Chamberlain La *KNTSWD* G13 .... 59 L4
Chamberlain Rd *KNTSWD* G13 .... 59 L4
Chancellor St *PTCK* G11 .... 60 B8
Chantinghall Rd *HMLTN* ML3 .... 119 H7
Chantinghall Ter *HMLTN* ML3 .... 119 H7
Chapelacre Gv *HBR/GL* G84 .... 10 E5
Chapel Ct *RUTH* G73 .... 95 M2
Chapel Crs *HMLTN* ML3 .... 129 K4
Chapelcross Av *AIRDRIE* ML6 .... 67 G8
Chapelhill Rd *PSLYS* PA2 .... 9 M9
Chapelknowe Rd *MTHW* ML1 .... 101 K8
Chapel Pl *BRHD/NEIL* G78 .... 111 K3
Chapel Rd *CLYDBK* G81 .... 40 A3
CRG/CRSL/HOU PA6 .... 55 H7
WISHAW ML2 .... 123 H8
Chapelside Av *AIRDRIE* ML6 .... 85 G1
Chapelside Rd *EKILN* G74 .... 117 H5
Chapel St *AIRDRIE* ML6 .... 85 G1
CARLUKE ML8 .... 133 H8
GRK PA19 .... 15 M2
KKNTL G66 .... 26 D2
MRYH/FIRH G20 .... 60 E5
MTHW ML1 .... 102 B8
RUTH G73 .... 95 M2
Chapelton Av *BSDN* G61 .... 41 M5
DMBTN G82 .... 21 G5
Chapelton Dr *LARGS* KA30 .... 106 F2
Chapelton Gdns *BSDN* G61 .... 41 M5
DMBTN G82 .... 21 G5
Chapelton Rd *CUMB* G67 .... 48 D3
Chapelton St *PGL* PA14 .... 18 A8
PPK/MIL G22 .... 61 J4
Chapelton Wy *LARGS* KA30 .... 106 F2
Chapland Rd *LNK/LMHG* ML11 .... 137 G4
Chaplet Av *KNTSWD* G13 .... 59 J1
Chapman Av *CTBR* ML5 .... 65 J4
Chapman St *GVH/MTFL* G42 .... 79 G8
Chappell St *BRHD/NEIL* G78 .... 92 B6
Charing Cross La *KVGV* G3 .... 4 A4
Charles Av *RNFRW* PA4 .... 58 D5
Charles Crs *CARLUKE* ML8 .... 133 K8
KKNTL G66 .... 45 K7
Charleson Rw *KSYTH* G65 .... 29 M7
Charles Pl *GRNK* PA15 .... 6 C3
Charles Qd *MTHW* ML1 .... 101 G4
Charles St *KSYTH* G65 .... 29 K1
LARGS KA30 .... 106 E6
SHOTTS ML7 .... 105 H5
SPRGB/BLRNK G21 .... 5 M2
WISHAW ML2 .... 121 J5
Charlotte Av *BSHPBGS* G64 .... 44 B2
Charlotte Pl *PSLYS* PA2 .... 75 L8
Charlotte St *CGLE* G1 .... 5 J9
DMBTN G82 .... 20 D6
HBR/GL G84 .... 10 E5
SHOTTS ML7 .... 105 G6
Charn Ter *MTHW* ML1 .... 121 J6
Charnwood Av *JNSTN* PA5 .... 89 K2
Chassels St *CTBR* ML5 .... 84 B1
Chateau Gv *HMLTN* ML3 .... 120 A7
Chatelherault Av
BLTYR/CAMB G72 .... 96 E5
Chatelherault Crs *HMLTN* ML3 .... 129 L2
Chatham *EKILS* G75 .... 126 F3
Chatton St *SMSTN* G23 .... 60 D1
Chatton Wk *CTBR* ML5 .... 84 D7
Cheapside St *KVGV* G3 .... 4 A7
Chelmsford Dr *KVD/HLHD* G12 .... 60 B5
Cherry Av *CUMB* G67 .... 31 L4
Cherry Bank *KKNTL* G66 .... 45 H5
Cherrybank Rd
PLKSW/MSWD G43 .... 94 F5
Cherrybank Wk *AIRDRIE* ML6 .... 84 D1
Cherry Crs *CLYDBK* G81 .... 40 A5
Cherry Gv *BAIL/MDB/MHD* G69 .... 83 H4
Cherryhill Vw *LRKH* ML9 .... 130 B7
Cherry Pl *BSHPBGS* G64 .... 62 B2
JNSTN PA5 .... 90 A1
KKNTL G66 .... 27 H5
MTHW ML1 .... 101 H5
UD/BTH/TAN G71 .... 99 K2
Cherryridge Dr
BAIL/MDB/MHD G69 .... 83 H4
Cherrytree Crs *LRKH* ML9 .... 130 C4
Cherrytree Dr *BLTYR/CAMB* G72 .... 97 L6
Cherrytree Wynd *EKILS* G75 .... 127 J3
Cherry Wk *MTHW* ML1 .... 120 E6
Cherrywood Dr *BEITH* KA15 .... 125 L3
Cherrywood Rd *JNSTN* PA5 .... 74 C8
Chesterfield Av *KVD/HLHD* G12 .... 60 A5
Chester Rd *GRNKW/INVK* PA16 .... 15 L5
Chesters Crs *MTHW* ML1 .... 120 C1
Chesters Pl *RUTH* G73 .... 95 M3
Chesters Rd *BSDN* G61 .... 41 J5
Chester St *CAR/SHTL* G32 .... 81 G5
Chestnut Av *BEITH* KA15 .... 125 J5
BSHPTN PA7 .... 37 M5
CUMB G67 .... 31 L4
Chestnut Ct *CUMB* G67 .... 31 L4
KKNTL G66 .... 27 H5
Chestnut Crs *EKILS* G75 .... 126 F4
HMLTN ML3 .... 119 L8
UD/BTH/TAN G71 .... 99 J3
Chestnut Dr *CLYDBK* G81 .... 40 A4
KKNTL G66 .... 45 H4
Chestnut Gv
BAIL/MDB/MHD G69 .... 65 J4
BLTYR/CAMB G72 .... 118 C2
CARLUKE ML8 .... 133 G8
LRKH ML9 .... 130 C4
MTHW ML1 .... 120 D5
Chestnut La *MLNGV* G62 .... 23 L6
Chestnut Pl *CUMB* G67 .... 31 L4
JNSTN PA5 .... 90 A2
Chestnut St *PPK/MIL* G22 .... 61 K5
Chestnut Wk *KKNTL* G66 .... 26 D3
Chestnut Wy *BLTYR/CAMB* G72 .... 97 L6
HMLTN ML3 .... 129 M6
Cheviot Av *BRHD/NEIL* G78 .... 92 C7
Cheviot Crs *EKILS* G75 .... 126 D6
WISHAW ML2 .... 121 M6
Cheviot Dr *NMRNS* G77 .... 113 J6
Cheviot Rd *HMLTN* ML3 .... 119 M8
LRKH ML9 .... 130 E7
PLKSW/MSWD G43 .... 94 C5
PSLYS PA2 .... 91 K2
Cheviot St *BLTYR/CAMB* G72 .... 118 C3
Chillin Pl *LRKH* ML9 .... 130 E7
Chirmorie Crs *PLK/PH/NH* G53 .... 77 G8
Chirmorie Pl *PLK/PH/NH* G53 .... 77 G8
Chirnside Pl
CARD/HILL/MSPK G52 .... 77 G3
Chirnside Rd
CARD/HILL/MSPK G52 .... 77 G3
Chisholm Av *BSHPTN* PA7 .... 38 C7
Chisholm Dr *NMRNS* G77 .... 113 L3
Chisholm Pl *MTHW* ML1 .... 121 H7
Chisholm St *CTBR* ML5 .... 84 B1
Chisolm St *CGLE* G1 .... 5 H8
Chrighton Gn *UD/BTH/TAN* G71 .... 99 G2
Chriss Av *HMLTN* ML3 .... 129 K3
Christchurch Pl *EKILS* G75 .... 126 E3
Christian St *PLKSW/MSWD* G43 .... 94 C3
Christie La *PSLYN/LNWD* PA3 .... 9 H3
Christie St *BLSH* ML4 .... 100 D5
PSLY PA1 .... 9 K4
Christopher St
SPRGB/BLRNK G21 .... 80 A1
Chromars Pl *GRNK* PA15 .... 6 A7
Chryston Rd
BAIL/MDB/MHD G69 .... 64 D2
KKNTL G66 .... 46 C4
Chuckie La *JNSTN* PA5 .... 73 J5
Church Av *DMBTN* G82 .... 19 G2
RUTH G73 .... 96 C5
STPS/GTHM/RID G33 .... 63 K4
WISHAW ML2 .... 122 F5
Church Ct *DMBTN* G82 .... 20 F7
HMLTN ML3 .... 119 L6
Church Crs *AIRDRIE* ML6 .... 67 L8
Church Hl *PSLY* PA1 .... 9 G4
Churchill Av *EKILN* G74 .... 3 H6
JNSTN PA5 .... 89 J2
Churchill Crs *UD/BTH/TAN* G71 .... 99 H7
Churchill Dr *BSHPTN* PA7 .... 38 B7
PTCK G11 .... 59 M5
Churchill Pl *KLBCH* PA10 .... 73 G8
Churchill Rd *KLMCLM* PA13 .... 53 J3
Churchill Sq *HBR/GL* G84 .... 11 G5
Church La *CTBR* ML5 .... 84 A2
Church Manse La *BRWEIR* PA11 .... 72 D2
Church Pl *AIRDRIE* ML6 .... 68 F5
OLDK G60 .... 39 G4
Church Rd *BAIL/MDB/MHD* G69 .... 64 C3
BRWEIR PA11 .... 53 L7
CRMNK/CLK/EAG G76 .... 114 F4
GIF/THBK G46 .... 94 C8
WISHAW ML2 .... 123 K3
Church St *ALEX/LLW* G83 .... 13 K6
BAIL/MDB/MHD G69 .... 82 C6
BLTYR/CAMB G72 .... 118 E3
CLYDBK G81 .... 40 A6
CTBR ML5 .... 84 A2
DMBTN G82 .... 20 F7
GRK PA19 .... 15 L1
HMLTN ML3 .... 119 L6
KLBCH PA10 .... 73 G7
KSYTH G65 .... 29 K2
LARGS KA30 .... 106 E5
LOCHW PA12 .... 109 J3
LRKH ML9 .... 130 C6
MTHW ML1 .... 101 M5
PGL PA14 .... 18 C8
PTCK G11 .... 78 C1
SHOTTS ML7 .... 71 J7
UD/BTH/TAN G71 .... 98 E5
Church Vw *BLTYR/CAMB* G72 .... 97 G3
CTBR ML5 .... 84 A2
Church View Gdns *BLSH* ML4 .... 100 A4
Circus Dr *DEN/PKHD* G31 .... 79 M3
Circus Place La *DEN/PKHD* G31 .... 79 M3
Citadel Pl *MTHW* ML1 .... 120 C1
Citizen La *CGLE* G1 .... 4 F6
Citrus Crs *UD/BTH/TAN* G71 .... 99 J2
Cityford Dr *RUTH* G73 .... 95 M4
Civic St *COWCAD* G4 .... 4 D2
Civic Wy *KKNTL* G66 .... 45 J3
Clachaig Pl *GRK* PA19 .... 14 F4
Clachan Dr *GOV/IBX* G51 .... 77 L1
The Clachan *WISHAW* ML2 .... 122 B6
Clachan Wy *CTBR* ML5 .... 83 L5
Claddens Pl *KKNTL* G66 .... 45 M6
PPK/MIL G22 .... 61 H4
Claddens Qd *PPK/MIL* G22 .... 61 J4
Claddens St *PPK/MIL* G22 .... 61 H4
Cladence Gv *EKILS* G75 .... 127 J5
Claire St *WISHAW* ML2 .... 122 F4
Clairinish *ALEX/LLW* G83 .... 13 J1
Clairinsh Gdns *RNFRW* PA4 .... 58 C8
Clairmont Gdns *KVGV* G3 .... 78 F1
Clair Rd *BSHPBGS* G64 .... 62 D1
Clamp Rd *WISHAW* ML2 .... 121 J5
Clamps Gv *EKILN* G74 .... 3 K8
Clamps Ter *EKILN* G74 .... 3 L8
Clamps Wd *EKILN* G74 .... 3 K8
Clanrye Dr *CTBR* ML5 .... 84 A5
Clapperhow Rd *MTHW* ML1 .... 101 G8
Claremont Av *KKNTL* G66 .... 45 H2
Claremont Dr *MLNGV* G62 .... 24 A8
Claremont Gdns *MLNGV* G62 .... 42 A1
Claremont Pas *KVGV* G3 .... 78 F1
Claremont Pl *KVGV* G3 .... 78 F1
Claremont St *KVGV* G3 .... 78 E2
Claremont Ter *KVGV* G3 .... 78 F1
Claremont Terrace La *KVGV* G3 .... 78 F1
Claremount Av *GIF/THBK* G46 .... 94 C8
Claremount Vw *CTBR* ML5 .... 84 C7
Clarence Dr *PSLY* PA1 .... 9 M4
PTCK G11 .... 60 A7
Clarence Gdns *PTCK* G11 .... 60 A7
Clarence La *KVD/HLHD* G12 .... 60 B7
Clarence St *CLYDBK* G81 .... 40 C7
GRNK PA15 .... 6 C1
PSLY PA1 .... 9 L4
Clarendon Pl *MRYH/FIRH* G20 .... 4 B1
Clarendon Rd *WISHAW* ML2 .... 121 L8
Clarendon St *MRYH/FIRH* G20 .... 4 B1
Clare St *SPRGB/BLRNK* G21 .... 80 A1
Clarinda Ct *KKNTL* G66 .... 28 A8
Clarinda Pl *MTHW* ML1 .... 101 J6
Clarion Crs *KNTSWD* G13 .... 59 G1
Clarion Rd *KNTSWD* G13 .... 59 G2
Clarkin Av *EKILS* G75 .... 126 D6
Clark Pl *NMRNS* G77 .... 113 H5
Clarkston Av *LNPK/KPK* G44 .... 94 F6
Clarkston Dr *AIRDRIE* ML6 .... 85 K2
Clarkston Rd
CRMNK/CLK/EAG G76 .... 114 E2
LNPK/KPK G44 .... 94 F7
Clark St *AIRDRIE* ML6 .... 85 H2
CLYDBK G81 .... 39 M6
JNSTN PA5 .... 73 M7
PSLYN/LNWD PA3 .... 8 D1
RNFRW PA4 .... 58 B6
WISHAW ML2 .... 122 F3
Clark Wy *BLSH* ML4 .... 99 M3
Clarkwell Rd *HMLTN* ML3 .... 118 E7
Clarkwell Ter *HMLTN* ML3 .... 118 F7
Clathic Av *BSDN* G61 .... 42 A7
Claude Av *BLTYR/CAMB* G72 .... 97 L7
Claude St *LRKH* ML9 .... 130 C6
Claud Rd *PSLYN/LNWD* PA3 .... 9 L1
Clavens Rd
CARD/HILL/MSPK G52 .... 76 E3
Claverhouse Pl *PSLYS* PA2 .... 9 M8
Claverhouse Rd
CARD/HILL/MSPK G52 .... 76 F2
Clavering St East *PSLY* PA1 .... 8 D4
Clavering St West *PSLY* PA1 .... 8 D5
Clay Ct *MTHW* ML1 .... 120 D5
Clay Crs *BLSH* ML4 .... 100 B2
Clayhouse Rd
STPS/GTHM/RID G33 .... 63 L6
Claymore Dr
CRG/CRSL/HOU PA6 .... 73 K2
Claypotts Pl
STPS/GTHM/RID G33 .... 81 G1
Claypotts Rd
STPS/GTHM/RID G33 .... 81 G1
Clay Rd *BLSH* ML4 .... 100 C2
Clayslaps Rd *KVGV* G3 .... 78 D1
Claythorn Av
DMNK/BRGTN G40 .... 79 L5
Claythorn Circ
DMNK/BRGTN G40 .... 5 K9
Claythorn Pk
DMNK/BRGTN G40 .... 79 L5
Claythorn Ter
DMNK/BRGTN G40 .... 5 L9
Clayton Ter *DEN/PKHD* G31 .... 79 M3
Clearfield Av *HMLTN* ML3 .... 119 H6
Cleddans Crs *CLYDBK* G81 .... 40 C3
Cleddans Rd *CLYDBK* G81 .... 40 C4
KKNTL G66 .... 45 L1
Cleddans Vw *AIRDRIE* ML6 .... 66 E5
Cleddens Ct *BSHPBGS* G64 .... 62 A1
Cleeves Qd *PLK/PH/NH* G53 .... 93 G4
Cleeves Rd *PLK/PH/NH* G53 .... 93 G4
Cleghorn Av *LNK/LMHG* ML11 .... 137 H4
Cleghorn Rd *LNK/LMHG* ML11 .... 137 G4
Cleghorn St *PPK/MIL* G22 .... 61 H7
Cleish Av *BSDN* G61 .... 41 J1
Cleland La *GBLS* G5 .... 79 J5
Cleland Pl *EKILN* G74 .... 3 K2
Cleland Rd *MTHW* ML1 .... 101 M7
WISHAW ML2 .... 122 A6
Cleland St *GBLS* G5 .... 79 J5
Clelland Av *BSHPBGS* G64 .... 62 A2
Clem Attlee Gdns *LRKH* ML9 .... 130 D8
Clerwood St *CAR/SHTL* G32 .... 80 D4
Cleuch Gdns
CRMNK/CLK/EAG G76 .... 114 D2
Clevans Rd *BRWEIR* PA11 .... 72 B3
Cleveden Crs *KVD/HLHD* G12 .... 60 B5
Cleveden Crescent La
KVD/HLHD G12 .... 60 C5
Cleveden Dr *KVD/HLHD* G12 .... 60 B5
RUTH G73 .... 96 C4
Cleveden Drive La
KVD/HLHD G12 .... 60 C6
Cleveden Gdns *KVD/HLHD* G12 .... 60 C5
Cleveden La *KVD/HLHD* G12 .... 60 B4
Cleveden Pl *KVD/HLHD* G12 .... 60 B4
Cleveden Rd *KVD/HLHD* G12 .... 60 B4
Cleveland La *KVGV* G3 .... 4 A4
Cleveland St *KVGV* G3 .... 4 A4
Clifford Gdns *GOV/IBX* G51 .... 78 B5
Clifford La *GOV/IBX* G51 .... 78 D5
Clifford St *GOV/IBX* G51 .... 78 C5
Cliff Rd *KVGV* G3 .... 78 F1
Cliff Terrace Rd *WMYSB* PA18 .... 50 B1
Clifton Pl *CTBR* ML5 .... 84 C3
KVGV G3 .... 78 E2
Clifton Rd *GIF/THBK* G46 .... 94 B7
Clifton St *KVGV* G3 .... 78 E1
Clifton Ter *BLTYR/CAMB* G72 .... 96 E7
Clincarthill Rd *RUTH* G73 .... 96 A3
Clincart Rd *GVH/MTFL* G42 .... 95 H2
Clippens Rd
CRG/CRSL/HOU PA6 .... 73 L2
PSLYN/LNWD PA3 .... 74 B5
Clive St *SHOTTS* ML7 .... 104 E4
Cloak Rd *KLMCLM* PA13 .... 35 H5
Cloan Av *DRUM* G15 .... 41 H7
Cloan Crs *BSHPBGS* G64 .... 44 B6
Clober Farm La *MLNGV* G62 .... 23 L6
Cloberfield *MLNGV* G62 .... 23 M5
Cloberfield Gdns *MLNGV* G62 .... 23 M6
Cloberhill Rd *KNTSWD* G13 .... 41 J8
Clober Rd *MLNGV* G62 .... 23 M6
Clochbar Av *MLNGV* G62 .... 23 M6
Clochbar Gdns *MLNGV* G62 .... 23 M7
Cloch Brae *GRK* PA19 .... 15 G3
Clochoderick Av *KLBCH* PA10 .... 73 H8
Cloch Rd *GRK* PA19 .... 14 F3
Cloch St *STPS/GTHM/RID* G33 .... 81 G2
Clockerhill Pl *MTHW* ML1 .... 101 L5
Cloister Av *AIRDRIE* ML6 .... 85 J5
Closeburn St *PPK/MIL* G22 .... 61 J5
Cloth St *BRHD/NEIL* G78 .... 92 C7
Clouden Rd *CUMB* G67 .... 31 J6
Cloudhowe Ter
BLTYR/CAMB G72 .... 118 C1
Clouston La *MRYH/FIRH* G20 .... 60 E6
Clouston St *MRYH/FIRH* G20 .... 60 D6
Clova Pl *UD/BTH/TAN* G71 .... 98 F4
Clova St *GIF/THBK* G46 .... 93 M5
Clove Mill Wynd *LRKH* ML9 .... 130 A7
Cloverbank Gdns
SPRGB/BLRNK G21 .... 80 A1
Cloverbank St
SPRGB/BLRNK G21 .... 80 A1
Clovergate *BSHPBGS* G64 .... 61 L1
Cloverhill Pl
BAIL/MDB/MHD G69 .... 64 C2
Cloverhill Ter *EKILN* G74 .... 2 E5
Cloverhill Vw *EKILN* G74 .... 2 D5
Clover Leaf Pth *ALEX/LLW* G83 .... 13 K6
Cluanie Av *SHOTTS* ML7 .... 104 E3
Clune Brae *PGL* PA14 .... 34 E2
Clune Park St *PGL* PA14 .... 34 E1
Clunie Pl *CTBR* ML5 .... 84 B6
WISHAW ML2 .... 122 F3
Clunie Rd *CARD/HILL/MSPK* G52 .... 77 L5
Cluny Av *BSDN* G61 .... 42 A8
CLYDBK G81 .... 40 C2
Cluny Dr *BSDN* G61 .... 42 A8
NMRNS G77 .... 113 H4
PSLYN/LNWD PA3 .... 9 M1
Cluny Gdns *SCOT* G14 .... 59 L5
Clutha Pl *EKILS* G75 .... 126 D3
Clutha St *GOV/IBX* G51 .... 78 D4
Clyde Arc *KVGV* G3 .... 78 E3
Clyde Av *BRHD/NEIL* G78 .... 92 D8
BSHPBGS G64 .... 44 B2
HMLTN ML3 .... 120 D8
UD/BTH/TAN G71 .... 118 F1
Clydebrae Dr
UD/BTH/TAN G71 .... 119 H2
Clydebrae St *GOV/IBX* G51 .... 78 B2
Clyde Crs *LNK/LMHG* ML11 .... 137 H4
Clyde Dr *BLSH* ML4 .... 100 C5
SHOTTS ML7 .... 105 H5
Clydeford Dr *CAR/SHTL* G32 .... 80 E7
UD/BTH/TAN G71 .... 98 D3
Clydeford Rd *BLTYR/CAMB* G72 .... 97 H4
Clydeholm Rd *SCOT* G14 .... 59 K7
Clydeholm Ter *CLYDBK* G81 .... 58 D2
Clydeneuk Dr *UD/BTH/TAN* G71 .... 98 D3
Clyde Pl *BLTYR/CAMB* G72 .... 97 K6
GBLS G5 .... 4 C8
JNSTN PA5 .... 89 J2
MTHW ML1 .... 101 G5
Clyde Rd *GRK* PA19 .... 15 M3
PSLYN/LNWD PA3 .... 76 B2
Clydesdale Av *HMLTN* ML3 .... 129 K4
PSLYN/LNWD PA3 .... 58 A8
WISHAW ML2 .... 121 K8
Clydesdale Pl *HMLTN* ML3 .... 129 K4
Clydesdale St *BLSH* ML4 .... 100 F5
HMLTN ML3 .... 119 J6
LRKH ML9 .... 130 C5
Clydesholm Ct
LNK/LMHG ML11 .... 136 D5
Clydeshore Rd *DMBTN* G82 .... 20 E8
Clydeside Rd *RUTH* G73 .... 79 M8
Clydesmill Dr *CAR/SHTL* G32 .... 97 G3
Clydesmill Gv *CAR/SHTL* G32 .... 97 G3
Clydesmill Pl *CAR/SHTL* G32 .... 97 G2
Clydesmill Rd *CAR/SHTL* G32 .... 97 G2
Clyde Sq *GRNK* PA15 .... 6 D4
Clyde St *CARLUKE* ML8 .... 133 G7
CGLE G1 .... 4 E8
CLYDBK G81 .... 58 C2
CTBR ML5 .... 84 C2
Clyde Ter *MTHW* ML1 .... 121 J7
UD/BTH/TAN G71 .... 119 G1
Clydevale *UD/BTH/TAN* G71 .... 119 H1
Clyde Valley Av *MTHW* ML1 .... 120 E5
Clyde Vw *HMLTN* ML3 .... 129 H1
PSLYS PA2 .... 76 B7
Clydeview *UD/BTH/TAN* G71 .... 119 J1
Clyde View Ct *OLDK* G60 .... 38 C2
Clydeview Rd *GRNK* PA15 .... 6 F8
PGL PA14 .... 34 E2
Clydeview Ter *CAR/SHTL* G32 .... 97 J2
Clyde Wynd *GRNK* PA15 .... 16 D6
Clynder Rd *GRNK* PA15 .... 17 J7
Clynder St *GOV/IBX* G51 .... 78 B4
Clyth Dr *GIF/THBK* G46 .... 94 D8
Coach Cl *KSYTH* G65 .... 30 A1
Coach Pl *KSYTH* G65 .... 29 L3
Coach Rd *KSYTH* G65 .... 29 L3
Coalburn Rd *UD/BTH/TAN* G71 .... 99 H5
Coalburn St *AIRDRIE* ML6 .... 49 M7
Coalhall Av *MTHW* ML1 .... 101 G8
Coalhill St *DEN/PKHD* G31 .... 80 B5
Coatbank St *CTBR* ML5 .... 84 B3
Coatbank Wy *CTBR* ML5 .... 84 B3
Coatbridge Rd *AIRDRIE* ML6 .... 66 E6
BAIL/MDB/MHD G69 .... 82 C5
Coathill St *CTBR* ML5 .... 84 B5
Coats Crs *BAIL/MDB/MHD* G69 .... 82 A5
Coats Dr *PSLYS* PA2 .... 8 A8
Coatshill Av *BLTYR/CAMB* G72 .... 118 C1
Coats St *CTBR* ML5 .... 84 B2
Cobbett Rd *MTHW* ML1 .... 120 B4
Cobbleton Rd *MTHW* ML1 .... 100 F7
Cobham St *GRNK* PA15 .... 17 L7
Cobington Pl
STPS/GTHM/RID G33 .... 81 H1
Cobinshaw St *CAR/SHTL* G32 .... 81 G4
Coburg St *GBLS* G5 .... 79 H5
Cochno Rd *CLYDBK* G81 .... 40 B2
Cochno St *CLYDBK* G81 .... 58 C1
Cochranemill Rd *JNSTN* PA5 .... 89 J1
Cochrane Pl *HBR/GL* G84 .... 11 G5
Cochrane Pl East *LARGS* KA30 .... 106 E4
Cochrane Sq *PSLYN/LNWD* PA3 .... 74 B4
Cochrane St *BLSH* ML4 .... 99 M4
BRHD/NEIL G78 .... 92 B7
CGLE G1 .... 5 G6
KBRN KA25 .... 124 C3
Cochran St *PSLY* PA1 .... 9 K5
Cockburn Pl *CTBR* ML5 .... 83 M6
Cockels Loan *RNFRW* PA4 .... 58 B8
Cockenzie St *CAR/SHTL* G32 .... 81 G5
Cockhill Wy *BLSH* ML4 .... 99 K4
Cockmuir St *SPRGB/BLRNK* G21 .... 62 A6
Coddington Crs *MTHW* ML1 .... 100 F2
Cogan Pl *BRHD/NEIL* G78 .... 92 B7
Cogan Rd *PLKSW/MSWD* G43 .... 94 C4
Cogan St *BRHD/NEIL* G78 .... 92 B7
PLKSW/MSWD G43 .... 94 C3
Colbert St *DMNK/BRGTN* G40 .... 79 M7
Colbreggan Ct *CLYDBK* G81 .... 40 C3
Colbreggan Gdns *CLYDBK* G81 .... 40 C3
Colchester Dr *KVD/HLHD* G12 .... 60 A4
Coldgreen Av *KBRN* KA25 .... 124 C4
Coldingham Av *SCOT* G14 .... 58 E3
Coldstream Crs *WISHAW* ML2 .... 122 C4
Coldstream Dr *PSLYS* PA2 .... 91 G1
RUTH G73 .... 96 D4
Coldstream Pl
SPRGB/BLRNK G21 .... 61 J7
Coldstream Rd *CLYDBK* G81 .... 40 B8
Coldstream St
BLTYR/CAMB G72 .... 118 D3
Colebrooke La *KVD/HLHD* G12 .... 60 E7
Colebrooke Pl *KVD/HLHD* G12 .... 60 E7
Colebrooke St
BLTYR/CAMB G72 .... 97 G4
KVD/HLHD G12 .... 60 E7
Colebrooke Ter *KVD/HLHD* G12 .... 60 F7
Coleridge *EKILS* G75 .... 126 D3
Coleridge Av *UD/BTH/TAN* G71 .... 99 H8
Colfin St *ESTRH* G34 .... 82 C1
Colgrain Av *MRYH/FIRH* G20 .... 61 G4
Colgrain St *MRYH/FIRH* G20 .... 61 G5
Colgrain Ter *MRYH/FIRH* G20 .... 60 F4
Colgrave Crs *CAR/SHTL* G32 .... 80 F7
Colinbar Cir *BRHD/NEIL* G78 .... 92 B8
Colinslee Av *PSLYS* PA2 .... 91 M1
Colinslee Crs *PSLYS* PA2 .... 91 M1
Colinslee Dr *PSLYS* PA2 .... 91 M1
Colinslie Rd *PLK/PH/NH* G53 .... 93 J1
Colinton Gdns
BAIL/MDB/MHD G69 .... 64 C1
Colinton Pl *CAR/SHTL* G32 .... 81 H3
Colintraive Av
STPS/GTHM/RID G33 .... 62 E7
Colintraive Crs
STPS/GTHM/RID G33 .... 62 E7
Coll *EKILN* G74 .... 127 M3
Collace Av *BRWEIR* PA11 .... 72 D3
Colla Gdns *BSHPBGS* G64 .... 44 D8
Coll Av *PGL* PA14 .... 35 H3
RNFRW PA4 .... 58 D8
Coll Dr *CTBR* ML5 .... 83 K6
College Ga *BSDN* G61 .... 41 J2
College St *DMBTN* G82 .... 20 F6
Collessie Dr
STPS/GTHM/RID G33 .... 63 J8
Collier St *JNSTN* PA5 .... 73 M7
Colliertree Rd *AIRDRIE* ML6 .... 85 K1
Collina St *MRYH/FIRH* G20 .... 60 C4
Collingwood Pl *HBR/GL* G84 .... 11 G5
Collins Rd *HBR/GL* G84 .... 11 G7
Collins St *CLYDBK* G81 .... 40 C3
COWCAD G4 .... 5 K6
Coll Pl *AIRDRIE* ML6 .... 85 J4
SPRGB/BLRNK G21 .... 62 B8
Collree Gdns *ESTRH* G34 .... 82 C3
Coll St *SPRGB/BLRNK* G21 .... 62 B8
WISHAW ML2 .... 122 F3
Collylinn Rd *BSDN* G61 .... 41 L5
Colmonell Av *KNTSWD* G13 .... 58 F2
Colonsay *EKILN* G74 .... 127 M3
Colonsay Av *PGL* PA14 .... 35 H3
RNFRW PA4 .... 58 C8
Colonsay Crs *CTBR* ML5 .... 83 K6
Colonsay Dr *NMRNS* G77 .... 113 H4
Colonsay Rd
CARD/HILL/MSPK G52 .... 77 L4
PSLYS PA2 .... 91 K3
Colquhoun *DMBTN* G82 .... 21 G6
Colquhoun Av
CARD/HILL/MSPK G52 .... 77 G2
Colquhoun Dr *ALEX/LLW* G83 .... 13 K3
BSDN G61 .... 41 K4
Colquhoun Rd *DMBTN* G82 .... 37 M1
Colquhoun Sq *HBR/GL* G84 .... 10 C6
Colquhoun St *DMBTN* G82 .... 21 H6
HBR/GL G84 .... 10 D5
Colson Pl *BLSH* ML4 .... 100 C6
Colston Av *BSHPBGS* G64 .... 61 M3
Colston Dr *BSHPBGS* G64 .... 61 M3
Colston Gdns *BSHPBGS* G64 .... 61 L3
Colston Gv *BSHPBGS* G64 .... 61 M3
Colston Pth *BSHPBGS* G64 .... 61 L3
Colston Pl *AIRDRIE* ML6 .... 85 J2
BSHPBGS G64 .... 61 L3
Colston Rd *AIRDRIE* ML6 .... 85 J2
BSHPBGS G64 .... 61 M3
Colston Ter *AIRDRIE* ML6 .... 85 J2
Colt Av *CTBR* ML5 .... 83 L1
Coltmuir Crs *BSHPBGS* G64 .... 61 L2
Coltmuir Dr *BSHPBGS* G64 .... 61 L2
Coltmuir Gdns *BSHPBGS* G64 .... 61 L2
Coltmuir St *PPK/MIL* G22 .... 61 J4
Coltness Av *SHOTTS* ML7 .... 123 M1
Coltness Dr *BLSH* ML4 .... 100 B5
Coltness La
STPS/GTHM/RID G33 .... 81 J3
Coltness Rd *WISHAW* ML2 .... 122 C5
Coltness St
STPS/GTHM/RID G33 .... 81 J2
Coltpark Av *BSHPBGS* G64 .... 61 L2
Coltpark La *BSHPBGS* G64 .... 61 L2
Colt Pl *CTBR* ML5 .... 84 A1
Coltsfoot Dr *PLK/PH/NH* G53 .... 93 H6
Coltswood Rd *CTBR* ML5 .... 66 A8
Colt Ter *CTBR* ML5 .... 84 A2
Columba Ct *UD/BTH/TAN* G71 .... 99 J3
Columba Crs *MTHW* ML1 .... 100 D8
Columba Pth
BLTYR/CAMB G72 .... 118 C2
Columba St *GOV/IBX* G51 .... 78 B3
GRNKW/INVK PA16 .... 16 D5
HBR/GL G84 .... 10 D5
Columbia Pl *EKILS* G75 .... 126 E2
Columbia Wy *EKILS* G75 .... 126 E2
Columbine Wy *CARLUKE* ML8 .... 134 F1
Colvend Dr *RUTH* G73 .... 96 B7
Colvend La *DMNK/BRGTN* G40 .... 79 M7
Colvend St *DMNK/BRGTN* G40 .... 79 M7
Colville Cl *BLTYR/CAMB* G72 .... 97 K5
Colville Ct *MTHW* ML1 .... 101 J8
Colville Dr *RUTH* G73 .... 96 D4
Colvilles Pl *EKILS* G75 .... 127 L4
Colvilles Rd *EKILS* G75 .... 127 K5
Colwood Av *PLK/PH/NH* G53 .... 93 G5
Colwood Gdns *PLK/PH/NH* G53 .... 93 G6
Colwood Pl *PLK/PH/NH* G53 .... 93 G6
Colwood Sq *PLK/PH/NH* G53 .... 93 G6
Colwyn Ct *AIRDRIE* ML6 .... 67 G8
Colzium Vw *KSYTH* G65 .... 29 L2

Combe Qd BLSH ML4 99 L7
Comedie Rd
STPS/GTHM/RID G33 63 L6
Comely Bank HMLTN ML3 118 F7
Comelybank La DMBTN G82 20 D6
Comelybank Rd DMBTN G82 20 D6
Comelypark St DEN/PKHD G31 79 M4
Commerce St GBLS G5 4 D9
Commercial Rd BRHD/NEIL G78 92 C6
GBLS G5 79 K5
Commoncraig Pl
GRNKW/INVK PA16 32 E5
Common Gn HMLTN ML3 119 L6
Commonhead Av AIRDRIE ML6 66 F8
Commonhead La AIRDRIE ML6 66 F8
Commonhead Rd ESTRH G34 82 D2
Commonhead St AIRDRIE ML6 66 F8
Commonside St AIRDRIE ML6 66 F8
Commore Av BRHD/NEIL G78 92 D8
Commore Dr KNTSWD G13 59 G2
Community Av BLSH ML4 100 A7
Community Pl BLSH ML4 100 B6
Community Rd BLSH ML4 99 M7
Comrie Crs HMLTN ML3 118 D7
Comrie Rd STPS/GTHM/RID G33 63 J5
Comrie St CAR/SHTL G32 81 H7
Cona St GIF/THBK G46 93 L5
Condor Gln MTHW ML1 100 E2
Condorrat Ring Rd CUMB G67 48 A3
Condorrat Rd AIRDRIE ML6 66 D2
CUMB G67 48 B5
Congress Rd KVGV G3 78 D3
Congress Wy KVGV G3 78 E3
Conifer Pl KKNTL G66 45 H4
Conisborough Cl ESTRH G34 82 A1
Conisborough Rd ESTRH G34 63 M8
Coniston EKILS G75 126 C5
Coniston Crs HMLTN ML3 129 J4
Coniston Dr BLSH ML4 100 B6
Conistone Crs
BAIL/MDB/MHD G69 81 M6
Connal St DMNK/BRGTN G40 80 B7
Connell Ct KBRN KA25 124 D4
Connell Crs MLNGV G62 42 C1
Conniston St CAR/SHTL G32 80 E3
Connor Rd BRHD/NEIL G78 92 B6
Connor St AIRDRIE ML6 67 L8
Conon Av BSDN G61 41 K6
Conservation Pl WISHAW ML2 122 B8
Consett La STPS/GTHM/RID G33 81 J2
Consett St STPS/GTHM/RID G33 81 J2
Constantine Rd MTHW ML1 100 C8
Constarry Rd KSYTH G65 29 M6
Consul Wy MTHW ML1 100 C8
Container Wy GRNK PA15 6 D2
Contin Pl MRYH/FIRH G20 60 D5
Cook Rd ALEX/LLW G83 13 M2
Cook St GBLS G5 79 G5
Coolgardie Pl EKILS G75 2 B9
Cooperage Ct SCOT G14 58 D3
Cooperage Yd LOCHW PA12 109 J3
Co-operative Ter JNSTN PA5 74 A7
Cooper Av CARLUKE ML8 133 G6
Copenhagen Av EKILS G75 127 H4
Copland Pl GOV/IBX G51 78 B4
Copland Qd GOV/IBX G51 78 B4
Copland Rd GOV/IBX G51 78 B5
Coplaw St GVH/MTFL G42 79 G7
Copperfield La
UD/BTH/TAN G71 99 G3
Copperwood Ct HMLTN ML3 119 H5
Copperwood Crs HMLTN ML3 119 H5
Copperwood Wynd
HMLTN ML3 119 H5
Coralmount Gdns KKNTL G66 45 L3
Corbett Ct CAR/SHTL G32 80 F7
Corbett St CAR/SHTL G32 81 G7
Corbie Pl MLNGV G62 23 L7
Cordale Av DMBTN G82 13 K8
Cordiner La LNPK/KPK G44 95 H3
Cordiner St LNPK/KPK G44 95 H3
Corkerhill Gdns
CARD/HILL/MSPK G52 77 L5
Corkerhill Pl
CARD/HILL/MSPK G52 77 K7
Corkerhill Rd PLK/PH/NH G53 77 K8
Corlaich Av GVH/MTFL G42 95 L3
Corlaich Dr GVH/MTFL G42 95 L3
Corless Ct UD/BTH/TAN G71 99 G5
Corlic St GRNK PA15 7 H9
Cormack Av BSHPBGS G64 44 C1
Cormorant Av
CRG/CRSL/HOU PA6 73 K2
Cornaig Rd PLK/PH/NH G53 93 H1
Cornalee Gdns PLK/PH/NH G53 93 G1
Cornalee Pl PLK/PH/NH G53 93 H2
Cornalee Rd PLK/PH/NH G53 93 H1
Cornelian Ter BLSH ML4 100 A5
Cornelia St MTHW ML1 100 B8
Cornhaddock St GRNK PA15 16 D5
Cornhill Dr CTBR ML5 83 M2
Cornhill St SPRGB/BLRNK G21 62 A5
Cornmill Ct CLYDBK G81 40 A3
Cornock Crs CLYDBK G81 40 B6
Cornock St CLYDBK G81 40 B6
Cornsilloch Brae LRKH ML9 131 J6
Corn St COWCAD G4 4 D1
Cornwall Av RUTH G73 96 D5
Cornwall St EKILN G74 2 E6
PLKSD/SHW G41 78 D5
Cornwall St South
PLKSD/SHW G41 78 D6
Coronation Ct MTHW ML1 100 F5
Coronation Pl
BAIL/MDB/MHD G69 64 E3
Coronation Rd MTHW ML1 100 F5
Coronation St WISHAW ML2 122 D6
Coronation Wy BSDN G61 41 M7
Corpach Pl ESTRH G34 82 D1
Corra Linn HMLTN ML3 119 G7
Corran Av NMRNS G77 113 J3
Corran St STPS/GTHM/RID G33 80 F2
Correen Gdns BSDN G61 41 H2
Corrie Brae KSYTH G65 29 J1
Corrie Ct HMLTN ML3 118 F8
Corrie Dr MTHW ML1 120 B2
PSLY PA1 76 E5
Corrie Gdns EKILS G75 126 E6
Corrie Gv LNPK/KPK G44 94 F6
Corrie Pl HBR/GL G84 10 F4
KKNTL G66 45 L6
Corrie Rd KSYTH G65 29 J1
Corrie Vw BALLOCH G68 47 M2
Corrie Wy LRKH ML9 130 D7
Corrour Rd NMRNS G77 113 J3
PLKSW/MSWD G43 94 D3
Corsebar Av PSLYS PA2 75 J8
Corsebar Crs PSLYS PA2 91 J1
Corsebar Dr PSLYS PA2 75 J8
Corsebar La PSLYS PA2 91 H1
Corsebar Rd PSLYS PA2 91 H1
Corsebar Wy PSLYS PA2 8 D8
Corse Dr BRHD/NEIL G78 92 B5
Corsefield Rd LOCHW PA12 108 E3
Corseford Av JNSTN PA5 89 J2
Corsehill Pl ESTRH G34 82 C2
Corsehill St ESTRH G34 82 C2
Corselet Rd PLK/PH/NH G53 93 G8
Corse Rd CARD/HILL/MSPK G52 76 E3
Corsewall Av CAR/SHTL G32 81 L7
Corsewall St CTBR ML5 83 L3
Corsford Dr PLK/PH/NH G53 93 J3
Corsliehill Rd
CRG/CRSL/HOU PA6 54 D3
Corsock Av HMLTN ML3 118 E8
Corsock St DEN/PKHD G31 80 B3
Corston St STPS/GTHM/RID G33 80 D2
Cortachy Pl BSHPBGS G64 62 D1
Cortmalaw Cl
STPS/GTHM/RID G33 62 E3
Cortmalaw Rd
STPS/GTHM/RID G33 62 E3
Coruisk Dr
CRMNK/CLK/EAG G76 114 D2
Corunna Ct CARLUKE ML8 133 K8
Corunna St KVGV G3 78 E2
Coshneuk Rd
STPS/GTHM/RID G33 63 H5
Cosy Neuk LRKH ML9 130 E8
Cottar St MRYH/FIRH G20 60 E3
Cotton Av PSLYN/LNWD PA3 74 B5
Cotton St DMNK/BRGTN G40 79 M8
PSLY PA1 9 J5
Cotton V MTHW ML1 121 L1
Coulin Gdns PPK/MIL G22 61 K6
Coulport Pl HBR/GL G84 10 B5
Coulter Av CTBR ML5 83 M2
WISHAW ML2 122 C2
Countess Ga UD/BTH/TAN G71 98 E7
County Av BLTYR/CAMB G72 96 D3
County Dr LNK/LMHG ML11 137 J6
County Pl PSLY PA1 9 H4
County Sq PSLY PA1 9 H4
Couper Pl COWCAD G4 5 H3
Couper St COWCAD G4 5 H3
Coursington Crs MTHW ML1 121 G2
Coursington Gdns MTHW ML1 120 F2
Coursington Pl MTHW ML1 120 F2
Coursington Rd MTHW ML1 120 E2
Courthill BSDN G61 41 K3
Courthill Av LNPK/KPK G44 95 H5
Courthill Crs KSYTH G65 29 L2
Courtrai Av HBR/GL G84 10 B5
Court Rd PGL PA14 34 C1
Court St LARGS KA30 106 E4
Coustonholm Rd
PLKSW/MSWD G43 94 D3
Couther Qd AIRDRIE ML6 66 F7
Covanburn Av HMLTN ML3 129 M1
Cove Crs SHOTTS ML7 104 E3
Covenant Crs LRKH ML9 130 D7
Covenanter Rd SHOTTS ML7 71 K7
Covenanters Wy WISHAW ML2 131 L3
Covenant Pl WISHAW ML2 121 J7
Coventry Dr DEN/PKHD G31 80 B2
Cove Pl HBR/GL G84 10 B5
Cove Rd GRK PA19 15 M2
Cowal Crs GRK PA19 15 H3
KKNTL G66 46 B1
Cowal Dr PSLYN/LNWD PA3 74 A5
Cowal Rd MRYH/FIRH G20 60 C3
Cowal St MRYH/FIRH G20 60 C3
Cowal Vw GRK PA19 15 H3
Cowan Crs BRHD/NEIL G78 92 D7
Cowan La KVD/HLHD G12 60 E8
Cowan Rd BALLOCH G68 30 C7
Cowan St KVD/HLHD G12 60 E8
Cowan Wilson Av
BLTYR/CAMB G72 118 D2
Cowan Wynd
UD/BTH/TAN G71 99 G2
WISHAW ML2 131 L2
Cowcaddens Rd COWCAD G4 4 D3
Cowcaddens St CGLW G2 4 E4
Cowdenhill Circ KNTSWD G13 59 K1
Cowdenhill Pl KNTSWD G13 59 K1
Cowdenhill Rd KNTSWD G13 59 K1
Cowden St GOV/IBX G51 77 K2
Cowdray Crs RNFRW PA4 58 D6
Cowgate KKNTL G66 45 J2
Cowglen Rd PLK/PH/NH G53 93 J2
Cowlairs Rd SPRGB/BLRNK G21 61 L6
Coxdale Av KKNTL G66 45 H2
Coxhill St SPRGB/BLRNK G21 61 K7
Coxton Pl STPS/GTHM/RID G33 81 K1
Coylton Crs HMLTN ML3 128 E1
Coylton Rd PLKSW/MSWD G43 94 F5
Crabb Qd MTHW ML1 100 C8
Cragdale EKILN G74 2 A2
Craggan Dr SCOT G14 58 F3
Crags Av PSLYS PA2 91 M1
Crags Crs PSLYS PA2 75 M8
Crags Rd PSLYS PA2 91 M1
Cragwell Pk
CRMNK/CLK/EAG G76 115 L3
Craigallian Av BLTYR/CAMB G72 97 K7
MLNGV G62 24 A7
Craiganour La
PLKSW/MSWD G43 94 C4
Craigard Pl RUTH G73 96 D7
Craigash Qd MLNGV G62 23 L7
Craigash Rd MLNGV G62 23 L7
Craig Av ALEX/LLW G83 13 H3
Craigbank Dr PLK/PH/NH G53 93 G3
Craigbarnet Av BSHPBGS G64 44 A2
Craigbarnet Crs
STPS/GTHM/RID G33 63 H6
Craigbarnet Rd MLNGV G62 23 K7
Craigbet Av BRWEIR PA11 53 L8
Craigbet Crs BRWEIR PA11 53 L8
Craigbet Pl BRWEIR PA11 53 L8
Craigbo Av SMSTN G23 60 D1
Craigbog Av JNSTN PA5 89 K2
Craigbo Rd SMSTN G23 60 D1
Craigbo St SMSTN G23 60 D1
Craigburn Av
CRG/CRSL/HOU PA6 73 L3
Craigburn Crs
CRG/CRSL/HOU PA6 73 K3
Craigburn Pl
CRG/CRSL/HOU PA6 73 L3
Craigburn St HMLTN ML3 129 K2
Craigdhu Av AIRDRIE ML6 85 L2
MLNGV G62 23 M8
Craigdhu Rd BSDN G61 41 K1
MLNGV G62 23 L8
Craigdonald Pl JNSTN PA5 73 M7
Craigellan Rd
PLKSW/MSWD G43 94 D4
Craigelvan Av CUMB G67 47 M4
Craigelvan Ct CUMB G67 47 M4
Craigelvan Dr CUMB G67 47 M4
Craigelvan Gdns CUMB G67 47 M4
Craigelvan Gv CUMB G67 47 M4
Craigelvan Pl CUMB G67 47 M4
Craigelvan Vw CUMB G67 47 M4
Craigenbay Crs KKNTL G66 45 L5
Craigenbay Rd KKNTL G66 45 K6
Craigenbay St
SPRGB/BLRNK G21 62 B6
Craigend Crs MLNGV G62 23 M7
Craigend Dr CTBR ML5 83 J6
Craigend Dr West MLNGV G62 23 L7
Craigendmuir Rd
STPS/GTHM/RID G33 63 L6
Craigendmuir St
STPS/GTHM/RID G33 62 D8
Craigendon Ov PSLYS PA2 91 J4
Craigendon Rd PSLYS PA2 91 J4
Craigendoran Av HBR/GL G84 10 F7
Craigend Pl KNTSWD G13 59 L3
Craigend Rd CUMB G67 47 M5
Craigends Av BRWEIR PA11 53 L7
Craigends Ct KSYTH G65 29 L2
Craigends Dr KLBCH PA10 73 H7
Craigends Pl BRWEIR PA11 53 L7
Craigends Rd
CRG/CRSL/HOU PA6 73 L2
GLGNK KA14 124 D7
Craigend St KNTSWD G13 59 L3
Craigend Vw CUMB G67 47 M5
Craigenfeoch Av JNSTN PA5 89 K1
Craigens Rd AIRDRIE ML6 85 M3
Craigfaulds Av PSLYS PA2 75 H8
Craigfell Ct HMLTN ML3 118 E8
Craigflower Gdns
PLK/PH/NH G53 93 G5
Craigflower Rd
PLK/PH/NH G53 93 G5
Craig Gdns NMRNS G77 113 J5
Craighalbert Rd BALLOCH G68 30 C6
Craighalbert Wy BALLOCH G68 30 C5
Craighall Qd BRHD/NEIL G78 111 K4
Craighall Rd COWCAD G4 4 E1
Craighaw St CLYDBK G81 40 D1
Craighead Av
STPS/GTHM/RID G33 62 D7
Craighead Dr MLNGV G62 23 K7
Craighead Rd BSHPTN PA7 38 B8
KKNTL G66 27 J4
Craighead St AIRDRIE ML6 85 L1
Craighead Wy BRHD/NEIL G78 92 B7
Craig Hl EKILS G75 126 F3
Craighill Dr
CRMNK/CLK/EAG G76 114 D4
Craighill Gv
CRMNK/CLK/EAG G76 114 D4
Craighill Vw BTHG/ARM EH48 71 L1
Craighirst Dr CLYDBK G81 40 A2
Craighirst Rd MLNGV G62 23 K7
Craighlaw Av
CRMNK/CLK/EAG G76 114 D8
Craighlaw Dr
CRMNK/CLK/EAG G76 114 D8
Craigholme
CRG/CRSL/HOU PA6 55 K8
Craighouse St
STPS/GTHM/RID G33 81 G1
Craighton Gdns KKNTL G66 26 F2
Craighurst Rd MLNGV G62 23 K7
Craigiebar Dr PSLYS PA2 91 J2
Craigieburn Gdns
MRYH/FIRH G20 60 B2
Craigieburn Rd CUMB G67 30 F8
Craigie Dr NMRNS G77 113 L6
Craigiehall Av ERSK PA8 57 G3
Craigiehall Crs ERSK PA8 57 G3
Craigiehall Pl GOV/IBX G51 78 D4
Craigiehall St GOV/IBX G51 78 D4
Craigiehall Wy ERSK PA8 57 H3
Craigieknowes St GRNK PA15 7 K8
Craigielea Crs MLNGV G62 23 L7
Craigielea Dr PSLYN/LNWD PA3 8 C2
Craigielea Pk RNFRW PA4 58 C6
Craigielea Rd CLYDBK G81 39 M3
RNFRW PA4 58 C6
Craigielea St DEN/PKHD G31 80 A2
Craigielinn Av PSLYS PA2 91 H4
Craigie Pk KKNTL G66 45 L5
Craigie Pl CTBR ML5 83 L5
Craigie St GVH/MTFL G42 79 G8
Craigievar Pl NMRNS G77 113 H4
Craigievar St
STPS/GTHM/RID G33 63 L8
Craiginn Ct BTHG/ARM EH48 71 K1
Craiginn Ter BTHG/ARM EH48 71 L1
Craiglea Pl AIRDRIE ML6 85 J1
Craiglea Ter AIRDRIE ML6 67 M6
Craiglee EKILS G75 127 H6
Craigleith St CAR/SHTL G32 80 E4
Craiglinn BALLOCH G68 30 A7
Craiglinn Park Rd BALLOCH G68 30 A8
Craiglockhart Dr
STPS/GTHM/RID G33 63 K8
Craiglockhart Pl
STPS/GTHM/RID G33 63 K8
Craiglockhart St
STPS/GTHM/RID G33 81 K1
Craiglomond Gdns
ALEX/LLW G83 13 J2
Craiglynn Gdns ALEX/LLW G83 13 L2
Craigmaddie Gdns
BSHPBGS G64 44 A2
Craigmaddie Rd MLNGV G62 24 F5
Craigmaddie Terrace La
KVGV G3 78 E1
Craigmarloch Av BSHPBGS G64 44 B2
Craigmillar Av MLNGV G62 24 B8
Craigmillar Pl
BAIL/MDB/MHD G69 64 E5
Craigmillar Rd GVH/MTFL G42 95 G3
Craigmochan Av AIRDRIE ML6 66 F7
Craigmont Dr MRYH/FIRH G20 60 E5
Craigmont St MRYH/FIRH G20 60 E4
Craigmore Rd BSDN G61 41 H2
Craigmore St DEN/PKHD G31 80 C4
Craigmount Av PSLYS PA2 91 J4
Craigmuir Crs
CARD/HILL/MSPK G52 76 F3
Craigmuir Gdns
BLTYR/CAMB G72 118 B4
Craigmuir Pl
CARD/HILL/MSPK G52 76 E3
Craigmuir Rd
BLTYR/CAMB G72 118 B4
CARD/HILL/MSPK G52 76 E3
Craigmuschat Rd GRK PA19 15 L2
Craigneil St
STPS/GTHM/RID G33 63 L8
Craigneith Ct EKILN G74 117 L6
Craignethan Rd CARLUKE ML8 133 G6
GIF/THBK G46 114 A3
Craigneuk Av AIRDRIE ML6 85 J3
Craigneuk Rd MTHW ML1 101 J8
Craigneuk St MTHW ML1 121 H4
Craignure Crs AIRDRIE ML6 85 L2
Craignure Rd RUTH G73 96 B7
Craigpark DEN/PKHD G31 80 A3
Craigpark Dr DEN/PKHD G31 80 A3
Craigpark St CLYDBK G81 40 D2
Craigpark Wy UD/BTH/TAN G71 99 G3
Craig Pl NMRNS G77 113 G4
Craig Rd BRHD/NEIL G78 111 K4
LNPK/KPK G44 95 G5
PSLYN/LNWD PA3 73 M3
Craigs Av CLYDBK G81 40 C3
Craigsheen Av
CRMNK/CLK/EAG G76 115 K3
Craigside Ct BALLOCH G68 47 M3
Craigside Rd BALLOCH G68 47 M3
Craigson Pl AIRDRIE ML6 85 M3
The Craigs GRNKW/INVK PA16 16 C2
Craigstone Vw KSYTH G65 29 M2
Craigston Rd JNSTN PA5 73 M8
Craig St AIRDRIE ML6 84 F2
BLTYR/CAMB G72 118 E3
BTHG/ARM EH48 71 L1
CTBR ML5 83 M6
Craigton Av BRHD/NEIL G78 92 E8
MLNGV G62 23 M7
Craigton Crs NMRNS G77 113 H4
Craigton Dr BRHD/NEIL G78 92 E8
GOV/IBX G51 77 M3
NMRNS G77 113 J4
Craigton Gdns MLNGV G62 23 M6
Craigton Pl BLTYR/CAMB G72 118 D1
GOV/IBX G51 77 L3
Craigton Rd GOV/IBX G51 77 M3
KBRN KA25 124 D5
MLNGV G62 23 M7
NMRNS G77 112 B6
Craigton St CLYDBK G81 40 D1
Craigvale Crs AIRDRIE ML6 85 L2
Craigvicar Gdns CAR/SHTL G32 81 K5
Craigview Av JNSTN PA5 89 K1
Craigview Rd MTHW ML1 120 F1
Craigview Ter JNSTN PA5 89 K1
Craigwell Av RUTH G73 96 D4
Crail Cl BLTYR/CAMB G72 118 D7
Crail St DEN/PKHD G31 80 D5
Crammond Av CTBR ML5 83 J6
Cramond Av RNFRW PA4 58 E7
Cramond St GBLS G5 79 K8
Cramond Ter CAR/SHTL G32 81 H5
Cranborne Rd KVD/HLHD G12 60 A5
Cranbrooke Dr MRYH/FIRH G20 60 D3
Crannog Rd DMBTN G82 37 L1
Cranston St KVGV G3 78 F3
Cranworth La KVD/HLHD G12 60 D7
Cranworth St KVD/HLHD G12 60 D7
Crarae Av BSDN G61 41 L7
Crarea Pl NMRNS G77 113 G4
Crathes Ct LNPK/KPK G44 94 E6
Crathie Dr AIRDRIE ML6 66 F5
PTCK G11 60 A8
Crathie Pl NMRNS G77 114 B6
Crathie Qd WISHAW ML2 122 B4
Crawberry Rd GRNK PA15 6 F9
Crawford Av KKNTL G66 45 L7
Crawford Crs
BLTYR/CAMB G72 118 D2
UD/BTH/TAN G71 98 E3
Crawford Dr DRUM G15 41 G8
EKILN G74 3 M3
HBR/GL G84 10 E4
Crawford Gdns MTHW ML1 120 C4
Crawford Hl EKILN G74 3 M3
Crawford Rd
CRG/CRSL/HOU PA6 73 K1
MLNGV G62 23 M5
Crawford St HMLTN ML3 119 G5
LARGS KA30 106 E5
MTHW ML1 120 D3
PGL PA14 18 C8
PTCK G11 60 A8
Crawfurd Av RUTH G73 96 B5
Crawfurd Dr PSLYN/LNWD PA3 8 A2
Crawfurd Gdns RUTH G73 96 C6
Crawfurd Rd RUTH G73 96 B6
Crawfurd St GRNK PA15 6 C2
Crawfurds Vw LOCHW PA12 109 K2
Crawhin Gdns GRNK PA15 16 D6
Craw Pl LOCHW PA12 109 J3
Crawriggs Av KKNTL G66 45 K4
Craw Rd PSLYS PA2 8 D7
Creamery Rd WISHAW ML2 122 C8
Crebar Dr BRHD/NEIL G78 92 C7
Crebar St GIF/THBK G46 93 L5
Credon Dr AIRDRIE ML6 85 G4
Credon Gdns RUTH G73 96 C6
Cree Av BSHPBGS G64 62 D1
Cree Gdns CAR/SHTL G32 80 F5
Cree Pl EKILS G75 126 E1
Creighton Gv EKILN G74 2 F5
Creran Ct HMLTN ML3 129 G1
Creran Dr RNFRW PA4 58 B5
Crescent Rd KNTSWD G13 59 H4
Crescent St GRNK PA15 7 G6
The Crescent CLYDBK G81 39 L7
CRMNK/CLK/EAG G76 115 G5
SKLM PA17 50 C5
Cressdale Ct CSMK G45 95 K8
Cressdale Dr CSMK G45 95 K8
Cresswell Gv NMRNS G77 113 K6
Cresswell La KVD/HLHD G12 60 D7
Cresswell Pl NMRNS G77 113 L7
Cresswell St KVD/HLHD G12 60 D7
Cressy St GOV/IBX G51 77 L1
Crest Av KNTSWD G13 59 H1
Crestlea Av PSLYS PA2 91 L2
Creveul Ct ALEX/LLW G83 13 K5
Crichton St CTBR ML5 84 A1
SPRGB/BLRNK G21 61 L6
Cricketfield La
CRG/CRSL/HOU PA6 55 H7
Crieff Av AIRDRIE ML6 85 K8
Criffell Gdns CAR/SHTL G32 81 K7
Criffell Rd CAR/SHTL G32 81 K6
Crighton Wynd BLSH ML4 99 J5
Crimea St CGLW G2 4 B7
Crimond Pl KSYTH G65 29 H1
Crinan Crs CTBR ML5 83 K1
Crinan Gdns BSHPBGS G64 62 C1
Crinan Pl BLSH ML4 100 B5
Crinan St DEN/PKHD G31 80 B2
Crindledyke Crs WISHAW ML2 123 G4
Cripps Av CLYDBK G81 40 D8
Crisswell Cl GRNKW/INVK PA16 15 J7
Croftbank Av
UD/BTH/TAN G71 119 H1
Croftbank Crs
UD/BTH/TAN G71 98 F4
Croftbank Ga
UD/BTH/TAN G71 119 H1
Croftbank St
SPRGB/BLRNK G21 61 M6
Croftburn Dr LNPK/KPK G44 95 K6
Croftcot Av BLSH ML4 99 M7
Croftcroighn Rd
STPS/GTHM/RID G33 81 H1
Croftend Av LNPK/KPK G44 95 L4
Croftend La LNPK/KPK G44 95 M5
Croftfoot Crs CSMK G45 96 A6
Croftfoot Dr CSMK G45 95 M6
Croftfoot Pl
BAIL/MDB/MHD G69 65 G4
Croftfoot Qd CSMK G45 95 L6
Croftfoot Rd CSMK G45 95 L6
Croftfoot St CSMK G45 96 A6
Croftfoot Ter CSMK G45 95 M6
Crofthead Crs BLSH ML4 99 M7
Crofthead Dr KKNTL G66 26 C1
Crofthead Pl BLSH ML4 99 M7
NMRNS G77 113 L6
Crofthead St UD/BTH/TAN G71 98 F5
Crofthill Av UD/BTH/TAN G71 98 F4
Crofthill Rd LNPK/KPK G44 95 L6
Crofthouse Dr LNPK/KPK G44 95 L6
Croftmont Av LNPK/KPK G44 95 L6
Croftmoraig Av
BAIL/MDB/MHD G69 47 G6
Crofton Av LNPK/KPK G44 95 K6
Croftpark Av LNPK/KPK G44 95 L5
Croftpark Crs
BLTYR/CAMB G72 118 E4
Croftpark Rd CLYDBK G81 40 B2
Croftpark St BLSH ML4 100 A3
Croft Pl LRKH ML9 130 B6
Croft Rd BLTYR/CAMB G72 97 H5
EKILS G75 2 E9
LRKH ML9 130 B6
Croftside Av LNPK/KPK G44 95 L6
Croftspar Av CAR/SHTL G32 81 K4
Croftspar Ct CAR/SHTL G32 81 K4
Croftspar Dr CAR/SHTL G32 81 J4
Croftspar Ga CAR/SHTL G32 81 K4
Croftspar Gv CAR/SHTL G32 81 J4
Croftspar Pl CAR/SHTL G32 81 J4
Croft St ALEX/LLW G83 13 L7
Croft Wy RNFRW PA4 58 E8
Croftwood Av LNPK/KPK G44 95 K6
Croftwood Rd HMLTN ML3 129 K1
Croft Wynd UD/BTH/TAN G71 99 G4
Crogal Crs AIRDRIE ML6 85 K7
Cromalt Av EKILS G75 126 E6
Cromalt Crs BSDN G61 41 J1
Cromarty Av BSHPBGS G64 44 D8
PLKSW/MSWD G43 94 F3
Cromarty Crs BSDN G61 41 M2
Cromarty Gdns
CRMNK/CLK/EAG G76 115 G1
Cromarty Pl
BAIL/MDB/MHD G69 64 D1
EKILN G74 117 J7
Cromarty Rd AIRDRIE ML6 84 F5
Crombie Gdns
BAIL/MDB/MHD G69 81 M7
Cromdale Rd PGL PA14 34 F4
Cromdale St GOV/IBX G51 77 L3
Cromdale Wy MTHW ML1 101 G7
Cromer Gdns MRYH/FIRH G20 60 F5
Cromlix Gv AIRDRIE ML6 68 B6
Crompton Av LNPK/KPK G44 95 H5
Cromptons Gv PSLY PA1 8 A7
Cromwell La COWCAD G4 4 B1
Cromwell St MRYH/FIRH G20 4 B1
Crona Dr HMLTN ML3 118 E6
Cronberry Qd
CARD/HILL/MSPK G52 76 F6
Cronberry Ter
CARD/HILL/MSPK G52 76 F6
Cronin Pl BLSH ML4 100 B2
Cronulla Pl KSYTH G65 29 M2
Crookedshields Rd EKILN G74 117 H3
Crookfur Rd NMRNS G77 113 K4
Crookhill Dr LOCHW PA12 109 J2
Crookhill Gdns LOCHW PA12 109 J2
Crookston Av
CARD/HILL/MSPK G52 77 G5
Crookston Ct
CARD/HILL/MSPK G52 77 G5
Crookston Dr
CARD/HILL/MSPK G52 76 F5
Crookston Gv
CARD/HILL/MSPK G52 77 G5
Crookston Pl
CARD/HILL/MSPK G52 76 F5
Crookston Qd
CARD/HILL/MSPK G52 76 F5
Crookston Rd
CARD/HILL/MSPK G52 76 F6
PLK/PH/NH G53 77 G8
Crookston Ter
CARD/HILL/MSPK G52 77 G5
Crosbie Dr PSLYS PA2 90 E3
Crosbie La MRYH/FIRH G20 60 C2
Crosbie St MRYH/FIRH G20 60 C2
Crosbie Wd PSLYS PA2 91 H1
Cross BEITH KA15 125 K5
Crossan Dr KKNTL G66 26 A1
Cross Arthurlie St
BRHD/NEIL G78 92 B6
Crossbank Av GVH/MTFL G42 95 L1
Crossbank Dr GVH/MTFL G42 95 K1
Crossbank Rd GVH/MTFL G42 95 K1
Crossbank Ter GVH/MTFL G42 95 K1
Crossburn Av MLNGV G62 23 M8
Crossclyde Vw CARLUKE ML8 134 C8
Crossdykes KKNTL G66 46 A3
Crossflat Crs PSLY PA1 9 L4
Crossford Dr SMSTN G23 60 E1
Cross Gates BLSH ML4 100 A5
Crossgates St LRKH ML9 130 B5
Crosshill Av GVH/MTFL G42 95 H1
KKNTL G66 45 K4

Crosshill Dr MTHW ML1 102 B6
RUTH G73 96 B4
Crosshill Pl PGL PA14 34 F3
Crosshill Rd BSHPBGS G64 44 D5
KKNTL G66 45 J7
KLMCLM PA13 34 F5
Crosshill St AIRDRIE ML6 84 F2
CTBR ML5 83 J6
KKNTL G66 26 D1
MTHW ML1 120 F3
Crosshouse Rd EKILS G75 126 C5
Crosslaw Av LNK/LMHG ML11 137 J6
Crosslea Gdns
CRG/CRSL/HOU PA6 73 H1
Crosslee Crs
CRG/CRSL/HOU PA6 73 J1
Crosslee Pk CRG/CRSL/HOU PA6 73 J2
Crosslee Rd BRWEIR PA11 72 F4
Crosslees Dr GIF/THBK G46 93 M6
Crosslees Pk GIF/THBK G46 93 M6
Crosslees Rd GIF/THBK G46 93 M7
Crosslee St
CARD/HILL/MSPK G52 77 K4
Crosslet Ct DMBTN G82 21 H7
Crosslet Pl DMBTN G82 21 H7
Crosslet Rd DMBTN G82 21 G7
Crossloan Rd GOV/IBX G51 77 M2
Crossloan Ter GOV/IBX G51 77 M2
Crossmill Av BRHD/NEIL G78 92 D5
Crossmyloof Gdns
PLKSD/SHW G41 94 D1
Crosspoint Dr SMSTN G23 60 E1
Cross Rd PSLYS PA2 8 B9
Cross Shore St GRNK PA15 6 E4
Cross Stone Pl MTHW ML1 120 F3
Cross St CAR/SHTL G32 97 J1
PSLY PA1 8 D5
Crosstobs Rd PLK/PH/NH G53 77 G8
Crossveggate MLNGV G62 42 B1
Crossview Av
BAIL/MDB/MHD G69 82 D5
Crossview Pl
BAIL/MDB/MHD G69 82 D5
Crossways
CRG/CRSL/HOU PA6 55 K8
Crovie Rd PLK/PH/NH G53 93 G2
Crow Av MTHW ML1 101 H4
Crowflats Rd UD/BTH/TAN G71 98 E4
Crowflat Vw UD/BTH/TAN G71 99 J1
Crowhill Crs AIRDRIE ML6 66 F7
Crowhill Dr
STPS/GTHM/RID G33 81 L4
Crowhill Rd BSHPBGS G64 61 M2
Crowhill St PPK/MIL G22 61 J4
Crow La KNTSWD G13 59 M4
Crowlin Crs
STPS/GTHM/RID G33 81 H2
Crown Av CLYDBK G81 40 A6
Crown Circ KVD/HLHD G12 60 C7
Crown Gdns KVD/HLHD G12 60 C7
Crownhall Pl CAR/SHTL G32 81 J5
Crownhall Rd CAR/SHTL G32 81 J5
Crownhill Ct AIRDRIE ML6 66 E6
Crownpoint Rd DEN/PKHD G31 80 A5
DMNK/BRGTN G40 79 M5
Crown Rd North
KVD/HLHD G12 60 B7
Crown Rd South
KVD/HLHD G12 60 C7
Crown St AIRDRIE ML6 85 H6
BAIL/MDB/MHD G69 81 M7
CTBR ML5 84 C2
GBLS G5 79 J6
GRNK PA15 6 D4
Crown Ter KVD/HLHD G12 60 B7
Crow Rd KKNTL G66 26 D1
PTCK G11 59 M5
Crow-wood Crs AIRDRIE ML6 85 H7
Crowwood Dr AIRDRIE ML6 85 K2
Crow-wood Rd AIRDRIE ML6 85 H7
Crow Wood Rd
BAIL/MDB/MHD G69 64 B3
Croy EKILN G74 2 D2
Croy Av NMRNS G77 114 A5
Croy Pl SPRGB/BLRNK G21 62 C5
Croy Rd CTBR ML5 83 L6
SPRGB/BLRNK G21 62 C5
Cruachan Av PSLYS PA2 91 L2
RNFRW PA4 58 C8
Cruachan Dr BRHD/NEIL G78 92 C8
NMRNS G77 113 M6
Cruachan Rd BSDN G61 41 H2
RUTH G73 96 D7
Cruachan St GIF/THBK G46 93 M5
Cruachan Wy BRHD/NEIL G78 92 C8
Cruden St GOV/IBX G51 77 M3
Crum Av GIF/THBK G46 94 A7
Crummock Gdns BEITH KA15 125 L4
Crummock St BEITH KA15 125 L4
Crusader Av KNTSWD G13 41 K8
Cubie St DMNK/BRGTN G40 79 M5
Cuckoo Wy MTHW ML1 101 H4
Cuff Crs BEITH KA15 125 J6
Cuilhill Rd BAIL/MDB/MHD G69 83 G4
Cuillin Pl AIRDRIE ML6 85 M8
Cuillins Av PGL PA14 34 F4
The Cuillins
BAIL/MDB/MHD G69 47 G6
UD/BTH/TAN G71 98 E1
Cuillin Wy BRHD/NEIL G78 92 C7
Cuilmuir Ter KSYTH G65 29 M6
Cuilmuir Vw KSYTH G65 29 M6
Culbin Dr KNTSWD G13 58 F1
Cullen Crs GRNKW/INVK PA16 32 E6
Cullen La EKILS G75 2 D9
Cullen Pl GRNKW/INVK PA16 32 E6
UD/BTH/TAN G71 99 G2
Cullen Rd EKILS G75 2 D9
MTHW ML1 120 C4
Cullen St ALEX/LLW G83 13 H3
CAR/SHTL G32 81 G6
Cullins Rd RUTH G73 96 D7
Cullion Wy MTHW ML1 101 M4
Cullochrig Rd AIRDRIE ML6 48 E7
Culloch Rd BSDN G61 41 J1
Culloden Av BLSH ML4 100 D5
Culloden St DEN/PKHD G31 80 B2
Culrain Gdns CAR/SHTL G32 81 G5
Culrain St CAR/SHTL G32 81 G5
Culross Hl EKILN G74 2 C5
Culross Pl CTBR ML5 83 M3
EKILN G74 2 C5
Culross St CAR/SHTL G32 81 J6
Culross Wy
BAIL/MDB/MHD G69 47 G7
Cult Rd KKNTL G66 45 L6
Cults St GOV/IBX G51 77 M3
Culvain Av BSDN G61 41 J2
Culzean AIRDRIE ML6 66 F4
Culzean Av CTBR ML5 83 L6
Culzean Crs
BAIL/MDB/MHD G69 82 A6
NMRNS G77 114 A5
Culzean Dr CAR/SHTL G32 81 K5
EKILN G74 2 C1
GRK PA19 14 F4
MTHW ML1 101 J6
Culzean Pl EKILN G74 2 C1
Cumberland Av HBR/GL G84 10 A4
Cumberland Pl CTBR ML5 83 J6
GBLS G5 79 J6
Cumberland Rd
GRNKW/INVK PA16 15 L5
Cumberland St GBLS G5 79 H5
Cumbernauld Rd
BAIL/MDB/MHD G69 47 G8
DEN/PKHD G31 80 C3
Cumbrae EKILN G74 127 M1
Cumbrae Av PGL PA14 35 H3
Cumbrae Ct CLYDBK G81 40 B7
Cumbrae Crs CTBR ML5 84 E4
Cumbrae Crs North
DMBTN G82 20 C5
Cumbrae Crs South
DMBTN G82 20 B5
Cumbrae Dr MTHW ML1 120 C2
Cumbrae Pl CTBR ML5 84 E5
GRK PA19 15 J3
Cumbrae Rd PSLYS PA2 91 L3
RNFRW PA4 58 D8
Cumbrae St
STPS/GTHM/RID G33 81 G2
Cumlodden Dr MRYH/FIRH G20 60 C3
Cumming Dr GVH/MTFL G42 95 H2
Cumnock Dr AIRDRIE ML6 85 G5
BRHD/NEIL G78 92 D8
HMLTN ML3 128 D1
Cumnock Rd
STPS/GTHM/RID G33 62 E4
Cumroch Rd KKNTL G66 26 C1
Cunard St CLYDBK G81 58 B1
Cuninghame Rd KLBCH PA10 73 H7
Cuningair Dr MTHW ML1 120 E5
Cunningham Dr GIF/THBK G46 94 E7
LARGS KA30 106 F6
SHOTTS ML7 71 K7
Cunninghame Rd EKILN G74 2 E4
RUTH G73 96 C2
Cunningham Gdns
CRG/CRSL/HOU PA6 73 K1
Cunningham Rd
CARD/HILL/MSPK G52 76 F1
Cunningham St MTHW ML1 120 D3
Cupar Dr GRNKW/INVK PA16 15 M6
Cuparhead Av CTBR ML5 83 K6
Cuppleton Brae HWWD PA9 88 B8
Curfew Rd KNTSWD G13 41 K8
Curle St SCOT G14 59 L7
Curlew Crs GRNKW/INVK PA16 16 B5
Curlew La GRNKW/INVK PA16 16 B5
Curlew Pl JNSTN PA5 89 J3
Curling Crs GVH/MTFL G42 95 J3
Curlinghall LARGS KA30 106 E6
Curlinghaugh Crs
WISHAW ML2 122 C6
Curlingmire EKILS G75 127 H4
Curran Av WISHAW ML2 121 L8
Currie Pl MRYH/FIRH G20 60 F5
Currieside Av SHOTTS ML7 104 D5
Currieside Pl SHOTTS ML7 104 D5
Currie St MRYH/FIRH G20 60 E4
Curtis Av LNPK/KPK G44 95 L3
Curzon St MRYH/FIRH G20 60 E4
Customhouse Pl GRNK PA15 6 F4
Custom House Wy GRNK PA15 6 D2
Cuthbertson St
PLKSD/SHW G41 79 G7
Cuthbert St UD/BTH/TAN G71 99 H3
Cuthelton Dr DEN/PKHD G31 80 E6
Cuthelton St DEN/PKHD G31 80 D6
Cuthelton Ter DEN/PKHD G31 80 D6
The Cut UD/BTH/TAN G71 98 F5
Cutty Sark Pl DMBTN G82 37 J1
Cypress Av BEITH KA15 125 L3
BLTYR/CAMB G72 118 C2
UD/BTH/TAN G71 99 H2
Cypress Ct EKILS G75 126 F5
HMLTN ML3 119 L8
KKNTL G66 45 H4
Cypress Crs EKILS G75 126 F5
Cypress Gv
BAIL/MDB/MHD G69 83 G4
BRWEIR PA11 53 M8
Cypress Pl EKILS G75 126 F5
Cypress St PPK/MIL G22 61 K5
Cypress Wy BLTYR/CAMB G72 97 M6
Cyprus Av JNSTN PA5 74 B8
Cyril St PSLY PA1 9 M5

D

Daer Av RNFRW PA4 58 E8
Daer Wy HMLTN ML3 119 G7
Daff Av GRNKW/INVK PA16 32 E4
Daffodil Wy MTHW ML1 120 E1
Dairsie Gdns BSHPBGS G64 62 D2
Dairsie St LNPK/KPK G44 94 F6
Daisybank GLGNK KA14 124 E7
Daisy St GVH/MTFL G42 95 H1
Dakala Ct WISHAW ML2 122 A7
Dalbeattie Braes AIRDRIE ML6 85 L8
Dalbeth Rd CAR/SHTL G32 80 F8
Dalcharn Pl ESTRH G34 82 A1
Dalcraig Crs BLTYR/CAMB G72 118 C1
Dalcross St PTCK G11 60 C8
Dalcruin Gdns
BAIL/MDB/MHD G69 47 G6
Daldowie Av CAR/SHTL G32 81 K7
Daldowie Rd UD/BTH/TAN G71 82 A8
Daldowie St CTBR ML5 83 L7
Dale Av EKILS G75 127 G4
Dale Ct WISHAW ML2 121 J7
Dale Dr MTHW ML1 101 G5
Dale St DMNK/BRGTN G40 79 M6
Daleview Av KVD/HLHD G12 60 B4
Daleview Dr
CRMNK/CLK/EAG G76 114 D4
Daleview Gv
CRMNK/CLK/EAG G76 114 D4
Dale Wy RUTH G73 96 A6
Dalfoil Ct PSLY PA1 76 F5
Dalgarroch Av CLYDBK G81 58 E1
Dalgleish Av CLYDBK G81 39 M4
Dalgraig Crs BLTYR/CAMB G72 98 C8
Dalhousie Gdns BSHPBGS G64 43 M8
Dalhousie La KVGV G3 4 C3
Dalhousie Rd KLBCH PA10 73 H8
Dalhousie St COWCAD G4 4 D3
Dalilea Dr ESTRH G34 82 D1
Dalilea Pl ESTRH G34 82 D1
Dalintober St GBLS G5 4 B9
Dalkeith Av BSHPBGS G64 44 B7
PLKSD/SHW G41 78 B6
Dalkeith Rd BSHPBGS G64 44 B6
Dalmacoulter Rd AIRDRIE ML6 67 H6
Dalmahoy Crs BRWEIR PA11 72 B4
Dalmahoy St CAR/SHTL G32 80 E3
Dalmally St GRNK PA15 17 M7
MRYH/FIRH G20 60 F7
Dalmarnock Ct
DMNK/BRGTN G40 80 B7
Dalmarnock Dr
DMNK/BRGTN G40 79 M6
Dalmarnock Rd
DMNK/BRGTN G40 79 M6
Dalmary Dr PSLY PA1 76 B3
Dalmellington Ct HMLTN ML3 128 D1
Dalmellington Dr EKILN G74 2 D3
PLK/PH/NH G53 93 G1
Dalmellington Rd
PLK/PH/NH G53 77 G8
Dalmeny Av GIF/THBK G46 94 C7
Dalmeny Dr BRHD/NEIL G78 92 A7
Dalmeny Rd HMLTN ML3 119 K8
Dalmeny St GBLS G5 79 L8
Dalmoak Rd GRNK PA15 17 J8
Dalmonach Rd ALEX/LLW G83 13 L6
Dalmore Crs HBR/GL G84 10 A4
MTHW ML1 101 G7
Dalmore Dr AIRDRIE ML6 85 G3
Dalnair Pl MLNGV G62 23 K8
Dalnair St KVGV G3 78 C1
Dalness St CAR/SHTL G32 81 G7
Dalnottar Av OLDK G60 39 H4
Dalnottar Dr OLDK G60 39 H5
Dalnottar Gdns OLDK G60 39 H5
Dalnottar Hill Rd OLDK G60 39 H5
Dalnottar Ter OLDK G60 39 H4
Dalquhurn La DMBTN G82 20 E2
Dalreoch Av
BAIL/MDB/MHD G69 82 C5
Dalreoch Ct DMBTN G82 20 D6
Dalriada Crs MTHW ML1 100 D8
Dalriada Dr BSHPBGS G64 44 C1
Dalriada Rd GRNKW/INVK PA16 15 K7
Dalriada St DMNK/BRGTN G40 80 C6
Dalry Gdns HMLTN ML3 118 D8
Dalrymple Dr CTBR ML5 83 M6
EKILN G74 2 F3
NMRNS G77 114 A6
Dalrymple St GRNK PA15 6 C2
Dalry Pl AIRDRIE ML6 101 L1
Dalry Rd BEITH KA15 125 J6
KBRN KA25 124 C6
LARGS KA30 107 G7
UD/BTH/TAN G71 99 H3
Dalry St CAR/SHTL G32 81 H6
Dalserf Crs GIF/THBK G46 114 B1
Dalserf Gdns DEN/PKHD G31 80 B5
Dalserf Pl DEN/PKHD G31 80 B5
Dalserf St DMNK/BRGTN G40 80 B5
Dalsetter Av DRUM G15 40 F7
Dalsetter Pl DRUM G15 41 G7
Dalshannon Pl CUMB G67 48 A2
Dalshannon Rd CUMB G67 48 B2
Dalshannon Vw CUMB G67 48 A2
Dalsholm Pl MRYH/FIRH G20 60 B2
Dalsholm Rd MRYH/FIRH G20 60 C2
Dalskeith Av PSLYN/LNWD PA3 75 G5
Dalskeith Crs PSLYN/LNWD PA3 75 G5
Dalskeith Rd PSLYN/LNWD PA3 75 G6
Dalswinton Pth ESTRH G34 82 C2
Dalswinton St ESTRH G34 82 C2
Dalton Av CLYDBK G81 40 E8
Dalton Hl HMLTN ML3 118 E8
Dalton St DEN/PKHD G31 80 E5
Dalvait Gdns ALEX/LLW G83 13 K2
Dalvait Rd ALEX/LLW G83 13 K2
Dalveen Ct BRHD/NEIL G78 92 C8
Dalveen Dr UD/BTH/TAN G71 98 E2
Dalveen Qd CTBR ML5 84 D4
Dalveen St CAR/SHTL G32 80 F5
Dalveen Wy RUTH G73 96 C7
Dalwhinnie Av
BLTYR/CAMB G72 98 C8
Daly Gdns BLTYR/CAMB G72 118 D1
Dalzell Av MTHW ML1 121 G5
Dalzell Dr MTHW ML1 121 G6
Dalziel Crs BLTYR/CAMB G72 97 K4
Dalziel Dr PLKSD/SHW G41 78 D7
Dalziel Gv BLTYR/CAMB G72 97 K4
Dalziel Pth BLTYR/CAMB G72 97 K4
Dalziel Rd
CARD/HILL/MSPK G52 76 F1
Dalziel St HMLTN ML3 119 H5
MTHW ML1 120 E2
Dalziel Wy BLTYR/CAMB G72 97 K5
Damshot Crs PLK/PH/NH G53 93 K1
Damshot Rd PLK/PH/NH G53 93 K2
Danby Rd BAIL/MDB/MHD G69 81 M6
Danefield Av LARGS KA30 106 D1
Danes Av SCOT G14 59 J5
Danes Crs SCOT G14 59 H4
Danes Dr SCOT G14 59 J5
Danes La North SCOT G14 59 J5
Danes La South SCOT G14 59 J5
Daniel McLaughlin Pl
KKNTL G66 45 L1
Dargarvel Av PLKSD/SHW G41 78 B6
Dargavel Av BSHPTN PA7 38 B8
Dargavel Rd ERSK PA8 56 D1
Dark Brig Rd CARLUKE ML8 134 B7
Darkwood Ct PSLYN/LNWD PA3 8 A2
Darkwood Crs PSLYN/LNWD PA3 8 A2
Darkwood Dr PSLYN/LNWD PA3 8 A2
Darleith Rd ALEX/LLW G83 13 K4
DMBTN G82 19 G1
Darleith St CAR/SHTL G32 80 F5
Darley Pl HMLTN ML3 129 G2
Darley Rd BALLOCH G68 30 E4
Darluith Rd PSLYN/LNWD PA3 73 L4
Darnaway Av
STPS/GTHM/RID G33 63 K8
Darnaway Dr
STPS/GTHM/RID G33 63 K8
Darnaway St
STPS/GTHM/RID G33 63 K8
Darndaff Rd GRNK PA15 6 F8
Darngaber Gdns HMLTN ML3 129 L7
Darngaber Rd HMLTN ML3 129 L7
Darngavil Rd AIRDRIE ML6 67 L3
Darnick St SPRGB/BLRNK G21 62 A8
Darnley Crs BSHPBGS G64 43 M7
Darnley Gdns PLKSD/SHW G41 78 E8
Darnley Mains Rd
PLK/PH/NH G53 93 J6
Darnley Pl PLKSD/SHW G41 78 E8
Darnley Rd BRHD/NEIL G78 92 E6
PLKSD/SHW G41 78 E8
Darnley St PLKSD/SHW G41 78 F7
Darragh Gn WISHAW ML2 123 G3
Darroch Av GRK PA19 15 L2
Darroch Dr ERSK PA8 38 F7
GRK PA19 15 L2
Darroch Wy CUMB G67 31 G6
Dartford St PPK/MIL G22 61 H7
Dartmouth Av GRK PA19 15 L4
Darvel Crs PSLY PA1 76 D5
Darvel Dr NMRNS G77 114 A5
Darvel Gv BLTYR/CAMB G72 118 D8
Darwin Pl CLYDBK G81 39 K7
Darwin Rd EKILS G75 2 A8
Davaar EKILN G74 127 M1
Davaar Dr CTBR ML5 83 K3
MTHW ML1 100 C7
PSLYS PA2 91 L3
Davaar Pl NMRNS G77 113 J3
Davaar Rd GRNKW/INVK PA16 15 J6
RNFRW PA4 58 D8
Davaar St DMNK/BRGTN G40 80 B6
Dave Barrie Av LRKH ML9 130 B4
Daventry Dr KVD/HLHD G12 60 A5
Davey St GRNKW/INVK PA16 16 B4
David Gray Dr KKNTL G66 46 A1
David Pl BAIL/MDB/MHD G69 81 M6
Davidson Av GLGNK KA14 124 F7
Davidson Crs KSYTH G65 28 F7
Davidson Dr GRK PA19 15 L2
Davidson Pl CAR/SHTL G32 81 J4
Davidson Qd CLYDBK G81 39 M3
Davidson Rd ALEX/LLW G83 13 L3
Davidson St CLYDBK G81 58 E1
CTBR ML5 84 B5
DMNK/BRGTN G40 80 A8
Davidston Pl KKNTL G66 45 M6
David St CTBR ML5 84 C2
DMNK/BRGTN G40 80 A5
SHOTTS ML7 87 H7
Davieland Rd GIF/THBK G46 114 A1
Davie's Acre EKILN G74 115 M6
Davies Dr ALEX/LLW G83 13 K4
Davies Qd MTHW ML1 100 D7
Davington Dr HMLTN ML3 118 D8
Daviot St GOV/IBX G51 77 K3
Dawson Av EKILS G75 126 E1
Dawson Pl COWCAD G4 61 H7
Dawson Rd COWCAD G4 61 H7
Deaconsbank Av GIF/THBK G46 93 K8
Deaconsbank Crs
GIF/THBK G46 93 L8
Deaconsbrook Rd
GIF/THBK G46 93 K8
Deaconsgrange Rd
GIF/THBK G46 93 K8
Deacons Rd KSYTH G65 29 K2
Deacons Vw GIF/THBK G46 93 K8
Dealston Rd BRHD/NEIL G78 92 B5
Deanbank Rd CTBR ML5 83 K3
Deanbrae St UD/BTH/TAN G71 98 F4
Dean Crs BAIL/MDB/MHD G69 64 D1
HMLTN ML3 129 J1
Deanfield Qd
CARD/HILL/MSPK G52 76 F3
Dean Park Av UD/BTH/TAN G71 99 G8
Dean Park Dr BLTYR/CAMB G72 97 K6
Dean Park Rd RNFRW PA4 58 D7
Dean Rd KBRN KA25 124 D3
Deans Av BLTYR/CAMB G72 97 K7
Deanside Rd
CARD/HILL/MSPK G52 77 G1
Deanston Av BRHD/NEIL G78 92 B8
Deanston Dr PLKSD/SHW G41 94 E2
Deanstone Pl CTBR ML5 84 D6
Deanstone Wk CTBR ML5 84 D7
Deanston Gv CTBR ML5 83 L7
Deanston Pk BRHD/NEIL G78 92 A8
Dean St BLSH ML4 100 B4
CLYDBK G81 40 C8
Deanwood Av LNPK/KPK G44 94 F7
Deanwood Rd LNPK/KPK G44 94 F7
Deas Rd SHOTTS ML7 104 C4
Dechmont EKILS G75 127 G5
Dechmont Av BLTYR/CAMB G72 97 K8
MTHW ML1 120 C2
Dechmont Gdns
BLTYR/CAMB G72 118 C1
Dechmont Pl BLTYR/CAMB G72 97 K7
Dechmont Rd UD/BTH/TAN G71 98 E1
Dechmont St DEN/PKHD G31 80 C6
HMLTN ML3 119 J8
Dechmont Vw
UD/BTH/TAN G71 99 G3
Dee Av PSLYS PA2 74 F8
RNFRW PA4 58 E6
Dee Crs PSLYS PA2 74 F8
Deedes St AIRDRIE ML6 84 D3
Dee Dr PSLYS PA2 90 F1
Deep Dl EKILN G74 2 B2
Deepdene Rd
BAIL/MDB/MHD G69 64 F1
BSDN G61 41 K7
Dee Pl EKILS G75 126 B3
JNSTN PA5 89 J2
Deerdykes Ct North
BALLOCH G68 47 L4
Deerdykes Ct South
BALLOCH G68 47 L5
Deerdykes Pl BALLOCH G68 47 L4
Deerdykes Rd BALLOCH G68 47 K5
Deerdykes Vw BALLOCH G68 47 K5
Deer Park Ct HMLTN ML3 129 K3
Deer Park Pl HMLTN ML3 129 L3
Deeside Dr CARLUKE ML8 133 J6
Dee St CTBR ML5 65 J8
SHOTTS ML7 104 D4
STPS/GTHM/RID G33 80 D2
Dee Ter HMLTN ML3 129 H2
Delfie Dr GRNKW/INVK PA16 16 B5
Delhi Av CLYDBK G81 39 J6
Dellburn St MTHW ML1 120 F4
Dellingburn St GRNK PA15 6 F5
The Dell BLSH ML4 100 D6
Delny Pl STPS/GTHM/RID G33 81 L3
Delves Rd LNK/LMHG ML11 137 G6
Delvin Rd LNPK/KPK G44 95 H5
De Morville Pl BEITH KA15 125 K5
Dempsey Rd BLSH ML4 99 M7
Dempster St GRNK PA15 6 A5
Denbak Av HMLTN ML3 119 G8
Denbeath Ct HMLTN ML3 120 C7
Denbeck St CAR/SHTL G32 80 F5
Denbrae St CAR/SHTL G32 80 F5
Denewood Av PSLYS PA2 91 K2
Denham St PPK/MIL G22 61 H7
Denholm Crs EKILS G75 2 F7
Denholm Dr GIF/THBK G46 114 C2
WISHAW ML2 122 C3
Denholm Gdns
GRNKW/INVK PA16 16 C4
HMLTN ML3 129 L7
Denholm Gn EKILS G75 3 G7
Denholm St GRNKW/INVK PA16 16 D3
Denholm Ter
GRNKW/INVK PA16 16 D4
HMLTN ML3 118 E7
Denholm Wy BEITH KA15 125 J6
Denmark St PPK/MIL G22 61 J6
Denmilne Rd
BAIL/MDB/MHD G69 82 D3
Denmilne St ESTRH G34 82 C3
Dennistoun Crs HBR/GL G84 11 G8
Dennistoun Rd PGL PA14 36 B3
Dennistoun St BLSH ML4 100 A4
Dennyholm Wynd KBRN KA25 124 D4
Dennystoun Forge DMBTN G82 20 E6
Dentdale EKILN G74 2 B2
Deramore Av GIF/THBK G46 114 A3
Derby St KVGV G3 78 E2
Derby Terrace La KVGV G3 78 D1
Derby Wynd MTHW ML1 101 H8
Derrywood Rd KKNTL G66 27 J4
Derwent Dr CTBR ML5 65 J8
Derwent St PPK/MIL G22 61 H6
Derwentwater EKILS G75 126 C4
Despard Av CAR/SHTL G32 81 K6
Despard Gdns CAR/SHTL G32 81 L6
Deveron Av GIF/THBK G46 94 D8
Deveron Crs HMLTN ML3 118 D6
Deveron Rd BSDN G61 41 J7
EKILN G74 3 L5
MTHW ML1 101 H4
Deveron St CTBR ML5 83 K1
STPS/GTHM/RID G33 80 D1
Devine Gv WISHAW ML2 123 G2
Devlin Ct BLTYR/CAMB G72 118 E3
Devlin Gv BLTYR/CAMB G72 118 E3
Devol Av PGL PA14 34 A1
Devol Crs PLK/PH/NH G53 93 H1
Devol Rd KLMCLM PA13 34 C5
Devondale Av
BLTYR/CAMB G72 118 C1
Devon Dr BSHPTN PA7 38 C7
Devon Gdns BSHPBGS G64 43 M7
CARLUKE ML8 133 G7
Devonhill Av HMLTN ML3 129 K3
Devon Pl PLKSD/SHW G41 79 H6
Devonport Pk EKILS G75 126 D3
Devon Rd GRNKW/INVK PA16 15 K5
Devonshire Gardens La
KVD/HLHD G12 60 B6
Devonshire Ter KVD/HLHD G12 60 B6
Devonshire Terrace La
KVD/HLHD G12 60 B6
Devon St GBLS G5 79 H6
Devonview Pl AIRDRIE ML6 84 F3
Devonview St AIRDRIE ML6 84 F2
Devon Wk BALLOCH G68 47 L2
Devon Wy MTHW ML1 120 B3
Dewar Cl UD/BTH/TAN G71 99 G1
Dewar Dr DRUM G15 41 G6
Dewar Ga DRUM G15 41 G6
Dewar Rd STPS/GTHM/RID G33 64 A6
Dhuhill Dr East HBR/GL G84 10 E3
Diamond St BLSH ML4 100 A5
Diana Av KNTSWD G13 59 H1
Diana Qd MTHW ML1 101 G4
Diana Vernon Ct HBR/GL G84 10 F7
Dickens Av CLYDBK G81 39 M6
Dickson St LRKH ML9 130 E8
Dicks Pk EKILS G75 2 D7
Dick St MRYH/FIRH G20 60 F7
Differ Av KSYTH G65 28 F8
Dillichip Cl ALEX/LLW G83 13 L8
Dillichip Gdns ALEX/LLW G83 13 L7
Dillichip Loan ALEX/LLW G83 13 K7
Dilwara Av SCOT G14 59 L7
Dimity St JNSTN PA5 73 M8
Dimsdale Crs WISHAW ML2 122 C8
Dimsdale Rd WISHAW ML2 122 C8
Dinard Dr GIF/THBK G46 94 C6
Dinart St STPS/GTHM/RID G33 80 D1
Dinduff St ESTRH G34 82 C1
Dingwall Dr GRNKW/INVK PA16 15 M6
Dinmont Av PSLYS PA2 90 F1
Dinmont Crs MTHW ML1 100 C7
Dinmont Rd PLKSD/SHW G41 94 D1
Dinwiddie St
SPRGB/BLRNK G21 62 C8
Dinyra Pl CTBR ML5 65 J4
Dipple Ct KBRN KA25 124 D3
Dipple Pl DRUM G15 41 H7
Dipple Rd KBRN KA25 124 D2
Dipple Vw KBRN KA25 124 D2
Dirleton Dr PLKSD/SHW G41 94 E2
PSLYS PA2 91 G1
Dirleton Ga BSDN G61 41 K7
Divernia Wy BRHD/NEIL G78 112 D1
Divert Rd GRK PA19 15 J3
Dixon Av DMBTN G82 20 E7
GVH/MTFL G42 79 G8
Dixon Dr DMBTN G82 20 D8
Dixon Pl EKILN G74 116 B7
Dixon Rd GVH/MTFL G42 95 J1
HBR/GL G84 10 E4
Dixon St CGLE G1 4 E8
CTBR ML5 84 B5
HMLTN ML3 119 K7
PSLY PA1 9 K5
Dickens Av MTHW ML1 101 K7
Dobbies Ct CARLUKE ML8 132 C3
Dobbie's Loan COWCAD G4 4 F2
Dobbie's Loan Pl COWCAD G4 5 H4
Dochart Av RNFRW PA4 58 E8
Dochart Dr CTBR ML5 65 J8
Dochart St
STPS/GTHM/RID G33 62 E8
Dock Breast GRNK PA15 6 F4
Dock St CLYDBK G81 58 D2
Dodhill Pl KNTSWD G13 59 H3
Dodside Gdns CAR/SHTL G32 81 J6
Dodside Pl CAR/SHTL G32 81 J6
Dodside Rd NMRNS G77 112 E5
Dodside St CAR/SHTL G32 81 J6

Dolan St BAIL/MDB/MHD G69 82 B5
Dollar Pk MTHW ML1 121 H6
Dollar Ter MRYH/FIRH G20 60 C2
Dolphin Rd PLKSD/SHW G41 78 D8
Dominica Gn EKILS G75 126 D1
Donaldfield Rd BRWEIR PA11 72 B3
Donaldson Av KSYTH G65 29 L3
Donaldson Crs KKNTL G66 45 J3
Donaldson Dr RNFRW PA4 58 D6
Donaldson Gn
UD/BTH/TAN G71 99 H2
Donaldson Rd LRKH ML9 130 E8
Donaldson St HMLTN ML3 119 G5
KKNTL G66 45 J3
Donaldswood Pk PSLYS PA2 91 J2
Donaldswood Rd PSLYS PA2 91 J2
Donald Ter HMLTN ML3 129 J1
Donald Wy UD/BTH/TAN G71 99 G3
Don Av RNFRW PA4 58 E7
Don Ct HMLTN ML3 129 G2
Don Dr PSLYS PA2 90 F1
Donhoe Ct BSHPBGS G64 62 A1
Donnelly Wy WISHAW ML2 123 H4
Donnies Brae BRHD/NEIL G78 111 M2
Don Pl JNSTN PA5 89 J2
Don St GRNKW/INVK PA16 16 C4
STPS/GTHM/RID G33 80 D2
Doon Crs BSDN G61 41 K6
Doonfoot Gdns EKILN G74 2 D3
Doonfoot Rd
PLKSW/MSWD G43 94 C4
Doon Pl KKNTL G66 27 M8
Doon Rd KKNTL G66 45 M1
Doon Side CUMB G67 31 H7
Doon St CLYDBK G81 40 C6
LRKH ML9 130 E7
MTHW ML1 121 G5
Doon Wy KKNTL G66 46 A1
Dorain Rd MTHW ML1 101 K6
Dora St DMNK/BRGTN G40 80 A7
Dorchester Av KVD/HLHD G12 60 A4
Dorchester Ct KVD/HLHD G12 60 A4
Dorchester Pl KVD/HLHD G12 60 A5
Dorian Dr
CRMNK/CLK/EAG G76 114 C2
Dorlin Rd STPS/GTHM/RID G33 63 L5
Dormanside Ct
PLK/PH/NH G53 77 H6
Dormanside Ga
PLK/PH/NH G53 77 H6
Dormanside Gv
PLK/PH/NH G53 77 H6
Dormanside Pl
PLK/PH/NH G53 77 J7
Dormanside Rd
PLK/PH/NH G53 77 H6
Dornal Av KNTSWD G13 58 F2
Dornford Av CAR/SHTL G32 81 K8
Dornford Rd CAR/SHTL G32 81 K8
Dornie Dr CAR/SHTL G32 97 H2
Dornoch Av GIF/THBK G46 114 C1
Dornoch Ct BLSH ML4 100 A4
Dornoch Pl
BAIL/MDB/MHD G69 64 D1
EKILN G74 2 C4
Dornoch Rd BSDN G61 41 K7
MTHW ML1 101 H4
Dornoch St DMNK/BRGTN G40 79 M5
Dornoch Wy AIRDRIE ML6 84 F4
BALLOCH G68 31 G4
BLTYR/CAMB G72 118 D6
Dorset Rd GRNKW/INVK PA16 15 L5
Dorset St KVGV G3 78 F2
Dosk Av KNTSWD G13 58 F1
Dosk Pl KNTSWD G13 58 F1
Double Hedges Rd
BRHD/NEIL G78 111 K4
Dougalston Av MLNGV G62 42 C1
Dougalston Crs MLNGV G62 42 B1
Dougalston Gdns North
MLNGV G62 42 B1
Dougalston Gdns South
MLNGV G62 42 B1
Dougalston Rd SMSTN G23 60 E1
Dougan Dr WISHAW ML2 123 H4
Douglas Av CAR/SHTL G32 97 H1
GIF/THBK G46 114 C1
JNSTN PA5 74 B8
KKNTL G66 45 K4
PGL PA14 36 C3
RUTH G73 96 C5
Douglas Crs AIRDRIE ML6 85 G3
ERSK PA8 38 F7
HMLTN ML3 129 K4
UD/BTH/TAN G71 99 H2
Douglasdale EKILN G74 2 C3
Douglas Dr
BAIL/MDB/MHD G69 81 M5
BLSH ML4 100 D5
BLTYR/CAMB G72 96 F6
DRUM G15 40 F8
EKILS G75 126 B3
HBR/GL G84 10 E4
NMRNS G77 113 L3
UD/BTH/TAN G71 119 G1
Douglas Dr East HBR/GL G84 10 E4
Douglas Drive La CSMK G45 95 K7
Douglas Gdns BSDN G61 41 M5
GIF/THBK G46 114 C1
UD/BTH/TAN G71 98 F5
Douglas Ga BLTYR/CAMB G72 97 G5
Douglas La CGLW G2 4 C5
Douglas Muir Dr MLNGV G62 23 J7
Douglas Muir Gdns MLNGV G62 23 J6
Douglas Muir Pl MLNGV G62 23 J6
Douglas Muir Rd CLYDBK G81 40 D2
MLNGV G62 23 K7
Douglas Park Crs BSDN G61 42 A4
Douglas Park La HMLTN ML3 119 J6
Douglas Pl BSDN G61 41 L4
HMLTN ML3 129 K4
KKNTL G66 45 K5
LARGS KA30 106 F3
Douglas Rd DMBTN G82 21 H7
PSLYN/LNWD PA3 75 H2
Douglas St AIRDRIE ML6 85 G3
BLTYR/CAMB G72 118 C4
CARLUKE ML8 133 G7
CGLW G2 4 C4
HMLTN ML3 119 J6
LARGS KA30 106 E3
LRKH ML9 130 C5
MLNGV G62 42 A1
MTHW ML1 120 D2
PSLY PA1 8 D4
UD/BTH/TAN G71 99 H3
WISHAW ML2 131 M2
Dougliehill Pl PGL PA14 34 C2
Dougliehill Rd PGL PA14 34 C2
Dougliehill Ter PGL PA14 34 C2
Dougray Pl BRHD/NEIL G78 92 C7
Dougrie Dr CSMK G45 95 L7
Dougrie Gdns CSMK G45 95 K8
Dougrie Pl CSMK G45 95 L7
Dougrie Rd CSMK G45 95 K7
Dougrie St CSMK G45 95 K7
Dougrie Ter CSMK G45 95 K7
Doune Crs AIRDRIE ML6 85 K8
BSHPBGS G64 44 B6
NMRNS G77 113 M4
Doune Gdns GRK PA19 14 F4
MRYH/FIRH G20 60 E7
Doune Gardens La
MRYH/FIRH G20 60 E7
Doune Park Wy CTBR ML5 83 M6
Doune Qd MRYH/FIRH G20 60 E7
Doune Ter CTBR ML5 83 K1
Dovecot PLKSW/MSWD G43 94 C2
Dovecote Vw KKNTL G66 45 M3
Dovecot La LNK/LMHG ML11 137 G5
Dovecotwood KSYTH G65 29 K1
Doveholm DMBTN G82 21 G5
Doveholm Av DMBTN G82 21 H5
Dove Pl EKILS G75 126 C4
Dover St CTBR ML5 65 K8
KVGV G3 78 F2
Dove St PLK/PH/NH G53 93 G4
Dove Wynd BLSH ML4 99 M3
Dowanfield Rd CUMB G67 30 D8
Dowanhill St PTCK G11 60 C8
Dowan Rd MLNGV G62 42 E3
Dowanside La KVD/HLHD G12 60 D7
Dowanside Rd KVD/HLHD G12 60 C7
Downcraig Dr CSMK G45 95 J8
Downcraig Gv CSMK G45 95 J8
Downcraig Rd CSMK G45 95 J8
Downcraig Ter CSMK G45 95 K8
Downfield Dr HMLTN ML3 129 H3
Downfield Gdns
UD/BTH/TAN G71 98 F8
Downfield St CAR/SHTL G32 80 E7
Downhill St KVD/HLHD G12 60 C7
Downiebrae Rd RUTH G73 80 B8
Downie Cl UD/BTH/TAN G71 99 H2
Downie St HMLTN ML3 129 K1
Downs St SPRGB/BLRNK G21 61 M6
Dowrie Crs PLK/PH/NH G53 77 H8
Draffen St MTHW ML1 120 F2
Drakemire Av CSMK G45 95 J6
Drakemire Dr CSMK G45 95 J8
Drake St DMNK/BRGTN G40 79 L5
Dreghorn St DEN/PKHD G31 80 C3
Dresling Rd GRNK PA15 6 A7
Drimnin Rd
STPS/GTHM/RID G33 63 M5
Drive Rd GOV/IBX G51 77 L1
Drochil St ESTRH G34 82 A1
Drove Hl BALLOCH G68 30 B6
Drumadoon Dr HBR/GL G84 10 F5
Drumbathie Rd AIRDRIE ML6 85 H1
Drumbeg Dr PLK/PH/NH G53 93 G3
Drumbeg Pth
BLTYR/CAMB G72 118 C7
Drumbeg Ter MLNGV G62 23 K7
Drumbottie Rd
SPRGB/BLRNK G21 62 A5
Drumbowie Crs SHOTTS ML7 87 H8
Drumby Crs
CRMNK/CLK/EAG G76 114 D1
Drumby Dr
CRMNK/CLK/EAG G76 114 D2
Drumcarn Dr MLNGV G62 23 M8
Drumcavel Rd
BAIL/MDB/MHD G69 64 D3
Drumchapel Gdns DRUM G15 41 G7
Drumchapel Pl DRUM G15 41 H7
Drumchapel Rd DRUM G15 41 H7
Drumclair Pl AIRDRIE ML6 85 K2
Drumclog Av MLNGV G62 24 A6
Drumclog Gdns
STPS/GTHM/RID G33 62 F4
Drumcross Rd BSHPTN PA7 38 D7
PLK/PH/NH G53 77 J8
Drumduff EKILS G75 127 G5
Drumfearn Rd MRYH/FIRH G20 61 H5
Drumfin Av AIRDRIE ML6 68 F5
Drumfork Ct HBR/GL G84 10 F7
Drumfork Rd HBR/GL G84 11 G8
Drumfrochar Pl GRNK PA15 6 C7
Drumfrochar Rd GRNK PA15 16 D6
Drumgelloch St AIRDRIE ML6 85 K1
Drumglass Steadings
KSYTH G65 29 K7
Drumglass Vw KSYTH G65 29 M6
Drumgray Gdns AIRDRIE ML6 49 K8
Drumgray La AIRDRIE ML6 49 K8
Drumhead Pl CAR/SHTL G32 96 F1
Drumhead Rd CAR/SHTL G32 96 F1
Drumhill KKNTL G66 28 B8
Drumilaw Rd RUTH G73 96 A5
Drumilaw Wy RUTH G73 96 A5
Drumillan Hl GRNKW/INVK PA16 15 J7
Drumkinnon Rd ALEX/LLW G83 13 J2
Drumlaken Av SMSTN G23 60 C1
Drumlaken Ct SMSTN G23 60 C1
Drumlaken St SMSTN G23 60 C1
Drumlanrig Av ESTRH G34 82 D2
Drumlanrig Crs
BAIL/MDB/MHD G69 64 E6
Drumlanrig Pl ESTRH G34 82 D2
Drumlin Dr MLNGV G62 41 M1
Drumloch Gdns EKILS G75 127 H5
Drumlochy Rd
STPS/GTHM/RID G33 81 G1
Drum Mains Pk BALLOCH G68 47 K2
Drummond Av RUTH G73 95 M2
Drummond Dr PSLY PA1 76 D5
WISHAW ML2 122 B7
Drummond Pl BTHG/ARM EH48 71 J1
EKILN G74 3 L1
Drummond St
GRNKW/INVK PA16 16 C5
Drummond Wy NMRNS G77 113 G4
Drummore Av CTBR ML5 84 D6
Drummore Rd DRUM G15 41 J5
Drumnessie Ct BALLOCH G68 * 47 M2
Drumnessie Rd BALLOCH G68 47 M2
Drumnessie Vw BALLOCH G68 47 M2
Drumore Av AIRDRIE ML6 85 K8
Drumover Dr DEN/PKHD G31 80 E6
Drumoyne Av GOV/IBX G51 77 L2
Drumoyne Circ GOV/IBX G51 77 L3
Drumoyne Dr GOV/IBX G51 77 L2
Drumoyne Pl GOV/IBX G51 77 L3
Drumoyne Qd GOV/IBX G51 77 L3
Drumoyne Rd GOV/IBX G51 77 L3
Drumoyne Sq GOV/IBX G51 77 L3
Drumpark St CTBR ML5 83 H6
GIF/THBK G46 93 M5
Drumpellier Av
BAIL/MDB/MHD G69 82 B7
CTBR ML5 83 K3
CUMB G67 48 C2
Drumpellier Ct CUMB G67 48 C2
Drumpellier Crs CTBR ML5 83 K4
Drumpellier Gdns CUMB G67 48 C2
Drumpellier Gv CUMB G67 48 C2
Drumpellier Pl
BAIL/MDB/MHD G69 82 B6
CUMB G67 48 C2
Drumpellier Rd
BAIL/MDB/MHD G69 82 A7
Drumpellier St
STPS/GTHM/RID G33 62 D8
Drumreoch Dr GVH/MTFL G42 95 L3
Drumreoch Pl GVH/MTFL G42 95 L2
Drumry Rd CLYDBK G81 40 C6
Drumry Rd East DRUM G15 40 F7
Drumsack Av
BAIL/MDB/MHD G69 64 C2
Drumsargard Rd RUTH G73 96 D5
Drums Av PSLYN/LNWD PA3 8 C3
Drums Crs PSLYN/LNWD PA3 8 C3
Drumshangie Pl AIRDRIE ML6 67 G7
Drumshangie St AIRDRIE ML6 67 G7
Drumshantie Rd GRK PA19 15 L3
Drumshaw Dr CAR/SHTL G32 97 J2
Drums Rd PLK/PH/NH G53 77 G7
Drums Ter GRNKW/INVK PA16 16 B1
Drumtrocher St KSYTH G65 29 K2
Drury St CGLW G2 4 E6
Dryad St GIF/THBK G46 93 L4
Dryburgh Av PSLYS PA2 91 G1
RUTH G73 96 B3
Dryburgh Gdns
MRYH/FIRH G20 60 F7
Dryburgh Hl EKILN G74 2 C5
Dryburgh La EKILN G74 2 D5
Dryburgh Pl CTBR ML5 83 M3
Dryburgh Rd BSDN G61 41 J3
WISHAW ML2 122 A5
Dryburgh St HMLTN ML3 119 H4
Dryburgh Wk
BAIL/MDB/MHD G69 47 G7
Dryburn Av
CARD/HILL/MSPK G52 77 G4
Dryden St HMLTN ML3 119 H4
Drygait HWWD PA9 89 G4
Drygate COWCAD G4 5 L7
Drygate St LRKH ML9 130 C5
Drygrange Rd
STPS/GTHM/RID G33 63 J8
Drymen Pl KKNTL G66 45 K7
Drymen Rd ALEX/LLW G83 13 K1
BSDN G61 41 K3
Drymen St
CARD/HILL/MSPK G52 77 L4
Drynoch Pl PPK/MIL G22 61 H3
Drysdale St SCOT G14 58 F4
Duart Dr EKILN G74 2 C1
JNSTN PA5 90 B1
NMRNS G77 114 A5
Duart St MRYH/FIRH G20 60 C2
Duart Wy BAIL/MDB/MHD G69 64 E6
Dubbs Rd PGL PA14 34 D2
Dubs Rd BRHD/NEIL G78 92 E6
Dubton St ESTRH G34 82 B1
Duchall Pl SCOT G14 59 H5
Duchal Rd KLMCLM PA13 53 K2
Duchal St PGL PA14 34 D2
Duchess Ct HMLTN ML3 120 A7
Duchess Dr HBR/GL G84 10 B3
Duchess Palace RUTH G73 96 C2
Duchess Pk HBR/GL G84 10 B4
Duchess Rd RUTH G73 96 C1
Duchray Dr PSLY PA1 76 F5
Duchray La
STPS/GTHM/RID G33 80 D1
Duchray St
STPS/GTHM/RID G33 80 D1
Dudhope St
STPS/GTHM/RID G33 63 K8
Dudley Dr CTBR ML5 65 J8
KVD/HLHD G12 60 A7
Dudley La KVD/HLHD G12 60 A7
Duffield Dr LARGS KA30 106 F6
Duff St GRNK PA15 6 E4
Duffus Pl CAR/SHTL G32 97 J2
Duffus St ESTRH G34 81 M1
Duffus Ter CAR/SHTL G32 97 J2
Duich Gdns SMSTN G23 60 E1
Duisdale Rd CAR/SHTL G32 97 J2
Dukes Ct LRKH ML9 130 C5
Dukes Ga UD/BTH/TAN G71 98 E6
Dukes Pl HMLTN ML3 129 K4
Dukes Rd BAIL/MDB/MHD G69 82 F5
RUTH G73 96 D5
Duke St COWCAD G4 5 L7
DEN/PKHD G31 80 B4
HMLTN ML3 119 L7
LRKH ML9 130 C5
MTHW ML1 120 F1
PSLYS PA2 75 L8
WISHAW ML2 122 F3
Dulnain St BLTYR/CAMB G72 97 K5
Dulsie Rd SPRGB/BLRNK G21 62 C4
Dumbain Crs ALEX/LLW G83 13 M1
Dumbain Rd ALEX/LLW G83 13 M1
Dumbarton Rd CLYDBK G81 39 K6
OLDK G60 38 D2
PTCK G11 59 M7
SCOT G14 58 E3
Dumbreck Av PLKSD/SHW G41 78 A7
Dumbreck Ct PLKSD/SHW G41 78 A7
Dumbreck Pl KKNTL G66 45 L6
PLKSD/SHW G41 78 A7
Dumbreck Rd PLKSD/SHW G41 78 A6
Dumbreck Sq PLKSD/SHW G41 78 A6
Dumbrock Rd MLNGV G62 23 K8
Dumbuck Crs DMBTN G82 21 J8
Dumbuck Gdns DMBTN G82 21 H8
Dumbuck Rd DMBTN G82 21 G5
Dumbuie Av DMBTN G82 21 H6
Dumfries Crs AIRDRIE ML6 84 F4
Dumgoyne Av MLNGV G62 23 M8
Dumgoyne Dr BSDN G61 41 K2
Dumgoyne Gdns MLNGV G62 23 M8
Dumgoyne Pl
CRMNK/CLK/EAG G76 114 C3
Dunagoil Rd CSMK G45 95 K8
Dunagoil St CSMK G45 95 L8
Dunagoil Ter CSMK G45 115 L1
Dunalastair Dr
STPS/GTHM/RID G33 63 H5
Dunan Pl STPS/GTHM/RID G33 81 L3
Dunard Rd RUTH G73 96 B3
Dunard St MRYH/FIRH G20 60 F7
Dunaskin St PTCK G11 78 C1
Dunavon Pl CTBR ML5 84 D5
Dunbar Av CTBR ML5 83 K6
JNSTN PA5 89 L2
RUTH G73 96 C3
Dunbar Dr MTHW ML1 121 G5
Dunbar Hl EKILN G74 2 A5
Dunbar La MTHW ML1 101 G7
Dunbar Pl EKILN G74 2 A5
Dunbar Rd PSLYS PA2 91 G1
Dunbar St HMLTN ML3 119 H5
Dunbeath Av NMRNS G77 113 M4
Dunbeath Gv
BLTYR/CAMB G72 118 C7
Dunbeith Pl MRYH/FIRH G20 60 D5
Dunbeth Av CTBR ML5 84 B2
Dunbeth Rd CTBR ML5 84 A1
Dunblane Dr EKILN G74 3 H3
Dunblane Pl EKILN G74 3 H3
Dunblane St COWCAD G4 4 E3
Dunbrach Rd BALLOCH G68 30 C7
Dunbreck Av AIRDRIE ML6 69 G4
Dunbritton Rd DMBTN G82 21 J7
Duncan Av SCOT G14 59 J6
Duncan Ct MTHW ML1 100 D8
Duncan Graham St LRKH ML9 130 D5
Duncan La SCOT G14 59 J6
Duncan La North SCOT G14 59 J5
Duncan La South SCOT G14 59 J6
Duncan McIntosh Rd
BALLOCH G68 31 J2
Duncann ERSK PA8 57 J3
Duncan Rd HBR/GL G84 10 E4
PGL PA14 34 B1
Duncansby Dr
BLTYR/CAMB G72 118 C7
Duncansby Rd
STPS/GTHM/RID G33 81 K4
Duncan St CLYDBK G81 40 A6
GRNK PA15 6 B5
Duncarnock Av
BRHD/NEIL G78 111 L3
Duncarnock Crs
BRHD/NEIL G78 111 M3
Dunchattan Pl DEN/PKHD G31 5 M8
Dunchattan St DEN/PKHD G31 5 M6
Dunchurch Rd PSLY PA1 76 D4
Duncluttha Dr
UD/BTH/TAN G71 119 G1
Duncluttha St
DMNK/BRGTN G40 80 B8
Duncolm Pl MLNGV G62 23 K7
Duncombe Av CLYDBK G81 40 B2
Duncombe St MRYH/FIRH G20 60 D3
Duncraig Crs JNSTN PA5 89 J2
Duncrub Dr BSHPBGS G64 61 L1
Duncruin St MRYH/FIRH G20 60 C3
Duncruin Ter MRYH/FIRH G20 60 C3
Duncryne Av CAR/SHTL G32 81 K6
Duncryne Gdns CAR/SHTL G32 81 L6
Duncryne Pl BSHPBGS G64 61 L2
Duncryne Rd ALEX/LLW G83 13 K4
CAR/SHTL G32 81 K6
Dundaff Hl BALLOCH G68 30 C7
Dundas Av BSHPBGS G64 44 B2
Dundas Ct EKILN G74 2 F3
Dundashill COWCAD G4 4 E1
Dundas La CGLE G1 4 F5
Dundas Pl EKILN G74 2 F3
Dundas St CGLE G1 4 F6
Dundee Dr
CARD/HILL/MSPK G52 77 H6
Dundonald Av JNSTN PA5 89 K1
Dundonald Crs CTBR ML5 83 M6
NMRNS G77 114 A6
Dundonald Dr HMLTN ML3 129 K3
Dundonald Pl BRHD/NEIL G78 111 K3
Dundonald Rd KVD/HLHD G12 60 C6
PSLYN/LNWD PA3 76 A2
Dundonald St
BLTYR/CAMB G72 118 C2
Dundrennan Dr AIRDRIE ML6 85 L7
Dundrennan Rd
GVH/MTFL G42 94 F3
Dundyvan Ga CTBR ML5 84 A4
Dundyvan La WISHAW ML2 121 M6
Dundyvan Rd CTBR ML5 83 M4
Dundyvan St WISHAW ML2 122 A7
Dundyvan Wy CTBR ML5 83 M5
Dunearn Pl PSLYS PA2 9 L8
Dunearn St COWCAD G4 4 A1
Dunedin Ct EKILS G75 126 D2
Dunedin Dr EKILS G75 126 D2
Dunedin Rd LRKH ML9 130 D8
Dunedin Ter CLYDBK G81 58 C1
Dunellan Av
BAIL/MDB/MHD G69 47 G8
Dunellan Ct
BAIL/MDB/MHD G69 47 G8
Dunellan Crs
BAIL/MDB/MHD G69 47 G8
Dunellan Dr CLYDBK G81 40 B2
Dunellan Gdns
BAIL/MDB/MHD G69 47 G8
Dunellan Gv
BAIL/MDB/MHD G69 46 F8
Dunellan Pl
BAIL/MDB/MHD G69 47 G8
Dunellan Rd MLNGV G62 23 J7
Dunellan St
CARD/HILL/MSPK G52 77 L4
Dungavel Gdns HMLTN ML3 129 L2
Dungeonhill Rd ESTRH G34 82 D2
Dunglass Av EKILN G74 3 G2
SCOT G14 59 J5
Dunglass La SCOT G14 59 J5
Dunglass La North SCOT G14 59 J5
Dunglass La South SCOT G14 59 J5
Dunglass Pl MLNGV G62 23 L6
NMRNS G77 113 G4
Dunglass Rd BSHPTN PA7 38 C8
Dungoil Av BALLOCH G68 30 B6
Dungoil Rd KKNTL G66 45 L6
Dungourney Dr
GRNKW/INVK PA16 16 C2
Dungoyne St MRYH/FIRH G20 60 C2
Dunira St CAR/SHTL G32 80 F7
Dunivaig Rd
STPS/GTHM/RID G33 81 L2
Dunkeld Av RUTH G73 96 B3
Dunkeld Dr BSDN G61 42 B6
Dunkeld Pl CTBR ML5 83 M7
HMLTN ML3 118 E7
NMRNS G77 114 B6
Dunkeld St DEN/PKHD G31 80 C6
Dunkenny Rd DRUM G15 40 F5
Dunkirk St AIRDRIE ML6 69 G4
Dunlin EKILN G74 2 E1
KVD/HLHD G12 60 A4
Dunlin Ct BLSH ML4 99 L2
Dunlin Crs CRG/CRSL/HOU PA6 73 J1
Dunlin Wy CTBR ML5 84 E7
Dunlop Ct HMLTN ML3 129 L3
Dunlop Crs UD/BTH/TAN G71 119 H1
Dunlop Gv UD/BTH/TAN G71 99 G1
Dunlop Pl MLNGV G62 23 M6
Dunlop St BLTYR/CAMB G72 97 L4
CGLE G1 4 F9
GRNKW/INVK PA16 16 D6
PSLYN/LNWD PA3 74 C4
RNFRW PA4 58 D5
Dunmore Dr MLNGV G62 42 C2
Dunmore St CLYDBK G81 58 C1
Dunnachie Dr CTBR ML5 83 H6
Dunnet Av AIRDRIE ML6 66 F4
Dunnet Ct BLTYR/CAMB G72 118 D6
Dunnet Dr CRG/CRSL/HOU PA6 73 H1
Dunnichen Gdns BSHPBGS G64 62 D1
Dunnikier Wk BALLOCH G68 47 L1
Dunning St DEN/PKHD G31 80 D6
Dunnock Gv GRNKW/INVK PA16 33 G4
Dunnock Pl CTBR ML5 84 E6
Dunnottar Ct EKILN G74 2 B1
Dunnottar Crs EKILN G74 2 B1
Dunnottar St BSHPBGS G64 44 D8
STPS/GTHM/RID G33 63 H8
Dunn St CLYDBK G81 39 L7
DMNK/BRGTN G40 79 M7
GRNK PA15 6 A6
PSLY PA1 9 L4
Dunns Wood Rd CUMB G67 31 L2
Dunn Ter SHOTTS ML7 71 L7
Dunollie Pl
BAIL/MDB/MHD G69 64 E5
Dunolly Dr NMRNS G77 113 M4
Dunolly St SPRGB/BLRNK G21 80 A1
Dunottar Av CTBR ML5 84 B7
Dunottar Pl CTBR ML5 84 B6
Dun Pk KKNTL G66 45 K2
Dunphail Dr ESTRH G34 82 D2
Dunphail Rd ESTRH G34 82 D2
Dunragit St DEN/PKHD G31 80 C3
Dunrobin Av JNSTN PA5 90 C1
Dunrobin Ct EKILN G74 2 D1
Dunrobin Crs EKILN G74 2 D1
Dunrobin Dr EKILN G74 2 D1
GRK PA19 14 F4
Dunrobin Pl CTBR ML5 83 M3
Dunrobin Rd AIRDRIE ML6 85 L2
Dunrobin St DEN/PKHD G31 80 B4
Dunrod Hl EKILN G74 3 G2
Dunrod Rd GRNKW/INVK PA16 33 H2
Dunrod St CAR/SHTL G32 81 H6
Dunscore Brae HMLTN ML3 118 E8
Duns Crs WISHAW ML2 122 C3
Dunside Dr PLK/PH/NH G53 93 G3
Dunsiston Rd AIRDRIE ML6 86 B5
Dunskaith Pl ESTRH G34 82 D3
Dunskaith St ESTRH G34 82 D2
Dunsmore Rd BSHPTN PA7 38 A6
Dunsmuir St GOV/IBX G51 78 B3
Duns Pth CTBR ML5 84 D6
Dunswin Av CLYDBK G81 39 L7
Dunsyre Pl SMSTN G23 60 E1
Dunsyre St
STPS/GTHM/RID G33 80 E2
Duntarvie Av ESTRH G34 82 C2
Duntarvie Cl ESTRH G34 82 C2
Duntarvie Crs ESTRH G34 82 C2
Duntarvie Dr ESTRH G34 82 B2
Duntarvie Gdns ESTRH G34 82 C2
Duntarvie Pl ESTRH G34 82 B2
Duntarvie Rd ESTRH G34 82 B2
Dunterlie Av KNTSWD G13 59 G3
Dunterlie Ct BRHD/NEIL G78 92 C6
Duntiblae KKNTL G66 46 A3
Duntiblae Rd KKNTL G66 46 A3
Duntiglennan Rd CLYDBK G81 40 A3
Duntilland Av SHOTTS ML7 87 H7
Duntilland Rd AIRDRIE ML6 86 E1
SHOTTS ML7 87 J4
Duntocher Rd BSDN G61 41 H3
CLYDBK G81 40 B4
Duntreath Av DRUM G15 40 F8
KNTSWD G13 58 E1
Duntreath Dr DRUM G15 40 F8
Duntreath Gdns DRUM G15 40 F7
Duntreath Gv DRUM G15 40 F8
Duntreath Ter KSYTH G65 29 K2
Duntroon St DEN/PKHD G31 80 B2
Dunure Dr HMLTN ML3 118 D8
NMRNS G77 114 A6
RUTH G73 95 M5
Dunure Pl CTBR ML5 83 L7
NMRNS G77 114 A6
Dunure St CTBR ML5 83 L7
MRYH/FIRH G20 60 D3
Dunvegan AIRDRIE ML6 66 E5
Dunvegan Av CTBR ML5 83 K1
GRK PA19 14 F4
JNSTN PA5 90 B1
Dunvegan Dr BSHPBGS G64 44 A6
NMRNS G77 114 A5
Dunvegan Pl EKILN G74 2 C1
UD/BTH/TAN G71 98 D2
Dunvegan Qd RNFRW PA4 58 B5
Dunwan Av KNTSWD G13 58 F2
Dunwan Pl KNTSWD G13 58 F2
Durban Av CLYDBK G81 39 K6
EKILS G75 126 E6
Durham Rd GRNKW/INVK PA16 15 L4
Durham St PLKSD/SHW G41 78 D5
Durisdeer Dr HMLTN ML3 128 E1
Durness Av BSDN G61 42 B5
Duror St CAR/SHTL G32 81 G4
Durris Gdns CAR/SHTL G32 81 K7
Durrockstock Crs PSLYS PA2 90 F3
Durrockstock Rd PSLYS PA2 90 F3
Durward EKILN G74 117 L6
Durward Av PLKSD/SHW G41 94 D1
Durward Ct PLKSD/SHW G41 94 D1
Durward Crs PSLYS PA2 90 F1
Duthie Park Gdns KNTSWD G13 59 K3
Duthie Rd GRK PA19 16 A3
Duthil St GOV/IBX G51 77 K3
Dyce Av AIRDRIE ML6 84 E5
Dyce La PTCK G11 60 A8
Dyer's La CGLE G1 5 H9

Dyfrig St BLTYR/CAMB G72 118 C2
SHOTTS ML7 104 E5
Dykebar Av KNTSWD G13 59 G3
Dykebar Crs PSLYS PA2 76 B7
Dykehead Crs AIRDRIE ML6 66 F7
Dykehead La
STPS/GTHM/RID G33 81 K3
Dykehead Rd AIRDRIE ML6 66 F7
BAIL/MDB/MHD G69 82 F5
BALLOCH G68 30 C3
KSYTH G65 28 E1
Dykehead Sq HMLTN ML3 118 F7
Dykehead St
STPS/GTHM/RID G33 81 K3
Dykemuir Pl
SPRGB/BLRNK G21 62 B6
Dykemuir Qd
SPRGB/BLRNK G21 62 A6
Dykemuir St
SPRGB/BLRNK G21 62 A6
Dykeneuk Rd PGL PA14 34 D3
Dyke Rd KNTSWD G13 58 F3
The Dykes KBRN KA25 124 C5
Dyke St BAIL/MDB/MHD G69 82 C5
CTBR ML5 83 H6
Dysart Ct BALLOCH G68 47 L1
Dysart Dr BLTYR/CAMB G72 118 D7
Dysart Wy AIRDRIE ML6 85 M3

E

Eagle Crs BSDN G61 41 H3
Eaglesham Ct EKILS G75 126 C1
GOV/IBX G51 78 E4
Eaglesham Pl GOV/IBX G51 78 E4
Eaglesham Rd
CRMNK/CLK/EAG G76 114 E6
EKILS G75 126 B1
NMRNS G77 113 K6
Eagle St COWCAD G4 61 J8
Earl Av AIRDRIE ML6 69 G4
Earlbank Av SCOT G14 59 J5
Earlbank La North SCOT G14 59 J5
Earlbank La South SCOT G14 59 J6
Earl Haig Rd
CARD/HILL/MSPK G52 76 F2
Earl La SCOT G14 59 J6
Earl Pl BRWEIR PA11 72 D4
SCOT G14 59 J5
Earlsburn Rd KKNTL G66 45 L6
Earlscourt
BAIL/MDB/MHD G69 64 F1
Earlsgate CRG/CRSL/HOU PA6 73 H1
Earl's Ga UD/BTH/TAN G71 98 E7
Earl's Hl BALLOCH G68 30 B7
Earlshill Dr HWWD PA9 88 E5
Earlspark Av
PLKSW/MSWD G43 94 F4
Earlston Av SPRGB/BLRNK G21 5 M3
Earlston Crs CTBR ML5 84 D6
Earlston Pl SPRGB/BLRNK G21 5 L3
Earlston St WISHAW ML2 122 C3
Earl St SCOT G14 59 J6
Earlybraes Gdns
STPS/GTHM/RID G33 81 K4
Earn Av BLSH ML4 99 L4
BSDN G61 42 B6
RNFRW PA4 58 E7
Earn Crs WISHAW ML2 122 B8
Earnhill La GRNKW/INVK PA16 15 J5
Earnhill Pl GRNKW/INVK PA16 15 K4
Earnhill Rd GRNKW/INVK PA16 15 K4
Earnock Av MTHW ML1 120 C2
Earnock Gdns HMLTN ML3 119 G8
Earnock Rd HMLTN ML3 118 D8
Earnock St HMLTN ML3 119 G6
STPS/GTHM/RID G33 62 D6
Earn Rd NMRNS G77 113 K2
Earnside St CAR/SHTL G32 81 H5
Earn St STPS/GTHM/RID G33 80 E1
Earn Ter SHOTTS ML7 104 E3
Easdale EKILN G74 3 L9
Easdale Dr CAR/SHTL G32 80 F6
Easdale Pth CTBR ML5 84 D5
Easdale Pl NMRNS G77 113 H4
Easdale Ri HMLTN ML3 118 E7
East Academy St WISHAW ML2 122 B7
East Argyle St HBR/GL G84 10 E6
East Av AIRDRIE ML6 68 A6
BLTYR/CAMB G72 118 E5
CARLUKE ML8 132 F7
MTHW ML1 101 H7
RNFRW PA4 58 D6
UD/BTH/TAN G71 99 J4
Eastbank Dr CAR/SHTL G32 81 J5
East Barmoss Av PGL PA14 34 F3
East Barns St CLYDBK G81 58 D1
East Bath La CGLW G2 4 F5
East Blackhall St GRNK PA15 6 F6
East Buchanan St PSLY PA1 9 J4
Eastburn Crs
SPRGB/BLRNK G21 62 B4
Eastburn Rd SPRGB/BLRNK G21 62 B5
East Burnside St KSYTH G65 29 K2
East Campbell St CGLE G1 5 K8
East Castle Av LARGS KA30 106 E5
East Clyde St HBR/GL G84 10 E6
Eastcote Av SCOT G14 59 L5
East Crawford St GRNK PA15 7 K8
Eastcroft RUTH G73 96 B2
Eastcroft Ter
SPRGB/BLRNK G21 62 A6
East Dean St BLSH ML4 100 B4
Eastend LOCHW PA12 109 K2
Eastend Av MTHW ML1 101 H8
Easterbrae MTHW ML1 120 D5
Easter Craigs DEN/PKHD G31 80 B2
Easter Crs WISHAW ML2 122 E5
Easter Garngaber Rd
KKNTL G66 45 L5
Easterhill Pl CAR/SHTL G32 80 F7
Easterhill Rd HBR/GL G84 10 E4
Easterhill St CAR/SHTL G32 80 F7
Easterhouse Pl ESTRH G34 82 C2
Easterhouse Rd
BAIL/MDB/MHD G69 82 B5
Eastermains KKNTL G66 28 B8
Easter Ms UD/BTH/TAN G71 98 E5
Eastern Av LARGS KA30 107 G5
Eastern Crs KBRN KA25 124 C6
Easter Queenslie Rd
STPS/GTHM/RID G33 81 L2
Easter Rd
CRMNK/CLK/EAG G76 115 G5
SHOTTS ML7 104 D4
Easterton Av
CRMNK/CLK/EAG G76 115 G5
Easter Wood Crs
UD/BTH/TAN G71 99 K1
Easterwood Pl CTBR ML5 84 A3
East Faulds Rd
LNK/LMHG ML11 137 M4
Eastfield Av BLTYR/CAMB G72 96 E5
Eastfield Crs DMBTN G82 21 H8
Eastfield Pl DMBTN G82 21 H8
Eastfield Rd AIRDRIE ML6 69 G5
BALLOCH G68 30 B6
CARLUKE ML8 135 G1
SPRGB/BLRNK G21 61 L6
Eastfield Ter BLSH ML4 100 D5
Eastgate BAIL/MDB/MHD G69 65 G5
East Ga CTBR ML5 65 K3
WISHAW ML2 122 D6
East George St CTBR ML5 84 B1
East Glebe Ter HMLTN ML3 119 K8
East Greenlees Av
BLTYR/CAMB G72 97 J7
East Greenlees Crs
BLTYR/CAMB G72 97 H7
East Greenlees Dr
BLTYR/CAMB G72 97 J7
East Greenlees Gv
BLTYR/CAMB G72 96 F8
East Greenlees Rd
BLTYR/CAMB G72 97 H7
East Hallhill Rd
STPS/GTHM/RID G33 81 M4
Easthall Pl STPS/GTHM/RID G33 81 M3
East Hamilton St GRNK PA15 7 K6
WISHAW ML2 122 B7
East High St AIRDRIE ML6 85 G1
KKNTL G66 45 J1
East India Breast GRNK PA15 6 F5
East Kilbride Rd
CRMNK/CLK/EAG G76 115 H5
RUTH G73 96 E6
East La PSLY PA1 76 B4
Eastlea Pl AIRDRIE ML6 85 H3
East Lennox Dr HBR/GL G84 10 E4
East Machan St LRKH ML9 130 D8
East Mains Rd EKILN G74 2 E3
East Main St SHOTTS ML7 71 M7
East Milton Gv EKILS G75 126 E1
East Montrose St HBR/GL G84 10 E5
Eastmuir St CAR/SHTL G32 81 H5
WISHAW ML2 122 E6
Easton Pl CTBR ML5 84 B4
East Princes St HBR/GL G84 10 E6
East Rd KLBCH PA10 73 G6
MTHW ML1 101 G5
East Rossdhu Dr HBR/GL G84 10 E4
East Scott Ter HMLTN ML3 129 K1
East Shaw St GRNK PA15 6 C4
Eastside KKNTL G66 45 K1
East Springfield Ter
BSHPBGS G64 62 B2
East Stewart Pl CTBR ML5 84 C3
East Stewart St CTBR ML5 84 C3
GRNK PA15 7 G6
East St GRNK PA15 17 M7
East Thomson St CLYDBK G81 40 B6
East Thornlie St WISHAW ML2 122 B7
Eastvale Pl KVGV G3 78 C2
East Wellbrae Crs HMLTN ML3 129 H1
East Wellington St
DEN/PKHD G31 80 D5
East William St GRNK PA15 7 J7
Eastwood Av GIF/THBK G46 94 C8
Eastwood Crs GIF/THBK G46 93 M5
Eastwood Dr WISHAW ML2 123 G4
Eastwood La HBR/GL G84 10 F7
Eastwoodmains Rd
GIF/THBK G46 114 C1
Eastwood Rd
BAIL/MDB/MHD G69 46 F8
East Woodside Av PGL PA14 34 F4
Eastwood Vw
BLTYR/CAMB G72 97 L4
Easwald Bank KLBCH PA10 73 H8
Ebroch Dr KSYTH G65 29 L2
Ebroch Pk KSYTH G65 29 L2
Eccles St PPK/MIL G22 61 L5
Eckford St CAR/SHTL G32 81 G6
Eday St PPK/MIL G22 61 K4
Edderton Pl ESTRH G34 82 A3
Edderton Wy ESTRH G34 82 A3
Eddington Dr NMRNS G77 113 J6
Eddlewood Ct
STPS/GTHM/RID G33 81 M3
Eddlewood Pth
STPS/GTHM/RID G33 81 M3
Eddlewood Pl
STPS/GTHM/RID G33 81 M3
Eddlewood Rd
STPS/GTHM/RID G33 81 M3
Eden Dr EKILS G75 126 C4
Eden Gdns EKILS G75 126 C3
Eden Gv EKILS G75 126 C3
Edenhall Ct NMRNS G77 113 K7
Edenhall Gv NMRNS G77 113 K7
Eden La STPS/GTHM/RID G33 80 D1
Eden Pk UD/BTH/TAN G71 98 F8
Eden Pl RNFRW PA4 58 B5
Edenside BALLOCH G68 31 H2
Eden St STPS/GTHM/RID G33 80 D1
Edenwood St DEN/PKHD G31 80 E5
Edgam Dr
CARD/HILL/MSPK G52 77 J4
Edgefauld Av
SPRGB/BLRNK G21 61 M7
Edgefauld Dr
SPRGB/BLRNK G21 61 M6
Edgefauld Pl
SPRGB/BLRNK G21 61 M5
Edgefauld Rd
SPRGB/BLRNK G21 61 M6
Edgehill La PTCK G11 60 A6
Edgehill Rd BSDN G61 41 L3
PTCK G11 59 M5
Edgemont Pk HMLTN ML3 129 J2
Edgemont St PLKSD/SHW G41 94 E2
Edinbeg Av GVH/MTFL G42 95 L2
Edinbeg Pl GVH/MTFL G42 95 L2
Edinburgh Dr GRK PA19 14 E4
Edinburgh Rd
BAIL/MDB/MHD G69 82 A4
CAR/SHTL G32 81 G3
MTHW ML1 101 L2
SHOTTS ML7 71 H7
STPS/GTHM/RID G33 80 E3
Edington Gdns
BAIL/MDB/MHD G69 46 F7
Edington St COWCAD G4 4 D1
Edison St CARD/HILL/MSPK G52 76 E1
Edmiston Dr GOV/IBX G51 78 A4
PSLYN/LNWD PA3 73 M4
Edmonstone Dr KSYTH G65 29 K3
Edmonton Ter EKILS G75 2 B7
Edmund Kean EKILN G74 117 J5
Edrom Ct CAR/SHTL G32 80 F5
Edrom St CAR/SHTL G32 80 F6
Edward Av RNFRW PA4 58 D5
Edward Dr HBR/GL G84 10 C4
Edward Pl STPS/GTHM/RID G33 63 K5
Edward St BAIL/MDB/MHD G69 82 F5
CLYDBK G81 58 E2
HMLTN ML3 119 K8
KSYTH G65 29 K1
MTHW ML1 120 F5
Edwin St GOV/IBX G51 78 D5
Edzell Ct SCOT G14 59 K7
Edzell Dr JNSTN PA5 74 D8
NMRNS G77 113 L5
Edzell Gdns BSHPBGS G64 62 C2
WISHAW ML2 122 A7
Edzell Pl SCOT G14 59 K6
Edzell St CTBR ML5 83 K6
SCOT G14 59 K7
Egidia Av GIF/THBK G46 94 B8
Egilsay Crs PPK/MIL G22 61 J2
Egilsay Pl PPK/MIL G22 61 J2
Egilsay St PPK/MIL G22 61 J2
Egilsay Ter PPK/MIL G22 61 J2
Eglinton Ct GBLS G5 79 H5
Eglinton Dr GIF/THBK G46 94 C8
SKLM PA17 50 C4
Eglinton Gdns SKLM PA17 50 C4
Eglinton St BEITH KA15 125 K5
CTBR ML5 84 B2
GBLS G5 79 H6
Eglinton Ter SKLM PA17 50 B6
Egmont Pk EKILS G75 126 D3
Eider KVD/HLHD G12 60 A3
Eider Av EKILS G75 126 D6
Eider Gv EKILS G75 126 D5
Eider Pl EKILS G75 126 D6
Eighth St UD/BTH/TAN G71 98 E1
Eildon Crs AIRDRIE ML6 85 M8
Eildon Dr BRHD/NEIL G78 92 C8
Eildon Rd KKNTL G66 45 M2
Eileen Gdns BSHPBGS G64 44 B8
Elcho St DMNK/BRGTN G40 5 M9
Elder Av BEITH KA15 125 J5
Elderbank BSDN G61 41 L6
Elder Crs BLTYR/CAMB G72 97 L6
Elder Dr BLTYR/CAMB G72 97 L6
Elder Gv UD/BTH/TAN G71 99 H3
Elder Grove Av GOV/IBX G51 77 K2
Elder Grove Ct GOV/IBX G51 77 K2
Elder Grove Pl GOV/IBX G51 77 K2
Elderpark Gdns GOV/IBX G51 77 M2
Elderpark Gv GOV/IBX G51 77 M2
Elderpark St GOV/IBX G51 77 M2
Elderslea Rd CARLUKE ML8 135 G1
Elderslie St KVGV G3 78 F2
Elder St GOV/IBX G51 77 M2
Elders Wy WISHAW ML2 122 D6
Elder Wy MTHW ML1 101 K7
Eldin Pl BRWEIR PA11 72 E4
JNSTN PA5 74 B8
Eldon Gdns BSHPBGS G64 61 L1
Eldon Pl GRNKW/INVK PA16 16 C1
Eldon St GRNKW/INVK PA16 16 B1
KVGV G3 60 E8
Elgin Av EKILN G74 3 H2
Elgin Gdns
CRMNK/CLK/EAG G76 114 F2
Elgin Pl CTBR ML5 84 B6
EKILN G74 3 H2
KSYTH G65 29 K1
Elgin Rd BSDN G61 41 M2
Elgin Ter HMLTN ML3 118 E6
Elgin Wy BLSH ML4 100 A3
Elibank St STPS/GTHM/RID G33 81 G1
Elie Rd BLTYR/CAMB G72 118 D7
Elie St PTCK G11 60 C8
Eliot Crs HMLTN ML3 129 K1
Eliot Ter HMLTN ML3 119 K8
Elizabeth Av KKNTL G66 27 H4
Elizabeth Crs GIF/THBK G46 94 A7
Elizabeth Qd MTHW ML1 100 F4
Elizabeth St GOV/IBX G51 78 C5
Elizabeth Wynd HMLTN ML3 129 K3
Ella Gdns BLSH ML4 100 C5
Ellangowan Ct MLNGV G62 24 A8
Ellangowan Rd MLNGV G62 24 A8
PLKSD/SHW G41 94 C2
Ellergreen Rd BSDN G61 41 L5
Ellerslie St JNSTN PA5 74 A7
Ellesmere St PPK/MIL G22 61 G7
Elliot Av GIF/THBK G46 94 C8
PSLYS PA2 90 E3
Elliot Ct MTHW ML1 100 D8
Elliot Crs EKILN G74 3 L3
Elliot Dr GIF/THBK G46 94 C7
Elliot St KVGV G3 78 F3
Ellisland EKILN G74 117 K7
KKNTL G66 28 B8
Ellisland Av CLYDBK G81 40 C6
Ellisland Crs RUTH G73 95 M5
Ellisland Dr BLTYR/CAMB G72 118 B4
KKNTL G66 28 A8
Ellisland Rd
CRMNK/CLK/EAG G76 114 E5
CUMB G67 31 H7
PLKSW/MSWD G43 94 D4
Ellismuir Farm Rd
BAIL/MDB/MHD G69 82 D6
Ellismuir Pl
BAIL/MDB/MHD G69 82 C6
Ellismuir Rd
BAIL/MDB/MHD G69 82 C6
Ellismuir St CTBR ML5 83 K7
Ellismuir Wy UD/BTH/TAN G71 99 G1
Ellis St CTBR ML5 84 A3
Elliston Av PLK/PH/NH G53 93 J4
Elliston Crs PLK/PH/NH G53 93 J4
Elliston Dr PLK/PH/NH G53 93 J4
Elliston Pl HWWD PA9 88 F5
Elliston Rd HWWD PA9 88 F5
Ellis Wy MTHW ML1 120 F4
Ellon Dr PSLYN/LNWD PA3 74 A5
Ellon Gv PSLYN/LNWD PA3 75 M3
Ellon Wy PSLYN/LNWD PA3 76 A2
Ellrig EKILS G75 127 G5
Elm Av KKNTL G66 45 J4
RNFRW PA4 58 C5
Elm Bank BSHPBGS G64 62 B1
KKNTL G66 45 K2
Elmbank Av UD/BTH/TAN G71 99 H3
Elmbank Crs CGLW G2 4 B4
HMLTN ML3 119 G6
Elmbank Dr ALEX/LLW G83 13 L5
LRKH ML9 130 E8
Elmbank Rd PGL PA14 36 C3
Elmbank St BLSH ML4 100 A4
CARLUKE ML8 135 G1
CGLW G2 4 B5
Elmbank Street La CGLW G2 4 B5
Elm Ct HMLTN ML3 129 M6
Elm Crs UD/BTH/TAN G71 99 K3
Elm Dr AIRDRIE ML6 85 L6
BLTYR/CAMB G72 97 J4
CUMB G67 31 M5
JNSTN PA5 89 M2
Elmfoot St GBLS G5 79 K8
Elm Gdns BSDN G61 41 L3
Elm Gv PGL PA14 36 C3
Elmhurst MTHW ML1 120 D5
Elmira Rd BAIL/MDB/MHD G69 64 C3
Elm La East SCOT G14 59 K6
Elm La West SCOT G14 59 K6
Elm Lea JNSTN PA5 74 B8
Elmore Av LNPK/KPK G44 95 J6
Elm Pl EKILS G75 126 F4
Elm Qd AIRDRIE ML6 85 K3
Elm Rd BRWEIR PA11 72 E2
CLYDBK G81 40 A4
DMBTN G82 20 F6
MTHW ML1 101 H4
PSLYS PA2 76 A8
RUTH G73 96 B6
Elmslie Ct BAIL/MDB/MHD G69 82 C6
Elms Pl BEITH KA15 125 K4
Elm St BLTYR/CAMB G72 118 E3
CRMNK/CLK/EAG G76 114 F4
CTBR ML5 84 C4
KKNTL G66 26 E2
MTHW ML1 120 D2
SCOT G14 59 K6
Elm Ter GRK PA19 15 L3
Elmvale Rw SPRGB/BLRNK G21 61 L6
Elmvale St SPRGB/BLRNK G21 61 L5
Elm View Ct BLSH ML4 100 D5
Elm Wk BSDN G61 41 L3
Elm Wy BLTYR/CAMB G72 97 L6
Elmway LRKH ML9 130 C4
Elmwood WISHAW ML2 121 L8
Elmwood Av NMRNS G77 113 M3
PTCK G11 59 M5
Elmwood Ct UD/BTH/TAN G71 99 G8
Elmwood La PTCK G11 59 M5
Elphinstone Crs EKILS G75 127 J4
Elphinstone Pl GOV/IBX G51 78 C3
Elphinstone Rd GIF/THBK G46 114 A3
Elphin St SMSTN G23 60 D1
Elrig Rd LNPK/KPK G44 94 F5
Elspeth Gdns BSHPBGS G64 44 C8
Elswick Dr AIRDRIE ML6 69 G5
Eltham St PPK/MIL G22 61 H7
Elvan Pl EKILS G75 126 B3
Elvan St CAR/SHTL G32 80 F5
MTHW ML1 120 D3
Embo Dr KNTSWD G13 59 H3
Emerald Ter BLSH ML4 100 A5
Emerson Rd BSHPBGS G64 62 A2
Emerson Rd West
BSHPBGS G64 62 A1
Emily Dr MTHW ML1 120 E5
Emma Jay Rd BLSH ML4 100 B4
Empire Ga SHOTTS ML7 104 F5
Empire Wy MTHW ML1 100 C8
Empress Ct GRNK PA15 7 G6
Empress Dr HBR/GL G84 10 A4
Endfield Av KVD/HLHD G12 60 B4
Endrick Bank BSHPBGS G64 44 A6
Endrick Dr ALEX/LLW G83 13 L1
BSDN G61 41 M5
PSLY PA1 8 B3
Endrick Rd GRNK PA15 17 H8
Endrick St SPRGB/BLRNK G21 61 K7
Endrick Wy ALEX/LLW G83 13 J4
Endrick Wynd HBR/GL G84 11 G7
Engels St ALEX/LLW G83 13 J3
English Rw AIRDRIE ML6 85 J7
English St WISHAW ML2 121 K6
Ennerdale EKILS G75 126 C4
Ennisfree Rd
BLTYR/CAMB G72 118 D2
Ensay St PPK/MIL G22 61 K3
Enterkin St CAR/SHTL G32 80 F6
Eriboll Pl PPK/MIL G22 61 H3
Eriboll St PPK/MIL G22 61 H3
Ericht Pl SHOTTS ML7 104 E3
Ericht Rd PLKSW/MSWD G43 94 C5
Eriska Av SCOT G14 59 G4
Eriskay Av HMLTN ML3 118 F8
NMRNS G77 113 H4
PGL PA14 35 H3
Eriskay Crs NMRNS G77 113 H4
Eriskay Dr OLDK G60 39 J4
Ermelo Gdns EKILS G75 126 E6
Erradale Pl PPK/MIL G22 61 G3
Erradale St PPK/MIL G22 61 G3
Errogie St ESTRH G34 82 B2
Errol Gdns GBLS G5 79 J6
Erskine Av PLKSD/SHW G41 78 B6
Erskine Br OLDK G60 39 G5
Erskine Crs AIRDRIE ML6 84 F4
Erskinefauld Rd
PSLYN/LNWD PA3 74 B4
Erskine Ferry Rd OLDK G60 39 G5
Erskine Rd GIF/THBK G46 114 B4
Erskine Sq
CARD/HILL/MSPK G52 76 F2
Erskine Wy SHOTTS ML7 104 E5
Ervie St ESTRH G34 82 C3
Escart Rd CARLUKE ML8 133 H6
Esdaile Ct MTHW ML1 101 G6
Esk Av RNFRW PA4 58 E7
Eskbank St CAR/SHTL G32 81 G4
Esk Dl EKILN G74 2 A2
Eskdale EKILN G74 2 C4
Eskdale Dr RUTH G73 96 D3
Eskdale Rd BSDN G61 41 K7
Eskdale St GVH/MTFL G42 95 H1
Esk Dr PSLYS PA2 90 E1
Esk St SCOT G14 58 F4
Esmond St KVGV G3 78 C1
Espedair St PSLYS PA2 9 H7
Espieside Crs CTBR ML5 83 L2
Esplanade GRNKW/INVK PA16 16 C1
Essenside Av DRUM G15 41 J7
Essex Dr SCOT G14 59 L5
Essex La SCOT G14 59 L6
Essex Rd GRNKW/INVK PA16 15 L5
Esslemont Av SCOT G14 59 H5
Estate Qd CAR/SHTL G32 97 J2
Estate Rd CAR/SHTL G32 97 J2
Etive Av BSDN G61 42 B6
HMLTN ML3 129 G1
Etive Ct CLYDBK G81 40 C4
CUMB G67 48 B3
Etive Crs BSHPBGS G64 62 B1
CUMB G67 48 B3
WISHAW ML2 131 K1
Etive Dr AIRDRIE ML6 85 J4
BSHPTN PA7 38 C8
CUMB G67 48 B3
GIF/THBK G46 114 D1
Etive Pl CUMB G67 48 C3
LRKH ML9 130 B4
Etive Rd WMYSB PA18 32 B8
Etive St CAR/SHTL G32 81 G5
WISHAW ML2 122 B8
Etna St WISHAW ML2 121 J5
Eton La KVD/HLHD G12 60 E8
Ettrick Av BLSH ML4 100 A2
RNFRW PA4 58 F7
Ettrick Crs RUTH G73 96 C3
Ettrick Dr BSDN G61 41 J2
BSHPTN PA7 38 C8
Ettrick Hl EKILN G74 3 K2
Ettrick Pl PLKSW/MSWD G43 94 D3
Ettrick St WISHAW ML2 122 A4
Ettrick Ter JNSTN PA5 89 J2
Evan Crs GIF/THBK G46 94 D8
Evan Dr GIF/THBK G46 114 D1
Evanton Dr GIF/THBK G46 93 L6
Evanton Pl GIF/THBK G46 93 L6
Everard Ct SPRGB/BLRNK G21 61 L3
Everard Dr SPRGB/BLRNK G21 61 L4
Everard Pl SPRGB/BLRNK G21 61 L3
Everard Qd SPRGB/BLRNK G21 61 L3
Eversley St CAR/SHTL G32 81 G7
Everton Rd PLK/PH/NH G53 77 J7
Ewart Crs HMLTN ML3 119 G8
Ewart Gdns HMLTN ML3 129 H1
Ewart Ter HMLTN ML3 119 G8
Ewing Ct HMLTN ML3 129 J3
Ewing Pl DEN/PKHD G31 80 C5
Ewing Rd LOCHW PA12 109 J2
Ewing St KLBCH PA10 73 G7
RUTH G73 96 A3
Ewing Wk MLNGV G62 42 C1
Excelsior St MTHW ML1 121 K6
Exchange Pl CGLE G1 4 F6
Exeter Dr PTCK G11 60 A8
Exeter La PTCK G11 60 A8
Exeter St CTBR ML5 84 A4
Exmouth Pl GRK PA19 15 L4
Eynort St PPK/MIL G22 61 G3
Eyrepoint Ct
STPS/GTHM/RID G33 81 G2

F

Factory Rd MTHW ML1 120 E4
Fagan Ct BLTYR/CAMB G72 118 E1
Faifley Rd CLYDBK G81 40 D2
Fairbairn Crs GIF/THBK G46 94 A8
Fairburn St CAR/SHTL G32 80 F6
Fairfax Av LNPK/KPK G44 95 J5
Fairfield Ct
CRMNK/CLK/EAG G76 114 E5
Fairfield Dr
CRMNK/CLK/EAG G76 114 E5
RNFRW PA4 58 D8
Fairfield Gdns GOV/IBX G51 77 M1
Fairfield Pl EKILN G74 116 B8
GOV/IBX G51 77 M1
HMLTN ML3 129 L1
UD/BTH/TAN G71 99 H8
Fairfield St GOV/IBX G51 77 M1
Fairford Dr CUMB G67 48 D3
Fairhaven Av AIRDRIE ML6 85 L3
Fairhaven Rd SMSTN G23 60 D2
Fairhill Av HMLTN ML3 129 J1
Fairhill Crs HMLTN ML3 129 J1
Fairhill Pl HMLTN ML3 129 H3
Fairholm Av HMLTN ML3 128 D8
Fairholm St CAR/SHTL G32 80 F6
LRKH ML9 130 B5
Fairley St GOV/IBX G51 78 B4
Fairlie EKILN G74 2 D3
Fairlie Park Dr PTCK G11 60 A8
Fair Oaks
CRMNK/CLK/EAG G76 115 L2
Fairrie St GRNK PA15 7 L8
Fair View Dr LNK/LMHG ML11 136 B5
Fairway BSDN G61 41 H4
Fair Wy DMBTN G82 19 G2
Fairway Av PSLYS PA2 91 K3
Fairways LRKH ML9 130 E6
The Fairways JNSTN PA5 89 K3
UD/BTH/TAN G71 99 G8
Fairways Vw CLYDBK G81 40 D3
Fairweather Pl NMRNS G77 113 J6
Fairyknowe Ct
UD/BTH/TAN G71 99 H8
Fairyknowe Gdns
UD/BTH/TAN G71 99 H8
Faith Av BRWEIR PA11 53 M8
Falconbridge Rd EKILN G74 117 J6
Falcon Crs GRNKW/INVK PA16 16 A3
PSLYN/LNWD PA3 8 A3
Falconer St PGL PA14 18 C8
Falconer Ter HMLTN ML3 129 J1
Falcon Rd JNSTN PA5 89 K3
Falcon Ter MRYH/FIRH G20 60 C2
Falcon Terrace La
MRYH/FIRH G20 60 C2
Falfield St GBLS G5 79 G6
Falkland Av NMRNS G77 114 A4
Falkland Crs BSHPBGS G64 62 D2
Falkland Dr EKILN G74 2 C5
Falkland La KVD/HLHD G12 60 B7
Falkland Pk EKILN G74 2 D6
Falkland Pl CTBR ML5 84 B6
EKILN G74 2 C4
Falkland St KVD/HLHD G12 60 B7
Falloch Pl WISHAW ML2 122 F3
Falloch Rd BSDN G61 41 J7
GVH/MTFL G42 95 G3
MLNGV G62 23 L6
Fallside Av UD/BTH/TAN G71 99 J4
Fallside Rd UD/BTH/TAN G71 99 G8
Falmouth Dr GRK PA19 15 M4
Falside Av PSLYS PA2 91 L1
Falside Rd CAR/SHTL G32 81 G8
PSLYS PA2 91 K1
Falstaff EKILN G74 117 J5

Fancy Farm Pl
GRNKW/INVK PA16 15 M5
Fancy Farm Rd
GRNKW/INVK PA16 15 M5
Faraday Av WISHAW ML2 122 C6
Fara St SMSTN G23 60 F2
Farie St RUTH G73 95 M2
Farm Ct UD/BTH/TAN G71 99 H6
Farm Crs MTHW ML1 101 M5
Farme Castle Ct RUTH G73 96 C1
Farmeloan Rd RUTH G73 96 B2
Farmgate Sq BLSH ML4 99 M6
Farmington Av CAR/SHTL G32 81 K5
Farmington Gdns
CAR/SHTL G32 81 K5
Farmington Gv CAR/SHTL G32 81 K5
Farm La BLSH ML4 99 M7
Farm Pk KKNTL G66 45 K6
Farm Rd BLTYR/CAMB G72 118 D1
CLYDBK G81 39 K7
PGL PA14 34 E3
PLKSD/SHW G41 78 B5
Farm St MTHW ML1 120 D2
Farm Ter HMLTN ML3 118 F6
Farndale EKILN G74 2 A1
Farne Dr LNPK/KPK G44 95 H6
Farnell St COWCAD G4 61 H8
Farquhar Rd PGL PA14 17 M7
Farrier Ct JNSTN PA5 73 M7
Faskally Av BSHPBGS G64 43 L7
Faskin Crs PLK/PH/NH G53 92 F2
Faskine Av AIRDRIE ML6 84 F4
Faskine Crs AIRDRIE ML6 84 F3
Faskin Pl PLK/PH/NH G53 92 F2
Faskin Rd PLK/PH/NH G53 92 F2
Fasque Pl DRUM G15 40 E5
Fauldhouse St GBLS G5 79 K7
Faulds BAIL/MDB/MHD G69 82 C5
Faulds Gdns
BAIL/MDB/MHD G69 82 C5
Fauldshead Rd RNFRW PA4 58 C6
Fauldspark Crs
BAIL/MDB/MHD G69 82 C4
Faulds Park Rd GRK PA19 14 E4
Faulds St CTBR ML5 83 L7
Fauldswood Crs PSLYS PA2 75 H8
Fauldswood Dr PSLYS PA2 75 H8
Faulkner Gv MTHW ML1 121 M1
Fearnach Pl MRYH/FIRH G20 60 B3
Fearnan Pl GRNKW/INVK PA16 16 A5
Fearnmore Rd MRYH/FIRH G20 60 D3
The Fells KKNTL G66 26 E2
Fellsview Av KKNTL G66 45 M1
Felton Pl KNTSWD G13 58 F2
Fendoch St CAR/SHTL G32 81 G6
Fenella St CAR/SHTL G32 81 H5
Fennsbank Av RUTH G73 96 D7
Fenwick Dr BRHD/NEIL G78 92 D8
HMLTN ML3 129 L3
Fenwick Pl GIF/THBK G46 114 B1
Fenwick Rd GIF/THBK G46 94 C7
Ferclay St CLYDBK G81 40 D2
Fereneze Av BRHD/NEIL G78 92 B6
CRMNK/CLK/EAG G76 114 C2
RNFRW PA4 76 A1
Fereneze Crs HMLTN ML3 118 F7
KNTSWD G13 58 F2
Fereneze Dr PSLYS PA2 91 J3
Fereneze Gv BRHD/NEIL G78 92 B6
Fereneze Rd BRHD/NEIL G78 110 F3
Fergus Av PSLYN/LNWD PA3 75 G5
Fergus Dr GRNKW/INVK PA16 16 A5
MRYH/FIRH G20 60 E6
PSLYN/LNWD PA3 75 G5
Fergus Gdns HMLTN ML3 119 M8
Fergus La MRYH/FIRH G20 60 F6
Ferguslie PSLY PA1 8 A6
Ferguslie Park Av
PSLYN/LNWD PA3 8 A1
Ferguslie Park Crs
PSLYN/LNWD PA3 75 G6
Ferguslie Wk PSLY PA1 8 B6
Ferguson Av MLNGV G62 42 A1
RNFRW PA4 58 D6
Ferguson Dr MTHW ML1 120 E6
Ferguson St JNSTN PA5 73 L7
RNFRW PA4 58 D6
Ferguson Wy AIRDRIE ML6 67 G7
Fergus Pl GRNKW/INVK PA16 16 A5
Fergus Rd GRNKW/INVK PA16 16 A5
Fergusson Pl EKILN G74 117 K5
Fergusson Rd CUMB G67 30 F7
Ferguston Rd BSDN G61 41 M5
Fernan St CAR/SHTL G32 80 F5
Fern Av BSHPBGS G64 62 B2
ERSK PA8 57 H3
KKNTL G66 45 J6
Fernbank Av BLTYR/CAMB G72 97 J6
Fernbank St PPK/MIL G22 61 L5
Fernbrae Av RUTH G73 96 C7
Fernbrae Wy RUTH G73 96 B7
Ferncroft Dr LNPK/KPK G44 95 K5
Ferndale LRKH ML9 130 C8
Ferndale Ct SMSTN G23 60 D2
Ferndale Dr SMSTN G23 60 C2
Ferndale Gdns SMSTN G23 60 D2
Ferndale Pl SMSTN G23 60 D2
Fern Dr BRHD/NEIL G78 92 B5
Ferness Ov SPRGB/BLRNK G21 62 C4
Ferness Pl SPRGB/BLRNK G21 62 C3
Ferness Rd SPRGB/BLRNK G21 62 C4
Fern Gv BAIL/MDB/MHD G69 65 G4
Ferngrove Av KVD/HLHD G12 60 B4
Fernhill Gra UD/BTH/TAN G71 119 G1
Fernhill Rd CSMK G45 96 A6
Ferniegair Av HBR/GL G84 10 A5
Fernie Gdns DMBTN G82 19 H2
MRYH/FIRH G20 60 E3
Fernieshaw Rd MTHW ML1 102 F6
Fernington Pl WISHAW ML2 122 B5
Fern La KKNTL G66 26 C1
KVD/HLHD G12 59 M4
Fernlea BSDN G61 41 L6
Fernleigh Rd
PLKSW/MSWD G43 94 D5
Fernslea Av BLTYR/CAMB G72 118 C2
Fern St MTHW ML1 121 G5
Ferryden St SCOT G14 59 L7
Ferryfield Gdns ALEX/LLW G83 13 L6
Ferry Loan ALEX/LLW G83 13 K5
Ferry Rd BSHPTN PA7 38 A6
DMBTN G82 19 H4
KVGV G3 78 C1
RNFRW PA4 58 D5
UD/BTH/TAN G71 98 E4
Fersit St PLKSW/MSWD G43 94 C4
Fetlar Dr LNPK/KPK G44 95 J5
Fetlar Rd BRWEIR PA11 72 D2
Fettercairn Av DRUM G15 40 E5
Fettes St STPS/GTHM/RID G33 80 F2
Fiddoch Ct WISHAW ML2 122 F2
Fidra St STPS/GTHM/RID G33 80 F2
Fielden Pl DMNK/BRGTN G40 80 A5
Fielden St DMNK/BRGTN G40 80 A5
Field Gv CRMNK/CLK/EAG G76 114 F5
Fieldhead Dr
PLKSW/MSWD G43 94 A5
Fieldhead Sq
PLKSW/MSWD G43 94 A5
Field Rd CLYDBK G81 40 D1
CRMNK/CLK/EAG G76 114 F5
LRKH ML9 130 D7
Fields La CRG/CRSL/HOU PA6 55 H7
Field St HMLTN ML3 129 K1
Fife Av AIRDRIE ML6 85 G4
CARD/HILL/MSPK G52 77 H5
Fife Crs UD/BTH/TAN G71 119 G1
Fife Dr GRNKW/INVK PA16 15 K4
MTHW ML1 100 D7
Fife Rd GRNKW/INVK PA16 15 K4
Fife Wy BSHPBGS G64 61 M3
Fifth Av AIRDRIE ML6 85 J1
KVD/HLHD G12 59 M4
RNFRW PA4 58 C7
STPS/GTHM/RID G33 63 H5
Fifth Rd BLTYR/CAMB G72 118 E5
Fifty Pitches Pl GOV/IBX G51 77 J2
Fifty Pitches Rd GOV/IBX G51 77 H3
Finart Dr PSLYS PA2 76 B8
Finaven Gdns BSDN G61 41 H1
Finbraken Dr GRK PA19 14 F4
Finch Dr KNTSWD G13 58 F1
Finch Gv CTBR ML5 84 E6
Finch Pl JNSTN PA5 89 K3
Finch Rd GRNKW/INVK PA16 16 B4
Finch Wy BLSH ML4 99 M2
Findhorn Av PSLYS PA2 90 F1
RNFRW PA4 58 E6
Findhorn Ct EKILS G75 126 A2
Findhorn Crs
GRNKW/INVK PA16 32 F6
Findhorn Pl EKILS G75 126 A2
GRNKW/INVK PA16 32 F5
Findhorn Rd GRNKW/INVK PA16 32 F6
Findhorn St
STPS/GTHM/RID G33 80 D2
Findlay St KSYTH G65 29 K2
MTHW ML1 120 F4
Findlay Ter BLTYR/CAMB G72 97 K4
Findochty St
STPS/GTHM/RID G33 81 L1
Fingal La MRYH/FIRH G20 60 C3
Fingal St MRYH/FIRH G20 60 D3
Fingalton Rd NMRNS G77 112 E4
Fingask St CAR/SHTL G32 81 J6
Finglas Av PSLYS PA2 76 B8
Finglen Pl PLK/PH/NH G53 93 H5
Fingleton Av BRHD/NEIL G78 92 D8
Finhaven St CAR/SHTL G32 80 E7
Finlarig St ESTRH G34 82 C3
Finlas Pl PPK/MIL G22 61 K5
Finlas St PPK/MIL G22 61 K6
Finlay Dr DEN/PKHD G31 80 A3
PSLYN/LNWD PA3 73 M5
Finlay Ri MLNGV G62 42 C2
Finlayson Dr AIRDRIE ML6 85 L2
Finlayson Qd AIRDRIE ML6 85 L2
Finlaystone Pl KLMCLM PA13 35 K8
Finlaystone Rd PGL PA14 35 G3
Finlaystone St CTBR ML5 83 L3
Finnart Crs GRK PA19 15 J3
Finnart Rd GRNKW/INVK PA16 16 D3
Finnart Sq DMNK/BRGTN G40 79 M7
Finnart St DMNK/BRGTN G40 79 M7
GRNKW/INVK PA16 6 A2
Finneston St GRNK PA15 7 H7
Finnieston Sq KVGV G3 78 E3
Finnieston St KVGV G3 78 E3
Finnie Ter GRK PA19 15 K3
Finnie Wynd MTHW ML1 121 H5
Finnockbog Dr
GRNKW/INVK PA16 32 E5
Finnockbog Rd
GRNKW/INVK PA16 32 E5
Finsbay St GOV/IBX G51 77 K3
Fintaig La WISHAW ML2 122 E6
Fintrie Ter HMLTN ML3 118 E6
Fintry Av PSLYS PA2 91 L2
Fintry Crs BRHD/NEIL G78 92 C8
BSHPBGS G64 62 C1
Fintry Dr LNPK/KPK G44 95 J3
Fintry Gdns BSDN G61 41 J1
Fintry Pl EKILS G75 126 E6
Fintry Rd GRNK PA15 17 H8
Firbank Av BSHPBGS G64 44 B2
Fir Bank Av LRKH ML9 130 D8
Firbank Qd AIRDRIE ML6 85 L6
Firbank Ter BRHD/NEIL G78 92 E8
Fir Ct BLTYR/CAMB G72 97 L6
Firdon Crs DRUM G15 41 G8
Fir Dr EKILS G75 126 E5
Fir Gv MTHW ML1 101 G7
UD/BTH/TAN G71 99 J3
Firhill Av AIRDRIE ML6 84 F3
Firhill Rd MRYH/FIRH G20 61 G6
Firhill St MRYH/FIRH G20 61 G6
Firlee EKILS G75 126 C3
Firpark Rd BSHPBGS G64 62 B2
Firpark St DEN/PKHD G31 5 M5
Fir Park St MTHW ML1 120 F5
Firpark Ter DEN/PKHD G31 5 M6
Fir Pl BAIL/MDB/MHD G69 82 A7
BLTYR/CAMB G72 97 H4
JNSTN PA5 90 A1
First Av ALEX/LLW G83 13 L5
BSDN G61 42 A7
DMBTN G82 21 J8
LNPK/KPK G44 94 F8
RNFRW PA4 58 C7
STPS/GTHM/RID G33 63 H5
UD/BTH/TAN G71 98 E2
First Gdns PLKSD/SHW G41 78 A6
Fir St GRNK PA15 17 L7
First Rd BLTYR/CAMB G72 118 E5
First St UD/BTH/TAN G71 98 F2
First Ter CLYDBK G81 40 A6
Fir Ter GRK PA19 15 K3
Firth Crs GRK PA19 15 H3
Firthview Ter DMBTN G82 20 C7
Firtree Pl WISHAW ML2 123 H3
Firtree Rd WISHAW ML2 123 H3
Fir Vw AIRDRIE ML6 85 H7
Firwood Cts NMRNS G77 113 M5
Firwood Dr LNPK/KPK G44 95 J4
Firwood Rd NMRNS G77 113 L4
Fischer Gdns PSLY PA1 74 F6
Fisher Av KSYTH G65 29 K2
PSLY PA1 74 F6
Fisher Crs CLYDBK G81 40 B4
Fisher Dr PSLY PA1 74 F6
Fisher Pl HBR/GL G84 11 G5
Fisher St LRKH ML9 130 D8
Fisher Wy PSLY PA1 74 F6
Fisherwood Rd ALEX/LLW G83 13 K2
Fishescoates Av RUTH G73 96 D5
Fishescoates Gdns RUTH G73 96 C5
Fitzalan Dr PSLYN/LNWD PA3 9 L1
Fitzalan Rd RNFRW PA4 58 A8
Fitzroy La KVGV G3 78 E2
Flakefield EKILN G74 116 B8
Flanders St CLYDBK G81 40 C2
Flatterton Rd
GRNKW/INVK PA16 15 J7
Flatt Rd LARGS KA30 106 F5
Flaxfield Gv MTHW ML1 100 D7
Flaxmill Av WISHAW ML2 121 K5
Flax Mill Rd SHOTTS ML7 71 L7
Flax Rd UD/BTH/TAN G71 99 G5
Fleet Av RNFRW PA4 58 E8
Fleet St CAR/SHTL G32 81 H6
Fleming Av
BAIL/MDB/MHD G69 64 C3
CLYDBK G81 58 D1
Fleming Ct CARLUKE ML8 133 G8
HMLTN ML3 118 E6
MTHW ML1 121 G5
Fleming Pl BTHG/ARM EH48 71 L1
EKILS G75 2 D7
Fleming Rd BLSH ML4 100 B3
BSHPTN PA7 38 B7
CRG/CRSL/HOU PA6 55 G8
CUMB G67 30 F7
Fleming St DEN/PKHD G31 80 B4
PSLYN/LNWD PA3 75 L3
Flemington St
SPRGB/BLRNK G21 61 M7
Flemington Wy
BAIL/MDB/MHD G69 64 C2
Fleming Wy HMLTN ML3 118 D6
Flenders Av
CRMNK/CLK/EAG G76 114 C4
Flenders Rd
CRMNK/CLK/EAG G76 114 C4
Fletcher Av GRK PA19 15 L3
Fleurs Av PLKSD/SHW G41 78 B7
Fleurs Rd PLKSD/SHW G41 78 B6
Flinders Pl EKILS G75 126 E3
Flint Mill La GRNK PA15 7 G9
Flloyd St CTBR ML5 83 M3
Floorsburn Crs JNSTN PA5 73 L8
Floors St JNSTN PA5 73 M8
Flora Gdns BSHPBGS G64 44 C8
Florence Dr GIF/THBK G46 94 C8
KLMCLM PA13 53 H2
Florence Gdns RUTH G73 96 C6
Florence St GBLS G5 79 J5
GRNKW/INVK PA16 16 B5
Florida Av GVH/MTFL G42 95 H2
Florida Crs GVH/MTFL G42 95 H2
Florida Dr GVH/MTFL G42 95 G2
Florida Gdns
BAIL/MDB/MHD G69 82 A5
Florida Sq GVH/MTFL G42 95 H2
Florida St GVH/MTFL G42 95 H2
Florish Rd ERSK PA8 57 K2
Flour Mill Wynd
BAIL/MDB/MHD G69 47 G7
Flowerdale Pl PLK/PH/NH G53 93 H6
Flowerhill St AIRDRIE ML6 85 H1
Fluchter Rd MLNGV G62 43 G1
Flures Av ERSK PA8 57 L2
Flures Crs ERSK PA8 57 L2
Flures Dr ERSK PA8 57 L2
Flures Pl ERSK PA8 57 L2
Fochabers Dr
CARD/HILL/MSPK G52 77 J3
Foinaven Dr GIF/THBK G46 93 M4
Foinaven Gdns GIF/THBK G46 93 M3
Foinaven Wy GIF/THBK G46 94 A4
Foinavon Rd HMLTN ML3 129 L7
Footfield Rd BLSH ML4 99 M7
Forbes Dr MTHW ML1 100 B7
Forbes Pl PSLY PA1 9 H5
Forbes St DMNK/BRGTN G40 5 M9
Fordneuk St
DMNK/BRGTN G40 80 A5
Fordoun St ESTRH G34 82 D2
Ford Rd KVD/HLHD G12 60 D6
NMRNS G77 113 K6
Fordyce St PTCK G11 60 B8
Forehouse Rd KLBCH PA10 72 C6
Foremount Terrace La
KVD/HLHD G12 60 C7
Fore Rw HMLTN ML3 119 L6
Forest Av BLSH ML4 100 C6
HMLTN ML3 129 K4
Forest Dr UD/BTH/TAN G71 99 G7
Forestfield Gdns AIRDRIE ML6 69 G5
Forest Gdns KKNTL G66 45 G6
Foresthall Crs
SPRGB/BLRNK G21 62 A7
Foresthall Dr
SPRGB/BLRNK G21 62 A7
Forest Kirk CARLUKE ML8 135 H1
Forest La HMLTN ML3 129 K4
Forest Pk WISHAW ML2 122 D4
Forest Pl CARLUKE ML8 134 B8
KKNTL G66 45 G6
PSLYS PA2 75 L8
Fore St PGL PA14 18 C8
SCOT G14 59 J6
Forest Rd CUMB G67 31 K7
LRKH ML9 130 D7
Forest Vw CUMB G67 31 J6
Forfar Av
CARD/HILL/MSPK G52 77 H5
Forfar Crs BSHPBGS G64 62 C2
Forfar Rd GRNKW/INVK PA16 15 M6
Forgan Gdns BSHPBGS G64 62 D2
Forge Dr CTBR ML5 83 M3
Forge Pl SPRGB/BLRNK G21 62 B8
Forge Rd AIRDRIE ML6 85 M3
Forge Rw AIRDRIE ML6 85 J6
Forge St SPRGB/BLRNK G21 62 B8
Forgewood Pth AIRDRIE ML6 85 M3
Forgewood Rd MTHW ML1 100 C7
Forglen St ESTRH G34 82 B1
Formby Dr SMSTN G23 60 D2
Forres Av GIF/THBK G46 94 D7
Forres Crs BLSH ML4 100 A3
Forres Ga GIF/THBK G46 94 D8
Forres Place
GRNKW/INVK PA16 32 F6
Forres Qd WISHAW ML2 122 B4
Forres St BLTYR/CAMB G72 118 C4
SMSTN G23 60 E1
Forrest Dr BSDN G61 23 H8
Forrester Ct BSHPBGS G64 61 M2
Forrestfield Crs NMRNS G77 113 L4
Forrestfield Gdns NMRNS G77 113 L4
Forrestfield Rd AIRDRIE ML6 69 L2
Forrestfield St
SPRGB/BLRNK G21 80 A1
Forrest Ga HMLTN ML3 129 H1
UD/BTH/TAN G71 99 H1
Forrestlea Rd CARLUKE ML8 135 G1
Forrest Pl SHOTTS ML7 71 L7
Forrest Rd AIRDRIE ML6 70 B3
LNK/LMHG ML11 137 H4
Forrest St AIRDRIE ML6 85 L1
BLTYR/CAMB G72 118 F3
DMNK/BRGTN G40 80 A5
SHOTTS ML7 104 E4
Forsa Ct EKILS G75 126 F6
Forsyth Ct LNK/LMHG ML11 137 J5
Forsyth Gv GRNKW/INVK PA16 16 D3
Forsyth St AIRDRIE ML6 85 H1
GRNKW/INVK PA16 16 D3
Forteviot Av
BAIL/MDB/MHD G69 82 C5
Forteviot Pl
BAIL/MDB/MHD G69 82 C5
Forth Av PSLYS PA2 90 F1
Forth Ct EKILS G75 126 B3
Forth Crs EKILS G75 126 B3
Forth Gv EKILS G75 126 B3
Forth Pl JNSTN PA5 89 J2
Forth Rd BLTYR/CAMB G72 118 E5
BSDN G61 41 K7
BSHPBGS G64 44 B2
Forth St CLYDBK G81 58 C1
PLKSD/SHW G41 78 F7
Forth Ter HMLTN ML3 129 H2
Forties Ct GIF/THBK G46 93 M4
Forties Crs GIF/THBK G46 93 M4
Forties Gdns GIF/THBK G46 94 A5
Forties Rd CRG/CRSL/HOU PA6 73 K2
Forties Wy GIF/THBK G46 94 A5
Fortieth Av EKILS G75 127 J5
Fortingall Av KVD/HLHD G12 60 C4
Fortingall Pl KVD/HLHD G12 60 C4
Fortingall Rd
BLTYR/CAMB G72 118 F5
Fortissat Av SHOTTS ML7 104 D4
Fortissat Rd SHOTTS ML7 104 B1
Fort Matilda Pl
GRNKW/INVK PA16 16 B2
Fortrose Ct BLTYR/CAMB G72 118 C7
Fortrose St PTCK G11 60 B8
Fort St LARGS KA30 106 E5
MTHW ML1 120 C1
Forum Pl MTHW ML1 100 C8
Fossil Gv KKNTL G66 46 A1
Fosterland SKLM PA17 50 C6
Foswell Dr DRUM G15 40 F4
Foswell Pl DRUM G15 40 F4
Fotheringay La
PLKSD/SHW G41 78 D8
Fotheringay Rd
PLKSD/SHW G41 78 D8
Foulburn Rd MTHW ML1 103 J7
Foulis La KNTSWD G13 59 M3
Foulis St KNTSWD G13 59 M3
Foulsykes Rd WISHAW ML2 122 E5
Foundry La BRHD/NEIL G78 92 C7
Foundry Rd MTHW ML1 102 C7
SHOTTS ML7 104 E5
Fountain Av RNFRW PA4 57 H6
Fountain Crs RNFRW PA4 57 H5
Fountain Dr RNFRW PA4 57 J6
Fountainwell Av
SPRGB/BLRNK G21 61 K8
Fountainwell Dr
SPRGB/BLRNK G21 61 K8
Fountainwell Pl
SPRGB/BLRNK G21 61 K8
Fountainwell Rd COWCAD G4 61 K8
Fountainwell Sq
SPRGB/BLRNK G21 61 L8
Fourth Av DMBTN G82 21 J8
RNFRW PA4 58 C7
STPS/GTHM/RID G33 63 H5
Fourth Gdns PLKSD/SHW G41 78 A6
Fourth St UD/BTH/TAN G71 98 F1
Four Windings
CRG/CRSL/HOU PA6 55 H8
Fowler Pl EKILS G75 127 K4
Fowlis Dr NMRNS G77 113 J3
Foxbar Crs PSLYS PA2 90 E3
Foxbar Dr KNTSWD G13 59 H3
PSLYS PA2 90 E3
Foxbar Rd PSLYS PA2 90 F3
Foxes Gv KKNTL G66 45 L5
Foxglove Pl PLK/PH/NH G53 93 H6
Fox Gv MTHW ML1 120 B2
Foxhills Pl SMSTN G23 60 E1
Foxknowe Gdns CLYDBK G81 40 D2
Foxley St CAR/SHTL G32 97 J1
Fox St CGLE G1 4 E8
GRNKW/INVK PA16 16 D2
Foyers Ter SPRGB/BLRNK G21 62 A6
Foy Gdn BLSH ML4 100 A1
Francis St GBLS G5 79 G6
Frankfield Rd
STPS/GTHM/RID G33 63 L5
Frankfield St
STPS/GTHM/RID G33 62 D8
Frankfort St PLKSD/SHW G41 94 E1
Franklin Pl EKILS G75 126 E1
Franklin St DMNK/BRGTN G40 79 M7
Fran Ter GRNKW/INVK PA16 32 E5
Fraser Av BSHPTN PA7 38 A6
DMBTN G82 21 J6
JNSTN PA5 74 A8
NMRNS G77 113 L3
RUTH G73 96 C3
Fraserburgh Pl
GRNKW/INVK PA16 32 E6
Fraser Crs HMLTN ML3 119 H8
Fraser Gdns KKNTL G66 45 H2
Fraser St BLTYR/CAMB G72 96 E4
MTHW ML1 102 B7
Frazer Av HBR/GL G84 10 A4
Frazer St DMNK/BRGTN G40 80 B5
LARGS KA30 106 E5
Frederick St CTBR ML5 83 L2
Freeland Ct PLK/PH/NH G53 93 J3
Freeland Crs PLK/PH/NH G53 93 H3
Freeland Dr BRWEIR PA11 72 D1
PLK/PH/NH G53 93 H3
RNFRW PA4 57 J4
Freeland Pl KKNTL G66 45 K2
Freeland Rd ERSK PA8 57 H3
Freelands Crs OLDK G60 39 H5
Freelands Rd OLDK G60 39 J6
Freeneuk La BLTYR/CAMB G72 97 H4
Freeneuk Wynd
BLTYR/CAMB G72 97 H4
Freesia Ct MTHW ML1 120 E4
French St CLYDBK G81 39 L7
DMNK/BRGTN G40 79 M7
RNFRW PA4 58 B7
WISHAW ML2 122 B6
Freuchie St
BAIL/MDB/MHD G69 82 B3
Frew St AIRDRIE ML6 85 G1
Friar Av BSHPBGS G64 44 B6
Friarscourt Av KNTSWD G13 59 K1
Friarscourt Rd
BAIL/MDB/MHD G69 64 B1
Friars Cft KKNTL G66 45 L2
Friarsdene LNK/LMHG ML11 136 F5
Friarsfield Rd LNK/LMHG ML11 136 F5
Friarshall Ga PSLYS PA2 75 K8
Friar's La LNK/LMHG ML11 136 F6
Friars Pl KNTSWD G13 59 K1
Friars Wy AIRDRIE ML6 85 J5
Friar's Wynd LNK/LMHG ML11 136 F5
Friarton Rd PLKSW/MSWD G43 94 F5
Frood St MTHW ML1 100 C8
Fruin Av NMRNS G77 113 L4
Fruin Dr WISHAW ML2 122 E6
Fruin La HBR/GL G84 11 G7
Fruin Ri HMLTN ML3 118 E8
Fruin Rd DRUM G15 40 F8
Fruin St PPK/MIL G22 61 J6
Fudstone Dr KBRN KA25 124 C5
Fulbar Av RNFRW PA4 58 C5
Fulbar Ct RNFRW PA4 58 C5
Fulbar Crs PSLYS PA2 74 F8
Fulbar Gdns PSLYS PA2 74 F8
Fulbar La RNFRW PA4 58 D5
Fulbar Rd GOV/IBX G51 77 J2
PSLYS PA2 74 F8
Fulbar St RNFRW PA4 58 D5
Fullarton Av CAR/SHTL G32 81 G8
Fullarton Dr CAR/SHTL G32 97 H1
Fullarton La CAR/SHTL G32 81 G8
Fullarton Pl CTBR ML5 83 K7
Fullarton Rd BALLOCH G68 30 E4
CAR/SHTL G32 97 G1
Fullarton St CTBR ML5 83 L7
Fullers Ga CLYDBK G81 40 C2
Fullerton La GRNK PA15 17 L6
Fullerton St PSLYN/LNWD PA3 75 K3
Fullerton Ter PSLYN/LNWD PA3 75 L3
Fulmar Pk EKILN G74 2 D2
Fulmar Pl JNSTN PA5 89 J4
Fulton Crs KLBCH PA10 73 G7
Fulton Dr CRG/CRSL/HOU PA6 73 L2
Fulton Gdns
CRG/CRSL/HOU PA6 73 L2
Fulton Rd MLNGV G62 42 B1
Fulton St KNTSWD G13 59 L2
Fulwood Av KNTSWD G13 58 F2
PSLYN/LNWD PA3 74 B4
Fulwood Pl KNTSWD G13 58 F2
The Furlongs HMLTN ML3 119 K6
Furnace Rd HMLTN ML3 129 M7
Fyfe Shore Rd PGL PA14 34 F1
Fyffe Park Rd PGL PA14 34 E1
Fyneart St WISHAW ML2 122 E5
Fyne Av BLSH ML4 99 L3
Fyne Ct HMLTN ML3 129 G1
Fyne Crs LRKH ML9 130 B4
Fynloch Pl CLYDBK G81 39 L3
Fyvie Av PLKSW/MSWD G43 94 A5
Fyvie Crs AIRDRIE ML6 85 L2

G

Gabriel St GRNK PA15 7 G9
Gadie Av RNFRW PA4 58 E7
Gadie St STPS/GTHM/RID G33 80 D2
Gadloch Av KKNTL G66 45 K8
Gadloch St PPK/MIL G22 61 J4
Gadloch Vw KKNTL G66 45 K8
Gadsburn Ct SPRGB/BLRNK G21 62 C4
Gadshill St SPRGB/BLRNK G21 5 M2
Gael St GRNKW/INVK PA16 16 C5
Gailes Pk UD/BTH/TAN G71 98 F8
Gailes Rd BALLOCH G68 30 F4
Gailes St DMNK/BRGTN G40 80 B6
Gain & Shankburn Rd
AIRDRIE ML6 48 C8
Gainburn Ct CUMB G67 47 M4
Gainburn Crs CUMB G67 47 M5
Gainburn Gdns CUMB G67 47 M5
Gainburn Pl CUMB G67 47 M4
Gainburn Vw CUMB G67 48 A3
Gain Rd CTBR ML5 65 M1
Gainside Rd CTBR ML5 65 J4
Gairbraid Av MRYH/FIRH G20 60 C4
Gairbraid Ct MRYH/FIRH G20 60 C4
Gairbraid Pl MRYH/FIRH G20 60 D4
Gairbraid Ter
BAIL/MDB/MHD G69 83 G5
Gair Crs CARLUKE ML8 133 J6
WISHAW ML2 122 B8
Gair Rd CARLUKE ML8 133 K4
Gaitskell Av ALEX/LLW G83 13 J3
Gala Av RNFRW PA4 58 E7
Gala Crs WISHAW ML2 122 A5
Gala St STPS/GTHM/RID G33 62 E8
Galbraith Crs CARLUKE ML8 132 C3
Galbraith Dr GOV/IBX G51 77 K1
MLNGV G62 41 M1
Galdenoch St
STPS/GTHM/RID G33 63 H8
Gallacher Av PSLYS PA2 91 G1
Gallacher Ct MTHW ML1 121 H6
Gallacher Crs ALEX/LLW G83 13 L2
Gallahill Av PGL PA14 35 G3
Gallan Av SMSTN G23 60 E1
Gallery Gv CTBR ML5 84 A3
Galloway Av HMLTN ML3 129 J3
PSLYN/LNWD PA3 75 K3
WISHAW ML2 122 C5
Galloway Dr RUTH G73 96 B7
Galloway Rd AIRDRIE ML6 84 F5
EKILN G74 117 J7
Galloway St SPRGB/BLRNK G21 61 M4
Galloway Ter PSLYN/LNWD PA3 75 K3

Gallowflat St RUTH G73 96 B2
Gallowgate CGLE G1 5 J8
DEN/PKHD G31 80 B5
Gallowgate La LARGS KA30 106 E5
Gallowgate St LARGS KA30 106 E5
Gallowhill LRKH ML9 130 C7
Gallowhill Av KKNTL G66 45 J4
Gallowhill Rd
CRMNK/CLK/EAG G76 115 L2
KKNTL G66 45 J4
LNK/LMHG ML11 137 G5
PSLYN/LNWD PA3 9 K2
Galston Av NMRNS G77 114 A5
Galston Ct HMLTN ML3 129 L3
Galston St PLK/PH/NH G53 92 F3
Galt Pl EKILS G75 127 G3
Galt St GRNK PA15 7 J7
Gamrie Dr PLK/PH/NH G53 93 G2
Gamrie Gdns PLK/PH/NH G53 93 G2
Gamrie Rd PLK/PH/NH G53 93 G1
Gannochy Dr BSHPBGS G64 62 C1
Gantock Crs
STPS/GTHM/RID G33 81 H3
Gara Rd AIRDRIE ML6 85 K4
Gardenhall EKILS G75 126 A2
Gardenhall Ct EKILS G75 126 B2
Gardenside Av CAR/SHTL G32 97 H2
UD/BTH/TAN G71 98 E4
Gardenside Crs CAR/SHTL G32 97 H2
Gardenside Gv CAR/SHTL G32 97 H2
Gardenside Pl CAR/SHTL G32 97 H2
Gardenside Rd HMLTN ML3 119 K8
Gardenside St
UD/BTH/TAN G71 98 E4
Garden Square Wk
AIRDRIE ML6 84 D1
Gardner Gv UD/BTH/TAN G71 99 G2
Gardner St PTCK G11 60 B8
Gardyne St ESTRH G34 82 A1
Gareloch Av AIRDRIE ML6 66 F7
PSLYS PA2 75 G8
Gareloch Ct GRNK PA15 6 F9
Gareloch La PGL PA14 34 D2
Gareloch Rd GRNK PA15 6 F8
PGL PA14 34 D2
Garfield Av BLSH ML4 100 C5
Garfield Dr BLSH ML4 100 C5
Garfield Pl STPS/GTHM/RID G33 63 L4
Garfield St DEN/PKHD G31 80 A4
Garforth Rd
BAIL/MDB/MHD G69 81 M6
Gargrave Av
BAIL/MDB/MHD G69 81 M6
Garion Dr KNTSWD G13 59 H4
Garlieston Rd
STPS/GTHM/RID G33 81 M4
Garmouth Ct GOV/IBX G51 78 A2
Garmouth Gdns GOV/IBX G51 77 M1
Garmouth St GOV/IBX G51 77 M1
Garnethill St KVGV G3 4 C3
Garnet St KVGV G3 4 B3
Garngaber Av KKNTL G66 45 K5
Garngaber Ct KKNTL G66 45 L5
Garnhall Farm Rd
BALLOCH G68 31 L1
Garnie Av ERSK PA8 57 K2
Garnieland Rd ERSK PA8 57 K2
Garnie La ERSK PA8 57 K2
Garnie Ov ERSK PA8 57 K1
Garnie Pl ERSK PA8 57 K1
Garnkirk La
STPS/GTHM/RID G33 63 L5
Garnock Ct KBRN KA25 124 C4
Garnock Pk EKILN G74 3 L5
Garnockside GLGNK KA14 124 D7
Garnock St KBRN KA25 124 D3
SPRGB/BLRNK G21 61 M8
Garnock Vw GLGNK KA14 124 D6
Garnqueen Crs CTBR ML5 65 K5
Garpel Wy LOCHW PA12 109 H2
Garrawy Rd HBR/GL G84 10 F5
Garrell Av KSYTH G65 29 K1
Garrell Pl KSYTH G65 29 J2
Garrell Rd KSYTH G65 29 J2
Garrell Wy CUMB G67 30 E7
KSYTH G65 29 J2
Garret Pl BALLOCH G68 30 D4
Garrick Av NMRNS G77 113 K7
Garrioch Crs MRYH/FIRH G20 60 D5
Garrioch Dr MRYH/FIRH G20 60 D5
Garrioch Ga MRYH/FIRH G20 60 D5
Garriochmill Rd KVD/HLHD G12 60 E7
Garrioch Qd MRYH/FIRH G20 60 D5
Garrioch Rd MRYH/FIRH G20 60 D6
Garrion Pl LRKH ML9 131 H8
Garrion St WISHAW ML2 131 L3
Garrowhill Dr
BAIL/MDB/MHD G69 81 M5
Garry Av BSDN G61 42 A8
Garry Dr PSLYS PA2 75 G8
Garry St LNPK/KPK G44 95 G3
Garscadden Rd DRUM G15 40 F7
Garscadden Rd South
DRUM G15 58 F1
KNTSWD G13 59 G1
Garscube Rd COWCAD G4 4 D3
MRYH/FIRH G20 61 G7
Garshake Av DMBTN G82 21 J5
Garshake Rd DMBTN G82 21 J6
Gartartan Rd PSLY PA1 76 F4
Gartcarron Hl BALLOCH G68 30 C6
Gartcloss Rd CTBR ML5 65 J8
Gartconnell Dr BSDN G61 41 L3
Gartconnell Gdns BSDN G61 41 L3
Gartconnell Rd BSDN G61 41 L3
Gartconner Av KKNTL G66 46 B2
Gartcosh Rd
BAIL/MDB/MHD G69 83 G2
Gartcosh Wk BLSH ML4 99 M5
Gartcraig Pl
STPS/GTHM/RID G33 80 F1
Gartcraig Rd
STPS/GTHM/RID G33 80 F2
Garten Dr SHOTTS ML7 105 H6
Gartferry Av
BAIL/MDB/MHD G69 46 E8
Gartferry Rd
BAIL/MDB/MHD G69 46 E7
Gartferry St SPRGB/BLRNK G21 62 A6
Gartfield St AIRDRIE ML6 85 H3
Gartgill Rd CTBR ML5 65 L8
Garthamlock Rd ESTRH G34 81 L1
Garthland Dr DEN/PKHD G31 80 A3
Garthland La PSLY PA1 9 K3
Garth St CGLE G1 5 G7
Gartlea Av AIRDRIE ML6 85 H2
Gartleahill AIRDRIE ML6 85 H3
Gartlea Rd AIRDRIE ML6 85 G2
Gartliston Rd CTBR ML5 65 M7
Gartliston Ter
BAIL/MDB/MHD G69 83 G5
Gartloch Rd
BAIL/MDB/MHD G69 64 E7
ESTRH G34 63 M8
STPS/GTHM/RID G33 80 F1
Gartly St LNPK/KPK G44 94 F6
Gartmore Gdns
UD/BTH/TAN G71 98 E2
Gartmore Rd PSLY PA1 76 C5
Gartmore Ter BLTYR/CAMB G72 96 E7
Gartness Dr AIRDRIE ML6 85 L4
Gartness Rd AIRDRIE ML6 86 A6
Gartocher Dr CAR/SHTL G32 81 J5
Gartocher Rd CAR/SHTL G32 81 J5
Gartocher Ter CAR/SHTL G32 81 J5
Gartons Rd SPRGB/BLRNK G21 62 C5
Gartsherrie Rd CTBR ML5 83 L2
Gartshore Crs KSYTH G65 28 F8
Gartshore Gdns BALLOCH G68 47 L1
Gartshore Rd BALLOCH G68 47 H4
Garturk St CTBR ML5 84 B5
GVH/MTFL G42 79 H8
Garvald St DMNK/BRGTN G40 80 B7
GRNK PA15 7 J7
Garve Av LNPK/KPK G44 95 G6
Garvel Crs STPS/GTHM/RID G33 81 L4
Garvel Dr GRNK PA15 16 D6
Garvel Pl MLNGV G62 23 K7
Garvel Rd MLNGV G62 23 K7
STPS/GTHM/RID G33 81 L4
Garvie Av GRK PA19 15 M3
Garvin Lea BLSH ML4 100 A1
Garvock Dr GRNK PA15 16 D6
PLKSW/MSWD G43 94 B5
Garwhitter Dr MLNGV G62 24 B8
Gascoyne EKILS G75 2 A9
Gask Pl KNTSWD G13 58 F1
Gas St JNSTN PA5 74 A7
Gasworks Rd CARLUKE ML8 132 E6
Gatehouse St CAR/SHTL G32 81 H5
Gateshead Pl KLBCH PA10 73 G7
Gateside Av BLTYR/CAMB G72 97 K5
GRNKW/INVK PA16 16 B5
KSYTH G65 29 H2
Gateside Crs AIRDRIE ML6 85 G1
BRHD/NEIL G78 92 A8
Gateside Gdns
GRNKW/INVK PA16 16 B5
Gateside Pk KSYTH G65 29 H2
Gateside Rd BRHD/NEIL G78 111 M1
WISHAW ML2 121 L5
Gateside St DEN/PKHD G31 80 B4
HMLTN ML3 119 L7
LARGS KA30 106 E5
Gates Rd LOCHW PA12 109 L2
The Gateway EKILN G74 117 G6
Gauldry Av
CARD/HILL/MSPK G52 77 J6
Gauze St PSLY PA1 9 H4
Gavel Gv LNK/LMHG ML11 137 J6
Gavell Rd KSYTH G65 28 F3
Gavinburn Gdns OLDK G60 38 F3
Gavinburn Pl OLDK G60 39 G3
Gavin's Mill Rd MLNGV G62 42 A1
Gavins Rd CLYDBK G81 40 B4
Gavin St MTHW ML1 120 E4
Gavinton St LNPK/KPK G44 94 F5
Gayne Dr CTBR ML5 65 J7
Gean Ct CUMB G67 31 M5
Geary St SMSTN G23 60 D1
Geddes Hl EKILN G74 117 H6
Geddes Rd SPRGB/BLRNK G21 62 C3
Geelong Gdns KKNTL G66 26 D1
Geils Av DMBTN G82 21 J8
Geilsland Rd BEITH KA15 125 M6
Geils Qd DMBTN G82 21 J8
Geilston Pk DMBTN G82 19 G3
Geirston Rd KBRN KA25 124 B3
Gelston St CAR/SHTL G32 81 H6
Gemmel Pl NMRNS G77 113 H5
General Roy Wy CARLUKE ML8 135 J1
Gentle Rw CLYDBK G81 39 M4
George Av CLYDBK G81 40 C6
George Crs CLYDBK G81 40 C6
George Gray St RUTH G73 96 C2
George La PSLY PA1 9 H6
George Mann Ter RUTH G73 96 A6
George Pl PSLY PA1 9 G6
George Reith Av
KVD/HLHD G12 59 M4
George Rd GRK PA19 15 L3
George Sq CGLE G1 4 F6
George St AIRDRIE ML6 84 E2
ALEX/LLW G83 13 L7
BAIL/MDB/MHD G69 82 B6
BRHD/NEIL G78 92 B6
CGLE G1 5 H6
HBR/GL G84 10 E6
HMLTN ML3 119 G5
HWWD PA9 88 F5
JNSTN PA5 73 M7
LARGS KA30 106 F4
MTHW ML1 120 E5
PSLY PA1 8 C6
George Street La
ALEX/LLW G83 13 L7
George V Br CGLE G1 4 D8
Gerard Pl BLSH ML4 100 B2
Germiston Ct EKILS G75 126 D6
Germiston Crs EKILS G75 126 D6
Gertrude Pl BRHD/NEIL G78 92 A7
Ghillies La MTHW ML1 100 C8
Gibbon Crs EKILN G74 117 J7
Gibbshill Pl SHOTTS ML7 71 K7
Gibb St AIRDRIE ML6 85 K6
MTHW ML1 102 B8
Gibshill Rd GRNK PA15 17 L7
Gibson Av DMBTN G82 21 H6
Gibson Crs JNSTN PA5 73 L8
Gibson La KLMCLM PA13 53 K1
Gibson Qd MTHW ML1 100 C8
Gibson Rd RNFRW PA4 76 B1
Gibson St COWCAD G4 5 K9
DMBTN G82 21 G6
GRNK PA15 17 L7
KVD/HLHD G12 60 E8
SHOTTS ML7 87 H7
Giffnock Park Av
GIF/THBK G46 94 C6
Gifford Dr
CARD/HILL/MSPK G52 77 G4
Gifford Pl CTBR ML5 83 L7
Gifford Wynd PSLYS PA2 74 F8
Gigha Gdns CARLUKE ML8 135 G1
Gigha Qd WISHAW ML2 121 L8
Gilbertfield Pl
STPS/GTHM/RID G33 63 H8
Gilbertfield Rd
BLTYR/CAMB G72 97 L7
Gilbertfield St
STPS/GTHM/RID G33 63 H8
Gilbert St KVGV G3 78 C2
Gilburn Pl SHOTTS ML7 104 F5
Gilchrist St CTBR ML5 84 B1
Gilchrist Wy WISHAW ML2 122 C8
Gilderdale EKILN G74 2 B3
Gilfillan Pl WISHAW ML2 131 L2
Gilhill St MRYH/FIRH G20 60 D3
Gillbank Av CARLUKE ML8 132 F7
Gillburn Rd KLMCLM PA13 53 K2
Gillburn St WISHAW ML2 131 L3
Gillespie Dr HBR/GL G84 10 D3
Gillies Crs EKILN G74 117 K5
Gillies La BAIL/MDB/MHD G69 82 C6
Gill Rd WISHAW ML2 131 M3
Gilmartin Rd PSLYN/LNWD PA3 73 M4
Gilmerton St CAR/SHTL G32 81 G6
Gilmour Av CLYDBK G81 40 B4
EKILN G74 115 H8
Gilmour Crs RUTH G73 95 M2
Gilmour Dr HMLTN ML3 118 F8
Gilmour Pl BLSH ML4 99 L5
CTBR ML5 83 L2
Gilmour St ALEX/LLW G83 13 J5
CLYDBK G81 40 C5
GRNK PA15 7 K8
PSLY PA1 9 H4
Gilmourton Crs NMRNS G77 113 K6
Gilroy Cl LNK/LMHG ML11 137 J4
Gimmerscroft Crs AIRDRIE ML6 85 M3
Girdons Wy UD/BTH/TAN G71 98 E4
Girthon St CAR/SHTL G32 81 J6
Girvan Crs AIRDRIE ML6 85 K8
Girvan St STPS/GTHM/RID G33 80 D1
The Glade LRKH ML9 130 D7
Gladney Av KNTSWD G13 58 E1
Gladsmuir Rd
CARD/HILL/MSPK G52 77 G3
Gladstone Av BRHD/NEIL G78 92 B7
JNSTN PA5 89 K3
Gladstone Ct HMLTN ML3 119 G5
Gladstone St BLSH ML4 100 B4
CLYDBK G81 39 L8
COWCAD G4 4 B1
Glaive Rd KNTSWD G13 41 K8
Glamis Av CARLUKE ML8 133 H7
JNSTN PA5 90 B1
NMRNS G77 113 M4
Glamis Ct MTHW ML1 101 J6
Glamis Crs BLTYR/CAMB G72 118 D7
Glamis Dr EKILN G74 3 H2
GRNKW/INVK PA16 16 A4
Glamis Pl GRNKW/INVK PA16 16 A4
Glamis Rd DEN/PKHD G31 80 D6
Glanderston Av
BRHD/NEIL G78 92 E7
NMRNS G77 113 H3
Glanderston Ct KNTSWD G13 59 G2
Glanderston Dr KNTSWD G13 59 G2
Glanderston Ga NMRNS G77 113 J3
Glanderston Rd NMRNS G77 112 D4
Glasgow & Edinburgh Rd
BAIL/MDB/MHD G69 82 C5
BAIL/MDB/MHD G69 83 G5
CTBR ML5 84 C7
MTHW ML1 101 J1
Glasgow Br GBLS G5 4 E8
KKNTL G66 44 F3
Glasgow Harbour Ter
PTCK G11 78 A1
Glasgow Rd
BAIL/MDB/MHD G69 81 M6
BLTYR/CAMB G72 116 F2
BLTYR/CAMB G72 118 B1
BRHD/NEIL G78 92 D5
CLYDBK G81 40 C3
CRMNK/CLK/EAG G76 114 D8
CUMB G67 48 C2
DMBTN G82 20 E7
EKILN G74 117 G3
KKNTL G66 45 G2
KSYTH G65 28 F3
LNK/LMHG ML11 136 E4
MLNGV G62 42 B2
PGL PA14 34 D1
PSLY PA1 9 J4
RNFRW PA4 58 E7
RUTH G73 95 M2
UD/BTH/TAN G71 98 E3
WISHAW ML2 121 K5
Glasgow St HBR/GL G84 10 C5
KBRN KA25 124 C3
KVD/HLHD G12 60 E7
Glassel Rd ESTRH G34 82 D1
Glasserton Pl
PLKSW/MSWD G43 94 F5
Glasserton Rd
PLKSW/MSWD G43 94 F5
Glassford St CGLE G1 5 G7
MTHW ML1 121 G5
Glaudhall Av
BAIL/MDB/MHD G69 64 E3
Glazert Dr KKNTL G66 26 A1
Glazert Meadow KKNTL G66 26 E3
Glazert Pl KKNTL G66 27 H5
Glebe Av CRMNK/CLK/EAG G76 115 K3
CTBR ML5 83 K7
UD/BTH/TAN G71 99 H8
Glebe Ct BEITH KA15 125 K5
COWCAD G4 5 J4
Glebe Crs AIRDRIE ML6 85 K1
EKILN G74 3 G5
HMLTN ML3 119 J8
Glebe Dr LNK/LMHG ML11 137 G5
Glebe Gdns ALEX/LLW G83 13 K6
CRG/CRSL/HOU PA6 55 H8
Glebe Hollow UD/BTH/TAN G71 99 H8
Glebelands Wy BEITH KA15 125 K6
Glebe La NMRNS G77 113 K5
Glebe Pk DMBTN G82 21 H5
Glebe Pl BLTYR/CAMB G72 97 H5
RUTH G73 95 M2
Glebe Rd BEITH KA15 125 K6
GRNKW/INVK PA16 32 F4
KLMCLM PA13 53 K2
NMRNS G77 113 K5
Glebe St BLSH ML4 99 M5
COWCAD G4 5 J3
EKILN G74 3 G5
HMLTN ML3 119 K8
RNFRW PA4 58 D6
The Glebe LNK/LMHG ML11 136 F5
UD/BTH/TAN G71 99 G8
Glebe Wynd UD/BTH/TAN G71 99 H8
Gleddoch Rd
CARD/HILL/MSPK G52 76 E3
Gleddoch Vw DMBTN G82 20 D8
Gleddoch Wynd PGL PA14 36 D5
Gledstane Rd BSHPTN PA7 38 B8
Glenacre Crs UD/BTH/TAN G71 98 E2
Glenacre Dr AIRDRIE ML6 85 K3
CSMK G45 95 K7
LARGS KA30 106 F4
Glenacre Rd CUMB G67 48 F1
Glenacre St CSMK G45 95 K7
Glenacre Ter CSMK G45 95 K7
Glenafeoch Rd CARLUKE ML8 133 J8
Glen Affric EKILN G74 3 M5
Glen Affric Av PLK/PH/NH G53 93 J5
Glen Affric Dr AIRDRIE ML6 85 K8
Glen Affric Wy AIRDRIE ML6 85 K8
Glenafton Gv CTBR ML5 83 M5
Glenafton Vw HMLTN ML3 129 H2
Glen Alby Pl PLK/PH/NH G53 93 J5
Glenallan Ter MTHW ML1 100 D7
Glen Almond EKILN G74 117 J8
Glenalmond St CAR/SHTL G32 81 G6
Glenalva Ct KSYTH G65 29 K1
Glenapp Av PSLYS PA2 76 C8
Glenapp Rd PSLYS PA2 76 B8
Glenapp St PLKSD/SHW G41 78 F7
Glenarklet Dr PSLYS PA2 76 A8
Glen Arroch EKILN G74 3 L6
Glenartney CRG/CRSL/HOU PA6 55 G8
Glenartney Rd
BAIL/MDB/MHD G69 64 C1
Glenashdale Wy PSLYS PA2 76 A8
Glen Av ALEX/LLW G83 13 M2
BAIL/MDB/MHD G69 46 F8
BRHD/NEIL G78 111 L3
CAR/SHTL G32 81 H4
GRK PA19 15 M3
LARGS KA30 106 F2
LRKH ML9 130 C8
PGL PA14 18 B8
Glenavon Ct HMLTN ML3 129 H2
Glen Avon Dr AIRDRIE ML6 85 K8
Glenavon Rd MRYH/FIRH G20 60 D3
Glenbank Av KKNTL G66 45 K6
Glenbank Dr GIF/THBK G46 93 M7
Glenbank Rd KKNTL G66 45 K6
Glenbarr St SPRGB/BLRNK G21 5 L2
Glen Bervie EKILN G74 3 M4
Glenbervie Pl GRK PA19 15 H3
NMRNS G77 113 G4
SMSTN G23 60 D1
Glenboig Farm Rd CTBR ML5 65 L4
Glenboig New Rd CTBR ML5 65 M4
Glenboig Rd
BAIL/MDB/MHD G69 65 H3
Glen Brae BRWEIR PA11 72 D2
Glenbrae Rd GRNK PA15 7 G9
PGL PA14 34 D3
Glenbrittle Dr PSLYS PA2 76 A8
Glenbrittle Wy PSLYS PA2 76 A8
Glenbuck Av
STPS/GTHM/RID G33 62 F4
Glenbuck Dr
STPS/GTHM/RID G33 62 F4
Glenburn Av
BAIL/MDB/MHD G69 82 C5
BLTYR/CAMB G72 96 D5
MTHW ML1 101 J5
Glenburn Cl AIRDRIE ML6 67 J1
Glenburn Crs KKNTL G66 27 J5
LARGS KA30 106 E4
PSLYS PA2 91 K3
UD/BTH/TAN G71 99 H2
Glenburn Gdns
BAIL/MDB/MHD G69 65 J4
BSHPBGS G64 43 M8
Glenburnie Pl ESTRH G34 82 A3
Glenburn La KLMCLM PA13 53 K1
MRYH/FIRH G20 60 E3
Glenburn Rd BSDN G61 41 K4
EKILN G74 116 A7
GIF/THBK G46 114 B1
HMLTN ML3 119 H7
KLMCLM PA13 53 K1
PSLYS PA2 91 H2
Glenburn St MRYH/FIRH G20 60 E3
PGL PA14 18 A8
Glenburn Ter CARLUKE ML8 134 E1
MTHW ML1 101 H8
Glenburn Wy EKILN G74 115 M7
Glencairn Av WISHAW ML2 121 K5
Glencairn Ct RUTH G73 95 M2
Glencairn Dr
BAIL/MDB/MHD G69 46 E8
CTBR ML5 83 M5
PLKSD/SHW G41 78 E8
RUTH G73 95 M2
Glencairn Gdns
BLTYR/CAMB G72 97 K5
PLKSD/SHW G41 78 E8
Glencairn La PLKSD/SHW G41 78 E8
Glencairn Rd CUMB G67 31 J7
DMBTN G82 20 C7
GRNKW/INVK PA16 15 L6
KLMCLM PA13 53 L3
PGL PA14 36 C3
PSLYN/LNWD PA3 76 A2
Glencairn St MTHW ML1 120 E4
Glencalder Crs BLSH ML4 100 C6
Glen Cally EKILN G74 3 M4
Glencally Av PSLYS PA2 76 B8
Glen Cannich EKILN G74 3 M6
Glen Carron EKILN G74 3 L6
Glencart Gv KLBCH PA10 89 J1
Glencleland Rd WISHAW ML2 121 K5
Glenclora Dr PSLYS PA2 76 A8
Glen Clova EKILN G74 3 M3
Glen Clova Dr BALLOCH G68 30 C5
Glencloy St MRYH/FIRH G20 60 C3
Glenclune Ct KLMCLM PA13 53 J3
Glen Clunie EKILN G74 117 K8
Glen Clunie Dr PLK/PH/NH G53 93 J5
Glen Clunie Pl PLK/PH/NH G53 93 J5
Glencoats Crs PSLYN/LNWD PA3 8 A4
Glencoats Dr PSLYN/LNWD PA3 8 A5
Glencoe Dr MTHW ML1 101 G4
Glencoe Pl HMLTN ML3 129 H2
KNTSWD G13 59 L2
Glencoe Rd CARLUKE ML8 135 G1
RUTH G73 96 D7
Glencoe St KNTSWD G13 59 M3
Glen Cona Dr PLK/PH/NH G53 93 J4
Glencorse Rd PSLYS PA2 8 C9
Glencorse St CAR/SHTL G32 80 E3
Glencraig St AIRDRIE ML6 84 E3
Glen Creran Crs
BRHD/NEIL G78 111 J4
Glen Crs GRNKW/INVK PA16 32 F5
KNTSWD G13 58 E2
Glencroft Av UD/BTH/TAN G71 98 E2
Glencroft Rd LNPK/KPK G44 95 K5
Glencryan Rd CUMB G67 31 H8
Glendale Av AIRDRIE ML6 85 K3
Glendale Crs BSHPBGS G64 62 C2
Glendale Dr BSHPBGS G64 62 C2
Glendale Gv CTBR ML5 83 L7
Glendale Pl BSHPBGS G64 62 C3
DEN/PKHD G31 80 B4
Glendale St DEN/PKHD G31 80 B4
Glendaruel Av BSDN G61 42 B6
Glendaruel Rd RUTH G73 96 E8
Glendarvel Gdns PPK/MIL G22 61 K6
Glendee Gdns RNFRW PA4 58 D7
Glendee Rd RNFRW PA4 58 D7
Glen Dene Wy PLK/PH/NH G53 93 J5
Glendentan Rd BRWEIR PA11 72 C4
Glen Derry EKILN G74 117 K7
Glen Dessary EKILN G74 3 L7
Glendeveron Wy MTHW ML1 101 H7
Glendevon Pl CLYDBK G81 39 M7
HMLTN ML3 129 H2
Glendevon Sq
STPS/GTHM/RID G33 63 H8
Glen Dewar Pl PLK/PH/NH G53 93 J5
Glendinning Rd KNTSWD G13 41 L8
Glen Dochart Dr BALLOCH G68 30 C5
Glendoick Pl NMRNS G77 113 G4
Glen Doll EKILN G74 3 M5
Glen Doll Rd BRHD/NEIL G78 111 J4
Glendorch Av WISHAW ML2 122 C2
Glendore St SCOT G14 59 L7
Glen Douglas Dr BALLOCH G68 30 D4
Glen Douglas Rd
GRNKW/INVK PA16 16 D6
Glendoune Rd
CRMNK/CLK/EAG G76 114 E5
Glen Dr HBR/GL G84 10 D3
MTHW ML1 101 H4
Glenduffhill Rd
BAIL/MDB/MHD G69 81 M5
Glen Dye EKILN G74 3 M4
Glen Eagles EKILN G74 127 M1
Gleneagles Av BALLOCH G68 31 G4
Gleneagles Dr GRK PA19 15 G3
NMRNS G77 114 B6
Gleneagles Gdns BSHPBGS G64 43 M7
Gleneagles Ga NMRNS G77 114 B6
Gleneagles La North SCOT G14 59 J5
Gleneagles La South SCOT G14 59 J6
Gleneagles Pk UD/BTH/TAN G71 98 F8
Glenelg Crs KKNTL G66 46 A1
Glenelg Qd ESTRH G34 82 D1
Glenelm Pl BLSH ML4 100 A3
Glen Esk EKILN G74 117 J8
Glenesk Crs PLK/PH/NH G53 93 J5
Glen Esk Dr PLK/PH/NH G53 93 J5
Glenesk Pl PLK/PH/NH G53 93 J5
Glen Etive Pl RUTH G73 96 E8
Glen Falloch EKILN G74 127 M1
Glen Falloch Crs
BRHD/NEIL G78 111 K5
Glen Falloch Wy BALLOCH G68 30 C4
Glen Farg EKILN G74 127 M1
Glenfarg Ct HMLTN ML3 129 H2
Glenfarg Crs BSDN G61 42 B6
Glenfarg Rd RUTH G73 96 B6
Glenfarg St MRYH/FIRH G20 4 B1
Glenfarm Rd MTHW ML1 101 L5
Glen Farrar EKILN G74 3 L5
Glen Feshie EKILN G74 3 M7
Glenfield Av PSLYS PA2 91 L4
Glenfield Crs PSLYS PA2 91 L4
Glenfield Gdns PSLYS PA2 91 K4
Glenfield Gv PSLYS PA2 91 K4
Glenfield Rd EKILS G75 127 K4
PSLYS PA2 91 K3
Glenfinlas St HBR/GL G84 10 E6
Glen Finlet Rd BRHD/NEIL G78 111 H5
Glenfinnan Dr BSDN G61 42 C7
MRYH/FIRH G20 60 D4
Glenfinnan Gv BLSH ML4 100 D5
Glenfinnan Pl MRYH/FIRH G20 60 D4
Glenfinnan Rd MRYH/FIRH G20 60 D5
Glenfruin Crs PSLYS PA2 76 B8
Glen Fruin Dr LRKH ML9 130 E8
Glen Fruin Pl AIRDRIE ML6 85 K8
Glenfruin Rd BLTYR/CAMB G72 118 C3
Glen Fruin Rd
GRNKW/INVK PA16 16 C6
Glen Fyne Rd BALLOCH G68 30 C5
Glen Gairn EKILN G74 117 K8
Glen Gairn Crs BRHD/NEIL G78 111 J4
Glen Gdns JNSTN PA5 74 C7
Glen Garrell Pl KSYTH G65 29 H1
Glengarriff Rd BLSH ML4 100 B1
Glen Garry EKILN G74 3 M7
Glengarry Dr
CARD/HILL/MSPK G52 77 J4
Glengavel Crs
STPS/GTHM/RID G33 62 F4
Glengavel Gdns WISHAW ML2 122 D2
Glen Gavin Wy PSLYS PA2 76 A8
Glengowan Rd AIRDRIE ML6 69 G5
BRWEIR PA11 72 C2
Glen Gv EKILS G75 2 C9
LARGS KA30 106 F2
Glengyre Pl ESTRH G34 82 D2
Glengyre St ESTRH G34 82 C2
Glenhead Crs CLYDBK G81 40 A2
PPK/MIL G22 61 J4
Glenhead Dr MTHW ML1 120 E5
Glenhead Rd CLYDBK G81 40 A4
KKNTL G66 45 J6
Glenhead St PPK/MIL G22 61 J4
Glenheath Dr CTBR ML5 65 J5
Glenholme Av PSLYS PA2 91 H1
Glenhove Rd CUMB G67 31 G7
Glenhuntly Rd PGL PA14 34 B1
Glenhuntly Ter PGL PA14 34 B1
Gleniffer Av KNTSWD G13 59 G3
Gleniffer Crs JNSTN PA5 90 C1
Gleniffer Dr BRHD/NEIL G78 92 A4
Gleniffer Rd PSLYS PA2 90 E5
RNFRW PA4 76 B1
Gleniffer Vw BRHD/NEIL G78 111 K2
Gleninver Rd
GRNKW/INVK PA16 15 M5
Glen Isla EKILN G74 117 J8
Glenisla Av BAIL/MDB/MHD G69 47 G7
Glen Isla Av BRHD/NEIL G78 111 J5

Glen Isla Qd MTHW ML1 122 B1
Glenisla St DEN/PKHD G31 80 D7
Glen Kinglas Av
GRNKW/INVK PA16 16 D7
Glen Kinglas Rd
GRNKW/INVK PA16 16 C7
Glenkirk Dr DRUM G15 41 H7
Glen Kyle Dr PLK/PH/NH G53 93 J5
Glen La BRHD/NEIL G78 110 A7
PSLYN/LNWD PA3 9 G3
Glen Lednock Dr BALLOCH G68 30 C5
Glen Lee EKILN G74 117 J8
Glenlee St HMLTN ML3 118 F5
Glen Lethnot EKILN G74 117 J8
Glen Livet Pl PLK/PH/NH G53 93 J5
Glenlivet Rd BRHD/NEIL G78 111 J4
Glen Lochay Gdns
BALLOCH G68 30 B5
Glenlora Dr PLK/PH/NH G53 93 G3
Glenlora Ter PLK/PH/NH G53 93 H2
Glen Loy Pl PLK/PH/NH G53 93 J5
Glen Luce Dr CAR/SHTL G32 81 K7
Glenluce Gdns
BAIL/MDB/MHD G69 47 G7
Glenluce Ter EKILN G74 2 B4
Glenluggie Rd KKNTL G66 46 A3
Glenlui Av RUTH G73 96 B5
Glen Luss Gdns BALLOCH G68 30 C5
Glen Luss Pl CTBR ML5 84 D4
PLK/PH/NH G53 93 J5
Glen Luss Rd
GRNKW/INVK PA16 16 C7
Glen Lyon EKILN G74 127 M1
Glen Lyon Ct BALLOCH G68 30 B5
Glenlyon Ct HMLTN ML3 129 H2
Glenlyon Pl RUTH G73 96 C8
Glen Lyon Rd BRHD/NEIL G78 111 J4
Glenmalloch Pl JNSTN PA5 74 C7
Glenmanor Av
BAIL/MDB/MHD G69 46 E7
Glen Mark EKILN G74 117 J8
Glenmarklet Crs PSLYS PA2 76 A8
Glen Mark Rd BRHD/NEIL G78 111 J4
Glenmavis Ct CARLUKE ML8 133 J8
Glenmavis Crs CARLUKE ML8 133 H8
Glenmavis Rd AIRDRIE ML6 66 E6
Glenmavis St COWCAD G4 4 E3
Glen Ms CARLUKE ML8 135 H1
Glen More CARLUKE ML8 135 J1
EKILN G74 3 L6
Glenmore Av ALEX/LLW G83 13 J4
BLSH ML4 100 B6
GVH/MTFL G42 95 L2
Glenmore Rd MTHW ML1 101 K6
Glen Moriston EKILN G74 3 M6
Glen Moriston Rd
BALLOCH G68 30 B5
PLK/PH/NH G53 93 K4
Glenmoss Av ERSK PA8 56 F1
Glenmosston Rd KLMCLM PA13 53 L2
Glen Moy EKILN G74 3 M6
Glenmuir Av PLK/PH/NH G53 93 K4
Glenmuir Ct PLK/PH/NH G53 93 K4
Glenmuir Crs PLK/PH/NH G53 93 J4
Glenmuir Dr PLK/PH/NH G53 93 H4
Glen Muir Rd BRHD/NEIL G78 111 J4
Glen Nevis EKILN G74 3 M7
Glen Nevis Pl RUTH G73 96 C8
Glen Noble MTHW ML1 122 B1
Glenochil Rd AIRDRIE ML6 85 K8
Glen Ogilvie EKILN G74 117 J8
Glen Ogle St CAR/SHTL G32 81 K6
Glenoran Rd HBR/GL G84 10 A3
Glenorchard Rd BSHPBGS G64 25 K7
Glen Orchy Ct BALLOCH G68 30 B4
Glen Orchy Dr BALLOCH G68 30 B5
PLK/PH/NH G53 93 K6
Glen Orchy Pl AIRDRIE ML6 85 K8
BALLOCH G68 30 B4
Glen Orchy Rd MTHW ML1 122 B1
Glen Ord Rd MTHW ML1 101 H7
Glenorrin Wy BRHD/NEIL G78 111 J4
Glenpark AIRDRIE ML6 85 L3
Glenpark Av GIF/THBK G46 93 M7
Glenpark Dr PGL PA14 18 A8
Glenpark Gdns
BLTYR/CAMB G72 96 E3
Glenpark Rd DEN/PKHD G31 80 B4
LOCHW PA12 109 J2
Glenpark St WISHAW ML2 122 A5
Glenpark Ter BLTYR/CAMB G72 96 E3
Glenpath DMBTN G82 21 J7
Glenpatrick Rd JNSTN PA5 90 C1
Glen Pl CRMNK/CLK/EAG G76 114 E3
LARGS KA30 106 F2
Glen Prosen EKILN G74 117 J8
Glen Quoich EKILN G74 117 K7
Glenraith Rd
STPS/GTHM/RID G33 63 H7
Glen Rannoch Dr AIRDRIE ML6 85 K8
Glenriddet Av KBRN KA25 124 D5
Glenrigg Ct AIRDRIE ML6 84 F4
Glen Rinnes Dr
BRHD/NEIL G78 111 K5
Glen Rd AIRDRIE ML6 68 F5
BSHPTN PA7 38 A6
CAR/SHTL G32 81 H3
CRMNK/CLK/EAG G76 115 L6
MTHW ML1 101 K2
OLDK G60 39 H4
SHOTTS ML7 104 F5
WISHAW ML2 122 A5
Glen Rosa Gdns BALLOCH G68 30 B5
Glen Roy Dr BRHD/NEIL G78 111 J4
Glen Sannox Dr BALLOCH G68 30 C5
Glen Sannox Gv BALLOCH G68 30 C5
Glen Sannox Loan
BALLOCH G68 30 B5
Glen Sannox Vw BALLOCH G68 30 B5
Glen Sannox Wy BALLOCH G68 30 B5
Glen Sannox Wynd
BALLOCH G68 30 C5
Glen Sax Dr RNFRW PA4 58 E8
Glen Shee EKILN G74 117 J8
Glen Shee Av BRHD/NEIL G78 111 J5
Glen Shee Ct CARLUKE ML8 135 H2
Glenshee Ct DEN/PKHD G31 80 D6
Glen Shee Crs AIRDRIE ML6 85 K8
Glen Shee Gdns CARLUKE ML8 135 J1
Glenshee Gdns DEN/PKHD G31 80 E7
Glenshee St DEN/PKHD G31 80 D6
Glenshee Ter HMLTN ML3 129 H2
Glenshiel Av PSLYS PA2 76 A8
Glenshira Av PSLYS PA2 76 A8
Glen Shirva Rd KSYTH G65 28 F6
Glenside Av PLK/PH/NH G53 77 H7
Glenside Dr RUTH G73 96 D4
Glenside Rd DMBTN G82 21 J4
PGL PA14 34 D3
Glenspean Pl CTBR ML5 84 D4
Glenspean St
PLKSW/MSWD G43 94 D4
Glen St BLTYR/CAMB G72 97 K6
BRHD/NEIL G78 92 C6
GRNKW/INVK PA16 16 D2
MTHW ML1 100 E8
PSLYN/LNWD PA3 9 G3
Glentanar Dr
BAIL/MDB/MHD G69 47 G8
Glentanar Pl PPK/MIL G22 61 H3
Glentanar Rd PPK/MIL G22 61 H3
Glen Tanner EKILN G74 117 K8
Glen Tarbert Dr
BRHD/NEIL G78 111 J4
Glentarbert Rd RUTH G73 96 D7
Glen Tennet EKILN G74 117 J8
Glen Ter AIRDRIE ML6 68 F5
Glentore Qd AIRDRIE ML6 67 G7
Glentrool Gdns
BAIL/MDB/MHD G69 47 G7
PPK/MIL G22 61 K6
Glen Turret EKILN G74 117 K8
Glenturret St CAR/SHTL G32 81 G6
Glentyan Av KLBCH PA10 73 G6
Glentyan Dr PLK/PH/NH G53 93 G2
Glentynan Pl PLK/PH/NH G53 93 G2
Glen Urquhart EKILN G74 3 M5
Glenview AIRDRIE ML6 85 K3
KKNTL G66 45 K2
LRKH ML9 130 B5
Glen Vw CUMB G67 31 J6
DMBTN G82 13 J8
HMLTN ML3 129 K4
Glenview Av AIRDRIE ML6 69 G5
Glenview Crs
BAIL/MDB/MHD G69 46 F7
Glenview Pl BLTYR/CAMB G72 118 D1
Glenview St AIRDRIE ML6 66 E5
Glenville Av GIF/THBK G46 94 B7
Glenville Ga
CRMNK/CLK/EAG G76 115 G5
Glenville Ter
CRMNK/CLK/EAG G76 115 G5
Glenward Av KKNTL G66 26 E2
Glenwell St AIRDRIE ML6 66 E6
Glenwood Av AIRDRIE ML6 85 J5
Glenwood Ct KKNTL G66 45 G5
Glenwood Dr GIF/THBK G46 93 M7
Glenwood Gdns KKNTL G66 45 G5
Glenwood Pth CSMK G45 95 L7
Glenwood Pl CSMK G45 95 L7
KKNTL G66 45 G5
Glenwood Rd KKNTL G66 45 G5
Glorat Av KKNTL G66 26 E2
Gloucester Av
CRMNK/CLK/EAG G76 114 D3
RUTH G73 96 D5
Gloucester St GBLS G5 79 G5
Gockston Rd PSLYN/LNWD PA3 75 K3
Gogar Pl STPS/GTHM/RID G33 80 E2
Gogar St STPS/GTHM/RID G33 80 E2
Gogoside Dr LARGS KA30 106 F5
Gogoside Rd LARGS KA30 106 F5
Gogo St LARGS KA30 106 E5
Goil Av BLSH ML4 99 K4
Goldberry Av SCOT G14 59 H4
Goldcrest Ct WISHAW ML2 121 M8
Goldenacre Pl AIRDRIE ML6 67 M6
Goldenlee Vw
CRG/CRSL/HOU PA6 73 G2
Goldie Rd UD/BTH/TAN G71 99 G6
Golf Av BLSH ML4 100 A6
Golf Course Rd BRWEIR PA11 72 B2
BSHPBGS G64 43 K2
SKLM PA17 50 C5
Golf Dr DRUM G15 40 F8
PGL PA14 34 D2
PSLY PA1 76 C5
Golf Gdns LRKH ML9 130 E7
Golfhill Dr ALEX/LLW G83 13 L5
DEN/PKHD G31 80 A2
HBR/GL G84 10 F5
Golfhill Qd AIRDRIE ML6 67 G7
Golfhill Rd WISHAW ML2 121 K5
Golf Pl BLSH ML4 100 B6
GRNKW/INVK PA16 16 C2
Golf Rd BSHPTN PA7 38 A5
CRMNK/CLK/EAG G76 114 D2
GRK PA19 15 J3
RUTH G73 96 B6
Golfview BSDN G61 41 H4
Golf Vw CLYDBK G81 39 M6
Golfview Dr CTBR ML5 83 J3
Golfview Pl CTBR ML5 83 J3
Golspie Av AIRDRIE ML6 84 E5
Golspie St GOV/IBX G51 78 A2
Golspie Wy BLTYR/CAMB G72 118 C7
Goodview Gdns LRKH ML9 130 E7
Goosedubbs CGLE G1 5 G9
Gooseholm Crs DMBTN G82 21 G5
Gooseholm Rd DMBTN G82 21 G5
Gopher Av UD/BTH/TAN G71 99 H2
Gorbals St GBLS G5 79 J5
Gordon Av BAIL/MDB/MHD G69 81 M5
BSHPTN PA7 38 A6
CARD/HILL/MSPK G52 76 E2
LNPK/KPK G44 94 E8
Gordon Crs NMRNS G77 113 L3
Gordon Dr EKILN G74 3 L1
LNPK/KPK G44 94 E7
Gordon La CGLE G1 4 E6
Gordon Pl BLSH ML4 99 M7
Gordon Rd HMLTN ML3 118 F6
LNPK/KPK G44 94 E8
Gordon St CGLE G1 4 E6
GRNK PA15 6 A6
Gordon Ter BLTYR/CAMB G72 98 C8
Gorebridge St CAR/SHTL G32 80 E3
Goremire Rd CARLUKE ML8 135 H1
Gorget Av KNTSWD G13 41 J8
Gorget Pl KNTSWD G13 41 J8
Gorget Qd KNTSWD G13 41 H8
Gorse Crs BRWEIR PA11 72 E3
Gorsehall St MTHW ML1 102 B7
Gorse Pl UD/BTH/TAN G71 99 H2
Gorsewood BSHPBGS G64 61 L1
Gorstan Pl MRYH/FIRH G20 60 C5
Gorstan St SMSTN G23 60 D2
Gosford La SCOT G14 59 G5
Goudie St PSLYN/LNWD PA3 75 K3
Gough St STPS/GTHM/RID G33 80 D2
Gourlay EKILN G74 117 K5
Gourlay Dr WISHAW ML2 131 L3
Gourlay St SPRGB/BLRNK G21 61 L6
Gourock St GBLS G5 79 G6
Govan Dr ALEX/LLW G83 13 J4
Govanhill St GVH/MTFL G42 79 J8
Govan Rd GOV/IBX G51 77 K1
Gowanbank Gdns JNSTN PA5 73 L8
Gowan Brae AIRDRIE ML6 69 H5
Gowanlea Av DRUM G15 41 G8
Gowanlea Dr GIF/THBK G46 94 D6
Gowanlea Ter UD/BTH/TAN G71 99 H3
Gowanside Pl CARLUKE ML8 132 F7
Gower St PLKSD/SHW G41 78 C5
Gower Ter PLKSD/SHW G41 78 C5
Gowkhall Av MTHW ML1 101 M6
Gowkhouse Rd KLMCLM PA13 53 L2
Goyle Av DRUM G15 41 J6
Grace Av BAIL/MDB/MHD G69 82 F5
Grace St KVGV G3 78 F3
Grace Wynd HMLTN ML3 119 L7
Graeme Ct MTHW ML1 100 D7
Graffham Av GIF/THBK G46 94 D7
Grafton Pl COWCAD G4 5 G5
Graham Av BLTYR/CAMB G72 97 K6
CLYDBK G81 40 B6
EKILN G74 2 F3
HMLTN ML3 129 K2
Graham Crs DMBTN G82 19 H3
Grahamfield Pl BEITH KA15 125 J6
Graham Pl HBR/GL G84 11 G5
LRKH ML9 131 H8
Graham Rd CARLUKE ML8 134 B8
DMBTN G82 20 D6
Grahams Av LOCHW PA12 109 K2
Grahamsdyke Rd KKNTL G66 45 L1
Grahamshill Av AIRDRIE ML6 85 K1
Grahamshill St AIRDRIE ML6 85 J1
Graham Sq DMNK/BRGTN G40 5 M9
Grahamston Av GLGNK KA14 124 D7
Grahamston Ct PSLYS PA2 92 C1
Grahamston Crs PSLYS PA2 92 C1
Grahamston Pk BRHD/NEIL G78 92 C4
Grahamston Pl PSLYS PA2 92 C1
Grahamston Rd PSLYS PA2 92 C3
Graham St AIRDRIE ML6 85 G2
BRHD/NEIL G78 92 B6
GRNKW/INVK PA16 16 C4
HMLTN ML3 119 L7
JNSTN PA5 73 L8
MTHW ML1 101 G4
WISHAW ML2 122 B7
Graham Ter BSHPBGS G64 62 B3
Graignestock Pl
DMNK/BRGTN G40 79 L5
Graigside Pl BALLOCH G68 47 M3
Grainger Rd BSHPBGS G64 62 D1
Grampian Av PSLYS PA2 91 K2
Grampian Ct BSDN G61 41 J1
Grampian Crs AIRDRIE ML6 85 M8
CAR/SHTL G32 81 H6
Grampian Dr EKILS G75 126 E6
Grampian Pl CAR/SHTL G32 81 H6
Grampian Rd PGL PA14 35 G4
WISHAW ML2 121 M5
Grampian St CAR/SHTL G32 81 H6
Grampian Wy BALLOCH G68 30 A7
BRHD/NEIL G78 92 C8
BSDN G61 41 J2
Granby La KVD/HLHD G12 60 D8
Grandtully Dr KVD/HLHD G12 60 C4
Grange Av MLNGV G62 24 B8
WISHAW ML2 121 L8
Grange Ct LNK/LMHG ML11 136 F4
Grange Gdns
UD/BTH/TAN G71 119 G1
Grangeneuk Gdns
BALLOCH G68 30 C8
Grange Pl ALEX/LLW G83 13 K5
Grange Rd BSDN G61 41 M4
GVH/MTFL G42 95 G2
Granger Rd ALEX/LLW G83 13 L2
Grange St MTHW ML1 121 G5
Grannoch Pl CTBR ML5 84 D7
Gran St CLYDBK G81 58 E1
Grant Ct HMLTN ML3 129 J4
Grant Crs DMBTN G82 20 D1
Grantholm Av MTHW ML1 101 H3
Grantlea Gv CAR/SHTL G32 81 K6
Grantlea Ter CAR/SHTL G32 81 K6
Grantley Gdns PLKSD/SHW G41 94 D2
Grantley St PLKSD/SHW G41 94 D2
Grantofften Pth EKILS G75 127 G5
Granton St GBLS G5 79 L8
Grantown Av AIRDRIE ML6 85 L3
Grantown Gdns AIRDRIE ML6 66 F4
Grants Av PSLYS PA2 91 J2
Grants Crs PSLYS PA2 91 K2
Grants Pl PSLYS PA2 91 K2
Grant St GRNK PA15 7 J7
HBR/GL G84 10 D6
KVGV G3 4 A2
Grants Wy PSLYS PA2 91 J1
Granville St CLYDBK G81 40 B6
HBR/GL G84 10 F6
KVGV G3 4 A4
Grasmere EKILS G75 126 C5
Grasmere Ct HMLTN ML3 129 K4
Grathellen Ct MTHW ML1 121 G1
Gray Dr BSDN G61 41 M6
Gray's Cl LNK/LMHG ML11 136 C5
Grayshill Rd BALLOCH G68 47 L4
Gray's Rd UD/BTH/TAN G71 99 H5
Graystonelee Rd SHOTTS ML7 104 D3
Grayston Mnr
BAIL/MDB/MHD G69 64 E1
Gray St ALEX/LLW G83 13 K5
GRNK PA15 7 H8
KKNTL G66 46 B3
KVGV G3 78 E1
LRKH ML9 130 C5
MTHW ML1 102 B8
SHOTTS ML7 105 G4
Great Dovehill CGLE G1 5 J8
Great George La
KVD/HLHD G12 60 D8
Great George St
KVD/HLHD G12 60 E8
Great Hamilton St PSLYS PA2 9 G9
Great Kelvin La KVD/HLHD G12 60 E8
Great Western Rd CLYDBK G81 39 M5
COWCAD G4 4 B1
KNTSWD G13 59 K2
KVD/HLHD G12 60 A5
OLDK G60 38 B2
Great Western Ter
KVD/HLHD G12 60 C6
Great Western Terrace La
KVD/HLHD G12 60 C6
Green LARGS KA30 106 E5
Greenacres MTHW ML1 120 C4
Greenacres Ct PLK/PH/NH G53 93 J5
Greenacres Dr PLK/PH/NH G53 93 J5
Greenacres Wy PLK/PH/NH G53 93 J5
Greenan Av LNPK/KPK G44 95 L3
Greenbank Av GIF/THBK G46 114 A3
Greenbank Dr PSLYS PA2 91 K3
Greenbank Ms
GRNKW/INVK PA16 16 D4
Green Bank Rd BALLOCH G68 30 C7
Greenbank Rd WISHAW ML2 122 C6
Greenbank Ter CARLUKE ML8 133 H7
Green Dl WISHAW ML2 122 D4
Greendyke St CGLE G1 5 H9
Greenend Av JNSTN PA5 89 K2
Greenend Pl CAR/SHTL G32 81 J3
Greenend Vw BLSH ML4 99 M6
Greenfarm Rd NMRNS G77 113 H4
Green Farm Rd
PSLYN/LNWD PA3 74 B4
Greenfaulds Crs CUMB G67 49 G1
Greenfaulds Rd CUMB G67 48 D2
Greenfield Crs WISHAW ML2 122 D5
Greenfield Dr WISHAW ML2 122 D5
Greenfield Qd MTHW ML1 101 M5
Greenfield Rd CAR/SHTL G32 81 J4
CARLUKE ML8 133 H6
CRMNK/CLK/EAG G76 114 E4
HMLTN ML3 119 G5
Greenfield St GOV/IBX G51 77 M2
WISHAW ML2 122 D5
Greengairs Av GOV/IBX G51 77 K2
Greengairs Rd AIRDRIE ML6 67 H1
Green Gdns MTHW ML1 102 C7
Greenhall Pl BLTYR/CAMB G72 118 C4
Greenhead Rd BSDN G61 41 M5
DMBTN G82 21 J7
RNFRW PA4 57 J3
WISHAW ML2 122 D6
Greenhead St
DMNK/BRGTN G40 79 L6
Greenhill BSHPBGS G64 62 C2
LARGS KA30 106 F5
Greenhill Av
BAIL/MDB/MHD G69 64 E3
GIF/THBK G46 114 C1
Greenhill Ct RUTH G73 96 A2
Greenhill Crs PSLYN/LNWD PA3 74 C4
Greenhill Dr PSLYN/LNWD PA3 74 C5
Greenhill Rd BTHG/ARM EH48 71 M1
MTHW ML1 102 F5
PSLYN/LNWD PA3 8 C2
RUTH G73 96 A3
Greenhills Crs EKILS G75 126 E5
Greenhills Rd EKILS G75 126 C4
Greenhill St RUTH G73 96 A3
Greenholm Av
CRMNK/CLK/EAG G76 114 E3
UD/BTH/TAN G71 98 E3
Greenholme St LNPK/KPK G44 95 G4
Greenknowe Dr CARLUKE ML8 132 B3
Greenknowe Rd
PLKSW/MSWD G43 94 B4
Greenknowe St WISHAW ML2 131 K3
Greenlady Wk
LNK/LMHG ML11 137 J5
Greenlaw Av PSLY PA1 9 L3
WISHAW ML2 122 C4
Greenlaw Ct SCOT G14 58 D3
Greenlaw Crs PSLY PA1 9 M2
Greenlaw Dr PSLY PA1 9 M4
Greenlaw Gdns PSLY PA1 9 M2
Greenlaw Rd NMRNS G77 113 K5
SCOT G14 58 E3
Greenlea Rd
BAIL/MDB/MHD G69 64 B2
Greenlea St KNTSWD G13 59 L3
Greenlees Gdns
BLTYR/CAMB G72 96 F7
Greenlees Gv CTBR ML5 84 D4
Greenlees Pk BLTYR/CAMB G72 97 G7
Greenlees Rd BLTYR/CAMB G72 96 F8
Greenloan Av GOV/IBX G51 77 L1
Greenmoss Pl BLSH ML4 100 B4
Greenmount PPK/MIL G22 61 G3
Greenock Av LNPK/KPK G44 95 H5
Greenock Rd BSHPTN PA7 38 B8
GRNK PA15 17 L6
LARGS KA30 106 C1
PGL PA14 18 B8
PGL PA14 37 H4
PSLYN/LNWD PA3 8 F1
RNFRW PA4 57 H4
Green Pl AIRDRIE ML6 85 H7
Greenrig UD/BTH/TAN G71 98 F4
Greenrigg Rd CUMB G67 31 H8
Greenrigg St UD/BTH/TAN G71 98 F4
Greenrig Rd LNK/LMHG ML11 136 C7
Greenrig St
STPS/GTHM/RID G33 62 D7
Green Rd PSLYS PA2 8 A8
Greens Av KKNTL G66 45 J3
Greens Crs KKNTL G66 45 J3
Greenshields Rd
BAIL/MDB/MHD G69 82 B5
Greenside
CRMNK/CLK/EAG G76 115 L2
Greenside Av KBRN KA25 124 C5
Greenside Crs
STPS/GTHM/RID G33 62 E7
Greenside La LNK/LMHG ML11 137 G5
Greenside Pl BSDN G61 41 H1
Greenside Rd CLYDBK G81 40 B2
MTHW ML1 101 J2
WISHAW ML2 122 C7
Greenside St CTBR ML5 84 B1
MTHW ML1 101 M5
STPS/GTHM/RID G33 62 E7
Greens Rd CUMB G67 48 F3
Green St CLYDBK G81 40 A6
DMNK/BRGTN G40 79 L5
UD/BTH/TAN G71 99 H8
The Green DMNK/BRGTN G40 79 L6
Greentowers Rd
LNK/LMHG ML11 135 K8
Greentree Dr
BAIL/MDB/MHD G69 81 M7
Greenview St
PLKSW/MSWD G43 94 C2
Greenways Av PSLYS PA2 75 G8
Greenways Ct PSLYS PA2 75 G8
Greenwood Av
BLTYR/CAMB G72 97 K4
Greenwood Crs CTBR ML5 84 C4
Greenwood Dr BSDN G61 42 A6
JNSTN PA5 89 L2
Greenwood Qd CLYDBK G81 40 D8
Greenwood Rd
CRMNK/CLK/EAG G76 114 D3
Greenwood St SHOTTS ML7 104 E5
Greer Qd CLYDBK G81 40 B5
Greeto Falls Av LARGS KA30 107 G4
Grenada Pl EKILS G75 126 D1
Grenadier Gdns MTHW ML1 120 D6
Grenadier Pk BLTYR/CAMB G72 97 G6
Grenville Dr BLTYR/CAMB G72 96 F6
Grenville Rd GRK PA19 15 M3
Gresham Vw MTHW ML1 121 H7
Greta Meek La KKNTL G66 27 J4
Gretna St DMNK/BRGTN G40 80 B6
Greyfriars Ct LNK/LMHG ML11 136 F5
Greyfriars Rd UD/BTH/TAN G71 98 C2
Greyfriars St CAR/SHTL G32 80 F3
Greystone Av RUTH G73 96 C4
Greystone Gdns RUTH G73 96 C4
Greywood St KNTSWD G13 59 L2
Grier Pl LRKH ML9 130 B7
Grierson La
STPS/GTHM/RID G33 80 D2
Grierson St
STPS/GTHM/RID G33 80 D2
Grieve Cft UD/BTH/TAN G71 118 F1
Grieve Rd CUMB G67 31 G6
GRNKW/INVK PA16 16 B4
Griffen Av PSLY PA1 74 E5
Griffin Pl BLSH ML4 100 A1
Griffiths Wy CARLUKE ML8 132 B5
Griqua Ter UD/BTH/TAN G71 99 H8
Grogarry Rd DRUM G15 41 G5
Grossart St SHOTTS ML7 87 G7
Grosvenor Crescent La
KVD/HLHD G12 60 D7
Grosvenor La KVD/HLHD G12 60 D7
Grosvenor Rd GRNK PA15 7 L8
Grosvenor Ter KVD/HLHD G12 60 D7
Groveburn Av GIF/THBK G46 94 A6
Grove Crs LRKH ML9 130 E7
Grove Pk KKNTL G66 45 K6
Grovepark Ct MRYH/FIRH G20 61 G8
Grove Park Gdns
MRYH/FIRH G20 61 G8
Grovepark Pl MRYH/FIRH G20 61 G7
Grovepark St MRYH/FIRH G20 61 G8
The Groves BSHPBGS G64 62 C2
The Grove BRHD/NEIL G78 111 J4
BRWEIR PA11 72 E4
BSHPTN PA7 38 A7
GIF/THBK G46 114 B2
KLBCH PA10 73 G7
Grove Wd UD/BTH/TAN G71 99 K1
Grudie St ESTRH G34 82 A2
Gryfebank Av
CRG/CRSL/HOU PA6 73 L1
Gryfebank Cl
CRG/CRSL/HOU PA6 73 L1
Gryfebank Crs
CRG/CRSL/HOU PA6 73 L1
Gryfebank Wy
CRG/CRSL/HOU PA6 73 L1
Gryfe Rd BRWEIR PA11 72 D3
PGL PA14 34 E3
Gryfe St GRNK PA15 7 H9
Gryfewood Crs
CRG/CRSL/HOU PA6 73 L1
Gryfewood Wy
CRG/CRSL/HOU PA6 73 L1
Gryffe Av BRWEIR PA11 72 D1
RNFRW PA4 58 B4
Gryffe Crs PSLYS PA2 90 F1
Gryffe Gv BRWEIR PA11 72 D2
Gryffe Rd KLMCLM PA13 53 L3
Gryffe St LNPK/KPK G44 95 G4
Guildford St
STPS/GTHM/RID G33 81 J1
Gullane Crs BALLOCH G68 30 F3
Gullane Dr CTBR ML5 83 L8
Gullane St PTCK G11 78 B1
Gullion Pk EKILN G74 117 G6
Gunn Ms WISHAW ML2 121 M7
Gunn Qd BLSH ML4 99 L7
Guschet Pl LNK/LMHG ML11 137 G6
Guthrie Dr UD/BTH/TAN G71 99 G1
Guthrie Pl BSHPBGS G64 44 C2
EKILN G74 3 H3
Guthrie St HMLTN ML3 119 K6
MRYH/FIRH G20 60 D4
Guy Mannering Rd
HBR/GL G84 10 F7
Gyle Pl WISHAW ML2 122 E6

H

Haberlea Av PLK/PH/NH G53 93 J6
Haberlea Gdns PLK/PH/NH G53 93 J7
Haco St LARGS KA30 106 F4
Haddington Wy CTBR ML5 83 L7
Haddow Gv UD/BTH/TAN G71 99 G2
Haddow St HMLTN ML3 119 L7
Hadrian Ter MTHW ML1 120 C1
Hagart Rd CRG/CRSL/HOU PA6 55 H8
Hagen Dr MTHW ML1 121 L1
Hagg Crs JNSTN PA5 73 L7
Hagg Pl JNSTN PA5 73 L7
Hagg Rd JNSTN PA5 73 L8
Haggs La PLKSD/SHW G41 78 C8
Haggs Rd PLKSD/SHW G41 94 C1
Haggswood Av
PLKSD/SHW G41 78 C8
Haghill Rd DEN/PKHD G31 80 C4
Hagholm Rd LNK/LMHG ML11 137 M2
Hagmill Crs CTBR ML5 84 C7
Hagmill Rd CTBR ML5 84 B7
Hagthorn Av KBRN KA25 124 C5
Haig Dr BAIL/MDB/MHD G69 81 M6
Haig St GRNK PA15 6 C2
SPRGB/BLRNK G21 61 M6
Hailes Av CAR/SHTL G32 81 K5
Haining Rd RNFRW PA4 58 D6
The Haining RNFRW PA4 58 D7
Hairmyres Dr EKILS G75 126 B2
Hairmyres La EKILS G75 126 B1
Hairmyres Pk EKILS G75 126 C2
Hairmyres St GVH/MTFL G42 79 J8
Hairst St RNFRW PA4 58 D5
Halbeath Av DRUM G15 40 F6
Halbert St PLKSD/SHW G41 94 E1
Haldane La SCOT G14 59 K6
Haldane Pl EKILS G75 3 G9
Haldane St SCOT G14 59 K6
Halfmerk North EKILN G74 3 K3
Halfmerk South EKILN G74 3 K3
Halgreen Av DRUM G15 40 E6

Halidon Av CUMB G67 48 F2
Halketburn Rd SKLM PA17 50 B6
Halketburn Ter SKLM PA17 50 C6
Halkett Crs ALEX/LLW G83 13 K3
Halkirk Ga BLTYR/CAMB G72 118 C6
Halkshill Dr LARGS KA30 107 G5
Hallbrae St
STPS/GTHM/RID G33 62 E8
Hallcraig St AIRDRIE ML6 85 G1
Halley Dr KNTSWD G13 58 E3
Halley Pl KNTSWD G13 58 E3
Halley St KNTSWD G13 58 E2
Hallforest St
STPS/GTHM/RID G33 63 H8
Hallgraig Pl CARLUKE ML8 132 F7
Hallhill Crs STPS/GTHM/RID G33 81 L4
Hallhill Rd BAIL/MDB/MHD G69 82 A4
CAR/SHTL G32 81 H5
JNSTN PA5 89 J3
Halliburton Crs ESTRH G34 81 M3
Halliburton Ter ESTRH G34 82 A3
Hallidale Crs RNFRW PA4 58 F7
Hallinan Gdns WISHAW ML2 121 M8
Hall Pl LNK/LMHG ML11 137 G5
STPS/GTHM/RID G33 63 M5
Hall Rd LNK/LMHG ML11 136 B4
Hallrule Dr
CARD/HILL/MSPK G52 77 J4
Hallside Av BLTYR/CAMB G72 97 L5
Hallside Bvd BLTYR/CAMB G72 97 M7
Hallside Crs BLTYR/CAMB G72 97 L5
Hallside Dr BLTYR/CAMB G72 97 L5
Hallside Gdns WISHAW ML2 122 E5
Hallside Pl GBLS G5 79 J6
Hallside Rd BLTYR/CAMB G72 97 M6
Hallside St HWWD PA9 88 F5
Hall St ALEX/LLW G83 13 L6
CLYDBK G81 40 B8
DMBTN G82 20 D2
HMLTN ML3 129 K1
MTHW ML1 101 G5
Hallydown Dr KNTSWD G13 59 J4
Halpin Cl BLSH ML4 99 K5
Halton Gdns
BAIL/MDB/MHD G69 81 M6
Haltons Pth UD/BTH/TAN G71 99 G4
Hamersley Pl EKILS G75 126 E3
Hamilcomb Rd BLSH ML4 100 A6
Hamill Dr KSYTH G65 29 M2
Hamilton Av PLKSD/SHW G41 78 B7
Hamilton Crs BLTYR/CAMB G72 97 J6
BSDN G61 41 L2
BSHPTN PA7 37 M7
CTBR ML5 84 A5
RNFRW PA4 58 D4
Hamilton Dr AIRDRIE ML6 67 H8
BLTYR/CAMB G72 118 B5
ERSK PA8 38 F7
GIF/THBK G46 94 D8
KVD/HLHD G12 60 F6
LARGS KA30 106 F5
MTHW ML1 120 F5
UD/BTH/TAN G71 119 H1
Hamilton Drive La
KVD/HLHD G12 60 E7
Hamiltonhill Crs PPK/MIL G22 61 H6
Hamiltonhill Rd PPK/MIL G22 61 H7
Hamilton Park Av
KVD/HLHD G12 60 E7
Hamilton Pk North
HMLTN ML3 119 K4
Hamilton Pk South
HMLTN ML3 119 K4
Hamilton Pl EKILS G75 2 E9
HMLTN ML3 129 K4
MTHW ML1 101 J5
Hamilton Rd BLSH ML4 99 M6
BLTYR/CAMB G72 118 A5
CAR/SHTL G32 81 K8
EKILN G74 117 H6
LRKH ML9 130 B4
MTHW ML1 120 D3
RUTH G73 96 B3
UD/BTH/TAN G71 119 H1
Hamilton St CARLUKE ML8 133 H8
CLYDBK G81 58 D2
GVH/MTFL G42 95 J1
LRKH ML9 130 B5
PSLYN/LNWD PA3 9 J3
Hamilton Ter CLYDBK G81 58 D2
Hamilton Vw UD/BTH/TAN G71 99 G3
Hamilton Wy GRNK PA15 6 D3
Hamlet EKILN G74 117 J5
Hampden Dr LNPK/KPK G44 95 H3
Hampden La GVH/MTFL G42 95 H2
Hampden Ter GVH/MTFL G42 95 H2
Handel Pl GBLS G5 79 J6
Hangingshaw Pl
GVH/MTFL G42 95 J2
Hannah Pl DMBTN G82 13 K8
Hanover Cl GVH/MTFL G42 95 G2
Hanover Ct CGLE G1 5 G5
Hanover St CGLE G1 4 F6
HBR/GL G84 10 E7
Hanson Pk DEN/PKHD G31 79 M2
Hanson St DEN/PKHD G31 79 M2
Hapland Av PLK/PH/NH G53 77 J7
Hapland Rd PLK/PH/NH G53 77 J7
Haran Rd ALEX/LLW G83 13 L1
Harbour La PSLYN/LNWD PA3 9 H3
Harbour Pl PTCK G11 78 A1
Harbour Rd PSLYN/LNWD PA3 75 L3
Harbourside GRNKW/INVK PA16 32 E4
Harbour Sq GRNKW/INVK PA16 32 D3
Harburn Pl SCOT G14 58 F3
SMSTN G23 60 E1
Harbury Pl SCOT G14 58 F3
Harcourt Dr DEN/PKHD G31 80 B2
Hardacres LNK/LMHG ML11 137 G4
Hardgate Dr GOV/IBX G51 77 J1
Hardgate Gdns GOV/IBX G51 77 J2
Hardgate Pl GOV/IBX G51 77 J2
Hardgate Rd GOV/IBX G51 77 J1
Hardie Av RUTH G73 96 C2
Hardie St ALEX/LLW G83 13 J3
BLTYR/CAMB G72 118 D3
HMLTN ML3 119 J8
MTHW ML1 120 E1
Hardmuir Gdns KKNTL G66 45 L1
Hardridge Av
CARD/HILL/MSPK G52 77 L7
Hardridge Pl
CARD/HILL/MSPK G52 77 L7
Hardridge Rd
CARD/HILL/MSPK G52 77 K7
Hardwood Ct
GRNKW/INVK PA16 16 E2
Hardy Hl HBR/GL G84 11 G5
Harefield Dr SCOT G14 59 H4
Harelaw Av BRHD/NEIL G78 92 D8
LNPK/KPK G44 94 E6
PGL PA14 34 D2
Harelaw Crs PSLYS PA2 91 J3
Hareleeshill Rd LRKH ML9 130 E7
Hareshaw Rd MTHW ML1 102 D4
Harestanes Gdns KKNTL G66 46 A1
Harestanes Rd CARLUKE ML8 134 E5
Harestone Crs WISHAW ML2 122 C7
Harestone Rd WISHAW ML2 122 C7
Harhill St GOV/IBX G51 78 A3
Harkins Av BLTYR/CAMB G72 118 C3
Harkness Av KKNTL G66 27 H5
Harland St SCOT G14 59 J6
Harley St GOV/IBX G51 78 C5
Harmetray St PPK/MIL G22 61 K4
Harmony Pl GOV/IBX G51 78 A3
Harmony Rw GOV/IBX G51 78 A3
Harmony Sq GOV/IBX G51 78 A3
Harmsworth St PTCK G11 59 L7
Harper Crs LARGS KA30 106 F5
WISHAW ML2 122 E5
Harport St GIF/THBK G46 93 L5
Harrier Wy GRNKW/INVK PA16 16 B5
Harriet Pl PLKSW/MSWD G43 94 B4
Harriet St RUTH G73 96 A2
Harrington Rd EKILN G74 2 E5
Harris Cl NMRNS G77 113 H3
Harris Crs OLDK G60 39 H5
Harris Dr OLDK G60 39 H5
Harris Gdns OLDK G60 39 J5
Harrison Dr GOV/IBX G51 78 B4
Harrison Pl DMBTN G82 13 J8
Harris Qd WISHAW ML2 122 E5
Harris Rd OLDK G60 39 H5
PGL PA14 35 H3
SMSTN G23 60 D1
Harrow Ct DRUM G15 40 F6
Harrow Pl DRUM G15 40 F6
Hartfield Ct DMBTN G82 21 G6
Hartfield Crs BRHD/NEIL G78 111 L3
Hartfield Ter PSLYS PA2 75 M8
Harthill Rd BTHG/ARM EH48 71 L3
Hartlaw Crs
CARD/HILL/MSPK G52 77 G3
Hartree Av KNTSWD G13 58 E1
Hartstone Rd PLK/PH/NH G53 93 H2
Hart St CLYDBK G81 40 D2
DEN/PKHD G31 80 E5
PSLYN/LNWD PA3 74 B5
Hartwood Gdns NMRNS G77 113 K7
SHOTTS ML7 103 M7
Hartwood Rd SHOTTS ML7 103 M6
Harvest Dr MTHW ML1 120 E5
Harvey Ct LOCHW PA12 109 J3
Harvey St COWCAD G4 61 J8
Harvey Ter LOCHW PA12 109 J3
Harvey Wy BLSH ML4 100 C2
Harvie Av NMRNS G77 113 K3
Harvie St GOV/IBX G51 78 D4
Harwood Gdns
BAIL/MDB/MHD G69 47 G7
Harwood St CAR/SHTL G32 80 E3
Hastie St KVGV G3 78 D1
Hastings EKILS G75 126 D3
Hatfield Dr KVD/HLHD G12 59 M4
Hathaway Dr GIF/THBK G46 94 B8
Hathaway La MRYH/FIRH G20 60 E5
Hathaway St MRYH/FIRH G20 60 E5
Hathersage Av
BAIL/MDB/MHD G69 82 B5
Hathersage Dr
BAIL/MDB/MHD G69 82 B5
Hathersage Gdns
BAIL/MDB/MHD G69 82 B5
Hatton Gdns
CARD/HILL/MSPK G52 77 G5
Hatton Pl MTHW ML1 101 J7
Hattonrigg Rd BLSH ML4 100 B2
Hatton Ter MTHW ML1 101 J7
Haughburn Pl PLK/PH/NH G53 93 H2
Haughburn Rd
PLK/PH/NH G53 93 H2
Haughburn Ter
PLK/PH/NH G53 93 J2
Haugh Pl HMLTN ML3 129 L1
Haugh Rd KSYTH G65 29 J2
KVGV G3 78 D2
Haughton Av KSYTH G65 29 L2
Haughview Rd MTHW ML1 120 B3
Havelock La PTCK G11 60 C8
Havelock Pk EKILS G75 126 D1
Havelock Pl HBR/GL G84 10 F5
Havelock St HBR/GL G84 10 E5
PTCK G11 60 C8
Haven Pk EKILS G75 126 C4
Havoc Rd DMBTN G82 20 B7
Hawbank Rd EKILN G74 116 A7
Hawick Av PSLYS PA2 91 H1
Hawick Ct GRNK PA15 7 G7
Hawick Crs LRKH ML9 130 C7
Hawick Dr CTBR ML5 84 D6
Hawick St KNTSWD G13 58 F2
WISHAW ML2 122 C4
Hawkhead Av PSLYS PA2 * 76 B8
Hawkhead Rd PSLY PA1 76 B5
Hawkwood EKILS G75 127 G6
Hawkwood Rd AIRDRIE ML6 66 F5
Hawthorn Av
BLTYR/CAMB G72 96 D5
BSDN G61 42 A3
BSHPBGS G64 62 B2
DMBTN G82 20 B6
ERSK PA8 57 L2
JNSTN PA5 90 A1
KKNTL G66 45 J5
WISHAW ML2 123 J3
Hawthorn Crs BEITH KA15 125 J5
ERSK PA8 57 L2
Hawthornden Gdns SMSTN G23 42 E8
Hawthorn Dr AIRDRIE ML6 85 K3
BRHD/NEIL G78 112 D1
CTBR ML5 84 D4
MTHW ML1 101 H6
SHOTTS ML7 105 H5
WISHAW ML2 122 C7
Hawthorne Pl GRK PA19 15 H3
Hawthorn Gdns BLSH ML4 100 C5
BLTYR/CAMB G72 97 L6
CRMNK/CLK/EAG G76 114 E4
LRKH ML9 130 E7
Hawthorn Hl HMLTN ML3 129 L1
Hawthornhill Rd DMBTN G82 20 B5
Hawthorn Pl SHOTTS ML7 123 M1
Hawthorn Qd PPK/MIL G22 61 J5
Hawthorn Rd
CRMNK/CLK/EAG G76 114 F5
CUMB G67 31 M5
ERSK PA8 57 L2
Hawthorn St BSHPBGS G64 44 C1
CLYDBK G81 40 A5
PPK/MIL G22 61 J5
Hawthorn Ter EKILS G75 126 E4
UD/BTH/TAN G71 99 H3
Hawthorn Wk
BLTYR/CAMB G72 96 D5
Hawthorn Wy
BLTYR/CAMB G72 96 E5
ERSK PA8 57 L2
Hay Av BSHPTN PA7 38 C7
Hayburn Crs PTCK G11 60 A7
Hayburn Ga PTCK G11 60 B8
Hayburn La KVD/HLHD G12 60 A7
Hayburn St PTCK G11 78 B1
Hayes Gv ALEX/LLW G83 13 K4
Hayfield St GBLS G5 79 K6
Hayle Gdns
BAIL/MDB/MHD G69 46 F7
Haylie Gdns LARGS KA30 106 F6
Haylie Neuk LARGS KA30 106 F6
Haymarket St CAR/SHTL G32 80 F3
Haystack Pl KKNTL G66 45 K6
Hayston Crs PPK/MIL G22 61 H5
Hayston Rd BALLOCH G68 30 F5
KKNTL G66 45 G2
Hayston St PPK/MIL G22 61 H5
Hay St GRNK PA15 6 D6
Hayward Av CARLUKE ML8 135 J1
Haywood St PPK/MIL G22 61 H4
Hazel Av BSDN G61 42 A3
DMBTN G82 20 A5
JNSTN PA5 90 A1
KKNTL G66 45 K4
LNPK/KPK G44 94 F6
Hazel Bank KKNTL G66 27 H6
Hazelbank Wk AIRDRIE ML6 84 D1
Hazeldean Crs WISHAW ML2 122 C4
Hazel Dene BSHPBGS G64 62 B1
Hazelden Pk LNPK/KPK G44 94 E6
Hazelfield Gv AIRDRIE ML6 85 L8
Hazel Gdns MTHW ML1 120 E6
Hazel Gv KKNTL G66 45 K4
Hazelhead EKILN G74 3 M3
Hazellea Dr GIF/THBK G46 94 D6
Hazelmere Rd KLMCLM PA13 53 H2
Hazel Pk HMLTN ML3 119 L8
Hazel Rd CUMB G67 31 K6
Hazel Ter GRK PA19 15 J3
UD/BTH/TAN G71 99 H3
Hazelton MTHW ML1 120 D4
Hazel Wd WISHAW ML2 122 D4
Hazelwood Av NMRNS G77 113 L5
PSLYS PA2 90 E3
Hazelwood Dr
BLTYR/CAMB G72 118 C2
Hazelwood Gdns RUTH G73 96 C6
Hazelwood Gv
BAIL/MDB/MHD G69 83 G4
Hazelwood La BRWEIR PA11 72 D3
Hazelwood Rd BRWEIR PA11 72 D4
PLKSD/SHW G41 78 C6
Hazlitt Gdns MRYH/FIRH G20 61 G4
Hazlitt Pl MRYH/FIRH G20 61 G4
Hazlitt St MRYH/FIRH G20 61 H4
Headhouse Ct EKILS G75 2 C8
Headlesscross Rd
WHIT/BBN/FH EH47 105 M7
Headsmuir Av CARLUKE ML8 132 F7
Head St BEITH KA15 125 L5
Heath Av BSHPBGS G64 62 B2
KKNTL G66 45 J6
Heathcliffe Av
BLTYR/CAMB G72 118 C1
Heathcot Av DRUM G15 40 E7
Heathcot Pl DRUM G15 40 D7
Heather Av ALEX/LLW G83 13 J4
BRHD/NEIL G78 92 A4
BSDN G61 41 K1
CLYDBK G81 40 A2
MTHW ML1 101 G4
Heatherbank Av
BAIL/MDB/MHD G69 64 C7
Heatherbank Dr
BAIL/MDB/MHD G69 64 B7
Heatherbank Gv
BAIL/MDB/MHD G69 64 C7
Heatherbank Wk AIRDRIE ML6 84 B1
Heatherbell Ct SHOTTS ML7 71 K7
Heatherbrae BSHPBGS G64 61 L1
Heather Dr KKNTL G66 45 G6
Heather Gdns KKNTL G66 45 G6
UD/BTH/TAN G71 99 J3
Heather Pl JNSTN PA5 90 A1
Heather Rd LNK/LMHG ML11 136 B3
Heather Rw CARLUKE ML8 133 G5
Heather St AIRDRIE ML6 69 G4
Heather Vw KKNTL G66 26 E1
Heatheryford Gdns
AIRDRIE ML6 68 B6
Heathery Knowe EKILS G75 2 E9
Heatheryknowe Rd
BAIL/MDB/MHD G69 82 F3
Heathery Lea Av CTBR ML5 84 D6
Heathery Rd WISHAW ML2 121 M6
Heathfield WISHAW ML2 131 J2
Heathfield Av
BAIL/MDB/MHD G69 47 G8
Heathfield Dr MLNGV G62 24 B7
Heathfield St
STPS/GTHM/RID G33 81 J2
Heath Rd LRKH ML9 130 D6
Heathside Rd GIF/THBK G46 94 D7
Heathwood Dr GIF/THBK G46 94 A7
Hebrides Gv GRNKW/INVK PA16 32 D3
Hecla Av DRUM G15 40 F6
Hecla Pl DRUM G15 40 F6
Hecla Sq DRUM G15 40 F7
Hector Rd PLKSD/SHW G41 94 D2
Heggies Av PGL PA14 35 G2
Heights Rd BTHG/ARM EH48 71 K1
Helensburgh Dr KNTSWD G13 59 K3
Helenslea BLTYR/CAMB G72 97 K6
Helenslea Pl BLSH ML4 99 M6
Helenslee Ct DMBTN G82 20 D7
Helenslee Crs DMBTN G82 20 D7
Helenslee Rd DMBTN G82 20 D7
PGL PA14 36 C3
Helen St GOV/IBX G51 77 M4
Helenvale Ct DEN/PKHD G31 80 D5
Helenvale St DEN/PKHD G31 80 C6
Helen Wy ALEX/LLW G83 13 L8
Helen Wynd LRKH ML9 130 C7
Helmsdale Av BLTYR/CAMB G72 98 C7
Helmsdale Cl
BLTYR/CAMB G72 118 D6
Helmsdale Dr PSLYS PA2 74 F8
Hemlock St KNTSWD G13 59 M2
Hemmingen Ct CARLUKE ML8 133 G6
Henderland Dr BSDN G61 41 L7
Henderland Rd BSDN G61 41 M8
Henderson Av
BLTYR/CAMB G72 97 K4
Henderson Ct MTHW ML1 120 D2
Henderson St AIRDRIE ML6 85 H1
CLYDBK G81 58 E1
CTBR ML5 83 M4
MRYH/FIRH G20 60 F7
PSLY PA1 8 E4
Henderson Ter GRK PA19 15 L2
Henrietta St SCOT G14 59 J6
Henry Bell St HBR/GL G84 10 E6
Henry Qd MTHW ML1 102 A4
Henry St BRHD/NEIL G78 92 B6
Hepburn Hl HMLTN ML3 129 H2
Hepburn Rd
CARD/HILL/MSPK G52 77 G2
Herald Av KNTSWD G13 41 K8
Herald Gv MTHW ML1 120 D5
Herbertson Gv
BLTYR/CAMB G72 118 B1
Herbertson St
BLTYR/CAMB G72 118 F3
Herbert St MRYH/FIRH G20 60 F7
Heriot Av PSLYS PA2 90 F2
Heriot Crs BSHPBGS G64 44 A7
Heriot Rd KKNTL G66 45 J7
Heritage Ct NMRNS G77 113 L4
Heritage Vw CTBR ML5 83 M2
Heritage Wy CTBR ML5 83 M2
Herma St SMSTN G23 60 E2
Hermes Wy BLSH ML4 100 F4
Hermiston Av CAR/SHTL G32 81 H4
Hermiston Rd CAR/SHTL G32 81 H4
Hermitage Av KNTSWD G13 59 J2
Hermitage Crs CTBR ML5 84 B6
Herndon Ct NMRNS G77 114 A4
Heron Ct CLYDBK G81 40 B4
Heron Pl JNSTN PA5 89 K3
Heron Rd GRNKW/INVK PA16 16 A5
Herries Rd PLKSD/SHW G41 94 C1
Herriet St PLKSD/SHW G41 78 F7
Herriot Av KBRN KA25 124 C1
Herriot St CTBR ML5 83 L2
Herschell St KNTSWD G13 59 M3
Hertford Av KVD/HLHD G12 60 B4
Hewett Crs CRG/CRSL/HOU PA6 73 J1
Hexham Gdns PLKSD/SHW G41 94 D1
Heys St BRHD/NEIL G78 92 C7
Heywood Gdns SKLM PA17 50 B6
Hibernia St GRNKW/INVK PA16 16 D5
Hickman St GVH/MTFL G42 95 H1
Hickman Ter GVH/MTFL G42 79 J8
Hickory Crs UD/BTH/TAN G71 99 J1
Hickory St PPK/MIL G22 61 L5
High Avon St LRKH ML9 130 B6
High Barholm KLBCH PA10 73 H7
High Barrwood Rd KSYTH G65 29 M2
High Beeches
CRMNK/CLK/EAG G76 115 L2
High Blantyre Rd HMLTN ML3 118 F5
Highburgh Av
LNK/LMHG ML11 137 H5
Highburgh Ct LNK/LMHG ML11 137 H5
Highburgh Dr RUTH G73 96 B5
Highburgh Rd KVD/HLHD G12 60 C8
High Burnside Av CTBR ML5 83 L5
High Calside PSLYS PA2 8 F7
High Carnegie Rd PGL PA14 34 F2
High Common Rd EKILN G74 3 M9
Highcraig Av JNSTN PA5 89 K1
High Craigends KSYTH G65 29 L2
High Craighall Rd COWCAD G4 4 E1
Highcroft Av LNPK/KPK G44 95 K5
Highcross Av CTBR ML5 83 K6
Higherness Wy CTBR ML5 83 L7
Highfield Av PSLYS PA2 91 K3
Highfield Ct KKNTL G66 45 M2
Highfield Crs MTHW ML1 121 G1
PSLYS PA2 91 K3
Highfield Dr
CRMNK/CLK/EAG G76 114 D3
KVD/HLHD G12 60 B4
RUTH G73 96 C7
Highfield Pl EKILN G74 3 H1
KVD/HLHD G12 60 B4
Highfield Rd KKNTL G66 45 L1
LRKH ML9 130 D6
High Flender Rd
CRMNK/CLK/EAG G76 114 D5
High Graighall Rd COWCAD G4 61 H8
Highgrove Rd RNFRW PA4 58 E6
Highholm Av PGL PA14 34 B1
Highholm St PGL PA14 18 B8
High Kirk Vw JNSTN PA5 73 M8
Highland Av BLTYR/CAMB G72 118 C2
Highland La GOV/IBX G51 78 C2
Highland Pk KSYTH G65 29 K1
High Mains Av DMBTN G82 21 J7
High Meadow CARLUKE ML8 135 H1
High Mill Rd CARLUKE ML8 133 J7
High Parksail ERSK PA8 57 J2
High Parks Crs HMLTN ML3 129 K4
High Patrick St HMLTN ML3 119 L8
High Pleasance LRKH ML9 130 C6
High Rd MTHW ML1 120 D2
PSLYS PA2 8 D7
Highstonehall Rd HMLTN ML3 128 F2
High St AIRDRIE ML6 84 F1
BRHD/NEIL G78 111 K3
CGLE G1 5 J7
DMBTN G82 20 E7
GRNK PA15 6 D4
JNSTN PA5 73 M7
KBRN KA25 124 C2
KLMCLM PA13 53 K1
LNK/LMHG ML11 137 G5
LOCHW PA12 109 J3
MTHW ML1 101 L5
PSLY PA1 8 F5
RNFRW PA4 58 D6
RUTH G73 96 A2
SHOTTS ML7 104 F5
High Whitehills Rd EKILS G75 127 H5
Hilary Dr BAIL/MDB/MHD G69 81 M5
Hillary Av RUTH G73 96 D4
Hill Av NMRNS G77 113 J5
Hillbank St ALEX/LLW G83 13 L6
Hillbare St GOV/IBX G51 77 K3
Hill Crs CRMNK/CLK/EAG G76 114 F4
Hillcrest BAIL/MDB/MHD G69 64 D2
CRMNK/CLK/EAG G76 115 K2
Hillcrest Av CAR/SHTL G32 97 H2
CLYDBK G81 40 A2
CTBR ML5 84 C3
CUMB G67 48 E1
LNPK/KPK G44 94 E6
PSLYS PA2 91 H4
WISHAW ML2 121 L6
Hillcrest Dr NMRNS G77 114 A5
Hillcrest Rd BSDN G61 41 M5
CAR/SHTL G32 97 J2
KSYTH G65 28 E2
UD/BTH/TAN G71 99 G3
Hillcrest St MLNGV G62 24 B8
Hillcrest Ter UD/BTH/TAN G71 99 H7
Hillcrest Vw LRKH ML9 130 D7
Hillcroft Ter BSHPBGS G64 61 M2
Hillend Crs CLYDBK G81 39 M3
CRMNK/CLK/EAG G76 114 C4
Hillend Dr GRNK PA15 7 J8
Hillend Pl GRNK PA15 7 J8
Hillend Rd
CRMNK/CLK/EAG G76 114 D4
PPK/MIL G22 61 G3
RUTH G73 96 B6
Hillfoot CRG/CRSL/HOU PA6 73 K2
DMBTN G82 13 J8
Hillfoot Av DMBTN G82 21 J6
RUTH G73 96 A3
WISHAW ML2 122 D2
Hillfoot Crs WISHAW ML2 122 D2
Hillfoot Dr BSDN G61 41 M4
CTBR ML5 83 K4
HWWD PA9 88 F5
WISHAW ML2 122 D2
Hillfoot Gdns UD/BTH/TAN G71 98 E2
WISHAW ML2 122 D2
Hillfoot Rd AIRDRIE ML6 85 H3
Hillfoot St DEN/PKHD G31 80 A3
Hillfoot Ter CARLUKE ML8 133 J8
Hillhead Av
BAIL/MDB/MHD G69 46 F8
CARLUKE ML8 133 J7
MTHW ML1 101 G7
RUTH G73 96 B6
Hillhead Crs HMLTN ML3 118 F7
MTHW ML1 101 G7
Hillhead Dr AIRDRIE ML6 85 G3
MTHW ML1 101 G8
Hillhead Pl RUTH G73 96 B6
Hillhead Rd KKNTL G66 45 K1
SPRGB/BLRNK G21 62 D3
Hillhead St KVD/HLHD G12 60 D8
MLNGV G62 24 A8
Hillhead Ter HMLTN ML3 118 E7
Hillhouse Crs HMLTN ML3 118 F7
Hillhouse Farm Ga
LNK/LMHG ML11 136 E4
Hillhouse Ga CARLUKE ML8 135 J1
Hillhouseridge Rd
SHOTTS ML7 104 D4
Hillhouse Rd BLTYR/CAMB G72 118 D6
Hillhouse St SPRGB/BLRNK G21 62 A6
Hillhouse Ter HMLTN ML3 * 118 F7
Hillington Gdns
CARD/HILL/MSPK G52 77 J5
Hillington Park Circ
CARD/HILL/MSPK G52 77 J4
Hillington Qd
CARD/HILL/MSPK G52 77 G4
Hillington Rd
CARD/HILL/MSPK G52 77 G2
Hillington Rd South
CARD/HILL/MSPK G52 77 G4
Hillington Ter
CARD/HILL/MSPK G52 77 G4
Hillkirk Pl SPRGB/BLRNK G21 61 M6
Hillkirk St SPRGB/BLRNK G21 61 M6
Hillneuk Av BSDN G61 41 M4
Hillneuk Dr BSDN G61 42 A5
Hillpark Av PSLYS PA2 91 K1
Hillpark Dr PLKSW/MSWD G43 94 C4
Hill Pl BLSH ML4 99 M7
MTHW ML1 101 J7
SHOTTS ML7 104 E4
Hillrigg AIRDRIE ML6 49 K8
Hillrigg Av AIRDRIE ML6 85 J1
Hill Rd CUMB G67 30 E7
GRNKW/INVK PA16 32 E5
HWWD PA9 88 F5
SHOTTS ML7 71 K6
Hillsborough La KVD/HLHD G12 60 E7
Hillsborough Rd
BAIL/MDB/MHD G69 81 M5
Hillside CRG/CRSL/HOU PA6 73 K2
KSYTH G65 29 M5
Hillside Av ALEX/LLW G83 13 J7
BSDN G61 41 M4
CRMNK/CLK/EAG G76 114 D3
KLMCLM PA13 53 K1
Hillside Ct GIF/THBK G46 93 M6
Hillside Crs BRHD/NEIL G78 111 K3
CTBR ML5 83 M6
HMLTN ML3 119 K8
MTHW ML1 101 K6
Hillside Dr BRHD/NEIL G78 92 A6
BSDN G61 42 A5
BSHPBGS G64 44 A8
BTHG/ARM EH48 71 K1
PGL PA14 34 B1
Hillside Gardens La PTCK G11 60 B7
Hillside Gv BRHD/NEIL G78 92 A7
Hillside La HMLTN ML3 119 K8
Hillside Pk CLYDBK G81 40 B3
Hillside Pl MTHW ML1 101 K6
Hillside Qd PLKSW/MSWD G43 94 B5
Hillside Rd BRHD/NEIL G78 111 K3
DMBTN G82 19 H1
GRK PA19 15 K2
GRNK PA15 7 H9
PLKSW/MSWD G43 94 B5
PSLYS PA2 76 A7
Hillside Ter HMLTN ML3 119 J8
KKNTL G66 27 H5
Hill St AIRDRIE ML6 68 F4
ALEX/LLW G83 13 J5
DMBTN G82 20 D7
GRNK PA15 6 E6
HMLTN ML3 118 F7
KVGV G3 4 C3
LARGS KA30 106 F6
LRKH ML9 130 C7
WISHAW ML2 122 A7
Hillswick Crs PPK/MIL G22 61 H2
Hill Ter MTHW ML1 101 J7
Hilltop Av BLSH ML4 100 A2

Hilltop Crs GRK PA19 15 M3
Hilltop Rd BAIL/MDB/MHD G69 46 F8
GRK PA19 15 L3
Hill Vw DMBTN G82 37 M1
EKILS G75 2 E8
Hillview AIRDRIE ML6 49 M7
SKLM PA17 50 C5
Hillview Av KKNTL G66 26 E3
KSYTH G65 29 K3
Hillview Ct CLYDBK G81 39 M7
Hillview Crs BLSH ML4 100 A1
LRKH ML9 130 D8
UD/BTH/TAN G71 98 E2
Hillview Dr BLTYR/CAMB G72 118 D1
CRMNK/CLK/EAG G76 114 D3
HBR/GL G84 10 D3
Hillview Gdns CLYDBK G81 39 M7
Hillview Pl
CRMNK/CLK/EAG G76 114 E3
NMRNS G77 113 K5
Hillview Rd BRWEIR PA11 72 E3
JNSTN PA5 74 C8
LNK/LMHG ML11 136 A6
Hillview St CAR/SHTL G32 80 F5
Hiltonbank St HMLTN ML3 119 J7
Hilton Gdns KNTSWD G13 59 M2
Hilton Pk BSHPBGS G64 43 M7
Hilton Rd BSHPBGS G64 43 M7
MLNGV G62 23 L7
Hilton Ter BLTYR/CAMB G72 96 E7
BSHPBGS G64 43 M7
KNTSWD G13 59 L2
Hilton Vw BLSH ML4 100 A1
Hindsland Rd LRKH ML9 130 D8
Hinshaw St MRYH/FIRH G20 61 G7
Hinshelwood Dr GOV/IBX G51 78 A5
Hinshelwood Pl GOV/IBX G51 78 B5
Hirst Gdns SHOTTS ML7 104 C4
Hirst Rd SHOTTS ML7 87 K7
Hobart Crs CLYDBK G81 39 K5
Hobart Qd WISHAW ML2 122 E6
Hobart Rd EKILS G75 2 A8
Hobart St PPK/MIL G22 61 H6
Hobden St SPRGB/BLRNK G21 62 A7
Hoddam Av CSMK G45 95 M7
Hoddam Ter CSMK G45 96 A7
Hoey Dr WISHAW ML2 131 L2
Hogan Wy MTHW ML1 121 L1
Hogarth Av CAR/SHTL G32 80 D3
Hogarth Ct ALEX/LLW G83 13 K4
Hogarth Dr CAR/SHTL G32 80 D3
Hogarth Gdns CAR/SHTL G32 80 D3
Hogganfield Ct
STPS/GTHM/RID G33 62 D8
Hogganfield St
STPS/GTHM/RID G33 62 D8
Hogg Av JNSTN PA5 89 L1
Hogg Rd AIRDRIE ML6 85 K5
Hogg St AIRDRIE ML6 85 G2
Holeburn La PLKSW/MSWD G43 94 C4
Holeburn Rd
PLKSW/MSWD G43 94 C4
Hole Farm Rd
GRNKW/INVK PA16 16 D6
Holehills Dr AIRDRIE ML6 67 H7
Holehills Pl AIRDRIE ML6 67 H7
Holehouse Brae
BRHD/NEIL G78 111 J3
Holehouse Ct LARGS KA30 107 G4
Holehouse Dr KBRN KA25 124 D3
KNTSWD G13 59 G3
Holehouse Rd LARGS KA30 107 G4
Holehouse Ter BRHD/NEIL G78 111 J3
Hollandbush Gv HMLTN ML3 129 K2
Hollandhurst Rd CTBR ML5 83 M1
Holland St CGLW G2 4 B5
Hollinwell Rd SMSTN G23 60 E1
Hollowglen Rd CAR/SHTL G32 81 H4
Hollows Av PSLYS PA2 90 F3
Hollows Crs PSLYS PA2 90 F3
Hollybank Pl BLTYR/CAMB G72 97 H6
Hollybank St
SPRGB/BLRNK G21 80 A1
Hollybrook Pl GVH/MTFL G42 79 H8
Hollybrook St GVH/MTFL G42 95 H1
Hollybush Av PSLYS PA2 91 H4
Hollybush Rd
CARD/HILL/MSPK G52 76 F4
Holly Dr DMBTN G82 20 B5
SPRGB/BLRNK G21 62 A7
Holly Gv BLSH ML4 100 F4
Hollyhill Gv
BAIL/MDB/MHD G69 83 G4
Hollymount BSDN G61 41 M7
Holly Pl JNSTN PA5 90 A2
Holly St AIRDRIE ML6 85 J2
CLYDBK G81 40 A5
Hollytree Gdns KKNTL G66 26 C2
Hollywood LARGS KA30 106 D1
Holm Av PSLYS PA2 9 J9
Holmbank Av PLKSD/SHW G41 94 D4
Holmbrae Av UD/BTH/TAN G71 98 F3
Holmbrae Rd UD/BTH/TAN G71 98 F3
Holmbyre Rd CSMK G45 115 H1
Holmbyre Ter CSMK G45 95 J8
Holm Crest CARLUKE ML8 134 B7
Holme Av UD/BTH/TAN G71 98 E3
Holmes Av RNFRW PA4 58 C8
Holmes Qd BLSH ML4 100 B6
Holmfauldhead Dr
GOV/IBX G51 77 L1
Holmfauldhead Pl
GOV/IBX G51 59 L8
Holmfauld Rd GOV/IBX G51 77 L1
Holm Gdns BLSH ML4 100 C5
Holmhead KBRN KA25 124 C5
Holmhead Crs LNPK/KPK G44 95 G4
Holmhead Pl LNPK/KPK G44 95 G4
Holmhead Rd LNPK/KPK G44 95 G5
Holmhill Av BLTYR/CAMB G72 97 G6
Holmhills Dr BLTYR/CAMB G72 96 F7
Holmhills Gdns
BLTYR/CAMB G72 96 F6
Holmhills Gv BLTYR/CAMB G72 96 F6
Holmhills Pl BLTYR/CAMB G72 96 F7
Holmhills Rd BLTYR/CAMB G72 96 F7
Holmhills Ter BLTYR/CAMB G72 96 F6
Holm La EKILN G74 2 E4
Holmlea Rd GVH/MTFL G42 95 G3
Holmpark BSHPTN PA7 38 A7
Holm Pl PSLYN/LNWD PA3 74 B3
Holm Rd CARLUKE ML8 134 B7
Holms Crs ERSK PA8 38 F8
Holmscroft Av GRNK PA15 6 A5
Holmscroft St GRNK PA15 6 A4
Holms Pl BAIL/MDB/MHD G69 64 E3
Holms Rd GLGNK KA14 124 D7
Holm St CARLUKE ML8 133 G7
CGLW G2 4 D7
MTHW ML1 101 G6
Holmswood Av
BLTYR/CAMB G72 118 D2
Holmwood Av
UD/BTH/TAN G71 98 F3
Holmwood Ct LARGS KA30 106 D1
Holmwood Gdns
UD/BTH/TAN G71 98 F4
Holmwood Pk CARLUKE ML8 134 A6
Holyknowe Crs KKNTL G66 26 E2
Holyknowe Rd KKNTL G66 26 E3
Holyrood Crs MRYH/FIRH G20 60 F8
Holyrood Qd MRYH/FIRH G20 60 F8
Holyrood St HMLTN ML3 119 G5
Holytown Rd BLSH ML4 100 E4
Holywell St DEN/PKHD G31 80 B5
Home Farm Rd SHOTTS ML7 103 M6
Homer Pl BLSH ML4 100 E4
Homeston Av
UD/BTH/TAN G71 99 G7
Home St LNK/LMHG ML11 137 J6
Honeybank Crs CARLUKE ML8 133 H6
Honeybog Rd
CARD/HILL/MSPK G52 76 E3
Honeyman Crs
LNK/LMHG ML11 137 J5
Honeysuckle La ALEX/LLW G83 13 K3
Honeywell Av
STPS/GTHM/RID G33 64 A6
Honeywell Ct
STPS/GTHM/RID G33 64 A6
Honeywell Crs AIRDRIE ML6 85 L8
Honeywell Dr
STPS/GTHM/RID G33 64 A6
Honeywell Gv
STPS/GTHM/RID G33 64 A5
Hood St CLYDBK G81 40 C7
GRNK PA15 6 C2
Hooper Pl BLSH ML4 100 B3
Hope Av BRWEIR PA11 53 L8
Hope Crs LRKH ML9 130 D6
Hopefield Av KVD/HLHD G12 60 C5
Hopehill Gdns MRYH/FIRH G20 61 G7
Hopehill Rd MRYH/FIRH G20 61 G7
Hopeman ERSK PA8 39 G7
Hopeman Av GIF/THBK G46 93 L5
Hopeman Dr GIF/THBK G46 93 L5
Hopeman Rd GIF/THBK G46 93 L5
Hopeman St GIF/THBK G46 93 L5
Hopepark Dr BALLOCH G68 29 L8
Hope St BLSH ML4 100 C4
CARLUKE ML8 133 J7
CGLW G2 4 E6
GRNK PA15 6 D6
HBR/GL G84 10 F7
HMLTN ML3 119 L7
LNK/LMHG ML11 137 G5
MTHW ML1 120 E2
WISHAW ML2 123 G5
Hopetoun Pl SMSTN G23 42 E8
Hopetoun Ter
SPRGB/BLRNK G21 62 A7
Horatius St MTHW ML1 100 B8
Hornal Rd UD/BTH/TAN G71 99 G6
Hornbeam Dr CLYDBK G81 39 M6
Hornbeam Rd CUMB G67 31 L4
UD/BTH/TAN G71 99 H2
Horne St PPK/MIL G22 61 L5
Hornock Rd CTBR ML5 83 M1
Hornshill Dr MTHW ML1 102 B7
Hornshill Farm Rd
STPS/GTHM/RID G33 63 L4
Hornshill St SPRGB/BLRNK G21 62 A6
Horsbrugh Av KSYTH G65 29 K1
Horse Shoe Rd BSDN G61 41 L5
Horsewood Rd BRWEIR PA11 72 C3
Horslethill Rd KVD/HLHD G12 60 D6
Horslet St CTBR ML5 83 J6
Horsley Brae WISHAW ML2 131 K5
Horton Pl HBR/GL G84 11 G4
Hospital Rd WISHAW ML2 122 C8
Hospital St CTBR ML5 84 A5
GBLS G5 79 H6
Hospitland Dr
LNK/LMHG ML11 137 H4
Hotspur St MRYH/FIRH G20 60 E6
Houldsworth La KVGV G3 78 E2
Househillmuir Crs
PLK/PH/NH G53 93 J3
Househillmuir Pl
PLK/PH/NH G53 93 J2
Househillmuir Rd
PLK/PH/NH G53 93 G4
Househillwood Crs
PLK/PH/NH G53 93 H2
Househillwood Rd
PLK/PH/NH G53 93 H3
Housel Av KNTSWD G13 59 H3
House O' Muir Rd SHOTTS ML7 70 B8
Houstonfield Qd
CRG/CRSL/HOU PA6 55 G8
Houston Pl GBLS G5 78 F4
JNSTN PA5 74 C8
Houston Rd BRWEIR PA11 72 E1
CRG/CRSL/HOU PA6 73 J1
KLMCLM PA13 55 J4
RNFRW PA4 57 G6
Houston St GBLS G5 78 F5
GRNKW/INVK PA16 6 B1
HMLTN ML3 129 K1
RNFRW PA4 58 D5
WISHAW ML2 122 D7
Houston Ter EKILN G74 2 D4
Houstoun Sq JNSTN PA5 73 M7
Howacre LNK/LMHG ML11 136 F4
Howard Av EKILN G74 117 G5
Howard Ct EKILN G74 117 G5
Howard St CGLE G1 4 F8
LRKH ML9 130 E8
PSLY PA1 9 L4
Howatshaws Rd DMBTN G82 21 H4
Howat St GOV/IBX G51 78 A2
Howburn Rd SHOTTS ML7 71 L6
Howden Av MTHW ML1 101 K1
Howden Dr PSLYN/LNWD PA3 74 A5
Howden Pl MTHW ML1 101 G4
Howe Gdns UD/BTH/TAN G71 99 G3
Howe Rd KSYTH G65 29 K3
Howes St CTBR ML5 84 B5
Howford Rd
CARD/HILL/MSPK G52 77 H5
Howgate Av DRUM G15 40 F6
Howgate Rd HMLTN ML3 129 J2
Howieshill Av
BLTYR/CAMB G72 97 H5
Howieshill Rd
BLTYR/CAMB G72 97 H6
Howie St LRKH ML9 130 D8
Howletnest Rd AIRDRIE ML6 85 J3
Howlet Pl HMLTN ML3 129 L1
Howson Lea MTHW ML1 121 H5
Howson Vw MTHW ML1 120 B2
Howth Dr KNTSWD G13 59 M1
Howth Ter KNTSWD G13 59 M1
Hoylake Pk UD/BTH/TAN G71 98 F8
Hoylake Pl SMSTN G23 60 E1
Hozier Crs UD/BTH/TAN G71 98 F2
Hozier St CARLUKE ML8 133 H7
CTBR ML5 84 A5
Hudson Ter EKILS G75 126 E2
Hudson Wy EKILS G75 2 A7
Hughenden Dr KVD/HLHD G12 60 B6
Hughenden Gdns
KVD/HLHD G12 60 B6
Hughenden La KVD/HLHD G12 60 B6
Hughenden Rd KVD/HLHD G12 60 B6
Hugh Murray Gv
BLTYR/CAMB G72 97 J5
Hugo St MRYH/FIRH G20 60 F5
Hulks Rd AIRDRIE ML6 49 H6
Humbie Ct NMRNS G77 113 L7
Humbie Ga NMRNS G77 113 L7
Humbie Gv NMRNS G77 113 L6
Humbie Lawns NMRNS G77 113 L7
Humbie Rd NMRNS G77 113 L7
Hume Dr UD/BTH/TAN G71 98 E3
Hume Pl EKILS G75 2 D8
Hume Rd CUMB G67 31 G6
Hume St CLYDBK G81 40 B8
Hunter Dr NMRNS G77 113 H6
Hunterfield Dr
BLTYR/CAMB G72 96 E5
Hunterhill Av PSLYS PA2 9 J8
Hunterhill Rd PSLYS PA2 9 J7
Hunter Pl KLBCH PA10 73 G8
MLNGV G62 23 L8
Hunter Rd HMLTN ML3 119 H4
MLNGV G62 23 L8
RUTH G73 96 C1
Hunter's Av DMBTN G82 21 K7
Hunters Crs EKILN G74 117 J8
Huntersfield Rd JNSTN PA5 89 J1
Hunters Gv EKILN G74 117 J7
Hunters Hill Ct
SPRGB/BLRNK G21 61 M4
Huntershill Rd BSHPBGS G64 61 M2
Huntershill St
SPRGB/BLRNK G21 61 L4
Huntershill Wy BSHPBGS G64 61 M1
Hunters Pl EKILN G74 117 J7
GRNK PA15 6 D3
Hunter St AIRDRIE ML6 66 F8
BLSH ML4 100 A4
COWCAD G4 5 L7
EKILN G74 3 G4
PSLY PA1 9 G4
SHOTTS ML7 104 D4
Hunt Hl BALLOCH G68 47 J1
Hunthill La BLTYR/CAMB G72 118 B4
Hunthill Pl
CRMNK/CLK/EAG G76 114 F5
Hunthill Rd BLTYR/CAMB G72 118 B4
Huntingdon Rd
SPRGB/BLRNK G21 5 K1
Huntingdon Sq
SPRGB/BLRNK G21 61 L8
Hunting Lodge Gdns
HMLTN ML3 120 A7
Huntingtower Rd
BAIL/MDB/MHD G69 81 M6
Huntley Gdns KVD/HLHD G12 60 D7
Huntly Av BLSH ML4 100 A3
GIF/THBK G46 94 D7
Huntly Ct BSHPBGS G64 62 A2
Huntly Dr BLTYR/CAMB G72 97 H6
BSDN G61 41 L2
CTBR ML5 83 K6
GRNKW/INVK PA16 15 M6
Huntly Gdns BLTYR/CAMB G72 118 D7
KVD/HLHD G12 60 D7
Huntly Pl PGL PA14 18 B8
Huntly Qd WISHAW ML2 122 B4
Huntly Rd
CARD/HILL/MSPK G52 76 F1
KVD/HLHD G12 60 C7
Huntly Ter PGL PA14 18 B8
PSLYS PA2 76 A8
SHOTTS ML7 105 H6
Hurlawcrook Pl EKILS G75 127 K7
Hurlawcrook Rd EKILS G75 127 J8
Hurlet Rd PSLYS PA2 92 C1
Hurlford Av KNTSWD G13 58 F2
Hurly Hawkin BSHPBGS G64 62 D2
Hutcheson Dr LARGS KA30 106 F7
Hutcheson Rd GIF/THBK G46 94 A8
Hutcheson St CGLE G1 5 G8
Hutchinson Pl
BLTYR/CAMB G72 97 L7
Hutchison Dr BSDN G61 42 A8
Hutchison Pl CTBR ML5 83 M4
Hutchison St HMLTN ML3 129 K2
WISHAW ML2 131 M2
Hutton KVD/HLHD G12 60 A4
Hutton Av CRG/CRSL/HOU PA6 73 J2
Hutton Dr EKILN G74 116 F6
GOV/IBX G51 77 L1
Hutton Park Crs LARGS KA30 106 E3
Huxley Pl MRYH/FIRH G20 60 F4
Huxley St MRYH/FIRH G20 60 F4
Hyacinth Wy CARLUKE ML8 134 F1
Hydepark St KVGV G3 78 F3
Hyndal Av PLK/PH/NH G53 77 J8
Hyndford Pl LNK/LMHG ML11 137 G5
Hyndford Rd LNK/LMHG ML11 137 H6
Hyndland Av PTCK G11 60 B8
Hyndland Rd KVD/HLHD G12 60 B8
Hyndland St PTCK G11 60 C8
Hyndlee Dr
CARD/HILL/MSPK G52 77 J4
Hyndshaw Rd CARLUKE ML8 133 H6
WISHAW ML2 132 E1
Hyndshaw Vw CARLUKE ML8 132 C5
Hyslop Pl CLYDBK G81 40 A6
Hyslop St AIRDRIE ML6 84 E1

I

Iain Dr BSDN G61 41 J3
Iain Rd BSDN G61 41 J3
Ian Smith Ct CLYDBK G81 58 D1
Ibroxholm Ov GOV/IBX G51 78 B5
Ibroxholm Pl GOV/IBX G51 78 B5
Ibrox St GOV/IBX G51 78 C4
Ibrox Ter GOV/IBX G51 78 B4
Ida Qd BLSH ML4 99 M5
Iddesleigh Av MLNGV G62 24 A8
Ilay Av BSDN G61 60 A2
Ilay Ct BSDN G61 60 A2
Ilay Rd BSDN G61 60 A2
Imlach Pl MTHW ML1 120 D4
Imperial Dr AIRDRIE ML6 84 F4
Imperial Wy UD/BTH/TAN G71 99 G8
Inchbrae Rd
CARD/HILL/MSPK G52 77 J5
Inchcolm Gdns
BAIL/MDB/MHD G69 46 F7
Inchcolm Pl EKILN G74 2 B3
Inchcruin ALEX/LLW G83 13 J2
Inchfad Crs DRUM G15 40 E6
Inchfad Dr DRUM G15 40 E6
Inchfad Pl DRUM G15 40 E6
Inchgower Rd
STPS/GTHM/RID G33 63 L4
Inchgreen St GRNK PA15 17 M7
Inchholm La PTCK G11 59 L7
Inchinnan Dr RNFRW PA4 57 J6
Inchinnan Rd BLSH ML4 99 M3
PSLYN/LNWD PA3 75 L3
RNFRW PA4 58 A5
Inchkeith Pl CAR/SHTL G32 81 H3
Inchlaggan Pl DRUM G15 40 E5
Inchlee St SCOT G14 59 L7
Inchlonaig Dr ALEX/LLW G83 13 K1
Inch Marnock EKILN G74 127 M2
Inchmurrin Av KKNTL G66 46 B2
Inchmurrin Crs ALEX/LLW G83 13 K1
Inchmurrin Dr RUTH G73 96 D8
Inchmurrin Gdns RUTH G73 96 D8
Inchmurrin Pl RUTH G73 96 D8
Inchneuk Rd CTBR ML5 65 L4
Inchnock Av
BAIL/MDB/MHD G69 65 G4
Inchoch Gv
STPS/GTHM/RID G33 63 L8
Inchoch St
STPS/GTHM/RID G33 63 L8
Inchrory Pl DRUM G15 40 E5
Inchtavannach ALEX/LLW G83 13 J2
Inchwood Ct BALLOCH G68 48 A2
Inchwood Pl BALLOCH G68 47 M3
Inchwood Rd BALLOCH G68 47 M3
Incle St PSLY PA1 9 J4
India Dr RNFRW PA4 57 J5
India St ALEX/LLW G83 13 K5
CGLW G2 4 B4
Industry St KKNTL G66 45 K3
Inga St MRYH/FIRH G20 60 E3
Ingerbreck Av RUTH G73 96 D5
Ingleby Dr DEN/PKHD G31 80 B3
Inglefield Ct AIRDRIE ML6 84 F3
Inglefield St GVH/MTFL G42 79 H8
Ingleneuk Av
STPS/GTHM/RID G33 63 H5
Inglestone Av GIF/THBK G46 94 A8
Ingleston St GRNK PA15 6 F7
Inglewood Crs EKILS G75 126 D2
PSLYS PA2 74 E8
Inglis Pl EKILS G75 127 H3
Inglis St DEN/PKHD G31 80 A4
WISHAW ML2 121 K8
Ingliston Dr BSHPTN PA7 37 M7
Ingram St CGLE G1 5 H7
Inishail Rd STPS/GTHM/RID G33 81 J1
Inkerman Rd
CARD/HILL/MSPK G52 76 F4
Innellan Crs SHOTTS ML7 104 E4
Innellan Gdns MRYH/FIRH G20 60 B3
Innellan Pl MRYH/FIRH G20 60 B3
Innellan Rd WMYSB PA18 32 B8
Innerleithen Dr WISHAW ML2 122 D3
Innermanse Qd MTHW ML1 101 M4
Innerwick Dr
CARD/HILL/MSPK G52 77 H4
Innes Ct EKILN G74 116 E6
Innes Park Rd SKLM PA17 50 C5
International Av
BLTYR/CAMB G72 118 D6
Inveraray Dr BSHPBGS G64 44 B6
Inveraray Gdns MTHW ML1 101 J7
Inverarish ERSK PA8 57 J3
Inverary Dr
BAIL/MDB/MHD G69 64 E6
Inveravon Dr MTHW ML1 120 B4
Invercanny Dr DRUM G15 41 G5
Invercanny Pl DRUM G15 41 G5
Invercargill EKILS G75 126 D3
Invercloy Ct EKILS G75 126 E6
Inverclyde Gdns RUTH G73 96 E7
Inverclyde Vw LARGS KA30 106 F2
Inveresk Pl CTBR ML5 84 A1
Inveresk Qd CAR/SHTL G32 81 G4
Inveresk St CAR/SHTL G32 81 G4
Inverewe Av GIF/THBK G46 93 K7
Inverewe Dr GIF/THBK G46 93 K7
Inverewe Gdns GIF/THBK G46 93 K7
Inverewe Pl GIF/THBK G46 93 K6
Inverewe Wy NMRNS G77 113 G4
Invergarry Av GIF/THBK G46 93 K8
Invergarry Ct GIF/THBK G46 93 L7
Invergarry Dr GIF/THBK G46 93 K7
Invergarry Gdns GIF/THBK G46 93 K8
Invergarry Gv GIF/THBK G46 93 K7
Invergarry Pl GIF/THBK G46 93 K7
Invergarry Quad GIF/THBK G46 93 L7
Invergarry Vw GIF/THBK G46 93 L7
Inverglas Av RNFRW PA4 58 F8
Invergordon Av
PLKSW/MSWD G43 94 F3
Invergordon Pl AIRDRIE ML6 85 G3
Invergyle Dr
CARD/HILL/MSPK G52 77 J4
Inverkar Dr PSLYS PA2 75 G8
Inverkip Dr SHOTTS ML7 104 E4
Inverkip Rd GRNKW/INVK PA16 32 F3
Inverkip St GRNK PA15 6 B4
Inverlair Av LNPK/KPK G44 95 G4
PLKSW/MSWD G43 94 F4
Inverleith St CAR/SHTL G32 80 E3
Inverlochy St
STPS/GTHM/RID G33 81 K1
Inverness St GOV/IBX G51 77 K3
Inveroran Dr BSDN G61 42 B6
Inver Rd STPS/GTHM/RID G33 81 L3
Invershiel Rd SMSTN G23 60 D1
Invershin Dr MRYH/FIRH G20 60 D5
Inverurie St SPRGB/BLRNK G21 61 K7
Invervale Av AIRDRIE ML6 85 M3
Inzievar Ter CAR/SHTL G32 97 H1
Iona Av EKILN G74 117 G6
Iona Crs GRK PA19 15 K3
OLDK G60 39 J5
Iona Dr PSLYS PA2 91 K3
Iona Gdns OLDK G60 39 J5
Iona Pl CTBR ML5 83 K1
Iona Qd WISHAW ML2 122 E4
Iona Rdg HMLTN ML3 128 F1
Iona Rd PGL PA14 35 G3
RNFRW PA4 58 C8
RUTH G73 96 E7
WISHAW ML2 122 F3
Iona St GOV/IBX G51 78 B3
GRNKW/INVK PA16 16 C5
MTHW ML1 100 D8
Iona Wk CTBR ML5 83 L6
Iona Wy KKNTL G66 46 A2
STPS/GTHM/RID G33 63 L6
Iona Wynd ALEX/LLW G83 20 F1
Iris Av CSMK G45 96 A7
Irongray St DEN/PKHD G31 80 C3
Irvine Ct DMNK/BRGTN G40 80 B7
Irvine Crs CTBR ML5 84 C2
Irvine Dr PSLYN/LNWD PA3 73 M3
Irvine Gdns KKNTL G66 27 H5
Irvine Pl KSYTH G65 29 H1
Irvine Rd LARGS KA30 106 F6
Irvine St AIRDRIE ML6 66 F5
DMNK/BRGTN G40 80 B7
Irvine Ter HMLTN ML3 129 K2
Irving Av CLYDBK G81 40 B4
Irving Ct CLYDBK G81 40 B3
Irving Qd CLYDBK G81 40 B3
Irwin St GRNK PA15 17 L7
Isabella Gdns HMLTN ML3 120 B8
Iser La PLKSD/SHW G41 94 E2
Isla Av WISHAW ML2 122 F3
Island Rd CUMB G67 48 D1
Islay Av PGL PA14 35 H3
RUTH G73 96 E7
Islay Ct HMLTN ML3 118 F8
Islay Crs OLDK G60 39 J5
PSLYS PA2 91 K3
Islay Dr NMRNS G77 113 H4
OLDK G60 39 J5
Islay Gdns CARLUKE ML8 134 F1
LRKH ML9 130 D7
Islay Qd WISHAW ML2 121 L8
Islay Rd KKNTL G66 46 A2
Islay Wy CTBR ML5 83 K6
Ivanhoe EKILN G74 117 K6
Ivanhoe Ct CARLUKE ML8 132 F8
Ivanhoe Crs WISHAW ML2 122 C6
Ivanhoe Dr KKNTL G66 45 L2
Ivanhoe Rd CUMB G67 48 F1
KNTSWD G13 59 K1
PSLYS PA2 90 E1
Ivybank Av BLTYR/CAMB G72 97 J6
Ivybank Crs PGL PA14 34 A1
Ivybank Rd PGL PA14 34 B1
Ivy Crs GRK PA19 15 L3
Ivy Gv CTBR ML5 84 C3
Ivy Pl BLTYR/CAMB G72 118 C2
MTHW ML1 101 G6
Ivy Rd UD/BTH/TAN G71 99 J2
Ivy Ter MTHW ML1 101 G4
Ivy Wy AIRDRIE ML6 85 L6

J

Jackson Dr
STPS/GTHM/RID G33 63 M6
Jackson Pl BSDN G61 41 L6
CARLUKE ML8 133 G6
DMBTN G82 13 J8
Jackson St CTBR ML5 84 B2
Jack's Rd UD/BTH/TAN G71 99 G6
Jack St HMLTN ML3 129 K2
MTHW ML1 121 H5
Jackton Rd EKILS G75 126 A5
Jacobite Pl BLSH ML4 100 D5
Jacobs Dr GRK PA19 15 K2
Jacob's Ladder Wy
WISHAW ML2 131 L3
Jagger Gdns
BAIL/MDB/MHD G69 81 M6
Jamaica Dr EKILS G75 126 E1
Jamaica La GRNKW/INVK PA16 6 B2
Jamaica St CGLE G1 4 E8
GRNK PA15 6 B2
James Dempsey Ct CTBR ML5 83 M4
James Dempsey Gdns
CTBR ML5 * 83 M4
James Dunlop Gdns
BSHPBGS G64 62 B3
James Gray St PLKSD/SHW G41 94 E2
James Hamilton Dr BLSH ML4 100 C3
James Healy Dr HMLTN ML3 129 J3
James Leeson Ct KKNTL G66 27 H4
James Morrison St CGLE G1 5 H9
James Nisbet St
SPRGB/BLRNK G21 5 M4
James St ALEX/LLW G83 13 K5
BLSH ML4 99 L3
CARLUKE ML8 133 H8
DMNK/BRGTN G40 79 L6
HBR/GL G84 10 D5
MTHW ML1 120 D2
James Vw MTHW ML1 100 F6
James Watt Av EKILS G75 3 H8
James Watt Pl EKILN G74 116 B7
James Watt Rd MLNGV G62 23 M6
James Watt St CGLW G2 4 C8
James Watt Wy GRNK PA15 7 K5
James Wilson Pl CARLUKE ML8 134 B7
Jamieson Ct CLYDBK G81 40 B2
GVH/MTFL G42 79 H8
Jamieson Dr EKILN G74 3 K4
Jamieson Gdns SHOTTS ML7 104 E4
Jamieson St GVH/MTFL G42 79 H8
Janebank Av BLTYR/CAMB G72 97 J6
Janefield Av JNSTN PA5 73 L8
Janefield Pl BEITH KA15 125 K4
BLTYR/CAMB G72 118 C4
KKNTL G66 26 D1
Janefield St DEN/PKHD G31 80 C6
Jane Pl GBLS G5 79 J6
Jane Rae Gdns CLYDBK G81 58 D1
Jane's Brae CUMB G67 48 F1
Janesmith St WISHAW ML2 121 J5
Janetta St CLYDBK G81 40 A6
Jardine St MRYH/FIRH G20 60 F7
Jardine Ter
BAIL/MDB/MHD G69 64 F5

Jarvie Av AIRDRIE ML6 68 B7
Jarvie Crs KSYTH G65 29 K3
Jarvie Wy PSLYS PA2 90 F2
Jasmine Pl CUMB G67 48 B2
Jasmine Wy CARLUKE ML8 134 E1
Java St MTHW ML1 100 C8
Jean Armour Dr CLYDBK G81 40 C6
Jean Armour Ter
GRNKW/INVK PA16 15 L6
Jeanette Av HMLTN ML3 129 K3
Jeanie Deans Dr HBR/GL G84 11 G7
Jean Maclean Pl BSHPBGS G64 44 B6
Jean St PGL PA14 18 B8
Jedburgh Av RUTH G73 96 B3
Jedburgh Dr PSLYS PA2 91 G1
Jedburgh Gdns
MRYH/FIRH G20 60 F7
Jedburgh Pl CTBR ML5 83 M7
EKILN G74 3 G3
Jedburgh St BLTYR/CAMB G72 118 D3
WISHAW ML2 122 C4
Jedworth Av DRUM G15 41 H6
Jedworth Rd DRUM G15 41 J6
Jeffrey Pl KSYTH G65 29 J1
Jellicoe Pl HBR/GL G84 11 G5
Jellicoe St CLYDBK G81 39 L7
Jennie Lee Dr WISHAW ML2 131 L2
Jennys Well Ct PSLYS PA2 76 B7
Jennys Well Rd PSLYS PA2 76 B7
Jervis Pl HBR/GL G84 11 G6
Jervis Ter EKILS G75 126 E3
Jerviston Ct MTHW ML1 101 G8
Jerviston Rd MTHW ML1 101 G8
STPS/GTHM/RID G33 63 J8
Jerviston St MTHW ML1 120 F1
Jerviswood MTHW ML1 101 G8
Jerviswood Dr
LNK/LMHG ML11 137 M2
Jerviswood Rd
LNK/LMHG ML11 137 G5
Jessie St GVH/MTFL G42 95 K1
Joanna Ter BLTYR/CAMB G72 118 D2
Jocelyn Sq CGLE G1 5 G9
John Bowman Gdns
BLSH ML4 100 B3
John Brannan Wy
UD/BTH/TAN G71 99 K4
John Brown Pl
BAIL/MDB/MHD G69 64 C2
John Burnside Dr CLYDBK G81 40 C2
John Campbell St GRK PA19 15 M2
John Clark St LARGS KA30 106 F4
John Ewing Gdns LRKH ML9 130 C5
John Gregor Pl LOCHW PA12 109 J3
John Hendry Rd
UD/BTH/TAN G71 99 G6
John Knox St CLYDBK G81 58 D2
COWCAD G4 5 L6
John Lang St JNSTN PA5 74 B7
John Marshall Dr BSHPBGS G64 61 L2
John Murray Ct MTHW ML1 120 E6
Johnsburn Dr PLK/PH/NH G53 93 H3
Johnsburn Rd PLK/PH/NH G53 93 H3
Johnshaven St
PLKSW/MSWD G43 94 C3
Johnshill LOCHW PA12 109 K2
John Smith Ct AIRDRIE ML6 84 F1
John Smith Gdns CTBR ML5 84 C3
John Smith Ga BRHD/NEIL G78 92 C5
Johnson Ct HBR/GL G84 10 F6
Johnson Dr BLTYR/CAMB G72 97 G5
Johnston Av KSYTH G65 29 K3
Johnstone Av
CARD/HILL/MSPK G52 77 H2
CLYDBK G81 58 D1
Johnstone Dr LOCHW PA12 109 J3
RUTH G73 96 A3
Johnstone Rd HMLTN ML3 119 L8
Johnstone St BLSH ML4 100 C4
Johnstone Ter KSYTH G65 28 F8
Johnston Rd
BAIL/MDB/MHD G69 65 G4
Johnston St AIRDRIE ML6 85 H1
GRNKW/INVK PA16 16 D2
PSLY PA1 9 H6
Johnston Ter
GRNKW/INVK PA16 16 D2
John St BLSH ML4 100 A4
BLTYR/CAMB G72 118 E3
BRHD/NEIL G78 92 B6
CARLUKE ML8 133 H8
CGLE G1 5 G7
DMBTN G82 20 D2
GRK PA19 15 L2
GRNK PA15 7 G7
HBR/GL G84 10 C6
HMLTN ML3 119 L7
KKNTL G66 45 K1
LARGS KA30 106 E6
LRKH ML9 130 C7
WISHAW ML2 121 J5
John Street La HBR/GL G84 10 C5
John Wilson Dr KSYTH G65 29 H1
John Wilson St GRNK PA15 7 M9
John Wood St PGL PA14 34 C1
Jones Wynd MTHW ML1 101 L8
Jonquil Wy CARLUKE ML8 134 F1
Joppa St STPS/GTHM/RID G33 80 E2
Jordanhill Crs KNTSWD G13 59 K4
Jordanhill Dr KNTSWD G13 59 K4
Jordanhill La KNTSWD G13 59 L4
Jordan St SCOT G14 59 K7
Jordanvale Av SCOT G14 59 K7
Jowitt Av CLYDBK G81 40 D8
Jubilee Ct
CARD/HILL/MSPK G52 76 F2
Jubilee Gdns BSDN G61 41 L5
Jubilee Ter JNSTN PA5 89 K1
Julian Av KVD/HLHD G12 60 C6
Julian La KVD/HLHD G12 60 C6
Juniper Av EKILS G75 127 G4
Juniper Ct KKNTL G66 45 H5
Juniper Dr HMLTN ML3 128 F3
KKNTL G66 27 H6
Juniper Gv HMLTN ML3 119 M8
Juniper Pl
BAIL/MDB/MHD G69 81 M6
JNSTN PA5 90 A2
UD/BTH/TAN G71 99 K2
Juniper Rd UD/BTH/TAN G71 99 K2
Juniper Ter CAR/SHTL G32 81 L6
Juno St MTHW ML1 100 D8
Juno Ter GRNKW/INVK PA16 15 K6
Jupiter St MTHW ML1 100 D8
Jupiter Ter GRNKW/INVK PA16 15 K6
Jura EKILN G74 3 M9
Jura Av RNFRW PA4 58 D8
Jura Dr BLTYR/CAMB G72 98 C7
NMRNS G77 113 H3
OLDK G60 39 J5
Jura Gdns CARLUKE ML8 134 F1
HMLTN ML3 119 G8
LRKH ML9 130 E6
Jura Qd WISHAW ML2 121 L8
Jura Rd OLDK G60 39 J5
PSLYS PA2 91 K3
Jura St CARD/HILL/MSPK G52 77 M4
GRNKW/INVK PA16 16 C5
Jura Wynd CTBR ML5 65 J4
Jutland Ct HBR/GL G84 10 A5

K

Kaim Dr PLK/PH/NH G53 93 K3
Kames Rd SHOTTS ML7 104 E3
Kane St DMBTN G82 13 J8
Karadale Gdns LRKH ML9 130 B7
Kateswell Dr SHOTTS ML7 87 H8
Katewell Av DRUM G15 40 E5
Katewell Pl DRUM G15 40 E5
Katherine Pl DMBTN G82 13 K8
Katherine St AIRDRIE ML6 85 L1
Kathleen Pk HBR/GL G84 10 A4
Katrine Av BLSH ML4 99 K4
BSHPBGS G64 62 B1
Katrine Crs AIRDRIE ML6 66 F8
Katrine Dr NMRNS G77 114 B6
PSLYS PA2 74 F8
Katrine Pl BLTYR/CAMB G72 97 G4
CTBR ML5 83 K1
Katrine Rd GRNK PA15 6 F8
SHOTTS ML7 104 E3
WMYSB PA18 50 B1
Kay Gdns MTHW ML1 120 B3
Kaystone Rd DRUM G15 41 G8
Kay St SPRGB/BLRNK G21 61 M6
Keal Av DRUM G15 59 H1
Keal Crs DRUM G15 59 G1
Keal Dr DRUM G15 59 G1
Keal Pl DRUM G15 59 G1
Kearn Av DRUM G15 41 H8
Kearn Pl DRUM G15 41 H8
Keats Pk UD/BTH/TAN G71 99 H7
Keil Crs DMBTN G82 20 D7
Keir Crs WISHAW ML2 122 B5
Keir Dr BSHPBGS G64 43 M8
Keir Hardie Av MTHW ML1 101 H4
Keir Hardie Dr BLSH ML4 99 M6
KBRN KA25 124 C4
KSYTH G65 29 K3
Keir Hardie Rd LRKH ML9 130 E8
Keir Hardie St GRNK PA15 17 L7
Keir St PLKSD/SHW G41 78 F7
Keir's Wk BLTYR/CAMB G72 97 G4
Keith Av GIF/THBK G46 94 D7
Keith Ct PTCK G11 78 B1
Keith Qd WISHAW ML2 122 B4
Keith St BLSH ML4 100 A3
HMLTN ML3 119 M6
PTCK G11 60 C8
Kelbourne Crs BLSH ML4 99 M5
Kelbourne St MRYH/FIRH G20 60 E6
Kelburn Ct LARGS KA30 106 E5
Kelburne Dr PSLY PA1 76 B4
Kelburne Gdns
BAIL/MDB/MHD G69 82 A7
PSLY PA1 9 M3
Kelburne Ov PSLY PA1 9 M4
Kelburn St BRHD/NEIL G78 92 B7
Kelburn Ter PGL PA14 34 F1
Kelhead Av
CARD/HILL/MSPK G52 76 F4
Kelhead Dr
CARD/HILL/MSPK G52 76 F4
Kelhead Pth
CARD/HILL/MSPK G52 76 F4
Kelhead Pl
CARD/HILL/MSPK G52 76 F4
Kellie Gv EKILN G74 2 D1
Kells Pl DRUM G15 40 E5
Kelly St GRNKW/INVK PA16 6 B2
Kelso Av BRWEIR PA11 72 C3
PSLYS PA2 91 G1
RUTH G73 96 B3
Kelso Crs WISHAW ML2 122 B3
Kelso Dr CARLUKE ML8 133 K8
EKILN G74 3 J1
Kelso Gdns
BAIL/MDB/MHD G69 46 F7
Kelso Pl DMBTN G82 13 K8
SCOT G14 58 E3
Kelso Qd CTBR ML5 83 M2
Kelso St KNTSWD G13 58 F2
Kelton St CAR/SHTL G32 81 H6
Kelvin Av
CARD/HILL/MSPK G52 76 F1
Kelvin Ct EKILS G75 127 K4
KKNTL G66 45 J1
Kelvin Crs BSDN G61 41 M7
Kelvindale Gdns
MRYH/FIRH G20 60 C4
Kelvindale Pl MRYH/FIRH G20 60 D4
Kelvindale Rd KVD/HLHD G12 60 C5
Kelvin Dr AIRDRIE ML6 67 H8
BAIL/MDB/MHD G69 64 E1
BRHD/NEIL G78 92 D8
BSHPBGS G64 44 A8
EKILS G75 127 J3
KKNTL G66 45 G2
MRYH/FIRH G20 60 D6
SHOTTS ML7 105 H5
Kelvin Gdns HMLTN ML3 118 E6
KSYTH G65 29 K3
LARGS KA30 106 E2
Kelvingrove St KVGV G3 78 E2
Kelvinhaugh Ga KVGV G3 78 D2
Kelvinhaugh Pl KVGV G3 78 D2
Kelvinhaugh St KVGV G3 78 D2
Kelvin Pk South EKILS G75 127 L6
Kelvin Pl EKILS G75 127 K3
Kelvin Rd BLSH ML4 100 B2
CUMB G67 49 G1
EKILS G75 3 H9
MLNGV G62 23 M7
UD/BTH/TAN G71 98 E3
Kelvin Rd North CUMB G67 49 G1
Kelvinside Av MRYH/FIRH G20 60 F6
Kelvinside Dr MRYH/FIRH G20 60 F6
Kelvinside Gdns
MRYH/FIRH G20 60 E6
Kelvinside Gdns East
MRYH/FIRH G20 60 F7
Kelvinside Gardens La
MRYH/FIRH G20 60 E7
Kelvinside Ter South
KVD/HLHD G12 60 E7
Kelvinside Ter West
MRYH/FIRH G20 60 E7
Kelvin St CTBR ML5 84 C4
LARGS KA30 106 F4
Kelvinvale KKNTL G66 45 K1
Kelvin Vw BSHPBGS G64 44 C2
KSYTH G65 28 F8
Kelvin Wk LARGS KA30 106 E2
Kelvin Wy KKNTL G66 45 G2
KSYTH G65 29 J1
KVGV G3 78 D1
Kemp Av PSLYN/LNWD PA3 58 A8
Kempock Pl GRK PA19 15 L1
Kempock St GRK PA19 15 L1
Kempsthorn Crs
PLK/PH/NH G53 77 H8
Kempsthorn Pl PLK/PH/NH G53 77 H8
Kempsthorn Rd
PLK/PH/NH G53 77 H8
Kemp St HMLTN ML3 119 K7
SPRGB/BLRNK G21 61 L6
Kenbank Crs BRWEIR PA11 72 D2
Kenbank Rd BRWEIR PA11 72 D2
Kendal Av GIF/THBK G46 94 C7
KVD/HLHD G12 60 A4
Kendal Dr KVD/HLHD G12 60 A4
Kendal Rd EKILS G75 126 C4
Kendoon Av DRUM G15 40 E6
Kenilburn Av AIRDRIE ML6 67 H7
Kenilburn Crs AIRDRIE ML6 67 H7
Kenilworth EKILN G74 117 K6
Kenilworth Av HBR/GL G84 11 G8
PLKSD/SHW G41 94 D2
PSLYS PA2 90 F2
WISHAW ML2 122 B6
Kenilworth Ct CARLUKE ML8 133 G8
CUMB G67 48 E1
Kenilworth Crs BLSH ML4 100 A3
BSDN G61 41 J3
GRNKW/INVK PA16 16 D6
HMLTN ML3 118 F6
Kenilworth Dr AIRDRIE ML6 85 J1
Kenilworth Rd KKNTL G66 45 L2
LNK/LMHG ML11 137 H5
Kenmar Gdns UD/BTH/TAN G71 98 E2
Kenmar Rd HMLTN ML3 119 H5
Kenmar Ter HMLTN ML3 119 H5
Kenmore Dr GRNKW/INVK PA16 16 A5
Kenmore Gdns BSDN G61 42 B5
Kenmore Pl GRNKW/INVK PA16 16 A5
Kenmore Rd CUMB G67 31 H7
KLMCLM PA13 53 J3
Kenmore St CAR/SHTL G32 81 G5
Kenmore Wy CTBR ML5 84 C6
Kenmuiraid Pl BLSH ML4 99 M7
Kenmuir Av CAR/SHTL G32 81 L7
Kenmuirhill Rd CAR/SHTL G32 81 K8
Kenmuir Rd CAR/SHTL G32 97 K2
Kenmuir St CTBR ML5 83 H6
Kenmure Av BSHPBGS G64 61 L1
Kenmure Crs BSHPBGS G64 61 M1
Kenmure Dr BSHPBGS G64 61 M1
Kenmure Gdns BSHPBGS G64 61 L1
Kenmure La BSHPBGS G64 61 M1
Kenmure Rd GIF/THBK G46 114 B4
Kenmure St PLKSD/SHW G41 78 F7
Kenmure Vw HWWD PA9 88 E5
Kenmure Wy RUTH G73 96 B7
Kennedar Dr GOV/IBX G51 77 L1
Kennedy Ct ALEX/LLW G83 13 H3
Kennedy Dr AIRDRIE ML6 84 E2
HBR/GL G84 10 D3
Kennedy Gdns WISHAW ML2 131 K2
Kennedy St COWCAD G4 5 J3
WISHAW ML2 122 C6
Kennelburn Rd AIRDRIE ML6 85 K8
Kenneth Rd MTHW ML1 120 C4
Kennihill AIRDRIE ML6 67 G8
Kennihill Qd AIRDRIE ML6 67 G8
Kennishead Av GIF/THBK G46 93 L4
Kennishead Pl GIF/THBK G46 93 L4
Kennishead Rd PLK/PH/NH G53 93 J4
PLKSW/MSWD G43 94 A4
Kennisholm Av GIF/THBK G46 93 L4
Kennoway Dr PTCK G11 59 M7
Kennyhill Sq DEN/PKHD G31 80 B2
Kensington Dr GIF/THBK G46 114 D1
Kensington Ga KVD/HLHD G12 60 C6
Kensington Gate La
KVD/HLHD G12 60 C6
Kensington Rd KVD/HLHD G12 60 C6
Kentallen Rd
STPS/GTHM/RID G33 81 K4
Kent Dr HBR/GL G84 11 G4
RUTH G73 96 D5
Kentigern Ter BSHPBGS G64 62 A2
Kentmere Cl EKILS G75 126 D4
Kentmere Dr EKILS G75 126 D4
Kentmere Pl EKILS G75 126 D4
Kent Pl EKILS G75 126 C4
Kent Rd BLSH ML4 99 K4
KVGV G3 78 F2
Kent St DMNK/BRGTN G40 5 K9
Keppel Dr LNPK/KPK G44 95 L3
Keppochhill Dr
SPRGB/BLRNK G21 61 K8
Keppochhill Pl
SPRGB/BLRNK G21 61 K8
Keppochhill Rd PPK/MIL G22 61 J7
Keppochhill Wy
SPRGB/BLRNK G21 61 K8
Keppoch St SPRGB/BLRNK G21 61 K7
Kerfield Pl DRUM G15 40 E5
Kerr Crs HMLTN ML3 129 J1
Kerr Dr DMNK/BRGTN G40 79 M5
MTHW ML1 120 C3
Kerrera Pl STPS/GTHM/RID G33 81 K4
Kerrera Rd
STPS/GTHM/RID G33 81 K4
Kerr Gdns UD/BTH/TAN G71 99 G2
Ker Rd MLNGV G62 23 L6
Kerr Pl DMNK/BRGTN G40 79 M5
Kerr St BLTYR/CAMB G72 118 E2
BRHD/NEIL G78 92 A7
DMNK/BRGTN G40 79 M5
KKNTL G66 45 J2
PSLYN/LNWD PA3 8 F3
Kerrycroy Av GVH/MTFL G42 95 K2
Kerrycroy Pl GVH/MTFL G42 95 K2
Kerrycroy St GVH/MTFL G42 95 K2
Kerrydale St
DMNK/BRGTN G40 80 B6
Kerrylamont Av GVH/MTFL G42 95 L3
Kerry Pl DRUM G15 40 E6
Kershaw St WISHAW ML2 131 L3
Kersland Dr MLNGV G62 24 B8
Kersland La KVD/HLHD G12 60 D7
MLNGV G62 24 B8
Kersland Rd GLGNK KA14 124 E7
Kersland St KVD/HLHD G12 60 D7
Ker St GRNK PA15 6 C1
Kerswinning Av KBRN KA25 124 C6
Kessington Dr BSDN G61 42 A6
Kessington Rd BSDN G61 42 B7
Kessington Sq BSDN G61 42 B7
Kessock Dr PPK/MIL G22 61 H7
Kessock Pl PPK/MIL G22 61 H7
Kessog Gdns ALEX/LLW G83 13 L2
Kestrel Ct CLYDBK G81 40 A4
CTBR ML5 84 E6
Kestrel Crs GRNKW/INVK PA16 16 A4
Kestrel Pl GRNKW/INVK PA16 16 A4
JNSTN PA5 89 K3
Kestrel Rd KNTSWD G13 59 J3
Kestrel Vw BLSH ML4 99 L1
Keswick Dr HMLTN ML3 129 J4
Keswick Rd EKILS G75 126 C4
Kethers La MTHW ML1 120 B3
Kethers St MTHW ML1 120 C2
Kew Gdns UD/BTH/TAN G71 99 H3
Kew La KVD/HLHD G12 60 D7
Kew Ter KVD/HLHD G12 60 D6
Keystone Av MLNGV G62 42 A2
Keystone Qd MLNGV G62 41 M1
Keystone Rd MLNGV G62 42 A2
Kibbleston Rd KLBCH PA10 73 G7
Kidston Dr HBR/GL G84 10 A5
Kidston Ter GBLS G5 79 J6
Kierhill Rd BALLOCH G68 30 B7
Kilallan Av BRWEIR PA11 72 D1
Kilallan Rd CRG/CRSL/HOU PA6 55 G6
KLMCLM PA13 53 M3
Kilbarchan Rd BRWEIR PA11 72 F4
JNSTN PA5 89 K1
KLBCH PA10 73 J8
Kilbeg Ter GIF/THBK G46 93 K6
Kilberry St SPRGB/BLRNK G21 80 A1
Kilbirnie Pl GBLS G5 79 G6
Kilbirnie St GBLS G5 79 G6
Kilblain St GRNK PA15 6 C3
Kilbowie Pl AIRDRIE ML6 85 K4
Kilbowie Rd CLYDBK G81 40 B3
CUMB G67 49 G1
Kilbrannan Dr
GRNKW/INVK PA16 16 B6
Kilbreck Gdns BSDN G61 41 J1
Kilbrennan Dr MTHW ML1 120 B2
Kilbrennan Rd
PSLYN/LNWD PA3 74 B4
Kilbride Dr HBR/GL G84 10 E4
Kilbride St GBLS G5 79 K7
Kilbride Vw UD/BTH/TAN G71 99 G3
Kilburn Gv BLTYR/CAMB G72 118 D1
Kilburn Pl KNTSWD G13 59 H3
Kilburn Water LARGS KA30 107 G1
Kilchattan Dr LNPK/KPK G44 95 J3
Kilchattan Pl WMYSB PA18 32 B8
Kilchoan Rd
STPS/GTHM/RID G33 63 J8
Kilcloy Av DRUM G15 41 G5
Kilcreggan Vw GRNK PA15 17 J7
Kildale Rd LOCHW PA12 109 H3
Kildale Wy RUTH G73 95 M2
Kildare Dr LNK/LMHG ML11 137 H5
Kildare Pl LNK/LMHG ML11 137 H5
Kildare Rd LNK/LMHG ML11 137 G5
Kildary Av LNPK/KPK G44 95 G5
Kildary Rd LNPK/KPK G44 95 G5
Kildermorie Rd ESTRH G34 81 M2
Kildonan Ct WISHAW ML2 122 F2
Kildonan Dr HBR/GL G84 10 F5
PTCK G11 60 A8
Kildonan Pl MTHW ML1 120 C2
Kildonan St CTBR ML5 84 C2
Kildrostan St PLKSD/SHW G41 78 F8
Kildrummy Dr
BAIL/MDB/MHD G69 64 F6
Kildrummy Pl EKILN G74 2 D1
Kildrum Rd CUMB G67 31 J7
Kilearn Rd PSLYN/LNWD PA3 76 B2
Kilearn Wy PSLYN/LNWD PA3 76 B2
Kilfinan Rd SHOTTS ML7 104 D3
Kilfinan St PPK/MIL G22 61 H3
Kilgarth St CTBR ML5 83 H6
Kilgraston Rd BRWEIR PA11 72 D4
Kilkerran Ct NMRNS G77 113 H5
Kilkerran Dr
STPS/GTHM/RID G33 62 F4
Kilkerran Pk NMRNS G77 113 H5
Kilkerran Wy NMRNS G77 113 H5
Killearn Crs AIRDRIE ML6 68 A6
Killearn Dr PSLY PA1 76 F5
Killearn Rd GRNK PA15 17 H7
Killearn St PPK/MIL G22 61 J6
Killellan Pl GRK PA19 14 F5
Killermont Av BSDN G61 42 B8
Killermont Mdw
UD/BTH/TAN G71 98 E8
Killermont Rd BSDN G61 41 M6
Killermont St CGLW G2 4 F4
Killermont Vw MRYH/FIRH G20 42 A8
Killiegrew Rd PLKSD/SHW G41 78 D8
Killin Dr PSLYN/LNWD PA3 73 M5
Killin Pl GRNKW/INVK PA16 16 A5
Killin St CAR/SHTL G32 81 H7
Killoch Av PSLYN/LNWD PA3 75 G5
Killoch Dr BRHD/NEIL G78 92 D8
KNTSWD G13 59 G2
Killochend Dr GRNK PA15 6 A7
Killoch La PSLYN/LNWD PA3 75 G5
Killoch Rd PSLYN/LNWD PA3 75 G5
Killoch Wy PSLYN/LNWD PA3 75 G5
Kilmacolm Pl GRNK PA15 17 J8
Kilmacolm Rd BRWEIR PA11 54 B8
CRG/CRSL/HOU PA6 55 H7
GRNK PA15 7 H9
PGL PA14 34 F3
Kilmahew Av DMBTN G82 19 G1
Kilmahew Ct DMBTN G82 19 G1
Kilmahew Dr DMBTN G82 19 G1
Kilmahew Gv DMBTN G82 19 H1
Kilmailing Rd LNPK/KPK G44 95 H5
Kilmair Pl MRYH/FIRH G20 60 D5
Kilmaluag Ter GIF/THBK G46 93 K6
Kilmany Dr CAR/SHTL G32 80 F5
Kilmany Gdns CAR/SHTL G32 80 F5
Kilmardinny Av BSDN G61 41 M3
Kilmardinny Crs BSDN G61 42 A4
Kilmardinny Dr BSDN G61 41 M3
Kilmardinny Ga BSDN G61 41 M4
Kilmardinny Gv BSDN G61 41 M3
Kilmari Gdns DRUM G15 40 E5
Kilmarnock Rd
PLKSW/MSWD G43 94 D4
Kilmartin Pl GIF/THBK G46 93 L5
UD/BTH/TAN G71 99 G1
Kilmaurs Dr GIF/THBK G46 94 E7
Kilmaurs St GOV/IBX G51 77 M3
Kilmeny Crs WISHAW ML2 122 C4
Kilmichael Av WISHAW ML2 123 G3
Kilmore Crs DRUM G15 40 E5
Kilmorie Dr RUTH G73 95 L3
Kilmory Av UD/BTH/TAN G71 99 G3
Kilmory Ct EKILS G75 126 F6
Kilmory Dr NMRNS G77 113 L3
Kilmory Gdns CARLUKE ML8 133 J6
SKLM PA17 50 B6
Kilmory Rd CARLUKE ML8 135 H1
Kilmuir Crs GIF/THBK G46 93 K5
Kilmuir Dr GIF/THBK G46 93 L5
Kilmuir Rd GIF/THBK G46 93 K6
UD/BTH/TAN G71 98 F1
Kilmun Rd GRNK PA15 6 E8
Kilmun St MRYH/FIRH G20 60 D3
Kilnburn Rd MTHW ML1 120 C2
Kilncadzow Rd CARLUKE ML8 133 K8
Kilncroft La PSLYS PA2 91 L1
Kilnside Rd PSLY PA1 9 K4
Kilnwell Qd MTHW ML1 120 D2
Kiloran Gv NMRNS G77 113 G5
Kiloran Pl NMRNS G77 113 G5
Kiloran St GIF/THBK G46 93 M5
Kilpatrick Av PSLYS PA2 8 B9
Kilpatrick Ct OLDK G60 39 G4
STPS/GTHM/RID G33 63 M5
Kilpatrick Crs PSLYS PA2 91 K1
Kilpatrick Dr BSDN G61 41 J1
EKILS G75 126 E7
ERSK PA8 39 H8
RNFRW PA4 76 B1
STPS/GTHM/RID G33 63 M5
Kilpatrick Gdns
CRMNK/CLK/EAG G76 114 D3
Kilpatrick Vw DMBTN G82 21 H6
Kilpatrick Wy UD/BTH/TAN G71 99 G2
Kilsyth Gdns EKILS G75 126 D7
Kilsyth Rd KKNTL G66 45 K1
KSYTH G65 28 E3
Kiltarie Crs AIRDRIE ML6 85 M3
Kiltearn Rd
STPS/GTHM/RID G33 81 M3
Kilvaxter Dr GIF/THBK G46 93 L6
Kilwinning Crs AIRDRIE ML6 67 L8
HMLTN ML3 128 E1
Kimberley Gdns EKILS G75 2 A8
Kimberley St CLYDBK G81 39 K5
WISHAW ML2 121 J6
Kinalty Rd LNPK/KPK G44 95 G5
Kinarvie Crs PLK/PH/NH G53 92 F2
Kinarvie Pl PLK/PH/NH G53 92 F2
Kinarvie Rd PLK/PH/NH G53 92 F2
Kinarvie Ter PLK/PH/NH G53 92 F2
Kinbuck St PPK/MIL G22 61 K6
Kincaid Ct GRNK PA15 7 K6
Kincaid Fld KKNTL G66 27 J5
Kincaid Gdns BLTYR/CAMB G72 97 G4
Kincaid St GRNKW/INVK PA16 16 B1
Kincaid Wy KKNTL G66 27 H5
Kincardine Dr BSHPBGS G64 62 B2
Kincardine Pl BSHPBGS G64 62 C3
EKILN G74 117 J7
Kincardine Sq
STPS/GTHM/RID G33 81 K1
Kincath Av RUTH G73 96 C7
Kinclaven Av DRUM G15 41 H6
Kinclaven Pl DRUM G15 41 H6
Kincraig St GOV/IBX G51 77 K3
Kinellan Rd BSDN G61 41 M8
Kinellar Dr SCOT G14 59 G3
Kinfauns Dr DRUM G15 40 F6
NMRNS G77 113 M4
Kingarth La GVH/MTFL G42 79 G8
Kingarth St HMLTN ML3 129 K2
PLKSD/SHW G41 79 G8
King Edward La KNTSWD G13 59 M4
King Edward Rd KNTSWD G13 59 M4
King Edward St ALEX/LLW G83 13 J5
Kingfisher Dr KNTSWD G13 58 F2
King George Ct RNFRW PA4 58 E8
King George Gdns RNFRW PA4 58 E7
King George Park Av
RNFRW PA4 58 E8
King George Pl RNFRW PA4 58 E8
King George Wy RNFRW PA4 58 E8
Kinghorn Dr LNPK/KPK G44 95 J4
Kinglas Rd BSDN G61 41 J7
King Pl BAIL/MDB/MHD G69 83 G5
Kingsacre Rd LNPK/KPK G44 95 J3
Kingsbarns Dr LNPK/KPK G44 95 H3
Kingsborough Gdns
KVD/HLHD G12 60 B6
Kingsborough Ga
KVD/HLHD G12 60 B7
Kingsborough La
KVD/HLHD G12 60 B7
Kingsborough La East
KVD/HLHD G12 60 B7
Kingsbrae Av LNPK/KPK G44 95 J3
Kingsbridge Crs LNPK/KPK G44 95 K4
Kingsbridge Dr LNPK/KPK G44 95 K4
Kingsburgh Dr PSLY PA1 76 B4
Kingsburn Dr RUTH G73 96 A4
Kingsburn Gv RUTH G73 96 A4
Kingscliffe Av LNPK/KPK G44 95 J4
King's Ct BEITH KA15 125 K4
Kingscourt Av LNPK/KPK G44 95 K3
Kings Cres BLTYR/CAMB G72 97 H5
King's Crs CARLUKE ML8 133 J7
HBR/GL G84 10 E6
JNSTN PA5 74 C7
Kingsdale Av LNPK/KPK G44 95 J3
King's Dr BALLOCH G68 30 F3
DMNK/BRGTN G40 79 L6
MTHW ML1 100 F6
NMRNS G77 113 M6
Kingsdyke Av LNPK/KPK G44 95 K3
Kingsford Av LNPK/KPK G44 94 E6
Kingsford Ct NMRNS G77 113 J3
King's Gdns NMRNS G77 114 A7
Kingsheath Av RUTH G73 95 L4
Kingshill Av BALLOCH G68 47 L1
Kingshill Dr LNPK/KPK G44 95 J4
Kingshill Vw CARLUKE ML8 132 C5
Kingshouse Av LNPK/KPK G44 95 J4
Kingshurst Av LNPK/KPK G44 95 J4
Kings Inch Dr GOV/IBX G51 59 H8
King's Inch Rd RNFRW PA4 58 F7

Kingsknowe Dr RUTH G73 95 L4
Kingsland Dr
CARD/HILL/MSPK G52 77 H3
Kingslea Rd
CRG/CRSL/HOU PA6 55 H8
Kingsley Av GVH/MTFL G42 95 H1
Kingsley Ct UD/BTH/TAN G71 99 G3
Kingslynn Dr LNPK/KPK G44 95 K4
Kingsmuir Dr BALLOCH G68 29 M8
Kings Myre LNK/LMHG ML11 137 J5
Kings Pk BSHPBGS G64 44 C1
King's Park Av LNPK/KPK G44 95 H4
King's Park Rd GVH/MTFL G42 95 H3
King's Pl PPK/MIL G22 61 H4
King's Rd BEITH KA15 125 K4
JNSTN PA5 74 B8
Kingston Av AIRDRIE ML6 85 K2
BRHD/NEIL G78 111 K4
UD/BTH/TAN G71 99 G2
Kingston Br GBLS G5 4 B8
Kingston Flats KSYTH G65 29 K1
Kingston Gv BSHPTN PA7 38 B7
Kingston Rd BRHD/NEIL G78 111 J5
BSHPTN PA7 38 B7
KSYTH G65 29 K1
Kingston St GBLS G5 4 C9
King St CGLE G1 5 G9
CLYDBK G81 58 D1
CTBR ML5 83 L4
DMBTN G82 20 D1
GRK PA19 15 L2
GRNK PA15 6 C4
HMLTN ML3 118 F6
KSYTH G65 29 K2
LRKH ML9 130 C6
PGL PA14 18 C8
PSLY PA1 8 C4
RUTH G73 96 A2
SHOTTS ML7 104 E4
WISHAW ML2 122 B7
King St East HBR/GL G84 10 E6
King Street La RUTH G73 96 A2
King's Vw BALLOCH G68 30 F3
King's Wy DMBTN G82 20 D5
Kingsway EKILN G74 3 K7
GRK PA19 15 K3
KKNTL G66 28 B8
KSYTH G65 29 K1
SCOT G14 59 H4
Kingsway Ct SCOT G14 59 H4
Kingswood Dr LNPK/KPK G44 95 J4
Kingswood Rd BSHPTN PA7 37 M6
Kingussie Dr LNPK/KPK G44 95 J4
Kiniver Dr DRUM G15 41 H8
Kinkell Gdns KKNTL G66 28 B8
Kinloch Av BLTYR/CAMB G72 97 H6
PSLYN/LNWD PA3 74 A5
Kinloch Dr MTHW ML1 100 D7
Kinloch Rd NMRNS G77 113 J3
RNFRW PA4 58 B8
Kinloch St DMNK/BRGTN G40 80 C6
Kinloch Ter GRNKW/INVK PA16 15 L6
Kinloss Pl EKILN G74 3 H3
Kinmount Av LNPK/KPK G44 95 H3
Kinnaird Av NMRNS G77 114 A5
Kinnaird Crs BSDN G61 42 B5
Kinnaird Dr PSLYN/LNWD PA3 74 B3
Kinnaird Pl BSHPBGS G64 62 B2
Kinnear Rd DMNK/BRGTN G40 80 B7
Kinneil Pl HMLTN ML3 118 F8
Kinnell Av
CARD/HILL/MSPK G52 77 J6
Kinnell Crs
CARD/HILL/MSPK G52 77 J6
Kinnell Pl CARD/HILL/MSPK G52 77 K6
Kinning St GBLS G5 78 F5
Kinnoul La KVD/HLHD G12 60 C7
Kinnoull Pl BLTYR/CAMB G72 118 D3
Kinpurnie Rd PSLY PA1 76 D4
Kinross Av
CARD/HILL/MSPK G52 77 H5
PGL PA14 34 C1
Kinross Pk EKILN G74 117 K7
Kinsail Dr CARD/HILL/MSPK G52 76 F3
Kinsbridge Park Ga
LNPK/KPK G44 95 K4
Kinstone Av SCOT G14 59 G4
Kintessack Pl BSHPBGS G64 44 D8
Kintillo Dr KNTSWD G13 59 H3
Kintore Pk HMLTN ML3 129 H3
Kintore Rd PLKSW/MSWD G43 94 F4
Kintra St GOV/IBX G51 78 B4
Kintyre Av PSLYN/LNWD PA3 74 A6
Kintyre Crs AIRDRIE ML6 67 M6
CTBR ML5 83 L6
NMRNS G77 113 J3
Kintyre Dr CTBR ML5 83 L6
Kintyre Gdns KKNTL G66 28 B8
Kintyre Rd BLTYR/CAMB G72 118 C2
Kintyre St SPRGB/BLRNK G21 80 A1
Kintyre Ter GRNKW/INVK PA16 15 K6
Kip Av GRNKW/INVK PA16 32 E5
Kipland Wk CTBR ML5 84 D4
Kippen Dr
CRMNK/CLK/EAG G76 115 H5
Kippen St AIRDRIE ML6 84 D3
PPK/MIL G22 61 K4
Kipperoch Rd DMBTN G82 20 A3
Kippford Pl AIRDRIE ML6 85 M8
Kippford St CAR/SHTL G32 81 J6
Kipps Av AIRDRIE ML6 84 E1
Kirkaig Av RNFRW PA4 58 F7
Kirkandrews Pl AIRDRIE ML6 85 M8
Kirkbean Av RUTH G73 96 A6
Kirkbriggs Gdns RUTH G73 96 B5
Kirkburn Av BLTYR/CAMB G72 97 G8
Kirkcaldy Rd PLKSD/SHW G41 78 D8
Kirkconnel Av BALLOCH G68 47 L1
KNTSWD G13 58 F3
Kirkconnel Dr RUTH G73 95 M5
Kirk Crs OLDK G60 39 G3
Kirkcudbright Pl EKILN G74 117 K6
Kirkdale Dr
CARD/HILL/MSPK G52 77 L5
Kirkdene Av NMRNS G77 114 B5
Kirkdene Bank NMRNS G77 114 B5
Kirkdene Crs NMRNS G77 114 B5
Kirkdene Gv NMRNS G77 114 B6
Kirkdene Pl NMRNS G77 114 B5
Kirkfieldbank Brae
LNK/LMHG ML11 136 D5
Kirkfield Bank Wy HMLTN ML3 119 G7
Kirkfield Rd LNK/LMHG ML11 136 D6
UD/BTH/TAN G71 99 G7
Kirkfield Wynd HWWD PA9 88 E5
Kirkford Rd
BAIL/MDB/MHD G69 46 E8
Kirkgate WISHAW ML2 122 F5
Kirkhall Rd MTHW ML1 101 K5
Kirkhill Av BLTYR/CAMB G72 97 G7
Kirkhill Crs BRHD/NEIL G78 111 L2
Kirkhill Dr MRYH/FIRH G20 60 D5
Kirkhill Gdns BLTYR/CAMB G72 97 G7
Kirkhill Ga NMRNS G77 114 B6
Kirkhill Gv BLTYR/CAMB G72 97 G7
Kirkhill Pl MRYH/FIRH G20 60 D5
WISHAW ML2 121 J7
Kirkhill Rd BAIL/MDB/MHD G69 64 F5
NMRNS G77 114 B5
UD/BTH/TAN G71 98 E2
WISHAW ML2 121 J8
Kirkhill St WISHAW ML2 121 K8
Kirkhill Ter BLTYR/CAMB G72 97 G7
Kirkhope Dr DRUM G15 41 H8
Kirkinner Rd CAR/SHTL G32 81 K7
Kirkintilloch Rd BSHPBGS G64 61 M2
KKNTL G66 27 G8
Kirkland Gv JNSTN PA5 73 M7
Kirkland La ALEX/LLW G83 13 K7
Kirklandneuk Rd RNFRW PA4 58 B5
Kirkland Rd KBRN KA25 124 D6
Kirklands RNFRW PA4 58 B6
Kirklands Crs KSYTH G65 29 K3
UD/BTH/TAN G71 99 G7
Kirklands Dr NMRNS G77 113 K7
Kirklands Pl NMRNS G77 113 K7
Kirklands Rd LNK/LMHG ML11 137 G6
NMRNS G77 113 K7
Kirkland St MRYH/FIRH G20 60 F7
MTHW ML1 120 D2
Kirk La BSDN G61 41 L4
PLKSW/MSWD G43 94 C3
Kirklea Gdns PSLYN/LNWD PA3 75 G5
Kirkle Dr NMRNS G77 114 B5
Kirklee Circ KVD/HLHD G12 60 D6
Kirklee Gdns KVD/HLHD G12 60 C6
Kirklee Gardens La
KVD/HLHD G12 60 C6
Kirklee Pl KVD/HLHD G12 60 D6
Kirklee Qd KVD/HLHD G12 60 D6
Kirklee Quadrant La
KVD/HLHD G12 60 D6
Kirklee Rd BLSH ML4 100 D5
KVD/HLHD G12 60 D5
Kirklee Ter KVD/HLHD G12 60 C6
Kirklee Terrace La
KVD/HLHD G12 60 D6
Kirklee Terrace Rd
KVD/HLHD G12 60 D6
Kirkliston St CAR/SHTL G32 80 F4
Kirkmaiden Wy
BLTYR/CAMB G72 118 D7
Kirkmichael Av PTCK G11 60 A7
Kirkmichael Gdns PTCK G11 60 A7
Kirkmichael Rd HBR/GL G84 10 F6
Kirkmuir Dr RUTH G73 96 B7
Kirkness St AIRDRIE ML6 85 G1
Kirknethan WISHAW ML2 121 J8
Kirknewton St CAR/SHTL G32 81 G4
Kirkoswald EKILN G74 117 K7
Kirkoswald Dr CLYDBK G81 40 D6
Kirkoswald Rd MTHW ML1 101 L5
PLKSW/MSWD G43 94 D4
Kirkpatrick Crs ALEX/LLW G83 13 J3
Kirkpatrick St
DMNK/BRGTN G40 80 A5
Kirk Pl BSDN G61 41 L4
CUMB G67 48 A2
Kirkriggs Av RUTH G73 96 B5
Kirk Rd BEITH KA15 125 L5
BSDN G61 41 L4
CARLUKE ML8 133 G7
CRG/CRSL/HOU PA6 55 H7
CRMNK/CLK/EAG G76 115 K3
LRKH ML9 131 K7
MTHW ML1 101 K2
SHOTTS ML7 104 F5
WISHAW ML2 122 D6
Kirkshaw Ct JNSTN PA5 73 M7
Kirkshaws Av CTBR ML5 83 L7
Kirkshaws Pl CTBR ML5 83 M7
Kirkshaws Rd CTBR ML5 83 L7
Kirkstall Gdns BSHPBGS G64 44 B6
Kirkstone Cl EKILS G75 126 C4
Kirk St CARLUKE ML8 133 G7
CTBR ML5 83 M4
MLNGV G62 23 L7
MTHW ML1 120 E2
Kirkstyle Av CARLUKE ML8 133 G8
Kirkstyle Crs AIRDRIE ML6 66 F7
BRHD/NEIL G78 111 K3
Kirkstyle La BRHD/NEIL G78 111 K3
Kirkstyle Pl AIRDRIE ML6 66 D5
Kirksyde Av KKNTL G66 45 K3
Kirkton ERSK PA8 39 G7
Kirkton Av BLTYR/CAMB G72 118 C5
BRHD/NEIL G78 92 B7
CARLUKE ML8 133 G8
KNTSWD G13 59 G3
Kirkton Ct CARLUKE ML8 133 G8
Kirkton Crs CTBR ML5 84 D5
DMBTN G82 19 G1
KKNTL G66 27 J5
KNTSWD G13 59 G3
Kirktonfield Crs
BRHD/NEIL G78 111 M3
Kirktonfield Dr
BRHD/NEIL G78 111 M3
Kirktonfield Pl
BRHD/NEIL G78 111 M3
Kirktonfield Rd
BRHD/NEIL G78 111 L3
Kirkton Ga EKILN G74 2 F4
Kirktonholme Crs EKILN G74 2 D4
Kirktonholme Rd EKILN G74 2 A4
Kirkton Pk EKILN G74 3 H4
Kirkton Pl CTBR ML5 84 D5
EKILN G74 3 H4
Kirkton Rd BLTYR/CAMB G72 97 H5
BRHD/NEIL G78 111 L4
DMBTN G82 19 G2
Kirktonside BRHD/NEIL G78 92 B8
Kirkton St CARLUKE ML8 133 H8
Kirkvale Ct NMRNS G77 114 B5
Kirkvale Crs NMRNS G77 114 B5
Kirkvale Dr NMRNS G77 114 B5
Kirk Vw BEITH KA15 125 K4
Kirkview CUMB G67 48 A3
Kirkview Av SHOTTS ML7 87 J7
Kirkview Ct CUMB G67 48 A3
Kirkview Crs NMRNS G77 113 L6
Kirkview Gdns
UD/BTH/TAN G71 98 E2
Kirkville Pl DRUM G15 41 H8
Kirkwall CUMB G67 31 H4
Kirkwall Av BLTYR/CAMB G72 98 C8
Kirkwall Rd GRNKW/INVK PA16 15 M6
Kirkwell Rd LNPK/KPK G44 95 H5
Kirkwood Av CLYDBK G81 40 E8
STPS/GTHM/RID G33 63 M5
Kirkwood Pl CTBR ML5 83 L6
Kirkwood Rd UD/BTH/TAN G71 98 F2
Kirkwood St CTBR ML5 83 L5
GOV/IBX G51 78 C5
RUTH G73 96 A2
Kirn Dr GRK PA19 15 J3
Kirn St MRYH/FIRH G20 60 C2
Kirriemuir EKILN G74 117 K5
Kirriemuir Av
CARD/HILL/MSPK G52 77 J6
Kirriemuir Gdns BSHPBGS G64 44 C8
Kirriemuir Pl
CARD/HILL/MSPK G52 77 J5
Kirriemuir Rd BSHPBGS G64 62 C1
Kirstie Pl ALEX/LLW G83 13 L8
Kirtle Dr RNFRW PA4 58 E7
Kirtle Pl EKILS G75 126 B3
Kishorn Pl
STPS/GTHM/RID G33 81 J1
Kishorn Rd WMYSB PA18 50 B1
Kitchener St WISHAW ML2 122 A6
Kittoch Pl EKILN G74 3 G4
Kittochside Rd
CRMNK/CLK/EAG G76 115 M4
Kittoch St EKILN G74 2 F4
Klondike Ct MTHW ML1 101 H6
Knapdale St PPK/MIL G22 61 G3
Knightsbridge St KNTSWD G13 59 K3
Knightscliffe Av KNTSWD G13 59 K1
Knights Ga UD/BTH/TAN G71 98 E5
Knightswood Ct KNTSWD G13 59 K3
Knightswood Rd KNTSWD G13 59 K2
Knightswood Ter
BLTYR/CAMB G72 118 E1
Knivysbridge Pl BLSH ML4 99 M7
Knockbuckle Av KLMCLM PA13 53 H1
Knockbuckle Rd KLMCLM PA13 53 H2
Knockburnie Rd
UD/BTH/TAN G71 99 G7
Knockdhu Pl GRK PA19 14 F4
Knockhall St
STPS/GTHM/RID G33 63 K8
Knockhill Dr LNPK/KPK G44 95 H3
Knockhill Rd RNFRW PA4 58 B8
Knockmilly Pl
BAIL/MDB/MHD G69 47 G7
Knocknair St PGL PA14 34 E2
Knockside Av PSLYS PA2 91 K3
Knoll Croft Rd SHOTTS ML7 105 G6
Knollpark Dr
CRMNK/CLK/EAG G76 114 D3
Knowe Crs MTHW ML1 101 K5
Knowehead Dr
UD/BTH/TAN G71 98 E4
Knowehead Gdns
PLKSD/SHW G41 78 F7
UD/BTH/TAN G71 98 E4
Knowehead Rd WISHAW ML2 122 C7
Knowehead Ter
PLKSD/SHW G41 78 E7
Knowenoble St MTHW ML1 102 B7
Knowe Rd BAIL/MDB/MHD G69 64 C3
GRNK PA15 7 H6
PSLYN/LNWD PA3 76 B2
Knowes Av NMRNS G77 113 L4
Knowes Rd NMRNS G77 113 M4
Knowe St MLNGV G62 23 M7
Knowetap St MRYH/FIRH G20 60 E3
Knowetop Av MTHW ML1 120 F4
Knowetop Crs DMBTN G82 20 C5
Knox Av BRWEIR PA11 72 C3
Knoxland Sq DMBTN G82 21 G7
Knox Pl NMRNS G77 113 H5
Knox St AIRDRIE ML6 85 H1
PSLY PA1 8 B6
Knoxville Rd KBRN KA25 124 D5
Kronborg Wy EKILS G75 127 H5
Kyleakin Dr BLTYR/CAMB G72 98 B8
Kyleakin Rd GIF/THBK G46 93 K6
Kyleakin Ter GIF/THBK G46 93 K6
Kyle Dr GIF/THBK G46 94 E7
Kyle Gv MTHW ML1 101 G6
Kylemore Crs MTHW ML1 100 D8
Kylemore Ter
GRNKW/INVK PA16 15 K6
Kylepark Av UD/BTH/TAN G71 98 D4
Kylepark Crs UD/BTH/TAN G71 98 D3
Kylepark Dr UD/BTH/TAN G71 98 D3
Kyle Qd WISHAW ML2 121 L8
Kylerhea Rd GIF/THBK G46 93 K6
Kyle Rd CUMB G67 31 H7
Kyle Sq RUTH G73 95 M5
The Kyles WMYSB PA18 50 B1
Kyle St COWCAD G4 5 G3
MTHW ML1 120 B2
Kyles Vw LARGS KA30 107 G4
Kyle Ter DMBTN G82 20 B6

L

La Belle Allee KVGV G3 78 E1
La Belle Pl KVGV G3 78 E1
Laberge Gdns MTHW ML1 101 H5
Laburnum Av BEITH KA15 125 J5
BLTYR/CAMB G72 97 L7
EKILS G75 126 F4
Laburnum Ct EKILS G75 126 F4
Laburnum Crs WISHAW ML2 122 B4
Laburnum Dr KKNTL G66 27 H5
Laburnum Gdns KKNTL G66 45 H5
Laburnum Gv CTBR ML5 84 B4
Laburnum Lea HMLTN ML3 129 L1
Laburnum Pl JNSTN PA5 90 A2
Laburnum Rd CUMB G67 31 K7
PLKSD/SHW G41 78 C6
UD/BTH/TAN G71 99 J1
Laburnum St GRNK PA15 17 M7
Lachlan Crs ERSK PA8 56 E1
Lacy St PSLY PA1 9 M4
Ladder Ct EKILS G75 126 E6
Lade Ct LOCHW PA12 109 J3
Ladeside Cl NMRNS G77 113 J3
Ladeside Ct KBRN KA25 124 C5
Ladeside Dr JNSTN PA5 73 K8
KSYTH G65 29 L1
Lade St LARGS KA30 106 E4
Lade Ter CARD/HILL/MSPK G52 77 G5
The Lade ALEX/LLW G83 13 L5
Ladhope Pl CLYDBK G81 58 E1
Ladyacre Rd LNK/LMHG ML11 137 H6
Ladyacres RNFRW PA4 57 K4
Ladyacres Wy RNFRW PA4 57 K4
Lady Ann Crs AIRDRIE ML6 85 J3
Ladybank BALLOCH G68 30 F3
Ladybank Ct EKILN G74 2 F4
Ladybank Dr
CARD/HILL/MSPK G52 77 L5
Ladybank Gdns EKILN G74 2 F4
Ladybank Pl EKILN G74 2 F4
Ladyburn St GRNK PA15 7 M9
PSLY PA1 9 L5
Ladyhill Dr BAIL/MDB/MHD G69 82 A6
Lady Isle Crs UD/BTH/TAN G71 98 E4
Lady Jane Ga UD/BTH/TAN G71 98 E6
Ladykirk Crs PSLYS PA2 9 K8
Ladykirk Dr
CARD/HILL/MSPK G52 77 H3
Ladykirk Wy EKILN G74 116 F6
Ladyland Dr KBRN KA25 124 D2
Lady La PSLY PA1 8 F6
Ladyloan Av DRUM G15 40 F5
Ladyloan Ct DRUM G15 40 F5
Ladyloan Gdns DRUM G15 40 F5
Ladymuir Cir ERSK PA8 56 F1
Ladymuir Crs PLK/PH/NH G53 77 J7
Lady's Ga ALEX/LLW G83 20 F1
Ladysmith Av KLBCH PA10 73 H8
Ladysmith Dr EKILS G75 126 D6
Ladysmith Rd KBRN KA25 124 C4
Ladysmith St WISHAW ML2 121 K5
Ladyton ALEX/LLW G83 13 L7
Lady Watson Gdns
HMLTN ML3 119 G8
Lady Well LNK/LMHG ML11 136 B4
Ladywell Rd MTHW ML1 120 B3
Ladywell St COWCAD G4 5 L6
Lady Wilson St AIRDRIE ML6 85 H2
Ladywood MLNGV G62 24 B8
Lagan Rd CARLUKE ML8 133 H8
Laggan Av SHOTTS ML7 105 H6
Laggan Qd AIRDRIE ML6 66 E8
Laggan Rd AIRDRIE ML6 66 F8
BSHPBGS G64 62 B1
NMRNS G77 113 K2
PLKSW/MSWD G43 94 E5
Laggan Ter RNFRW PA4 58 B5
Laidlaw Av MTHW ML1 100 F6
Laidlaw Gdns UD/BTH/TAN G71 98 F1
Laidlaw St GBLS G5 4 B9
Laidon Rd AIRDRIE ML6 66 F8
Laighcartside St JNSTN PA5 74 A7
Laigh Ct BEITH KA15 125 K4
Laighlands Rd
UD/BTH/TAN G71 99 H8
Laighmuir St UD/BTH/TAN G71 98 F5
Laighpark Av BSHPTN PA7 38 B7
Laighpark Vw
PSLYN/LNWD PA3 75 L3
Laigh Rd BEITH KA15 125 K4
NMRNS G77 114 B6
Laighstonehall Rd HMLTN ML3 119 H8
Laightoun Ct CUMB G67 48 A3
Laightoun Dr CUMB G67 48 A3
Laightoun Gdns CUMB G67 48 A3
Lainshaw Dr CSMK G45 95 H8
Laird Gv UD/BTH/TAN G71 99 G2
Laird Pl DMNK/BRGTN G40 79 M6
Lairds Ga UD/BTH/TAN G71 98 D5
Lairds Hl CUMB G67 30 E7
Laird's Hill Ct KSYTH G65 29 G2
Laird's Hill Pl KSYTH G65 29 G2
Laird St CTBR ML5 84 B2
GRNK PA15 6 D2
Lairg Dr BLTYR/CAMB G72 98 C8
Lairhills Rd EKILS G75 2 F9
Lake Av LNK/LMHG ML11 137 K6
Lamberton Dr
CARD/HILL/MSPK G52 77 J4
Lambhill Qd PLKSD/SHW G41 78 E5
Lambhill St PLKSD/SHW G41 78 D5
Lambie Crs NMRNS G77 113 J4
Lamb St HMLTN ML3 119 L7
PPK/MIL G22 61 H4
Lamerton Rd CUMB G67 31 J7
Lamington Rd
CARD/HILL/MSPK G52 77 H5
Lamlash Crs
STPS/GTHM/RID G33 81 H2
Lamlash Pl EKILS G75 126 E6
HBR/GL G84 10 F5
MTHW ML1 120 C2
STPS/GTHM/RID G33 81 H2
Lammermoor EKILN G74 117 L6
Lammermoor Av
CARD/HILL/MSPK G52 77 J6
Lammermoor Crs KKNTL G66 45 M2
Lammermoor Dr CUMB G67 48 E2
Lammermoor Rd KKNTL G66 45 M3
Lammermoor Ter
WISHAW ML2 122 B6
Lammermuir Ct PSLYS PA2 91 L2
Lammermuir Dr PSLYS PA2 91 K2
Lammermuir Gdns BSDN G61 41 J2
Lammermuir Wy AIRDRIE ML6 85 M8
Lammermuir Wynd LRKH ML9 130 B4
Lamont Av BSHPTN PA7 38 C7
Lamont Crs DMBTN G82 13 J8
Lamont Rd SPRGB/BLRNK G21 62 B4
Lanark Av AIRDRIE ML6 84 F5
Lanark Rd CARLUKE ML8 134 A6
CARLUKE ML8 135 G4
LNK/LMHG ML11 136 D3
LRKH ML9 130 A2
Lanark St CGLE G1 5 J9
Lancaster Av AIRDRIE ML6 85 K6
BEITH KA15 125 K6
Lancaster Crs KVD/HLHD G12 60 C6
Lancaster Crescent La
KVD/HLHD G12 60 C6
Lancaster Rd BSHPBGS G64 44 B6
Lancefield Quay KVGV G3 78 E3
Lancefield St KVGV G3 78 F3
Landemer Dr RUTH G73 95 M4
Landemer Gait RUTH G73 96 A4
Landressy Pl DMNK/BRGTN G40 79 M6
Landressy St DMNK/BRGTN G40 79 M6
Landsdowne Gdns
HMLTN ML3 119 M7
Landsdowne Rd LRKH ML9 130 E7
The Lane BALLOCH G68 30 D3
SKLM PA17 50 C5
Lanfine Rd PSLY PA1 76 C5
Langa St MRYH/FIRH G20 60 E3
Lang Av BSHPTN PA7 38 C7
RNFRW PA4 58 D8
Langbank Dr KLMCLM PA13 53 L1
Langbank Ri KLMCLM PA13 53 K1
Langbar Crs
STPS/GTHM/RID G33 81 L3
Langbar Gdns
STPS/GTHM/RID G33 81 M3
Langbyres Rd MTHW ML1 102 D8
Langcraigs Ct PSLYS PA2 91 J2
Langcraigs Dr PSLYS PA2 91 J4
Langcraigs Ter PSLYS PA2 91 J4
Langcroft Dr BLTYR/CAMB G72 97 J6
Langcroft Pl GOV/IBX G51 77 J2
Langcroft Rd GOV/IBX G51 77 K2
Langcroft Ter GOV/IBX G51 77 K2
Langdale EKILN G74 2 A2
Langdale Av
STPS/GTHM/RID G33 62 E7
Langdales Av BALLOCH G68 30 D7
Langdale St
STPS/GTHM/RID G33 62 E7
Langfaulds Crs CLYDBK G81 40 E3
Langford Dr PLK/PH/NH G53 93 G6
Langford Pl PLK/PH/NH G53 93 H6
Langhaul Av PLK/PH/NH G53 76 F8
Langhaul Ct PLK/PH/NH G53 76 F8
Langhaul Pl PLK/PH/NH G53 76 F8
Langhaul Rd PLK/PH/NH G53 76 F8
Langhill Dr BALLOCH G68 30 D6
Langholm EKILS G75 126 C4
Langholm Crs WISHAW ML2 122 B3
Langholm Dr PSLYN/LNWD PA3 74 C5
Langhouse Av
GRNKW/INVK PA16 32 F4
Langhouse Pl
GRNKW/INVK PA16 32 F4
Langhouse Rd
GRNKW/INVK PA16 32 F4
Langlands Av EKILS G75 127 J6
GOV/IBX G51 77 K2
Langlands Ct EKILS G75 127 K6
GOV/IBX G51 77 M1
Langlands Dr EKILS G75 127 J6
GOV/IBX G51 77 J1
Langlands Pl EKILS G75 127 J6
Langlands Rd EKILS G75 127 H8
GOV/IBX G51 77 K2
Langlands Sq EKILS G75 127 J7
Langlands Ter DMBTN G82 21 H4
Langlea Av BLTYR/CAMB G72 96 D6
Langlea Ct BLTYR/CAMB G72 96 E6
Langlea Dr BLTYR/CAMB G72 96 E5
Langlea Gdns BLTYR/CAMB G72 96 E5
Langlea Gv BLTYR/CAMB G72 96 E6
Langlea Rd BLTYR/CAMB G72 96 E6
Langlees Av NMRNS G77 114 B6
Langley Av KNTSWD G13 59 H2
Langloan Crs CTBR ML5 83 L5
Langloan Pl CTBR ML5 83 L4
Langloan St CTBR ML5 83 L5
Langlook Rd PLK/PH/NH G53 76 F8
Langmuir Av KKNTL G66 45 M1
Langmuirhead Rd KKNTL G66 45 K8
STPS/GTHM/RID G33 63 G2
Langmuir Rd
BAIL/MDB/MHD G69 83 G5
KKNTL G66 45 M1
Langmuir Wy
BAIL/MDB/MHD G69 83 H5
Langness Rd
STPS/GTHM/RID G33 81 H2
Langoreth Av HMLTN ML3 118 F8
Lang Pl JNSTN PA5 73 L7
Langrig Rd NMRNS G77 113 J6
SPRGB/BLRNK G21 62 A6
Langshaw Crs CARLUKE ML8 133 H7
Langshot St GOV/IBX G51 78 D5
Langside Av PLKSD/SHW G41 94 E1
UD/BTH/TAN G71 99 J4
Langside Ct UD/BTH/TAN G71 119 H1
Langside Dr BTHG/ARM EH48 71 H1
KLBCH PA10 73 G8
PLKSW/MSWD G43 94 E6
Langside Gdns GVH/MTFL G42 95 G3
Langside La GVH/MTFL G42 95 G1
Langside Pk KLBCH PA10 73 G8
Langside Pl KBRN KA25 124 C4
PLKSD/SHW G41 94 F2
Langside Rd GVH/MTFL G42 95 G2
UD/BTH/TAN G71 119 H1
Langside St CLYDBK G81 40 D3
Langside Ter PGL PA14 34 D2
Langstile Rd
CARD/HILL/MSPK G52 76 F4
Lang St PSLY PA1 9 L5
Langton Crs BRHD/NEIL G78 92 D8
PLK/PH/NH G53 77 J8
Langton Gdns
BAIL/MDB/MHD G69 81 M6
Langton Ga NMRNS G77 113 J4
Langton Pl NMRNS G77 113 J4
Langton Rd PLK/PH/NH G53 93 J1
Langtree Av GIF/THBK G46 114 A1
Lanrig Pl BAIL/MDB/MHD G69 64 C2
Lanrig Rd BAIL/MDB/MHD G69 64 C2
Lansbury Gdns
PSLYN/LNWD PA3 75 K3
Lansbury St ALEX/LLW G83 13 J2
GRNK PA15 17 M7
Lansbury Ter LRKH ML9 130 E8
Lansdowne Crs
MRYH/FIRH G20 60 F8
SHOTTS ML7 105 H6
Lansdowne Crescent La
MRYH/FIRH G20 60 F8
Lansdowne Dr BALLOCH G68 30 F5
Lantana Gv MTHW ML1 120 D1
Lanton Dr
CARD/HILL/MSPK G52 77 H4
Lanton Pth AIRDRIE ML6 85 L8
Lanton Rd PLKSW/MSWD G43 94 E5
Lappin St CLYDBK G81 58 D1
Lapwing Rd RNFRW PA4 58 E5
Larbert St COWCAD G4 4 E3
Larch Av BSHPBGS G64 62 B2
KKNTL G66 45 J5
Larch Cl BLTYR/CAMB G72 97 L7
Larch Ct BLTYR/CAMB G72 97 L7
BLTYR/CAMB G72 118 C2
CUMB G67 31 L5
EKILS G75 126 E5
Larch Crs KKNTL G66 45 J4
Larch Dr EKILS G75 126 E5
The Larches
BAIL/MDB/MHD G69 47 G6
Larchfield HBR/GL G84 10 D5
Larchfield Av NMRNS G77 113 L5
SCOT G14 59 H5
Larchfield Ct NMRNS G77 113 L5

Larchfield Crs WISHAW ML2 122 C3
Larchfield Dr RUTH G73 96 C6
Larchfield Gdns WISHAW ML2 122 D3
Larchfield Gv WISHAW ML2 122 D2
Larchfield Pl SCOT G14 59 H5
WISHAW ML2 122 D3
Larchfield Rd
BAIL/MDB/MHD G69 46 F8
BSDN G61 41 M8
Larch Gv CUMB G67 31 K5
HMLTN ML3 119 L8
KKNTL G66 27 H5
Larchgrove Av CAR/SHTL G32 81 J4
Larchgrove Pl CAR/SHTL G32 81 J3
Larchgrove Rd CAR/SHTL G32 81 J3
Larch Pl BLTYR/CAMB G72 97 L7
CUMB G67 31 K5
EKILS G75 126 F5
JNSTN PA5 89 M2
UD/BTH/TAN G71 99 K2
Larch Rd CUMB G67 31 K5
PLKSD/SHW G41 78 B6
Larch Ter BEITH KA15 125 L5
Larch Wy HMLTN ML3 129 M6
Larchwood Ter BRHD/NEIL G78 92 D8
Largie Rd PLKSW/MSWD G43 94 F5
Largo La BLTYR/CAMB G72 118 D7
Largo Pl GOV/IBX G51 77 L2
Larkfield Ct BLTYR/CAMB G72 118 C4
Larkfield Dr BLTYR/CAMB G72 118 D4
Larkfield Gv GRNKW/INVK PA16 15 M5
Larkfield Rd GRK PA19 15 M4
KKNTL G66 45 L5
Larkfield St GVH/MTFL G42 79 H7
Larkin Gdns PSLYN/LNWD PA3 75 K3
Larkin Wy BLSH ML4 99 M3
Larksfield Dr CARLUKE ML8 135 G1
Larkspur Dr EKILN G74 116 C6
Larkspur Wy CARLUKE ML8 134 F1
Lark Wy BLSH ML4 99 M2
Lashley Gv WISHAW ML2 131 L2
Lasswade St SCOT G14 58 E3
Latherton Dr MRYH/FIRH G20 60 D5
Latimer Gdns
CARD/HILL/MSPK G52 77 G5
Latta St DMBTN G82 21 G6
Lauchope Rd MTHW ML1 101 K2
Lauchope St AIRDRIE ML6 85 L7
Lauder Crs WISHAW ML2 122 B3
Lauderdale Dr NMRNS G77 113 J6
Lauderdale Gdns
KVD/HLHD G12 60 B6
Lauderdale La KVD/HLHD G12 60 B7
Lauder Dr PSLYN/LNWD PA3 74 B5
RUTH G73 96 D4
Lauder Gdns BLTYR/CAMB G72 98 C8
CTBR ML5 84 D6
Lauder Gn EKILN G74 117 H6
Laudervale Gdns ALEX/LLW G83 13 J1
Laughland Dr MTHW ML1 101 K6
Laundry La
STPS/GTHM/RID G33 63 J5
Lauranne Pl BLSH ML4 99 L5
Laurel Av CLYDBK G81 39 K6
KKNTL G66 45 K4
Laurelbank CTBR ML5 84 A1
Laurel Bank HMLTN ML3 129 J2
Laurelbank Rd
BAIL/MDB/MHD G69 64 B3
CAR/SHTL G32 97 J2
Laurel Ct BLTYR/CAMB G72 97 L7
EKILS G75 127 G5
Laurel Dr EKILS G75 127 G5
LRKH ML9 130 E7
WISHAW ML2 121 K5
Laurel Gait BLTYR/CAMB G72 97 L7
Laurel Gdns AIRDRIE ML6 85 L7
UD/BTH/TAN G71 98 F2
Laurel Gv AIRDRIE ML6 49 M7
Laurel La BLTYR/CAMB G72 97 L7
Laurel Park Gdns KNTSWD G13 59 J4
Laurel Pl EKILS G75 127 G5
PTCK G11 60 A8
The Laurels MTHW ML1 101 H7
NMRNS G77 113 K4
Laurel St PTCK G11 60 A8
Laurel Wy BRHD/NEIL G78 92 B6
Laurel Wynd BLTYR/CAMB G72 97 M7
Laurence Ct DRUM G15 40 E6
Laurence Dr BSDN G61 41 K3
DRUM G15 40 E6
Laurence Gdns DRUM G15 40 E6
Lauren Vw AIRDRIE ML6 84 F2
Lauren Wy PSLYS PA2 90 F1
Laurieston Crs AIRDRIE ML6 85 K8
Laurieston Pl CTBR ML5 84 D6
Laurieston Rd GBLS G5 79 J5
Laurieston Wy RUTH G73 96 A6
Lauriston Gv NMRNS G77 113 H4
Lavelle Dr CTBR ML5 84 C2
Lavender Ct UD/BTH/TAN G71 99 J3
Lavender Dr EKILS G75 127 G5
Lavender La CARLUKE ML8 134 E1
Laverock Av GRNK PA15 16 D6
HMLTN ML3 120 A7
Laverock Dr LARGS KA30 106 F3
Laverockhall LNK/LMHG ML11 137 H4
Laverockhall St
SPRGB/BLRNK G21 61 M7
Laverock Rd AIRDRIE ML6 67 H7
Laverock Ter
BAIL/MDB/MHD G69 64 F1
Law Dr MTHW ML1 101 J5
Lawers Dr BSDN G61 41 J3
Lawers Pl GRNKW/INVK PA16 16 A5
Lawers Rd PLKSW/MSWD G43 94 B5
RNFRW PA4 58 B8
Lawfield Av NMRNS G77 114 B5
Lawhill Av LNPK/KPK G44 95 K6
Lawhill Rd CARLUKE ML8 132 C5
Lawhope Mill Rd AIRDRIE ML6 85 M6
Lawmarnock Crs BRWEIR PA11 72 C3
Lawmarnock Rd BRWEIR PA11 72 C4
Lawmoor Av GBLS G5 79 J8
Lawmoor Pl GBLS G5 79 J8
Lawmoor Rd GBLS G5 79 J7
Lawmoor St GBLS G5 79 J7
Lawmuir Crs CLYDBK G81 40 A2
Lawmuir Pl BLSH ML4 100 A7
Lawmuir Rd BLSH ML4 100 A6
CARLUKE ML8 132 B3
Lawnmoor Rd GBLS G5 79 J7
Lawn Pk MLNGV G62 42 C1
Lawn St PSLY PA1 9 J4
Law Pl EKILN G74 116 F6
Lawrence Av GIF/THBK G46 114 D1
HBR/GL G84 11 G8
Lawrence Dr ALEX/LLW G83 13 L1
Lawrence St PTCK G11 60 C8
Lawrie Pl MTHW ML1 101 L8
Lawrie St PTCK G11 60 B8
WISHAW ML2 122 F4
Lawson Av MTHW ML1 120 E6
Law St DMNK/BRGTN G40 80 A5
Law Vw WISHAW ML2 131 L3
Laxford Av LNPK/KPK G44 95 G6
Laxford Pl CTBR ML5 84 D4
Laxford Rd ERSK PA8 56 E1
Laxton Dr KKNTL G66 45 L6
Lea Av BRHD/NEIL G78 111 K3
Leabank Av PSLYS PA2 91 L2
Leadburn Rd
SPRGB/BLRNK G21 62 C6
Leadburn St
STPS/GTHM/RID G33 80 E3
Leader St STPS/GTHM/RID G33 80 D1
Leaend Rd AIRDRIE ML6 84 E1
Leander Crs BLSH ML4 100 E4
RNFRW PA4 58 E7
Leapmoor Dr WMYSB PA18 32 A8
Learigg Rd AIRDRIE ML6 68 B6
Learmont Pl MLNGV G62 23 M7
Leathem Pl WISHAW ML2 121 J8
Leathen Pl ERSK PA8 56 E1
Leckethill Av BALLOCH G68 47 M3
Leckethill Ct BALLOCH G68 47 M3
Leckethill Pl BALLOCH G68 47 M3
Leckethill Vw BALLOCH G68 47 M3
Leckie Dr HMLTN ML3 119 J7
Leckie Pl ALEX/LLW G83 13 K4
Leckie St PLKSD/SHW G41 94 C2
Ledaig Pl DEN/PKHD G31 80 C3
Ledaig St DEN/PKHD G31 80 C3
Ledard Rd GVH/MTFL G42 94 F3
Ledcameroch Crs BSDN G61 41 K5
Ledcameroch Pk BSDN G61 41 K5
Ledcameroch Rd BSDN G61 41 K5
Ledgate KKNTL G66 45 K1
Ledgowan Pl MRYH/FIRH G20 60 D2
Ledi Dr BSDN G61 41 H2
Ledi Rd PLKSW/MSWD G43 94 C5
Ledmore Dr DRUM G15 40 F5
Lednock Rd
CARD/HILL/MSPK G52 77 G4
STPS/GTHM/RID G33 63 J5
Ledvinka Crs HMLTN ML3 119 G4
Lee Av STPS/GTHM/RID G33 80 E1
Leebank Dr LNPK/KPK G44 114 F1
Leeburn Av
CRG/CRSL/HOU PA6 73 J1
Leeburn Gdns
CRG/CRSL/HOU PA6 73 J1
Leechford LNK/LMHG ML11 137 H4
Leechlee Rd HMLTN ML3 119 L7
Lee Crs BSHPBGS G64 61 M2
Leefield Dr LNPK/KPK G44 94 F8
Leehill Rd SPRGB/BLRNK G21 61 L3
Leemuir Vw CARLUKE ML8 135 H1
Lee Pl BLSH ML4 100 D5
Leesburn Pl EKILN G74 116 F6
Lee's Ct CTBR ML5 84 A4
Leesland UD/BTH/TAN G71 99 G2
Leeward Cir EKILS G75 126 D1
Lewood Dr LNPK/KPK G44 95 G8
Le Froy Gdns EKILS G75 2 A7
Le Froy La EKILS G75 2 B7
Lefroy St CTBR ML5 83 L3
Legbrannock Av MTHW ML1 101 K3
Legbrannock Crs MTHW ML1 101 K5
Legbrannock Rd MTHW ML1 101 L3
Leggate Wy BLSH ML4 100 A1
Leggatston Rd PLK/PH/NH G53 93 J6
Leglen Wood Crs
SPRGB/BLRNK G21 62 D4
Leglen Wood Dr
SPRGB/BLRNK G21 62 D4
Leglen Wood Pl
SPRGB/BLRNK G21 62 E4
Leglen Wood Rd
SPRGB/BLRNK G21 62 D4
Leicester Av KVD/HLHD G12 60 B5
Leighton St MRYH/FIRH G20 60 E4
WISHAW ML2 122 B7
Leishman Ct BTHG/ARM EH48 71 K2
Leitchland Rd JNSTN PA5 90 D2
Leitch St GRNK PA15 7 M8
Leithland Av PLK/PH/NH G53 93 H1
Leithland Rd PLK/PH/NH G53 77 H8
Leith St STPS/GTHM/RID G33 80 D2
Leman Dr CRG/CRSL/HOU PA6 73 K2
Leman Gv CRG/CRSL/HOU PA6 73 K2
Lembert Dr
CRMNK/CLK/EAG G76 114 D2
Lemmon St GRNK PA15 16 D6
Lendale La BSHPBGS G64 44 A7
Lendalfoot Gdns HMLTN ML3 128 D1
Lendal Pl EKILS G75 126 B4
Lendel Pl GOV/IBX G51 78 D5
Lenihall Dr CSMK G45 95 L8
Lenihall Ter CSMK G45 95 L8
Lennox Av BSHPTN PA7 38 B7
CTBR ML5 83 L5
MLNGV G62 42 A1
SCOT G14 59 J6
Lennox Ct KSYTH G65 29 K2
Lennox Crs BSHPBGS G64 61 M2
Lennox Dr BSDN G61 41 M3
CLYDBK G81 40 D2
NMRNS G77 113 L7
Lennox Gdns DMBTN G82 20 A6
SCOT G14 59 K6
Lennox La East SCOT G14 59 K6
Lennox La West SCOT G14 59 K5
Lennox Rd CUMB G67 30 F7
DMBTN G82 21 H7
KKNTL G66 26 C1
Lennox St ALEX/LLW G83 13 K5
DMBTN G82 20 D2
MRYH/FIRH G20 60 C3
WISHAW ML2 122 E5
Lennox Ter PSLYN/LNWD PA3 76 A1
Lentran St ESTRH G34 82 D3
Lenwood Gdns ALEX/LLW G83 13 L7
Leny St MRYH/FIRH G20 60 F6
Lenziemill Rd CUMB G67 48 F2
Lenzie Pl SPRGB/BLRNK G21 61 M4
Lenzie Rd KKNTL G66 45 K3
STPS/GTHM/RID G33 63 K3
Lenzie St SPRGB/BLRNK G21 61 M5
Lenzie Ter SPRGB/BLRNK G21 61 M4
Leonard Gv MTHW ML1 101 L8
Leperstone Av KLMCLM PA13 35 K8
PGL PA14 34 E3
Lesley Qd BLSH ML4 99 M8
Leslie Av BSHPTN PA7 38 B7
NMRNS G77 113 L2
Leslie Rd PLKSD/SHW G41 78 E8
Leslie St MTHW ML1 120 F2
PLKSD/SHW G41 78 F7
Lesmahagow Rd
LNK/LMHG ML11 136 A5
Lesmuir Dr SCOT G14 59 G4
Lesmuir Pl SCOT G14 58 F4
Letham Ct PLKSW/MSWD G43 94 E5
Letham Dr BSHPBGS G64 62 C2
PLKSW/MSWD G43 94 E5
Letham Gra BALLOCH G68 30 F5
Lethamhill Pl
STPS/GTHM/RID G33 80 E1
Lethamhill Rd
STPS/GTHM/RID G33 80 F1
Letham Ov BSHPBGS G64 62 D2
Lethbridge Pl EKILS G75 2 B7
Letherby Dr LNPK/KPK G44 95 H3
Letheron Dr WISHAW ML2 122 B4
Lethington Av
PLKSD/SHW G41 94 F2
Lethington Pl PLKSD/SHW G41 94 E2
Lethington Rd GIF/THBK G46 114 A3
Letterfearn Rd SMSTN G23 42 D8
Letterickhills Crs
BLTYR/CAMB G72 97 L7
Levanne Gdns GRK PA19 14 F3
Levanne Pl GRK PA19 14 F3
Leven Av BSHPBGS G64 62 B1
HBR/GL G84 11 G7
Levenbank Gdns
ALEX/LLW G83 13 L3
Leven Ct BRHD/NEIL G78 92 B4
Levencroft Ms ALEX/LLW G83 13 L6
Leven Dr BSDN G61 41 M5
HMLTN ML3 129 H2
Levenford Ter DMBTN G82 20 E7
Levenhowe Pl ALEX/LLW G83 13 K3
Levenhowe Rd ALEX/LLW G83 13 K3
Leven Pl ERSK PA8 56 E1
GRNK PA15 17 J8
SHOTTS ML7 104 E3
Leven Qd AIRDRIE ML6 66 F7
Leven Rd CTBR ML5 83 J1
GRNK PA15 17 H7
PGL PA14 36 C3
WMYSB PA18 50 B1
Leven St ALEX/LLW G83 13 K6
DMBTN G82 20 D2
MTHW ML1 120 E4
PLKSD/SHW G41 78 F7
Leven Ter MTHW ML1 101 J7
Leven Wy EKILS G75 126 C4
Levern Bridge Ct
PLK/PH/NH G53 92 F2
Levern Bridge Gv
PLK/PH/NH G53 92 F3
Levern Bridge Pl
PLK/PH/NH G53 92 F3
Levern Bridge Rd
PLK/PH/NH G53 93 G3
Levern Bridge Wy
PLK/PH/NH G53 92 F3
Levern Crs BRHD/NEIL G78 92 B8
Leverndale Ct PLK/PH/NH G53 76 F8
Leverndale Rd PLK/PH/NH G53 76 F8
Levern Gdns BRHD/NEIL G78 92 B6
Levern Grove Ct
PLK/PH/NH G53 92 F3
Levernside Av BRHD/NEIL G78 92 A7
PLK/PH/NH G53 93 J1
Levernside Crs PLK/PH/NH G53 77 H8
Levernside Rd PLK/PH/NH G53 77 H8
Lever Rd HBR/GL G84 10 F4
Lewis Av RNFRW PA4 58 D8
WISHAW ML2 122 E4
Lewis Crs KLBCH PA10 73 J8
OLDK G60 39 J5
Lewis Dr OLDK G60 39 H5
Lewis Gdns BSDN G61 41 H3
OLDK G60 39 J5
Lewis Gv OLDK G60 39 J5
Lewis Pl AIRDRIE ML6 85 K4
NMRNS G77 113 H3
OLDK G60 39 J5
Lewis Rd GRNKW/INVK PA16 16 C5
PGL PA14 35 H3
Lewiston Dr SMSTN G23 60 D1
Lewiston Pl SMSTN G23 60 D1
Lewiston Rd SMSTN G23 60 D1
Lexwell Av JNSTN PA5 74 D7
Leyden Gdns MRYH/FIRH G20 60 E5
Leyden St MRYH/FIRH G20 60 E5
Leyland Av HMLTN ML3 129 G2
Leys Pk HMLTN ML3 119 G6
The Leys BSHPBGS G64 62 A1
Libberton Wy HMLTN ML3 119 G7
Liberton St
STPS/GTHM/RID G33 80 E2
Liberty Av
BAIL/MDB/MHD G69 82 F5
Liberty Rd AIRDRIE ML6 69 G4
BLSH ML4 100 A6
Libo Av BRHD/NEIL G78 110 A7
PLK/PH/NH G53 77 K8
Libo Pl ERSK PA8 38 E8
Library Gdns BLTYR/CAMB G72 96 F4
Library La GIF/THBK G46 93 M6
Library Rd WISHAW ML2 122 B6
Lickprivick Rd EKILS G75 126 E3
Liddell Gv EKILS G75 127 G3
Liddells Ct BSHPBGS G64 62 A3
Liddell St CAR/SHTL G32 97 J1
Liddel Rd CUMB G67 30 E8
Liddesdale Av PSLYS PA2 90 D3
Liddesdale Pl PPK/MIL G22 61 L3
Liddesdale Rd PPK/MIL G22 61 J3
Liddesdale Sq PPK/MIL G22 61 K3
Liddesdale Ter PPK/MIL G22 61 L3
Liddoch Wy RUTH G73 95 M2
Liff Gdns BSHPBGS G64 62 D2
Liff Pl ESTRH G34 82 C1
Lightburn Pl CAR/SHTL G32 81 H3
Lightburn Rd BLTYR/CAMB G72 97 K6
Lilac Av CLYDBK G81 39 L6
CUMB G67 31 L4
Lilac Ct CUMB G67 31 L4
Lilac Crs UD/BTH/TAN G71 99 J2
Lilac Gdns BSHPBGS G64 62 B2
Lilac Gv WISHAW ML2 121 M8
Lilac Hl CUMB G67 31 M4
HMLTN ML3 119 M8
Lilac Pl CUMB G67 31 M4
Lilac Wynd BLTYR/CAMB G72 97 M6
Lillyburn Pl DRUM G15 40 E5
Lilybank Av AIRDRIE ML6 67 H7
BAIL/MDB/MHD G69 64 C3
BLTYR/CAMB G72 97 H6
Lilybank Gdns KVD/HLHD G12 60 D8
Lilybank Gardens La
KVD/HLHD G12 60 D8
Lilybank Rd GRNK PA15 17 M7
Lilybank St HMLTN ML3 119 J6
Lilybank Ter KVD/HLHD G12 60 D8
Lilybank Terrace La
KVD/HLHD G12 60 D8
Lily St DMNK/BRGTN G40 80 A7
Limecraigs Av PSLYS PA2 91 J3
Limecraigs Crs PSLYS PA2 91 J3
Limecraigs Rd PSLYS PA2 91 J3
Lime Crs AIRDRIE ML6 85 J2
CUMB G67 31 L6
Lime Gv BLTYR/CAMB G72 118 C1
KKNTL G66 45 K5
MTHW ML1 120 E5
Limegrove St BLSH ML4 100 A2
Limekilnburn Rd HMLTN ML3 129 H8
Limekilns Rd CUMB G67 48 F3
Limekilns St CLYDBK G81 40 D3
Limelands Qd AIRDRIE ML6 68 F5
Lime La SCOT G14 59 K6
Lime Loan MTHW ML1 101 H5
Lime Rd DMBTN G82 20 F6
Limeside Av RUTH G73 96 C3
Limeside Gdns RUTH G73 96 C3
Lime St GRNK PA15 6 A6
SCOT G14 59 K6
Limetree Av UD/BTH/TAN G71 99 H2
Limetree Ct HMLTN ML3 119 G5
Limetree Crs NMRNS G77 113 K5
Limetree Dr CLYDBK G81 40 A5
Limetree Qd UD/BTH/TAN G71 99 J3
Limetree Wk KKNTL G66 27 H6
Limeview Av PSLYS PA2 91 H3
Limeview Crs PSLYS PA2 91 H3
Limeview Wy PSLYS PA2 91 H3
Limewood Pl
BAIL/MDB/MHD G69 83 G4
Limpetlaw LNK/LMHG ML11 137 H4
Linacre Dr CAR/SHTL G32 81 J5
Linacre Gdns CAR/SHTL G32 81 K5
Linburn Pl
CARD/HILL/MSPK G52 77 G3
Linburn Rd
CARD/HILL/MSPK G52 76 F2
ERSK PA8 56 E1
Lincoln Av KNTSWD G13 59 J2
UD/BTH/TAN G71 98 F1
Lincoln Ct CTBR ML5 84 A1
Lincoln Rd GRNKW/INVK PA16 15 K5
Lincuan Av GIF/THBK G46 114 C2
Lindams UD/BTH/TAN G71 98 F5
Linden Av WISHAW ML2 122 C3
Linden Dr CLYDBK G81 40 A3
Linden Lea HMLTN ML3 119 H6
KKNTL G66 27 H5
Linden Pl KNTSWD G13 59 M2
Linden St KNTSWD G13 59 M2
Lindon Aisle LARGS KA30 106 E5
Lindon Ct LARGS KA30 106 E5
Lindores Av RUTH G73 96 B3
Lindores Dr EKILN G74 126 E1
Lindores Pl EKILN G74 2 A5
Lindores St GVH/MTFL G42 95 H2
Lindrick Dr SMSTN G23 60 D2
Lindsay Av KBRN KA25 124 D2
Lindsaybeg Ct
BAIL/MDB/MHD G69 64 C2
Lindsaybeg Rd
BAIL/MDB/MHD G69 46 B8
KKNTL G66 45 L6
Lindsay Crs LARGS KA30 106 F4
Lindsay Dr KVD/HLHD G12 60 B4
Lindsayfield Av EKILS G75 126 F6
Lindsayfield Rd EKILS G75 126 E6
Lindsay Gdns ALEX/LLW G83 13 J4
Lindsay Gv EKILN G74 3 H4
Lindsay Pl EKILN G74 3 J5
KVD/HLHD G12 60 B4
Lindsay Qd ALEX/LLW G83 13 M2
Lindsay Rd EKILN G74 3 H5
Lindsay Ter KKNTL G66 26 E2
Lindum Crs MTHW ML1 120 C1
Lindum St MTHW ML1 120 B1
Linfern Rd KVD/HLHD G12 60 C7
Linghope Pl WISHAW ML2 131 H1
Lingley Av AIRDRIE ML6 85 G3
Linhead Dr PLK/PH/NH G53 93 J3
Linhope Pl EKILS G75 126 C3
Linister Crs HWWD PA9 88 E5
Links Rd CAR/SHTL G32 81 K7
The Links BALLOCH G68 31 H3
Links Vw LRKH ML9 130 E7
Linksview Rd MTHW ML1 101 H8
Linkwood Av DRUM G15 41 G5
Linkwood Crs DRUM G15 41 G6
Linkwood Dr DRUM G15 40 F6
Linkwood Gdns DRUM G15 41 H6
Linkwood Pl DRUM G15 40 F6
Linlithgow Gdns
CAR/SHTL G32 81 K5
Linlithgow Pl
BAIL/MDB/MHD G69 64 E5
Linn Av LARGS KA30 107 G5
Linn Crs LNK/LMHG ML11 136 A5
PSLYS PA2 91 J3
Linn Dr LNPK/KPK G44 94 F7
Linnet Av JNSTN PA5 89 J3
Linnet Pl KNTSWD G13 58 F2
Linnet Rd BLSH ML4 100 B5
GRNKW/INVK PA16 16 B5
Linnet Wy BLSH ML4 99 M2
Linn Gdns BALLOCH G68 29 M8
Linn Ga BALLOCH G68 30 A7
Linn Gln KKNTL G66 26 F2
Linnhead Dr PLK/PH/NH G53 93 H4
Linnhead Pl SCOT G14 59 H5
Linnhe Av BSHPBGS G64 62 B1
HMLTN ML3 129 G1
LNPK/KPK G44 95 G6
Linnhe Ct LRKH ML9 130 B4
Linnhe Crs WISHAW ML2 131 K1
Linnhe Dr BRHD/NEIL G78 92 B4
Linnhe Pl BLTYR/CAMB G72 98 C8
ERSK PA8 56 E1
Linnhe Rd WMYSB PA18 32 B8
Linnpark Av LNPK/KPK G44 94 F8
Linn Park Gdns JNSTN PA5 74 A8
Linnvale Wy BALLOCH G68 30 C3
Linn Valley Vw CSMK G45 95 K7
Linnwell Crs PSLYS PA2 91 K3
Linrigg Rd MTHW ML1 102 C1
Linside Av PSLY PA1 76 B5
Linthaugh Rd PLK/PH/NH G53 77 J6
Linthaugh Ter PLK/PH/NH G53 77 K8
Linthill LNK/LMHG ML11 137 H4
Linthouse Buildings
GOV/IBX G51 77 L1
Linthouse Rd GOV/IBX G51 59 K8
Lintie Rd MTHW ML1 101 J5
Lintlaw BLTYR/CAMB G72 98 D8
Lintlaw Dr
CARD/HILL/MSPK G52 77 H3
Lintmill Ter BRHD/NEIL G78 111 J4
Lint Mill Wy BALLOCH G68 30 A7
Linton St STPS/GTHM/RID G33 80 E2
Lintwhite Crs BRWEIR PA11 72 E3
Linwood Av
CRMNK/CLK/EAG G76 114 F3
EKILN G74 115 M8
Linwood Ct LNPK/KPK G44 95 G5
Linwood Rd PSLY PA1 74 F6
Linwood Ter HMLTN ML3 119 H6
Lion Bank KKNTL G66 45 K1
Lismore EKILN G74 127 M2
Lismore Av MTHW ML1 120 B1
PGL PA14 35 H3
RNFRW PA4 58 D8
Lismore Dr CTBR ML5 83 L6
PSLYN/LNWD PA3 73 M5
PSLYS PA2 91 K3
Lismore Gdns KLBCH PA10 89 J1
Lismore Hl HMLTN ML3 118 D7
Lismore Pl AIRDRIE ML6 85 J4
BAIL/MDB/MHD G69 47 G7
NMRNS G77 113 H4
Lismore Rd KVD/HLHD G12 60 B5
Lister Gdns
CRMNK/CLK/EAG G76 115 G5
Lister Pl CARD/HILL/MSPK G52 77 G2
Lister Rd CARD/HILL/MSPK G52 76 F2
Lister St COWCAD G4 5 J3
Lister Wy BLTYR/CAMB G72 118 C5
Lithgow Av PGL PA14 36 B3
Lithgow Crs PSLYS PA2 76 A7
Lithgow Dr MTHW ML1 102 B8
Lithgow Pl EKILN G74 116 B8
Little Dovehill CGLE G1 5 J8
Littlehill St SPRGB/BLRNK G21 62 A6
Littleholm Pl CLYDBK G81 39 L6
Little John Gdns WISHAW ML2 122 F5
Littlemill Av BALLOCH G68 47 L1
Littlemill Crs PLK/PH/NH G53 93 H1
Littlemill Dr PLK/PH/NH G53 93 G1
Littlemill Gdns PLK/PH/NH G53 93 G1
Littlemill La OLDK G60 38 C2
Littlemill Wy MTHW ML1 101 H8
Littleston Gdns ERSK PA8 56 F1
Little St KVGV G3 78 F3
Littleton St SMSTN G23 60 D1
Livingstone Dr AIRDRIE ML6 68 A7
Livingstone Av
CARD/HILL/MSPK G52 77 G1
Livingstone Bvd
BLTYR/CAMB G72 118 C5
Livingstone Crs
BLTYR/CAMB G72 118 D1
EKILS G75 2 D9
Livingstone Dr EKILS G75 2 D7
Livingstone Gdns LRKH ML9 130 D6
Livingstone La
BLTYR/CAMB G72 97 G7
Livingstone Pl AIRDRIE ML6 85 H3
Livingstone Qd SHOTTS ML7 71 K8
Livingstone St CLYDBK G81 40 D8
HMLTN ML3 118 F6
Lloyd Av CAR/SHTL G32 81 G8
Lloyd Dr MTHW ML1 101 G8
Lloyd St CTBR ML5 84 A4
Lloyd St DEN/PKHD G31 80 A2
MTHW ML1 101 G8
RUTH G73 96 B1
Llynallan Rd SHOTTS ML7 70 F8
Loadingbank KBRN KA25 124 C6
Loanbank Pl GOV/IBX G51 78 A3
Loanbank Qd GOV/IBX G51 78 A3
Loancroft Av
BAIL/MDB/MHD G69 82 C7
Loancroft Gdns
UD/BTH/TAN G71 98 E5
Loancroft Ga UD/BTH/TAN G71 98 E5
Loancroft Pl
BAIL/MDB/MHD G69 82 B7
Loanfoot Av BRHD/NEIL G78 111 K4
KNTSWD G13 59 G2
Loanfoot Gdns CARLUKE ML8 134 F4
Loanfoot Rd BLTYR/CAMB G72 118 D5
Loanhead Av MTHW ML1 101 K6
PSLYN/LNWD PA3 74 A4
RNFRW PA4 58 D6
Loanhead Crs MTHW ML1 101 K6
Loanhead Rd MTHW ML1 101 H6
PSLYN/LNWD PA3 74 A4
Loanhead St CAR/SHTL G32 80 F3
CTBR ML5 83 L7
Loaninghead Dr DMBTN G82 21 H4
The Loaning GIF/THBK G46 114 A3
KKNTL G66 45 J3
MTHW ML1 120 C2
Loan Lea Crs LRKH ML9 130 D8
Loan Pl SHOTTS ML7 71 L6
The Loan MLNGV G62 23 J5
Lobnitz Av RNFRW PA4 58 D6
Lochaber Crs SHOTTS ML7 105 G6
Lochaber Dr RUTH G73 96 D6
Lochaber Pl EKILN G74 3 H1
Lochaber Rd BSDN G61 42 B8
Loch Achray St CAR/SHTL G32 81 J6
Lochaline Av PSLYS PA2 75 G8
Lochaline Dr LNPK/KPK G44 95 G6
Lochalsh Crs KKNTL G66 27 J3
Lochalsh Dr PSLYS PA2 74 F8
Lochalsh Pl BLTYR/CAMB G72 98 B8
Lochar Crs PLK/PH/NH G53 77 K7
Lochard Dr PSLYS PA2 91 G1
Lochar Pl EKILS G75 126 B3
Loch Assynt EKILN G74 3 L7
Loch Av CARLUKE ML8 134 E5
Loch Awe EKILN G74 3 K7
Loch Awe Pl CTBR ML5 83 M4
Lochay St CAR/SHTL G32 81 J6
Lochbrae Dr RUTH G73 96 D6
Lochbridge Rd ESTRH G34 82 A3
Lochbroom Dr NMRNS G77 113 M3
PSLYS PA2 75 G8
Loch Brora Crs CTBR ML5 83 L4
Lochbuie La AIRDRIE ML6 66 E5
Lochburn Crs MRYH/FIRH G20 60 E3
Lochburn Pass MRYH/FIRH G20 60 E3

Lochburn Rd MRYH/FIRH G20 60 E3
Lochdochart Rd ESTRH G34 82 D2
Loch Dr HBR/GL G84 10 A5
Lochearn Crs AIRDRIE ML6 66 F7
PSLYS PA2 75 G8
Lochend Av
BAIL/MDB/MHD G69 64 E4
Lochend Crs BSDN G61 41 K6
Lochend Dr BSDN G61 41 K6
Lochend Rd
BAIL/MDB/MHD G69 64 F5
BSDN G61 41 L6
ESTRH G34 82 B1
GLGNK KA14 124 E6
Lochend St MTHW ML1 120 F3
Locher Av CRG/CRSL/HOU PA6 73 L1
Locherburn Av
CRG/CRSL/HOU PA6 73 K2
Locherburn Pl
CRG/CRSL/HOU PA6 73 L2
Locher Crs CRG/CRSL/HOU PA6 73 L2
Locher Gait
CRG/CRSL/HOU PA6 73 L2
Locher Gdns
CRG/CRSL/HOU PA6 73 L2
Locher Pl CTBR ML5 84 D6
Locher Rd BRWEIR PA11 72 F5
Locher Wk CTBR ML5 84 C6
Locher Wy CRG/CRSL/HOU PA6 73 L2
Lochfauld Rd SMSTN G23 43 H8
Lochfield Crs PSLYS PA2 91 M1
Lochfield Dr PSLYS PA2 76 A8
Lochfield Rd PSLYS PA2 91 M1
Lochgarry Wy CTBR ML5 83 K6
Lochgilp St MRYH/FIRH G20 60 C3
Loch Goil EKILN G74 3 K6
Lochgoin Av DRUM G15 40 E5
Lochgreen Pl CTBR ML5 65 J8
HMLTN ML3 129 H3
Lochgreen St
STPS/GTHM/RID G33 62 D7
Lochhead Av PSLYN/LNWD PA3 74 B5
Lochiel Dr KKNTL G66 27 J4
Lochiel Rd GIF/THBK G46 93 M5
Lochinch Pl NMRNS G77 113 G4
Lochinvar Rd CUMB G67 48 D2
Lochinver Crs
BLTYR/CAMB G72 118 C7
PSLYS PA2 75 G8
Lochinver Dr LNPK/KPK G44 95 G5
Lochinver Gv BLTYR/CAMB G72 97 H5
Lochknowe St CARLUKE ML8 134 F4
Loch Laidon St CAR/SHTL G32 81 K6
Lochlands Gv BEITH KA15 125 K5
Loch Laxford EKILN G74 3 L8
Lochlea EKILN G74 117 K6
Loch Lea KKNTL G66 45 M1
Lochlea Av CLYDBK G81 40 C6
Lochlea Rd
CRMNK/CLK/EAG G76 114 E5
CUMB G67 31 H6
PLKSW/MSWD G43 94 D4
RUTH G73 95 M5
Lochlea Wy MTHW ML1 101 L5
Lochleven La GVH/MTFL G42 95 G3
Lochleven Rd GVH/MTFL G42 95 G3
Lochlibo Av KNTSWD G13 58 F3
Lochlibo Crs BRHD/NEIL G78 92 A8
Lochlibo Rd BRHD/NEIL G78 92 A7
Lochlibo Ter BRHD/NEIL G78 92 A8
Lochlip Rd LOCHW PA12 109 K3
Loch Long EKILN G74 3 K7
Loch Loyal EKILN G74 3 M8
Lochmaben Rd
BAIL/MDB/MHD G69 64 F6
CARD/HILL/MSPK G52 76 F5
Lochmaddy Av LNPK/KPK G44 95 G6
Loch Maree EKILN G74 3 L7
Loch Meadie EKILN G74 3 M7
Lochnagar Dr BSDN G61 41 H2
Loch Naver EKILN G74 3 M8
Lochore Av PSLYN/LNWD PA3 76 A2
Loch Pk WISHAW ML2 122 C6
Loch Park Av CARLUKE ML8 134 F1
Loch Park Pl LRKH ML9 130 C8
Loch Pl BRWEIR PA11 72 D2
Lochranza Dr EKILS G75 126 E6
HBR/GL G84 10 F5
Lochranza La EKILS G75 126 F6
Loch Rd AIRDRIE ML6 85 K7
BRWEIR PA11 72 D2
KKNTL G66 45 L3
MLNGV G62 24 B7
STPS/GTHM/RID G33 63 K5
Loch Shin EKILN G74 3 M8
Lochside BAIL/MDB/MHD G69 64 F4
BSDN G61 41 M6
Lochside Crs AIRDRIE ML6 67 G6
Lochside St PLKSD/SHW G41 94 E1
Loch St AIRDRIE ML6 85 H7
Loch Striven EKILN G74 3 K6
Loch Torridon EKILN G74 3 L8
Loch Vw AIRDRIE ML6 69 G4
AIRDRIE ML6 85 H7
Lochview Av GRK PA19 16 A2
Lochview Crs
STPS/GTHM/RID G33 62 F7
Lochview Dr
STPS/GTHM/RID G33 62 F7
Lochview Gdns
STPS/GTHM/RID G33 62 F7
Lochview Pl
STPS/GTHM/RID G33 62 F7
Lochview Qd BLSH ML4 99 M7
Lochview Rd BEITH KA15 125 H6
BSDN G61 41 L6
CTBR ML5 83 J1
PGL PA14 34 B1
Loch Voil St CAR/SHTL G32 81 K6
Lochwinnoch Rd
KLMCLM PA13 53 H3
Lochwood Loan
BAIL/MDB/MHD G69 47 G7
Lochwood St
STPS/GTHM/RID G33 62 E8
Lochy Av RNFRW PA4 58 F8
Lochy Pl ERSK PA8 38 E8
Lochy St WISHAW ML2 122 B8
Locke Gv MTHW ML1 101 M8
Lockerbie Av
PLKSW/MSWD G43 94 F4
Locket Yett Vw BLSH ML4 99 M5
Lockhart Av BLTYR/CAMB G72 97 K4
Lockhart Ct NMRNS G77 113 K7
Lockhart Dr BLTYR/CAMB G72 97 K4
LNK/LMHG ML11 136 E4
NMRNS G77 113 K7
Lockhart Pl UD/BTH/TAN G71 * 82 B8
WISHAW ML2 122 E5
Lockhart St CARLUKE ML8 133 H7
HMLTN ML3 129 J4
SPRGB/BLRNK G21 62 B8
Lockhart Ter EKILN G74 3 L3
Locksley Av CUMB G67 48 E3
KNTSWD G13 59 J1
Locksley Ct CUMB G67 48 E3
Locksley Crs CUMB G67 48 E3
Locksley Pl CUMB G67 48 E3
Locksley Rd CUMB G67 48 E3
PSLYS PA2 90 F1
Locks St CTBR ML5 84 D3
Lodge Crs KLMCLM PA13 53 L2
Lodge Gdns KLMCLM PA13 53 L1
Lodge Gv KLMCLM PA13 53 L1
Lodge Pk KLMCLM PA13 53 L1
Logan Av NMRNS G77 113 J3
Logandale Av WISHAW ML2 122 F3
Logan Dr BALLOCH G68 30 D6
PSLYN/LNWD PA3 8 C2
Logan Gdns MTHW ML1 122 B1
Loganlea Dr MTHW ML1 101 G8
Logans Rd MTHW ML1 120 B1
Logan St BLTYR/CAMB G72 118 E3
GBLS G5 79 K8
Loganswell Dr GIF/THBK G46 93 L7
Loganswell Gdns GIF/THBK G46 93 L7
Loganswell Pl GIF/THBK G46 93 L7
Loganswell Rd GIF/THBK G46 93 L7
Logie Pk EKILN G74 3 J2
Logie Sq EKILN G74 3 J2
Lomax St STPS/GTHM/RID G33 80 D2
Lomond EKILS G75 127 H5
Lomond Av PGL PA14 34 D2
RNFRW PA4 58 B8
Lomond Ct BRHD/NEIL G78 92 C7
CTBR ML5 84 D2
CUMB G67 48 C2
Lomond Crs ALEX/LLW G83 13 J3
BEITH KA15 125 L3
BRWEIR PA11 72 C2
CUMB G67 48 C2
PSLYS PA2 91 K2
Lomond Dr AIRDRIE ML6 66 F7
ALEX/LLW G83 13 J3
BRHD/NEIL G78 92 B5
BSHPBGS G64 43 M7
CUMB G67 48 B2
DMBTN G82 21 H4
NMRNS G77 113 K2
UD/BTH/TAN G71 99 H7
WISHAW ML2 122 A8
Lomond Gdns JNSTN PA5 74 C8
Lomond Gv CUMB G67 48 C2
HBR/GL G84 11 G6
Lomond Pl CTBR ML5 83 L1
CUMB G67 48 B2
ERSK PA8 56 E1
STPS/GTHM/RID G33 63 K6
Lomond Rd ALEX/LLW G83 13 J3
BSDN G61 41 L7
CTBR ML5 65 K8
GRNK PA15 6 F8
KKNTL G66 45 K5
SHOTTS ML7 104 D3
UD/BTH/TAN G71 98 F1
WMYSB PA18 50 B1
Lomondside Av
CRMNK/CLK/EAG G76 114 C2
Lomond St HBR/GL G84 10 E6
PPK/MIL G22 61 H5
Lomond Vw CUMB G67 48 C2
HMLTN ML3 118 F8
London Dr CAR/SHTL G32 81 L8
London La CGLE G1 5 H9
London Rd CAR/SHTL G32 81 H1
DMNK/BRGTN G40 5 K9
London St LRKH ML9 130 C5
RNFRW PA4 58 D4
Lonend PSLY PA1 9 J7
Longay Pl PPK/MIL G22 61 J2
Longay St PPK/MIL G22 61 J2
Longbar Av GLGNK KA14 124 F7
Long Crags Vw DMBTN G82 21 J4
Longcroft Dr RNFRW PA4 58 C6
Longden St CLYDBK G81 58 D1
Long Dr EKILS G75 127 K3
Longford St
STPS/GTHM/RID G33 80 D2
Long Hl SKLM PA17 50 B5
Longlee BAIL/MDB/MHD G69 82 B6
Longmeadow JNSTN PA5 89 J1
Longmorn Pl MTHW ML1 101 H8
Long Rw BAIL/MDB/MHD G69 82 C4
KKNTL G66 46 B3
Longstone Rd
STPS/GTHM/RID G33 81 H2
Longwill Ter CUMB G67 31 H5
Lonmay Dr
STPS/GTHM/RID G33 81 K2
Lonmay Rd
STPS/GTHM/RID G33 81 K2
Lonsdale Av GIF/THBK G46 94 C7
Loom Wk KLBCH PA10 73 G7
Lora Dr CARD/HILL/MSPK G52 77 L5
Loretto Pl STPS/GTHM/RID G33 80 F2
Loretto St STPS/GTHM/RID G33 80 F2
Lorimer Crs EKILS G75 127 G3
Lorn Av BAIL/MDB/MHD G69 64 D2
Lorn Dr ALEX/LLW G83 13 K1
Lorne Crs BSHPBGS G64 44 D8
Lorne Dr MTHW ML1 100 D7
PSLYN/LNWD PA3 74 A5
Lorne Gdns SHOTTS ML7 87 G7
Lorne Pl CTBR ML5 84 D5
Lorne Rd CARD/HILL/MSPK G52 76 F1
Lorne St GOV/IBX G51 78 D4
HBR/GL G84 10 D5
HMLTN ML3 119 J6
Lorne Ter BLTYR/CAMB G72 96 F7
Lorn Pl KKNTL G66 46 C1
Lorraine Gdns KVD/HLHD G12 60 C6
Lorraine Gardens La
KVD/HLHD G12 60 C6
Lorraine Rd KVD/HLHD G12 60 C6
Lorraine Wy ALEX/LLW G83 20 F1
Loskin Dr PPK/MIL G22 61 H3
Lossie Crs RNFRW PA4 58 F7
Lossie St STPS/GTHM/RID G33 80 D1
Lothain St
CARD/HILL/MSPK G52 76 E1
Lothian Crs PSLYS PA2 91 K1
Lothian Dr
CRMNK/CLK/EAG G76 114 D2
Lothian Gdns MRYH/FIRH G20 60 E7
Lothian Rd GRNKW/INVK PA16 15 K5
Lothian St
CARD/HILL/MSPK G52 76 F1
Lothian Wy EKILN G74 117 J7
Louburn BTHG/ARM EH48 71 J1
Louden Hill Pl
STPS/GTHM/RID G33 * 62 E4
Louden Hill Rd
STPS/GTHM/RID G33 62 E4
Louden Hill Wy
SPRGB/BLRNK G21 62 E4
Loudon EKILS G75 127 H5
Loudon Gdns JNSTN PA5 74 A7
Loudonhill Av HMLTN ML3 129 K2
Loudon Rd
STPS/GTHM/RID G33 63 H6
Loudon St WISHAW ML2 122 B3
Louise Gdns BLSH ML4 100 F4
Louisville Av WISHAW ML2 122 D4
Lounsdale Av PSLYS PA2 8 A8
Lounsdale Crs PSLYS PA2 75 G8
Lounsdale Dr PSLYS PA2 8 A9
Lounsdale Pl SCOT G14 59 H5
Lounsdale Rd PSLYS PA2 8 B8
Lourdes Av
CARD/HILL/MSPK G52 77 K5
Lovat Av BSDN G61 41 L2
Lovat Dr KKNTL G66 45 H2
Lovat Pl CARD/HILL/MSPK G52 76 E2
RUTH G73 96 D6
Lovat St LARGS KA30 106 F5
Love Av BRWEIR PA11 53 L8
Love Dr BLSH ML4 100 B3
Love St PSLYN/LNWD PA3 9 G1
Low Barholm KLBCH PA10 73 H8
Low Broadlie Rd
BRHD/NEIL G78 111 K2
Low Craigends KSYTH G65 29 L2
Low Crs CLYDBK G81 58 E1
Lower Auchingramont Rd
HMLTN ML3 119 L6
Lower Bourtree Dr RUTH G73 96 C6
Lower Bouverie St PGL PA14 34 D1
Lower Millgate
UD/BTH/TAN G71 98 F4
Lower Mill Rd
CRMNK/CLK/EAG G76 114 F4
Lower Stoneymollan Rd
ALEX/LLW G83 13 H2
Lower Sutherland Crs
HBR/GL G84 10 B4
Low Flender Rd
CRMNK/CLK/EAG G76 114 D5
Lowndes St BRHD/NEIL G78 92 C7
Low Parksail ERSK PA8 57 J2
Low Patrick St HMLTN ML3 119 M7
Low Pleasance LRKH ML9 130 D6
Low Rd PSLYS PA2 8 D7
Lowther Av BSDN G61 41 J2
Lowther Ter KVD/HLHD G12 60 C6
Low Waters Rd HMLTN ML3 129 K2
Loyal Av ERSK PA8 56 F1
Loyal Gdns BSDN G61 41 H1
Loyal Pl ERSK PA8 56 F1
Loyne Dr RNFRW PA4 58 F8
Luath St GOV/IBX G51 78 A2
Lubas Av GVH/MTFL G42 95 K3
Lubas Pl GVH/MTFL G42 95 K3
Lubnaig Dr ERSK PA8 56 E1
Lubnaig Gdns BSDN G61 41 J2
Lubnaig Pl AIRDRIE ML6 66 E7
Lubnaig Rd PLKSW/MSWD G43 94 E5
Luckiesfauld BRHD/NEIL G78 111 K3
Luckingsford Av RNFRW PA4 57 K3
Luckingsford Dr RNFRW PA4 57 J3
Luckingsford Rd RNFRW PA4 57 J3
Lucy Brae UD/BTH/TAN G71 98 E2
Luffness Gdns CAR/SHTL G32 81 H8
Lugar Dr
CARD/HILL/MSPK G52 77 L5
Lugar Pl LNPK/KPK G44 95 L5
Lugar St CTBR ML5 84 B1
Luggiebank Pl
BAIL/MDB/MHD G69 83 G6
Luggiebank Rd KKNTL G66 45 K2
Luggieburn Wk CTBR ML5 83 M5
Luggie Rd CARLUKE ML8 132 F7
Luggie Vw CUMB G67 48 A2
Luing Rd CARD/HILL/MSPK G52 77 L4
Luma Gdns GOV/IBX G51 77 J2
Lumloch St SPRGB/BLRNK G21 62 A6
Lumsden La KVGV G3 78 D1
Lumsden St KVGV G3 78 D2
Lunan Dr BSHPBGS G64 62 C2
Lunan Pl GOV/IBX G51 77 L2
Luncarty Pl CAR/SHTL G32 81 G7
Luncarty St CAR/SHTL G32 81 G7
Lunderston Dr PLK/PH/NH G53 93 G2
Lundie Gdns BSHPBGS G64 62 D2
Lundie St CAR/SHTL G32 80 E7
Lurg St PGL PA14 34 D2
Luss Av GRNK PA15 17 H8
Luss Brae HMLTN ML3 118 E8
Lusset Gln OLDK G60 39 H4
Lusset Rd OLDK G60 39 H4
Lusshill Ter UD/BTH/TAN G71 82 B8
Luss Pl GRNK PA15 17 J8
Luss Rd ALEX/LLW G83 13 J3
GOV/IBX G51 77 M2
HBR/GL G84 11 G2
Lybster Wy BLTYR/CAMB G72 118 C7
Lye Brae CUMB G67 31 G7
Lyell Gv EKILN G74 2 E2
Lyell Pl EKILN G74 2 E2
Lyle Crs BSHPTN PA7 37 M6
Lylefoot Crs GRNKW/INVK PA16 16 B2
Lylefoot Pl GRNKW/INVK PA16 16 B2
Lyle Gv GRNKW/INVK PA16 16 B2
Lyle Pl GRNKW/INVK PA16 16 A2
PSLYS PA2 75 M8
Lyle Rd AIRDRIE ML6 85 M2
GRNKW/INVK PA16 16 B2
KLMCLM PA13 53 K2
Lylesland Ct PSLYS PA2 9 H9
Lyle Sq MLNGV G62 23 L7
Lyle St GRNK PA15 6 E6
Lyman Dr WISHAW ML2 122 C2
Lymburn St KVGV G3 78 D2
Lymekilns Rd EKILN G74 2 C3
Lyndale Pl MRYH/FIRH G20 60 D2
Lyndale Rd MRYH/FIRH G20 60 D2
Lyndhurst Gdns
MRYH/FIRH G20 60 F7
Lyndhurst Gardens La
MRYH/FIRH G20 60 F7
Lynebank Gv NMRNS G77 113 K7
Lynebank Pl NMRNS G77 113 K7
Lyne Cft BSHPBGS G64 44 A6
Lynedoch Crs KVGV G3 78 F1
Lynedoch Crescent La KVGV G3 4 A2
Lynedoch Pl KVGV G3 78 F1
Lynedoch St GRNK PA15 6 E5
KVGV G3 78 F1
Lynedoch Ter KVGV G3 78 F1
Lyne St WISHAW ML2 122 A4
Lynmouth Pl GRK PA19 15 L4
Lynnburn Av BLSH ML4 100 A4
Lynn Ct LRKH ML9 130 C7
Lynn Dr KBRN KA25 124 D2
MLNGV G62 24 C8
Lynne Dr SMSTN G23 60 E1
Lynnhurst UD/BTH/TAN G71 98 F3
Lynnwood Rd WISHAW ML2 123 J3
Lynton Av GIF/THBK G46 114 A1
Lyoncross Av BRHD/NEIL G78 92 D7
Lyoncross Crs BRHD/NEIL G78 92 D6
Lyoncross Rd PLK/PH/NH G53 77 H7
Lyon Rd ERSK PA8 56 E1
PSLYN/LNWD PA3 74 B6
PSLYS PA2 90 F1
Lyons Qd WISHAW ML2 121 K5
Lysa Vale Pl BLSH ML4 99 L5
Lytham Dr SMSTN G23 60 E1
Lytham Mdw UD/BTH/TAN G71 98 E8
Lythgow Wy LNK/LMHG ML11 137 J4
Lyttelton EKILS G75 126 E3

M

Mabel St MTHW ML1 120 E4
Macadam Gdns BLSH ML4 100 A3
Macadam Pl EKILS G75 2 F8
Macallan Ms MTHW ML1 101 H7
Macarthur Av AIRDRIE ML6 66 D6
Macarthur Ct EKILN G74 2 A1
Macarthur Crs EKILN G74 116 C6
Macarthur Dr EKILN G74 2 A1
Macarthur Gdns EKILN G74 2 A1
Macarthur Wynd
BLTYR/CAMB G72 97 J5
Macaulay Pl HBR/GL G84 10 A5
Macbeth EKILN G74 117 H5
Macbeth Pl DEN/PKHD G31 80 D6
Macbeth Rd GRNKW/INVK PA16 16 A4
Macbeth St DEN/PKHD G31 80 D6
Mac Callum Dr
BLTYR/CAMB G72 97 J5
Maccrimmon Pk EKILN G74 116 B6
Macdairmid Dr HMLTN ML3 129 H3
Macdonald Av EKILN G74 116 A6
Macdonald Ct BEITH KA15 125 J6
Macdonald Gv BLSH ML4 99 M8
Macdonald St MTHW ML1 120 F4
RUTH G73 96 A2
Macdougal Dr
BLTYR/CAMB G72 97 J5
Macdougall St GRNK PA15 7 L7
PLKSW/MSWD G43 94 C3
Macdougal Qd BLSH ML4 99 M8
Macdowall St JNSTN PA5 73 M7
PSLYN/LNWD PA3 8 E2
Macduff Pl DEN/PKHD G31 80 D6
Macduff St DEN/PKHD G31 80 D6
Macedonian Gv MTHW ML1 101 J5
Mace Rd KNTSWD G13 41 J8
Macfarlane Crs
BLTYR/CAMB G72 97 K5
Macfarlane Rd BSDN G61 41 M6
Macfie Pl EKILN G74 116 B6
Macgillvary Av GRNK PA15 17 L6
Macgregor Ct BLTYR/CAMB G72 97 J5
Machan Av LRKH ML9 130 C6
Machanhill LRKH ML9 130 E7
Machanhill Vw LRKH ML9 130 D7
Machan Rd LRKH ML9 130 C7
Machrie Dr CSMK G45 95 M6
HBR/GL G84 10 F4
NMRNS G77 113 L3
Machrie Gn EKILS G75 126 E6
Machrie Rd CSMK G45 95 M6
Machrie St CSMK G45 95 M6
MTHW ML1 120 B2
Macinnes Dr MTHW ML1 102 A4
Macintosh Pl EKILS G75 126 F3
Macintyre St KVGV G3 4 A6
Macivor Crs EKILN G74 116 A6
Mackean St PSLYN/LNWD PA3 8 D1
Mackeith St DMNK/BRGTN G40 79 M6
Mackenzie Dr KLBCH PA10 89 H1
Mackenzie Gdns EKILN G74 116 A6
Mackenzie St GRNK PA15 7 L7
Mackenzie Ter BLSH ML4 100 A3
Mackerston Pl LARGS KA30 106 E6
Mackie Av PGL PA14 34 A1
Mackie's Mill Rd JNSTN PA5 90 D3
Mackinlay Pl NMRNS G77 113 K5
Mackintosh Ct
BLTYR/CAMB G72 97 G7
Mack St AIRDRIE ML6 85 G1
Maclachlan Pl HBR/GL G84 10 E4
Maclachlan Rd HBR/GL G84 10 E4
Maclay Pk KLBCH PA10 73 G8
Maclean Ct EKILN G74 116 B6
Maclean Gv EKILN G74 116 B6
Maclean Pl EKILN G74 116 B6
Maclean Sq GOV/IBX G51 78 D4
Maclean St CLYDBK G81 58 E1
GOV/IBX G51 78 D4
Maclehose Rd CUMB G67 31 J6
Maclellan Rd BRHD/NEIL G78 111 L4
Maclellan St PLKSD/SHW G41 78 D5
Macleod Crs HBR/GL G84 10 B3
Macleod Dr HBR/GL G84 10 C3
Macleod Pl EKILN G74 3 L2
Macleod St COWCAD G4 5 K6
Macleod Wy BLTYR/CAMB G72 97 J5
Macmillan Dr GRK PA19 15 K3
Macmillan Gdns
UD/BTH/TAN G71 99 G2
Macmillan St LRKH ML9 130 B7
Macneill Dr EKILN G74 116 B6
Macneill Gdns EKILN G74 116 A6
Macneil St LRKH ML9 130 B6
Macneish Wy EKILN G74 116 C6
Macnicol Ct EKILN G74 116 A6
Macnicol Pk EKILN G74 116 A6
Macnicol Pl EKILN G74 116 A6
Macpherson Pk EKILN G74 2 A1
Macphie Rd DMBTN G82 21 J5
Macrae Gdns EKILN G74 2 A1
Macrimmon Pl EKILS G75 2 E7
Mactaggart Rd CUMB G67 48 E1
Madeira La GRNKW/INVK PA16 16 D2
Madeira St GRNKW/INVK PA16 16 D2
Madison Av LNPK/KPK G44 95 H5
Madras Pl BRHD/NEIL G78 111 L3
Madras St DMNK/BRGTN G40 79 M7
Mafeking St GOV/IBX G51 78 B4
WISHAW ML2 121 K5
Mafeking Ter BRHD/NEIL G78 111 J4
Magna St MTHW ML1 120 B1
Magnolia Dr BLTYR/CAMB G72 97 M7
Magnolia Gdns LRKH ML9 131 G8
MTHW ML1 101 H6
Magnolia Pl UD/BTH/TAN G71 99 J2
Magnolia St WISHAW ML2 122 B4
Magnolia Ter
BLTYR/CAMB G72 97 M7
Magnus Crs LNPK/KPK G44 95 H6
Magnus Rd CRG/CRSL/HOU PA6 73 K1
Magpie Crs GRNKW/INVK PA16 32 F4
Mahon Ct BAIL/MDB/MHD G69 64 F1
Maidens EKILN G74 2 C2
Maidens Av NMRNS G77 114 A5
Maidland Rd PLK/PH/NH G53 93 J2
Mailerbeg Gdns
BAIL/MDB/MHD G69 46 F7
Mailing Av BSHPBGS G64 44 B8
Mainhill Av
BAIL/MDB/MHD G69 82 D5
Mainhill Dr BAIL/MDB/MHD G69 82 C5
Mainhill Pl BAIL/MDB/MHD G69 82 C5
Mainhill Rd
BAIL/MDB/MHD G69 82 F5
Main Rd CUMB G67 47 M5
DMBTN G82 19 H2
JNSTN PA5 74 C7
KBRN KA25 124 D4
PGL PA14 36 B3
PSLYS PA2 8 E7
Mains Av BEITH KA15 125 J4
GIF/THBK G46 114 B1
HBR/GL G84 10 A4
Mains Ct LNK/LMHG ML11 137 J3
Mainscroft ERSK PA8 57 J1
Mains Dr ERSK PA8 57 J2
Mains Hl ERSK PA8 57 J1
Mainshill Av ERSK PA8 57 H1
Mainshill Gdns ERSK PA8 57 H1
Mains Pl BLSH ML4 100 A6
Mains River ERSK PA8 57 J1
Mains Rd BEITH KA15 125 J4
EKILN G74 116 E5
SHOTTS ML7 71 L7
Main St AIRDRIE ML6 68 A7
AIRDRIE ML6 69 G1
AIRDRIE ML6 85 L6
ALEX/LLW G83 13 J6
BAIL/MDB/MHD G69 82 C6
BEITH KA15 125 K4
BLSH ML4 99 M5
BLTYR/CAMB G72 118 C4
BRHD/NEIL G78 111 K3
BRWEIR PA11 72 D2
BSDN G61 42 A3
BSHPBGS G64 44 B2
BTHG/ARM EH48 71 H1
CRG/CRSL/HOU PA6 55 G7
CTBR ML5 65 K5
CUMB G67 31 H4
DMBTN G82 13 J8
DMNK/BRGTN G40 79 M7
EKILN G74 3 G3
GIF/THBK G46 93 M6
GLGNK KA14 124 D7
GRNK PA15 7 H6
GRNKW/INVK PA16 32 E4
HWWD PA9 88 F5
KKNTL G66 26 D2
KSYTH G65 28 F6
LARGS KA30 106 E5
LOCHW PA12 109 J3
MLNGV G62 42 A1
MTHW ML1 122 B1
RUTH G73 96 C2
SHOTTS ML7 105 G6
UD/BTH/TAN G71 98 E4
WISHAW ML2 123 G6
WISHAW ML2 131 L2
Mains Wd ERSK PA8 57 K1
Mair St GOV/IBX G51 78 E4
Maitland Bank LRKH ML9 130 E6
Maitland Dr BSHPBGS G64 44 B1
Maitland Pl RNFRW PA4 58 B7
Maitland St COWCAD G4 4 E2
HBR/GL G84 10 D6
Malborough La North
PTCK G11 59 M6
Malborough La South
PTCK G11 59 M6
Malcolm Gdns EKILN G74 2 A4
Malcolm Pl HBR/GL G84 10 F5
Malcolm St MTHW ML1 120 C3
Malin Pl STPS/GTHM/RID G33 80 F2
Mallaig Pl GOV/IBX G51 77 K2
Mallaig Rd GOV/IBX G51 77 K2
PGL PA14 34 F3
Mallard Crs EKILS G75 126 D5
GRNKW/INVK PA16 16 A3
Mallard Pl EKILS G75 126 D5
Mallard Rd CLYDBK G81 40 B4
Mallard Ter EKILS G75 126 D5
Mallard Wy BLSH ML4 99 M2
Malleable Gdns MTHW ML1 100 C7
Malleny Gv NMRNS G77 113 H6
Malletsheugh Rd NMRNS G77 113 H6
Malloch Crs JNSTN PA5 74 B8
Malloch Pl EKILN G74 3 L4
Malloch St MRYH/FIRH G20 60 E5
Mallot's Vw NMRNS G77 113 H6
Malov Ct EKILS G75 127 H5
Malplaquet Ct CARLUKE ML8 133 K8
Malta Ter GBLS G5 79 H6
Maltbarns St MRYH/FIRH G20 61 G7
Mambeg Dr GOV/IBX G51 77 L1
Mamore Pl PLKSW/MSWD G43 94 C4
Mamore St PLKSW/MSWD G43 94 C4
Manchester Dr KVD/HLHD G12 60 A4
Manderston Meadow
NMRNS G77 113 H5
Mandora Ct CARLUKE ML8 133 K8
Manitoba Crs EKILS G75 126 E1
Mannering EKILN G74 117 K6
Mannering Ct PLKSD/SHW G41 94 C2
Mannering Rd PLKSD/SHW G41 94 C2
PSLYS PA2 90 E2
Mannoch Pl CTBR ML5 84 D6
Mannofield BSDN G61 41 K5
Manor Crs GRK PA19 15 M2

Manor Dr AIRDRIE ML6 84 E1
CTBR ML5 83 K3
Manor Ga NMRNS G77 113 M6
Manor Park Av PSLYS PA2 91 H1
Manor Rd BAIL/MDB/MHD G69 64 F5
DRUM G15 40 F8
PSLYS PA2 90 F1
SCOT G14 59 L5
Manor Vw AIRDRIE ML6 85 H7
LRKH ML9 130 E7
Manor Wy RUTH G73 96 C6
Manresa Pl COWCAD G4 4 D1
Manse Av BSDN G61 41 M4
CTBR ML5 83 K6
UD/BTH/TAN G71 99 G8
Manse Brae LNPK/KPK G44 95 H4
LRKH ML9 131 L8
Manse Ct BRHD/NEIL G78 92 D6
CARLUKE ML8 132 C5
KSYTH G65 29 K3
LARGS KA30 106 E5
Manse Crs CRG/CRSL/HOU PA6 55 H8
Manse Dr ALEX/LLW G83 13 M2
Mansefield Av
BLTYR/CAMB G72 97 G6
Mansefield Crs LARGS KA30 106 E3
OLDK G60 39 G4
Manse Gdns ALEX/LLW G83 13 L2
Manse La EKILN G74 3 G2
Mansel St SPRGB/BLRNK G21 61 M5
Manse Pl AIRDRIE ML6 84 F2
Manse Rd BAIL/MDB/MHD G69 82 E4
BRHD/NEIL G78 111 K3
BSDN G61 41 M4
CAR/SHTL G32 81 K6
CRMNK/CLK/EAG G76 115 K3
KSYTH G65 29 L3
LNK/LMHG ML11 136 F5
MTHW ML1 120 F6
OLDK G60 38 D2
SHOTTS ML7 87 K8
SHOTTS ML7 105 G6
WISHAW ML2 122 F5
Manse Road Gdns BSDN G61 41 M4
Manse St CTBR ML5 83 M4
KLMCLM PA13 53 K2
RNFRW PA4 58 D5
Manseview LRKH ML9 130 D7
Manse Vw MTHW ML1 101 M5
Mansewood Dr DMBTN G82 21 H5
Mansewood Rd GIF/THBK G46 94 B6
Mansfield Crs
CRMNK/CLK/EAG G76 114 D4
Mansfield Rd BLSH ML4 99 M6
CARD/HILL/MSPK G52 76 F2
CRMNK/CLK/EAG G76 114 E4
HMLTN ML3 129 L4
LOCHW PA12 109 J2
Mansfield St PTCK G11 60 C8
Mansion Av PGL PA14 35 G2
Mansion Ct BLTYR/CAMB G72 97 G4
Mansionhouse Av
CAR/SHTL G32 97 J2
Mansionhouse Dr
CAR/SHTL G32 81 J4
Mansionhouse Gdns
PLKSD/SHW G41 94 E3
Mansionhouse Gv
CAR/SHTL G32 81 L7
Mansionhouse Rd
CAR/SHTL G32 81 L7
PLKSD/SHW G41 94 E3
PSLY PA1 9 L4
Mansion St BLTYR/CAMB G72 97 G4
PPK/MIL G22 61 H4
Manson Pl EKILS G75 127 K5
Manuel Av BEITH KA15 125 J6
Manuel Ct KBRN KA25 124 C5
Maple Av DMBTN G82 20 B5
KKNTL G66 27 H5
NMRNS G77 113 K5
Maple Bank HMLTN ML3 119 M8
Maple Ct CUMB G67 31 M4
Maple Crs BLTYR/CAMB G72 97 M7
Maple Dr BEITH KA15 125 K3
BRHD/NEIL G78 112 D1
CLYDBK G81 39 M5
JNSTN PA5 89 M2
KKNTL G66 45 G5
LRKH ML9 130 C4
Maple Gv BAIL/MDB/MHD G69 83 G4
Maple Pl EKILS G75 126 E4
UD/BTH/TAN G71 99 K2
Maple Qd AIRDRIE ML6 85 K3
Maple Rd CUMB G67 31 M4
GRNKW/INVK PA16 16 B6
MTHW ML1 101 H4
PLKSD/SHW G41 78 B6
Maple Ter EKILS G75 126 E4
Maplewood WISHAW ML2 121 K8
Mar Av BSHPTN PA7 38 B7
Marchbank Gdns PSLY PA1 76 D5
The Marches LNK/LMHG ML11 137 H4
Marchfield Av
PSLYN/LNWD PA3 75 K2
Marchglen Pl GOV/IBX G51 77 K2
Marchmont Gdns
BSHPBGS G64 43 M8
Marchmont Ter KVD/HLHD G12 60 C7
March St PLKSD/SHW G41 78 F8
Marcus Wy MTHW ML1 120 D1
Mardale EKILN G74 2 A2
Mar Dr BSDN G61 41 M2
Maree Dr CARD/HILL/MSPK G52 77 L5
CUMB G67 48 B2
Maree Gdns BSHPBGS G64 62 B1
Maree Rd PSLYS PA2 75 G8
Marfield St CAR/SHTL G32 80 E3
Mar Gdns RUTH G73 96 D6
Margaret Av SHOTTS ML7 87 H7
Margaret Dr ALEX/LLW G83 13 J5
MTHW ML1 121 H6
Margaret Gdns HMLTN ML3 119 H4
Margaret Pl BLSH ML4 99 L5
Margaret Rd HMLTN ML3 119 H4
Margaret's Pl LRKH ML9 130 C6
Margaret St CTBR ML5 84 A5
GRK PA19 15 M2
GRNKW/INVK PA16 16 D2
Margaretvale Dr LRKH ML9 130 C8
Marguerite Av KKNTL G66 45 J4
Marguerite Gdns
UD/BTH/TAN G71 99 H8
Marian Dr MTHW ML1 101 J7
Marigold Av MTHW ML1 120 E1
Marigold Wy CARLUKE ML8 134 F1
Marina Ct BLSH ML4 99 M7
Marine Crs GOV/IBX G51 78 E4
Marine Gdns GOV/IBX G51 78 F4
Mariner Ct CLYDBK G81 40 A7
Marion St BLSH ML4 100 D4
Mariscat Rd PLKSD/SHW G41 78 E8
Marius Crs MTHW ML1 120 C1
Marjory Dr PSLYN/LNWD PA3 76 A2
Marjory Rd RNFRW PA4 58 A8
Markdow Av PLK/PH/NH G53 77 G8
Market Cl KSYTH G65 29 K2
Market End LNK/LMHG ML11 137 G5
Markethill Rd EKILN G74 2 F1
Market Pl CARLUKE ML8 133 H7
Market Rd CARLUKE ML8 133 H7
KKNTL G66 46 A3
UD/BTH/TAN G71 99 J3
Market St AIRDRIE ML6 85 G2
KSYTH G65 29 K2
UD/BTH/TAN G71 99 J3
Markinch Rd PGL PA14 34 F4
Marlach Pl PLK/PH/NH G53 93 G1
Marlborough Av PTCK G11 59 M6
Marlborough Pk EKILS G75 126 D3
Marldon La PTCK G11 59 M6
Marley Wy KKNTL G66 27 G4
Marlfield Gdns BLSH ML4 100 A2
Marloch Av PGL PA14 34 F4
Marlow St PLKSD/SHW G41 78 E6
Marlow Ter PLKSD/SHW G41 78 E6
Marmion Av HBR/GL G84 11 G8
Marmion Crs MTHW ML1 100 D7
Marmion Dr KKNTL G66 45 M2
Marmion Pl CUMB G67 48 E2
Marmion Rd CUMB G67 48 E2
PSLYS PA2 90 E2
Marne St DEN/PKHD G31 80 B3
Marnoch Dr CTBR ML5 65 K4
Marnock Ter PSLYS PA2 9 L9
Marquis Av HMLTN ML3 119 H5
Marrswood Gn HMLTN ML3 119 H6
Marrs Wynd LNK/LMHG ML11 137 J4
Marrwood Av KKNTL G66 46 B4
Marshall Gv HMLTN ML3 119 H7
Marshall La WISHAW ML2 122 A6
Marshall's La PSLY PA1 9 H5
Marshall St CTBR ML5 83 K6
LRKH ML9 130 C6
WISHAW ML2 121 M7
Mars Rd GRNKW/INVK PA16 15 J6
Martha St CGLE G1 5 G5
Martin Av ALEX/LLW G83 13 M2
Martin Ct HMLTN ML3 119 J7
Martin Crs
BAIL/MDB/MHD G69 82 C5
Martin Pl MTHW ML1 101 J6
Martinside EKILS G75 127 H5
Martin St CTBR ML5 84 D2
DMNK/BRGTN G40 79 M7
Martlet Dr JNSTN PA5 89 J3
Mart St CGLE G1 5 G9
Martyn St AIRDRIE ML6 85 E3
Martyrs Pl BSHPBGS G64 62 A2
Marwick St DEN/PKHD G31 80 B3
Mary Dr BLSH ML4 99 L7
Mary Fisher Crs DMBTN G82 21 J8
Mary Gln WISHAW ML2 122 D4
Maryhill Rd BSDN G61 42 A8
COWCAD G4 4 B2
MRYH/FIRH G20 60 D3
Maryknowe Rd MTHW ML1 101 J8
Maryland Dr
CARD/HILL/MSPK G52 77 L4
Maryland Gdns
CARD/HILL/MSPK G52 77 L4
Maryland Rd DMBTN G82 21 J4
Marypark Rd PGL PA14 36 B3
Mary Rae Rd BLSH ML4 99 L8
Maryston St
STPS/GTHM/RID G33 62 D8
Mary St GRNKW/INVK PA16 16 C5
HMLTN ML3 119 K8
JNSTN PA5 74 A7
PGL PA14 18 A8
PSLYS PA2 75 L8
Maryville Av GIF/THBK G46 94 C8
Maryville Gdns GIF/THBK G46 94 C8
Maryville Vw UD/BTH/TAN G71 98 D1
Marywell Pth BALLOCH G68 29 M8
Marywood Sq PLKSD/SHW G41 78 F8
Mary Young Pl
CRMNK/CLK/EAG G76 114 F4
Masonfield Av BALLOCH G68 30 D7
Mason La MTHW ML1 120 E3
Mason St LRKH ML9 130 E8
Masterton St COWCAD G4 61 J7
Masterton Wy
UD/BTH/TAN G71 99 H1
Matherton Av NMRNS G77 114 B5
Mathie Crs GRK PA19 15 L3
Mathieson Crs
STPS/GTHM/RID G33 63 M5
Mathieson Rd RUTH G73 96 C1
Mathieson St PSLY PA1 76 B4
Matilda Rd PLKSD/SHW G41 78 E7
Matthew McWhirter Pl
LRKH ML9 130 D5
Mauchline EKILN G74 117 K7
Mauchline Av KKNTL G66 28 A8
Mauchline Ct HMLTN ML3 118 D8
Mauchline St GBLS G5 79 G6
Mauchline Ter
GRNKW/INVK PA16 15 L6
Maukinfauld Ct CAR/SHTL G32 80 D7
Maukinfauld Gdns
DEN/PKHD G31 80 E6
Maukinfauld Rd CAR/SHTL G32 80 E7
Mauldslie Dr CARLUKE ML8 132 B3
Mauldslie Rd CARLUKE ML8 131 M6
Mauldslie St BLSH ML4 100 A5
CTBR ML5 84 A4
DMNK/BRGTN G40 80 B6
Maule Dr PTCK G11 60 A8
Mausoleum Dr HMLTN ML3 119 M5
Mavis Bank BSHPBGS G64 61 M2
Mavisbank Gdns BLSH ML4 100 A3
GOV/IBX G51 78 E4
Mavisbank Rd GOV/IBX G51 78 D4
Mavisbank St AIRDRIE ML6 84 F1
WISHAW ML2 123 J3
Mavisbank Ter JNSTN PA5 73 M8
PSLY PA1 9 K7
Mavis Rd GRNKW/INVK PA16 16 A4
Mavor Av EKILN G74 116 F6
Maxton Av BRHD/NEIL G78 92 A6
Maxton Crs WISHAW ML2 122 C3
Maxton Gv BRHD/NEIL G78 92 A7
Maxton Ter BLTYR/CAMB G72 96 F7
Maxwell Av
BAIL/MDB/MHD G69 82 A6
BSDN G61 41 L7
PLKSD/SHW G41 78 E6
Maxwell Ct BEITH KA15 125 J6
Maxwell Crs BLTYR/CAMB G72 118 D4
Maxwell Dr
BAIL/MDB/MHD G69 81 M5
EKILN G74 3 J4
ERSK PA8 38 F7
PLKSD/SHW G41 78 C6
Maxwell Gdns PLKSD/SHW G41 78 D6
Maxwell Gv PLKSD/SHW G41 78 D6
Maxwell La PLKSD/SHW G41 78 E6
Maxwell Pl BRWEIR PA11 72 D2
PLKSD/SHW G41 79 G7
UD/BTH/TAN G71 99 G4
Maxwell Rd BSHPTN PA7 38 B7
PLKSD/SHW G41 78 F6
Maxwell St
BAIL/MDB/MHD G69 82 B6
CGLE G1 4 F8
CLYDBK G81 39 M6
PGL PA14 34 E1
PSLYN/LNWD PA3 9 H3
Maxwellton Av EKILN G74 3 K3
Maxwellton Rd EKILN G74 117 J6
PGL PA14 34 F4
PSLY PA1 8 B7
Maxwellton St PSLY PA1 8 D6
Maxwelton Rd
STPS/GTHM/RID G33 62 D8
Maybank La GVH/MTFL G42 95 G1
Maybank St GVH/MTFL G42 95 G1
Mayberry Crs CAR/SHTL G32 81 J5
Mayberry Gdns CAR/SHTL G32 81 K5
Mayberry Gv CAR/SHTL G32 81 K5
Mayberry Pl BLTYR/CAMB G72 118 D2
Maybole Crs NMRNS G77 114 A6
Maybole Dr AIRDRIE ML6 85 G5
Maybole Gdns HMLTN ML3 118 D8
Maybole Gv NMRNS G77 114 A6
Maybole Pl CTBR ML5 84 D6
Maybole Rd PGL PA14 34 F4
Maybole St PLK/PH/NH G53 92 F3
Mayfield Av
CRMNK/CLK/EAG G76 114 E3
Mayfield Ct HWWD PA9 88 F5
Mayfield Crs HWWD PA9 88 F4
Mayfield Dr HWWD PA9 88 F4
Mayfield Gdns CARLUKE ML8 135 G2
Mayfield Pl CTBR ML5 84 A6
Mayfield Rd HMLTN ML3 118 F6
Mayfield St MRYH/FIRH G20 60 F5
May Gdns WISHAW ML2 122 A6
May Rd PSLYS PA2 91 L3
May St HMLTN ML3 119 K5
LARGS KA30 106 F6
May Ter GIF/THBK G46 94 C7
GVH/MTFL G42 95 H2
May Wynd HMLTN ML3 119 J5
Mc Alister Rd ALEX/LLW G83 13 K5
McAlister Rd ALEX/LLW G83 13 K5
McAllister Av AIRDRIE ML6 85 K1
McAlpine St CGLW G2 4 B8
WISHAW ML2 122 B7
McArdle Av MTHW ML1 120 B2
McArthur Pk KKNTL G66 45 J3
McArthur St PLKSW/MSWD G43 94 C3
McAslin Ct COWCAD G4 5 J4
McAslin St COWCAD G4 5 K4
McAuslan Pl HBR/GL G84 10 F5
McBride Pth
STPS/GTHM/RID G33 63 L5
McCallum Av RUTH G73 96 B3
McCallum Ct EKILN G74 116 B6
McCallum Crs GRK PA19 15 L2
McCallum Gdns BLSH ML4 99 M8
McCallum Gv EKILN G74 116 A6
McCallum Pl EKILN G74 116 B6
McCallum Rd LRKH ML9 130 D8
McCarrison Rd WISHAW ML2 123 G3
McCash Pl KKNTL G66 45 J3
McCloy Gdns PLK/PH/NH G53 92 F4
McClue Av RNFRW PA4 58 B5
McClue Rd RNFRW PA4 58 B5
McColl Pl ALEX/LLW G83 13 H4
McConnell Rd LOCHW PA12 109 H3
McCormack Gdns MTHW ML1 101 L5
McCracken Av RNFRW PA4 58 B7
McCracken Dr UD/BTH/TAN G71 99 J2
McCreery St CLYDBK G81 58 D1
McCrorie Pl KLBCH PA10 73 G6
Mc Culloch Av
UD/BTH/TAN G71 99 J4
McCulloch St PLKSD/SHW G41 78 F6
McCulloch Wy BRHD/NEIL G78 111 K3
McDonald Av JNSTN PA5 89 L1
McDonald Crs CLYDBK G81 58 D1
McDonald Pl BRHD/NEIL G78 111 L3
MTHW ML1 101 G4
McEwan Dr HBR/GL G84 10 F4
McEwan Gdns EKILN G74 116 A6
McFarlane Rd ALEX/LLW G83 13 M2
McFarlane St COWCAD G4 5 K9
PSLYN/LNWD PA3 75 J3
Mc Ghee St CLYDBK G81 40 B6
McGoldrick Pl
STPS/GTHM/RID G33 63 M5
McGowan Pl HMLTN ML3 119 G5
McGown St PSLYN/LNWD PA3 8 E1
McGregor Av AIRDRIE ML6 85 K1
ALEX/LLW G83 13 M2
RNFRW PA4 58 B7
McGregor Dr DMBTN G82 21 J6
McGregor Rd CUMB G67 30 E8
McGregor St CLYDBK G81 58 D1
GOV/IBX G51 77 M3
WISHAW ML2 121 K6
McGrigor Rd MLNGV G62 23 M6
McGurk Wy BLSH ML4 99 K4
McInnes Ct WISHAW ML2 122 B7
McInnes Pl WISHAW ML2 131 K2
McInnes St ALEX/LLW G83 13 M2
McIntosh Qd BLSH ML4 99 M8
McIntosh St DEN/PKHD G31 5 M7
McIntosh Wy MTHW ML1 120 C5
McIntyre Pl PSLYS PA2 8 F9
McIntyre Ter BLTYR/CAMB G72 97 G4
McIver St BLTYR/CAMB G72 97 K4
McKay Crs JNSTN PA5 74 B8
McKay Gv BLSH ML4 99 M5
McKay Pl EKILN G74 116 A6
NMRNS G77 113 J5
McKechnie St GOV/IBX G51 78 A2
McKenna Dr AIRDRIE ML6 84 E1
McKenzie Av CLYDBK G81 40 B5
McKenzie St PSLYN/LNWD PA3 8 C3
McKeown Gdns BLSH ML4 100 D5
McKerrell St PSLY PA1 9 L4
McKinlay Av ALEX/LLW G83 13 M2
McLaren Av RNFRW PA4 58 C8
McLaren Ct GIF/THBK G46 114 B1
McLaren Crs MRYH/FIRH G20 60 E3
McLaren Dr BLSH ML4 100 D5
McLaren Gdns MRYH/FIRH G20 60 E3
McLaren Gv EKILN G74 116 A6
McLaren Pl DMBTN G82 13 J8
McLauchlan Vw SHOTTS ML7 71 M7
Mc Laurin Crs JNSTN PA5 89 K1
McLean Crs ALEX/LLW G83 13 L1
McLean Dr BLSH ML4 99 M8
McLean Pl PSLYN/LNWD PA3 75 K3
McLees La MTHW ML1 120 B2
Mc Lelland Dr AIRDRIE ML6 68 B7
McLennan St GVH/MTFL G42 95 G2
McLeod Rd DMBTN G82 21 J6
McLeod St GRNK PA15 7 M8
McMahon Dr WISHAW ML2 123 G3
McMahon Gv BLSH ML4 100 B3
McMillan Crs BEITH KA15 125 J6
McMillan Rd WISHAW ML2 121 K7
McMillan Wy CARLUKE ML8 132 B4
McNair St CAR/SHTL G32 81 G5
McNeil Av CLYDBK G81 40 E8
McNeil Dr MTHW ML1 100 E2
McNeil Gdns GBLS G5 79 K6
Mc Neil Pl WISHAW ML2 131 L2
McNeil St GBLS G5 79 K6
McPhail Av MTHW ML1 101 M4
McPhail St DMNK/BRGTN G40 79 L6
Mc Phail St GRNK PA15 7 L8
McPhater St COWCAD G4 4 E3
McPherson Crs AIRDRIE ML6 85 L8
McPherson Dr GRK PA19 15 K3
UD/BTH/TAN G71 99 H7
McPherson St BLSH ML4 100 D4
McShannon Gv BLSH ML4 100 A6
McSparran Rd KSYTH G65 29 M6
McUlloch Wy
STPS/GTHM/RID G33 63 L5
Meadow Av BLTYR/CAMB G72 118 D4
ERSK PA8 57 J1
Meadowbank Pl NMRNS G77 113 K4
Meadowbank Rd LARGS KA30 107 G4
Meadowbank St DMBTN G82 20 F6
Meadowburn BSHPBGS G64 43 M7
Meadowburn Av KKNTL G66 45 L5
NMRNS G77 113 K4
Meadowburn Rd WISHAW ML2 122 C6
Meadow Cl EKILS G75 126 D6
Meadow Ct CARLUKE ML8 133 L8
DMBTN G82 20 F5
Meadowfield Pl WISHAW ML2 123 J3
Meadowhead Av
BAIL/MDB/MHD G69 46 F8
Meadowhead Rd AIRDRIE ML6 67 M6
WISHAW ML2 121 K5
Meadowhill NMRNS G77 113 K4
Meadowhill St LRKH ML9 130 D6
Meadow La RNFRW PA4 58 D4
Meadowpark St
DEN/PKHD G31 80 B3
Meadow Ri NMRNS G77 113 J4
Meadow Rd CARLUKE ML8 135 G5
DMBTN G82 21 G6
MTHW ML1 121 G4
PTCK G11 78 A1
Meadows Av LRKH ML9 130 D6
Meadows Dr ERSK PA8 57 J1
Meadowside BEITH KA15 125 J5
HMLTN ML3 129 K4
Meadowside Av JNSTN PA5 74 D8
Meadowside Gdns AIRDRIE ML6 85 K2
Meadowside Pl AIRDRIE ML6 85 K2
Meadowside Rd KSYTH G65 28 E2
Meadowside St GOV/IBX G51 78 A1
RNFRW PA4 58 D4
The Meadows
CRG/CRSL/HOU PA6 73 L1
HBR/GL G84 10 F3
Meadow St CTBR ML5 84 B5
Meadow Vw AIRDRIE ML6 68 A6
CUMB G67 31 J6
Meadow Wk CTBR ML5 84 B4
Meadow Wy NMRNS G77 113 K4
Meadowwell St CAR/SHTL G32 81 H5
Meadside Av KLBCH PA10 73 G6
Meadside Rd KLBCH PA10 73 G6
Mealkirk St CLYDBK G81 40 C2
Mealybrae Rd BSHPBGS G64 25 K7
Mearns Ct HMLTN ML3 129 L3
Mearnscroft Gdns NMRNS G77 113 M6
Mearnscroft Rd NMRNS G77 113 M6
Mearnskirk Rd NMRNS G77 113 K8
Mearns Rd
CRMNK/CLK/EAG G76 114 D3
MTHW ML1 120 C1
NMRNS G77 113 L7
Mearns St GRNK PA15 6 D5
Mearns Ter GRNK PA15 6 C5
Medine Av BEITH KA15 125 K4
Medine Ct BEITH KA15 125 K4
Medlar Ct BLTYR/CAMB G72 97 M7
Medlar Rd CUMB G67 31 K7
Medrox Gdns CUMB G67 47 M5
Medwin Ct EKILS G75 126 B3
Medwin Gdns EKILS G75 126 B3
Medwin St BLTYR/CAMB G72 97 K5
Medwyn St SCOT G14 59 L7
Meek Pl BLTYR/CAMB G72 97 H5
Meetinghouse La PSLY PA1 9 G4
Megan St DMNK/BRGTN G40 79 M6
Meikle Av RNFRW PA4 58 C7
Meikle Bin Brae KKNTL G66 26 E3
Meikle Crs AIRDRIE ML6 67 K1
HMLTN ML3 129 J3
Meikle Drumgray Rd
AIRDRIE ML6 67 K1
Meikle Earnock Rd
HMLTN ML3 128 F4
Meiklehill Ct KKNTL G66 45 L1
Meiklehill Rd KKNTL G66 45 L1
Meiklerig Crs PLK/PH/NH G53 77 J7
Meikleriggs Dr PSLYS PA2 91 G1
Meikle Rd PLK/PH/NH G53 93 J1
Meiklewood Rd GOV/IBX G51 77 K3
Melbourne Av CLYDBK G81 39 K5
EKILS G75 2 A8
Melbourne Ct GIF/THBK G46 94 D7
Melbourne Gn EKILS G75 2 A8
Melbourne St DMNK/BRGTN G40 5 M8
Meldon Pl GOV/IBX G51 77 K2
Meldrum Gdns PLKSD/SHW G41 78 D8
Meldrum Mains AIRDRIE ML6 66 E5
Meldrum St CLYDBK G81 58 D1
Melford Av GIF/THBK G46 94 D8
KKNTL G66 45 H2
SHOTTS ML7 105 H6
Melford Rd BLSH ML4 99 L4
Melfort Av CLYDBK G81 40 C6
PLKSD/SHW G41 78 B6
Melfort Gdns KLBCH PA10 89 J1
Melfort Rd HMLTN ML3 118 E7
WMYSB PA18 50 B1
Mellerstain Dr SCOT G14 58 E3
Melness Pl GOV/IBX G51 77 K2
Melrose Av AIRDRIE ML6 85 K7
BAIL/MDB/MHD G69 82 F5
MTHW ML1 101 H4
PSLYN/LNWD PA3 74 B5
PSLYS PA2 91 G2
RUTH G73 96 B3
Melrose Crs WISHAW ML2 122 A4
Melrose Gdns MRYH/FIRH G20 60 F7
Melrose Pl BLTYR/CAMB G72 118 C1
CTBR ML5 83 M3
LRKH ML9 130 C8
Melrose Rd CUMB G67 48 E2
PGL PA14 34 F3
Melrose St COWCAD G4 4 B2
HMLTN ML3 119 H5
Melrose Ter EKILN G74 3 G3
HMLTN ML3 119 H4
Melvaig Pl MRYH/FIRH G20 60 D5
Melvick Pl GOV/IBX G51 77 K2
Melville Crs MTHW ML1 120 E3
Melville Gdns BSHPBGS G64 44 A8
Melville Pk EKILN G74 3 M1
Melville Pl CARLUKE ML8 133 G7
Melville St PLKSD/SHW G41 78 F7
Melvinhall Rd LNK/LMHG ML11 137 G4
Memel St PPK/MIL G22 61 L5
Memorial Wy MTHW ML1 101 J3
Memus Av
CARD/HILL/MSPK G52 77 J5
Mendip La EKILS G75 126 D6
Mennock Ct HMLTN ML3 118 E8
Mennock Dr BSHPBGS G64 44 A6
Mennock St MTHW ML1 102 C7
Menock Rd LNPK/KPK G44 95 H4
Menteith Av BSHPBGS G64 62 B1
Menteith Dr RUTH G73 96 D8
Menteith Gdns BSDN G61 41 J1
Menteith Pl RUTH G73 96 D8
Menteith Rd MTHW ML1 120 E3
Menzies Dr SPRGB/BLRNK G21 62 A5
Menzies Pl SPRGB/BLRNK G21 62 A5
Menzies Rd SPRGB/BLRNK G21 62 A5
Merchant La CGLE G1 5 G9
Merchants Cl KLBCH PA10 73 G7
Merchiston Av
PSLYN/LNWD PA3 73 M5
Merchiston Dr JNSTN PA5 73 K5
Merchiston St CAR/SHTL G32 80 E3
Mere Ct BALLOCH G68 30 D3
Merkins Av DMBTN G82 21 H4
Merkland Dr KKNTL G66 46 A1
Merkland Pl KKNTL G66 45 M1
Merkland Rd CTBR ML5 65 J8
Merkland St PTCK G11 60 B8
Merkland Wy EKILS G75 126 F6
Merlewood Av
UD/BTH/TAN G71 99 H6
Merlin Av BLSH ML4 100 A1
GRNKW/INVK PA16 16 B3
Merlinford Av RNFRW PA4 58 E6
Merlinford Crs RNFRW PA4 58 E6
Merlinford Dr RNFRW PA4 58 E6
Merlinford Wy RNFRW PA4 58 E6
Merlin La GRNKW/INVK PA16 16 A4
Merlin Wy PSLYN/LNWD PA3 76 B2
Merrick Gdns BSDN G61 41 J2
GOV/IBX G51 78 B5
HMLTN ML3 129 L7
Merrick Ter UD/BTH/TAN G71 99 H3
Merrick Wy RUTH G73 96 B7
Merryburn Av GIF/THBK G46 94 D6
Merry Ct BLTYR/CAMB G72 118 E4
Merrycrest Av GIF/THBK G46 94 D6
Merrycroft Av GIF/THBK G46 94 D6
Merryflats KSYTH G65 28 F6
Merryland Pl GOV/IBX G51 78 C3
Merryland St GOV/IBX G51 78 C3
Merrylee Av PGL PA14 34 D3
Merrylee Crs GIF/THBK G46 94 C5
Merrylee Pk GIF/THBK G46 94 C5
Merrylee Park Av GIF/THBK G46 94 D6
Merrylee Rd PLKSW/MSWD G43 94 E5
Merrylees Rd
BLTYR/CAMB G72 118 C3
Merrystone St CTBR ML5 83 M3
Merry St MTHW ML1 120 F1
Merryton Av DRUM G15 41 H6
GIF/THBK G46 94 C6
Merryton Gdns DRUM G15 41 H6
Merryton Pl DRUM G15 41 H6
Merryton Rd LRKH ML9 130 B4
MTHW ML1 121 H7
Merryton St LRKH ML9 130 B4
Merryvale Av GIF/THBK G46 94 D6
Merryvale Pl GIF/THBK G46 94 C5
Merton Dr
CARD/HILL/MSPK G52 77 G4
Meryon Gdns CAR/SHTL G32 81 K8
Meryon Rd CAR/SHTL G32 81 K7
Methil Rd PGL PA14 34 F4
Methil St SCOT G14 59 J6
Methil Wy BLTYR/CAMB G72 118 D8
Methlan Park Gdns
DMBTN G82 20 D8
Methlick Av AIRDRIE ML6 84 E5
Methuen Rd PSLYN/LNWD PA3 75 M2
Methven Av BSDN G61 42 B5
Methven Pl EKILN G74 2 B4
Methven Rd GIF/THBK G46 114 A4
Methven St CLYDBK G81 39 M6
DEN/PKHD G31 80 D7
Metropole La CGLE G1 4 F9
Mews La GRNKW/INVK PA16 16 C1
PSLYN/LNWD PA3 75 M3
Mey Ct NMRNS G77 113 G5
Mey Pl NMRNS G77 113 G5
Mharie Pl ALEX/LLW G83 13 L8
Michael McParland Dr
BSHPBGS G64 44 B2
Michael Ter AIRDRIE ML6 85 K8
Micklehouse Ov
BAIL/MDB/MHD G69 82 B4
Micklehouse Pl
BAIL/MDB/MHD G69 82 B4

Micklehouse Rd
BAIL/MDB/MHD G69 ... 82 B4
Micklehouse Wynd
BAIL/MDB/MHD G69 ... 82 B4
Midas Pl *BLSH* ML4 ... 100 E4
Mid Av *PGL* PA14 ... 34 F2
Mid Barrwood Rd *KSYTH* G65 ... 29 M3
Mid Barwood Rd *KSYTH* G65 ... 30 A1
Mid Carbarns *WISHAW* ML2 ... 121 K8
Midcroft Av *LNPK/KPK* G44 ... 95 L5
Middlefield *EKILS* G75 ... 127 H5
Middlehouse Ct *CARLUKE* ML8 ... 132 F7
Middlemuir Rd *KKNTL* G66 ... 45 K4
Middlepenny Pl *PGL* PA14 ... 36 B3
Middlepenny Rd *PGL* PA14 ... 36 B3
Middlerigg Rd *BALLOCH* G68 ... 30 D7
Middlesex Gdns
PLKSD/SHW G41 ... 78 E5
Middlesex St *PLKSD/SHW* G41 ... 78 E5
Middleton Crs *PSLYN/LNWD* PA3 ... 8 B1
Middleton Dr *HBR/GL* G84 ... 10 F8
LARGS KA30 ... 106 F4
MLNGV G62 ... 24 B8
Middleton La *HBR/GL* G84 ... 10 F7
Middleton Pl *BALLOCH* G68 ... 29 M8
Middleton Rd *PSLYN/LNWD* PA3 ... 8 B1
PSLYN/LNWD PA3 ... 74 C3
Middleton St *ALEX/LLW* G83 ... 13 J6
GOV/IBX G51 ... 78 C4
Middle Ward St *CLYDBK* G81 ... 40 D2
Midfaulds Av *RNFRW* PA4 ... 58 E7
Midland St *CGLE* G1 ... 4 E8
Midlem Dr
CARD/HILL/MSPK G52 ... 77 J4
Midlem Ov
CARD/HILL/MSPK G52 ... 77 J4
Mid-loan St *CARLUKE* ML8 ... 134 E5
Midlock St *GOV/IBX* G51 ... 78 C5
Midlothian Dr *PLKSD/SHW* G41 ... 94 D1
Mid Pk *EKILS* G75 ... 2 E7
Mid Rd *BEITH* KA15 ... 125 J4
CUMB G67 ... 48 F3
Midton Rd *HWWD* PA9 ... 89 H4
Midton St *SPRGB/BLRNK* G21 ... 61 M7
Mid-wharf St *COWCAD* G4 ... 4 F1
Migvie Pl *MRYH/FIRH* G20 ... 60 C5
Milford *EKILS* G75 ... 126 E3
Milford St *STPS/GTHM/RID* G33 ... 81 G2
Millands Av *BLTYR/CAMB* G72 ... 118 C1
Millarbank St
SPRGB/BLRNK G21 ... 61 L6
Millard Av *MTHW* ML1 ... 101 H7
Millar Gv *HMLTN* ML3 ... 119 H7
Millar Pl *BSHPBGS* G64 ... 62 D2
Millars Pl *KKNTL* G66 ... 45 K6
Millarston Av *PSLY* PA1 ... 75 G6
Millarston Dr *PSLY* PA1 ... 75 G6
Millar St *GRNK* PA15 ... 7 H9
PSLY PA1 ... 9 K4
Millbank Av *BLSH* ML4 ... 100 B6
Millbank Ct *CTBR* ML5 ... 83 M7
Millbank Rd *PGL* PA14 ... 34 C2
WISHAW ML2 ... 121 M7
Millbeg Crs
STPS/GTHM/RID G33 ... 81 M5
Millbeg Pl *STPS/GTHM/RID* G33 ... 81 L5
Mill Brae *BRWEIR* PA11 ... 72 D2
Millbrae Av
BAIL/MDB/MHD G69 ... 64 D2
Millbrae Crs *CLYDBK* G81 ... 58 D2
GVH/MTFL G42 ... 94 E3
Millbrae Gdns *GVH/MTFL* G42 ... 94 F3
Millbrae Rd *GVH/MTFL* G42 ... 94 F3
Millbrix Av *SCOT* G14 ... 59 G4
Millbrook *EKILN* G74 ... 126 D1
Millburn Av *RNFRW* PA4 ... 58 D6
RUTH G73 ... 96 A4
Millburn Ct *EKILS* G75 ... 126 B3
Millburn Crs *DMBTN* G82 ... 21 H7
Millburn Dr *KLMCLM* PA13 ... 53 H2
RNFRW PA4 ... 58 E6
Millburn Gdns *EKILS* G75 ... 126 B3
LARGS KA30 ... 106 F5
Millburn Ga *LRKH* ML9 ... 131 H8
Millburn Rd *ALEX/LLW* G83 ... 13 J7
DMBTN G82 ... 21 H7
LRKH ML9 ... 131 H8
PGL PA14 ... 34 C2
RNFRW PA4 ... 58 E6
Millburn St *KKNTL* G66 ... 26 D2
MTHW ML1 ... 120 E2
SPRGB/BLRNK G21 ... 80 A1
Millburn Wy *EKILS* G75 ... 126 B3
RNFRW PA4 ... 58 E6
Mill Ct *HMLTN* ML3 ... 119 J8
KBRN KA25 ... 124 D4
RUTH G73 ... 96 A2
Mill Crs *BSHPBGS* G64 ... 44 C1
DMNK/BRGTN G40 ... 79 M7
Millcroft Rd *AIRDRIE* ML6 ... 49 G5
CUMB G67 ... 48 E5
RUTH G73 ... 79 M8
Milldam Rd *CLYDBK* G81 ... 40 C2
Millenium Gv *ESTRH* G34 ... 82 C3
Millennium Ct *ESTRH* G34 ... 82 C2
Millennium Gdns *ESTRH* G34 ... 82 C3
Miller Cl *BSHPBGS* G64 ... 62 D2
Miller Ct *DMBTN* G82 ... 21 H6
Miller Dr *BSHPBGS* G64 ... 62 D2
Millerfield Pl *DMNK/BRGTN* G40 ... 80 B7
Miller Field Pl *HMLTN* ML3 ... 119 M7
Millerfield Rd
DMNK/BRGTN G40 ... 80 B7
Miller Gdns *BSHPBGS* G64 ... 62 D2
Miller Pl *SHOTTS* ML7 ... 71 M6
Miller Rd *ALEX/LLW* G83 ... 13 M2
Millerslea Gdns *HBR/GL* G84 ... 10 F6
Millersneuk Av *KKNTL* G66 ... 45 K6
Millersneuk Ct *KKNTL* G66 ... 45 K6
Millersneuk Crs
STPS/GTHM/RID G33 ... 63 G5
Millersneuk Dr *KKNTL* G66 ... 45 K6
Millersneuk Rd *KKNTL* G66 ... 45 K6
Miller's Pl *AIRDRIE* ML6 ... 85 H2
Millerston St *DEN/PKHD* G31 ... 80 B4
Miller St *BAIL/MDB/MHD* G69 ... 82 B6
CARLUKE ML8 ... 133 J7
CGLW G2 ... 4 F7
CLYDBK G81 ... 40 B8
CTBR ML5 ... 84 B4
DMBTN G82 ... 21 H6
HMLTN ML3 ... 119 M7
JNSTN PA5 ... 74 B7
LRKH ML9 ... 130 C6
SHOTTS ML7 ... 71 L6
WISHAW ML2 ... 122 A6
Miller Wk *BSHPBGS* G64 ... 62 D2
Millfield Av *ERSK* PA8 ... 56 F1
MTHW ML1 ... 120 F1
Millfield Crs *ERSK* PA8 ... 57 G1
Millfield Dr *ERSK* PA8 ... 57 G2
Millfield Gdns *ERSK* PA8 ... 57 G1
Millfield Hl *ERSK* PA8 ... 56 F1
Millfield Mdw *ERSK* PA8 ... 56 F1
Millfield Pl *ERSK* PA8 ... 56 F1
Millfield Vw *ERSK* PA8 ... 56 F1
Millfield Wk *ERSK* PA8 ... 57 G2
Millfield Wynd *ERSK* PA8 ... 56 F2
Millford Dr *PSLYN/LNWD* PA3 ... 74 B5
Millgate Av *UD/BTH/TAN* G71 ... 98 F2
Millgate Ct *UD/BTH/TAN* G71 ... 98 F3
Millgate Rd *HMLTN* ML3 ... 129 J1
Mill Gv *BLTYR/CAMB* G72 ... 97 K5
HMLTN ML3 ... 119 J8
Millhall Rd
CRMNK/CLK/EAG G76 ... 126 A8
Millheugh Brae *LRKH* ML9 ... 130 A7
Millheugh Pl *BLTYR/CAMB* G72 ... 118 C4
Millheugh Rd *LRKH* ML9 ... 130 A8
Millholm Rd *LNPK/KPK* G44 ... 95 H6
Millhouse Crs *MRYH/FIRH* G20 ... 60 B3
Millhouse Dr *MRYH/FIRH* G20 ... 60 C3
Millhouse Rd
GRNKW/INVK PA16 ... 32 F4
Millichen Rd *SMSTN* G23 ... 42 C5
Millig St *HBR/GL* G84 ... 10 C4
Milliken Dr *KLBCH* PA10 ... 73 J8
Milliken Park Rd *KLBCH* PA10 ... 89 J1
Milliken Rd *KLBCH* PA10 ... 73 J8
Mill Loan *AIRDRIE* ML6 ... 85 G1
Mill of Gryffe La *BRWEIR* PA11 ... 72 D2
Mill of Gryffe Rd *BRWEIR* PA11 ... 72 D2
Mill Pl *PSLYN/LNWD* PA3 ... 74 A4
UD/BTH/TAN G71 ... 98 F4
Millport Av *LNPK/KPK* G44 ... 95 J3
Millport Rd *PGL* PA14 ... 34 F4
Mill Rig *EKILS* G75 ... 127 G5
Mill Ri *KKNTL* G66 ... 45 K6
Mill Rd *AIRDRIE* ML6 ... 67 G8
BLTYR/CAMB G72 ... 97 J4
CARLUKE ML8 ... 133 H8
CLYDBK G81 ... 58 D2
DMBTN G82 ... 19 G1
HMLTN ML3 ... 129 J1
KBRN KA25 ... 124 D4
KSYTH G65 ... 28 E3
MTHW ML1 ... 120 F1
SHOTTS ML7 ... 71 M7
UD/BTH/TAN G71 ... 119 G1
WISHAW ML2 ... 123 J6
Millroad Dr *DMNK/BRGTN* G40 ... 5 M9
Millroad St *DMNK/BRGTN* G40 ... 5 L9
Millstream Ct *PSLY* PA1 ... 9 L6
Millstream Crs *AIRDRIE* ML6 ... 68 F5
Mill St *AIRDRIE* ML6 ... 68 F4
DMNK/BRGTN G40 ... 79 M7
GRNK PA15 ... 6 B6
PSLY PA1 ... 9 J5
RUTH G73 ... 96 A4
Millview *BRHD/NEIL* G78 ... 92 D6
Millview Mdw *BRHD/NEIL* G78 ... 111 J3
Millview Pl *PLK/PH/NH* G53 ... 93 H5
Millview Ter *BRHD/NEIL* G78 ... 111 J3
Mill Wk *BLTYR/CAMB* G72 ... 97 K5
Mill Wy *KKNTL* G66 ... 46 A3
Millwood St *PLKSD/SHW* G41 ... 94 E2
Milnbank St *DEN/PKHD* G31 ... 80 A2
Milncroft Pl
STPS/GTHM/RID G33 ... 81 G1
Milncroft Rd
STPS/GTHM/RID G33 ... 81 G1
Milner La *KNTSWD* G13 ... 59 L4
Milner Rd *KNTSWD* G13 ... 59 L4
Milne Wy *UD/BTH/TAN* G71 ... 99 G4
Milngavie Rd *BSDN* G61 ... 41 M6
Milnpark Gdns *PLKSD/SHW* G41 ... 78 D5
Milnpark St *PLKSD/SHW* G41 ... 78 E5
Milnwood Dr *MTHW* ML1 ... 100 C7
Milovaig Av *SMSTN* G23 ... 42 D8
Milovaig St *SMSTN* G23 ... 60 D1
Milrig Rd *RUTH* G73 ... 95 M3
Milroy Gdns *BLSH* ML4 ... 100 A1
Milton Av *BLTYR/CAMB* G72 ... 96 E5
Milton Brae *DMBTN* G82 ... 21 K7
Milton Ct *DMBTN* G82 ... 21 M8
Milton Crs *CARLUKE* ML8 ... 133 G8
Milton Douglas Rd *CLYDBK* G81 ... 40 B4
Milton Dr *BSHPBGS* G64 ... 61 L3
Milton Gdns *UD/BTH/TAN* G71 ... 98 E2
Milton Hl *DMBTN* G82 ... 37 M1
Milton Mains Rd *CLYDBK* G81 ... 40 A4
Milton Pk *KBRN* KA25 ... 124 D3
Milton Qd *KBRN* KA25 ... 124 C2
Milton Rd *CARLUKE* ML8 ... 134 C2
EKILN G74 ... 116 A8
KBRN KA25 ... 124 C3
KKNTL G66 ... 26 E3
PGL PA14 ... 34 E4
Milton St *AIRDRIE* ML6 ... 85 G1
CARLUKE ML8 ... 133 G7
COWCAD G4 ... 4 F3
HMLTN ML3 ... 119 G5
MTHW ML1 ... 120 E1
Milton Ter *HMLTN* ML3 ... 119 G5
Milverton Av *BSDN* G61 ... 41 J3
Milverton Rd *GIF/THBK* G46 ... 114 A1
Mimosa Rd *BRWEIR* PA11 ... 72 D2
Minard Rd *PGL* PA14 ... 34 E4
PLKSD/SHW G41 ... 94 E1
SHOTTS ML7 ... 104 D3
Minard Wy *UD/BTH/TAN* G71 ... 99 G3
Mincher Crs *MTHW* ML1 ... 120 E5
Minch Wy *AIRDRIE* ML6 ... 85 K4
Minella Gdns *BLSH* ML4 ... 100 A1
Minerva St *KVGV* G3 ... 78 E2
Minerva Ter *GRNKW/INVK* PA16 ... 15 K6
Minerva Wy *KVGV* G3 ... 78 D2
Mingarry La *MRYH/FIRH* G20 ... 60 E6
Mingarry St *MRYH/FIRH* G20 ... 60 E6
Mingulay Crs *PPK/MIL* G22 ... 61 K2
Mingulay Pl *PPK/MIL* G22 ... 61 L2
Mingulay St *PPK/MIL* G22 ... 61 L2
Ministers Pk *EKILN* G74 ... 115 M6
Minmoir Rd *PLK/PH/NH* G53 ... 92 F2
Minstrel Rd *KNTSWD* G13 ... 41 K8
Minthill Pl *SHOTTS* ML7 ... 71 K7
Minto Av *RUTH* G73 ... 96 D6
Minto Crs *CARD/HILL/MSPK* G52 ... 77 M4
Minto Pk *WISHAW* ML2 ... 122 C3
Minto St *CARD/HILL/MSPK* G52 ... 77 M4
GRNKW/INVK PA16 ... 16 D5
Mireton St *PPK/MIL* G22 ... 61 H5
Mirin Dr *PSLYN/LNWD* PA3 ... 75 L3
Mirren Dr *CLYDBK* G81 ... 39 M3
Mirren's Shore *PGL* PA14 ... 18 C8
Mirrin Wynd *PSLYN/LNWD* PA3 ... 75 K3
Mirrlees Dr *KVD/HLHD* G12 ... 60 C6
Mirrlees La *KVD/HLHD* G12 ... 60 C6
Mission Pl *MTHW* ML1 ... 120 E1
Mitchell Av *BLTYR/CAMB* G72 ... 97 L4
RNFRW PA4 ... 58 B7
Mitchell Dr *DMBTN* G82 ... 19 H4
MLNGV G62 ... 42 C1
RUTH G73 ... 96 B4
Mitchell Gv *EKILN* G74 ... 2 A3
Mitchell Hill Rd *CSMK* G45 ... 95 M8
Mitchell La *CGLE* G1 ... 4 E7
Mitchell Rd *CUMB* G67 ... 30 F7
Mitchell St *AIRDRIE* ML6 ... 84 F1
BEITH KA15 ... 125 K4
CGLE G1 ... 4 E7
CTBR ML5 ... 83 H5
GRNK PA15 ... 17 M7
Mitchell Wy *ALEX/LLW* G83 ... 13 K5
Mitchison Rd *CUMB* G67 ... 31 G6
Mitre Ct *PTCK* G11 ... 59 M6
Mitre La *SCOT* G14 ... 59 K5
Mitre La West *SCOT* G14 ... 59 K5
Mitre Rd *PTCK* G11 ... 59 M5
Moat Av *KNTSWD* G13 ... 59 J2
Mochrum Rd
PLKSW/MSWD G43 ... 94 E4
Moffat Ct *EKILS* G75 ... 126 B3
Moffathill *AIRDRIE* ML6 ... 85 L5
Moffat Pl *BLTYR/CAMB* G72 ... 118 D1
CTBR ML5 ... 84 D5
EKILS G75 ... 126 B3
Moffat Rd *AIRDRIE* ML6 ... 85 M2
Moffat St *GBLS* G5 ... 79 K6
GRNK PA15 ... 7 K8
Moffat Vw *AIRDRIE* ML6 ... 68 A7
Mogarth Av *PSLYS* PA2 ... 90 F2
Moidart Av *RNFRW* PA4 ... 58 B5
Moidart Ct *BRHD/NEIL* G78 ... 92 B5
Moidart Crs
CARD/HILL/MSPK G52 ... 77 L4
Moidart Gdns *KKNTL* G66 ... 46 B1
NMRNS G77 ... 113 L3
Moidart Pl
CARD/HILL/MSPK G52 ... 77 L4
Moidart Rd
CARD/HILL/MSPK G52 ... 77 L4
PGL PA14 ... 34 E3
Moir St *CGLE* G1 ... 5 J9
Molendinar St *CGLE* G1 ... 5 J8
Molendinar Ter
BRHD/NEIL G78 ... 111 J4
Mollinsburn Rd *AIRDRIE* ML6 ... 66 C3
CTBR ML5 ... 65 M2
CUMB G67 ... 47 L7
Mollinsburn St
SPRGB/BLRNK G21 ... 61 L7
Mollins Ct *BALLOCH* G68 ... 47 K5
Mollins Rd *BALLOCH* G68 ... 47 H1
Mollison Av *SHOTTS* ML7 ... 71 L6
Monach Rd *PGL* PA14 ... 35 G3
STPS/GTHM/RID G33 ... 81 J2
Monaebrook Pl *HBR/GL* G84 ... 10 F7
Monar Dr *PPK/MIL* G22 ... 61 H7
Monar St *PPK/MIL* G22 ... 61 H7
Monart Pl *MRYH/FIRH* G20 ... 60 F6
Moncrieff Av *KKNTL* G66 ... 45 K5
Moncrieffe Rd *AIRDRIE* ML6 ... 85 K5
Moncrieff Gdns *KKNTL* G66 ... 45 K5
Moncrieff St *PSLYN/LNWD* PA3 ... 9 G3
Moncur St *DMNK/BRGTN* G40 ... 5 L9
Moness Dr
CARD/HILL/MSPK G52 ... 77 L5
Money Gv *MTHW* ML1 ... 121 H5
Monieburgh Crs *KSYTH* G65 ... 29 L1
Monieburgh Rd *KSYTH* G65 ... 29 L1
Monifieth Av
CARD/HILL/MSPK G52 ... 77 K6
Monikie Gdns *BSHPBGS* G64 ... 62 D1
Monkcastle Dr
BLTYR/CAMB G72 ... 97 G4
Monkland Av *KKNTL* G66 ... 45 K4
Monkland St *AIRDRIE* ML6 ... 85 H2
Monkland Ter *CTBR* ML5 ... 65 K4
Monkland Vw *AIRDRIE* ML6 ... 85 H7
UD/BTH/TAN G71 ... 99 G1
Monkland View Crs
BAIL/MDB/MHD G69 ... 83 G5
Monksbridge Av *KNTSWD* G13 ... 41 K8
Monkscourt Av *AIRDRIE* ML6 ... 84 E1
Monkscroft Av *PTCK* G11 ... 60 A7
Monkscroft Ct *PTCK* G11 ... 60 A8
Monks La *CARLUKE* ML8 ... 134 E5
Monks Rd *AIRDRIE* ML6 ... 85 J5
Monkton Brae
BAIL/MDB/MHD G69 ... 64 C1
Monkton Crs *CTBR* ML5 ... 83 L6
Monkton Dr *DRUM* G15 ... 41 H8
Monkton Gdns *NMRNS* G77 ... 114 A6
Monmouth Av *KVD/HLHD* G12 ... 60 A5
Monreith Av *BSDN* G61 ... 41 L7
Monreith Rd *PLKSW/MSWD* G43 ... 94 E4
Monreith Rd East
LNPK/KPK G44 ... 95 G5
Monroe Dr *UD/BTH/TAN* G71 ... 98 F1
Monroe Pl *UD/BTH/TAN* G71 ... 98 F1
Montague La *KVD/HLHD* G12 ... 60 B6
Montague St *COWCAD* G4 ... 60 F8
Montalto Av *MTHW* ML1 ... 101 G8
Montclair Pl *PSLYN/LNWD* PA3 ... 74 A4
Montego Gn *EKILS* G75 ... 126 D1
Monteith Dr
CRMNK/CLK/EAG G76 ... 115 G2
Monteith Gdns
CRMNK/CLK/EAG G76 ... 114 F2
Monteith Pl *DMNK/BRGTN* G40 ... 79 L5
Monteith Rw *CGLE* G1 ... 5 J9
DMNK/BRGTN G40 ... 79 L5
Montford Av *LNPK/KPK* G44 ... 95 L3
Montgarrie St *GOV/IBX* G51 ... 77 K3
Montgomerie Dr *SKLM* PA17 ... 50 C4
Montgomerieston Pl
KBRN KA25 ... 124 C4
Montgomerieston St
KBRN KA25 ... 124 C4
Montgomerie St *PGL* PA14 ... 34 D1
Montgomerie Ter *SKLM* PA17 ... 50 B5
Montgomery Av *BEITH* KA15 ... 125 L5
CTBR ML5 ... 83 M2
PSLYN/LNWD PA3 ... 76 B1
Montgomery Crs
WISHAW ML2 ... 121 L8
Montgomery Dr *GIF/THBK* G46 ... 114 C1
KLBCH PA10 ... 73 G6
Montgomery Pl *EKILN* G74 ... 2 F4
LRKH ML9 ... 130 D7
Montgomery Rd
PSLYN/LNWD PA3 ... 76 A1
Montgomery St
BLTYR/CAMB G72 ... 97 K5
DMNK/BRGTN G40 ... 80 A6
EKILN G74 ... 3 G4
LRKH ML9 ... 130 C5
Montgomery Ter *KKNTL* G66 ... 27 H5
Montport Ga *BRHD/NEIL* G78 ... 92 E6
Montraive St *RUTH* G73 ... 96 C1
Montrave St
CARD/HILL/MSPK G52 ... 77 K5
Montreal Pk *EKILS* G75 ... 2 B6
Montrose Av *CAR/SHTL* G32 ... 97 H1
CARD/HILL/MSPK G52 ... 76 F2
PGL PA14 ... 34 E3
Montrose Crs *HMLTN* ML3 ... 119 K6
Montrose Dr *BSDN* G61 ... 41 L2
Montrose Gdns
BLTYR/CAMB G72 ... 98 C8
KSYTH G65 ... 29 J1
MLNGV G62 ... 24 A7
Montrose Pl *PSLYN/LNWD* PA3 ... 74 A4
Montrose Rd *PSLYS* PA2 ... 90 F2
Montrose St *CGLE* G1 ... 5 H7
CLYDBK G81 ... 40 B7
MTHW ML1 ... 100 D8
Montrose Ter *BRWEIR* PA11 ... 72 D3
BSHPBGS G64 ... 62 C3
Monymusk Gdns *BSHPBGS* G64 ... 44 D8
Monymusk Pl *DRUM* G15 ... 40 E4
Moodiesburn St
STPS/GTHM/RID G33 ... 62 D8
Moorburn Av *GIF/THBK* G46 ... 94 B7
Moorburn Pl *PSLYN/LNWD* PA3 ... 73 M4
Moorburn Rd *LARGS* KA30 ... 106 F4
Moorcroft Dr *AIRDRIE* ML6 ... 85 L2
Moorcroft Rd *NMRNS* G77 ... 113 J6
Moore Dr *BSDN* G61 ... 41 M6
HBR/GL G84 ... 11 G8
Moore Gdns *HMLTN* ML3 ... 129 L3
Moore St *DMNK/BRGTN* G40 ... 5 M8
MTHW ML1 ... 101 G6
Moorfield Av *PGL* PA14 ... 34 D3
Moorfield Crs *AIRDRIE* ML6 ... 85 L2
Moorfield La *GRK* PA19 ... 15 J3
Moorfield Rd
BLTYR/CAMB G72 ... 118 C4
GRK PA19 ... 15 J3
Moorfoot Av *GIF/THBK* G46 ... 94 A7
PSLYS PA2 ... 91 K1
Moorfoot Dr *GRK* PA19 ... 15 J3
WISHAW ML2 ... 121 M6
Moorfoot Gdns *EKILS* G75 ... 126 E7
Moorfoot St *CAR/SHTL* G32 ... 80 E4
Moorfoot Wy *BSDN* G61 ... 41 J1
Moorhill Crs *NMRNS* G77 ... 113 J6
Moorhill Rd *NMRNS* G77 ... 113 J5
Moorhouse Av *KNTSWD* G13 ... 58 F3
PSLYS PA2 ... 75 H8
Moorhouse St *BRHD/NEIL* G78 ... 92 C7
The Moorings *PSLYS* PA2 ... 8 B7
Moorland Dr *AIRDRIE* ML6 ... 85 L2
Moorlands Wk
UD/BTH/TAN G71 ... 99 G5
Moorpark Av *AIRDRIE* ML6 ... 85 L2
BAIL/MDB/MHD G69 ... 64 C3
CARD/HILL/MSPK G52 ... 76 F3
Moorpark Ct *GOV/IBX* G51 ... 78 A3
Moorpark Dr
CARD/HILL/MSPK G52 ... 77 G3
Moorpark Sq *RNFRW* PA4 ... 58 B7
Moor Rd *LNK/LMHG* ML11 ... 135 K8
MLNGV G62 ... 24 B8
Moorside St *CARLUKE* ML8 ... 133 J7
Morag Av *BLTYR/CAMB* G72 ... 118 C1
Moraine Av *DRUM* G15 ... 41 G8
Moraine Circ *DRUM* G15 ... 41 G8
Moraine Dr
CRMNK/CLK/EAG G76 ... 114 C2
DRUM G15 ... 41 G8
Moraine Pl *DRUM* G15 ... 41 H8
Morar Av *CLYDBK* G81 ... 40 B5
Morar Ct *CUMB* G67 ... 48 B1
HMLTN ML3 ... 129 G1
LRKH ML9 ... 130 B4
Morar Crs *AIRDRIE* ML6 ... 66 E8
BSHPBGS G64 ... 43 M8
BSHPTN PA7 ... 38 C8
CLYDBK G81 ... 40 B5
CTBR ML5 ... 83 K1
Morar Dr *BSDN* G61 ... 42 B7
CLYDBK G81 ... 40 B5
CUMB G67 ... 48 C1
PSLYS PA2 ... 74 F8
RUTH G73 ... 96 B7
Morar Pl *CLYDBK* G81 ... 40 B5
EKILN G74 ... 3 H1
NMRNS G77 ... 113 K2
RNFRW PA4 ... 58 B5
Morar Rd *CARD/HILL/MSPK* G52 ... 77 L4
CLYDBK G81 ... 40 B5
PGL PA14 ... 34 E3
WMYSB PA18 ... 50 B1
Morar St *WISHAW* ML2 ... 122 A8
Morar Ter *RUTH* G73 ... 96 D7
UD/BTH/TAN G71 ... 99 H3
Moravia Av *UD/BTH/TAN* G71 ... 99 G7
Moray Av *AIRDRIE* ML6 ... 85 G4
Moray Ct *RUTH* G73 ... 96 A2
Moray Dr *BSHPBGS* G64 ... 44 B1
CRMNK/CLK/EAG G76 ... 114 F3
Moray Gdns *BALLOCH* G68 ... 30 F4
CRMNK/CLK/EAG G76 ... 114 F2
UD/BTH/TAN G71 ... 98 F2
Moray Ga *UD/BTH/TAN* G71 ... 98 F6
Moray Pl *BAIL/MDB/MHD* G69 ... 64 D2
BLTYR/CAMB G72 ... 118 C4
BSHPBGS G64 ... 62 C1
KKNTL G66 ... 46 A1
PLKSD/SHW G41 ... 78 E8
PSLYN/LNWD PA3 ... 74 A4
Moray Qd *BLSH* ML4 ... 100 A4
Moray Rd *PGL* PA14 ... 34 C1
Mordaunt St *DMNK/BRGTN* G40 ... 80 A7
Moredun Crs *CAR/SHTL* G32 ... 81 J3
Moredun Dr *PSLYS* PA2 ... 91 H1
Moredun Rd *PSLYS* PA2 ... 91 H1
Moredun St *CAR/SHTL* G32 ... 81 J3
Morefield Rd *GOV/IBX* G51 ... 77 K2
Morgan Ms *GVH/MTFL* G42 ... 79 H8
Morgan St *HMLTN* ML3 ... 119 K8
LRKH ML9 ... 130 B6
Morina Gdns *PLK/PH/NH* G53 ... 93 J7
Morion Rd *KNTSWD* G13 ... 59 K1
Moriston Ct *WISHAW* ML2 ... 122 F3
Morland *EKILN* G74 ... 117 K5
Morley St *GVH/MTFL* G42 ... 95 G3
Morna La *SCOT* G14 ... 59 L7
Morningside Rd *WISHAW* ML2 ... 123 G5
Morningside St
STPS/GTHM/RID G33 ... 80 E2
Morrin St *SPRGB/BLRNK* G21 ... 61 L7
Morris Crs *BLTYR/CAMB* G72 ... 118 D3
MTHW ML1 ... 101 L8
Morrishall Rd *EKILN* G74 ... 117 J8
Morrishill Dr *BEITH* KA15 ... 125 J6
Morrison Dr *KKNTL* G66 ... 26 E3
Morrison Qd *CLYDBK* G81 ... 40 E8
Morrison St *CLYDBK* G81 ... 39 M4
GBLS G5 ... 4 B9
Morris St *GRNK* PA15 ... 7 K8
HMLTN ML3 ... 129 K1
LARGS KA30 ... 106 E5
LRKH ML9 ... 130 E8
Morriston Crs *RNFRW* PA4 ... 58 F8
Morriston Park Dr
BLTYR/CAMB G72 ... 97 G3
Morriston St *BLTYR/CAMB* G72 ... 97 G4
Morton Gdns *PLKSD/SHW* G41 ... 94 C1
Morton St *MTHW* ML1 ... 120 E1
Morven Av *BLTYR/CAMB* G72 ... 118 C1
BSHPBGS G64 ... 62 C1
PSLYS PA2 ... 91 K2
Morven Dr
CRMNK/CLK/EAG G76 ... 114 D2
PSLYN/LNWD PA3 ... 74 A5
Morven Gait *ERSK* PA8 ... 57 L2
Morven Gdns
UD/BTH/TAN G71 ... 98 F2
Morven Rd *BLTYR/CAMB* G72 ... 96 F7
BSDN G61 ... 41 L3
Morven St
CARD/HILL/MSPK G52 ... 77 L4
CTBR ML5 ... 84 A1
Mosesfield St
SPRGB/BLRNK G21 ... 61 M5
Mosque Av *GBLS* G5 ... 79 J5
Mossacre Rd *WISHAW* ML2 ... 122 C5
Moss Av *AIRDRIE* ML6 ... 68 F4
PSLYN/LNWD PA3 ... 74 B4
Mossband La *SHOTTS* ML7 ... 104 E3
Mossbank *BLTYR/CAMB* G72 ... 118 D4
EKILS G75 ... 126 C2
Mossbank Av
STPS/GTHM/RID G33 ... 62 F6
Mossbank Crs *MTHW* ML1 ... 101 M5
Mossbank Dr
STPS/GTHM/RID G33 ... 62 F6
Mossbank Rd *WISHAW* ML2 ... 122 C5
Mossbell Rd *BLSH* ML4 ... 99 M4
Mossblown St *LRKH* ML9 ... 130 B6
Mossburn Av *ALEX/LLW* G83 ... 13 L1
SHOTTS ML7 ... 71 K7
Mossburn Rd *WISHAW* ML2 ... 122 D6
Mossburn St *WISHAW* ML2 ... 122 D8
Mosscastle Rd
STPS/GTHM/RID G33 ... 63 J8
Mossdale *EKILN* G74 ... 2 A2
Mossdale Gdns *HMLTN* ML3 ... 118 E8
Moss Dr *BRHD/NEIL* G78 ... 92 A4
ERSK PA8 ... 57 H3
Mossend Av *HBR/GL* G84 ... 10 F6
KBRN KA25 ... 124 C5
Mossend La
STPS/GTHM/RID G33 ... 81 K2
Mossend St
STPS/GTHM/RID G33 ... 81 K3
Mossgiel *EKILS* G75 ... 126 E3
Mossgiel Av *RUTH* G73 ... 96 A5
Mossgiel Crs
CRMNK/CLK/EAG G76 ... 114 F5
Mossgiel Dr *CLYDBK* G81 ... 40 C6
Mossgiel Gdns *KKNTL* G66 ... 45 M1
UD/BTH/TAN G71 ... 98 E2
Mossgiel Pl *RUTH* G73 ... 96 A5
Mossgiel Rd *CUMB* G67 ... 31 H7
PLKSW/MSWD G43 ... 94 D4
Mossgiel Ter *BLTYR/CAMB* G72 ... 98 C8
Mosshall Gv *MTHW* ML1 ... 101 M5
Mosshall Rd *MTHW* ML1 ... 101 K2
Mosshall St *MTHW* ML1 ... 101 M6
Mosshead Rd *BSDN* G61 ... 41 M2
Moss Heights Av
CARD/HILL/MSPK G52 ... 77 K4
Mosshill Rd *BLSH* ML4 ... 100 B2
Moss Knowe *CUMB* G67 ... 31 H7
Mossland Dr *WISHAW* ML2 ... 122 C5
Mossland Rd
CARD/HILL/MSPK G52 ... 76 D1
Mosslands Rd
PSLYN/LNWD PA3 ... 75 K3
Mosslingal *EKILS* G75 ... 127 H5
Mossmulloch *EKILS* G75 ... 127 G5
Mossneuk Av *EKILS* G75 ... 126 B3
Mossneuk Crs *WISHAW* ML2 ... 122 C5
Mossneuk Dr *EKILS* G75 ... 126 C3
PSLYS PA2 ... 91 J2
WISHAW ML2 ... 122 C5
Mossneuk Pk *WISHAW* ML2 ... 122 C5
Mossneuk Rd *EKILS* G75 ... 126 D2
Mossneuk St *CTBR* ML5 ... 83 M7
Mosspark Av
CARD/HILL/MSPK G52 ... 77 M6
MLNGV G62 ... 24 A7
Mosspark Bvd
CARD/HILL/MSPK G52 ... 77 M6
Mosspark Dr
CARD/HILL/MSPK G52 ... 77 J6
Mosspark Ov
CARD/HILL/MSPK G52 ... 77 L6
Mosspark Rd *CTBR* ML5 ... 83 K2
MLNGV G62 ... 24 A7
Mosspark Sq
CARD/HILL/MSPK G52 ... 77 L6
Moss Rd *AIRDRIE* ML6 ... 85 G3
BAIL/MDB/MHD G69 ... 64 C3
BRWEIR PA11 ... 72 E3
CRG/CRSL/HOU PA6 ... 74 B2
CUMB G67 ... 31 L5
EKILS G75 ... 126 F6
GOV/IBX G51 ... 77 K1
KKNTL G66 ... 45 H4
KLMCLM PA13 ... 53 K2
PGL PA14 ... 34 F3
PSLYN/LNWD PA3 ... 74 C4
WISHAW ML2 ... 122 E6
Moss Side Av *AIRDRIE* ML6 ... 84 E1
Moss-side Av *CARLUKE* ML8 ... 132 F7
Moss-side Rd *PLKSD/SHW* G41 ... 94 E1
Moss St *PSLY* PA1 ... 9 H4
Mossvale La *PSLYN/LNWD* PA3 ... 8 F1
Mossvale Rd
STPS/GTHM/RID G33 ... 63 J8

Mossvale Sq
STPS/GTHM/RID G33 63 H8
Mossvale St PSLYN/LNWD PA3 75 K3
Mossvale Ter
BAIL/MDB/MHD G69 47 G7
Mossview Crs AIRDRIE ML6 85 G3
Mossview La
CARD/HILL/MSPK G52 77 J4
Mossview Qd
CARD/HILL/MSPK G52 77 K4
Mossview Rd
STPS/GTHM/RID G33 63 L5
Mosswater Wynd BALLOCH G68 29 M8
Mosswell Rd MLNGV G62 24 B7
Mossyde Av PGL PA14 34 F3
Mossywood Ct BALLOCH G68 47 M3
Mossywood Pl BALLOCH G68 47 M3
Mossywood Rd BALLOCH G68 47 M3
Mote Hl HMLTN ML3 119 L6
Mote Hill Ct HMLTN ML3 119 L5
Mote Hill Gv HMLTN ML3 119 L5
Mote Hill Rd PSLYN/LNWD PA3 9 M1
Motehill Rd PSLYN/LNWD PA3 76 B2
Motherwell Rd HMLTN ML3 119 M7
MTHW ML1 100 B8
Motherwell St AIRDRIE ML6 67 J8
Moulin Circ
CARD/HILL/MSPK G52 77 H5
Moulin Pl CARD/HILL/MSPK G52 77 G5
Moulin Rd
CARD/HILL/MSPK G52 77 G5
Moulin Ter
CARD/HILL/MSPK G52 77 G6
Mountainblue St
DEN/PKHD G31 80 A5
Mount Annan Dr
LNPK/KPK G44 95 H3
Mountblow Rd CLYDBK G81 39 L4
Mount Cameron Dr North
EKILN G74 3 L7
Mount Cameron Dr South
EKILN G74 3 K8
Mountgarrie Rd GOV/IBX G51 77 K2
Mount Harriet Av
STPS/GTHM/RID G33 63 L4
Mount Harriet Dr
STPS/GTHM/RID G33 63 L4
Mountherrick EKILS G75 127 H5
Mount Lockhart
UD/BTH/TAN G71 82 B8
Mount Lockhart Pl
UD/BTH/TAN G71 82 B8
Mount Pleasant Crs KKNTL G66 27 H4
Mount Pleasant Dr OLDK G60 39 H3
Mount Pleasant St GRNK PA15 6 A5
Mount Stewart St
CARLUKE ML8 133 G7
Mount St MRYH/FIRH G20 60 F7
Mount Stuart Dr WMYSB PA18 32 C8
Mount Stuart Rd LARGS KA30 107 G4
Mount Stuart St
PLKSD/SHW G41 94 E2
Mount Vernon Av
BAIL/MDB/MHD G69 81 L7
CTBR ML5 83 L3
Mournian Wy HMLTN ML3 129 K1
Mousebank Rd
LNK/LMHG ML11 136 D4
Mousemill Rd LNK/LMHG ML11 136 D4
Mowbray EKILN G74 117 J6
Mowbray Av
BAIL/MDB/MHD G69 64 F5
Moyne Rd PLK/PH/NH G53 77 G7
Muckcroft Rd
BAIL/MDB/MHD G69 46 B6
Mugdock Rd MLNGV G62 24 A5
Muirbank Av RUTH G73 95 M3
Muirbank Gdns RUTH G73 95 M3
Muirbrae Rd RUTH G73 96 B6
Muirbrae Wy RUTH G73 96 B6
Muirburn Rd BEITH KA15 125 J2
Muircroft Dr MTHW ML1 102 B7
Muirdrum Av
CARD/HILL/MSPK G52 77 K6
Muirdyke Rd AIRDRIE ML6 66 A4
CTBR ML5 83 K2
Muirdykes Av
CARD/HILL/MSPK G52 77 G4
PGL PA14 34 D3
Muirdykes Crs PSLYN/LNWD PA3 8 B1
Muirdykes Rd
CARD/HILL/MSPK G52 77 G4
PSLYN/LNWD PA3 8 A1
Muiredge & Jersy Rd
MTHW ML1 103 H6
Muiredge Ct UD/BTH/TAN G71 98 F4
Muiredge Ter
BAIL/MDB/MHD G69 82 B6
Muirend Av LNPK/KPK G44 94 F5
Muirend Rd DMBTN G82 19 G2
LNPK/KPK G44 94 E6
Muirend St KBRN KA25 124 D3
Muirfield Ct LNPK/KPK G44 94 F6
Muirfield Crs SMSTN G23 60 E1
Muirfield Mdw
UD/BTH/TAN G71 98 E8
Muirfield Rd BALLOCH G68 31 G4
Muirhall Ter SHOTTS ML7 87 H7
Muirhead Dr CARLUKE ML8 132 C3
MTHW ML1 101 M5
PSLYN/LNWD PA3 74 A5
Muirhead Gdns
BAIL/MDB/MHD G69 82 C7
SHOTTS ML7 87 H7
Muirhead Ga UD/BTH/TAN G71 99 G2
Muirhead Gv
BAIL/MDB/MHD G69 82 C6
Muirhead Pl SHOTTS ML7 71 J8
Muirhead Rd
BAIL/MDB/MHD G69 82 B7
Muirhead St LOCHW PA12 109 J3
Muirhead Ter MTHW ML1 120 E5
Muirhead Wy BSHPBGS G64 62 D1
Muirhill Av LNPK/KPK G44 94 E6
Muirhill Ct HMLTN ML3 119 K6
Muirhill Crs KNTSWD G13 58 F2
Muirhouse Av MTHW ML1 121 H6
WISHAW ML2 123 H3
Muirhouse Dr MTHW ML1 121 J7
Muirhouse La EKILS G75 3 G8
Muirhouse Pk BSDN G61 41 K1
Muirhouse Rd MTHW ML1 121 H7
Muirhouse St PLKSD/SHW G41 79 G7
Muirkirk Dr HMLTN ML3 118 D8
KNTSWD G13 59 M2
Muirlee Rd CARLUKE ML8 133 K8
Muirlees Crs MLNGV G62 23 L7
Muirmadkin Rd BLSH ML4 100 B4
Muirmaillen Av MTHW ML1 102 C8
Muirpark Av RNFRW PA4 58 C7
Muirpark Dr BSHPBGS G64 62 A2
Muirpark Rd BEITH KA15 125 K4
Muirpark St PTCK G11 60 B8
Muirpark Ter BSHPBGS G64 62 A2
Muir Rd DMBTN G82 21 J4
Muirshiel Av PLK/PH/NH G53 93 J3
Muirshiel Ct PLK/PH/NH G53 93 J4
Muirshiel Crs PLK/PH/NH G53 93 J3
Muirshiel La PGL PA14 34 D2
Muirshiel Rd PGL PA14 34 D2
Muirshot Rd LRKH ML9 130 D5
Muirside Av CAR/SHTL G32 81 L7
KKNTL G66 46 A2
Muirside Pl WISHAW ML2 122 F3
Muirside Rd
BAIL/MDB/MHD G69 82 B6
Muirside St
BAIL/MDB/MHD G69 82 B6
Muirskeith Crs
PLKSW/MSWD G43 94 F4
Muirskeith Pl
PLKSW/MSWD G43 94 F4
Muirskeith Rd
PLKSW/MSWD G43 94 F4
Muir St ALEX/LLW G83 13 J2
BLTYR/CAMB G72 118 D4
BSHPBGS G64 62 A1
CARLUKE ML8 132 B3
CTBR ML5 83 L3
HMLTN ML3 119 L6
LRKH ML9 130 C6
MTHW ML1 120 D1
RNFRW PA4 58 D5
Muir Ter PSLYN/LNWD PA3 76 A2
Muirton Dr BSHPBGS G64 43 M7
Muiryfauld Dr DEN/PKHD G31 80 E6
Muiryhall St CTBR ML5 84 B2
Muiryhall St East CTBR ML5 84 C2
Mulben Crs PLK/PH/NH G53 92 F2
Mulben Pl PLK/PH/NH G53 92 F2
Mulben Ter PLK/PH/NH G53 92 F2
Mulberry Crs AIRDRIE ML6 85 L6
Mulberry Dr EKILS G75 126 F5
Mulberry Rd
PLKSW/MSWD G43 94 D5
UD/BTH/TAN G71 99 J1
Mulberry Wy EKILS G75 126 F5
Mulberry Wynd
BLTYR/CAMB G72 97 M7
Muldron Ter SHOTTS ML7 105 H7
Mull EKILN G74 127 M3
Mullardoch St SMSTN G23 60 D1
Mull Av PGL PA14 35 G3
PSLYS PA2 91 L3
RNFRW PA4 58 C8
Mull Ct HMLTN ML3 128 F1
Mullen Ct STPS/GTHM/RID G33 63 M5
Mull Qd WISHAW ML2 122 E4
Mull St SPRGB/BLRNK G21 62 B8
Mulvey Crs AIRDRIE ML6 84 E2
Mungo Pk EKILS G75 2 C8
Mungo Pl UD/BTH/TAN G71 99 G1
Munlochy Rd GOV/IBX G51 77 K2
Munro Ct CLYDBK G81 39 M4
Munro Dr KBRN KA25 124 D5
KKNTL G66 27 H5
Munro Dr East HBR/GL G84 10 E4
Munro Dr West HBR/GL G84 10 D4
Munro La KNTSWD G13 59 L4
Munro La East KNTSWD G13 59 L4
Munro Pl EKILN G74 3 M1
KNTSWD G13 59 L2
Munro Rd KNTSWD G13 59 L4
Munro St ALEX/LLW G83 13 K5
GRNKW/INVK PA16 16 A5
Murano Pl MRYH/FIRH G20 60 F6
Murano St MRYH/FIRH G20 60 F6
Murchison KVD/HLHD G12 60 A4
Murchison Dr EKILS G75 126 E2
Murchison Rd
CRG/CRSL/HOU PA6 73 J1
Murdieston St GRNK PA15 16 D5
Murdoch Dr MLNGV G62 42 D2
Murdoch Pl MTHW ML1 100 F6
Murdoch Rd EKILS G75 2 F8
Murdoch Sq BLSH ML4 100 C2
Murdostoun Crs SHOTTS ML7 71 M6
Murdostoun Gdns
WISHAW ML2 122 B4
Murdostoun Rd WISHAW ML2 103 J8
Murdostoun Ter MTHW ML1 102 E8
Murdostoun Vw WISHAW ML2 122 F3
Mure Pl BRHD/NEIL G78 110 A7
Murial Blue Ct GRK PA19 15 M2
Muriel La BRHD/NEIL G78 92 C6
Muriel St BRHD/NEIL G78 92 C6
Murray Av KSYTH G65 29 K2
Murray Ct HMLTN ML3 119 G7
Murray Crs BLTYR/CAMB G72 118 E4
WISHAW ML2 123 G2
Murrayfield Dr BSDN G61 41 L8
Murrayfield St CAR/SHTL G32 80 E3
Murray Gv BSDN G61 41 H1
Murrayhill EKILS G75 2 C7
Murray Pl BLSH ML4 99 L3
BRHD/NEIL G78 92 D5
DMBTN G82 21 J7
GRK PA19 15 L3
Murray Rd CARLUKE ML8 132 C5
UD/BTH/TAN G71 99 G7
The Murray Rd EKILS G75 2 C9
The Murray Sq EKILS G75 127 H3
Murray St GRNKW/INVK PA16 16 C4
PSLYN/LNWD PA3 8 C2
RNFRW PA4 58 C6
Murray Ter MTHW ML1 120 B2
Murray Wk BLTYR/CAMB G72 118 E4
Murrin Av BSHPBGS G64 62 D1
Murroch Av DMBTN G82 21 J4
Murroch Crs ALEX/LLW G83 13 M8
Murroes Rd GOV/IBX G51 77 K2
Musgrove Pl EKILS G75 2 A8
Muslin St DMNK/BRGTN G40 79 M6
Muttonhole Rd HMLTN ML3 128 B2
Mybster Pl GOV/IBX G51 77 K2
Myers Ct BLSH ML4 99 K4
Myers Crs UD/BTH/TAN G71 99 G5
Myreside Pl CAR/SHTL G32 80 D4
Myreside St CAR/SHTL G32 80 E4
Myres Rd PLK/PH/NH G53 93 K1
Myreton Av KLMCLM PA13 53 J3
Myrie Gdns BSHPBGS G64 44 B8
Myrtle Av KKNTL G66 45 J5
Myrtle Bank BEITH KA15 125 J5
Myrtle Dr MTHW ML1 101 H4
WISHAW ML2 121 K5
Myrtle Hill La GVH/MTFL G42 95 J2
Myrtle La LRKH ML9 130 D8
Myrtle Pk GVH/MTFL G42 95 H1
Myrtle Pl GVH/MTFL G42 95 J2
Myrtle Rd CLYDBK G81 39 K6
UD/BTH/TAN G71 99 H2
Myrtle Sq BSHPBGS G64 62 A2
Myrtle St BLTYR/CAMB G72 118 D1
Myrtle View Rd GVH/MTFL G42 95 J2
Myrtle Wk BLTYR/CAMB G72 96 F4
Myvot Av CUMB G67 48 B3
Myvot Rd CUMB G67 47 L6

N

Naburn Ga GBLS G5 79 J6
Nagle Gdns MTHW ML1 121 M1
Nairn Av BLSH ML4 100 A3
BLTYR/CAMB G72 98 C8
Nairn Crs AIRDRIE ML6 85 G5
Nairn Dr GRNKW/INVK PA16 15 K4
Nairn Pl CLYDBK G81 39 M7
EKILN G74 117 J7
Nairn Qd WISHAW ML2 122 B4
Nairn Rd GRNKW/INVK PA16 15 K5
Nairnside Rd
SPRGB/BLRNK G21 62 C3
Nairn St BLTYR/CAMB G72 118 C4
CLYDBK G81 39 M7
KVGV G3 78 D1
LRKH ML9 130 B7
Nairn Wy BALLOCH G68 31 G4
Naismith St CAR/SHTL G32 97 J2
Naismith Wk BLSH ML4 100 C2
Nansen St MRYH/FIRH G20 61 G7
Napier Av DMBTN G82 19 H2
Napier Ct BALLOCH G68 31 K1
DMBTN G82 19 H2
OLDK G60 39 J5
Napier Crs DMBTN G82 20 D7
Napier Dr GOV/IBX G51 78 B2
Napier Gdns PSLYN/LNWD PA3 74 C4
Napier Hl EKILS G75 2 F8
Napier La EKILS G75 2 F8
Napier Pk BALLOCH G68 31 J3
Napier Pl BALLOCH G68 31 J1
GOV/IBX G51 78 B2
OLDK G60 39 J5
Napier Rd BALLOCH G68 31 K2
CARD/HILL/MSPK G52 58 F8
GOV/IBX G51 78 B2
Napiershall La MRYH/FIRH G20 60 F8
Napiershall Pl MRYH/FIRH G20 60 F8
Napiershall St MRYH/FIRH G20 60 F8
Napier Sq BLSH ML4 100 C2
Napierston Rd ALEX/LLW G83 13 L5
Napier St CLYDBK G81 58 D2
GOV/IBX G51 78 B2
JNSTN PA5 73 L7
PSLYN/LNWD PA3 74 C4
Napier Ter GOV/IBX G51 78 B2
Napier Wy BALLOCH G68 31 J2
Naproch Pl NMRNS G77 114 C5
Naseby Av PTCK G11 59 M6
Naseby La PTCK G11 59 M6
Nasmyth Av BSDN G61 41 H1
EKILS G75 3 H9
Nasmyth Pl EKILS G75 3 H9
Nasmyth Rd
CARD/HILL/MSPK G52 77 G2
Nasmyth Rd North
CARD/HILL/MSPK G52 77 G2
Nasmyth Rd South
CARD/HILL/MSPK G52 77 G2
Nassau Pl EKILS G75 126 D1
National Bank La CGLE G1 4 E6
Navar Ct SHOTTS ML7 105 G6
Navar Pl PSLYS PA2 76 A7
Naver St STPS/GTHM/RID G33 80 E1
Naylor La AIRDRIE ML6 85 H1
Naysmyth Bank EKILS G75 3 G8
Needle Gn CARLUKE ML8 133 H7
Neidpath Av CTBR ML5 84 A6
Neidpath Pl CTBR ML5 84 A6
Neidpath Rd CARLUKE ML8 133 G6
Neidpath Rd East
GIF/THBK G46 114 A4
Neidpath Rd West
GIF/THBK G46 114 A3
Neilsland Dr HMLTN ML3 129 J3
MTHW ML1 120 B3
Neilsland Ov PLK/PH/NH G53 93 K1
Neilsland Rd HMLTN ML3 119 H8
Neilsland Sq HMLTN ML3 129 J1
PLK/PH/NH G53 77 K8
Neilsland St HMLTN ML3 129 J1
Neilson Ct HMLTN ML3 119 L8
Neilson St BLSH ML4 100 A4
Neilston Av PLK/PH/NH G53 93 J5
Neilston Pl KSYTH G65 29 H1
Neilston Rd BRHD/NEIL G78 110 A7
PSLYS PA2 9 H9
Neilston Wk KSYTH G65 29 K1
Neil St GRNKW/INVK PA16 16 A5
RNFRW PA4 58 D4
Neilvaig Dr RUTH G73 96 C7
Neistpoint Dr
STPS/GTHM/RID G33 81 G2
Nellfield Ct CARLUKE ML8 135 G5
Nellfield Gdns CARLUKE ML8 135 G5
Nelson Av CTBR ML5 83 L6
Nelson Crs MTHW ML1 121 H5
Nelson Mandela Pl CGLE G1 4 F5
Nelson Pl BAIL/MDB/MHD G69 82 B6
HBR/GL G84 11 G5
Nelson Rd GRK PA19 15 M3
Nelson St BAIL/MDB/MHD G69 82 B6
GBLS G5 4 C9
GRNK PA15 6 B3
LARGS KA30 106 E4
Nelson Ter EKILN G74 3 K8
Nemphlar Moor Rd
CARLUKE ML8 134 D8
Nemphlar Rd
LNK/LMHG ML11 136 B3
Nemphlat Hl LNK/LMHG ML11 136 B4
Neptune St GOV/IBX G51 78 B3
Neptune Wy BLSH ML4 100 E4
Nerston Rd EKILN G74 116 E4
Ness Av JNSTN PA5 89 J2
Ness Dr BLTYR/CAMB G72 118 E1
EKILN G74 3 L5
Ness Gdns BSHPBGS G64 62 B1
Ness Rd GRNKW/INVK PA16 16 C4
RNFRW PA4 58 B5
Ness St STPS/GTHM/RID G33 80 E1
WISHAW ML2 131 K1
Ness Ter HMLTN ML3 129 G1
Nethan Av WISHAW ML2 121 J7
Nethanfoot Rd CARLUKE ML8 134 B7
Nethan Ga HMLTN ML3 119 J7
Nethan Gln CARLUKE ML8 134 A7
Nethan Pl HMLTN ML3 129 K4
Nethan St GOV/IBX G51 78 A2
MTHW ML1 100 C7
Nether Auldhouse Rd
PLKSW/MSWD G43 94 C4
Netherbank Rd WISHAW ML2 121 K7
Netherbog Rd DMBTN G82 21 H6
Netherburn Av
CRG/CRSL/HOU PA6 73 L3
LNPK/KPK G44 94 F8
Netherburn Gdns
CRG/CRSL/HOU PA6 73 L2
Netherby Dr PLKSD/SHW G41 78 D6
Nethercairn Pl NMRNS G77 114 C5
Nethercairn Rd
PLKSW/MSWD G43 94 C6
Nethercliffe Av LNPK/KPK G44 94 F8
Nethercraigs Dr PSLYS PA2 91 J2
Nethercraigs Rd PSLYS PA2 91 H3
Nethercroy Rd KSYTH G65 29 L5
Netherdale Crs MTHW ML1 121 J7
Netherdale Dr PSLY PA1 76 F6
Netherdale Rd WISHAW ML2 121 L7
Netherfield St DEN/PKHD G31 80 C4
Nethergreen Crs RNFRW PA4 58 B6
Nethergreen Wynd
RNFRW PA4 58 B6
Netherhall Rd WISHAW ML2 121 L7
Netherhill Av LNPK/KPK G44 114 F1
Netherhill Crs PSLYN/LNWD PA3 9 L1
Netherhill Rd
BAIL/MDB/MHD G69 64 F1
PSLYN/LNWD PA3 9 K2
Netherhouse Av CTBR ML5 83 M7
KKNTL G66 45 L6
Netherhouse Pl ESTRH G34 82 E2
Netherhouse Rd
BAIL/MDB/MHD G69 82 E3
Nether Kirkton Av
BRHD/NEIL G78 111 L2
Netherlee Pl LNPK/KPK G44 95 G6
Netherlee Rd LNPK/KPK G44 95 G7
Nethermains Rd MLNGV G62 42 A2
Netherpark Av LNPK/KPK G44 114 F1
Netherpark Crs LARGS KA30 106 E2
Netherplace Crs NMRNS G77 113 J5
PLK/PH/NH G53 93 H1
Netherplace Rd NMRNS G77 112 F5
PLK/PH/NH G53 93 H1
Netherton Av KNTSWD G13 59 L2
PGL PA14 35 G3
Netherton Ct NMRNS G77 113 M3
Netherton Dr BRHD/NEIL G78 92 D7
Netherton Farm La
KNTSWD G13 59 M1
Netherton Hl KKNTL G66 26 B2
Netherton Ov KKNTL G66 26 B2
Netherton Rd EKILS G75 126 C6
KNTSWD G13 59 M2
NMRNS G77 113 M3
WISHAW ML2 121 K7
Netherton St SHOTTS ML7 71 K7
WISHAW ML2 121 M7
Nethervale Av LNPK/KPK G44 114 F1
Netherview Rd LNPK/KPK G44 115 G1
Netherway LNPK/KPK G44 114 F1
Netherwood Av BALLOCH G68 47 M2
Netherwood Ct BALLOCH G68 48 A1
Netherwood Gv BALLOCH G68 48 A1
Netherwood Rd BALLOCH G68 47 M2
MTHW ML1 121 H6
Netherwood Wy BALLOCH G68 48 A1
Neuk Av BAIL/MDB/MHD G69 64 C3
CRG/CRSL/HOU PA6 73 J1
Neuk Crs CRG/CRSL/HOU PA6 55 J8
The Neuk WISHAW ML2 121 L6
Neville EKILN G74 117 J5
Nevis Av HMLTN ML3 129 G1
Nevis Ct BRHD/NEIL G78 92 C8
MTHW ML1 120 E5
Nevis Dr BSHPBGS G64 44 B1
MTHW ML1 121 J7
Nevison St LRKH ML9 130 D7
Nevis Pl SHOTTS ML7 105 H6
Nevis Rd BSDN G61 41 H2
PLKSW/MSWD G43 94 B5
RNFRW PA4 58 B8
Nevis Wy PSLYN/LNWD PA3 75 L1
Newark Av GRNKW/INVK PA16 16 C2
Newark Dr PLKSD/SHW G41 78 E7
PSLYS PA2 91 J2
WISHAW ML2 122 C3
Newark Ga SHOTTS ML7 123 M1
Newark Pl PGL PA14 34 D1
WISHAW ML2 122 D3
Newark St GRNKW/INVK PA16 16 B1
PGL PA14 34 D1
Newarthill Rd MTHW ML1 101 J7
New Ashtree St WISHAW ML2 121 L6
New Av HWWD PA9 88 F5
Newbank Ct DEN/PKHD G31 80 E6
Newbank Gdns DEN/PKHD G31 80 D6
Newbank Rd DEN/PKHD G31 80 D6
Newbarns St CARLUKE ML8 133 H6
Newbattle Av AIRDRIE ML6 85 H7
Newbattle Ct CAR/SHTL G32 81 H8
Newbattle Gdns CAR/SHTL G32 81 H8
Newbattle Pl CAR/SHTL G32 81 H8
Newbattle Rd CAR/SHTL G32 97 G1
Newbold Av SPRGB/BLRNK G21 61 L3
Newburgh St
PLKSW/MSWD G43 94 D3
Newcastleton Dr SMSTN G23 60 E1
New City Rd COWCAD G4 4 D2
New Cordale Rd DMBTN G82 13 J8
Newcraigs Drive
CRMNK/CLK/EAG G76 115 K3
Newcroft Dr LNPK/KPK G44 95 K5
New Dock La GRNK PA15 6 F4
Newdyke Rd KKNTL G66 45 M2
New Edinburgh Rd
UD/BTH/TAN G71 98 E3
Newfield Crs HMLTN ML3 119 H6
Newfield Pl GIF/THBK G46 93 M7
RUTH G73 95 L3
Newfield Sq PLK/PH/NH G53 93 G3
Newford Gv
CRMNK/CLK/EAG G76 114 E5
Newgrove Gdns
BLTYR/CAMB G72 97 G4
Newhall St DMNK/BRGTN G40 79 L7
Newhaven Gv LARGS KA30 106 D2
Newhaven Rd
STPS/GTHM/RID G33 81 H2
Newhaven St CAR/SHTL G32 81 G3
Newhills Rd
STPS/GTHM/RID G33 81 L3
Newhouse Dr KBRN KA25 124 B5
Newhousemill Rd EKILN G74 127 M3
HMLTN ML3 128 C1
Newhut Rd MTHW ML1 120 D1
New Inchinnan Rd
PSLYN/LNWD PA3 75 L3
Newington St CAR/SHTL G32 80 F4
New Kirk Rd BSDN G61 41 L4
New Lairdsland Rd KKNTL G66 45 K2
New Lanark Rd
LNK/LMHG ML11 136 F7
Newlands Dr HMLTN ML3 129 K2
Newlandsfield Rd
PLKSW/MSWD G43 94 D3
Newlands Gdns JNSTN PA5 90 C1
Newlandsmuir Rd EKILS G75 126 C4
Newlands Pl EKILN G74 2 F6
Newlands Rd EKILS G75 126 B6
PLKSW/MSWD G43 94 F4
UD/BTH/TAN G71 98 F2
Newlands St CTBR ML5 84 A5
LNK/LMHG ML11 137 J6
Newlands Ter CARLUKE ML8 133 H7
New La AIRDRIE ML6 85 H7
Newliston Dr GBLS G5 79 K7
New Luce Dr CAR/SHTL G32 81 K7
Newmains Av RNFRW PA4 57 G5
Newmains Rd RNFRW PA4 58 C8
Newmill & Canthill Rd
SHOTTS ML7 87 M8
SHOTTS ML7 104 A5
Newmill Gdns SHOTTS ML7 103 M7
Newmill Rd SPRGB/BLRNK G21 62 C5
Newmilns Gdns HMLTN ML3 118 D8
Newmilns St PLK/PH/NH G53 92 F3
Newnham Rd PSLY PA1 76 E5
Newpark Crs BLTYR/CAMB G72 97 G3
New Park St HMLTN ML3 119 J5
New Plymouth EKILS G75 126 D3
New Rd BLTYR/CAMB G72 97 L6
Newrose Av BLSH ML4 100 B2
Newshot Dr ERSK PA8 57 K2
New Sneddon St
PSLYN/LNWD PA3 9 H2
Newstead Gdns SMSTN G23 60 E1
New Stevenston Rd
MTHW ML1 101 H7
New St BEITH KA15 125 L5
BLTYR/CAMB G72 118 C3
CLYDBK G81 40 A3
KLBCH PA10 73 G7
LARGS KA30 106 F5
LOCHW PA12 109 J3
PSLY PA1 9 H5
Newton Av BLTYR/CAMB G72 97 K4
BRHD/NEIL G78 112 D1
JNSTN PA5 74 E7
Newton Brae BLTYR/CAMB G72 97 M5
Newton Ct BLTYR/CAMB G72 97 K4
NMRNS G77 113 K6
Newton Dr JNSTN PA5 74 E7
UD/BTH/TAN G71 99 G3
WISHAW ML2 123 G4
Newton Farm Rd
BLTYR/CAMB G72 97 M4
Newtongrange Av
CAR/SHTL G32 81 H8
Newtongrange Gdns
CAR/SHTL G32 81 H8
Newton Gv NMRNS G77 113 K6
Newtonlea Av NMRNS G77 113 M5
Newton of Barr LOCHW PA12 109 J4
Newton Pl KVGV G3 4 A3
NMRNS G77 113 L6
Newton Rd BSHPTN PA7 37 M7
KKNTL G66 45 L6
Newton St CGLW G2 4 A4
Newton Station Rd
BLTYR/CAMB G72 97 L6
Newton St GRNK PA15 6 A4
GRNKW/INVK PA16 6 A3
KBRN KA25 124 D4
PSLY PA1 8 C6
Newton Ter PSLYS PA2 74 F7
Newton Terrace La KVGV G3 78 F2
Newtown St KSYTH G65 29 K2
Newtyle Dr PLK/PH/NH G53 76 F8
Newtyle Pl BSHPBGS G64 62 D1
PLK/PH/NH G53 76 F8
Newtyle Rd PSLY PA1 76 C5
New View Dr BLSH ML4 100 A6
New View Pl BLSH ML4 100 A6
New Wynd CGLE G1 5 G8
Niamh Ct RNFRW PA4 57 J3
Nicholas St CGLE G1 5 J6
Nicholson St GBLS G5 4 E9
Nicklaus Wy MTHW ML1 101 L2
Nicol Dr GRNKW/INVK PA16 16 B4
Nicolson Ct
STPS/GTHM/RID G33 63 K5
Nicolson St GRNK PA15 6 C3
Nicol St AIRDRIE ML6 67 J8
GRNKW/INVK PA16 16 B5
Niddrie Rd GVH/MTFL G42 78 F8
Niddrie Sq GVH/MTFL G42 94 F1
Niddry St PSLYN/LNWD PA3 9 H3
Nigel Gdns PLKSD/SHW G41 94 D1
Nigel St MTHW ML1 120 D3
Nigg Pl ESTRH G34 82 A2
Nightingale Pl JNSTN PA5 89 K3
Nile St GRNK PA15 6 C6
Nimmo Dr GOV/IBX G51 77 L2
Nimmo Pl CARLUKE ML8 133 G6
WISHAW ML2 122 C6
Nimmo St GRNKW/INVK PA16 16 C5
Ninian Av CRG/CRSL/HOU PA6 73 J2
Ninian Rd AIRDRIE ML6 85 J4
Ninian's Ri KKNTL G66 45 M3
Nisbet St DEN/PKHD G31 80 D5
Nisbett Pl AIRDRIE ML6 85 L6
Nisbett St AIRDRIE ML6 85 L7
Nissen Pl PLK/PH/NH G53 76 F8
Nith Av PSLYS PA2 90 F1
Nith Dr HMLTN ML3 129 G2
RNFRW PA4 58 E7
Nith Qd MTHW ML1 101 J6
Nithsdale EKILN G74 117 K7
Nithsdale Crs BSDN G61 41 J3

Nithsdale Dr PLKSD/SHW G41 78 F8
Nithsdale Pl PLKSD/SHW G41 78 F7
Nithsdale Rd PLKSD/SHW G41 78 C6
Nithsdale St PLKSD/SHW G41 78 F8
SHOTTS ML7 104 D4
Nith St STPS/GTHM/RID G33 80 D1
Nitshill Rd PLK/PH/NH G53 92 F3
PLK/PH/NH G53 93 G4
Niven St MRYH/FIRH G20 60 C4
Noble Rd BLSH ML4 100 A4
Nobles Pl BLSH ML4 99 M6
Nobleston ALEX/LLW G83 13 M8
Nobles Vw BLSH ML4 99 M6
Noddleburn Lea LARGS KA30 106 F2
Noddleburn Meadow
LARGS KA30 106 E2
Noddleburn Pl LARGS KA30 106 E2
Noddleburn Rd LARGS KA30 106 E3
Noldrum Av CAR/SHTL G32 97 J2
Noldrum Gdns CAR/SHTL G32 97 J2
Norbreck Dr GIF/THBK G46 94 C6
Norby Rd PTCK G11 59 M6
Nordic Crs BLTYR/CAMB G72 118 E3
Nordic Gdns BLTYR/CAMB G72 118 E3
Nordic Gv BLTYR/CAMB G72 118 E4
Noremac Wy BLSH ML4 99 M3
Norfield Dr LNPK/KPK G44 95 H3
Norfolk Ct GBLS G5 79 H5
Norfolk Crs BSHPBGS G64 43 L7
Norfolk Rd GRNKW/INVK PA16 15 L5
Norfolk St GBLS G5 79 H5
Norham St PLKSD/SHW G41 94 E1
Norman St DMNK/BRGTN G40 79 M7
Norse La North SCOT G14 59 J5
Norse La South SCOT G14 59 J5
Norse Pl SCOT G14 59 J5
Norse Rd SCOT G14 59 J5
Northall Qd MTHW ML1 101 G8
Northampton Dr
KVD/HLHD G12 60 B4
North & South Rd MTHW ML1 122 E1
North Av BLTYR/CAMB G72 96 F4
CARLUKE ML8 132 F7
CLYDBK G81 40 A7
Northbank Av
BLTYR/CAMB G72 97 K4
North Bank Pl CLYDBK G81 58 C1
Northbank Rd KKNTL G66 45 J2
Northbank St BLTYR/CAMB G72 97 K4
North Bank St CLYDBK G81 58 C1
North Barr Av ERSK PA8 39 G8
North Berwick Av
BALLOCH G68 30 F4
North Berwick Crs EKILS G75 126 D4
North Biggar Rd AIRDRIE ML6 85 H1
North Birbiston Rd KKNTL G66 26 D2
Northbrae Pl KNTSWD G13 59 H3
North Bridge St AIRDRIE ML6 84 F1
North British Rd
UD/BTH/TAN G71 98 F4
Northburn Av AIRDRIE ML6 67 H8
Northburn Pl AIRDRIE ML6 67 H7
Northburn Rd CTBR ML5 66 C8
Northburn St AIRDRIE ML6 68 B7
North Bute St CTBR ML5 84 B5
North Caldeen Rd CTBR ML5 84 C4
North Calder Dr AIRDRIE ML6 85 K3
North Calder Gv
UD/BTH/TAN G71 82 B8
North Calder Pl
UD/BTH/TAN G71 82 B8
North Calder Rd
UD/BTH/TAN G71 99 J1
North Campbell Av MLNGV G62 23 M8
North Canal Bank St
COWCAD G4 4 F1
North Carbrain Rd CUMB G67 48 F1
North Claremont La
MLNGV G62 24 A8
North Claremont St KVGV G3 78 E1
North Corsebar Rd PSLYS PA2 75 J8
North Ct CGLE G1 4 F6
North Court La CGLE G1 4 F6
Northcroft Rd
BAIL/MDB/MHD G69 46 E8
North Croft St PSLYN/LNWD PA3 9 H3
North Dean Park Av
UD/BTH/TAN G71 99 G7
North Douglas St CLYDBK G81 58 C1
North Dr CGLW G2 4 E7
KBRN KA25 124 C5
PSLYN/LNWD PA3 74 B4
North Dryburgh Rd
WISHAW ML2 122 A4
North Dumgoyne Av
MLNGV G62 23 M7
North Elgin Pl CLYDBK G81 58 C2
North Elgin St CLYDBK G81 58 D1
North Erskine Pk BSDN G61 41 K4
North Faulds Rd
LNK/LMHG ML11 137 L4
Northfield EKILS G75 126 C3
Northfield Av PGL PA14 34 F2
SHOTTS ML7 105 H7
Northfield Dr ALEX/LLW G83 13 L5
Northfield Pk LARGS KA30 106 D2
Northfield Rd ALEX/LLW G83 13 M5
KSYTH G65 29 H1
Northfield St MTHW ML1 120 E1
Northflat Pl CARLUKE ML8 135 J1
North Frederick St CGLE G1 5 G6
North Gardner St PTCK G11 60 B8
Northgate Qd
SPRGB/BLRNK G21 62 C4
Northgate Rd
SPRGB/BLRNK G21 62 C3
North Gower St GOV/IBX G51 78 C5
North Grange Rd BSDN G61 41 L3
North Hanover St CGLE G1 5 G5
Northinch St SCOT G14 59 K7
North Iverton Park Rd
JNSTN PA5 74 A7
North Kilmeny Crs
WISHAW ML2 122 C3
Northland Av SCOT G14 59 J4
Northland Dr SCOT G14 59 J5
Northland Gdns SCOT G14 59 J5
Northland La SCOT G14 59 J5
North La PSLYN/LNWD PA3 74 C4
North Lodge Av MTHW ML1 120 E6
North Lodge Rd RNFRW PA4 58 C5
North Main St ALEX/LLW G83 13 J4
North Middleton Dr
LARGS KA30 106 F4
Northmuir Dr WISHAW ML2 122 D5
Northmuir Rd DRUM G15 41 H5
North Orchard St MTHW ML1 120 D2
North Park Av BRHD/NEIL G78 92 B6
GIF/THBK G46 93 M5
Northpark St MRYH/FIRH G20 60 F6
North Portland St COWCAD G4 5 H6
North Porton Rd BSHPTN PA7 38 C6
North Rd BALLOCH G68 48 A2
BLSH ML4 100 A4
JNSTN PA5 73 L8
PGL PA14 34 E2
North St ALEX/LLW G83 13 K5
CRG/CRSL/HOU PA6 55 H7
GRNKW/INVK PA16 16 C1
KVGV G3 4 A5
LRKH ML9 130 C5
MTHW ML1 120 F1
PSLYN/LNWD PA3 9 G2
Northumberland St
MRYH/FIRH G20 60 E6
North Vennel LNK/LMHG ML11 137 G5
North Vw BSDN G61 41 K7
North View Rd BRWEIR PA11 72 F3
North Wallace St COWCAD G4 5 H3
Northway BLTYR/CAMB G72 118 C1
Northwood Dr WISHAW ML2 123 G3
North Woodside Rd
MRYH/FIRH G20 60 F8
Norval St PTCK G11 60 A8
Norwich Dr KVD/HLHD G12 60 B5
Norwood Av KKNTL G66 45 H1
Norwood Dr GIF/THBK G46 114 A1
Norwood Pk BSDN G61 41 M6
Norwood Ter UD/BTH/TAN G71 99 G3
Nottingham Av KVD/HLHD G12 60 B4
Nottingham La KVD/HLHD G12 60 B4
Novar Dr KVD/HLHD G12 60 A6
Novar Gdns BSHPBGS G64 61 L1
Novar St HMLTN ML3 119 K8
Nuneaton St DMNK/BRGTN G40 80 A7
Nurseries Rd
BAIL/MDB/MHD G69 81 M4
Nursery Av BSHPTN PA7 38 E6
Nursery Ct CARLUKE ML8 133 G6
Nursery Gv KLMCLM PA13 53 J1
Nursery La KLMCLM PA13 53 J1
PLKSD/SHW G41 78 F8
Nursery Pk CARLUKE ML8 133 G7
Nursery Pl BLTYR/CAMB G72 118 D4
Nursery St HBR/GL G84 10 F7
PLKSD/SHW G41 79 G7
Nutberry Ct GVH/MTFL G42 95 H1

O

Oak Av BSDN G61 41 M2
EKILS G75 126 E4
Oakbank Av WISHAW ML2 121 L8
Oakbank Dr BRHD/NEIL G78 112 E1
Oakbank Rd PGL PA14 34 F2
Oakbank St AIRDRIE ML6 85 K2
Oakburn Av MLNGV G62 23 M8
Oakburn Crs MLNGV G62 23 M8
Oakburn Gdns ALEX/LLW G83 13 L5
Oakburn Wk ALEX/LLW G83 13 L4
Oak Crs BAIL/MDB/MHD G69 82 A6
Oakdene Av BLSH ML4 100 A2
UD/BTH/TAN G71 99 H3
Oakdene Crs MTHW ML1 101 J5
Oak Dr BLTYR/CAMB G72 97 J6
KKNTL G66 45 H5
Oak Fern Dr EKILN G74 116 D6
Oak Fern Gv EKILN G74 2 C1
Oakfield Av KVD/HLHD G12 60 E8
Oakfield Dr ALEX/LLW G83 13 L5
MTHW ML1 120 E3
Oakfield La KVD/HLHD G12 60 E8
Oakfield Rd MTHW ML1 120 E4
Oakfield Ter GRNK PA15 7 K6
Oak Gv AIRDRIE ML6 85 L6
Oakhill Av BAIL/MDB/MHD G69 81 M7
Oak Lea HMLTN ML3 119 M8
Oaklea Crs BLTYR/CAMB G72 118 C2
Oakleigh Dr GRNKW/INVK PA16 16 D2
Oakley Dr LNPK/KPK G44 94 F7
Oakley Ter DEN/PKHD G31 79 M3
Oak Pk BSHPBGS G64 62 B1
MTHW ML1 120 D5
Oak Pl CTBR ML5 84 C4
EKILS G75 126 E4
UD/BTH/TAN G71 99 J3
Oakridge Crs PSLYN/LNWD PA3 8 A4
Oakridge Rd
BAIL/MDB/MHD G69 83 H4
Oak Rd CLYDBK G81 39 M5
CUMB G67 31 L5
PSLYS PA2 76 A8
Oakshaw Brae PSLY PA1 8 E4
Oakshawhead PSLY PA1 8 E4
Oakshaw St East PSLY PA1 8 F4
Oakshaw St West PSLY PA1 8 F4
The Oaks JNSTN PA5 73 K8
Oak St CGLW G2 4 B6
Oaktree Gdns CSMK G45 95 M6
DMBTN G82 21 J8
Oakwood Av PSLYS PA2 91 H1
Oakwood Crs ESTRH G34 82 D2
Oakwood Dr BEITH KA15 125 J5
CTBR ML5 83 K5
NMRNS G77 113 M5
Oak Wynd BLTYR/CAMB G72 97 M7
Oates Gdns MTHW ML1 121 H5
Oatfield St SPRGB/BLRNK G21 62 B6
Oban Dr MRYH/FIRH G20 60 E6
Oban La MRYH/FIRH G20 60 E6
Oban Pl AIRDRIE ML6 85 K3
Obiston Gdns CAR/SHTL G32 81 G5
Observatory Rd KVD/HLHD G12 60 D7
Ocean Fld CLYDBK G81 39 M5
Ochil Ct EKILS G75 126 E6
Ochil Dr BRHD/NEIL G78 92 C8
PSLYS PA2 91 K2
Ochil Pl CAR/SHTL G32 81 G6
Ochil Rd BSDN G61 41 H2
BSHPBGS G64 62 C1
RNFRW PA4 58 B8
Ochil St CAR/SHTL G32 81 G6
WISHAW ML2 121 M5
Ochiltree Av KNTSWD G13 59 M2
Ochiltree Crs CTBR ML5 83 L6
Ochiltree Dr HMLTN ML3 128 E1
Ochil Vw UD/BTH/TAN G71 99 G2
Octavia Ter GRNKW/INVK PA16 16 B1
Odense Ct EKILS G75 127 H4
Ogilface Crs BTHG/ARM EH48 71 J2
Ogilvie Pl DEN/PKHD G31 80 D6
Ogilvie St DEN/PKHD G31 80 D6
O'Hare ALEX/LLW G83 13 M7
Oki Wy BALLOCH G68 31 J2
Old Aisle Rd KKNTL G66 45 M3
Old Avon Rd HMLTN ML3 120 A7
Old Balmore Rd BSHPBGS G64 43 M2
Old Bars Dr
BAIL/MDB/MHD G69 47 G7
Old Biggar Rd AIRDRIE ML6 67 H1
Old Bore Rd AIRDRIE ML6 85 K1
Old Bothwell Rd
UD/BTH/TAN G71 119 H2
Old Bridgend CARLUKE ML8 133 H8
Old Bridge of Weir Rd
CRG/CRSL/HOU PA6 55 G8
Old Castle Gdns LNPK/KPK G44 95 H4
Old Castle Rd LNPK/KPK G44 95 G4
Old Church Gdns
BAIL/MDB/MHD G69 83 G5
Old Coach Rd EKILN G74 3 G2
Old Dalmarnock Rd
DMNK/BRGTN G40 79 M6
Old Dalnottar Rd OLDK G60 39 H5
Old Dullatur Rd BALLOCH G68 30 D3
Old Dumbarton Rd KVGV G3 78 D1
Old Eastfield St SHOTTS ML7 71 K8
Old Edinburgh Rd
UD/BTH/TAN G71 98 E1
UD/BTH/TAN G71 99 H3
Old Farm Rd BSDN G61 59 M1
Old Gartloch Rd
BAIL/MDB/MHD G69 64 F6
Old Glasgow Rd CUMB G67 31 G5
UD/BTH/TAN G71 98 D2
Old Govan Rd RNFRW PA4 58 F6
Old Greenock Rd BSHPTN PA7 37 L6
BSHPTN PA7 38 D8
ERSK PA8 57 G2
PGL PA14 35 L3
RNFRW PA4 56 F2
Oldhall Dr KLMCLM PA13 53 K1
Oldhall Rd PSLY PA1 76 D4
Old Humbie Rd NMRNS G77 113 L7
Old Inverkip Rd
GRNKW/INVK PA16 16 C5
Old Lanark Rd CARLUKE ML8 133 H8
LNK/LMHG ML11 136 E1
Old Largs Rd
GRNKW/INVK PA16 6 B9
Old Luss Rd ALEX/LLW G83 13 G1
HBR/GL G84 10 F7
Old Manse Gdns CTBR ML5 84 A2
Old Manse Rd CAR/SHTL G32 81 K6
WISHAW ML2 131 G1
Old Market Rd
LNK/LMHG ML11 137 H6
Old Mill Ct CLYDBK G81 40 A4
Old Mill La UD/BTH/TAN G71 98 F4
Old Mill Rd BLTYR/CAMB G72 97 K5
CLYDBK G81 40 A4
EKILN G74 3 H3
PSLY PA1 8 A7
SHOTTS ML7 104 B8
UD/BTH/TAN G71 98 F5
Old Mill Vw KSYTH G65 29 M7
Old Monkland Rd CTBR ML5 83 K7
Old Mugdock Rd
CMPF/LLE G63 24 C2
Old Playfield Rd
CRMNK/CLK/EAG G76 115 K2
Old Quarry Rd BALLOCH G68 47 K5
Old Renfrew Rd GOV/IBX G51 59 G7
Old Rd JNSTN PA5 74 C7
Old Rutherglen Rd GBLS G5 79 K6
Old Schoolhouse La
CRG/CRSL/HOU PA6 55 H7
Old School Sq KLBCH PA10 73 G7
Old Shettleston Rd
CAR/SHTL G32 81 G5
Old Sneddon St
PSLYN/LNWD PA3 9 H3
Old Stable Rw CTBR ML5 84 B2
Old St CLYDBK G81 39 M4
Old Union St AIRDRIE ML6 85 H2
Old Willowyard Rd
BEITH KA15 125 J6
Old Wood Rd
BAIL/MDB/MHD G69 82 A7
Old Wynd CGLE G1 5 G8
Olifard Av UD/BTH/TAN G71 99 H7
Oliphant Crs
CRMNK/CLK/EAG G76 114 E5
PSLYS PA2 90 F3
Olive Bank UD/BTH/TAN G71 99 J1
Olive St STPS/GTHM/RID G33 62 D6
Olympia EKILN G74 3 G7
Olympia Ct EKILN G74 3 G7
Olympia St DMNK/BRGTN G40 79 M5
Omoa Rd MTHW ML1 102 A8
O'Neill Av BSHPBGS G64 62 B2
O'Neil Ter ALEX/LLW G83 13 K6
Onich Pl SHOTTS ML7 105 H6
Onslow EKILS G75 2 A9
Onslow Dr DEN/PKHD G31 80 A3
Onslow Rd CLYDBK G81 40 D7
Onslow Sq DEN/PKHD G31 80 A3
Ontario Pk EKILS G75 126 E1
Ontario Pl EKILS G75 126 E1
Onyx St BLSH ML4 100 A5
Open Shore GRNK PA15 6 F4
Oran Gdns MRYH/FIRH G20 60 E5
Oran Ga MRYH/FIRH G20 60 E5
Orangefield La
GRNKW/INVK PA16 6 A4
Oran Pl MRYH/FIRH G20 60 E6
Oran St MRYH/FIRH G20 60 E6
Orbiston Dr BLSH ML4 100 B6
CLYDBK G81 40 D2
Orbiston Pl CLYDBK G81 40 D2
Orbiston Rd BLSH ML4 99 M6
Orbiston Sq BLSH ML4 99 M7
Orbiston St MTHW ML1 120 F4
Orcades Dr LNPK/KPK G44 95 H6
Orchard Av UD/BTH/TAN G71 119 H1
Orchard Brae HMLTN ML3 119 K7
Orchard Ct CAR/SHTL G32 97 H2
GIF/THBK G46 94 A7
Orchard Dr BLTYR/CAMB G72 118 D2
GIF/THBK G46 94 B7
RUTH G73 95 M2
Orchard Fld KKNTL G66 45 K6
Orchard Ga LRKH ML9 130 C7
Orchard Gn EKILN G74 117 H6
Orchard Gv CTBR ML5 84 B3
GIF/THBK G46 94 B6
KLMCLM PA13 53 J2
Orchard Pk GIF/THBK G46 94 C7
Orchard Park Av GIF/THBK G46 94 B7
Orchard Pl BLSH ML4 99 M7
HMLTN ML3 119 K7
KKNTL G66 45 M3
Orchard St
BAIL/MDB/MHD G69 81 M7
CARLUKE ML8 133 H8
GRNK PA15 7 G7
HMLTN ML3 119 L7
MTHW ML1 120 D2
PSLY PA1 9 H5
RNFRW PA4 58 D5
WISHAW ML2 131 K3
Orchardton Rd BALLOCH G68 47 K3
Orchard View Dr
LNK/LMHG ML11 136 B5
Orchid Pl KKNTL G66 26 C2
Orchill Dr AIRDRIE ML6 68 B6
Orchy Av
CRMNK/CLK/EAG G76 114 F2
Orchy Ct CLYDBK G81 40 C4
Orchy Crs AIRDRIE ML6 85 J4
BSDN G61 41 K8
PSLYS PA2 90 F1
Orchy Dr
CRMNK/CLK/EAG G76 114 F1
Orchy Gdns
CRMNK/CLK/EAG G76 114 F1
Orchy St LNPK/KPK G44 95 G4
Orefield Pl EKILN G74 2 F1
Oregon Pl GBLS G5 79 J6
Orion Pl BLSH ML4 100 E4
Orion Wy BLTYR/CAMB G72 97 G4
CARLUKE ML8 132 F7
Orkney Pl GOV/IBX G51 78 B3
Orkney Qd WISHAW ML2 122 D5
Orkney St GOV/IBX G51 78 B3
Orlando EKILN G74 117 J5
Orleans Av SCOT G14 59 L6
Orleans La SCOT G14 59 L6
Ormiston Av SCOT G14 59 J5
Ormiston Dr HMLTN ML3 129 J2
Ormiston La SCOT G14 59 J5
Ormiston La North SCOT G14 59 J5
Ormiston La South SCOT G14 59 J5
Ormonde Av LNPK/KPK G44 94 F7
Ormonde Ct LNPK/KPK G44 94 E7
Ormonde Crs LNPK/KPK G44 94 F7
Ormonde Dr LNPK/KPK G44 94 F7
Ornsay St PPK/MIL G22 61 K3
Oronsay Av PGL PA14 35 G4
Oronsay Crs BSDN G61 42 B7
OLDK G60 39 J4
Oronsay Gdns OLDK G60 39 J4
Oronsay Pl OLDK G60 39 J4
WISHAW ML2 122 B8
Oronsay Rd AIRDRIE ML6 85 K4
Orr Sq PSLY PA1 9 G4
Orr St DMNK/BRGTN G40 79 M5
PSLY PA1 8 F4
PSLYS PA2 9 H8
Orr Ter BRHD/NEIL G78 111 J4
SHOTTS ML7 71 J7
Orton Pl GOV/IBX G51 78 A4
Osborne Crs EKILN G74 115 H7
Osborne St CGLW G2 4 F8
CLYDBK G81 40 A6
Osprey Crs WISHAW ML2 122 A5
Osprey Dr UD/BTH/TAN G71 99 G3
Osprey Rd GRNKW/INVK PA16 16 A5
PSLYN/LNWD PA3 75 K2
Osprey Vw PSLYN/LNWD PA3 75 K3
Ossian Av PSLY PA1 76 F4
Ossian Rd PLKSW/MSWD G43 94 E4
Oss Qd MTHW ML1 121 J7
Oswald St CGLE G1 4 D8
Oswald Wk MLNGV G62 42 C2
Otago La KVD/HLHD G12 60 E8
Otago Pk EKILS G75 126 D1
Otago Pl DMBTN G82 21 J8
Otago St KVD/HLHD G12 60 E8
Othello EKILN G74 117 H5
Otterburn Dr GIF/THBK G46 94 C8
Otterswick Pl
STPS/GTHM/RID G33 63 J8
Oudenarde Ct CARLUKE ML8 133 K8
The Oval CRMNK/CLK/EAG G76 114 F1
CTBR ML5 65 J4
Overbrae Gdns DRUM G15 40 F4
Overbrae Pl DRUM G15 40 F4
Overburn Av DMBTN G82 20 F6
Overburn Crs DMBTN G82 20 F5
Overdale Av GVH/MTFL G42 94 F2
Overdale Gdns GVH/MTFL G42 94 F2
Overdale Pl WISHAW ML2 131 L3
Overdale St GVH/MTFL G42 94 F2
Overjohnstone Dr
WISHAW ML2 121 K5
Overlea Av RUTH G73 96 D4
Overlee Rd
CRMNK/CLK/EAG G76 114 E3
Overnewton Pl KVGV G3 78 D2
Overnewton Sq KVGV G3 78 D2
Overnewton St KVGV G3 78 D1
Overton Crs GRNK PA15 16 D6
JNSTN PA5 74 B8
Overton Gdns KLMCLM PA13 53 L1
Overton Gv KLMCLM PA13 53 L1
Overton Rd ALEX/LLW G83 13 J6
BLTYR/CAMB G72 97 L6
JNSTN PA5 74 A8
Overton St ALEX/LLW G83 13 J6
BLTYR/CAMB G72 97 K6
Overtoun Av DMBTN G82 21 H8
Overtoun Dr CLYDBK G81 39 M6
RUTH G73 96 A3
Overtoun Rd CLYDBK G81 39 M6
Overtown Av PLK/PH/NH G53 93 G3
Overtown Pl DEN/PKHD G31 80 A5
Overtown Rd WISHAW ML2 122 F8
Overtown St DEN/PKHD G31 80 A5
Overwood Dr DMBTN G82 21 H6
LNPK/KPK G44 95 J4
Owen Av EKILS G75 126 F3
Owendale Av BLSH ML4 100 B2
Owen Pk EKILS G75 126 F3
Owen St MTHW ML1 120 E1
O'Wood Av MTHW ML1 101 H3
Oxford Av GRK PA19 16 A3
Oxford Dr PSLYN/LNWD PA3 74 B4
Oxford La GBLS G5 79 H5
RNFRW PA4 58 C6
Oxford Rd GRNKW/INVK PA16 15 K5
RNFRW PA4 58 C6
Oxford St CTBR ML5 83 M4
GBLS G5 4 E9
KKNTL G66 45 J2
Oxgang Pl KKNTL G66 45 L3
Oxhill Pl DMBTN G82 20 D7
Oxhill Rd DMBTN G82 20 D7
Oxton Dr CARD/HILL/MSPK G52 77 H4

P

Pacemuir Rd KLMCLM PA13 53 H2
Pacific Dr GOV/IBX G51 78 D4
Paddockdyke SKLM PA17 50 C6
Paddockholm Rd KBRN KA25 124 D4
Paddock St CTBR ML5 84 E5
The Paddock
CRMNK/CLK/EAG G76 115 G5
HMLTN ML3 119 J4
LNK/LMHG ML11 137 K2
Paduff Pl KBRN KA25 124 C3
Paidmyre Crs NMRNS G77 113 K6
Paidmyre Gdns NMRNS G77 113 K6
Paidmyre Rd NMRNS G77 113 K6
Paisley Rd BRHD/NEIL G78 92 B5
GBLS G5 4 B9
PLKSD/SHW G41 78 E4
PSLYN/LNWD PA3 76 A1
RNFRW PA4 58 B8
Paisley Rd West
CARD/HILL/MSPK G52 77 G5
Palacecraig St CTBR ML5 84 A6
Palace Grounds Rd
HMLTN ML3 119 M6
Paladin Av KNTSWD G13 59 H1
Palladium Pl SCOT G14 59 K6
Palmer Av KNTSWD G13 41 K8
Palmerston EKILS G75 126 D3
Palmerston Pl JNSTN PA5 89 J3
KVGV G3 78 D2
Palm Pl UD/BTH/TAN G71 99 H1
Pandora Wy UD/BTH/TAN G71 99 G3
Pankhurst Pl EKILN G74 3 G4
Panmure Pth BALLOCH G68 29 L8
Panmure Pl PPK/MIL G22 61 G5
Panmure St MRYH/FIRH G20 61 G6
Papermill Rd
GRNKW/INVK PA16 16 D7
Pappert ALEX/LLW G83 13 M6
Parkandarroch Crs
CARLUKE ML8 133 J8
Park Av ALEX/LLW G83 13 K1
BEITH KA15 125 K4
BRHD/NEIL G78 92 B8
BSHPBGS G64 44 A7
CARLUKE ML8 133 H6
DMBTN G82 21 H7
GRK PA19 16 A2
JNSTN PA5 74 C8
KKNTL G66 45 J2
KSYTH G65 28 E6
KVGV G3 60 F8
MLNGV G62 42 A1
MTHW ML1 101 G4
PSLYS PA2 91 K1
Park Bank ERSK PA8 57 H1
Park Brae ERSK PA8 57 J2
Parkbrae Av MRYH/FIRH G20 61 G4
Parkbrae Gdns MRYH/FIRH G20 61 G4
Parkbrae La MRYH/FIRH G20 61 G4
Parkburn Av KKNTL G66 45 J4
Park Burn Ct HMLTN ML3 119 G4
Parkburn Rd KSYTH G65 29 K1
Park Circ CARLUKE ML8 133 H6
KVGV G3 78 E1
Park Circus La KVGV G3 78 F1
Park Circus Pl KVGV G3 78 F1
Park Ct BEITH KA15 125 L5
BSHPBGS G64 44 B7
GIF/THBK G46 94 B7
Park Crs BLTYR/CAMB G72 118 C4
BSDN G61 41 J4
BSHPBGS G64 44 A7
DMBTN G82 20 F5
RNFRW PA4 57 J3
Park Dr BLSH ML4 100 A5
EKILN G74 115 J7
ERSK PA8 57 J2
HMLTN ML3 120 C8
KVGV G3 60 F8
LNK/LMHG ML11 136 F5
RUTH G73 96 A3
WISHAW ML2 123 G4
Parker Pl KSYTH G65 29 K2
LRKH ML9 130 D5
Parkfield EKILS G75 127 H5
Parkfoot St KSYTH G65 29 K1
Park Gdns KLBCH PA10 73 H6
KVGV G3 78 E1
Park Ga ERSK PA8 57 H2
KVGV G3 78 E1
Park Gate Pl BLSH ML4 99 M5
Park Gld ERSK PA8 57 J2
Park Gn ERSK PA8 57 H2
Park Gv DMBTN G82 19 H2
ERSK PA8 57 J2
Parkgrove Av GIF/THBK G46 94 D7
Parkgrove Ter KVGV G3 78 E1
Parkgrove Terrace La KVGV G3 78 E1
Parkhall Rd CLYDBK G81 39 M6
Parkhall St EKILN G74 2 F3
Parkhall Ter CLYDBK G81 39 M5
Parkhead St AIRDRIE ML6 85 G1
MTHW ML1 120 F4
Park Hl ERSK PA8 57 H1
Parkhill Av PGL PA14 35 G2
Parkhill Dr LOCHW PA12 109 K2
RUTH G73 96 A3
Parkhill Rd PLKSW/MSWD G43 94 C2
Parkholm Dr PLK/PH/NH G53 93 G6
Park Holme Ct HMLTN ML3 119 K5
Parkholm Gdns
PLK/PH/NH G53 93 G6
Parkholm La GBLS G5 78 F4
Parkholm Qd PLK/PH/NH G53 93 G6
Parkhouse Dr KBRN KA25 124 C4
Parkhouse Rd PLK/PH/NH G53 93 G5
Parkinch ERSK PA8 57 J3
Parklands Ov PLK/PH/NH G53 76 F7
Parklands Rd LNPK/KPK G44 94 F7
Parklands Vw PLK/PH/NH G53 76 F7
Park La BLTYR/CAMB G72 118 D2
CARLUKE ML8 133 G8
DMNK/BRGTN G40 79 M5
KSYTH G65 29 K2
Park Lea AIRDRIE ML6 68 F5
Parklee Dr
CRMNK/CLK/EAG G76 115 L3
Parkmanor Av PLK/PH/NH G53 92 F6
Parkmanor Gn PLK/PH/NH G53 92 F6

Park Moor ERSK PA8 57 H2
Parkneuk Rd
BLTYR/CAMB G72 118 A8
PLKSW/MSWD G43 94 C6
Parkneuk St MTHW ML1 120 E1
Park Pl BLSH ML4 99 L7
EKILN G74 115 J7
LNK/LMHG ML11 136 F5
Park Qd KVGV G3 78 E1
WISHAW ML2 121 L8
Park Rd AIRDRIE ML6 85 H7
BAIL/MDB/MHD G69 64 C2
BLSH ML4 100 A5
BRWEIR PA11 72 D1
BSHPBGS G64 44 A8
CAR/SHTL G32 97 J2
CLYDBK G81 39 M7
COWCAD G4 60 E8
GIF/THBK G46 94 C8
HMLTN ML3 119 K7
JNSTN PA5 89 M1
KLMCLM PA13 53 J2
MLNGV G62 42 A1
PSLYS PA2 91 K2
RNFRW PA4 57 K3
SHOTTS ML7 104 D4
Parksail ERSK PA8 57 J3
Parksail Dr ERSK PA8 57 J2
Parkside Gdns MRYH/FIRH G20 61 G4
Parkside Pl MRYH/FIRH G20 61 G4
Parkside Rd MTHW ML1 120 C3
SHOTTS ML7 104 D5
Park St ALEX/LLW G83 13 J5
CARLUKE ML8 133 H8
CTBR ML5 84 B2
DMBTN G82 21 G7
KKNTL G66 46 B3
MTHW ML1 120 E2
Park St South KVGV G3 78 E1
Parks Vw HMLTN ML3 129 K4
Park Ter DMBTN G82 19 G2
EKILN G74 2 E5
GRK PA19 15 L2
KVGV G3 78 E1
Park Terrace East La KVGV G3 78 F1
Park Terrace La KVGV G3 78 E1
Park Top ERSK PA8 57 J1
Parkvale Av ERSK PA8 57 K2
Parkvale Crs ERSK PA8 57 K2
Parkvale Dr ERSK PA8 57 K2
Parkvale Gdns ERSK PA8 57 K2
Parkvale Wy ERSK PA8 57 K2
Park Vw AIRDRIE ML6 69 G4
KBRN KA25 124 C4
KLBCH PA10 73 G6
LARGS KA30 106 F5
LRKH ML9 130 D7
PSLYS PA2 75 K8
Parkview Av KKNTL G66 45 K3
Parkview Ct KKNTL G66 45 K3
Parkview Crs WISHAW ML2 123 G5
Parkview Dr CTBR ML5 83 L3
STPS/GTHM/RID G33 63 L4
Parkville Dr BLTYR/CAMB G72 118 F4
Parkville Rd BLSH ML4 100 C2
Park Wy CUMB G67 31 H5
Parkway ERSK PA8 57 H3
Parkway Ct
BAIL/MDB/MHD G69 82 B3
CTBR ML5 83 L4
Parkway Pl CTBR ML5 83 L5
Park Winding ERSK PA8 57 J2
Park Wd ERSK PA8 57 J1
Parlament Rd KKNTL G66 45 K3
Parnell St AIRDRIE ML6 84 F4
Parnie St CGLE G1 5 H8
Parry Ter EKILS G75 126 E1
Parsonage Rw COWCAD G4 5 J7
Parsonage Sq CGLE G1 5 J7
Partick Bridge St PTCK G11 78 C1
Partickhill Av PTCK G11 60 B8
Partickhill Rd PTCK G11 60 B8
Partick St CTBR ML5 84 C4
Partridge Rd
GRNKW/INVK PA16 16 A3
Paterson Dr HBR/GL G84 10 B3
Paterson Pl BSDN G61 41 J1
Paterson's Laun BSHPBGS G64 43 L3
Paterson St GBLS G5 79 G5
MTHW ML1 120 E2
Paterson Ter EKILS G75 2 C9
Pather St WISHAW ML2 122 B7
Pathhead Gdns
STPS/GTHM/RID G33 62 F4
Pathhead Rd
CRMNK/CLK/EAG G76 115 K3
Patna Ct HMLTN ML3 128 E1
Patna St DMNK/BRGTN G40 80 B7
Paton Qd LARGS KA30 107 G4
Paton St DEN/PKHD G31 80 B3
GRNKW/INVK PA16 16 C5
Patrickbank Crs JNSTN PA5 90 D1
Patrick St GRNKW/INVK PA16 6 B2
PSLYS PA2 9 J7
Patterson Dr CARLUKE ML8 132 C3
Patterton Dr BRHD/NEIL G78 92 D8
Pattison St CLYDBK G81 39 L7
Paxstone Dr SHOTTS ML7 71 K7
Paxton Ct EKILN G74 116 F6
Paxton Crs EKILN G74 116 F6
Payne St COWCAD G4 4 F2
Peace Av BRWEIR PA11 53 M8
Peach Ct MTHW ML1 101 K7
Peacock Av PSLYS PA2 74 F8
Peacock Ct CARLUKE ML8 135 H1
Peacock Dr HMLTN ML3 119 J6
PSLYS PA2 74 F8
Pearce La GOV/IBX G51 78 A2
Pearce St GOV/IBX G51 78 A2
Pear Gv MTHW ML1 101 K7
Pearl St BLSH ML4 100 B6
Pearson Dr RNFRW PA4 58 D7
Pearson Pl PSLYN/LNWD PA3 74 B5
Peathill Av BAIL/MDB/MHD G69 64 B2
Peathill St SPRGB/BLRNK G21 61 J7
Peat Rd BRWEIR PA11 72 E3
GRNK PA15 16 D6
PLK/PH/NH G53 93 H3
Peden St SHOTTS ML7 71 J7
Pedmyre La
CRMNK/CLK/EAG G76 115 J3
Peebles Dr RUTH G73 96 D3
Peebles Pth CTBR ML5 84 D6
Peel Av MTHW ML1 120 E5
Peel Glen Gdns DRUM G15 41 G4
Peel Glen Rd BSDN G61 41 G3
Peel La PTCK G11 60 A8
Peel Park Pl EKILN G74 126 C1
Peel Pl CTBR ML5 83 K5
UD/BTH/TAN G71 99 G7
Peel Rd EKILN G74 126 A2
Peel St DMBTN G82 19 H3
PTCK G11 60 B8
Pegasus Av CARLUKE ML8 133 G7
PSLY PA1 74 D5
Pegasus Rd BLSH ML4 100 E4
Peile St GRNKW/INVK PA16 16 C3
Pembroke EKILN G74 117 J6
Pembroke Rd
GRNKW/INVK PA16 15 K5
Pembroke St KVGV G3 78 F2
Pembury Crs HMLTN ML3 128 F3
Pencaitland Dr CAR/SHTL G32 81 G7
Pencaitland Gv CAR/SHTL G32 81 G8
Pencaitland Pl SMSTN G23 60 E1
Pencil Vw LARGS KA30 106 F8
Pendale Ri CSMK G45 95 K7
Pendeen Crs
STPS/GTHM/RID G33 81 L5
Pendeen Pl
STPS/GTHM/RID G33 81 M4
Pendeen Rd
STPS/GTHM/RID G33 81 M5
Pendicle Crs BSDN G61 41 K6
Pendicle Rd BSDN G61 41 K6
Pendle Ct BAIL/MDB/MHD G69 64 F4
Penfold Crs EKILS G75 2 C7
Penilee Rd
CARD/HILL/MSPK G52 76 E2
Penilee Ter
CARD/HILL/MSPK G52 76 E3
Peninver Dr GOV/IBX G51 77 K1
Penman Av RUTH G73 95 M2
Pennan Pl SCOT G14 59 G4
Penneld Rd
CARD/HILL/MSPK G52 76 F4
Penniecroft Av DMBTN G82 21 J5
Pennine Gv AIRDRIE ML6 85 M8
Pennyfern Dr
GRNKW/INVK PA16 16 B6
Pennyfern Rd
GRNKW/INVK PA16 16 B6
Pennyroyal Ct EKILN G74 2 C1
Penrioch Dr EKILS G75 126 F6
Penrith Av GIF/THBK G46 94 C8
Penrith Dr KVD/HLHD G12 60 A4
Penrith Pl EKILS G75 126 C4
Penryn Gdns CAR/SHTL G32 81 K7
Penston Rd
STPS/GTHM/RID G33 81 K2
Pentland Av PGL PA14 34 F4
PSLYN/LNWD PA3 74 A5
Pentland Crs LRKH ML9 130 B4
PSLYS PA2 91 K2
Pentland Dr BRHD/NEIL G78 92 C8
BSHPBGS G64 44 D8
RNFRW PA4 76 B1
Pentland Gdns LRKH ML9 130 B4
Pentland Pl BSDN G61 41 H2
Pentland Rd
BAIL/MDB/MHD G69 64 D2
EKILS G75 126 D7
PLKSW/MSWD G43 94 C5
WISHAW ML2 121 L5
Pentland Wy HMLTN ML3 129 G3
Penzance Wy
BAIL/MDB/MHD G69 46 F8
Peockland Gdns JNSTN PA5 74 A7
Peockland Pl JNSTN PA5 74 A7
Peploe Dr EKILN G74 117 K5
Perchy Vw WISHAW ML2 122 C8
Percy Dr GIF/THBK G46 114 C1
Percy Rd PSLYN/LNWD PA3 76 A1
Percy St GOV/IBX G51 78 C5
LRKH ML9 130 C5
Perran Gdns
BAIL/MDB/MHD G69 46 E8
Perray Av DMBTN G82 20 B5
Perrays Crs DMBTN G82 20 A5
Perrays Dr DMBTN G82 20 A5
Perrays Gv DMBTN G82 20 A5
Perrays Wy DMBTN G82 20 A5
Perth Av AIRDRIE ML6 85 G4
Perth Crs CLYDBK G81 39 K5
Perth St KVGV G3 4 A6
Peter D. Stirling Rd KKNTL G66 45 K1
Peters Av ALEX/LLW G83 13 M2
Petersburn Pl AIRDRIE ML6 85 K3
Petersburn Rd AIRDRIE ML6 85 K3
Petershill Ct
SPRGB/BLRNK G21 62 B7
Petershill Dr
SPRGB/BLRNK G21 62 C7
Petershill Pl SPRGB/BLRNK G21 62 B6
Petershill Rd
SPRGB/BLRNK G21 61 M7
Peterson Dr KNTSWD G13 58 E1
Peterson Gdns KNTSWD G13 58 E1
Petition Pl UD/BTH/TAN G71 99 G5
Pettigrew St CAR/SHTL G32 81 G5
Peveril Av PLKSD/SHW G41 94 D1
RUTH G73 96 C5
Pharonhill St DEN/PKHD G31 80 E5
Philip Ct BLSH ML4 100 A5
Philip Murray Rd BLSH ML4 99 K4
Philipshill Ga EKILN G74 115 L7
Philipshill Rd EKILN G74 115 L7
Phillips Av LARGS KA30 107 G4
Phoenix Crs BLSH ML4 99 M2
Phoenix Pl JNSTN PA5 74 D7
MTHW ML1 101 G6
Phoenix Rd BLSH ML4 100 E4
Piccadilly St KVGV G3 4 A7
Pickerstonhill MTHW ML1 101 L5
Picketlaw Dr
CRMNK/CLK/EAG G76 115 K3
Picketlaw Farm Rd
CRMNK/CLK/EAG G76 115 J3
Pienchorran ERSK PA8 57 J3
Pier Rd ALEX/LLW G83 13 J1
Piershill St CAR/SHTL G32 80 F3
Pikeman Rd KNTSWD G13 59 J3
Pillans Ct HMLTN ML3 119 G4
Pilmuir Av LNPK/KPK G44 94 F6
Pilrig St CAR/SHTL G32 80 E3
Pilton Rd DRUM G15 41 G6
Pine Av BLTYR/CAMB G72 97 M7
Pine Cl CUMB G67 31 L5
Pine Ct CUMB G67 31 L5
EKILS G75 126 E5
Pine Crs CUMB G67 31 L5
EKILS G75 126 E5
HMLTN ML3 129 G3
JNSTN PA5 90 A1
Pine Gv AIRDRIE ML6 85 H7
BAIL/MDB/MHD G69 83 G4
CUMB G67 31 L5
UD/BTH/TAN G71 99 H2
Pine Lawn WISHAW ML2 122 D4
Pine Pk HMLTN ML3 129 L1
Pine Pl CUMB G67 31 L5
GBLS G5 79 J6
Pine Qd AIRDRIE ML6 85 L6
Pine Rd CLYDBK G81 39 K6
CUMB G67 31 L5
DMBTN G82 20 F6
Pine St AIRDRIE ML6 85 K2
GRNK PA15 6 A7
KKNTL G66 26 E2
PSLYS PA2 76 A7
Pinewood Av KKNTL G66 45 G5
Pinewood Ct DMBTN G82 21 J5
KKNTL G66 45 G5
Pinewood Pl KKNTL G66 45 G5
Pinewood Sq DRUM G15 41 H6
Pinkerton Av RUTH G73 95 M2
Pinkerton La RNFRW PA4 58 D8
Pinkston Dr
SPRGB/BLRNK G21 5 K1
Pinkston Rd COWCAD G4 61 K8
SPRGB/BLRNK G21 5 J1
Pinmore Pl PLK/PH/NH G53 92 F4
Pinmore St PLK/PH/NH G53 92 F4
Pinwherry Dr
STPS/GTHM/RID G33 62 F4
Pinwherry Pl UD/BTH/TAN G71 99 G7
Piper Av CRG/CRSL/HOU PA6 73 J2
Piper Rd AIRDRIE ML6 85 J4
CRG/CRSL/HOU PA6 73 J2
Pirnie Pl KSYTH G65 29 K2
Pirnmill Av EKILS G75 126 E6
MTHW ML1 120 B2
Pirnmill Pl HBR/GL G84 10 F5
Pitcairn Crs EKILS G75 126 C2
Pitcairn Gv EKILS G75 126 D2
Pitcairn Pl EKILS G75 126 C2
Pitcairn St DEN/PKHD G31 80 E6
Pitcairn Ter HMLTN ML3 119 G6
Pitcaple Dr
PLKSW/MSWD G43 94 B4
Pitlochry Dr
CARD/HILL/MSPK G52 77 H5
LRKH ML9 130 E8
Pitmedden Rd BSHPBGS G64 44 D8
Pitmilly Rd DRUM G15 41 J5
Pitreavie Ct HMLTN ML3 129 H2
Pitreavie Pl
STPS/GTHM/RID G33 63 J8
Pit Rd BLSH ML4 99 M4
KKNTL G66 46 B3
Pittenweem Pth
BLTYR/CAMB G72 118 D7
Pitt St CGLW G2 4 C4
Place of Bonhill DMBTN G82 13 J7
Place Vw KBRN KA25 124 B4
Pladda Av PGL PA14 35 H3
Pladda Rd RNFRW PA4 58 D8
Pladda St MTHW ML1 120 B1
Pladda Wy HBR/GL G84 10 F5
Plaintrees Ct PSLYS PA2 91 L1
Plane Pl UD/BTH/TAN G71 99 H1
Planetree Pl JNSTN PA5 90 A1
Planetree Rd CLYDBK G81 40 A5
Plantation Av MTHW ML1 101 H3
Plantation Park Gdns
GOV/IBX G51 78 D5
Plantation Sq GOV/IBX G51 78 E4
Plant St DEN/PKHD G31 80 C4
Plan Vw KBRN KA25 124 D2
Platthorn Dr EKILN G74 3 H5
Platthorn Rd EKILN G74 3 H6
Playfair St DMNK/BRGTN G40 80 A7
Plaza EKILN G74 2 F7
Pleaknowe Crs
BAIL/MDB/MHD G69 46 E8
Pleamuir Pl BALLOCH G68 30 C8
Plean St SCOT G14 59 G4
Pleasance St
PLKSW/MSWD G43 94 C2
Pleasance Wy
PLKSW/MSWD G43 94 C3
Pleasantside Av PGL PA14 35 G2
Plover Dr EKILS G75 126 D5
Plover Pl JNSTN PA5 89 J3
Plymouth Av GRK PA19 15 L4
Pochard Wy BLSH ML4 99 M2
Poet's Vw KKNTL G66 45 M3
Poindfauld Ter DMBTN G82 21 G6
Pointhouse Rd KVGV G3 78 C2
Polden Av EKILS G75 126 D7
Polden Ct EKILS G75 126 D7
Polkemmet Dr SHOTTS ML7 71 M6
Polkemmet Rd SHOTTS ML7 71 M6
Pollick Av BRHD/NEIL G78 110 B7
Pollick Farm La
BRHD/NEIL G78 110 A8
Pollock Av HMLTN ML3 119 G7
Pollock Rd BSDN G61 42 A7
NMRNS G77 113 J5
Pollock St BLSH ML4 100 C4
Pollok Dr BSHPBGS G64 61 L1
Pollok La EKILN G74 3 M1
Pollok Pl EKILN G74 3 M1
Pollokshaws Rd
GVH/MTFL G42 79 G7
PLKSW/MSWD G43 94 C3
Pollokshields Sq
PLKSD/SHW G41 78 E8
Polmadie Av GBLS G5 79 K8
Polmadie Rd GBLS G5 79 L7
GVH/MTFL G42 95 K1
Polmadie St GVH/MTFL G42 95 J1
Polnoon Av KNTSWD G13 59 G3
Polquhap Ct PLK/PH/NH G53 93 G1
Polquhap Gdns
PLK/PH/NH G53 93 G1
Polquhap Pl PLK/PH/NH G53 93 G1
Polquhap Rd PLK/PH/NH G53 93 G1
Polson Dr JNSTN PA5 73 L8
Polsons Crs PSLYS PA2 8 F9
Polwarth La KVD/HLHD G12 60 B7
Polwarth St KVD/HLHD G12 60 B7
Pomona Pl HMLTN ML3 118 F8
Poplar Av BSHPTN PA7 38 B8
JNSTN PA5 90 A1
NMRNS G77 113 L6
PTCK G11 59 M5
Poplar Crs BSHPTN PA7 38 B8
Poplar Dr CLYDBK G81 39 M5
KKNTL G66 45 G5
Poplar Gdns EKILS G75 126 F5
Poplar Pl BLTYR/CAMB G72 118 C1
GRK PA19 15 J3
MTHW ML1 101 H5
UD/BTH/TAN G71 99 K2
Poplar Rd DMBTN G82 20 F6
The Poplars BSDN G61 41 K1
Poplar St AIRDRIE ML6 85 J2
GRNK PA15 17 M7
Poplar Wy BLTYR/CAMB G72 97 M7
MTHW ML1 101 K7
Poplin St DMNK/BRGTN G40 79 M7
Porchester St
STPS/GTHM/RID G33 63 K8
Portal Rd KNTSWD G13 59 J1
Port Dundas Pl CGLW G2 4 F4
Port Dundas Rd COWCAD G4 4 E2
Porterfield Rd KLMCLM PA13 53 K3
RNFRW PA4 58 B7
Porter St GOV/IBX G51 78 C5
Porters Well UD/BTH/TAN G71 98 E5
Portessie ERSK PA8 39 G8
Port Glasgow Rd GRNK PA15 17 M7
KLMCLM PA13 53 J1
Portia Pl MTHW ML1 120 E2
Portland Pk HMLTN ML3 119 L8
Portland Pl HMLTN ML3 119 L8
LNK/LMHG ML11 137 H6
Portland Rd BALLOCH G68 30 F4
PSLYS PA2 76 B6
Portland Sq HMLTN ML3 119 L8
Portland St CTBR ML5 84 B1
Portman St PLKSD/SHW G41 78 E5
Portmarnock Dr SMSTN G23 60 E2
Portpatrick Rd OLDK G60 38 F3
Portreath Rd
BAIL/MDB/MHD G69 46 F7
Portree Av CTBR ML5 83 L6
Portree Pl DRUM G15 40 E5
Portsmouth Dr GRK PA19 15 L4
Portsoy Av KNTSWD G13 58 E1
Portsoy Pl KNTSWD G13 58 F1
Port St KVGV G3 78 F3
Portugal St GBLS G5 79 H5
Portwell HMLTN ML3 119 L6
Possil Rd COWCAD G4 61 H8
Postgate HMLTN ML3 119 L6
Potassels Rd
BAIL/MDB/MHD G69 64 C3
Potrail Pl HMLTN ML3 119 G7
Potter Cl CAR/SHTL G32 80 E7
Potter Gv CAR/SHTL G32 80 E7
Potterhill Av PSLYS PA2 91 L2
Potterhill Rd PLK/PH/NH G53 77 G7
Potter Pl CAR/SHTL G32 80 E7
Potter St CAR/SHTL G32 80 E7
Potters Wynd
LNK/LMHG ML11 137 J4
Pottery St GRNK PA15 17 L6
Potts Wy MTHW ML1 100 C8
Powbrone EKILS G75 127 H5
Powburn Crs
UD/BTH/TAN G71 98 D3
Powfoot St DEN/PKHD G31 80 D5
Powforth Cl LRKH ML9 130 A6
Powgree Crs BEITH KA15 125 L8
Powrie St
STPS/GTHM/RID G33 63 J7
Prentice La UD/BTH/TAN G71 99 G2
Prentice Rd MTHW ML1 120 B4
Prestonfield MLNGV G62 41 L1
Preston Pl GRK PA19 15 K3
GVH/MTFL G42 79 H8
Preston St GVH/MTFL G42 79 H8
Prestwick Ct BALLOCH G68 30 F5
Prestwick Pl NMRNS G77 114 A6
Prestwick St PLK/PH/NH G53 93 G3
Pretoria Ct EKILS G75 126 E6
Priestfield St
BLTYR/CAMB G72 118 C4
Priesthill Av PLK/PH/NH G53 93 J3
Priesthill Crs PLK/PH/NH G53 93 J3
Priesthill Gdns PLK/PH/NH G53 93 J3
Priesthill Rd PLK/PH/NH G53 93 H3
Prieston Rd BRWEIR PA11 72 D3
Primrose Av BLSH ML4 100 A2
GRNKW/INVK PA16 32 F4
Primrose Crs
GRNKW/INVK PA16 32 F4
MTHW ML1 120 E4
Primrose Pl CUMB G67 48 B2
GRNKW/INVK PA16 32 F4
UD/BTH/TAN G71 99 J2
Primrose St SCOT G14 59 J6
Primrose Wy CARLUKE ML8 134 E1
KKNTL G66 26 E3
Prince Albert Rd
KVD/HLHD G12 60 B7
Prince Edward St
GVH/MTFL G42 79 G8
Prince of Wales Gdns
MRYH/FIRH G20 60 C2
Prince Pl WISHAW ML2 123 G3
Prince's Gdns KVD/HLHD G12 60 B7
Prince's Gardens La
KVD/HLHD G12 60 B7
Princes Ga RUTH G73 96 A2
UD/BTH/TAN G71 98 E6
Princes Ml EKILN G74 3 G6
Princes Pk BSHPTN PA7 38 E6
Prince's Pl KVD/HLHD G12 60 C7
Princess Crs PSLY PA1 76 B3
Princess Dr
BAIL/MDB/MHD G69 83 G5
Princes Sq BRHD/NEIL G78 92 D6
EKILN G74 2 F6
Princess Rd MTHW ML1 100 F5
Princes St AIRDRIE ML6 69 G4
GRNK PA15 6 B3
MTHW ML1 120 E1
PGL PA14 18 C8
RUTH G73 96 A2
Princes St East HBR/GL G84 10 E6
Prince's Ter KVD/HLHD G12 60 C7
Prince's Terrace La
KVD/HLHD G12 60 C7
Printers Lea KKNTL G66 26 C2
Priorwood Gdns KNTSWD G13 59 K3
Priorwood Ga NMRNS G77 113 H5
Priorwood Pl KNTSWD G13 59 K3
Priorwood Rd NMRNS G77 113 G5
Priorwood Wy NMRNS G77 113 G5
Priory Av PSLYN/LNWD PA3 76 A2
Priory Dr UD/BTH/TAN G71 98 D3
Priory Ga WISHAW ML2 131 K2
Priory Pl BALLOCH G68 47 L1
KNTSWD G13 59 K2
Priory Rd KNTSWD G13 59 K2
Priory St BLTYR/CAMB G72 118 D3
Priory Ter WISHAW ML2 121 J7
Procession Rd PSLYS PA2 91 K5
Progress Dr AIRDRIE ML6 68 F4
Prosen St CAR/SHTL G32 80 E7
Prospect Av BLTYR/CAMB G72 96 F4
UD/BTH/TAN G71 98 E4
Prospect Ct BLTYR/CAMB G72 118 D5
Prospecthill Circ
GVH/MTFL G42 95 L1
Prospecthill Crs GVH/MTFL G42 95 L2
Prospecthill Dr GVH/MTFL G42 95 J2
Prospecthill Gv GVH/MTFL G42 95 G2
Prospecthill Pl GRNK PA15 6 B5
GVH/MTFL G42 95 L2
Prospecthill Rd GVH/MTFL G42 95 H2
Prospecthill Sq GVH/MTFL G42 95 K2
Prospecthill St GRNK PA15 6 A6
Prospecthill Wy GVH/MTFL G42 95 G2
Prospect Rd BALLOCH G68 30 C3
PLKSD/SHW G41 94 D2
Provand Hall Crs
BAIL/MDB/MHD G69 82 B7
Provanhill St
SPRGB/BLRNK G21 5 M2
Provanmill Rd
STPS/GTHM/RID G33 62 E8
Provan Rd STPS/GTHM/RID G33 80 C1
Provost Driver Ct RNFRW PA4 58 D8
Provost Ga LRKH ML9 130 C6
Pundeavon Av KBRN KA25 124 C3
Purdie EKILN G74 117 K5
Purdie St HMLTN ML3 119 G5
Purdon St PTCK G11 60 B8
Pyatshaw Rd LRKH ML9 130 D8

Q

Quadrant Rd
PLKSW/MSWD G43 94 E5
The Quadrant
CRMNK/CLK/EAG G76 114 F2
Quantock Dr EKILS G75 126 D7
Quarrelton Gv JNSTN PA5 89 M1
Quarrelton Rd JNSTN PA5 73 L8
Quarrier St GRNK PA15 7 M8
Quarry Av BLTYR/CAMB G72 97 K7
Quarrybank KLBCH PA10 73 J8
Quarrybrae Av
CRMNK/CLK/EAG G76 114 D3
Quarrybrae Gdns
UD/BTH/TAN G71 99 J4
Quarrybrae St DEN/PKHD G31 80 E5
Quarry Dr KKNTL G66 45 M2
KLMCLM PA13 35 K8
Quarry Knowe DMBTN G82 20 D5
Quarryknowe
LNK/LMHG ML11 137 G5
RUTH G73 95 M3
Quarryknowe Gdns
DEN/PKHD G31 80 E5
Quarry Knowe Pl BLSH ML4 99 M7
Quarryknowe St CLYDBK G81 40 E2
DEN/PKHD G31 80 E5
Quarry La KKNTL G66 26 D1
Quarry Pk EKILS G75 2 E8
Quarry Pl BLTYR/CAMB G72 96 E4
DMBTN G82 20 D5
SHOTTS ML7 104 D4
Quarry Rd AIRDRIE ML6 66 F8
BRHD/NEIL G78 92 B5
CARLUKE ML8 132 C6
EKILS G75 127 G5
LRKH ML9 130 C7
PGL PA14 34 F3
PSLYS PA2 91 M1
SHOTTS ML7 104 D4
Quarryside St AIRDRIE ML6 66 E5
Quarry St CTBR ML5 84 D3
HMLTN ML3 119 L7
JNSTN PA5 73 M7
LRKH ML9 130 D8
MTHW ML1 101 G5
SHOTTS ML7 104 D4
WISHAW ML2 122 A6
Quarrywood Av
SPRGB/BLRNK G21 62 C6
Quarrywood Rd
SPRGB/BLRNK G21 62 D6
Quay Pend DMBTN G82 20 E7
Quay Rd RUTH G73 96 A2
Quay Rd North RUTH G73 96 A1
Quay St DMBTN G82 20 F7
Quebec Dr EKILS G75 2 A6
Quebec Wynd CAR/SHTL G32 97 J2
Queen Elizabeth Av
CARD/HILL/MSPK G52 76 E2
Queen Elizabeth Ct
CLYDBK G81 40 A6
Queen Elizabeth Gdns
CLYDBK G81 40 A6
GBLS G5 79 J6
Queen Elizabeth Sq GBLS G5 79 J6
Queen Margaret Dr
KVD/HLHD G12 60 E7
Queen Margaret Rd
MRYH/FIRH G20 60 E7
Queen Mary Av CLYDBK G81 40 D7
GVH/MTFL G42 95 H1
Queen Mary Gdns CLYDBK G81 40 A6
Queen Mary St
DMNK/BRGTN G40 80 A6
Queen's Av BLTYR/CAMB G72 97 H4
LARGS KA30 106 F4
Queensbank Av
BAIL/MDB/MHD G69 64 E3
Queensberry Av BSDN G61 41 L2
CARD/HILL/MSPK G52 76 F2
CRMNK/CLK/EAG G76 114 E3
Queensborough Gdns
KVD/HLHD G12 60 A6
Queensby Av
BAIL/MDB/MHD G69 82 B5
Queensby Pl
BAIL/MDB/MHD G69 82 C4
Queensby Rd
BAIL/MDB/MHD G69 82 B4
Queen's Ct MLNGV G62 42 A2
Queen's Crs AIRDRIE ML6 85 K6
BAIL/MDB/MHD G69 82 F5
BLSH ML4 99 M6
CARLUKE ML8 133 J7
COWCAD G4 4 B1
MTHW ML1 100 F6
MTHW ML1 102 B7

Queen's Dr ALEX/LLW G83 13 J7
BALLOCH G68 30 F3
BSHPTN PA7 38 C7
GVH/MTFL G42 78 F8
HMLTN ML3 129 K4
Queen's Drive La
GVH/MTFL G42 95 H1
Queensferry St GBLS G5 79 L8
Queen's Gdns KVD/HLHD G12 60 C7
Queen's Ga
CRMNK/CLK/EAG G76 114 E2
Queens Gate La
KVD/HLHD G12 60 C7
Queens Gv KKNTL G66 45 J6
Queenside Crs ERSK PA8 56 F1
Queensland Dr
CARD/HILL/MSPK G52 77 J3
Queensland Gdns
CARD/HILL/MSPK G52 77 J3
Queensland La East
CARD/HILL/MSPK G52 77 J4
Queensland La West
CARD/HILL/MSPK G52 77 J3
Queenslie St
STPS/GTHM/RID G33 62 D8
Queen's Park Av GVH/MTFL G42 95 H1
Queen's Pl KVD/HLHD G12 60 C7
Queen Sq PLKSD/SHW G41 78 F8
Queen's Rd JNSTN PA5 74 C8
Queen St ALEX/LLW G83 13 J6
CGLW G2 4 F7
HBR/GL G84 10 C4
HMLTN ML3 119 G5
KKNTL G66 45 J2
MTHW ML1 120 E2
PGL PA14 18 C8
PSLY PA1 8 D5
RNFRW PA4 58 D6
RUTH G73 96 A2
WISHAW ML2 122 F3
Queens Vw BSHPBGS G64 44 B2
Queens Wy ALEX/LLW G83 13 J6
Queensway EKILN G74 2 A5
GRK PA19 15 J3
Queen Victoria Dr SCOT G14 59 J5
Queen Victoria Ga KNTSWD G13 59 J4
Queen Victoria St AIRDRIE ML6 84 F2
Quendale Dr CAR/SHTL G32 80 F7
Quentin St PLKSD/SHW G41 94 E1
Quinton Gdns
BAIL/MDB/MHD G69 82 A5

R

Raasay Crs AIRDRIE ML6 85 L3
Raasay Dr PSLYS PA2 91 K3
Raasay Gdns NMRNS G77 113 H4
Raasay St PPK/MIL G22 61 J2
Racecourse Vw HMLTN ML3 119 L5
Rachan St ESTRH G34 82 D1
Radnor St CLYDBK G81 40 B6
KVGV G3 78 D1
Raeberry St MRYH/FIRH G20 60 F7
Raebog Crs AIRDRIE ML6 66 F7
Raebog Rd AIRDRIE ML6 67 G4
Raeburn Av EKILN G74 117 H6
PSLY PA1 9 K6
Raeburn Crs HMLTN ML3 118 E7
Raeburn Pl EKILN G74 117 H6
Raeside Av NMRNS G77 113 K6
Raes Rd CARLUKE ML8 134 B1
Raeswood Dr PLK/PH/NH G53 92 F1
Raeswood Rd PLK/PH/NH G53 92 F1
Raewell Crs BLSH ML4 99 M7
Raglan St ALEX/LLW G83 13 L7
COWCAD G4 4 C1
Raglan Street La ALEX/LLW G83 13 L7
Raillies Av LARGS KA30 106 F2
Raillies Rd LARGS KA30 106 F2
Railway Rd AIRDRIE ML6 84 D2
Raith Av CSMK G45 95 K6
Raithburn Av CSMK G45 95 J6
Raithburn Rd CSMK G45 95 J7
Raith Dr BALLOCH G68 47 K1
BLSH ML4 100 B5
Ralston Av PSLY PA1 76 F6
Ralston Ct
CARD/HILL/MSPK G52 76 F5
Ralston Dr
CARD/HILL/MSPK G52 76 F5
Ralston Pl
CARD/HILL/MSPK G52 76 F5
Ralston Rd BRHD/NEIL G78 92 C7
BSDN G61 41 L4
Ralston St AIRDRIE ML6 84 E2
PSLY PA1 9 M6
Ramage Rd CARLUKE ML8 133 K8
Ramillies Ct CARLUKE ML8 133 J8
Ramoth LNK/LMHG ML11 136 D5
Rampart Av KNTSWD G13 59 G1
Ramsay Av JNSTN PA5 89 L1
Ramsay Ct NMRNS G77 113 L6
Ramsay Crs KLBCH PA10 73 H8
Ramsay Hl EKILN G74 3 K2
Ramsay Pl CTBR ML5 83 K5
JNSTN PA5 89 L1
Ramsay St CLYDBK G81 39 M7
Ram St CAR/SHTL G32 80 F5
Ranald Gdns RUTH G73 96 D7
Randolph Av
CRMNK/CLK/EAG G76 114 F1
Randolph Dr
CRMNK/CLK/EAG G76 114 F1
Randolph Gdns
CRMNK/CLK/EAG G76 114 F1
Randolph Ga PTCK G11 59 M5
Randolph La PTCK G11 59 M6
Randolph Rd PTCK G11 59 M6
Ranfurly Dr BALLOCH G68 30 E5
Ranfurly Pl BRWEIR PA11 72 D3
Ranfurly Rd BRWEIR PA11 72 E4
CARD/HILL/MSPK G52 76 F4
Range Av MTHW ML1 121 J6
Range Pl HMLTN ML3 129 L1
Rangerhouse Rd EKILS G75 127 J5
Range Rd MTHW ML1 121 H5
Range St MTHW ML1 121 H5
Rankin Crs AIRDRIE ML6 49 M7
Rankin Dr LARGS KA30 106 F3
NMRNS G77 113 J3
Rankine Av EKILS G75 3 K9
Rankine Pl EKILS G75 3 K9
JNSTN PA5 73 M7
Rankine St JNSTN PA5 73 M7
Rankin Rd WISHAW ML2 122 E5
Rankin St CARLUKE ML8 133 H7
GRNKW/INVK PA16 16 C5
Rannoch Av BSHPBGS G64 62 B1
CTBR ML5 83 K1
HMLTN ML3 129 G1
NMRNS G77 113 K2
Rannoch Ct CUMB G67 48 B3
Rannoch Dr BSDN G61 42 B7
CUMB G67 48 B3
KKNTL G66 46 B1
RNFRW PA4 58 C5
WISHAW ML2 131 K1
Rannoch Gn EKILN G74 3 G1
Rannoch Pl PSLYS PA2 9 L8
SHOTTS ML7 104 E3
Rannoch Rd AIRDRIE ML6 66 F8
JNSTN PA5 89 M1
KLMCLM PA13 53 J3
UD/BTH/TAN G71 98 E1
WMYSB PA18 50 B1
Rannoch St LNPK/KPK G44 95 G4
Rannoch Ter LRKH ML9 130 E8
Raploch Av SCOT G14 59 H5
Raploch La SCOT G14 59 H5
Raploch Rd LRKH ML9 130 B7
Raploch St LRKH ML9 130 B6
Rashielee ERSK PA8 39 G8
Rashielee Av ERSK PA8 39 H8
Rashielee Rd ERSK PA8 39 G8
Rathlin St GOV/IBX G51 78 A2
Rathlin Ter DMBTN G82 20 D5
Ratho Dr BALLOCH G68 30 E4
SPRGB/BLRNK G21 61 L6
Ratho Pk HMLTN ML3 129 H3
Ratho St GRNK PA15 7 K6
Rattray St CAR/SHTL G32 80 E7
Ravel Rw DEN/PKHD G31 80 D5
Ravelston Rd BSDN G61 41 L7
Ravelston St CAR/SHTL G32 80 D4
Ravel Wynd UD/BTH/TAN G71 99 H2
Raven Rd GRNKW/INVK PA16 16 A4
Ravenscliffe Dr GIF/THBK G46 94 B7
Ravenscourt EKILN G74 115 J7
Ravenscraig Av PSLYS PA2 75 J8
Ravenscraig Ct BLSH ML4 100 B4
Ravenscraig Dr
PLK/PH/NH G53 93 H3
Ravenscraig Ter
PLK/PH/NH G53 93 J4
Ravenshall MTHW ML1 122 B1
Ravenshall Rd
PLKSD/SHW G41 94 C2
Ravenshill Dr MTHW ML1 102 C8
Ravenstone Dr GIF/THBK G46 94 C6
Ravenswood Av PSLYS PA2 90 E3
Ravenswood Dr
PLKSD/SHW G41 94 D1
Ravenswood Rd
BAIL/MDB/MHD G69 82 C6
Raven Wynd WISHAW ML2 122 B6
Rawyards Av AIRDRIE ML6 67 H7
Raymond Pl EKILS G75 2 B6
Rayne Pl DRUM G15 41 H5
Ream Av AIRDRIE ML6 85 M3
Reay Av DMBTN G82 19 G2
EKILN G74 116 B8
Reay Gdns EKILN G74 116 B8
Redan St DMNK/BRGTN G40 79 M5
Redbrae Rd KKNTL G66 45 L2
Redburn ALEX/LLW G83 13 M8
Redburn Av GIF/THBK G46 114 B2
Redburn Ct CUMB G67 31 M3
Redburn Pl CUMB G67 31 M4
Redburn Rd BTHG/ARM EH48 71 H1
CUMB G67 31 M3
Redcastle Sq
STPS/GTHM/RID G33 81 K1
Redcliffe Dr EKILS G75 126 E2
Redclyffe Gdns HBR/GL G84 10 D3
Red Deer Rd EKILS G75 2 A7
Rederech Crs HMLTN ML3 118 F8
Redford St
STPS/GTHM/RID G33 80 D2
Red Fox Dr ALEX/LLW G83 13 K2
Redgate Pl SCOT G14 59 H5
Redgauntlet Rd HBR/GL G84 10 F7
Redgrave EKILN G74 117 J5
Redhaws Rd SHOTTS ML7 105 G6
Redheugh Av KBRN KA25 124 D2
Redhill Rd BALLOCH G68 30 D6
Redhills Vw KKNTL G66 26 F3
Redhurst Crs PSLYS PA2 91 H3
Redhurst La PSLYS PA2 91 H3
Redhurst Wy PSLYS PA2 91 J3
Redlands La KVD/HLHD G12 60 C6
Redlands Rd KVD/HLHD G12 60 C6
Redlands Ter KVD/HLHD G12 60 C6
Redlands Terrace La
KVD/HLHD G12 60 C6
Redlawood Pl
BLTYR/CAMB G72 98 A4
Redlawood Rd
BLTYR/CAMB G72 98 A4
Redmoss Rd CLYDBK G81 39 M4
KKNTL G66 27 H5
Redmoss St PPK/MIL G22 61 H5
Rednock St PPK/MIL G22 61 J6
Redpath Dr BLTYR/CAMB G72 97 K4
CARD/HILL/MSPK G52 77 H3
Red Rd SPRGB/BLRNK G21 62 B6
Red Road Ct SPRGB/BLRNK G21 62 B7
Red Rw DMBTN G82 13 J8
Redshank Av RNFRW PA4 58 E5
Redwing Crs CTBR ML5 84 E7
Redwing Gdns WISHAW ML2 122 A8
Redwood Av EKILN G74 126 B1
Redwood Cl HMLTN ML3 128 F3
Redwood Ct EKILN G74 126 B1
Redwood Crs BLTYR/CAMB G72 97 M6
BSHPTN PA7 38 C7
EKILN G74 115 L8
HMLTN ML3 128 F3
UD/BTH/TAN G71 99 J2
Redwood Dr EKILN G74 126 B1
SPRGB/BLRNK G21 62 A7
Redwood Gv CTBR ML5 84 B3
Redwood Pl EKILN G74 115 M8
UD/BTH/TAN G71 99 J2
Redwood Rd CUMB G67 31 K7
MTHW ML1 101 H4
Redwood Wy BLTYR/CAMB G72 97 M7
Reelick Av KNTSWD G13 58 E1
Reelick Qd KNTSWD G13 58 E1
Reema Rd BLSH ML4 100 C3
Reen Pl UD/BTH/TAN G71 99 H6
Reform St BEITH KA15 125 K4
Regal Gv SHOTTS ML7 104 E5
Regency Wy HMLTN ML3 120 A7
MTHW ML1 100 F5
Regent Dr RUTH G73 96 A2
Regent Moray St KVGV G3 78 D1
Regent Park Sq
PLKSD/SHW G41 78 F8
Regent Pl CLYDBK G81 39 M6
Regents Ga UD/BTH/TAN G71 98 D6
Regent Sq KKNTL G66 45 J6
Regent St CLYDBK G81 39 M7
GRNK PA15 6 E5
KKNTL G66 45 J2
PSLY PA1 76 B4
Register Av BLSH ML4 100 A6
Register Rd KSYTH G65 29 L2
Regwood St PLKSD/SHW G41 94 D2
Reid Av BSDN G61 42 A4
PSLYN/LNWD PA3 74 B5
Reid Ct RUTH G73 96 B2
Reid Gv MTHW ML1 121 H5
Reidhouse St
SPRGB/BLRNK G21 61 M6
Reid Pl DMNK/BRGTN G40 79 M6
Reid St AIRDRIE ML6 67 H8
CTBR ML5 84 A1
DMNK/BRGTN G40 79 M7
HMLTN ML3 118 F5
RUTH G73 96 B2
SHOTTS ML7 87 H7
Reidvale St DEN/PKHD G31 79 M4
Reilly Rd CRG/CRSL/HOU PA6 55 J2
Reith Dr EKILS G75 127 G3
Remus Pl BLSH ML4 100 E4
Renfield La CGLW G2 4 E6
Renfield St CGLW G2 4 E4
RNFRW PA4 58 D5
Renfrew Ct CGLW G2 4 F4
Renfrew Rd
CARD/HILL/MSPK G52 59 G8
PSLYN/LNWD PA3 9 J2
Renfrew St CTBR ML5 83 J6
KVGV G3 4 C3
Rennie Pl EKILN G74 116 A7
Rennie Rd KSYTH G65 29 H1
Renshaw Dr
CARD/HILL/MSPK G52 77 H3
Renshaw Pl MTHW ML1 100 F1
Renshaw Rd BSHPTN PA7 38 B7
JNSTN PA5 90 C1
Renton Rd DMBTN G82 20 D4
GRNK PA15 17 J8
Renton St COWCAD G4 4 F2
Reservoir Rd GRK PA19 15 M3
Resipol Rd STPS/GTHM/RID G33 63 L5
Reston Dr
CARD/HILL/MSPK G52 77 H3
Reuther Av RUTH G73 96 B3
Revoch Dr KNTSWD G13 59 G2
Reynolds Av EKILS G75 3 K9
Reynolds Dr
STPS/GTHM/RID G33 63 M5
Reynolds Pth WISHAW ML2 122 D8
Rhannan Rd LNPK/KPK G44 95 G5
Rhannan Ter LNPK/KPK G44 95 G5
Rhindhouse Pl
BAIL/MDB/MHD G69 82 D5
Rhindhouse Rd
BAIL/MDB/MHD G69 82 D5
Rhindmuir Av
BAIL/MDB/MHD G69 82 C5
Rhindmuir Ct
BAIL/MDB/MHD G69 82 C4
Rhindmuir Crs
BAIL/MDB/MHD G69 82 D4
Rhindmuir Dr
BAIL/MDB/MHD G69 82 C4
Rhindmuir Gdns
BAIL/MDB/MHD G69 82 C4
Rhindmuir Pth
BAIL/MDB/MHD G69 82 D4
Rhindmuir Pl
BAIL/MDB/MHD G69 82 D4
Rhindmuir Rd
BAIL/MDB/MHD G69 82 C4
Rhindmuir Wynd
BAIL/MDB/MHD G69 82 D4
Rhindsdale Crs
BAIL/MDB/MHD G69 82 C5
Rhinds St CTBR ML5 83 H6
Rhu Road Higher HBR/GL G84 10 A4
Rhu Road Lower HBR/GL G84 10 A5
Rhyber Av LNK/LMHG ML11 137 H4
Rhymer St SPRGB/BLRNK G21 5 L3
Rhymie Rd CAR/SHTL G32 81 K7
Rhynie Dr GOV/IBX G51 78 B5
Riach Gdns MTHW ML1 100 C8
Ribblesdale EKILN G74 2 B1
Riccarton EKILS G75 126 E3
Riccarton St GVH/MTFL G42 79 J8
Riccartsbar Av PSLYS PA2 8 D8
Rice Wy MTHW ML1 121 H5
Richie Av DMBTN G82 19 G2
Richmond Av
CRMNK/CLK/EAG G76 114 E3
Richmond Ct RUTH G73 96 C2
Richmond Dr PSLYN/LNWD PA3 74 A3
RUTH G73 96 D3
Richmond Gdns
BAIL/MDB/MHD G69 64 B1
Richmond Gv RUTH G73 96 C3
Richmond Pl RUTH G73 96 C2
Richmond Rd BLTYR/CAMB G72 96 D3
Richmond St CGLE G1 5 H6
CLYDBK G81 40 C8
Riddell St CLYDBK G81 40 C6
CTBR ML5 84 C2
Riddon Av KNTSWD G13 58 E1
Riddon Pl KNTSWD G13 58 E1
Riddrie Crs
STPS/GTHM/RID G33 80 E2
Riddrie Knowes
STPS/GTHM/RID G33 80 E2
Riddrievale Ct
STPS/GTHM/RID G33 80 E1
Riddrievale St
STPS/GTHM/RID G33 80 E1
Ridgepark Dr LNK/LMHG ML11 136 F4
Rigby St CAR/SHTL G32 80 D4
Rigghead Av CUMB G67 31 H4
Rigg Pl STPS/GTHM/RID G33 81 L3
Riggside Rd
STPS/GTHM/RID G33 63 J8
The Riggs MLNGV G62 24 A7
Riglands Ga RNFRW PA4 58 C5
Riglaw Pl KNTSWD G13 59 G2
Rimmon Crs SHOTTS ML7 104 E3
Rimsdale St DMNK/BRGTN G40 80 A5
Ringford St SPRGB/BLRNK G21 61 M7
Ripon Dr KVD/HLHD G12 60 A4
Risk St CLYDBK G81 39 M6
DMBTN G82 20 E7
Ritchie Crs JNSTN PA5 74 C7
Ritchie Pk JNSTN PA5 74 B7
Ritchie Pl NMRNS G77 113 J5
Ritchie St GBLS G5 79 G6
WISHAW ML2 121 K6
Riverbank Dr BLSH ML4 100 D6
Riverbank St
PLKSW/MSWD G43 94 C3
River Ct CRMNK/CLK/EAG G76 114 F4
Riverdale Gdns HMLTN ML3 129 L1
River Dr RNFRW PA4 57 J5
Riverford Rd
PLKSW/MSWD G43 94 C3
RUTH G73 96 C1
River Pl KBRN KA25 124 D4
River Rd CAR/SHTL G32 97 H2
Riversdale La SCOT G14 59 G4
Riverside ALEX/LLW G83 13 K2
CRG/CRSL/HOU PA6 73 L1
KKNTL G66 26 B1
MLNGV G62 24 A8
Riverside Ct LNPK/KPK G44 94 F8
Riverside Gdns
CRMNK/CLK/EAG G76 114 F5
Riverside La DMBTN G82 20 F7
Riverside Pl BLTYR/CAMB G72 97 L4
KBRN KA25 124 D4
Riverside Rd GRNK PA15 6 F8
KBRN KA25 124 D4
LNK/LMHG ML11 136 B5
PLKSW/MSWD G43 94 E3
Riverside Ter
CRMNK/CLK/EAG G76 114 F5
Riverside Wk MTHW ML1 120 F1
Riverton Dr EKILS G75 126 E2
River View Crs DMBTN G82 19 H2
Riverview Dr GBLS G5 4 B8
Riverview Gdns GBLS G5 4 C8
Riverview Pl GBLS G5 4 B9
Roaden Av PSLYS PA2 90 F3
Roaden Rd PSLYS PA2 90 F3
Roadside CUMB G67 31 H4
Roadside Pl AIRDRIE ML6 67 K1
Robert Burns Av CLYDBK G81 40 C6
MTHW ML1 101 L5
Robert Burns Ct BEITH KA15 125 K5
Robert Burns Qd BLSH ML4 99 M5
Robert Dr GOV/IBX G51 78 A3
Robert Gilson Gdns CTBR ML5 84 B4
Robertland Av PLKSD/SHW G41 78 C8
Roberton St AIRDRIE ML6 85 L7
Robert Smillie Crs LRKH ML9 130 C8
Robertson Av RNFRW PA4 58 B6
Robertson Cl RNFRW PA4 58 B6
Robertson Crs
BRHD/NEIL G78 111 K3
Robertson Dr BLSH ML4 100 A5
EKILN G74 3 M3
RNFRW PA4 58 B6
Robertson Gait PSLYS PA2 9 G7
Robertson St AIRDRIE ML6 84 E1
BRHD/NEIL G78 92 B6
CGLW G2 4 D8
GRNKW/INVK PA16 16 D3
HMLTN ML3 118 F5
Roberts Qd BLSH ML4 100 B6
Roberts St WISHAW ML2 122 A6
Robert St GOV/IBX G51 78 A3
PGL PA14 34 E1
SHOTTS ML7 104 E5
Robert Templeton Dr
BLTYR/CAMB G72 97 H5
Robert Wynd WISHAW ML2 123 G2
Robin Pl WISHAW ML2 122 B6
Robin Rd GRNKW/INVK PA16 16 B4
Robroyston Av
STPS/GTHM/RID G33 62 E7
Robroyston Rd
STPS/GTHM/RID G33 62 D7
Robslee Crs GIF/THBK G46 94 A7
Robslee Dr GIF/THBK G46 94 B7
Robslee Rd GIF/THBK G46 94 A7
Robson Gv GVH/MTFL G42 79 H8
Rochsoles Crs AIRDRIE ML6 67 G7
Rochsoles Dr AIRDRIE ML6 66 F7
Rochsolloch Rd AIRDRIE ML6 84 D3
Rockall Dr LNPK/KPK G44 95 H6
Rockbank Crs CTBR ML5 65 L4
Rockbank Pl DMNK/BRGTN G40 80 A5
Rockbank St DMNK/BRGTN G40 80 A5
Rockburn Crs BLSH ML4 100 A2
Rockburn Dr
CRMNK/CLK/EAG G76 114 C2
Rockcliffe Pth AIRDRIE ML6 85 M8
Rockcliffe St DMNK/BRGTN G40 79 M7
Rock Dr KLBCH PA10 73 H8
Rockfield Pl SPRGB/BLRNK G21 62 C5
Rockfield Rd
SPRGB/BLRNK G21 62 C5
Rockhampton Av EKILS G75 126 E3
Rockland Pk LARGS KA30 106 F8
Rockmount Av BRHD/NEIL G78 92 D8
GIF/THBK G46 94 A7
Rockwell Av PSLYS PA2 91 J2
Rockwood Pl AIRDRIE ML6 68 D5
Roddinghead Rd
GIF/THBK G46 114 A4
The Rodding LNK/LMHG ML11 137 H4
Rodger Av NMRNS G77 113 J4
Rodger Dr RUTH G73 96 A4
Rodger Pl RUTH G73 96 A4
Rodil Av LNPK/KPK G44 95 J6
Rodney Pl HBR/GL G84 11 G5
Rodney Rd GRK PA19 15 M3
Rodney St MRYH/FIRH G20 61 H7
Roebank Dr BRHD/NEIL G78 92 C8
Roebank Rd BEITH KA15 125 L4
Roebank St DEN/PKHD G31 80 B2
Roffey Park Rd PSLY PA1 76 D4
Rogart St DMNK/BRGTN G40 79 M5
Rogerfield Rd ESTRH G34 82 C3
Rokeby La KVD/HLHD G12 60 E7
Roland Crs NMRNS G77 113 M6
Roman Av DRUM G15 41 G8
Roman Ct BSDN G61 41 L4
CLYDBK G81 40 A3
LNK/LMHG ML11 137 M2
Roman Crs OLDK G60 38 F3
Roman Dr BLSH ML4 100 B5
BSDN G61 41 M4
Roman Gdns BSDN G61 41 M4
Roman Hill Rd CLYDBK G81 40 B2
Roman Pl BLSH ML4 99 L7
Roman Rd BSDN G61 41 M5
CLYDBK G81 40 A3
KKNTL G66 45 H2
MTHW ML1 120 E2
Roman Wy UD/BTH/TAN G71 99 J4
Romney Av LNPK/KPK G44 95 J5
Romulus Ct MTHW ML1 100 C8
Rona Av PGL PA14 35 H3
Ronaldsay Dr BSHPBGS G64 44 D8
Ronaldsay Pl CUMB G67 48 D1
Ronaldsay St PPK/MIL G22 61 J3
Ronald St CTBR ML5 84 A1
Rona St SPRGB/BLRNK G21 62 B8
Rona Ter BLTYR/CAMB G72 96 F7
Ronay St PPK/MIL G22 61 K3
WISHAW ML2 122 E4
Rook Rd GRNKW/INVK PA16 16 A4
Rooksdell Av PSLYS PA2 91 J1
Ropework La CGLE G1 4 F9
Rorison Pl LRKH ML9 131 H8
Rosa Burn Av EKILS G75 126 E6
Rosebank Av
BLTYR/CAMB G72 118 E1
KKNTL G66 45 L2
Rosebank Dr BLTYR/CAMB G72 97 J6
UD/BTH/TAN G71 99 J3
Rosebank Gdns
UD/BTH/TAN G71 82 B8
Rosebank Pl BALLOCH G68 30 C3
HMLTN ML3 119 G7
Rosebank Rd BLSH ML4 100 B1
WISHAW ML2 131 L3
Rosebank St AIRDRIE ML6 85 L1
Rosebank Ter
BAIL/MDB/MHD G69 82 F6
KLMCLM PA13 53 K2
Roseberry La AIRDRIE ML6 85 L6
Roseberry Pl HMLTN ML3 119 G6
Roseberry Rd AIRDRIE ML6 85 K5
Roseberry St GBLS G5 79 L8
Roseburn Ct CUMB G67 31 M4
Rose Crs GRK PA19 15 K3
HMLTN ML3 118 F6
Rose Dl BSHPBGS G64 * 62 B2
Rosedale EKILN G74 2 B2
Rosedale Av PSLYS PA2 90 D4
Rosedale Dr
BAIL/MDB/MHD G69 82 A6
Rosedale Gdns HBR/GL G84 10 F7
MRYH/FIRH G20 60 C2
Rosedale St LNK/LMHG ML11 136 F7
Rosedene Ter BLSH ML4 100 A3
Rosefield Gdns
UD/BTH/TAN G71 98 E3
Rose Gdns CTBR ML5 83 M7
Rosegreen Crs BLSH ML4 100 A1
Rosehall Av CTBR ML5 84 B5
Rosehall Rd BLSH ML4 99 M4
SHOTTS ML7 104 D6
Rosehall Ter WISHAW ML2 121 L8
Rosehill Dr CUMB G67 48 A3
Rosehill Rd BSHPBGS G64 44 C2
Rose Knowe Rd GVH/MTFL G42 95 L2
Roselea Dr MLNGV G62 24 B7
Roselea Gdns KNTSWD G13 59 M2
Roselea Pl BLTYR/CAMB G72 118 C1
Roselea Rd UD/BTH/TAN G71 98 E2
Roselea St LRKH ML9 130 D5
Rosemarkie Pl
GRNKW/INVK PA16 32 E6
Rosemary Crs EKILN G74 116 D6
Rosemary Pl EKILN G74 116 D6
Rosemount BALLOCH G68 30 F4
Rosemount Av NMRNS G77 113 K7
Rose Mount Ct AIRDRIE ML6 85 J1
Rosemount Ct NMRNS G77 113 K8
Rosemount La BRWEIR PA11 72 B4
Rosemount Mdw
UD/BTH/TAN G71 98 F8
Rosemount Pl GRK PA19 15 H3
Rosemount St
SPRGB/BLRNK G21 80 A2
Rosendale Wy
BLTYR/CAMB G72 118 E3
Roseneath Dr HBR/GL G84 10 B5
Roseneath St
GRNKW/INVK PA16 16 C1
Roseness Pl
STPS/GTHM/RID G33 81 G2
Rosenheath Ga EKILN G74 2 B3
Rosepark Av UD/BTH/TAN G71 99 J4
Rose St CGLW G2 4 D4
CUMB G67 48 B3
GRNKW/INVK PA16 16 C5
KKNTL G66 45 K2
MTHW ML1 121 G4
Rosevale Crs BLSH ML4 100 C5
HMLTN ML3 119 H8
Rosevale Rd BSDN G61 41 M5
Rosevale St PTCK G11 60 A8
Rosewood Av BLSH ML4 100 B2
PSLYS PA2 91 H1
Rosewood Pth BLSH ML4 99 L5
Rosewood Pl
BAIL/MDB/MHD G69 83 G4
Rosewood St KNTSWD G13 59 L2
Roseyard Pl PGL PA14 34 C1
Roslea Dr DEN/PKHD G31 80 A3
Roslin Ct KLMCLM PA13 53 J3
Roslin Pl AIRDRIE ML6 85 L7
Roslin St GRNK PA15 6 C2
Roslyn Dr BAIL/MDB/MHD G69 82 F5
Rosneath Rd PGL PA14 34 D2
Rosneath St GOV/IBX G51 78 A2
Ross Av KKNTL G66 45 M2
RNFRW PA4 58 A8
Rossbank Rd PGL PA14 18 A8
Ross Crs MTHW ML1 120 C4
Ross Dr AIRDRIE ML6 84 E5
MTHW ML1 120 C4
UD/BTH/TAN G71 99 J1
Rossendale Ct
PLKSW/MSWD G43 94 C2
Rossendale Rd
PLKSW/MSWD G43 94 C2
Ross Gdns MTHW ML1 120 C4
Rosshall Av PSLY PA1 76 C5
Rosshall Pl RNFRW PA4 58 D6
Rosshill Av
CARD/HILL/MSPK G52 76 F4
Rosshill Rd
CARD/HILL/MSPK G52 76 F4
Rossie Crs BSHPBGS G64 62 C2
Rossie Gv NMRNS G77 113 H4
Rossland Crs BSHPTN PA7 38 A7
Rossland Gdns BSHPTN PA7 38 A7
Rosslea Dr GIF/THBK G46 94 C8

Rosslyn Av EKILN G74 3 H2
RUTH G73 96 C3
Rosslyn Ct HMLTN ML3 119 G6
Rosslyn Rd BSDN G61 41 H3
Rosslyn Ter KVD/HLHD G12 60 C6
Ross Pl RUTH G73 96 D6
Ross St CTBR ML5 84 A2
DMNK/BRGTN G40 5 J9
PSLY PA1 9 L7
Ross Ter HMLTN ML3 120 C8
Rostan Rd PLKSW/MSWD G43 94 C5
Rosyth Rd GBLS G5 79 L8
Rosyth St GBLS G5 79 L8
Rotherwick Dr PSLY PA1 76 E5
Rotherwood Av KNTSWD G13 41 J8
PSLYS PA2 90 F2
Rotherwood La KNTSWD G13 41 J7
Rotherwood Pl KNTSWD G13 59 K1
Rothesay Crs CTBR ML5 84 C5
Rothesay Pl CTBR ML5 84 B5
Rothesay Rd
GRNKW/INVK PA16 15 M6
Rothesay St EKILS G75 2 E6
Rothes Dr SMSTN G23 60 D2
Rothes Pl SMSTN G23 60 C1
Rottenrow CGLE G1 5 H5
Rottenrow East COWCAD G4 5 J6
Roughcraig St AIRDRIE ML6 67 G7
Roughrigg Rd AIRDRIE ML6 86 A3
Roukenburn St GIF/THBK G46 93 L5
Rouken Glen Rd GIF/THBK G46 93 M7
The Roundel LARGS KA30 107 G5
WISHAW ML2 122 C6
Roundhill Dr JNSTN PA5 74 E7
Roundknowe Rd
UD/BTH/TAN G71 98 C1
Round Riding Rd DMBTN G82 21 H6
Rowallan Gdns PTCK G11 59 M6
Rowallan La
CRMNK/CLK/EAG G76 114 E3
PTCK G11 59 M6
Rowallan La East PTCK G11 60 A7
Rowallan Rd GIF/THBK G46 93 M7
Rowallan St HBR/GL G84 10 B4
Rowallan Ter
STPS/GTHM/RID G33 63 H6
Rowan Av KKNTL G66 27 H5
RNFRW PA4 58 C5
Rowanbank Pl AIRDRIE ML6 84 D2
Rowan Ct WISHAW ML2 121 K7
Rowan Crs AIRDRIE ML6 85 L6
KKNTL G66 45 J5
SHOTTS ML7 105 H4
Rowandale Av
BAIL/MDB/MHD G69 82 A6
Rowand Av GIF/THBK G46 94 C8
Rowanden Av BLSH ML4 100 A3
Rowan Dr BSDN G61 41 M2
CLYDBK G81 39 M6
DMBTN G82 20 A6
Rowan Gdns PLKSD/SHW G41 78 B6
Rowan Gv HMLTN ML3 129 M7
Rowanlea Av PSLYS PA2 90 D3
Rowanlea Dr GIF/THBK G46 94 D6
Rowanpark Dr BRHD/NEIL G78 92 A4
Rowan Pl BLTYR/CAMB G72 97 J4
BLTYR/CAMB G72 118 D2
CTBR ML5 83 L6
Rowan Ri HMLTN ML3 119 L8
Rowan Rd CUMB G67 31 K6
PLKSD/SHW G41 78 B6
PSLYN/LNWD PA3 73 M3
Rowans Gdns UD/BTH/TAN G71 99 H6
Rowans Ga PSLYS PA2 75 M8
The Rowans BSHPBGS G64 43 M8
Rowan St BEITH KA15 125 L5
GRNKW/INVK PA16 16 C4
PSLYS PA2 75 M8
WISHAW ML2 122 B4
Rowantree Av MTHW ML1 101 K2
RUTH G73 96 B6
UD/BTH/TAN G71 98 E3
Rowantree Gv ALEX/LLW G83 13 K6
Rowantreehill Rd
KLMCLM PA13 53 K2
Rowantree Pl JNSTN PA5 * 89 M1
KKNTL G66 26 F3
LRKH ML9 130 F7
Rowantree Rd JNSTN PA5 89 M1
Rowantree Ter KKNTL G66 26 E3
MTHW ML1 101 H4
Rowanwood Crs CTBR ML5 83 K5
Rowena Av KNTSWD G13 41 K8
Roxburgh Av GRNK PA15 6 B5
Roxburgh Dr BSDN G61 41 L2
CTBR ML5 84 D5
Roxburgh Pk EKILN G74 3 H6
Roxburgh Rd PSLYS PA2 90 D3
Roxburgh St GRNK PA15 6 C5
KVD/HLHD G12 60 D7
Royal Av LARGS KA30 106 F4
Royal Bank Pl CGLE G1 4 F6
Royal Crs KVGV G3 78 E2
Royal Dr HMLTN ML3 120 A7
Royal Exchange Ct CGLE G1 4 F6
Royal Exchange Sq CGLE G1 4 F6
Royal Gdns UD/BTH/TAN G71 98 E8
Royal Inch Crs RNFRW PA4 58 D4
Royal St GRK PA19 15 L1
Royal Ter KVGV G3 78 E1
WISHAW ML2 122 C2
Royal Terrace La KVGV G3 78 E1
Royellen Av HMLTN ML3 118 F8
Roystonhill SPRGB/BLRNK G21 5 M3
Roystonhill Pl
SPRGB/BLRNK G21 5 M3
Royston Rd SPRGB/BLRNK G21 5 L3
STPS/GTHM/RID G33 62 F6
Royston Sq SPRGB/BLRNK G21 5 L2
Roy St SPRGB/BLRNK G21 61 K7
Roy Young Av ALEX/LLW G83 13 M2
Rozelle Av DRUM G15 41 H6
NMRNS G77 113 H5
Rozelle Dr NMRNS G77 113 H5
Rozelle Pl NMRNS G77 113 H5
Rubislaw Dr BSDN G61 41 L6
Ruby St DMNK/BRGTN G40 80 A6
Ruby Ter BLSH ML4 100 A5
Ruchazie Pl
STPS/GTHM/RID G33 80 F2
Ruchazie Rd CAR/SHTL G32 80 F4
Ruchill Pl MRYH/FIRH G20 60 F5
Ruchill St MRYH/FIRH G20 60 E5
Rue End St GRNK PA15 6 F5
Ruel St LNPK/KPK G44 95 G3
Rufflees Av BRHD/NEIL G78 92 D6
Rugby Av KNTSWD G13 59 H1
Rullion Pl STPS/GTHM/RID G33 80 F2
Rumford St DMNK/BRGTN G40 79 M7
Runciman Pl EKILN G74 117 H6
Rundell Dr KKNTL G66 27 J5
Rupert St COWCAD G4 4 A1
Rushyhill St SPRGB/BLRNK G21 62 A6
Ruskin La KVD/HLHD G12 60 E7
Ruskin Pl KSYTH G65 29 K2
Ruskin Ter KVD/HLHD G12 60 E7
Russell Colt St CTBR ML5 84 A1
Russell Dr ALEX/LLW G83 13 H3
BSDN G61 41 M3
Russell Gdns UD/BTH/TAN G71 99 G2
Russell La WISHAW ML2 122 A7
Russell Pl
CRMNK/CLK/EAG G76 115 G5
EKILS G75 126 F3
PSLYN/LNWD PA3 73 M4
Russell Rd CLYDBK G81 39 L3
LNK/LMHG ML11 137 H4
Russell St AIRDRIE ML6 85 L7
BLSH ML4 100 D4
HMLTN ML3 118 F5
JNSTN PA5 74 A7
PSLYN/LNWD PA3 75 K3
WISHAW ML2 122 A7
Rutherford Av BSDN G61 41 H1
Rutherford Ct CLYDBK G81 40 A7
Rutherford Gra KKNTL G66 45 J4
Rutherford La EKILS G75 3 G8
Rutherford Sq EKILS G75 2 F8
Rutherglen Rd GBLS G5 79 K7
Ruthven Av GIF/THBK G46 114 D1
Ruthven La KVD/HLHD G12 60 C7
Ruthven Pl BSHPBGS G64 62 C2
Ruthven St KVD/HLHD G12 60 C7
Rutland Ct GOV/IBX G51 78 E4
Rutland Crs GOV/IBX G51 78 E4
Rutland Pl GOV/IBX G51 78 E4
Ryan Rd BSHPBGS G64 62 B1
WMYSB PA18 50 B1
Ryan Wy RUTH G73 96 C7
Ryat Dr NMRNS G77 113 J3
Ryat Gn NMRNS G77 113 J4
Ryatt Linn ERSK PA8 56 F1
Rydal Gv EKILS G75 126 C4
Rydal Pl EKILS G75 126 C4
Ryden Mains Rd AIRDRIE ML6 66 E5
Ryde Rd WISHAW ML2 122 C6
Rye Crs SPRGB/BLRNK G21 62 B5
Ryecroft Dr
BAIL/MDB/MHD G69 82 B5
Ryedale Pl DRUM G15 41 G5
Rye Dr SPRGB/BLRNK G21 62 B5
Ryefield Av CTBR ML5 83 K3
JNSTN PA5 89 K1
Ryefield Pl JNSTN PA5 89 K1
Ryefield Rd SPRGB/BLRNK G21 62 B5
Ryehill Pl SPRGB/BLRNK G21 62 C5
Ryehill Rd SPRGB/BLRNK G21 62 C5
Ryemount Rd
SPRGB/BLRNK G21 62 C5
Rye Rd SPRGB/BLRNK G21 62 C6
Ryeside Rd SPRGB/BLRNK G21 62 B6
Ryewraes Rd PSLYN/LNWD PA3 74 B5
Rylands Dr CAR/SHTL G32 81 K6
Rylands Gdns CAR/SHTL G32 81 L6
Rylees Crs
CARD/HILL/MSPK G52 76 E2
Rylees Rd
CARD/HILL/MSPK G52 76 E3
Rysland Av NMRNS G77 113 L4
Rysland Crs NMRNS G77 113 L4
Ryvra Rd KNTSWD G13 59 K3

S

Sachelcourt Av BSHPTN PA7 56 B1
Sackville Av KNTSWD G13 59 M4
Sackville La KNTSWD G13 59 M4
Saddell Rd DRUM G15 41 H5
Saffron Crs WISHAW ML2 121 K8
Saffronhall Crs HMLTN ML3 119 K6
Saffronhall La HMLTN ML3 119 K6
St Abb's Dr PSLYS PA2 91 G1
St Aidan's Pth WISHAW ML2 * 122 C3
St Andrew's Av BSHPBGS G64 43 L8
UD/BTH/TAN G71 119 G1
St Andrew's Brae DMBTN G82 21 H4
St Andrews Ct EKILS G75 126 F4
St Andrew's Crs DMBTN G82 21 H5
PLKSD/SHW G41 78 E6
PSLYN/LNWD PA3 75 J1
St Andrews Dr BALLOCH G68 31 H3
BRWEIR PA11 72 B4
BSDN G61 41 K2
GRK PA19 15 G3
HMLTN ML3 118 D6
PLKSD/SHW G41 78 C8
PSLYN/LNWD PA3 75 L1
St Andrew's Dr West
PSLYN/LNWD PA3 75 J2
St Andrew's Gdns AIRDRIE ML6 85 H1
St Andrew's La CGLE G1 5 H8
GRK PA19 15 G3
St Andrews Pl BEITH KA15 125 J6
KSYTH G65 29 J1
St Andrew's Rd
PLKSD/SHW G41 78 F6
RNFRW PA4 58 C6
St Andrew's Sq CGLE G1 5 H9
St Andrew's St CGLE G1 5 H9
MTHW ML1 101 G4
St Andrew St GRNK PA15 7 G6
St Andrew's Wy WISHAW ML2 122 C3
St Andrews Wynd HBR/GL G84 10 E4
St Annes Av ERSK PA8 57 K2
St Anne's Ct HMLTN ML3 129 K2
St Annes Wynd ERSK PA8 57 K2
St Ann's Dr GIF/THBK G46 94 C8
St Barchan's Rd KLBCH PA10 73 H8
St Blane's Dr RUTH G73 95 L4
St Boswell's Crs PSLYS PA2 91 G1
St Boswells Dr CTBR ML5 84 D5
St Bride's Av UD/BTH/TAN G71 99 J3
St Bride's Rd
PLKSW/MSWD G43 94 D4
St Brides Wy UD/BTH/TAN G71 99 G6
St Bryde St EKILN G74 3 G4
St Catherines Crs SHOTTS ML7 104 D3
St Catherine's Rd GIF/THBK G46 94 C8
St Clair HWWD PA9 88 F5
St Clair Av GIF/THBK G46 94 C7
St Clair St MRYH/FIRH G20 60 F8
St Colms Pl LARGS KA30 106 E4
St Columba Dr KKNTL G66 45 L3
St Cuthbert Wy HMLTN ML3 118 F5
St Cyrus Gdns BSHPBGS G64 62 C1
St Cyrus Rd BSHPBGS G64 62 C1
St Davids Dr AIRDRIE ML6 85 J5
St David's Pl LRKH ML9 130 C6
St Denis Wy CTBR ML5 83 M2
St Edmunds Gv MLNGV G62 24 A7
St Enoch Av UD/BTH/TAN G71 99 J2
St Enoch Sq CGLE G1 4 E8
St Fillans Dr
CRG/CRSL/HOU PA6 55 G8
St Fillans Rd
STPS/GTHM/RID G33 63 J5
St Flanan Rd KKNTL G66 28 D8
St Francis Rigg GBLS G5 79 K6
St George's Pl MRYH/FIRH G20 4 B1
St George's Rd KVGV G3 4 A3
St Germains BSDN G61 41 L5
St Giles Pk HMLTN ML3 119 H8
St Giles Wy HMLTN ML3 119 H8
St Helena Crs CLYDBK G81 40 C3
St Helens Gdns
PLKSD/SHW G41 94 E2
St Inan's Dr BEITH KA15 125 L4
St Ives Rd BAIL/MDB/MHD G69 46 F7
St James Av PSLYN/LNWD PA3 75 H3
St James Ct CTBR ML5 83 L7
St James Rd COWCAD G4 5 J5
St James' St PSLYN/LNWD PA3 8 F3
St James Wy CTBR ML5 83 L7
St Johns Bvd UD/BTH/TAN G71 99 G4
St John's Ct PLKSD/SHW G41 78 E6
St John's Qd PLKSD/SHW G41 78 E6
St John's Rd GRK PA19 15 L1
PLKSD/SHW G41 78 E7
St John St CTBR ML5 84 A2
St Johns Wy KSYTH G65 28 F7
St Joseph's Ct
SPRGB/BLRNK G21 79 M1
St Joseph's Vw
SPRGB/BLRNK G21 79 M2
St Kenneth Dr GOV/IBX G51 77 K1
St Kentigerns Rd
LNK/LMHG ML11 137 H4
St Kilda Dr SCOT G14 59 L5
St Kilda Wy WISHAW ML2 122 E4
St Lawrence Pk EKILS G75 2 B6
St Lawrence St GRNK PA15 7 J6
St Leonard's Dr GIF/THBK G46 94 C7
St Leonards Rd EKILN G74 3 L5
LNK/LMHG ML11 137 H5
St Leonard St LNK/LMHG ML11 137 H5
St Leonards Wk CTBR ML5 84 C6
St Luke's Av CARLUKE ML8 134 E1
St Lukes Pl GBLS G5 79 J5
St Lukes Ter GBLS G5 79 J5
St Machan's Wy KKNTL G66 26 D1
St Machars Rd BRWEIR PA11 72 E3
St Margarets Av
PSLYN/LNWD PA3 75 M3
St Margaret's Dr WISHAW ML2 121 L8
St Margaret's Pl CGLE G1 5 G9
St Mark Gdns CAR/SHTL G32 80 F5
St Mark's Ct WISHAW ML2 122 C3
St Mark St CAR/SHTL G32 80 E5
St Marnock St
DMNK/BRGTN G40 80 A5
St Martins Ga CTBR ML5 84 A5
St Mary's Crs BRHD/NEIL G78 92 C7
St Marys Gdns BRHD/NEIL G78 92 C7
St Mary's La CGLW G2 4 E6
St Mary's Rd BLSH ML4 99 L5
BSHPBGS G64 43 L8
St Mary's Wy DMBTN G82 20 F7
St Michael Dr HBR/GL G84 10 E5
St Michael Rd WISHAW ML2 121 J8
St Michael's La DEN/PKHD G31 80 C5
St Mirren's Rd KSYTH G65 29 L2
St Mirren St PSLY PA1 9 H5
St Monance St
SPRGB/BLRNK G21 61 M5
St Mungo Av COWCAD G4 5 G4
St Mungo Ct BRWEIR PA11 72 E2
St Mungo Pl COWCAD G4 5 J4
HMLTN ML3 118 D6
St Mungo's LNK/LMHG ML11 137 G6
St Mungos Crs MTHW ML1 101 H7
St Mungo's Rd CUMB G67 30 F8
St Mungo St BSHPBGS G64 61 M2
St Nicholas Rd
LNK/LMHG ML11 137 H4
St Ninian's LNK/LMHG ML11 137 H4
St Ninian's Crs PSLYS PA2 75 M8
St Ninian's Pl HMLTN ML3 118 F7
St Ninian's Rd HMLTN ML3 118 E7
PSLYS PA2 9 K9
St Ninian Ter GBLS G5 79 J5
St Patrick's Ct
LNK/LMHG ML11 136 F5
St Patrick's Rd
LNK/LMHG ML11 136 F6
St Peter's La CGLW G2 4 C6
St Roberts Gdns
PLK/PH/NH G53 93 J4
St Ronan's Dr HMLTN ML3 129 J2
PLKSD/SHW G41 94 D1
RUTH G73 96 C5
St Stephens Av RUTH G73 96 C7
St Stephens Ct CLYDBK G81 39 M7
St Stephen's Crs RUTH G73 96 D7
St Teiling LNK/LMHG ML11 137 H3
St Valentine Ter GBLS G5 79 K6
St Vigeans Av NMRNS G77 113 H6
St Vigeans Pl NMRNS G77 113 J6
St Vincent Crs KVGV G3 78 D2
St Vincent Crescent La
KVGV G3 78 D2
St Vincent La CGLW G2 4 C5
St Vincent Pl CGLE G1 4 F6
EKILS G75 126 D2
LNK/LMHG ML11 137 H5
MTHW ML1 120 E2
St Vincent St CGLW G2 4 D6
KVGV G3 78 F2
St Vincent Ter KVGV G3 4 A5
St Winifred's Wy WISHAW ML2 122 A5
St Winnoc Rd LOCHW PA12 109 K2
Salamanca St DEN/PKHD G31 80 D5
Salasaig Ct
STPS/GTHM/RID G33 81 G3
Salen St CARD/HILL/MSPK G52 77 M4
Saline St AIRDRIE ML6 84 D3
Salisbury EKILN G74 117 K6
Salisbury Crs MTHW ML1 100 B8
Salisbury Pl CLYDBK G81 39 K5
Salisbury St PLKSD/SHW G41 79 H6
Salkeld St GBLS G5 79 G6
Salmona St PPK/MIL G22 61 H6
Salmon St GRNK PA15 6 B4
Saltaire Av UD/BTH/TAN G71 99 G5
Salterland Rd PLK/PH/NH G53 92 E4
Saltire Crs LRKH ML9 130 E7
Saltmarket CGLE G1 5 G9
Saltmarket Pl CGLE G1 * 5 G9
Saltoun La KVD/HLHD G12 60 D7
Saltoun St KVD/HLHD G12 60 D7
Salvia St BLTYR/CAMB G72 96 E4
Samson Crs CARLUKE ML8 135 J1
Sandaig Rd
STPS/GTHM/RID G33 81 L5
Sandalwood Av EKILN G74 116 D6
Sandalwood Ct EKILN G74 116 D6
Sanda St MRYH/FIRH G20 60 E6
Sandbank Av MRYH/FIRH G20 60 D3
Sandbank Crs ALEX/LLW G83 13 L5
MRYH/FIRH G20 60 D4
Sandbank Dr MRYH/FIRH G20 60 D3
Sandbank St MRYH/FIRH G20 60 D4
Sandbank Ter MRYH/FIRH G20 60 D3
Sandend Pl GRNKW/INVK PA16 32 E5
Sandend Rd PLK/PH/NH G53 93 G2
Sanderling Pl JNSTN PA5 89 K4
Sanderling Rd
PSLYN/LNWD PA3 75 K2
Sanders Ct BRHD/NEIL G78 92 B6
Sanderson Av UD/BTH/TAN G71 99 K4
Sandfield Av MLNGV G62 24 A7
Sandfield St MRYH/FIRH G20 60 E5
Sandgate Av CAR/SHTL G32 81 K7
Sandhaven Pl
GRNKW/INVK PA16 32 F6
PLK/PH/NH G53 93 G2
Sandhaven Rd PLK/PH/NH G53 93 G2
Sandhead Crs AIRDRIE ML6 85 L8
Sandhead Ter
BLTYR/CAMB G72 118 D8
Sandholes Rd JNSTN PA5 73 J5
Sandholes St PSLY PA1 8 D5
Sandholm Pl SCOT G14 58 F4
Sandholm Ter SCOT G14 58 F4
Sandiefield Rd GBLS G5 79 J6
Sandielands Av ERSK PA8 57 K3
Sandilands Crs MTHW ML1 120 B4
Sandilands St CAR/SHTL G32 81 H5
Sandmill St SPRGB/BLRNK G21 80 A1
Sandpiper Crs CTBR ML5 84 D7
Sandpiper Dr EKILS G75 126 D5
Sandpiper Pl EKILS G75 126 D5
Sandpiper Rd LOCHW PA12 109 J3
Sandpiper Wy BLSH ML4 99 L2
Sandra Rd BSHPBGS G64 44 C8
Sandray Av PGL PA14 35 H4
Sandringham Av NMRNS G77 114 A4
Sandringham Dr JNSTN PA5 90 B1
Sandringham La
KVD/HLHD G12 60 D7
Sandwood Rd
CARD/HILL/MSPK G52 77 G4
Sandybrae Rd SKLM PA17 50 C5
Sandyfaulds St GBLS G5 79 K6
Sandyford Av MTHW ML1 101 K1
Sandyford Pl MTHW ML1 101 K2
Sandyford Place La KVGV G3 78 E2
Sandyford Rd MTHW ML1 101 L2
PSLYN/LNWD PA3 75 M2
Sandyford St KVGV G3 78 C2
Sandyhill Av SHOTTS ML7 105 G6
Sandyhills Crs CAR/SHTL G32 81 H7
Sandyhills Dr CAR/SHTL G32 81 H7
Sandyhills Gv CAR/SHTL G32 81 J8
Sandyhills Pl CAR/SHTL G32 81 H7
Sandyhills Rd CAR/SHTL G32 81 K6
Sandyknowes Rd CUMB G67 48 F1
Sandy Rd CARLUKE ML8 133 H7
PTCK G11 78 A1
RNFRW PA4 58 C8
Sandyvale Pl SHOTTS ML7 105 G6
Sanford Pl KVGV G3 78 F2
Sannox Dr MTHW ML1 120 B2
Sannox Gdns DEN/PKHD G31 80 B2
Sannox Pl EKILS G75 126 E6
HBR/GL G84 10 F4
Sanquhar Dr PLK/PH/NH G53 93 G1
Sanquhar Gdns
BLTYR/CAMB G72 98 B8
PLK/PH/NH G53 93 G1
Sanquhar Pl PLK/PH/NH G53 93 G1
Sanquhar Rd PLK/PH/NH G53 93 G1
Sanson La CARLUKE ML8 135 J1
Sapphire Rd BLSH ML4 100 B6
Saracen Head Rd CGLE G1 5 K8
Saracen St PPK/MIL G22 61 J6
Sarazen Ct MTHW ML1 121 L1
Sardinia La KVD/HLHD G12 60 D7
Saskatoon Pl EKILS G75 126 E1
Saturn Av PSLY PA1 74 E6
Saucel Crs PSLY PA1 9 H6
Saucel Hill Ter PSLYS PA2 9 H8
Saucel Pl PSLY PA1 9 H7
Saucel St PSLY PA1 9 H6
Sauchenhall Pth
BAIL/MDB/MHD G69 47 G7
Sauchiehall La CGLW G2 4 B4
Sauchiehall St CGLW G2 4 B4
KVGV G3 78 D1
Sauchiesmoor Rd
CARLUKE ML8 135 G1
Saughs Av STPS/GTHM/RID G33 62 F4
Saughs Dr STPS/GTHM/RID G33 62 F4
Saughs Ga STPS/GTHM/RID G33 62 F4
Saughs Pl STPS/GTHM/RID G33 62 F4
Saughs Rd STPS/GTHM/RID G33 62 F4
Saughton St CAR/SHTL G32 80 E3
Savoy St DMNK/BRGTN G40 79 M6
Sawmillfield St COWCAD G4 4 D1
Saxon Rd KNTSWD G13 59 K2
Scadlock Rd PSLYN/LNWD PA3 8 A2
Scalloway Rd
BAIL/MDB/MHD G69 64 E6
BLTYR/CAMB G72 96 E7
Scalpay EKILN G74 127 M1
Scalpay Pl PPK/MIL G22 61 K3
Scalpay St PPK/MIL G22 61 K3
Scapa St SMSTN G23 60 E2
Scapa Wy STPS/GTHM/RID G33 63 L4
Scaraway Dr PPK/MIL G22 61 K2
Scaraway Pl PPK/MIL G22 61 K2
Scaraway St PPK/MIL G22 61 J2
Scaraway Ter PPK/MIL G22 61 K2
Scarba Dr PLKSW/MSWD G43 94 B4
Scarba Qd WISHAW ML2 121 L8
Scarffe Av PSLYN/LNWD PA3 73 M5
Scarhill Av AIRDRIE ML6 84 F4
Scarhill La AIRDRIE ML6 85 G4
Scarhill St CTBR ML5 83 M7
MTHW ML1 102 B7
Scarletmuir LNK/LMHG ML11 136 F4
Scarlow St PGL PA14 18 C8
Scarrel Dr CSMK G45 96 A6
Scarrel Gdns CSMK G45 96 A6
Scarrel Rd CSMK G45 96 A7
Scarrel Ter CSMK G45 96 A6
Scavaig Crs DRUM G15 40 E5
Schaw Dr BSDN G61 41 L3
CLYDBK G81 40 D3
Schaw Rd PSLYN/LNWD PA3 9 L1
Scholar's Ga EKILS G75 127 G4
School Av BLTYR/CAMB G72 97 H5
Schoolhouse La
BLTYR/CAMB G72 118 C4
School La BLTYR/CAMB G72 97 L6
CARLUKE ML8 133 G8
DMBTN G82 20 D6
KKNTL G66 26 D2
School Qd AIRDRIE ML6 66 F7
School Rd BSHPBGS G64 44 C1
KBRN KA25 124 C3
NMRNS G77 113 K5
PSLY PA1 76 E4
SHOTTS ML7 87 K6
STPS/GTHM/RID G33 63 L4
WISHAW ML2 123 H6
School St AIRDRIE ML6 85 K7
CTBR ML5 84 A5
HMLTN ML3 129 K1
LARGS KA30 106 E4
SHOTTS ML7 104 F5
School Wynd BRWEIR PA11 53 L7
KBRN KA25 124 C3
LARGS KA30 106 E4
PSLY PA1 9 G4
Scioncroft Av RUTH G73 96 C3
Scone Pl EKILN G74 2 C2
NMRNS G77 114 B6
Scone St SPRGB/BLRNK G21 61 J7
Sconser ERSK PA8 57 J3
Sconser St SMSTN G23 60 E1
Scorton Gdns
BAIL/MDB/MHD G69 81 M6
Scotia Crs LRKH ML9 130 C8
Scotia Gdns HMLTN ML3 129 J3
Scotia St MTHW ML1 120 C2
Scotland St GBLS G5 78 F5
Scotland St West
PLKSD/SHW G41 78 D5
Scotlaw Dr LARGS KA30 106 F4
Scotsblair Av KKNTL G66 45 J3
Scotsburn Rd
SPRGB/BLRNK G21 62 C6
Scotstoun St SCOT G14 59 J6
Scott Av JNSTN PA5 89 L2
KKNTL G66 27 J4
OLDK G60 38 D2
Scott Ct HBR/GL G84 10 C6
Scott Crs CUMB G67 48 D2
LARGS KA30 107 G6
Scott Dr BSDN G61 41 J3
CUMB G67 48 D2
LARGS KA30 107 G6
Scott Gv HMLTN ML3 119 K8
Scott Hl EKILN G74 3 K1
Scott Pl BLSH ML4 100 B2
Scott Rd CARD/HILL/MSPK G52 76 F1
Scott's Pl AIRDRIE ML6 85 H1
Scott's Rd PSLYS PA2 76 C6
Scott St ALEX/LLW G83 13 L6
BAIL/MDB/MHD G69 82 B6
CLYDBK G81 39 L6
GRNK PA15 6 E6
HMLTN ML3 129 K1
KVGV G3 4 C3
LARGS KA30 106 F6
LRKH ML9 130 D7
MTHW ML1 120 F2
Seabank Av LARGS KA30 106 F7
Seafar Rd CUMB G67 30 F7
Seafield Av BSDN G61 41 M2
Seafield Cottage La
GRNKW/INVK PA16 16 D2
Seafield Crs BALLOCH G68 47 L1
Seafield Dr RUTH G73 96 D7
Seaforth Crs BRHD/NEIL G78 92 B4
Seaforth Pl BLSH ML4 99 M8
Seaforth Rd
CARD/HILL/MSPK G52 77 G2
CLYDBK G81 40 B8
Seaforth Rd North
CARD/HILL/MSPK G52 77 G2
Seaforth Rd South
CARD/HILL/MSPK G52 77 G2
Seagrove St CAR/SHTL G32 80 D4
Seamill Gdns EKILN G74 2 D3
Seamill St PLK/PH/NH G53 92 F4
Seamore St LARGS KA30 106 E4
MRYH/FIRH G20 60 F8
Seath Av AIRDRIE ML6 84 E1
PGL PA14 36 C4
Seath Rd RUTH G73 96 A1
Seath St GVH/MTFL G42 79 J8
Seaton Ter HMLTN ML3 119 G6
Seaward La PLKSD/SHW G41 78 E5
Seaward Pl PLKSD/SHW G41 78 F5
Seaward St PLKSD/SHW G41 78 F5
Second Av ALEX/LLW G83 13 L5
BSDN G61 42 A7
CLYDBK G81 40 B7
DMBTN G82 21 J8
LNPK/KPK G44 95 H4
RNFRW PA4 58 C8
STPS/GTHM/RID G33 63 H5
UD/BTH/TAN G71 98 E1
Second Gdns PLKSD/SHW G41 78 A6
Second Rd BLTYR/CAMB G72 118 E5
Second St UD/BTH/TAN G71 98 F2
Seedhill PSLY PA1 9 J6
Seedhill Rd PSLY PA1 9 K5
Seggielea La KNTSWD G13 59 K3
Seggielea Rd KNTSWD G13 59 K3
Seil Dr LNPK/KPK G44 95 H6
Selborne Pl KNTSWD G13 59 L4
Selborne Place La
KNTSWD G13 59 L4
Selborne Rd KNTSWD G13 59 L4
Selby Gdns CAR/SHTL G32 81 K5
Selby Pl CTBR ML5 65 K8
Selby St CTBR ML5 65 K8
Selkirk Av
CARD/HILL/MSPK G52 77 J5
PSLYS PA2 91 G2
Selkirk Dr RUTH G73 96 C3

Selkirk Pl EKILN G74 117 K7
HMLTN ML3 119 L8
Selkirk Rd PGL PA14 34 D2
Selkirk St BLTYR/CAMB G72 118 D3
WISHAW ML2 122 C4
Selkirk Wy CTBR ML5 84 E6
Sella Rd BSHPBGS G64 44 D8
Selvieland Rd
CARD/HILL/MSPK G52 76 E4
Semphill Gdns EKILN G74 3 L4
Semple St HMLTN ML3 118 F6
Sempill Av ERSK PA8 38 F8
Semple Av BSHPTN PA7 38 B7
LOCHW PA12 109 J2
Semple Pl PSLYN/LNWD PA3 74 C3
Semple Vw HWWD PA9 88 F5
Senate Pl MTHW ML1 100 C8
Senga Crs BLSH ML4 100 A2
Seres Rd CRMNK/CLK/EAG G76 114 D2
Sergeantlaw Rd
BRHD/NEIL G78 110 B3
PSLYS PA2 90 F5
Serpentine Wk GRNK PA15 7 H7
Sersley Dr KBRN KA25 124 B5
Service St KKNTL G66 26 C1
Seton Ter DEN/PKHD G31 79 M3
SKLM PA17 50 C5
Settle Gdns
BAIL/MDB/MHD G69 81 M6
Seven Sisters KKNTL G66 45 L5
Seventh Av UD/BTH/TAN G71 98 F2
Seventh Rd BLTYR/CAMB G72 118 E5
Severn Rd EKILS G75 126 B3
Seymour Gn EKILS G75 126 E2
Seyton Av GIF/THBK G46 114 C1
Seyton Ct GIF/THBK G46 114 C1
Seyton La EKILN G74 2 F2
Shaftesbury St CLYDBK G81 39 M8
KVGV G3 4 A5
Shafton Pl KNTSWD G13 59 L1
Shafton Rd KNTSWD G13 59 L1
Shakespeare Av CLYDBK G81 39 M6
Shakespeare St
MRYH/FIRH G20 60 E5
Shamrock St COWCAD G4 4 C2
KKNTL G66 45 K2
Shandon Brae ALEX/LLW G83 13 L2
Shandon Crs ALEX/LLW G83 13 L2
BLSH ML4 100 A2
Shandon Pl GRNK PA15 17 J8
Shandon Ter HMLTN ML3 118 F8
Shand St WISHAW ML2 122 C7
Shandwick Pl
GRNKW/INVK PA16 32 F6
Shandwick St ESTRH G34 82 A2
Shankland La GRNK PA15 17 M7
Shankland Rd GRNK PA15 17 M7
Shanks Av BRHD/NEIL G78 92 C7
Shanks Crs JNSTN PA5 73 L8
Shanks St AIRDRIE ML6 67 G8
MRYH/FIRH G20 60 E5
Shanks Wy BRHD/NEIL G78 92 C4
Shannon St MRYH/FIRH G20 60 F5
Shantron Rd ALEX/LLW G83 13 K4
Shapinsay St PPK/MIL G22 61 K2
Sharp Av CTBR ML5 83 J6
Sharp St GRK PA19 15 M2
MTHW ML1 120 B2
Shaw Av BSHPTN PA7 38 C7
Shawbridge St
PLKSW/MSWD G43 94 C3
Shawburn St HMLTN ML3 119 H6
Shaw Ct ERSK PA8 38 F7
Shawfield Crs CARLUKE ML8 132 B4
Shawfield Dr GBLS G5 79 M8
Shawfield Rd GBLS G5 79 M7
Shawfoot Rd MTHW ML1 100 F1
Shawgill Ct CARLUKE ML8 132 B5
Shawhead Av CTBR ML5 84 B5
Shawhill Ct PLKSD/SHW G41 94 D2
Shawhill Crs NMRNS G77 113 L6
Shawhill Rd PLKSW/MSWD G43 94 D2
Shawholm Crs
PLKSW/MSWD G43 94 B3
Shawmoss Rd PLKSD/SHW G41 94 C1
Shawpark St MRYH/FIRH G20 60 E4
Shaw Pl GRNK PA15 6 D4
PSLYN/LNWD PA3 74 B5
Shawrigg Rd LRKH ML9 130 E7
Shaw Rd MLNGV G62 42 A2
NMRNS G77 113 L5
Shawsgate LRKH ML9 130 F8
Shaws Rd LRKH ML9 130 F8
Shawstonfoot Rd MTHW ML1 103 G8
Shaw St GOV/IBX G51 78 A2
Shawwood Crs NMRNS G77 113 L6
Shearer Dr HMLTN ML3 129 J3
Shearer Qd ALEX/LLW G83 13 M2
Sheddens Pl CAR/SHTL G32 80 F5
Sheena Dr ALEX/LLW G83 13 L8
Sheepburn Rd
UD/BTH/TAN G71 98 E3
Sheila St STPS/GTHM/RID G33 62 E6
Sheiling Hl HMLTN ML3 119 L6
Sheldaig Rd PPK/MIL G22 61 J2
Sheldrake Pl JNSTN PA5 89 K4
Shelley Dr CLYDBK G81 40 A5
UD/BTH/TAN G71 99 H8
Shelley Rd KVD/HLHD G12 59 M4
Shells Rd KKNTL G66 45 L1
Shepford Pl CTBR ML5 83 K3
Sherbrooke Av
PLKSD/SHW G41 78 C8
Sherbrooke Dr PLKSD/SHW G41 78 C6
Sherbrooke Gdns
PLKSD/SHW G41 78 C7
Sherbrooke Pl EKILS G75 2 B6
Sherburn Gdns
BAIL/MDB/MHD G69 81 M6
Sherdale Av AIRDRIE ML6 85 K7
Sheriff Park Av RUTH G73 96 A3
Sherry Av MTHW ML1 100 F4
Sherry Dr HMLTN ML3 129 G1
Sherwood Av PSLY PA1 9 M2
UD/BTH/TAN G71 99 G5
Sherwood Dr GIF/THBK G46 94 A7
Sherwood Pl DRUM G15 41 H6
Sherwood Rd CTBR ML5 65 L4
Shetland Dr LNPK/KPK G44 95 H6
Shettleston Rd DEN/PKHD G31 80 E5
Shiel Av EKILN G74 3 G1
Shielbridge Gdns SMSTN G23 60 E1
Shiel Ct BRHD/NEIL G78 92 B4
Shieldaig Dr RUTH G73 96 B6
Shieldburn Rd GOV/IBX G51 77 J3
Shieldhall Gdns GOV/IBX G51 77 J2
Shieldhall Rd GOV/IBX G51 77 J2
Shieldhill Rd CARLUKE ML8 134 F1
Shieldmuir St WISHAW ML2 121 J5
Shiel Dr LRKH ML9 130 B4
Shields Ct MTHW ML1 121 H6
Shields Dr MTHW ML1 121 H6
Shields Loan LNK/LMHG ML11 136 F4
Shields Rd EKILS G75 126 B8
MTHW ML1 121 H6
PLKSD/SHW G41 78 E8
Shiel Gdns SHOTTS ML7 105 G6
Shiel Pl CTBR ML5 84 D4
EKILN G74 3 G1
Shiel Rd BSHPBGS G64 62 B1
Shiel Ter WISHAW ML2 122 F3
Shilford Av KNTSWD G13 59 G2
Shilford Rd BRHD/NEIL G78 110 B1
Shillay St PPK/MIL G22 61 L2
Shillingworth Pl BRWEIR PA11 72 D4
Shilton Dr PLK/PH/NH G53 93 J4
Shilton La BSHPTN PA7 38 E8
Shinwell Av CLYDBK G81 40 D8
Shipbank La CGLE G1 5 G9
Shira Ter EKILN G74 3 L5
Shirley Qd MTHW ML1 120 D6
Shirrel Av BLSH ML4 100 A2
Shirrel Rd MTHW ML1 101 G5
Shirva Lea KSYTH G65 28 F6
Shiskine Dr MRYH/FIRH G20 60 C2
Shiskine Pl HBR/GL G84 10 F5
MRYH/FIRH G20 60 C2
Shiskine St MRYH/FIRH G20 60 C2
Sholto Crs BLSH ML4 99 K3
Shore Rd SKLM PA17 50 B6
The Shores SKLM PA17 50 B8
Shore St DMNK/BRGTN G40 79 M6
GRK PA19 15 L1
PGL PA14 18 B8
Shortridge St MRYH/FIRH G20 60 E5
Shortroods Rd
PSLYN/LNWD PA3 75 K3
Shottskirk Rd SHOTTS ML7 104 D4
Shotts St STPS/GTHM/RID G33 81 K2
Shuna Crs MRYH/FIRH G20 60 F5
Shuna Gdns MRYH/FIRH G20 60 E5
Shuna Pl MRYH/FIRH G20 60 E5
NMRNS G77 113 H3
Shuna St MRYH/FIRH G20 60 E4
Shuttle St CGLE G1 5 J7
KLBCH PA10 73 G6
KSYTH G65 29 K2
PSLY PA1 9 G5
Sidehead Rd SHOTTS ML7 71 L7
Sidland Rd SPRGB/BLRNK G21 62 C5
Sidlaw Av BRHD/NEIL G78 92 C8
HMLTN ML3 118 F8
PGL PA14 34 F4
Sidlaw Dr WISHAW ML2 121 M6
Sidlaw Rd BSDN G61 41 H3
Sidlaw Wy AIRDRIE ML6 85 M8
LRKH ML9 130 B4
Sielga Pl ESTRH G34 82 A2
Siemens Pl SPRGB/BLRNK G21 62 B8
Siemens St SPRGB/BLRNK G21 62 A8
Sievewright St RUTH G73 96 C1
Sighthill Ter SHOTTS ML7 87 H7
Sikeside Pl CTBR ML5 84 D4
Sikeside St CTBR ML5 84 D4
Silkin Av CLYDBK G81 40 D8
Silk St PSLY PA1 9 J4
Silvan Pl CRMNK/CLK/EAG G76 115 G5
Silverae Ct LARGS KA30 106 F6
Silver Birch Dr GOV/IBX G51 77 K2
Silver Birch Gdns GOV/IBX G51 77 K2
Silverbirch Gv HMLTN ML3 129 M7
Silverburn Crs MTHW ML1 101 K6
Silverburn St
STPS/GTHM/RID G33 80 E2
Silverdale EKILN G74 2 A1
Silverdale Ct LNK/LMHG ML11 136 F5
Silverdale Gdns LARGS KA30 106 F5
Silverdale St DEN/PKHD G31 80 C6
Silverdale Ter AIRDRIE ML6 67 M6
Silver Firs MTHW ML1 101 H6
Silverfir St GBLS G5 79 K7
Silvergrove St
DMNK/BRGTN G40 79 L6
Silvermuir Av LNK/LMHG ML11 137 M2
Silverton Av DMBTN G82 21 H7
Silvertonhill Av HMLTN ML3 129 L2
Silvertonhill La DMBTN G82 21 H7
Silvertonhill Pl HMLTN ML3 129 K3
Silverwells UD/BTH/TAN G71 119 G1
Silverwells Crs
UD/BTH/TAN G71 119 G1
Simons Crs RNFRW PA4 58 D4
Simpson Ct CLYDBK G81 40 A7
UD/BTH/TAN G71 98 F4
Simpson Dr EKILS G75 2 C9
Simpson Qd ALEX/LLW G83 13 M2
Simpson St MRYH/FIRH G20 60 F7
Simpson Wy BLSH ML4 100 C2
Simshill Rd LNPK/KPK G44 95 H7
Sinclair Av BSDN G61 41 L3
Sinclair Dr CTBR ML5 83 K3
GVH/MTFL G42 94 F3
HBR/GL G84 10 E4
LARGS KA30 106 F3
Sinclair Gdns BSHPBGS G64 62 B2
Sinclair Gv BLSH ML4 99 M8
Sinclair La HBR/GL G84 10 E3
Sinclair Pk EKILS G75 3 G7
Sinclair Pl EKILS G75 3 G8
Sinclair St CLYDBK G81 58 D1
GRNK PA15 7 L9
HBR/GL G84 10 D5
MLNGV G62 24 A8
Sinclair Ter LARGS KA30 106 F3
Singer Rd CLYDBK G81 39 M7
EKILS G75 127 J4
Singer St CLYDBK G81 40 B6
Sir Michael Pl GRNK PA15 6 C4
PSLY PA1 8 F6
Sir Michael St GRNK PA15 6 C4
Siskin Wy CTBR ML5 84 D6
Sixth Av RNFRW PA4 58 C8
Sixth St UD/BTH/TAN G71 98 E1
Skaethorn Rd MRYH/FIRH G20 60 B3
Skaterigg La KNTSWD G13 59 L4
Skelbo Pl ESTRH G34 82 D1
Skellyton Crs LRKH ML9 130 D8
Skelmorlie Castle Rd
SKLM PA17 50 B4
Skelmorlie Cross SKLM PA17 50 C5
Skene Rd GOV/IBX G51 78 A5
Skerne Gv EKILS G75 126 C4
Skerray Qd PPK/MIL G22 61 J2
Skerray St PPK/MIL G22 61 J2
Skerryvore Pl
STPS/GTHM/RID G33 81 H2
Skerryvore Rd
STPS/GTHM/RID G33 81 H2
Skibo La GIF/THBK G46 93 L6
Skimmers Hl KKNTL G66 27 H6
Skipness Av CARLUKE ML8 135 G1
Skipness Dr GOV/IBX G51 77 K1
Skirsa Ct SMSTN G23 61 G2
Skirsa Pl SMSTN G23 60 F3
Skirsa Sq SMSTN G23 61 G3
Skirsa St SMSTN G23 60 F2
Skirving St PLKSD/SHW G41 94 E2
Skovlunde Wy EKILS G75 127 H4
Skye EKILN G74 127 M1
Skye Av RNFRW PA4 58 C8
Skye Ct CUMB G67 48 D1
Skye Crs GRK PA19 15 K3
OLDK G60 39 J5
PSLYS PA2 91 K3
Skye Dr CUMB G67 48 D1
OLDK G60 39 J5
Skye Gdns BSDN G61 41 H3
Skye Pl AIRDRIE ML6 85 K3
CUMB G67 48 D1
Skye Qd WISHAW ML2 122 E4
Skye Rd CUMB G67 48 D1
PGL PA14 35 H4
RUTH G73 96 D7
Skye St GRNKW/INVK PA16 16 C5
Skye Wynd HMLTN ML3 128 F1
Skylands Gv HMLTN ML3 129 G2
Skylands Ri HMLTN ML3 129 G2
Slaemuir Av PGL PA14 34 F4
Slaemuir Gdns PGL PA14 34 F4
Slakiewood Av
BAIL/MDB/MHD G69 64 E3
Slatefield KKNTL G66 26 D2
Slatefield St DEN/PKHD G31 80 A4
Sleaford Av MTHW ML1 120 D5
Slenavon Av RUTH G73 96 D7
Slessor Dr EKILS G75 127 H3
Sloy St PPK/MIL G22 61 K6
WISHAW ML2 122 A8
Small Crs BLTYR/CAMB G72 118 D3
Smeaton Av BSHPBGS G64 44 B2
Smeaton Dr BSHPBGS G64 44 A6
Smeaton Gv MRYH/FIRH G20 60 F4
Smeaton St MRYH/FIRH G20 60 F4
Smiddy Ct LNK/LMHG ML11 137 G5
Smillie St GRNK PA15 17 L7
Smith Av GLGNK KA14 124 F7
WISHAW ML2 131 J2
Smith Cl BSHPBGS G64 62 D2
Smith Crs CLYDBK G81 40 B4
Smith Gdns BSHPBGS G64 62 D2
Smith Gv BSHPBGS G64 62 D2
Smithhills St PSLY PA1 9 H4
Smith Qd CTBR ML5 84 C2
Smith's La PSLYN/LNWD PA3 9 H2
Smithstone Crs KSYTH G65 29 L5
Smithstone Rd BALLOCH G68 29 M8
Smith St GRNK PA15 6 D4
SCOT G14 59 L7
Smithview WISHAW ML2 131 L2
Smith Wy BSHPBGS G64 62 D2
Smithy Ct DMBTN G82 19 G2
GRNKW/INVK PA16 32 E4
Smithycroft HMLTN ML3 120 A7
Smithycroft Rd
STPS/GTHM/RID G33 80 E1
Smithyends CUMB G67 31 H4
Smithy Rd DMBTN G82 19 G2
Smollett Rd DMBTN G82 21 H7
Smollett St ALEX/LLW G83 13 J5
Smugglers Brig Rd
CARLUKE ML8 134 B7
Smyllum Pk LNK/LMHG ML11 137 J5
Smyllum Rd LNK/LMHG ML11 137 J5
Snaefell Av RUTH G73 96 C6
Snaefell Crs RUTH G73 96 C5
Snead Vw MTHW ML1 101 L8
Sneddon Av WISHAW ML2 122 C8
Sneddon St HMLTN ML3 118 G4
Sneddon Ter HMLTN ML3 118 F4
Snowdon St GBLS G5 79 K6
Snuff Mill Rd LNPK/KPK G44 95 H5
Society St DEN/PKHD G31 80 B5
Sollas Pl KNTSWD G13 58 E1
Solsgirth Gdns KKNTL G66 46 B1
Solway Ct HMLTN ML3 129 H2
Solway Pl BAIL/MDB/MHD G69 64 D1
Solway Rd BSHPBGS G64 44 D8
Solway St DMNK/BRGTN G40 79 M8
Somerford Rd BSDN G61 41 M8
Somerled Av PSLYN/LNWD PA3 75 M1
Somerset Av HMLTN ML3 119 H6
Somerset Pl KVGV G3 78 F1
Somerset Place Ms KVGV G3 78 F1
Somervell St BLTYR/CAMB G72 96 F4
Somerville Ct BEITH KA15 125 K4
Somerville Dr EKILS G75 127 J3
GVH/MTFL G42 95 H2
Somerville La EKILS G75 127 J3
Somerville Pl HBR/GL G84 10 E7
Sorby St DEN/PKHD G31 80 D5
Sorley St PTCK G11 59 M7
Sorn St DMNK/BRGTN G40 80 B7
Souterhouse Pth CTBR ML5 83 M5
Souterhouse Rd CTBR ML5 83 M5
Southampton Dr
KVD/HLHD G12 60 B4
Southampton La
KVD/HLHD G12 60 B4
South Annandale St
GVH/MTFL G42 79 H8
South Av BLTYR/CAMB G72 118 E5
CARLUKE ML8 133 G8
CLYDBK G81 40 A7
PSLYS PA2 91 M2
RNFRW PA4 58 D6
Southbank Dr KKNTL G66 45 J2
Southbank Rd KKNTL G66 45 H3
South Bank St CLYDBK G81 58 C2
Southbank St DEN/PKHD G31 80 D5
Southbar Av KNTSWD G13 59 G2
Southbar Rd ERSK PA8 57 G3
South Barrwood Rd KSYTH G65 29 M3
South Biggar Rd AIRDRIE ML6 85 H2
South Brae KKNTL G66 26 C3
Southbrae Av BRWEIR PA11 72 B3
Southbrae Dr KNTSWD G13 59 K5
Southbrae Gdns KNTSWD G13 59 K4
Southbrae La KNTSWD G13 59 L4
South Bridge St AIRDRIE ML6 85 G1
South Burn Rd AIRDRIE ML6 84 D2
South Caldeen Rd CTBR ML5 84 C4
South Campbell St PSLYS PA2 9 H8
South Carbrain Rd CUMB G67 49 G1
South Chester St CAR/SHTL G32 81 G5
South Church Pl ALEX/LLW G83 13 L7
South Circular Rd CTBR ML5 84 B3
South Claremont La
MLNGV G62 42 A1
South Commonhead Av
AIRDRIE ML6 66 F8
Southcroft Rd RUTH G73 95 L1
Southcroft St GOV/IBX G51 78 B3
South Crosshill Rd
BSHPBGS G64 62 A1
South Dean Park Av
UD/BTH/TAN G71 99 G8
Southdeen Av DRUM G15 41 H6
Southdeen Rd DRUM G15 41 G6
South Douglas St CLYDBK G81 58 C1
South Dr KBRN KA25 124 B5
PSLYN/LNWD PA3 74 B4
South Dumbreck Rd
KSYTH G65 29 J2
South Elgin Pl CLYDBK G81 58 C2
South Elgin St CLYDBK G81 58 C2
Southend Pl BLSH ML4 99 M6
Southend Rd CLYDBK G81 40 B4
Southern Av RUTH G73 96 B5
Southerness Dr BALLOCH G68 31 G4
South Erskine Pk BSDN G61 41 K4
Southesk Av BSHPBGS G64 43 M7
South Exchange Ct CGLE G1 4 F7
Southfield CTBR ML5 84 C4
Southfield Av PGL PA14 34 F2
PSLYS PA2 91 L2
SHOTTS ML7 105 H5
Southfield Crs CTBR ML5 84 C4
PLK/PH/NH G53 93 J1
SHOTTS ML7 105 H5
Southfield Rd BALLOCH G68 30 C8
SHOTTS ML7 105 H5
South Frederick St CGLE G1 5 G7
Southgate EKILN G74 2 F7
MLNGV G62 42 A1
South Glassford St MLNGV G62 42 B1
Southhill Av RUTH G73 96 C5
Southinch Av SCOT G14 58 E3
Southinch La SCOT G14 58 E3
South King St HBR/GL G84 10 F7
Southlea Av GIF/THBK G46 94 A7
South Line Vw WISHAW ML2 121 L7
Southloch Gdns
SPRGB/BLRNK G21 61 M7
Southloch St
SPRGB/BLRNK G21 61 M7
South Mains Rd MLNGV G62 23 M8
South Medrox St CTBR ML5 65 J3
South Mound
CRG/CRSL/HOU PA6 55 G8
South Muirhead Rd CUMB G67 31 G7
Southmuir Pl MRYH/FIRH G20 60 D5
South Neuk KBRN KA25 124 C6
South Nimmo St AIRDRIE ML6 85 H2
South Park Av BRHD/NEIL G78 92 B6
Southpark Av KVD/HLHD G12 60 E8
South Park Dr PSLYS PA2 75 L8
South Park Gv HMLTN ML3 119 K7
Southpark La KVD/HLHD G12 60 E8
South Park Rd HMLTN ML3 119 K8
South Pl BLSH ML4 99 M6
South Portland St GBLS G5 4 E9
South Rd
CRMNK/CLK/EAG G76 115 G5
PGL PA14 34 E2
South Robertson Pl
AIRDRIE ML6 84 E2
South Scott St
BAIL/MDB/MHD G69 82 B6
Southside Crs GBLS G5 79 H6
South St CRG/CRSL/HOU PA6 55 H8
GRNKW/INVK PA16 16 D4
RNFRW PA4 57 H6
SCOT G14 59 G5
South Vennel LNK/LMHG ML11 137 G5
South Vesalius St
CAR/SHTL G32 81 G5
South Vw BLSH ML4 99 L6
BLTYR/CAMB G72 118 C1
CLYDBK G81 39 M7
Southview BSDN G61 41 J4
Southview Av
CRMNK/CLK/EAG G76 114 E5
Southview Ct BSHPBGS G64 61 M3
Southview Crs BRWEIR PA11 72 D1
Southview Gv BSDN G61 41 J4
Southview Pl
BAIL/MDB/MHD G69 64 E4
Southview Ter BSHPBGS G64 61 M3
South William St JNSTN PA5 73 M8
Southwold Rd PSLY PA1 76 E4
Southwood Dr LNPK/KPK G44 95 J5
South Woodside Rd
COWCAD G4 60 E8
Soutra Pl STPS/GTHM/RID G33 81 H2
Spairdrum Rd AIRDRIE ML6 48 F5
Spalding Dr LARGS KA30 106 F3
Spalehall Dr MTHW ML1 101 M6
Spateston Rd JNSTN PA5 89 K3
Spean Av EKILN G74 3 L5
Spean St LNPK/KPK G44 95 G3
Speirsfield Gdns PSLYS PA2 8 F7
Speirshall Cl SCOT G14 58 F4
Speirshall Ter SCOT G14 58 E3
Speirs Pl PSLYN/LNWD PA3 74 C4
Speirs Rd BSDN G61 42 A7
Spencer Dr PSLYS PA2 90 D3
Spencer Field Gdns
HMLTN ML3 119 M7
Spencer St CLYDBK G81 40 A6
KNTSWD G13 59 M2
Spence St MRYH/FIRH G20 60 C2
Spey Av PSLYS PA2 90 E1
Speyburn Pl AIRDRIE ML6 67 G7
STPS/GTHM/RID G33 63 L4
Spey Ct AIRDRIE ML6 85 J4
Spey Dr CTBR ML5 83 L6
RNFRW PA4 58 E7
Spey Gdns HMLTN ML3 129 H2
Spey Gv EKILS G75 126 C3
Spey Pl JNSTN PA5 89 J2
Spey Rd BSDN G61 41 J7
Spey St STPS/GTHM/RID G33 80 F2
Spey Ter EKILS G75 126 C3
Spiers Av BEITH KA15 125 J6
Spiersbridge Av GIF/THBK G46 93 M6
Spiersbridge La GIF/THBK G46 93 L6
Spiersbridge Rd GIF/THBK G46 93 M7
Spiersbridge Ter GIF/THBK G46 93 L6
Spiersbridge Wy GIF/THBK G46 93 M6
Spiers Gv GIF/THBK G46 93 M6
Spiersland Wy BEITH KA15 125 L6
Spiers Pl BEITH KA15 125 J6
Spiers Rd CRG/CRSL/HOU PA6 55 H8
JNSTN PA5 74 B7
LOCHW PA12 109 H2
Spindlehowe Rd
UD/BTH/TAN G71 99 G4
Spindleside Rd MTHW ML1 102 D8
Spinners Gdns PSLYS PA2 8 A8
Spinners La CLYDBK G81 40 B2
Spittal Rd RUTH G73 95 M6
Spoolers Rd PSLY PA1 8 C7
Spoutmouth CGLE G1 5 J8
Sprig Wy SHOTTS ML7 71 L7
Springbank Crs HMLTN ML3 129 G3
MTHW ML1 101 G8
Springbank Rd
PSLYN/LNWD PA3 75 K3
SHOTTS ML7 104 C3
Springbank St MRYH/FIRH G20 60 F6
Springbank Ter AIRDRIE ML6 67 M6
PSLYN/LNWD PA3 75 K3
Springbank Vw AIRDRIE ML6 67 M6
Springboig Av CAR/SHTL G32 81 J4
Springboig Rd CAR/SHTL G32 81 J3
Springburn Pl EKILN G74 116 A7
Springburn Rd
SPRGB/BLRNK G21 5 L2
SPRGB/BLRNK G21 61 L7
Springburn Wy
SPRGB/BLRNK G21 61 M6
Springcroft Av
BAIL/MDB/MHD G69 82 B4
Springcroft Crs
BAIL/MDB/MHD G69 82 B4
Springcroft Dr
BAIL/MDB/MHD G69 82 B4
Springcroft Gdns
BAIL/MDB/MHD G69 82 C4
Springcroft Gv ALEX/LLW G83 13 L7
BAIL/MDB/MHD G69 82 B4
Springcroft Rd
BAIL/MDB/MHD G69 82 B4
Springcroft Wynd
BAIL/MDB/MHD G69 82 B4
Springfield Av BSHPBGS G64 62 A2
PSLY PA1 76 B5
UD/BTH/TAN G71 98 F5
Springfield Ct CGLE G1 4 F7
Springfield Crs
BLTYR/CAMB G72 118 C4
BSHPBGS G64 62 A2
CARLUKE ML8 134 F1
UD/BTH/TAN G71 98 F5
Springfield Dr BRHD/NEIL G78 92 E8
Springfield Gdns
LNK/LMHG ML11 136 F4
Springfield Gv
BRHD/NEIL G78 112 D1
Springfield Pk JNSTN PA5 74 A8
Springfield Park Rd RUTH G73 96 C4
Springfield Quay GBLS G5 4 A9
Springfield Rd AIRDRIE ML6 85 L1
BRHD/NEIL G78 111 M3
BSHPBGS G64 62 A1
CUMB G67 31 G5
DEN/PKHD G31 80 C6
SHOTTS ML7 86 F8
Springfields Gdns LARGS KA30 106 F7
Springfield Sq BSHPBGS G64 62 A2
Springfield Woods JNSTN PA5 74 A8
Springhill & Leadloch Rd
SHOTTS ML7 105 J6
Springhill Av AIRDRIE ML6 85 H1
CTBR ML5 83 J6
Springhill Dr North
BAIL/MDB/MHD G69 82 A3
Springhill Dr South
BAIL/MDB/MHD G69 82 A4
Springhill Farm Gv
BAIL/MDB/MHD G69 82 A4
Springhill Farm Pl
BAIL/MDB/MHD G69 82 A4
Springhill Farm Rd
BAIL/MDB/MHD G69 82 A4
Springhill Farm Wy
BAIL/MDB/MHD G69 82 A4
Springhill Gdns
PLKSD/SHW G41 94 E1
Springhill Pkwy
BAIL/MDB/MHD G69 82 B3
Springhill Pl CTBR ML5 83 J6
Springhill Rd
BAIL/MDB/MHD G69 81 M5
BRHD/NEIL G78 112 A4
CRMNK/CLK/EAG G76 114 F3
PGL PA14 34 C1
SHOTTS ML7 105 H6
Springholm Dr AIRDRIE ML6 66 F7
Springkell Av PLKSD/SHW G41 78 B7
Springkell Dr PLKSD/SHW G41 78 B8
Springkell Gdns
PLKSD/SHW G41 78 C8
Springkell Ga PLKSD/SHW G41 78 D8
Springkell St GRNK PA15 7 G6
Springside Gdns DRUM G15 41 G4
Springside Pl DRUM G15 41 G5
Springvale Dr PSLYS PA2 74 F8
Springvale Ter
SPRGB/BLRNK G21 61 L6
Springwell Crs
BLTYR/CAMB G72 118 F3
Springwells Av AIRDRIE ML6 85 J1
Springwells Crs AIRDRIE ML6 85 J1
Springwood Dr
KLMCLM PA13 35 K8
Spring Wynd GBLS G5 79 J6
Spruce Av BLTYR/CAMB G72 118 C2
HMLTN ML3 129 L1
JNSTN PA5 90 A1
Spruce Ct HMLTN ML3 129 L1
Spruce Dr BLTYR/CAMB G72 97 M6
KKNTL G66 45 G5
Spruce Rd CUMB G67 31 K5
UD/BTH/TAN G71 99 J1
Spruce St PPK/MIL G22 61 K5
Spruce Wy BLTYR/CAMB G72 97 M6
Squire St SCOT G14 59 K7
Stable Gv PSLY PA1 8 A7
Stable Pl MLNGV G62 23 M6
Stable Rd MLNGV G62 23 M6
SHOTTS ML7 105 G5
Staffa EKILN G74 127 M2
Staffa Av PGL PA14 35 G3
RNFRW PA4 58 C8

Staffa Dr AIRDRIE ML6 85 M2
KKNTL G66 46 B2
PSLYS PA2 91 L3
Staffa Rd BLTYR/CAMB G72 96 F7
Staffa St DEN/PKHD G31 80 B2
GRK PA19 15 K3
Staffin Dr SMSTN G23 60 D1
Staffin St SMSTN G23 60 E1
Stafford Crs GRNKW/INVK PA16 15 M5
Stafford Rd GRNKW/INVK PA16 15 M5
Stafford St BLSH ML4 99 M6
COWCAD G4 5 H3
HBR/GL G84 10 D5
Stafford St West HBR/GL G84 10 C4
Staffordway South
GRNKW/INVK PA16 15 L5
Stag Ct UD/BTH/TAN G71 99 J4
Stag St GOV/IBX G51 78 B3
Staig Wynd MTHW ML1 121 G5
Staikhill LNK/LMHG ML11 136 F4
Staineybraes Pl AIRDRIE ML6 66 F7
Stakehill LARGS KA30 106 F5
Stalker St WISHAW ML2 121 J5
Stamford Ga DEN/PKHD G31 80 B5
Stamford Pl DEN/PKHD G31 80 B5
Stamford Rd DEN/PKHD G31 80 B5
Stamford St DEN/PKHD G31 80 B5
Stamperland Av
CRMNK/CLK/EAG G76 114 F2
Stamperland Dr
CRMNK/CLK/EAG G76 114 F3
Stamperland Gdns
CRMNK/CLK/EAG G76 114 F3
Stamperland Hl
CRMNK/CLK/EAG G76 114 F1
Stanalane St GIF/THBK G46 93 M5
Standburn Rd
SPRGB/BLRNK G21 62 D4
Staneacre Pk HMLTN ML3 119 M7
Stanecraigs Pl WISHAW ML2 122 F3
Stanefield Dr MTHW ML1 101 L5
Stane Gv SHOTTS ML7 105 G6
Stanely Av PSLYS PA2 91 H1
Stanely Crs PSLYS PA2 91 H2
Stanely Dr PSLYS PA2 91 J1
Stanely Gra PSLYS PA2 91 H3
Stanely Gv PSLYS PA2 91 H2
Stanely Rd PSLYS PA2 91 J1
Stane Rd PGL PA14 34 E2
SHOTTS ML7 105 G7
Stanford St CLYDBK G81 40 C8
Stanhope Dr RUTH G73 96 D5
Stanhope Pl WISHAW ML2 131 J1
Stanistone Rd CARLUKE ML8 133 J7
Stanlane Pl LARGS KA30 106 E5
Stanley Bvd BLTYR/CAMB G72 118 D6
Stanley Dr BLSH ML4 100 A3
BSHPBGS G64 44 B8
JNSTN PA5 73 J5
Stanley La JNSTN PA5 73 J5
Stanley Pl BLTYR/CAMB G72 118 D1
Stanley St HMLTN ML3 118 F6
PLKSD/SHW G41 78 E5
Stanley Street La
PLKSD/SHW G41 78 E5
Stanmore Av LNK/LMHG ML11 137 H5
Stanmore Crs LNK/LMHG ML11 137 J4
Stanmore Rd GVH/MTFL G42 95 H2
LNK/LMHG ML11 137 K4
Stanners La GRNK PA15 7 G6
Stanrigg St AIRDRIE ML6 68 A7
Stark Av CLYDBK G81 39 L4
Starling Wy BLSH ML4 99 L2
Starryshaw Rd SHOTTS ML7 104 E3
Startpoint St
STPS/GTHM/RID G33 81 G2
Station Av GRNK PA15 6 E5
GRNKW/INVK PA16 32 E5
HWWD PA9 88 F5
Station Brae BRHD/NEIL G78 111 J2
Station Ct GLGNK KA14 124 E7
Station Crs RNFRW PA4 58 E5
Station Pk BAIL/MDB/MHD G69 82 C6
Station Pl CARLUKE ML8 132 C3
Station Ri LOCHW PA12 109 J3
Station Rd AIRDRIE ML6 68 B7
AIRDRIE ML6 85 L1
BAIL/MDB/MHD G69 82 C6
BLTYR/CAMB G72 118 E2
BRHD/NEIL G78 111 K3
BSDN G61 41 J6
BSHPTN PA7 38 B8
BTHG/ARM EH48 71 K2
CARLUKE ML8 132 C3
CRMNK/CLK/EAG G76 115 G5
DMBTN G82 19 G3
GIF/THBK G46 94 C7
GRK PA19 15 L1
GRNKW/INVK PA16 32 E4
HBR/GL G84 10 F7
HWWD PA9 88 E4
KKNTL G66 26 D2
KLBCH PA10 88 D4
KSYTH G65 29 K1
LRKH ML9 130 D5
MLNGV G62 42 B1
MRYH/FIRH G20 60 C2
MTHW ML1 101 H6
OLDK G60 39 H4
PGL PA14 34 C1
PSLY PA1 75 G7
PSLYS PA2 8 A7
RNFRW PA4 58 E5
SHOTTS ML7 104 F5
SKLM PA17 50 B4
STPS/GTHM/RID G33 63 G5
UD/BTH/TAN G71 98 E4
WISHAW ML2 122 A7
Station Rw CARLUKE ML8 132 C3
Station St DMBTN G82 20 D1
Station Wynd KLBCH PA10 73 H8
Staybrae Dr PLK/PH/NH G53 76 F8
Staybrae Gv PLK/PH/NH G53 76 F8
Steading Dr ALEX/LLW G83 13 M4
The Steading WISHAW ML2 122 B4
Steele Crs ALEX/LLW G83 13 M3
Steele Wk ALEX/LLW G83 13 M2
Steel Pl WISHAW ML2 121 L7
Steel St CGLE G1 5 H9
GRK PA19 15 M2
WISHAW ML2 122 B7
Steeple St KLBCH PA10 73 G7
Stenhouse Av
BAIL/MDB/MHD G69 64 C3
Stenton Crs WISHAW ML2 121 K8
Stenton Pl WISHAW ML2 121 K8
Stenton St CAR/SHTL G32 80 E3
Stenzel Pl STPS/GTHM/RID G33 63 M5
Stepends Rd AIRDRIE ML6 86 B3
Stepford Pl
STPS/GTHM/RID G33 81 M3
Stepford Rd
STPS/GTHM/RID G33 81 M3
Stephen Crs
BAIL/MDB/MHD G69 81 M5
Stephens Av AIRDRIE ML6 68 F5
Stephenson Pl EKILS G75 2 C8
Stephenson St
CARD/HILL/MSPK G52 76 E1
Stephenson Ter EKILS G75 2 C8
Stepps Rd KKNTL G66 45 L8
STPS/GTHM/RID G33 81 J1
Steven Pl KBRN KA25 124 D3
Stevenson Pl BLSH ML4 100 B2
Stevenson St CARLUKE ML8 133 G7
CLYDBK G81 39 M6
DMNK/BRGTN G40 5 K9
PSLYS PA2 9 G7
Stevens Pl GRK PA19 15 L3
Stevenston Ct MTHW ML1 101 G5
Stevenston St MTHW ML1 101 G5
Steven St ALEX/LLW G83 13 K5
Stewart Av BLTYR/CAMB G72 118 C3
HMLTN ML3 128 F2
NMRNS G77 113 L3
RNFRW PA4 58 A8
Stewart Centre GRNK PA15 6 C3
Stewart Ct BRHD/NEIL G78 92 C5
Stewart Crs BRHD/NEIL G78 92 D5
WISHAW ML2 123 G3
Stewart Dr
BAIL/MDB/MHD G69 83 H4
CLYDBK G81 40 B3
CRMNK/CLK/EAG G76 114 D2
Stewartfield Crs EKILN G74 2 D2
Stewartfield Dr EKILN G74 116 D6
Stewartfield Rd EKILN G74 2 B2
Stewartfield Wy EKILN G74 115 M6
Stewartgill Pl LRKH ML9 131 H8
Stewart Gv SHOTTS ML7 71 M7
Stewarton Dr
BLTYR/CAMB G72 96 E5
Stewarton Rd NMRNS G77 113 J2
Stewarton St WISHAW ML2 122 C7
Stewart Pl BRHD/NEIL G78 92 D5
CARLUKE ML8 133 H7
Stewart Qd MTHW ML1 101 H3
Stewart Rd PSLYS PA2 91 M2
Stewarts La WISHAW ML2 122 C6
Stewart St BLSH ML4 100 D4
BRHD/NEIL G78 92 D5
CARLUKE ML8 133 H7
CLYDBK G81 39 L7
COWCAD G4 4 E2
CTBR ML5 84 A1
HMLTN ML3 119 G5
MLNGV G62 42 A1
Stewartville St PTCK G11 60 B8
Stirling Av BSDN G61 41 L7
EKILN G74 3 J1
Stirling Dr BSDN G61 41 J3
BSHPBGS G64 43 L7
GRK PA19 14 F4
HMLTN ML3 118 E6
JNSTN PA5 73 K8
RUTH G73 96 B5
Stirlingfauld Pl GBLS G5 79 H6
Stirling Gdns BSHPBGS G64 43 L7
Stirling Ga PSLYN/LNWD PA3 73 M4
Stirling Pl KKNTL G66 26 E2
Stirling Rd AIRDRIE ML6 49 G7
CARLUKE ML8 133 G5
COWCAD G4 5 J5
CUMB G67 49 G3
DMBTN G82 21 G3
KSYTH G65 29 M1
Stirling St AIRDRIE ML6 84 F2
CTBR ML5 83 K6
CUMB G67 31 H5
DMBTN G82 13 J8
MTHW ML1 121 H5
Stirrat St MRYH/FIRH G20 60 C4
PSLYN/LNWD PA3 73 M3
Stobcross Rd KVGV G3 78 C2
Stobcross St CTBR ML5 84 A3
Stobcross Wynd KVGV G3 78 C2
Stobhill Rd SPRGB/BLRNK G21 61 M3
Stobo EKILN G74 117 J6
Stobo Ct EKILN G74 117 J6
Stobo St WISHAW ML2 122 C4
Stobs Dr BRHD/NEIL G78 92 B5
Stock Av PSLYS PA2 9 H9
Stockbridge Crs KBRN KA25 124 C1
Stockholm Crs PSLYS PA2 9 J8
Stockiemuir Av BSDN G61 41 L2
Stockiemuir Rd BSDN G61 23 J8
Stocks Rd MTHW ML1 102 F8
Stock St PSLYS PA2 9 G9
Stockwell Pl CGLE G1 4 F8
Stockwell St CGLE G1 5 G9
Stonebank Gv CSMK G45 95 K7
Stonebyres Ct HMLTN ML3 119 G7
Stonecraig Rd WISHAW ML2 122 C7
Stonedyke Crs CARLUKE ML8 133 J6
Stonedyke Gv DRUM G15 41 H7
Stonedyke Rd CARLUKE ML8 133 J6
Stonefield Av KVD/HLHD G12 60 B4
PSLYS PA2 91 M1
Stonefield Crs
BLTYR/CAMB G72 118 C4
CRMNK/CLK/EAG G76 114 C2
PSLYS PA2 91 M1
Stonefield Dr PSLYS PA2 91 M1
Stonefield Gdns PSLYS PA2 91 L1
Stonefield Pk PSLYS PA2 91 L1
Stonefield Park Gdns
BLTYR/CAMB G72 118 E2
Stonefield Pl
BLTYR/CAMB G72 118 B4
Stonefield Rd
BLTYR/CAMB G72 118 C3
Stonefield St AIRDRIE ML6 67 G8
Stonehall Av HMLTN ML3 119 H8
Stonehaven Crs AIRDRIE ML6 84 E4
Stonehaven Rd
GRNKW/INVK PA16 15 M6
Stonelaw Dr RUTH G73 96 B3
Stonelaw Rd RUTH G73 96 B3
Stoneleigh Rd
GRNKW/INVK PA16 16 C2
Stoneside Dr
PLKSW/MSWD G43 94 B4
Stoneside Sq
PLKSW/MSWD G43 94 A4
Stoney Brae PSLYN/LNWD PA3 9 G3
PSLYS PA2 91 L2
Stoneyetts Rd
BAIL/MDB/MHD G69 46 F8
Stoneyholm Rd KBRN KA25 124 E3
Stoneymeadow Rd EKILN G74 117 H5
Stonyflatt Av DMBTN G82 21 H5
Stonyflatt Rd DMBTN G82 21 H5
Stonyhurst St PPK/MIL G22 61 J6
Stonylee Rd CUMB G67 31 G8
Storie St PSLY PA1 9 G5
Stormyland Wy
BRHD/NEIL G78 92 C7
Stornoway Crs WISHAW ML2 122 E5
Stornoway St PPK/MIL G22 61 J2
Stow Brae PSLY PA1 9 G7
Stow St PSLY PA1 9 H6
Strachan Pl BLTYR/CAMB G72 118 D7
Strachan St BLSH ML4 100 A5
Strachur Crs PPK/MIL G22 61 G3
Strachur St PPK/MIL G22 61 G3
Strain Crs AIRDRIE ML6 85 H3
Straiton Dr HMLTN ML3 118 D8
Straiton St
STPS/GTHM/RID G33 80 E3
Stranka Av PSLYS PA2 8 C8
Stranraer Dr DRUM G15 41 J7
Stratford EKILN G74 117 K5
Stratford St MRYH/FIRH G20 60 E5
Strathallan Av EKILS G75 126 D2
Strathallan Crs AIRDRIE ML6 67 G6
Strathallan Ga EKILS G75 126 D2
Strathallan Wynd EKILS G75 126 C1
Strathallon Pl RUTH G73 96 D7
Strathaven Rd EKILN G74 3 K8
EKILS G75 127 L5
HMLTN ML3 129 H7
Strathavon Crs AIRDRIE ML6 67 G7
Strathblane Crs AIRDRIE ML6 67 G6
Strathblane Dr EKILS G75 126 B2
Strathblane Gdns KNTSWD G13 59 M1
Strathblane Rd MLNGV G62 24 B8
Strathbran St DEN/PKHD G31 80 D6
Strathcairn Crs AIRDRIE ML6 67 G6
Strath Carron CARLUKE ML8 132 C3
Strathcarron Crs PSLYS PA2 92 B1
Strathcarron Dr PSLYS PA2 76 C8
Strathcarron Pl
MRYH/FIRH G20 60 D5
PSLYS PA2 92 B1
Strathcarron Rd PSLYS PA2 92 B1
Strathcarron Wy PSLYS PA2 76 B8
Strathclyde Dr RUTH G73 96 A4
Strathclyde Gdns
BLTYR/CAMB G72 97 L7
Strathclyde Pl HBR/GL G84 10 B5
Strathclyde Rd DMBTN G82 21 G5
MTHW ML1 120 B3
Strathclyde St
DMNK/BRGTN G40 80 A8
Strathclyde Vw
UD/BTH/TAN G71 119 H1
Strathclyde Wy BLSH ML4 100 C2
Strathcona Dr KNTSWD G13 59 M2
Strathcona Gdns KNTSWD G13 60 A3
Strathcona La EKILS G75 127 H3
Strathcona Pl EKILS G75 127 H3
RUTH G73 96 D6
Strathcona St KNTSWD G13 59 M3
Strathconon Gdns EKILS G75 126 B1
Strath Dearn CARLUKE ML8 132 C4
Strathdearn Gv EKILS G75 126 B2
Strathdee Av CLYDBK G81 40 B4
Strathdee Rd LNPK/KPK G44 94 E8
Strathdon Av LNPK/KPK G44 94 F8
PSLYS PA2 8 C9
Strathdon Dr LNPK/KPK G44 94 F8
Strathdon Pl EKILS G75 126 B2
Strathearn Gv KKNTL G66 46 B1
Strathearn Rd
CRMNK/CLK/EAG G76 114 E4
Strath Elgin CARLUKE ML8 132 B4
Strathendrick Dr
LNPK/KPK G44 94 E6
Strathfillan Rd EKILN G74 2 D4
Strathgoil Crs AIRDRIE ML6 67 G6
Strathgryffe Crs BRWEIR PA11 72 C1
Strath Halladale CARLUKE ML8 132 C4
Strathhalladale Ct EKILS G75 126 B2
Strathisla Wy MTHW ML1 101 H7
Strathkelvin Av BSHPBGS G64 61 M3
Strathkelvin La EKILS G75 126 B2
Strathlachlan Av
CARLUKE ML8 133 J8
Strathleven Dr ALEX/LLW G83 20 F1
Strathmiglo Ct EKILS G75 126 B2
Strathmore Av
BLTYR/CAMB G72 118 C1
PSLY PA1 76 D5
Strathmore Crs AIRDRIE ML6 * 67 G7
Strathmore Gdns RUTH G73 96 D6
Strathmore Gv EKILS G75 126 B2
Strathmore Pl CTBR ML5 * 84 D4
Strathmore Rd HMLTN ML3 119 L7
PPK/MIL G22 61 H3
Strathmore Wk CTBR ML5 84 D4
Strathmungo Crs AIRDRIE ML6 66 F7
Strath Nairn CARLUKE ML8 132 C4
Strathnairn Av EKILS G75 126 B2
Strathnairn Ct EKILS G75 126 B2
Strathnairn Dr EKILS G75 126 B2
Strathnairn Wy EKILS G75 126 B2
Strath Naver CARLUKE ML8 132 C4
Strathnaver Crs AIRDRIE ML6 67 G6
Strathnaver Gdns EKILS G75 126 B2
Strathord Pl
BAIL/MDB/MHD G69 47 G7
Strathord St CAR/SHTL G32 81 G7
Strath Peffer CARLUKE ML8 132 B4
Strathpeffer Crs AIRDRIE ML6 67 G7
Strathrannoch Wy EKILS G75 126 B2
Strathspey Av EKILS G75 126 B2
Strathspey Crs AIRDRIE ML6 67 G6
Strathtay Av EKILS G75 126 C1
LNPK/KPK G44 94 E8
Strathtummel Crs AIRDRIE ML6 67 G6
Strathview Gv LNPK/KPK G44 94 E8
Strathview Pk LNPK/KPK G44 94 E8
Strathview Rd BLSH ML4 99 M7
Strathvithie Gv EKILS G75 126 B2
Strathyre Ct EKILS G75 126 B2
Strathyre Gdns AIRDRIE ML6 66 F4
BSDN G61 42 B5
EKILS G75 126 B2
Strathyre Rd
BLTYR/CAMB G72 118 F4
Strathyre St PLKSD/SHW G41 94 E2
Stratton Dr GIF/THBK G46 94 B8
Strauss Av CLYDBK G81 40 E8
Stravaig Pth PSLYS PA2 91 G3
Stravaig Wk PSLYS PA2 91 G3
Stravanan Ct CSMK G45 95 L8
Stravanan Gdns CSMK G45 95 K8
Stravanan Pl CSMK G45 95 L8
Stravanan Rd CSMK G45 95 K8
Stravanan St CSMK G45 95 K8
Stravanan Ter CSMK G45 95 K8
Stravenhouse Rd
CARLUKE ML8 132 A5
Strawberry Field Rd
CRG/CRSL/HOU PA6 73 H1
Strawhill Rd
CRMNK/CLK/EAG G76 114 F3
Streamfield Gdns
STPS/GTHM/RID G33 62 E3
Streamfield Ga
STPS/GTHM/RID G33 62 D3
Streamfield Lea
STPS/GTHM/RID G33 62 E2
Streamfield Pl
STPS/GTHM/RID G33 62 E3
Strenabey Av RUTH G73 96 D6
Striven Crs WISHAW ML2 122 A8
Striven Gdns MRYH/FIRH G20 60 F7
Striven Rd WMYSB PA18 50 B1
Striven Ter HMLTN ML3 129 G1
Stroma Av PGL PA14 35 H4
Stroma St SPRGB/BLRNK G21 62 B8
Stromness St GBLS G5 79 G6
Strone Crs GRNK PA15 7 G9
Strone Gdns KSYTH G65 29 H2
Stronend St PPK/MIL G22 61 H5
Strone Rd ALEX/LLW G83 13 L4
STPS/GTHM/RID G33 81 H3
Stronsay St SPRGB/BLRNK G21 62 B8
Stronvar Dr SCOT G14 59 H5
Stroud Rd EKILS G75 126 F5
Strowan Crs CAR/SHTL G32 81 H6
Strowan's Rd DMBTN G82 21 J7
Strowan St CAR/SHTL G32 81 H6
Strowan's Well Rd DMBTN G82 21 J7
Struan Av GIF/THBK G46 94 C7
Struan Gdns LNPK/KPK G44 95 G5
Struan Rd LNPK/KPK G44 95 G5
Struie St ESTRH G34 82 A2
Struma Dr
CRMNK/CLK/EAG G76 114 C2
Struthers Crs EKILN G74 117 H6
Stuart Av OLDK G60 39 H5
RUTH G73 96 B5
Stuart Dr BSHPBGS G64 61 L2
LNK/LMHG ML11 137 H4
LRKH ML9 130 E8
Stuarton Pk EKILN G74 2 F3
Stuart Qd WISHAW ML2 121 L8
Stuart Rd BSHPTN PA7 38 B6
CRMNK/CLK/EAG G76 115 K2
DMBTN G82 21 J6
Stuart St EKILN G74 3 G4
OLDK G60 39 H5
Stuckleckie Rd HBR/GL G84 10 F6
Succoth St KNTSWD G13 59 M2
Sudbury Crs EKILS G75 126 E1
Suffolk Rd GRNKW/INVK PA16 15 L5
Suffolk St DMNK/BRGTN G40 5 J9
HBR/GL G84 10 B5
Sugworth Av
BAIL/MDB/MHD G69 82 B5
Suisnish ERSK PA8 57 J3
Sumburgh St
STPS/GTHM/RID G33 80 F3
Summerfield Rd CUMB G67 48 A3
Summerfield St
DMNK/BRGTN G40 80 B8
Summerhill & Garngibbock Rd
CUMB G67 48 D6
Summerhill Av LRKH ML9 130 C7
Summerhill Dr DRUM G15 41 H5
Summerhill Gdns DRUM G15 41 H5
Summerhill Pl DRUM G15 41 H5
Summerhill Rd
CRMNK/CLK/EAG G76 114 F3
DRUM G15 41 H5
Summerlea Rd GIF/THBK G46 93 M6
Summerlee Rd LRKH ML9 130 B4
WISHAW ML2 121 J5
Summerlee St CTBR ML5 83 M3
STPS/GTHM/RID G33 81 J2
Summer St DMNK/BRGTN G40 79 M5
Summertown Rd GOV/IBX G51 78 B3
Sunart Av RNFRW PA4 58 B5
Sunart Gdns BSHPBGS G64 62 C1
Sunart Rd BSHPBGS G64 62 C1
CARD/HILL/MSPK G52 77 L4
WMYSB PA18 32 B8
Sunart St WISHAW ML2 122 A8
Sunbury Av
CRMNK/CLK/EAG G76 114 C3
Sundale Av
CRMNK/CLK/EAG G76 114 D4
Sunderland Av DMBTN G82 20 C6
Sunflower Gdns MTHW ML1 120 D1
Sunningdale Av NMRNS G77 113 M4
Sunningdale Dr BRWEIR PA11 72 B4
Sunningdale Rd SMSTN G23 60 D2
Sunningdale Wynd
UD/BTH/TAN G71 98 E7
Sunnybank Dr
CRMNK/CLK/EAG G76 114 D4
Sunnybank Gv
CRMNK/CLK/EAG G76 114 D4
Sunnydale Dr BTHG/ARM EH48 71 M1
Sunnyhill KSYTH G65 28 F7
Sunnylaw Dr PSLYS PA2 75 H8
Sunnylaw St PPK/MIL G22 61 H6
Sunnyside Av MTHW ML1 101 H4
PGL PA14 35 G2
UD/BTH/TAN G71 98 F5
Sunnyside Crs MTHW ML1 101 H4
Sunnyside Dr
BAIL/MDB/MHD G69 82 F5
CRMNK/CLK/EAG G76 114 D2
DRUM G15 41 G8
Sunnyside Ga MTHW ML1 101 G4
Sunnyside Ov PSLYS PA2 91 L1
Sunnyside Pl BRHD/NEIL G78 92 B7
DRUM G15 41 G8
MTHW ML1 101 G4
Sunnyside Rd CTBR ML5 84 A2
LNK/LMHG ML11 136 D4
MTHW ML1 122 B1
PSLYS PA2 91 K1
Sunnyside St LRKH ML9 130 B5
Sunnyside Ter MTHW ML1 101 G4
Surrey La GBLS G5 79 H6
Surrey St GBLS G5 79 H6
Susannah St ALEX/LLW G83 13 K5
Sussex St PLKSD/SHW G41 78 E5
Sutcliffe Ct KNTSWD G13 59 L2
Sutcliffe Rd KNTSWD G13 59 M2
Sutherland Av BSDN G61 41 L2
PLKSD/SHW G41 78 C7
Sutherland Crs HMLTN ML3 119 G6
Sutherland Dr AIRDRIE ML6 84 F4
GIF/THBK G46 114 D1
Sutherland La KVD/HLHD G12 60 D8
Sutherland Pl BLSH ML4 99 M8
Sutherland Rd CLYDBK G81 40 B7
GRNKW/INVK PA16 16 A5
Sutherland St
BLTYR/CAMB G72 118 C5
HBR/GL G84 10 B5
PSLY PA1 8 E4
Sutherland Wy EKILN G74 117 J7
Sutherness Dr
STPS/GTHM/RID G33 81 G3
Swaledale EKILN G74 2 B2
Swallow Brae
GRNKW/INVK PA16 32 F4
Swallow Crs
GRNKW/INVK PA16 33 G3
Swallow Dr JNSTN PA5 89 J3
Swallow Gdns KNTSWD G13 58 F2
Swallow Rd CLYDBK G81 40 D2
WISHAW ML2 122 B6
Swan Pl JNSTN PA5 89 J3
Swanson Rd ALEX/LLW G83 13 J3
Swanston St DMNK/BRGTN G40 80 A8
Swan St CLYDBK G81 39 M7
COWCAD G4 5 G2
Swan Wy CARLUKE ML8 132 B5
Sween Av LNPK/KPK G44 95 G6
Sween Dr HMLTN ML3 129 G1
Sweethope Gdns
UD/BTH/TAN G71 99 H8
Sweethope Pl
UD/BTH/TAN G71 99 G7
Swift Av GRNKW/INVK PA16 33 G4
Swift Bank HMLTN ML3 128 E1
Swift Cl WISHAW ML2 122 B6
Swift Crs KNTSWD G13 58 F2
Swift Pl EKILS G75 126 B4
JNSTN PA5 89 K3
Swindon St CLYDBK G81 39 L7
Swinstie Rd MTHW ML1 122 C1
Swinstie Vw MTHW ML1 102 C8
Swinton Av
BAIL/MDB/MHD G69 82 D5
Swinton Crs
BAIL/MDB/MHD G69 82 C5
CTBR ML5 83 H6
Swinton Dr
CARD/HILL/MSPK G52 77 H4
Swinton Gdns
BAIL/MDB/MHD G69 82 D5
Swinton Pth
BAIL/MDB/MHD G69 82 D5
Swinton Pl
CARD/HILL/MSPK G52 77 H4
Swinton Rd
BAIL/MDB/MHD G69 82 C5
Swinton Vw
BAIL/MDB/MHD G69 82 C5
Swisscot Av HMLTN ML3 129 H2
Swisscot Wk HMLTN ML3 129 H2
Switchback Rd BSDN G61 41 M8
Swordale Pl ESTRH G34 82 A2
Sword St AIRDRIE ML6 84 F2
DEN/PKHD G31 79 M4
Sycamore Av BEITH KA15 125 K3
JNSTN PA5 90 A1
KKNTL G66 45 K5
UD/BTH/TAN G71 99 J3
Sycamore Ct EKILS G75 127 G4
Sycamore Crs AIRDRIE ML6 85 K3
EKILS G75 127 G4
Sycamore Dr AIRDRIE ML6 85 K3
CLYDBK G81 39 M6
HMLTN ML3 119 M8
Sycamore Gv
BLTYR/CAMB G72 118 C2
Sycamore Pl EKILS G75 127 G4
GRK PA19 15 J3
MTHW ML1 101 J6
Sycamore Wy BLTYR/CAMB G72 97 M6
CRMNK/CLK/EAG G76 115 K3
KKNTL G66 27 J6
Sydenham Rd KVD/HLHD G12 60 C7
Sydes Brae BLTYR/CAMB G72 118 B6
Sydney Dr EKILS G75 2 B9
Sydney Pl EKILS G75 2 B8
Sydney St CLYDBK G81 39 K6
DMNK/BRGTN G40 5 L8
Sykehead Av BLSH ML4 100 B4
Sykeside Rd AIRDRIE ML6 84 E5
Symington Dr CLYDBK G81 40 B7
Syriam Pl SPRGB/BLRNK G21 61 M6
Syriam St SPRGB/BLRNK G21 61 M5

T

Tabard Pl KNTSWD G13 59 J1
Tabard Rd KNTSWD G13 59 J1
Tabernacle La BLTYR/CAMB G72 97 G5
Tabernacle St BLTYR/CAMB G72 97 G5
Taggart Rd KSYTH G65 29 M7
Taig Rd KKNTL G66 46 B3
Tain Ter BLTYR/CAMB G72 118 C7
Tait Av BRHD/NEIL G78 92 D5
Tait Wk CARLUKE ML8 134 B8
Talbot EKILN G74 117 J6
Talbot Ct KNTSWD G13 59 H4
Talbot Crs CTBR ML5 83 L6
Talbot Dr KNTSWD G13 59 H4
Talbot Pl KNTSWD G13 59 H4
Talbot Rd ALEX/LLW G83 13 M2
Talbot Ter KNTSWD G13 59 H4
UD/BTH/TAN G71 98 E2
Talisman Av DMBTN G82 20 C6
Talisman Crs HBR/GL G84 10 F7
MTHW ML1 100 D7
Talisman Rd KNTSWD G13 59 J3
PSLYS PA2 90 E3
Tallant Rd DRUM G15 41 H6
Tallant Ter DRUM G15 41 J6
Talla Rd CARD/HILL/MSPK G52 77 H4
Tamarack Crs UD/BTH/TAN G71 99 J1
Tamar Dr EKILS G75 126 C4
Tambowie Av MLNGV G62 23 M7

Tambowie Crs MLNGV G62 23 M7
Tambowie St KNTSWD G13 59 L2
Tamshill St MRYH/FIRH G20 60 F4
Tanar Av RNFRW PA4 58 F8
Tandlehill Rd KLBCH PA10 89 H1
Tanera Av LNPK/KPK G44 95 J6
Tanfield Pl CAR/SHTL G32 81 J3
Tanfield St CAR/SHTL G32 81 J3
Tankerland Rd LNPK/KPK G44 95 G4
Tannadice Av
CARD/HILL/MSPK G52 77 J6
Tanna Dr CARD/HILL/MSPK G52 77 M6
Tannahill Crs JNSTN PA5 89 M1
Tannahill Rd EKILN G74 117 J7
Tannahill Rd PLKSW/MSWD G43 94 F4
PSLYN/LNWD PA3 8 B2
Tannahill Ter PSLYN/LNWD PA3 8 B2
Tannoch Dr CUMB G67 48 F2
MLNGV G62 24 B7
Tannoch Pl CUMB G67 48 F2
Tannoch Rd BRHD/NEIL G78 110 B7
Tannochside Dr
UD/BTH/TAN G71 99 H1
Tannock St PPK/MIL G22 61 H6
Tantallon Av GRK PA19 14 F4
Tantallon Ct CARLUKE ML8 133 G6
Tantallon Dr CTBR ML5 83 J1
PSLYS PA2 91 G1
Tantallon Pk EKILN G74 2 C4
Tantallon Rd
BAIL/MDB/MHD G69 82 A7
PLKSD/SHW G41 94 E3
Tanzieknowe Av
BLTYR/CAMB G72 97 H7
Tanzieknowe Dr
BLTYR/CAMB G72 97 H7
Tanzieknowe Pl
BLTYR/CAMB G72 97 G7
Tanzieknowe Rd
BLTYR/CAMB G72 97 H7
Taransay St GOV/IBX G51 77 M1
Tarbert Av BLTYR/CAMB G72 98 C8
WISHAW ML2 122 A8
Tarbert Ct HMLTN ML3 129 G1
Tarbert Pl CARLUKE ML8 133 J8
Tarbert Wy CTBR ML5 83 L6
Tarbet St GRK PA19 15 M2
Tarbolton EKILN G74 117 K7
Tarbolton Crs AIRDRIE ML6 85 K8
Tarbolton Dr CLYDBK G81 40 C6
Tarbolton Pth LRKH ML9 130 B6
Tarbolton Rd CUMB G67 31 H7
PLKSW/MSWD G43 94 D4
Tarbrax Wy HMLTN ML3 119 G7
Tarfside Av
CARD/HILL/MSPK G52 77 K5
Tarfside Gdns
CARD/HILL/MSPK G52 77 K5
Tarfside Ov
CARD/HILL/MSPK G52 77 K6
Target Rd AIRDRIE ML6 85 H3
Tarland St GOV/IBX G51 77 M3
Tarn Gv STPS/GTHM/RID G33 62 E2
Tarquin Pl MTHW ML1 120 C1
Tarras Dr RNFRW PA4 58 E8
Tasker St GRNKW/INVK PA16 16 B4
Tasman Dr EKILS G75 126 E3
Tasmania Qd WISHAW ML2 122 E6
Tassie Pl EKILN G74 3 K4
Tassie St PLKSD/SHW G41 94 D2
Tattershall Rd
STPS/GTHM/RID G33 63 J8
Tavistock Dr PLKSW/MSWD G43 94 D5
Tay Av RNFRW PA4 58 E6
Tay Ct EKILS G75 126 B2
Tay Crs BSHPBGS G64 62 B1
STPS/GTHM/RID G33 80 E1
Tay Gv EKILS G75 126 B3
Tayinloan Dr CARLUKE ML8 135 H1
Taylor Av KLBCH PA10 72 F7
MTHW ML1 101 K7
Taylor Pl COWCAD G4 5 J5
Taylor St ALEX/LLW G83 13 H3
CLYDBK G81 58 C1
COWCAD G4 5 J6
Taymouth Dr GRK PA19 14 F4
Taymouth St CAR/SHTL G32 81 H7
Taynish Dr LNPK/KPK G44 95 J6
Tay Pl DMBTN G82 21 H3
EKILS G75 126 B3
JNSTN PA5 89 J2
SHOTTS ML7 104 E3
Tay Rd BSDN G61 41 K7
BSHPBGS G64 62 B1
Tayside AIRDRIE ML6 66 F8
Tay St CTBR ML5 83 J1
GRNKW/INVK PA16 16 B4
Tay Ter EKILS G75 126 B2
Teak Pl UD/BTH/TAN G71 99 K1
Teal Ct BLSH ML4 99 L2
Teal Crs EKILS G75 126 C5
Teal Dr GRNKW/INVK PA16 33 G3
KNTSWD G13 59 G2
Tealing Av
CARD/HILL/MSPK G52 77 J5
Tealing Crs
CARD/HILL/MSPK G52 77 J5
Teasel Av PLK/PH/NH G53 93 H6
Teawell Rd NMRNS G77 113 K4
Technology Av
BLTYR/CAMB G72 118 C6
Teesdale EKILN G74 2 B2
Teign Gv EKILS G75 126 C4
Teith Av RNFRW PA4 58 F7
Teith Dr BSDN G61 41 J6
Teith St STPS/GTHM/RID G33 80 E1
Telegraph Rd AIRDRIE ML6 69 H1
Telephone La KVD/HLHD G12 60 C8
Telford Pl CUMB G67 49 G2
Telford Rd CUMB G67 49 G1
EKILS G75 2 E7
Telford St BLSH ML4 100 A3
Teme Pl EKILS G75 126 C3
Templar Av KNTSWD G13 59 K1
Temple Gdns KNTSWD G13 59 M2
Templeland Rd PLK/PH/NH G53 77 J7
Temple Locks Ct KNTSWD G13 59 M2
Temple Locks Pl KNTSWD G13 59 M2
Temple Rd KNTSWD G13 60 A3
Templeton Ct
DMNK/BRGTN G40 79 L5
Templeton St
DMNK/BRGTN G40 79 L5
Tennant Av EKILN G74 116 A8
Tennant St RNFRW PA4 58 D5
Tennant Wynd BLSH ML4 100 A1
Tennent St CTBR ML5 84 B4
Tennyson Dr DEN/PKHD G31 80 E6
Tennyson Gdns
BLTYR/CAMB G72 118 D3
Tenters Wy PSLYS PA2 8 B7
Tern Pl JNSTN PA5 89 K3
Tern Wy CTBR ML5 84 E6
Terrace Rd GRNK PA15 6 E4
Terregles Av PLKSD/SHW G41 78 C8
Terregles Crs PLKSD/SHW G41 78 C8
Terregles Dr PLKSD/SHW G41 78 C8
Teviot Av BSHPBGS G64 44 A7
PSLYS PA2 90 E2
Teviot Crs BSDN G61 41 K7
Teviot Dr BSHPTN PA7 38 C8
Teviot Rd PGL PA14 34 F4
Teviot St CTBR ML5 65 K8
KVGV G3 78 D2
Teviot Ter JNSTN PA5 89 J2
Tewkesbury Rd EKILN G74 117 K5
Thane Rd KNTSWD G13 59 J3
Thanes Ga UD/BTH/TAN G71 98 E5
Thankerton Av MTHW ML1 100 F4
Thankerton Rd LRKH ML9 130 D8
Tharsis St SPRGB/BLRNK G21 79 M1
Thimble St DMBTN G82 13 J8
Third Av ALEX/LLW G83 13 L5
DMBTN G82 21 J8
LNPK/KPK G44 95 H3
RNFRW PA4 58 C7
STPS/GTHM/RID G33 63 H5
Third Gdns PLKSD/SHW G41 78 A6
Thirdpart Crs KNTSWD G13 58 E2
Third Rd BLTYR/CAMB G72 118 E5
Third St UD/BTH/TAN G71 98 F2
Thirlmere EKILS G75 126 C5
Thistle Bank KKNTL G66 45 K6
Thistlebank Gdns CTBR ML5 83 L7
Thistle Crs LRKH ML9 130 D7
Thistledown Gv CTBR ML5 84 C3
Thistle Gdns MTHW ML1 101 G5
Thistle Neuk OLDK G60 39 G3
Thistle Pl EKILN G74 2 D2
Thistle Qd AIRDRIE ML6 67 H8
Thistle Rd MTHW ML1 101 G6
Thistle St AIRDRIE ML6 67 H8
GBLS G5 79 J5
KKNTL G66 45 J2
MTHW ML1 102 C8
PSLYS PA2 8 C9
Thistle Ter GBLS G5 79 H6
Thomas Muir Av BSHPBGS G64 62 A2
Thomas Muir La GRNK PA15 17 M7
Thomas Muir St GRNK PA15 17 M7
Thomas St ALEX/LLW G83 13 K6
PSLY PA1 8 B6
Thompson Brae PSLY PA1 9 H7
Thompson Pl CLYDBK G81 40 C3
Thompson St DEN/PKHD G31 80 A4
Thomson Av JNSTN PA5 73 L7
KKNTL G66 45 L2
WISHAW ML2 121 K8
Thomson Dr AIRDRIE ML6 84 F3
BLSH ML4 99 K5
BSDN G61 41 M3
Thomson Gv BLTYR/CAMB G72 97 G3
Thomson's Cl LNK/LMHG ML11 137 G5
Thomson St CARLUKE ML8 133 H8
JNSTN PA5 73 L8
RNFRW PA4 58 C7
Thomson Ter SHOTTS ML7 104 D4
Thom St GRNKW/INVK PA16 16 C5
Thorn Av EKILN G74 115 J7
Thornbank St KVGV G3 78 C2
Thorn Brae JNSTN PA5 74 A7
Thornbridge Av
BAIL/MDB/MHD G69 82 B5
KVD/HLHD G12 60 C5
Thornbridge Gdns
BAIL/MDB/MHD G69 82 A5
Thornbridge Rd
BAIL/MDB/MHD G69 82 A5
Thorncliffe Gdns
PLKSD/SHW G41 78 E8
Thorncroft Dr LNPK/KPK G44 95 K6
Thorndean Av BLSH ML4 100 B5
Thorndean Crs BLSH ML4 100 B5
Thorndene JNSTN PA5 74 B7
Thorndene Av MTHW ML1 101 J7
Thornden La SCOT G14 59 G5
Thorn Dr BSDN G61 41 K4
RUTH G73 96 C6
Thorndyke EKILN G74 117 J5
Thornhill JNSTN PA5 74 A8
Thornhill Av BLTYR/CAMB G72 118 D2
JNSTN PA5 74 B8
Thornhill Dr JNSTN PA5 74 B8
Thornhill Gdns JNSTN PA5 74 A7
NMRNS G77 113 K7
Thornhill Rd HMLTN ML3 118 E6
Thornhill Wy CTBR ML5 84 D5
Thorniecroft Dr CUMB G67 48 C3
Thorniecroft Pl CUMB G67 48 C3
Thorniewood Gdns
UD/BTH/TAN G71 99 G4
Thorniewood Rd
UD/BTH/TAN G71 98 F2
Thornkip Pl CTBR ML5 84 D4
Thornlea Dr GIF/THBK G46 94 D6
Thornlea Pl LNK/LMHG ML11 137 M2
Thornlea St CARLUKE ML8 135 G1
Thornley Av KNTSWD G13 59 H3
Thornliebank Rd
PLKSW/MSWD G43 94 B5
Thornlie Gill WISHAW ML2 122 B7
Thornly Park Av PSLYS PA2 91 M2
Thornly Park Dr PSLYS PA2 91 M2
Thornly Park Gdns PSLYS PA2 91 M1
Thornly Park Rd PSLYS PA2 91 M1
Thorn Rd BLSH ML4 100 B4
BSDN G61 41 J4
Thornside Rd JNSTN PA5 74 A7
Thornton La MRYH/FIRH G20 60 E3
Thornton Pl HMLTN ML3 129 K4
Thornton Rd EKILN G74 115 J8
Thornton St CTBR ML5 65 K8
MRYH/FIRH G20 60 E3
Thorntree Av BEITH KA15 125 K3
HMLTN ML3 118 F5
Thorntree Dr CTBR ML5 83 L5
Thorntree Wy UD/BTH/TAN G71 99 H7
Thornwood Av KKNTL G66 45 G5
PTCK G11 60 A8
Thornwood Crs PTCK G11 59 M7
Thornwood Dr BRWEIR PA11 72 B3
PSLYS PA2 91 H1
PTCK G11 59 M7
Thornwood Gdns PTCK G11 59 M7
Thornwood Pl PTCK G11 59 M6
Thornwood Rd PTCK G11 59 M7
Thornwood Ter PTCK G11 59 M7
Thornyburn Dr
BAIL/MDB/MHD G69 82 D6
Thornyburn Pl
BAIL/MDB/MHD G69 82 C6
Thrashbush Av WISHAW ML2 122 D5
Thrashbush Crs WISHAW ML2 122 D5
Thrashbush La AIRDRIE ML6 67 H7
Thrashbush Rd AIRDRIE ML6 67 G7
WISHAW ML2 122 D5
Thread St PSLY PA1 9 J7
Threave Ct CARLUKE ML8 133 G6
Threave Pl
BAIL/MDB/MHD G69 64 E6
NMRNS G77 113 H4
Threepwood Rd BEITH KA15 125 M4
Threestonehill Av
CAR/SHTL G32 81 H4
Threshold EKILN G74 3 J4
Threshold Pk EKILN G74 3 J4
Thriplee Rd BRWEIR PA11 72 C2
Thrums EKILN G74 117 K5
Thrums Av BSHPBGS G64 62 C1
Thrushbush Qd AIRDRIE ML6 67 G7
Thrushcraig Crs PSLYS PA2 75 M8
Thrush Pl JNSTN PA5 89 K3
Thurso St PTCK G11 78 C1
Thurston Rd
CARD/HILL/MSPK G52 77 G4
Thyme Sq MTHW ML1 120 E1
Tibbermore Rd PTCK G11 60 A7
Tiber Av MTHW ML1 100 C8
Tillanburn Rd MTHW ML1 101 M6
Tillet Ov PSLYN/LNWD PA3 75 K3
Tillie St MRYH/FIRH G20 60 F7
Till St WISHAW ML2 122 B3
Tillycairn Av
STPS/GTHM/RID G33 63 K8
Tillycairn Dr
STPS/GTHM/RID G33 63 K8
Tillycairn Pl
STPS/GTHM/RID G33 63 L8
Tillycairn Rd
STPS/GTHM/RID G33 63 K8
Tillycairn St
STPS/GTHM/RID G33 63 L8
Tilt Rd WISHAW ML2 122 F3
Tilt St STPS/GTHM/RID G33 62 E8
Timmons Gv BLSH ML4 100 D4
Timmons Ter AIRDRIE ML6 85 K8
Tinker's La MTHW ML1 120 C3
Tintagel Gdns
BAIL/MDB/MHD G69 46 F7
Tintock Pl BALLOCH G68 30 D3
Tintock Rd KKNTL G66 28 B8
Tinto Crs WISHAW ML2 122 C7
Tinto Dr BALLOCH G68 30 D7
BRHD/NEIL G78 112 C1
Tinto Rd AIRDRIE ML6 85 H3
BAIL/MDB/MHD G69 83 H4
BSDN G61 41 H3
PLKSW/MSWD G43 94 C5
Tinto St WISHAW ML2 122 C7
Tinto Vw HMLTN ML3 129 L2
Tinto View Rd LRKH ML9 131 G8
Tinto Wy EKILS G75 126 E5
Tinwald Pth
CARD/HILL/MSPK G52 77 G4
Tiree EKILN G74 127 M3
Tiree Av PGL PA14 35 G3
RNFRW PA4 76 C1
Tiree Ct CUMB G67 48 D1
Tiree Crs WISHAW ML2 122 F2
Tiree Dr CUMB G67 48 D1
Tiree Gdns AIRDRIE ML6 66 F4
BSDN G61 41 H3
OLDK G60 39 J4
Tiree Gra HMLTN ML3 128 F1
Tiree Pl CTBR ML5 * 83 L6
NMRNS G77 113 H4
OLDK G60 39 J4
Tiree Rd CUMB G67 48 D1
Tiree St SPRGB/BLRNK G21 62 C8
Tirry Av RNFRW PA4 58 F7
Titwood Rd NMRNS G77 113 L8
PLKSD/SHW G41 78 C8
Tiverton Av CAR/SHTL G32 81 K7
Tivoli Ct EKILS G75 127 H4
Tobago Pl DMNK/BRGTN G40 79 M5
EKILS G75 126 D1
Tobago St DMNK/BRGTN G40 79 L5
GRNK PA15 6 C4
Tobermory Gdns AIRDRIE ML6 67 G6
Tobermory Rd RUTH G73 96 D7
Todburn Dr PSLYS PA2 91 M3
Todd St DEN/PKHD G31 80 C3
Todhills North EKILS G75 3 G8
Todhills South EKILS G75 3 G8
Todholm Crs PSLYS PA2 76 B7
Todholm Rd PSLYS PA2 76 B7
Todholm Ter PSLYS PA2 9 M9
Tofthill Av BSHPBGS G64 43 M8
Tofthill Gdns BSHPBGS G64 43 L8
Togo Pl GRNK PA15 6 B6
Tollbrae Av AIRDRIE ML6 85 H2
Tollcross Park Gdns
CAR/SHTL G32 80 E7
Tollcross Park Gv
CAR/SHTL G32 * 80 F7
Tollcross Park Vw
CAR/SHTL G32 80 F7
Tollcross Rd DEN/PKHD G31 80 D5
Tollhouse Gdns BLSH ML4 100 C6
Toll La GOV/IBX G51 78 E4
Tollpark Crs WISHAW ML2 123 G4
Tollpark Pl BALLOCH G68 31 L1
Tollpark Rd BALLOCH G68 31 L1
Toll St MTHW ML1 120 F4
Toll Wynd HMLTN ML3 129 J3
Tolsta St SMSTN G23 60 E1
Tomtain Brae BALLOCH G68 47 M3
Tomtain Ct BALLOCH G68 47 M3
Toner Gdns WISHAW ML2 131 K2
Tontine Crs DMBTN G82 20 D2
Tontine La CGLE G1 5 H8
Tontine Pk DMBTN G82 20 D2
Tontine Pl RUTH G73 96 E6
Topaz Ter BLSH ML4 100 A6
Toppersfield KLBCH PA10 73 J8
Torbeg Gdns EKILS G75 126 E6
Torbothie Rd SHOTTS ML7 105 G5
Torbracken HWWD PA9 89 G4
Torbreck St
CARD/HILL/MSPK G52 77 M4
Torbrex Rd CUMB G67 31 G8
Torburn Av GIF/THBK G46 94 B6
Tordene Pth BALLOCH G68 30 D6
Torgyle St SMSTN G23 60 D1
Tormeadow Rd NMRNS G77 113 K4
Tormore Ct
STPS/GTHM/RID G33 63 L4
Tormore St GOV/IBX G51 77 K3
Tormusk Dr CSMK G45 96 A6
Tormusk Gdns CSMK G45 96 A6
Tormusk Gv CSMK G45 96 A6
Tormusk Rd CSMK G45 96 A7
Torness St PTCK G11 60 C8
Torogay Pl PPK/MIL G22 61 L2
Torogay St PPK/MIL G22 61 J3
Torogay Ter PPK/MIL G22 61 J2
Torphin Crs CAR/SHTL G32 81 G3
Torrance Av AIRDRIE ML6 85 K2
EKILS G75 127 L5
Torrance Ct EKILS G75 127 L6
Torrance Gait EKILS G75 127 L6
Torrance La EKILS G75 127 L6
Torrance Rd BSHPBGS G64 44 C3
EKILN G74 2 F4
GRNK PA15 17 J8
Torrance Wynd EKILS G75 127 L5
Torran Dr ERSK PA8 57 L3
Torran Rd STPS/GTHM/RID G33 81 M3
Torranyard Ter HMLTN ML3 128 E1
Torr Av BRWEIR PA11 53 L8
Torr Gdns PPK/MIL G22 61 K6
Torriden Pl CTBR ML5 83 L5
Torriden St CTBR ML5 83 K5
Torridon Av MTHW ML1 101 K6
PLKSD/SHW G41 78 B7
Torridon Gdns NMRNS G77 114 B6
Torrington Av GIF/THBK G46 114 A2
Torrington Crs CAR/SHTL G32 81 K7
Torrin Rd SMSTN G23 60 D1
Torrisdale Pl CTBR ML5 83 L3
Torrisdale St CTBR ML5 83 L3
PLKSD/SHW G41 78 F8
Torr La BRWEIR PA11 53 L8
Torr Pl PPK/MIL G22 61 K6
Torr Rd BRWEIR PA11 72 C2
BSHPBGS G64 62 D1
Torr St PPK/MIL G22 61 K6
Torryburn Rd
SPRGB/BLRNK G21 62 C6
Torwood Brae HMLTN ML3 118 F8
Toryglen Rd RUTH G73 95 L2
Toryglen St GBLS G5 79 L8
Tourmaline Ter BLSH ML4 100 B6
Toward Ct BLTYR/CAMB G72 118 E1
Toward Rd
STPS/GTHM/RID G33 81 J3
WMYSB PA18 32 B8
Toward Vw SKLM PA17 50 C5
Tower Av BRHD/NEIL G78 92 D5
Tower Crs RNFRW PA4 58 B7
Tower Dr GRK PA19 15 K3
RNFRW PA4 58 B7
Towerhill Rd KNTSWD G13 41 J8
Tower Pl JNSTN PA5 89 M1
MLNGV G62 24 B8
Tower Rd BSHPBGS G64 25 J7
CUMB G67 49 G3
JNSTN PA5 89 M1
MLNGV G62 24 F7
Towerside Crs PLK/PH/NH G53 77 G7
Towerside Rd PLK/PH/NH G53 77 G7
Towers Rd AIRDRIE ML6 85 M2
Tower St PLKSD/SHW G41 78 E5
Tower Ter PSLY PA1 8 F6
Towie Pl UD/BTH/TAN G71 98 F4
Townend Rd DMBTN G82 21 G5
Townhead BEITH KA15 125 K5
KBRN KA25 124 D3
Townhead Av MTHW ML1 100 E2
Townhead Cl LARGS KA30 106 E5
Townhead Dr MTHW ML1 101 M6
Townhead Pl UD/BTH/TAN G71 99 G2
Townhead Rd CTBR ML5 83 G1
NMRNS G77 113 J5
Townhead St HMLTN ML3 119 M7
KSYTH G65 29 K3
Townhead Ter PSLY PA1 8 F5
Townhill Rd HMLTN ML3 118 E7
Townhill Ter HMLTN ML3 118 E7
Townmill Rd DEN/PKHD G31 80 A2
Townsend St COWCAD G4 4 F2
Tradeston St GBLS G5 4 C9
Trafalgar Ct BALLOCH G68 30 D3
Trafalgar St CLYDBK G81 39 M7
DMNK/BRGTN G40 79 M7
GRNK PA15 6 D5
Trainard Av CAR/SHTL G32 80 F6
Tranent Pl MTHW ML1 102 C7
STPS/GTHM/RID G33 80 E2
Traquair Av WISHAW ML2 122 C4
Traquair Dr
CARD/HILL/MSPK G52 77 H5
Treeburn Av GIF/THBK G46 94 B7
Treemain Rd GIF/THBK G46 114 A2
Treespark Av BRHD/NEIL G78 92 B5
Trefoil Av PLKSD/SHW G41 94 D2
Trent Pl EKILS G75 126 B4
Trent St CTBR ML5 65 K8
Tresta Rd SMSTN G23 60 F2
Tribboch St LRKH ML9 130 B6
Trigoni Ct LARGS KA30 106 F7
Trinidad Gn EKILS G75 126 D1
Trinity Av
CARD/HILL/MSPK G52 77 J5
Trinity Crs BEITH KA15 125 L4
Trinity Dr BLTYR/CAMB G72 97 J7
Trinley Rd KNTSWD G13 41 K8
Triton Pl BLSH ML4 100 F4
Trondra Pth ESTRH G34 81 M2
Trondra Pl ESTRH G34 81 M2
Trongate CGLE G1 5 H8
Tron Pl LARGS KA30 106 E5
Troon Av EKILS G75 126 D4
Troon Ct EKILS G75 126 E4
Troon Dr BRWEIR PA11 72 C3
Troon Gdns BALLOCH G68 30 F3
Troon Pl NMRNS G77 114 A6
Troon St DMNK/BRGTN G40 80 B7
Trossachs Av MTHW ML1 101 G4
Trossachs Ct MRYH/FIRH G20 61 G7
Trossachs Rd RUTH G73 96 D8
Trossachs St MRYH/FIRH G20 61 G7
Troubridge Av KLBCH PA10 89 H1
Troubridge Crs KLBCH PA10 73 H8
Trovaig ERSK PA8 57 J3
Trows Rd WISHAW ML2 131 K3
Truce Rd KNTSWD G13 59 H1
Truro Av BAIL/MDB/MHD G69 46 F7
Tryst Rd CUMB G67 30 F8
Tudor La South SCOT G14 59 L6
Tudor Rd SCOT G14 59 L6
Tudor St BAIL/MDB/MHD G69 81 M7
Tulley Wynd MTHW ML1 100 D7
Tulliallan Pl EKILN G74 3 K8
Tullichewan Crs ALEX/LLW G83 13 J3
Tullichewan Dr ALEX/LLW G83 13 J3
Tullichewan Rd ALEX/LLW G83 13 J2
Tullis Ct DMNK/BRGTN G40 79 L6
Tullis St DMNK/BRGTN G40 79 L6
Tulloch-ard Pl RUTH G73 96 D7
Tulloch Gdns MTHW ML1 121 H5
Tulloch Rd SHOTTS ML7 105 H6
Tulloch St LNPK/KPK G44 95 G4
Tullymet Rd HMLTN ML3 129 K2
Tummel Dr AIRDRIE ML6 66 F7
Tummel Gn EKILN G74 2 F1
Tummel Rd WMYSB PA18 50 B1
Tummel St STPS/GTHM/RID G33 80 E1
Tummel Wy CUMB G67 31 G7
Tunnel St KVGV G3 78 E3
Tuphall Rd HMLTN ML3 119 K8
Turnberry Av GRK PA19 15 G3
PTCK G11 60 B7
Turnberry Crs AIRDRIE ML6 85 L8
CTBR ML5 83 L6
Turnberry Dr BRWEIR PA11 72 C4
HMLTN ML3 128 D1
NMRNS G77 114 A6
RUTH G73 95 M6
Turnberry Gdns BALLOCH G68 30 F4
Turnberry Pl EKILS G75 126 E4
RUTH G73 95 M5
Turnberry Rd PTCK G11 60 B7
Turnberry Wynd
UD/BTH/TAN G71 98 E7
Turnbull Av ALEX/LLW G83 13 J7
Turnbull Crs ALEX/LLW G83 13 J7
Turnbull St CGLE G1 5 H9
Turner Rd PSLYN/LNWD PA3 75 M2
Turners Av PSLY PA1 8 A7
Turner St CTBR ML5 83 M4
Turnhill Av ERSK PA8 57 G3
Turnhill Crs ERSK PA8 57 H3
Turnhill Dr ERSK PA8 57 H3
Turnhill Gdns ERSK PA8 57 H3
Turningshaw Rd
CRG/CRSL/HOU PA6 55 L4
Turnlaw EKILS G75 127 G5
Turnlaw Rd BLTYR/CAMB G72 97 G8
Turnlaw St GBLS G5 79 K6
Turnyland Mdw ERSK PA8 57 H3
Turnyland Wy ERSK PA8 57 H3
Turquoise Ter BLSH ML4 100 A6
Turret Crs KNTSWD G13 59 J1
Turret Rd KNTSWD G13 59 J1
Turriff St GBLS G5 79 H6
Tweed Av PSLYS PA2 74 F8
Tweed Ct AIRDRIE ML6 85 J4
Tweed Crs RNFRW PA4 58 E7
STPS/GTHM/RID G33 80 D1
WISHAW ML2 122 C4
Tweed Dr BSDN G61 41 K6
Tweedmuir Pl CTBR ML5 84 C6
Tweed Pl JNSTN PA5 89 J2
Tweedsmuir BSHPBGS G64 44 C8
Tweedsmuir Crs BSDN G61 41 L2
Tweedsmuir Pk HMLTN ML3 129 J2
Tweedsmuir Rd
CARD/HILL/MSPK G52 77 H5
Tweed St CTBR ML5 84 A6
EKILS G75 126 B3
GRNKW/INVK PA16 16 B4
LRKH ML9 130 C8
Tweedvale Av SCOT G14 58 E3
Tweedvale Pl SCOT G14 58 E3
Twinlaw St ESTRH G34 82 D1
Tylney Rd PSLY PA1 76 D4
Tyndrum Rd BSDN G61 42 B5
Tyndrum St COWCAD G4 4 F2
Tynecastle Crs CAR/SHTL G32 81 H3
Tynecastle Pl CAR/SHTL G32 81 H3
Tynecastle St CAR/SHTL G32 81 H3
Tyne Pl EKILS G75 126 B4
Tynron Ct HMLTN ML3 128 E1
Tynwald Av RUTH G73 95 C6

U

Udston Rd HMLTN ML3 118 E6
Udston Ter HMLTN ML3 118 F5
Uig Pl STPS/GTHM/RID G33 81 L4
Uist Av PGL PA14 35 G3
Uist Crs STPS/GTHM/RID G33 63 L6
Uist Dr KKNTL G66 46 A2
Uist Pl AIRDRIE ML6 85 K3
Uist St GOV/IBX G51 77 M2
Uist Wy WISHAW ML2 122 E4
Ullswater EKILS G75 126 C5
Ulundi Rd JNSTN PA5 73 L8
Ulva St CARD/HILL/MSPK G52 77 M4
Ulverston Ter HMLTN ML3 129 K4
Umachan ERSK PA8 57 J3
Underbank LARGS KA30 106 D1
Undercliffe Rd WMYSB PA18 50 A1
Underwood Ct
PSLYN/LNWD PA3 8 E3
Underwood Dr WISHAW ML2 122 F2
Underwood La PSLY PA1 8 E4
Underwood Rd
PSLYN/LNWD PA3 8 E3
RUTH G73 96 C4
Underwood St PLKSD/SHW G41 94 E4
Union Pl CGLE G1 4 E6
Union St ALEX/LLW G83 13 L6
CARLUKE ML8 133 H8
CGLE G1 4 E7
GRNKW/INVK PA16 6 B2
HMLTN ML3 119 K6
KKNTL G66 45 J2
LARGS KA30 106 E5
LRKH ML9 130 C6
MTHW ML1 101 G5
PSLYS PA2 9 G9
SHOTTS ML7 104 D4
Union Street La ALEX/LLW G83 13 L6
Unitas Crs CARLUKE ML8 134 E1
Unitas Rd BLSH ML4 100 C4
Unity Pk SHOTTS ML7 104 D5
Unity Pl COWCAD G4 4 C1
University Av KVD/HLHD G12 60 D8
University Gdns KVD/HLHD G12 60 D8
University Pl KVD/HLHD G12 60 D8
Unsted Pl PSLY PA1 9 L5

170 Uns - Wes

Unst La BLTYR/CAMB G72 96 E8
Unthank Rd BLSH ML4 100 C4
Uphall Pl STPS/GTHM/RID G33 80 E2
Upland La SCOT G14 59 J5
Upland Rd SCOT G14 59 J5
U.P. La KSYTH G65 29 K2
Uplawmoor Rd
BRHD/NEIL G78 110 C6
Upper Adelaide St HBR/GL G84 10 F6
Upper Arthur St ALEX/LLW G83 13 J6
Upper Bourtree Ct RUTH G73 96 C6
Upper Bourtree Dr RUTH G73 96 B6
Upper Bridge St ALEX/LLW G83 13 J6
Upper Carman Rd DMBTN G82 20 D1
Upper Cartsburn St GRNK PA15 6 F8
Upper Colquhoun St
HBR/GL G84 10 D4
Upper Glenburn Rd BSDN G61 41 K4
Upper Glenfinlas St
HBR/GL G84 10 E5
Upper Mill St AIRDRIE ML6 85 G1
Upper Smollett St
ALEX/LLW G83 13 J6
Upper Stoneymollan Rd
ALEX/LLW G83 12 F2
Upper Sutherland Crs
HBR/GL G84 10 B4
Upper Sutherland St
HBR/GL G84 10 B4
U.P. Rd KSYTH G65 29 K2
Urquhart Crs RNFRW PA4 58 C7
Urquhart Dr EKILN G74 3 K1
GRK PA19 14 F4
Urquhart Pl
BAIL/MDB/MHD G69 64 E6
HBR/GL G84 10 D3
Urrdale Rd PLKSD/SHW G41 78 B5
Usmore Pl STPS/GTHM/RID G33 81 L5

V

Vaila La BLTYR/CAMB G72 96 F7
Vaila St SMSTN G23 60 F3
Valerio Ct BLTYR/CAMB G72 118 D2
Valetta Pl CLYDBK G81 39 K7
Valeview Ter DMBTN G82 21 G4
GVH/MTFL G42 95 G2
Vallantine Crs UD/BTH/TAN G71 99 G2
Vallay St PPK/MIL G22 61 K2
Valley Ct HMLTN ML3 119 J8
Valleyfield EKILS G75 2 C6
KKNTL G66 27 G4
Valleyfield Dr BALLOCH G68 47 L1
Valleyfield St
SPRGB/BLRNK G21 61 L7
Valley Vw MTHW ML1 121 H6
Vancouver Dr EKILS G75 126 E1
Vancouver La SCOT G14 59 K5
Vancouver Pl CLYDBK G81 39 K7
Vancouver Rd SCOT G14 59 J6
Vanguard St CLYDBK G81 40 D7
Vardar Av
CRMNK/CLK/EAG G76 114 C2
Vardon Lea MTHW ML1 101 L8
Varna La SCOT G14 59 L6
Varna Rd SCOT G14 59 L5
Varnsdorf Wy AIRDRIE ML6 85 K3
Vassart Pl MRYH/FIRH G20 60 F6
Veir Ter DMBTN G82 20 E7
Veitches Ct CLYDBK G81 40 A3
Veitch Pl KKNTL G66 26 D2
Vennachar St SHOTTS ML7 104 E3
Vennacher Rd RNFRW PA4 58 A5
Vennard Gdns PLKSD/SHW G41 78 F8
Vermont Av RUTH G73 96 A3
Vermont St PLKSD/SHW G41 78 E5
Vernon Bank EKILN G74 2 F2
Vernon Dr PSLYN/LNWD PA3 74 A4
Verona Av SCOT G14 59 J5
Verona Gdns SCOT G14 59 J5
Verona La SCOT G14 59 J5
Vesalius St CAR/SHTL G32 81 G5
Viaduct Rd
CRMNK/CLK/EAG G76 114 F4
Vicarfield St GOV/IBX G51 78 B3
Vicarland Rd BLTYR/CAMB G72 97 G5
Vicars Wk BLTYR/CAMB G72 97 H5
Vickers St MTHW ML1 120 B1
Victoria Av BRHD/NEIL G78 92 B5
CARLUKE ML8 133 G8
Victoria Br GBLS G5 4 F9
Victoria Circ KVD/HLHD G12 60 C7
Victoria Ct LRKH ML9 130 C5
Victoria Crs AIRDRIE ML6 84 F3
BRHD/NEIL G78 92 B5
CRMNK/CLK/EAG G76 114 F3
KSYTH G65 29 H2
WISHAW ML2 121 K5
Victoria Crescent La
KVD/HLHD G12 60 C7
Victoria Crescent Pl
KVD/HLHD G12 60 C7
Victoria Crescent Rd
KVD/HLHD G12 60 C7
Victoria Dr BRHD/NEIL G78 92 B5
Victoria Dr East RNFRW PA4 58 C7
Victoria Dr West RNFRW PA4 58 B6
Victoria Gdns BRHD/NEIL G78 92 B5
KLMCLM PA13 53 J1
PSLYS PA2 8 C9
Victoria Gv BRHD/NEIL G78 92 B5
Victoria La NMRNS G77 113 K7
Victoria Pk KSYTH G65 29 H2
Victoria Park Cnr SCOT G14 59 K5
Victoria Park Dr North
SCOT G14 59 L6
Victoria Park Dr South
SCOT G14 59 L6
Victoria Park Gdns North
PTCK G11 59 M6
Victoria Park Gdns South
PTCK G11 59 M6
Victoria Park La South
SCOT G14 59 K6
Victoria Park St SCOT G14 59 K6
Victoria Pl AIRDRIE ML6 84 F3
BLSH ML4 99 M6
BRHD/NEIL G78 92 C5
KSYTH G65 29 J2
MLNGV G62 42 B1
Victoria Qd MTHW ML1 100 F4
Victoria Rd BALLOCH G68 30 D3
BRHD/NEIL G78 92 B5
GRK PA19 15 J2
GVH/MTFL G42 95 G1
HBR/GL G84 10 E5
JNSTN PA5 73 K5
KKNTL G66 45 J6
PSLYS PA2 75 J8
RUTH G73 96 B4
SHOTTS ML7 71 L7
STPS/GTHM/RID G33 63 K5
Victoria St ALEX/LLW G83 13 K6
BLTYR/CAMB G72 118 D4
DMBTN G82 21 G8
HMLTN ML3 119 H4
KKNTL G66 45 J2
LRKH ML9 130 C6
RUTH G73 96 A2
SHOTTS ML7 71 L7
WISHAW ML2 123 G5
Victor St AIRDRIE ML6 68 A7
Victory Dr KLBCH PA10 73 G6
Viewbank GIF/THBK G46 94 A7
Viewbank Av AIRDRIE ML6 85 H7
Viewbank St CTBR ML5 65 M5
Viewfield AIRDRIE ML6 84 E2
Viewfield Av
BAIL/MDB/MHD G69 81 M5
BLTYR/CAMB G72 118 E1
BSHPBGS G64 61 L2
KKNTL G66 27 H5
LOCHW PA12 109 H3
Viewfield Dr
BAIL/MDB/MHD G69 81 L5
Viewfield La KVD/HLHD G12 60 E8
Viewfield Rd BLSH ML4 99 M7
BSHPBGS G64 61 L2
CTBR ML5 83 J6
Viewfield St SHOTTS ML7 71 M6
Viewglen Ct CSMK G45 115 K1
Viewmount Dr MRYH/FIRH G20 60 D3
Viewpark Av DEN/PKHD G31 80 B2
Viewpark Dr RUTH G73 96 B4
Viewpark Gdns RNFRW PA4 58 B7
Viewpark Pl MTHW ML1 120 C3
Viewpark Rd MTHW ML1 120 C3
Viking Crs CRG/CRSL/HOU PA6 73 K2
Viking Rd AIRDRIE ML6 85 H4
Viking Ter EKILS G75 127 H4
Viking Wy GIF/THBK G46 93 M4
LARGS KA30 107 G5
Villafield Av BSHPBGS G64 44 A7
Villafield Dr BSHPBGS G64 44 A7
Village Gdns BLTYR/CAMB G72 118 E1
Village Rd BLTYR/CAMB G72 97 L5
Vine St PTCK G11 60 B8
Vinicombe La KVD/HLHD G12 60 D7
Vinicombe St KVD/HLHD G12 60 D7
Viola Pl BSHPBGS G64 44 C2
Violet Gdns CARLUKE ML8 134 E1
Violet Pl MTHW ML1 101 H3
Violet St PSLY PA1 9 L5
Virginia Ct CGLE G1 4 F7
Virginia Gdns MLNGV G62 42 C2
Virginia Gv HMLTN ML3 128 F2
Virginia Pl CGLE G1 5 G7
Virginia St CGLW G2 5 G7
GRNK PA15 6 F5
Virtue Well Vw AIRDRIE ML6 66 E6
Viscount Av RNFRW PA4 58 C8
Viscount Ga UD/BTH/TAN G71 98 E5
Vivian Av MLNGV G62 23 M8
Voil Dr LNPK/KPK G44 95 G6
Vorlich Ct BRHD/NEIL G78 92 C8
Vorlich Gdns BSDN G61 41 J2
Vryburg Crs EKILS G75 126 D6
Vulcan St MTHW ML1 120 E1
SPRGB/BLRNK G21 61 L6

W

Waddell Av AIRDRIE ML6 66 D5
Waddell St AIRDRIE ML6 67 G8
GBLS G5 79 K6
Waid Av NMRNS G77 113 J3
Waldemar Rd KNTSWD G13 59 J2
Waldo St KNTSWD G13 59 M2
Walkerburn Dr WISHAW ML2 122 D3
Walkerburn Rd
CARD/HILL/MSPK G52 77 H5
Walker Ct PTCK G11 78 B1
Walker Dr JNSTN PA5 74 B8
Walker Pth UD/BTH/TAN G71 99 G9
Walkerston Av LARGS KA30 106 F7
Walker St GRNKW/INVK PA16 16 C5
KBRN KA25 124 C4
PSLY PA1 8 E5
PTCK G11 78 B1
Walkinshaw Crs
PSLYN/LNWD PA3 8 A1
Walkinshaw Rd RNFRW PA4 57 H7
Walkinshaw St
DMNK/BRGTN G40 80 A6
JNSTN PA5 73 M7
Wallace Av BSHPTN PA7 38 B7
JNSTN PA5 74 C8
Wallace Ct LNK/LMHG ML11 137 G5
Wallace Dr BSHPBGS G64 62 D2
LRKH ML9 130 E7
Wallace Ga BSHPBGS G64 62 D2
Wallace Pl BLTYR/CAMB G72 118 E1
BSHPBGS G64 62 D2
GRNK PA15 6 D4
HMLTN ML3 120 A7
Wallace Rd MTHW ML1 101 H7
RNFRW PA4 58 A7
WMYSB PA18 50 B1
Wallace St AIRDRIE ML6 68 A7
CLYDBK G81 58 B1
CTBR ML5 84 A4
DMBTN G82 21 G8
GBLS G5 79 G5
GRNKW/INVK PA16 16 D5
MTHW ML1 120 D2
PGL PA14 34 E1
PSLYN/LNWD PA3 9 G2
RUTH G73 96 A3
Wallace Wy LNK/LMHG ML11 137 J5
Wallacewell Crs
SPRGB/BLRNK G21 62 B5
Wallacewell Pl
SPRGB/BLRNK G21 62 B5
Wallacewell Qd
SPRGB/BLRNK G21 62 C4
Wallacewell Rd
SPRGB/BLRNK G21 62 C4
Wallace Wynd
BLTYR/CAMB G72 97 G7
CARLUKE ML8 132 C3
Wallbrae Rd CUMB G67 48 F1
Wallneuk PSLY PA1 9 J3
Wallneuk Rd PSLYN/LNWD PA3 9 K3
Walls St CGLE G1 5 H7
Walmer Crs GOV/IBX G51 78 C5
Walnut Cl EKILS G75 126 F4
Walnut Crs JNSTN PA5 90 B2
PPK/MIL G22 61 K5
Walnut Dr KKNTL G66 45 H4
Walnut Ga BLTYR/CAMB G72 97 M6
Walnut Gv EKILS G75 126 F4
Walnut Pl UD/BTH/TAN G71 99 J2
Walnut Rd PPK/MIL G22 61 J5
Walpole Pl JNSTN PA5 89 J3
Walter St DEN/PKHD G31 80 B3
WISHAW ML2 122 D6
Walton Av NMRNS G77 113 J3
Walton St BRHD/NEIL G78 92 C6
PLKSD/SHW G41 94 E2
Wamba Av KNTSWD G13 59 L1
Wamphray Pl EKILS G75 126 A3
Wandilla Av CLYDBK G81 40 D7
Wanlock St GOV/IBX G51 78 A1
Wardend Rd BSHPBGS G64 44 B1
Warden Rd KNTSWD G13 59 K2
Wardhill Rd SPRGB/BLRNK G21 62 B5
Wardhouse Rd PSLYS PA2 91 J3
Wardie Pl STPS/GTHM/RID G33 81 M3
Wardie Rd ESTRH G34 82 A3
Wardlaw Av RUTH G73 96 B3
Wardlaw Crs EKILS G75 127 J4
Wardlaw Dr RUTH G73 96 B2
Wardlaw Rd BSDN G61 41 M8
Wardpark Ct CUMB G67 31 K3
Wardpark Pl CUMB G67 31 K3
Wardpark Rd CUMB G67 31 K3
Wardrop Pl EKILN G74 3 G2
Wardrop St BEITH KA15 125 L5
GOV/IBX G51 78 A2
PSLY PA1 9 G6
Wards Crs CTBR ML5 83 L5
Ware Rd ESTRH G34 81 M3
Warilda Av CLYDBK G81 40 C7
Warlock Dr BRWEIR PA11 72 D1
Warlock Rd BRWEIR PA11 54 C5
Warnock Crs BLSH ML4 100 B5
Warnock Rd NMRNS G77 113 J2
Warnock St DEN/PKHD G31 5 L5
Warren Park Ms LARGS KA30 106 F7
Warrenpark Rd LARGS KA30 106 F7
Warren Rd HMLTN ML3 129 K2
Warren St GVH/MTFL G42 95 J1
Warren Wk KKNTL G66 26 E3
Warriston Crs
STPS/GTHM/RID G33 80 E2
Warriston Pl CAR/SHTL G32 81 H3
Warriston St
STPS/GTHM/RID G33 80 D2
Warroch St KVGV G3 4 A7
Warwick EKILN G74 117 J6
Warwick Gv HMLTN ML3 118 E6
Warwick Rd GRNKW/INVK PA16 15 L5
Washington Rd KKNTL G66 45 H2
PSLYN/LNWD PA3 75 M2
Washington St KVGV G3 4 B8
Watchmeal Crs CLYDBK G81 40 C2
Waterbank Rd
CRMNK/CLK/EAG G76 115 K4
Waterfoot Av PLK/PH/NH G53 93 J1
Waterfoot Rd NMRNS G77 113 M6
Waterfoot Rw
CRMNK/CLK/EAG G76 114 E7
Waterfoot Ter PLK/PH/NH G53 93 J1
Waterford Rd GIF/THBK G46 94 B7
Waterhaughs Gdns
STPS/GTHM/RID G33 62 D3
Waterhaughs Gv
STPS/GTHM/RID G33 62 D3
Waterlands Gdns
CARLUKE ML8 133 J6
Waterlands Pl CARLUKE ML8 132 C5
Waterlands Rd CARLUKE ML8 132 D3
Waterloo Cl KKNTL G66 45 K1
Waterloo Dr LNK/LMHG ML11 137 G4
Waterloo La CGLW G2 4 D6
Waterloo Rd LNK/LMHG ML11 136 F3
Waterloo St CGLW G2 4 C6
Watermill Av KKNTL G66 45 L6
Water Rd BRHD/NEIL G78 92 C6
Water Rw GOV/IBX G51 78 B2
Watersaugh Dr MTHW ML1 102 B7
Waterside Av NMRNS G77 113 J5
Waterside Dr NMRNS G77 113 J5
Waterside Gdns
BLTYR/CAMB G72 97 L7
CRMNK/CLK/EAG G76 115 K3
HMLTN ML3 129 L1
Waterside Rd
CRMNK/CLK/EAG G76 115 K5
KKNTL G66 45 L3
Waterside St GBLS G5 79 K6
LARGS KA30 106 F5
Waterston Wy LOCHW PA12 109 J2
Water St PGL PA14 18 C8
Wateryetts Dr KLMCLM PA13 53 K1
Watling Pl EKILS G75 126 D1
Watling St MTHW ML1 100 C8
UD/BTH/TAN G71 98 E1
Watson Av PSLYN/LNWD PA3 74 B5
RUTH G73 95 M3
Watson Crs KSYTH G65 29 L2
Watson Pl BLTYR/CAMB G72 118 B3
Watson St BLTYR/CAMB G72 118 C3
CGLE G1 5 H8
LRKH ML9 130 B6
MTHW ML1 120 E4
UD/BTH/TAN G71 98 F5
Watsonville Pk MTHW ML1 120 E3
Watt Av STPS/GTHM/RID G33 63 M5
Watt Crs BLSH ML4 100 B2
Watt La BRWEIR PA11 72 E3
Watt Low Av RUTH G73 95 M4
Watt Pl GRNK PA15 6 E4
MLNGV G62 23 M6
Watt Rd BRWEIR PA11 72 E3
CARD/HILL/MSPK G52 76 F2
Watt St AIRDRIE ML6 67 J8
GBLS G5 78 F5
GRNKW/INVK PA16 6 B2
Waukglen Av PLK/PH/NH G53 93 H7
Waukglen Crs PLK/PH/NH G53 93 J6
Waukglen Dr PLK/PH/NH G53 93 H6
Waukglen Gdns
PLK/PH/NH G53 93 H7
Waukglen Pth PLK/PH/NH G53 93 H6
Waukglen Pl PLK/PH/NH G53 93 H6
Waukglen Rd PLK/PH/NH G53 93 H6
Waulking Mill Rd CLYDBK G81 40 C2
Waulkmill Av BRHD/NEIL G78 92 D5
Waulkmill La CLYDBK G81 40 B3
Waulkmill St GIF/THBK G46 93 L5
Waulkmill Wy BRHD/NEIL G78 92 D5
Waverley EKILN G74 117 K6
Waverley Av HBR/GL G84 11 G8
Waverley Ct UD/BTH/TAN G71 99 G8
Waverley Crs CUMB G67 48 D2
HMLTN ML3 118 F6
KKNTL G66 45 L2
LNK/LMHG ML11 137 J4
Waverley Dr AIRDRIE ML6 67 H8
RUTH G73 96 C3
WISHAW ML2 122 C5
Waverley Gdns JNSTN PA5 74 D8
PLKSD/SHW G41 94 E1
Waverley Pk KKNTL G66 45 L2
Waverley Rd PSLYS PA2 90 F2
Waverley St CTBR ML5 66 B8
GRNKW/INVK PA16 16 C6
HMLTN ML3 118 F6
PLKSD/SHW G41 94 E1
Waverley Ter
BLTYR/CAMB G72 118 C5
DMBTN G82 20 B6
Weardale La
STPS/GTHM/RID G33 81 J2
Weardale St
STPS/GTHM/RID G33 81 J2
Weaver Av NMRNS G77 113 K3
Weaver Crs AIRDRIE ML6 85 G4
Weaver Pl EKILS G75 126 B3
Weavers Av PSLYS PA2 8 B8
Weavers Ct KLBCH PA10 73 G7
Weavers Rd PSLYS PA2 8 B8
Weaver St COWCAD G4 5 J6
Weavers Wk LNK/LMHG ML11 137 G6
Weaver Ter PSLYS PA2 9 L8
Webster Groves WISHAW ML2 122 D4
Webster St CLYDBK G81 58 E1
DMNK/BRGTN G40 80 A7
Wedderlea Dr
CARD/HILL/MSPK G52 77 J4
Wee Cl BEITH KA15 125 K5
Weensmoor Rd
PLK/PH/NH G53 93 G5
Weeple Dr PSLYN/LNWD PA3 74 A4
Weighhouse Cl PSLY PA1 9 G5
Weighhouse Rd CARLUKE ML8 133 G6
Weir Av BRHD/NEIL G78 92 C7
Weir Pl CARLUKE ML8 132 B5
GRNK PA15 7 M9
KBRN KA25 124 D4
Weir St CTBR ML5 84 A2
GRNK PA15 7 M8
PSLYN/LNWD PA3 9 J4
Weirwood Av
BAIL/MDB/MHD G69 81 M6
Weirwood Gdns
BAIL/MDB/MHD G69 81 M5
Welbeck Rd PLK/PH/NH G53 93 H5
Welbeck St GRNKW/INVK PA16 16 C1
Weldon Pl KSYTH G65 29 M7
Welfare Av BLTYR/CAMB G72 97 K6
Welland Pl EKILS G75 126 B3
Wellbank Pl UD/BTH/TAN G71 98 F5
Wellbrae LRKH ML9 130 C7
Wellbrae Rd HMLTN ML3 129 H1
Wellbuttslea Dr
LNK/LMHG ML11 136 E6
Wellcroft Pl GBLS G5 79 H6
Wellcroft Rd HMLTN ML3 118 E7
Wellcroft Ter HMLTN ML3 118 E7
Welldale La LNK/LMHG ML11 136 B4
Wellesley Crs BALLOCH G68 47 K1
EKILS G75 126 D3
Wellesley Dr BALLOCH G68 47 K1
EKILS G75 126 C2
Wellfield Av GIF/THBK G46 94 B7
Wellfield St SPRGB/BLRNK G21 61 M6
Wellgate Ct LRKH ML9 130 C5
Wellgatehead
LNK/LMHG ML11 137 G6
Wellgate St LRKH ML9 130 C5
Well Gn PLKSW/MSWD G43 94 C2
Wellhall Ct HMLTN ML3 119 H6
Wellhall Rd HMLTN ML3 118 F8
Wellhead Ct LNK/LMHG ML11 137 H5
Wellhouse Crs
STPS/GTHM/RID G33 81 L3
Wellhouse Gdns
STPS/GTHM/RID G33 81 M3
Wellhouse Gv
STPS/GTHM/RID G33 81 M3
Wellhouse Rd
STPS/GTHM/RID G33 81 M2
Wellington EKILS G75 126 E3
Wellington La CGLW G2 4 C6
Wellington Pl CLYDBK G81 39 K7
CTBR ML5 83 J5
WISHAW ML2 131 M1
Wellington Rd BSHPBGS G64 44 C6
Wellington St AIRDRIE ML6 67 G8
CGLW G2 4 D6
GRNK PA15 6 A5
PSLYN/LNWD PA3 8 F3
WISHAW ML2 121 J4
Wellington Ter
LNK/LMHG ML11 136 F4
Wellknowe Av EKILN G74 115 J8
Wellknowe Pl EKILN G74 115 H7
Wellknowe Rd EKILN G74 115 J7
Well La KKNTL G66 26 D2
Wellmeadow Cl NMRNS G77 113 K4
Wellmeadow Gn NMRNS G77 113 K4
Wellmeadow Rd
PLKSW/MSWD G43 94 A4
Wellmeadows La HMLTN ML3 119 G8
Wellmeadow St PSLY PA1 8 E5
Wellmeadow Wy NMRNS G77 113 K4
Wellpark Rd MTHW ML1 120 C3
Wellpark St COWCAD G4 5 L7
Wellpark Ter BRHD/NEIL G78 111 K4
Well Rd KLBCH PA10 73 G7
LNK/LMHG ML11 137 H6
Wellshot Dr BLTYR/CAMB G72 96 F5
Wellshot Rd CAR/SHTL G32 80 F6
Wellside Av AIRDRIE ML6 67 G8
Wellside Dr BLTYR/CAMB G72 97 J6
Wellside La AIRDRIE ML6 67 G8
Wellside Qd AIRDRIE ML6 67 G7
Wellsquarry Rd EKILN G74 116 C6
Wells St CLYDBK G81 39 M7
Well St PSLY PA1 8 D4
Wellview Dr MTHW ML1 120 D2
Wellwood Av LNK/LMHG ML11 137 H4
Wellwynd AIRDRIE ML6 84 F1
Wellyard La GRNKW/INVK PA16 15 J7
Wellyard Wy GRNKW/INVK PA16 15 J7
Wellyard Wynd
GRNKW/INVK PA16 15 J7
Welsh Dr BLTYR/CAMB G72 118 D4
HMLTN ML3 129 J3
Welsh Rw AIRDRIE ML6 85 J6
Wemyss Av NMRNS G77 113 J2
Wemyss Bay Rd WMYSB PA18 50 B2
Wemyss Bay St GRNK PA15 6 A7
Wemyss Ct WMYSB PA18 32 A8
Wemyss Dr BALLOCH G68 47 L1
Wemyss Gdns
BAIL/MDB/MHD G69 82 A7
Wenlock Rd PSLYS PA2 9 K9
Wensleydale EKILN G74 2 B1
Wentworth Dr SMSTN G23 60 E1
Wesley St AIRDRIE ML6 84 F2
West Abercromby St
HBR/GL G84 10 D4
West Academy St
WISHAW ML2 121 L6
Westacres Rd NMRNS G77 113 H5
West Av AIRDRIE ML6 68 A6
BLTYR/CAMB G72 118 E5
CARLUKE ML8 132 F8
PSLYN/LNWD PA3 74 D6
RNFRW PA4 58 C6
STPS/GTHM/RID G33 63 K5
UD/BTH/TAN G71 99 H4
West Balgrochan Rd
BSHPBGS G64 44 B1
Westbank La KVD/HLHD G12 60 E8
Westbank Qd KVD/HLHD G12 60 E8
West Barmoss Av PGL PA14 34 F3
West Blackhall St GRNK PA15 6 C3
Westbourne Crs BSDN G61 41 J4
Westbourne Dr BSDN G61 41 J4
Westbourne Gardens La
KVD/HLHD G12 60 B6
Westbourne Gdns South
KVD/HLHD G12 60 C6
Westbourne Gdns West
KVD/HLHD G12 60 C6
Westbourne Rd KVD/HLHD G12 60 B6
Westbourne Terrace La North
KVD/HLHD G12 60 C6
Westbourne Terrace La South
KVD/HLHD G12 60 B6
West Brae PSLY PA1 8 E5
Westbrae Dr KNTSWD G13 59 L5
Westbrae Rd NMRNS G77 113 M3
West Bridgend DMBTN G82 20 E6
Westburn Av BLTYR/CAMB G72 97 K4
PSLYN/LNWD PA3 75 G5
Westburn Crs CLYDBK G81 40 B2
RUTH G73 95 M3
Westburn Farm Rd
BLTYR/CAMB G72 97 H4
Westburn Rd BLTYR/CAMB G72 97 J4
West Burnside St KSYTH G65 29 K2
West Burn St GRNK PA15 6 C3
West Campbell St CGLW G2 4 C7
PSLY PA1 8 B6
West Canal St CTBR ML5 83 M4
Westcastle Ct CSMK G45 95 K7
Westcastle Crs CSMK G45 95 K7
Westcastle Gdns CSMK G45 95 K7
Westcastle Gv CSMK G45 95 K7
West Chapelton Av BSDN G61 41 M5
West Chapelton Crs BSDN G61 41 M5
West Chapelton Dr BSDN G61 41 M5
West Chapelton La BSDN G61 41 M5
Westcliff DMBTN G82 20 B6
West Clyde St HBR/GL G84 10 B6
LRKH ML9 130 D7
Westclyffe St PLKSD/SHW G41 94 E1
West Coats Rd
BLTYR/CAMB G72 96 F6
Westcott Pl LNK/LMHG ML11 137 J4
Westcraigs Pk BTHG/ARM EH48 71 J1
Westcraigs Rd BTHG/ARM EH48 71 K1
Westdale Dr
BAIL/MDB/MHD G69 47 H7
West Dhuhill Dr HBR/GL G84 10 D3
West Dr AIRDRIE ML6 85 L3
Westend Ct CARLUKE ML8 132 B4
West End Dr BLSH ML4 99 M6
Westend Park St KVGV G3 4 A2
West End Pl BLSH ML4 99 M6
Westerburn St CAR/SHTL G32 80 F4
Wester Carriagehill PSLYS PA2 8 F9
Wester Cleddens Rd
BSHPBGS G64 44 A8
Wester Common Dr
PPK/MIL G22 61 G6
Wester Common Rd
PPK/MIL G22 61 H6
Westercraigs DEN/PKHD G31 79 M3
Westercraigs Ct
DEN/PKHD G31 79 M3
Westerdale EKILN G74 2 A2
Westerfield Rd EKILN G74 115 K6
Westergill Av AIRDRIE ML6 85 L3
Westergreens Av KKNTL G66 45 J4
Westerhill Rd BSHPBGS G64 44 C7
Westerhouse Ct CARLUKE ML8 132 F7
Westerhouse Rd ESTRH G34 82 B2
Westerkirk Dr SMSTN G23 60 F1
Westerlands KVD/HLHD G12 59 M3
Westerlands Dr NMRNS G77 113 H5
Westerlands Gv NMRNS G77 113 H5
Westerlands Pl NMRNS G77 113 H4
Westermains Av KKNTL G66 45 H3
Wester Mavisbank Av
AIRDRIE ML6 84 F1
Wester Moffat Av AIRDRIE ML6 85 L1
Wester Moffat Crs AIRDRIE ML6 85 L2
Wester Myvot Rd CUMB G67 48 B5
Western Av RUTH G73 95 M2
Western Crs KBRN KA25 124 C6
Western Isles Rd OLDK G60 39 J5
Western Rd BLTYR/CAMB G72 96 F7
Westerpark Av
BLTYR/CAMB G72 118 C7
Wester Rd CAR/SHTL G32 81 K7
Westerton KKNTL G66 26 E2
Westerton Av BSDN G61 59 M1
CRMNK/CLK/EAG G76 115 G5
LRKH ML9 130 C8
Westerton La
CRMNK/CLK/EAG G76 115 G5
Westerton Rd BALLOCH G68 30 D3
West Fairholm St LRKH ML9 130 B4
Westfarm Crs BLTYR/CAMB G72 97 K4
Westfarm Gv BLTYR/CAMB G72 97 K4

Westfarm Wynd
BLTYR/CAMB G72 97 K3
West Faulds Rd
LNK/LMHG ML11 137 L4
Westfield DMBTN G82 20 C6
KBRN KA25 124 D5
Westfield Av RUTH G73 95 M3
Westfield Crs BSDN G61 41 L7
Westfield Dr BALLOCH G68 47 M3
BSDN G61 41 L7
CARD/HILL/MSPK G52 77 G4
GRNKW/INVK PA16 16 C1
KLMCLM PA13 53 H2
Westfield Pl BALLOCH G68 47 K4
Westfield Rd BALLOCH G68 30 A8
GIF/THBK G46 94 A8
KSYTH G65 29 H1
MTHW ML1 101 J2
PGL PA14 34 F2
Westfields BSHPBGS G64 43 L7
Westgarth Pl EKILN G74 116 A7
West Ga WISHAW ML2 122 D6
West George La CGLW G2 4 C5
West George St CGLW G2 4 B5
CTBR ML5 84 A1
West Glebe Ter HMLTN ML3 119 J8
West Glen Rd KLMCLM PA13 53 L1
PGL PA14 54 B1
West Graham St COWCAD G4 4 C3
West Greenhill Pl KVGV G3 78 E2
West Highland Wy MLNGV G62 23 K3
West High St KKNTL G66 45 J1
Westhorn Dr CAR/SHTL G32 97 G1
Westhouse Av RUTH G73 95 L3
Westhouse Gdns RUTH G73 95 L3
West King St HBR/GL G84 10 B5
West Kirk St AIRDRIE ML6 84 F2
Westland Dr SCOT G14 59 K6
Westlands Gdns PSLYS PA2 8 F9
West La PSLY PA1 8 A7
Westlea Pl AIRDRIE ML6 85 G3
West Lennox Dr HBR/GL G84 10 D4
West Lodge Rd RNFRW PA4 58 B5
West Mains Rd EKILN G74 2 C3
West Main St SHOTTS ML7 71 K7
West Montrose St HBR/GL G84 10 C5
Westmoreland St
GVH/MTFL G42 79 G8
Westmorland Rd
GRNKW/INVK PA16 15 L5
Westmuir Pl RUTH G73 95 L2
Westmuir St DEN/PKHD G31 80 D5
West Nemphlar Rd
LNK/LMHG ML11 136 C3
West Nile St CGLE G1 4 E6
Westpark Dr PSLYN/LNWD PA3 8 A3
West Pl WISHAW ML2 123 G4
Westport EKILS G75 126 C1
West Port LNK/LMHG ML11 136 F5
Westport St KSYTH G65 29 K2
West Princes St HBR/GL G84 10 B5
COWCAD G4 60 F8
KVGV G3 4 A1
West Quay PGL PA14 18 C8
Westray Av NMRNS G77 113 J2
PGL PA14 35 H4
Westray Circ PPK/MIL G22 61 J4
Westray Ct CUMB G67 48 D1
Westray Pl PPK/MIL G22 61 K3
Westray Rd CUMB G67 48 E1
Westray Sq PPK/MIL G22 61 K3
Westray St PPK/MIL G22 61 J3
West Regent St CGLW G2 4 D5
West Rd BSHPBGS G64 44 B1
KLBCH PA10 73 G6
PGL PA14 34 E2
West Rossdhu Dr HBR/GL G84 10 D4
West Scott Ter HMLTN ML3 129 K1
West Shaw St GRNK PA15 6 B3
West Stewart St GRNK PA15 6 C2
HMLTN ML3 119 J6
West St CLYDBK G81 58 E1
GBLS G5 79 G6
PSLY PA1 8 C6
West Thomson St CLYDBK G81 40 A6
West Thornlie St WISHAW ML2 122 A7
West Wellbrae Crs
HMLTN ML3 129 J2
West Whitby St
DEN/PKHD G31 80 C6
Westwood Av GIF/THBK G46 94 C7
Westwood Crs HMLTN ML3 119 J8
Westwood Dr MTHW ML1 102 E8
Westwood Gdns
PSLYN/LNWD PA3 8 A3
Westwood Hl EKILS G75 2 B9
Westwood Qd CLYDBK G81 40 D8
Westwood Rd EKILS G75 2 A7
PLKSW/MSWD G43 94 B4
WISHAW ML2 122 F2
West Woodside Av PGL PA14 34 F3
Weymouth Crs GRK PA19 15 L4
Weymouth Dr KVD/HLHD G12 60 A4
Weymouth La KVD/HLHD G12 60 B5
Whamflet Av
BAIL/MDB/MHD G69 82 C3
Wheatfield Rd BSDN G61 41 K7
Wheatholm St AIRDRIE ML6 67 H8
Wheatland Av
BLTYR/CAMB G72 118 C2
Wheatland Dr
LNK/LMHG ML11 136 F5
Wheatlandhead Ct
BLTYR/CAMB G72 118 C2
Wheatlands Dr KLBCH PA10 73 G6
Wheatlands Farm Rd
KLBCH PA10 73 G6
Wheatlandside
LNK/LMHG ML11 136 F4
Wheatley Ct CAR/SHTL G32 81 G5
Wheatley Crs KSYTH G65 29 K3
Wheatley Dr CAR/SHTL G32 81 G5
Wheatley Loan BSHPBGS G64 62 C2
Wheatley Pl CAR/SHTL G32 81 G5
Wheatpark Rd
LNK/LMHG ML11 136 F5
Whifflet St CTBR ML5 84 A6
Whimbrel Wy RNFRW PA4 58 E5
Whin Av BRHD/NEIL G78 92 A5
Whinfell Dr EKILS G75 126 D4
Whinfell Gdns EKILS G75 126 D4
Whinfield Rd PLK/PH/NH G53 93 G5
Whinhall Av AIRDRIE ML6 66 E8
Whinhall Rd AIRDRIE ML6 66 E8
Whin Hl EKILN G74 117 H6
Whinhill Av LARGS KA30 106 F5
Whinhill Crs GRNK PA15 6 F9
Whinhill Rd GRNK PA15 6 F8
PLK/PH/NH G53 77 G6
PSLYS PA2 76 B7
Whin Loan KSYTH G65 28 D2
Whinney Gv WISHAW ML2 122 E5
Whinnie Knowe LRKH ML9 130 B8
Whinny Burn Ct MTHW ML1 121 H6
Whinpark Av BLSH ML4 99 M7
Whin Pl EKILN G74 117 H5
Whins Rd PLKSD/SHW G41 94 C1
Whin St CLYDBK G81 40 A5
Whirlie Dr CRG/CRSL/HOU PA6 73 H2
Whirlie Rd CRG/CRSL/HOU PA6 73 J2
Whirlow Gdns
BAIL/MDB/MHD G69 82 A5
Whirlow Rd
BAIL/MDB/MHD G69 82 A5
Whistleberry Crs HMLTN ML3 119 G3
Whistleberry Dr HMLTN ML3 119 H4
Whistleberry La HMLTN ML3 119 H4
Whistleberry Pk HMLTN ML3 119 G3
Whistleberry Rd HMLTN ML3 119 G3
Whistlefield Ct BSDN G61 41 L6
Whitacres Rd PLK/PH/NH G53 92 F5
Whitburn St CAR/SHTL G32 80 F3
Whiteadder Pl EKILS G75 126 A3
White Av DMBTN G82 21 H7
White Cart Ct
PLKSW/MSWD G43 94 D3
White Cart Rd
PSLYN/LNWD PA3 75 L2
Whitecraigs Ct GIF/THBK G46 114 A2
Whitecraigs Pl SMSTN G23 60 E2
Whitecrook St CLYDBK G81 58 C1
Whitefield Av
BLTYR/CAMB G72 97 G6
Whitefield Rd GOV/IBX G51 78 C4
Whitefield Ter KKNTL G66 26 C1
Whiteford Av DMBTN G82 21 H4
Whiteford Ct HMLTN ML3 129 J4
Whiteford Crs DMBTN G82 21 J5
Whiteford Pl DMBTN G82 21 J5
Whiteford Rd PSLYS PA2 9 M9
STPS/GTHM/RID G33 63 M5
Whitehall St KVGV G3 4 A7
Whitehaugh Av PSLY PA1 76 B4
Whitehaugh Crs
PLK/PH/NH G53 93 G5
Whitehaugh Dr PSLY PA1 76 B4
Whitehaugh Rd
PLK/PH/NH G53 93 G5
Whitehill Av AIRDRIE ML6 67 G7
BALLOCH G68 30 D7
KKNTL G66 45 L1
STPS/GTHM/RID G33 63 K4
Whitehill Ct DEN/PKHD G31 80 A3
Whitehill Crs CARLUKE ML8 133 H6
CLYDBK G81 40 E2
KKNTL G66 45 M1
LNK/LMHG ML11 136 F5
Whitehill Farm Rd
STPS/GTHM/RID G33 63 K4
Whitehill Gdns DEN/PKHD G31 80 A3
Whitehill Gv NMRNS G77 113 M7
Whitehill La BSDN G61 41 K5
Whitehill Pl DEN/PKHD G31 80 A3
Whitehill Rd BSDN G61 41 K5
HMLTN ML3 119 H5
Whitehills Dr EKILS G75 127 H3
Whitehills Pl EKILS G75 127 H3
Whitehills Ter EKILS G75 127 H4
Whitehill St DEN/PKHD G31 80 A3
Whitehill Street La
DEN/PKHD G31 80 A3
Whitehill Ter LNK/LMHG ML11 136 F5
Whitehurst BSDN G61 41 J3
Whitehurst Pk BSDN G61 41 J3
Whitekirk Pl DRUM G15 41 G7
Whitelaw Av CTBR ML5 65 M5
Whitelaw Crs BLSH ML4 100 D5
Whitelaw Gdns BSHPBGS G64 44 A7
Whitelaw St BTHG/ARM EH48 71 K3
MRYH/FIRH G20 60 C3
Whitelaw Ter KSYTH G65 28 F6
Whitelea Av KLMCLM PA13 53 J2
Whitelea Crs KLMCLM PA13 53 K2
Whitelea Rd KLMCLM PA13 53 J2
Whitelee EKILS G75 127 G5
Whitelee Crs NMRNS G77 113 H3
Whitelee Ga NMRNS G77 113 H3
Whitelees Rd CUMB G67 31 M3
GRNK PA15 17 M7
LNK/LMHG ML11 137 H5
Whiteloans UD/BTH/TAN G71 99 H7
Whitemoss Av EKILN G74 3 H5
LNPK/KPK G44 94 F6
Whitemoss Gv EKILN G74 3 J4
Whitemoss Rd EKILN G74 3 H5
Whitepond Av BLSH ML4 99 M7
Whites Bridge Av
PSLYN/LNWD PA3 74 F6
Whites Bridge Cl
PSLYN/LNWD PA3 74 F5
Whiteshaw Av CARLUKE ML8 132 F8
Whiteshaw Dr CARLUKE ML8 132 F7
Whiteshaw Rd CARLUKE ML8 132 D6
White St CLYDBK G81 58 D2
PTCK G11 60 B8
Whitevale St DEN/PKHD G31 80 A3
Whithope Rd PLK/PH/NH G53 92 F4
Whithorn Crs
BAIL/MDB/MHD G69 46 F7
Whiting Rd WMYSB PA18 32 B8
Whitlawburn Av
BLTYR/CAMB G72 96 E6
Whitlawburn Rd
BLTYR/CAMB G72 96 E6
Whitlawburn Ter
BLTYR/CAMB G72 96 E6
Whitriggs Rd PLK/PH/NH G53 92 F5
Whitslade Pl ESTRH G34 82 A1
Whitslade St ESTRH G34 82 A1
Whitsun Dl EKILN G74 2 B2
Whittagreen Av MTHW ML1 101 K6
Whittagreen Crs MTHW ML1 101 K7
Whittingehame Dr
KVD/HLHD G12 59 M4
Whittingehame La
KNTSWD G13 59 M4
Whittingehame Pk
KVD/HLHD G12 59 M4
Whittington St CTBR ML5 84 A4
Whittlemuir Av LNPK/KPK G44 94 F6
Whitton Dr GIF/THBK G46 94 D6
Whitton St MRYH/FIRH G20 60 C2
Whitworth Dr CLYDBK G81 40 A7
MRYH/FIRH G20 61 G4
Whitworth Gdns
MRYH/FIRH G20 60 F4
Whitworth Ga MRYH/FIRH G20 60 F5
Whyte Av BLTYR/CAMB G72 96 E4
Whyte Cnr DMBTN G82 37 M1
Whyte St SHOTTS ML7 71 M6
Wick Av AIRDRIE ML6 84 E5
The Wickets PSLY PA1 9 M7
Wickham Av NMRNS G77 113 K3
Wide Cl LNK/LMHG ML11 137 G5
Wigton Av NMRNS G77 113 J2
Wigtoun Pl CUMB G67 31 H5
Wildman Rd CARLUKE ML8 132 D2
Wilfred Av KNTSWD G13 59 K2
Wilkie Crs LRKH ML9 130 D7
Wilkie Rd UD/BTH/TAN G71 99 G5
William Dr HMLTN ML3 129 K3
William Mann Dr NMRNS G77 113 J5
Williamsburgh Ter PSLY PA1 9 M4
Williamson Av DMBTN G82 21 G6
Williamson Dr HBR/GL G84 10 F6
Williamson Pl JNSTN PA5 74 B8
Williamson St CLYDBK G81 40 B5
DMNK/BRGTN G40 80 C6
William Spiers Pl LRKH ML9 130 D8
William St CLYDBK G81 40 A3
CTBR ML5 84 B5
GRNK PA15 6 E4
HBR/GL G84 10 C6
HMLTN ML3 119 H5
JNSTN PA5 73 M8
KSYTH G65 29 K2
KVGV G3 4 A5
PGL PA14 18 B8
PSLY PA1 8 C5
William Ure Pl BSHPBGS G64 44 B5
William Wilson Ct KSYTH G65 29 K1
Williamwood Dr LNPK/KPK G44 94 E8
Williamwood Pk LNPK/KPK G44 94 F8
Williamwood Pk West
LNPK/KPK G44 94 F8
Willie Ross La RUTH G73 96 B1
Willison's La PGL PA14 34 C1
Willock Pl MRYH/FIRH G20 60 E3
Willoughby Dr KNTSWD G13 59 M3
Willoughby La KNTSWD G13 59 M3
Willow Av BSHPBGS G64 62 A2
JNSTN PA5 74 C8
KKNTL G66 45 J5
MTHW ML1 101 G7
Willowbank Crs KVGV G3 60 F8
Willowbank Gdns KKNTL G66 45 K2
Willowbank St KVGV G3 78 F1
Willowburn Rd BEITH KA15 125 H6
Willow Ct EKILS G75 126 E4
Willow Crs CTBR ML5 83 M6
Willowdale Crs
BAIL/MDB/MHD G69 82 A6
Willowdale Gdns
BAIL/MDB/MHD G69 82 A6
Willow Dr AIRDRIE ML6 85 K2
BLTYR/CAMB G72 118 C2
JNSTN PA5 89 M1
KKNTL G66 27 J5
Willowford Rd PLK/PH/NH G53 92 F5
Willow Gv MTHW ML1 101 H4
Willow La CAR/SHTL G32 81 H8
Willow Pl GRNKW/INVK PA16 32 E5
JNSTN PA5 74 A8
UD/BTH/TAN G71 99 K2
The Willows
CRMNK/CLK/EAG G76 115 L2
Willow St KNTSWD G13 59 M2
Willow Wy HMLTN ML3 129 L1
Willowyard Rd BEITH KA15 125 H5
Willwood Dr WISHAW ML2 122 C2
Wilmot Rd KNTSWD G13 59 K3
Wilsgait St MTHW ML1 102 C7
Wilson Av PSLYN/LNWD PA3 74 A4
Wilson Ct BLSH ML4 99 M5
Wilson Pl EKILN G74 117 G6
NMRNS G77 113 J5
Wilson Rd SHOTTS ML7 123 M1
Wilsons Rd MTHW ML1 102 E2
Wilson St ALEX/LLW G83 13 J5
BEITH KA15 125 L4
CGLE G1 5 G7
CTBR ML5 84 C2
HMLTN ML3 119 G5
LARGS KA30 106 F5
LRKH ML9 130 D8
MTHW ML1 120 F2
PGL PA14 34 D1
RNFRW PA4 58 D5
Wiltonburn Rd PLK/PH/NH G53 93 G5
Wilton Crescent La
MRYH/FIRH G20 60 F7
Wilton Dr MRYH/FIRH G20 60 F7
Wilton Rd CARLUKE ML8 135 G1
Wilton St CTBR ML5 65 K8
MRYH/FIRH G20 60 E7
Wilverton Rd KNTSWD G13 59 L1
Winburne Crs HMLTN ML3 119 H6
Winchester Dr KVD/HLHD G12 60 B4
Windemere Gdns HMLTN ML3 129 J5
Winderemere St BLSH ML4 99 M6
Windermere EKILS G75 126 C5
Windhill Crs PLKSW/MSWD G43 94 B5
Windhill Rd PLKSW/MSWD G43 94 B5
Windlaw Gdns LNPK/KPK G44 94 F7
Windlaw Park Gdns
LNPK/KPK G44 94 F6
Windlaw Rd CSMK G45 115 K1
Windmill Ct HMLTN ML3 119 K6
MTHW ML1 120 F4
Windmillhill St MTHW ML1 120 F4
Windmill Rd HMLTN ML3 119 K6
Windrow Ter WISHAW ML2 122 C2
Windsor Av NMRNS G77 113 M4
Windsor Ct CARLUKE ML8 133 H7
Windsor Crs CLYDBK G81 40 A6
JNSTN PA5 90 B1
PSLY PA1 9 M2
Windsor Crescent La
CLYDBK G81 40 A6
Windsor Dr AIRDRIE ML6 66 F5
Windsor Gdns HMLTN ML3 119 G5
LARGS KA30 106 F2
Windsor Qd CARLUKE ML8 * 133 H7
Windsor Rd MTHW ML1 101 G4
RNFRW PA4 58 C7
Windsor St CTBR ML5 83 L7
MRYH/FIRH G20 61 G8
SHOTTS ML7 104 E4
Windsor Ter MRYH/FIRH G20 61 G8
Windward Rd EKILS G75 126 D1
Windyedge Crs KNTSWD G13 59 J4
Windyedge Pl KNTSWD G13 59 J4
Windyedge Rd MTHW ML1 102 C6
Windyridge Pl
BLTYR/CAMB G72 118 C3
Windy Yetts KSYTH G65 28 F7
Winfield Av BLTYR/CAMB G72 96 E3
Wingate Crs EKILN G74 117 J6
Wingate Dr EKILN G74 117 J6
Wingate Pk EKILN G74 117 J6
Wingate St WISHAW ML2 121 K5
Wingfield Gdns
UD/BTH/TAN G71 119 H1
Winifred St
STPS/GTHM/RID G33 62 D6
Winning Ct BLTYR/CAMB G72 118 E1
Winning Rw DEN/PKHD G31 80 D5
Winnipeg Dr EKILS G75 126 E2
Winston Crs KKNTL G66 26 C1
Winston Rd HBR/GL G84 11 G5
Wintergreen Ct EKILN G74 116 D6
Wintergreen Dr EKILN G74 116 D6
Winter St COWCAD G4 61 J8
Winton Av GIF/THBK G46 94 C8
Winton Crs BLTYR/CAMB G72 118 D3
Winton Dr KVD/HLHD G12 60 C5
SKLM PA17 50 C4
Winton Gdns UD/BTH/TAN G71 98 F3
Winton La KVD/HLHD G12 60 C5
Winton Pk EKILS G75 126 C1
Wirran Pl KNTSWD G13 58 E1
Wishart Av CLYDBK G81 40 C2
Wishart La CARLUKE ML8 132 C4
Wishart St COWCAD G4 5 L5
Wishaw High Rd MTHW ML1 122 C1
Wishawhill St WISHAW ML2 121 M6
Wishaw Low Rd MTHW ML1 122 B2
Wishaw Rd WISHAW ML2 132 B1
Wisner Ct GIF/THBK G46 93 M6
Wisteria La CARLUKE ML8 134 F1
Wiston St BLTYR/CAMB G72 97 K5
Witcutt Wy WISHAW ML2 121 L8
Woddrop St
DMNK/BRGTN G40 80 B8
Wolcott Dr BLTYR/CAMB G72 118 D2
Wolfe Av NMRNS G77 113 J2
Wolseley St GBLS G5 79 K7
Wood Aven Dr EKILN G74 116 D6
Woodbank Crs
CRMNK/CLK/EAG G76 114 E4
JNSTN PA5 73 M8
Woodbank Gdns
ALEX/LLW G83 13 H3
LARGS KA30 106 D2
Woodburn Av AIRDRIE ML6 84 F3
ALEX/LLW G83 13 L3
BLTYR/CAMB G72 118 E2
CRMNK/CLK/EAG G76 114 E4
Woodburn Ct
LNK/LMHG ML11 137 J7
RUTH G73 96 B4
Woodburn Gv HMLTN ML3 119 K7
Woodburn Pl
CRG/CRSL/HOU PA6 73 L3
Woodburn Rd BEITH KA15 125 L5
MTHW ML1 101 K2
PLKSW/MSWD G43 94 D5
Woodburn St MTHW ML1 120 E1
Woodburn Ter LRKH ML9 130 E7
Woodburn Wy BALLOCH G68 30 C7
MLNGV G62 42 A1
Wood Crs MTHW ML1 120 E1
Woodcroft Av LARGS KA30 107 G5
PTCK G11 59 M5
Wooddale MTHW ML1 120 D5
Woodend Ct CAR/SHTL G32 81 L8
Woodend Dr AIRDRIE ML6 67 J8
KNTSWD G13 59 L4
PSLY PA1 76 D5
Woodend Gdns CAR/SHTL G32 81 K8
Woodend La KNTSWD G13 59 L4
Woodend Pl JNSTN PA5 74 B8
Woodend Rd CAR/SHTL G32 81 K8
CARLUKE ML8 133 J7
RUTH G73 96 B6
Woodend St HBR/GL G84 10 B4
Wood Farm Rd GIF/THBK G46 114 A1
Woodfield UD/BTH/TAN G71 99 J4
Woodfield Av BSHPBGS G64 62 B2
Woodfoot Rd HMLTN ML3 119 H8
Woodford Pl PSLYN/LNWD PA3 74 A4
Woodford St
PLKSW/MSWD G43 94 D3
Woodgreen Av LNPK/KPK G44 95 H4
Woodhall MTHW ML1 101 H1
Woodhall Av AIRDRIE ML6 85 H7
CTBR ML5 83 M7
HMLTN ML3 119 H6
MTHW ML1 100 F4
Woodhall Cottage Rd
AIRDRIE ML6 85 J8
Woodhall Mill Rd AIRDRIE ML6 101 J1
Woodhall Pl CTBR ML5 83 M7
Woodhall Rd AIRDRIE ML6 85 H8
CARLUKE ML8 134 E5
WISHAW ML2 122 F6
Woodhall St AIRDRIE ML6 85 K8
DMNK/BRGTN G40 80 A8
Woodhall Ter PGL PA14 35 H2
Woodhead Av BALLOCH G68 47 M3
KKNTL G66 45 K3
UD/BTH/TAN G71 119 H2
Woodhead Ct BALLOCH G68 47 M3
Woodhead Crs AIRDRIE ML6 66 E6
HMLTN ML3 129 G2
UD/BTH/TAN G71 98 F2
Woodhead Gdns
UD/BTH/TAN G71 119 H2
Woodhead Gv BALLOCH G68 47 M3
Woodhead Pl BALLOCH G68 47 M3
Woodhead Rd
BAIL/MDB/MHD G69 64 B4
BALLOCH G68 47 M3
PLK/PH/NH G53 92 F4
Woodhead Ter
BAIL/MDB/MHD G69 64 B3
Woodhead Vw BALLOCH G68 47 M3
Woodhill Rd BTHG/ARM EH48 71 H1
SPRGB/BLRNK G21 62 B4
Woodholm Av LNPK/KPK G44 95 J4
Woodhouse St KNTSWD G13 59 L2
Woodilee Rd KKNTL G66 45 L4
MTHW ML1 101 L5
Woodland Av AIRDRIE ML6 85 J5
KKNTL G66 45 H2
PSLYS PA2 91 L2
Woodland Crs
BLTYR/CAMB G72 97 H6
Woodland Gdns
CRMNK/CLK/EAG G76 115 K3
HMLTN ML3 119 L8
Woodlands Av
BAIL/MDB/MHD G69 64 E3
CARLUKE ML8 132 B3
LNK/LMHG ML11 137 J6
UD/BTH/TAN G71 99 G7
Woodlands Ct ALEX/LLW G83 13 H3
GIF/THBK G46 93 M7
Woodlands Crs GIF/THBK G46 93 M6
JNSTN PA5 89 K1
UD/BTH/TAN G71 99 G7
Woodlands Dr COWCAD G4 60 F8
CTBR ML5 83 K3
MTHW ML1 100 F4
Woodlands Gdns
UD/BTH/TAN G71 98 F7
Woodlands Ga GIF/THBK G46 93 M6
KVGV G3 78 F1
Woodlands Gv MLNGV G62 24 A7
Woodlands Pk GIF/THBK G46 93 M7
Woodlands Pl CTBR ML5 83 K3
Woodlands Rd GIF/THBK G46 93 M7
KVGV G3 60 F8
MTHW ML1 120 F6
Woodlands St MLNGV G62 24 A8
MTHW ML1 120 F5
Woodlands Ter KVGV G3 78 E1
The Woodlands BLSH ML4 100 D6
Woodland Ter LRKH ML9 130 E8
Woodland Wy CUMB G67 31 H6
Woodlark Gv
GRNKW/INVK PA16 33 G4
Woodlea Av AIRDRIE ML6 85 J5
Woodlea Dr GIF/THBK G46 94 D6
HMLTN ML3 129 K2
Woodlea La GRK PA19 16 A2
Woodlea Pl AIRDRIE ML6 67 J8
Woodlinn Av LNPK/KPK G44 95 H5
Woodmill Dr BSHPBGS G64 44 C1
Woodmill Gdns CUMB G67 47 M4
Woodneuk Rd
BAIL/MDB/MHD G69 64 F5
PLK/PH/NH G53 93 H4
Woodneuk St AIRDRIE ML6 85 K8
Woodneuk Ter
BAIL/MDB/MHD G69 64 F5
Wood Qd CLYDBK G81 58 E1
Woodrow MTHW ML1 101 H1
Woodrow Av KLMCLM PA13 53 K1
MTHW ML1 101 H7
Woodrow Circ PLKSD/SHW G41 78 D6
Woodrow Pl PLKSD/SHW G41 78 C6
Woodrow Rd PLKSD/SHW G41 78 D6
Woodside CRG/CRSL/HOU PA6 73 K1
MTHW ML1 100 E1
Woodside Av BRWEIR PA11 72 D2
GIF/THBK G46 94 A7
HMLTN ML3 119 L8
KKNTL G66 45 K5
KSYTH G65 29 M2
RUTH G73 96 C3
Woodside Crs ALEX/LLW G83 13 L4
BRHD/NEIL G78 92 D7
KVGV G3 4 A3
PSLY PA1 8 C5
WISHAW ML2 123 H3
Woodside Dr AIRDRIE ML6 85 G7
CRMNK/CLK/EAG G76 114 D8
Woodside Gdns
CRMNK/CLK/EAG G76 114 D3
CRMNK/CLK/EAG G76 115 K3
CTBR ML5 83 K6
Woodside La JNSTN PA5 73 J4
LNK/LMHG ML11 137 J7
Woodside Pl KVGV G3 78 F1
UD/BTH/TAN G71 99 J2
Woodside Place La KVGV G3 78 F1
Woodside Rd AIRDRIE ML6 70 A1
BEITH KA15 125 K4
CRMNK/CLK/EAG G76 115 K3
JNSTN PA5 73 K4
Woodside St AIRDRIE ML6 85 K7
CTBR ML5 83 K7
MTHW ML1 121 H5
Woodside Ter KVGV G3 78 F1
Woodside Terrace La KVGV G3 78 F1
Woodside Wk HMLTN ML3 119 L8
Woodside Gv RUTH G73 96 C3
Woodstock Av KKNTL G66 45 M2
LNK/LMHG ML11 137 H5
PLKSD/SHW G41 94 D2
PSLYS PA2 90 E2
Woodstock Dr WISHAW ML2 122 C5
Woodstock Rd
GRNKW/INVK PA16 16 C6
LNK/LMHG ML11 137 H5
Wood St AIRDRIE ML6 67 J8
CTBR ML5 83 L3
DEN/PKHD G31 80 B2
GRNKW/INVK PA16 16 B1
MTHW ML1 120 F1
PSLYS PA2 76 B6
Woodvale Av AIRDRIE ML6 85 K5
BSDN G61 42 B8
GIF/THBK G46 114 B2
Woodvale Dr PSLYN/LNWD PA3 75 G5
Woodview UD/BTH/TAN G71 99 K2
Woodview Dr AIRDRIE ML6 85 G4
BLSH ML4 100 C2
Woodview Ter HMLTN ML3 119 H6
Woodville Pk GOV/IBX G51 78 B4
Woodville St GOV/IBX G51 78 B4
Woodyard Rd DMBTN G82 20 E7
Woodyett Pk
CRMNK/CLK/EAG G76 114 F5
Woodyett Rd
CRMNK/CLK/EAG G76 114 F5
Wordsworth Wy
UD/BTH/TAN G71 99 H7
Worrall Gdns HMLTN ML3 120 B7
Worsley Crs NMRNS G77 113 J3
Wotherspoon Dr BEITH KA15 125 K3
Wraes Av BRHD/NEIL G78 92 D5
Wraes Vw BRHD/NEIL G78 111 M1
Wraisland Crs BSHPTN PA7 37 M6
Wrangholm Crs MTHW ML1 101 H6
Wrangholm Dr MTHW ML1 101 G6
Wren Ct BLSH ML4 99 L2
Wren Pl JNSTN PA5 89 K3
Wren Rd GRNKW/INVK PA16 16 A5
Wright Av BRHD/NEIL G78 92 A7
Wrightlands Crs ERSK PA8 57 L2
Wright St RNFRW PA4 75 M1
Wye Crs CTBR ML5 83 K1
Wykeham Pl KNTSWD G13 59 J3

Wykeham Rd KNTSWD G13 59 J3
Wylie EKILN G74 117 K5
Wylie Av ALEX/LLW G83 13 J7
NMRNS G77 113 K2
Wylie Pl DMBTN G82 13 K8
Wylie St HMLTN ML3 119 K8
Wyndford Dr MRYH/FIRH G20 60 D5
Wyndford Pl MRYH/FIRH G20 60 D5
Wyndford Rd BALLOCH G68 31 K1
MRYH/FIRH G20 60 C5
Wyndford Ter UD/BTH/TAN G71 99 H3
Wyndham Ct KVD/HLHD G12 60 D6
Wyndham St KVD/HLHD G12 60 D6
The Wynd CUMB G67 31 H4
Wynyard Gn EKILS G75 126 E3
Wyper Pl DEN/PKHD G31 80 A4
Wyvil Av KNTSWD G13 41 L8
Wyvis Av BSDN G61 41 J2
KNTSWD G13 58 F1
Wyvis Ct NMRNS G77 113 J7
Wyvis Pl KNTSWD G13 58 F1
NMRNS G77 113 K7
SHOTTS ML7 105 H6
Wyvis Qd KNTSWD G13 58 F1
Wyvis Wy MTHW ML1 121 K6

Y

Yair Dr CARD/HILL/MSPK G52 77 G3
Yarrow Crs BSHPTN PA7 38 C8
WISHAW ML2 122 B5
Yarrow Gdns MRYH/FIRH G20 60 F7
Yarrow Gardens La MRYH/FIRH G20 60 F7
Yarrow Pk EKILN G74 3 K6
Yarrow Rd BSHPBGS G64 44 A6
Yate Gv DEN/PKHD G31 80 B5
Yate Rd DEN/PKHD G31 80 B5
Yate St DEN/PKHD G31 80 B5
Yetholm Gdns EKILN G74 116 F6
Yetholm St SCOT G14 58 F4
Yetholm Ter HMLTN ML3 118 E7
Yett Rd MTHW ML1 101 K6
Yetts Av KLMCLM PA13 53 K1
Yetts Crs KKNTL G66 45 M2
Yetts Hole Rd AIRDRIE ML6 66 B4
Yew Dr SPRGB/BLRNK G21 62 A7
Yew Pl JNSTN PA5 89 M1
Yieldshields Rd CARLUKE ML8 135 K1
Yokerburn Pl KNTSWD G13 58 E2
Yokerburn Ter CLYDBK G81 58 D2
Yoker Ferry Rd SCOT G14 58 E3
Yoker Mill Gdns KNTSWD G13 58 E2
Yoker Mill Rd KNTSWD G13 58 F1
York Dr RUTH G73 96 D5
Yorkhill Pde KVGV G3 78 C1
Yorkhill St KVGV G3 78 D2
York Rd AIRDRIE ML6 101 K1
GRNKW/INVK PA16 15 L4
York St CGLW G2 4 C7
CLYDBK G81 40 D7
WISHAW ML2 122 B7
Young Pl EKILS G75 127 L5
UD/BTH/TAN G71 99 G2
WISHAW ML2 123 H4
Young Rd LNK/LMHG ML11 137 L4
Young St CLYDBK G81 40 B5
WISHAW ML2 122 C6
Young Ter SPRGB/BLRNK G21 62 A6
Young Wynd BLSH ML4 100 A1
Yukon Ter EKILS G75 126 E2
Yule Wy CUMB G67 31 G7
Yvetot Av LNK/LMHG ML11 137 H5
Yvetot Ct CARLUKE ML8 133 G6

Z

Zambesi Dr BLTYR/CAMB G72 118 C1
Zena Crs STPS/GTHM/RID G33 62 C6
Zena Pl SPRGB/BLRNK G21 62 D6
Zena St STPS/GTHM/RID G33 62 D6
Zetland Rd CARD/HILL/MSPK G52 76 F1

Index - featured places

Abbey Cemetery JNSTN PA5 74 C8
Abbey Mill Business Centre PSLY PA1 9 J6
ABC Cinema LNPK/KPK G44 94 F6
Abercorn Industrial Estate PSLYN/LNWD PA3 9 H3
Abercorn School COWCAD G4 4 D1
Abode Hotel CGLW G2 4 D5
Abronhill Health Centre CUMB G67 31 L5
Abronhill High School CUMB G67 31 L5
Abronhill Primary School CUMB G67 31 K6
Agricultural Museum CRMNK/CLK/EAG G76 115 M5
Airdrie Academy AIRDRIE ML6 66 F8
Airdrie Golf Club AIRDRIE ML6 66 F7
Airdrie Health Centre AIRDRIE ML6 84 E2
Airdrie United FC (Excelsior Stadium) AIRDRIE ML6 85 J3
Air Link Industrial Estate PSLYN/LNWD PA3 75 L2
Aitkenbar Primary School DMBTN G82 21 J5
Aitkenhead Primary School UD/BTH/TAN G71 98 F1
Albert Primary School AIRDRIE ML6 85 H1
SPRGB/BLRNK G21 61 M5
Albion Rovers FC (Cliftonhill) CTBR ML5 84 C3
Alexander Hospital CTBR ML5 83 L2
Alexander Peden Primary School SHOTTS ML7 71 L7
Alexandra Golf Club DEN/PKHD G31 80 B2
Alexandra Parade Primary School DEN/PKHD G31 80 A3
Alexandra Primary School AIRDRIE ML6 85 G2
Alexandria Medical Centre ALEX/LLW G83 13 J5
Allandar Sports Centre BSDN G61 42 B3
Allanshaw Industrial Estate HMLTN ML3 119 J6
All Saints Secondary School SPRGB/BLRNK G21 62 C5
AMF Bowling KVGV G3 78 F3
The Anderson Doe Podiatry Clinic PTCK G11 59 M5
Anderson Primary School KVGV G3 78 F2
Anderston Medical Centre KVGV G3 78 E2
Annette Street Primary School GVH/MTFL G42 79 G8
Annfield Medical Centre DEN/PKHD G31 80 A3
Anniesland College KVD/HLHD G12 60 A5
MRYH/FIRH G20 60 E4
PPK/MIL G22 61 L3
PTCK G11 59 M7
Anniesland Industrial Estate KNTSWD G13 59 L1
The Antonine Sports Centre CLYDBK G81 40 A3
Antonine Wall: Bearsden Bath-House BSDN G61 41 M5
Aquatec Leisure Centre MTHW ML1 120 E2
Arcadia Business Centre CLYDBK G81 40 A8
Arches Theatre CGLE G1 4 D8
Arden Primary School GIF/THBK G46 93 K5
Ardgowan Bowling & Tennis Club GRNKW/INVK PA16 6 A1
Ardgowan Primary School GRNKW/INVK PA16 16 D3
Ardoch Medical Centre BLTYR/CAMB G72 96 F4
Argo Sports Centre DRUM G15 40 E6
Arkleston Primary School RNFRW PA4 58 D8
Arts Guild Theatre GRNKW/INVK PA16 6 A1
Ashcraig School STPS/GTHM/RID G33 63 H7
Ashfield Medical Practice MLNGV G62 42 A1
Atholl Preparatory School MLNGV G62 24 A7
Auchenback Primary School BRHD/NEIL G78 92 D8
Auchenlodment Primary School JNSTN PA5 90 A1
Auchinairn Primary School BSHPBGS G64 62 B2
Auchinloch Primary School KKNTL G66 45 K8
Auchinraith Primary School BLTYR/CAMB G72 118 D3
Auldhouse Retail Park PLKSW/MSWD G43 94 C4
Auld Kirk Museum KKNTL G66 45 J1
The Avenue Shopping Centre NMRNS G77 113 J5
Baillieston FC BAIL/MDB/MHD G69 82 C6
Baillieston Health Centre BAIL/MDB/MHD G69 82 B6
Baird Memorial Primary School CUMB G67 48 C2
Baldernock Primary School BSHPBGS G64 25 H8
Baljaffray Primary School BSDN G61 41 J1
Baljaffray Shopping Centre BSDN G61 41 J1
Balmalloch Primary School KSYTH G65 29 J1
Balmore Golf Club BSHPBGS G64 43 K2
Balmuildy Primary School BSHPBGS G64 43 M7
Balornock Primary School SPRGB/BLRNK G21 62 A6
Balrossie School KLMCLM PA13 53 G3
Bankhead Primary School KNTSWD G13 59 G3
RUTH G73 95 M3
Bannerman High School BAIL/MDB/MHD G69 82 A6
Bargarran Primary School ERSK PA8 38 F7
Bargeddie Primary School BAIL/MDB/MHD G69 83 G4
Barlanark Primary School STPS/GTHM/RID G33 81 L4
Barmulloch Primary School SPRGB/BLRNK G21 62 C6
Barncluith Business Centre HMLTN ML3 119 M7
Barratt Trading Estate COWCAD G4 4 D1
Barrhead Bowling Club BRHD/NEIL G78 92 C6
Barrhead High School BRHD/NEIL G78 92 D6
Barrhead Sports Centre BRHD/NEIL G78 92 C6
Barsail Primary School ERSK PA8 57 J2
Battlefield Primary School GVH/MTFL G42 94 F3
BBC Scotland GOV/IBX G51 78 D3
Beardmore Hotel CLYDBK G81 39 K7
Bearsden Academy BSDN G61 41 L3
Bearsden Golf Club BSDN G61 41 J4
Bearsden Primary School BSDN G61 41 L4
The Beatson West of Scotland Cancer Centre KVD/HLHD G12 60 A6
Beckford Primary School HMLTN ML3 119 J5
Beckford Street Business Centre HMLTN ML3 119 J5
Beith Health Centre BEITH KA15 125 K4
Beith Primary School BEITH KA15 125 K5
Bellahouston Academy PLKSD/SHW G41 78 C5
Bellahouston Leisure Centre CARD/HILL/MSPK G52 77 M5
Bellahouston Primary School GOV/IBX G51 78 C4
Bell College HMLTN ML3 119 K6
The Bell Leisure Centre DMBTN G82 20 E7
Bellshill Academy BLSH ML4 100 B4
Bellshill Golf Club BLSH ML4 100 B6
Bellshill Industrial Estate BLSH ML4 99 M4
Belmont House School NMRNS G77 113 M3
Belvidere Primary School BLSH ML4 100 A5
Benburb FC GOV/IBX G51 77 L3
Bent Cemetery HMLTN ML3 119 J7
Berryhill Primary School WISHAW ML2 121 L6
Best Western Garfield House Hotel STPS/GTHM/RID G33 63 M3
Bewleys Hotel CGLW G2 4 E5
Birkenshaw Industrial Estate UD/BTH/TAN G71 98 E1
Bishopbriggs Golf Club BSHPBGS G64 43 M8
Bishopbriggs High School BSHPBGS G64 62 A1
Bishopbriggs Sports Centre BSHPBGS G64 43 L6
Bishoploch Primary School ESTRH G34 82 C1
Bishopton Health Centre BSHPTN PA7 38 B8
Bishopton Primary School BSHPTN PA7 38 A7
Blackfriars Primary School GBLS G5 79 J6
Blacklaw Primary School EKILN G74 3 M6
Blackridge Primary School BTHG/ARM EH48 71 J1
Blackwoods Medical Centre BAIL/MDB/MHD G69 46 F7
Blairbeth Golf Club CSMK G45 96 A7
Blairdardie Primary School DRUM G15 41 H8
Blairtummock Primary School ESTRH G34 82 B2
Blantyre Cemetery BLTYR/CAMB G72 118 C4
Blantyre High School BLTYR/CAMB G72 118 D3
Blantyre Victoria FC BLTYR/CAMB G72 118 F3
Blawarthill Hospital KNTSWD G13 59 G3
Blythswood Estate RNFRW PA4 58 B5
Bobbys Leisure Centre CUMB G67 30 F7
Boclair Academy BSDN G61 42 C6
Bonhill Primary School ALEX/LLW G83 13 K7
Bothwell Bridge Hotel UD/BTH/TAN G71 99 G8
Bothwell Castle UD/BTH/TAN G71 98 D7
Bothwell Castle Golf Club UD/BTH/TAN G71 98 F8
Bothwell Cemetery BLSH ML4 99 K5
Bothwell Medical Centre UD/BTH/TAN G71 99 G8
Bothwell Park High School MTHW ML1 121 G5
Bothwell Park Industrial Estate UD/BTH/TAN G71 99 G6
Bothwell Primary School UD/BTH/TAN G71 99 G8
Bowfield Hotel HWWD PA9 88 E7
Braehead Arena RNFRW PA4 58 F5
Braehead Business Park RNFRW PA4 58 F6
Braehead Primary School DMBTN G82 21 G6
Braehead Retail Park GOV/IBX G51 59 H7
Braehead Shopping Centre GOV/IBX G51 59 G6
Braidbar Primary School GIF/THBK G46 94 D7
Braidcraft Medical Centre PLK/PH/NH G53 77 J8
Braidfield High School CLYDBK G81 40 C7
Braidhurst Business Centre MTHW ML1 100 C7
Braidhurst High School MTHW ML1 100 D8
Braidhurst Industrial Estate MTHW ML1 120 D1
Braidwood Primary School CARLUKE ML8 134 F5
Brannock High School MTHW ML1 101 J6
Brediland Primary School PSLYS PA2 91 G1
Bridge of Weir Primary School BRWEIR PA11 72 D1
Bridgeton Business Centre DMNK/BRGTN G40 79 L5
Bridgeton Health Centre DMNK/BRGTN G40 79 M5
The Bridgewater Shopping Centre ERSK PA8 39 H8
Brisbane Primary School LARGS KA30 107 G4
Broomhill Industrial Estate KKNTL G66 27 L8
Broomhill Primary School PTCK G11 59 M5
Broomlea School PTCK G11 59 M7
Brownsburn Industrial Estate AIRDRIE ML6 85 H4
Bruce Medical Centre BLSH ML4 100 B4
Buchanan Business Park STPS/GTHM/RID G33 63 M4
Buchanan Galleries & Shopping Centre CGLE G1 4 F5
Burgh Primary School RUTH G73 96 A2
Burnbank Medical Centre HMLTN ML3 119 G5
Burnbrae Primary School PLK/PH/NH G53 93 K4
Burnhead Primary School UD/BTH/TAN G71 99 K2
Burnhill Sports Centre RUTH G73 95 M2
Burnside Primary School RUTH G73 96 B5
Burrell Collection PLKSW/MSWD G43 94 B1
Busby Primary School CRMNK/CLK/EAG G76 114 F4
Bushes Primary School PSLYS PA2 91 K2
Butterbiggins Medical Centre GVH/MTFL G42 79 H7
Cadder Primary School SMSTN G23 60 F3
Cadzow Business Centre HMLTN ML3 119 K6
Cadzow Health Centre HMLTN ML3 129 K2
Cadzow Industrial Estate HMLTN ML3 129 K2
Cairnbrook Industrial Estate ESTRH G34 82 B2
Cairnhill Industrial Estate AIRDRIE ML6 85 G3
Cairnhill Trading Estate AIRDRIE ML6 85 G3
Cairns Primary School BLTYR/CAMB G72 97 J6
Calderbank Primary School AIRDRIE ML6 85 J6
Calderbraes Golf Club UD/BTH/TAN G71 98 C1
Caldercuilt Primary School SMSTN G23 60 E1
Calderglen Country Park EKILS G75 127 M4
Calderhead High School SHOTTS ML7 104 F4
Calder Primary School MTHW ML1 120 F2
Caldervale High School AIRDRIE ML6 85 M2
Calderwood Lodge Jewish Primary School PLKSW/MSWD G43 94 E5
Calderwood Primary School RUTH G73 96 C4
Caldwellside Industrial Estate LNK/LMHG ML11 137 L4
Caledonian University CGLW G2 4 E4
Caledonia Primary School BAIL/MDB/MHD G69 82 B7
Callander Street Clinic MRYH/FIRH G20 61 G7
Cambuslang Avory Club BLTYR/CAMB G72 97 G6
Cambuslang College BLTYR/CAMB G72 97 H5
EKILN G74 3 G3
Cambuslang Golf Club BLTYR/CAMB G72 97 H3
Cambuslang Rangers FC BLTYR/CAMB G72 96 F4
Cambuslang Recreation Centre BLTYR/CAMB G72 97 K5
Cambuslang RFC RUTH G73 96 D5
Cambusnethan Primary School WISHAW ML2 122 D5
Campanile Hotel KVGV G3 78 E3
Campsie Recreation Centre KKNTL G66 26 D2
Campsie View School KKNTL G66 45 G5
Canberra Primary School EKILS G75 126 E2
Canniesburn Hospital BSDN G61 41 L7
Carbrain Primary School CUMB G67 31 H7
Cardinal Newman High School BLSH ML4 99 L5
Cardonald Clinic CARD/HILL/MSPK G52 77 J4
Cardonald College CARD/HILL/MSPK G52 77 K6
Cardonald Primary School CARD/HILL/MSPK G52 77 H5
Cardross Golf Club DMBTN G82 19 H3
Cardross Primary School DMBTN G82 19 G1
Carfin Industrial Estate MTHW ML1 101 G6
Carleith Primary School CLYDBK G81 39 L4
Carlibar Primary School BRHD/NEIL G78 92 C6
Carluke Golf Club CARLUKE ML8 132 D7
Carluke Health Centre CARLUKE ML8 133 H7
Carluke High School CARLUKE ML8 133 J7
Carluke Leisure Centre CARLUKE ML8 133 J7
Carluke Primary School CARLUKE ML8 133 J6
Carman Leisure Centre DMBTN G82 13 J8
Carmichael Hall GIF/THBK G46 94 B8
Carmunnock Cemetery CSMK G45 115 H1
Carmunnock Primary School CRMNK/CLK/EAG G76 115 K3
Carmyle Medical Centre CAR/SHTL G32 97 H2
Carmyle Primary School CAR/SHTL G32 97 J1
Carnbooth Residential School CRMNK/CLK/EAG G76 115 H3
Carnbroe Primary School CTBR ML5 84 D5
Carntyne Primary School STPS/GTHM/RID G33 80 D2
Carnwadric Primary School GIF/THBK G46 93 M5
Carolside Medical Centre CRMNK/CLK/EAG G76 114 E3
Carolside Primary School CRMNK/CLK/EAG G76 114 E4
Carsemeadow School BRWEIR PA11 53 K8
Cartland Bridge Hotel LNK/LMHG ML11 136 E3
Cart Vale Secondary School GOV/IBX G51 78 B3
Castlebank Industrial Estate PTCK G11 78 A1
Castlefield Primary School EKILS G75 126 E5
Castlehead High School PSLYS PA2 8 E7
Castle Hill Fort LARGS KA30 107 G6
Castlehill Industrial Estate CARLUKE ML8 133 G6
Castlehill Primary School BSDN G61 41 H3
WISHAW ML2 131 J1
Castlemilk Health Centre CSMK G45 95 L7
Castlemilk High School CSMK G45 95 L8
Castlemilk Pool CSMK G45 95 L7
Castlemilk Sports Centre CSMK G45 95 L7
Castle Semple Country Park LOCHW PA12 109 L1
Castle Semple Sailing Club LOCHW PA12 109 K2
Castleton Primary School CSMK G45 95 J7
Cathcart Castle Golf Club CRMNK/CLK/EAG G76 114 C3
Cathedral Primary School MTHW ML1 120 E2
Cathkin Braes Country Park CSMK G45 115 M1
Cathkin Braes Golf Club RUTH G73 116 B1
Cathkin High School BLTYR/CAMB G72 96 E6
Cathkin Primary School RUTH G73 96 D7
Cawder Golf Club BSHPBGS G64 43 M4
Cedars School of Excellence GRNKW/INVK PA16 6 A2
Celtic FC (Celtic Park) DEN/PKHD G31 80 B5
Central College of Commerce CGLE G1 5 G5
Central Health Centre CUMB G67 30 F8
Chapelgreen Primary School KSYTH G65 28 E3
Chapelhall Industrial Estate AIRDRIE ML6 85 K6
Chapelhall Primary School AIRDRIE ML6 85 K7
Chapelside Primary School AIRDRIE ML6 67 G8
Chapel Street Industrial Estate MRYH/FIRH G20 60 E4
Charing Cross Clinic KVGV G3 4 A3
Chatelherault Primary School HMLTN ML3 129 L1
Child Health Clinic PLKSW/MSWD G43 94 C2
Chirnsyde Primary School PPK/MIL G22 61 K4

Christie Park Primary School *ALEX/LLW* G83 13 J5
Christ the King Primary School *MTHW* ML1 101 H3
Chryston High School *BAIL/MDB/MHD* G69 64 C2
Chryston Primary School *BAIL/MDB/MHD* G69 64 C2
Chryston Valley Business Centre *BAIL/MDB/MHD* G69 64 C2
Cineworld *CGLW* G2 4 E4
DEN/PKHD G31 80 C5
City Chambers *CGLE* G1 5 G6
Claremont High School *EKILN* G74 127 M2
Clarkston Primary School *AIRDRIE* ML6 85 K1
Cleland Athletics Track *MTHW* ML1 121 L1
Cleland Hospital *MTHW* ML1 102 C8
Cleland Primary School *MTHW* ML1 102 B8
Cleveden Secondary School *KVD/HLHD* G12 60 B5
MRYH/FIRH G20 60 E6
Clippens Special School *PSLYN/LNWD* PA3 74 C4
Clober Golf Club *MLNGV* G62 23 M6
Clober Primary School *MLNGV* G62 23 L7
Clune Park Primary School *PGL* PA14 34 D1
Clyde Auditorium *KVGV* G3 78 D3
Clydebank Business Centre *CLYDBK* G81 58 C1
Clydebank College *CLYDBK* G81 40 B6
DMBTN G82 20 D6
Clydebank Crematorium *CLYDBK* G81 39 K4
Clydebank & District Golf Course *CLYDBK* G81 40 C3
Clydebank Health Centre *CLYDBK* G81 40 B5
Clydebank High School *CLYDBK* G81 40 A5
Clydebuilt *GOV/IBX* G51 59 G6
Clyde FC (Broadwood Stadium) *BALLOCH* G68 47 M1
Clyde Industrial Estate *RUTH* G73 96 D2
Clydemuir Primary School *CLYDBK* G81 39 K6
Clydesdale Business Centre *LNK/LMHG* ML11 137 J6
Clydesdale CC *PLKSD/SHW* G41 78 D8
Clyde Tunnel *SCOT* G14 59 L8
Clyde Valley High School *WISHAW* ML2 131 K2
'Clyde Valley Woodlands' National Nature Reserve *LNK/LMHG* ML11 136 E3
Clydeview Primary School *MTHW* ML1 120 B1
Clydeview Shopping Centre *BLTYR/CAMB* G72 118 D3
Clydeway Business Centre *KVGV* G3 78 E3
Coatbridge Business Centre *CTBR* ML5 84 C3
Coatbridge College *CTBR* ML5 84 B2
Coatbridge Health Centre *CTBR* ML5 84 A3
Coatbridge High School *CTBR* ML5 84 A2
Coatbridge Outdoor Sports Complex Track *CTBR* ML5 83 M5
Coathill Hospital *CTBR* ML5 84 A5
Coats Observatory *PSLY* PA1 8 F4
Cochrane Castle Golf Club *JNSTN* PA5 89 L2
Cochrane Castle Primary School *JNSTN* PA5 89 K2
Colgrain Primary School *HBR/GL* G84 11 G6
College of Building & Printing *CGLE* G1 5 G5
Colquhoun Park Primary School *BSDN* G61 41 J6
Coltness High School *WISHAW* ML2 122 D5
Coltness Primary School *WISHAW* ML2 122 C3
Columba High School *CTBR* ML5 84 A5
Colville Park Golf Club *MTHW* ML1 100 F8
Commonhead Primary School *ESTRH* G34 82 D2
Condorrat Health Centre *CUMB* G67 48 A3
Condorrat Primary School *CUMB* G67 48 B2
Copeland Primary School *GOV/IBX* G51 78 B3
Corpus Christi Primary School *AIRDRIE* ML6 85 H6
KNTSWD G13 59 J3
Corseford School *KLBCH* PA10 89 H3
Cotton Street Business Park *DMNK/BRGTN* G40 80 A8
Cowglen Golf Club *PLKSW/MSWD* G43 93 M2
Cowglen Hospital *PLK/PH/NH* G53 93 K2
Craigdhu Primary School *MLNGV* G62 41 M1
Craighead Primary School *KKNTL* G66 27 J4
Craighead School *HMLTN* ML3 119 H3
Craigholme School *PLKSD/SHW* G41 78 C7
Craigielea Primary School *PSLYN/LNWD* PA3 75 G4
Craigton Crematorium *CARD/HILL/MSPK* G52 77 K4
Craigton Primary School *CARD/HILL/MSPK* G52 77 L4
Crawforddyke Primary School *CARLUKE* ML8 135 G1
Croftcroighn Special School *STPS/GTHM/RID* G33 81 L1
Crofthead Industrial Estate *BRHD/NEIL* G78 111 J3
Crookfur Primary School *NMRNS* G77 113 K2
Crookston Castle (NTS) *PLK/PH/NH* G53 77 H7
Cross Arthurlie Primary School *BRHD/NEIL* G78 92 A5
Crosshouse Primary School *EKILS* G75 126 D5
Crowne Plaza Hotel *KVGV* G3 78 D3
Crowngate Business Centre *DMNK/BRGTN* G40 79 M5
Crownpoint Sports Complex *DMNK/BRGTN* G40 79 M4
Crow Wood Golf Club *BAIL/MDB/MHD* G69 64 A2
Cumbernauld Airport *BALLOCH* G68 31 J1
Cumbernauld College *CUMB* G67 30 F8
Cumbernauld High School *CUMB* G67 31 J8
Cumbernauld Primary School *BALLOCH* G68 31 H3
Cumbernauld Shopping Centre *CUMB* G67 30 F8
Cumbernauld Theatre *CUMB* G67 31 H5
Cunard Primary School *CLYDBK* G81 40 C8
Cuthbertson Primary School *PLKSD/SHW* G41 79 G7
Daily Record & Sunday Mail Offices *KVGV* G3 78 F3
Dairsie House School *PLKSW/MSWD* G43 94 E4
Daldowie Crematorium *UD/BTH/TAN* G71 98 B2
Dalmarnock Industrial Estate *RUTH* G73 80 B8
Dalmarnock Primary School *DMNK/BRGTN* G40 80 A6
Dalmarnock Primary School Annexe *DMNK/BRGTN* G40 80 A6
Dalmarnock Trading Estate *RUTH* G73 96 A1
Dalmuir Municipal Golf Club *CLYDBK* G81 39 L6
Dalreoch Primary School *DMBTN* G82 20 C5
Dalsholm Industrial Estate *MRYH/FIRH* G20 60 B3
Dalzell House *MTHW* ML1 121 G7
Dalziel Business Centre *MTHW* ML1 120 E3
Dalziel High School *MTHW* ML1 120 D3
Darnley Outdoor Recreation Centre *BSHPBGS* G64 61 M2
Darnley Primary School *PLK/PH/NH* G53 93 J5
Darrows Estate *BLSH* ML4 99 K4
David Dale College *DMNK/BRGTN* G40 79 M5
David Livingstone Centre (NTS) *UD/BTH/TAN* G71 98 E8
David Livingstone Primary School *BLTYR/CAMB* G72 118 D1
David Lloyd Sports Centre *PSLYN/LNWD* PA3 76 A1
Dental Hospital & School *CGLW* G2 4 C4
Devol Industrial Estate *PGL* PA14 34 D2
The Dollan Aqua Centre *EKILN* G74 2 E6
Donald Dewar Leisure Centre *DRUM* G15 41 G7
Douglas Academy *MLNGV* G62 23 K6
Douglas Inch Centre *KVGV* G3 4 A3
Douglas Park Golf Club *BSDN* G61 42 A5
Dowanhill Primary School *PTCK* G11 60 C8
Drumchapel Health Centre *DRUM* G15 40 F6
Drumchapel High School *DRUM* G15 41 G5
Drumchapel Hospital *DRUM* G15 41 G7
Drumchapel Pool *DRUM* G15 40 F7
Drummore School *DRUM* G15 41 J5
Drumoyne Industrial Estate *GOV/IBX* G51 77 L3
Drumoyne Primary School *GOV/IBX* G51 77 L2
Drumpark School *BAIL/MDB/MHD* G69 83 H4
Drumpellier Country Park *CTBR* ML5 83 J2
Drumpellier CC *CTBR* ML5 83 K4
Drumpellier Golf Club *CTBR* ML5 83 J4
Drumry Primary School *DRUM* G15 40 E7
Drumry Primary School Annexe *DRUM* G15 40 F5
Duchess Industrial Estate *RUTH* G73 96 C1
Dullatur Golf Club *BALLOCH* G68 30 D3
Dumbarton Academy *DMBTN* G82 21 G6
Dumbarton Castle *DMBTN* G82 21 G8
Dumbarton FC (Strathclyde Homes Stadium) *DMBTN* G82 20 F8
Dumbarton Golf Club *DMBTN* G82 20 F5
Dumbarton Health Centre *DMBTN* G82 20 E6
Dumbarton Joint Hospital *DMBTN* G82 20 C6
Dumbarton Peoples Theatre *DMBTN* G82 21 H7
Dunard Primary School *MRYH/FIRH* G20 60 F6
Duncanrig Secondary School *EKILS* G75 126 E1
Duncanrig Sports Centre *EKILS* G75 126 E2
Dundas Business Centre *COWCAD* G4 4 D2
Dundyvan Industrial Estate *CTBR* ML5 83 M6
Dunrobin Primary School *AIRDRIE* ML6 85 L2
Dykebar Hospital *PSLYS* PA2 92 B2
Dykehead Primary School *SHOTTS* ML7 104 D4
Earnhill Primary School *GRK* PA19 15 L5
Earnock High School *HMLTN* ML3 119 G8
Eastbank Academy *CAR/SHTL* G32 81 H6
Eastbank Primary School *CAR/SHTL* G32 81 J5
Easterhouse Day Care *ESTRH* G34 82 B2
Easterhouse Pool *ESTRH* G34 82 A2
Easterhouse Sports Centre *ESTRH* G34 81 M1
Easter Moffat Golf Club *AIRDRIE* ML6 68 B8
Eastfield Primary School *BALLOCH* G68 30 B8
East Fulton Primary School *PSLYN/LNWD* PA3 73 M4
Easthall Primary School *ESTRH* G34 81 M3
East Kilbride Arts Centre Cinema *EKILN* G74 3 H1
East Kilbride Golf Club *EKILN* G74 117 H4
East Kilbride Ice Rink *EKILN* G74 3 G7
East Kilbride Shopping Centre *EKILN* G74 2 E6
East Kilbride Sports Club *EKILS* G75 127 M4
East Kilbride Stadium *EKILN* G74 3 K4
East Milton Primary School *EKILS* G75 2 A6
Eastmuir Special School *CAR/SHTL* G32 81 K4
East Park Home School *MRYH/FIRH* G20 60 E5
Eastside Industrial Estate *KKNTL* G66 45 K1
Eastwood High School *NMRNS* G77 113 L2
Eastwood Recreation Centre *GIF/THBK* G46 94 B8
Eastwood Theatre *GIF/THBK* G46 94 B8
Edinbarnet Primary School *CLYDBK* G81 40 C1
Elderpark Clinic *GOV/IBX* G51 77 M2
Elder Park Primary School *GOV/IBX* G51 77 L1
Elderslie Cottage Hospital *JNSTN* PA5 74 B8
Elderslie Golf Club *JNSTN* PA5 74 E7
Elise Hospital *BRWEIR* PA11 53 L7
Elmvale Primary School *SPRGB/BLRNK* G21 61 L6
Elmwood Medical Centre *NMRNS* G77 113 M3
Empire Cinema *CLYDBK* G81 40 B7
Empire Theatre *LRKH* ML9 130 C6
Erskine Golf Club *BSHPTN* PA7 38 B5
Erskine Health Centre *ERSK* PA8 39 G7
Erskine Hospital *BSHPTN* PA7 38 E5
Erskine Swimming Pool *ERSK* PA8 39 H8
Erskine View Clinic *OLDK* G60 39 G4
Esporta, Dougalston Golf Club *MLNGV* G62 24 D7
Eurocentral International Freight Terminal *MTHW* ML1 100 F2
Fallside Secondary School *UD/BTH/TAN* G71 99 K4
Falls of Clyde Nature Reserve *LNK/LMHG* ML11 136 F8
Faraday Retail Park *CTBR* ML5 84 A3
Farm Castle Industrial Estate *RUTH* G73 96 C2
Farmeloan Industrial Estate *RUTH* G73 96 B2
Fereneze Golf Club *BRHD/NEIL* G78 92 A6
Ferguslie CC *PSLYS* PA2 8 C8
Ferguslie Primary School *PSLYN/LNWD* PA3 8 A2
Fernhill School *RUTH* G73 96 C7
Festival Business Centre *GOV/IBX* G51 78 C4
Finlaystone Country Estate *PGL* PA14 35 L2
Firhill Business Centre *MRYH/FIRH* G20 61 G6
Firpark School *MTHW* ML1 120 F5
Flemington Industrial Estate *BLTYR/CAMB* G72 97 L6
Florence Street Clinic *GBLS* G5 79 J5
Flowerhill Industrial Estate *AIRDRIE* ML6 85 H1
Fordbank Primary School *JNSTN* PA5 89 J2
Forge Shopping Centre *DEN/PKHD* G31 80 C4
Fort Matilda Industrial Estate *GRNKW/INVK* PA16 16 A1
The Fort Theatre *BSHPBGS* G64 61 M1
Fountain Business Centre *CTBR* ML5 84 A2
French Street Industrial Estate *RNFRW* PA4 58 B7
Fullwood Health Centre *MTHW* ML1 101 G5
Fullwood Industrial Estate *HMLTN* ML3 119 H6
Gadburn Special School *SPRGB/BLRNK* G21 62 C5
The Gait *CGLE* G1 5 H7
Gallery of Modern Art *CGLE* G1 4 F6
Gallowhill Primary School *PSLYN/LNWD* PA3 76 B2
Garnetbank Primary School *KVGV* G3 4 B3
Garnock Academy *KBRN* KA25 124 C3
Garnock Swimming Pool *KBRN* KA25 124 C5
Garrell Business Centre *KSYTH* G65 29 J2
Garrion Business Park *WISHAW* ML2 131 J1
Garrowhill Primary School *BAIL/MDB/MHD* G69 82 A5
Garscadden Primary School *KNTSWD* G13 58 F2
Gartconner Primary School *KKNTL* G66 46 C2
Gartcosh Primary School *BAIL/MDB/MHD* G69 64 F5
Gartcosh Works Sports Club *BAIL/MDB/MHD* G69 65 G5
Garthamlock Primary School *STPS/GTHM/RID* G33 81 J1
Garthamlock Secondary School *STPS/GTHM/RID* G33 63 K8
Gartnavel General Hospital *KVD/HLHD* G12 60 A6
Gartnavel Royal Hospital *KVD/HLHD* G12 60 A6
Gartsherrie Industrial Estate *CTBR* ML5 83 M1
Gartsherrie Primary School *CTBR* ML5 83 L2
Gask House School *BSHPBGS* G64 61 M3
Gavinburn Primary School *OLDK* G60 38 F3
Geilsland School *BEITH* KA15 125 L5
Geilston Garden (NTS) *DMBTN* G82 19 G2
Georgian Hotel *CTBR* ML5 83 L3
GHK RFC *KNTSWD* G13 59 M3
Giffnock Primary School *GIF/THBK* G46 94 C7
The Glasgow Academy *KVD/HLHD* G12 60 E7
Glasgow Airport *RNFRW* PA4 57 K8
Glasgow Airport Terminals *PSLYN/LNWD* PA3 75 K1
Glasgow Botanic Gardens *KVD/HLHD* G12 60 D6
Glasgow Caledonian University *COWCAD* G4 4 F3
KVD/HLHD G12 60 A4
KVGV G3 78 E1
Glasgow Cathedral *COWCAD* G4 5 K5
Glasgow College of Nautical Studies *GBLS* G5 79 J5
Glasgow Cross *CGLE* G1 5 H8
The Glasgow Gaelic School *KVGV* G3 78 E2
Glasgow Golf Club *BSDN* G61 42 C8
Glasgow Marriott Hotel *KVGV* G3 4 B6
Glasgow Metropolitan College *CGLE* G1 5 G5
DMNK/BRGTN G40 79 M5
Glasgow Museums Resource Centre (The Open Museum) *PLK/PH/NH* G53 92 F4
Glasgow Necropolis *COWCAD* G4 5 L6
Glasgow Nuffield Hospital *KVD/HLHD* G12 60 B5
Glasgow Royal Infirmary *DEN/PKHD* G31 5 K4
Glasgow School of Art *CGLW* G2 4 C4
Glasgow Science Centre & IMAX Theatre *GOV/IBX* G51 78 D3
Glasgow Ski & Snowboard Centre *PLKSD/SHW* G41 78 A6
Glasgow Tower *GOV/IBX* G51 78 C3
Gleddoch Golf & Country Club *PGL* PA14 36 C5
Glenboig Primary School *CTBR* ML5 65 M5
Glenburn Clinic *PSLYS* PA2 91 K2
Glenburn School *GRNKW/INVK* PA16 15 L7
Glencairn Primary School *MTHW* ML1 120 F4
Glencryan School *CUMB* G67 48 E2
Glendale Primary School *PLKSD/SHW* G41 78 F6
Glenduffhill Cemetery *CAR/SHTL* G32 81 K4
Glen Family Centre *GIF/THBK* G46 94 A8
Glengarnock Primary School *KBRN* KA25 124 D6
Glengowan Primary School *AIRDRIE* ML6 69 G5
LRKH ML9 130 C6
Glenhead Primary School *CUMB* G67 31 L4
Gleniffer Braes Country Park *PSLYS* PA2 91 G4
Gleniffer High School *PSLYS* PA2 91 G2
Glenlee Primary School *HMLTN* ML3 119 G5
Glenmanor Primary School *BAIL/MDB/MHD* G69 46 E8
Glenpark Industrial Estate *DEN/PKHD* G31 80 B4
Glenvale FC *PSLY* PA1 8 D5
Glenwood Business Centre *CSMK* G45 95 L7
Glenwood Business Park *CSMK* G45 95 L7
Glynhill Hotel *RNFRW* PA4 58 B8
Goethe Institute *KVGV* G3 78 E1
Goldenhill Primary School *CLYDBK* G81 40 B3
Golfhill Primary School *AIRDRIE* ML6 66 E7
DEN/PKHD G31 5 M5
Gorbals Health Centre *GBLS* G5 79 J6
Gorbals Leisure Centre *GBLS* G5 79 K5
Gourock Golf Club *GRK* PA19 15 H3
Gourock Health Centre *GRK* PA19 15 L1
Gourock High School *GRK* PA19 15 K2
Gourock Primary School *GRK* PA19 15 K1
Govan Health Centre *GOV/IBX* G51 77 L1
Govan High School *GOV/IBX* G51 77 L2
Govanhill Health Centre *GVH/MTFL* G42 79 H8
Gowanbank Primary School *PLK/PH/NH* G53 93 G3
Greenbank Garden (NTS) *CRMNK/CLK/EAG* G76 114 B4
Greenburn Primary School *EKILN* G74 3 L3
Greenfaulds High School *CUMB* G67 48 D2
Greenfield Primary School *GOV/IBX* G51 77 M2
Greengairs Primary School *AIRDRIE* ML6 49 L7
Greenhill Industrial Estate *CTBR* ML5 66 A8
Greenhill Primary School *CTBR* ML5 84 A1
Greenhills Health Centre *EKILS* G75 126 D4
Greenhills Primary School *EKILS* G75 126 F5
Greenock Academy *GRNKW/INVK* PA16 16 D2
Greenock Crematorium *GRNKW/INVK* PA16 16 D4
Greenock CC *GRNKW/INVK* PA16 16 D2
Greenock Golf Club *GRNKW/INVK* PA16 16 C3
Greenock Health Centre *GRNK* PA15 6 B4
Greenock High School *GRNKW/INVK* PA16 15 K7
Greenock Sports Centre *GRNKW/INVK* PA16 6 A3
Greenock Wanderers RFC *GRNKW/INVK* PA16 16 B1
Greenock Whinhill Golf Club *GRNKW/INVK* PA16 6 C9
Greenrigg Primary School *SHOTTS* ML7 71 M6
Greenview School *PPK/MIL* G22 61 K4
Grovewood Business Centre *BLSH* ML4 99 L2
Gryffe High School *CRG/CRSL/HOU* PA6 55 G8
Haggs Castle Golf Club *CARD/HILL/MSPK* G52 78 A7
Haghill Park Primary School *DEN/PKHD* G31 80 B3
Hairmyres & Stonehouse Hospitals *EKILS* G75 126 C1
Haldane Primary School *ALEX/LLW* G83 13 L2
Halfmerke Primary School *EKILN* G74 3 J2
Hallside Primary School *BLTYR/CAMB* G72 97 L6
Hamilton Academical FC (New Douglas Park) *HMLTN* ML3 119 J5
Hamilton Business Park *HMLTN* ML3 119 K5
Hamilton College *HMLTN* ML3 119 K5
Hamilton Grammar School *HMLTN* ML3 119 K7
Hamiltonhill Industrial Estate *PPK/MIL* G22 61 H6
Hamilton Park Racecourse *HMLTN* ML3 119 K3
Hamilton Public Baths *HMLTN* ML3 119 K6
Hamilton School for the Deaf *HMLTN* ML3 119 G8
Hamilton Water Palace *HMLTN* ML3 119 K5
Hampden Special School *GVH/MTFL* G42 95 K2
Hampden (Scotland's National Stadium) *GVH/MTFL* G42 95 J2

Hareleeshill Primary School LRKH ML9 130 E7
Harestanes Industrial Estate CARLUKE ML8 134 F4
Harestanes Primary School KKNTL G66 46 A1
Hartfield Clinic DMBTN G82 21 G6
Harthill Industrial Estate SHOTTS ML7 71 K7
Harthill Royal FC SHOTTS ML7 71 M7
Hartwoodhill Hospital SHOTTS ML7 104 B5
The Harvest Clinic COWCAD G4 4 B2
Hawkhead Cemetery PSLYS PA2 76 C6
Hawkhead Hospital PSLYS PA2 76 C7
Hayston Golf Club KKNTL G66 27 H8
Healthcare International (HCI) CLYDBK G81 39 M8
Heathery Knowe Primary School EKILS G75 127 G3
Helensburgh Golf Club HBR/GL G84 10 F4
Helensburgh Medical Centre HBR/GL G84 10 D6
Helensburgh Swimming Pool HBR/GL G84 10 D6
The Henderson Theatre SHOTTS ML7 104 F5
Heriot Primary School PSLYS PA2 90 F2
Hermitage Academy HBR/GL G84 11 G7
Hermitage Primary School HBR/GL G84 10 D5
High Blantyre Primary School BLTYR/CAMB G72 118 B3
Highholm Primary School PGL PA14 34 B1
Highlanders Academy Primary School GRNK PA15 16 D5
High Mill Primary School CARLUKE ML8 133 H7
High School of Glasgow BSDN G61 41 K5
The High School of Glasgow KNTSWD G13 59 L3
High Street Industrial Estate KKNTL G66 45 J1
Hillhead High School KVD/HLHD G12 60 E8
Hillhead Primary School
KKNTL G66 45 L2
KVD/HLHD G12 60 E7
Hillhead RFC KVD/HLHD G12 60 B6
The Hill House (NTS) HBR/GL G84 10 E3
Hillington Industrial Estate CARD/HILL/MSPK G52 76 F2
Hillington Park Retail & Amenities Centre CARD/HILL/MSPK G52 77 G1
Hillington Primary School CARD/HILL/MSPK G52 77 G3
Hillpark Secondary School PLKSW/MSWD G43 94 C5
Hill's Trust Primary School GOV/IBX G51 77 M1
Hilton Park Golf Club MLNGV G62 23 H1
HM Prison
BSHPBGS G64 44 D5
GRNKW/INVK PA16 16 C5
STPS/GTHM/RID G33 80 F1
Hollybrook Special School GVH/MTFL G42 79 H8
Hollywood Bowl BAIL/MDB/MHD G69 83 J7
Holm Industrial Estate PSLYS PA2 9 J9
Holmwood House (NTS) LNPK/KPK G44 95 H6
Holy Cross High School HMLTN ML3 119 L6
Holy Cross Primary School
GVH/MTFL G42 79 H8
KSYTH G65 29 M6
Holy Family Primary School
BLSH ML4 100 C4
KKNTL G66 45 H4
Holyrood Secondary School & Sports Centre GVH/MTFL G42 95 J1
Holytown Primary School MTHW ML1 101 H4
Hotel 377 CGLW G2 4 C7
Hotel du Vin KVD/HLHD G12 60 B6
Hotel Ibis CGLW G2 4 C4
House for an Art Lover PLKSD/SHW G41 78 A5
Househillmuir Primary School PLK/PH/NH G53 93 H4
Houston Primary School CRG/CRSL/HOU PA6 73 H1
Howford Special School PLK/PH/NH G53 77 G7
Howwood Primary School HWWD PA9 88 F5
The Hunter Health Centre EKILN G74 3 G5
Hunter High School EKILN G74 117 J8
Hunterhill Tutorial Centre PSLYS PA2 9 M7
Hunterian Museum KVD/HLHD G12 60 D8
Hunter Primary School EKILN G74 3 M2
Hutchesons Grammar Junior School KVD/HLHD G12 60 D8
Hutchesons Grammar Preparatory School GVH/MTFL G42 79 G8
Hutchesons Grammar School PLKSD/SHW G41 78 E8
Hutchesons' Hall CGLE G1 5 G7
Hutchesons St Aloysians RFC GIF/THBK G46 94 A5
Hyndland Primary School PTCK G11 60 B8
Hyndland Secondary School KVD/HLHD G12 60 A7
Ibrox Industrial Estate GOV/IBX G51 78 B4
Ibrox Primary School GOV/IBX G51 78 A5
IKEA Store Glasgow GOV/IBX G51 59 G7
Inchinnan Business Park RNFRW PA4 57 J6
Inchinnan Primary School RNFRW PA4 57 K3
Industrial Estate DMBTN G82 20 F3
Innkeeper's Lodge
ALEX/LLW G83 13 K1
BALLOCH G68 30 C8
HBR/GL G84 10 B5
MTHW ML1 119 K1
International Christian College COWCAD G4 5 J5
Inverclyde Royal Hospital GRK PA19 15 M5
Inverkip Primary School GRNKW/INVK PA16 32 E4
Isobel Mair School CRMNK/CLK/EAG G76 114 D1
Italian Centre CGLE G1 5 G7
James Aiton Primary School BLTYR/CAMB G72 97 G4
James Hamilton Heritage Park EKILN G74 116 D5
Jamestown Industrial Estate ALEX/LLW G83 13 L3
Jamestown Primary School ALEX/LLW G83 13 L3
James Watt College
GRNK PA15 6 F3
GRNKW/INVK PA16 6 A3
John Hillhouse Industrial Estate BLTYR/CAMB G72 96 D3
John Logie Baird Primary School HBR/GL G84 10 F5
John Ogilvie High School HMLTN ML3 118 E6
John Paul Academy SMSTN G23 60 C1
John Paul II Primary School
CSMK G45 95 M8
UD/BTH/TAN G71 99 J3
John Smith Memorial Swimming Pool AIRDRIE ML6 85 G2
Johnstone Health Centre JNSTN PA5 73 M8
Johnstone High School JNSTN PA5 89 K2
Johnstone Hospital JNSTN PA5 74 A6
Johnstone Swimming Pool JNSTN PA5 73 M7
John Street Clinic DMBTN G82 20 D2
John Wheatley College
CAR/SHTL G32 81 H5
STPS/GTHM/RID G33 81 J3
The John Wright Sports Centre EKILN G74 3 K4
Jordanhill School KNTSWD G13 59 L4
Keil School DMBTN G82 20 D7
Keir Hardie Memorial Primary School MTHW ML1 101 K6
Keir Hardie Sports Centre MTHW ML1 101 G3
Kelbourne School MRYH/FIRH G20 60 E5
Kelburn Business Park PGL PA14 35 H1
Kelburne CC PSLY PA1 9 M3
Kelburn Primary School LARGS KA30 106 F5
Kelvindale Primary School KVD/HLHD G12 60 A5
Kelvingrove Art Gallery & Museum PTCK G11 78 D1
Kelvin Hall International Sports Arena KVGV G3 78 C1
Kelvinhaugh Primary School KVGV G3 78 C2
Kelvin School KVGV G3 78 C1
Kelvinside Academy KVD/HLHD G12 60 D6
Kenilworth Medical Centre CUMB G67 48 E1
Kennyhill School DEN/PKHD G31 80 C2
Kersland School PSLYS PA2 76 C8
Kibble Education & Care Centre PSLYN/LNWD PA3 75 J2
Kilbarchan Cemetery JNSTN PA5 73 H5
Kilbarchan Primary School KLBCH PA10 73 G6
Kilbirnie Place Golf Club KBRN KA25 124 B4
Kilbowie Cemetery CLYDBK G81 40 C7
Kilbowie Primary School CLYDBK G81 40 B6
Kilbowie Retail Park CLYDBK G81 40 C7
Kildrum Primary School CUMB G67 31 H7
Killermont Primary School BSDN G61 42 A6
Kilmacolm Golf Club KLMCLM PA13 53 L3
Kilmacolm Primary School KLMCLM PA13 53 J3
Kilpatrick School CLYDBK G81 39 L4
Kilsyth Academy KSYTH G65 29 J1
Kilsyth Health Centre KSYTH G65 29 L2
Kilsyth Primary School KSYTH G65 29 K2
Kilsyth Swimming Pool KSYTH G65 29 J1
Kingsgate Retail Park EKILN G74 116 F4
Kings Oak Primary School GRNK PA15 17 K7
Kings Park Secondary School LNPK/KPK G44 95 J5
Kings Theatre CGLW G2 4 B4
Kingston Business Park PGL PA14 18 A8
Kingston Industrial Estate PGL PA14 18 A8
Kinning Park Medical Centre PLKSD/SHW G41 78 E4
Kirkfieldbank Primary School LNK/LMHG ML11 136 D5
Kirkhill Golf Club BLTYR/CAMB G72 97 G7
Kirkhill Primary School NMRNS G77 114 B5
Kirkintilloch Foot Clinic KKNTL G66 45 J2
Kirkintilloch Golf Club KKNTL G66 45 G1
Kirkintilloch High School KKNTL G66 45 M2
Kirkintilloch Industrial Estate KKNTL G66 27 K8
Kirkintilloch Leisure Centre KKNTL G66 45 K3
Kirkland Hospital UD/BTH/TAN G71 99 H6
Kirklandneuk Primary School RNFRW PA4 58 B6
Kirk Lane Cemetery PLKSW/MSWD G43 94 C3
Kirk O'Shotts Primary School SHOTTS ML7 87 K6
Kirkriggs School CSMK G45 96 A5
Kirkshaws Primary School CTBR ML5 83 L6
Kirktonholme Primary School EKILN G74 2 C3
Kirkton Primary School CARLUKE ML8 133 G8
Kirkwood Health Clinic CTBR ML5 83 J6
Kittoch School EKILS G75 2 D9
Knightswood Golf Club KNTSWD G13 59 H2
Knightswood Primary School KNTSWD G13 59 L2
Knightswood Secondary School KNTSWD G13 59 K3
Knockburn Primary School SPRGB/BLRNK G21 62 C3
Knocknairshill Cemetery GRNK PA15 17 K8
Knowetop Primary School MTHW ML1 120 F5
Knoxland Primary School DMBTN G82 21 G7
Lady Alice Primary School GRNKW/INVK PA16 16 C5
Ladyburn Business Park GRNK PA15 17 L6
Lady Octavia Recreation Centre GRNK PA15 7 K9
Ladyton Primary School ALEX/LLW G83 13 M7
Ladyton Shopping Centre ALEX/LLW G83 13 M7
Ladywell Primary School MTHW ML1 120 D2
Ladywell School SCOT G14 59 K7
Lagoon Leisure Centre PSLY PA1 9 K4
Laigh Bent Sports Club HMLTN ML3 119 M6
Laird Business Park DMNK/BRGTN G40 80 A8
Lairdsland Primary School KKNTL G66 45 J2
Lambhill Cemetery SMSTN G23 60 F1
Lamlash Primary School STPS/GTHM/RID G33 81 H2
Lammermoor Primary School WISHAW ML2 122 B5
Lanark Golf Club LNK/LMHG ML11 137 K6
Lanark Grammar School LNK/LMHG ML11 137 G6
Lanark Moor Country Park LNK/LMHG ML11 137 L7
Lanark Primary School LNK/LMHG ML11 137 H4
Lanarkshire Ice Rink HMLTN ML3 119 L6
Lanark Tennis Club LNK/LMHG ML11 137 G4
Langbank Primary School PGL PA14 36 B3
Langcraigs Primary School PSLYS PA2 91 J3
Langfaulds Primary School DRUM G15 40 F5
Langlands School GOV/IBX G51 77 L2
Langloan Primary School CTBR ML5 83 L4
Langs Hotel CGLW G2 4 F4
Langside College
CSMK G45 95 M7
GVH/MTFL G42 95 G2
RUTH G73 96 C3
Langside Primary School PLKSD/SHW G41 94 D2
Lansdowne Clinic KVD/HLHD G12 60 A5
Largs Academy LARGS KA30 106 F5
Largs Golf Club LARGS KA30 107 G7
Largs Sailing Club LARGS KA30 106 F8
Larkfield Industrial Estate GRNKW/INVK PA16 15 J4
Larkfield Primary School GRNKW/INVK PA16 15 L5
Larkhall Academy LRKH ML9 130 B8
Larkhall Golf Club LRKH ML9 130 E6
Larkhall Leisure Centre & Baths LRKH ML9 130 B7
Lawmuir Primary School BLSH ML4 100 A6
Law Primary School CARLUKE ML8 132 C4
Lennoxtown Primary School KKNTL G66 26 D2
Lenzie Academy KKNTL G66 45 J4
Lenzie Golf Club KKNTL G66 45 K7
Lenzie Hospital KKNTL G66 45 L7
Lenzie Moss Primary School KKNTL G66 45 H5
Lenzie Primary School KKNTL G66 45 J5
Lethamhill Golf Club STPS/GTHM/RID G33 62 F7
Levenvale Primary School ALEX/LLW G83 13 J3
Leverndale Hospital PLK/PH/NH G53 76 F7
Lightburn Hospital CAR/SHTL G32 81 H3
The Lighthouse CGLE G1 4 E7
Lilybank School GRNK PA15 17 M7
Linburn Special School CARD/HILL/MSPK G52 76 F3
The Linn Cemetery CSMK G45 115 H1
The Linn Crematorium CSMK G45 95 G8
Linn Park Gardens LNPK/KPK G44 95 G7
Linn Park Golf Club LNPK/KPK G44 95 H6
Linnpark Industrial Estate CSMK G45 95 H8
Linnvale Primary School CLYDBK G81 40 D8
Linwood Health Centre PSLYN/LNWD PA3 74 C5
Linwood High School PSLYN/LNWD PA3 73 M4
Linwood Moss Sports Centre PSLYN/LNWD PA3 74 A3
Littlehill Golf Club BSHPBGS G64 62 A3
Lochend Community High School ESTRH G34 82 C2
Lochend Secondary School ESTRH G34 82 C2
Lochfield Primary School PSLYS PA2 91 M1
Lochinch Playing Fields & Sports Club PLKSD/SHW G41 77 M8
Lochpark Stadium CARLUKE ML8 134 F1
Loch Primary School RUTH G73 96 D6
Lochshore Industrial Estate GLGNK KA14 124 E6
Lochwinnoch Community Museum LOCHW PA12 109 J2
Lochwinnoch Golf Club LOCHW PA12 109 H3
Lochwinnoch Primary School LOCHW PA12 109 H2
Lockhart Hospital LNK/LMHG ML11 137 J6
Logans Primary School MTHW ML1 120 B1
Lomond Industrial Estate ALEX/LLW G83 13 K4
Lomond School HBR/GL G84 10 D4
Lomond Woods Holiday Park ALEX/LLW G83 13 H2
Long Calderwood Primary School EKILN G74 117 J5
Lorne Street Primary School GOV/IBX G51 78 D4
Lourdes Primary School CARD/HILL/MSPK G52 77 J5
Lourdes Secondary School CARD/HILL/MSPK G52 77 K5
Low Parks Museum HMLTN ML3 119 L5
Low Waters Medical Centre HMLTN ML3 129 J2
Lyle Hill Viewpoint GRNKW/INVK PA16 16 B2
Lynedoch Industrial Estate GRNK PA15 6 D6
Macdonald Crutherland House Hotel EKILS G75 127 M6
Machanhill Primary School LRKH ML9 130 D6
Macmillan School of Music & Drama PSLY PA1 8 C6
Madhok Medical Centre GVH/MTFL G42 95 G3
Maiden Castle KKNTL G66 27 G1
Malmaison Hotel CGLW G2 4 C5
Manse Road Medical Centre WISHAW ML2 123 G4
Martyr's Public School COWCAD G4 5 J4
Maryhill Crematorium SMSTN G23 60 E2
Maryhill FC MRYH/FIRH G20 60 E4
Maryhill Health Centre MRYH/FIRH G20 60 E4
Maryhill Primary School MRYH/FIRH G20 60 D3
The Mary Russell School PSLYS PA2 76 C7
Mavisbank Special School AIRDRIE ML6 84 F1
Maxwelton Primary School EKILN G74 3 L3
McGill Primary Annexe Bonnyholm Campus CARD/HILL/MSPK G52 77 G6
McGill Primary Annexe Leithland Campus PLK/PH/NH G53 93 H1
McGill Primary School PLK/PH/NH G53 77 J7
McLean Museum & Art Gallery GRNKW/INVK PA16 6 B2
McLellan Galleries KVGV G3 4 C4
Meadowburn Primary School BSHPBGS G64 44 A7
Meadowside Industrial Estate RNFRW PA4 58 D3
Mearns Castle High School NMRNS G77 114 A7
Mearns Cemetery NMRNS G77 113 M7
Mearns Primary School NMRNS G77 113 J6
Megabowl CLYDBK G81 40 C8
Merchiston Hospital CRG/CRSL/HOU PA6 73 L5
Merkland School KKNTL G66 45 M1
Merrylee Annex LNPK/KPK G44 95 H6
Merrylee Primary School PLKSW/MSWD G43 94 F5
Middlefield Residential School PTCK G11 60 B8
Middlemuir School CLYDBK G81 39 M7
Midlock Medical Centre GOV/IBX G51 78 B5
Millarston Industrial Estate PSLY PA1 75 G7
Millennium Hotel CGLE G1 4 F6
Millersneuk Primary School KKNTL G66 45 L6
Milncroft Primary School STPS/GTHM/RID G33 81 J2
Milngavie & Bearsden Sports Club MLNGV G62 42 D3
Milngavie Business Centre MLNGV G62 24 A8
Milngavie Golf Club MLNGV G62 23 L4
Milngavie Primary School MLNGV G62 24 A8
Miltonbank Primary School PPK/MIL G22 61 J2
Milton Clinic PPK/MIL G22 61 J3
Miltonhead CARLUKE ML8 134 A1
Milton School PPK/MIL G22 61 L3
Mitchell Theatre & Library KVGV G3 4 A4
Modryvale Medical Centre MTHW ML1 120 F4
Monklands District General Hospital AIRDRIE ML6 84 D2
Monklands Industrial Estate CTBR ML5 83 M8
Moorfoot Primary School GRK PA19 15 J3
Moorpark Primary School
KBRN KA25 124 C2
RNFRW PA4 58 B7
Morningside Primary School WISHAW ML2 123 H5
Morton FC (Cappielow Park) GRNK PA15 7 L7
Mossburn Industrial Estate SHOTTS ML7 71 J7
Mossedge Industrial Estate PSLYN/LNWD PA3 74 C3
Mossend Primary School BLSH ML4 100 C5
Mosshead Primary School BSDN G61 41 L2
Mossneuk Primary School EKILS G75 126 C3
Mosspark Primary School CARD/HILL/MSPK G52 77 L6
Mossvale Primary School PSLYN/LNWD PA3 75 K3
Motherwell Business Centre MTHW ML1 120 F2
Motherwell CC MTHW ML1 121 G6
Motherwell College MTHW ML1 120 F6
Motherwell FC (Fir Park) MTHW ML1 120 F5
Motherwell Heritage Centre MTHW ML1 120 D2
Mount Cameron Primary School EKILN G74 3 M9
Mount Ellen Golf Club BAIL/MDB/MHD G69 65 H4
Mount Florida Medical Centre GVH/MTFL G42 95 G2
Mount Florida Primary School GVH/MTFL G42 95 H3
Mount Manor Business Park KVGV G3 78 D2
Mount Vernon Primary School CAR/SHTL G32 81 K7
M8 Trading Estate PLKSD/SHW G41 78 E5
Mugdock Castle MLNGV G62 23 M2
Mugdock Country Park MLNGV G62 24 A3
Muiredge Primary School UD/BTH/TAN G71 98 F4
Muirhouse Primary School MTHW ML1 121 J7
Muir Street Primary School MTHW ML1 120 D1
Munro Business Centre KNTSWD G13 59 L2
Murano Medical Centre MRYH/FIRH G20 60 F6
Murray Primary School EKILS G75 2 F8
Museum of Scottish Country Life CRMNK/CLK/EAG G76 115 M6

Museum of Scottish Football
 GVH/MTFL G42 .... 95 H3
Museum of Transport
 PTCK G11 .... 78 C1
National Piping Centre
 COWCAD G4 .... 4 F3
National Swimming Centre at
 Tollcross Leisure Centre
 CAR/SHTL G32 .... 80 F6
Neilsland Primary School
 HMLTN ML3 .... 129 G1
Neilston Cemetery
 BRHD/NEIL G78 .... 92 A8
Neilston Primary School
 BRHD/NEIL G78 .... 111 L3
Neilston Swimming Pool
 BRHD/NEIL G78 .... 111 L3
Nellfield House
 CARLUKE ML8 .... 135 G4
Nerston Residential School
 EKILN G74 .... 117 G3
Nethercommon Industrial
 Estate *PSLYN/LNWD* PA3 .... 75 L3
Nethercraigs
 Sports Centre
 PLK/PH/NH G53 .... 77 K7
Netherlee Primary School
 LNPK/KPK G44 .... 94 F8
Netherton Primary School
 WISHAW ML2 .... 121 L8
Netherton School
 CSMK G45 .... 95 J8
New Albion Industrial Estate
 KNTSWD G13 .... 58 L2
Newark Castle
 PGL PA14 .... 18 D8
Newarthill Primary School
 MTHW ML1 .... 101 L1
Newhills School
 STPS/GTHM/RID G33 .... 81 L3
Newhouse Industrial Estate
 MTHW ML1 .... 101 J2
 MTHW ML1 .... 120 D2
New Lanark Mill Hotel
 LNK/LMHG ML11 .... 136 F7
New Lanark Primary School
 LNK/LMHG ML11 .... 137 G3
New Lanark Visitor Centre
 LNK/LMHG ML11 .... 136 F8
Newmains Primary School
 RNFRW PA4 .... 58 C8
 WISHAW ML2 .... 122 H1
New Monkland Primary
 School *AIRDRIE* ML6 .... 66 E5
New Stevenston Primary
 School *MTHW* ML1 .... 100 F5
The Nicholas Geraghty Clinic
 MTHW ML1 .... 120 F2
Nitshill Primary School
 PLK/PH/NH G53 .... 93 G5
Noble Primary School
 BLSH ML4 .... 100 A2
North Glasgow College
 SPRGB/BLRNK G21 .... 61 M6
North Woodside Swimming
 Pool *COWCAD* G4 .... 4 C1
Notre Dame High School
 GRNKW/INVK PA16 .... 16 D5
 KVD/HLHD G12 .... 60 C7
Notre Dame Primary School
 KVD/HLHD G12 .... 60 C7
Novotel
 CGLW G2 .... 4 C4
Nuneaton Industrial Estate
 DMNK/BRGTN G40 .... 80 A7
Oakbank Industrial Estate
 MRYH/FIRH G20 .... 61 G7
Oakgrove Primary School
 COWCAD G4 .... 4 C1
Oak Mall Shopping Centre
 GRNK PA15 .... 6 C3
Odeon Cinema
 CGLW G2 .... 4 E5
 EKILN G74 .... 3 G6
 GOV/IBX G51 .... 78 F4
Ogilvie Primary School
 STPS/GTHM/RID G33 .... 81 M3
Old Aisle Cemetery
 KKNTL G66 .... 45 M4
Old Course Ranfurly Golf Club
 BRWEIR PA11 .... 72 C3
Old Kilpatrick Cemetery
 OLDK G60 .... 39 G3
Old Monkland Cemetery
 CTBR ML5 .... 83 K7
Old Monkland Primary School
 CTBR ML5 .... 83 J6
Optimax Laser Eye Clinic
 KVGV G3 .... 4 A3
Orbiston Business Centre
 BLSH ML4 .... 100 C4
Our Holy Redeemers Primary
 School *CLYDBK* G81 .... 58 D2
Our Lady of Loretto Primary
 School *CLYDBK* G81 .... 39 K7
Our Lady of Lourdes Primary
 School *EKILS* G75 .... 2 D1
Our Lady of Peace Primary
 School *PSLYN/LNWD* PA3 ... 74 A5
Our Lady of the Annunciation
 Primary School
 PLKSW/MSWD G43 .... 94 E5
Our Lady of the Assumption
 Primary School
 MRYH/FIRH G20 .... 61 G6
Our Lady of the Missions
 Primary School
 GIF/THBK G46 .... 94 A8
Our Lady of the Rosary
 Primary School
 CARD/HILL/MSPK G52 .... 77 K5
Our Lady & St Francis Primary
 School *MTHW* ML1 .... 101 J7
Our Lady & St Patricks High
 School *DMBTN* G82 .... 20 L4
Our Ladys High School
 CUMB G67 .... 30 D8
 MTHW ML1 .... 121 G6
Overton Primary School
 GRNKW/INVK PA16 .... 16 D6
Overtown Primary School
 WISHAW ML2 .... 131 G2
Oxgang Primary School
 KKNTL G66 .... 45 M2
Paisley Abbey
 PSLY PA1 .... 9 J4

Paisley Crematorium
 PSLY PA1 .... 8 C4
Paisley Golf Club
 PSLYS PA2 .... 91 H5
Paisley Grammar School
 PSLY PA1 .... 9 L4
Paisley Maternity Hospital
 PSLYS PA2 .... 8 C9
Paisley Museum & Art Galleries
 PSLY PA1 .... 8 F5
Palacerigg Country Park
 CUMB G67 .... 49 M1
Palacerigg Golf Club
 CUMB G67 .... 49 H2
Parkburn Industrial Estate
 BLTYR/CAMB G72 .... 118 F4
Parkhead Hospital
 DEN/PKHD G31 .... 80 D5
Parklands School
 HBR/GL G84 .... 10 L5
Park Lodge School
 HBR/GL G84 .... 10 L6
Park Mains High School
 ERSK PA8 .... 57 H1
Parkview Business Centre
 KVGV G3 .... 4 A3
Parkview Primary School
 SMSTN G23 .... 60 D2
Partick Market
 PTCK G11 .... 60 C8
Partick Thistle FC
 (Firhill Stadium)
 MRYH/FIRH G20 .... 61 G6
The Pavilion Theatre
 CGLW G2 .... 4 E4
Peacock Cross Industrial
 Estate *HMLTN* ML3 .... 119 J5
Penilee Secondary School
 CARD/HILL/MSPK G52 .... 76 F3
Pentagon Business Centre
 KVGV G3 .... 4 B7
Pentland School
 CTBR ML5 .... 83 J1
People's Palace
 DMNK/BRGTN G40 .... 79 L5
Petersburn Primary School
 AIRDRIE ML6 .... 85 J4
Petershill FC
 SPRGB/BLRNK G21 .... 61 M7
Petershill Recreation Centre
 SPRGB/BLRNK G21 .... 62 B7
Phoenix Business Park
 PSLYN/LNWD PA3 .... 74 D6
Phoenix Industrial Estate
 PSLYN/LNWD PA3 .... 75 L3
Phoenix Retail
 & Business Park
 PSLY PA1 .... 74 E5
Pierhead Clinic
 GRK PA19 .... 15 K1
Pinewood Primary School
 DRUM G15 .... 41 J6
Plains Country Park
 AIRDRIE ML6 .... 68 B8
Plains Primary School
 AIRDRIE ML6 .... 68 A7
The Play Drome
 CLYDBK G81 .... 40 B8
Pollock Leisure Centre
 PLK/PH/NH G53 .... 93 J2
Pollock Shopping Centre
 PLK/PH/NH G53 .... 93 J2
Pollok Country Park
 PLKSD/SHW G41 .... 94 A1
Pollok Golf Club
 PLKSW/MSWD G43 .... 94 A3
Pollok House
 PLKSW/MSWD G43 .... 93 M1
Pollokshields Primary School
 PLKSD/SHW G41 .... 78 B2
Port Glasgow Baths
 PGL PA14 .... 18 C8
Port Glasgow Golf Club
 PGL PA14 .... 34 D3
Port Glasgow Health Centre
 PGL PA14 .... 18 C8
Port Glasgow High School
 PGL PA14 .... 35 G4
Port Glasgow Juniors FC
 PGL PA14 .... 35 G1
Port Glasgow Protestant
 Athletic Club *PGL* PA14 ..... 18 A8
Portland High School
 CTBR ML5 .... 84 B2
Portland Park Medical Centre
 HMLTN ML3 .... 119 L8
Possil Marsh Nature Reserve
 SMSTN G23 .... 61 H2
Possilpark Health Centre
 PPK/MIL G22 .... 61 J6
Premier Travel Inn
 BSDN G61 .... 42 A3
 CAR/SHTL G32 .... 97 C1
 CGLE G1 .... 5 H6
 CUMB G67 .... 31 G7
 EKILS G75 .... 126 E1
 GRNK PA15 .... 7 K5
 HMLTN ML3 .... 119 L4
 KVGV G3 .... 4 B4
 MLNGV G62 .... 42 A2
 MTHW ML1 .... 102 A2
 PSLY PA1 .... 74 D5
 PSLYN/LNWD PA3 .... 75 L2
 STPS/GTHM/RID G33 .... 63 M4
 UD/BTH/TAN G71 .... 98 B1
Priestfield Industrial Estate
 BLTYR/CAMB G72 .... 118 D5
Prince's Square Shopping
 Centre *CGLE* G1 .... 4 E7
Princess Royal
 Maternity Hospital
 DEN/PKHD G31 .... 5 L4
Pro Bowl
 KKNTL G66 .... 27 J8
Pro Lane Bowl
 EKILS G75 .... 127 K4
Provand's Lordship
 COWCAD G4 .... 5 J5
Provan Hall (NTS)
 STRH G34 .... 81 M1
Provanhall Primary School
 STRH G34 .... 82 A1
Quadrant Shopping Centre
 CTBR ML5 .... 84 A2
Quality Hotel
 CGLE G1 .... 4 D6

Quarry Brae Primary School
 DEN/PKHD G31 .... 80 E5
Quarter Primary School
 HMLTN ML3 .... 129 M7
Queen Margaret Hall of
 Residence *KVD/HLHD* G12 ... 60 C5
Queenslie Industrial Estate
 STPS/GTHM/RID G33 .... 81 L2
Queen's Park FC
 (Hampden Park)
 GVH/MTFL G42 .... 95 J2
Radisson SAS Glasgow
 CGLE G1 .... 4 D7
Ralston Golf Club
 PSLY PA1 .... 76 D5
Ralston Primary School
 PSLY PA1 .... 76 E4
Ramada Hotel
 CGLE G1 .... 4 F7
 GRK PA19 .... 14 E4
 PSLYN/LNWD PA3 .... 75 K2
Ramoy Business Centre
 PSLY PA1 .... 8 D5
Ramshorn Theatre
 CGLE G1 .... 5 H6
Ranfurly Castle Golf Club
 BRWEIR PA11 .... 72 B3
Range Road
 Industrial Estate
 MTHW ML1 .... 121 J5
Rangers FC
 GOV/IBX G51 .... 78 A4
Rashielea Primary School
 ERSK PA8 .... 39 H7
Ravenscraig Hospital
 GRNKW/INVK PA16 .... 16 A6
Ravenscraig Primary School
 GRNKW/INVK PA16 .... 15 L6
Ravenscraig Stadium
 GRNKW/INVK PA16 .... 15 L6
Ravenswood Primary School
 CUMB G67 .... 48 E1
Redburn School
 CUMB G67 .... 31 J7
Red Deer Day Hospital
 EKILS G75 .... 2 A7
Regency Medical Clinic
 KVGV G3 .... 78 E1
Reid Kerr College
 PSLYN/LNWD PA3 .... 9 J1
Reid Kerr Learning Centre
 PSLYN/LNWD PA3 .... 75 G4
Renfrew District
 Welfare Clinic
 PSLYS PA2 .... 90 F1
Renfrew Golf Club
 RNFRW PA4 .... 58 B4
Renfrew Health Centre
 RNFRW PA4 .... 58 C7
Renfrew High School
 RNFRW PA4 .... 58 D7
Renton Primary School
 DMBTN G82 .... 20 D1
Richmond Park School
 GBLS G5 .... 79 K7
Riddrie Park Cemetery
 STPS/GTHM/RID G33 .... 62 E7
Ridgepark School
 LNK/LMHG ML11 .... 136 F3
Righead Industrial Estate
 BLSH ML4 .... 99 L4
Roadmeetings Hospital
 CARLUKE ML8 .... 135 J1
Robert Owen Memorial
 Primary School
 LNK/LMHG ML11 .... 137 J5
Robert Smillie Memorial
 Primary School
 LRKH ML9 .... 130 B8
Robertsons Sports Centre
 PSLYS PA2 .... 91 M3
Rob Roy FC
 KKNTL G66 .... 45 G2
Robslee Primary School
 GIF/THBK G46 .... 94 B8
Rochsolloch Primary School
 AIRDRIE ML6 .... 84 E3
Rogerfield Primary School
 ESTRH G34 .... 82 C2
Rosehall High School
 CTBR ML5 .... 83 M7
Rosehall Industrial Estate
 CTBR ML5 .... 83 M7
Rosevale School
 PPK/MIL G22 .... 61 K3
Rosshall Academy
 CARD/HILL/MSPK G52 .... 77 G5
Ross Hall Hospital
 CARD/HILL/MSPK G52 .... 77 G6
Rouken Glen Park
 GIF/THBK G46 .... 93 M8
Routenburn Golf Club
 LARGS KA30 .... 106 E2
Royal Alexandra Hospital
 PSLYS PA2 .... 8 E9
Royal College of Nursing
 KVGV G3 .... 78 F1
Royal Concert Hall
 CGLE G1 .... 4 F5
Royal Gourock Yacht Club
 GRK PA19 .... 15 J2
Royal Highland Fusiliers
 Museum *KVGV* G3 .... 4 B3
Royal Hospital for Sick Children
 & Maternity Hospital
 KVGV G3 .... 78 C1
Royal Scottish Academy of
 Music *CGLE* G1 .... 4 E3
Royston Primary School
 SPRGB/BLRNK G21 .... 5 M2
RSPB Lochwinnoch Nature
 Reserve *LOCHW* PA12 .... 109 J5
RSPB Nature Reserve
 MTHW ML1 .... 120 E7
Ruchazie Primary School
 STPS/GTHM/RID G33 .... 81 G1
Ruchill Primary School
 MRYH/FIRH G20 .... 60 F4
Rutherglen Cemetery
 DEN/PKHD G31 .... 80 B3
Rutherglen Health Centre
 RUTH G73 .... 96 B3
Rutherglen High School
 RUTH G73 .... 96 B2
Rutherglen Swimming Pool
 RUTH G73 .... 96 A3

Sacred Heart Primary School
 BLSH ML4 .... 100 A6
 DMNK/BRGTN G40 .... 79 M6
 GRNKW/INVK PA16 .... 15 L5
SAE Institute
 PLKSD/SHW G41 .... 78 C5
St Agathas Primary School
 KKNTL G66 .... 46 B2
St Agnes Primary School
 SMSTN G23 .... 60 E2
St Aidans High School
 WISHAW ML2 .... 122 B6
St Aidans Primary School
 WISHAW ML2 .... 122 C3
St Aidans School
 CAR/SHTL G32 .... 80 D4
St Alberts Primary School
 PLKSD/SHW G41 .... 78 D6
St Aloysius College
 KVGV G3 .... 4 D3
St Aloysius Preparatory School
 KVGV G3 .... 4 D3
St Aloysius Primary School
 AIRDRIE ML6 .... 85 L7
 PPK/MIL G22 .... 61 L5
St Ambrose High School
 CTBR ML5 .... 83 L2
St Andrews Academy
 PSLYS PA2 .... 76 C8
St Andrews Cathedral
 CGLE G1 .... 4 E6
St Andrews Clinics for Children
 KVD/HLHD G12 .... 60 D7
St Andrews High School
 CLYDBK G81 .... 58 C1
 EKILS G75 .... 127 C4
St Andrews Primary RC School
 BALLOCH G68 .... 31 H3
St Andrews Primary School
 AIRDRIE ML6 .... 66 E8
 BSDN G61 .... 41 J3
St Andrews RC Secondary
 School *CAR/SHTL* G32 .... 81 C3
St Angelas Primary School
 PLK/PH/NH G53 .... 93 J6
St Annes Primary School
 DEN/PKHD G31 .... 80 A4
 ERSK PA8 .... 57 J2
 HMLTN ML3 .... 129 K1
St Anthonys FC
 GOV/IBX G51 .... 78 A4
St Anthonys Primary School
 GOV/IBX G51 .... 77 M1
 HWWD PA9 .... 89 J3
 RUTH G73 .... 96 C6
St Athanasius Primary School
 CARLUKE ML8 .... 133 H8
St Augustine's Primary School
 CTBR ML5 .... 83 M4
St Augustines Primary School
 PPK/MIL G22 .... 61 J3
St Barbaras Primary School
 BAIL/MDB/MHD G69 .... 64 D3
St Bartholomews Primary
 School *CTBR* ML5 .... 83 J1
St Benedicts Primary School
 ESTRH G34 .... 82 D2
St Bernadette's Primary
 School *MTHW* ML1 .... 120 B1
St Bernards Primary School
 CTBR ML5 .... 84 B6
 PLK/PH/NH G53 .... 92 F4
St Blanes Primary School
 BLTYR/CAMB G72 .... 118 D2
 SMSTN G23 .... 60 D1
St Brendans High School
 PSLYN/LNWD PA3 .... 74 C4
St Brendan's Primary School
 KNTSWD G13 .... 58 E2
 MTHW ML1 .... 121 H7
St Brides High School
 EKILN G74 .... 3 J6
St Bride's Primary School
 BLTYR/CAMB G72 .... 97 G5
St Brides RC Primary School
 GVH/MTFL G42 .... 79 G8
 UD/BTH/TAN G71 .... 99 G6
St Bridgets Primary School
 BAIL/MDB/MHD G69 .... 82 B5
 KBRN KA25 .... 124 B5
St Brigids Primary School
 GVH/MTFL G42 .... 95 K2
 WISHAW ML2 .... 123 G4
St Cadoc's Primary School
 BLTYR/CAMB G72 .... 97 J6
St Cadocs Primary School
 NMRNS G77 .... 113 J4
St Catherine's Primary School
 PSLYN/LNWD PA3 .... 9 L1
St Catherines Primary School
 SPRGB/BLRNK G21 .... 62 C5
St Charles Primary School
 BLTYR/CAMB G72 .... 97 M4
 MRYH/FIRH G20 .... 60 F6
St Charles's Primary School
 PSLYS PA2 .... 91 M1
St Clares Primary School
 DRUM G15 .... 41 G5
St Columbas High School
 CLYDBK G81 .... 40 C5
 GRK PA19 .... 16 A3
St Columbas Primary School
 KLMCLM PA13 .... 53 J2
St Columbas School
 KLMCLM PA13 .... 53 K2
St Columbkilles Primary School
 RUTH G73 .... 96 A3
St Convals Primary School
 PLKSW/MSWD G43 .... 94 D2
St Cuthberts High School
 KLBCH PA10 .... 89 J3
St Cuthberts Primary School
 HMLTN ML3 .... 119 G5
 PPK/MIL G22 .... 61 H6
St David's Primary School
 AIRDRIE ML6 .... 67 M7
 JNSTN PA5 .... 89 K1
St Denis Primary School
 DEN/PKHD G31 .... 80 B3
St Dominic's RC
 Primary School
 AIRDRIE ML6 .... 85 J3
St Edmunds Primary School
 PLK/PH/NH G53 .... 77 K8
St Edwards Primary School
 AIRDRIE ML6 .... 85 J2

St Elizabeth Seton Primary
 School *STPS/GTHM/RID* G33 .... 81 H2
St Elizabeths Primary School
 HMLTN ML3 .... 129 K3
St Enoch Business Centre
 CGLE G1 .... 4 E8
St Enoch Shopping Centre
 CGLE G1 .... 4 F8
St Eunans Primary School
 CLYDBK G81 .... 40 C7
St Fergus Primary School
 PSLYN/LNWD PA3 .... 8 B3
St Fillan's Primary School
 CRG/CRSL/HOU PA6 .... 73 H1
St Fillans Primary School
 LNPK/KPK G44 .... 95 H4
St Flannans Primary School
 KKNTL G66 .... 45 M1
St Francis of Assisi Primary
 School *BAIL/MDB/MHD* G69 .. 81 M7
 BALLOCH G68 .... 48 A2
St Francis Primary School
 GBLS G5 .... 79 K6
 PGL PA14 .... 34 F3
St Gabriels Primary School
 CRNKW/INVK PA16 .... 15 K6
St Gabriel's Primary School
 UD/BTH/TAN G71 .... 99 K2
St Georges Medical Centre
 KVGV G3 .... 4 A2
St Georges Primary School
 CARD/HILL/MSPK G52 .... 76 F4
St George's Primary School
 CARD/HILL/MSPK G52 .... 77 G4
St Gerards Primary School
 BLSH ML4 .... 100 A2
St Gilberts Primary School
 SPRGB/BLRNK G21 .... 62 C7
St Gregorys Primary School
 MRYH/FIRH G20 .... 60 D5
St Helens Primary School
 BSHPBGS G64 .... 44 C8
 CUMB G67 .... 48 B2
St Hilarys Primary School
 EKILN G74 .... 3 M7
St Ignatius Primary School
 WISHAW ML2 .... 122 C6
St James Primary School
 DMNK/BRGTN G40 .... 79 L5
St Jamess Primary School
 RNFRW PA4 .... 58 C6
St James Street Health Centre
 PSLYN/LNWD PA3 .... 8 F3
St Jerome's Primary School
 GOV/IBX G51 .... 77 L2
St Joachims Catholic Primary
 School *CAR/SHTL* G32 .... 97 J1
St Joan of Arc Secondary
 School *PPK/MIL* G22 .... 61 H3
St John Bosco Primary School
 ERSK PA8 .... 38 F8
St John Ogilvie
 Primary School
 PSLY PA1 .... 76 B5
St Johns Primary School
 BRHD/NEIL G78 .... 92 C5
 GBLS G5 .... 79 H5
 HMLTN ML3 .... 119 K7
 PGL PA14 .... 18 A8
St John the Baptist Primary
 School *UD/BTH/TAN* G71 .... 99 G4
St Josephs Primary School
 BLTYR/CAMB G72 .... 118 D2
 CLYDBK G81 .... 40 C4
 COWCAD G4 .... 4 C1
 CRMNK/CLK/EAG G76 .... 114 E4
 HBR/GL G84 .... 10 F5
 MLNGV G62 .... 23 M8
 MRYH/FIRH G20 .... 61 G8
 STPS/GTHM/RID G33 .... 63 J8
St Joseph's Primary School
 GRNKW/INVK PA16 .... 16 A5
St Judes Primary School
 STPS/GTHM/RID G33 .... 81 L4
St Julies Primary School
 LNPK/KPK G44 .... 95 K6
St Kenneths Primary School
 EKILN G74 .... 2 E3
St Kessogs Primary School
 ALEX/LLW G83 .... 13 L2
St Kevins Primary School
 BAIL/MDB/MHD G69 .... 83 G5
St Laurences Primary School
 GRNK PA15 .... 7 G7
St Leonards Primary School
 EKILN G74 .... 117 K7
St Louise Primary School
 GIF/THBK G46 .... 93 K5
St Louises Primary School
 EKILS G75 .... 127 G3
St Lucys Primary School
 CUMB G67 .... 31 L5
St Lukes High School
 BRHD/NEIL G78 .... 112 C1
St Machans RC
 Primary School
 KKNTL G66 .... 26 D1
St Margaret Marys Secondary
 School *CSMK* G45 .... 95 K8
St Margaret of Scotland
 Primary School *CUMB* G67 ... 31 G8
St Margarets High School
 AIRDRIE ML6 .... 85 H1
St Margarets Primary School
 JNSTN PA5 .... 73 L8
St Marks Primary School
 BRHD/NEIL G78 .... 92 C8
St Mark's Primary School
 DEN/PKHD G31 .... 80 E5
St Marks Primary School
 HMLTN ML3 .... 128 F1
 RUTH G73 .... 96 B5
St Marnock's Primary School
 PLK/PH/NH G53 .... 77 J8
St Marthas RC Primary School
 SPRGB/BLRNK G21 .... 62 B5
St Martins Primary School
 DMBTN G82 .... 13 K7
St Marys Cathedral
 MRYH/FIRH G20 .... 60 F8
St Marys Hospital
 LNK/LMHG ML11 .... 137 K4
St Mary's Kenmure School
 BSHPBGS G64 .... 61 L1
St Marys (Maryhill) Primary
 School *MRYH/FIRH* G20 ...... 60 C3

St Marys Primary School
AIRDRIE ML6 .... 68 F4
ALEX/LLW G83 .... 13 K6
CLYDBK G81 .... 39 M4
CTBR ML5 .... 84 A4
CUMB G67 .... 30 E8
GRNKW/INVK PA16 .... 6 B2
HMLTN ML3 .... 119 K6
KKNTL G66 .... 45 G2
LARGS KA30 .... 106 F4
LNK/LMHG ML11 .... 137 J5
MTHW ML1 .... 102 B8
PSLY PA1 .... 8 C7
St Mary's Primary School
LRKH ML9 .... 130 B7
St Matthews Primary School
BSHPBGS G64 .... 44 B8
St Matthew's Primary School
WISHAW ML2 .... 121 L5
St Maurices High School
BALLOCH G68 .... 48 A1
St Michaels Primary School
BAIL/MDB/MHD G69 .... 47 G8
DMBTN G82 .... 20 C6
PGL PA14 .... 35 G2
St Michael's Primary School
DEN/PKHD G31 .... 80 C5
St Mirins High School
PSLY PA1 .... 8 A6
St Mirins Primary School
LNPK/KPK G44 .... 95 J5
St Mirren FC (St Mirren Park)
PSLYN/LNWD PA3 .... 9 C1
St Modans Primary School
STPS/GTHM/RID G33 .... 81 G2
St Monicas Primary School
CTBR ML5 .... 83 J6
PLK/PH/NH G53 .... 77 G8
St Mungo Museum of Religious
Life & Art COWCAD G4 .... 5 K5
St Mungo's Academy
DEN/PKHD G31 .... 80 A4
St Ninians High School
GIF/THBK G46 .... 93 M7
KKNTL G66 .... 45 H2
St Ninians Primary School
CRK PA19 .... 15 K3
HMLTN ML3 .... 118 E6
St Ninian's Primary School
KNTSWD G13 .... 41 J8
St Oswald's School
LNPK/KPK G44 .... 95 G5
St Patrick's Cemetery
MTHW ML1 .... 100 F6
St Patricks High School
CTBR ML5 .... 84 B2
St Patrick's Primary School
MTHW ML1 .... 100 C4
St Patricks Primary School
CTBR ML5 .... 84 B2
DMBTN G82 .... 21 G6
GRNK PA15 .... 6 A4
KSYTH G65 .... 29 K3
KVGV G3 .... 4 A5
SHOTTS ML7 .... 104 F5
St Paul's High School
PLK/PH/NH G53 .... 93 K1
St Pauls Primary School
CAR/SHTL G32 .... 81 G7
HMLTN ML3 .... 119 H4
PSLYS PA2 .... 90 F1
SCOT G14 .... 59 J6
St Peters Primary School
DMBTN G82 .... 21 H4
HMLTN ML3 .... 129 H1
St Peter's Primary School
PSLYS PA2 .... 91 J2
PTCK G11 .... 60 C8
St Philip's Primary School
STPS/GTHM/RID G33 .... 81 G1
St Philips School
AIRDRIE ML6 .... 67 M8
St Philomena's Primary School
STPS/GTHM/RID G33 .... 62 D7
St Pius Primary School
DRUM G15 .... 41 G5
St Raymond's Special School
CSMK G45 .... 95 H8
St Robert's Primary School
PLK/PH/NH G53 .... 93 J3
St Rochs Primary School
SPRGB/BLRNK G21 .... 61 M8
St Rochs Secondary School
SPRGB/BLRNK G21 .... 5 L3
St Ronans Primary School
ALEX/LLW G83 .... 13 M7
St Rose of Lima Primary School
STPS/GTHM/RID G33 .... 63 H8
St Saviours Primary School
GOV/IBX G51 .... 78 B3
St Serfs Primary School
AIRDRIE ML6 .... 67 H7
St Stephens High School
PGL PA14 .... 35 G3
St Stephens Primary School
CLYDBK G81 .... 39 M7
St Stephen's Primary School
SPRGB/BLRNK G21 .... 5 K1
St Teresas Primary School
MTHW ML1 .... 101 K6
St Teresa's Primary School
SPRGB/BLRNK G21 .... 61 J7
St Thomas Aquinas RC
Secondary School SCOT G14 .... 59 L5
St Thomas Primary School
BRHD/NEIL G78 .... 111 K2
STPS/GTHM/RID G33 .... 80 E1
St Thomas' Primary School
WISHAW ML2 .... 121 M7
St Timothys Primary School
CAR/SHTL G32 .... 81 G3
CTBR ML5 .... 83 M6
St Vincents Primary School
EKILS G75 .... 126 E5
St Vincent's Primary School
GIF/THBK G46 .... 93 L5
St Vincents School Tollcross
CAR/SHTL G32 .... 81 G3
Sandaig Primary School
STPS/GTHM/RID G33 .... 81 L4
Sanderson High School
EKILN G74 .... 127 M2
Sandwood Primary School
CARD/HILL/MSPK G52 .... 77 G4
Saracen Health Centre
PPK/MIL G22 .... 61 H6

Saracen Primary School
PPK/MIL G22 .... 61 H6
School of Art
KVGV G3 .... 4 C3
Scotland's Theme park
MTHW ML1 .... 119 L1
Scotland Street School
Museum GBLS G5 .... 78 F5
Scotstoun Leisure Centre
SCOT G14 .... 59 K5
Scotstoun Primary School
SCOT G14 .... 59 J5
Scotstoun Stadium
SCOT G14 .... 59 J5
The Scottish Centre for Children
with Motor Impairments
BALLOCH G68 .... 30 C6
Scottish Exhibition &
Conference Centre
KVGV G3 .... 78 D3
The Scottish Hotel School
COWCAD G4 .... 5 J5
Scottish Maritime Museum
DMBTN G82 .... 21 G7
Scottish School of Herbal
Medicine
GOV/IBX G51 .... 59 L8
Scottish TV
CGLW G2 .... 4 E4
Scottish Youth Theatre
CGLE G1 .... 4 E6
Scotus College
BSDN G61 .... 41 J5
Shawbridge
Industrial Estate
PLKSW/MSWD G43 .... 94 C3
Shawhead Industrial Estate
CTBR ML5 .... 84 B7
Shawhead Primary School
CTBR ML5 .... 84 B6
Shawlands Academy
PLKSD/SHW G41 .... 94 D1
Shawlands Primary School
PLKSD/SHW G41 .... 94 D1
Shettleston Day Hospital
CAR/SHTL G32 .... 80 F6
Shettleston Health Centre
CAR/SHTL G32 .... 81 G5
Shotts Bon Accord FC
SHOTTS ML7 .... 104 D3
Shotts Golf Club
SHOTTS ML7 .... 105 G5
Shotts Health Centre
SHOTTS ML7 .... 105 G5
Shotts Leisure Centre
SHOTTS ML7 .... 105 G5
Showcase Cinema
BAIL/MDB/MHD G69 .... 83 H6
PSLY PA1 .... 74 F5
Sighthill Cemetery
SPRGB/BLRNK G21 .... 61 L7
Sighthill Primary School
SPRGB/BLRNK G21 .... 61 K7
Sikeside Primary School
CTBR ML5 .... 84 D4
Sir John Maxwell
Primary School
PLKSW/MSWD G43 .... 94 C3
Sir Matt Busby Sports
Complex BLSH ML4 .... 99 M5
Skelmorlie Aisle
LARGS KA30 .... 106 E3
Skelmorlie Golf Club
SKLM PA17 .... 50 D6
Skelmorlie Primary School
SKLM PA17 .... 50 C4
Slaemuir Primary School
PGL PA14 .... 35 G4
Smithycroft
Secondary School
STPS/GTHM/RID G33 .... 80 E1
Somerset Eye Clinic
KVGV G3 .... 78 E2
Southern General Hospital
GOV/IBX G51 .... 77 K1
South Lanarkshire College
BLTYR/CAMB G72 .... 97 H5
EKILN G74 .... 3 G4
South Lanarkshire Lifestyle
Leisure Centre RUTH G73 .... 96 E4
South Park Primary School
EKILS G75 .... 126 F4
South Primary School
PSLYS PA2 .... 75 L8
Spark of Genius
PSLY PA1 .... 9 L4
Spectrum Business Centre
RUTH G73 .... 96 A2
Spiersbridge Business Park
GIF/THBK G46 .... 93 L6
Spittal Primary School
RUTH G73 .... 95 M5
Springboig St Johns School
STPS/GTHM/RID G33 .... 81 K3
Springburn Academy
SPRGB/BLRNK G21 .... 61 M5
Springburn Health Centre
SPRGB/BLRNK G21 .... 61 M6
Springburn Sports Centre
SPRGB/BLRNK G21 .... 61 M6
Springhill Primary School
BRHD/NEIL G78 .... 92 B8
Stanmore House School
LNK/LMHG ML11 .... 137 K3
Stepps Primary School
STPS/GTHM/RID G33 .... 63 L4
Stirling Road Industrial Estate
AIRDRIE ML6 .... 67 H6
Stirling's Library
CGLE G1 .... 5 G7
Stobcross Street Industrial
Estate CTBR ML5 .... 84 A3
Stobhill General Hospital
SPRGB/BLRNK G21 .... 62 A4
Stonedyke Primary School
DRUM G15 .... 41 H7
Stonelaw High School
RUTH G73 .... 96 C4
Stow College
COWCAD G4 .... 4 C1
Strathclyde Art Centre
KVGV G3 .... 4 B7
Strathclyde Business Centre
GOV/IBX G51 .... 78 D4
GRNK PA15 .... 17 L6
MTHW ML1 .... 100 F5

Strathclyde Country Park
MTHW ML1 .... 119 M2
Strathclyde Country Park
Camping & Caravan Site
MTHW ML1 .... 120 A3
Strathclyde Hospital
MTHW ML1 .... 120 C4
Strathclyde Park Golf Club
HMLTN ML3 .... 119 L5
Strathkelvin Retail Park
BSHPBGS G64 .... 44 B6
Strutherhill Industrial Estate
LRKH ML9 .... 130 D8
Student Study Base
CLYDBK G81 .... 40 B6
Summerhill Primary School
DRUM G15 .... 41 H5
Summerlee Heritage Trust
CTBR ML5 .... 83 M3
Sunnyside Primary School
STPS/GTHM/RID G33 .... 63 H7
Swinton Primary School
BAIL/MDB/MHD G69 .... 82 D4
The Tall Ship at Glasgow
Harbour KVGV G3 .... 78 C2
Tannochside Primary School
UD/BTH/TAN G71 .... 99 G2
Taylor High School
MTHW ML1 .... 101 G6
Temple Primary School
KNTSWD G13 .... 59 M2
Templeton Business Centre
DMNK/BRGTN G40 .... 79 L5
Tenement House
KVGV G3 .... 4 B3
Tennant Caledonian Brewery
COWCAD G4 .... 5 L6
Thames Open College
CGLW G2 .... 4 D6
Thistle Hotel
CGLW G2 .... 4 D4
Thomas Muir High School
BSHPBGS G64 .... 62 D1
Thorniewood FC
UD/BTH/TAN G71 .... 99 H3
Thornliebank Health Centre
GIF/THBK G46 .... 93 M5
Thornliebank
Industrial Estate
GIF/THBK G46 .... 93 K7
Thornliebank Primary School
GIF/THBK G46 .... 94 A6
Thornlie Primary School
WISHAW ML2 .... 122 A7
Thorn Primary School
JNSTN PA5 .... 74 A8
Thorntree Primary School
CAR/SHTL G32 .... 81 G4
Thornwood Primary School
PTCK G11 .... 59 M7
Tinto Primary School
PLKSW/MSWD G43 .... 94 C4
Todholm Primary School
PSLYS PA2 .... 76 B7
Tolbooth Steeple
CGLE G1 .... 5 H8
Tollbrae Primary School
AIRDRIE ML6 .... 85 J2
Tollcross Industrial Estate
CAR/SHTL G32 .... 81 G7
Tormusk Primary School
CSMK G45 .... 96 A7
Torrance House Golf Club
EKILS G75 .... 127 M4
Torrance Primary School
BSHPBGS G64 .... 44 B1
Toryglen Primary School
GVH/MTFL G42 .... 95 L2
Toss Theatre
BLSH ML4 .... 100 C4
Town Hall Business Centre
MTHW ML1 .... 120 D3
Townhead Clinic
CTBR ML5 .... 83 L2
KKNTL G66 .... 45 K3
Townhead Health Centre
DEN/PKHD G31 .... 5 L4
Townhead Primary School
CTBR ML5 .... 65 K8
Townhill Primary School
HMLTN ML3 .... 118 E8
Trades Hall
CGLE G1 .... 5 G7
Travelodge
DMBTN G82 .... 37 M1
GBLS G5 .... 4 A9
KVGV G3 .... 4 B8
PSLYN/LNWD PA3 .... 75 K2
The Triangle
Shopping Centre
BSHPBGS G64 .... 62 A1
Trinity High School
RNFRW PA4 .... 58 D5
RUTH G73 .... 96 E3
Tron Steeple
CGLE G1 .... 5 G8
Tron Theatre
CGLE G1 .... 5 H8
Tryst Sports Centre
CUMB G67 .... 31 G8
Tulip Inn
GBLS G5 .... 79 J5
Turnbull High School
BSHPBGS G64 .... 43 L8
Turret Theatre
KKNTL G66 .... 45 J1
Twechar Primary School
KSYTH G65 .... 28 F7
Uddingston Cricket
& Sports Club
UD/BTH/TAN G71 .... 98 E5
Uddingston Grammar School
UD/BTH/TAN G71 .... 98 E4
Udston Hospital
HMLTN ML3 .... 118 F6
Udston Primary School
HMLTN ML3 .... 118 E6
University of Glasgow
BSDN G61 .... 60 A2
CGLW G2 .... 4 C5
KNTSWD G13 .... 59 L2
KVD/HLHD G12 .... 60 E8
KVGV G3 .... 60 E8
PTCK G11 .... 60 C8
University of Glasgow Visitor
Centre PTCK G11 .... 60 D8

University of Paisley
PSLY PA1 .... 8 F7
University of Strathclyde
CGLE G1 .... 4 E8
CGLW G2 .... 4 E8
COWCAD G4 .... 5 H6
KNTSWD G13 .... 59 K4
University of Strathclyde RFC
STPS/GTHM/RID G33 .... 63 H6
Uplawmoor Hotel
BRHD/NEIL G78 .... 110 D2
Uplawmoor Primary School
BRHD/NEIL G78 .... 110 D2
Vale of Leven Academy
ALEX/LLW G83 .... 13 K4
Vale of Leven Cemetery
ALEX/LLW G83 .... 13 H6
Vale of Leven District General
Hospital ALEX/LLW G83 .... 13 J4
Vale of Leven Golf Club
ALEX/LLW G83 .... 13 M5
Vale of Leven Industrial Estate
DMBTN G82 .... 20 D1
Vale of Leven Swimming Pool
ALEX/LLW G83 .... 13 J4
Victoria Buildings Business
Centre PSLY PA1 .... 9 M5
Victoria Industrial Estate
PSLY PA1 .... 9 M5
Victoria Infirmary
HBR/GL G84 .... 10 F6
PLKSD/SHW G41 .... 94 F2
Victoria Memorial Cottage
Hospital KSYTH G65 .... 29 H2
Victoria Park School
CARLUKE ML8 .... 133 H7
Victoria Primary School
AIRDRIE ML6 .... 84 D2
GVH/MTFL G42 .... 79 H8
Victory Baths
RNFRW PA4 .... 58 D5
Vikingar Cinema
LARGS KA30 .... 106 E3
Vikingar! Viking & Leisure
Centre LARGS KA30 .... 106 E3
Village Theatre
EKILN G74 .... 3 H4
Walker Clinic
KVGV G3 .... 78 F2
Wallace Primary School
JNSTN PA5 .... 74 D8
Wallacewell Primary
School Annexe
STPS/GTHM/RID G33 .... 62 D8
Waterfront Cinema
GRNK PA15 .... 6 D2
Waterfront Leisure Complex
GRNK PA15 .... 6 E3
Waverley Park Day Hospital
KKNTL G66 .... 45 K1
Waygateshaw House
CARLUKE ML8 .... 134 A4
Weaver's Cottage (NTS)
KLBCH PA10 .... 73 G7
Wellgreen Health Centre
PLKSW/MSWD G43 .... 94 C2
Wellhall Medical Centre
HMLTN ML3 .... 119 G7
Wellhouse Primary School
STPS/GTHM/RID G33 .... 81 L3
Wellington Academy
GRNK PA15 .... 6 C5
Wellpark Clinic
GRNK PA15 .... 6 D5
Wellshot Primary School
CAR/SHTL G32 .... 80 F6
Wemyss Bay Primary School
WMYSB PA18 .... 32 B8
Westburn Cemetery
BLTYR/CAMB G72 .... 97 J4
West Cemetery
HMLTN ML3 .... 119 G7
West Coats Primary School
BLTYR/CAMB G72 .... 96 F5
Wester Cleddens Primary
School BSHPBGS G64 .... 44 A8
Westercommon Primary
School MRYH/FIRH G20 .... 61 G6
Western Infirmary & Accident
& Emergency
KVD/HLHD G12 .... 60 C7
Westerton Primary School
BSDN G61 .... 41 K7
The Westerwood Hotel
BALLOCH G68 .... 31 H3
Westfield Health Clinic
CARD/HILL/MSPK G52 .... 77 G4
Westfield Industrial Estate
BALLOCH G68 .... 47 J4
Westfield Primary School
BALLOCH G68 .... 47 M3
West Mains School
EKIL G74 .... 3 J2
Westmuir Medical Centre
DEN/PKHD G31 .... 80 D5
West of Scotland CC
PTCK G11 .... 60 B8
West of Scotland Science Park
MRYH/FIRH G20 .... 60 A1
West of Scotland
Snowports Centre
BSDN G61 .... 41 L1
West Primary School
PSLY PA1 .... 8 B6
Westwood Business Centre
ESTRH G34 .... 82 B2
Whistleberry Industrial Park
HMLTN ML3 .... 119 G4
The Whitecraigs Golf Club
NMRNS G77 .... 114 A3
Whitecraigs RFC
NMRNS G77 .... 113 L4
Whitecrook Business Centre
CLYDBK G81 .... 40 C8
Whitehill Pool
DEN/PKHD G31 .... 80 D3
Whitehill Secondary School
DEN/PKHD G31 .... 80 D3
Whiteinch Business Park
SCOT G14 .... 59 K7
Whiteinch Indoor Bowling
Stadium SCOT G14 .... 59 L7
Whiteinch Primary School
SCOT G14 .... 59 L6
Whitelees Primary School
CUMB G67 .... 31 M4

Whitlawburn Shopping Centre
BLTYR/CAMB G72 .... 96 E7
Williamsburgh Primary School
PSLY PA1 .... 9 M5
William Street Clinic
KVGV G3 .... 4 A5
Williamwood Golf Club
LNPK/KPK G44 .... 114 E1
Williamwood High School
CRMNK/CLK/EAG G76 .... 114 D2
Williamwood Medical Centre
CRMNK/CLK/EAG G76 .... 114 D2
Willowbank Hotel
LARGS KA30 .... 106 D2
Willowbank Primary School
COWCAD G4 .... 60 E8
Willowbank Special School
CTBR ML5 .... 83 K4
Windlaw Primary School
CSMK G45 .... 115 L1
Windyhill Golf Club
BSDN G61 .... 41 G1
Wishaw Academy Primary
School WISHAW ML2 .... 122 B7
Wishaw General Hospital
WISHAW ML2 .... 121 L6
Wishaw Health Centre
WISHAW ML2 .... 122 B6
Wishaw Sports Centre
WISHAW ML2 .... 121 M7
Woodfarm High School
GIF/THBK G46 .... 94 A7
Woodhead Primary School
HMLTN ML3 .... 129 G2
Woodhill Primary School
BSHPBGS G64 .... 44 C8
Woodilee Industrial Estate
KKNTL G66 .... 45 L4
Woodlands Primary School
CUMB G67 .... 48 E2
PSLYN/LNWD PA3 .... 74 A5
Woodside Place Business
Centre KVGV G3 .... 4 A3
Woodside Primary School
HMLTN ML3 .... 119 L8
Woodville Park Industrial
Estate GOV/IBX G51 .... 78 A4
World Heritage Village
LNK/LMHG ML11 .... 137 G7
Wyndford Primary School
MRYH/FIRH G20 .... 60 D4
Wyndford Recreation Centre
KVD/HLHD G12 .... 60 D5
Xscape
RNFRW PA4 .... 58 F5
XS Superbowl
PSLYN/LNWD PA3 .... 9 K2
Yoker Primary School
SCOT G14 .... 58 F3
Yoker Sports Centre
SCOT G14 .... 58 F3

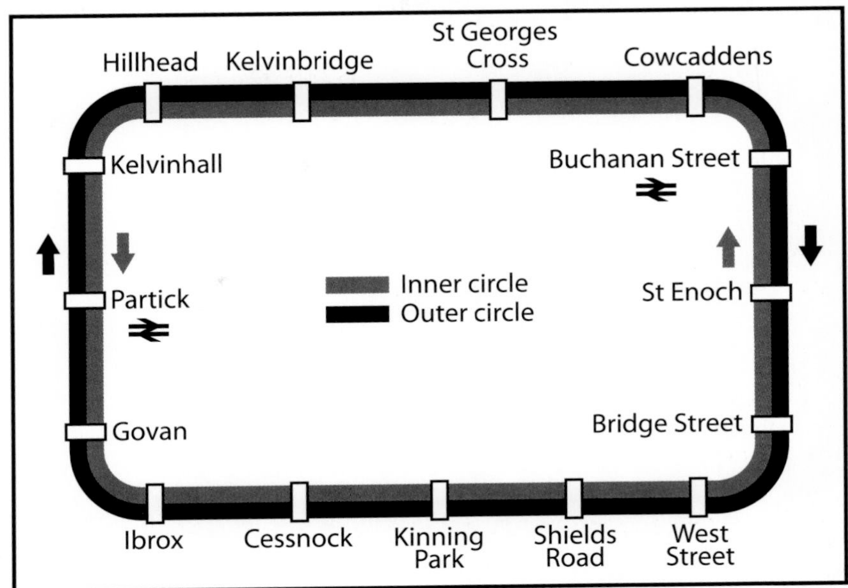

Hillhead Kelvinbridge St Georges Cross Cowcaddens

Kelvinhall

Buchanan Street

Partick

St Enoch

| | Inner circle |
| | Outer circle |

Govan

Bridge Street

Ibrox Cessnock Kinning Park Shields Road West Street

Acknowledgements

Schools address data provided by Education Direct

Petrol station information supplied by Johnsons

Garden centre information provided by:

Garden Centre Association Britains best garden centres

Wyevale Garden Centres

The statement on the front cover of this atlas is sourced, selected and quoted from a reader comment and feedback form received in 2004

How do I find the perfect place?

AA Street by Street QUESTIONNAIRE

Dear Atlas User
Your comments, opinions and recommendations are very important to us.
So please help us to improve our street atlases by taking a few minutes to
complete this simple questionnaire.

You do not need a stamp (unless posted outside the UK). If you do not want to remove this page from your street atlas, then photocopy it or write your answers on a plain sheet of paper.

Send to: Marketing Assistant, AA Publishing, 14th Floor Fanum House,
Freepost SCE 4598, Basingstoke RG21 4GY

ABOUT THE ATLAS...

Please state which city / town / county street atlas you bought:

_____

_____

Where did you buy the atlas? (City, Town, County)

_____

For what purpose? (please tick all applicable)

To use in your own local area ☐   **To use on business or at work** ☐

Visiting a strange place ☐   **In the car** ☐   **On foot** ☐

Other (please state)

_____

Have you ever used any street atlases other than AA Street by Street?

Yes ☐   No ☐

If so, which ones?

_____

Is there any aspect of our street atlases that could be improved?
(Please continue on a separate sheet if necessary)

_____

_____

_____

_____

_____

MX71z

continued overleaf

Please list the features you found most useful:

_____
_____

Please list the features you found least useful:

_____
_____
_____
_____

LOCAL KNOWLEDGE...

Local knowledge is invaluable. Whilst every attempt has been made to make the information contained in this atlas as accurate as possible, should you notice any inaccuracies, please detail them below (if necessary, use a blank piece of paper) or e-mail us at *streetbystreet@theAA.com*

_____
_____
_____
_____

ABOUT YOU...

Name (Mr/Mrs/Ms) _____

Address _____

_____ **Postcode** _____

Daytime tel no _____

E-mail address _____

Which age group are you in?

Under 25 ☐   **25-34** ☐   **35-44** ☐   **45-54** ☐   **55-64** ☐   **65+** ☐

Are you an AA member?   Yes ☐   No ☐

Do you have Internet access?   Yes ☐   No ☐

Thank you for taking the time to complete this questionnaire. Please send it to us as soon as possible, and remember, you do not need a stamp (unless posted outside the UK).

We may use information we hold about you to, telephone or email you about other products and services offered by the AA, we do NOT disclose this information to third parties.

Please tick here if you do not wish to hear about products and services from the AA. ☐

MX71z